OUR NATIONAL INCOME ACCOUNTS AND CHAIN-WEIGHTED REAL GDP

In this table we see historical data for the various components of GDP. These are given in the first four columns. We then show the rest of the national income accounts going from GDP to NDP to NI to PI to DPI. The last column gives chain-weighted real GDP.

	The Sum of These Expenditures				Equals	Less	Equals	Plus	Less	Equals	Less			Plus	Equals	Less	Equals	
Year	Personal Consumption Expenditures	Gross Private Domestic Investment	Government Purchases of Goods and Services	Net Exports	Gross Domestic Product	Depreciation	Net Domestic Product	Net U.S. Income Earned Abroad	Indirect Business Taxes, Transfers, Adjustments	National Income	Undistributed Corporate Profits	Social Security Taxes	Corporate Income Taxes	Transfer Payments and Net Interest Earnings	Personal Income	Personal Income Taxes and Nontax Payments	Disposable Personal Income	Chain-Weighted Real GDP (2000 dollars)
1984	2503.3	735.6	797.0	−102.7	3933.2	472.6	3460.6	36.3	14.6	3482.3	130.3	257.5	97.5	292.5	3289.5	377.5	2912.0	5813.6
1985	2720.3	736.2	879.0	−115.2	4220.3	506.7	3713.6	26.5	16.7	3723.4	133.4	281.4	99.4	317.5	3526.7	417.4	3109.3	6053.7
1986	2899.7	746.5	949.3	−132.7	4462.8	531.1	3931.7	17.8	47.2	3902.3	103.7	303.4	109.7	336.9	3722.4	437.3	3285.1	6263.6
1987	3100.2	785.0	999.5	−145.2	4739.5	561.9	4177.6	17.9	21.8	4173.7	126.1	323.1	130.4	353.3	3947.4	489.1	3458.3	6475.1
1988	3353.6	821.6	1039.0	−110.4	5103.8	597.6	4506.2	23.6	−19.6	4549.4	161.1	361.5	141.6	368.5	4253.7	505.0	3748.7	6742.7
1989	3598.5	874.9	1099.1	−88.2	5484.4	644.3	4840.1	26.2	39.7	4826.6	122.6	385.2	146.1	415.1	4587.8	566.1	4021.7	6981.4
1990	3839.9	861.0	1180.2	−78.0	5803.1	682.5	5120.6	34.8	66.3	5089.1	123.3	410.1	145.4	468.3	4878.6	592.8	4285.8	7112.5
1991	3986.1	802.9	1234.4	−27.5	5995.9	725.9	5270.0	30.4	72.5	5227.9	131.9	430.2	138.6	523.8	5051.0	586.7	4464.3	7100.5
1992	4235.3	864.8	1271.0	−33.2	6337.7	751.9	5585.8	29.7	102.7	5512.8	142.7	455.0	148.7	595.6	5362.0	610.6	4751.4	7336.6
1993	4477.9	953.4	1291.2	−65.0	6657.4	776.4	5881.0	31.9	139.5	5773.4	168.1	477.7	171.0	601.9	5558.5	646.6	4911.9	7532.7
1994	4743.3	1097.1	1325.5	−93.6	7072.2	833.7	6238.5	26.2	142.4	6122.3	171.8	508.2	193.7	593.9	5842.5	690.7	5151.8	7835.5
1995	4975.8	1144.0	1369.2	−91.4	7397.7	878.4	6519.3	35.8	101.2	6453.9	223.8	532.8	218.7	673.7	6152.3	744.1	5408.2	8031.7
1996	5256.8	1240.3	1416.0	−96.2	7816.9	918.1	6898.8	35.0	93.7	6840.1	256.9	555.5	231.7	724.3	6520.6	832.1	5688.5	8328.9
1997	5547.4	1389.8	1468.7	−101.6	8304.3	974.4	7329.9	33.0	70.7	7292.2	287.9	587.2	246.1	744.1	6915.1	926.3	5988.8	8703.5
1998	5879.5	1509.1	1518.3	−159.9	8747.0	1030.2	7716.8	21.3	−14.7	7752.8	201.7	624.2	248.3	744.4	7423.0	1028.0	6395.0	9066.9
1999	6282.5	1625.7	1620.8	−260.5	9268.4	1101.3	8167.1	33.8	−35.8	8236.7	255.3	661.4	258.6	741.0	7802.4	1107.4	6695.0	9470.3
2000	6739.4	1735.5	1721.6	−379.5	9817.0	1187.8	8629.2	39.0	−127.0	8795.2	174.8	691.7	265.2	766.2	8429.7	1235.7	7194.0	9817.0
2001	7055.0	1614.3	1825.7	−367.0	10128.0	1281.5	8846.5	43.6	−89.7	8979.8	196.0	728.5	201.1	869.9	8724.1	1237.3	7486.8	9890.7
2002	7350.7	1582.1	1961.1	−424.3	10469.6	1292.0	9177.6	30.7	−21.0	9229.3	310.8	732.2	195.0	890.6	8881.9	1051.8	7830.1	10048.8
2003	7703.6	1664.1	2092.5	−499.4	10960.8	1331.3	9629.5	68.1	36.7	9660.9	376.5	759.1	232.1	875.9	9169.1	999.9	8169.2	10320.6
2004	8211.5	1888.0	2226.2	−613.2	11712.5	1435.3	10277.2	53.7	55.0	10275.9	397.3	802.5	271.1	908.3	9713.3	1049.1	8664.2	10755.7
2005	8742.4	2057.4	2372.8	−716.7	12455.9	1675.2	10780.7	45.9	−52.6	10879.2	415.3	862.4	295.3	932.0	10238.2	1206.9	9031.3	11134.8
2006[a]	9364.2	2263.2	2422.5	−833.8	13216.1	1832.4	11383.7	55.8	−20.1	11459.6	440.2	949.2	310.9	942.5	10701.8	1138.6	9563.2	11464.0
2007[a]	9957.6	2384.2	2636.7	−953.7	14024.8	2124.8	11900.0	64.4	−117.7	12082.1	480.3	985.3	332.8	928.1	11211.8	1068.6	10143.2	11776.8

Note: Some rows may not add up due to rounding errors.
[a] Author's estimates.

MACROECONOMIC PRINCIPLES

Nominal versus Real Interest Rate

$i_n = i_r +$ expected rate of inflation

where $i_n =$ nominal rate of interest
$i_r =$ real rate of interest

Marginal versus Average Tax Rates

$$\text{Marginal tax rate} = \frac{\text{change in taxes due}}{\text{change in taxable income}}$$

$$\text{Average tax rate} = \frac{\text{total taxes due}}{\text{total taxable income}}$$

GDP—The Expenditure and Income Approaches

$GDP = C + I + G + X$

where $C =$ consumption expenditures
$I =$ investment expenditures
$G =$ government expenditures
$X =$ net exports

$GDP =$ wages $+$ rent $+$ interest $+$ profits

Say's Law

Supply creates its own demand, or *desired* aggregate expenditures will equal *actual* aggregate expenditures.

Saving, Consumption, and Investment

Consumption $+$ saving $=$ disposable income

Saving $=$ disposable income $-$ consumption

Average and Marginal Propensities

$$APC = \frac{\text{real consumption}}{\text{real disposable income}}$$

$$APS = \frac{\text{real saving}}{\text{real disposable income}}$$

$$MPC = \frac{\text{change in real consumption}}{\text{change in real disposable income}}$$

$$MPS = \frac{\text{change in real saving}}{\text{change in real disposable income}}$$

The Multiplier Formula

$$\text{Multiplier} = \frac{1}{MPS} = \frac{1}{1 - MPC}$$

Multiplier $\times$ change in autonomous spending $=$ change in equilibrium level of national income

Relationship Between Bond Prices and Interest Rates

The market price of existing (old) bonds is inversely related to "the" rate of interest prevailing in the economy.

Government Spending and Taxation Multipliers

$$M_g = \frac{1}{MPS}$$

$$M_t = -MPC \times \frac{1}{MPS}$$

Economics Today

14th Edition

Roger LeRoy Miller
Institute for University Studies, Arlington, Texas

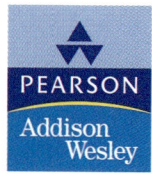

Boston San Francisco New York
London Toronto Sydney Tokyo Singapore Madrid
Mexico City Munich Paris Cape Town Hong Kong Montreal

Dedication

To Barry Zwick,

You are still the only friend who can understand everything that I write. Keep reading this for another several decades.
—R. L. M.

Publisher: Greg Tobin
Editor in Chief: Denise Clinton
Acquisitions Editor: Roxanne Hoch
Sponsoring Editor: Noel Kamm
Director of Development: Kay Ueno
Development Editor: Julie Z. Lindstrom
Assistant Editor: Julia Boyles
Managing Editor: Nancy Fenton
Senior Production Supervisor: Kathryn Dinovo
Digital Assets Manager: Marianne Groth
Supplements Production Coordinator: Heather McNally
Director of Media: Michelle Neil

Senior Media Producer: Melissa Honig
Content Lead, MyEconLab: Douglas A. Ruby
Senior Marketing Manager: Roxanne Hoch
Senior Manufacturing Buyer: Carol Melville
Senior Media Buyer: Ginny Michaud
Design Manager: Chuck Spaulding
Text Designer: Lisa Buckley
Cover Designer: Ejyo Katagiri, VisualVoices.net
Production Coordinator: Orr Book Services
Compositor: Nesbitt Graphics
Art Studio: ElectraGraphics, Inc.

Cover images: © Corbis. All rights reserved.

Photo Credits

Pages 1 and 12, © Don Mason/ CORBIS; Pages 26 and 44, © Publiphoto / Photo Researchers, Inc.; Pages 51 and 75, Bruce Bennett/ Getty Images; Pages 82 and 99, Getty Images/ Stockbyte; Pages 107 and 126, © Kim Kulish/ Corbis; Pages 134 and 153, Don Klumpp/ Getty Images/ The Image Bank; Pages 159 and 178, William Thomas Cain/ Getty Images; Pages 184 and 205, Getty Images/ Photodisc; Pages 213 and 233, © Cindy Charles / PhotoEdit; Pages 239 and 254, AP/ Wide World Photos; Pages 261 and 280, Digital Vision/ Getty Images; Pages 287 and 310, Marcus Mok/ Getty Images/ Asia Images; Pages 318 and 332, AP/ Wide World Photos; Pages 342 and 359, Gerard Cerles/AFP/ Getty Images; Pages 365 and 386, © Jose Luis Pelaez, Inc./ CORBIS; Pages 392 and 416, © Eliane Farray-Sulle / Alamy; Pages 422 and 440, AP/ Wide World Photos;

Pages 449 and 471, © James Leynse/ CORBIS; Pages 477 and 493, © Viviane Moos/ CORBIS; Pages 500 and 514, © Michael Newman / PhotoEdit; Pages 527 and 546, AP/ Wide World Photos; Pages 552 and 571, Doug Kanter/AFP/Getty Images; Pages 578 and 599, © Bill Aron / PhotoEdit; Pages 605 and 627, AP/ Wide World Photos; Pages 633 and 653, Bill Pugliano/ Getty Images; Pages 661 and 672, Roland Magunia/AFP/ Getty Images; Pages 682 and 698, © Steve Skjold / Alamy; Pages 705 and 725, Getty Images/ Photodisc Red; Pages 732 and 753, © Sherwin Crasto/Reuters/ Corbis; Pages 759 and 777, AP/ Wide World Photos; Pages 783 and 807, Michael Melford/ Getty Images/ The Image Bank; Pages 813 and 827, © Royalty-Free/ Corbis; Pages 833 and 852, © Royalty-Free/ Corbis; Pages 858 and 880, Toshifumi Kitamura/AFP/ Getty Images.

Library of Congress Cataloging-in-Publication Data

Miller, Roger LeRoy.
   Economics today/Roger LeRoy Miller—14th ed.
     p.cm. — (Addison-Wesley series in economics)
   Includes bibliographical references and index.
   ISBN 0-321-42827-7 (main volume; chapters 1-34) — ISBN 0-321-42145-0
   (the macro view; chapters 1-19; 33-34) — ISBN 0-321-42507-3 (the micro
   view: chapters 1-6; 20-34)
   I. Economics. 2. Microeconomics. 3. Macroeconomics. I. Title.
HB171.5.M642 2008
330—dc22
                                            2006037226

Copyright © 2008 Pearson Education, Inc.

All rights reserved. No part of this publication may be reproduced, stored in a retrieval system, or transmitted, in any form or by any means, electronic, mechanical, photocopying, recording, or otherwise, without the prior written permission of the publisher. Printed in the United States of America.

For information on obtaining permission for use of material in this work, please submit a written request to Pearson Education, Inc., Rights and Contracts Department, 75 Arlington Street, Suite 30, Boston, MA 02116, fax your request to 617-848-7047, or e-mail at http://www.pearsoned.com/legal/permissions.htm.

ISBN-13: 978-0-321-42827-1
ISBN-10: 0-321-42827-7

1 2 3 4 5 6 7 8 9 10–CRK–10 09 08 07 06

The Addison-Wesley Series in Economics

Abel/Bernanke/Croushore
Macroeconomics

Bade/Parkin
Foundations of Economics

Bierman/Fernandez
Game Theory with Economic Applications

Binger/Hoffman
Microeconomics with Calculus

Boyer
Principles of Transportation Economics

Branson
Macroeconomic Theory and Policy

Bruce
Public Finance and the American Economy

Byrns/Stone
Economics

Carlton/Perloff
Modern Industrial Organization

Caves/Frankel/Jones
World Trade and Payments: An Introduction

Chapman
Environmental Economics: Theory, Application, and Policy

Cooter/Ulen
Law and Economics

Downs
An Economic Theory of Democracy

Ehrenberg/Smith
Modern Labor Economics

Ekelund/Ressler/Tollison
Economics: Private Markets and Public Choice

Fusfeld
The Age of the Economist

Gerber
International Economics

Ghiara
Learning Economics

Gordon
Macroeconomics

Gregory
Essentials of Economics

Gregory/Stuart
Russian and Soviet Economic Performance and Structure

Hartwick/Olewiler
The Economics of Natural Resource Use

Hoffman/Averett
Women and the Economy: Family, Work, and Pay

Holt
Markets, Games, and Strategic Behavior

Hubbard
Money, the Financial System, and the Economy

Hughes/Cain
American Economic History

Husted/Melvin
International Economics

Jehle/Reny
Advanced Microeconomic Theory

Johnson-Lans
A Health Economics Primer

Klein
Mathematical Methods for Economics

Krugman/Obstfeld
International Economics: Theory and Policy

Laidler
The Demand for Money

Leeds/von Allmen/Schiming
Economics

Leeds/von Allmen
The Economics of Sports

Lipsey/Courant/Ragan
Economics

Melvin
International Money and Finance

Miller
Economics Today

Miller
Understanding Modern Economics

Miller/Benjamin
The Economics of Macro Issues

Miller/Benjamin/North
The Economics of Public Issues

Mills/Hamilton
Urban Economics

Mishkin
The Economics of Money, Banking, and Financial Markets

Mishkin
The Economics of Money, Banking, and Financial Markets, Alternate Edition

Murray
Econometrics: A Modern Introduction

Parkin
Economics

Perloff
Microeconomics

Perman/Common/McGilvray/Ma
Natural Resources and Environmental Economics

Phelps
Health Economics

Riddell/Shackelford/Stamos/Schneider
Economics: A Tool for Critically Understanding Society

Ritter/Silber/Udell
Principles of Money, Banking, and Financial Markets

Rohlf
Introduction to Economic Reasoning

Ruffin/Gregory
Principles of Economics

Sargent
Rational Expectations and Inflation

Scherer
Industry Structure, Strategy, and Public Policy

Stock/Watson
Introduction to Econometrics

Studenmund
Using Econometrics

Tietenberg
Environmental and Natural Resource Economics

Tietenberg
Environmental Economics and Policy

Todaro/Smith
Economic Development

Waldman
Microeconomics

Waldman/Jensen
Industrial Organization: Theory and Practice

Weil
Economic Growth

Williamson
Macroeconomics

Contents in Brief

	Preface		xx
PART I	**INTRODUCTION**		**1**
	1	The Nature of Economics	1
	2	Scarcity and the World of Trade-Offs	26
	3	Demand and Supply	51
	4	Extensions of Demand and Supply Analysis	82
	5	Public Spending and Public Choice	107
	6	Funding the Public Sector	134
PART II	**INTRODUCTION TO MACROECONOMICS AND ECONOMIC GROWTH**		**159**
	7	The Macroeconomy: Unemployment, Inflation, and Deflation	159
	8	Measuring the Economy's Performance	184
	9	Global Economic Growth and Development	213
PART III	**REAL GDP DETERMINATION AND FISCAL POLICY**		**239**
	10	Real GDP and the Price Level in the Long Run	239
	11	Classical and Keynesian Macro Analyses	261
	12	Consumption, Real GDP, and the Multiplier	287
	13	Fiscal Policy	318
	14	Deficit Spending and the Public Debt	342
PART IV	**MONEY, STABILIZATION, AND GROWTH**		**365**
	15	Money, Banking, and Central Banking	365
	16	Money Creation and Deposit Insurance	392
	17	Domestic and International Dimensions of Monetary Policy	422
	18	Stabilization in an Integrated World Economy	449
	19	Policies and Prospects for Global Economic Growth	477
PART V	**DIMENSIONS OF MICROECONOMICS**		**500**
	20	Consumer Choice	500
	21	Demand and Supply Elasticity	527
	22	Rents, Profits, and the Financial Environment of Business	552
PART VI	**MARKET STRUCTURE, RESOURCE ALLOCATION, AND REGULATION**		**578**
	23	The Firm: Cost and Output Determination	578
	24	Perfect Competition	605
	25	Monopoly	633
	26	Monopolistic Competition	661
	27	Oligopoly and Strategic Behavior	682
	28	Regulation and Antitrust Policy in a Globalized Economy	705
PART VII	**LABOR RESOURCES AND THE ENVIRONMENT**		**732**
	29	The Labor Market: Demand, Supply, and Outsourcing	732
	30	Unions and Labor Market Monopoly Power	759
	31	Income, Poverty, and Health Care	783
	32	Environmental Economics	813
PART VIII	**GLOBAL ECONOMICS**		**833**
	33	Comparative Advantage and the Open Economy	833
	34	Exchange Rates and the Balance of Payments	858
	Answers to Odd-Numbered Problems		A-1
	Glossary		G-1
	Index		I-1

Contents in Detail

Preface xx

PART I INTRODUCTION 1

Chapter 1 The Nature of Economics 1

The Power of Economic Analysis 2
Defining Economics 2
Microeconomics versus Macroeconomics 3
The Economic Person: Rational Self-Interest 3
Economics as a Science 7
Positive versus Normative Economics 10
CASE STUDY: Economics Front and Center *Time to Fight Spam with E-Mail Postage Charges?* 11
ISSUES AND APPLICATIONS *Do People Engage in Conspicuous Consumption?* 12
Summary: What You Should Know/Key Terms and Key Figures/ Where to Go to Practice 14
Problems 15
Economics on the Net *The Usefulness of Studying Economics* 16
Answers to Quick Quizzes 16
Appendix A *Reading and Working with Graphs* 17
Direct and Inverse Relationships 17
Constructing a Graph 18
Graphing Numbers in a Table 19
The Slope of a Line (A Linear Curve) 20
Summary: What You Should Know/Key Terms and Key Figures/ Where to Go to Practice 24
Problems 25

Chapter 2 Scarcity and the World of Trade-Offs 26

Scarcity 27
Wants and Needs 29
Scarcity, Choice, and Opportunity Cost 29
The World of Trade-Offs 31
The Choices Society Faces 33
Economic Growth and the Production Possibilities Curve 37
The Trade-Off Between the Present and the Future 38
Specialization and Greater Productivity 39
Comparative Advantage and Trade Among Nations 42
CASE STUDY: Economics Front and Center *The Opportunity Cost of Declaring a Wrecked Car a "Total Loss"* 43
ISSUES AND APPLICATIONS *An Economic Theory of the Neanderthals' Extinction* 44
Summary: What You Should Know/Key Terms and Key Figures/ Where to Go to Practice 46
Problems 48
Economics on the Net *Opportunity Cost and Labor Force Participation* 50
Answers to Quick Quizzes 50

EXAMPLES
"Pay for Performance" Bonuses Give Health Care a Booster Shot 4
"Neuroeconomics" Explores the Rationality Assumption 5
The Perceived Value of Gifts 6
Getting Directions 7
Insurers That Know Exactly How You Drive 9

E-COMMERCE EXAMPLE
Playing the Float with Plastic Instead of Checks 5

EXAMPLES
Small-Business Entrepreneurs Create Most New Jobs for Workers 28
A Comparative Advantage in Holiday Spirit 41

E-COMMERCE EXAMPLE
Making It Easier to Get to the "Submit Order" Button 30

POLICY EXAMPLE
The Opportunity Cost of Time Stuck in Traffic 32

INTERNATIONAL EXAMPLE
Making Death Illegal—At Least, Inside City Limits 34

Chapter 3 Demand and Supply — 51

Demand — 52
The Demand Schedule — 54
Shifts in Demand — 57
The Law of Supply — 62
The Supply Schedule — 63
Shifts in Supply — 65
Putting Demand and Supply Together — 69
CASE STUDY: Economics Front and Center *A Higher-Priced Substitute Creates a Market Opportunity* — 74
ISSUES AND APPLICATIONS *The Market Clearing Prices of Baseball Cards* — 75
Summary: What You Should Know/Key Terms and Key Figures/
    Where to Go to Practice — 77
Problems — 79
Economics on the Net *The U. S. Nursing Shortage* — 81
Answers to Quick Quizzes — 81

EXAMPLES
Brunettes Now Have More Fun — 59
Kids Give Barbie Dolls and Legos the Boot — 60
Building Two-Way Transcontinental Railroads — 63
Forest Fires Boost Productivity in Mushroom Harvesting — 67

E-COMMERCE EXAMPLE
Why RFID Tags Are Catching On Fast — 55

POLICY EXAMPLES
Import Restrictions Reduce the Supply of Cement — 68
Should Shortages in the Ticket Market Be Solved by Scalpers? — 72

INTERNATIONAL EXAMPLE
Thai Gadget Makers Raise Production When LCD Prices Fall — 67

Chapter 4 Extensions of Demand and Supply Analysis — 82

The Price System and Markets — 83
Changes in Demand and Supply — 85
The Rationing Function of Prices — 88
The Policy of Government-Imposed Price Controls — 90
The Policy of Controlling Rents — 92
Price Floors in Agriculture — 94
Price Floors in the Labor Market — 96
Quantity Restrictions — 97
CASE STUDY: Economics Front and Center *Using Auctions to Bypass the Army's Chain of Command* — 98
ISSUES AND APPLICATIONS *Coping with a Growing Global Demand for Freshwater* — 99
Summary: What You Should Know/Key Terms and Key Figures/
    Where to Go to Practice — 102
Problems — 103
Economics on the Net *The Floor on Milk Prices* — 105
Answers to Quick Quizzes — 106

EXAMPLES
Why Cheese Prices Have Jumped — 86
Why Gasoline Prices Have Increased — 87

E-COMMERCE EXAMPLE
What's New on the Web: Very Old Auto Parts — 84

POLICY EXAMPLES
Profiting by Lowering the Transaction Costs of Junking Computers — 84
Preventing Price Gouging Promotes Black Markets in Florida — 91

INTERNATIONAL POLICY EXAMPLES
The High Cost of European Sugar Subsidies — 95
Germany Looks to the Minimum Wage to Crowd Out Migrants — 97

Chapter 5 Public Spending and Public Choice — 107

What a Price System Can and Cannot Do — 108
Correcting for Externalities — 108
The Other Economic Functions of Government — 113
The Political Functions of Government — 115
Public Spending and Transfer Programs — 117
Collective Decision Making: The Theory of Public Choice — 122

E-COMMERCE EXAMPLE
Property Rights Resolve the Airport Wi-Fi Spillover Problem — 109

POLICY EXAMPLES
Civic Centers Grow as Exhibition Attendance Declines — 116

CASE STUDY: Economics Front and Center *Is It Time to Move Space Exploration to the Marketplace?* ... 125
ISSUES AND APPLICATIONS *Why Can Inoculations Against Disease Be Hard to Obtain?* ... 126
Summary: What You Should Know/Key Terms and Key Figures/ Where to Go to Practice ... 128
Problems ... 130
Economics on the Net *Putting Tax Dollars to Work* ... 132
Answers to Quick Quizzes ... 133

POLICY EXAMPLES
Is the Medicare Program on a Fast Track to Bankruptcy? ... 120
What Have Public Schools Done with Subsidies? ... 122

INTERNATIONAL EXAMPLE
Canada Opts Out of Paying for North American Missile Defense ... 114

INTERNATIONAL POLICY EXAMPLE
Italy's Ineffective Program for Reducing Smoking Spillovers ... 111

Chapter 6 Funding the Public Sector ... 134

Paying for the Public Sector ... 135
Systems of Taxation ... 136
The Most Important Federal Taxes ... 138
Tax Rates and Tax Revenues ... 141
Taxation from the Point of View of Producers and Consumers ... 145
Financing Social Security ... 147
CASE STUDY: Economics Front and Center *Combating Declining State Tax Revenues* ... 152
ISSUES AND APPLICATIONS *Can Social Security Learn from the Private Sector?* ... 153
Summary: What You Should Know/Key Terms and Key Figures/ Where to Go to Practice ... 155
Problems ... 156
Economics on the Net *Social Security Privatization* ... 158
Answers to Quick Quizzes ... 158

EXAMPLE
Incorporating a Business Could Dodge a Broadened Payroll Tax ... 149

E-COMMERCE EXAMPLE
Even During a Revenue Boom, States Seek to Tax Internet Sales ... 143

POLICY EXAMPLE
How State Trucking Fees Push Up Highway Maintenance Costs ... 135

INTERNATIONAL EXAMPLE
The Age for Receiving State Retirement Benefits Begins Rising in Europe ... 150

INTERNATIONAL POLICY EXAMPLE
Eastern Europe Discovers Proportional Income Taxation ... 137

PART II INTRODUCTION TO MACROECONOMICS AND ECONOMIC GROWTH ... 159

Chapter 7 The Macroeconomy: Unemployment, Inflation, and Deflation ... 159

Unemployment ... 160
The Major Types of Unemployment ... 164
Full Employment and the Natural Rate of Unemployment ... 166
Inflation and Deflation ... 167
Anticipated versus Unanticipated Inflation ... 172
Changing Inflation and Unemployment: Business Fluctuations ... 174
CASE STUDY: Economics Front and Center *Looking to France for Answers* ... 177
ISSUES AND APPLICATIONS *Wal-Mart, Product Quality, and the CPI* ... 178
Summary: What You Should Know/Key Terms and Key Figures/ Where to Go to Practice ... 180
Problems ... 181
Economics on the Net *Looking at the Unemployment and Inflation Data* ... 183
Answers to Quick Quizzes ... 183

EXAMPLES
Why the U.S. Labor Force Participation Rate Has Dipped ... 164
So Far, Higher Prices for Services Trump Goods Deflation ... 170

POLICY EXAMPLE
How Pervasive Is "Inflation Inequality" in the United States? ... 174

INTERNATIONAL EXAMPLE
Challenges of Measuring the Unemployment Rate in China ... 166

INTERNATIONAL POLICY EXAMPLE
Policymakers Promote Measured Full Employment in India ... 167

viii CONTENTS IN DETAIL

Chapter 8 Measuring the Economy's Performance — 184

The Simple Circular Flow — 185
National Income Accounting — 187
Two Main Methods of Measuring GDP — 191
Other Components of National Income Accounting — 198
Distinguishing Between Nominal and Real Values — 199
Comparing GDP Throughout the World — 202
CASE STUDY: Economics Front and Center *Just How Poor Is Zimbabwe, Really?* — 204
ISSUES AND APPLICATIONS *The Art of Estimating GDP Often Requires Touch-Ups* — 205
Summary: What You Should Know/Key Terms and Key Figures/
 Where to Go to Practice — 208
Problems — 209
Economics on the Net *Tracking the Components of Gross Domestic Product* — 211
Answers to Quick Quizzes — 212

EXAMPLES
Personal Computers Depreciate Rapidly — 194
Correcting GDP for Price Index Changes, 1997–2007 — 200
E-COMMERCE EXAMPLE
Microsoft Single-Handedly Boosts U.S. Personal Income — 198
INTERNATIONAL EXAMPLES
World GDP May Be Understated — 196
Purchasing Power Parity Comparisons of World Incomes — 203

Chapter 9 Global Economic Growth and Development — 213

How Do We Define Economic Growth? — 214
Productivity Increases: The Heart of Economic Growth — 219
Saving: A Fundamental Determinant of Economic Growth — 220
New Growth Theory and the Determinants of Growth — 221
Immigration, Property Rights, and Growth — 226
Economic Development — 228
CASE STUDY: Economics Front and Center *The Congressman Wants to Know the Facts—Or Does He?* — 232
ISSUES AND APPLICATIONS *Winners and Losers in the Brain-Drain Game* — 233
Summary: What You Should Know/Key Terms and Key Figures/
 Where to Go to Practice — 235
Problems — 236
Economics on the Net *Multifactor Productivity and Its Growth* — 238
Answers to Quick Quizzes — 238

EXAMPLES
Is Official Labor Productivity Growth Overstated? — 219
Putting in a Cellphone Call for Growth — 222
All That Stands in the Way of This Energy Source Is a City — 227
INTERNATIONAL EXAMPLES
Growth Rates Around the World — 216
Europe Tries to Play Catch-Up — 218

PART III REAL GDP DETERMINATION AND FISCAL POLICY — 239

Chapter 10 Real GDP and the Price Level in the Long Run — 239

Output Growth and the Long-Run Aggregate Supply Curve — 240
Total Expenditures and Aggregate Demand — 243
Shifts in the Aggregate Demand Curve — 246
Long-Run Equilibrium and the Price Level — 247
Causes of Inflation — 250
CASE STUDY: Economics Front and Center *Searching for Answers in Africa* — 253
ISSUES AND APPLICATIONS *Why the 2004 Tsunami Did Not Swamp Asian Economies* — 254
Summary: What You Should Know/Key Terms and Key Figures/
 Where to Go to Practice — 256
Problems — 258
Economics on the Net *Wages, Productivity, and Aggregate Supply* — 259
Answers to Quick Quizzes — 260

POLICY EXAMPLE
Regulation and Economic Growth — 242
INTERNATIONAL EXAMPLE
Deflation Is the Norm in Japan — 249
INTERNATIONAL POLICY EXAMPLE
The People's Bank of China Rediscovers How to Create Inflation — 252

CONTENTS IN DETAIL ix

Chapter 11 Classical and Keynesian Macro Analyses — 261

The Classical Model — 262
Keynesian Economics and the Keynesian Short-Run Aggregate Supply Curve — 268
Output Determination Using Aggregate Demand and Aggregate Supply: Fixed versus Changing Price Levels in the Short Run — 270
Shifts in the Aggregate Supply Curve — 272
Consequences of Changes in Aggregate Demand — 274
Explaining Short-Run Variations in Inflation — 276
CASE STUDY: Economics Front and Center *A Student Intern Is Put on the Spot* — 279
ISSUES AND APPLICATIONS *Oil Prices Still Matter but Not As Much As Before* — 280
Summary: What You Should Know/Key Terms and Key Figures/Where to Go to Practice — 283
Problems — 284
Economics on the Net *Money, the Price Level, and Real GDP* — 286
Answers to Quick Quizzes — 286

EXAMPLE
Bringing Keynesian Short-Run Aggregate Supply Back to Life — 270
INTERNATIONAL EXAMPLE
A Global Credit Market Awash in Saving — 265
INTERNATIONAL POLICY EXAMPLE
Can Iran's Vicious Cycle of Supply Shocks Be Smoothed? — 277

Chapter 12 Consumption, Real GDP, and the Multiplier — 287

Some Simplifying Assumptions in a Keynesian Model — 288
Determinants of Planned Consumption and Planned Saving — 290
Determinants of Investment — 295
Determining Equilibrium Real GDP — 297
Keynesian Equilibrium with Government and the Foreign Sector Added — 301
The Multiplier — 304
How a Change in Autonomous Spending Affects Real GDP When the Price Level Can Change — 306
The Relationship Between Aggregate Demand and the $C + I + G + X$ Curve — 307
CASE STUDY: Economics Front and Center *Considering an Investment in Internet Telephony* — 309
ISSUES AND APPLICATIONS *Is the U.S. Average Propensity to Save Really As Low As 0.01?* — 310
Summary: What You Should Know/Key Terms and Key Figures/Where to Go to Practice — 312
Problems — 314
Economics on the Net *The Relationship Between Consumption and Real GDP* — 316
Answers to Quick Quizzes — 316
Appendix B *The Keynesian Cross and the Multiplier* — 317

EXAMPLE
Information-Technology Investment Continues to Lag — 297
POLICY EXAMPLE
Spending on Human Capital: Investment or Consumption? — 289

Chapter 13 Fiscal Policy — 318

Discretionary Fiscal Policy — 319
Possible Offsets to Fiscal Policy — 322
Discretionary Fiscal Policy in Practice: Coping with Time Lags — 328
Automatic Stabilizers — 329
What Do We Really Know About Fiscal Policy? — 330
CASE STUDY: Economics Front and Center *Budget Surplus or Bust!* — 331
ISSUES AND APPLICATIONS *The Roller Coaster of Japanese Tax Policy* — 332
Summary: What You Should Know/Key Terms and Key Figures/Where to Go to Practice — 334
Problems — 336
Economics on the Net *Federal Government Spending and Taxation* — 338
Answers to Quick Quizzes — 338

POLICY EXAMPLES
A Millionaire Tax Morphs into a Tax on Middle-Income Workers — 321
A Laffer Curve in the Mid-2000s — 327
INTERNATIONAL POLICY EXAMPLE
Britain Pays Up but Receives Little Economic Payoff — 326

Appendix C *Fiscal Policy: A Keynesian Perspective* — 339
Changes in Government Spending — 339
Changes in Taxes — 340
The Balanced-Budget Multiplier — 340
The Fixed Price Level Assumption — 341
Problems — 341

Chapter 14 Deficit Spending and the Public Debt — 342

Public Deficits and Debts: Flows versus Stocks — 343
Government Finance: Spending More Than Tax Collections — 344
Evaluating the Rising Public Debt — 347
Federal Budget Deficits in an Open Economy — 351
Growing U.S. Government Deficits: Implications for U.S. Economic Performance — 352
CASE STUDY: Economics Front and Center *The Public Debt—Public Enemy Number One* — 358
ISSUES AND APPLICATIONS *Budget Deficit Rules Made to Be Broken?* — 359
Summary: What You Should Know/Key Terms and Key Figures/ Where to Go to Practice — 361
Problems — 362
Economics on the Net *The Public Debt* — 364
Answers to Quick Quizzes — 364

POLICY EXAMPLES
Explaining a $109 Billion Deficit Projection Turnaround — 346
How Rich Taxpayers Avoid Part of a Tax-Rate Increase — 356

INTERNATIONAL EXAMPLE
Where Are Most U.S. Treasury Securities Held Abroad? — 350

PART IV MONEY, STABILIZATION, AND GROWTH — 365

Chapter 15 Money, Banking, and Central Banking — 365

The Functions of Money — 366
Liquidity — 368
Monetary Standards, or What Backs Money — 369
Defining Money — 370
Financial Intermediation and Banks — 375
Banking Structures Throughout the World — 379
The Federal Reserve System — 381
CASE STUDY: Economics Front and Center *A Well-Intentioned Law Creates Problems in Japan* — 385
ISSUES AND APPLICATIONS *Check Clearing—A Rapidly Diminishing Fed Function* — 386
Summary: What You Should Know/Key Terms and Key Figures/ Where to Go to Practice — 387
Problems — 389
Economics on the Net *What's Happened to the Money Supply?* — 391
Answers to Quick Quizzes — 391

EXAMPLE
Why McDonald's Wants Your Card, Not Your Cash — 372

E-COMMERCE EXAMPLES
E-Gold–Backed Money — 369
Why Banks Want Their Customers to Go Online — 376

INTERNATIONAL EXAMPLE
Converting Dollars into African Vouchers on the Web — 368

Chapter 16 Money Creation and Deposit Insurance — 392

Links Between Changes in the Money Supply and Other Economic Variables — 393
Depository Institution Reserves — 394
The Relationship Between Legal Reserves and Total Deposits — 396
The Fed's Direct Effect on the Overall Level of Reserves — 398
Money Expansion by the Banking System — 400
The Money Multiplier — 405
Federal Deposit Insurance — 410
CASE STUDY: Economics Front and Center *A Job Enjoyed by No One at the Fed* — 415

EXAMPLE
Debiting with a PIN May Double-Debit Your Account — 398

E-COMMERCE EXAMPLE
Remote Capture Speeds the Check-Clearing Process — 403

POLICY EXAMPLE
Extending the Scope of FDIC Insurance with Stored-Value Cards — 413

ISSUES AND APPLICATIONS *Smart Cards, Digital Cash, and the Money Supply* 416
Summary: What You Should Know/Key Terms and Key Figures/
    Where to Go to Practice 418
Problems 420
Economics on the Net *E-Checks and the Money Supply* 421
Answers to Quick Quizzes 421

Chapter 17 Domestic and International Dimensions of Monetary Policy 422

What's So Special About Money? 423
The Tools of Monetary Policy 425
Effects of an Increase in the Money Supply 428
Open Economy Transmission of Monetary Policy 430
Monetary Policy and Inflation 432
Monetary Policy in Action: The Transmission Mechanism 434
Fed Target Choice: Interest Rates or Money Supply? 435
The Way Fed Policy Is Currently Implemented 436

CASE STUDY: Economics Front and Center *Predicting the Finicky U.S. Demand for Money* 439

ISSUES AND APPLICATIONS *How the Fed Pursues "Neutral" Monetary Policymaking* 440

Summary: What You Should Know/Key Terms and Key Figures/
    Where to Go to Practice 442
Problems 443
Economics on the Net *The Fed's Policy Report to Congress* 445
Answers to Quick Quizzes 445

Appendix D *Monetary Policy: A Keynesian Perspective* 446
Increasing the Money Supply 446
Decreasing the Money Supply 447
Arguments Against Monetary Policy 447
Problems 447

POLICY EXAMPLE
Should the Fed Use a Computer to Set Its Interest Rate Target? 437
INTERNATIONAL POLICY EXAMPLE
The People's Bank of China Learns About the Real Interest Rate 430
Zeroing Out Multiple Zeros 433

Chapter 18 Stabilization in an Integrated World Economy 449

Active versus Passive Policymaking 450
The Natural Rate of Unemployment 451
Rational Expectations and the Policy Irrelevance Proposition 458
Another Challenge to Policy Activism: Real Business Cycles 463
Modern Approaches to Rationalizing Active Policymaking 465
Summing Up: Economic Factors Favoring Active versus Passive Policymaking 469

CASE STUDY: Economics Front and Center *A Federal Reserve Board Governor in Search of a Theory* 470

ISSUES AND APPLICATIONS *Can Active Policymaking Take Credit for the "Great Moderation"?* 471

Summary: What You Should Know/Key Terms and Key Figures/
    Where to Go to Practice 473
Problems 475
Economics on the Net *The Inflation-Unemployment Relationship* 476
Answers to Quick Quizzes 476

EXAMPLES
The U.S. Natural Rate of Unemployment 451
Tracking Inflation Expectations 459
U.S. Price Stickiness—In the Eye of the Beholder? 466
POLICY EXAMPLE
Will the Bernanke Fed Opt for Passivity via Inflation Targeting? 450
INTERNATIONAL POLICY EXAMPLE
The Effects of Higher Inflation on Inflation Expectations 457

Chapter 19 Policies and Prospects for Global Economic Growth — 477

Labor Resources and Economic Growth — 478
Capital Goods and Economic Growth — 482
Private International Financial Flows as a Source of Global Growth — 484
International Institutions and Policies for Global Growth — 487
CASE STUDY: Economics Front and Center *Trying to Start a Business in Kenya* — 492
ISSUES AND APPLICATIONS *Bogging Down Business in Brazil* — 493
Summary: What You Should Know/Key Terms and Key Figures/
  Where to Go to Practice — 494
Problems — 496
Economics on the Net *Book Prices and Consumer Optimum* — 499
Answers to Quick Quizzes — 499

INTERNATIONAL EXAMPLES
The Rule of Law and Per Capita Real GDP — 481
Investing in the Usual Places — 486

INTERNATIONAL POLICY EXAMPLE
Using Catastrophe Bonds to Aid Drought-Stricken Nations — 490

PART V DIMENSIONS OF MICROECONOMICS — 500

Chapter 20 Consumer Choice — 500

Utility Theory — 501
Graphical Analysis — 502
Diminishing Marginal Utility — 505
Optimizing Consumption Choices — 506
How a Price Change Affects Consumer Optimum — 508
The Demand Curve Revisited — 510
Behaviorial Economics and Consumer Choice Theory — 512
CASE STUDY: Economics Front and Center *An Open Secret for Success in the "Dollar-Store" Business* — 513
ISSUES AND APPLICATIONS *The Upside of Taking Off from a Less Convenient Airport* — 514
Summary: What You Should Know/Key Terms and Key Figures/
  Where to Go to Practice — 516
Problems — 517
Economics on the Net *Book Prices and Consumer Optimum* — 519
Answers to Quick Quizzes — 519
Appendix E *More Advanced Consumer Choice Theory* — 520
On Being Indifferent — 520
Properties of Indifference Curves — 521
The Marginal Rate of Substitution — 523
The Indifference Map — 523
The Budget Constraint — 524
Consumer Optimum Revisited — 525

EXAMPLES
The High Cost of Certain Sources of Negative Marginal Utility — 504
Newspaper Vending Machines versus Candy Vending Machines — 505

E-COMMERCE EXAMPLE
Have You Got My Size? — 511

Chapter 21 Demand and Supply Elasticity — 527

Price Elasticity — 528
Price Elasticity Ranges — 530
Elasticity and Total Revenues — 532
Determinants of the Price Elasticity of Demand — 536
Cross Price Elasticity of Demand — 539
Income Elasticity of Demand — 540
Price Elasticity of Supply — 542

EXAMPLES
The Price Elasticity of Demand for Gasoline — 530
What Do Real-World Price Elasticities of Demand Look Like? — 538
Do People Substitute Wireless Phone Services for Wired Services? — 540
Good News for Sheep, but Bad News for the U.S. Lamb Industry — 541

CONTENTS IN DETAIL **xiii**

CASE STUDY: Economics Front and Center *Total Revenues and the Price Elasticity of Demand for Dog Food* 545
ISSUES AND APPLICATIONS *The Price Elasticity of Demand for Illicit Drugs* 546
Summary: What You Should Know/Key Terms and Key Figures/ Where to Go to Practice 548
Problems 549
Economics on the Net *Price Elasticity and Consumption of Illegal Drugs* 551
Answers to Quick Quizzes 551

POLICY EXAMPLE
Who Pays Higher Cigarette Taxes? 532
INTERNATIONAL EXAMPLE
Low Short- and Long-Run Price Elasticities of Oil Supply 544

Chapter 22 Rents, Profits, and the Financial Environment of Business 552

Economic Rent 553
Firms and Profits 555
Interest 561
Corporate Financing Methods 566
The Markets for Stocks and Bonds 567
CASE STUDY: Economics Front and Center *Earning Economic Rents from Beyond the Grave* 570
ISSUES AND APPLICATIONS *Downs and Ups in Seats on the New York Stock Exchange* 571
Summary: What You Should Know/Key Terms and Key Figures/ Where to Go to Practice 573
Problems 575
Economics on the Net *How the New York Stock Exchange Operates* 577
Answers to Quick Quizzes 577

EXAMPLES
Do Entertainment Superstars Make Super Economic Rents? 555
No Interest for the Life of the Loan, but with Strings Attached 562
How to Read the Financial Press: Stock Prices 569
E-COMMERCE EXAMPLES
Two Firms Find Different Uses for Big Loads of Cash 563
"Program Trading" Takes Center Stage in U.S. Stock Markets 568
INTERNATIONAL EXAMPLE
Aiming to Duplicate Nasdaq's Successes in China 567

PART VI MARKET STRUCTURE, RESOURCE ALLOCATION, AND REGULATION 578

Chapter 23 The Firm: Cost and Output Determination 578

Short Run versus Long Run 579
The Relationship Between Output and Inputs 580
Diminishing Marginal Product 581
Short-Run Costs to the Firm 584
The Relationship Between Diminishing Marginal Product and Cost Curves 590
Long-Run Cost Curves 593
Why the Long-Run Average Cost Curve Is U-Shaped 594
Minimum Efficient Scale 596
CASE STUDY: Economics Front and Center *I've Been Working on the Railroad—But Inefficiently, So Far* 598
ISSUES AND APPLICATIONS *Book Publishers Search for a Lower-Cost Business Model* 599
Summary: What You Should Know/Key Terms and Key Figures/ Where to Go to Practice 601
Problems 602
Economics on the Net *Industry-Level Capital Expenditures* 604
Answers to Quick Quizzes 604

EXAMPLES
Reducing the Marginal Cost of Air Transport with "Winglets" 588
A Company Thinks Smaller to Boost Its Minimum Efficient Scale 597
E-COMMERCE EXAMPLES
Put Away the Clay and Turn On the Holographic Camera 580
High-Tech Canines Help Reduce Theft Costs 589
POLICY EXAMPLE
Economies of Scale in Payment Processing 596

Chapter 24 Perfect Competition   605

Characteristics of a Perfectly Competitive Market Structure   606
The Demand Curve of the Perfect Competitor   607
How Much Should the Perfect Competitor Produce?   608
Using Marginal Analysis to Determine the Profit-Maximizing Rate of Production   610
Short-Run Profits   612
The Short-Run Break-Even Price and the Short-Run Shutdown Price   614
The Supply Curve for a Perfectly Competitive Industry   616
Price Determination Under Perfect Competition   619
The Long-Run Industry Situation: Exit and Entry   620
Long-Run Equilibrium   624
Competitive Pricing: Marginal Cost Pricing   624
CASE STUDY: Economics Front and Center *Confronting Lower Crop Prices*   626
ISSUES AND APPLICATIONS *The Big Rush to Provide Digital Snaps in a Snap*   627

Summary: What You Should Know/Key Terms and Key Figures/
    Where to Go to Practice   629
Problems   630
Economics on the Net *The Cost Structure of the Movie Theater Business*   632
Answers to Quick Quizzes   632

EXAMPLE
Decreasing Costs and the Market for Transistors   623

E-COMMERCE EXAMPLE
A Monastery Takes Advantage of Unhindered Entry   607

INTERNATIONAL EXAMPLES
In South Africa, Gold Does Not Glitter Unless the Price Is Right   615
Pressuring Japanese Retailers to Equalize Price and Average Total Cost   625

Chapter 25 Monopoly   633

Definition of a Monopolist   634
Barriers to Entry   634
The Demand Curve a Monopolist Faces   639
Elasticity and Monopoly   641
Costs and Monopoly Profit Maximization   642
Calculating Monopoly Profit   646
On Making Higher Profits: Price Discrimination   648
The Social Cost of Monopolies   650
CASE STUDY: Economics Front and Center *Entry Barriers in the Diamond Industry: Cracking or Crystallizing?*   652
ISSUES AND APPLICATIONS *For This Monopoly, Location Is the Key*   653

Summary: What You Should Know/Key Terms and Key Figures/
    Where to Go to Practice   654
Problems   656
Economics on the Net *Patents, Trademarks, and Intellectual Property*   657
Answers to Quick Quizzes   657

Appendix F Consumer Surplus and Losses Resulting from Monopoly   658
Consumer Surplus   658
Consumer Surplus in a Perfectly Competitive Market   659
How Society Loses from Monopoly   660

EXAMPLES
Go Away, Kids, You Bother Me!   636
Why Students Pay Different Prices to Attend College   649

E-COMMERCE EXAMPLE
The Airport Security Monopoly and Demand Elasticity   642

INTERNATIONAL EXAMPLES
Looking for Lots of Tungsten? The Choices Are Limited   635
Germany's Economics Cartel Breaks Down   638

INTERNATIONAL POLICY EXAMPLE
Malaysia's Drug-Labeling Monopoly   637
Forcing People to Reveal How Much They Are Willing to Pay   646

Chapter 26 Monopolistic Competition   661

Monopolistic Competition   662
Price and Output for the Monopolistic Competitor   665
Comparing Perfect Competition with Monopolistic Competition   667
Brand Names and Advertising   668
Information Products and Monopolistic Competition   671
CASE STUDY: Economics Front and Center *Trying to Generate a Surging Demand for Surge Protectors*   675
ISSUES AND APPLICATIONS *Paying for the Right to Produce Realistic Model Trains*   676

EXAMPLES
What Else Besides a Tart Taste Do Cranberries Have to Offer?   663
Half the Calories, but a Tiny Fraction of the Revenues   664

Summary: What You Should Know/Key Terms and Key Figures/ Where to Go to Practice	678
Problems	679
Economics on the Net *Legal Services on the Internet*	681
Answers to Quick Quizzes	681

Chapter 27 Oligopoly and Strategic Behavior — 682

Oligopoly	683
Strategic Behavior and Game Theory	687
Price Rigidity and the Kinked Demand Curve	690
Strategic Behavior with Implicit Collusion: A Model of Price Leadership	693
Deterring Entry into an Industry	694
Network Effects	696
Comparing Market Structures	697
CASE STUDY: Economics Front and Center *A No-Frills Airline Contemplates Adding Some Frills*	698
ISSUES AND APPLICATIONS *The Network Economics of Languages*	699
Summary: What You Should Know/Key Terms and Key Figures/ Where to Go to Practice	701
Problems	703
Economics on the Net *Current Concentration Ratios in U.S. Manufacturing Industries*	704
Answers to Quick Quizzes	704

EXAMPLES

DHL Flies Over a Barrier in the Overnight Delivery Industry	684
Using Experiments to Find Cooperative Players	687
The Prisoners' Dilemma	688
Switching Costs Keep the HDTV Market on a Dim Setting	695

E-COMMERCE EXAMPLES

Market Concentration in the Computer Printer Industry	686
Jumping on the "i" Bandwagon	696

Chapter 28 Regulation and Antitrust Policy in a Globalized Economy — 705

Forms of Industry Regulation	706
Regulating Natural Monopolies	709
Regulating Nonmonopolistic Industries	713
Incentive and Costs of Regulation	715
Antitrust Policy	719
Antitrust Enforcement	721
CASE STUDY: Economics Front and Center *Balancing Auto Sales and Fuel Economy Is a High-Wire Act*	724
ISSUES AND APPLICATIONS *Identifying the Relevant Telecommunications Market*	725
Summary: What You Should Know/Key Terms and Key Figures/ Where to Go to Practice	727
Problems	729
Economics on the Net *Guidelines for U.S. Antitrust Merger Enforcement*	731
Answers to Quick Quizzes	731

E-COMMERCE EXAMPLES

Vying to Offer VOIP	712
Microsoft's Market Shares	722

POLICY EXAMPLE

How Dare You Get Ahead of Me in That HOV Lane?	716

INTERNATIONAL POLICY EXAMPLE

Time to Break Up the Irish Cellphone Duopoly?	711

PART VII LABOR RESOURCES AND THE ENVIRONMENT — 732

Chapter 29 The Labor Market: Demand, Supply, and Outsourcing — 732

Labor Demand for a Perfectly Competitive Firm	733
The Market Demand for Labor	738
Wage Determination in a Perfectly Competitive Labor Market	740
Labor Outsourcing, Wages, and Employment	743
Monopoly in the Product Market	748
The Utilization of Other Factors of Production	750

EXAMPLE

Choosing the Nuclear Option	742

E-COMMERCE EXAMPLE

Outsourcing Computer Programming Very Close to the Border	747

CONTENTS IN DETAIL

CASE STUDY: Economics Front and Center *Efforts to Protect Maine Logging Jobs May Destroy Them* ... 752
ISSUES AND APPLICATIONS *Now Indian Outsourcing Specialists Are Also Outsourcing* ... 753
Summary: What You Should Know/Key Terms and Key Figures/ Where to Go to Practice ... 754
Problems ... 756
Economics on the Net *Current Trends in U.S. Labor Markets* ... 758
Answers to Quick Quizzes ... 758

Chapter 30 Unions and Labor Market Monopoly Power ... 759

Industrialization and Labor Unions ... 760
Union Goals and Strategies ... 764
Economic Effects of Labor Unions ... 769
Monopsony: A Buyer's Monopoly ... 771
CASE STUDY: Economics Front and Center *A Psychologist Contemplates Union "Affiliation"* ... 776
ISSUES AND APPLICATIONS *Big Labor Breaks Up* ... 777
Summary: What You Should Know/Key Terms and Key Figures/ Where to Go to Practice ... 779
Problems ... 781
Economics on the Net *Evaluating Union Goals* ... 782
Answers to Quick Quizzes ... 782

Chapter 31 Income, Poverty, and Health Care ... 783

Income ... 784
Determinants of Income Differences ... 788
Theories of Desired Income Distribution ... 793
Poverty and Attempts to Eliminate It ... 794
Health Care ... 799
CASE STUDY: Economics Front and Center *Competing to Inform Owners of Health Savings Accounts* ... 806
ISSUES AND APPLICATIONS *Is the United States No Longer an Income-Mobile Nation?* ... 807
Summary: What You Should Know/Key Terms and Key Figures/ Where to Go to Practice ... 809
Problems ... 810
Economics on the Net *Measuring Poverty* ... 812
Answers to Quick Quizzes ... 812

Chapter 32 Environmental Economics ... 813

Private versus Social Costs ... 814
Correcting for Externalities ... 815
Pollution ... 818
Common Property ... 821
Wild Species, Common Property, and Trade-Offs ... 823
Recycling ... 824
CASE STUDY: Economics Front and Center *Reducing the Marginal Cost of Cleaning Up Nuclear Waste* ... 826
ISSUES AND APPLICATIONS *The Government's Climbing Costs to Protect Wild Horses* ... 827

INTERNATIONAL EXAMPLES
A Global Shortage Hits the Market for Mining Workers ... 741
How Tsunami Relief Efforts Boosted Indonesian Wages ... 742
The Widening Expanse of Labor Outsourcing ... 745

EXAMPLE
To Save Members' Jobs, the UAW Agrees to a Two-Tier Pay Scale ... 767
POLICY EXAMPLES
Higher FDIC Wages for Some Means Fewer FDIC Jobs for Others ... 766
Can Minimum Wage Laws Ever Boost Employment? ... 774
INTERNATIONAL POLICY EXAMPLE
The Canadian Wheat Export Monopsony ... 771

EXAMPLES
Why It Is Misleading to Examine Only Wages and Salaries ... 787
More of the "Self-Made" Rise to the Top ... 791
Do Employers Favor Minority Female Graduates? ... 792
To Some Physicians, the "M" in Medicaid Stands for "Markup" ... 803
POLICY EXAMPLES
What Are Food Stamps Worth? ... 798
How "Elder Law" Fuels the Growth of Medicaid ... 802

E-COMMERCE EXAMPLE
Boom Times in Personal Computer Recycling ... 824
POLICY EXAMPLE
How Much Does Society Pay to Protect Endangered Species? ... 823
INTERNATIONAL EXAMPLE
Profiting by Generating Electricity from Thin Air in Ireland ... 822

Summary: What You Should Know/Key Terms and Key Figures/ Where to Go to Practice	828
Problems	830
Economics on the Net *Economic Analysis at the Environmental Protection Agency*	832
Answers to Quick Quizzes	832

PART VIII GLOBAL ECONOMICS — 833

Chapter 33 Comparative Advantage and the Open Economy — 833

The Worldwide Importance of International Trade	834
Why We Trade: Comparative Advantage and Mutual Gains from Exchange	834
The Relationship Between Imports and Exports	842
International Competitiveness	843
Arguments Against Free Trade	843
Ways to Restrict Foreign Trade	845
International Trade Organizations	848
CASE STUDY: Economics Front and Center *How Tariffs Complicate the Global Battle Against Malaria*	851
ISSUES AND APPLICATIONS *Do Regional Trade Blocs Encourage "Trade Deflection"?*	852
Summary: What You Should Know/Key Terms and Key Figures/ Where to Go to Practice	854
Problems	855
Economics on the Net *How the World Trade Organization Settles Trade Disputes*	857
Answers to Quick Quizzes	857

Chapter 34 Exchange Rates and the Balance of Payments — 858

The Balance of Payments and International Capital Movements	859
Determining Foreign Exchange Rates	866
The Gold Standard and the International Monetary Fund	874
Fixed versus Floating Exchange Rates	875
CASE STUDY: Economics Front and Center *A Big Buildup of Dollars at the Bank of Mexico*	879
ISSUES AND APPLICATIONS *The Currency Most Traded in Foreign Exchange Markets*	880
Summary: What You Should Know/Key Terms and Key Figures/ Where to Go to Practice	882
Problems	883
Economics on the Net *Daily Exchange Rates*	885
Answers to Quick Quizzes	885
Answers to Odd-Numbered Problems	A-1
Glossary	G-1
Index	I-1

INTERNATIONAL POLICY EXAMPLES

Belgian Governments Forgo a Uniform Tax and Kill Off Jobs	817
A Dutch Gain from a Lower Marginal Cost of Pollution Abatement in Brazil	819
Canada Confronts a High Marginal Cost of Pollution Abatement	820

E-COMMERCE EXAMPLES

U.S. Consumers Go Online to Import Canadian Pharmaceuticals	834
Japan Loses Its Electronics Advantage to the United States	841

INTERNATIONAL EXAMPLES

Kenya's Green Thumb in Exporting Green Beans	836
U.S. Exports Pay for More Oil Imports	842

INTERNATIONAL POLICY EXAMPLES

To the French, the Name of This Traded Good Is All Important	847
Twin Growth Paths in World Trade	850

EXAMPLES

Taking Multinational Firms into Account in Trade Statistics	862
One U.S. Firm's Key Role in the Market for Chinese Yuan	872

INTERNATIONAL EXAMPLE

Central European Currency Values Are Up, So Exports Are Down	868

One-Semester Course Outline

MACROECONOMIC EMPHASIS
THE MACRO VIEW
1. The Nature of Economics
2. Scarcity and the World of Trade-Offs
3. Demand and Supply
4. Extensions of Demand and Supply Analysis
5. Public Spending and Public Choice
6. Funding the Public Sector
7. The Macroeconomy: Unemployment, Inflation, and Deflation
8. Measuring the Economy's Performance
9. Global Economic Growth and Development
10. Real GDP and the Price Level in the Long Run
11. Classical and Keynesian Macro Analyses
12. Consumption, Real GDP, and the Multiplier
13. Fiscal Policy
14. Deficit Spending and the Public Debt
15. Money, Banking, and Central Banking
16. Money Creation and Deposit Insurance
17. Domestic and International Dimensions of Monetary Policy
18. Stabilization in an Integrated World Economy
19. Policies and Prospects for Global Economic Growth
33. Comparative Advantage and the Open Economy
34. Exchange Rates and the Balance of Payments

MICROECONOMIC EMPHASIS
THE MICRO VIEW
1. The Nature of Economics
2. Scarcity and the World of Trade-Offs
3. Demand and Supply
4. Extensions of Demand and Supply Analysis
5. Public Spending and Public Choice
6. Funding the Public Sector
20. Consumer Choice
21. Demand and Supply Elasticity
22. Rents, Profits, and the Financial Environment of Business
23. The Firm: Cost and Output Determination
24. Perfect Competition
25. Monopoly
26. Monopolistic Competition
27. Oligopoly and Strategic Behavior
28. Regulation and Antitrust Policy in a Globalized Economy
29. The Labor Market: Demand, Supply, and Outsourcing
30. Unions and Labor Market Monopoly Power
31. Income, Poverty, and Health Care
32. Environmental Economics
33. Comparative Advantage and the Open Economy
34. Exchange Rates and the Balance of Payments

BALANCED MICRO–MACRO
1. The Nature of Economics
2. Scarcity and the World of Trade-Offs
3. Demand and Supply
4. Extensions of Demand and Supply Analysis
5. Public Spending and Public Choice
6. Funding the Public Sector
21. Demand and Supply Elasticity
22. Rents, Profits, and the Financial Environment of Business
23. The Firm: Cost and Output Determination
24. Perfect Competition
25. Monopoly
29. The Labor Market: Demand, Supply, and Outsourcing
30. Unions and Labor Market Monopoly Power
7. The Macroeconomy: Unemployment, Inflation, and Deflation
10. Real GDP and the Price Level in the Long Run
11. Classical and Keynesian Macro Analyses
13. Fiscal Policy
14. Deficit Spending and the Public Debt
15. Money, Banking, and Central Banking
16. Money Creation and Deposit Insurance
33. Comparative Advantage and the Open Economy
34. Exchange Rates and the Balance of Payments

Preface

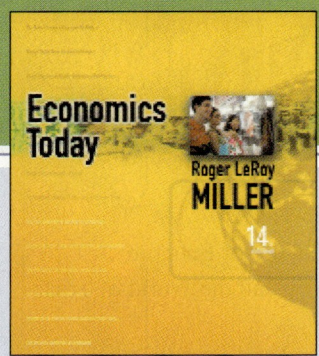

Miller's *Economics Today*—
Relevant Topics, Current Applications

Student learning is at the heart of every author's process. Every word, feature, and graph must motivate a student to appreciate and retain the concept being presented. My goal for the Fourteenth Edition is to continue to create an environment where students can actively learn, practice, and apply economics.

In doing so, I took a broad view of the text to streamline the writing and present topics with an active voice throughout. I want to connect the students to their learning, and solidify this connection through the pedagogical features in each chapter. By providing all the necessary tools, learning is then placed in the hands of the student.

The currency of the text is important to students, so I have updated all relevant material to reflect the latest issues and research. New topic areas include applications of behavioral economics in utility theory and new Keynesian models of sticky prices; the growing use of debit cards and other electronic payments processing; a revamp of federal deposit insurance; the splintering of the AFL-CIO; and changes in the status of industries traditionally regarded as natural monopolies.

> *Students learn most efficiently when concepts relate to their lives and when they are able to apply these concepts as they read.*

The plethora of examples illustrates economic theory through attention-grabbing issues and applications that students are eager to read and discuss. Each chapter contains opportunities for students to check their understanding, and critical analysis questions ask them to think like economists. Changing labels on more graphs from variables to actual numbers reiterates my desire to make difficult concepts as concrete as possible.

> *The latest issues and research allow students to be on the cutting edge of economic theory and research.*

In reading *Economics Today,* I want students to learn not only the basic tenets of the discipline, but also to begin to recognize that economics is integrated into nearly every aspect of their lives. Once they reach this realization, they will begin to notice economic principles themselves and truly be able to analyze today's economic landscape.

— Roger LeRoy Miller

New to this Edition

The Fourteenth Edition presents the latest topics with students' learning in mind, relating each concept to students' lives and then checking their understanding throughout the chapter.

The most recent developments in the field have been integrated, including:
- **Behavioral economics** applied through utility theory and new Keynesian models of sticky prices.
- **Property rights** as an important development in research on externalities.
- **Gains from trade** generated from comparative advantage.

Information technology plays a key role in the daily lives of students. Coverage of cutting-edge technology enlivens the Fourteenth Edition through an evaluation of how the Fed conducts open market operations electronically, a discussion of downloaded music to illustrate utility and the consumer optimum, and all new e-commerce, international, and policy examples.

In the macro half, Chapter 7 tackles the misconceptions surrounding the government's task of compiling accurate aggregate price and employment data. Chapters 15 and 16 treat debit cards and checks as equally important means of transferring funds, especially to today's students. Coverage in Chapter 17 of the Fed's interest rate targeting practices is expanded to include computer models, with a discussion of the Taylor rule. Chapter 18 broaches the new Keynesian theories of sticky prices as a source of inflation dynamics and as a rationale for policy activism.

On the micro side, utility theory is covered in Chapter 20 with applications of behavioral economics. The applicability of price elasticities to energy issues is added to Chapter 21. A new appendix following Chapter 25 carefully explains consumer surplus under perfect competition versus monopoly. Chapter 28 reflects new regulatory policies in the electricity, natural gas, and telecommunications industries. Structural changes in the U.S. union movement are covered in Chapter 30. In Chapter 31, controversies around income mobility are examined.

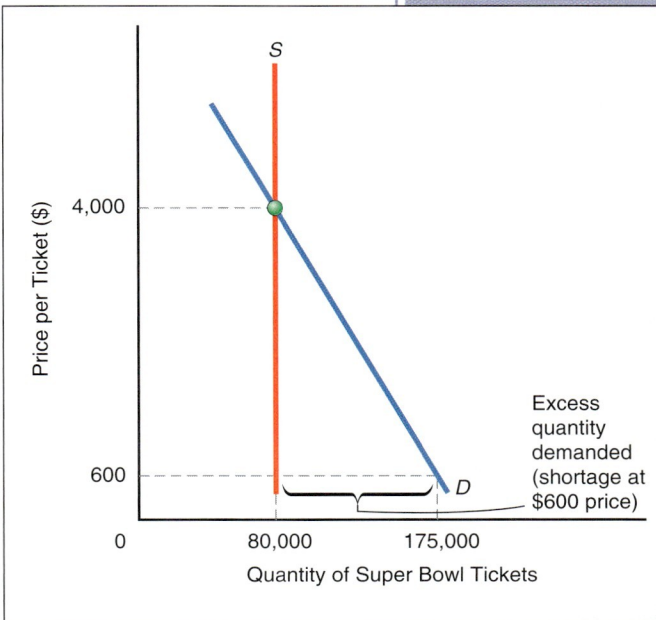

Where possible, figures have been revised to use actual numbers rather than variables.

Making the connection— from the classroom to the real world

Today's students need to connect economic theory with their lives. *Economics Today* gives students the tools necessary to learn and retain lessons in the book so they can apply economics to the real world.

EXAMPLE
Kids Give Barbie Dolls and Legos the Boot

For years, Barbie dolls and Lego building blocks were among the most popular toys in the United States. Since the early 2000s, however, annual purchases of Barbie dolls and Legos have fallen by as much as 25 percent. Indeed, the demand for *all* toys has decreased.

Are today's kids studying so much that they have no time to play? Probably not. A more likely explanation for the decrease in the demand for toys is that the prices of substitute forms of children's entertainment, such as video games, computer software, and mobile phones and digital-text-messaging services, have declined. As prices of these substitute means of entertainment for kids have declined, consumers have substituted away from Barbie dolls, Legos, and other toys—the demand for toys has fallen.

FOR CRITICAL ANALYSIS
In what direction has the demand curve for toys shifted as the prices of substitute forms of childhood entertainment have declined?

Relentlessly current examples
By effectively demonstrating economic principles, real-world examples in policy, international, and e-commerce topics help students understand why economic concepts are important in their lives. Every example has been updated for the Fourteenth Edition.

72 PART 1 *Introduction*

POLICY EXAMPLE
Should Shortages in the Ticket Market Be Solved by Scalpers?

If you have ever tried to get tickets to a playoff game in sports, a popular Broadway play, or a superstar's rap concert, you know about "shortages." The standard Super Bowl ticket situation is shown in Figure 3-11. At the face-value price of Super Bowl tickets ($600), the quantity demanded (175,000) greatly exceeds the quantity supplied (80,000). Because shortages last only so long as prices and quantities do not change, markets tend to exhibit a movement out of this disequilibrium toward equilibrium. Obviously, the quantity of Super Bowl tickets cannot change, but the price can go as high as $4,000.

Enter the scalper. This colorful term is used because when you purchase a ticket that is being resold at a price higher than face value, the seller is skimming an extra profit off the top ("taking your scalp"). If an event sells out and people who wished to purchase tickets at current prices were unable to do so, ticket prices by definition were lower than market clearing prices. People without tickets may be willing to buy high-priced tickets because they place a greater value on the entertainment event than the face value of the ticket. Without scalpers, those individuals would not be able to attend the event. In the case of the Super Bowl, various forms of scalping occur nationwide. Tickets for a seat on the 50-yard line have been sold for as much as $4,000 apiece. In front of every Super Bowl arena, you can find ticket scalpers hawking their wares.

In most states, scalping is illegal. In Pennsylvania, convicted scalpers are either fined $5,000 or sentenced to two years behind bars. For an economist, such legislation seems strange. As one New York ticket broker said, "I look at scalping like working as a stockbroker, buying low and selling high. If people are willing to pay me the money, what kind of problem is that?"

FOR CRITICAL ANALYSIS
What happens to ticket scalpers who are still holding tickets after an event has started?

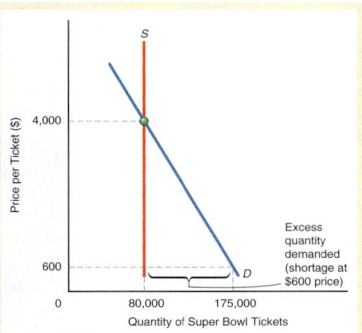

FIGURE 3-11
Shortages of Super Bowl Tickets
The quantity of tickets for a Super Bowl game is fixed at 80,000. At the price per ticket of $600, the quantity demanded is 175,000. Consequently, there is an excess quantity demanded at the below–market clearing price. In this example, prices can go as high as $4,000 in the scalpers' market.

Domestic topics and events are presented through thought-provoking discussions, including:

- Small-Business Entrepreneurs Create Most New Jobs for Workers
- A Comparative Advantage in Holiday Spirit
- Brunettes Now Have More Fun
- Kids Give Barbie Dolls and Legos the Boot

Important policy questions help students see how they can evaluate public debates, including:

- The Opportunity Cost of Time Stuck in Traffic
- Should Shortages in the Ticket Market Be Solved by Scalpers?
- Preventing Price Gouging Promotes Black Markets in Florida
- Is the Medicare Program on a Fast Track to Bankruptcy?

Global examples emphasize the continued importance of international perspectives, including:
- Thai Gadget Makers Raise Production When LCD Prices Fall
- Germany Looks to the Minimum Wage to Crowd Out Migration
- Italy's Ineffective Program for Reducing Smoking Spillovers
- Canada Opts Out of Paying for North American Missile Defense

INTERNATIONAL POLICY EXAMPLE
Germany Looks to the Minimum Wage to Crowd Out Migrants

Germany has no nationwide minimum wage. Instead, the nation's 1949 Collective Bargaining Act permits the government to issue a "declaration of general applicability" extending collective bargaining contracts to many industries. In effect, such a declaration requires all firms in an industry to pay union-negotiated wages to their employees, even if the firms are not unionized. At present, such declarations cover only about 5 percent of the German labor force.

In 2004, the European Union expanded to include several nations in Central and Eastern Europe. Many migrant workers from these regions now can work in Germany, and many have proved willing to accept lower wages than German workers. In a number of industries, such as hotels and meat packing, more migrant workers are employed than Germans.

In 2005, in an effort to prevent migrant workers from taking so many jobs in Germany, the nation's government proposed extending collective bargaining applicability to most industries. If adopted, this policy effectively would create a minimum wage system in Germany.

Most economists agree that such a policy undoubtedly would discourage German firms from hiring as many migrant workers. Another effect, however, would be to induce firms to stop hiring as many Germans.

FOR CRITICAL ANALYSIS
Which German workers would gain from establishment of a minimum wage system in that nation, and which would lose?

Information technology is presented in relevant e-commerce examples, including:
- Playing the Float with Plastic Instead of Checks
- Making It Easier to Get to the "Submit Order" Button
- What's New on the Web: Very Old Car Parts
- Even During a Revenue Boom, States Seek to Tax Internet Sales

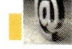

E-COMMERCE EXAMPLE
Making It Easier to Get to the "Submit Order" Button

About half of all consumers who place items in online "shopping carts" abandon the carts before authorizing payment. In some cases, people fail to authorize payment when they learn of unexpected taxes or shipping costs. Web retailers have found, however, that most people fail to finalize an online order simply because they become frustrated with complicated and lengthy checkout procedures.

In an effort to reduce the opportunity cost of purchasing an item online, many Internet sellers are striving to limit all tasks associated with submitting an order to a single Web page. For instance, Internet sellers increasingly utilize software that enables an online shopper to change her order—say, by altering the color or size of an article of clothing—without having to click back and forth among Web pages. Simplifying the online checkout process, these retailers hope, will induce more Internet consumers to decide to click on the "submit order" icon.

FOR CRITICAL ANALYSIS
For an Internet retailer, what is the opportunity cost of not devoting resources to make software simplifications that encourages consumers to finalize online orders?

Economics Front and Center case studies

At key points, marginal notes lead students to a case study at the end of each chapter. These newly revised cases place students in real-world situations requiring them to apply what they have studied in the chapter, including subjects such as:

- Time To Fight Spam with E-Mail Postage Charges?
- The Opportunity Cost of Declaring a Wrecked Car a "Total Loss"
- Using Auctions to Bypass the Army's Chain of Command

---

114 PART 1 Introduction

Principle of rival consumption
The recognition that individuals are rivals in consuming private goods because one person's consumption reduces the amount available for others to consume.

Public goods
Goods for which the principle of rival consumption does not apply; they can be jointly consumed by many individuals simultaneously at no additional cost and with no reduction in quality or quantity. Also no one who fails to help pay for the good can be denied the benefit of the good.

Exclusion principle
The principle that no one can be excluded from the benefits of a public good, even if that person has not paid for it.

ECONOMICS FRONT AND CENTER
To contemplate whether space exploration is a public good, read **Is It Time to Move Space Exploration to the Marketplace?** on page 125.

Free-rider problem
A problem that arises when individuals presume that others will pay for public goods so that, individually, they can escape paying for their portion without causing a reduction in production.

The **principle of rival consumption** applies to all private goods by definition. Rival consumption is easy to understand. Either you use private goods, or I use them.

There is an entire class of goods that are not private goods. These are called **public goods**. The principle of rival consumption does not apply to them. They can be consumed *jointly* by many individuals simultaneously, and no one can be excluded from consuming these goods even if...

legal system, for ex...

Characteristics o...
set them apart from...

1. *Public goods c...*
   and without de...
   been spent on n...
   amount of prote...
   national defens...
   protect you, it a...

2. *It is difficult to...*
   individuals use...
   pay for that pu...

One of the probl...
possible, time prov...
to offer public good...
cannot be excluded...
ernment. Note, thou...
ply because the gov...

Free Riders. The...
which some individ...
paying for public go...
in proportion to ho...
people who actually...
value to them—they...
all want to be free...
question that we act...

The free-rider pr...
defense. A country t...
North Atlantic Treat...
ing funds to the orga...
were attacked but wo...

Which nation's...
America from one p...

INTERNATIONAL EXAMPLE

Canada Opts Out of Paying for North American Missile Defense

The North American Aerospace Defense (NORAD) system uses satellites and ground-based and air-based radar systems to detect attacks aimed at the United States and Canada. In the past, both countries have contributed to the operation of NORAD. Indeed, on the morning of September 11, 2001,
(continued)

CASE STUDY — **ECONOMICS FRONT AND CENTER**

Is It Time to Move Space Exploration to the Marketplace?

Braddock is an engineer who formerly worked for the National Aeronautics and Space Administration (NASA). Today, he heads a company that hopes someday to rocket tens of thousands of people on suborbital sight-seeing trips. He is in his office, drafting a proposal for a cooperative effort with two other firms to build the first generation of suborbital spacecraft.

"There is a market," Braddock writes, "for space tourism." More generally, he writes:

> Moving space travel to the private market is more likely to lead to exploration beyond Earth's orbit. NASA is operating under the false impression that it will remain the sole provider of space travel, which it also incorrectly believes is a public good. In fact, the principle of rival consumption applies to space travel just as to other private goods. Only three or four people can fly at one time in the suborbital vehicle we plan to build. Two will be required to pilot it, but on each trip the other two will be paying passengers.
>
> Profiting from suborbital space tourism in the near term will be an important first step toward the long-run dream of regularly traveling to other locales beyond Earth. And profits can be earned in this proposed joint endeavor. NASA earns no revenues while spending $500 million on each shuttle mission. In contrast, my proposed suborbital vehicle will cost only $25 million to $30 million to build and maintain over the next several years.

"Furthermore," Braddock concludes, "my company has already managed to earn $200,000 from sales of advance tickets for a vehicle that does not even exist yet—proof of a significant demand for the space tourism that our companies can provide."

CRITICAL ANALYSIS QUESTIONS

1. *Is government support for space travel the provision of a public good, or is its spending on transporting astronauts beyond the atmosphere the provision of a merit good? (Hint: Does space travel satisfy either of the characteristics of public goods?)*

2. *Could NASA supporters make a case that some form of externality is associated with space travel that might justify government involvement? (Hint: Are any potential positive or negative spillovers associated with the market for space travel?)*

xxiv

For Critical Analysis questions

At the end of each boxed example and case study, students are asked to "think like economists" as they answer For Critical Analysis questions. These probing questions are effective tools for sharpening students' analytical skills. Suggested answers to all questions are found in the *Instructor's Manual*.

INTERNATIONAL EXAMPLE

Europe Tries to Play Catch-Up

Per capita real GDP in the European Union (EU) is less than 75 percent of the U.S. level. As a consequence, the average U.S. resident is able to spend nearly $10,000 more on consumption per year than the average EU resident.

How much faster would EU nations' economies have to grow for real GDP per capita to catch up with the U.S. level? Suppose that U.S. per capita real GDP is frozen for the next couple of decades. At a sustained annual growth rate of 4 percent, EU per capita real GDP could reach equality with the U.S. level within seven years.

Of course, U.S. per capita real GDP is not frozen in time. In recent years, it has been growing at an annual rate of 3 to 4 percent per year. Thus, EU nations would have to achieve a sustained annual rate of economic growth of 5 to 10 percent for EU per capita real GDP to rise to the U.S. level within seven years. In fact, the rate of economic growth in the European Union in recent years has been closer to 1 percent. Consequently, the gap between U.S. per capita real GDP and EU per capita real GDP is actually more likely to *increase* during the coming years.

FOR CRITICAL ANALYSIS
If U.S. per capita real GDP were frozen and each EU nation grew at its current pace, per capita real GDP in Germany would take twice as long to reach the U.S. level as in Ireland. If both Germany and Ireland began near the EU average per capita real GDP, what would this imply about Ireland's rate of economic growth compared with the rate of economic growth in Germany?

Helping students focus

A clear, timely, and thoughtful presentation, coupled with revised and new pedagogy, helps students to focus on the central ideas in economics today.

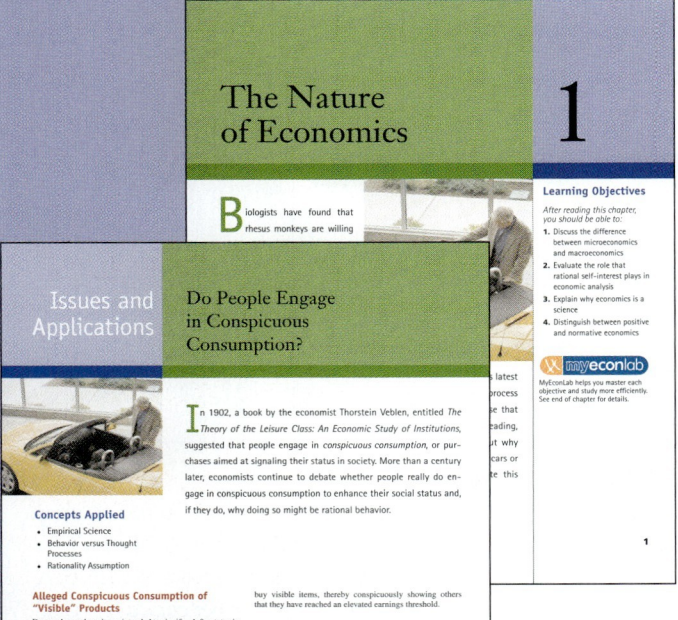

Chapter openers tie to Issues and Applications at the end of each chapter
The current applications in this book—all new to this edition—get students' attention right at the beginning of each chapter, then follow through at the end of the chapter with a two-page Issues and Applications section that presents a more in-depth discussion of the issue.

Each Issues and Applications concludes by encouraging students to visit **MyEconLab** for additional news coverage of the topic. For Critical Analysis questions, Web Resources, and a suggested Research Project give students opportunities for in-depth discussion and exploration of the application. (Suggested answers to critical-thinking questions appear in the *Instructor's Manual*.)

Provocative Did You Know That... questions begin each chapter by involving students and leading them into the content of the chapter.

New Quick Quizzes replace the previous edition's Concepts in Brief and allow students to interact with the text and quickly judge their understanding of a section through fill-in-the-blank concept checks. Answers to Quick Quizzes at the end of each chapter provide immediate feedback. To further test their understanding of the concepts covered, students are encouraged to go to **MyEconLab**.

xxvi

A variety of end-of-chapter problems offer opportunities to test knowledge and review chapter concepts. Many new end-of-chapter problems have been added, including a number of questions involving working with diagrams. Answers for all odd-numbered problems are provided at the back of this textbook, and select questions are assignable as homework questions in **MyEconLab**.

Marginal URLs direct students to topic-related Web sites to illustrate chapter topics and build students' research skills.

> Go to www.econtoday.com/ch03 to see how the U.S. Department of Agriculture seeks to estimate demand and supply conditions for major agricultural products.

Economics on the Net activities are designed to build student research skills and reinforce key concepts. The activities guide students to a Web site and provide structured assignments for both individual and group work.

A new treatment to the end-of-chapter summary makes *Economics Today* an efficient study tool by integrating chapter content with online learning resources available in **MyEconLab**. A thorough summary of the key concepts—What You Should Know—is directly linked with text and online resources—Where to Go to Practice.

Where students go to practice

myeconlab is the premier student and instructor tool, integrating lessons from the text into a powerful online learning and teaching resource.

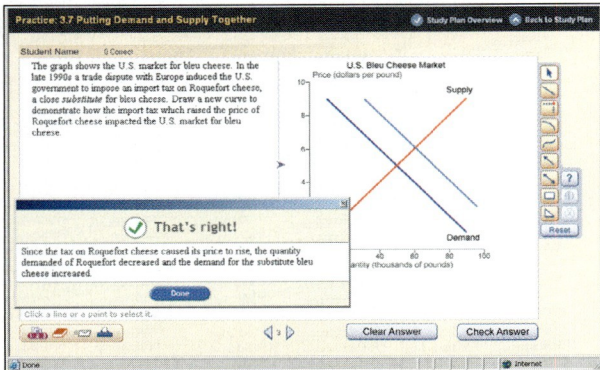

Students control their learning through a variety of features unique to **MyEconLab**.

- **Sample Tests,** two for every chapter of the book, ask students to test their understanding of concepts and graphs. The powerful graphing application allows students to draw graphs themselves, and **MyEconLab** evaluates and grades them automatically.
- **Personalized Study Plans** analyze students' performance on Sample Tests, identify areas where students need further study, then offer additional exercises to reinforce learning.
- **Tutorial instruction,** launched from the personalized Study Plans, provides additional practice, targeted learning aids, and step-by-step explanations.
- **An integrated eText** allows students access to their textbook on any computer. The eText comes complete with an audio clip for each glossary term and other learning aids.
- **The Econ Tutor Center,** staffed by experienced college economics instructors, is open five days a week, seven hours a day, to assist students one-on-one with examples, related exercises, and problems. Tutors can be reached by phone, fax, e-mail, or White Board technology. Designed to meet students' needs, the Econ Tutor Center is open during evening hours Sunday through Thursday.

- **Animated figures** present audio explanations for each step in the graph.
- **Video clips** of author Roger LeRoy Miller review key points in every chapter.
- **Glossary flashcards** allow students to review key terms from one or more chapters at a time.
- **Weekly News** updates, linked to the each chapter's Issues and Applications section, feature new microeconomic and macroeconomic current events. Discussion questions posed online weekly by Andrew J. Dane of Angelo State University test students' knowledge of relevant issues. Instructor answer keys are available.
- **eThemes of the Times** articles from the *New York Times* are correlated to each textbook chapter and paired with critical thinking questions. Instructor answer keys are available.
- **Research Navigator** develops students' research skills by offering exclusive access to databases of the *New York Times*, the *Financial Times*, and peer-reviewed journals. This is available with **MyEconLab** in CourseCompass™.

Instructors save time and gain flexibility with **MyEconLab**'s unmatched instructor features.

- **Problems assignable in MyEconLab** are directly correlated with Test Bank 1 and end-of-chapter problems. Instructors can design their own quizzes, tests, or homework assignments from the significant bank of questions or assign pre-loaded Sample Tests.
- **The Gradebook** automatically grades tests, quizzes, or homework assigned in **MyEconLab**—including graphing questions—and tracks the results in an online gradebook.
- For more information about **MyEconLab**, or to request an Instructor Access Code, visit www.myeconlab.com

Supplemental materials

Student and instructor resources provide tools for success.

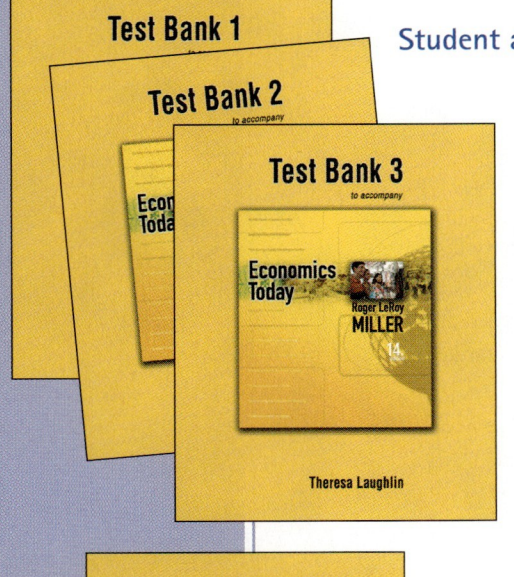

Meticulously Revised and Updated! Test Banks 1, 2, and 3 offer over 10,000 questions, all of which are available in computerized format in the TextGen® software or in **MyEconLab**. The significant review process by authors David VanHoose of Baylor University, Mitchell B. Fisher of the College of DuPage, M. James Kahiga and Gregory Okoro of Georgia Perimeter College, and Theresa Laughlin of Palomar College ensures the accuracy of problems and solutions in these heavily revised and updated test banks.

The Instructor's Manual, prepared by Andrew J. Dane of Angelo State University, offers instructors materials to make the course successful. Features include lecture-ready examples; chapter overviews, objectives, and outlines; points to emphasize; answers to Issues and Applications critical-thinking questions; answers to all end-of-chapter problems; step-by-step analyses of end-of-chapter questions; suggested answers to Economics Front and Center case study questions; annotated answers to selected student learning questions; and selected references.

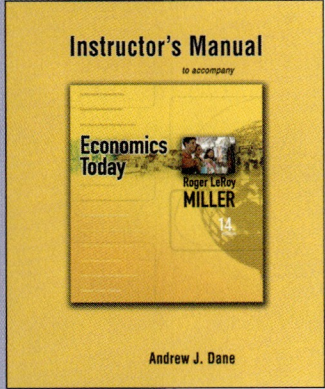

The Instructor's Resource Disk offers instructors electronic supplements conveniently packaged on a CD-ROM. **PowerPoint® lecture presentations** for each chapter, revised by Bruce W. Bellner of the Ohio State University, include graphs from the text and outline key terms, concepts, and figures from the text. The entire **Instructor's Manual** is included as Microsoft® Word files, and all three **Computerized Test Banks** are offered with TestGen® software for simple test preparation.

Four-color Overhead Transparencies reproduce one hundred of the most important graphs and figures from the text, and many contain multiple overlays.

Clicker PowerPoint® Slides allow professors to instantly quiz students in class and receive immediate feedback through Clicker Response System technology.

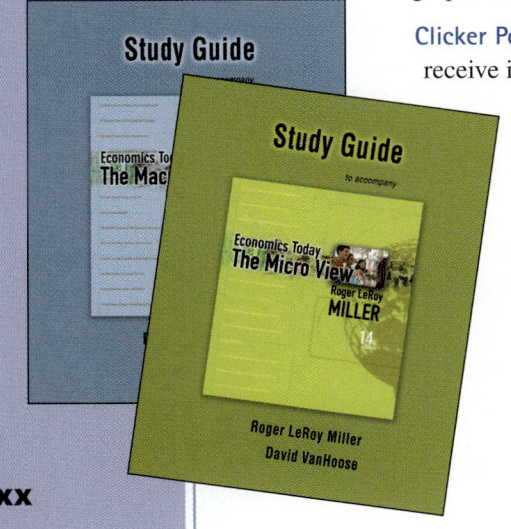

The Instructor Resource Center puts supplements right at instructors' fingertips. By registering for the Instructor Resource Center, instructors can download supplements directly from the Internet. Visit www.aw-bc.com/irc to register.

The Study Guide offers the practice and review students need to excel. Written by Roger LeRoy Miller and updated by David VanHoose, the study guide has been thoroughly revised to take into account changes to the Fourteenth Edition.

PearsonChoices

A variety of options for students and instructors provide convenience and flexibility.

The Books à la Carte Edition is created for today's students on the go. These highly portable versions of *Economics Today* are three-hole punched so students can take only what they need to class, incorporate their own notes—and save money!

Economist.com provides your students with the premier online source of news analysis, insight, and opinion on current economic events. When packaged with the text, students receive a low-cost subscription to Economist.com for three months, including the complete text of the current issue and access to searchable archives. Professors receive a complimentary one-year subscription to Economist.com.

The *Wall Street Journal* can be packaged with the text, and a 10- or 15-week subscription to the print and interactive editions of the *Wall Street Journal* is available at a reduced cost to students. Professors receive a complimentary one-year subscription to the print and interactive editions.

The *Financial Times* features international news and analysis from journalists in more than 50 countries. For a small charge, a 15-week student subscription to the *Financial Times* can be included with the text. Professors will receive a complimentary one-year print subscription, as well as access to the online edition at FT.com.

The Dismal Scientist provides real-time monitoring of the global economy, allowing students to go beyond theory and into application. For a nominal fee, a 15-week student subscription to the Dismal Scientist can be included with the text. Professors will receive a complimentary one-year subscription.

Acknowledgments

I am the most fortunate of economics textbook writers, for I receive the benefit of literally hundreds of suggestions from those of you who use *Economics Today*. I continue to be fully appreciative of the constructive criticisms that you offer. There are some professors who have been asked by my publisher to participate in a more detailed reviewing process of this edition. I list them below. I hope that each one of you so listed accepts my sincere appreciation for the fine work that you have done.

Rebecca Abraham, Nova Southeastern University
John W. Allen, Texas A & M University
Rebecca Arnold, San Diego Mesa College
Daniel K. Benjamin, Clemson University
Julia G. Derrick, Brevard Community College
Mitchell Fisher, College of DuPage
Michael G. Goode, Central Piedmont Community College
Anthony J. Greco, University of Louisiana
Philip J. Grossman, St. Cloud State University
William Gunther, University of Southern Mississippi
Paul J. Kubik, DePaul University

Theresa Laughlin, Palomar College
John Marangos, Colorado State University
Solomon Namala, Cerritos College
William Nook, Milwaukee Area Technical College
Greg Okoro, Georgia Perimeter College
Greg Pratt, Mesa Community College
Amanda Stallings-Wood, ITT-Technical Institute
Roger E. Wehr, University of Texas at Arlington
James Wetzel, Virginia Commonwealth University
Sourushe Zandvakili, University of Cincinnati

I also thank the reviewers of previous editions:

Cinda J. Adams
Esmond Adams
John Adams
Bill Adamson
Carlos Aguilar
John R. Aidem
Mohammed Akacem
E. G. Aksoy
M. C. Alderfer
John Allen
Ann Al-Yasiri
Charles Anderson
Leslie J. Anderson
Fatma W. Antar
Mohammad Ashraf
Aliakbar Ataiifar
Leonard Atencio
John M. Atkins
Glen W. Atkinson
Thomas R. Atkinson
James Q. Aylesworth
John Baffoe-Bonnie
Kevin Baird
Charley Ballard
Maurice B. Ballabon
G. Jeffrey Barbour
Daniel Barszcz
Robin L. Bartlett
Kari Battaglia
Robert Becker
Charles Beem
Glen Beeson
Bruce W. Bellner
Daniel K. Benjamin
Charles Berry
Abraham Bertisch
John Bethune
R.A. Blewett
Scott Bloom

M. L. Bodnar
Mary Bone
Karl Bonnhi
Thomas W. Bonsor
John M. Booth
Wesley F. Booth
Thomas Borcherding
Melvin Borland
Tom Boston
Barry Boyer
Maryanna Boynton
Ronald Brandolini
Fenton L. Broadhead
Elba Brown
William Brown
Michael Bull
Maureen Burton
Conrad P. Caligaris
Kevin Carey
James Carlson
Robert Carlsson
Dancy R. Carr
Scott Carson
Doris Cash
Thomas H. Cate
Richard J. Cebula
Catherine Chanbers
K. Merry Chambers
Richard Chapman
Ronald Cherry
Young Back Choi
Marc Chopin
Carol Cies
Joy L. Clark
Curtis Clarke
Gary Clayton
Marsha Clayton
Dale O. Cloninger
Warren L. Coats

Ed Coen
Pat Conroy
James Cox
Stephen R. Cox
Eleanor D. Craig
Peggy Crane
Jerry Crawford
Joanna Cruse
John P. Cullity
Will Cummings
Thomas Curtis
Margaret M. Dalton
Andrew J. Dane
Mahmoud Davoudi
Diana Denison
Edward Dennis
Carol Dimamro
William Dougherty
Barry Duman
Diane Dumont
Floyd Durham
G. B. Duwaji
James A. Dyal
Ishita Edwards
Robert P. Edwards
Alan E. Ellis
Mike Ellis
Steffany Ellis
Frank Emerson
Carl Enomoto
Zaki Eusufzai
Sandy Evans
John L. Ewing-Smith
Frank Falero
Frank Fato
Abdollah Ferdowsi
Grant Ferguson
David Fletcher
James Foley

John Foreman
Diana Fortier
Ralph G. Fowler
Arthur Friedberg
Peter Frost
Tom Fullerton
E. Gabriel
James Gale
Byron Gangnes
Steve Gardner
Peter C. Garlick
Neil Garston
Alexander Garvin
Joe Garwood
Doug Gehrke
J. P. Gilbert
Otis Gilley
Frank Glesber
Jack Goddard
Michael Goode
Allen C. Goodman
Richard J. Gosselin
Paul Graf
Edward Greenberg
Gary Greene
Nicholas Grunt
William Gunther
Kwabena Gyimah-Brempong
Demos Hadjiyanis
Martin D. Haney
Mehdi Haririan
Ray Harvey
E. L. Hazlett
Sanford B. Helman
William Henderson
John Hensel
Robert Herman
Gus W. Herring

Charles Hill
John M. Hill
Morton Hirsch
Benjamin Hitchner
Charles W. Hockert
R. Bradley Hoppes
James Horner
Grover Howard
Nancy Howe-Ford
Yu-Mong Hsiao
Yu Hsing
James Hubert
Joseph W. Hunt Jr.
Scott Hunt
John Ifediora
R. Jack Inch
Christopher Inya
Tomotaka Ishimine
E. E. Jarvis
Parvis Jenab
Allan Jenkins
Mark Jensen
S. D. Jevremovic
J. Paul Jewell
Frederick Johnson
David Jones
Lamar B. Jones
Paul A. Joray
Daniel A. Joseph
Craig Justice
M. James Kahiga
Septimus Kai Kai
Devajyoti Kataky
Timothy R. Keely
Ziad Keilany
Norman F. Keiser
Randall G. Kesselring
Alan Kessler
E. D. Key

Saleem Khan
M. Barbara Killen
Bruce Kimzey
Philip G. King
Terrence Kinal
E. R. Kittrell
David Klingman
Charles Knapp
Jerry Knarr
Faik Koray
Janet Koscianski
Marie Kratochvil
Peter Kressler
Michael Kupilik
Larry Landrum
Margaret Landman
Richard LaNear
Keith Langford
Anthony T. Lee
Loren Lee
Bozena Leven
Donald Lien
George Lieu
Stephen E. Lile
Lawrence W. Lovick
Marty Ludlum
G. Dirk Mateer
Robert McAuliffe
James C. McBrearty
Howard J. McBride
Bruce McClung
John McDowell
E. S. McKuskey
James J. McLain
John L. Madden
Mary Lou Madden
Glen Marston
John M. Martin
Paul J. Mascotti

James D. Mason	Claron Nelson	Robert Posatko	William Schaniel	Diane L. Stehman	Craig Walker
Paul M. Mason	Douglas Nettleton	Reneé Prim	David Schauer	Columbus Stephens	Robert F. Wallace
Tom Mathew	Gerald T. O'Boyle	Robert W. Pulsinelli	A. C. Schlenker	William Stine	Henry C. Wallich
Warren Matthews	Gregory Okoro	Rod D. Raehsler	David Schlow	Allen D. Stone	Milledge Weathers
Warren T. Matthews	Richard E. O'Neill	Kambriz Raffiee	Scott J. Schroeder	Osman Suliman	Robert G. Welch
Akbar Marvasti	Lucian T. Orlowski	Sandra Rahman	William Scott	J. M. Sullivan	Terence West
G. Hartley Mellish	Diane S. Osborne	Jaishankar Raman	Dan Segebarth	Rebecca Summary	Wylie Whalthall
Mike Melvin	Melissa A. Osborne	John Rapp	Paul Seidenstat	Joseph L. Swaffar	James H. Wheeler
Diego Mendez-Carbajo	James O'Toole	Richard Rawlins	Swapan Sen	Thomas Swanke	Everett E. White
Dan C. Messerschmidt	Jan Palmer	Gautam Raychaudhuri	Augustus Shackelford	Frank D. Taylor	Michael D. White
Michael Metzger	Zuohong Pan	Ron Reddall	Richard Sherman Jr.	Daniel Teferra	Mark A. Wilkening
Herbert C. Milikien	Gerald Parker	Mitchell Redlo	Liang-rong Shiau	Lea Templer	Raburn M. Williams
Joel C. Millonzi	Ginger Parker	Charles Reichhelu	David Shorow	Gary Theige	James Willis
Glenn Milner	Randall E. Parker	Robert S. Rippey	Vishwa Shukla	Dave Thiessen	George Wilson
Daniel Mizak	Kenneth Parzych	Charles Roberts	R. J. Sidwell	Robert P. Thomas	Travis Wilson
Khan Mohabbat	Norm Paul	Ray C. Roberts	David E. Sisk	Deborah Thorsen	Mark Wohar
Thomas Molloy	Wesley Payne	Richard Romano	Alden Smith	Richard Trieff	Ken Woodward
Margaret D. Moore	Raymond A. Pepin	Judy Roobian-Mohr	Garvin Smith	George Troxler	Tim Wulf
William E. Morgan	Martin M. Perline	Duane Rosa	Howard F. Smith	William T. Trulove	Peter R. Wyman
Stephen Morrell	Timothy Perri	Richard Rosenberg	Lynn A. Smith	William N. Trumbull	Whitney Yamamura
Irving Morrissett	Jerry Petr	Larry Ross	Phil Smith	Arianne K. Turner	Donald Yankovic
James W. Moser	Bruce Pietrykowski	Barbara Ross-Pfeiffer	Steve Smith	Kay Unger	Alex Yguado
Thaddeaus Mounkurai	Maurice Pfannesteil	Philip Rothman	William Doyle Smith	Anthony Uremovic	Paul Young
Martin F. Murray	James Phillips	John Roufagalas	Lee Spector	John Vahaly	Shik Young
Densel L. Myers	Raymond J. Phillips	Stephen Rubb	George Spiva	Jim Van Beek	Mohammed Zaheer
George L. Nagy	I. James Pickl	Henry Ryder	Richard L. Sprinkle	David VanHoose	Ed Zajicek
Solomon Namala	Dennis Placone	Patricia Sanderson	Alan Stafford	Lee J. Van Scyoc	Paul Zarembka
Jerome Neadly	Mannie Poen	Thomas N. Schaap	Herbert F. Steeper	Roy Van Til	William J. Zimmer Jr.
James E. Needham	William L. Polvent	William A. Schaeffer			

When I undertake a major revision of *Economics Today*, I start the process almost immediately after I've published the previous edition. So, what you are about to read has its roots in editorial meetings that started almost three years ago.

I am fortunate to have an incredibly imaginative and knowledgeable editorial team at Addison Wesley, with which I have worked during these last several years. They include Adrienne D'Ambrosio, Rebecca Ferris-Caruso, Roxanne Hoch, Julie Z. Lindstrom, Julia Boyles, and Denise Clinton. Of course, they have accused me of monopolizing their time. In any event, I thank them for all of the meetings, phone calls, e-mails, and faxes that, if properly recorded, would fill up more pages than the resulting text.

On the design and production side, I feel fortunate to have worked with John Orr of Orr Book Services. I thank his staff and him for their creative and professional services as well as Kathryn Dinovo, my production supervisor at Addison Wesley, and Lisa Buckley, my talented designer. I also very much appreciate the efforts of Marianne Groth and Heather McNally in coordinating the production process of the many print supplements.

I had more than my deserved amount of constant comments and criticisms from my colleagues David VanHoose and Dan Benjamin. I hope they will accept this sentence of appreciation in the manner in which it is offered—with utmost sincerity.

I have been blessed with a powerhouse of talented colleagues who have created or revised the extensive supplements package. So, thank you David VanHoose of Baylor University for the Study Guides; Andrew J. Dane of Angelo State University for the *Instructor's Manual*; Bruce W. Bellner of the Ohio State University for the PowerPoint® slides; Mitchell Fisher of the College of DuPage for Test Bank 1; M. James Kahiga and Gregory Okoro of Georgia Perimeter College for Test Bank 2; and Theresa Laughlin of Palomar College for Test Bank 3.

I also must extend my gratitude to the multimedia developers who created and refined all of the online services for this edition of *Economics Today*. At Addison Wesley, Melissa Honig and Michelle Neil deftly coordinated the efforts of the content and multimedia developers. I am especially appreciative of the efforts of Doug Ruby, who heads the MyEconLab content development team.

Finally, Sue Jasin probably could teach a course in economics after typing, retyping, and even retyping again various drafts of this revision. Thank you, Sue, for everything, including the many weekends you worked on this project.

I welcome comments and ideas from professors and students. After all, by the time you read this, I will already be working on the next edition.

R. L. M.

The Nature of Economics

1

Biologists have found that rhesus monkeys are willing to forgo 10 percent of their "income" of cherry juice to examine photos of leading and attractive members of their group. This behavior, the biologists suggest, mirrors the willingness of human beings to pay for magazines displaying photos of a Donald Trump wedding extravaganza or of Paris Hilton's latest fashion statement. Nevertheless, some *economists*, who study the process of making choices in response to rewards or inducements, propose that human beings may also be willing to pay to be *viewed by others* as leading, attractive members of society. What can economists tell us about why people purchase items that attract attention, such as flashy sports cars or designer clothing? This chapter will prepare you to contemplate this question.

Learning Objectives

After reading this chapter, you should be able to:

1. Discuss the difference between microeconomics and macroeconomics
2. Evaluate the role that rational self-interest plays in economic analysis
3. Explain why economics is a science
4. Distinguish between positive and normative economics

MyEconLab helps you master each objective and study more efficiently. See end of chapter for details.

Did You Know That...

six of the seven main U.S. railroad lines meet in Chicago and that about 1,200 trains accounting for one-third of all U.S. railroad traffic transit the city each day? Multiple trains seeking to use the same tracks through town commonly create bottlenecks. Consequently, a freight train passing through Chicago often requires several days just to get across town. These delays impose costs on rail transport customers, who must wait longer to obtain items carried on or in freight cars. The delays also inconvenience railroad companies, which incur higher labor and other costs per mile of freight transported. Railroad firms have responded in two ways. In an effort to separate freight and passenger traffic and thereby prevent passenger trains from slowing down freight trains, the companies have laid more track within the city of Chicago. Several firms have also constructed more rail beds outside Chicago, so that more trains can bypass the city entirely.

In this chapter, you will learn why studying the nature of self-interested responses to **incentives** is the starting point for analyzing choices people make in all walks of life. After all, just as rail firms have responded to the cost incentives they face in Chicago by laying more track, how much time you devote to studying economics depends in part on the incentives established by your instructor's grading system. As you will see, self-interest and incentives are the underpinnings for all the decisions you and others around you make each day.

Incentives
Rewards for engaging in a particular activity.

THE POWER OF ECONOMIC ANALYSIS

Simply knowing that self-interest and incentives are central to any decision-making process is not sufficient for predicting the choices that people will actually make. You also have to develop a framework that will allow you to analyze solutions to each economic problem—whether you are trying to decide how much to study, which courses to take, whether to finish school, or whether the U.S. government should send troops abroad or raise taxes. The framework that you will learn in this text is the *economic way of thinking*.

This framework gives you power—the power to reach informed conclusions about what is happening in the world. You can, of course, live your life without the power of economic analysis as part of your analytical framework. Indeed, most people do. But economists believe that economic analysis can help you make better decisions concerning your career, your education, financing your home, and other important matters. In the business world, the power of economic analysis can help you increase your competitive edge as an employee or as the owner of a business. As a voter, for the rest of your life you will be asked to make judgments about policies that are advocated by political parties. Many of these policies will deal with questions related to international economics, such as whether the U.S. government should encourage or discourage immigration, prevent foreign residents and firms from investing in domestic oil companies or aerospace firms, or restrict other countries from selling their goods here.

Finally, just as taking an art, music, or literature appreciation class increases the pleasure you receive when you view paintings, listen to concerts, or read novels, taking an economics course will increase your understanding when watching the news on TV or reading articles in the newspaper or at Web sites.

DEFINING ECONOMICS

Economics
The study of how people allocate their limited resources to satisfy their unlimited wants.

Economics is part of the social sciences and as such seeks explanations of real events. All social sciences analyze human behavior, as opposed to the physical sciences, which generally analyze the behavior of electrons, atoms, and other nonhuman phenomena.

Economics is the study of how people allocate their limited resources in an attempt to satisfy their unlimited wants. As such, economics is the study of how people make choices.

To understand this definition fully, two other words need explaining: *resources* and *wants*. **Resources** are things that have value and, more specifically, are used to produce things that satisfy people's wants. **Wants** are all of the items that people would purchase if they had unlimited income.

Whenever an individual, a business, or a nation faces alternatives, a choice must be made, and economics helps us study how those choices are made. For example, you have to choose how to spend your limited income. You also have to choose how to spend your limited time. You may have to choose how much of your company's limited funds to spend on advertising and how much to spend on new-product research. In economics, we examine situations in which individuals choose how to do things, when to do things, and with whom to do them. Ultimately, the purpose of economics is to explain choices.

Resources
Things used to produce other things to satisfy people's wants.

Wants
What people would buy if their incomes were unlimited.

MICROECONOMICS VERSUS MACROECONOMICS

Economics is typically divided into two types of analysis: **microeconomics** and **macroeconomics.**

Microeconomics is the part of economic analysis that studies decision making undertaken by individuals (or households) and by firms. It is like looking through a microscope to focus on the small parts of our economy.

Macroeconomics is the part of economic analysis that studies the behavior of the economy as a whole. It deals with economywide phenomena such as changes in unemployment, in the general price level, and in national income.

Microeconomic analysis, for example, is concerned with the effects of changes in the price of gasoline relative to that of other energy sources. It examines the effects of new taxes on a specific product or industry. If price controls were reinstituted in the United States, how individual firms and consumers would react to them would be in the realm of microeconomics. The effects of higher wages brought about by an effective union strike would also be analyzed using the tools of microeconomics.

In contrast, issues such as the rate of inflation, the amount of economywide unemployment, and the yearly growth in the output of goods and services in the nation all fall into the realm of macroeconomic analysis. In other words, macroeconomics deals with **aggregates,** or totals—such as total output in an economy.

Be aware, however, of the blending of microeconomics and macroeconomics in modern economic theory. Modern economists are increasingly using microeconomic analysis—the study of decision making by individuals and by firms—as the basis of macroeconomic analysis. They do this because even though macroeconomic analysis focuses on aggregates, those aggregates are the result of choices made by individuals and firms.

Microeconomics
The study of decision making undertaken by individuals (or households) and by firms.

Macroeconomics
The study of the behavior of the economy as a whole, including such economywide phenomena as changes in unemployment, the general price level, and national income.

Aggregates
Total amounts or quantities; aggregate demand, for example, is total planned expenditures throughout a nation.

THE ECONOMIC PERSON: RATIONAL SELF-INTEREST

Economists assume that individuals act *as if* motivated by self-interest and respond predictably to opportunities for gain. This central insight of economics was first clearly articulated by Adam Smith in 1776. Smith wrote in his most famous book, *An Inquiry into the*

Go to www.econtoday.com/ch01 to access the eCommerce Info Center and explore whether it is in a consumer's self-interest to shop on the Internet. Click on "To e-shoppers," and then click on "Consumer Info."

Nature and Causes of the Wealth of Nations, that "it is not from the benevolence of the butcher, the brewer, or the baker that we expect our dinner, but from their regard to their own interest." Thus, the typical person about whom economists make behavioral predictions is assumed to act as though motivated by self-interest. Because monetary benefits and costs of actions are often the most easily measured, economists make behavioral predictions about individuals' responses to opportunities to increase their wealth, measured in money terms.

Is it possible to apply the theory of rational self-interest to explain why dozens of U.S. health plans now pay bonuses to physicians who meet specific health care goals?

EXAMPLE

"Pay for Performance" Bonuses Give Health Care a Booster Shot

When large employers such as General Electric and Ford have studied factors contributing to higher costs for employee health plans, they consistently find that one stands out: physicians' failures to provide care as efficiently as possible. To encourage physicians to provide lower-cost care, dozens of health plans now offer cash bonuses to physicians who push preventive care, implement systems to track patients' health, and ensure that patients pursue recommended treatments. Physicians who meet goals for improved efficiency receive annual bonuses as high as $25,000. Thus, it is now in the self-interest of tens of thousands of U.S. physicians to attain health plans' objectives for more efficient provision of medical care.

FOR CRITICAL ANALYSIS
Why might it be in the self-interest of some physicians to turn down the opportunity to earn bonuses from health plans? (Hint: Promoting preventive care and tracking patients can be costly endeavors.)

The Rationality Assumption

Rationality assumption
The assumption that people do not intentionally make decisions that would leave them worse off.

The **rationality assumption** of economics, simply stated, is as follows:

> *We assume that individuals do not intentionally make decisions that would leave them worse off.*

The distinction here is between what people may think—the realm of psychology and psychiatry and perhaps sociology—and what they do. Economics does *not* involve itself in analyzing individual or group thought processes. Economics looks at what people actually do in life with their limited resources. It does little good to criticize the rationality assumption by stating, "Nobody thinks that way" or "I never think that way" or "How unrealistic! That's as irrational as anyone can get!"

Take the example of driving. When you consider passing another car on a two-lane highway with oncoming traffic, you have to make very quick decisions: You must estimate the speed of the car that you are going to pass, the speed of the oncoming cars, the distance between your car and the oncoming cars, and your car's potential rate of acceleration. If we were to apply a model to your behavior, we would use the rules of calculus. In actual fact, you and most other drivers in such a situation do not actually think of using the rules of calculus, but to predict your behavior, we could make the prediction *as if* you understood those rules.

How might magnetic resonance imaging (MRI) scans help in evaluating the rationality assumption of economics?

EXAMPLE

"Neuroeconomics" Explores the Rationality Assumption

In recent years, some economists have developed a field of study known as *neuroeconomics*. Typically, these economists work with medical researchers to conduct brain scans of people as they make economic decisions. The aim is to determine which part of the brain plays the greater role in determining an individual's choices: the *limbic system*, a brain region that governs emotions, or the *prefrontal cortex*, a portion of the brain associated with reason and calculation.

A typical individual's brain reacts to the prospect of short-term gains or losses mainly in the limbic system, implying that purely immediate rewards trigger emotional responses. The prospect of longer-lasting gains or losses induces more brain activity in the prefrontal cortex, meaning that the possibility of future gains or losses sets off a reasoned, calculating response. Most economic decision making entails balancing immediate and longer-term gains or losses. In such cases, brain scans reveal considerable coordination between the limbic system and the prefrontal cortex. Thus, there is evidence that the human brain naturally attempts to factor in reasoned calculations aimed at making a choice consistent with the "best" overall outcome. This conclusion, of course, supports the rationality assumption.

FOR CRITICAL ANALYSIS
Why might a person rationally pass up a choice that would yield a significant immediate gain in favor of a choice that would yield a series of smaller future gains?

Responding to Incentives

If it can be assumed that individuals never intentionally make decisions that would leave them worse off, then almost by definition they will respond to changes in incentives. Indeed, much of human behavior can be explained in terms of how individuals respond to changing incentives over time.

Schoolchildren are motivated to do better by a variety of incentive systems, ranging from gold stars and certificates of achievement when they are young, to better grades with accompanying promises of a "better life" as they get older. Of course, negative incentives affect our behavior, too. Penalties, punishments, and other forms of negative incentives can raise the cost of engaging in various activities. Why do you suppose that a decline in the time it takes for checks to clear created a negative incentive to use checks and a positive incentive to use credit cards?

> **ECONOMICS FRONT AND CENTER**
>
> To see why incentives are important in dealing with the problem of unwanted commercial e-mails commonly known as *spam*, contemplate **Time to Fight Spam with E-Mail Postage Charges?** on page 11.

E-COMMERCE EXAMPLE

Playing the Float with Plastic Instead of Checks

In years past, a person could rest assured that she could safely write a check even if there were insufficient funds in her bank account. The check, after all, would take several days to clear. The period between when the check was written and when it cleared—commonly called check *float*—provided time to deposit sufficient funds to avoid overdraft penalties. Even today, about one in five U.S. residents admits to having raced to make a deposit to avoid an overdraft at least once during the preceding year.

Technological developments in banking are rapidly reducing check float, however. Increasingly, rather than transporting physical checks to be cleared, banks scan checks and transmit digital images instead. As a result, checks that once took four to six days to clear are now being cleared within a couple of days.

The drop in check float has given many people a greater incentive to buy items with credit cards, which allow people to

(*continued*)

postpone payment, just as they previously could by writing a check. Credit-card issuers report that the majority of people who have increased their use of credit cards in recent years have done so in response to the decline in check float.

FOR CRITICAL ANALYSIS
How might relatively high interest rates charged on credit-card balances not paid by the monthly payment due date influence the incentive to use credit cards?

Defining Self-Interest

Self-interest does not always mean increasing one's wealth measured in dollars and cents. We assume that individuals seek many goals, not just increased wealth measured in monetary terms. Thus, the self-interest part of our economic-person assumption includes goals relating to prestige, friendship, love, power, helping others, creating works of art, and many other matters. We can also think in terms of enlightened self-interest, whereby individuals, in the pursuit of what makes them better off, also achieve the betterment of others around them. In brief, individuals are assumed to want the right to further their goals by making decisions about how things around them are used. The head of a charitable organization will usually not turn down an additional contribution, because accepting it yields control over how those funds are used, even if it is for other people's benefit.

Thus, self-interest does not rule out doing charitable acts. Giving gifts to relatives can be considered a form of charity that is nonetheless in the self-interest of the giver. But how efficient is such gift giving?

EXAMPLE

The Perceived Value of Gifts

Every holiday season, aunts, uncles, grandparents, mothers, and fathers give gifts to their college-aged loved ones. Joel Waldfogel, an economist at Yale University, surveyed several thousand college students after Christmas to find out the value of holiday gifts. He found that compact discs and outerwear (coats and jackets) had a perceived intrinsic value about equal to their actual cash equivalent. By the time he got down the list to socks, underwear, and cosmetics, the students' valuation was only about 85 percent of the cash value of the gift. He found out that aunts, uncles, and grandparents gave the "worst" gifts and friends, siblings, and parents gave the "best."

FOR CRITICAL ANALYSIS
What argument could you use against the idea of substituting cash or gift cards for physical gifts?

QUICK QUIZ

Economics is a social science that involves the study of how individuals choose among alternatives to satisfy their _____, which are what people would buy if their incomes were _____.

_____, the study of the decision-making processes of individuals (or households) and firms, and _____, the study of the performance of the economy as a whole, are the two main branches into which the study of economics is divided.

In economics, we assume that people do not intentionally make decisions that will leave them worse off. This is known as the _____ assumption.

_____ is not confined to material well-being but also involves any action that makes a person feel better off, such as having more friends, love, power, affection, or providing more help to others.

See page 16 for the answers. Review concepts from this section in MyEconLab.

ECONOMICS AS A SCIENCE

Economics is a social science that employs the same kinds of methods used in other sciences, such as biology, physics, and chemistry. Like these other sciences, economics uses models, or theories. Economic **models, or theories,** are simplified representations of the real world that we use to help us understand, explain, and predict economic phenomena in the real world. There are, of course, differences between sciences. The social sciences—especially economics—make little use of laboratory experiments in which changes in variables are studied under controlled conditions. Rather, social scientists, and especially economists, usually have to test their models, or theories, by examining what has already happened in the real world.

Models, or theories
Simplified representations of the real world used as the basis for predictions or explanations.

Models and Realism

At the outset it must be emphasized that no model in *any* science, and therefore no economic model, is complete in the sense that it captures *every* detail or interrelationship that exists. Indeed, a model, by definition, is an abstraction from reality. It is conceptually impossible to construct a perfectly complete realistic model. For example, in physics we cannot account for every molecule and its position and certainly not for every atom and subparticle. Not only is such a model impossibly expensive to build, but working with it would be impossibly complex.

The nature of scientific model building is that the model should capture only the *essential* relationships that are sufficient to analyze the particular problem or answer the particular question with which we are concerned. *An economic model cannot be faulted as unrealistic simply because it does not represent every detail of the real world.* A map of a city that shows only major streets is not faulty if, in fact, all you need to know is how to pass through the city using major streets. As long as a model is able to shed light on the *central* issue at hand or forces at work, it may be useful.

A map is the quintessential model. It is always a simplified representation. It is always unrealistic. But it is also useful in making predictions about the world. If the model—the map—predicts that when you take Campus Avenue to the north, you always run into the campus, that is a prediction. If a simple model can explain observed behavior in repeated settings just as well as a complex one, the simple model has some value and is probably easier to use.

Assumptions

Every model, or theory, must be based on a set of assumptions. Assumptions define the array of circumstances in which our model is most likely to be applicable. When scientists predicted that sailing ships would fall off the edge of the earth, they used the *assumption* that the earth was flat. Columbus did not accept the implications of such a model because he did not accept its assumptions. He assumed that the world was round. The real-world test of his own model refuted the flat-earth model. Indirectly, then, it was a test of the assumption of the flat-earth model.

Is it possible to use our knowledge about assumptions to understand why driving directions sometimes contain very few details?

 EXAMPLE

Getting Directions

Assumptions are a shorthand for reality. Imagine that you have decided to drive from your home in San Diego to downtown San Francisco. Because you have never driven this route, you decide to get directions from the local office of the American Automobile Association (AAA).

(continued)

When you ask for directions, the travel planner could give you a set of detailed maps that shows each city through which you will travel—Oceanside, San Clemente, Irvine, Anaheim, Los Angeles, Bakersfield, Modesto, and so on—and then, opening each map, show you exactly how the freeway threads through each of these cities. You would get a nearly complete description of reality because the AAA travel planner will not have used many simplifying assumptions. It is more likely, however, that the travel planner will simply say, "Get on Interstate 5 going north. Stay on it for about 500 miles. Follow the signs for San Francisco. After crossing the toll bridge, take any exit marked 'Downtown.'" By omitting all of the trivial details, the travel planner has told you all that you really need and want to know. The models you will be using in this text are similar to the simplified directions on how to drive from San Diego to San Francisco—they focus on what is relevant to the problem at hand and omit what is not.

FOR CRITICAL ANALYSIS
In what way do small talk and gossip represent the use of simplifying assumptions?

Ceteris paribus [KAY-ter-us PEAR-uh-bus] **assumption**
The assumption that nothing changes except the factor or factors being studied.

The *Ceteris Paribus* Assumption: All Other Things Being Equal. Everything in the world seems to relate in some way to everything else in the world. It would be impossible to isolate the effects of changes in one variable on another variable if we always had to worry about the many other variables that might also enter the analysis. Like other sciences, economics uses the **ceteris paribus assumption.** *Ceteris paribus* means "other things constant" or "other things equal."

Consider an example taken from economics. One of the most important determinants of how much of a particular product a family buys is how expensive that product is relative to other products. We know that in addition to relative prices, other factors influence decisions about making purchases. Some of them have to do with income, others with tastes, and yet others with custom and religious beliefs. Whatever these other factors are, we hold them constant when we look at the relationship between changes in prices and changes in how much of a given product people will purchase.

Deciding on the Usefulness of a Model

We generally do not attempt to determine the usefulness, or "goodness," of a model merely by evaluating how realistic its assumptions are. Rather, we consider a model "good" if it yields usable predictions and implications for the real world. In other words, can we use the model to predict what will happen in the world around us? Does the model provide useful implications about how things happen in our world?

Once we have determined that the model does predict real-world phenomena, the scientific approach to the analysis of the world around us requires that we consider evidence. Evidence is used to test the usefulness of a model. This is why we call economics an **empirical** science. *Empirical* means that evidence (data) is looked at to see whether we are right. Economists are often engaged in empirically testing their models.

Empirical
Relying on real-world data in evaluating the usefulness of a model.

Models of Behavior, Not Thought Processes

Take special note of the fact that economists' models do not relate to the way people *think;* they relate to the way people *act,* to what they do in life with their limited resources. Normally, the economist does not attempt to predict how people will think about a particular topic, such as a higher price of oil products, accelerated inflation, or higher taxes. Rather, the task at hand is to predict how people will behave, which may be quite different from what they *say* they will do (much to the consternation of poll takers and market researchers). The people involved in examining thought processes are psychologists and psychiatrists, not typically economists.

When you ask people what they thought and how they behaved in a certain situation, they may have trouble remembering or may not reveal all the details. How do you think auto insurers are adjusting to the fact that people have imperfect recollections and, in some instances, do not reveal their true actions?

EXAMPLE

Insurers That Know Exactly How You Drive

Traditionally, insurance companies have relied on data from police reports to determine causes of accidents. Those reports, however, depend on recollections of drivers and witnesses and on postaccident investigations by public safety officers. To get more reliable information about exactly what motorists did before and during an accident, insurers have begun offering policies that require policyholders to have global-positioning-system (GPS) receivers in their automobiles. The receivers transmit information to the insurers, via satellites, regarding a driver's speed, acceleration, and braking. In the event of an accident, this information can supplement police reports. In some instances, the data show that a policyholder was not at fault, thereby protecting both the policyholder and the insurer from risks of loss.

Some insurance companies also use information from GPS receivers in deciding what premiums to charge their customers. An insurer that discovers a customer is driving more miles each week than he claimed when he applied for his insurance policy will adjust the customer's premium rate upward to reflect the higher risk of loss. Thus, the insurer is basing its premiums on how the policyholder *actually* behaves instead of how he *says* he behaves.

FOR CRITICAL ANALYSIS
Why might an insurance customer have an incentive to say that he drives fewer miles per week than he actually drives? (Hint: Insurers typically charge lower premiums to people who indicate that they drive their cars a limited number of miles each week or for "pleasure" only.)

Behavioral Economics and Bounded Rationality

In recent years, some economists have proposed paying more attention to psychologists and psychiatrists. They have suggested an alternative approach to economic analysis. Their approach, which is known as **behavioral economics,** examines consumer behavior in the face of psychological limitations and complications that may interfere with rational decision making.

Bounded Rationality. Proponents of behavioral economics suggest that traditional economic models assume that people exhibit three "unrealistic" characteristics:

1. *Unbounded selfishness.* People are interested only in their own satisfaction.
2. *Unbounded willpower.* Their choices are always consistent with their long-term goals.
3. *Unbounded rationality.* They are able to consider every relevant choice.

Instead, advocates of behavioral economics have proposed replacing the rationality assumption with the assumption of **bounded rationality,** which assumes that people cannot examine and think through every possible choice they confront. As a consequence, behavioral economists suggest, people cannot always pursue their long-term personal interests. From time to time, they must also rely on other people and take into account other people's interests as well as their own.

Behavioral economics
An approach to the study of consumer behavior that emphasizes psychological limitations and complications that potentially interfere with rational decision making.

Bounded rationality
The hypothesis that people are *nearly*, but not fully, rational, so that they cannot examine every possible choice available to them but instead use simple rules of thumb to sort among the alternatives that happen to occur to them.

Rules of Thumb. A key behavioral implication of the bounded rationality assumption is that people should use so-called *rules of thumb:* Because every possible choice cannot be considered, an individual will tend to fall back on methods of making decisions that are simpler than trying to sort through every possibility.

A problem confronting advocates of behavioral economics is that people who *appear* to use rules of thumb may in fact behave *as if* they are fully rational. For instance, if a person faces persistently predictable ranges of choices for a time, the individual may rationally settle into repetitive behaviors that an outside observer might conclude to be consistent with a rule of thumb. The bounded rationality assumption indicates that the person should continue to rely on a rule of thumb even if there is a major change in the environment that the individual faces. Time and time again, however, economists find that people respond to altered circumstances by fundamentally changing their behaviors. Economists also generally observe that people make decisions that are consistent with their own self-interest and long-term objectives.

Behavioral Economics: A Work in Progress. It remains to be seen whether the application of the assumption of bounded rationality proposed by behavioral economists will truly alter the manner in which economists construct models intended to better predict human decision making. So far, proponents of behavioral economics have not conclusively demonstrated that paying closer attention to psychological thought processes can improve economic predictions.

As a consequence, the bulk of economic analysis continues to rely on the rationality assumption as the basis for constructing economic models. As you will learn in Chapters 18 and 20, advocates of behavioral economics continue to explore ways in which psychological elements might improve analysis of both macroeconomic and microeconomic phenomena.

POSITIVE VERSUS NORMATIVE ECONOMICS

Economics uses *positive analysis,* a value-free approach to inquiry. No subjective or moral judgments enter into the analysis. Positive analysis relates to statements such as "If A, then B." For example, "If the price of gasoline goes up relative to all other prices, then the amount of it that people will buy will fall." That is a positive economic statement. It is a statement of *what is.* It is not a statement of anyone's value judgment or subjective feelings.

Distinguishing Between Positive and Normative Economics

For many problems analyzed in the hard sciences such as physics and chemistry, the analyses are considered to be virtually value-free. After all, how can someone's values enter into a theory of molecular behavior? But economists face a different problem. They deal with the behavior of individuals, not molecules. That makes it more difficult to stick to what we consider to be value-free or **positive economics** without reference to our feelings.

When our values are interjected into the analysis, we enter the realm of **normative economics,** involving *normative analysis.* A positive economic statement is "If the price of gas rises, people will buy less." If we add to that analysis the statement "so we should not allow the price to go up," we have entered the realm of normative economics—we have expressed a value judgment. In fact, any time you see the word *should,* you will know that values are entering into the discussion. Just remember that positive statements are concerned with *what is,* whereas normative statements are concerned with *what ought to be.*

Each of us has a desire for different things. That means that we have different values. When we express a value judgment, we are simply saying what we prefer, like, or desire. Because individual values are diverse, we expect—and indeed observe—people expressing widely varying value judgments about how the world ought to be.

Positive economics
Analysis that is *strictly* limited to making either purely descriptive statements or scientific predictions; for example, "If A, then B." A statement of *what is.*

Normative economics
Analysis involving value judgments about economic policies; relates to whether things are good or bad. A statement of *what ought to be.*

A Warning: Recognize Normative Analysis

It is easy to define positive economics. It is quite another matter to catch all unlabeled normative statements in a textbook, even though an author goes over the manuscript many times before it is printed. Therefore, do not get the impression that a textbook author will be able to keep all personal values out of the book. They will slip through. In fact, the very choice of which topics to include in an introductory textbook involves normative economics. There is no value-free way to decide which topics to use in a textbook. The author's values ultimately make a difference when choices have to be made. But from your own standpoint, you might want to be able to recognize when you are engaging in normative as opposed to positive economic analysis. Reading this text will help equip you for that task.

QUICK QUIZ

A _____, or _____, uses assumptions and is by nature a simplification of the real world. The usefulness of a _____ can be evaluated by bringing empirical evidence to bear on its predictions.

Most models use the _____ _____ assumption that all other things are held constant, or equal.

_____ economics emphasizes psychological constraints and complexities that potentially interfere with rational decision making. This approach utilizes the _____ _____ hypothesis that people are not quite rational, because they cannot study every possible alternative but instead use simple rules of thumb to decide among choices.

_____ economics is value-free and relates to statements that can be refuted, such as "If A, then B."

_____ economics involves people's values and typically uses the word *should*.

See page 16 for the answers. Review concepts from this section in MyEconLab.

CASE STUDY
ECONOMICS FRONT AND CENTER

Time to Fight Spam with E-Mail Postage Charges?

Chang is employed by an Internet retailer, PurchaseOnTheWeb (POTW). POTW is facing problems created by *spam*, or unwanted e-mail messages that now account for more than 60 percent of e-mails. To limit spam, Internet service providers increasingly use spam-blocking systems. These systems have been blocking a significant portion of POTW's legitimate e-mail messages, such as order confirmations and answers to customer-service inquiries. The resulting breakdown in POTW's communications is alienating its customers. Using telephone and fax messages is driving up the company's costs.

Chang has been assigned to solve the company's communications problems. Initially, he is discouraged by what he learns about the economics of spam. Sending spam is a very low-cost activity, and spammers can profit if only one spam message out of a million generates sales. Recent anti-spam laws have simply given many spammers an incentive to move abroad, and spam-blocking technology is unlikely to improve dramatically any time soon.

Chang develops a proposal to use the services of an "e-mail postage" firm called Goodmail Systems. At a charge of 1 cent per e-mail message, Goodmail adds electronic "stamps" as encrypted headers to e-mail messages. Internet service providers do not automatically block such e-mails as spam. Goodmail shares revenues earned from its postage services with the Internet service providers, which in turn transmit the "stamped" e-mail messages directly to consumers' inboxes. Paying to e-mail all POTW customers, Chang has determined, would be less expensive than the costs it is incurring to communicate with them in other ways.

CRITICAL ANALYSIS QUESTIONS

1. *Why does "free" e-mail provide an incentive for spammers to transmit millions of unsolicited e-mail messages?*
2. *Why might the total volume of spam decline considerably if everyone using e-mail had to pay 1 cent to send every e-mail message?*

Issues and Applications

Do People Engage in Conspicuous Consumption?

Concepts Applied
- Empirical Science
- Behavior versus Thought Processes
- Rationality Assumption

In 1902, a book by the economist Thorstein Veblen, entitled *The Theory of the Leisure Class: An Economic Study of Institutions*, suggested that people engage in *conspicuous consumption*, or purchases aimed at signaling their status in society. More than a century later, economists continue to debate whether people really do engage in conspicuous consumption to enhance their social status and, if they do, why doing so might be rational behavior.

Alleged Conspicuous Consumption of "Visible" Products

Do people purchase items intended to signify a lofty status in society? To try to determine if there is empirical evidence supporting Veblen's idea, Ori Heffetz of Princeton University identified products that a large sample of people indicated cause individuals to stand out conspicuously in a crowd. These products included such items as relatively expensive automobiles, jewelry, and wristwatches. Thus, one motivation for buying such items, which Heffetz called *visible products*, may be to signal to others that the buyer has "made it" in society.

Heffetz then examined data on purchases of visible products by nearly 4,000 U.S. consumers. He found that among the higher-income half of this large set of consumers, a given proportionate increase in income generated a more-than-proportionate increase in spending on these products. This, he concluded, is evidence that higher-income people buy visible items, thereby conspicuously showing others that they have reached an elevated earnings threshold.

Higher Incomes Translate into More Purchases of Most Items

Is conspicuous consumption for real? Certainly, many entertainers and performers purchase fancy clothing, jewelry, and automobiles to increase the likelihood that they will be noticed by the general public. Consuming conspicuously can thereby contribute to their celebrity status and help them land their next "gig." For these individuals, conspicuous consumption is clearly rational.

But purchasing more units of most items, ranging from cheese to books to earrings, is also a rational response to earning a higher income. Consumer purchases of only a few items—such as powdered milk and packaged macaroni and cheese dinners—decrease when incomes rise. Thus, it is not surprising that when people's incomes increase, they begin buying more expensive items, such as fine wines and expensive steaks. Receiving higher incomes also induces people to buy automobiles with higher-performance engines, including sports cars, and jewelry and higher-quality wristwatches.

Empirical evidence indicating that some particularly visible items account for larger shares of consumers' budgets when their incomes increase does not necessarily reveal the *thought processes* that motivate consumers' choices. The evidence only indicates how people *behave* when their incomes rise. Indeed, as you learned in this chapter, economists are not very well qualified to try to analyze how people think. What economists *can* do is predict how much consumption of items is likely to respond to an increase in income. What economists *cannot* do is determine the thought processes driving consumers' choices.

Log in to MyEconLab, click on "Economic News," and test your understanding of the chapter by answering interactive questions that relate directly to this issue.

For Critical Analysis

1. Why might it be rational for certain entertainers to go out of their way to try to attract attention by wearing very expensive clothing and jewelry at public events yet try to look plain and ordinary while grocery shopping?
2. Why might an individual's purchases of certain items *decline* when his income increases?

Web Resources

1. To learn more about Ori Heffetz's research on conspicuous consumption, go to www.econtoday.com/ch01.
2. To learn about economist Edward Miller's study of conspicuous consumption of "status goods," go to www.econtoday.com/ch01.

Research Project

Economists suggest that understanding the *thought processes* that lead a person to purchase a particular item is less important than being able to identify observable factors that predict whether the person will actually *purchase* the item. Take the perspective of a businessperson trying to market a new product. In such a role, are you more likely to profit from knowing about a customer's thought processes or about observable factors that can help predict whether a customer will buy your product?

Here is what you should know after reading this chapter. MyEconLab will help you identify what you know, and where to go when you need to practice.

WHAT YOU SHOULD KNOW		WHERE TO GO TO PRACTICE
Microeconomics versus Macroeconomics In general, economics is the study of how individuals make choices to satisfy wants. Economics is usually divided into microeconomics, which is the study of decision making by individual households and individual firms, and macroeconomics, which is the study of nationwide phenomena, such as inflation and unemployment.	incentives, 2 economics, 2 resources, 3 wants, 3 microeconomics, 3 macroeconomics, 3 aggregates, 3	• **MyEconLab** Study Plans 1.1, 1.2, 1.3 • Audio introduction to Chapter 1 • Video: The Difference Between Microeconomics and Macroeconomics
Self-Interest in Economic Analysis Rational self-interest is the assumption that individuals never intentionally make decisions that would leave them worse off. Instead, they are motivated primarily by their self-interest, keeping in mind that self-interest can relate to monetary and nonmonetary objectives, such as love, prestige, and helping others.	rationality assumption, 4	• **MyEconLab** Study Plan 1.4 • Video: The Economic Person: Rational Self-Interest
Economics as a Science Like other scientists, economists use models, or theories, that are simplified representations of the real world to analyze and make predictions about the real world. Economic models are never completely realistic because by definition they are simplifications using assumptions that are not directly testable. Nevertheless, economists can subject the predictions of economic theories to empirical tests in which real-world data are used to decide whether or not to reject the predictions.	models, or theories, 7 *ceteris paribus* assumption, 8 empirical, 8 behavioral economics, 9 bounded rationality, 9	• **MyEconLab** Study Plan 1.5
Positive and Normative Economics Positive economics deals with *what is*, whereas normative economics deals with *what ought to be*. Positive economic statements are of the "if . . . then" variety; they are descriptive and predictive and are not related to what "should" happen. By contrast, whenever statements embodying values are made, we enter the realm of normative economics, or how individuals and groups think things ought to be.	positive economics, 10 normative economics, 10	• **MyEconLab** Study Plan 1.6 • Video: Difference Between Normative and Positive Economics

Log in to MyEconLab, take a chapter test, and get a personalized Study Plan that tells you which concepts you understand and which ones you need to review. From there, MyEconLab will give you further practice, tutorials, animations, videos, and guided solutions.
Log in to www.myeconlab.com

PROBLEMS

*Select problems, indicated by a blue oval, are assignable in **MyEconLab**.*
Answers to the odd-numbered problems appear at the back of the book.

1-1. Define economics. Explain briefly how the economic way of thinking—in terms of rational, self-interested people responding to incentives—relates to each of the following situations.
   a. A student deciding whether to purchase a textbook for a particular class
   b. Government officials seeking more funding for mass transit through higher taxes
   c. A municipality taxing hotel guests to obtain funding for a new sports stadium

1-2. Some people claim that the "economic way of thinking" does not apply to issues such as health care. Explain how economics does apply to this issue by developing a "model" of an individual's choice.

1-3. Does the phrase "unlimited wants and limited resources" apply to both a low-income household and a middle-income household? Can the same phrase be applied to a very high-income household?

1-4. In a single sentence, contrast microeconomics and macroeconomics. Next, categorize each of the following issues as either a microeconomic issue, a macroeconomic issue, or not an economic issue.
   a. The national unemployment rate
   b. The decision of a worker to work overtime or not
   c. A family's choice of having a baby
   d. The rate of growth of the money supply
   e. The national government's budget deficit
   f. A student's allocation of study time across two subjects

1-5. One of your classmates, Sally, is a hardworking student, serious about her classes, and conscientious about her grades. Sally is also involved, however, in volunteer activities and an extracurricular sport. Is Sally displaying rational behavior? Based on what you read in this chapter, construct an argument supporting the conclusion that she is.

1-6. Explain, in your own words, the rationality assumption, and contrast it with the assumption of bounded rationality proposed by adherents of behavioral economics.

1-7. Why does the assumption of bounded rationality suggest that people might use rules of thumb to guide their decision making instead of considering every possible choice available to them?

1-8. Under what circumstances might people appear to use rules of thumb, as suggested by the assumption of bounded rationality, even though they really were behaving in a manner suggested by the rationality assumption?

1-9. Which of the following predictions appears to follow from a model based on the assumption that rational, self-interested individuals respond to incentives?
   a. For every 10 exam points Myrna must earn in order to pass her economics course and meet her graduation requirements, she will study one additional hour for her economics test next week.
   b. A coin toss will best predict Leonardo's decision about whether to purchase an expensive business suit or an inexpensive casual outfit to wear next week when he interviews for a high-paying job he is seeking.
   c. Celeste, who uses earnings from her regularly scheduled hours of part-time work to pay for her room and board at college, will decide to buy a newly released DVD this week only if she is able to work two additional hours.

1-10. Consider two models for estimating, in advance of an election, the shares of votes that will go to rival candidates. According to one model, pollsters' surveys of a randomly chosen set of registered voters before an election can be used to forecast the percentage of votes that each candidate will receive. This first model relies on the assumption that unpaid survey respondents will give truthful responses about how they will vote and that they will actually cast a ballot in the election. The other model uses prices of financial assets (legally binding IOUs) issued by the Iowa Electronic Market, operated by the University of Iowa, to predict electoral outcomes. The final payments received by owners of these assets, which can be bought or sold during the weeks and days preceding an election, depend on the shares of votes the candidates actually end up receiving. This second model assumes that owners of these assets wish to earn the highest possible returns, and it indicates that the market prices of these assets provide an indication of the percentage of votes that

16 PART 1 Introduction

each candidate will actually receive on the day of the election.

a. Which of these two models for forecasting electoral results is more firmly based on the rationality assumption of economics?

b. How would an economist evaluate which is the better model for forecasting electoral outcomes?

1-11. Write a sentence contrasting positive and normative economic analysis.

1-12 Based on your answer to Problem 1-11, categorize each of the following conclusions as being the result of positive analysis or normative analysis.

a. A higher minimum wage will reduce employment opportunities for minimum wage workers.

b. Increasing the earnings of minimum wage employees is desirable, and raising the minimum wage is the best way to accomplish this.

c. Everyone should enjoy open access to health care.

d. Heath care subsidies will increase the consumption of health care.

1-13 Consider the following statements, based on a positive economic analysis that assumes that all other things remain constant. For each, list one other thing that might change and thus offset the outcome stated.

a. Increased demand for laptop computers will drive up their price.

b. Falling gasoline prices will result in additional vacation travel.

c. A reduction of income tax rates will result in more people working.

1-14. Alan Greenspan, chairman of the U.S. Federal Reserve between 1987 and 2006, once said the high stock market prices of the late 1990s were a result of "irrational exuberance." Counter this statement by considering the rationality of stock market investors.

ECONOMICS ON THE NET

The Usefulness of Studying Economics This application helps you see how accomplished people benefited from their study of economics. It also explores ways in which these people feel others of all walks of life can gain from learning more about the economics field.

Title: How Taking an Economics Course Can Lead to Becoming an Economist

Navigation: Go to www.econtoday.com/ch01 to visit the Federal Reserve Bank of Minneapolis publication, *The Region*. Select the last article of the issue, Economists in *The Region* on Their Student Experiences and the Need for Economic Literacy.

Application Read the interviews of the six economists, and answer the following questions.

1. Based on your reading, what economists do you think other economists regard as influential? What educational institutions do you think are the most influential in economics?

2. Which economists do you think were attracted to microeconomics and which to macroeconomics?

For Group Study and Analysis Divide the class into three groups, and assign the groups the Blinder, Yellen, and Rivlin interviews. Have each group use the content of its assigned interview to develop a statement explaining why the study of economics is important, regardless of a student's chosen major.

ANSWERS TO QUICK QUIZZES

p. 6: (i) wants . . . unlimited; (ii) Microeconomics . . . macroeconomics; (iii) rationality; (iv) Self-interest

p. 11: (i) model . . . theory . . . model; (ii) *ceteris paribus;* (iii) Behavioral . . . bounded rationality; (iv) Positive . . . Normative

Reading and Working with Graphs

Appendix A

A graph is a visual representation of the relationship between variables. In this appendix, we'll stick to just two variables: an **independent variable,** which can change in value freely, and a **dependent variable**, which changes only as a result of changes in the value of the independent variable. For example, if nothing else is changing in your life, your weight depends on your intake of calories. The independent variable is caloric intake and the dependent variable is weight.

A table is a list of numerical values showing the relationship between two (or more) variables. Any table can be converted into a graph, which is a visual representation of that list. Once you understand how a table can be converted to a graph, you will understand what graphs are and how to construct and use them.

Consider a practical example. A conservationist may try to convince you that driving at lower highway speeds will help you conserve gas. Table A-1 shows the relationship between speed—the independent variable—and the distance you can go on a gallon of gas at that speed—the dependent variable. This table does show a pattern. As the data in the first column get larger in value, the data in the second column get smaller.

Now let's take a look at the different ways in which variables can be related.

Independent variable
A variable whose value is determined independently of, or outside, the equation under study.

Dependent variable
A variable whose value changes according to changes in the value of one or more independent variables.

TABLE A-1
Gas Mileage as a Function of Driving Speed

Miles per Hour	Miles per Gallon
45	25
50	24
55	23
60	21
65	19
70	16
75	13

DIRECT AND INVERSE RELATIONSHIPS

Two variables can be related in different ways, some simple, others more complex. For example, a person's weight and height are often related. If we measured the height and weight of thousands of people, we would surely find that taller people tend to weigh more than shorter people. That is, we would discover that there is a **direct relationship** between height and weight. By this we simply mean that an *increase* in one variable is usually associated with an *increase* in the related variable. This can easily be seen in panel (a) of Figure A-1.

Direct relationship
A relationship between two variables that is positive, meaning that an increase in one variable is associated with an increase in the other and a decrease in one variable is associated with a decrease in the other.

FIGURE A-1
Direct and Indirect Relationships

Panel (a) Direct Relationship

Panel (b) Inverse Relationship

Inverse relationship
A relationship between two variables that is negative, meaning that an increase in one variable is associated with a decrease in the other and a decrease in one variable is associated with an increase in the other.

Let's look at another simple way in which two variables can be related. Much evidence indicates that as the price of a specific commodity rises, the amount purchased decreases—there is an **inverse relationship** between the variable's price per unit and quantity purchased. Such a relationship indicates that for higher and higher prices, smaller and smaller quantities will be purchased. We see this relationship in panel (b) of Figure A-1 on the previous page.

CONSTRUCTING A GRAPH

Let us now examine how to construct a graph to illustrate a relationship between two variables.

A Number Line

Number line
A line that can be divided into segments of equal length, each associated with a number.

The first step is to become familiar with what is called a **number line.** One is shown in Figure A-2. You should know two things about it:

1. The points on the line divide the line into equal segments.
2. The numbers associated with the points on the line increase in value from left to right; saying it the other way around, the numbers decrease in value from right to left. However you say it, what you're describing is formally called an *ordered set of points*.

On the number line, we have shown the line segments—that is, the distance from 0 to 10 or the distance between 30 and 40. They all appear to be equal and, indeed, are each equal to $\frac{1}{2}$ inch. When we use a distance to represent a quantity, such as barrels of oil, graphically, we are *scaling* the number line. In the example shown, the distance between 0 and 10 might represent 10 barrels of oil, or the distance from 0 to 40 might represent 40 barrels. Of course, the scale may differ on different number lines. For example, a distance of 1 inch could represent 10 units on one number line but 5,000 units on another. Notice that on our number line, points to the left of 0 correspond to negative numbers and points to the right of 0 correspond to positive numbers.

Of course, we can also construct a vertical number line. Consider the one in Figure A-3. As we move up this vertical number line, the numbers increase in value; conversely, as we descend, they decrease in value. Below 0 the numbers are negative, and above 0 the numbers are positive. And as on the horizontal number line, all the line segments are equal. This line is divided into segments such that the distance between -2 and -1 is the same as the distance between 0 and 1.

Combining Vertical and Horizontal Number Lines

By drawing the horizontal and vertical lines on the same sheet of paper, we are able to express the relationships between variables graphically. We do this in Figure A-4.

We draw them (1) so that they intersect at each other's 0 point and (2) so that they are perpendicular to each other. The result is a set of coordinate axes, where each line is called an *axis*. When we have two axes, they span a *plane*.

FIGURE A-2
Horizontal Number Line

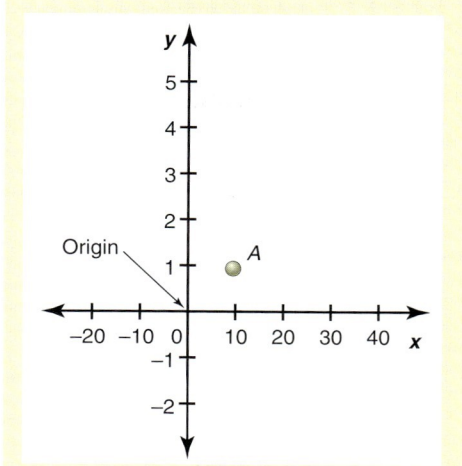

FIGURE A-4
A Set of Coordinate Axes

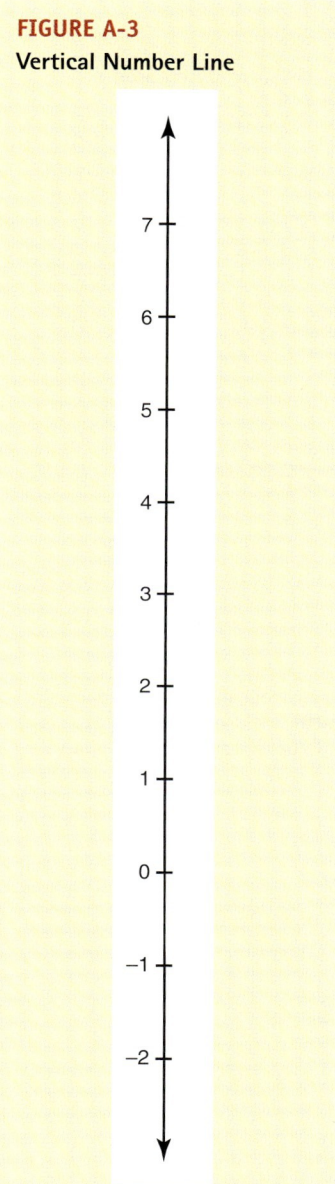

FIGURE A-3
Vertical Number Line

For one number line, you need only one number to specify any point on the line; equivalently, when you see a point on the line, you know that it represents one number or one value. With a coordinate value system, you need two numbers to specify a single point in the plane; when you see a single point on a graph, you know that it represents two numbers or two values.

The basic things that you should know about a coordinate number system are that the vertical number line is referred to as the **y axis,** the horizontal number line is referred to as the **x axis,** and the point of intersection of the two lines is referred to as the **origin.**

Any point such as A in Figure A-4 represents two numbers—a value of x and a value of y. But we know more than that: We also know that point A represents a positive value of y because it is above the x axis, and we know that it represents a positive value of x because it is to the right of the y axis.

Point A represents a "paired observation" of the variables x and y; in particular, in Figure A-4, A represents an observation of the pair of values $x = 10$ and $y = 1$. Every point in the coordinate system corresponds to a paired observation of x and y, which can be simply written (x, y)—the x value is always specified first and then the y value. When we give the values associated with the position of point A in the coordinate number system, we are in effect giving the coordinates of that point. A's coordinates are $x = 10$, $y = 1$, or $(10, 1)$.

GRAPHING NUMBERS IN A TABLE

Consider Table A-2 on page 20. Column 1 shows different prices for T-shirts, and column 2 gives the number of T-shirts purchased per week at these prices. Notice the pattern of these numbers. As the price of T-shirts falls, the number of T-shirts purchased per week increases. Therefore, an inverse relationship exists between these two variables, and as soon as we represent it on a graph, you will be able to see the relationship. We can graph this relationship using a coordinate number system—a vertical and horizontal number line for each of these two variables. Such a graph is shown in panel (b) of Figure A-5 on the next page.

In economics, it is conventional to put dollar values on the y axis. We therefore construct a vertical number line for price and a horizontal number line, the x axis, for quantity of T-shirts purchased per week. The resulting coordinate system allows the plotting of each of the paired observation points; in panel (a), we repeat Table A-2, with a column added

y axis
The vertical axis in a graph.

x axis
The horizontal axis in a graph.

Origin
The intersection of the y axis and the x axis in a graph.

TABLE A-2
T–Shirts Purchased

(1) Price of T-Shirts	(2) Number of T-Shirts Purchased per Week
$10	20
9	30
8	40
7	50
6	60
5	70

Slope
The change in the y value divided by the corresponding change in the x value of a curve; the "incline" of the curve.

expressing these points in paired-data (x, y) form. For example, point J is the paired observation (30, 9). It indicates that when the price of a T-shirt is $9, 30 will be purchased per week.

If it were possible to sell parts of a T-shirt ($\frac{1}{2}$ or $\frac{1}{20}$ of a shirt), we would have observations at every possible price. That is, we would be able to connect our paired observations, represented as lettered points. Let's assume that we can make T-shirts perfectly divisible so that the linear relationship shown in Figure A-5 also holds for fractions of dollars and T-shirts. We would then have a line that connects these points, as shown in the graph in Figure A-6.

In short, we have now represented the data from the table in the form of a graph. Note that an inverse relationship between two variables shows up on a graph as a line or curve that slopes *downward* from left to right. (You might as well get used to the idea that economists call a straight line a "curve" even though it may not curve at all. Economists' data frequently turn out to be curves, so they refer to everything represented graphically, even straight lines, as curves.)

THE SLOPE OF A LINE (A LINEAR CURVE)

An important property of a curve represented on a graph is its *slope*. Consider Figure A-7, which represents the quantities of shoes per week that a seller is willing to offer at different prices. Note that in panel (a) of Figure A-7, as in Figure A-5, we have expressed the coordinates of the points in parentheses in paired-data form.

The **slope** of a line is defined as the change in the y values divided by the corresponding change in the x values as we move along the line. Let's move from point E to point D in panel (b) of Figure A-7. As we move, we note that the change in the y values, which is the change in price, is +$20, because we have moved from a price of $20 to a price of $40 per pair. As we move from E to D, the change in the x values is +80; the number of pairs of

FIGURE A-5
Graphing the Relationship Between T-Shirts Purchased and Price

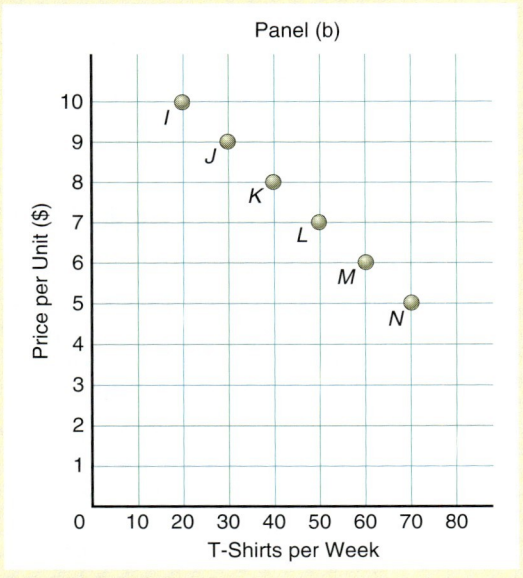

Panel (a)

Price per T-Shirt	T-Shirts Purchased per Week	Point on Graph
$10	20	I (20, 10)
9	30	J (30, 9)
8	40	K (40, 8)
7	50	L (50, 7)
6	60	M (60, 6)
5	70	N (70, 5)

FIGURE A-6
Connecting the Observation Points

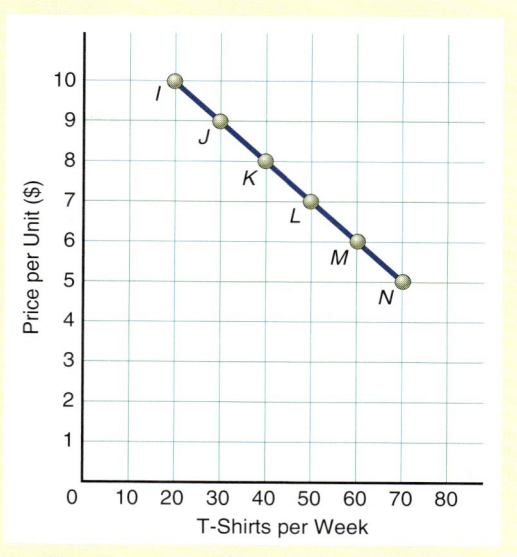

shoes willingly offered per week rises from 80 to 160 pairs. The slope calculated as a change in the *y* values divided by the change in the *x* values is therefore

$$\frac{20}{80} = \frac{1}{4}$$

It may be helpful for you to think of slope as a "rise" (movement in the vertical direction) over a "run" (movement in the horizontal direction). We show this abstractly in Figure A-8 on the following page. The slope is the amount of rise divided by the amount of run. In the example in Figure A-8, and of course in Figure A-7, the amount of rise is

FIGURE A-7
A Positively Sloped Curve

Panel (a)

Price per Pair	Pairs of Shoes Offered per Week	Point on Graph
$100	400	A (400, 100)
80	320	B (320, 80)
60	240	C (240, 60)
40	160	D (160, 40)
20	80	E (80, 20)

FIGURE A-8
Figuring Positive Slope

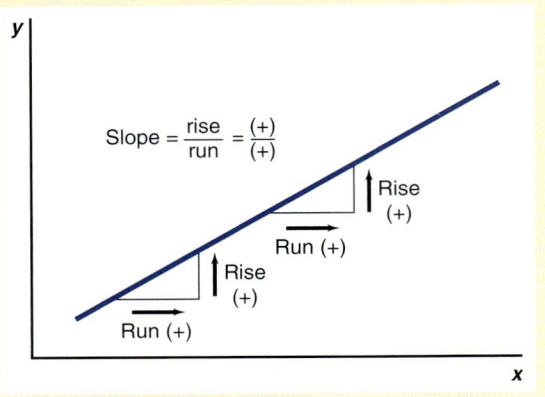

positive and so is the amount of run. That's because it's a direct relationship. We show an inverse relationship in Figure A-9. The slope is still equal to the rise divided by the run, but in this case the rise and the run have opposite signs because the curve slopes downward. That means that the slope is negative and that we are dealing with an inverse relationship.

Now let's calculate the slope for a different part of the curve in panel (b) of Figure A-7 on the previous page. We will find the slope as we move from point *B* to point *A*. Again, we note that the slope, or rise over run, from *B* to *A* equals

$$\frac{20}{80} = \frac{1}{4}$$

A specific property of a straight line is that its slope is the same between any two points; in other words, the slope is constant at all points on a straight line in a graph.

We conclude that for our example in Figure A-7, the relationship between the price of a pair of shoes and the number of pairs of shoes willingly offered per week is *linear,* which simply means "in a straight line," and our calculations indicate a constant slope. Moreover, we calculate a direct relationship between these two variables, which turns out to be an upward-sloping (from left to right) curve. Upward-sloping curves have positive slopes—in this case, the slope is $+\frac{1}{4}$.

We know that an inverse relationship between two variables shows up as a downward-sloping curve—rise over run will be negative because the rise and run have opposite signs, as shown in Figure A-9. When we see a negative slope, we know that increases in one vari-

FIGURE A-9
Figuring Negative Slope

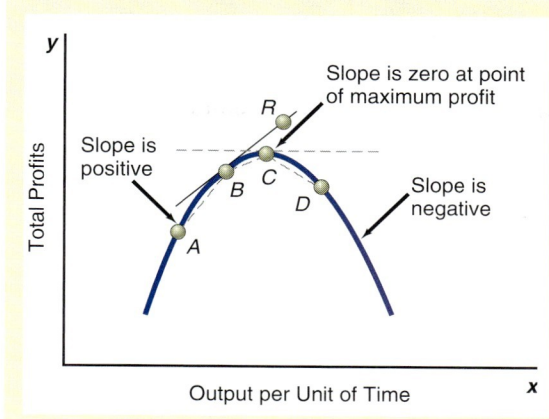

FIGURE A-10
The Slope of a Nonlinear Curve

able are associated with decreases in the other. Therefore, we say that downward-sloping curves have negative slopes. Can you verify that the slope of the graph representing the relationship between T-shirt prices and the quantity of T-shirts purchased per week in Figure A-6 on page 21 is $-\frac{1}{10}$?

Slopes of Nonlinear Curves

The graph presented in Figure A-10 indicates a *nonlinear* relationship between two variables, total profits and output per unit of time. Inspection of this graph indicates that at first, increases in output lead to increases in total profits; that is, total profits rise as output increases. But beyond some output level, further increases in output cause decreases in total profits.

Can you see how this curve rises at first, reaches a peak at point C, and then falls? This curve relating total profits to output levels appears mountain-shaped.

Considering that this curve is nonlinear (it is obviously not a straight line), should we expect a constant slope when we compute changes in y divided by corresponding changes in x in moving from one point to another? A quick inspection, even without specific numbers, should lead us to conclude that the slopes of lines joining different points in this curve, such as between A and B, B and C, or C and D, will *not* be the same. The curve slopes upward (in a positive direction) for some values and downward (in a negative direction) for other values. In fact, the slope of the line between any two points on this curve will be different from the slope of the line between any two other points. Each slope will be different as we move along the curve.

Instead of using a line between two points to discuss slope, mathematicians and economists prefer to discuss the slope *at a particular point*. The slope at a point on the curve, such as point B in the graph in Figure A-10, is the slope of a line tangent to that point. A tangent line is a straight line that touches a curve at only one point. For example, it might be helpful to think of the tangent at B as the straight line that just "kisses" the curve at point B.

To calculate the slope of a tangent line, you need to have some additional information besides the two values of the point of tangency. For example, in Figure A-10, if we knew that the point R also lay on the tangent line and we knew the two values of that point, we could calculate the slope of the tangent line. We could calculate rise over run between points B and R, and the result would be the slope of the line tangent to the one point B on the curve.

24 PART 1 Introduction

Here is what you should know after reading this appendix. MyEconLab will help you identify what you know, and where to go when you need to practice.

WHAT YOU SHOULD KNOW		WHERE TO GO TO PRACTICE
Direct and Inverse Relationships Direct relationships involve a dependent variable changing in the same direction as the change in the independent variable. Inverse relationships involve the dependent variable changing in the opposite direction of the change in the independent variable.	independent variable, 17 dependent variable, 17 direct relationship, 17 inverse relationship, 18	• **MyEconLab** Study Plan 1.7
Constructing a Graph When we draw a graph showing the relationship between two economic variables, we are holding all other things constant (the Latin term for which is *ceteris paribus*).	number line, 18 *y* axis, 19 *x* axis, 19 origin, 19	• **MyEconLab** Study Plan 1.8
Graphing Numbers We obtain a set of coordinates by putting vertical and horizontal number lines together. The vertical line is called the *y* axis; the horizontal line, the *x* axis.		• **MyEconLab** Study Plan 1.9
The Slope of a Linear Curve The slope of any linear (straight-line) curve is the change in the y values divided by the corresponding change in the x values as we move along the line. Otherwise stated, the slope is calculated as the amount of rise over the amount of run, where rise is movement in the vertical direction and run is movement in the horizontal direction.	slope, 20 **Key figures** Figures A-8 and A-9, 22	• **MyEconLab** Study Plan 1.10 • Animated Figures A-8 and A-9
The Slope of a Nonlinear Curve The slope of a nonlinear curve changes; it is positive when the curve is rising and negative when the curve is falling. At a maximum or minimum point, the slope of the nonlinear curve is zero.	**Key figure** Figure A-10, 23	• **MyEconLab** Study Plan 1.10 • Animated Figure A-10

Log in to MyEconLab, take an appendix test, and get a personalized Study Plan that tells you which concepts you understand and which ones you need to review. From there, MyEconLab will give you further practice, tutorials, animations, videos, and guided solutions.
Log in to www.myeconlab.com

PROBLEMS

Select problems, indicated by a blue oval ⬤ *, are assignable in **MyEconLab**.*
Answers to the odd-numbered problems appear at the back of the book.

A-1 Explain which is the independent variable and which is the dependent variable for each of the following examples.
   a. Once you determine the price of a notebook at the college bookstore, you will decide how many notebooks to buy.
   b. You will decide how many credit hours to register for this semester once the university tells you how many work-study hours you will be assigned.
   c. You anticipate earning a higher grade on your next economics exam because you studied more hours in the weeks preceding the exam.

A-2 For each of the following items, state whether a direct or an inverse relationship is likely to exist.
   a. The number of hours you study for an exam and your exam score
   b. The price of pizza and the quantity purchased
   c. The number of games the university basketball team won *last* year and the number of season tickets sold *this* year

A-3 Review Figure A-4, and then state whether each of the following paired observations is on, above, or below the x axis and on, to the left of, or to the right of the y axis.
   a. $(-10, 4)$
   b. $(20, -2)$
   c. $(10, 0)$

A-4 State whether each of the following functions is linear or nonlinear.
   a. $y = 5x$
   b. $y = 5x^2$
   c. $y = 3 + x$
   d. $y = -3x$

A-5 Given the function $y = 5x$, complete the following schedule and plot the curve.

y	x
	−4
	−2
	0
	2
	4

A-6 Given the function $y = 5x^2$, complete the following schedule and plot the curve.

y	x
	−4
	−2
	0
	2
	4

A-7 Calculate the slope of the function you graphed in Problem A-5.

A-8 Indicate at each ordered pair whether the slope of the curve you plotted in Problem A-6 is positive, negative, or zero.

A-9 State whether each of the following functions implies a positive or negative relationship between x and y.
   a. $y = 5x$
   b. $y = 3 + x$
   c. $y = -3x$

2 Scarcity and the World of Trade-Offs

Learning Objectives

After reading this chapter, you should be able to:

1. Evaluate whether even affluent people face the problem of scarcity
2. Understand why economics considers individuals' "wants" but not their "needs"
3. Explain why the scarcity problem induces individuals to consider opportunity costs
4. Discuss why obtaining increasing increments of any particular good typically entails giving up more and more units of other goods
5. Explain why society faces a trade-off between consumption goods and capital goods
6. Distinguish between absolute and comparative advantage

MyEconLab helps you master each objective and study more efficiently. See end of chapter for details.

Homo neanderthalensis, or "Neanderthal man," flourished about 200,000 years ago. Yet, within 6,000 years after the arrival of Cro-Magnon man, the *Homo sapiens* ancestors of modern humans, Neanderthals disappeared. During their overlap, the two human species competed for food. Anthropologists realized long ago that biological differences could not explain why *Homo sapiens* alone survived this competition. If anything, the Neanderthals' stockier build, stubbier extremities, and broader noses and nasal passages were better suited to the climates prevailing at the time. Recently, economists have proposed a possible explanation: *Homo sapiens* had a winning talent for specializing and trading. In this chapter, you will learn about how today's human societies continue to gain from specialization and trade.

Did You Know That...

there are more than 105 million parking spaces in the United States? Although parking spaces vary in size, the typical space is about 19 feet long and 8 feet wide and takes up an area of about 152 square feet. Consequently, U.S. parking spaces occupy almost 16 billion square feet of space, or almost 575 square miles.

All of this land devoted to parking spaces could, of course, be allocated to numerous alternative uses, such as housing developments, office buildings, city parks, and playgrounds. These alternative uses of land now occupied by parking spaces could yield benefits to numerous members of society. Because this land does not yield these benefits, the allocation of land to parking spaces entails costs. Consequently, we know that land, like all other resources, is scarce.

SCARCITY

Whenever individuals or communities cannot obtain everything they desire simultaneously, they must make choices. Choices occur because of *scarcity*. **Scarcity** is the most basic concept in all of economics. Scarcity means that we do not ever have enough of everything, including time, to satisfy our *every* desire. Scarcity exists because human wants always exceed what can be produced with the limited resources and time that nature makes available.

Scarcity
A situation in which the ingredients for producing the things that people desire are insufficient to satisfy all wants.

What Scarcity Is Not

Scarcity is not a shortage. After a hurricane hits and cuts off supplies to a community, TV newscasts often show people standing in line to get minimum amounts of cooking fuel and food. A news commentator might say that the line is caused by the "scarcity" of these products. But cooking fuel and food are always scarce—we cannot obtain all that we want at a zero price. Therefore, do not confuse the concept of scarcity, which is general and all-encompassing, with the concept of shortages as evidenced by people waiting in line to obtain a particular product.

Scarcity is not the same thing as poverty. Scarcity occurs among the poor and among the rich. Even the richest person on earth faces scarcity. For instance, even the world's richest person has only limited time available. Low income levels do not create more scarcity. High income levels do not create less scarcity.

Scarcity is a fact of life, like gravity. And just as physicists did not invent gravity, economists did not invent scarcity—it existed well before the first economist ever lived. It has existed at all times in the past and will exist at all times in the future.

Scarcity and Resources

Scarcity exists because resources are insufficient to satisfy our every desire. Resources are the inputs used in the production of the things that we want. **Production** can be defined as virtually any activity that results in the conversion of resources into products that can be used in consumption. Production includes delivering things from one part of the country to another. It includes taking ice from an ice tray to put it in your soft-drink glass. The resources used in production are called *factors of production*, and some economists use the terms *resources* and *factors of production* interchangeably. The total quantity of all resources that an economy has at any one time determines what that economy can produce.

Production
Any activity that results in the conversion of resources into products that can be used in consumption.

Land
The natural resources that are available from nature. Land as a resource includes location, original fertility and mineral deposits, topography, climate, water, and vegetation.

Labor
Productive contributions of humans who work, involving both mental and physical activities.

Physical capital
All manufactured resources, including buildings, equipment, machines, and improvements to land that are used for production.

Human capital
The accumulated training and education of workers.

Entrepreneurship
The component of human resources that performs the functions of raising capital, organizing, managing, and assembling other factors of production, making basic business policy decisions, and taking risks.

Factors of production can be classified in many ways. Here is one such classification:

1. *Land*. **Land** encompasses all the nonhuman gifts of nature, including timber, water, fish, minerals, and the original fertility of land. It is often called the *natural resource*.
2. *Labor*. **Labor** is the *human resource*, which includes all productive contributions made by individuals who work, such as Web page designers, ballet dancers, and professional football players.
3. *Physical capital*. **Physical capital** consists of the factories and equipment used in production. It also includes improvements to natural resources, such as irrigation ditches.
4. *Human capital*. **Human capital** is the economic characterization of the education and training of workers. How much the nation produces depends not only on how many hours people work but also on how productive they are, and that in turn depends in part on education and training. To become more educated, individuals have to devote time and resources, just as a business has to devote resources if it wants to increase its physical capital. Whenever a worker's skills increase, human capital has been improved.
5. *Entrepreneurship*. **Entrepreneurship** (actually a subdivision of labor) is the component of human resources that performs the functions of organizing, managing, and assembling the other factors of production to create and operate business ventures. Entrepreneurship also encompasses taking risks that involve the possibility of losing large sums of wealth on new ventures. It includes new methods of doing common things and generally experimenting with any type of new thinking that could lead to making more income. Without entrepreneurship, virtually no business organization could operate.

How much do you suppose that the formation of new small-business ventures by entrepreneurs contributes to U.S. labor employment each year?

EXAMPLE

Small-Business Entrepreneurs Create Most New Jobs for Workers

Small, entrepreneur-headed companies employing fewer than 500 workers account for about 99.7 percent of all U.S. businesses and employ nearly half of all U.S. workers. Entrepreneurs' efforts to create new small enterprises or to expand existing businesses account for between 1 million and 3 million new jobs each year. As a consequence, the enterprise-establishing and business-expanding efforts of entrepreneurs account for about 75 percent of the net increase in U.S. employment.

FOR CRITICAL ANALYSIS
Why do you suppose that the U.S. states with laws promoting entrepreneurial activity, such as Arizona, Colorado, and Oklahoma, typically experience the largest employment gains each year?

Goods versus Economic Goods

Goods
All things from which individuals derive satisfaction or happiness.

Economic goods
Goods that are scarce, for which the quantity demanded exceeds the quantity supplied at a zero price.

Goods are defined as all things from which individuals derive satisfaction or happiness. Goods therefore include air to breathe and the beauty of a sunset as well as food, cars, and iPods.

Economic goods are a subset of all goods—they are scarce goods, about which we must constantly make decisions regarding their best use. By definition, the desired quantity of an economic good exceeds the amount that is available at a zero price. Virtually every example we use in economics concerns economic goods—cars, DVD players, computers, socks, baseball bats, and corn. Weeds are a good example of *bads*—goods for which the desired quantity is much *less* than what nature provides at a zero price.

Sometimes you will see references to "goods and services." **Services** are tasks that are performed for someone else, such as laundry, Internet access, hospital care, restaurant meal preparation, car polishing, psychological counseling, and teaching. One way of looking at services is to think of them as *intangible goods*.

Services
Mental or physical labor or help purchased by consumers. Examples are the assistance of physicians, lawyers, dentists, repair personnel, housecleaners, educators, retailers, and wholesalers; items purchased or used by consumers that do not have physical characteristics.

WANTS AND NEEDS

Wants are not the same as needs. Indeed, from the economist's point of view, the term *needs* is objectively undefinable. When someone says, "I need some new clothes," there is no way to know whether that person is stating a vague wish, a want, or a lifesaving necessity. If the individual making the statement were dying of exposure in a northern country during the winter, we might argue that indeed the person does need clothes—perhaps not new ones, but at least some articles of warm clothing. Typically, however, the term *need* is used very casually in conversation. What people mean, usually, is that they desire something that they do not currently have.

Humans have unlimited wants. Just imagine that every single material want that you might have was satisfied. You could have all of the clothes, cars, houses, DVDs, yachts, and other things that you want. Does that mean that nothing else could add to your total level of happiness? Undoubtedly, you might continue to think of new goods and services that you could obtain, particularly as they came to market. You would also still be lacking in fulfilling all of your wants for compassion, friendship, love, affection, prestige, musical abilities, sports abilities, and so on.

In reality, every individual has competing wants but cannot satisfy all of them, given limited resources. This is the reality of scarcity. Each person must therefore make choices. Whenever a choice is made to produce or buy something, something else that is also desired is not produced or not purchased. In other words, in a world of scarcity, every want that ends up being satisfied causes one or more other wants to remain unsatisfied or to be forfeited.

> ### QUICK QUIZ
>
> _____ is the situation in which human wants always exceed what can be produced with the limited resources and time that nature makes available.
>
> We use scarce resources, such as _____, _____, _____ and _____ capital, and _____, to produce economic goods—goods that are desired but are not directly obtainable from nature to the extent demanded or desired at a zero price.
>
> _____ are unlimited; they include all material desires and all nonmaterial desires, such as love, affection, power, and prestige.
>
> The concept of _____ is difficult to define objectively for every person; consequently, we simply consider every person's wants to be unlimited. In a world of **scarcity,** satisfaction of one want necessarily means nonsatisfaction of one or more other wants.
>
> See page 50 for the answers. Review concepts from this section in MyEconLab.

SCARCITY, CHOICE, AND OPPORTUNITY COST

The natural fact of scarcity implies that we must make choices. One of the most important results of this fact is that every choice made (or not made, for that matter) means that some opportunity must be sacrificed. Every choice involves giving up an opportunity to produce or consume something else.

Valuing Forgone Alternatives

Consider a practical example. Every choice you make to study economics for one more hour requires that you give up the opportunity to engage in any of the following activities: study more of another subject, listen to music, sleep, browse at a local store, read a novel, or work out at the gym. The most highly valued of these opportunities is forgone if you choose to study economics an additional hour.

Because there were so many alternatives from which to choose, how could you determine the value of what you gave up to engage in that extra hour of studying economics? First of all, no one else can tell you the answer because only *you* can put a value on the alternatives forgone. Only you know the value of another hour of sleep or of an hour looking for the latest digital music downloads. That means that only you can determine the highest-valued, next-best alternative that you had to sacrifice in order to study economics one more hour. Only you can determine the value of the next-best alternative.

Opportunity Cost

Opportunity cost
The highest-valued, next-best alternative that must be sacrificed to obtain something or to satisfy a want.

The value of the next-best alternative is called **opportunity cost.** The opportunity cost of any action is the value of what is given up—the next-highest-ranked alternative—because a choice was made. When you study one more hour, there may be many alternatives available for the use of that hour, but assume that you can do only one other thing in that hour—your next-highest-ranked alternative. What is important is the choice that you would have made if you hadn't studied one more hour. Your opportunity cost is the *next-highest-ranked* alternative, not *all* alternatives.

In economics, cost is always a forgone opportunity.

One way to think about opportunity cost is to understand that when you choose to do something, you lose something else. What you lose is being able to engage in your next-highest-valued alternative. The cost of your chosen alternative is what you lose, which is by definition your next-highest-valued alternative. This is your opportunity cost.

Why are Internet sellers trying to reduce the opportunity cost of submitting online orders?

ECONOMICS FRONT AND CENTER

For an example of how the concept of opportunity cost can matter in a realistic business context, consider **The Opportunity Cost of Declaring a Wrecked Car a "Total Loss,"** on page 43.

E-COMMERCE EXAMPLE

Making It Easier to Get to the "Submit Order" Button

About half of all consumers who place items in online "shopping carts" abandon the carts before authorizing payment. In some cases, people fail to authorize payment when they learn of unexpected taxes or shipping costs. Web retailers have found, however, that most people fail to finalize an online order simply because they become frustrated with complicated and lengthy checkout procedures.

In an effort to reduce the opportunity cost of purchasing an item online, many Internet sellers are striving to limit all tasks associated with submitting an order to a single Web page. For instance, Internet sellers increasingly utilize software that enables an online shopper to change her order—say, by altering the color or size of an article of clothing—without having to click back and forth among Web pages. Simplifying the online checkout process, these retailers hope, will induce more Internet consumers to decide to click on the "submit order" icon.

FOR CRITICAL ANALYSIS
For an Internet retailer, what is the opportunity cost of not devoting resources to make software simplifications that encourage consumers to finalize online orders?

THE WORLD OF TRADE-OFFS

Whenever you engage in any activity using any resource, even time, you are *trading off* the use of that resource for one or more alternative uses. The extent of the trade-off is represented by the opportunity cost. The opportunity cost of studying economics has already been mentioned—it is the value of the next-best alternative. When you think of any alternative, you are thinking of trade-offs.

Let's consider a hypothetical example of a trade-off between the results of spending time studying economics and mathematics. For the sake of this argument, we will assume that additional time studying either economics or mathematics will lead to a higher grade in the subject to which more study time is allocated. One of the best ways to examine this trade-off is with a graph. (If you would like a refresher on graphical techniques, study Appendix A at the end of Chapter 1 before going on.)

Graphical Analysis

In Figure 2-1, the expected grade in mathematics is measured on the vertical axis of the graph, and the expected grade in economics is measured on the horizontal axis. We simplify the world and assume that you have a maximum of 12 hours per week to spend studying these two subjects and that if you spend all 12 hours on economics, you will get an A in the course. You will, however, fail mathematics, Conversely, if you spend all of your 12 hours studying mathematics, you will get an A in that subject, but you will flunk economics. Here the trade-off is a special case: one to one. A one-to-one trade-off means that the opportunity cost of receiving one grade higher in economics (for example, improving from a C to a B) is one grade lower in mathematics (falling from a C to a D).

FIGURE 2-1
Production Possibilities Curve for Grades in Mathematics and Economics (Trade-Offs)
We assume that only 12 hours can be spent per week on studying. If the student is at point x, equal time (6 hours a week) is spent on both courses, and equal grades of C will be received. If a higher grade in economics is desired, the student may go to point y, thereby receiving a B in economics but a D in mathematics. At point y, 3 hours are spent on mathematics and 9 hours on economics.

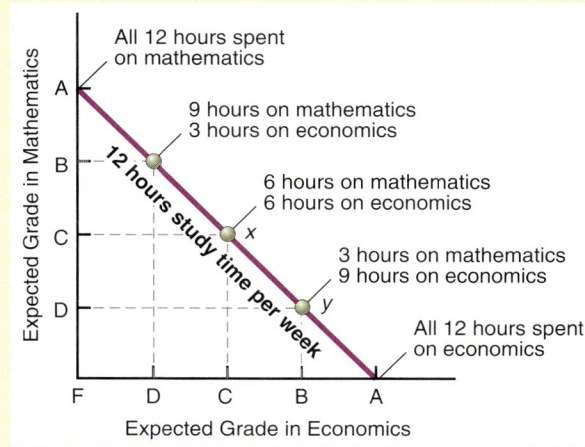

The Production Possibilities Curve (PPC)

The graph in Figure 2-1 on the previous page illustrates the relationship between the possible results that can be produced in each of two activities, depending on how much time you choose to devote to each activity. This graph shows a representation of a **production possibilities curve (PPC).**

Consider that you are producing a grade in economics when you study economics and a grade in mathematics when you study mathematics. Then the line that goes from A on one axis to A on the other axis therefore becomes a production possibilities curve. It is defined as the maximum quantity of one good or service that can be produced, given that a specific quantity of another is produced. It is a curve that shows the possibilities available for increasing the output of one good or service by reducing the amount of another. In the example in Figure 2-1, your time for studying was limited to 12 hours per week. The two possible outputs were your grade in mathematics and your grade in economics. The particular production possibilities curve presented in Figure 2-1 is a graphical representation of the opportunity cost of studying one more hour in one subject. It is a *straight-line production possibilities curve*, which is a special case. (The more general case will be discussed next.) If you decide to be at point *x* in Figure 2-1, you will devote 6 hours of study time to mathematics and 6 hours to economics. The expected grade in each course will be a C. If you are more interested in getting a B in economics, you will go to point *y* on the production possibilities curve, spending only 3 hours on mathematics but 9 hours on economics. Your expected grade in mathematics will then drop from a C to a D.

Note that these trade-offs between expected grades in mathematics and economics are the result of *holding constant* total study time as well as all other factors that might influence a student's ability to learn, such as computerized study aids. Quite clearly, if you were able to spend more total time studying, it would be possible to have higher grades in both economics and mathematics. In that case, however, we would no longer be on the specific production possibilities curve illustrated in Figure 2-1. We would have to draw a new curve, farther to the right, to show the greater total study time and a different set of possible trade-offs.

What trade-off does society face because so many people spend so much time waiting in traffic jams?

> **Production possibilities curve (PPC)**
> A curve representing all possible combinations of maximum outputs that could be produced assuming a fixed amount of productive resources of a given quality.

POLICY EXAMPLE

The Opportunity Cost of Time Stuck in Traffic

Every year, U.S. motorists spend more than 3.7 billion hours waiting in gridlocked traffic. Policymakers commonly argue that the explicit cost of time spent in traffic jams—at least $6 billion spent on the 2.3 billion gallons of fuel burned while engines idle—is sufficiently high to justify building more highways. The implicit opportunity cost is much higher, however. The average U.S. worker earns just over $16 per hour, so the implicit opportunity cost of all those hours stuck in traffic is nearly $60 billion per year. Thus, the annual (total) social cost of U.S. traffic gridlock exceeds $66 billion.

FOR CRITICAL ANALYSIS

Why do economists use hourly wage to measure the opportunity cost of the time a person spends in gridlocked traffic, even if that person is stuck on the highway during weekend or vacation hours?

QUICK QUIZ

Scarcity requires us to choose. Whenever we choose, we lose the _____-_____-valued alternative.

Cost is always a forgone _____.

Another way to look at **opportunity cost** is the trade-off that occurs when one activity is undertaken rather than the _____-_____ alternative activity.

A _____ _____ curve graphically shows the trade-off that occurs when more of one output is obtained at the sacrifice of another. This curve is a graphical representation of, among other things, opportunity cost.

See page 50 for the answers. Review concepts from this section in MyEconLab.

THE CHOICES SOCIETY FACES

The straight-line production possibilities curve presented in Figure 2-1 can be generalized to demonstrate the related concepts of scarcity, choice, and trade-offs that our entire nation faces. As you will see, the production possibilities curve is a simple but powerful economic model because it can demonstrate these related concepts.

A Two-Good Example

The example we will use is the choice between the production of digital cameras and pocket personal computers (pocket PCs). We assume for the moment that these are the only two goods that can be produced in the nation.

Panel (a) of Figure 2-2 on page 34 gives the various combinations of digital cameras and pocket PCs that are possible. If all resources are devoted to camera production, 50 million per year can be produced. If all resources are devoted to production of pocket PCs, 60 million per year can be produced. In between are various possible combinations.

Production Trade-Offs

The nation's production combinations are plotted as points *A, B, C, D, E, F,* and *G* in panel (b) of Figure 2-2. If these points are connected with a smooth curve, the nation's production possibilities curve (PPC) is shown, demonstrating the trade-off between the production of digital cameras and pocket PCs. These trade-offs occur *on* the PPC.

Notice the major difference in the shape of the production possibilities curves in Figure 2-1 on page 31 and Figure 2-2 on the next page. In Figure 2-1, there is a constant trade-off between grades in economics and in mathematics. In Figure 2-2, the trade-off between digital camera production and pocket PC production is not constant, and therefore the PPC is a *bowed* curve. To understand why the production possibilities curve for a society is typically bowed outward, you must understand the assumptions underlying the PPC.

Go to www.econtoday.com/ch02 for one perspective, offered by the National Center for Policy Analysis, on whether society's production decisions should be publicly or privately coordinated.

Assumptions Underlying the Production Possibilities Curve

When we draw the curve that is shown in Figure 2-2, we make the following assumptions:

1. Resources are fully employed.
2. Production takes place over a specific time period—for example, one year.

FIGURE 2-2

Society's Trade-Off Between Digital Cameras and Pocket PCs

The production of digital cameras and pocket PCs is measured in millions of units per year. The various combinations are given in panel (a) and plotted in panel (b). Connecting the points A–G with a relatively smooth line gives the society's production possibilities curve for digital cameras and pocket PCs. Point R lies outside the production possibilities curve and is therefore unattainable at the point in time for which the graph is drawn. Point S lies inside the production possibilities curve and therefore entails unemployed or underemployed resources.

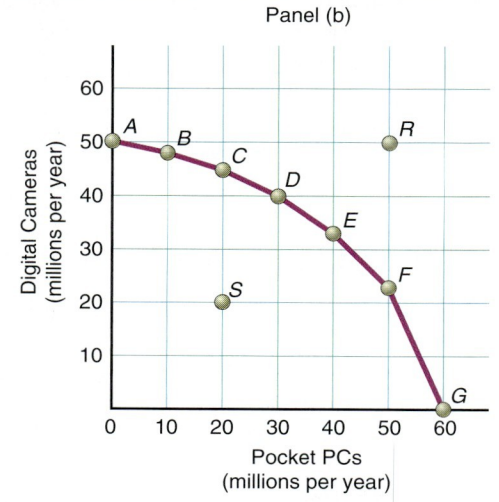

Panel (a)

Combination	Digital Cameras (millions per year)	Pocket PCs (millions per year)
A	50.0	0
B	48.0	10
C	45.0	20
D	40.0	30
E	33.0	40
F	22.5	50
G	0.0	60

3. The resource inputs, in both quantity and quality, used to produce digital cameras or pocket PCs are fixed over this time period.
4. Technology does not change over this time period.

Technology
Society's pool of applied knowledge concerning how goods and services can be produced.

Technology is defined as society's pool of applied knowledge concerning how goods and services can be produced by managers, workers, engineers, scientists, and artisans, using land, physical and human capital, and entrepreneurship. You can think of technology as the formula or recipe used to combine factors of production. (When better formulas are developed, more production can be obtained from the same amount of resources.) The level of technology sets the limit on the amount and types of goods and services that we can derive from any given amount of resources. The production possibilities curve is drawn under the assumption that we use the best technology that we currently have available and that this technology doesn't change over the time period under study.

The land available to a town with established borders is an example of a fixed resource that is fully employed and used with available technology along a production possibilities curve. Why do you suppose that deciding how to allocate a fixed amount of land recently posed "grave" problems for a town in France?

INTERNATIONAL EXAMPLE

Making Death Illegal—At Least, Inside City Limits

Le Lavandou, France, a Riviera community known for breathtaking views of a rocky coastline along a clear-blue section of the Mediterranean Sea, recently drew international ridicule when it passed a law that appeared aimed at regulating death. Specifically, the law stated, "It is forbidden without a cemetery plot to die on the territory of the commune."

(continued)

Of course, it is not possible for a law to prevent someone from dying inside a town. The purpose of the law was to indicate a permissible choice along a production possibilities curve. Land is a scarce resource with many alternative uses, so trade-offs involving different productive uses of land arise everywhere on the planet where people establish communities. Le Lavandou is no exception. The town's cemetery filled up, and the townspeople had to decide whether to allocate more land to cemetery plots, thereby providing a service for deceased individuals and for their family and friends, or to continue allocating remaining land resources to the production of other goods and services. The point of the legal requirement was to emphasize that the town had decided not to incur an opportunity cost by allocating more space to cemetery plots.

Nonetheless, it was still true that someone who happened to die in Le Lavandou without first buying an existing cemetery plot was technically breaking the law.

FOR CRITICAL ANALYSIS
What is likely to happen to the opportunity cost of cemetery services as the world's population continues to increase and spread over available land resources?

Being off the Production Possibilities Curve

Look again at panel (b) of Figure 2-2. Point *R* lies *outside* the production possibilities curve and is *impossible* to achieve during the time period assumed. By definition, the PPC indicates the *maximum* quantity of one good, given the quantity produced of the other good.

It is possible, however, to be at point *S* in Figure 2-2. That point lies beneath the production possibilities curve. If the nation is at point *S*, it means that its resources are not being fully utilized. This occurs, for example, during periods of relatively high unemployment. Point *S* and all such points inside the PPC are always attainable but imply unemployed or underemployed resources.

Efficiency

The production possibilities curve can be used to define the notion of efficiency. Whenever the economy is operating on the PPC, at points such as *A, B, C,* or *D*, we say that its production is efficient. Points such as *S* in Figure 2-2, which lie beneath the PPC, are said to represent production situations that are not efficient.

Efficiency can mean many things to many people. Even in economics, there are different types of efficiency. Here we are discussing *productive efficiency*. An economy is productively efficient whenever it is producing the maximum output with given technology and resources.

A simple commonsense definition of efficiency is getting the most out of what we have. Clearly, we are not getting the most out of what we have if we are at point *S* in panel (b) of Figure 2-2. We can move from point *S* to, say, point *C*, thereby increasing the total quantity of digital cameras produced without any decrease in the total quantity of pocket PCs produced. Alternatively, we can move from point *S* to point *E*, for example, and have both more digital cameras and more pocket PCs. Point *S* is called an **inefficient point,** which is defined as any point below the production possibilities curve.

Efficiency
The case in which a given level of inputs is used to produce the maximum output possible. Alternatively, the situation in which a given output is produced at minimum cost.

Inefficient point
Any point below the production possibilities curve at which the use of resources is not generating the maximum possible output.

The Law of Increasing Relative Cost

In the example in Figure 2-1 on page 31, the trade-off between a grade in mathematics and a grade in economics was one to one. The trade-off ratio was constant. That is, the production possibilities curve was a straight line. The curve in Figure 2-2 is a more general case.

FIGURE 2-3
The Law of Increasing Relative Cost

Consider equal increments of production of pocket PCs, as measured on the horizontal axis. All of the horizontal arrows—*aB*, *bC*, and so on—are of equal length (10 million). In contrast, the length of each vertical arrow—*Aa*, *Bb*, and so on—increases as we move down the production possibilities curve. Hence, the opportunity cost of going from 50 million pocket PCs per year to 60 million (*Ff*) is much greater than going from zero units to 10 million (*Aa*). The opportunity cost of each additional equal increase in production of pocket PCs rises.

We have re-created the curve in Figure 2-2 as Figure 2-3. Each combination, *A* through *G*, of digital cameras and pocket PCs is represented on the production possibilities curve. Starting with the production of zero pocket PCs, the nation can produce 50 million digital cameras with its available resources and technology.

Increasing Relative Costs. When we increase production of pocket PCs from zero to 10 million per year, the nation has to give up in digital cameras an amount shown by that first vertical arrow, *Aa*. From panel (a) of Figure 2-2 on page 34 you can see that this is 2 million per year (50 million minus 48 million). Again, if we increase production of pocket PCs by another 10 million units per year, we go from *B* to *C*. In order to do so, the nation has to give up the vertical distance *Bb*, or 3 million digital cameras per year. By the time we go from 50 million to 60 million pocket PCs, to obtain that 10 million increase, we have to forgo the vertical distance *Ff*, or 22.5 million digital cameras. In other words, we see that the opportunity cost of the last 10 million pocket PCs has increased to 22.5 million digital cameras, compared to 2 million digital cameras for the same increase in pocket PCs when we started with none at all being produced.

Law of increasing relative cost
The fact that the opportunity cost of additional units of a good generally increases as society attempts to produce more of that good. This accounts for the bowed-out shape of the production possibilities curve.

What we are observing is called the **law of increasing relative cost.** When society takes more resources and applies them to the production of any specific good, the opportunity cost increases for each additional unit produced.

Explaining the Law of Increasing Relative Cost. The reason that as a nation we face the law of increasing relative cost (shown as a production possibilities curve that is bowed outward) is that certain resources are better suited for producing some goods than they are for other goods. Generally, resources are not *perfectly* adaptable for alternative uses. When increasing the output of a particular good, producers must use less suitable resources than those already used in order to produce the additional output. Hence the cost of producing the additional units increases.

With respect to our hypothetical example here, at first the optical imaging specialists at digital camera firms would shift over to producing pocket PCs. After a while, though, lens-crafting technicians, workers who normally build cameras, and others would be asked to help design and manufacture pocket PC components. Clearly, they would be less effective in making pocket PCs than the people who previously specialized in this task.

In general, *the more specialized the resources, the more bowed the production possibilities curve*. At the other extreme, if all resources are equally suitable for digital camera production or production of pocket PCs, the curves in Figures 2-2 and 2-3 would approach the straight line shown in our first example in Figure 2-1 on page 31.

> ## QUICK QUIZ
>
> Trade-offs are represented graphically by a _____ _____ curve showing the maximum quantity of one good or service that can be produced, given a specific quantity of another, from a given set of resources over a specified period of time—for example, one year.
>
> A **production possibilities curve** is drawn holding the quantity and quality of all resources _____ over the time period under study.
>
> Points _____ the **production possibilities curve** are unattainable; points _____ are attainable but represent an inefficient use or underuse of available resouces.
>
> Because many resources are better suited for certain productive tasks than for others, society's production possibilities curve is bowed _____, reflecting the law of increasing relative cost.
>
> See page 50 for the answers. Review concepts from this section in MyEconLab.

ECONOMIC GROWTH AND THE PRODUCTION POSSIBILITIES CURVE

At any particular point in time, a society cannot be outside the production possibilities curve. *Over time*, however, it is possible to have more of everything. This occurs through economic growth. (An important reason for economic growth, capital accumulation, is discussed next. A more complete discussion of why economic growth occurs appears in Chapter 9.) Figure 2-4 shows the production possibilities curve for digital cameras and pocket PCs shifting outward. The two additional curves shown represent new choices open to an economy that has experienced economic growth. Such economic growth occurs because of many things, including increases in the number of workers and productive investment in equipment.

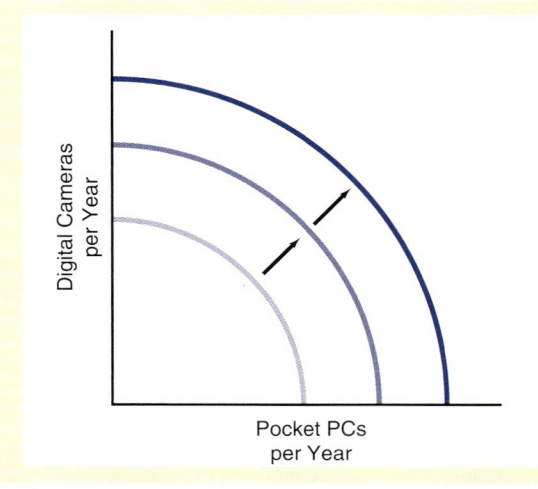

FIGURE 2-4

Economic Growth Allows for More of Everything

If the nation experiences economic growth, the production possibilities curve between digital cameras and pocket PCs will move out as shown. This takes time, however, and it does not occur automatically. This means, therefore, that we can have more of both digital cameras and pocket PCs only after a period of time during which we have experienced economic growth.

Scarcity still exists, however, no matter how much economic growth there is. At any point in time, we will always be on some production possibilities curve; thus, we will always face trade-offs. The more we have of one thing, the less we can have of others.

If a nation experiences economic growth, the production possibilities curve between digital cameras and pocket PCs will move outward, as shown in Figure 2-4. This takes time and does not occur automatically. One reason it will occur involves the choice about how much to consume today.

THE TRADE-OFF BETWEEN THE PRESENT AND THE FUTURE

The production possibilities curve and economic growth can be combined to examine the trade-off between present **consumption** and future consumption. When we consume today, we are using up what we call consumption or consumer goods—food and clothes, for example.

Consumption
The use of goods and services for personal satisfaction.

Why We Make Capital Goods

Why would we be willing to use productive resources to make things—capital goods—that we cannot consume directly? For one thing, capital goods enable us to produce larger quantities of consumer goods or to produce them less expensively than we otherwise could. Before fish are "produced" for the market, equipment such as fishing boats, nets, and poles is produced first. Imagine how expensive it would be to obtain fish for market without using these capital goods. Catching fish with one's hands is not an easy task. The cost per fish would be very high if capital goods weren't used.

Forgoing Current Consumption

Whenever we use productive resources to make capital goods, we are implicitly forgoing current consumption. We are waiting for some time in the future to consume the fruits that will be reaped from the use of capital goods. In effect, when we forgo current consumption to invest in capital goods, we are engaging in an economic activity that is forward-looking—we do not get instant utility or satisfaction from our activity.

The Trade-Off Between Consumption Goods and Capital Goods

To have more consumer goods in the future, we must accept fewer consumer goods today, because resources must be used in producing capital goods instead of consumer goods. In other words, an opportunity cost is involved. Every time we make a choice for more goods today, we incur an opportunity cost of fewer goods tomorrow, and every time we make a choice of more goods in the future, we incur an opportunity cost of fewer goods today. With the resources that we don't use to produce consumer goods for today, we invest in capital goods that will produce more consumer goods for us later. The trade-off is shown in Figure 2-5. On the left in panel (a), you can see this trade-off depicted as a production possibilities curve between capital goods and consumption goods.

Assume that we are willing to give up $1 trillion worth of consumption today. We will be at point A in the left-hand diagram of panel (a). This will allow the economy to grow. We will have more future consumption because we invested in more capital goods today. In the right-hand diagram of panel (a), we see two goods represented, food and entertainment. The production possibilities curve will move outward if we collectively decide to restrict consumption each year and invest in capital goods.

In panel (b), we show the results of our willingness to forgo even more current consumption. We move to point C, where we have many fewer consumer goods today but

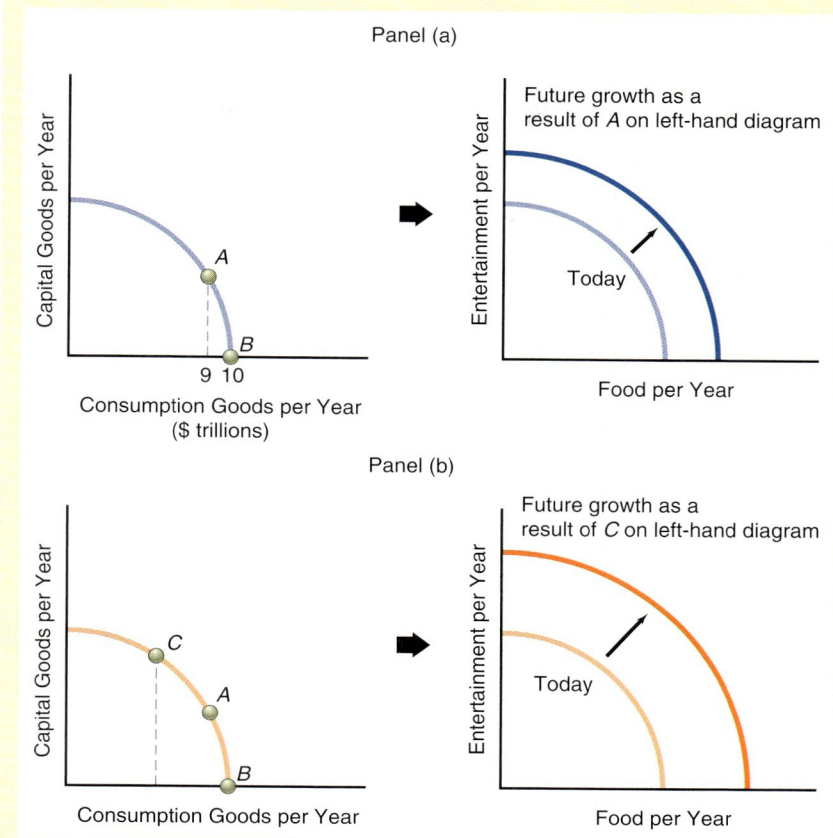

FIGURE 2-5

Capital Goods and Growth

In panel (a), the nation chooses not to consume $1 trillion, so it invests that amount in capital goods. As a result, more of all goods may be produced in the future, as shown in the right-hand diagram in panel (a). In panel (b), society chooses even more capital goods (point C). The result is that the PPC moves even more to the right on the right-hand diagram in panel (b).

produce many more capital goods. This leads to more future growth in this simplified model, and thus the production possibilities curve in the right-hand side of panel (b) shifts outward more than it did in the right-hand side of panel (a).

In other words, the more we give up today, the more we can have tomorrow, provided, of course, that the capital goods are productive in future periods.

QUICK QUIZ

_____ goods are goods that will later be used to produce consumer goods.

A trade-off is involved between current consumption and capital goods or, alternatively, between current consumption and future consumption. The _____ we invest in capital goods today, the greater the amount of consumer goods we can produce in the future and the _____ the amount of consumer goods we can produce today.

See page 50 for the answers. Review concepts from this section in MyEconLab.

SPECIALIZATION AND GREATER PRODUCTIVITY

Specialization involves working at a relatively well-defined, limited endeavor, such as accounting or teaching. It involves the organization of economic activity among different individuals and regions. Most individuals do specialize. For example, you could change the

Specialization
The organization of economic activity so that what each person (or region) consumes is not identical to what that person (or region) produces. An individual may specialize, for example, in law or medicine. A nation may specialize in the production of coffee, computers, or cameras.

oil in your car if you wanted to. Typically, though, you take your car to a garage and let the mechanic change the oil. You benefit by letting the garage mechanic specialize in changing the oil and in doing other repairs on your car. The specialist normally will get the job finished sooner than you could and has the proper equipment to make the job go more smoothly. Specialization usually leads to greater productivity, not only for each individual but also for the nation.

Comparative Advantage

Specialization occurs because different individuals experience different costs when they engage in the same activities. Some individuals can accurately solve mathematical problems at lower cost than others who might try to solve the same problems. Thus, those who solve math problems at lower cost sacrifice production of fewer alternative items. Some people can develop more high-quality computer programs than others while giving up less production of other items, such as clean houses and neatly manicured yards.

Comparative advantage
The ability to produce a good or service at a lower opportunity cost compared to other producers.

Comparative advantage is the ability to perform an activity *at a lower opportunity cost*. You have a comparative advantage in one activity whenever you have a lower opportunity cost of performing that activity. Comparative advantage is always a *relative* concept. You may be able to change the oil in your car; you might even be able to change it faster than the local mechanic. But if the opportunity cost you face by changing the oil exceeds the mechanic's opportunity cost, the mechanic has a comparative advantage in changing the oil. The mechanic faces a lower opportunity cost for that activity.

You may be convinced that everybody can do more of everything during the same period of time and using the same resources than you can. In this extreme situation, do you still have a comparative advantage? The answer is yes. You do not have to be a mathematical genius to figure this out. The market tells you so very clearly by offering you the highest income for the job for which you have a comparative advantage. Stated differently, to find your comparative advantage, simply find the job that maximizes your income.

Absolute Advantage

Suppose that, conversely, you have a job at a firm and are convinced that you have the ability to do every job in that company at a lower cost than everyone else who works there. You might be able to keyboard documents into a computer faster than any of the other employees, file documents in order in a file cabinet faster than any of the file clerks, and wash windows faster than any of the window washers. Indeed, you might even be able to manage the firm just as effectively as the current company president but at even lower time cost than the president incurs in performing that function.

Absolute advantage
The ability to produce more units of a good or service using a given quantity of labor or resource inputs. Equivalently, the ability to produce the same quantity of a good or service using fewer units of labor or resource inputs.

If all of these self-perceptions were really true, then you would have an **absolute advantage** in all of these endeavors. In other words, if you were to spend a given amount of time in any one of them, you could produce more than anyone else in the company. Nonetheless, you would not spend your time doing these other activities. Why not? Because your cost advantage in undertaking the president's managerial duties is even greater. Therefore, you would find yourself specializing in that particular task even though you have an *absolute* advantage in all these other tasks. Indeed, absolute advantage is irrelevant in predicting how you will allocate your time. Only *comparative advantage* matters.

The coaches of sports teams often have to determine the comparative advantage of an individual player who has an absolute advantage in every aspect of the sport in question. Babe Ruth, who could hit more home runs and pitch more strikeouts per game than other players on the Boston Red Sox, was a pitcher on that professional baseball team. After he was traded to the New York Yankees, the owner and the manager decided to make him an outfielder, even though he could also hurl more strikeouts per game than other Yankees. They wanted "The Babe" to concentrate on his hitting because a home-run king would bring in more fans than a good pitcher would. Babe Ruth had an absolute advantage in both aspects of the game of baseball, but his comparative advantage was clearly in hitting homers rather than in practicing and developing his pitching game.

When contemplating how to decorate their homes for the Christmas holidays, some people find that doing their own decorating entails a higher opportunity cost than others face. How has this given entrepreneurs an opportunity to profit from providing holiday-decorating services?

EXAMPLE

A Comparative Advantage in Holiday Spirit

Putting up a Christmas tree, winding lights around the tree, and decorating it with ornaments and other trimmings are activities that require hours of time to complete. So do wrapping garlands around mantels, hanging wreaths, and stringing lights across the front porch and around the roof.

Increasingly, people are determining that holiday decorating is a next-best alternative. These individuals devote their time to other activities, such as earning additional income, and pay a professional decorator to spruce up their homes for the holidays. One company, Christmas Décor, Inc., now has 268 franchise operations that provide professional holiday-decorating services at prices ranging from $500 to $3,000 per home. Owners of such businesses have a comparative advantage in holiday decorating, so they specialize in this activity.

FOR CRITICAL ANALYSIS
Why do you think that holiday-decorating businesses charge the highest fees for providing the most elaborate decorations? (Hint: How could owners of holiday-decorating businesses alternatively allocate the time they spend putting up the most elaborate decorations at one house, when others are willing to pay for less ornate decorations?)

Scarcity, Self-Interest, and Specialization

In Chapter 1, you learned about the assumption of rational self-interest. To repeat, for the purposes of our analyses we assume that individuals are rational in that they will do what is in their own self-interest. They will not consciously carry out actions that will make them worse off. In this chapter, you learned that scarcity requires people to make choices. We assume that they make choices based on their self-interest. When they make these choices, they attempt to maximize benefits net of opportunity cost. In so doing, individuals choose their comparative advantage and end up specializing.

The Division of Labor

In any firm that includes specialized human and nonhuman resources, there is a **division of labor** among those resources. The best-known example comes from Adam Smith, who in *The Wealth of Nations* illustrated the benefits of a division of labor in the making of pins, as depicted in the following example:

> One man draws out the wire, another straightens it, a third cuts it, a fourth points it, a fifth grinds it at the top for receiving the head; to make the head requires two or three distinct operations; to put it on is a peculiar business, to whiten the pins is another; it is even a trade by itself to put them into the paper.

Division of labor
The segregation of a resource into different specific tasks; for example, one automobile worker puts on bumpers, another doors, and so on.

Making pins this way allowed 10 workers without very much skill to make almost 48,000 pins "of a middling size" in a day. One worker, toiling alone, could have made perhaps 20 pins a day; therefore, 10 workers could have produced 200. Division of labor allowed for an increase in the daily output of the pin factory from 200 to 48,000! (Smith did not attribute all of the gain to the division of labor but credited also the use of machinery and the fact that less time was spent shifting from task to task.)

What we are discussing here involves a division of the resource called labor into different uses of labor. The different uses of labor are organized in such a way as to increase the amount of output possible from the fixed resources available. We can therefore talk about an organized division of labor within a firm leading to increased output.

COMPARATIVE ADVANTAGE AND TRADE AMONG NATIONS

Most of our analysis of absolute advantage, comparative advantage, and specialization has dealt with individuals. Nevertheless, it is equally applicable to nations.

Trade Among Regions

Consider the United States. The Plains states have a comparative advantage in the production of grains and other agricultural goods. Relative to the Plains states, the states to the north and east tend to specialize in industrialized production, such as automobiles. Not surprisingly, grains are shipped from the Plains states to the northern states, and automobiles are shipped in the reverse direction. Such specialization and trade allow for higher incomes and standards of living.

If both the Plains states and the northern states were separate nations, the same analysis would still hold, but we would call it international trade. Indeed, the European Union (EU) is comparable to the United States in area and population, but instead of one nation, the EU has 25. What U.S. residents call *interstate* trade, Europeans call *international* trade. There is no difference, however, in the economic results—both yield greater economic efficiency and higher average incomes.

International Aspects of Trade

Political problems that do not normally occur within a particular nation often arise between nations. For example, if California avocado growers develop a cheaper method of producing a tastier avocado than growers in southern Florida use, the Florida growers will lose out. They cannot do much about the situation except try to lower their own costs of production or improve their product.

If avocado growers in Mexico, however, develop a cheaper method of producing better-tasting avocados, both California and Florida growers can (and likely will) try to raise political barriers that will prevent Mexican avocado growers from freely selling their product in the United States. U.S. avocado growers will use such arguments as "unfair" competition and loss of U.S. jobs. Certainly, avocado-growing jobs may decline in the United States, but there is no reason to believe that U.S. jobs will decline overall. Instead, former U.S. avocado workers will move into alternative employment—something that 1 million people do every *week* in the United States. If the argument of U.S. avocado growers had any validity, every time a region in the United States developed a better way to produce a product manufactured somewhere else in the country, U.S. employment would decline. That has never happened and never will.

Go to www.econtoday.com/ch02 to find out from the World Trade Organization how much international trade takes place. Under "Resources," click on "Trade statistics" and then click on "International Trade Statistics" for the most recent year.

When nations specialize where they have a comparative advantage and then trade with the rest of the world, the average standard of living in the world rises. In effect, international trade allows the world to move from inside the global production possibilities curve toward the curve itself, thereby improving worldwide economic efficiency. Thus, all countries that engage in trade can benefit from comparative advantage, just as regions in the United States benefit from interregional trade.

QUICK QUIZ

With a given set of resources, specialization results in _____ output; in other words, there are gains to specialization in terms of greater material well-being.

Individuals and nations specialize in their areas of _____ advantage in order to reap the gains of specialization.

Comparative advantages are found by determining which activities have the _____ opportunity cost—that is, which activities yield the highest return for the time and resources used.

A _____ of labor occurs when different workers are assigned different tasks. Together, the workers produce a desired product.

See page 50 for the answers. Review concepts from this section in MyEconLab.

CASE STUDY — ECONOMICS FRONT AND CENTER

The Opportunity Cost of Declaring a Wrecked Car a "Total Loss"

Rhodes works for a major automobile insurance company. She is investigating a sharp increase in the rate at which the company's claims adjusters are determining that cars damaged in accidents are "total losses" beyond repair. Her boss worries that the company is writing too many checks to policyholders rather than paying body shops to repair the cars.

Rhodes knows that during the past three years, the percentage of automobiles written off by insurers as total losses following accidents has more than doubled. She also knows that her company, like most others in the industry, typically chooses not to pay for a car to be repaired if the repair bill exceeds 65 percent of the market value of the automobile. After some study of recent company experience and industry reports, Rhodes discovers that even "minor" collisions often generate expensive repairs. Just replacing air bags entails an expense as high as $6,000, and a number of autos now have side impact bags and curtains that must be replaced at a cost of several thousand more dollars. An increasing number of cars also have headlight assemblies and magnesium radiators that crumple easily, generating further repair bills of at least $5,000.

In her report to her boss, Rhodes points out that the next-best alternative to the company's current procedure would be to declare fewer wrecked cars to be total losses and to repair them instead. The cost of this next-best alternative is much higher today than in years past, she reports. Given the current nature of the trade-off between declaring cars total losses and repairing the cars, she concludes that declaring a car a total loss truly is often the company's best choice, because it minimizes the firm's overall expenses.

CRITICAL ANALYSIS QUESTIONS

1. How might the terms of the trade-off faced by Rhodes's company change if more automakers started using more durable steel frames in automobile bodies instead of frames composed of light metal alloys?

2. Why might an insured policyholder prefer for a heavily damaged car to be declared a total loss than to be repaired? (Hint: Think in terms of the policyholder's opportunity cost, and keep in mind that a body shop can take weeks to repair a heavily damaged car.)

Issues and Applications

An Economic Theory of the Neanderthals' Extinction

Concepts Applied
- Technology
- Specialization
- Division of Labor

The extinction of the Neanderthals has long been a mystery to anthropologists and archaeologists. Throughout much of the twentieth century, scientists speculated that the Neanderthals died out because they had less cohesive families and because the members of *Homo sapiens* were more intelligent and agile hunters. Recent evidence has cast considerable doubt on these hypotheses, however. Neanderthals appear to have had family support structures as sophisticated as those of the Cro-Magnon version of humans with whom they competed. In addition, findings of remains of Neanderthal hunters alongside remains of their prey indicate that they were as good at hunting live game as *Homo sapiens*. Analysis of the physical characteristics of Neanderthal skeletons also indicates that they were probably every bit as agile as *Homo sapiens*. Why, then, did Cro-Magnon humans win out over Neanderthals?

Strike One: Failure to Develop New Technology

Even though both Neanderthals and *Homo sapiens* were socially sophisticated and physically agile, the anthropological and archaeological evidence reveals some key differences. Study of Neanderthal remains shows that they appear to have suffered more hunting injuries than Cro-Magnon humans, even though they were just as agile.

One possible explanation for why the Neanderthals suffered more injuries was that the Neanderthals fell behind *Homo sapiens* in their technological sophistication. While the Neanderthals continued to rely on spears to hunt, Cro-Magnon humans gradually developed better technologies, such as harpoons, tools, and fishing nets. The use of these improved technologies allowed Cro-Magnon humans to build traps and fish safely from the shore, so that they came into less direct contact with the game they hunted. As a consequence, *Homo sapiens* hunters were more likely to avoid injuries and deaths as both species competed for the same food sources.

Strike Two: Failure to Specialize

Another difference between Neanderthals and Cro-Magnon humans has been revealed by their dwellings. In contrast to Neanderthals, Cro-Magnon humans set aside spaces for different uses. Some parts of human dwellings, for instance, were devoted to handling foods, while others were set aside for crafting pottery and tools.

Thus, it appears that Cro-Magnon humans engaged in division of labor, with different members of households specializing in different tasks. Perhaps those with a comparative advantage in crafts stayed at home to make harpoons and tools, while those with a comparative advantage in hunting searched for game—which might further help to explain why *Homo sapiens* hunters appear to have sustained fewer injuries than Neanderthal hunters.

Strike Three: Failure to Trade

A final difference is revealed by study of the items found in human and Neanderthal dwellings. Human tools often contain metals that could only have been obtained from areas far distant. Jewelry of people who lived far from oceans often contained seashells. These and other bits of evidence suggest that *Homo sapiens* groups in diverse regions engaged in trade. In contrast, there is no evidence that Neanderthal groups in different areas traded with one another.

An Economic Solution to the Neanderthal Puzzle

Economics, therefore, may provide the solution to the long-standing puzzle of the demise of the Neanderthals, who fell behind technologically, did not engage in division of labor and specialize in different tasks, and failed to trade. Neanderthals, according to this view, struck out as a species because their Cro-Magnon human cousins experienced rapid rates of economic growth—and, in the end, population growth—that the Neanderthals could not match.

Log in to **MyEconLab**, click on "Economic News," and test your understanding of the chapter by answering interactive questions that relate directly to this issue.

For Critical Analysis

1. Why might the *Homo sapiens* production possibilities curves have shifted outward to the right much more rapidly than those of the Neanderthals?
2. Why might failure to specialize explain why Neanderthal groups in different areas did not trade? (Hint: Remember that comparative advantage is the key basis for trade.)

Web Resources

1. For a review of the economic theory of the demise of the Neanderthals, go to www.econtoday.com/ch02.
2. To review the main arguments against the idea that economic failings were the main source of the Neanderthals' extinction, go to www.econtoday.com/ch02.

Research Project

Failure to advance technologically, to specialize, and to trade appear to have helped doom the Neanderthals. Discuss why failure to engage in any one of these three economic behaviors complicates engaging in either of the other two. Why might this help explain why the Neanderthals did not exhibit any of these three economic characteristics?

Here is what you should know after reading this chapter. MyEconLab will help you identify what you know, and where to go when you need to practice.

WHAT YOU SHOULD KNOW		WHERE TO GO TO PRACTICE
The Problem of Scarcity, Even for the Affluent Scarcity is very different from poverty. No one can obtain all one desires from nature without sacrifice. Thus, even the richest people face scarcity because they have to make choices among alternatives. Despite their high levels of income or wealth, affluent people, like everyone else, want more than they can have (in terms of goods, power, prestige, and so on).	scarcity, 27 production, 27 land, 28 labor, 28 physical capital, 28 human capital, 28 entrepreneurship, 28 goods, 28 economic goods, 28 services, 29	• **MyEconLab** Study Plan 2.1 • Audio introduction to Chapter 2 • Video: Scarcity, Resources, and Production
Why Economists Consider Individuals' Wants but Not Their "Needs" Goods are all things from which individuals derive satisfaction. Economic goods are those for which the desired quantity exceeds the amount that is directly available from nature at a zero price. To economists, the term *need* is undefinable, whereas humans have unlimited *wants*, which are defined as the goods and services on which we place a positive value.		• **MyEconLab** Study Plan 2.2
Why Scarcity Leads People to Evaluate Opportunity Costs We measure the opportunity cost of anything by the highest-valued alternative that one must give up to obtain it. The trade-offs that we face as individuals and as a society can be represented by a production possibilities curve (PPC), and moving from one point on a PPC to another entails incurring an opportunity cost. The reason is that along a PPC, all currently available resources and technology are being used, so obtaining more of one good requires shifting resources to production of that good and away from production of another. That is, there is an opportunity cost of allocating scarce resources toward producing one good instead of another good.	opportunity cost, 30 production possibilities curve (PPC), 32 **Key figure** Figure 2-1, 31	• **MyEconLab** Study Plans 2.3 and 2.4 • Animated Figure 2-1

CHAPTER 2   *Scarcity and the World of Trade-Offs*   **47**

WHAT YOU SHOULD KNOW		**WHERE TO GO TO PRACTICE**

Why Obtaining Increasing Increments of a Good Requires Giving Up More and More Units of Other Goods Typically, resources are specialized. Thus, when society allocates additional resources to producing more and more of a single good, it must increasingly employ resources that would be better suited for producing other goods. As a result, the law of increasing relative cost holds. Each additional unit of a good can be obtained only by giving up more and more of other goods, which means that the production possibilities curve that society faces is bowed outward.	technology, 34
	efficiency, 35
	inefficient point, 35
	law of increasing
	   relative cost, 36
	Key figures
	   Figure 2-3, 36
	   Figure 2-4, 37
		• **MyEconLab** Study
		   Plan 2.5
		• Animated Figures
		   2-3, 2-4
		• Weblink

The Trade-Off Between Consumption Goods and Capital Goods If we allocate more resources to producing capital goods today, then, other things being equal, the economy will grow faster than it would have otherwise. Thus, the production possibilities curve will shift outward by a larger amount in the future, which means that we can have more consumption goods in the future. The trade-off, however, is that producing more capital goods today entails giving up consumption goods today.	consumption, 38	• **MyEconLab** Study Plans 2.6 and 2.7

Absolute Advantage versus Comparative Advantage A person has an absolute advantage if she can produce more of a specific good than someone else who uses the same amount of resources. Nevertheless, the individual can gain from specializing in producing a different good if she has a comparative advantage in producing that good, meaning that she can produce the good at a lower opportunity cost than someone else. By specializing in producing the good for which she has a comparative advantage, she assures herself of reaping gains from specialization in the form of a higher income.	specialization, 40
	comparative
	   advantage, 40
	absolute advantage, 40
	division of labor, 41
		• **MyEconLab** Study
		   Plans 2.8 and 2.9
		• Video: Absolute versus
		   Comparative Advantage
		• Weblink

Log in to MyEconLab, take a chapter test, and get a personalized Study Plan that tells you which concepts you understand and which ones you need to review. From there, MyEconLab will give you further practice, tutorials, animations, videos, and guided solutions.

Log in to www.myeconlab.com

PROBLEMS

Select problems, indicated by a blue oval, are assignable in MyEconLab.
Answers to the odd-numbered problems appear at the back of the book.

2-1 Define opportunity cost. What is your opportunity cost of attending a class at 11:00 A.M.? How does it differ from your opportunity cost of attending a class at 8:00 A.M.?

2-2 If you receive a free ticket to a concert, what, if anything, is your opportunity cost of attending the concert? How does your opportunity cost change if miserable weather on the night of the concert requires you to leave much earlier for the concert hall and greatly extends the time it takes to get home afterward?

2-3 The following table illustrates the points a student can earn on examinations in economics and biology if the student uses all available hours for study.

Economics	Biology
100	40
90	50
80	60
70	70
60	80
50	90
40	100

Plot this student's production possibilities curve. Does the PPC illustrate the law of increasing relative cost?

2-4 Based on the information provided in Problem 2-3, what is the opportunity cost to this student of allocating enough additional study time on economics to move her grade up from a 90 to a 100?

2-5 Consider a change in the table in Problem 2-3. The student's set of opportunities is now as follows:

Economics	Biology
100	40
90	60
80	75
70	85
60	93
50	98
40	100

Plot this student's production possibilities curve. Does the PPC illustrate the law of increasing relative cost? What is the opportunity cost to this student for the additional amount of study time on economics required to move her grade from 60 to 70? From 90 to 100?

2-6 Construct a production possibilities curve (PPC) for a nation facing increasing opportunity costs for producing food and video games. Show how the PPC changes given the following events.

a. A new and better fertilizer is invented.
b. Immigration occurs, and immigrants' labor can be employed in both the agricultural sector and the video game sector.
c. A new programming language is invented that is less costly to code and is more memory-efficient, enabling the use of smaller game cartridges.
d. A heat wave and drought result in a 10 percent decrease in usable farmland.

2-7 A nation's residents can allocate their scarce resources either to producing consumption goods or to producing human capital—that is, providing themselves with training and education. The following table displays the production possibilities for this nation:

Production Combination	Units of Consumption Goods	Units of Human Capital
A	0	100
B	10	97
C	20	90
D	30	75
E	40	55
F	50	30
G	60	0

a. Suppose that the nation's residents currently produce combination A. What is the opportunity cost of increasing production of consumption goods by 10 units? By 60 units?
b. Does the law of increasing relative cost hold true for this nation? Why or why not?

2-8 Like physical capital, human capital produced in the present can be applied to the production of future goods and services. Consider the table in Problem 2-7, and suppose that the nation's residents are trying to choose between combination C and combination F. Other things being equal, will the future production possibilities curve for this nation be located farther outward if the nation chooses combination F instead of combination C? Explain.

2-9 You can wash, fold, and iron a basket of laundry in two hours and prepare a meal in one hour. Your roommate can wash, fold, and iron a basket of laundry in three hours and prepare a meal in one hour. Who has the absolute advantage in laundry, and who has an absolute advantage in meal preparation? Who has the comparative advantage in laundry, and who has a comparative advantage in meal preparation?

2-10 Based on the information in Problem 2–9, should you and your roommate specialize in a particular task? Why? And if so, who should specialize in which task? Show how much labor time you save if you choose to "trade" an appropriate task with your roommate as opposed to doing it yourself.

2-11. On the one hand, Canada goes to considerable lengths to protect its television program and magazine producers from U.S. competitors. The United States, on the other hand, often seeks protection from food imports from Canada. Construct an argument showing that from an economywide viewpoint, these efforts by both nations are misguided.

2-12. Using only the concept of comparative advantage, evaluate this statement: "A professor with a Ph.D. in economics should never mow his or her own lawn, because this would fail to take into account the professor's comparative advantage."

2-13 Country A and country B produce the same consumption goods and capital goods and currently have *identical* production possibilities curves. They also have the same resources at present, and they have access to the same technology.
  a. At present, does either country have a comparative advantage in producing capital goods? Consumption goods?
  b. Currently, country A has chosen to produce more consumption goods, compared with country B.

Other things being equal, which country will experience the larger outward shift of its PPC during the next year?

Consider the following diagram when answering Problems 2-14, 2-15, and 2-16

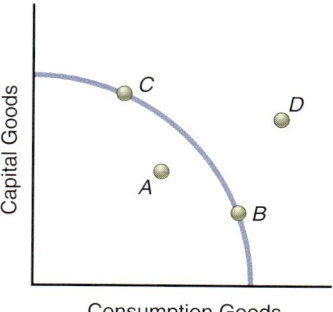

2-14 During a debate on the floor of the U.S. Senate, Senator Creighton states, "Our nation should not devote so many of its fully employed resources to producing capital goods because we already are not producing enough consumption goods for our citizens." Compared with the other labeled points on the diagram, which one could be consistent with the *current* production combination choice that Senator Creighton believes the nation has made?

2-15 In response to Senator Creighton's statement reported in Problem 2-14, Senator Long replies, "We must remain at our current production combination if we want to be able to produce more consumption goods in the future." Of the labeled points on the diagram, which one could depict the *future* production combination Senator Long has in mind?

2-16 Senator Borman interjects the following comment after the statements by Senators Creighton and Long reported in Problems 2-14 and 2-15: "In fact, both of my esteemed colleagues are wrong, because an unacceptably large portion of our nation's resources is currently unemployed." Of the labeled points on the diagram, which one is consistent with Senator Borman's position?

ECONOMICS ON THE NET

Opportunity Cost and Labor Force Participation Many students choose to forgo full-time employment to concentrate on their studies, thereby incurring a sizable opportunity cost. This application explores the nature of this opportunity cost.

Title: College Enrollment and Work Activity of High School Graduates

Navigation: Go to www.econtoday.com/ch02 to visit the Bureau of Labor Statistics (BLS) home page. Select A–Z Index and then click on *Educational Attainment, Statistics*. Finally, under the heading "Economic News Releases," click on *College Enrollment and Work Activity of High School Graduates*.

Application Read the abbreviated report on college enrollment and work activity of high school graduates. Then answer the following questions.

1. Based on the article, explain who the BLS considers to be in the labor force and who it does not view as part of the labor force.

2. What is the difference in labor force participation rates between high school students entering four-year universities and those entering two-year universities? Using the concept of opportunity cost, explain the difference.

3. What is the difference in labor force participation rates between part-time college students and full-time college students? Using the concept of opportunity cost, explain the difference.

For Group Study and Analysis Read the last paragraph of the article. Then divide the class into two groups. The first group should explain, based on the concept of opportunity cost, the difference in labor force participation rates between youths not in school but with a high school diploma and youths not in school and without a high school diploma. The second half should explain, based on opportunity cost, the difference in labor force participation rates between men and women not in school but with a high school diploma and men and women not in school and without a high school diploma.

ANSWERS TO QUICK QUIZZES

p. 29: (i) Scarcity; (ii) land . . . labor . . . physical . . . human . . . entrepreneurship; (iii) Wants; (iv) need
p. 33: (i) next-highest; (ii) opportunity; (iii) next-best; (iv) production possibilities
p. 37: (i) production possibilities; (ii) fixed; (iii) outside . . . inside; (iv) outward
p. 39: (i) Capital; (ii) more . . . smaller
p. 43: (i) higher; (ii) comparative; (iii) lowest; (iv) division

Demand and Supply 3

They are small, thin, and lightweight, and some people are not even aware of their existence. Nevertheless, many other individuals allocate hundreds of dollars per month to purchasing these items, and all buyers together spend hundreds of millions to billions of dollars on them each year. The items in question are sports trading cards, such as baseball cards that display photos of professional baseball players along with key statistics about the players' careers. Most sports trading cards can be purchased for a few dollars or less, but many cost $50 or more. A few cards can be obtained only at a price of several thousand dollars. In this chapter, you will learn why the prices of sports trading cards vary so widely.

Learning Objectives

After reading this chapter, you should be able to:

1. Explain the law of demand
2. Discuss the difference between money prices and relative prices
3. Distinguish between changes in demand and changes in quantity demanded
4. Explain the law of supply
5. Distinguish between changes in supply and changes in quantity supplied
6. Understand how the interaction of the demand for and supply of a commodity determines the market price of the commodity and the equilibrium quantity of the commodity that is produced and consumed

MyEconLab helps you master each objective and study more efficiently. See end of chapter for details.

Did You Know That...

since the end of 2003, the average price of an apartment-sized condominium has often exceeded the average price of a stand-alone house? This is just one example of how the relative physical size of items does not determine the prices at which people exchange them. As another example, consider that a high-quality diamond no more than a fraction of an inch in diameter often sells at a much higher price than a computer or a high-definition television set.

If we use the economist's primary set of tools, *demand* and *supply*, we can develop a better understanding of why the relative size of an item typically has little to do with the price at which the item sells. Demand and supply are two ways of categorizing the influences on the prices of goods that you buy and the quantities available. Indeed, demand and supply characterize much economic analysis of the world around us.

As you will see throughout this text, the operation of the forces of demand and supply takes place in *markets*. A **market** is an abstract concept summarizing all the arrangements individuals have for exchanging with one another. Goods and services are sold in markets, such as the automobile market, the health care market, and the market for Internet telephone services. Workers offer their services in the labor market. Companies, or firms, buy workers' labor services in the labor market. Firms also buy other inputs in order to produce the goods and services that you buy as a consumer. Firms purchase machines, buildings, and land. These markets are in operation at all times. One of the most important activities in these markets is the determination of the prices of all of the inputs and outputs that are bought and sold in our complicated economy. To understand the determination of prices, you first need to look at the law of demand.

Market
All of the arrangements that individuals have for exchanging with one another. Thus, for example, we can speak of the labor market, the automobile market, and the credit market.

DEMAND

Demand
A schedule showing how much of a good or service people will purchase at any price during a specified time period, other things being constant.

Demand has a special meaning in economics. It refers to the quantities of specific goods or services that individuals, taken singly or as a group, will purchase at various possible prices, other things being constant. We can therefore talk about the demand for microprocessor chips, french fries, multifunction printer-copiers, children, and criminal activities.

The Law of Demand

Law of demand
The observation that there is a negative, or inverse, relationship between the price of any good or service and the quantity demanded, holding other factors constant.

Associated with the concept of demand is the **law of demand,** which can be stated as follows:

When the price of a good goes up, people buy less of it, other things being equal. When the price of a good goes down, people buy more of it, other things being equal.

The law of demand tells us that the quantity demanded of any commodity is inversely related to its price, other things being equal. In an inverse relationship, one variable moves up in value when the other moves down. The law of demand states that a change in price causes a change in the quantity demanded in the *opposite* direction.

Notice that we tacked on to the end of the law of demand the statement "other things being equal." We referred to this in Chapter 1 as the *ceteris paribus* assumption. It means, for example, that when we predict that people will buy fewer DVD players if their price goes up, we are holding constant the price of all other goods in the economy as well as people's incomes. Implicitly, therefore, if we are assuming that no other prices change when we examine the price behavior of DVD players, we are looking at the *relative* price of DVD players.

The law of demand is supported by millions of observations of people's behavior in the marketplace. Theoretically, it can be derived from an economic model based on rational behavior, as was discussed in Chapter 1. Basically, if nothing else changes and the price of a good falls, the lower price induces us to buy more over a certain period of time because we can enjoy additional net gains that were unavailable at the higher price. If you examine your own behavior, you will see that it generally follows the law of demand.

Relative Prices versus Money Prices

The **relative price** of any commodity is its price in terms of another commodity. The price that you pay in dollars and cents for any good or service at any point in time is called its **money price**. You might hear from your grandparents, "My first new car cost only fifteen hundred dollars." The implication, of course, is that the price of cars today is outrageously high because the average new car may cost $32,000. But that is not an accurate comparison. What was the price of the average house during that same year? Perhaps it was only $12,000. By comparison, then, given that the average price of houses today is close to $270,000, the price of a new car today doesn't sound so far out of line, does it?

The point is that money prices during different time periods don't tell you much. You have to calculate relative prices. Consider an example of the price of prerecorded DVDs versus prerecorded videocassettes from last year and this year. In Table 3-1, we show the money prices of DVDs and videocassettes for two years during which they have both gone up. That means that we have to pay out in today's dollars more for DVDs and more for videocassettes. If we look, though, at the relative prices of DVDs and videocassettes, we find that last year, DVDs were twice as expensive as videocassettes, whereas this year they are only $1\frac{3}{4}$ times as expensive. Conversely, if we compare videocassettes to DVDs, last year the price of videocassettes was half the price of DVDs, but today the price of videocassettes is about 57 percent of the DVD price. In the one-year period, though both prices have gone up in money terms, the relative price of DVDs has fallen (and equivalently, the relative price of videocassettes has risen).

Sometimes relative price changes occur because the quality of a product improves, thereby bringing about a decrease in the item's effective *price per constant-quality unit*. The price of an item may decrease simply because producers have reduced the item's quality. Thus, when evaluating the effects of price changes, we must always compare *price per constant-quality unit*.

Relative price
The money price of one commodity divided by the money price of another commodity; the number of units of one commodity that must be sacrificed to purchase one unit of another commodity.

Money price
The price that we observe today, expressed in today's dollars; also called the *absolute* or *nominal price*.

TABLE 3-1
Money Price versus Relative Price

The money prices of both digital videodiscs (DVDs) and videocassettes have risen. But the relative price of DVDs has fallen (or conversely, the relative price of videocassettes has risen).

	Money Price		Relative Price	
	Price Last Year	Price This Year	Price Last Year	Price This Year
DVDs	$20	$28	$\frac{\$20}{\$10} = 2.0$	$\frac{\$28}{\$16} = 1.75$
Videocassettes	$10	$16	$\frac{\$10}{\$20} = 0.5$	$\frac{\$16}{\$28} = 0.57$

QUICK QUIZ

The **law of demand** posits a(n) _____ relationship between the quantity demanded of a good and its price, other things being equal.

The law of _____ applies when other things, such as income and the prices of all other goods and services, are held constant.

See page 81 for the answers. Review concepts from this section in MyEconLab.

THE DEMAND SCHEDULE

Let's take a hypothetical demand situation to see how the inverse relationship between the price and the quantity demanded looks (holding other things equal). We will consider the quantity of 64-megabyte, computer flash memory pen drives (also known as "flash pen drives") demanded *per year*. Without stating the *time dimension*, we could not make sense out of this demand relationship because the numbers would be different if we were talking about the quantity demanded per month or the quantity demanded per decade.

In addition to implicitly or explicitly stating a time dimension for a demand relationship, we are also implicitly referring to *constant-quality units* of the good or service in question. Prices are always expressed in constant-quality units in order to avoid the problem of comparing commodities that are in fact not truly comparable.

In panel (a) of Figure 3-1, we see that if the price is $1 apiece, 50 flash pen drives will be bought each year by our representative individual, but if the price is $5 apiece,

FIGURE 3-1
The Individual Demand Schedule and the Individual Demand Curve

In panel (a), we show combinations *A* through *E* of the quantities of flash memory pen drives demanded, measured in constant-quality units at prices ranging from $5 down to $1 apiece. These combinations are points on the demand schedule. In panel (b), we plot combinations *A* through *E* on a grid. The result is the individual demand curve for flash memory pen drives.

Panel (a)

Combination	Price per Constant-Quality Flash Memory Pen Drive	Quantity of Constant-Quality Flash Memory Pen Drives per Year
A	$5	10
B	4	20
C	3	30
D	2	40
E	1	50

only 10 flash pen drives will be bought each year. This reflects the law of demand. Panel (a) is also called simply demand, or a *demand schedule*, because it gives a schedule of alternative quantities demanded per year at different possible prices.

The Demand Curve

Tables expressing relationships between two variables can be represented in graphical terms. To do this, we need only construct a graph that has the price per constant-quality flash memory pen drive on the vertical axis and the quantity measured in constant-quality flash memory pen drives per year on the horizontal axis. All we have to do is take combinations A through E from panel (a) of Figure 3-1 and plot those points in panel (b). Now we connect the points with a smooth line, and *voilà*, we have a **demand curve.** It is downward sloping (from left to right) to indicate the inverse relationship between the price of flash pen drives and the quantity demanded per year. Our presentation of demand schedules and curves applies equally well to all commodities, including dental floss, bagels, textbooks, credit, and labor. Remember, the demand curve is simply a graphical representation of the law of demand.

What do you suppose has happened to the quantity of radio frequency identification (RFID) tags demanded as an RFID tag's price has declined?

Demand curve
A graphical representation of the demand schedule; a negatively sloped line showing the inverse relationship between the price and the quantity demanded (other things being equal).

E-COMMERCE EXAMPLE

Why RFID Tags Are Catching On Fast

An RFID tag contains a tiny microchip and a radio antenna, and it emits a unique signal that a computer-operated reader can use to track any item to which the tag is attached. In principle, any tagged item can be tracked as it travels in planes, trucks, and ships, through ports and warehouses, onto retailers' shelves and through their checkout lines, and into homes and offices.

Just a couple of years ago, the price of an RFID tag was about 30 cents. It has now dropped to 15 cents, and in just a few more years, the price is likely to decline to not much more than a nickel.

As the price of an RFID tag has fallen, an increasing number of tags have been put to use by retailers, hospitals, trucking firms, airlines, railroads, and shipping lines. Thus, the quantity of RFID tags demanded has increased in response to the price decrease, consistent with the law of demand.

FOR CRITICAL ANALYSIS
Why do you suppose that the European Central Bank, which already embeds RFID tags in the largest-denomination euro notes to help deter theft and counterfeiting, is now contemplating placing the tags in smaller-denomination notes?

Individual versus Market Demand Curves

The demand schedule shown in panel (a) of Figure 3-1 and the resulting demand curve shown in panel (b) are both given for an individual. As we shall see, the determination of price in the marketplace depends on, among other things, the **market demand** for a particular commodity. The way in which we measure a market demand schedule and derive a market demand curve for flash pen drives or any other good or service is by summing (at each price) the individual quantities demanded by all buyers in the market. Suppose that the market demand for flash pen drives consists of only two buyers: buyer 1, for whom we've already shown the demand schedule, and buyer 2, whose demand schedule

Market demand
The demand of all consumers in the marketplace for a particular good or service. The summation at each price of the quantity demanded by each individual.

FIGURE 3-2

The Horizontal Summation of Two Demand Curves

Panel (a) shows how to sum the demand schedule for one buyer with that of another buyer. In column 2 is the quantity demanded by buyer 1, taken from panel (a) of Figure 3-1 on page 54. Column 4 is the sum of columns 2 and 3. We plot the demand curve for buyer 1 in panel (b) and the demand curve for buyer 2 in panel (c). When we add those two demand curves horizontally, we get the market demand curve for two buyers, shown in panel (d).

is displayed in column 3 of panel (a) of Figure 3-2. Column 1 shows the price, and column 2 shows the quantity demanded by buyer 1 at each price. These data are taken directly from Figure 3-1 on page 54. In column 3, we show the quantity demanded by buyer 2. Column 4 shows the total quantity demanded at each price, which is obtained by simply adding columns 2 and 3. Graphically, in panel (d) of Figure 3-2, we add the demand curves of buyer 1 [panel (b)] and buyer 2 [panel (c)] to derive the market demand curve.

There are, of course, numerous potential consumers of flash memory pen drives. We'll simply assume that the summation of all of the consumers in the market results in a demand schedule, given in panel (a) of Figure 3-3, and a demand curve, given in panel (b). The quantity demanded is now measured in millions of units per year. Remember, panel (b) in Figure 3-3 shows the market demand curve for the millions of users of flash pen drives. The "market" demand curve that we derived in Figure 3-2 was undertaken assuming that there were only two buyers in the entire market. That's why we assume that the "market" demand curve for two buyers in panel (d) of Figure 3-2 is not a smooth line, whereas the true market demand curve in panel (b) of Figure 3-3 is a smooth line with no kinks.

FIGURE 3-3
The Market Demand Schedule for Flash Memory Pen Drives

In panel (a), we add up the existing demand schedules for flash pen drives. In panel (b), we plot the quantities from panel (a) on a grid; connecting them produces the market demand curve for flash pen drives.

Panel (a)

Price per Constant-Quality Flash Memory Pen Drive	Total Quantity Demanded of Constant-Quality Flash Memory Pen Drives per Year (millions)
$5	2
4	4
3	6
2	8
1	10

QUICK QUIZ

We measure the **demand schedule** in terms of a time dimension and in _____-quality units.

The _____ _____ curve is derived by summing the quantity demanded by individuals at each price. Graphically, we add the individual demand curves horizontally to derive the total, or market, demand curve.

See page 81 for the answers. Review concepts from this section in MyEconLab.

SHIFTS IN DEMAND

Assume that the federal government gives every student registered in a college, university, or technical school in the United States a laptop computer. The demand curve presented in panel (b) of Figure 3-3 would no longer be an accurate representation of total market demand for flash memory pen drives. What we have to do is shift the curve outward, or to the right, to represent the rise in demand that would result from this program. There will now be an increase in the number of flash pen drives demanded at *each and every possible price*. The demand curve shown in Figure 3-4 on the following page will shift from D_1 to D_2. Take any price, say, $3 per flash pen drive. Originally, before the federal government giveaway of laptop computers, the amount demanded at $3 was 6 million flash pen drives per year. After the government giveaway of laptop computers, however, the new amount demanded at the $3 price is 10 million flash pen drives per year. What we have seen is a shift in the demand for flash pen drives.

FIGURE 3-4

A Shift in the Demand Curve

If some factor other than price changes, we can show its effect by moving the entire demand curve, say, from D_1 to D_2. We have assumed in our example that this move was precipitated by the government's giving a free laptop computer to every registered college student in the United States. Thus, at *all* prices, a larger number of flash memory pen drives would be demanded than before. Curve D_3 represents reduced demand compared to curve D_1, caused by a prohibition of laptop computers on campus.

Under different circumstances, the shift can also go in the opposite direction. What if colleges uniformly prohibited the use of laptop computers by any of their students? Such a regulation would cause a shift inward—to the left—of the demand curve for flash pen drives. In Figure 3-4, the demand curve would shift to D_3; the number demanded would now be less at each and every possible price.

The Other Determinants of Demand

The demand curve in panel (b) of Figure 3-3 on the previous page is drawn with other things held constant, specifically all of the other factors that determine how many flash pen drives will be bought. There are many such determinants. We refer to these determinants as ***ceteris paribus* conditions,** and they include consumers' income; tastes and preferences; the prices of related goods; expectations regarding future prices and future incomes; and market size (number of buyers). Let's examine each of these determinants more closely.

***Ceteris paribus* conditions**
Determinants of the relationship between price and quantity that are unchanged along a curve; changes in these factors cause the curve to shift.

Income. For most goods, an increase in income will lead to an increase in demand. That is, an increase in income will lead to a rightward shift in the position of the demand curve from, say, D_1 to D_2 in Figure 3-4. You can avoid confusion about shifts in curves by always relating a rise in demand to a rightward shift in the demand curve and a fall in demand to a leftward shift in the demand curve. Goods for which the demand rises when consumer income rises are called **normal goods.** Most goods, such as shoes, computers, and DVDs, are "normal goods." For some goods, however, demand *falls* as income rises. These are called **inferior goods.** Beans might be an example. As households get richer, they tend to purchase fewer and fewer beans and purchase more and more meat. (The terms *normal* and *inferior* are merely part of the economist's lexicon; no value judgments are associated with them.)

Normal goods
Goods for which demand rises as income rises. Most goods are normal goods.

Inferior goods
Goods for which demand falls as income rises.

Remember, a shift to the left in the demand curve represents a decrease in demand, and a shift to the right represents an increase in demand.

Tastes and Preferences. A change in consumer tastes in favor of a good can shift its demand curve outward to the right. When Pokémon trading cards became the rage, the demand curve for them shifted outward to the right; when the rage died out, the demand curve shifted inward to the left. Fashions depend to a large extent on people's tastes and preferences. Economists have little to say about the determination of tastes; that is, they don't have any "good" theories of taste determination or why people buy one brand of product rather than others. Advertisers, however, have various theories that they use to try to make consumers prefer their products over those of competitors.

What do you think has happened to the demand for brown hair dyes since more women have decided that they prefer to be brunettes?

EXAMPLE

Brunettes Now Have More Fun

In the 1960s, manufacturers of hair dye aired television and radio commercials claiming that "Blondes Have More Fun" and that "Gentlemen Prefer Blondes." For years thereafter, purchases of blonde hair colorings were a significantly higher share of total U.S. expenditures on hair dyes.

Women's tastes in hair color began to change in the mid-2000s, however. More of the top female stars of stage and screen are brunettes, such as Jennifer Lopez and Catherine Zeta-Jones. In addition, there has been an increase in U.S. populations of Hispanic, Asian, and Arabic women, whose natural hair shades tend to be brunette colors. Finally, graying women from the baby boom generation born between the mid-1940s and the late 1950s have found that darker shades better cover gray and require less maintenance. Together, these factors have contributed to a change in tastes favoring brown hair dyes. Consequently, the demand for brown shades of hair dye has risen sharply.

FOR CRITICAL ANALYSIS

What do you suppose has happened to the demand for blonde hair dyes since the mid-2000s?

Prices of Related Goods: Substitutes and Complements. Demand schedules are always drawn with the prices of all other commodities held constant. That is to say, when deriving a given demand curve, we assume that only the price of the good under study changes. For example, when we draw the demand curve for butter, we assume that the price of margarine is held constant. When we draw the demand curve for home cinema speakers, we assume that the price of surround-sound amplifiers is held constant. When we refer to *related goods*, we are talking about goods for which demand is interdependent. If a change in the price of one good shifts the demand for another good, those two goods have interdependent demands. There are two types of demand interdependencies: those in which goods are *substitutes* and those in which goods are *complements*. We can define and distinguish between substitutes and complements in terms of how the change in price of one commodity affects the demand for its related commodity.

Butter and margarine are **substitutes.** Either can be consumed to satisfy the same basic want. Let's assume that both products originally cost $2 per pound. If the price of butter remains the same and the price of margarine falls from $2 per pound to $1 per pound, people will buy more margarine and less butter. The demand curve for butter shifts inward to the left. If, conversely, the price of margarine rises from $2 per pound to $3 per pound, people will buy more butter and less margarine. The demand curve for butter shifts

Substitutes
Two goods are substitutes when a change in the price of one causes a shift in demand for the other in the same direction as the price change.

> **ECONOMICS FRONT AND CENTER**
>
> To contemplate a real-world example of the effect on demand of an increase in the price of a substitute, read **A Higher-Priced Substitute Creates a Market Opportunity,** on page 74.

outward to the right. In other words, an increase in the price of margarine will lead to an increase in the demand for butter, and an increase in the price of butter will lead to an increase in the demand for margarine. For substitutes, a change in the price of a substitute will cause a change in demand *in the same direction.*

Why do you suppose that decreases in the prices of computer software and other information-technology products have contributed to a significant fall in the demand for toys?

EXAMPLE

Kids Give Barbie Dolls and Legos the Boot

For years, Barbie dolls and Lego building blocks were among the most popular toys in the United States. Since the early 2000s, however, annual purchases of Barbie dolls and Legos have fallen by as much as 25 percent. Indeed, the demand for *all* toys has decreased.

Are today's kids studying so much that they have no time to play? Probably not. A more likely explanation for the decrease in the demand for toys is that the prices of substitute forms of children's entertainment, such as video games, computer software, and mobile phones and digital-text-messaging services, have declined. As prices of these substitute means of entertainment for kids have declined, consumers have substituted away from Barbie dolls, Legos, and other toys—the demand for toys has fallen.

FOR CRITICAL ANALYSIS

In what direction has the demand curve for toys shifted as the prices of substitute forms of childhood entertainment have declined?

Complements
Two goods are complements when a change in the price of one causes an opposite shift in the demand for the other.

For **complements,** goods typically consumed together, the situation is reversed. Consider desktop computers and printers. We draw the demand curve for printers with the price of desktop computers held constant. If the price per constant-quality unit of computers decreases from, say, $1,500 to $1,200, that will encourage more people to purchase computer peripheral devices. They will now buy more printers, at any given printer price, than before. The demand curve for printers will shift outward to the right. If, by contrast, the price of desktop computers increases from $1,100 to $1,400, fewer people will purchase computer peripheral devices. The demand curve for printers will shift inward to the left. To summarize, a decrease in the price of computers leads to an increase in the demand for printers. An increase in the price of computers leads to a decrease in the demand for printers. Thus, for complements, a change in the price of a product will cause a change in demand *in the opposite direction.*

Expectations. Consumers' expectations regarding future prices and future incomes will prompt them to buy more or less of a particular good without a change in its current money price. For example, consumers getting wind of a scheduled 100 percent increase in the price of flash memory pen drives next month will buy more of them today at today's prices. Today's demand curve for flash pen drives will shift from D_1 to D_2 in Figure 3-4 on page 58. The opposite would occur if a decrease in the price of flash pen drives were scheduled for next month (from D_1 to D_3).

Expectations of a rise in income may cause consumers to want to purchase more of everything today at today's prices. Again, such a change in expectations of higher future income will cause a shift in the demand curve from D_1 to D_2 in Figure 3-4 on page 58.

Finally, expectations that goods will not be available at any price will induce consumers to stock up now, increasing current demand.

Market Size (Number of Buyers). An increase in the number of buyers (holding buyers' incomes constant) at any given price shifts the market demand curve outward. Conversely, a reduction in the number of buyers at any given price shifts the market demand curve inward.

Changes in Demand versus Changes in Quantity Demanded

We have made repeated references to demand and to quantity demanded. It is important to realize that there is a difference between a *change in demand* and a *change in quantity demanded*.

Demand refers to a schedule of planned rates of purchase and depends on a great many *ceteris paribus* conditions, such as incomes, expectations, and the prices of substitutes or complements. Whenever there is a change in a *ceteris paribus* condition, there will be a change in demand—a shift in the entire demand curve to the right or to the left.

A quantity demanded is a specific quantity at a specific price, represented by a single point on a demand curve. When price changes, quantity demanded changes according to the law of demand, and there will be a movement from one point to another along the same demand curve. Look at Figure 3-5. At a price of $3 per flash memory pen drive, 6 million flash pen drives per year are demanded. If the price falls to $1, quantity demanded increases to 10 million per year. This movement occurs because the current market price for the product changes. In Figure 3-5, you can see the arrow pointing down the given demand curve D.

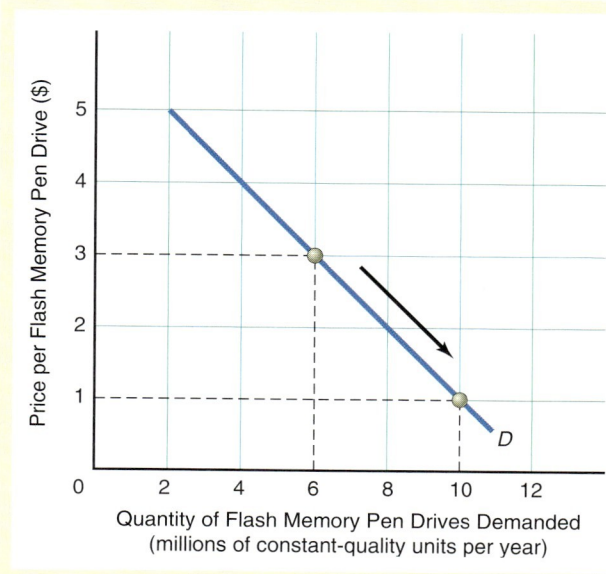

FIGURE 3-5

Movement Along a Given Demand Curve

A change in price changes the quantity of a good demanded. This can be represented as movement along a given demand schedule. If, in our example, the price of flash memory pen drives falls from $3 to $1 apiece, the quantity demanded will increase from 6 million to 10 million units per year.

When you think of demand, think of the entire curve. Quantity demanded, in contrast, is represented by a single point on the demand curve.

A change or shift in demand is a movement of the **entire** *curve. The* **only** *thing that can cause the entire curve to move is a change in a determinant* **other than its own price.**

In economic analysis, we cannot emphasize too much the following distinction that must constantly be made:

A change in a good's own price leads to a change in quantity demanded for any given demand curve, other things held constant. This is a movement **on** *the curve.*

A change in any of the **ceteris paribus** *conditions for demand leads to a change in demand. This causes a movement* **of** *the curve.*

QUICK QUIZ

Demand curves are drawn with determinants other than the price of the good held constant. These other determinants, called *ceteris paribus* **conditions**, are (1) _____; (2) _____; (3) _____; (4) _____, _____, and _____; and (5) _____ at any given price. If any one of these determinants changes, the demand curve will shift to the right or to the left.

A change in demand comes about only because of a change in the _____ _____ conditions of demand. This change in demand is a shift in the demand curve to the left or to the right.

A change in the quantity demanded comes about when there is a change in the price of the good (other things held constant). Such a change in quantity demanded involves _____ _____ a given demand curve.

See page 81 for the answers. Review concepts from this section in MyEconLab.

THE LAW OF SUPPLY

The other side of the basic model in economics involves the quantities of goods and services that firms will offer for sale to the market. The **supply** of any good or service is the amount that firms will produce and offer for sale under certain conditions during a specified time period. The relationship between price and quantity supplied, called the **law of supply,** can be summarized as follows:

Supply
A schedule showing the relationship between price and quantity supplied for a specified period of time, other things being equal.

Law of supply
The observation that the higher the price of a good, the more of that good sellers will make available over a specified time period, other things being equal.

At higher prices, a larger quantity will generally be supplied than at lower prices, all other things held constant. At lower prices, a smaller quantity will generally be supplied than at higher prices, all other things held constant.

There is generally a direct relationship between price and quantity supplied. For supply, as the price rises, the quantity supplied rises; as price falls, the quantity supplied also falls. Producers are normally willing to produce and sell more of their product at a higher price than at a lower price, other things being constant. At $5 per flash pen drive, manufacturers would almost certainly be willing to supply a larger quantity than at $1 per flash pen drive, assuming, of course, that no other prices in the economy had changed.

As with the law of demand, millions of instances in the real world have given us confidence in the law of supply. On a theoretical level, the law of supply is based on a model in which producers and sellers seek to make the most gain possible from their activities. For example, as a manufacturer attempts to produce more and more flash pen drives over the same time period, it will eventually have to hire more workers, pay overtime wages (which are higher), and overutilize its machines. Only if offered a higher price per flash pen drive will the manufacturer be willing to incur these higher costs. That is why the law of supply implies a direct relationship between price and quantity supplied.

How do you suppose that U.S. railroads responded when the prices they received for cross-country rail transportation services increased significantly during the 2000s?

EXAMPLE

Building Two-Way Transcontinental Railroads

In 1869, the first U.S. transcontinental railroad was completed when representatives from the Union Pacific and Central Pacific railroads drove a ceremonial golden spike into the last tie linking a single line of track connecting east and west. Some years later, the Union Pacific and Central Pacific companies merged, and eventually the Santa Fe railroad (which later merged with Burlington Northern) built another line of track stretching from Los Angeles to Chicago. Throughout the twentieth century, each company moved its trains back and forth along a single line of track by shunting eastbound trains onto side tracks to allow westbound trains to pass, and vice versa.

Since the early 2000s, the price of rail freight services has increased significantly. In response, Union Pacific and Burlington Northern Santa Fe have sought to increase the amount of rail traffic moving between Los Angeles and Chicago. To make this possible, the two rail companies are laying track parallel to their existing transcontinental lines. Adding these parallel tracks will allow unhindered two-way movement of trains across the nation, which will enable the firms to increase the quantity of rail transportation services supplied.

FOR CRITICAL ANALYSIS
How do you think that rail companies would respond to a temporary reduction in the price of rail transportation services?

THE SUPPLY SCHEDULE

Just as we were able to construct a demand schedule, we can construct a *supply schedule*, which is a table relating prices to the quantity supplied at each price. A supply schedule can also be referred to simply as *supply*. It is a set of planned production rates that depends on the price of the product. We show the individual supply schedule for a hypothetical producer in panel (a) of Figure 3-6 on page 64. At $1 per flash pen drive, for example, this producer will supply 20,000 flash pen drives per year; at $5, this producer will supply 55,000 flash pen drives per year.

The Supply Curve

We can convert the supply schedule in panel (a) of Figure 3-6 into a **supply curve,** just as we earlier created a demand curve in Figure 3-1. All we do is take the price-quantity combinations from panel (a) of Figure 3-6 and plot them in panel (b). We have labeled these combinations F through J. Connecting these points, we obtain an upward-sloping curve that shows the typically direct relationship between price and quantity supplied. Again, we have to remember that we are talking about quantity supplied *per year,* measured in constant-quality units.

Supply curve
The graphical representation of the supply schedule; a line (curve) showing the supply schedule, which generally slopes upward (has a positive slope), other things being equal.

The Market Supply Curve

Just as we summed the individual demand curves to obtain the market demand curve, we sum the individual producers' supply curves to obtain the market supply curve. Look at Figure 3-7 on page 65, in which we horizontally sum two typical supply curves for manufac-

FIGURE 3-6
The Individual Producer's Supply Schedule and Supply Curve for Flash Memory Pen Drives

Panel (a) shows that at higher prices, a hypothetical supplier will be willing to provide a greater quantity of flash memory pen drives. We plot the various price-quantity combinations in panel (a) on the grid in panel (b). When we connect these points, we create the individual supply curve for flash pen drives. It is positively sloped.

Panel (a)

Combination	Price per Constant-Quality Flash Memory Pen Drive	Quantity of Flash Memory Pen Drives Supplied (thousands of constant-quality units per year)
F	$5	55
G	4	40
H	3	35
I	2	25
J	1	20

turers of flash pen drives. Supplier 1's data are taken from Figure 3-6; supplier 2 is added. The numbers are presented in panel (a). The graphical representation of supplier 1 is in panel (b), of supplier 2 in panel (c), and of the summation in panel (d). The result, then, is the supply curve for flash pen drives for suppliers 1 and 2. We assume that there are more suppliers of flash pen drives, however. The total market supply schedule and total market supply curve for flash pen drives are represented in Figure 3-8 on page 66, with the curve in panel (b) obtained by adding all of the supply curves such as those shown in panels (b) and (c) of Figure 3-7. Notice the difference between the market supply curve with only two suppliers in Figure 3-7 and the one with a large number of suppliers—the entire true market—in panel (b) of Figure 3-8. (For simplicity, we assume that the true total market supply curve is a straight line.)

Note what happens at the market level when price changes. If the price is $3, the quantity supplied is 6 million. If the price goes up to $4, the quantity supplied increases to 8 million per year. If the price falls to $2, the quantity supplied decreases to 4 million per year. Changes in quantity supplied are represented by movements along the supply curve in panel (b) of Figure 3-8.

QUICK QUIZ

There is normally a _____ relationship between price and quantity of a good supplied, other things held constant.

The _____ curve normally shows a direct relationship between price and quantity supplied. The _____ _____ curve is obtained by horizontally adding individual supply curves in the market.

See page 81 for the answers. Review concepts from this section in MyEconLab.

FIGURE 3-7

Horizontal Summation of Supply Curves

In panel (a), we show the data for two individual suppliers of flash pen drives. Adding how much each is willing to supply at different prices, we come up with the combined quantities supplied in column 4. When we plot the values in columns 2 and 3 on grids in panels (b) and (c) and add them horizontally, we obtain the combined supply curve for the two suppliers in question, shown in panel (d).

SHIFTS IN SUPPLY

When we looked at demand, we found out that any change in anything relevant besides the price of the good or service caused the demand curve to shift inward or outward. The same is true for the supply curve. If something besides price changes and alters the willingness of suppliers to produce a good or service, we will see the entire supply curve shift.

Consider an example. There is a new method of manufacturing flash memory pen drives that significantly reduces the cost of production. In this situation, producers of flash pen drives will supply more product at *all* prices because their cost of so doing has fallen dramatically. Competition among manufacturers to produce more at each and every price will shift the supply curve outward to the right from S_1 to S_2 in Figure 3-9 on the following page. At a price of $3, the number supplied was originally 6 million per year, but now the amount supplied (after the reduction in the costs of production) at $3 per flash memory pen drive will be 9 million a year. (This is similar to what has happened to the supply curve of personal computers and fax machines in recent years as computer memory chip prices have fallen.)

FIGURE 3-8
The Market Supply Schedule and the Market Supply Curve for Flash Memory Pen Drives

In panel (a), we show the summation of all the individual producers' supply schedules; in panel (b), we graph the resulting supply curve. It represents the market supply curve for flash memory pen drives and is upward sloping.

Panel (a)

Price per Constant-Quality Flash Memory Pen Drive	Quantity of Flash Memory Pen Drives Supplied (millions of constant-quality units per year)
$5	10
4	8
3	6
2	4
1	2

FIGURE 3-9
A Shift in the Supply Curve

If the cost of producing flash memory pen drives were to fall dramatically, the supply curve would shift rightward from S_1 to S_2 such that at all prices, a larger quantity would be forthcoming from suppliers. Conversely, if the cost of production rose, the supply curve would shift leftward to S_3.

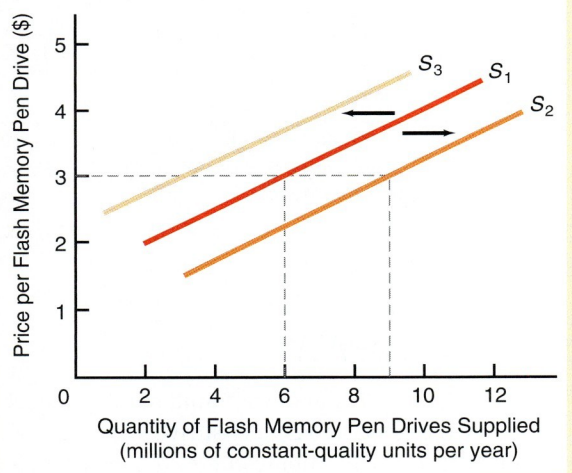

Consider the opposite case. If the cost of making flash pen drives increases, the supply curve in Figure 3-9 will shift from S_1 to S_3. At each and every price, the quantity of flash pen drives supplied will fall due to the increase in the price of raw materials.

The Other Determinants of Supply

When supply curves are drawn, only the price of the good in question changes, and it is assumed that other things remain constant. The other things assumed constant are the *ceteris paribus* conditions of supply. They include the prices of resources (inputs) used to produce the product, technology and productivity, taxes and subsidies, producers' price expectations, and the number of firms in the industry. If *any* of these *ceteris paribus* conditions changes, there will be a shift in the supply curve.

Cost of Inputs Used to Produce the Product. If one or more input prices fall, production costs fall, and the supply curve will shift outward to the right; that is, more will be supplied at each and every price. The opposite will be true if one or more inputs become more expensive. For example, when we draw the supply curve of new laptop computers, we are holding the price of microprocessors (and other inputs) constant. When we draw the supply curve of blue jeans, we are holding the cost of cotton fabric fixed.

In recent years, firms based in Thailand have become major producers of various electronic devices. How do you suppose that Thai companies responded to a significant decline in world prices of liquid crystal displays (LCDs) used in many such devices?

INTERNATIONAL EXAMPLE

Thai Gadget Makers Raise Production When LCD Prices Fall

Beginning in 2004, the prices of liquid crystal displays (LCDs), which are key components in many electronic devices, plummeted. As LCD prices declined by as much as 20 percent per month, Thailand-based manufacturers of cellphones, handheld computers, and laptop computers dramatically increased production of electronic devices that used LCDs. Thai companies such as AU Optronics, Chi Mei Optoelectronics, and Chunghwa Picture Tubes also responded to the lower LCD prices by increasing production of portable DVD players for automobiles.

FOR CRITICAL ANALYSIS

How do you predict that Thai producers of items that use LCDs as inputs would react to a significant increase in LCD prices?

Technology and Productivity. Supply curves are drawn by assuming a given technology, or "state of the art." When the available production techniques change, the supply curve will shift. For example, when a better production technique for flash pen drives becomes available, production costs decrease, and the supply curve will shift to the right. A larger quantity will be forthcoming at each and every price because the cost of production is lower.

How can destructive forest fires cause productivity in harvesting certain mushrooms to rise and thereby increase market supply?

EXAMPLE

Forest Fires Boost Productivity in Mushroom Harvesting

Morels are spongy mushrooms prized by gourmets because of their nutty flavor and ability to soak up sauces. Morels particularly thrive in burnt-out woodlands along riverbanks, so morel hunters descend on areas charred by forest fires. Following a recent fire that destroyed nearly a quarter of a million acres of forested lands in Montana, morel pickers converged on the area to harvest an unusually large bounty of morels. This boost in harvesting productivity generated a sudden increase in the market supply of morels.

FOR CRITICAL ANALYSIS

What would you speculate happens to the market supply of morels, other things being equal, when there are long periods with few forest fires?

Subsidy
A negative tax; a payment to a producer from the government, usually in the form of a cash grant per unit.

Taxes and Subsidies. Certain taxes, such as a per-unit tax, are effectively an addition to production costs and therefore reduce the supply. If the supply curve were S_1 in Figure 3-9 on page 66, a per-unit tax increase would shift it to S_3. A per-unit **subsidy** would do the opposite; it would shift the curve to S_2. Every producer would get a "gift" from the government for each unit produced.

How does a per-unit tax on an imported item, known as a *tariff*, affect the supply of that item in the United States?

POLICY EXAMPLE

Import Restrictions Reduce the Supply of Cement

U.S. cement manufacturers produce more than 80 million metric tons of cement each year. The rest of the cement supplied to the U.S. market—typically 15 to 20 million metric tons—is produced by firms located outside the United States, mostly in Mexico. During the 1990s, the U.S. government began imposing a special import duty, or tariff, on U.S. imports of cement from Mexico. Continuation of this tariff during the 2000s has induced Mexican producers to limit sales of cement in the United States at any given price. Consequently, the government's policy has had the effect of reducing the U.S. supply of cement.

FOR CRITICAL ANALYSIS
Who likely benefits from U.S. government restrictions on imports of cement from Mexico?

Price Expectations. A change in the expectation of a future relative price of a product can affect a producer's current willingness to supply, just as price expectations affect a consumer's current willingness to purchase. For example, suppliers of flash memory pen drives may withhold from the market part of their current supply if they anticipate higher prices in the future. The current amount supplied at each and every price will decrease.

Number of Firms in the Industry. In the short run, when firms can change only the number of employees they use, we hold the number of firms in the industry constant. In the long run, the number of firms may change. If the number of firms increases, the supply curve will shift outward to the right. If the number of firms decreases, it will shift inward to the left.

Changes in Supply versus Changes in Quantity Supplied

We cannot overstress the importance of distinguishing between a movement along the supply curve—which occurs only when the price changes for a given supply curve—and a shift in the supply curve—which occurs only with changes in *ceteris paribus* conditions. A change in the price of the good in question always (and only) brings about a change in the quantity supplied along a given supply curve. We move to a different point on the existing supply curve. This is specifically called a *change in quantity supplied*. When price changes, quantity supplied changes—there is a movement from one point to another along the same supply curve.

When you think of *supply*, think of the entire curve. Quantity supplied is represented by a single point on the supply curve.

*A change or shift in supply is a movement of the entire curve. The **only** thing that can cause the entire curve to move is a change in one of the **ceteris paribus** conditions.*

Consequently,

*A change in the price leads to a change in the quantity supplied, other things being constant. This is a movement **on** the curve.*

*A change in any **ceteris paribus** conditon for supply leads to a change in supply. This causes a movement **of** the curve.*

QUICK QUIZ

If the price changes, we _____ _____ a curve—there is a change in quantity demanded or supplied. If some other determinant changes, we _____ a curve—there is a change in demand or supply.

The **supply curve** is drawn with other things held constant. If these *ceteris paribus* conditions of supply change, the supply curve will shift. The major *ceteris paribus* conditions are (1) _____, (2) _____, (3) _____, (4) _____, and (5) _____.

See page 81 for the answers. Review concepts from this section in MyEconLab.

PUTTING DEMAND AND SUPPLY TOGETHER

In the sections on demand and supply, we tried to confine each discussion to demand or supply only. But you have probably already realized that we can't view the world just from the demand side or just from the supply side. There is interaction between the two. In this section, we will discuss how they interact and how that interaction determines the prices that prevail in our economy and other economies in which the forces of demand and supply are allowed to work.

Let's first combine the demand and supply schedules and then combine the curves.

Go to www.econtoday.com/ch03 to see how the U.S. Department of Agriculture seeks to estimate demand and supply conditions for major agricultural products.

Demand and Supply Schedules Combined

Let's place panel (a) from Figure 3-3 (the market demand schedule) on page 57 and panel (a) from Figure 3-8 (the market supply schedule) on page 66 together in panel (a) of Figure 3-10 on the next page. Column 1 shows the price; column 2, the quantity supplied per year at any given price; and column 3, the quantity demanded. Column 4 is the difference between columns 2 and 3, or the difference between the quantity supplied and the quantity demanded. In column 5, we label those differences as either excess quantity supplied (called a *surplus*, which we shall discuss shortly) or excess quantity demanded (commonly known as a *shortage*, also discussed shortly). For example, at a price of $1, only 2 million flash memory pen drives would be supplied, but the quantity demanded would be 10 million. The difference would be −8 million,

FIGURE 3-10

Putting Demand and Supply Together

In panel (a), we see that at the price of $3, the quantity supplied and the quantity demanded are equal, resulting in neither an excess quantity demanded nor an excess quantity supplied. We call this price the equilibrium, or market clearing, price. In panel (b), the intersection of the supply and demand curves is at *E*, at a price of $3 and a quantity of 6 million per year. At point *E*, there is neither an excess quantity demanded nor an excess quantity supplied. At a price of $1, the quantity supplied will be only 2 million per year, but the quantity demanded will be 10 million. The difference is excess quantity demanded at a price of $1. The price will rise, so we will move from point *A* up the supply curve and from point *B* up the demand curve to point *E*. At the other extreme, $5 elicits a quantity supplied of 10 million but a quantity demanded of only 2 million. The difference is excess quantity supplied at a price of $5. The price will fall, so we will move down the demand curve and the supply curve to the equilibrium price, $3 per flash pen drive.

Panel (a)

(1) Price per Constant-Quality Flash Memory Pen Drive	(2) Quantity Supplied (flash memory pen drives per year)	(3) Quantity Demanded (flash memory pen drives per year)	(4) Difference (2) − (3) (flash memory pen drives per year)	(5) Condition
$5	10 million	2 million	8 million	Excess quantity supplied (surplus)
4	8 million	4 million	4 million	Excess quantity supplied (surplus)
3	6 million	6 million	0	Market clearing price—equilibrium (no surplus, no shortage)
2	4 million	8 million	−4 million	Excess quantity demanded (shortage)
1	2 million	10 million	−8 million	Excess quantity demanded (shortage)

Panel (b)

which we label excess quantity demanded (a shortage). At the other end, a price of $5 would elicit 10 million in quantity supplied, but quantity demanded would drop to 2 million, leaving a difference of +8 million units, which we call excess quantity supplied (a surplus).

Now, do you notice something special about the price of $3? At that price, both the quantity supplied and the quantity demanded per year are 6 million. The difference then is zero. There is neither excess quantity demanded (shortage) nor excess quantity supplied (surplus). Hence the price of $3 is very special. It is called the **market clearing price**—it clears the market of all excess quantities demanded or supplied. There are no willing consumers who want to pay $3 per flash pen drive but are turned away by sellers, and there are no willing suppliers who want to sell flash pen drives at $3 who cannot sell all they want at that price. Another term for the market clearing price is the **equilibrium price,** the price at which there is no tendency for change. Consumers are able to get all they want at that price, and suppliers are able to sell all they want at that price.

Market clearing, or equilibrium, price
The price that clears the market, at which quantity demanded equals quantity supplied; the price where the demand curve intersects the supply curve.

Equilibrium

We can define **equilibrium** in general as a point at which quantity demanded equals quantity supplied at a particular price. There tends to be no movement of the price or the quantity away from this point unless demand or supply changes. Any movement away from this point will set into motion forces that will cause movement back to it. Therefore, equilibrium is a stable point. Any point that is not at equilibrium is unstable and will not persist.

Equilibrium
The situation when quantity supplied equals quantity demanded at a particular price.

The equilibrium point occurs where the supply and demand curves intersect. The equilibrium price is given on the vertical axis directly to the left of where the supply and demand curves cross. The equilibrium quantity is given on the horizontal axis directly underneath the intersection of the demand and supply curves.

Panel (b) in Figure 3-3 and panel (b) in Figure 3-8 are combined as panel (b) in Figure 3-10. The only difference now is that the horizontal axis measures both the quantity supplied and the quantity demanded per year. Everything else is the same. The demand curve is labeled *D*, the supply curve *S*. We have labeled the intersection of the supply curve with the demand curve as point *E*, for equilibrium. That corresponds to a market clearing price of $3, at which both the quantity supplied and the quantity demanded are 6 million units per year. There is neither excess quantity supplied nor excess quantity demanded. Point *E*, the equilibrium point, always occurs at the intersection of the supply and demand curves. This is the price *toward which* the market price will automatically tend to gravitate, because there is no outcome better than this price for both consumers and producers.

Shortages

The price of $3 depicted in Figure 3-10 represents a situation of equilibrium. If there were a non-market-clearing, or disequilibrium, price, this would put into play forces that would cause the price to change toward the market clearing price at which equilibrium would again be sustained. Look again at panel (b) in Figure 3-10. Suppose that instead of being at the equilibrium price of $3, for some reason the market price is $1. At this price, the quantity demanded of 10 million per year exceeds the quantity supplied of 2 million per year. We

Shortage
A situation in which quantity demanded is greater than quantity supplied at a price below the market clearing price.

have a situation of excess quantity demanded at the price of $1. This is usually called a **shortage.** Consumers of flash memory pen drives would find that they could not buy all that they wished at $1 apiece. But forces will cause the price to rise: Competing consumers will bid up the price, and suppliers will increase output in response. (Remember, some buyers would pay $5 or more rather than do without flash memory pen drives. They do not want to be left out.) We would move from points A and B toward point E. The process would stop when the price again reached $3 per flash pen drive.

At this point, it is important to recall a distinction made in Chapter 2:

Shortages and scarcity are not the same thing.

A shortage is a situation in which the quantity demanded exceeds the quantity supplied at a price that is somehow kept *below* the market clearing price. Our definition of scarcity was much more general and all-encompassing: a situation in which the resources available for producing output are insufficient to satisfy all wants. Any choice necessarily costs an opportunity, and the opportunity is lost. Hence we will always live in a world of scarcity because we must constantly make choices, but we do not necessarily have to live in a world of shortages.

Surpluses

Now let's repeat the experiment with the market price at $5 rather than at the market clearing price of $3. Clearly, the quantity supplied will exceed the quantity demanded at that price. The result will be an excess quantity supplied at $5 per unit. This excess quantity supplied is often called a **surplus.** Given the curves in panel (b) in Figure 3-10 on page 70, however, there will be forces pushing the price back down toward $3 per flash memory pen drive: Competing suppliers will cut prices and reduce output, and consumers will purchase more at these new lower prices. If the two forces of supply and demand are unrestricted, they will bring the price back to $3 per flash pen drive.

Surplus
A situation in which quantity supplied is greater than quantity demanded at a price above the market clearing price.

Shortages and surpluses are resolved in unfettered markets—markets in which price changes are free to occur. The forces that resolve them are those of competition: In the case of shortages, consumers competing for a limited quantity supplied drive up the price; in the case of surpluses, sellers compete for the limited quantity demanded, thus driving prices down to equilibrium. The equilibrium price is the only stable price, and the (unrestricted) market price tends to gravitate toward it.

What happens when the price is set below the equilibrium price? Here come the scalpers.

POLICY EXAMPLE

Should Shortages in the Ticket Market Be Solved by Scalpers?

If you have ever tried to get tickets to a playoff game in sports, a popular Broadway play, or a superstar's rap concert, you know about "shortages." The standard Super Bowl ticket situation is shown in Figure 3-11. At the face-value price of Super Bowl tickets ($600), the quantity demanded (175,000) greatly exceeds the quantity supplied (80,000). Because shortages last only so long as prices and quantities do not change, markets tend to exhibit a movement out of this disequilibrium toward equilibrium. Obviously, the quantity of Super Bowl tickets cannot change, but the price can go as high as $4,000. *(continued)*

Enter the scalper. This colorful term is used because when you purchase a ticket that is being resold at a price higher than face value, the seller is skimming an extra profit off the top ("taking your scalp"). If an event sells out and people who wished to purchase tickets at current prices were unable to do so, ticket prices by definition were lower than market clearing prices. People without tickets may be willing to buy high-priced tickets because they place a greater value on the entertainment event than the face value of the ticket. Without scalpers, those individuals would not be able to attend the event. In the case of the Super Bowl, various forms of scalping occur nationwide. Tickets for a seat on the 50-yard line have been sold for as much as $4,000 apiece. In front of every Super Bowl arena, you can find ticket scalpers hawking their wares.

In most states, scalping is illegal. In Pennsylvania, convicted scalpers are either fined $5,000 or sentenced to two years behind bars. For an economist, such legislation seems strange. As one New York ticket broker said, "I look at scalping like working as a stockbroker, buying low and selling high. If people are willing to pay me the money, what kind of problem is that?"

FOR CRITICAL ANALYSIS
What happens to ticket scalpers who are still holding tickets after an event has started?

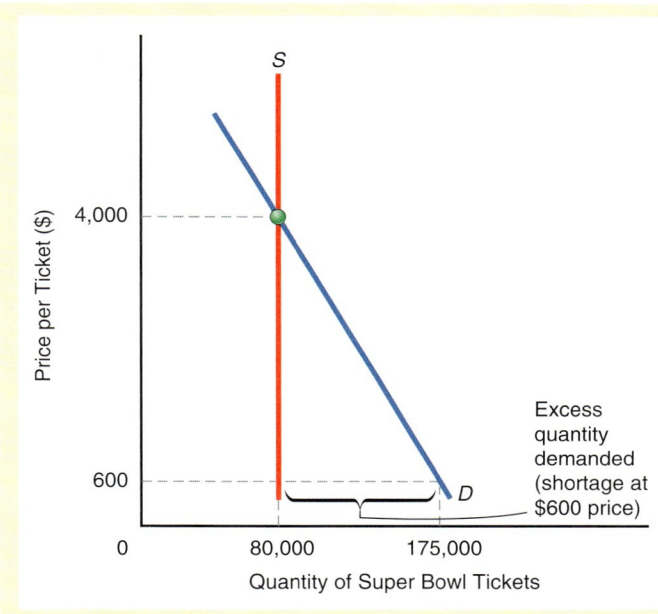

FIGURE 3-11

Shortages of Super Bowl Tickets

The quantity of tickets for a Super Bowl game is fixed at 80,000. At the price per ticket of $600, the quantity demanded is 175,000. Consequently, there is an excess quantity demanded at the below–market clearing price. In this example, prices can go as high as $4,000 in the scalpers' market.

QUICK QUIZ

The market clearing price occurs at the _____ of the market demand curve and the market supply curve. It is also called the _____ price, the price from which there is no tendency to change unless there is a change in demand or supply.

Whenever the price is _____ than the equilibrium price, there is an excess quantity supplied (a **surplus**).

Whenever the price is _____ than the equilibrium price, there is an excess quantity demanded (a **shortage**).

See page 81 for the answers. Review concepts from this section in MyEconLab.

CASE STUDY: ECONOMICS FRONT AND CENTER

A Higher-Priced Substitute Creates a Market Opportunity

Levitt is an engineer with Security Systems, Inc., an antiterrorism security firm. Levitt and his colleagues have spent the past several years developing a handheld bomb-sniffing device they have named Bulldog. The Bulldog uses molecules called chromophores to detect explosive compounds. When waved over the hands and clothing of suspects who have actually been handling explosives, the chromophores in the Bulldog stop glowing, causing the device to sound an alarm. Nevertheless, the company has had difficulty convincing potential users to purchase the Bulldog at a per-unit price of $15,000.

The military, the Department of Homeland Security, and transportation firms have traditionally used bomb-sniffing dogs to detect explosives. Dogs' noses have more than 2 billion odor receptors—greater than 40 times the number in a human nose—and trained dogs can be used in groups to reduce the risk of error by a dog having an "off day."

During the past four years, however, the price of a well-trained bomb-sniffing dog has jumped by more than 50 percent, to at least $12,000 per dog. As a result, the demand for Security Systems' Bulldog has increased considerably. Levitt's current task is to expand production lines for the device, now that the company has accepted several hundred orders.

CRITICAL ANALYSIS QUESTIONS

1. *In the market for the Bulldog and similar devices, has the increase in the price of bomb-sniffing dogs generated an increase in demand for electronic bomb sniffers or an increase in quantity demanded?*

2. *What is likely to happen to the market clearing price of the Bulldog and similar devices as a result of the increase in the price of bomb-sniffing dogs?*

Issues and Applications

The Market Clearing Prices of Baseball Cards

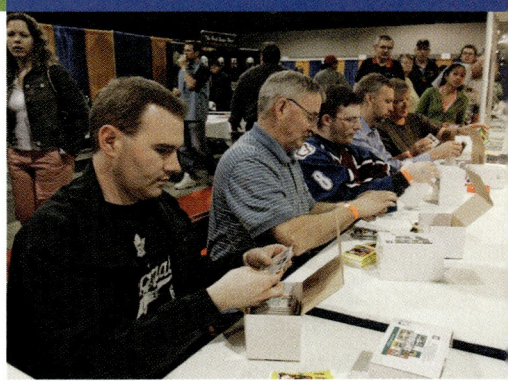

Concepts Applied
- Market Clearing Price
- Demand
- Supply

Various companies, such as Topps and Upper Deck, print sports trading cards that provide photos and statistics of professional athletes at various stages in their careers. For instance, companies print a number of cards for each new professional baseball player, or rookie. Manufacturers of items such as bubble gum and candies purchase the cards to package with those items to sell as bundled products. A consumer of the bundled product thereby obtains one item, such as bubble gum, that can be consumed immediately, and another, the baseball trading card, that can be collected or sold to other collectors.

The first modern-style baseball card, issued in 1909 and packaged with cigarettes, featured Honus Wagner, a talented second baseman with the Pittsburgh Pirates. As indicated in Table 3-2, a single Honus Wagner trading card trades today at a market clearing price of more than a quarter of a million dollars!

TABLE 3-2
Baseball Cards with the Highest Market Clearing Prices

Baseball cards for top baseball players such as Joe DiMaggio, Ted Williams, and Willie Mays typically have market clearing prices of at least $2,000. The cards with the highest market clearing prices, however, are for players who were stars much earlier in baseball history, such as Honus Wagner and Nap Lajoie.

Player	Year Issued	Price Range (mid-2000s)
Honus Wagner	1909	$250,000–$400,000
Lawrence "Nap" Lajoie	1933	$20,000–$30,000
Mickey Mantle	1952	$12,000–$18,000
"Shoeless" Joe Jackson	1914	$5,000–$9,000
Ty Cobb	1914	$3,600–$6,000
Leroy "Satchel" Paige	1949	$3,500–$6,000
Babe Ruth	1933	$3,500–$5,000
Joe DiMaggio	1938	$2,000–$3,500
Ted Williams	1954	$2,000–$3,500
Willie Mays	1951	$2,000–$3,000

Source: Beckette.com.

Why Market Clearing Prices of Some Cards Are So High

Why do some baseball cards have market clearing prices in the thousands—or tens or hundreds of thousands—of dollars? The answer has to do with demand and supply. For many cards, such as those featuring popular baseball greats including Mickey Mantle, Leroy "Satchel" Paige, and Ty Cobb, relatively high demands for the cards account for their relatively high market clearing prices.

In the case of the cards featuring Honus Wagner, both demand and supply factors are at work. The Wagner cards were the very first baseball cards ever printed, so many collectors of sports trading cards would like to own the card, thereby creating a relatively high demand for the card. At the same time, however, the market supply of cards featuring Wagner is relatively low. Only about 100 of the Wagner cards are believed to exist, and only 10 are in very good condition.

A relatively low supply also helps explain the relatively high market clearing price of the cards featuring Lawrence "Nap" Lajoie, who spent most of his stellar career with the Cleveland Indians in the early 1900s. The company that printed a special 1933 set of cards summarizing top players' careers accidentally left the Lajoie card out of the set. Only the few people who wrote to the company specially requesting the card received copies, and the company destroyed all the remaining cards.

Baseball Scandals and Market Clearing Prices

One of the highest-priced cards listed in Table 3-2 features the great Chicago White Sox player "Shoeless" Joe Jackson. In 1919, Jackson and seven other players were implicated in the infamous "Black Sox" scandal, in which gamblers paid White Sox players to play poorly so that the Cincinnati Reds could win the World Series. In disgust, many fans discarded cards featuring Jackson, thereby reducing the supply of Jackson cards. Nevertheless, because Jackson was an outstanding player and his role in the scandal was tangential, today many people wish to own Jackson cards. Together, relatively low supply and relatively high demand boost the card's price.

A player's involvement in scandals typically does not push up the market clearing price of his card, however. When allegations surfaced that recent top players such as Sammy Sosa, Mark McGwire, and Jason Giambi might have used steroids to artificially enhance their hitting performances, the demand for each player's cards plummeted. Consequently, the market clearing prices of cards featuring these players declined more than 50 percent.

Log in to **MyEconLab**, click on "Economic News," and test your understanding of the chapter by answering interactive questions that relate directly to this issue.

For Critical Analysis

1. Why might the market clearing price of a baseball card featuring a particular player be relatively low even if many people wish to purchase the card?
2. Why might the market clearing price of a baseball card featuring a particular player be relatively high even if relatively few people wish to purchase the card?

Web Resources

1. For a look at a Web site that facilitates the market for sports trading cards, go to www.econtoday.com/ch03.
2. To see how traders of baseball cards track the market clearing prices of the cards, go to www.econtoday.com/ch03.

Research Project

Sports trading cards feature athletes in a variety of men's and women's professional sports, including auto racing, basketball, boxing, football, golf, hockey, soccer, tennis, and wrestling. Consider factors that might push the average price of a trading card in one sport above the average price of a trading card in another sport. Why might the equilibrium price of a trading card for an athlete in a sport with a relatively low average equilibrium price be much higher than the equilibrium price of an athlete in another sport in which the average equilibrium price is relatively high?

CHAPTER 3 **Demand and Supply** **77**

Here is what you should know after reading this chapter. MyEconLab will help you identify what you know, and where to go when you need to practice.

WHAT YOU SHOULD KNOW		WHERE TO GO TO PRACTICE
The Law of Demand According to the law of demand, other things being equal, individuals will purchase fewer units of a good at a higher price, and they will purchase more units of a good at a lower price.	market, 52 demand, 52 law of demand, 52	• **MyEconLab** Study Plan 3.1 • Audio introduction to Chapter 3
Relative Prices versus Money Prices When determining the quantity of a good to purchase, people respond to changes in its relative price, which is the price of the good in terms of other goods. If the price of a unit of health care services rises by 50 percent next year while at the same time all other prices, including your wages, also increase by 50 percent, then the relative price of the health care services has not changed. Thus, in a world of generally rising prices, you have to compare the price of one good with the general level of prices of other goods in order to decide whether the relative price of that one good has gone up, gone down, or stayed the same.	relative price, 53 money price, 53	• **MyEconLab** Study Plan 3.1 • Video: The Difference Between Relative and Absolute Prices and the Importance of Looking at Only Relative Prices
A Change in Quantity Demanded versus a Change in Demand The demand schedule shows the relationship between various possible prices and respective quantities purchased per unit of time. Graphically, the demand schedule is a downward-sloping demand curve. A change in the price of the good generates a change in the quantity demanded, which is a movement along the demand curve. Factors other than the price of the good that affect the amount demanded are (1) income, (2) tastes and preferences, (3) the prices of related goods, (4) expectations, and (5) market size (the number of buyers). Whenever any of these *ceteris paribus* conditions of demand changes, there is a change in the demand for the good, and the demand curve shifts to a new position.	demand curve, 55 market demand, 55 *ceteris paribus* conditions, 58 normal goods, 58 inferior goods, 58 substitutes, 59 complements, 60 **Key figures** Figure 3-2, 56 Figure 3-4, 58 Figure 3-5, 61	• **MyEconLab** Study Plans 3.2 and 3.3 • Video: The Importance of Distinguishing Between a Shift in a Demand Curve and a Move Along the Demand Curve • Animated Figures 3-2, 3-4, 3-5
The Law of Supply According to the law of supply, sellers will produce and offer for sale more units of a good at a higher price, and they will produce and offer for sale fewer units of the good at a lower price.	supply, 62 law of supply, 62	• **MyEconLab** Study Plan 3.4

WHAT YOU SHOULD KNOW		WHERE TO GO TO PRACTICE
A Change in Quantity Supplied versus a Change in Supply The supply schedule shows the relationship between various possible prices and respective quantities produced and sold per unit of time. On a graph, the supply schedule is a supply curve that slopes upward. A change in the price of the good generates a change in the quantity supplied, which is a movement along the supply curve. Factors other than the price of the good that affect the amount supplied are (1) input prices, (2) technology and productivity, (3) taxes and subsidies, (4) price expectations, and (5) the number of sellers. Whenever any of these *ceteris paribus* conditions changes, there is a change in the supply of the good, and the supply curve shifts to a new position.	supply curve, 63 subsidy, 68 **Key figures** Figure 3-6, 64 Figure 3-7, 65 Figure 3-9, 66	• **MyEconLab** Study Plans 3.5, 3.6 • Video: The Importance of Distinguishing Between a Change in Supply versus a Change in Quantity Supplied • Animated Figures 3-6, 3-7, 3-9
Determining the Market Price and the Equilibrium Quantity The equilibrium price of a good and the equilibrium quantity of the good that is produced and sold are determined by the intersection of the demand and supply curves. At this intersection point, the quantity demanded by buyers of the good just equals the quantity supplied by sellers. At the equilibrium price at this point of intersection, the plans of buyers and sellers mesh exactly. Hence there is neither an excess quantity of the good supplied (surplus) nor an excess quantity of the good demanded (shortage) at this equilibrium point.	market clearing, or equilibrium, price, 71 equilibrium, 71 shortage, 72 surplus, 72 **Key figure** Figure 3-11, 73	• **MyEconLab** Study Plan 3.7 • Animated Figure 3-11

Log in to MyEconLab, take a chapter test, and get a personalized Study Plan that tells you which concepts you understand and which ones you need to review. From there, MyEconLab will give you futher practice, tutorials, animations, videos, and guided solutions.

Log in to www.myeconlab.com

PROBLEMS

*Select problems, indicated by a blue oval, are assignable in **MyEconLab**.*
Answers to the odd-numbered problems appear at the back of the book.

3-1 Suppose that in a recent market period, an industry-wide survey determined the following relationship between the price of prerecorded movie DVDs and the quantity supplied and quantity demanded.

Price	Quantity Demanded	Quantity Supplied
$19	100 million	40 million
$20	90 million	60 million
$21	80 million	80 million
$22	70 million	100 million
$23	60 million	120 million

Illustrate the supply and demand curves for movie DVDs given the information in the table. What are the equilibrium price and quantity? If the industry price is $20, is there a shortage or surplus of DVDs? How much is the shortage or surplus?

3-2 Suppose that a survey for a later market period indicates that the quantities supplied in the table in Problem 3-1 are unchanged. The quantity demanded, however, has increased by 30 million at each price. Construct the resulting demand curve in the illustration you made for Problem 3-1. Is this an increase or a decrease in demand? What are the new equilibrium quantity and the new market price? Give two examples of changes in *ceteris paribus* conditions that might cause such a change.

3-3 Consider the market for DSL high-speed Internet access service, which is a normal good. Explain whether the following events would cause an increase or a decrease in demand or an increase or a decrease in the quantity demanded.
  a. Firms providing cable Internet access services reduce their prices.
  b. Firms providing DSL high-speed Internet access services reduce their prices.
  c. There is a decrease in the incomes earned by consumers of DSL high-speed Internet access services.
  d. Consumers of DSL high-speed Internet access services anticipate a decline in the future price of these services.

3-4 In the market for rewritable DVDs, explain whether the following events would cause an increase or a decrease in demand or an increase or a decrease in the quantity demanded. Also explain what happens to the equilibrium quantity and the market clearing price.
  a. There are increases in the prices of storage racks and boxes for rewritable DVDs.
  b. There is a decrease in the price of computer drives that read the information contained on rewritable DVDs.
  c. There is a dramatic increase in the price of flash memory drives that can be used to store digital data.
  d. A booming economy increases the income of the typical buyer of rewritable DVDs.
  e. Consumers of rewritable DVDs anticipate that the price of this good will decline in the future.

3-5. Give an example of a complement and a substitute in consumption for each of the following items.
  a. Bacon
  b. Tennis racquets
  c. Coffee
  d. Automobiles

3-6 At the beginning of the 2000s, the United States imposed high import taxes on a number of European goods due to a trade dispute. One of these goods was Roquefort cheese. Show how this tax affects the market for Roquefort cheese in the United States, shifting the appropriate curve and indicating a new equilibrium quantity and market price.

3-7 Consider the diagram at the top of page 80 of a market for one-bedroom rental apartments in a college community.
  a. At a rental rate of $1,000 per month, is there an excess quantity supplied, or is there an excess quantity demanded? What is the amount of the excess quantity supplied or demanded?
  b. If the present rental rate of one-bedroom apartments is $1,000 per month, through what mechanism will the rental rate adjust to the equilibrium rental rate of $800?

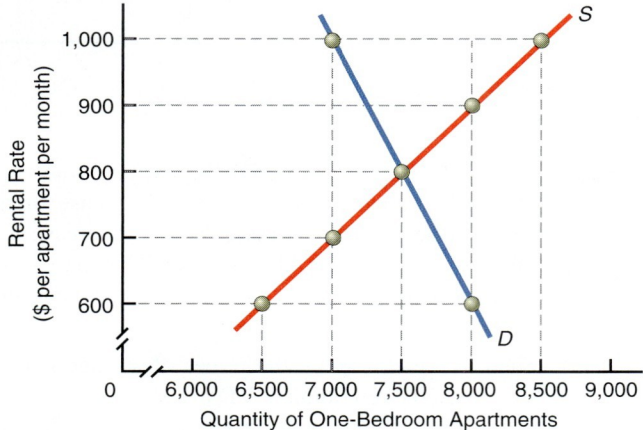

c. At a rental rate of $600 per month, is there an excess quantity supplied, or is there an excess quantity demanded? What is the amount of the excess quantity supplied or demanded?

d. If the present rental rate of one-bedroom apartments is $600 per month, through what mechanism will the rental rate adjust to the equilibrium rental rate of $800?

3-8 Consider the market for economics textbooks. Explain whether the following events would cause an increase or a decrease in supply or an increase or a decrease in the quantity supplied.

a. The market price of paper increases.
b. The market price of economics textbooks increases.
c. The number of publishers of economics textbooks increases.
d. Publishers expect that the market price of economics textbooks will increase next month.

3-9 Consider the market for laptop computers. Explain whether the following events would cause an increase or a decrease in supply or an increase or a decrease in the quantity supplied. Illustrate each, and show what would happen to the equilibrium quantity and the market price.

a. The price of memory chips used in laptop computers declines.
b. The price of machinery used to produce laptop computers increases.
c. The number of manufacturers of laptop computers increases.
d. There is a decrease in the demand for laptop computers.

3-10 The U.S. government offers significant per-unit subsidy payments to U.S. sugar growers. Describe the effects of the introduction of such subsidies on the market for sugar and the market for artificial sweeteners. Explain whether the demand curve or the supply curve shifts in each market, and if so, in which direction. Also explain what happens to the equilibrium quantity and the market price in each market.

3-11 The supply curve for season tickets for basketball games for your school's team is vertical because there are a fixed number of seats in the school's gymnasium. Before preseason practice sessions begin, your school's administration commits itself to selling season tickets the day before the first basketball game at a predetermined price that happens to equal last season's market price. The school will not change that price at any time prior to and including the day tickets go on sale. Illustrate, within a supply and demand framework, the effect of each of the following events on the market for season tickets on the day the school opens ticket sales, and indicate whether a surplus or a shortage would result.

a. The school's star player breaks a leg during preseason practice.
b. During preseason practice, a published newspaper poll of coaches of teams in your school's conference surprises everyone by indicating that your school's team is predicted to win the conference championship.
c. At a preseason practice session that is open to the public, the school president announces that all refreshments served during games will be free of charge throughout the season.
d. Most of your school's basketball fans enjoy an up-tempo, "run and gun" approach to basketball, but after the team's coach quits following the first preseason practice, the school's administration immediately hires a new coach who believes in a deliberate style of play that relies heavily on a slow-tempo, four-corners offense.

3-12 Recent advances in telecommunications and computer technologies now allow individuals to transmit telephone calls from their homes and offices using the Internet. Explain the impact of this technological advance on the market for traditional telephone services.

3-13 Ethanol is a motor fuel manufactured from corn, barley, or wheat, and it can be used to power the engines of many autos and trucks. Suppose that the government decides to provide a large per-unit subsidy to ethanol producers. Explain the effects in the markets for the following items:

a. Corn
b. Gasoline
c. Automobiles

3-14 If the price of processor chips used in manufacturing personal computers decreases, what will happen in the market for personal computers? How will the equilibrium price and equilibrium quantity of personal computers change?

3-15 Assume that the cost of aluminum used by soft-drink companies increases. Which of the following correctly describes the resulting effects in the market for soft drinks distributed in aluminum cans? (More than one statement may be correct.)

a. The demand for soft drinks decreases.
b. The quantity of soft drinks demanded decreases.
c. The supply of soft drinks decreases.
d. The quantity of soft drinks supplied decreases.

ECONOMICS ON THE NET

The U.S. Nursing Shortage For some years media stories have discussed a shortage of qualified nurses in the United States. This application explores some of the factors that have caused the quantity of newly trained nurses demanded to tend to exceed the quantity of newly trained nurses supplied.

Title: Nursing Shortage Resource Web Link

Navigation: Go to the Nursing Shortage Resource Web Link at **www.econtoday.com/ch03**, and click on *Enrollment Increase Insufficient to Meet the Projected Increase in Demand for New Nurses*.

Application Read the discussion, and answer the following questions.

1. What has happened to the demand for new nurses in the United States? What has happened to the supply of new nurses? Why has the result been a shortage?

2. If there is a free market for the skills of new nurses, what can you predict is likely to happen to the wage rate earned by individuals who have just completed their nursing training?

For Group Study and Analysis Discuss the pros and cons of high schools and colleges trying to factor predictions about future wages into student career counseling. How might this potentially benefit students? What problems might high schools and colleges face in trying to assist students in evaluating the future earnings prospects of various jobs?

ANSWERS TO QUICK QUIZZES

p. 54: (i) negative; (ii) demand
p. 57: (i) constant; (ii) market demand
p. 62: (i) income . . . tastes and preferences . . . prices of related goods . . . expectations about future prices and incomes . . . market size (the number of buyers in the market); (ii) *ceteris paribus*; (iii) movement along
p. 64: (i) direct; (ii) supply . . . market supply
p. 69: (i) move along . . . shift; (ii) input prices . . . technology and productivity . . . taxes and subsidies . . . expectations of future relative prices . . . the number of firms in the industry
p. 73: (i) intersection . . . equilibrium; (ii) greater; (iii) less

4 Extensions of Demand and Supply Analysis

Learning Objectives

After reading this chapter, you should be able to:

1. Discuss the essential features of the price system
2. Evaluate the effects of changes in demand and supply on the market price and equilibrium quantity
3. Understand the rationing function of prices
4. Explain the effects of price ceilings
5. Explain the effects of price floors
6. Describe various types of government-imposed quantity restrictions on markets

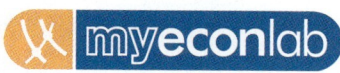

MyEconLab helps you master each objective and study more efficiently. See end of chapter for details.

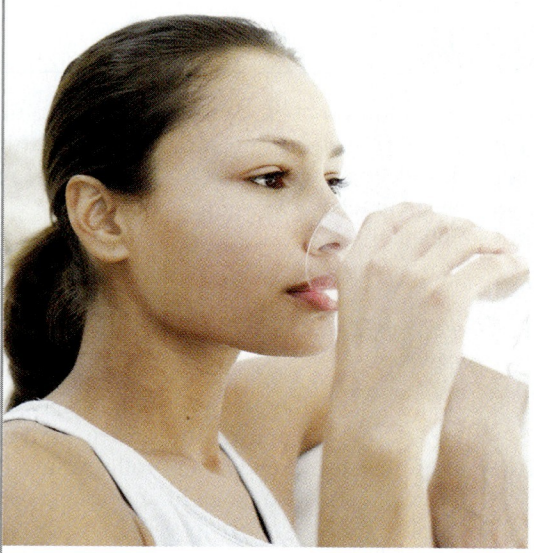

Water covers about 71 percent of the surface of planet Earth. Only 2.5 percent of all that water is fresh water, however. Furthermore, only a very small fraction of this fresh water is in a purified, healthful state at any given moment.

People in many locales complain that there are "shortages" of safe drinking water. That is, at current water prices, there is less treated water available than they wish to consume. In this chapter, you will learn more about shortages. You will discover why a shortage eventually should disappear in an unregulated market. Understanding how government regulation of prices can result in shortages will enable you to explain why a shortage of healthful drinking water has been a persistent problem in many of the world's nations.

Did You Know That...

the inflation-adjusted value of the U.S. minimum wage rate, measured in 2006 dollars, peaked at just over $8 per hour back in 1964? Congress has acted to increase the absolute minimum wage rate at various times since 1964. Nevertheless, failure of these boosts in the absolute minimum wage to keep pace with inflation has caused the inflation-adjusted minimum wage to drift generally downward since the mid-1960s.

What effects does a minimum wage have on employment in the United States? As you will learn in this chapter, we can use the supply and demand analysis developed in Chapter 3 to answer this question. You will find that a minimum wage can sometimes lead to "surplus" labor, or unemployment. Similarly, in this chapter you will learn how we can use supply and demand analysis to examine the "surplus" of various agricultural products, the "shortage" of apartments in certain cities, and many other phenomena. All of these examples are part of our economy, which we characterize as a *price system*.

ECONOMICS FRONT AND CENTER

To consider how the U.S. military has used the price system to allocate its personnel to vacant positions in units based in locales around the globe, contemplate **Using Auctions to Bypass the Army's Chain of Command,** on page 98.

THE PRICE SYSTEM AND MARKETS

In a **price system,** otherwise known as a *market system,* relative prices are constantly changing to reflect changes in supply and demand for different commodities. The prices of those commodities are the signals to everyone within the system as to what is relatively scarce and what is relatively abundant. In this sense, prices provide information.

Indeed, it is the *signaling* aspect of the price system that provides the information to buyers and sellers about what should be bought and what should be produced. In a price system, there is a clear-cut chain of events in which any changes in demand and supply cause changes in prices that in turn affect the opportunities that businesses and individuals have for profit and personal gain. Such changes influence our use of resources.

Price system
An economic system in which relative prices are constantly changing to reflect changes in supply and demand for different commodities. The prices of those commodities are signals to everyone within the system as to what is relatively scarce and what is relatively abundant.

Exchange and Markets

The price system features **voluntary exchange,** acts of trading between individuals that make both parties to the trade subjectively better off. The **terms of exchange**—the prices we pay for the desired items—are determined by the interaction of the forces underlying supply and demand. In our economy, the majority of exchanges take place voluntarily in markets. A market encompasses the exchange arrangements of both buyers and sellers that underlie the forces of supply and demand. Indeed, one definition of a market is that it is a low-cost institution for facilitating exchange. A market increases incomes by helping resources move to their highest-valued uses.

Voluntary exchange
An act of trading, done on an elective basis, in which both parties to the trade are better off after the exchange.

Terms of exchange
The conditions under which trading takes place. Usually, the terms of exchange are equal to the price at which a good is traded.

Transaction Costs

Individuals turn to markets because markets reduce the cost of exchanges. These costs are sometimes referred to as **transaction costs,** which are broadly defined as the costs associated with finding out exactly what is being transacted as well as the cost of enforcing contracts. If you were Robinson Crusoe and lived alone on an island, you would never incur a transaction cost. For everyone else, transaction costs are just as real as the costs of production. Today, high-speed computers have allowed us to reduce transaction costs by increasing our ability to process information and keep records.

How can people obtain information about how much they will have to spend to keep aging vehicles operating?

Transaction costs
All of the costs associated with exchange, including the informational costs of finding out the price and quality, service record, and durability of a product, plus the cost of contracting and enforcing that contract.

E-COMMERCE EXAMPLE

What's New on the Web: Very Old Auto Parts

Direct your Web browser to sites such as allamericanclassics.com, azclassics.com, or autoranch.com, and you will be able to access databases on thousands of junked cars. Some of the cars and trucks featured at such sites are recent models, but many are several years or even decades old. In addition to the prices they wish to obtain, junkyards post photos of their auto parts, such as chrome hood ornaments, interior lamp fixtures, and rusted alternators. Using these sites, people can find out just how many resources they will have to give up to satisfy their desire to keep old-model vehicles in operation.

FOR CRITICAL ANALYSIS

Why do photos supplement information about prices at junk-auto Web sites? (Hint: Recall from Chapter 3 that it is the quality-adjusted price that is important in determining the quantity demanded of any product.)

Consider some simple examples of transaction costs. A club warehouse such as Sam's Club or Costco reduces the transaction costs of having to go to numerous specialty stores to obtain the items you desire. Financial institutions, such as commercial banks, have reduced the transaction costs of directing funds from savers to borrowers. In general, the more organized the market, the lower the transaction costs. A group of individuals who constantly attempt to lower transaction costs includes the much maligned middlemen.

The Role of Middlemen

As long as there are costs of bringing together buyers and sellers, there will be an incentive for intermediaries, normally called middlemen, to lower those costs. This means that middlemen specialize in lowering transaction costs. Whenever producers do not sell their products directly to the final consumer, by definition, one or more middlemen are involved. Farmers typically sell their output to distributors, who are usually called wholesalers, who then sell those products to retailers such as supermarkets.

How can laws aimed at protecting the environment from pollutants lurking in old computers create opportunities for middlemen?

POLICY EXAMPLE

Profiting by Lowering the Transaction Costs of Junking Computers

Have you ever had a personal computer so out of date that you simply wanted to give it away or throw it out? If so, you may have experienced difficulties. Upgrading old computers so that they will operate the latest software is so much trouble that few people want old computers even free of charge. Putting an old computer out in the trash is not a solution either: cathode-ray tubes and other parts in old computers contain lead and other potentially harmful sources of pollution, so most states have laws against throwing computers away.

This is the point at which middlemen have entered the picture. For fees ranging from a few dollars to $50, companies such as RetroBox and Market Velocity now accept obsolete computing equipment. They refurbish computers that can be upgraded for resale and sell off usable parts from computers that are too old to effectively operate modern software. In this way, middlemen profit from reducing the transaction costs consumers face in discarding old computer equipment.

FOR CRITICAL ANALYSIS

What would happen to the demand for the services of computer-recycling middlemen if computer manufacturers found a way to produce computers without pollution-causing components?

CHANGES IN DEMAND AND SUPPLY

It is in markets that we see the results of changes in demand and supply. Market equilibrium can change whenever there is a *shock* caused by a change in a *ceteris paribus* condition for demand or supply. A shock to the supply and demand system can be represented by a shift in the supply curve, a shift in the demand curve, or a shift in both curves. Any shock to the system will result in a new set of supply and demand relationships and a new equilibrium. Forces will come into play to move the system from the old price-quantity equilibrium (now a disequilibrium situation) to the new equilibrium, where the new demand and supply curves intersect.

Effects of Changes in Either Demand or Supply

In certain situations, it is possible to predict what will happen to both equilibrium price and equilibrium quantity when demand or supply changes. Specifically, whenever one curve is stable while the other curve shifts, we can tell what will happen to both price and quantity. Consider the possibilities in Figure 4-1. In panel (a), the supply curve remains unchanged, but demand increases from D_1 to D_2. Note that the results are an increase in

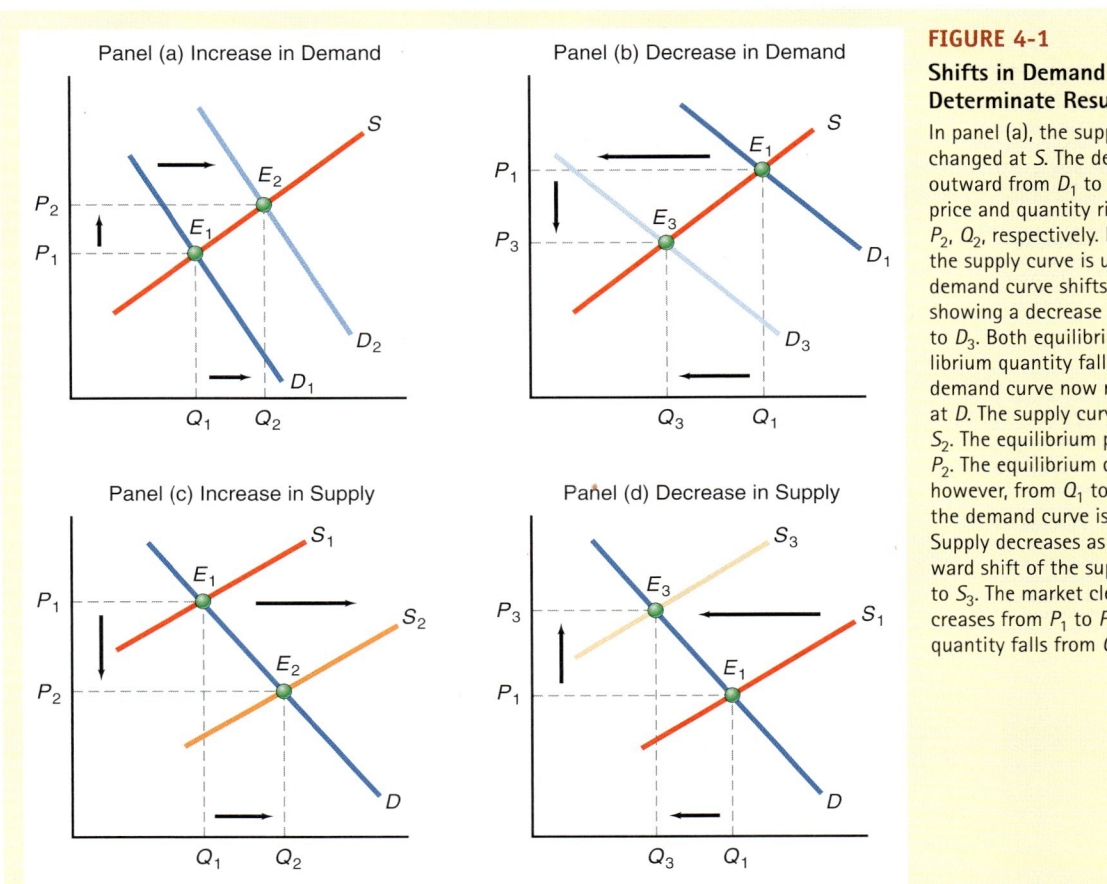

FIGURE 4-1

Shifts in Demand and in Supply: Determinate Results

In panel (a), the supply curve is unchanged at S. The demand curve shifts outward from D_1 to D_2. The equilibrium price and quantity rise from P_1, Q_1 to P_2, Q_2, respectively. In panel (b), again the supply curve is unchanged at S. The demand curve shifts inward to the left, showing a decrease in demand from D_1 to D_3. Both equilibrium price and equilibrium quantity fall. In panel (c), the demand curve now remains unchanged at D. The supply curve shifts from S_1 to S_2. The equilibrium price falls from P_1 to P_2. The equilibrium quantity increases, however, from Q_1 to Q_2. In panel (d), the demand curve is unchanged at D. Supply decreases as shown by a leftward shift of the supply curve from S_1 to S_3. The market clearing price increases from P_1 to P_3. The equilibrium quantity falls from Q_1 to Q_3.

the market clearing price from P_1 to P_2 and an increase in the equilibrium quantity from Q_1 to Q_2.

In panel (b), there is a decrease in demand from D_1 to D_3. This results in a decrease in both the relative price of the good and the equilibrium quantity. Panels (c) and (d) show the effects of a shift in the supply curve while the demand curve is unchanged. In panel (c), the supply curve has shifted rightward. The relative price of the product falls; the equilibrium quantity increases. In panel (d), supply has shifted leftward—there has been a supply decrease. The product's relative price increases, and the equilibrium quantity decreases.

Why has the market supply curve for cheese shifted leftward in recent years, thereby pushing up the equilibrium price of cheese?

EXAMPLE

Why Cheese Prices Have Jumped

Two events have affected cheese prices since the mid-2000s. First, factory problems at one of the top sellers of a hormone that stimulates milk production in dairy cows have resulted in a cutback in production. This has reduced the supply of the hormone and caused its market clearing price to rise. Second, a big increase in beef prices has induced many farmers to sell off more than 200,000 dairy cows to be used for beef. Both of these events have reduced the supply of milk since the mid-2000s and pushed up the market clearing price of milk, which is a key input in the production of cheese. The resulting decrease in cheese supply has generated higher market clearing prices of cheese. For instance, during a single two-month period, the price of mozzarella cheese rose by nearly 70 percent, from just over $1.30 per pound to more than $2.20 per pound.

FOR CRITICAL ANALYSIS
If dairy farmers are successful in convincing government officials to adopt proposed policies limiting the number of milk producers, how could this ultimately affect the market clearing price of cheese?

Situations in Which Both Demand and Supply Shift

The examples in Figure 4-1 on the preceding page show a theoretically determinate outcome of a shift either in the demand curve, holding the supply curve constant, or in the supply curve, holding the demand curve constant. When both supply and demand curves change, the outcome is indeterminate for either equilibrium price or equilibrium quantity.

When both demand and supply increase, all we can be certain of is that equilibrium quantity will increase. We do not know what will happen to equilibrium price until we determine whether demand increased relative to supply (equilibrium price will rise) or supply increased relative to demand (equilibrium price will fall). The same analysis applies to decreases in both demand and supply, except that in this case equilibrium quantity falls.

We can be certain that when demand decreases and supply increases at the same time, the equilibrium price will fall, but we do not know what will happen to the equilibrium quantity unless we actually draw the new curves. If supply decreases and demand increases at the same time, we can be sure that equilibrium price will rise, but again we do not know what happens to equilibrium quantity without drawing the curves. In every situation in which both supply and demand change, you should always draw graphs to determine the resulting change in equilibrium price and quantity.

Why do you suppose that gasoline prices have increased so much?

EXAMPLE

Why Gasoline Prices Have Increased

Although many people complained about "high" gasoline prices in the 1990s and 2000s, except for a brief period during 2005 the inflation-adjusted price of regular gasoline remained well below the 1981 level of $3.03 (in 2006 dollars). Two factors, shown in Figure 4-2, contributed to the significant rise in gasoline prices that occurred in the mid-2000s. One was an increase in the amount of gasoline demanded at any given price, "fueled" in part by the public's desire to fill the tanks of gas-guzzling sport utility vehicles (SUVs) that had come into favor during the preceding years. This implied a rightward shift in the demand curve for gasoline, as shown in the figure. Another factor was a reduction in supply, shown by the leftward shift in the supply curve in Figure 4-2. This decrease in supply was generated by a higher price for the oil that is refined to produce gasoline, increased gasoline taxes, tougher antipollution regulations, and events such as Hurricanes Katrina and Rita that disrupted fuel refining and distribution. On net, the equilibrium quantity of gasoline consumed in the United States could have risen or fallen. On balance, it increased slightly. As predicted in the figure, the market clearing price of gasoline increased.

FOR CRITICAL ANALYSIS
How do you suppose that growing demand for gasoline in China, India, and other nations affects the market for gasoline in the United States? (Hint: If gasoline firms sell more of the gasoline they produce to other nations, what happens to the supply of gasoline in the U.S. market?)

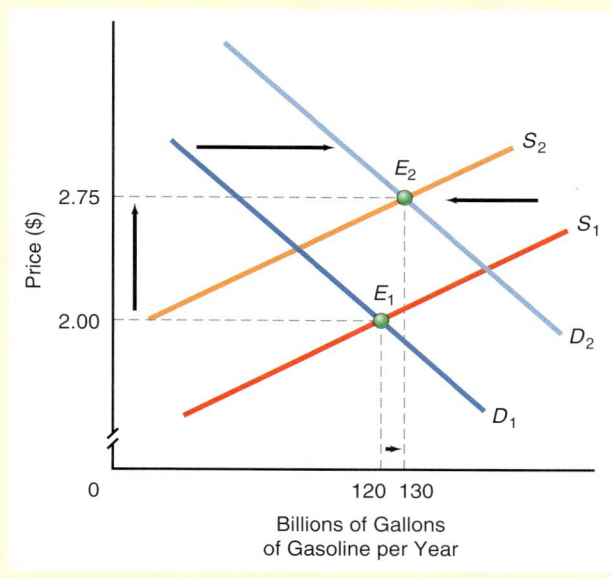

FIGURE 4-2

The Effects of a Simultaneous Decrease in Gasoline Supply and Increase in Gasoline Demand

In the mid-2000s, various factors contributed to a reduction in the supply of gasoline in the United States, depicted by the leftward shift in the gasoline supply curve from S_1 to S_2. At the same time, there was an increase in the demand for gasoline, as shown by the shift in the gasoline demand curve from D_1 to D_2. On net, the equilibrium quantity of gasoline produced and consumed rose only slightly, from 120 billion gallons per year at point E_1, to 130 billion gallons per year at point E_2, but the equilibrium price of gasoline increased significantly, from about $2.00 per gallon to about $2.75 per gallon.

Price Flexibility and Adjustment Speed

We have used as an illustration for our analysis a market in which prices are quite flexible. Some markets are indeed like that. In others, however, price flexibility may take the form of indirect adjustments such as hidden payments or quality changes. For example, although the published price of bouquets of flowers may stay the same, the freshness of the flowers may change, meaning that the price per constant-quality unit changes. The published price of French bread might stay the same, but the quality could go up or down, thereby changing the price per constant-quality unit. There are many ways to implicitly change prices without actually changing the published price for a *nominal* unit of a product or service.

We must also note that markets do not always return to equilibrium immediately. There may be a significant adjustment time. A shock to the economy in the form of an oil embargo, a drought, or a long strike will not be absorbed overnight. This means that even in unfettered market situations, in which there are no restrictions on changes in prices and quantities, temporary excess quantities supplied or excess quantities demanded may appear. Our analysis simply indicates what the market clearing price and equilibrium quantity ultimately will be, given a demand curve and a supply curve. Nowhere in the analysis is there any indication of the speed with which a market will get to a new equilibrium after a shock. The price may overshoot the equilibrium level. Remember this warning when we examine changes in demand and in supply due to changes in their *ceteris paribus* conditions.

QUICK QUIZ

The _____ of _____ in a voluntary exchange are determined by the interaction of the forces underlying demand and supply. These forces take place in markets, which tend to minimize _____ costs.

When the _____ curve shifts outward or inward with an unchanged _____ curve, equilibrium price and quantity increase or decrease, respectively. When the _____ curve shifts outward or inward given an unchanged _____ curve, equilibrium price moves in the direction opposite to equilibrium quantity.

When there is a shift in demand or supply, the new equilibrium price is not obtained _____. Adjustment takes _____.

See page 106 for the answers. Review concepts from this section in MyEconLab.

THE RATIONING FUNCTION OF PRICES

The synchronization of decisions by buyers and sellers that leads to equilibrium is called the *rationing function of prices*. Prices are indicators of relative scarcity. An equilibrium price clears the market. The plans of buyers and sellers, given the price, are not frustrated. It is the free interaction of buyers and sellers that sets the price that eventually clears the market. Price, in effect, rations a good to demanders who are willing and able to pay the highest price. Whenever the rationing function of prices is frustrated by government-enforced price ceilings that set prices below the market clearing level, a prolonged shortage results.

Methods of Nonprice Rationing

There are ways other than price to ration goods. *First come, first served* is one method. *Political power* is another. *Physical force* is yet another. Cultural, religious, and physical differences have been and are used as rationing devices throughout the world.

Rationing by Waiting.   Consider first come, first served as a rationing device. We call this *rationing by queues,* where *queue* means "line." Whoever is willing to wait in line the longest obtains the good that is being sold at less than the market clearing price. All who wait in line are paying a higher *total* price than the money price paid for the good. Personal time has an opportunity cost. To calculate the total price of the good, we must add up the money price plus the opportunity cost of the time spent waiting.

Rationing by waiting may occur in situations in which entrepreneurs are free to change prices to equate quantity demanded with quantity supplied but choose not to do so. This results in queues of potential buyers. It may seem to be that the price in the market is being held below equilibrium by some noncompetitive force. That is not true, however. Such queuing may arise in a free market when the demand for a good is subject to large or unpredictable fluctuations, and the additional costs to firms (and ultimately to consumers) of constantly changing prices or of holding sufficient inventories or providing sufficient excess capacity to cover peak demands are greater than the costs to consumers of waiting for the good. Common examples are waiting in line to purchase a fast-food lunch and queuing to purchase a movie ticket a few minutes before the next show.

Rationing by Random Assignment or Coupons.   *Random assignment* is another way to ration goods. You may have been involved in a rationing-by-random-assignment scheme in college if you were assigned a housing unit. Sometimes rationing by random assignment is used to fill slots in popular classes.

Rationing by *coupons* has also been used, particularly during wartime. In the United States during World War II, families were allotted coupons that allowed them to purchase specified quantities of rationed goods, such as meat and gasoline. To purchase such goods, they had to pay a specified price *and* give up a coupon.

The Essential Role of Rationing

In a world of scarcity, there is, by definition, competition for what is scarce. After all, any resources that are not scarce can be had by everyone at a zero price in as large a quantity as everyone wants, such as air to burn in internal combustion engines. Once scarcity arises, there has to be some method to ration the available resources, goods, and services. The price system is one form of rationing; the others that we mentioned are alternatives. Economists cannot say which system of rationing is "best." They can, however, say that rationing via the price system leads to the most efficient use of available resources. This means that generally in a freely functioning price system, all of the gains from mutually beneficial trade will be captured.

QUICK QUIZ

Prices in a market economy perform a rationing function because they reflect relative scarcity, allowing the market to clear. Other ways to ration goods include _____, _____ _____; _____ _____; _____ _____; _____; and _____.

Even when businesspeople can change prices, some rationing by waiting may occur. Such _____ arises when there are large changes in demand coupled with high costs of satisfying those changes immediately.

See page 106 for the answers. Review concepts from this section in MyEconLab.

THE POLICY OF GOVERNMENT-IMPOSED PRICE CONTROLS

Price controls
Government-mandated minimum or maximum prices that may be charged for goods and services.

Price ceiling
A legal maximum price that may be charged for a particular good or service.

Price floor
A legal minimum price below which a good or service may not be sold. Legal minimum wages are an example.

The rationing function of prices is prevented when governments impose price controls. **Price controls** often involve setting a **price ceiling**—the maximum price that may be allowed in an exchange. The world has had a long history of price ceilings applied to product prices, wages, rents, and interest rates. Occasionally, a government will set a **price floor**—a minimum price below which a good or service may not be sold. Price floors have most often been applied to wages and agricultural products. Let's first consider price ceilings.

Price Ceilings and Black Markets

As long as a price ceiling is below the market clearing price, imposing a price ceiling creates a shortage, as can be seen in Figure 4-3. At any price below the market clearing, or equilibrium, price of $1,000, there will always be a larger quantity demanded than quantity supplied—a shortage, as you will recall from Chapter 3. Normally, whenever quantity demanded exceeds quantity supplied—that is, when a shortage exists—there is a tendency for the price to rise to its equilibrium level. But with a price ceiling, this tendency cannot be fully realized because everyone is forbidden to trade at the equilibrium price.

Nonprice rationing devices
All methods used to ration scarce goods that are price-controlled. Whenever the price system is not allowed to work, nonprice rationing devices will evolve to ration the affected goods and services.

The result is fewer exchanges and **nonprice rationing devices.** Figure 4-3 illustrates the situation for portable electricity generators after a natural disaster: the equilibrium quantity of portable generators demanded and supplied (or traded) would be 10,000 units, and the market clearing price would be $1,000 per generator. But, if the government essentially imposes a price ceiling by requiring the price of portable generators to remain at the predisaster level of $600, the equilibrium quantity offered is only 5,000. Because frustrated consumers will be able to purchase only 5,000 units, there is a shortage. The most obvious nonprice rationing device to help clear the market is queuing, or long lines, which we have already discussed. To avoid physical lines, waiting lists may be established.

FIGURE 4-3
Black Markets

The demand curve is D. The supply curve is S. The equilibrium price is $1,000. The government, however, steps in and imposes a maximum price of $600. At that lower price, the quantity demanded will be 15,000, but the quantity supplied will be only 5,000. There is a "shortage." The implicit price (including time costs) tends to rise to $1,400. If black markets arise, as they generally will, the equilibrium black market price will end up somewhere between $600 and $1,400. The actual quantity transacted will be between 5,000 and 10,000.

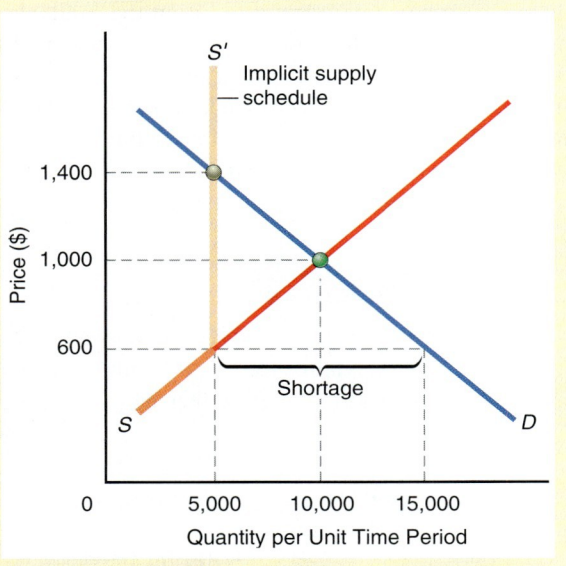

Typically, an effective price ceiling leads to a **black market.** A black market is a market in which the price-controlled good is sold at an illegally high price through various methods. For example, if the price of gasoline is controlled at lower than the market clearing price, drivers who wish to fill up their cars may offer the gas station attendant a cash payment on the side (as happened in the United States in the 1970s and in China and India in the mid-2000s during price controls on gasoline). If the price of beef is controlled at below its market clearing price, a customer who offers the butcher good tickets to an upcoming football game may be allocated otherwise unavailable beef. Indeed, the true implicit price of a price-controlled good or service can be increased in an infinite number of ways, limited only by the imagination. (Black markets also occur when goods are made illegal.)

Governments sometimes adopt "antigouging laws" to prevent prices of goods from rising in the wake of a disaster. How can such laws encourage black markets?

Black market
A market in which goods are traded at prices above their legal maximum prices or in which illegal goods are sold.

POLICY EXAMPLE

Preventing Price Gouging Promotes Black Markets in Florida

In several U.S. states, it is illegal to engage in *price gouging.* Florida's antigouging law penalizes a seller for any "gross disparity" between the quoted price of a "necessity item," such as water, and the item's price on the date the state's governor declares an emergency. The law provides for penalties during a 30-day period following such a declaration, which typically occurs any time a natural disaster strikes.

Of course, Florida is susceptible to hurricanes. In the aftermath of these storms, the demands for drinking water, gasoline, and plywood increase. In an unregulated market, such increases in demand would result in temporary shortages at prehurricane prices, thereby causing prices to rise. The resulting price increases would, in turn, induce producers to increase the quantities supplied to stricken regions.

Antigouging laws aim to prevent such price increases from occurring. When an unprecedented three successive hurricanes hit Florida in 2004, there were also unprecedented shortages. With prices fixed at predisaster levels, producers had little incentive to rush bottled water, gasoline, and plywood to these locales. Many families and businesses resorted to black market transactions by offering under-the-table inducements to sellers.

FOR CRITICAL ANALYSIS
Who gains and who loses when antigouging laws contribute to shortages of items such as bottled water and plywood? (Hint: When shortages occur, some people obtain bottled water and plywood they wish to buy at current prices, but others do not.)

QUICK QUIZ

Governments sometimes impose **price controls** in the form of price _____ and price _____.

An effective price _____ is one that sets the legal price below the market clearing price and is enforced. Effective price _____ lead to nonprice rationing devices and black markets.

See page 106 for the answers. Review concepts from this section in MyEconLab.

THE POLICY OF CONTROLLING RENTS

More than 200 U.S. cities and towns, including Berkeley, California, and New York City, operate under some kind of rent control. **Rent control** is a system under which the local government tells building owners how much they can charge their tenants for rent. In the United States, rent controls date back to at least World War II. The objective of rent control is to keep rents below levels that would be observed in a freely competitive market.

Rent control
Price ceilings on rents.

The Functions of Rental Prices

In any housing market, rental prices serve three functions: (1) to promote the efficient maintenance of existing housing and stimulate the construction of new housing, (2) to allocate existing scarce housing among competing claimants, and (3) to ration the use of existing housing by current demanders.

Rent Controls and Construction. Rent controls have discouraged the construction of new rental units. Rents are the most important long-term determinant of profitability, and rent controls have artificially depressed them. Consider some examples. In a recent year in Dallas, Texas, with a 16 percent rental vacancy rate but no rent control laws, 11,000 new rental housing units were built. In the same year in San Francisco, California, only 2,000 units were built, despite a mere 1.6 percent vacancy rate. The major difference? San Francisco has had stringent rent control laws. In New York City, until changes in the law in 1997 and 2003, the only rental units being built were luxury units, which were exempt from controls.

Effects on the Existing Supply of Housing. When rental rates are held below equilibrium levels, property owners cannot recover the cost of maintenance, repairs, and capital improvements through higher rents. Hence they curtail these activities. In the extreme situation, taxes, utilities, and the expenses of basic repairs exceed rental receipts. The result is abandoned buildings from Santa Monica, California, to New York City. Some owners have resorted to arson, hoping to collect the insurance on their empty buildings before the city claims them for back taxes.

Rationing the Current Use of Housing. Rent controls also affect the current use of housing because they restrict tenant mobility. Consider a family whose children have gone off to college. That family might want to live in a smaller apartment. But in a rent-controlled environment, giving up a rent-controlled unit can entail a substantial cost. In most rent-controlled cities, rents can be adjusted only when a tenant leaves. That means that a move from a long-occupied rent-controlled apartment to a smaller apartment can involve a hefty rent hike. In New York, this artificial preservation of the status quo came to be known as "housing gridlock."

Attempts to Evade Rent Controls

The distortions produced by rent controls lead to efforts by both property owners and tenants to evade the rules. This leads to the growth of expensive government bureaucracies whose job it is to make sure that rent controls aren't evaded. In New York City, because rent can be raised only if the tenant leaves, property owners have had an incentive to make life unpleasant for tenants in order to drive them out or to evict them on the

Go to www.econtoday.com/ch04 to learn more about New York City's rent controls from Tenant.net.

slightest pretext. The city has responded by making evictions extremely costly for property owners. Eviction requires a tedious and expensive judicial proceeding. Tenants, for their part, routinely try to sublet all or part of their rent-controlled apartments at fees substantially above the rent they pay to the owner. Both the city and the property owners try to prohibit subletting and often end up in the city's housing courts—an entire judicial system developed to deal with disputes involving rent-controlled apartments. The overflow and appeals from the city's housing courts sometimes clog the rest of New York's judicial system.

Who Gains and Who Loses from Rent Controls?

The big losers from rent controls are clearly property owners. But there is another group of losers—low-income individuals, especially single mothers, trying to find their first apartment. Some observers now believe that rent controls have worsened the problem of homelessness in cities such as New York.

Often, owners of rent-controlled apartments charge "key money" before allowing a new tenant to move in. This is a large up-front cash payment, usually illegal but demanded nonetheless—just one aspect of the black market in rent-controlled apartments. Poor individuals cannot afford a hefty key money payment, nor can they assure the owner that their rent will be on time or even paid each month. Because controlled rents are usually below market clearing levels, apartment owners have little incentive to take any risk on low-income individuals as tenants. This is particularly true when a prospective tenant's chief source of income is a welfare check. Indeed, a large number of the litigants in the New York housing courts are welfare mothers who have missed their rent payments due to emergency expenses or delayed welfare checks. Their appeals often end in evictions and a new home in a temporary public shelter—or on the streets.

Who benefits from rent control? Ample evidence indicates that upper-income professionals benefit the most. These people can use their mastery of the bureaucracy and their large network of friends and connections to exploit the rent control system. Consider that in New York, actresses Mia Farrow and Cicely Tyson live in rent-controlled apartments, paying well below market rates. So do the director of the Metropolitan Museum of Art, the chairman of Pathmark Stores, and singer and children's book author Carly Simon.

QUICK QUIZ

_____ prices perform three functions: (1) allocating existing scarce housing among competing claimants, (2) promoting efficient maintenance of existing houses and stimulating new housing construction, and (3) rationing the use of existing houses by current demanders.

Effective rent _____ impede the functioning of rental prices. Construction of new rental units is discouraged. Rent _____ decrease spending on maintenance of existing ones and also lead to "housing gridlock."

There are numerous ways to evade rent controls; _____ _____ is one.

See page 106 for the answers. Review concepts from this section in MyEconLab.

PRICE FLOORS IN AGRICULTURE

Another way that government can affect markets is by imposing price floors or price supports. In the United States, price supports are most often associated with agricultural products.

Price Supports

During the Great Depression, the federal government swung into action to help farmers. In 1933, it established a system of price supports for many agricultural products. Since then, there have been price supports for wheat, feed grains, cotton, rice, soybeans, sorghum, and dairy products, among other foodstuffs. The nature of the supports is quite simple: The government simply chooses a *support price* for an agricultural product and then acts to ensure that the price of the product never falls below the support level. Figure 4-4 shows the market demand for and supply of peanuts. Without a price support program, competitive forces would yield an equilibrium price of $250 per ton and an equilibrium quantity of 1.4 million tons per year. Clearly, if the government were to set the support price at or below $250 per ton, the quantity of peanuts demanded would equal the quantity of peanuts supplied at point E, because farmers could sell all they wanted at the market clearing price of $250 per ton.

But what happens when the government sets the support price *above* the market clearing price, at $350 per ton? At a support price of $350 per ton, the quantity demanded is only 1.0 million tons, but the quantity supplied is 2.2 million tons. The 1.2-million-ton difference between them is called the *excess quantity supplied,* or *surplus.* As simple as this program seems, its existence creates a fundamental question: How can the government agency charged with administering the price-support program prevent market forces from pushing the actual price down to $250 per ton?

If production exceeds the amount that consumers want to buy at the support price, what happens to the surplus? Quite simply, if the price-support program is to work, the government has to buy the surplus—the 1.2-million-ton difference. As a practical matter, the gov-

FIGURE 4-4
Agricultural Price Supports

Free market equilibrium occurs at E, with an equilibrium price of $250 per ton and an equilibrium quantity of 1.4 million tons. When the government sets a support price at $350 per ton, the quantity demanded is 1.0 million tons, and the quantity supplied is 2.2 million tons. The difference is the surplus, which the government buys. Farmers' income from consumers equals $350 × 1.0 million = $350 million. Farmers' additional income from taxpayers equals $350 × (2.2 million − 1.0 million) = $420 million.

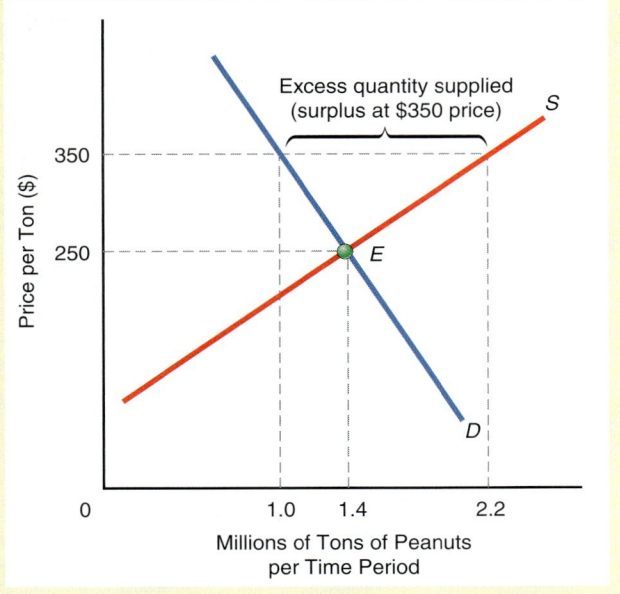

ernment acquires the 1.2-million-ton surplus indirectly through a government agency. The government either stores the surplus or sells it to foreign countries at a greatly reduced price (or gives it away free of charge) under the Food for Peace program.

Who Benefits from Agricultural Price Supports?

Although agricultural price supports have traditionally been promoted as a way to guarantee decent earnings for low-income farmers, most of the benefits have in fact gone to the owners of very large farms. Price-support payments are made on a per-bushel basis, not on a per-farm basis. Thus, traditionally, the larger the farm, the bigger the benefit from agricultural price supports. In addition, *all* of the benefits from price supports ultimately accrue to *landowners* on whose land price-supported crops grow.

Back in the early 1990s, Congress indicated an intention to phase out most agricultural subsidies by the early 2000s. What Congress actually *did* throughout the 1990s, however, was to pass a series of "emergency laws" keeping farm subsidies alive. Some of these laws aimed to replace agricultural price supports with payments to many farmers for growing no crops at all, thereby boosting the market prices of crops by reducing supply. Nevertheless, the federal government and a number of state governments have continued to support prices of a number of agricultural products, such as peanuts, through "marketing loan" programs. These programs advance funds to farmers to help them finance the storage of some or all of their crops. The farmers can then use the stored produce as collateral for borrowing or sell it to the government and use the proceeds to repay debts. Marketing loan programs raise the effective price that farmers receive for their crops and commit federal and state governments to purchasing surplus production. Consequently, they lead to outcomes similar to traditional price-support programs.

In 2002, Congress enacted the Farm Security Act, which has perpetuated these and other subsidy and price-support programs for such farm products as wheat, corn, rice, cotton, and soybeans. All told, government payments for these and other products amount to about 20 percent of the annual market value of all U.S. farm production.

European government price-support payments are even more extensive, accounting for almost twice as much of the total value of European agricultural output. How much do you suppose it costs European residents to support the production of sugar in their countries?

INTERNATIONAL POLICY EXAMPLE

The High Cost of European Sugar Subsidies

Sugar is most efficiently extracted from sugarcane, which can be grown at lowest cost in warm, moist climates. This helps explain why much of the world's sugar is produced in Brazil, India, Malawi, Thailand, and Zambia. Extracting sugar from sugar beets, which can be grown in cooler drier climates, is four times more costly than extracting sugar from sugarcane. Nevertheless, Europe, where only sugar beets can be grown, is the second-largest sugar-producing region of the world. Europe's governments buy much of this sugar at a price of about 25 cents per pound and then proceed to sell it outside Europe at a price of about 6 cents per pound. The cost to European taxpayers of supporting all this beet sugar production is at least $1.5 billion per year.

FOR CRITICAL ANALYSIS
Why do you suppose that governments of developing countries, such as Malawi and Zambia, commonly complain that Europe's sugar subsidy program enriches European sugar beet farmers at the expense of poorer farmers in their nations?

Minimum wage
A wage floor, legislated by government, setting the lowest hourly rate that firms may legally pay workers.

PRICE FLOORS IN THE LABOR MARKET

The **minimum wage** is the lowest hourly wage rate that firms may legally pay their workers. Proponents want higher minimum wages to ensure low-income workers a "decent" standard of living. Opponents counter that higher minimum wages cause increased unemployment, particularly among unskilled minority teenagers.

Minimum Wages in the United States

The federal minimum wage started in 1938 at 25 cents an hour, about 40 percent of the average manufacturing wage at the time. Typically, its level has stayed at about 40 to 50 percent of average manufacturing wages. It was increased to $5.15 in 1997 and may be higher by the time you read this.

Many states and cities have their own minimum wage laws that exceed the federal minimum. A number of municipalities refer to their minimum wage rules as "living wage" laws. Governments of these municipalities seek to set minimum wages consistent with a socially acceptable living standard—that is, overall wage income judged to be sufficient to purchase basic items such as housing and food.

Economic Effects of a Minimum Wage

What happens when the government establishes a floor on wages? The effects can be seen in Figure 4-5. We start off in equilibrium with the equilibrium wage rate of W_e and the equilibrium quantity of labor equal to Q_e. A minimum wage, W_m, higher than W_e, is imposed. At W_m, the quantity demanded for labor is reduced to Q_d, and some workers now become unemployed. Note that the reduction in employment from Q_e to Q_d, or the distance from B to A, is less than the excess quantity of labor supplied at wage rate W_m. This excess quantity supplied is the distance between A and C, or the distance between Q_d and Q_s. The reason the reduction in employment is smaller than the excess quantity of labor

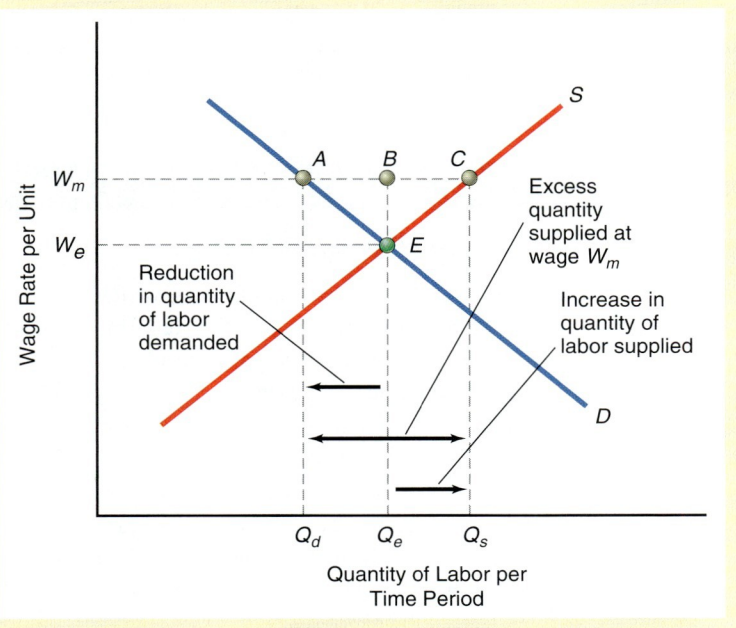

FIGURE 4-5

The Effect of Minimum Wages

The market clearing wage rate is W_e. The market clearing quantity of employment is Q_e, determined by the intersection of supply and demand at point E. A minimum wage equal to W_m is established. The quantity of labor demanded is reduced to Q_d. The reduction in employment from Q_e to Q_d is equal to the distance between B and A. That distance is smaller than the excess quantity of labor supplied at wage rate W_m. The distance between B and C is the increase in the quantity of labor supplied that results from the higher minimum wage rate.

supplied at the minimum wage is that the excess quantity of labor supplied also includes the *additional* workers who would like to work more hours at the new, higher minimum wage. Some workers will become unemployed as a result of the minimum wage, but others will move to sectors where minimum wage laws do not apply; wages will be pushed down in these uncovered sectors.

In the long run (a time period that is long enough to allow for full adjustment by workers and firms), some of the reduction in the quantity of labor demanded will result from a reduction in the number of firms, and some will result from changes in the number of workers employed by each firm. Economists estimate that a 10 percent increase in the minimum wage relative to the average prices of goods and services decreases total employment of those affected by 1 to 2 percent.

We can conclude from application of demand and supply analysis that a minimum wage established above the equilibrium wage rate typically has two fundamental effects. On the one hand, it boosts the wage earnings of those people who obtain employment. On the other hand, the minimum wage results in unemployment for other individuals. Thus, demand and supply analysis implies that the minimum wage makes some people better off while making others worse off.

What rationale has the German government offered for minimum wages?

Go to www.econtoday.com/ch04 for information from the U.S. Department of Labor about recent developments concerning the federal minimum wage.

INTERNATIONAL POLICY EXAMPLE

Germany Looks to the Minimum Wage to Crowd Out Migrants

Germany has no nationwide minimum wage. Instead, the nation's 1949 Collective Bargaining Act permits the government to issue a "declaration of general applicability" extending collective bargaining contracts to many industries. In effect, such a declaration requires all firms in an industry to pay union-negotiated wages to their employees, even if the firms are not unionized. At present, such declarations cover only about 5 percent of the German labor force.

In 2004, the European Union expanded to include several nations in Central and Eastern Europe. Many migrant workers from these regions now can work in Germany, and many have proved willing to accept lower wages than German workers. In a number of industries, such as hotels and meat packing, more migrant workers are employed than Germans.

In 2005, in an effort to prevent migrant workers from taking so many jobs in Germany, the nation's government proposed extending collective bargaining applicability to most industries. If adopted, this policy effectively would create a minimum wage system in Germany.

Most economists agree that such a policy undoubtedly would discourage German firms from hiring as many migrant workers. Another effect, however, would be to induce firms to stop hiring as many Germans.

FOR CRITICAL ANALYSIS
Which German workers would gain from establishment of a minimum wage system in that nation, and which would lose?

QUANTITY RESTRICTIONS

Governments can impose quantity restrictions on a market. The most obvious restriction is an outright ban on the ownership or trading of a good. It is currently illegal to buy and sell human organs. It is also currently illegal to buy and sell certain psychoactive drugs such as cocaine, heroin, and marijuana. In some states, it is illegal to start a new hospital without obtaining a license for a particular number of beds to be offered to patients. This licensing requirement effectively limits the quantity of hospital beds in some states. From 1933 to

1973, it was illegal for U.S. citizens to own gold except for manufacturing, medicinal, or jewelry purposes.

Some of the most common quantity restrictions exist in the area of international trade. The U.S. government, as well as many foreign governments, imposes import quotas on a variety of goods. An **import quota** is a supply restriction that prohibits the importation of more than a specified quantity of a particular good in a one-year period. The United States has had import quotas on tobacco, sugar, and immigrant labor. For many years, there were import quotas on oil coming into the United States. There are also "voluntary" import quotas on certain goods. For instance, in 2005 the Chinese government agreed to "voluntarily" restrict the amount of textile products China sends to the United States and the European Union.

Import quota
A physical supply restriction on imports of a particular good, such as sugar. Foreign exporters are unable to sell in the United States more than the quantity specified in the import quota.

QUICK QUIZ

With a price-_____ system, the government sets a minimum price at which, say, qualifying farm products can be sold. Any farmers who cannot sell at that price in the market can "sell" their surplus to the government. The only way a price-_____ system can survive is for the government or some other entity to buy up the excess quantity supplied at the support price.

When a _____ is placed on wages at a rate that is above market equilibrium, the result is an excess quantity of labor supplied at that minimum wage.

Quantity restrictions may take the form of _____ _____, which are limits on the quantity of specific foreign goods that can be brought into the United States for resale purposes.

See page 106 for the answers. Review concepts from this section in MyEconLab.

CASE STUDY

ECONOMICS FRONT AND CENTER

Using Auctions to Bypass the Army's Chain of Command

U.S. Army General Alvarez has been charged with finding a better way to allocate available personnel to vacant positions. She knows that decisions about which enlisted personnel to move into open positions have been made through the chain of command. "Personnel officers" comb through soldiers' records to find possible matches for vacant positions but give little attention to the soldiers' interests.

General Alvarez and her task force have concluded that this system helps explain why many soldiers shuffled into vacant positions have not renewed their enlistments in the nation's all-volunteer Army. Her job is to find a method for filling vacancies that increases the job satisfaction of soldiers, thereby encouraging them to remain in the military. Otherwise, the Army will soon face shortages of qualified personnel in a number of important positions throughout the ranks.

General Alvarez decides to see what she can learn from another branch of the military, the U.S. Navy, which has experimented with using a price system to allocate personnel. Sailors are able to bid for jobs, and ships are able to bid for the best-qualified sailors. In some cases, ships grant sailors considerable wage increases and assign enlisted sailors, such as petty officers, to tasks normally reserved for officers. After reviewing the Navy's experience with allowing sailors and ships to engage in voluntary exchanges and to establish the terms of exchange via auctions, General Alvarez makes a decision. The Army, she concludes, should develop a system closely modeled on the Navy's auction method.

CRITICAL ANALYSIS QUESTIONS

1. *In the Army's current system, who are middlemen in filling open positions?*
2. *From an economic perspective, why does a failure to rely on a price system for allocating personnel lead to frequent shortages in certain military positions?*

Coping with a Growing Global Demand for Freshwater

Issues and Applications

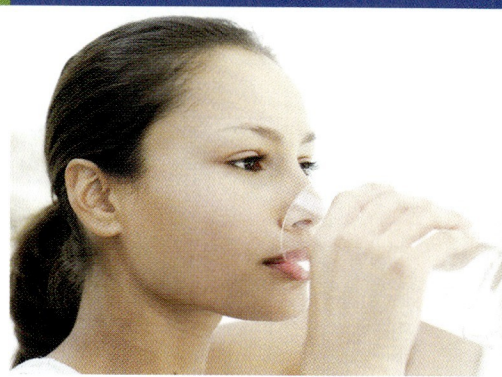

Today, about 2.5 billion people around the world consume safe drinking water. For the rest of the world's population, however—about 4 billion people—healthful water can be a rare commodity. Two billion tons of human waste are released into the world's rivers and streams each year, and the use of untreated water from these sources leads to nearly 2 million deaths annually.

What rationing method can best ensure greater access to safe drinking water? Traditionally, nations have utilized price controls to ration treated water. Increasingly, however, nations are concluding that a less hindered price system can best direct purified water to their residents.

Concepts Applied
- Price System
- Price Controls
- Price Ceilings

Price Controls Make a Scarce Resource Harder to Obtain

For years, people around the world have clamored for "low-cost" or even "free" drinking water. Many governments have attempted to oblige.

The problem is that the purification, storage, and delivery of healthful drinking water require the utilization of other scarce resources, such as labor and capital. Owners of these resources who direct them to the production of safe drinking water are willing to produce additional units of healthful water only if the price of water rises sufficiently to justify allocating more labor and capital to water production. Thus, the supply curve for drinkable water slopes upward, as shown in Figure 4-6 on page 100. If a nation's government allows water to be sold only at a very low price, such as 5 cents per unit, the result is predictable. The quantity of treated drinking water demanded exceeds the quantity of safe drinkable water supplied. There is a shortage of purified water at this below-market price—exactly the situation most of the world's people face today.

With projections indicating that the global amount of drinking water demanded at current prices is likely to rise by 40 percent during the next decade, it is little wonder that each year the United Nations classifies more of the world's nations as "water stressed." In China, for instance, a top political priority for the government has been to keep cities such as Beijing supplied with "cheap"—that is, below-market-price—drinking water. Producers of healthful water route purified water to these cities, but at ceiling prices, there is insufficient water available to channel to other parts of the country. Thus, water "shortages" in the world's most populous nation are becoming acute.

Letting the Price System Work

The vast majority of the world's households receive their water from municipal water authorities—government-controlled producers of treated water that set ceiling prices. In a growing number of locales, however, water production has moved to the unregulated private sector. For instance, in the United States, a number of municipalities have sold their water treatment oper-

99

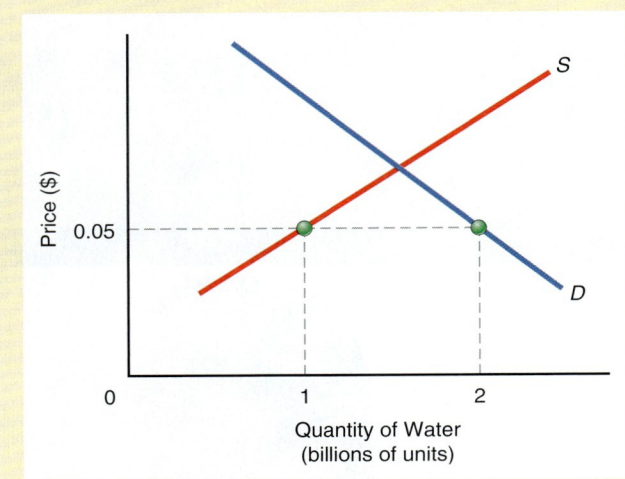

FIGURE 4-6

How to Generate a Water Shortage

In many nations, governments set the price of treated water at a price, such as 5 cents per unit, which is well below the market clearing price of purified water. As a result, the quantity of water demanded, 2 billion units, significantly exceeds the quantity of water supplied, 1 billion units.

ations to privately owned companies such as Aqua America and American States Water Company. Furthermore, governments in developed nations increasingly are deregulating water prices. This has allowed the price of treated water to move closer to the market clearing price, and quantities of safe water produced in these countries are moving nearer to equality with the quantities of safe water people wish to consume.

Even developing nations have begun privatizing the activities of water purification and storage. Multinational companies such as General Electric, ITT Industries, Siemens, and Tyco International now compete to sell water desalination, purification, storage, and transportation equipment around the world at unregulated prices. What remains to be seen is whether governments will allow market-determined prices to ration treated water or continue to require "low-priced" or "free" water. The decisions these governments make today will determine just how "water stressed" much of the world's population will be in the years to come.

Log in to **MyEconLab,** click on "Economic News," and test your understanding of the chapter by answering interactive questions that relate directly to this issue.

For Critical Analysis

1. Why do you suppose that when governments set a ceiling price and own or regulate firms that produce treated water, rationing by political power, random assignment, or queues is commonplace?
2. Who benefits and who loses when legal ceilings on prices of purified water create market shortages?

Web Resources

1. Review the status of private water production at www.econtoday.com/ch04.
2. Learn more about the results of privatization of the production of drinking water at www.econtoday.com/ch04.

Research Project

Discuss why the total stock of water on planet Earth is different from the global supply of healthful drinking water. Explain in your own words why this implies that the supply curve slopes upward in the market for purified drinking water. In what sense can a ceiling price set below the equilibrium price of treated water be blamed for adding to the world's "water stress"? Speculate about types of policies that national governments might consider implementing to try to push the *market clearing* prices of water to lower levels. (Hint: What factor or factors must change in the market for any item in order for its market clearing price to decrease?)

Here is what you should know after reading this chapter. MyEconLab will help you identify what you know, and where to go when you need to practice.

WHAT YOU SHOULD KNOW		WHERE TO GO TO PRACTICE
Essential Features of the Price System The price system, otherwise called the market system, allows prices to respond to changes in supply and demand for different commodities. Consumers' and business managers' decisions on resource use depend on what happens to prices. In the price system, exchange takes place in markets. The terms of exchange are communicated by prices in the marketplace, where middlemen reduce transaction costs by bringing buyers and sellers together.	price system, 83 voluntary exchange, 83 terms of exchange, 83 transaction costs, 83	• **MyEconLab** Study Plan 4.1 • Audio introduction to Chapter 4
How Changes in Demand and Supply Affect the Market Price and Equilibrium Quantity With a given supply curve, an increase in demand causes a rise in the market price and an increase in the equilibrium quantity, and a decrease in demand induces a fall in the market price and a decline in the equilibrium quantity. With a given demand curve, an increase in supply causes a fall in the market price and an increase in the equilibrium quantity, and a decrease in supply causes a rise in the market price and a decline in the equilibrium quantity. When both demand and supply shift at the same time, indeterminate results may occur. We must know the direction and degree of each shift in order to predict the change in the market price and the equilibrium quantity.	**Key figure** Figure 4-1, 85	• **MyEconLab** Study Plan 4.2 • Animated Figure 4-1
The Rationing Function of Prices In the market system, prices perform a rationing function—they ration scarce goods and services. Other ways of rationing include first come, first served; political power; physical force; random assignment; and coupons.		• **MyEconLab** Study Plan 4.3
The Effects of Price Ceilings Government-imposed price controls that require prices to be no higher than a certain level are price ceilings. If a government sets a price ceiling below the market price, then at the ceiling price the quantity of the good demanded will exceed the quantity supplied. There will be a shortage of the good at the ceiling price. For instance, rent controls place a ceiling on permitted rental prices and create shortages in housing markets. Price ceilings can lead to nonprice rationing devices and black markets.	price controls, 90 price ceiling, 90 price floor, 90 nonprice rationing devices, 90 black market, 91 rent control, 92 **Key figure** Figure 4-3, 90	• **MyEconLab** Study Plans 4.4 and 4.5 • Video: Price Flexibility, the Essential Role of Rationing via Price and Alternative Rationing Systems • Animated Figure 4-3

CHAPTER 4 Extensions of Demand and Supply Analysis

WHAT YOU SHOULD KNOW / WHERE TO GO TO PRACTICE

The Effects of Price Floors Government-mandated price controls that require prices to be no lower than a certain level are price floors. If a government sets a price floor above the market price, then at the floor price the quantity of the good supplied will exceed the quantity demanded. There will be a surplus of the good at the floor price. For instance, minimum wage laws that establish a price floor in the labor market and government price support policies that set price floors in markets for agricultural goods often generate surpluses in these markets.

minimum wage, 96
Key figures
Figure 4-4, 94
Figure 4-5, 96

- **MyEconLab** Study Plans 4.6 and 4.7
- Video: Minimum Wages
- Animated Figures 4-4, 4-5

Government-Imposed Restrictions on Market Quantities Quantity restrictions can take the form of outright government bans on the sale of certain goods, such as human organs or various psychoactive drugs. They can also arise from licensing requirements that limit the number of producers and thereby restrict the amount supplied of a good or service. Another example is an import quota, which limits the number of units of a foreign-produced good that can legally be sold domestically.

import quota, 98

- **MyEconLab** Study Plan 4.8

Log in to MyEconLab, take a chapter test, and get a personalized Study Plan that tells you which concepts you understand and which ones you need to review. From there, MyEconLab will give you futher practice, tutorials, animations, videos, and guided solutions.

Log in to www.myeconlab.com

PROBLEMS

Select problems, indicated by a blue oval ●, *are assignable in MyEconLab.*
Answers to the odd-numbered problems appear at the back of the book.

4-1 In recent years, technological improvements have greatly reduced the costs of producing music CDs, and a number of new firms have entered the music CD industry. At the same time, prices of substitutes for music CDs, such as Internet downloads and music DVDs, have declined considerably. Construct a supply and demand diagram of the market for music CDs. Illustrate the impacts of these developments, and evaluate the effects on the market price and equilibrium quantity.

4-2 The pharmaceutical industry has benefited from advances in research and development that enable manufacturers to identify potential cures more quickly and therefore at lower cost. At the same time, the aging of our society has increased the demand for new drugs. Construct a supply and demand diagram of the market for pharmaceutical drugs. Illustrate the impacts of these developments, and evaluate the effects on the market price and the equilibrium quantity.

4-3 The following table depicts the quantity demanded and quantity supplied of studio apartments in a small college town.

Monthly Rent	Quantity Demanded	Quantity Supplied
$400	3,000	1,600
$450	2,500	1,800
$500	2,000	2,000
$550	1,500	2,200
$600	1,000	2,400

What are the market price and equilibrium quantity of apartments in this town? If this town imposes a rent control of $450 per month, how many studio apartments will be rented?

4-4 The U.S. government imposes a price floor for U.S. sugar that is above the market clearing price. Illustrate the U.S. sugar market with the price floor in place. Discuss the effects of the price floor on conditions in the market for sugar in the United States.

4-5 The Canadian sugar industry has complained that U.S. sugar manufacturers "dump" sugar surpluses in the Canadian market. U.S. chocolate manufacturers have also complained about the high U.S. price of sugar. Explain how the imposition of a price floor for U.S. sugar, as described in Problem 4-4, affects each of these markets. What are the changes in equilibrium quantities and market prices?

4-6 Suppose that the U.S. government places a ceiling on the price of Internet access.

a. Show why there is a shortage of Internet access at the legal price.
b. Suppose that a black market for Internet providers arises, with Internet service providers developing hidden connections. Illustrate the black market for Internet access, including the implicit supply schedule, the legal price, the black market supply and demand, and the highest feasible black market price.

4-7 The table below illustrates the demand and supply schedules for seats on air flights between two cities:

Price	Quantity Demanded	Quantity Supplied
$200	2,000	1,200
$300	1,800	1,400
$400	1,600	1,600
$500	1,400	1,800
$600	1,200	2,000

What are the market price and equilibrium quantity in this market? Now suppose that federal authorities limit the number of flights between the two cities to ensure that no more than 1,200 passengers can be flown. Evaluate the effects of this quota. (Hint: How much are the 1,200 passengers willing to pay for their flights?)

4-8. The consequences of decriminalizing illegal drugs have long been debated. Some claim that legalization will lower the price of these drugs and reduce related crime. Others claim that more people will use these drugs. Suppose that some of these drugs are legalized so that anyone may sell them and use them. Now consider the two claims—that price will fall and quantity demanded will increase. Based on positive economic analysis, are these claims sound?

4-9 In recent years, the government of Pakistan has established a support price for wheat of about $0.20 per kilogram of wheat. At this price, consumers are willing to purchase 10 billion kilograms of wheat per year, while Pakistani farmers are willing to grow and harvest 18 billion kilograms of wheat per year. The government purchases and stores all surplus wheat.

a. What are annual consumer expenditures on the Pakistani wheat crop?
b. What are annual government expenditures on the Pakistani wheat crop?
c. How much, in total, do Pakistani wheat farmers receive for the wheat they produce?

4-10 Consider the information in Problem 4-9 and your answers to that question. Suppose that the market clearing price of Pakistani wheat in the absence of price supports is equal to $0.10 per kilogram. At this price, the quantity of wheat demanded is 12 billion kilograms. Under the government wheat price-support program, how much more is spent each year on wheat harvested in Pakistan than otherwise would have been spent in an unregulated market for Pakistani wheat?

4-11 Consider the diagram below, which depicts the labor market in a city that has adopted a "living wage law" requiring employers to pay a minimum wage rate of $9 per hour. Answer the questions that follow.

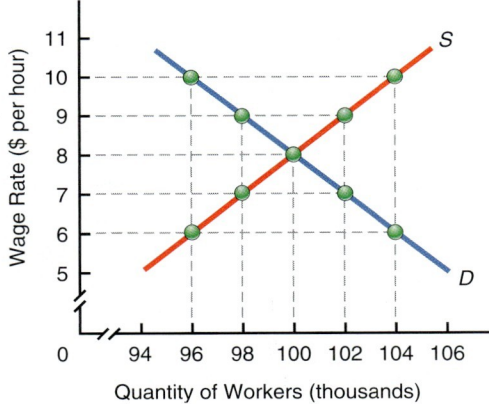

a. What condition exists in this city's labor market at the present minimum wage of $9 per hour? How many people are unemployed at this wage?
b. A city councilwoman has proposed amending the living wage law. She suggests reducing the minimum wage to $6 per hour. Assuming that the

labor demand and supply curves were to remain in their present positions, how many people would be unemployed at a $6 minimum wage?

c. A councilman has offered a counterproposal. In his view, the current minimum wage is too low and should be increased to $10 per hour. Assuming that the labor demand and supply curves were to remain in their present positions, how many people would be unemployed at a $10 minimum wage?

4-12 Suppose that owners of high-rise office buildings are the main employers of custodial workers in a city. The city has decided to impose rent controls, and it has established a rent ceiling below the previous equilibrium rental rate for offices throughout the city.

a. How will the quantity of offices the building owners lease change?
b. How will the market wage and equilibrium quantity of labor services provided by custodial workers be affected by the imposition of rent controls?

4-13 In 2005, the government of a nation established a price support for wheat. The government's support price has been above the equilibrium price each year since, and the government has purchased all wheat over and above the amounts that consumers have bought at the support price. Every year since 2005, there has been an increase in the number of wheat producers in the market. No other factors affecting the market for wheat have changed. Predict what has happened every year since 2005 to each of the following:

a. Quantity of wheat supplied by wheat producers
b. Quantity of wheat demanded by wheat consumers
c. Quantity of wheat purchased by the government

4-14 The government of a large U.S. city recently established a "living wage law" that, beginning January 1 of next year, will require all businesses operating within city limits to pay their workers a wage no lower than $8.50 per hour. The current equilibrium wage for fast-food workers is $7.50 per hour in this city. Predict what will happen to each of the following beginning on January 1 of next year:

a. The quantity of labor supplied by fast-food workers
b. The quantity of labor demanded by fast-food producers
c. The number of unemployed fast-food workers in this city

ECONOMICS ON THE NET

The Floor on Milk Prices At various times, the U.S. government has established price floors for milk. This application gives you an opportunity to apply what you have learned in this chapter to this real-world issue.

Title: Northeast Dairy Compact Commission

Navigation: Go to www.econtoday.com/ch04 to visit the Web site of the Northeast Dairy Compact Commission.

Application Read the contents and answer these questions.

1. Based on the government-set price control concepts discussed in Chapter 4, explain the Northeast Dairy Compact that was once in place in the northeastern United States.
2. Draw a diagram illustrating the supply of and demand for milk in the Northeast Dairy Compact and the supply of and demand for milk outside the Northeast Dairy Compact. Illustrate how the compact affected the quantities demanded and supplied for participants in the compact. In addition, show how this affected the market for milk produced by those producers outside the dairy compact.
3. Economists have found that while the Northeast Dairy Compact functioned, midwestern dairy farmers lost their dominance of milk production and sales. In light of your answer to Question 2, explain how this occurred.

For Group Discussion and Analysis Discuss the impact of congressional failure to reauthorize the compact based on your above answers. Identify which arguments in your debate are based on positive economic analysis and which are normative arguments.

ANSWERS TO QUICK QUIZZES

p. 88: (i) terms . . . exchange . . . transaction; (ii) demand . . . supply . . . supply . . . demand; (iii) immediately . . . time
p. 89: (i) first come, first served . . . political power . . . physical force . . . random assignment . . . coupons; (ii) queuing
p. 91: (i) ceilings . . . floors; (ii) ceiling . . . controls
p. 93: (i) Rental; (ii) controls . . . controls; (iii) key money
p. 98: (i) support . . . support; (ii) floor; (iii) import quotas

Public Spending and Public Choice

5

Vaccines, which are the first line of defense against many communicable diseases, protect not only those who are inoculated but also others who might be exposed to more infected individuals. In recent years, shortages of vaccines have been so acute and widespread that the U.S. government has instructed medical professionals not to inoculate people deemed to be at "low risk" of becoming infected with diseases such as influenza or measles. Why have shortages existed in markets for vaccines, even though society as a whole benefits if more people receive them? Why might the government have a legitimate role to perform in trying to correct this situation? In this chapter, you will learn the answers to these questions.

Learning Objectives

After reading this chapter, you should be able to:

1. Explain how market failures such as externalities might justify economic functions of government
2. Distinguish between private goods and public goods and explain the nature of the free-rider problem
3. Describe political functions of government that entail its involvement in the economy
4. Analyze how Medicare affects the incentives to consume medical services
5. Explain why increases in government spending on public education have not been associated with improvements in measures of student performance
6. Discuss the central elements of the theory of public choice

MyEconLab helps you master each objective and study more efficiently. See end of chapter for details.

107

Did You Know That...

during the past five years, more than 60 percent of U.S. corporations paid no federal taxes? Since 2003, corporate income taxes have accounted for less than 8 percent of the federal government's overall receipts. This historically low rate of corporate income taxation has been decried by many members of Congress, a body that devotes considerable time and effort to looking for new ways to fund the federal government's operations. The U.S. government collects more than $1 trillion annually in income taxes alone. Local, state, and federal governments additionally raise more than $1 trillion in miscellaneous other taxes, such as sales and excise taxes. Clearly, we cannot ignore the presence of government in our society. One of the reasons the government exists is to take care of the functions that people argue the price system does not do well.

WHAT A PRICE SYSTEM CAN AND CANNOT DO

Throughout the book so far, we have alluded to the benefits of a price system. High on the list is economic efficiency. In its most ideal form, a price system allows resources to move from lower-valued uses to higher-valued uses through voluntary exchange. Economic efficiency arises when all mutually advantageous trades have taken place. In a price system, consumers are sovereign; that is to say, they have the individual freedom to decide what they wish to purchase. Politicians and even business managers do not ultimately decide what is produced; consumers decide. Some proponents of the price system argue that this is its most important characteristic. A market organization of economic activity generally prevents one person from illegally interfering with most of other people's activities. Competition among sellers protects consumers from coercion by one seller, and sellers are protected from coercion by one consumer because other consumers are available.

Sometimes the price system does not generate these results, and too few or too many resources go to specific economic activities. Such situations are called **market failures.** Market failures prevent the price system from attaining economic efficiency and individual freedom. Market failures offer one of the strongest arguments in favor of certain economic functions of government, which we now examine.

Market failure
A situation in which the market economy leads to too few or too many resources going to a specific economic activity.

CORRECTING FOR EXTERNALITIES

In a pure market system, competition generates economic efficiency only when individuals know and must bear the true opportunity cost of their actions. In some circumstances, the price that someone actually pays for a resource, good, or service is higher or lower than the opportunity cost that all of society pays for that same resource, good, or service.

Externalities

Consider a hypothetical world in which there is no government regulation against pollution. You are living in a town that until now has had clean air. A steel mill moves into town. It produces steel and has paid for the inputs—land, labor, capital, and entrepreneurship. The price the mill charges for the steel reflects, in this example, only the costs that it incurs. In the course of production, however, the mill utilizes one input—clean air—by simply using it. This is indeed an input because in making steel, the furnaces emit smoke. The steel mill doesn't have to pay the cost of using the clean air. Rather, it is the people in the community who incur that cost in the form of dirtier clothes, dirtier cars and houses, and more respiratory illnesses. The effect is similar to what would happen if the steel mill could take coal or oil or workers' services for free. There is an **externality,** an external cost. Some of the costs associated with the production of the steel have "spilled over" to affect **third parties,** parties other than the buyer and the seller of the steel.

A fundamental reason that air pollution creates external costs is that the air belongs to everyone and hence to no one in particular. Lack of clearly assigned **property rights,** or the rights of an owner to use and exchange property, prevents market prices from reflecting all the costs created by activities that generate spillovers onto third parties.

How has assigning property rights to local airwaves addressed spillovers among wireless Internet and e-mail systems at U.S. airports?

Externality
A consequence of an economic activity that spills over to affect third parties. Pollution is an externality.

Third parties
Parties who are not directly involved in a given activity or transaction.

Property rights
The rights of an owner to use and to exchange property.

E-COMMERCE EXAMPLE

Property Rights Resolve the Airport Wi-Fi Spillover Problem

To encourage travelers to use their facilities, various U.S. airports have constructed wireless, or Wi-Fi, systems. Antennas broadcast radio signals that allow travelers to use electronic devices, such as laptops and Blackberries, to access the Internet and e-mail accounts. Before the Wi-Fi systems were installed, a number of airlines had already set up their own wireless communications systems to process passenger tickets and to track baggage. When the airport Wi-Fi systems began operating, their radio signals interfered with some airlines' wireless communications systems, causing ticketing and baggage data transmissions to be blocked or garbled. At the same time, transmissions from the airlines' wireless systems impeded the smooth operations of the airport Wi-Fi systems.

Under the airlines' contracts with the airports, the airports had the right to utilize the wireless frequencies on which conflicts had arisen. Thus, the airlines had to incur costs to recalibrate their wireless systems or, in some cases, replace their systems entirely to eliminate wavelength "pollution" created by competing signals.

FOR CRITICAL ANALYSIS
Why is it that an external cost would be created if transmissions from a company's Wi-Fi system garbled the signals of the wireless computer networks in a nearby residential neighborhood?

External Costs in Graphical Form

To consider how market prices fail to take into account external costs in situations in which third-party spillovers exist without a clear assignment of property rights, look at panel (a) in Figure 5-1 on the following page. Here we show the demand curve for steel as D. The supply curve is S_1. The supply curve includes only the costs that the firms have to pay. Equilibrium occurs at point E, with a price of $500 per ton and a quantity equal to 110 million tons per year. But producing steel also involves externalities—the external costs that you and your neighbors pay in the form of dirtier clothes, cars, and houses and increased respiratory disease due to the air pollution emitted from the steel mill. In this case, the producers of steel use clean air without having to pay for it. Let's include these external costs in our graph to find out what the full cost of steel production would really be if property rights to the air around the steel mill could generate payments for "owners" of that air. We do this by imagining that steel producers have to pay the "owners" of the air for the input—clean air—that the producers previously used at a zero price.

FIGURE 5-1

External Costs and Benefits

In panel (a), we show a situation in which the production of steel generates external costs. If the steel mills ignore pollution, at equilibrium the quantity of steel will be 110 million tons. If the steel mills had to pay for the external costs that are caused by the mills' production but are currently borne by nearby residents, the supply curve would shift the vertical distance A–E_1, to S_2. If consumers of steel were forced to pay a price that reflected the spillover costs, the quantity demanded would fall to 100 million tons. In panel (b), we show a situation in which inoculations against communicable diseases generate external benefits to those individuals who may not be inoculated but who will benefit because epidemics will not occur. If each individual ignores the external benefit of inoculations, the market clearing quantity will be 150 million. If external benefits are taken into account by purchasers of inoculations, however, the demand curve would shift to D_2. The new equilibrium quantity would be 200 million inoculations, and the price of an inoculation would rise from $10 to $15.

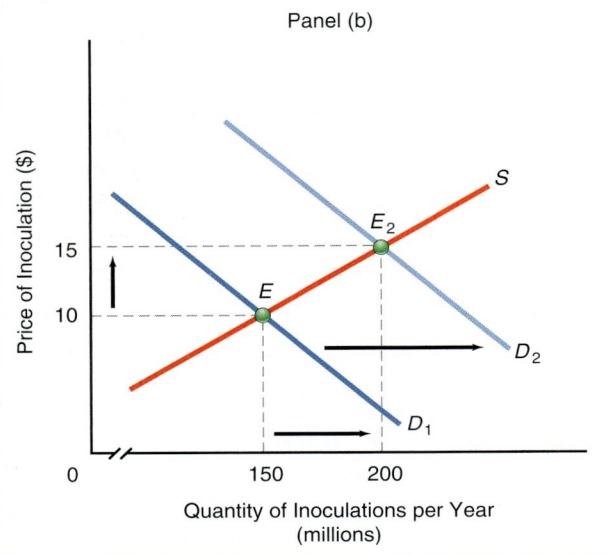

Recall from Chapter 3 that an increase in input prices shifts the supply curve. Thus, in panel (a) of the figure, the supply curve shifts from S_1 to S_2; the external costs equal the vertical distance between A and E_1. In this example, if steel firms had to take into account these external costs, the equilibrium quantity would fall to 100 million tons per year, and the price would rise to $600 per ton. Equilibrium would shift from E to E_1. In contrast, if the price of steel does not account for external costs, third parties bear those costs—represented by the distance between A and E_1—in the form of dirtier clothes, houses, and cars and increased respiratory illnesses.

External Benefits in Graphical Form

Externalities can also be positive. To demonstrate external benefits in graphical form, we will use the example of inoculations against communicable disease. In panel (b) of Figure 5-1, we show the demand curve as D_1 (without taking account of any external benefits) and the supply curve as S. The equilibrium price is $10 per inoculation, and the equilibrium quantity is 150 million inoculations.

We assume, however, that inoculations against communicable diseases generate external benefits to individuals who may not be inoculated but will benefit nevertheless because epidemics will not break out. If such external benefits were taken into account by those who purchase inoculations, the demand curve would shift from D_1 to D_2.

As a consequence of this shift in demand, the new equilibrium quantity would be 200 million inoculations, and the new equilibrium price would be $15 per inoculation. If people who consider getting inoculations fail to take external benefits into account, this society is not devoting enough resources to inoculations against communicable diseases.

Resource Misallocations of Externalities

When there are external costs, the market will tend to *overallocate* resources to the production of the good or service in question, for those goods or services are implicitly priced deceptively low. In the steel example, too much will be produced because the steel mill owners and managers are not required to take account of the external cost that steel production is imposing on the rest of society. In essence, the full cost of production is not borne by the owners and managers, so the price they charge the public for steel is lower than it would otherwise be. And, of course, the lower price means that buyers are willing and able to buy more. More steel is produced and consumed than if the sellers were to bear external costs.

When there are external benefits, the price is too low to induce suppliers to allocate resources to the production of that good or service (because the demand, which fails to reflect the external benefits, is relatively too low). Thus, the market *underallocates* resources to producing the good or service. In a market system, too many of the goods that generate external costs are produced, and too few of the goods that generate external benefits are produced.

How the Government Can Correct Negative Externalities

In theory, the government can take action to try to correct situations in which a lack of property rights allows third-party spillovers to create an externality. In the case of negative externalities, at least two avenues are open to the government: special taxes and legislative regulation or prohibition.

Special Taxes. In our example of the steel mill, the externality problem arises because using the air as a waste disposal place is costless to the firm but not to society. The government could make the steel mill pay a tax for dumping its pollutants into the air. The government could attempt to tax the steel mill commensurate with the cost to third parties from smoke in the air. This, in effect, would be a pollution tax or an **effluent fee**. The ultimate effect would be to reduce the supply of steel and raise the price to consumers, ideally making the price equal to the full cost of production to society.

Why do you suppose that an effort to impose an effluent-fee system intended to reduce emissions of cigarette smoke in Italian restaurants has not proved successful?

Effluent fee
A charge to a polluter that gives the right to discharge into the air or water a certain amount of pollution; also called a *pollution tax*.

INTERNATIONAL POLICY EXAMPLE

Italy's Ineffective Program for Reducing Smoking Spillovers

In most systems for reducing pollution using an effluent fee, the government is directly involved as a fee collector. When the Italian government decided to implement an effluent-fee system aimed at reducing secondhand smoke in restaurants, however, it put the restaurants at the center of enforcement efforts. If a customer lights up a cigarette in a smoke-free zone in a restaurant in Italy, its managers are legally bound to charge the violator a fine as part of the bill and to transmit the amount of the fine to the government.

(*continued*)

Many restaurant owners have refused to participate in the government's program. Some worry about losing customers they penalize. Others simply do not want to go to the trouble to collect the government's fees without receiving compensation for the tax-collecting expenses they would incur. Consequently, the Italian government's effluent-fee system so far has largely failed to reduce secondhand smoke in restaurants.

FOR CRITICAL ANALYSIS
How might the Italian government redesign its effluent-fee system so that it more effectively cuts down on the spillover costs incurred by nonsmoking patrons of restaurants?

Go to www.econtoday.com/ch05 to learn more about how the Environmental Protection Agency uses regulations to try to protect the environment.

Regulation. Alternatively, to correct a negative externality arising from steel production, the government could specify a maximum allowable rate of pollution. This regulation would require that the steel mill install pollution abatement equipment at its facilities, reduce its rate of output, or some combination of the two. Note that the government's job would not be simple, for it would have to determine the appropriate level of pollution and then measure the pollutants emitted in order to enforce the regulation.

How the Government Can Correct Positive Externalities

What can the government do when the production of one good spills *benefits* over to third parties? It has several policy options: financing the production of the good or producing the good itself, subsidies (negative taxes), and regulation.

Government Financing and Production. If the positive externalities seem extremely large, the government has the option of financing the desired additional production facilities so that the "right" amount of the good will be produced. Again consider inoculations against communicable diseases. The government could—and often does—finance campaigns to inoculate the population. It could (and does) even produce and operate inoculation centers where inoculations are given at no charge.

Subsidies. A subsidy is a negative tax; it is a payment made either to a business or to a consumer when the business produces or the consumer buys a good or a service. To generate more inoculations against communicable diseases, the government could subsidize everyone who obtains an inoculation by directly reimbursing those inoculated or by making payments to private firms that provide inoculations. Subsidies reduce the net price to consumers, thereby causing a larger quantity to be demanded.

Regulation. In some cases involving positive externalities, the government can require by law that individuals in the society undertake a certain action. For example, regulations require that all school-age children be inoculated before entering public and private schools. Some people believe that a basic school education itself generates positive externalities. Perhaps as a result of this belief, we have regulations—laws—that require all school-age children to be enrolled in a public or private school.

QUICK QUIZ

External _____ lead to an overallocation of resources to the specific economic activity. Two possible ways of correcting these spillovers are _____ and _____.

External _____ result in an underallocation of resources to the specific activity. Three possible government corrections are _____ the production of the activity, _____ private firms or consumers to engage in the activity, and _____.

See page 133 for the answers. Review concepts from this section in MyEconLab.

THE OTHER ECONOMIC FUNCTIONS OF GOVERNMENT

Besides correcting for externalities, the government performs many other economic functions that affect the way exchange is carried out. In contrast, the political functions of government have to do with deciding how income should be redistributed among households and selecting which goods and services have special merits and should therefore be treated differently. The economic and political functions of government can and do overlap.

Let's look at four more economic functions of government.

Providing a Legal System

The courts and the police may not at first seem like economic functions of government. Their activities nonetheless have important consequences for economic activities in any country. You and I enter into contracts constantly, whether they be oral or written, expressed or implied. When we believe that we have been wronged, we seek redress of our grievances through our legal institutions. Moreover, consider the legal system that is necessary for the smooth functioning of our economic system. Our system has defined quite explicitly the legal status of businesses, the rights of private ownership, and a method of enforcing contracts. All relationships among consumers and businesses are governed by the legal rules of the game. In its judicial function, then, the government serves as the referee for settling disputes in the economic arena. In this role, the government often imposes penalties for violations of legal rules.

Much of our legal system is involved with defining and protecting property rights. One might say that property rights are really the rules of our economic game. When property rights are well defined, owners of property have an incentive to use that property efficiently. Any mistakes in their decisions about the use of property have negative consequences that the owners suffer. Furthermore, when property rights are well defined, owners of property have an incentive to maintain that property so that if they ever desire to sell it, it will fetch a better price.

Promoting Competition

Many people believe that the only way to attain economic efficiency is through competition. One of the roles of government is to serve as the protector of a competitive economic system. Congress and the various state governments have passed **antitrust legislation.** Such legislation makes illegal certain (but not all) economic activities that might restrain trade—that is, that might prevent free competition among actual and potential rival firms in the marketplace. The avowed aim of antitrust legislation is to reduce the power of **monopolies**—firms that can determine the market price of the goods they sell. A large number of antitrust laws have been passed that prohibit specific anticompetitive actions. Both the Antitrust Division of the Department of Justice and the Federal Trade Commission attempt to enforce these antitrust laws. Various state judicial agencies also expend efforts at maintaining competition.

Antitrust legislation
Laws that restrict the formation of monopolies and regulate certain anticompetitive business practices.

Monopoly
A firm that can determine the market price of a good. In the extreme case, a monopoly is the only seller of a good or service.

Providing Public Goods

The goods used in our examples up to this point have been **private goods.** When I eat a cheeseburger, you cannot eat the same one. So you and I are rivals for that cheeseburger, just as much as rivals for the title of world champion are. When I use a DVD player, you cannot play some other disc at the same time. When I use the services of an auto mechanic, that person cannot work at the same time for you. That is the distinguishing feature of private goods—their use is exclusive to the people who purchase or rent them.

Private goods
Goods that can be consumed by only one individual at a time. Private goods are subject to the principle of rival consumption.

Principle of rival consumption
The recognition that individuals are rivals in consuming private goods because one person's consumption reduces the amount available for others to consume.

Public goods
Goods for which the principle of rival consumption does not apply; they can be jointly consumed by many individuals simultaneously at no additional cost and with no reduction in quality or quantity. Also no one who fails to help pay for the good can be denied the benefit of the good.

Exclusion principle
The principle that no one can be excluded from the benefits of a public good, even if that person has not paid for it.

ECONOMICS FRONT AND CENTER

To contemplate whether space exploration is a public good, read **Is It Time to Move Space Exploration to the Marketplace?** on page 125.

Free-rider problem
A problem that arises when individuals presume that others will pay for public goods so that, individually, they can escape paying for their portion without causing a reduction in production.

The **principle of rival consumption** applies to all private goods by definition. Rival consumption is easy to understand. Either you use private goods, or I use them.

There is an entire class of goods that are not private goods. These are called **public goods.** The principle of rival consumption does not apply to them. They can be consumed *jointly* by many individuals simultaneously, and no one can be excluded from consuming these goods even if they fail to pay to do so. National defense, police protection, and the legal system, for example, are public goods.

Characteristics of Public Goods.
Two fundamental characteristics of public goods set them apart from all other goods:

1. *Public goods can be used by more and more people at no additional opportunity cost and without depriving others of any of the services of the goods.* Once funds have been spent on national defense, the defense protection you receive does not reduce the amount of protection bestowed on anyone else. The opportunity cost of your receiving national defense once it is in place is zero because once national defense is in place to protect you, it also protects others.
2. *It is difficult to design a collection system for a public good on the basis of how much individuals use it.* No one can be denied the benefits of national defense for failing to pay for that public good. This is often called the **exclusion principle.**

One of the problems of public goods is that the private sector has a difficult, if not impossible, time providing them. Individuals in the private sector have little or no incentive to offer public goods. It is difficult for them to make a profit doing so, because nonpayers cannot be excluded. Consequently, true public goods must necessarily be provided by government. Note, though, that economists do not categorize something as a public good simply because the government provides it.

Free Riders.
The nature of public goods leads to the **free-rider problem,** a situation in which some individuals take advantage of the fact that others will assume the burden of paying for public goods such as national defense. Suppose that citizens were taxed directly in proportion to how much they tell an interviewer that they value national defense. Some people who actually value national defense will probably tell interviewers that it has no value to them—they don't want any of it. Such people are trying to be free riders. We may all want to be free riders if we believe that someone else will provide the commodity in question that we actually value.

The free-rider problem often arises in connection with sharing the burden of international defense. A country may choose to belong to a multilateral defense organization, such as the North Atlantic Treaty Organization (NATO), but then consistently attempt to avoid contributing funds to the organization. The nation knows it would be defended by others in NATO if it were attacked but would rather not pay for such defense. In short, it seeks a free ride.

Which nation's taxpayers have effectively become free riders in defending North America from one possible form of terrorist attack?

INTERNATIONAL EXAMPLE

Canada Opts Out of Paying for North American Missile Defense

The North American Aerospace Defense (NORAD) system uses satellites and ground-based and air-based radar systems to detect attacks aimed at the United States and Canada. In the past, both countries have contributed to the operation of NORAD. Indeed, on the morning of September 11, 2001,

(*continued*)

when terrorists took over planes and aimed them at the World Trade Center and the Pentagon, a Canadian general at NORAD was in charge of the military response.

Nevertheless, when the U.S. government asked the Canadian government to contribute to a new missile defense system that would supplement NORAD's activities, the Canadians declined. At the time, joining with the U.S. government in a missile defense system was politically unpopular in Canada. Canadian government officials realized that the U.S. military could deploy an effective missile defense system without Canada's assistance. The Canadian officials also knew that the U.S. military would attempt to shoot down any missile that might land in Canada and thereby expose U.S. residents to radiation fallout or disease. Thus, the Canadian government could act as a free rider, and it did.

FOR CRITICAL ANALYSIS
In a world in which terrorists might be able to load nuclear or biological weapons on missiles, why might missile defense systems be categorized as public goods?

Ensuring Economywide Stability

Our economy sometimes faces the problems of undesired unemployment and rising prices. The government, especially the federal government, has made an attempt to solve these problems by trying to stabilize the economy by smoothing out the ups and downs in overall business activity. The notion that the federal government should undertake actions to stabilize business activity is a relatively new idea in the United States, encouraged by high unemployment rates during the Great Depression of the 1930s and subsequent theories about possible ways that government could reduce unemployment. In 1946, Congress passed the Full-Employment Act, a landmark law concerning government responsibility for economic performance. It established three goals for government stabilization policy: full employment, price stability, and economic growth. These goals have provided the justification for many government economic programs during the post–World War II period.

QUICK QUIZ

The economic activities of government include (1) correcting for _____, (2) providing a _____ _____, (3) promoting _____, (4) producing _____ goods, and (5) ensuring _____ _____.

The principle of _____ _____ does not apply to public goods as it does to private goods.

Public goods have two characteristics: (1) Once they are produced, there is no additional _____ _____ when additional consumers use them, because your use of a public good does not deprive others of its simultaneous use; and (2) consumers cannot conveniently be _____ on the basis of use.

See page 133 for the answers. Review concepts from this section in MyEconLab.

THE POLITICAL FUNCTIONS OF GOVERNMENT

At least two functions of government are political or normative functions rather than economic ones like those discussed in the first part of this chapter. These two areas are (1) the regulation and provision of merit and demerit goods and (2) income redistribution.

Merit and Demerit Goods

Certain goods are considered to have special merit. A **merit good** is defined as any good that the political process has deemed socially desirable. (Note that nothing inherent in any particular good makes it a merit good. The designation is entirely subjective.) Some examples of

Merit good
A good that has been deemed socially desirable through the political process. Museums are an example.

merit goods in our society are sports stadiums, museums, ballets, plays, and concerts. In these areas, the government's role is the provision of merit goods to the people in society who would not otherwise purchase them at market clearing prices or who would not purchase an amount of them judged to be sufficient. This provision may take the form of government production and distribution of merit goods. It can also take the form of reimbursement for spending on merit goods or subsidies to producers or consumers for part of the cost of merit goods. Governments do indeed subsidize such merit goods as professional sports, concerts, ballets, museums, and plays. In most cases, those goods would not be so numerous without subsidization.

Why do critics of government funding of civic centers argue that the per-unit merits of government-funded civic centers are declining?

POLICY EXAMPLE

Civic Centers Grow as Exhibition Attendance Declines

Recently, Carmel, Indiana, a town with a population of about 40,000, broke ground on a civic center that will provide 100,000 square feet of space to be used for exhibitions such as concerts, conventions, and displays. In building a government-funded civic center, Carmel joined the ranks of municipalities across the land. More than 50 new government-funded civic centers are under construction in the United States, from Spokane, Washington, and Jackson, Mississippi, to Peoria, Illinois, and Albany, New York. Many other towns and cities, including Portland, Oregon, are expanding existing civic centers. All told, 7 million square feet of new civic-center space will be added to the 64 million square feet already in existence.

Between 1991 and 1995, total admissions at events held at U.S. municipal civic centers rose from 3.8 million to 5.2 million. Since 1995, however, total attendance at civic-center events across the United States has fallen to about 4 million, and admissions per square foot of space in U.S. civic centers have declined by 50 percent. Thus, even as governments continue to build new and larger civic centers, one measure of merit—attendance per square foot of space—is declining.

FOR CRITICAL ANALYSIS
Who ultimately bears most of the costs of constructing and maintaining civic centers? (Hint: Most municipalities fund at least part of the expenses associated with building and maintaining civic centers from sales, property, and other taxes.)

Demerit good
A good that has been deemed socially undesirable through the political process. Heroin is an example.

Demerit goods are the opposite of merit goods. They are goods that, through the political process, are deemed socially undesirable. Heroin, cigarettes, gambling, and cocaine are examples. The government exercises its role in the area of demerit goods by taxing, regulating, or prohibiting their manufacture, sale, and use. Governments justify the relatively high taxes on alcohol and tobacco by declaring them demerit goods. The best-known example of governmental exercise of power in this area is the stance against certain psychoactive drugs. Most psychoactives (except nicotine, caffeine, and alcohol) are either expressly prohibited, as is the case for heroin, cocaine, and opium, or heavily regulated, as in the case of prescription psychoactives.

Transfer payments
Money payments made by governments to individuals for which no services or goods are rendered in return. Examples are Social Security old-age and disability benefits and unemployment insurance benefits.

Income Redistribution

Another relatively recent political function of government has been the explicit redistribution of income. This redistribution uses two systems: the progressive income tax (described in Chapter 6) and transfer payments. **Transfer payments** are payments made to individuals for which no services or goods are rendered in return. The two primary money transfer payments in our system are Social Security old-age and disability benefits and unemployment insurance benefits. Income redistribution also includes a large amount of income **transfers in kind,** rather than money transfers. Some income transfers in kind are food stamps, Medicare and Medicaid, government health care services, and subsidized public housing.

The government has also engaged in other activities as a form of redistribution of income. For example, the provision of public education is at least in part an attempt to redistribute income by making sure that the poor have access to education.

Transfers in kind
Payments that are in the form of actual goods and services, such as food stamps, subsidized public housing, and medical care, and for which in return no goods or services are rendered in return.

QUICK QUIZ

Political, or normative, activities of the government include the provision and regulation of _____ and _____ goods and _____ redistribution.

Merit and demerit goods do not have any inherent characteristics that qualify them as such; rather, collectively, through the _____ process, we make judgments about which goods and services are "good" for society and which are "bad."

Income redistribution can be carried out by a system of progressive taxation, coupled with _____ payments, which can be made in money or in kind, such as food stamps and Medicare.

See page 133 for the answers. Review concepts from this section in MyEconLab.

PUBLIC SPENDING AND TRANSFER PROGRAMS

The size of the public sector can be measured in many different ways. One way is to count the number of public employees. Another is to look at total government outlays. Government outlays include all government expenditures on employees, rent, electricity, and the like. In addition, total government outlays include transfer payments, such as welfare and Social Security. In Figure 5-2, you see that government outlays prior to World War I did

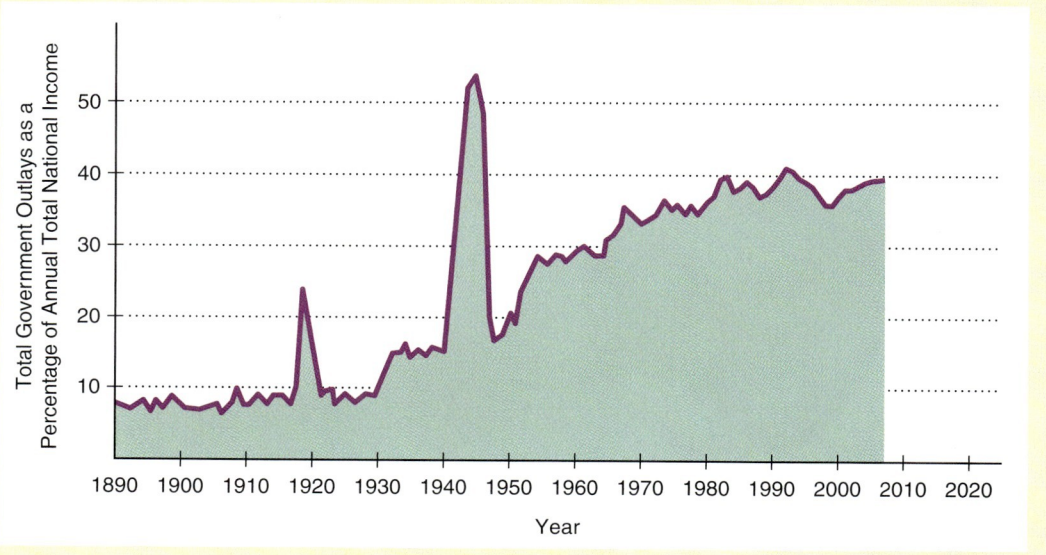

FIGURE 5-2

Total Government Outlays over Time

Total government outlays (federal, state, and local combined) remained small until the 1930s, except during World War I. Since World War II, government outlays have not fallen back to their historical average.

Sources: *Facts and Figures on Government Finance*, various issues; *Economic Indicators*, various issues.

not exceed 10 percent of annual national income. There was a spike during World War I, a general increase during the Great Depression, and then a huge spike during World War II. Contrary to previous postwar periods, after World War II government outlays as a percentage of total national income rose steadily before dropping in the 1990s and rising again in the 2000s.

How do federal and state governments allocate their spending on public goods and merit goods? A typical federal government budget is shown in panel (a) of Figure 5-3. The three largest categories are Medicare and other health-related spending, Social Security and other income-security programs, and national defense, which together constitute 77.6 percent of the total federal budget.

The makeup of state and local expenditures is quite different. As panel (b) shows, education is the biggest category, accounting for 34.1 percent of all expenditures.

Publicly Subsidized Health Care: Medicare

Go to www.econtoday.com/ch05 to visit the U.S. government's official Medicare Web site.

Figure 5-3 shows that health-related spending is a significant portion of total government expenditures. Certainly, medical expenses are a major concern for many elderly people. Since 1965, that concern has been reflected in the existence of the Medicare program, which pays hospital and physicians' bills for U.S. residents over the age of 65 (and for those younger than 65 in some instances). In return for paying a tax on their earnings while in the workforce (currently set at 2.9 percent of wages and salaries), retirees are

---

FIGURE 5-3

Federal Government Spending Compared to State and Local Spending

The federal government's spending habits are quite different from those of the states and cities. In panel (a), you can see that the categories of most importance in the federal budget are Medicare and other health-related spending, Social Security and other income-security programs, and national defense, which make up 77.6 percent. In panel (b), the most important category at the state and local level is education, which makes up 34.1 percent. "Other" includes expenditures in such areas as waste treatment, garbage collection, mosquito abatement, and the judicial system.

Sources: *Budget of the United States Government; Government Finances.*

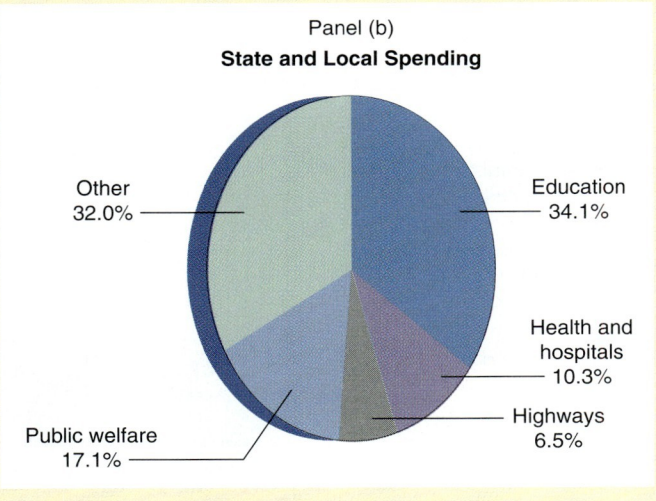

ensured that the majority of their hospital and physicians' bills will be paid for with public monies.

The Simple Economics of Medicare. To understand how, in less than 40 years, Medicare became the second-biggest domestic government spending program in existence, a bit of economics is in order. Consider Figure 5-4, which shows the demand for and supply of medical care.

The initial equilibrium price is P_0 and equilibrium quantity is Q_0. Perhaps because the government believes that Q_0 is not enough medical care for these consumers, suppose that the government begins paying a subsidy that eventually is set at M for each unit of medical care consumed. This will simultaneously tend to raise the price per unit of care received by providers (physicians, hospitals, and so on) and lower the perceived price per unit that consumers see when they make decisions about how much medical care to consume. As presented in the figure, the price received by providers rises to P_s, while the price paid by consumers falls to P_d. As a result, consumers of medical care want to purchase Q_m units, and suppliers are quite happy to provide it for them.

Medicare Incentives at Work. We can now understand the problems that plague the Medicare system today. First, one of the things that people observed during the 20 years after the founding of Medicare was a huge upsurge in physicians' incomes and medical school applications, the spread of private for-profit hospitals, and the rapid proliferation of new medical tests and procedures. All of this was being encouraged by the rise in the price of medical services from P_0 to P_s, which encouraged entry into this market.

Second, government expenditures on Medicare have routinely turned out to be far in excess of the expenditures forecast at the time the program was put in place or was expanded. The reasons for this are easy to see. Bureaucratic planners often fail to recognize the incentive effects of government programs. On the demand side, they fail to account for

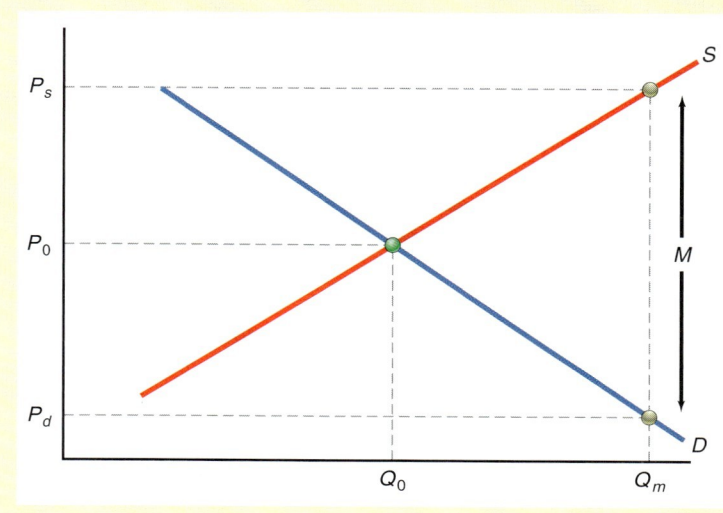

FIGURE 5-4

The Economic Effects of Medicare Subsidies

When the government pays a per-unit subsidy M for medical care, consumers pay the price of services P_d for the quantity of services Q_m. Providers receive the price P_s for supplying this quantity. Originally, the federal government projected that its total spending on Medicare would equal an amount such as the area $Q_0 \times (P_0 - P_d)$. Because actual consumption equals Q_m, however, the government's total expenditures actually equal $Q_m \times M$.

the huge increase in consumption (from Q_0 to Q_m) that will result from a subsidy like Medicare. On the supply side, they fail to recognize that the larger amount of services can only be extracted from suppliers at a higher price, P_s. Consequently, original projected spending on Medicare was an area like $Q_0 \times (P_0 - P_d)$, because original plans for the program only allowed for consumption of Q_0 and assumed that the subsidy would have to be only $P_0 - P_d$ per unit. In fact, consumption rises to Q_m, and marginal cost per unit of service rises to P_s, necessitating an increase in the per-unit subsidy to M. Hence actual expenditures turn out to be the far larger number $Q_m \times M$. Every expansion of the program, including the extension of Medicare to cover patients' prescription drug expenses beginning in 2006 and the 2004 broadening to cover obesity as a new illness eligible for coverage, has followed the same pattern.

Third, total spending on medical services soars, consuming far more income than initially expected. Originally, total spending on medical services was $P_0 \times Q_0$. In the presence of Medicare, spending rises to $P_s \times Q_m$.

Health Care Subsidies Continue to Grow. Just how fast are Medicare subsidies growing? Medicare's cost has risen from 0.7 percent of U.S. national income in 1970 to more than 2.8 percent today, which amounts to nearly $400 billion per year. Because Medicare spending is growing much faster than total employer and employee contributions, future spending guarantees far outstrip the taxes to be collected in the future to pay for the system. (The current Medicare tax rate is 2.9 percent on all earnings, with 1.45 percent paid by the employee and 1.45 percent paid by the employer.) Currently, unfunded guarantees of Medicare spending in the future are estimated at more than $25 trillion (in today's dollars).

These amounts fail to reflect the costs of another federal health program called Medicaid. The Medicaid program is structured similarly to Medicare, in that the government also pays per-unit subsidies for health care to qualifying patients. Medicaid, however, provides subsidies only to people who qualify because they have lower incomes. At present, about 50 million people, or about one out of every six U.S. residents, qualify for Medicaid coverage. Medicaid is administered by state governments, but the federal government pays about 57 percent of the program's total cost from general tax revenues. The current cost of the program is more than $300 billion per year. In recent years, Medicaid spending has grown even faster than expenditures on Medicare, rising by more than 75 percent since 2000 alone. Current estimates indicate that spending on Medicaid is likely to increase at an annual rate of nearly 8 percent for the foreseeable future.

Unlike Medicaid, which is funded from general tax collections, Medicare is supposed to be fully funded by collections from employers and employees. How soon will the current 2.9 percent rate imposed on total earnings fail to cover the program's expenses?

POLICY EXAMPLE

Is the Medicare Program on a Fast Track to Bankruptcy?

After prescription drug assistance was added as a Medicare benefit beginning in 2006, the rate at which Medicare spending is growing increased substantially. At the current rate of growth, expenditures on Medicare as a share of total national income will expand from just over 2.6 percent today to nearly 6 percent by 2026 and to close to 9 percent by 2050. If both Medicare and federal tax collections continue to grow at present rates until 2050, by that year Medicare taxes will account for *half* of *all* federal tax collections.

The program's moment of truth is likely to arrive much sooner, however. Because Medicare spending is growing so much faster than employer and employee contributions to the program, the program will lack sufficient financial

(continued)

resources to cover promised benefits by 2019, if not sooner. To prevent the program from going into the red, which would require a bailout from general tax revenues, Congress will have to increase the Medicare payroll tax or reduce Medicare benefits.

FOR CRITICAL ANALYSIS
How do increasing life expectancies contribute to Medicare's funding difficulties?

Economic Issues of Public Education

In the United States, government involvement in health care is a relatively recent phenomenon. In contrast, state and local governments have assumed primary responsibility for public education for many years. Currently, these governments spend well over $625 billion on education—more than 4 percent of total U.S. national income. State and local sales, excise, property, and income taxes finance the bulk of these expenditures. In addition, each year the federal government provides tens of billions of dollars of support for public education through grants and other transfers to state and local governments.

The Now-Familiar Economics of Public Education.
State and local governments around the United States have developed a variety of complex mechanisms for funding public education. What all public education programs have in common, however, is the provision of educational services to primary, secondary, and college students at prices well below those that would otherwise prevail in the marketplace for these services.

So how do state and local governments accomplish this? The answer is that they operate public education programs that are very similar to government-subsidized health care programs such as Medicare. Analogously to Figure 5-4 on page 119, public schools provide educational services at a price below the market price. They are willing to produce the quantity of educational services demanded at this below-market price as long as they receive a sufficiently high per-unit subsidy from state and local governments.

The Incentive Problems of Public Education.
Since the 1960s, various measures of the performance of U.S. primary and secondary students have failed to increase even as public spending on education has risen. Some measures of student performance have even declined.

Many economists argue that the incentive effects that have naturally arisen as government subsidies for public education have increased help to explain this lack of improvement in student performance. A higher per-pupil subsidy creates a difference between the relatively high per-unit costs to schools of providing the amount of educational services that parents and students are willing to purchase and the relatively lower valuations of those services. As a consequence, schools may have provided services, such as after-school babysitting and various social services, which have contributed relatively little to student learning.

A factor that complicates efforts to assess the effects of education subsidies is that the public schools often face little or no competition from unsubsidized providers of educational services. In addition, public schools rarely compete against each other. In most locales, therefore, parents who are unhappy with the quality of services provided at the subsidized price cannot transfer their child to a different public school.

How does the mismatch between the cost of subsidized public educational services and the valuation of those services by consumers help explain trends in how public schools spend government subsidies?

POLICY EXAMPLE

What Have Public Schools Done with Subsidies?

Since 1960, U.S. public school enrollments have increased by about 40 percent. During the same period, inflation-adjusted spending per public school student has increased by nearly 200 percent. Most of this substantial increase in spending has shown up in larger school payrolls. The number of public school teachers has increased by more than 60 percent. Because the number of students has grown by only 40 percent, having more teachers has allowed schools to provide more instruction per student.

A significant fraction of the increased payroll expenditures of public schools, however, has gone to larger staffs of nonteaching personnel. The number of principals, vice principals, and other administrators, most of whom do not teach, has risen by 80 percent since 1960. Overall, the number of nonteaching staff employed at public schools has increased by *500 percent*. As predicted by the basic economics of subsidies, schools have allocated a portion of the increased public funds to activities that contribute relatively little to student learning.

FOR CRITICAL ANALYSIS
Why are people who engage in "home schooling" by teaching their children themselves or in cooperation with other parents likely to spend a per-unit amount (including opportunity costs) close to their valuation of home schooling provided?

QUICK QUIZ

Medicare subsidizes the consumption of medical care by the elderly, thus increasing the amount of such care consumed. People tend to purchase large amounts of _____-value, _____-cost services in publicly funded health care programs such as Medicare, because they do not directly bear the full cost of their decisions.

Basic economic analysis indicates that higher subsidies for public education have widened the differential between parents' and students' relatively _____ per-unit valuations of the educational services of public schools and the _____ costs that schools incur in providing those services.

See page 133 for the answers. Review concepts from this section in MyEconLab.

COLLECTIVE DECISION MAKING: THE THEORY OF PUBLIC CHOICE

Collective decision making
How voters, politicians, and other interested parties act and how these actions influence nonmarket decisions.

Governments consist of individuals. No government actually thinks and acts; rather, government actions are the result of decision making by individuals in their roles as elected representatives, appointed officials, and salaried bureaucrats. Therefore, to understand how government works, we must examine the incentives of the people in government as well as those who would like to be in government—avowed or would-be candidates for elective or appointed positions—and special-interest lobbyists attempting to get government to do something. At issue is the analysis of **collective decision making.** Collective decision making involves the actions of voters, politicians, political parties, interest groups, and many other groups and individuals. The analysis of collective decision making is usually called the **theory of public choice.** It has been given this name because it involves hypotheses about how choices are made in the public sector, as opposed to the private sector. The foundation of public-choice theory is the assumption that individuals will act within the political process to maximize their *individual* (not collective) well-being. In that sense, the theory is similar to our analysis of the market economy, in which we also assume that individuals act as though they are motivated by self-interest.

Theory of public choice
The study of collective decision making.

To understand public-choice theory, it is necessary to point out other similarities between the private market sector and the public, or government, sector; then we will look at the differences.

Similarities in Market and Public-Sector Decision Making

In addition to the assumption of self-interest being the motivating force in both sectors, there are other similarities.

Opportunity Cost. Everything that is spent by all levels of government plus everything that is spent by the private sector must add up to the total income available at any point in time. Hence every government action has an opportunity cost, just as in the market sector.

Competition. Although we typically think of competition as a private-market phenomenon, it is also present in collective action. Given the scarcity constraint government faces, bureaucrats, appointed officials, and elected representatives will always be in competition for available government funds. Furthermore, the individuals within any government agency or institution will act as individuals do in the private sector: They will try to obtain higher wages, better working conditions, and higher job-level classifications. We assume that they will compete and act in their own interest, not society's.

Similarity of Individuals. Contrary to popular belief, the types of individuals working in the private sector and working in the public sector are not inherently different. The difference, as we shall see, is that the individuals in government face a different **incentive structure** than those in the private sector. For example, the costs and benefits of being efficient or inefficient differ in the private and public sectors.

Incentive structure
The system of rewards and punishments individuals face with respect to their own actions.

One approach to predicting government bureaucratic behavior is to ask what incentives bureaucrats face. Take the United States Postal Service (USPS) as an example. The bureaucrats running that government corporation are human beings with IQs not dissimilar to those possessed by workers in similar positions at Microsoft or American Airlines. Yet the USPS does not function like either of these companies. The difference can be explained in terms of the incentives provided for managers in the two types of institutions. When the bureaucratic managers and workers at Microsoft make incorrect decisions, work slowly, produce shoddy products, and are generally "inefficient," the profitability of the company declines. The owners—millions of shareholders—express their displeasure by selling some of their shares of company stock. The market value, as tracked on the stock exchange, falls. This induces owners of shares of stock to pressure managers to pursue strategies more likely to boost revenues and reduce costs.

But what about the USPS? If a manager, a worker, or a bureaucrat in the USPS gives shoddy service, the organization's owners—the taxpayers—have no straightforward mechanism for expressing their dissatisfaction. Despite the postal service's status as a "government corporation," taxpayers as shareholders do not really own shares of stock in the organization that they can sell.

Thus, to understand purported inefficiency in the government bureaucracy, we need to examine incentives and institutional arrangements—not people and personalities.

Differences Between Market and Collective Decision Making

There are probably more dissimilarities between the market sector and the public sector than there are similarities.

Government Goods at Zero Price.
The majority of goods that governments produce are furnished to the ultimate consumers without payment required. **Government, or political, goods** can be either private or public goods. The fact that they are furnished to the ultimate consumer free of charge does *not* mean that the cost to society of those goods is zero, however; it only means that the price *charged* is zero. The full opportunity cost to society is the value of the resources used in the production of goods produced and provided by the government.

For example, none of us pays directly for each unit of consumption of defense or police protection. Rather, we pay for all these things indirectly through the taxes that support our governments—federal, state, and local. This special feature of government can be looked at in a different way. There is no longer a one-to-one relationship between consumption of a government-provided good and payment for that good. Indeed, most taxpayers will find that their tax bill is the same whether or not they consume government-provided goods.

Use of Force.
All governments can resort to using force in their regulation of economic affairs. For example, governments can use *expropriation,* which means that if you refuse to pay your taxes, your bank account and other assets may be seized by the Internal Revenue Service. In fact, you have no choice in the matter of paying taxes to governments. Collectively, we decide the total size of government through the political process, but individually, we cannot determine how much service we pay for just for ourselves during any one year.

Voting versus Spending.
In the private market sector, a dollar voting system is in effect. This dollar voting system is not equivalent to the voting system in the public sector. There are at least three differences:

1. In a political system, one person gets one vote, whereas in the market system, each dollar one spends counts separately.
2. The political system is run by **majority rule,** whereas the market system is run by **proportional rule.**
3. The spending of dollars can indicate intensity of want, whereas because of the all-or-nothing nature of political voting, a vote cannot.

Ultimately, the main distinction between political votes and dollar votes is that political outcomes may differ from economic outcomes. Remember that economic efficiency is a situation in which, given the prevailing distribution of income, consumers obtain the economic goods they want. There is no corresponding situation when political voting determines economic outcomes. Thus, we can never assume that a political voting process will lead to the same decisions that a dollar voting process will lead to in the marketplace.

Indeed, consider the dilemma every voter faces. Usually, a voter is not asked to decide on a single issue (although this happens); rather, a voter is asked to choose among candidates who present a large number of issues and state a position on each of them. Just consider the average U.S. senator, who has to vote on several thousand different issues during a six-year term. When you vote for that senator, you are voting for a person who must make thousands of decisions during the next six years.

Government, or political, goods
Goods (and services) provided by the public sector; they can be either private or public goods.

Majority rule
A collective decision-making system in which group decisions are made on the basis of more than 50 percent of the vote. In other words, whatever more than half of the electorate votes for, the entire electorate has to accept.

Proportional rule
A decision-making system in which actions are based on the proportion of the "votes" cast and are in proportion to them. In a market system, if 10 percent of the "dollar votes" are cast for blue cars, 10 percent of the output will be blue cars.

QUICK QUIZ

The theory of _____ _____ examines how voters, politicians, and other parties collectively reach decisions in the public sector of the economy.

As in private markets, _____ _____ and _____ have incentive effects that influence public-sector decision making. In contrast to private market situations, however, there is not a one-to-one relationship between consumption of a publicly provided good and the payment for that good.

See page 133 for the answers. Review concepts from this section in MyEconLab.

CASE STUDY — ECONOMICS FRONT AND CENTER

Is It Time to Move Space Exploration to the Marketplace?

Braddock is an engineer who formerly worked for the National Aeronautics and Space Administration (NASA). Today, he heads a company that hopes someday to rocket tens of thousands of people on suborbital sightseeing trips. He is in his office, drafting a proposal for a cooperative effort with two other firms to build the first generation of suborbital spacecraft.

"There is a market," Braddock writes, "for space tourism." More generally, he writes:

> Moving space travel to the private market is more likely to lead to exploration beyond Earth's orbit. NASA is operating under the false impression that it will remain the sole provider of space travel, which it also incorrectly believes is a public good. In fact, the principle of rival consumption applies to space travel just as to other private goods. Only three or four people can fly at one time in the suborbital vehicle we plan to build. Two will be required to pilot it, but on each trip the other two will be paying passengers.
>
> Profiting from suborbital space tourism in the near term will be an important first step toward the long-run dream of regularly traveling to other locales beyond Earth. And profits can be earned in this proposed joint endeavor. NASA earns no revenues while spending $500 million on each shuttle mission. In contrast, my proposed suborbital vehicle will cost only $25 million to $30 million to build and maintain over the next several years.

"Furthermore," Braddock concludes, "my company has already managed to earn $200,000 from sales of advance tickets for a vehicle that does not even exist yet—proof of a significant demand for the space tourism that our companies can provide."

CRITICAL ANALYSIS QUESTIONS

1. *Is government support for space travel the provision of a public good, or is its spending on transporting astronauts beyond the atmosphere the provision of a merit good? (Hint: Does space travel satisfy either of the characteristics of public goods?)*

2. *Could NASA supporters make a case that some form of externality is associated with space travel that might justify government involvement? (Hint: Are any potential positive or negative spillovers associated with the market for space travel?)*

Issues and Applications

Why Can Inoculations Against Disease Be Hard to Obtain?

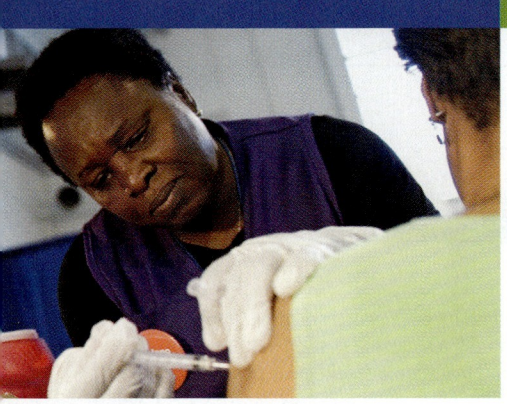

Concepts Applied
- External Benefits
- Positive Externality
- Property Rights

Every fall, millions of U.S. residents stand in line to obtain their "flu shots"—inoculations intended to ward off the influenza virus. Each of these inoculations contains vaccines against strains of the infectious virus that medical scientists determine in the preceding spring are most likely to appear during the coming fall and winter months.

During the mid-2000s, significant shortages of flu vaccines developed. In response, the U.S. government ordered doctors and hospitals to inoculate only people regarded as most at risk of dying from influenza in the event of a widespread outbreak. Since then, what some immunization experts call "feeding frenzies" have occurred each spring, as vaccine buyers, hoping to avoid running out of vaccine during autumn months, have rushed to place big orders. And every fall, local shortages of the vaccine have developed.

Flu vaccines are not the only vaccines that can be difficult to obtain. Since the mid-1990s, physicians and hospitals have experienced difficulties keeping in stock vaccines for most childhood diseases. At various times of the year, many pediatricians around the United States maintain waiting lists to ration vaccines among children in families covered by private health insurance plans.

Why Vaccine Shortages Are Occurring

What accounts for the shortages of vaccines for influenza and childhood diseases? Somewhat paradoxically, the answer is that the U.S. government has become involved in purchasing inoculations against diseases. Since 1993, for instance, a federal program called Vaccines for Children has existed to ensure that as many children as possible are inoculated against childhood diseases. Under the program, manufacturers must sell one-third of all the vaccines they produce to the government at a 50 percent discount. The government provides the vaccines at no charge to children in households without private health insurance.

In the years since 1993, the government has expanded its efforts to generate positive externalities from wider use of vaccines. Today, the government provides more than 60 percent of all childhood vaccines, and it purchases and oversees inoculations of ever-growing shares of other vaccines, such as influenza vaccines. To limit its costs, the government insists on purchasing vaccines from manufacturers at heavily discounted prices. In many cases, the government requires manufacturers to contribute vaccines to government stockpiles but does not pay for the vaccines until the inoculations are administered. Thus, manufacturers receive lower prices and often must wait for weeks or months before receiving any payment at all. Not surprisingly, many vaccine manufacturers have responded by cutting back on production. Some have stopped producing vaccines at all.

In short, the vaccine shortages are easy to explain. At government-mandated prices set below market prices, the quantities of vaccines supplied often fall short of the quantities demanded.

An Alternative Method of Reaping Vaccines' External Benefits

Is there a better way for the U.S. government to help society reap the external benefits of vaccines against various diseases? According to critics of the government's current approach, the fundamental problems are obvious: The price that vaccine manufacturers receive for their products is too low. If anything, critics argue, the government should implement policies aimed at *pushing up* prices received by vaccine producers. After all, the traditional correction for a positive externality is to induce an increase in the demand for the affected item, thereby causing the market price to *rise* and giving sellers an incentive to produce more of that item.

These critics propose that the government provide consumers with direct subsidies, perhaps by offering vouchers or "rebate coupons," for flu shots, childhood vaccinations, and other inoculations aimed at warding off diseases. Providing direct subsidies to consumers would reduce their out-of-pocket costs and thereby induce them to consume more vaccines at any given price. Thus, the demand for vaccines would rise, thereby boosting the market price of vaccines. In turn, a higher market price would encourage manufacturers to *increase* production of vaccines, countering the recent production reductions and consequent shortages that have occurred under current government programs.

Log in to **MyEconLab,** click on "Economic News," and test your understanding of the chapter by answering interactive questions that relate directly to this issue.

For Critical Analysis

1. From the perspective of demand and supply analysis, why have current government vaccine programs intended to increase inoculations actually had the opposite effect?

2. How might providing vouchers, rebates, or other subsidy payments to those obtaining inoculations better enable the government to address the positive externalities associated with vaccinations against diseases?

Web Resources

1. To see information about shortages of vaccines for childhood diseases, go to www.econtoday.com/ch05.

2. For updates about vaccine shortages from the U.S. government's Centers for Disease Control, go to www.econtoday.com/ch05.

Research Project

A major concern for world health officials is the potential for an outbreak of "avian flu"—a new flu virus that spreads directly from birds to people and has the potential to mutate and spread from person to person. Imagine being an economist who has been asked for advice about how national governments can best address positive externalities associated with people obtaining inoculations against the avian flu. Develop a proposal for how governments might ensure that society would reap the full external benefits associated with the vaccine.

Here is what you should know after reading this chapter. MyEconLab will help you identify what you know, and where to go when you need to practice.

WHAT YOU SHOULD KNOW		WHERE TO GO TO PRACTICE
How Market Failures Such as Externalities Might Justify Economic Functions of Government A market failure is a situation in which an unhindered free market gives rise to too many or too few resources being directed to a specific form of economic activity. A good example of a market failure is an externality, which is a spillover effect on third parties not directly involved in producing or purchasing a good or service. In the case of a negative externality, firms do not pay for the costs arising from spillover effects that their production of a good imposes on others, so they produce too much of the good in question. Government may be able to improve on the situation by restricting production or by imposing fees on producers. In the case of a positive externality, buyers fail to take into account the benefits that their consumption of a good yields to others, so they purchase too little of the good. Government may be able to induce more consumption of the good by regulating the market or subsidizing consumption. It can also provide a legal system to adjudicate disagreements about property rights, conduct antitrust policies to discourage monopoly and promote competition, provide public goods, and engage in policies designed to promote economic stability.	market failure, 108 externality, 109 third parties, 109 property rights, 109 effluent fee, 111 antitrust legislation, 113 monopoly, 113 **Key figure** Figure 5-1, 110	• **MyEconLab** Study Plans 5.1, 5.2 • Audio introduction to Chapter 5 • Animated Figure 5-1
Private Goods versus Public Goods and the Free-Rider Problem Private goods are subject to the principle of rival consumption, meaning that one person's consumption of such a good reduces the amount available for another person to consume. This is not so for public goods, which can be consumed by many people simultaneously at no additional opportunity cost and with no reduction in the quality or quantity of the good. In addition, public goods are subject to the exclusion principle: No individual can be excluded from the benefits of a public good even if that person fails to help pay for it. This leads to the free-rider problem, which occurs when a person who thinks that others will pay for a public good seeks to avoid contributing to financing production of the good.	private goods, 113 principle of rival consumption, 114 public goods, 114 exclusion principle, 114 free-rider problem, 114	• **MyEconLab** Study Plan 5.3 • Video: Private Goods and Public Goods
Political Functions of Government That Lead to Its Involvement in the Economy Through the political process, people may decide that certain goods are merit goods, which they deem socially desirable, or demerit goods, which they feel are socially undesirable. They may call on government to promote the production of merit goods but to restrict or even ban the production and sale of demerit goods. In addition, the political process may determine that income redistribution is socially desirable, and governments may become involved in supervising transfer payments or in-kind transfers in the form of nonmoney payments.	merit good, 115 demerit good, 116 transfer payments, 116 transfers in kind, 117	• **MyEconLab** Study Plan 5.4

WHAT YOU SHOULD KNOW		WHERE TO GO TO PRACTICE
The Effect of Medicare on the Incentives to Consume Medical Services Medicare subsidizes the consumption of medical services by the elderly. As a result, the quantity consumed is higher, as is the price sellers receive per unit of those services. Medicare also encourages people to consume medical services that are very low in per-unit value relative to the cost of providing them. Medicare thereby places a substantial tax burden on other sectors of the economy.	**Key figure** Figure 5-2, 117	• **MyEconLab** Study Plan 5.5 • Video: Medicare • Animated Figure 5-2
Why Bigger Subsidies for Public Schools Do Not Necessarily Translate into Improved Student Performance When governments subsidize public schools, the last unit of educational services provided by public schools is likely to cost more than its valuation by parents and students. Public schools therefore provide services in excess of those best suited to promoting student learning. This may help explain why measures of overall U.S. student performance have stagnated even as per-pupil subsidies to public schools have increased significantly.		• **MyEconLab** Study Plan 5.5
Central Elements of the Theory of Public Choice The theory of public choice is the study of collective decision making, or the process through which voters, politicians, and other interested parties interact to influence nonmarket choices. Public-choice theory emphasizes the incentive structures, or system of rewards or punishments, that affect the provision of government goods by the public sector of the economy. This theory points out that certain aspects of public-sector decision making, such as scarcity and competition, are similar to those that affect private-sector choices. Others, however, such as legal coercion and majority-rule decision making, differ from those involved in the market system.	collective decision making, 122 theory of public choice, 123 incentive structure, 123 government, or political, goods, 124 majority rule, 124 proportional rule, 124	• **MyEconLab** Study Plan 5.6

Log in to MyEconLab, take a chapter test, and get a personalized Study Plan that tells you which concepts you understand and which ones you need to review. From there, MyEconLab will give you futher practice, tutorials, animations, videos, and guided solutions.
Log in to www.myeconlab.com

PROBLEMS

*Select problems, indicated by a blue oval, are assignable in MyEconLab.
Answers to the odd-numbered problems appear at the back of the book.*

5-1 Many people who do not smoke cigars are bothered by the odor of cigar smoke. In the absence of any government involvement in the market for cigars, will too many or too few cigars be produced and consumed? From society's point of view, will the market price of cigars be too high or too low?

5-2 Suppose that repeated application of a pesticide used on orange trees causes harmful contamination of groundwater. The pesticide is applied annually in virtually all of the orange groves throughout the world. Most orange growers regard the pesticide as a key input in their production of oranges.

   a. Use a diagram of the market for the pesticide to illustrate the implications of a failure of orange producers' costs to reflect the social costs of groundwater contamination.

   b. Use your diagram from part (a) to explain a government policy that might be effective in achieving the amount of orange production that fully reflects all social costs.

5-3 Now draw a diagram of the market for oranges. Explain how the government policy you discussed in part (b) of Problem 5-2 is likely to affect the market price and equilibrium quantity in the orange market. In what sense do consumers of oranges now "pay" for dealing with the spillover costs of pesticide production?

5-4. Suppose that the U.S. government determines that cigarette smoking creates social costs not reflected in the current market price and equilibrium quantity of cigarettes. A study has recommended that the government can correct for the externality effect of cigarette consumption by paying farmers *not* to plant tobacco used to manufacture cigarettes. It also recommends raising the funds to make these payments by increasing taxes on cigarettes. Assuming that the government is correct that cigarette smoking creates external costs, evaluate whether the study's recommended policies might help correct this negative externality.

5-5 The government of a major city in the United States has determined that mass transit, such as bus lines, helps alleviate traffic congestion, thereby benefiting both individual auto commuters and companies that desire to move products and factors of production speedily along streets and highways. Nevertheless, even though several private bus lines are in service, commuters in the city are failing to take the social benefits of the use of mass transit into account.

   a. Discuss, in the context of demand-supply analysis, the essential implications of commuters' failure to take into account the social benefits associated with bus ridership.

   b. Explain a government policy that might be effective in achieving the socially efficient use of bus services.

5-6 Draw a diagram of the market for automobiles, which are a substitute means of transit. Explain how the government policy you discussed in part (b) of Problem 5-5 is likely to affect the market price and equilibrium quantity in the auto market. How are auto consumers affected by this policy to attain the spillover benefits of bus transit?

5-7 Displayed below are conditions in the market for residential Internet access in a U.S. state. The government of this state has determined that access to the Internet improves the learning skills of children, which it has concluded is an external benefit of Internet access. The government has also concluded that if these external benefits were to be taken into account, 3 million residences would have Internet access. Suppose that the state government's judgments about the benefits of Internet access are correct and that it wishes to offer a per-unit subsidy just sufficient to increase total Internet access to 3 million residences. What per-unit subsidy should it offer? Use the diagram to explain how providing this subsidy would affect conditions in the state's market for residential Internet access.

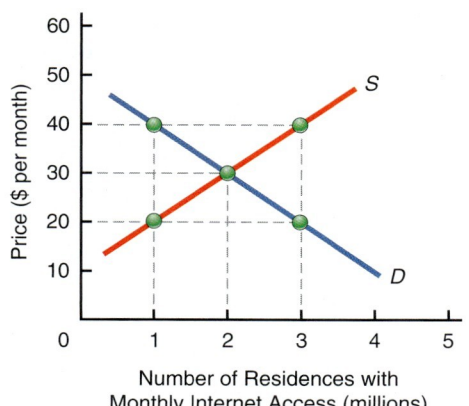

5-8 Does a tennis court provided by a local government agency satisfy both key characteristics of a public good? Why or why not? Based on your answer, is a public tennis court a public good or a merit good?

5-9 To promote increased use of port facilities in a major coastal city, a state government has decided to construct a state-of-the-art lighthouse at a projected cost of $10 million. The state proposes to pay half this cost and asks the city to raise the additional funds. Rather than raise its $5 million in funds via an increase in city taxes and fees, however, the city's government asks major businesses in and near the port area to contribute voluntarily to the project. Discuss key problems that the city is likely to face in raising the funds.

5-10 Governments of country A and country B spend the same amount each year. Spending on functions relating to dealing with market externalities and public goods accounts for 25 percent of government expenditures in country A but makes up 75 percent of government expenditures in country B. Funding to provide merit goods and efforts to restrict the production of demerit goods account for 75 percent of government expenditures in country A but only 25 percent of government expenditures in country B. Which country's government is more heavily involved in the economy through economic functions of government as opposed to political functions? Explain.

5-11. A government offers to let a number of students at a public school transfer to a private school under two conditions: It will transmit to the private school the same per-pupil subsidy it currently provides the public school, and the private school will be required to admit the students at a below-market tuition rate. Will the economic outcome be the same as the one that would have arisen if the government instead simply provided students with grants to cover the current market tuition rate at the private school? (Hint: Does it matter if schools receive payments directly from the government or from consumers?)

5-12. After a government implements a voucher program, granting funds that families can spend at schools of their choice, numerous students in public schools switch to private schools. Parents' and students' valuations of the services provided at both private and public schools adjust to equality with the true market price of educational services. Is anyone likely to lose out nonetheless? If so, who?

5-13 Suppose that the current price of a DVD drive is $100 and that people are buying 1 million drives per year. In order to improve computer literacy, the government decides to begin subsidizing the purchase of new DVD drives. The government believes that the appropriate price is $60 per drive, so the program offers to send people cash for the difference between $60 and whatever the people pay for each drive they buy.

a. If no consumers change their drive-buying behavior, how much will this program cost the taxpayers?
b. Will the subsidy cause people to buy more, less, or the same number of drives? Explain.
c. Suppose that people end up buying 1.5 million drives once the program is in place. If the market price of drives does not change, how much will this program cost the taxpayers?
d. Under the assumption that the program causes people to buy 1.5 million drives and also causes the market price of drives to rise to $120, how much will this program cost the taxpayers?

5-14 Scans of internal organs using magnetic resonance imaging (MRI) devices are often covered by subsidized health insurance programs such as Medicare. Consider the following table illustrating hypothetical quantities of individual MRI testing procedures demanded and supplied at various prices, and then answer the questions that follow.

Price	Quantity Demanded	Quantity Supplied
$100	100,000	40,000
$300	90,000	60,000
$500	80,000	80,000
$700	70,000	100,000
$900	60,000	120,000

a. In the absence of a government-subsidized health plan, what is the equilibrium price of MRI tests? What is the amount of society's total spending on MRI tests?
b. Suppose that the government establishes a health plan guaranteeing that all qualified participants can purchase MRI tests at an effective price (that is, out-of-pocket cost) to the individual of $100 per test. How many MRI tests will people consume?
c. What is the per-unit price that induces producers to provide the amount of MRI tests demanded at the government-guaranteed price of $100? What is society's total spending on MRI tests?
d. Under the government's coverage of MRI tests, what is the per-unit subsidy it provides? What is the total subsidy that the government pays to support MRI testing at its guaranteed price?

5-15 Suppose that, as part of an expansion of its State Care health system, a state government decides to offer a $50 subsidy to all people who, according to their physicians, should have their own blood pressure monitoring devices. Prior to this governmental decision, the market clearing price of blood pressure monitoring devices in this state was $50, and the equilibrium quantity purchased was 20,000 per year.

   a. After the government expands its State Care plan, people in this state desire to purchase 40,000 devices each year. Manufacturers of blood pressure monitoring devices are willing to provide 40,000 devices at a price of $60 per device. What out-of-pocket price does each consumer pay for a blood pressure monitoring device?
   b. What is the dollar amount of the increase in total expenditures on blood pressure monitoring devices in this state following the expansion in the State Care program?
   c. Following the expansion of the State Care program, what *percentage* of total expenditures on blood pressure monitoring devices is paid by the government? What percentage of total expenditures is paid by consumers of these devices?

5-16. A government agency is contemplating launching an effort to expand the scope of its activities. One rationale for doing so is that another government agency might make the same effort and, if successful, receive larger budget allocations in future years. Another rationale for expanding the agency's activities is that this will make the jobs of its workers more interesting, which may help the agency attract better-qualified employees. Nevertheless, to broaden its legal mandate, the agency will have to convince more than half of the House of Representatives and the Senate to approve a formal proposal to expand its activities. In addition, to expand its activities, the agency must have the authority to force private companies it does not currently regulate to be officially licensed by agency personnel. Identify which aspects of this problem are similar to those faced by firms that operate in private markets and which aspects are specific to the public sector.

ECONOMICS ON THE NET

Putting Tax Dollars to Work In this application, you will learn about how the U.S. government allocates its expenditures. This will enable you to conduct an evaluation of the current functions of the federal government.

Title: Historical Tables: Budget of the United States Government

Navigation: Go to www.econtoday.com/ch05 to visit the home page of the U.S. Government Printing Office. Select the most recent budget available, and then click on *Historical Tables*.

Application After the document downloads, examine Section 3, Federal Government Outlays by Function, and in particular Table 3.1, Outlays by Superfunction and Function. Then answer the following questions:

1. What government functions have been capturing growing shares of government spending in recent years? Which of these do you believe are related to the problem of addressing externalities, providing public goods, or dealing with other market failures? Which appear to be related to political functions instead of economic functions?
2. Which government functions are receiving declining shares of total spending? Are any of these related to the problem of addressing externalities, providing public goods, or dealing with other market failures? Are any related to political functions instead of economic functions?

For Group Study and Analysis Assign groups to the following overall categories of government functions: national defense, health, income security, and Social Security. Have each group prepare a brief report concerning long-term and recent trends in government spending on each category. Each group should take a stand on whether specific spending on items in its category is likely to relate to resolving market failures, public funding of merit goods, regulating the sale of demerit goods, and so on.

ANSWERS TO QUICK QUIZZES

p. 112: (i) costs . . . taxation . . . regulation; (ii) benefits . . . financing . . . subsidizing . . . regulation

p. 115: (i) externalities . . . legal system . . . competition . . . public . . . economywide stability; (ii) rival consumption; (iii) opportunity cost . . . charged

p. 117: (i) merit . . . demerit . . . income; (ii) political; (iii) transfer

p. 122: (i) low . . . high; (ii) low . . . higher

p. 125: (i) public choice; (ii) opportunity cost . . . competition

6 Funding the Public Sector

Learning Objectives

After reading this chapter, you should be able to:

1. Distinguish between average tax rates and marginal tax rates
2. Explain the structure of the U.S. income tax system
3. Understand the key factors influencing the relationship between tax rates and the tax revenues governments collect
4. Explain how the taxes governments levy on purchases of goods and services affect market prices and equilibrium quantities
5. Understand how the Social Security system works and explain the nature of the problems it poses for today's students

MyEconLab helps you master each objective and study more efficiently. See end of chapter for details.

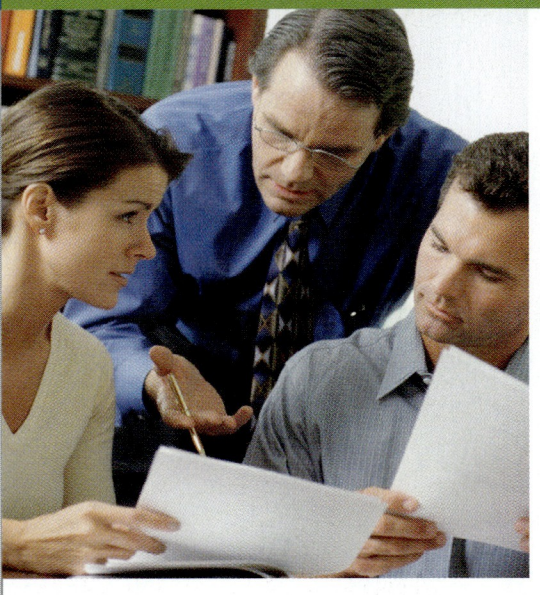

In 2005, President George W. Bush proposed that younger workers be allowed to direct a portion of their current Social Security contributions to so-called private accounts. Implementing this idea, the president argued, would help save the Social Security system from long-term financial problems. Critics of the president's suggestion argued that the Social Security system actually is very healthy, as evidenced by a projected $2 trillion increase in the "Social Security trust fund" over the coming decade. Is the Social Security system really in trouble? Why would President Bush—or anyone else, for that matter—see private accounts as a possible way to shore up the financial health of the Social Security system? After you have completed your study of this chapter, you will know the answers to these questions.

Did You Know That...

each year, a typical individual who buys a ticket from Amtrak, the company that operates most U.S. passenger trains, receives a subsidy of nearly $50 from the federal government? The average government subsidy for a new Amtrak route from Oklahoma to Texas exceeds $225 per passenger. Critics have argued that it would be less costly for the government to hire a limousine and chauffeur to transport each passenger—and thereby get the passenger to the final destination faster than Amtrak typically does.

In total, the government contributes more than $1 billion in subsidies to Amtrak every year. Passenger rail service is just one of a number of goods and services currently subsidized by the government. Others include education, police protection, and access to health care. To obtain all the funds required to provide these subsidies, state and local governments assess sales taxes, property taxes, income taxes, airline taxes, hotel occupancy taxes, and electricity, gasoline, water, and sewage taxes. At the federal level, there are income taxes, Social Security taxes, Medicare taxes, and so-called excise taxes. When a person dies, state and federal governments also collect estate and inheritance taxes. Clearly, the subsidization role of governments is associated with their role as tax collectors.

PAYING FOR THE PUBLIC SECTOR

There are three sources of funding available to governments. One source is explicit fees, called user *charges,* for government services. The second and main source of government funding is taxes. Nevertheless, sometimes federal, state, and local governments spend more than they collect in taxes. To do this, they must rely on a third source of financing, which is borrowing. During a specific interval, the **government budget constraint** expresses the fundamental limitation on public expenditures. It states that the sum of public spending on goods and services and transfer payments during a given period cannot exceed tax revenues plus borrowed funds.

A government cannot borrow unlimited amounts, however. After all, a government, like an individual or a firm, can convince others to lend it funds only if it can provide evidence that it will repay its debts. A government must ultimately rely on taxation and user charges, the sources of its own current and future revenues, to repay its debts. Over the long run, therefore, taxes and user charges are any government's *fundamental* sources of revenues. This long-term constraint indicates that the total amount that a government plans to spend and transfer today and into the future cannot exceed the total taxes and user charges that it currently earns and can reasonably anticipate collecting in future years. Taxation dwarfs user charges as a source of government resources, so let's begin by looking at taxation from a government's perspective.

How does the system of highway fees (user charges) that state governments charge operators of freight-hauling trucks influence how much the governments end up spending on highway maintenance?

Government budget constraint
The limit on government spending and transfers imposed by the fact that every dollar the government spends, transfers, or uses to repay borrowed funds must ultimately be provided by the taxes it collects.

POLICY EXAMPLE

How State Trucking Fees Push Up Highway Maintenance Costs

Oregon is the only U.S. state that bases the highway fees charged to truckers on the amount of weight carried per truck axle. Having more axles better distributes cargo weight and reduces pressure on the highway, so wear and tear on the roads is minimized. Thus, Oregon's system of highway

(continued)

fees gives truckers who haul freight only within Oregon an incentive to drive trucks with more axles, thereby reducing damage to the state's roads and helping hold down state highway spending.

In contrast, every other state bases highway fees on a truck's fuel consumption. Driving trucks with fewer axles reduces tire friction on the road surface, which increases fuel efficiency and thereby reduces the fees truckers must pay to use highways. Naturally, freight haulers in states outside Oregon have an incentive to drive trucks with fewer axles. As a result, roads in these states suffer greater damage, which, in turn, ultimately generates more spending on highway maintenance.

FOR CRITICAL ANALYSIS
If a trucking firm based in Oregon sends most of its trucks on long-distance trips outside the state, is it more likely to use trucks with four or five axles?

SYSTEMS OF TAXATION

In light of the government budget constraint, a major concern of any government is how to collect taxes. Jean-Baptiste Colbert, the seventeenth-century French finance minister, said the art of taxation was in "plucking the goose so as to obtain the largest amount of feathers with the least possible amount of hissing." In the United States, governments have designed a variety of methods of plucking the private-sector goose.

The Tax Base and the Tax Rate

Tax base
The value of goods, services, wealth, or incomes subject to taxation.

Tax rate
The proportion of a tax base that must be paid to a government as taxes.

To collect a tax, a government typically establishes a **tax base,** which is the value of goods, services, wealth, or incomes subject to taxation. Then it assesses a **tax rate,** which is the proportion of the tax base that must be paid to the government as taxes.

Federal, state, and local governments have established a number of tax bases and tax rates. As we discuss shortly, for the federal government and many state governments, incomes are key tax bases. Therefore, to discuss tax rates and the structure of taxation systems in more detail, let's focus for now on income taxation.

Marginal and Average Tax Rates

If somebody says, "I pay 28 percent in taxes," you cannot really tell what that person means unless you know whether he or she is referring to average taxes paid or the tax rate on the last dollars earned. The latter concept refers to the **marginal tax rate,** where the word *marginal* means "incremental."

The marginal tax rate is expressed as follows:

Marginal tax rate
The change in the tax payment divided by the change in income, or the percentage of additional dollars that must be paid in taxes. The marginal tax rate is applied to the highest tax bracket of taxable income reached.

$$\text{Marginal tax rate} = \frac{\text{change in taxes due}}{\text{change in taxable income}}$$

It is important to understand that the marginal tax rate applies only to the income in the highest **tax bracket** reached, where a tax bracket is defined as a specified range of taxable income to which a specific and unique marginal tax rate is applied.

Tax bracket
A specified interval of income to which a specific and unique marginal tax rate is applied.

The marginal tax rate is not the same thing as the **average tax rate,** which is defined as follows:

Average tax rate
The total tax payment divided by total income. It is the proportion of total income paid in taxes.

$$\text{Average tax rate} = \frac{\text{total taxes due}}{\text{total taxable income}}$$

Taxation Systems

No matter how governments raise revenues—from income taxes, sales taxes, or other taxes—all of those taxes fit into one of three types of taxation systems: proportional, progressive, or regressive, according to the relationship between the tax rate and income.

To determine whether a tax system is proportional, progressive, or regressive, we simply ask, What is the relationship between the average tax rate and the marginal tax rate?

Proportional Taxation.
Proportional taxation means that regardless of an individual's income, taxes comprise exactly the same proportion. In a proportional taxation system, the marginal tax rate is always equal to the average tax rate. If every dollar is taxed at 20 percent, then the average tax rate is 20 percent, and so is the marginal tax rate.

Under a proportional system of taxation, taxpayers at all income levels end up paying the same *percentage* of their income in taxes. With a proportional tax rate of 20 percent, an individual with an income of $10,000 pays $2,000 in taxes, while an individual making $100,000 pays $20,000. Thus, the identical 20 percent rate is levied on both taxpayers.

Proportional taxation
A tax system in which, regardless of an individual's income, the tax bill comprises exactly the same proportion.

Progressive Taxation.
Under **progressive taxation,** as a person's taxable income increases, the percentage of income paid in taxes increases. In a progressive system, the marginal tax rate is above the average tax rate. If you are taxed 5 percent on the first $10,000 you earn, 10 percent on the next $10,000 you earn, and 30 percent on the last $10,000 you earn, you face a progressive income tax system. Your marginal tax rate is always above your average tax rate.

Progressive taxation
A tax system in which, as income increases, a higher percentage of the additional income is paid as taxes. The marginal tax rate exceeds the average tax rate as income rises.

Regressive Taxation.
With **regressive taxation,** a smaller percentage of taxable income is taken in taxes as taxable income increases. The marginal rate is *below* the average rate. As income increases, the marginal tax rate falls, and so does the average tax rate. The U.S. Social Security tax is regressive. Once the legislative maximum taxable wage base is reached, no further Social Security taxes are paid. Consider a simplified hypothetical example: Suppose that every dollar up to $50,000 is taxed at 10 percent. After $50,000 there is no Social Security tax. Someone making $100,000 still pays only $5,000 in Social Security taxes. That person's average Social Security tax is 5 percent. The person making $50,000, by contrast, effectively pays 10 percent. The person making $1 million faces an average Social Security tax rate of only 0.5 percent in our simplified example.

Regressive taxation
A tax system in which as more dollars are earned, the percentage of tax paid on them falls. The marginal tax rate is less than the average tax rate as income rises.

In what part of the world have proportional income tax systems become particularly popular in recent years?

INTERNATIONAL POLICY EXAMPLE

Eastern Europe Discovers Proportional Income Taxation

In most nations, income tax systems are progressive. Nevertheless, governments of several Eastern European nations have recently opted for proportional taxation. Most of these nations were formerly part of the Soviet Union, such as Russia and Estonia, or were its satellites, such as Romania. Beginning in the mid-1990s, the governments of Estonia, Lithuania, and Latvia introduced tax systems that apply the same income tax rate to all levels of income. The Russian government established a proportional income tax system in 2001. Since then, the governments of Serbia, Ukraine, Slovakia, Georgia, and Romania have followed suit.

FOR CRITICAL ANALYSIS
What is true of average and marginal tax rates in Eastern European countries that have adopted proportional income tax systems?

QUICK QUIZ

Governments collect taxes by applying a tax _____ to a tax _____, which refers to the value of goods, services, wealth, or incomes. Income tax rates are applied to tax brackets, which are ranges of income over which the tax rate is constant.

The _____ tax rate is the total tax payment divided by total income, and the _____ tax rate is the change in the tax payment divided by the change in income.

Tax systems can be _____, _____, or _____, depending on whether the marginal tax rate is the same as, greater than, or less than the average tax rate as income rises.

See page 158 for the answers. Review concepts from this section in MyEconLab.

THE MOST IMPORTANT FEDERAL TAXES

What types of taxes do federal, state, and local governments collect? The two pie diagrams in Figure 6-1 show the percentage of receipts from various taxes obtained by the federal government and by state and local governments. For the federal government, key taxes are individual income taxes, corporate income taxes, Social Security taxes, and taxes on imported goods and excise taxes on items such as gasoline and alcoholic beverages. For state and local governments, sales taxes, property taxes, and personal and corporate income taxes are the main types of taxes.

The Federal Personal Income Tax

The most important tax in the U.S. economy is the federal personal income tax, which, as Figure 6-1 indicates, accounts for about 43.6 percent of all federal revenues. All U.S. citi-

FIGURE 6-1

Sources of Government Tax Receipts

As panel (a) shows, about 80 percent of federal revenues comes from income and Social Security taxes. State government revenues, shown in panel (b), are spread more evenly across sources, with less emphasis on taxes based on individual income.

Source: U.S. Department of Commerce, Bureau of Economic Analysis.

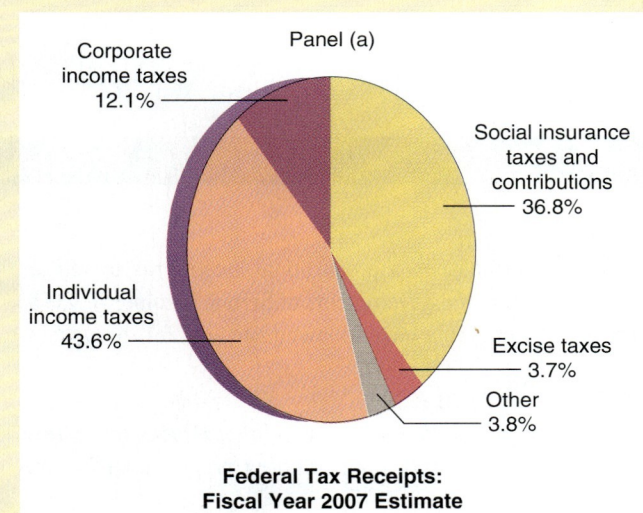
Federal Tax Receipts: Fiscal Year 2007 Estimate

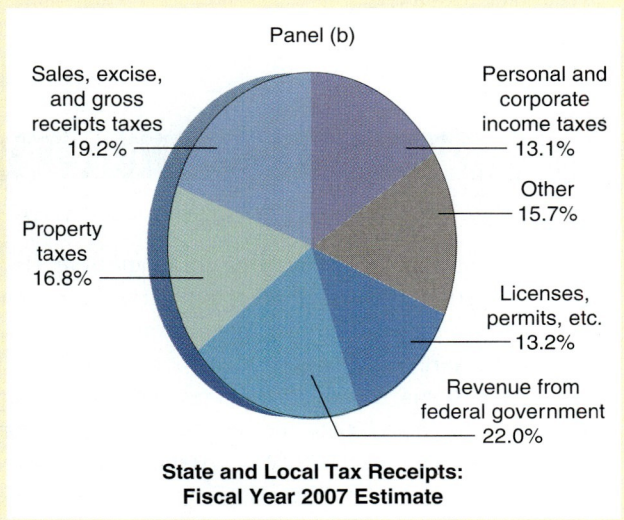
State and Local Tax Receipts: Fiscal Year 2007 Estimate

TABLE 6-1
Federal Marginal Income Tax Rates
These rates became effective in 2006.

Single Persons		Married Couples	
Marginal Tax Bracket	Marginal Tax Rate	Marginal Tax Bracket	Marginal Tax Rate
$0–$7,550	10%	$0–$15,100	10%
$7,551–$30,650	15%	$15,101–$61,300	15%
$30,651–$74,200	25%	$61,301–$123,700	25%
$74,201–$154,800	28%	$123,701–$188,450	28%
$154,801–$336,550	33%	$188,451–$336,550	33%
$336,551 and up	35%	$336,551 and up	35%

Source: U.S. Department of the Treasury.

zens, resident aliens, and most others who earn income in the United States are required to pay federal income taxes on all taxable income, including income earned abroad.

The rates that are paid rise as income increases, as can be seen in Table 6-1. Marginal income tax rates at the federal level have varied from as low as 1 percent after the 1913 passage of the Sixteenth Amendment, which made the individual income tax constitutional, to as high as 94 percent (reached in 1944). There were 14 separate tax brackets prior to the Tax Reform Act of 1986, which reduced the number to three (now six, as shown in Table 6-1).

Advocates of a more progressive income tax system in the United States argue that such a system redistributes income from the rich to the poor, taxes people according to their ability to pay, and taxes people according to the benefits they receive from government. Although there is much controversy over the redistributional nature of our progressive tax system, there is no strong evidence that the tax system has actually ever done much income redistribution in this country. Currently, about 85 percent of all taxpaying U.S. residents pay roughly the same proportion of their total income in federal taxes.

Go to www.econtoday.com/ch06 to learn from the National Center for Policy Analysis about what distinguishes recent flat tax proposals from a truly proportional income tax system. Next, click on "Flat Tax Proposals."

The Treatment of Capital Gains

The difference between the purchase price and sale price of an asset, such as a share of stock or a plot of land, is called a **capital gain** if it is a profit and a **capital loss** if it is not. The federal government taxes capital gains, and as of 2007, there were several capital gains tax rates.

What appear to be capital gains are not always real gains. If you pay $100,000 for a financial asset in one year and sell it for 50 percent more 10 years later, your nominal capital gain is $50,000. But what if during those 10 years inflation has driven average asset prices up by 50 percent? Your *real* capital gain would be zero, but you would still have to pay taxes on that $50,000. To counter this problem, many economists have argued that capital gains should be indexed to the rate of inflation. This is exactly what is done with the marginal tax brackets in the federal income tax code. Tax brackets for the purposes of calculating marginal tax rates each year are expanded at the rate of inflation, that is, the rate at which the average of all prices is rising. So, if the rate of inflation is 10 percent, each tax bracket is moved up by 10 percent. The same concept could be applied to capital gains and financial assets. So far, Congress has refused to enact such a measure.

Capital gain
The positive difference between the purchase price and the sale price of an asset. If a share of stock is bought for $5 and then sold for $15, the capital gain is $10.

Capital loss
The negative difference between the purchase price and the sale price of an asset.

The Corporate Income Tax

Figure 6-1 on page 138 shows that corporate income taxes account for about 12 percent of all federal taxes collected and about 2 percent of all state and local taxes collected. Corporations are generally taxed on the difference between their total revenues (or receipts) and their expenses. The federal corporate income tax structure is given in Table 6-2.

Double Taxation. Because individual stockholders must pay taxes on the dividends they receive, and those dividends are paid out of *after-tax* profits by the corporation, corporate profits are taxed twice. If you receive $1,000 in dividends, you have to declare them as income, and you must pay taxes on them. Before the corporation was able to pay you those dividends, it had to pay taxes on all its profits, including any that it put back into the company or did not distribute in the form of dividends. Eventually, the new investment made possible by those **retained earnings**—profits not given out to stockholders—along with borrowed funds will be reflected in the increased value of the stock in that company. When you sell your stock in that company, you will have to pay taxes on the difference between what you paid for the stock and what you sold it for. In both cases, dividends and retained earnings (corporate profits) are taxed twice. In 2003, Congress reduced the double taxation effect somewhat by enacting legislation that allows most dividends to be taxed at lower rates than are applied to regular income.

Retained earnings
Earnings that a corporation saves, or retains, for investment in other productive activities; earnings that are not distributed to stockholders.

Who Really Pays the Corporate Income Tax? Corporations can exist only as long as consumers buy their products, employees make their goods, stockholders (owners) buy their shares, and bondholders buy their bonds. Corporations per se do not do anything. We must ask, then, who really pays the tax on corporate income? This is a question of **tax incidence.** (The question of tax incidence applies to all taxes, including sales taxes and Social Security taxes.) The incidence of corporate taxation is the subject of considerable debate. Some economists suggest that corporations pass their tax burdens on to consumers by charging higher prices. Other economists argue that it is the stockholders who bear most of the tax. Still others contend that employees pay at least part of the tax by receiving lower wages than they would otherwise. Because the debate is not yet settled, we will not hazard a guess here as to what the correct conclusion may be. Suffice it to say that you should be cautious when you advocate increasing corporation income taxes. *People*—whether owners, consumers, or workers—ultimately end up paying the increase.

Tax incidence
The distribution of tax burdens among various groups in society.

TABLE 6-2
Federal Corporate Income Tax Schedule
These corporate tax rates were in effect through 2007.

Corporate Taxable Income	Corporate Tax Rate
$0–$50,000	15%
$50,001–$75,000	25%
$75,001–$100,000	34%
$100,001–$335,000	39%
$335,001–$10,000,000	34%
$10,000,001–$15,000,000	35%
$15,000,001–$18,333,333	38%
$18,333,334 and up	35%

Source: Internal Revenue Service.

Social Security and Unemployment Taxes

Each year, payroll taxes levied on payrolls account for an increasing percentage of federal tax receipts. These taxes, which are distinct from personal income taxes, are for Social Security, retirement, survivors' disability, and old-age medical benefits (Medicare). Today, the Social Security tax is imposed on earnings up to roughly $98,000 at a rate of 6.2 percent on employers and 6.2 percent on employees. That is, the employer matches your "contribution" to Social Security. (The employer's contribution is really paid, at least in part, in the form of a reduced wage rate paid to employees.) As Chapter 5 explained, a Medicare tax is imposed on all wage earnings at a combined rate of 2.9 percent. These taxes and the base on which they are levied are slated to rise in the next decade. Social Security taxes came into existence when the Federal Insurance Contributions Act (FICA) was passed in 1935. The future of Social Security is addressed later in this chapter.

There is also a federal unemployment tax, which helps pay for unemployment insurance. This tax rate is 0.8 percent on the first $7,000 of annual wages of each employee who earns more than $1,500. Only the employer makes the direct tax payment. This tax covers the costs of the unemployment insurance system. In addition to this federal tax, some states with an unemployment system impose their own tax of up to about 3 percent, depending on the past record of the particular employer. An employer who frequently lays off workers typically will have a slightly higher state unemployment tax rate than an employer who never lays off workers.

QUICK QUIZ

The federal government raises most of its revenues through _____ taxes and social insurance taxes and contributions, and state and local governments raise most of their revenues from _____ taxes, _____ taxes, and income taxes.

Because corporations must first pay an income tax on most earnings, the personal income tax shareholders pay on dividends received (or realized capital gains) constitutes _____ taxation.

Both employers and employees must pay _____ _____ taxes and contributions at rates of 6.2 percent on roughly the first $98,000 in wage earnings, and a 2.9 percent _____ tax rate is applied to all wage earnings. The federal government and some state governments also assess taxes to pay for _____ insurance systems.

See page 158 for the answers. Review concepts from this section in MyEconLab.

TAX RATES AND TAX REVENUES

For most state and local governments, income taxes yield fewer revenues than taxes imposed on sales of goods and services. Figure 6-1 on page 138 shows that sales taxes, gross receipts taxes, and excise taxes generate almost one-fifth of the total funds available to state and local governments. Thus, from the perspective of many state and local governments, a fundamental issue is how to set tax rates on sales of goods and services to extract the largest possible tax payments.

Sales Taxes

Governments levy **sales taxes** on the prices that consumers pay to purchase each unit of a broad range of goods and services. Sellers collect sales taxes and transmit them to the government. Sales taxes are levied under a system of **ad valorem taxation**, which means

Sales taxes
Taxes assessed on the prices paid on a large set of goods and services.

***Ad valorem* taxation**
Assessing taxes by charging a tax rate equal to a fraction of the market price of each unit purchased.

that the tax is applied "to the value" of the good. Thus, a government using a system of *ad valorem* taxation charges a tax rate equal to a fraction of the market price of each unit that a consumer buys. For instance, if the tax rate is 8 percent and the market price of an item is $100, then the amount of the tax on the item is $8.

A sales tax is therefore a proportional tax. The total amount of sales taxes a government collects equals the sales tax rate times the sales tax base, which is the market value of total purchases.

Static Tax Analysis

There are two approaches to evaluating how changes in tax rates affect government tax collections. **Static tax analysis** assumes that changes in the tax rate have no effect on the tax base. Thus, this approach implies that if a state government desires to increase its sales tax collections, it can simply raise the tax rate. Multiplying the higher tax rate by the tax base thereby produces higher tax revenues.

Governments often rely on static tax analysis. Sometimes this yields unpleasant surprises. Consider, for instance, what happened in 1992 when Congress implemented a federal "luxury tax" on purchases of new pleasure boats priced at $100,000 or more. Applying the 10 percent luxury tax rate to the anticipated tax base—sales of new boats during previous years—produced a forecast of hundreds of million of dollars in revenues from the luxury tax. What actually happened, however, was an 80 percent plunge in sales of new luxury boats. People postponed boat purchases or bought used boats instead. Consequently, the tax base all but disappeared, and the federal government collected only a few tens of millions of dollars in taxes on boat sales. Congress repealed the tax a year later.

Dynamic Tax Analysis

The problem with static tax analysis is that it ignores incentive effects created by new taxes or hikes in existing tax rates. According to **dynamic tax analysis,** a likely response to an increase in a tax rate is a decrease in the tax base. When a government pushes up its sales tax rate, for example, consumers have an incentive to cut back on their purchases of goods and services subjected to the higher rate, perhaps by buying them in a locale where there is a lower sales tax rate or perhaps no tax rate at all. As shown in Figure 6-2, the maximum sales tax rate varies considerably from state to state. Consider someone who lives in a state bordering Oregon. In such a border state, the sales tax rate can be as high as 8 percent, so a resident of that state has a strong incentive to buy higher-priced goods and services in Oregon, where there is no sales tax. Someone who lives in a high-tax county in Alabama has an incentive to buy an item online from an out-of-state firm and also avoid paying sales taxes. Such shifts in expenditures in response to higher relative tax rates can reduce a state's sales tax base and thereby result in lower sales tax collections than the levels predicted by static tax analysis.

Dynamic tax analysis recognizes that increasing the tax rate could actually cause the government's total tax collections to *decline* if a sufficiently large number of consumers react to the higher sales tax rate by cutting back on purchases of goods and services included in the state's tax base. Some residents who live close to other states with lower sales tax rates might, for instance, drive across the state line to do more of their shopping. Other residents might place more orders with catalog companies or online firms located in other legal jurisdictions where this state's sales tax does not apply.

Static tax analysis
Economic evaluation of the effects of tax rate changes under the assumption that there is no effect on the tax base, meaning that there is an unambiguous positive relationship between tax rates and tax revenues.

Dynamic tax analysis
Economic evaluation of tax rate changes that recognizes that the tax base eventually declines with ever-higher tax rates, so that tax revenues may eventually decline if the tax rate is raised sufficiently.

ECONOMICS **FRONT AND CENTER**

To think about how static tax analysis and dynamic tax analysis apply in a real-world context, read **Combating Declining State Tax Revenues,** on page 152.

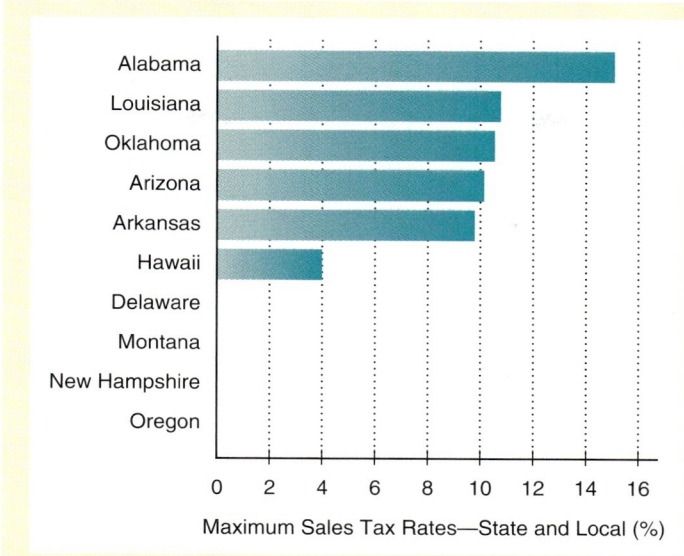

FIGURE 6-2

States with the Highest and Lowest Sales Tax Rates

A number of states allow counties and cities to collect their own sales taxes in addition to state sales taxes. This figure shows the maximum sales tax rates for selected states, including county and municipal taxes. Delaware, Montana, New Hampshire, and Oregon have no sales taxes. All other states besides those in the figure and the District of Columbia have maximum sales tax rates between the 4 percent rate of Hawaii and the 9.875 percent rate in Arkansas.

Source: U.S. Department of Commerce.

How are states trying to collect sales taxes on consumers' out-of-state purchases?

E-COMMERCE EXAMPLE

Even During a Revenue Boom, States Seek to Tax Internet Sales

Since the end of 2003, the tax revenues received by state governments have increased at an annual rate exceeding 6 percent. In spite of this revenue increase, however, state governments are seeking to expand their sales tax bases by applying sales tax rates to items shipped from other states, including items ordered online.

According to the National Governors Association, failure to collect sales taxes on online purchases results in annual tax revenue losses of at least $35 billion. State governments are unable to apply sales tax rates to most Internet orders of out-of-state goods and services, but this has not stopped many of them from trying to do so after the fact. Twenty state income tax forms now include a line on which taxpayers are supposed to report sales taxes owed on out-of-state purchases.

To induce people to report out-of-state purchases, states threaten audits that would uncover credit-card records. So far, most states conduct audits of out-of-state purchases only if taxpayers are already under investigation for tax evasion. Nevertheless, most state governments are becoming more serious about broadening the sales tax base to include Internet purchases.

FOR CRITICAL ANALYSIS

Why do you suppose that states with lines on tax forms that "require" taxpayers to enter sales taxes due on out-of-state purchases do not audit every taxpayer who chooses to leave the line blank? (Hint: Engaging in any activity, including conducting audits of taxpayers, entails an opportunity cost.)

Maximizing Tax Revenues

Dynamic tax analysis indicates that whether a government's tax revenues ultimately rise or fall in response to a tax rate increase depends on exactly how much the tax base declines in response to the higher tax rate. On the one hand, the tax base may decline by a relatively small amount following an increase in the tax rate, or perhaps even imperceptibly, so that

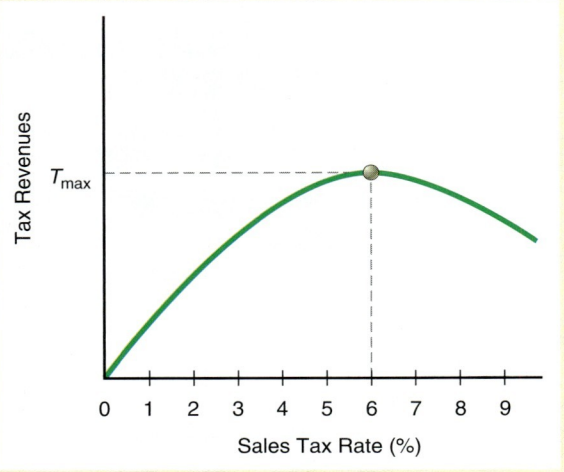

FIGURE 6-3

Maximizing the Government's Sales Tax Revenues

Dynamic tax analysis predicts that ever-higher tax rates bring about declines in the tax base, so that at sufficiently high tax rates the government's tax revenues begin to fall off. This implies that there is a tax rate, 6 percent in this example, at which the government can collect the maximum possible revenues, T_{max}.

tax revenues rise. For instance, in the situation we imagine a government facing in Figure 6-3, a rise in the tax rate from 5 percent to 6 percent causes tax revenues to increase. Along this range, static tax analysis can provide a good approximation of the revenue effects of an increase in the tax rate. On the other hand, the tax base may decline so much that total tax revenues decrease. In Figure 6-3, for example, increasing the tax rate from 6 percent to 7 percent causes tax revenues to *decline*.

What is most likely is that when the tax rate is already relatively low, increasing the tax rate causes relatively small declines in the tax base. Within a range of relatively low sales tax rates, therefore, increasing the tax rate generates higher sales tax revenues, as illustrated along the upward-sloping portion of the curve depicted in Figure 6-3. If the government continues to push up the tax rate, however, people increasingly have an incentive to find ways to avoid purchasing taxable goods and services. Eventually, the tax base decreases sufficiently that the government's tax collections decline with ever-higher tax rates.

Consequently, governments that wish to maximize their tax revenues should not necessarily assess a high tax rate. In the situation illustrated in Figure 6-3, the government maximizes its tax revenues at T_{max} by establishing a sales tax rate of 6 percent. If the government were to raise the rate above 6 percent, it would induce a sufficient decline in the tax base that its tax collections would decline. If the government wishes to collect more than T_{max} in revenues to fund various government programs, it must somehow either expand its sales tax base or develop another tax.

QUICK QUIZ

The _____ view of the relationship between tax rates and tax revenues implies that higher tax rates always generate increased government tax collections.

According to _____ tax analysis, higher tax rates cause the tax base to decrease. Tax collections will rise less than predicted by _____ tax analysis.

Dynamic tax analysis indicates that there is a tax rate that maximizes the government's tax collections. Setting the tax rate any higher would cause the tax base to _____ sufficiently that the government's tax revenues will _____.

See page 158 for the answers. Review concepts from this section in MyEconLab.

TAXATION FROM THE POINT OF VIEW OF PRODUCERS AND CONSUMERS

Governments collect taxes on product sales at the source. They require producers to charge these taxes when they sell their output. This means that taxes on sales of goods and services affect market prices and quantities. Let's consider why this is so.

Taxes and the Market Supply Curve

Imposing taxes on final sales of a good or service affects the position of the market supply curve. To see why, consider panel (a) of Figure 6-4, which shows a gasoline market supply curve S_1 in the absence of taxation. At a price of $2.35 per gallon, gasoline producers are willing and able to supply 180,000 gallons of gasoline per week. If the price increases to $2.45 per gallon, firms increase production to 200,000 gallons of gasoline per week.

Both federal and state governments assess **excise taxes**—taxes on sales of particular commodities—on sales of gasoline. They levy gasoline excise taxes as a **unit tax,** or a constant tax per unit sold. On average, combined federal and state excise taxes on gasoline are about $0.40 per gallon.

Excise tax
A tax levied on purchases of a particular good or service.

Unit tax
A constant tax assessed on each unit of a good that consumers purchase.

FIGURE 6-4

The Effects of Excise Taxes on the Market Supply and Equilibrium Price and Quantity of Gasoline

Panel (a) shows what happens if the government requires gasoline sellers to collect and transmit a $0.40 unit excise tax on gasoline. To be willing to continue supplying a given quantity, sellers must receive a price that is $0.40 higher for each gallon they sell, so the market supply curve shifts vertically by the amount of the tax. As illustrated in panel (b), this decline in market supply causes a reduction in the equilibrium quantity of gasoline produced and purchased. It also causes a rise in the market clearing price, to $2.75, so that consumers pay part of the tax. Sellers pay the rest in higher costs.

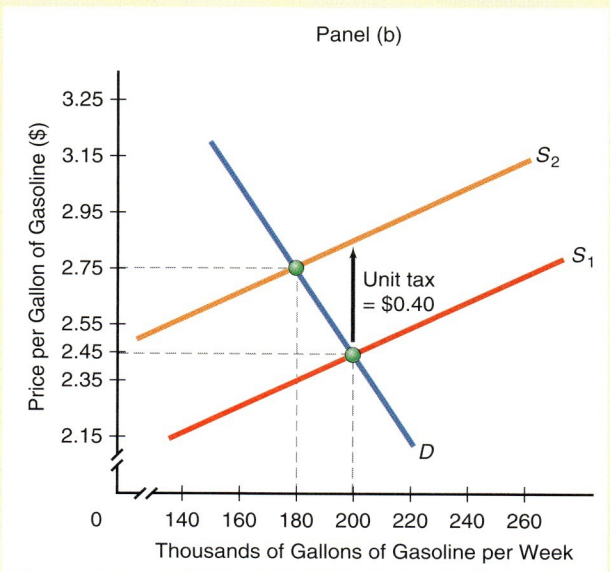

Let's suppose, therefore, that a gasoline producer must transmit a total of $0.40 per gallon to federal and state governments for each gallon sold. Producers must continue to receive a net amount of $2.35 per gallon to induce them to supply 180,000 gallons each week, so they must now receive $2.75 per gallon to supply that weekly quantity. Likewise, gasoline producers now will be willing to supply 200,000 gallons each week only if they receive $0.40 more per gallon, or a total amount of $2.85 per gallon.

As you can see, imposing the combined $0.40 per gallon excise taxes on gasoline shifts the supply curve vertically by exactly that amount to S_2. Thus, the effect of levying excise taxes on gasoline is to shift the supply curve vertically by the total per-unit taxes levied on gasoline sales. Hence there is a decrease in supply. (In the case of an *ad valorem* sales tax, the supply curve would shift vertically by a proportionate amount equal to the tax rate.)

How Taxes Affect the Market Price and Equilibrium Quantity

Panel (b) of Figure 6-4 on the preceding page shows how imposing $0.40 per gallon in excise taxes affects the market price of gasoline and the equilibrium quantity of gasoline produced and sold. In the absence of excise taxes, the market supply curve S_1 crosses the demand curve D at a market price of $2.45 per gallon. At this market price, the equilibrium quantity of gasoline is 200,000 gallons of gasoline per week.

The excise tax levy of $0.40 per gallon shifts the supply curve to S_2. At the original $2.45 per gallon price, there is now an excess quantity of gasoline demanded, so the market price of gasoline rises to $2.75 per gallon. At this market price, the equilibrium quantity of gasoline produced and consumed each week is 180,000 gallons.

What factors determine how much the equilibrium quantity of a good or service declines in response to taxation? The answer to this question depends on how responsive quantities demanded and supplied are to changes in price.

Who Pays the Tax?

In our example, imposing excise taxes of $0.40 per gallon of gasoline causes the market price to rise from $2.45 per gallon to $2.75 per gallon. Thus, the price that each consumer pays is $0.30 per gallon higher. Consumers pay three-fourths of the excise tax levied on each gallon of gasoline produced and sold.

Gasoline producers must pay the rest of the tax. Their profits decline by $0.10 per gallon because costs have increased by $0.40 per gallon while consumers pay $0.30 more per gallon.

In the gasoline market, as in other markets for products subject to excise taxes and other taxes on sales, the shapes of the market demand and supply curves determine who pays most of a tax. The reason is that the shapes of these curves reflect the responsiveness to price changes of the quantity demanded by consumers and of the quantity supplied by producers.

In the example illustrated in Figure 6-4, the fact that consumers pay most of the excise taxes levied on gasoline reflects a relatively low responsiveness of quantity demanded by consumers to a change in the price of gasoline. Consumers pay most of the excise taxes on each gallon produced and sold because in this example the amount of gasoline they desire to purchase is relatively unresponsive to a change in the market price induced by excise taxes. We will revisit the issue of who pays excise taxes in Chapter 21.

QUICK QUIZ

When the government levies a tax on sales of a particular product, firms must receive a higher price to continue supplying the same quantity as before, so the supply curve shifts _____. If the tax is a unit excise tax, the supply curve shifts _____ by the amount of the tax.

Imposing a tax on sales of an item _____ the equilibrium quantity produced and consumed and _____ the market price.

When a government assesses a unit excise tax, the market price of the good or service typically rises by an amount _____ than the per-unit tax. Hence consumers pay a portion of the tax, and firms pay the remainder.

See page 158 for the answers. Review concepts from this section in MyEconLab.

FINANCING SOCIAL SECURITY

In Chapter 5, you learned about Medicare, which is one of two major federal transfer programs. The other is Social Security, the federal system that transfers portions of the incomes of working-age people to elderly and disabled individuals. If current laws are maintained, Medicare's share of total national income will double over the next 20 years, as will the number of "very old" people—those over 85 and most in need of care. When Social Security is also taken into account, probably *half* of all federal government spending will go to the elderly by 2025. In a nutshell, senior citizens are the beneficiaries of an expensive and rapidly growing share of all federal spending.

Good Times for the First Retirees

The Social Security system was founded in 1935, as the United States was recovering from the Great Depression. The decision was made to establish Social Security as a means of guaranteeing a minimum level of pension benefits to all residents. Today, many people regard Social Security as a kind of "social compact"—a national promise to successive generations that they will receive support in their old age.

Big Payoffs for the Earliest Recipients.
The first Social Security taxes (called "contributions") were collected in 1937, but it was not until 1940 that retirement benefits were first paid. Ida May Fuller was the first person to receive a regular Social Security pension. She had paid a total of $25 in **Social Security contributions** before she retired. By the time she died in 1975 at age 100, she had received benefits totaling $23,000. Although Fuller did perhaps better than most, for the average retiree of 1940, the Social Security system was still more generous than any private investment plan anyone is likely to devise: After adjusting for inflation, the implicit **rate of return** on their contributions was an astounding 135 percent. (Roughly speaking, every $100 of combined employer and employee contributions yielded $135 *per year* during each and every year of that person's retirement. This is also called the **inflation-adjusted return.**)

Ever since the early days of Social Security, however, the rate of return has decreased. Nonetheless, Social Security was an excellent deal for most retirees during

Social Security contributions
The mandatory taxes paid out of workers' wages and salaries. Although half are supposedly paid by employers, in fact the net wages of employees are lower by the full amount.

Rate of return
The proportional annual benefit that results from making an investment.

Inflation-adjusted return
A rate of return that is measured in terms of real goods and services; that is, after the effects of inflation have been factored out.

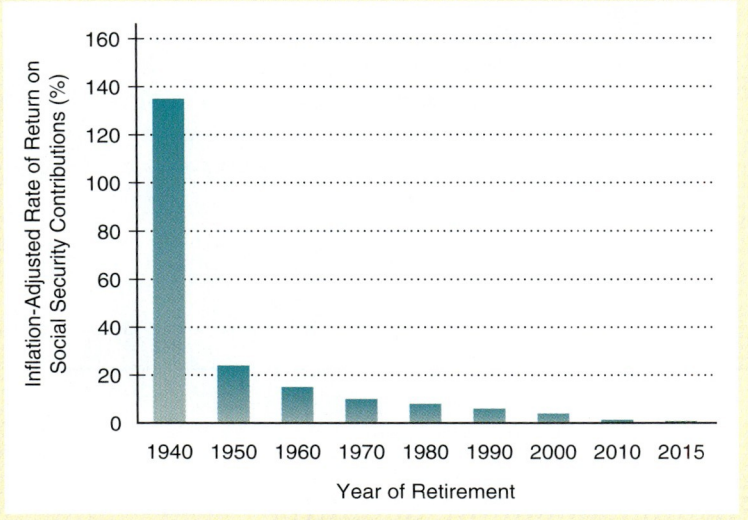

FIGURE 6-5
Private Rates of Return on Social Security Contributions, by Year of Retirement
The rate of return on Social Security contributions has steadily declined.
Sources: Social Security Administration and author's estimates.

the twentieth century. Figure 6-5 shows the implicit rate of return for people retiring in different years.

Given that the inflation-adjusted long-term rate of return on the stock market is about 7 to 9 percent, it is clear that for retirees, Social Security was a good deal until at least 1970. In fact, because Social Security benefits are a lot less risky than stocks, Social Security actually remained a pretty good "investment" for many people until around 1990.

Slowing Membership Growth. Social Security has managed to pay such high returns because at each point in time, current retirees are paid benefits out of the contributions of individuals who are currently working. (The contributions of today's retirees were long ago used to pay the benefits of previous retirees.) As long as Social Security was pulling in growing numbers of workers, either through a burgeoning workforce or by expanding its coverage of individuals in the workforce, the impressive rates of return during the early years of the program were possible.

But as membership growth slowed as the post–World War II baby boom generation began to reach retirement age, the rate of return fell. Moreover, because the early participants received more than they contributed, it follows that if the number of participants stops growing, later participants must receive less—and that ultimately means a *negative* rate of return. And for today's college students—indeed for most people now under the age of 40 or so—that negative rate of return is what lies ahead, unless reforms are implemented.

What Will It Take to Salvage Social Security?

The United States now finds itself with a social compact—the Social Security system—that entails a flow of promised benefits that could exceed the inflow of taxes sometime between 2010 and 2015. What, if anything, might be done about this? There are five relevant options to consider.

1. **Raise Taxes.** The history of Social Security has been one of steadily increasing tax rates applied to an ever-larger portion of workers' wages. In 1935, a Social Security payroll tax rate of 2 percent was applied to the first $3,000 of an individual's earnings (more than $36,000 in today's dollars). Now the Social Security payroll tax rate is 10.4 percentage points higher, and the government applies this tax rate to roughly an additional $60,000 of a worker's wages measured in today's dollars.

   One prominent proposal promises an $80 billion increase in contributions via a 2.2 percentage-point hike in the payroll tax rate, to an overall rate of 14.6 percent. Another proposal is to eliminate the current cap on the level of wages to which the payroll tax is applied, which would also generate about $80 billion per year in additional tax revenues. Nevertheless, even a combined policy of eliminating the wage cap and implementing a 2.2 percentage-point tax increase would not, by itself, keep tax collections above benefit payments over the long run.

   Why might eliminating the wage cap for the Social Security payroll tax encourage many professionals to form corporations?

Go to www.econtoday.com/ch06 to learn more about Social Security at the official Web site of the Social Security Administration.

EXAMPLE

Incorporating a Business Could Dodge a Broadened Payroll Tax

The Social Security payroll tax rate applies only to the first $98,000 of income earned each year. A professional, such as a physician or lawyer, who earns $1 million in annual income pays Social Security payroll taxes equal to 12.4 percent of $98,000, or $12,152. If the $98,000 limit were removed, the annual tax bill for Social Security would increase by more than 1,000 percent, to $124,000.

To avoid paying the higher tax bill, a professional could instead establish a legal entity called an "S corporation" and work as an employee. She could pay herself a salary of, say, $98,000, thereby holding her Social Security tax bill at $12,152, and report the rest of her annual income as corporate profits. Under present rules, she would still have to pay income taxes on the remaining $902,000 in income, but she would not have to pay an additional $111,848 in Social Security taxes.

Thus, raising the income limit for payroll taxes is unlikely to increase revenues for Social Security as much as proponents suggest. High-income professionals are likely to respond to the economic incentives created by a higher legal limit for payroll taxes, thereby undercutting the rationale for the proposed change.

FOR CRITICAL ANALYSIS
Why would professionals who earn not much more than $98,000 be less likely to incorporate to avoid higher Social Security payroll taxes? (Hint: Incorporating entails legal and accounting expenses.)

2. **Reduce Retirement Benefit Payouts.** Proposals are on the table to increase the age of full benefit eligibility, perhaps to as high as 70. Another option is to cut benefits to nonworking spouses. A third proposal is to impose "means testing" on some or all Social Security benefits. As things stand now, all individuals covered by the system collect benefits when they retire, regardless of their assets or other sources of retirement income. Under a system of means testing, individuals with substantial amounts of alternative sources of retirement income would receive reduced Social Security benefits.

Why do you suppose that the European workforce is likely to include a larger number of older people in future years?

INTERNATIONAL EXAMPLE

The Age for Receiving State Retirement Benefits Begins Rising in Europe

In the United States, about 68 percent of the population between the ages of 50 and 64 are either working or looking for jobs. In Germany and France, only slightly more than 50 percent of people in this age group are part of their nations' workforces. In Belgium and Italy, the percentages are not much above 40 percent.

The percentages of older people who are actively working or interested in employment are so much smaller in these European nations because their Social Security systems have lower retirement ages. Retirement ages range from as low as age 57 in Italy to age 63 in Germany.

Legal retirement ages are beginning to rise in Europe, however. The German government recently raised the retirement age for its version of Social Security, and other European nations are considering following suit. Motivating these actual and contemplated changes is a population bulge of aging residents, which is placing pressure on publicly funded retirement systems throughout Europe. Pushing up the retirement age is a way to reduce total benefit payouts and add to the number of years that the systems can remain financially viable.

FOR CRITICAL ANALYSIS
Based on the U.S. example, what other approaches can governments of European nations evaluate for shoring up their financially pressed old-age retirement systems? (Hint: Review the various proposals for salvaging the U.S. Social Security system, and contemplate how they might be applied in Europe.)

3. **Reduce Disability Benefits.** In addition to old-age pension payments, the U.S. Social Security system also offers benefits to people with various types of disabilities. In 1984, Congress greatly liberalized the definition of "disability" for purposes of qualifying for these benefits, and the result has been a near doubling of disability beneficiaries, from 2.6 million to more than 5 million today. One way to help shore up Social Security's financial situation would be to tighten requirements for this program or perhaps separate it from the Social Security system.

4. **Reform Immigration Policies.** Many experts believe that significant changes in U.S. immigration laws could offer the best hope of dealing with the tax burdens and workforce shrinkage of the future. Currently, however, more than 90 percent of new immigrants are admitted on the basis of a selection system unchanged since 1952. This system ties immigration rights to family preference. That is why most people admitted to the United States happen to be the spouses, children, or siblings of earlier immigrants. Unless Congress makes skills or training that are highly valued in the U.S. workplace a criterion in the U.S. immigration preference system, new immigrants are unlikely to contribute significant resources to Social Security, because their incomes will remain relatively low. Without reforms, it is unlikely that immigration will relieve much of the pressure building due to our aging population.

5. **Find a Way to Increase Social Security's Rate of Return.** As noted earlier, a major current problem for Social Security is a low implicit rate of return. Looking into the future, however, the situation looks even worse. As Figure 6-6 indicates, implicit rates of return for the system will be *negative* by 2020.

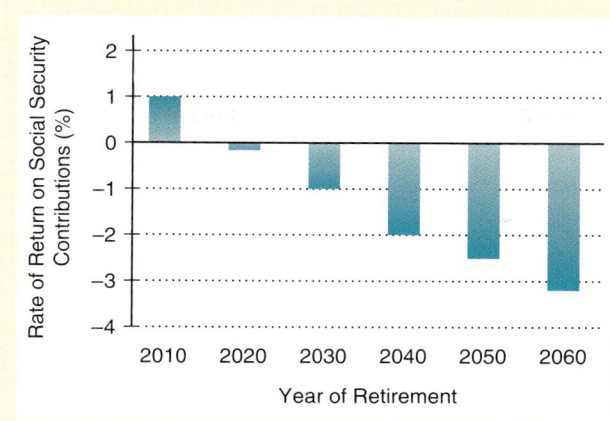

FIGURE 6-6

Projected Social Security Rates of Return for Future Retirees

Whereas workers who paid into Social Security in earlier years got a good deal, those who are now paying in and those who will pay in the future are facing low or negative implicit rates of return.

Sources: Social Security Administration and author's estimates.

The long-term inflation-adjusted return available in the stock market has been 7 to 9 percent since the 1930s. It is not surprising, therefore, that some observers have advocated that the Social Security system purchase stocks rather than Treasury bonds with the current excess of payroll taxes over current benefit payments. (Because this would necessitate the Treasury's borrowing more from the public, this amounts to having the government borrow from the public for purposes of investing in the stock market.)

Although the added returns on stock investments could help stave off tax increases or benefit cuts, there are a few potential problems with this proposal. Despite the stock market's higher long-term returns, the inherent uncertainty of those returns is not entirely consistent with the function of Social Security as a source of *guaranteed* retirement income. Another issue is what stocks would be purchased. Political pressure to invest in companies that happened to be politically popular and to refrain from investing in those that were unpopular, regardless of their returns, would reduce the expected returns from the government's stock portfolio—possibly even below the returns on Treasury bonds.

QUICK QUIZ

Social Security and Medicare payments are using up a large and _____ portion of the federal budget. Because of a shrinking number of workers available to support each retiree, the per capita expense for future workers to fund these programs will _____ rapidly unless reforms are made.

During the early years of the Social Security system, taxes were _____ relative to benefits, resulting in a _____ rate of return for retirees. As taxes have risen relative to benefits, the rate of return on Social Security has _____ steadily.

There are only five options—or combinations of these five options—for preserving the current social compact: _____ taxes, _____ retirement benefit payouts, _____ disability benefits, reform _____ policies, or _____ Social Security's rate of return.

See page 158 for the answers. Review concepts from this section in MyEconLab.

CASE STUDY: ECONOMICS FRONT AND CENTER

Combating Declining State Tax Revenues

Khadiija works for the department of revenue of a midwestern state. In recent years, the state government has sought to boost its sales and income tax collections via a series of tax rate increases. Nevertheless, the general trend in the state's sales and income tax revenues, after taking into account cyclical changes due to variations in statewide purchases and incomes, has been downward.

Khadiija has been appointed to a task force charged with developing a plan for increasing the state's tax receipts. Her immediate job is to develop possible options for the task force to explore. She jots down a list:

- *Find ways to broaden the sales tax base. Perhaps develop methods for requiring out-of-state companies to report sales to residents of this state to simplify audits of residents' reports of sales taxes due on their out-of-state purchases.*
- *Reduce the sales tax rate to try to encourage a sufficient increase in purchases within the state to push up net sales tax revenues.*
- *Reduce the income tax rate in an effort to boost the income tax base and increase income tax revenues. Reducing the tax rate could give more people an incentive to live and work in this state and give more companies an incentive to locate here.*

Khadiija realizes that several of her task force colleagues will react negatively to her ideas. Nevertheless, she begins putting together a more formal draft of a document outlining the three options she has listed.

CRITICAL ANALYSIS QUESTIONS

1. What economic argument could Khadiija give for doubting that further increases in sales and income tax rates will actually lead to higher sales and income tax receipts?
2. Based on the items in Khadiija's list, does she appear to be more influenced by static or dynamic tax analysis?

Can Social Security Learn from the Private Sector?

Issues and Applications

The largest component of the U.S. Social Security program is the retirement system that it operates. In certain ways, the Social Security retirement system is similar to private pensions, which provide retirement benefits for retirees from private companies.

There is an obvious difference between Social Security and private pensions, however. Social Security is operated by the federal government, while private pensions are privately owned and managed. Social Security is most like one particular type of private pension, called the *pay-as-you-go pension*, which is not fully funded when employees retire.

Some policymakers have recently suggested that reforming Social Security will require making the system function more like a *terminally funded pension*. Employees who participate in a terminally funded pension ultimately receive benefits from a pool of funds that has accumulated after years of contributions by the employee, the employer, or both.

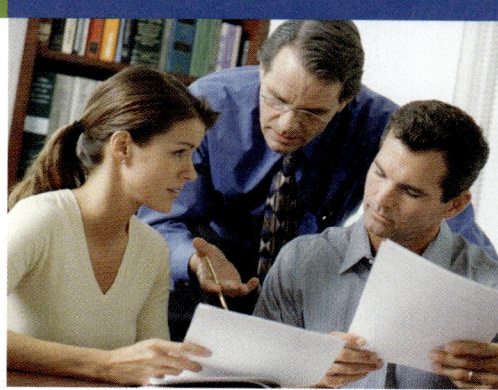

Concepts Applied
- Social Security Contributions
- Rate of Return
- Inflation-Adjusted Returns

Lessons from Private Pension Plans

Employers offering pay-as-you-go pensions finance benefits for retirees largely out of current earnings. Prominent employers offering pensions with pay-as-you-go characteristics include automakers, such as General Motors and Ford Motor Company, and airline firms, such as American Airlines and Delta Airlines.

These and other companies do not operate purely pay-as-you-go systems because they commonly set aside reserves of funds to help cover anticipated future retirement benefits. In good times, when revenues are flowing and business is growing, the companies add to their reserves. In bad times, when revenues are flat or decreasing, they do not. When companies with pay-as-you-go pensions experience particularly bad times, they often dip into their pension reserves. Sometimes they even stop payments to their retirees, as United Airlines did in 2005 after it declared bankruptcy.

Social Security is modeled on the pay-as-you-go pension. Congress has established what it calls a Social Security *trust fund* that is analogous to the pools of reserves that companies with pay-as-you-go plans typically establish. Unlike most companies, however, Congress dips into its trust fund every year, by "borrowing" from the trust fund to obtain funds that help cover government spending not fully financed by regular tax receipts. Congress does this even in good years when the U.S. economy is doing well and federal tax receipts are booming.

Is It Time to Alter the Pension Model for Social Security?

In contrast to a pay-as-you-go pension, a terminally funded pension is essentially a savings account. Contributions accumulate in the account during working years, and withdrawals are deferred until retirement. Employee and employer contributions build up during working years, and these funds are used to buy government and corporate bonds and stocks. Hence terminally funded pensions accumulate interest from bonds and capital gains from rising values of stocks. When a worker retires, funds are then available to draw upon during retirement.

In 2005, President George W. Bush suggested allowing people born after 1965 to divert a portion of their Social Security contributions to *private Social Security accounts*. People would be able to allocate funds in these accounts to both corporate bonds and stocks. This potentially would allow individuals to earn higher rates of return than those offered by the Social Security trust fund, which allocates its funds only to holdings of U.S. government bonds paying historically lower inflation-adjusted returns.

Effectively, the Bush administration's suggestion is to make the Social Security system offer a terminally funded pension plan alongside the traditional pay-as-you-go arrangement. So far, Congress has not acted on this proposal. Nevertheless, modeling Social Security on terminally funded pension plans in the private sector ultimately may prove to be one way to make the program economically sound.

Log in to **MyEconLab**, click on "Economic News," and test your understanding of the chapter by answering interactive questions that relate directly to this issue.

For Critical Analysis

1. Who provides the funds that Congress "borrows" year after year from the Social Security trust fund?
2. In what sense do critics of President Bush's proposal have a point when they argue that private accounts represent a fundamental break with past operations of the Social Security system?

Web Resources

1. For a brief overview of the Bush administration's suggestions for private Social Security accounts, go to www.econtoday.com/ch06.
2. To obtain more details about the Bush administration's private-accounts plan, read the documents available through the links provided at www.econtoday.com/ch06.

Research Project

Explain why a pay-as-you-go Social Security system might have appeared attractive to policymakers in the late 1930s, when U.S. population growth appeared unlikely to level off for years to come. Evaluate whether a terminally funded Social Security old-age benefit plan might be more appropriate in today's environment, in which the U.S. population is growing at a slower rate.

CHAPTER 6 *Funding the Public Sector* 155

Here is what you should know after reading this chapter. MyEconLab will help you identify what you know, and where to go when you need to practice.

WHAT YOU SHOULD KNOW		WHERE TO GO TO PRACTICE
Average Tax Rates versus Marginal Tax Rates The average tax rate is the ratio of total tax payments to total income. By contrast, the marginal tax rate is the change in tax payments induced by a change in total taxable income. Thus, the marginal tax rate applies to the last dollar that a person earns.	government budget constraint, 135 tax base, 136 tax rate, 136 marginal tax rate, 136 tax bracket, 136 average tax rate, 136 proportional taxation, 137 progressive taxation, 137 regressive taxation, 137	• **MyEconLab** Study Plans 6.1, 6.2 • Audio introduction to Chapter 6 • Video: Types of Tax Systems
The U.S. Income Tax System The U.S. income tax system assesses taxes against both personal and business income. It is designed to be a progressive tax system, in which the marginal tax rate increases as income rises, so that the marginal tax rate exceeds the average tax rate. This contrasts with a regressive tax system, in which higher-income people pay lower marginal tax rates, resulting in a marginal tax rate that is less than the average tax rate. The marginal tax rate equals the average tax rate only under proportional taxation, in which the marginal tax rate does not vary with income.	capital gain, 139 capital loss, 139 retained earnings, 140 tax incidence, 140	• **MyEconLab** Study Plan 6.3 • Video: The Corporate Income Tax
The Relationship Between Tax Rates and Tax Revenues Static tax analysis assumes that the tax base does not respond significantly to an increase in the tax rate, so it seems to imply that a tax rate hike must always boost a government's total tax collections. Dynamic tax analysis reveals, however, that increases in tax rates cause the tax base to decline. Thus, there is a tax rate that maximizes the government's tax revenues. If the government pushes the tax rate higher, tax collections decline.	sales taxes, 141 *ad valorem* taxation, 141 static tax analysis, 142 dynamic tax analysis, 142 **Key figure** Figure 6-3, 144	• **MyEconLab** Study Plan 6.4 • Animated Figure 6-3
How Taxes on Purchases of Goods and Services Affect Market Prices and Quantities When a government imposes a per-unit tax on a good or service, a seller is willing to supply any given quantity only if the seller receives a price that is higher by exactly the amount of the tax. Hence the supply curve shifts vertically by the amount of the tax per unit. In a market with typically shaped demand and supply curves, this results in a fall in the equilibrium quantity and an increase in the market price. To the extent that the market price rises, consumers pay a portion of the tax on each unit they buy. Sellers pay the remainder in higher per-unit production costs.	excise tax, 145 unit tax, 145 **Key figure** Figure 6-4, 145	• **MyEconLab** Study Plan 6.5 • Animated Figure 6-4

WHAT YOU SHOULD KNOW

How Social Security Works and Why It Poses Problems for Today's Students Since its inception, Social Security benefits have been paid out of taxes. Because of the growing mismatch between elderly and younger citizens, future scheduled benefits vastly exceed future scheduled taxes, so some combination of higher taxes and lower benefits will have to be implemented to maintain the current system. The situation might also be eased a bit if more immigration of skilled workers were permitted and if Social Security contributions were invested in the stock market, where they could earn higher rates of return.

Social Security contributions, 147
rate of return, 147
inflation-adjusted return, 147

Key figure
Figure 6-6, 151

WHERE TO GO TO PRACTICE

- **MyEconLab** Study Plan 6.6
- Animated Figure 6-6

Log in to MyEconLab, take a chapter test, and get a personalized Study Plan that tells you which concepts you understand and which ones you need to review. From there, MyEconLab will give you further practice, tutorials, animations, videos, and guided solutions.
Log in to www.myeconlab.com

PROBLEMS

Select problems, indicated by a blue oval, are assignable in MyEconLab.
Answers to the odd-numbered problems appear at the back of the book.

6-1 A senior citizen gets a part-time job at a fast-food restaurant. She earns $8 per hour for each hour she works, and she works exactly 25 hours per week. Thus, her total pretax weekly income is $200. Her total income tax assessment each week is $40, but she has determined that she is assessed $3 in taxes for the final hour she works each week.

  a. What is this person's average tax rate each week?
  b. What is the marginal tax rate for the last hour she works each week?

6-2 For purposes of assessing income taxes, there are three official income levels for workers in a small country: high, medium, and low. For the last hour on the job during a 40-hour workweek, a high-income worker pays a marginal income tax rate of 15 percent, a medium-income worker pays a marginal tax rate of 20 percent, and a low-income worker is assessed a 25 percent marginal income tax rate. Based only on this information, does this nation's income tax system appear to be progressive, proportional, or regressive?

6-3 Suppose that a state has increased its sales tax rate every other year since 1999. Assume that the state collected all sales taxes that residents legally owed. The following table summarizes its experience. What were total taxable sales in this state during each year displayed in the table?

Year	Sales Tax Rate	Sales Tax Collections
1999	0.03 (3 percent)	$9.0 million
2001	0.04 (4 percent)	$14.0 million
2003	0.05 (5 percent)	$20.0 million
2005	0.06 (6 percent)	$24.0 million
2007	0.07 (7 percent)	$29.4 million

6-4 The sales tax rate applied to all purchases within a state was 0.04 (4 percent) throughout 2006 but increased to 0.05 (5 percent) during all of 2007. The state government collected all taxes due, but its tax revenues were equal to $40 million each year. What happened to the sales tax base between 2006 and 2007? What could account for this result?

6-5 A city government imposes a proportional income tax on all people who earn income within its city limits. In 2006, the city's income tax rate was 0.05 (5 percent), and it collected $20 million in income taxes. In 2007, it raised the income tax rate to 0.06 (6 percent), and its income tax collections declined to $19.2 million. What happened to the city's income tax base between 2006 and 2007? How could this have occurred?

6-6 To raise funds aimed at providing more support for public schools, a state government has just imposed a unit excise tax equal to $4 for each monthly unit of telephone services sold by each telephone company operating in the state. The diagram below depicts the positions of the demand and supply curves for telephone services *before* the unit excise tax was imposed. Use this diagram to determine the position of the new market supply curve now that the tax hike has gone into effect.

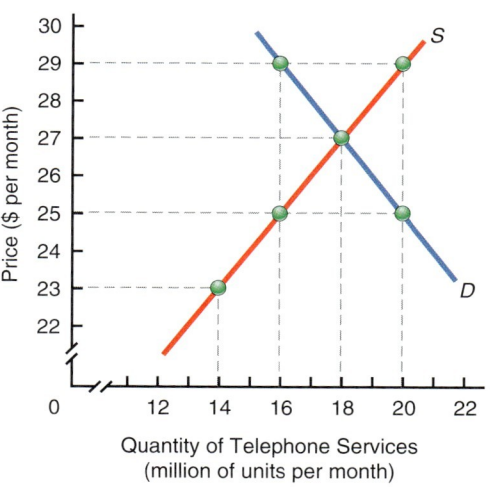

a. Does imposing the $4-per-month unit excise tax cause the market price of telephone services to rise by $4 per month? Why or why not?
b. What portion of the $4-per-month unit excise tax is paid by consumers? What portion is paid by providers of telephone services?

6-7 Suppose that the federal government imposes a unit excise tax of $2 per month on the rates that Internet service providers charge for providing DSL high-speed Internet access to households and businesses. Draw a diagram of normally shaped market demand and supply curves for DSL Internet access services. Use this diagram to make predictions about how the Internet service tax is likely to affect the market price and market quantity.

6-8 Consider the $2 per month tax on DSL Internet access in Problem 6-7. Suppose that in the market for DSL Internet access services provided to households, the market price increases by $2 per month after the unit excise tax is imposed. If the market supply curve slopes upward, what can you say about the shape of the market demand curve over the relevant ranges of prices and quantities? Who pays the excise tax in this market?

6-9 Consider once more the DSL Internet access tax of $2 per month discussed in Problem 6-7. Suppose that in the market for DSL Internet access services provided to businesses, the market price does not change after the unit excise tax is imposed. If the market supply curve slopes upward, what can you say about the shape of the market demand curve over the relevant ranges of prices and quantities? Who pays the excise tax in this market?

6-10 The following information applies to the market for a particular item in the *absence* of a unit excise tax:

Price ($ per unit)	Quantity Supplied	Quantity Demanded
4	50	200
5	75	175
6	100	150
7	125	125
8	150	100
9	175	75

a. According to the information above, in the *absence* of a unit excise tax, what is the market price? What is the equilibrium quantity?
b. Suppose that the government decides to subject producers of this item to a unit excise tax equal to $2 per unit sold. What is the new market price? What is the new equilibrium quantity?
c. What portion of the tax is paid by producers? What portion of the tax is paid by consumers?

6-11 In the following situations, what is the rate of return on the investment? (Hint: In each case, what is the percentage by which next year's benefit exceeds—or falls short of—this year's cost?)

a. You invest $100 today and receive in return $150 exactly one year from now.

b. You invest $100 today and receive in return $80 exactly one year from now.

6-12. Suppose that the following Social Security reform became law: All current Social Security recipients will continue to receive their benefits, but no increase will be made other than cost-of-living adjustments; U.S. citizens between age 40 and retirement not yet receiving Social Security can opt to continue with the current system; those who opt out can place what they would have contributed to Social Security into one or more government-approved mutual funds; and those under 40 must place their contributions into one or more government-approved mutual funds.

Now answer the following questions:

a. Who will be in favor of this reform and why?
b. Who will be against this reform and why?
c. What might happen to stock market indexes?
d. What additional risk is involved for those who end up in the private system?
e. What additional benefits are possible for the people in the private system?
f. Which firms in the mutual fund industry might not be approved by the federal government and why?

ECONOMICS ON THE NET

Social Security Privatization There are many proposals for reforming Social Security, but only one fundamentally alters the nature of the current system: privatization. The purpose of this exercise is to learn more about what would happen if Social Security were privatized.

Title: Social Security Privatization

Navigation: Go to www.econtoday.com/ch06 to learn about Social Security privatization. Click on *FAQ on Social Security* in the left-hand column.

Application For each of the three entries noted here, read the entry and answer the question.

1. Click on *How would individual accounts affect women?* According to this article, what are the likely consequences of Social Security privatization for women? Why?

2. Click on *I'm a low-wage worker. How would individual accounts affect me?* What does this article contend are the likely consequences of Social Security privatization for low-wage workers? Why?

3. Click on *I've heard that individual accounts would help minorities. Is that true?* Why does this article argue that African Americans in particular would benefit from a privatized Social Security system?

For Group Study and Analysis Taking into account the characteristics of your group as a whole, is it likely to be made better off or worse off if Social Security is privatized? Should your decision to support or oppose privatization be based solely on how it affects you personally? Or should your decision take into account how it might affect others in your group?

It will be worthwhile for those not nearing retirement age to examine what the "older" generation thinks about the idea of privatizing the Social Security system in the United States. So create two groups—one for and one against privatization. Each group will examine the following Web site and come up with arguments in favor or against the ideas expressed on it.

Go to www.econtoday.com/ch06 to read a proposal for Social Security reform. Accept or rebut the proposal, depending on the side to which you have been assigned. Be prepared to defend your reasons with more than just your feelings. At a minimum, be prepared to present arguments that are logical, if not entirely backed by facts.

ANSWERS TO QUICK QUIZZES

p. 138: (i) rate . . . base; (ii) average . . . marginal; (iii) proportional . . . progressive . . . regressive
p. 141: (i) income . . . sales . . . property; (ii) double; (iii) Social Security . . . Medicare . . . unemployment
p. 144: (i) static; (ii) dynamic . . . static; (iii) fall . . . decline
p. 147: (i) vertically . . . vertically; (ii) reduces . . . raises; (iii) less
p. 151: (i) rising . . . grow; (ii) low . . . high . . . decreased; (iii) raise . . . reduce . . . reduce . . . immigration . . . increase

The Macroeconomy: Unemployment, Inflation, and Deflation

7

Last week, a Wal-Mart supercenter opened its doors and began selling grocery items at lower prices than a traditional grocery store in a U.S. community. This morning, a government worker visited both stores and recorded the prices of a variety of grocery items. This afternoon, she has forwarded the data to her supervisor in Washington, D.C., who is charged with tracking the U.S. inflation rate. The supervisor notes that many of the prices in the report were for items sold at Wal-Mart. Following established policy, instead of recording Wal-Mart's prices for the items, he enters the prices charged by the traditional grocer.

How does the U.S. government measure the overall level of prices? Why does the government replace prices charged by Wal-Mart supercenters with higher prices charged by traditional grocers? This chapter will answer these questions.

Learning Objectives

After reading this chapter, you should be able to:

1. Explain how the U.S. government calculates the official unemployment rate
2. Discuss the types of unemployment
3. Describe how price indexes are calculated and define the key types of price indexes
4. Distinguish between nominal and real interest rates
5. Evaluate who loses and who gains from inflation
6. Understand key features of business fluctuations

MyEconLab helps you master each objective and study more efficiently. See end of chapter for details.

> ### Did You Know That...
> in recent years, the U.S. government's two approaches to estimating the growth of labor employment during a given year have differed by an amount larger than the entire population of Baltimore, Maryland? In an effort to track trends in labor employment from month to month, the government relies on two employment surveys conducted by the Bureau of Labor Statistics. One, the *employment (payroll) survey*, estimates U.S. employment based on responses from about 400,000 businesses that account for about a third of nonfarm payroll employment. The other, the *household survey*, estimates employment using responses from about 60,000 households. The payroll survey provides information about the number of jobs, so a person with multiple jobs is counted more than once in the payroll survey. In contrast, this same person is counted only once in the household survey. Nevertheless, since 2001, the household survey has persistently tended to yield higher employment estimates than the payroll survey—as many as 680,000 more over a one-year period.
>
> Although several factors account for the difference in the estimates derived from the two surveys, one factor consistently stands out. Because the payroll survey by definition measures only employment of individuals who are on firms' payrolls, it fails to include people who are self-employed. In contrast, the household survey includes self-employed individuals. In recent years, an increasing number of people have become self-employed, pushing the household survey's employment estimate above the payroll survey's estimated level of employment.
>
> Trying to understand and better forecast labor employment and the overall performance of the national economy is a central objective of macroeconomics. This branch of economics seeks to explain and predict movements in unemployment, the average level of prices, and the total production of goods and services. This chapter introduces you to these key issues of macroeconomics.

UNEMPLOYMENT

Unemployment
The total number of adults (aged 16 years or older) who are willing and able to work and who are actively looking for work but have not found a job.

Unemployment is normally defined as the number of adults who are actively looking for work but do not have a job. Unemployment creates a cost to the entire economy in terms of lost output. One estimate indicates that at the beginning of the 2000s, when the unemployment rate rose by nearly 2 percentage points and firms were operating below 80 percent of their capacity, the amount of output that the economy lost due to idle resources was roughly 2 percent of the total production throughout the United States. (In other words, we were somewhere inside the production possibilities curve that we talked about in Chapter 2.) That was the equivalent of more than an inflation-adjusted $200 billion of schools, houses, restaurant meals, cars, and movies that *could have been* produced. It is no wonder that policymakers closely watch the unemployment figures published by the Department of Labor's Bureau of Labor Statistics.

On a more personal level, the state of being unemployed often results in hardship and failed opportunities as well as a lack of self-respect. Psychological researchers believe that being fired creates at least as much stress as the death of a close friend. The numbers that we present about unemployment can never fully convey its true cost to the people of this or any other nation.

Labor force
Individuals aged 16 years or older who either have jobs or who are looking and available for jobs; the number of employed plus the number of unemployed.

Historical Unemployment Rates

The unemployment rate, defined as the proportion of the measured **labor force** that is unemployed, reached a low of 1.2 percent of the labor force at the end of World War II, after having

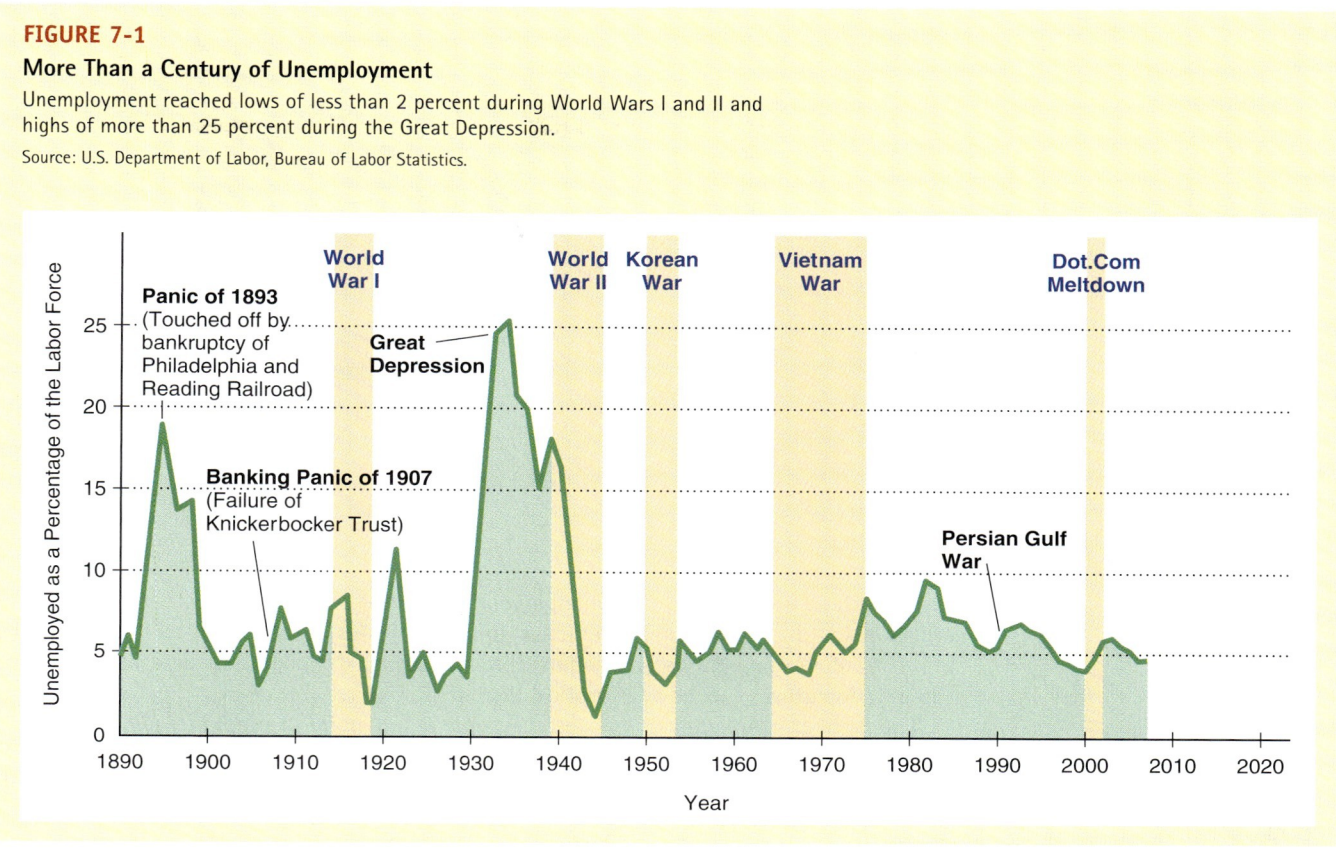

FIGURE 7-1

More Than a Century of Unemployment

Unemployment reached lows of less than 2 percent during World Wars I and II and highs of more than 25 percent during the Great Depression.

Source: U.S. Department of Labor, Bureau of Labor Statistics.

reached 25 percent during the Great Depression in the 1930s. You can see in Figure 7-1 what has happened to the unemployment rate in the United States since 1890. The highest level ever was reached in the Great Depression, but the unemployment rate was also high during the Panic of 1893.

Employment, Unemployment, and the Labor Force

Figure 7-2 on the following page presents the population of individuals 16 years of age or older broken into three segments: (1) employed, (2) unemployed, and (3) not in the civilian labor force (a category that includes homemakers, full-time students, military personnel, persons in institutions, and retired persons). The employed and the unemployed, added together, make up the labor force. In 2007, the labor force amounted to 145.4 million + 7.3 million = 152.7 million people. To calculate the unemployment rate, we simply divide the number of unemployed by the number of people in the labor force and multiply by 100: 7.3 million/152.7 million × 100 = 4.8 percent.

The Arithmetic Determination of Unemployment

Because there is a transition between employment and unemployment at any point in time—people are leaving jobs and others are finding jobs—there is a simple relationship

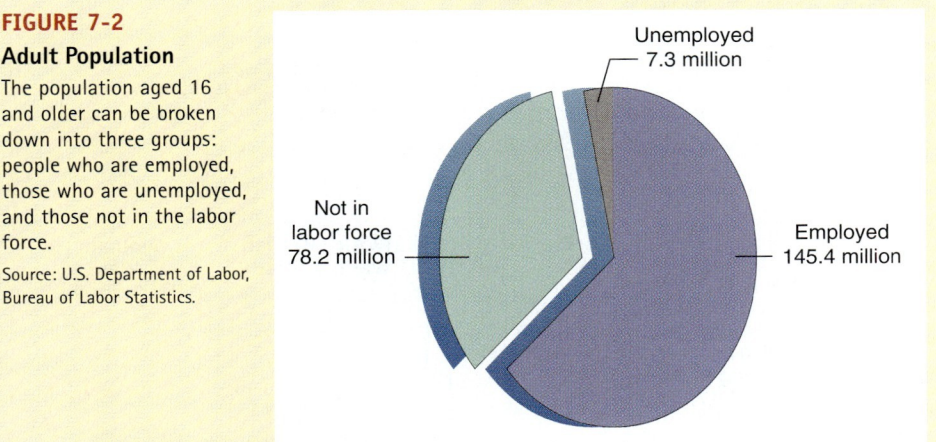

FIGURE 7-2

Adult Population

The population aged 16 and older can be broken down into three groups: people who are employed, those who are unemployed, and those not in the labor force.

Source: U.S. Department of Labor, Bureau of Labor Statistics.

between the employed and the unemployed, as can be seen in Figure 7-3. Job departures are shown at the top of the diagram, and job acquisitions are shown at the bottom. If the numbers of job departures and acquisitions are equal, the unemployment rate stays the same. If departures exceed acquisitions, the unemployment rate rises.

The number of unemployed is some number at any point in time. It is a **stock** of individuals who do not have a job but are actively looking for one. The same is true for the number of employed. The number of people departing jobs, whether voluntarily or involuntarily, is a **flow,** as is the number of people acquiring jobs.

Categories of Individuals Who Are Without Work.

According to the Bureau of Labor Statistics, an unemployed individual will fall into any of four categories:

1. A **job loser,** whose employment was involuntarily terminated or who was laid off (40 to 60 percent of the unemployed)
2. A **reentrant,** who worked a full-time job before but has been out of the labor force (20 to 30 percent of the unemployed)
3. A **job leaver,** who voluntarily ended employment (less than 10 to around 15 percent of the unemployed)
4. A **new entrant,** who has never worked a full-time job for two weeks or longer (10 to 15 percent of the unemployed)

Duration of Unemployment.

If you are out of a job for a week, your situation is typically much less serious than if you are out of a job for, say, 14 weeks. An increase in the duration of unemployment can increase the unemployment rate because workers stay unemployed longer, thereby creating a greater number of them at any given time. The most recent information on duration of unemployment paints the following picture: more than a third of those who become unemployed acquire a new job by the end of one month, approximately one-third more acquire a job by the end of two months, and only about a sixth are still unemployed after six months. The average duration of unemployment for all unemployed has been just over 15 weeks for the past 15 years.

When overall business activity goes into a downturn, the duration of unemployment tends to rise, thereby causing much of the increase in the estimated unemployment rate. In

---

Stock
The quantity of something, measured at a given point in time—for example, an inventory of goods or a bank account. Stocks are defined independently of time, although they are assessed at a point in time.

Flow
A quantity measured per unit of time; something that occurs over time, such as the income you make per week or per year or the number of individuals who are fired every month.

Job loser
An individual in the labor force whose employment was involuntarily terminated.

Reentrant
An individual who used to work full-time but left the labor force and has now reentered it looking for a job.

Job leaver
An individual in the labor force who quits voluntarily.

New entrant
An individual who has never held a full-time job lasting two weeks or longer but is now seeking employment.

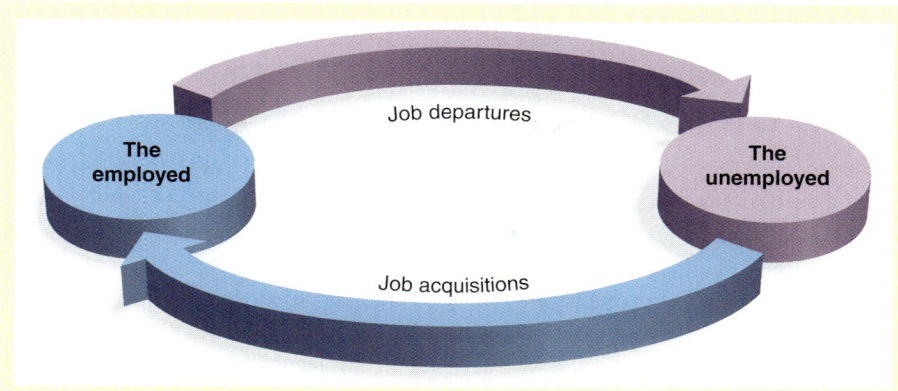

FIGURE 7-3

The Logic of the Unemployment Rate
Individuals who depart jobs but remain in the labor force are subtracted from the employed and added to the unemployed. When the unemployed acquire jobs, they are subtracted from the unemployed and added to the employed. In an unchanged labor force, if both flows are equal, the unemployment rate is stable. If more people depart jobs than acquire them, the unemployment rate increases, and vice versa.

a sense, then, it is the increase in the *duration* of unemployment during a downturn in national economic activity that generates the bad news that concerns policymakers in Washington, D.C. Furthermore, the individuals who stay unemployed longer than six months are the ones who create the pressure on Congress to "do something." What Congress does, typically, is extend and supplement unemployment benefits.

The Discouraged Worker Phenomenon. Critics of the published unemployment rate calculated by the federal government believe that it fails to reflect the true numbers of **discouraged workers** and "hidden unemployed." Though there is no agreed-on method to measure discouraged workers, the Department of Labor defines them as people who have dropped out of the labor force and are no longer looking for a job because they believe that the job market has little to offer them. To what extent do we want to include in the measured labor force individuals who voluntarily choose not to look for work or those who take only a few minutes a day to scan the want ads and then decide that there are no jobs?

Some economists argue that people who work part-time but are willing to work full-time should be classified as "semihidden" unemployed. Estimates range as high as 6 million workers at any one time. Offsetting this factor, though, is *overemployment*. An individual working 50 or 60 hours a week is still counted as only one full-time worker. Some people work two or three jobs.

Discouraged workers
Individuals who have stopped looking for a job because they are convinced that they will not find a suitable one.

Labor Force Participation. The way in which we define unemployment and membership in the labor force will affect what is known as the **labor force participation rate**. It is defined as the proportion of noninstitutionalized (i.e., not in prisons, mental institutions, etc.) working-age individuals who are employed or seeking employment.

The U.S. labor force participation rate has risen somewhat over time, from 60 percent in 1950 to slightly less than 66 percent today. The gender composition of the U.S. labor force has changed considerably during this time. In 1950, more than 83 percent of men and fewer than 35 percent of women participated in the U.S. labor force. Today, fewer than 75 percent of men and more than 60 percent of women are U.S. labor force participants. The present labor force participation rate of just below 66 percent is down slightly from 2000, when the rate was above 67 percent. What accounts for the slight decrease in the labor force participation rate during the 2000s?

Labor force participation rate
The percentage of noninstitutionalized working-age individuals who are employed or seeking employment.

EXAMPLE

Why the U.S. Labor Force Participation Rate Has Dipped

In 2000, the U.S. labor force participation rate was 67.3 percent. Since then, it has steadily dipped, to slightly less than 66 percent today. A less than 1.4-percentage-point drop in the labor force participation rate does not seem large until it is multiplied by just over 230 million people. This yields an absolute drop in the labor force of roughly 3 million people, or an amount close to the population of Chicago.

Why are fewer people in the labor force? One contributing factor has been that new female entrants have been insufficient to replace women who have departed the labor force. Another is that many middle-aged workers have taken early retirements. Finally, legal changes have made it easier for workers to receive disability benefits. There is some evidence that these changes have encouraged people who otherwise might have worked with back pain or other problems to accept benefits and leave the labor force. Some estimates indicate that greater access to disability benefits may account for as much as half of the decrease in the labor force during the 2000s.

FOR CRITICAL ANALYSIS
Why are people receiving disability benefits not counted as part of the labor force?

QUICK QUIZ

_____ persons are adults who are willing and able to work and are actively looking for a job but have not found one. The unemployment rate is computed by dividing the number of unemployed by the total _____ _____, which is equal to those who are employed plus those who are unemployed.

The unemployed are classified as _____ _____, _____, _____ _____, and _____ _____ to the labor force. The flow of people departing jobs and people acquiring jobs determines the stock of unemployed as well as the stock of employed.

The duration of unemployment affects the unemployment rate. The number of unemployed workers can remain the same, but if the duration of unemployment increases, the measured unemployment rate will _____.

Whereas overall labor force participation has risen only modestly since World War II, there has been a major increase in _____ labor force participation.

See page 183 for the answers. Review concepts from this section in MyEconLab.

THE MAJOR TYPES OF UNEMPLOYMENT

Unemployment has been categorized into four basic types: frictional, structural, cyclical, and seasonal.

Frictional Unemployment

Of the more than 152 million people in the labor force, more than 50 million will have either changed jobs or taken new jobs during the year; every single month, about one worker in 20 will have quit, been laid off (told to expect to be rehired later), or been permanently fired; another 6 percent will have gone to new jobs or returned to old ones. In the process, more than 22 million persons will have reported themselves unemployed at one time or another. This continuous flow of individuals from job to job and in and out of employment is called **frictional unemployment.** There will always be some frictional unemployment as resources are redirected in the market, because job-hunting costs are

Frictional unemployment
Unemployment due to the fact that workers must search for appropriate job offers. This takes time, and so they remain temporarily unemployed.

never zero, and workers never have full information about available jobs. To eliminate frictional unemployment, we would have to prevent workers from leaving their present jobs until they had already lined up other jobs at which they would start working immediately. And we would have to guarantee first-time job seekers a job *before* they started looking.

Structural Unemployment

Structural changes in our economy cause some workers to become unemployed permanently or for very long periods of time because they cannot find jobs that use their particular skills. This is called **structural unemployment.** Structural unemployment is not caused by general business fluctuations, although business fluctuations may affect it. And unlike frictional unemployment, structural unemployment is not related to the movement of workers from low-paying to high-paying jobs.

At one time, economists thought about structural unemployment only from the perspective of workers. The concept applied to workers who did not have the ability, training, and skills necessary to obtain available jobs. Today, it still encompasses these workers. In addition, however, economists increasingly look at structural unemployment from the viewpoint of employers, many of whom face government mandates to provide funds for social insurance programs for their employees, to announce plant closings months or even years in advance, and so on. There is now considerable evidence that government labor market policies influence how many positions businesses wish to create, thereby affecting structural unemployment. In the United States, many businesses appear to have adjusted to these policies by hiring more "temporary workers" or establishing short-term contracts with "private consultants," which may have reduced the extent of U.S. structural unemployment in recent years.

> **Structural unemployment**
> Unemployment resulting from a poor match of workers' abilities and skills with current requirements of employers.

Cyclical Unemployment

Cyclical unemployment is related to business fluctuations. It is defined as unemployment associated with changes in business conditions—primarily recessions and depressions. The way to lessen cyclical unemployment would be to reduce the intensity, duration, and frequency of downturns of business activity. Economic policymakers attempt, through their policies, to reduce cyclical unemployment by keeping business activity on an even keel.

> **Cyclical unemployment**
> Unemployment resulting from business recessions that occur when aggregate (total) demand is insufficient to create full employment.

Seasonal Unemployment

Seasonal unemployment comes and goes with seasons of the year in which the demand for particular jobs rises and falls. In northern states, construction workers can often work only during the warmer months; they are seasonally unemployed during the winter. Summer resort workers can usually get jobs in resorts only during the summer season. They, too, become seasonally unemployed during the winter; the opposite is true for ski resort workers.

The unemployment rate that the Bureau of Labor Statistics releases each month is "seasonally adjusted." This means that the reported unemployment rate has been adjusted to remove the effects of variations in seasonal unemployment. Thus, the unemployment rate that the media dutifully announce reflects only the sum of frictional unemployment, structural unemployment, and cyclical unemployment.

Why is the unemployment rate so difficult to measure in China?

> **Seasonal unemployment**
> Unemployment resulting from the seasonal pattern of work in specific industries. It is usually due to seasonal fluctuations in demand or to changing weather conditions, rendering work difficult, if not impossible, as in the agriculture, construction, and tourist industries.

INTERNATIONAL EXAMPLE

Challenges of Measuring the Unemployment Rate in China

In recent years, the Chinese government's official estimate of the unemployment rate has hovered between 4 and 5 percent. This figure takes into account only members of the nation's labor force who permanently reside in urban areas, however. Measurement of China's labor force and unemployment rate fails to encompass all of the roughly 115 million people who migrate each year from rural areas in search of jobs in cities. Most of these migrant workers do find jobs in urban areas, but millions do not. In addition, China's government has not yet developed a way to determine how many of the millions of people laid off from state-owned firms have obtained positions with private firms.

Studies of unemployment in China suggest that the average annual unemployment rate for the nation as a whole during the mid-2000s has actually been somewhere between 7 and 13 percent. In a nation with a labor force exceeding 760 million people, this means that it is likely that between 15 million and 60 million more residents of China are unemployed than government figures indicate.

FOR CRITICAL ANALYSIS
Why might total unemployment of migrant workers in China be likely to reflect all four major types of unemployment?

FULL EMPLOYMENT AND THE NATURAL RATE OF UNEMPLOYMENT

Does full employment mean that everybody has a job? Certainly not, for not everyone is looking for a job—full-time students and full-time homemakers, for example, are not. Is it possible for everyone who is looking for a job always to find one? No, because transaction costs in the labor market are not zero. Transaction costs are those associated with any activity whose goal is to enter into, carry out, or terminate contracts. In the labor market, these costs involve time spent looking for a job, being interviewed, negotiating the terms of employment, and so on.

Full Employment

Full employment
An arbitrary level of unemployment that corresponds to "normal" friction in the labor market. In 1986, a 6.5 percent rate of unemployment was considered full employment. Today, it is assumed to be around 5 percent.

We will always have some frictional unemployment as individuals move in and out of the labor force, seek higher-paying jobs, and move to different parts of the country. **Full employment** is therefore a concept implying some sort of balance or equilibrium in an ever-shifting labor market. Of course, this general notion of full employment must somehow be put into numbers so that economists and others can determine whether the economy has reached the full-employment point.

The Natural Rate of Unemployment

Natural rate of unemployment
The rate of unemployment that is estimated to prevail in long-run macroeconomic equilibrium, when all workers and employers have fully adjusted to any changes in the economy.

To try to assess when a situation of balance has been attained in the labor market, economists estimate the **natural rate of unemployment,** the rate that is expected to prevail in the long run once all workers and employers have fully adjusted to any changes in the economy. If correctly estimated, the natural rate of unemployment should not include cyclical unemployment. When seasonally adjusted, the natural unemployment rate should include only frictional and structural unemployment.

A long-standing difficulty, however, has been a lack of agreement about how to estimate the natural unemployment rate. From the mid-1980s to the early 1990s, the President's Council of Economic Advisers (CEA) consistently estimated that the natural unemployment rate in the United States was about 6.5 percent. Even into the 2000s, Federal Reserve staff economists, employing an approach to estimating the natural rate of unemployment that was intended to improve on the CEA's traditional method, have arrived at a natural rate just over 6 percent. When the measured unemployment rate fell to 4 percent in 2000, however, economists began to rethink their approach to estimating the natural unemployment rate. This led some to alter their estimation methods to take into account such factors as greater rivalry among domestic businesses and increased international competition, which led to an estimated natural rate of unemployment of roughly 5 percent. We shall return to the concept of the natural unemployment rate in Chapter 10.

How has the government of India sought to come closer to artificially attaining "full employment"?

> **ECONOMICS FRONT AND CENTER**
>
> To learn about how at least one country has experimented with limiting the legal workweek to try to reduce its unemployment rate, read **Looking to France for Answers,** on page 177.

INTERNATIONAL POLICY EXAMPLE

Policymakers Promote Measured Full Employment in India

Since 2005, the Indian government has extended a standing guarantee of employment, at a government-established wage, to one person per household for at least 100 days per year. Those employed under this policy engage in such activities as building rural roads and planting mango and orange groves. During the time that the government honors its commitment, those people put to work on such tasks are no longer unemployed. Consequently, the measured unemployment rate in India has been reduced.

FOR CRITICAL ANALYSIS
Who provides the funds required to honor the government's guarantee and reduce India's unemployment rate?

QUICK QUIZ

_____ unemployment occurs because of transaction costs in the labor market. For example, workers do not have full information about vacancies and must search for jobs.

_____ unemployment occurs when there is a poor match of workers' skills and abilities with available jobs, perhaps because workers lack appropriate training or government labor rules reduce firms' willingness to hire.

The levels of frictional and structural unemployment are used in part to determine our (somewhat arbitrary) measurement of the _____ rate of unemployment.

See page 183 for the answers. Review concepts from this section in MyEconLab.

INFLATION AND DEFLATION

During World War II, you could buy bread for 8 to 10 cents a loaf and have milk delivered fresh to your door for about 25 cents a half gallon. The average price of a new car was less than $700, and the average house cost less than $3,000. Today, bread, milk, cars, and houses all cost more—a lot more. Prices are more than 12 times what they were in 1940.

Inflation
A sustained increase in the average of all prices of goods and services in an economy.

Deflation
A sustained decrease in the average of all prices of goods and services in an economy.

Clearly, this country has experienced quite a bit of *inflation* since then. We define **inflation** as an upward movement in the average level of prices. The opposite of inflation is **deflation,** defined as a downward movement in the average level of prices. Notice that these definitions depend on the *average* level of prices. This means that even during a period of inflation, some prices can be falling if other prices are rising at a faster rate. The prices of electronic equipment have dropped dramatically since the 1960s, even though there has been general inflation.

To discuss what has happened to prices here and in other countries, we have to know how to measure inflation.

Inflation and the Purchasing Power of Money

The value of a dollar does not stay constant when there is inflation. The value of money is usually talked about in terms of **purchasing power.** A dollar's purchasing power is the real goods and services that it can buy. Consequently, another way of defining inflation is as a decline in the purchasing power of money. The faster the rate of inflation, the greater the rate of decline in the purchasing power of money.

Purchasing power
The value of money for buying goods and services. If your money income stays the same but the price of one good that you are buying goes up, your effective purchasing power falls, and vice versa.

One way to think about inflation and the purchasing power of money is to discuss dollar values in terms of *nominal* versus *real* values. The nominal value of anything is simply its price expressed in today's dollars. In contrast, the real value of anything is its value expressed in purchasing power, which varies with the overall price level. Let's say that you received a $100 bill from your grandparents this year. One year from now, the nominal value of that bill will still be $100. The real value will depend on what the purchasing power of money is after one year's worth of inflation. Obviously, if there is inflation during the year, the real value of that $100 bill will have diminished. For example, if you keep the $100 bill in your pocket for a year during which the rate of inflation is 3 percent, at the end of the year you will have to come up with $3 more to buy the same amount of goods and services that the $100 bill can purchase today.

Measuring the Rate of Inflation

How can we measure the rate of inflation? This is a thorny problem for government statisticians. It is easy to determine how much the price of an individual commodity has risen: If last year a light bulb cost 50 cents and this year it costs 75 cents, there has been a 50 percent rise in the price of that light bulb over a one-year period. We can express the change in the individual light bulb price in one of several ways: The price has gone up 25 cents; the price is one and a half (1.5) times as high; the price has risen by 50 percent. An *index number* of this price rise is simply the second way (1.5) multiplied by 100, meaning that the index today would stand at 150. We multiply by 100 to eliminate decimals because it is easier to think in terms of percentage changes using integers. This is the standard convention adopted for convenience in dealing with index numbers or price levels.

Price index
The cost of today's market basket of goods expressed as a percentage of the cost of the same market basket during a base year.

Base year
The year that is chosen as the point of reference for comparison of prices in other years.

Computing a Price Index. The measurement problem becomes more complicated when it involves a large number of goods, especially if some prices have risen faster than others and some have even fallen. What we have to do is pick a representative bundle, a so-called market basket, of goods and compare the cost of that market basket of goods over time. When we do this, we obtain a **price index,** which is defined as the cost of a market basket of goods today, expressed as a percentage of the cost of that identical market basket of goods in some starting year, known as the **base year.**

$$\text{Price index} = \frac{\text{cost today of market basket}}{\text{cost of market basket in base year}} \times 100$$

TABLE 7-1
Calculating a Price Index for a Two-Good Market Basket

In this simplified example, there are only two goods—corn and computers. The quantities and base-year prices are given in columns 2 and 3. The cost of the 1999 market basket, calculated in column 4, comes to $1,400. The 2009 prices are given in column 5. The cost of the market basket in 2009, calculated in column 6, is $1,650. The price index for 2009 compared with 1999 is 117.86.

(1) Commodity	(2) Market Basket Quantity	(3) 1999 Price per Unit	(4) Cost of Market Basket in 1999	(5) 2009 Price per Unit	(6) Cost of Market Basket in 2009
Corn	100 bushels	$ 4	$ 400	$ 8	$ 800
Computers	2	500	1,000	425	850
Totals			$1,400		$1,650

$$\text{Price index} = \frac{\text{cost of market basket in 2009}}{\text{cost of market basket in base year 1999}} \times 100 = \frac{\$1,650}{\$1,400} \times 100 = 117.86$$

In the base year, the price index will always be 100, because the year in the numerator and in the denominator of the fraction is the same; therefore, the fraction equals 1, and when we multiply it by 100, we get 100. A simple numerical example is given in Table 7-1. In the table, there are only two goods in the market basket—corn and computers. The *quantities* in the basket are the same in the base year, 1999, and the current year, 2009; only the *prices* change. Such a *fixed-quantity* price index is the easiest to compute because the statistician need only look at prices of goods and services sold every year rather than actually observing how much of these goods and services consumers actually purchase each year.

Real-World Price Indexes. Government statisticians calculate a number of price indexes. The most often quoted are the **Consumer Price Index (CPI),** the **Producer Price Index (PPI),** the **GDP deflator,** and the **Personal Consumption Expenditure (PCE) Index.** The CPI attempts to measure changes only in the level of prices of goods and services purchased by consumers. The PPI attempts to show what has happened to the average price of goods and services produced and sold by a typical firm. (There are also *wholesale price indexes* that track the price level for commodities that firms purchase from other firms.) The GDP deflator is the most general indicator of inflation because it measures changes in the level of prices of all new goods and services produced in the economy. The PCE Index measures average prices using weights from consumer-spending surveys.

The CPI. The Bureau of Labor Statistics (BLS) has the task of identifying a market basket of goods and services of the typical consumer. Today, the BLS uses the time period 1982–1984 as its base of market prices. It intends to change the base to 1993–1995 but has yet to do so. It has, though, updated the expenditure weights for its market basket of goods to reflect consumer spending patterns in 1993–1995. All CPI numbers since February 1998 reflect the new expenditure weights.

Economists have known for years that the way the BLS measures changes in the Consumer Price Index is flawed. Specifically, the BLS has been unable to account for the way consumers substitute less expensive items for higher-priced items. The reason is that the CPI is a fixed-quantity price index, meaning that the BLS implicitly ignores changes in consumption patterns that occur between years in which it revises the index. Until recently, the BLS has been unable to take quality changes into account as they occur. Now, though, it is subtracting from certain list prices estimated effects of qualitative improvements and adding to other list prices to account for deteriorations in quality. An additional flaw is that the CPI usually ignores successful new products until long after they have been introduced. Despite these flaws, the CPI is widely followed because its level is calculated and published monthly.

Consumer Price Index (CPI)
A statistical measure of a weighted average of prices of a specified set of goods and services purchased by typical consumers in urban areas.

Producer Price Index (PPI)
A statistical measure of a weighted average of prices of goods and services that firms produce and sell.

GDP deflator
A price index measuring the changes in prices of all new goods and services produced in the economy.

Personal Consumption Expenditure (PCE) Index
A statistical measure of average prices that uses annually updated weights based on surveys of consumer spending.

The PPI. There are a number of Producer Price Indexes, including one for foodstuffs, another for intermediate goods (goods used in the production of other goods), and one for finished goods. Most of the producer prices included are in mining, manufacturing, and agriculture. The PPIs can be considered general-purpose indexes for nonretail markets.

Although in the long run the various PPIs and the CPI generally show the same rate of inflation, such is not the case in the short run. Most often the PPIs increase before the CPI because it takes time for producer price increases to show up in the prices that consumers pay for final products. Often changes in the PPIs are watched closely as a hint that inflation is going to increase or decrease.

Go to www.econtoday.com/ch07 to obtain information about inflation and unemployment in other countries from the International Monetary Fund. Click on "World Economic Outlook Databases."

The GDP Deflator. The broadest price index reported in the United States is the GDP deflator, where GDP stands for gross domestic product, or annual total national income. Unlike the CPI and the PPIs, the GDP deflator is *not* based on a fixed market basket of goods and services. The basket is allowed to change with people's consumption and investment patterns. In this sense, the changes in the GDP deflator reflect both price changes and the public's market responses to those price changes. Why? Because new expenditure patterns are allowed to show up in the GDP deflator as people respond to changing prices.

The PCE Index. Another price index that takes into account changing expenditure patterns is the Personal Consumption Expenditure (PCE) Index. The Bureau of Economic Analysis, an agency of the U.S. Department of Commerce, uses continuously updated annual surveys of consumer purchases to construct the weights for the PCE Index. Thus, an advantage of the PCE Index is that weights in the index are updated every year. The Federal Reserve has used the rate of change in the PCE Index as its primary inflation indicator because Fed officials believe that the updated weights in the PCE Index make it more accurate than the CPI as a measure of consumer price changes. Nevertheless, the CPI remains the most widely reported price index, and the U.S. government continues to use the CPI to adjust the value of Social Security benefits to account for inflation.

What do you suppose that the PCE Index measure of inflation has revealed about recent year-to-year movements in the level of prices of services compared with the level of prices of physical goods?

EXAMPLE

So Far, Higher Prices for Services Trump Goods Deflation

The PCE Index measure of the price level reveals that since the mid-1960s, the inflation rate for services has, on average, been 2.6 percentage points higher than the inflation rate for physical goods. During the last 10 years, the difference between the rate of inflation for services and the inflation rate for goods has widened to nearly 5 percentage points.

The key factor accounting for the rising gap between inflation rates for services relative to goods has been a decrease in the rate of inflation for goods. Indeed, except for a brief period during early 2000, the overall level of prices of goods measured using the PCE Index has *declined* since the mid-1990s. According to the PCE Index, therefore, goods *deflation* has occurred.

Spending on services makes up 60 percent of personal expenditures on all goods and services. Consequently, the average level of prices that people pay for *all* items has increased each year. Nevertheless, goods deflation has contributed to keeping overall inflation lower than it would otherwise have been.

FOR CRITICAL ANALYSIS
Other things being equal, what would happen to the overall rate of inflation if goods deflation ended and goods inflation began?

Historical Changes in the CPI. Until the mid-1990s, the Consumer Price Index showed a fairly dramatic trend upward since about World War II. Figure 7-4 shows the annual rate of change in the CPI since 1860. Prior to World War II, there were numerous periods of deflation along with periods of inflation. Persistent year-in and year-out inflation seems to be a post–World War II phenomenon, at least in this country. As far back as before the American Revolution, prices used to rise during war periods but then would fall back toward prewar levels afterward. This occurred after the Revolutionary War, the War of 1812, the Civil War, and to a lesser extent World War I. Consequently, the overall price level in 1940 wasn't much different from 150 years earlier.

FIGURE 7-4

Inflation and Deflation in U.S. History

For 80 years after the Civil War, the United States experienced alternating inflation and deflation. Here we show them as reflected by changes in the Consumer Price Index. Since World War II, the periods of inflation have not been followed by periods of deflation; that is, even during peacetime, the price index has continued to rise. The shaded areas represent wartime.

Source: U.S. Department of Labor, Bureau of Labor Statistics.

QUICK QUIZ

Once we pick a market basket of goods, we can construct a **price index** that compares the cost of that market basket today with the cost of the same market basket in a _____ year.

The _____ _____ Index is the most often used price index in the United States. The Producer Price Index (PPI) is also widely mentioned.

The _____ _____ measures what is happening to the average price level of *all* new, domestically produced final goods and services in our economy.

The _____ _____ _____ Index uses annually updated weights from consumer spending surveys to measure average prices faced by consumers.

See page 183 for the answers. Review concepts from this section in MyEconLab.

ANTICIPATED VERSUS UNANTICIPATED INFLATION

To determine who is hurt by inflation and what the effects of inflation are in general, we have to distinguish between anticipated and unanticipated inflation. We will see that the effects on individuals and the economy are vastly different, depending on which type of inflation exists.

Anticipated inflation is the rate of inflation that most individuals believe will occur. If the rate of inflation this year turns out to be 10 percent, and that's about what most people thought it was going to be, we are in a situation of fully anticipated inflation.

Unanticipated inflation is inflation that comes as a surprise to individuals in the economy. For example, if the inflation rate in a particular year turns out to be 10 percent when on average people thought it was going to be 5 percent, there was unanticipated inflation—inflation greater than anticipated.

Some of the problems caused by inflation arise when it is unanticipated, because when it is anticipated, many people are able to protect themselves from its ravages. Keeping the distinction between anticipated and unanticipated inflation in mind, we can easily see the relationship between inflation and interest rates.

Inflation and Interest Rates

Let's start in a hypothetical world in which there is no inflation and anticipated inflation is zero. In that world, you may be able to borrow funds—to buy a house or a car, for example—at a **nominal rate of interest** of, say, 6 percent. If you borrow the funds to purchase a house or a car and your anticipation of inflation turns out to be accurate, neither you nor the lender will have been fooled. Each dollar you pay back in the years to come will be just as valuable in terms of purchasing power as the dollar that you borrowed.

What you ordinarily want to know when you borrow is the *real* rate of interest that you will have to pay. The **real rate of interest** is defined as the nominal rate of interest minus the anticipated rate of inflation. If you are able to borrow funds at 6 percent and you anticipated an inflation rate of 6 percent, your real rate of interest would be zero—lucky you, particularly if the actual rate of inflation turned out to be 6 percent. In effect, we can say that the nominal rate of interest is equal to the real rate of interest plus an *inflationary*

Anticipated inflation
The inflation rate that we believe will occur; when it does, we are in a situation of fully anticipated inflation.

Unanticipated inflation
Inflation at a rate that comes as a surprise, either higher or lower than the rate anticipated.

Nominal rate of interest
The market rate of interest expressed in today's dollars.

Real rate of interest
The nominal rate of interest minus the anticipated rate of inflation.

premium to take account of anticipated inflation. That inflationary premium covers depreciation in the purchasing power of the dollars repaid by borrowers. (Whenever there are relatively high rates of anticipated inflation, we must add an additional factor to the inflationary premium—the product of the real rate of interest times the anticipated rate of inflation. Usually, this last term is omitted because the anticipated rate of inflation is not high enough to make much of a difference.)

Does Inflation Necessarily Hurt Everyone?

Most people think that inflation is bad. After all, inflation means higher prices, and when we have to pay higher prices, are we not necessarily worse off? The truth is that inflation affects different people differently. Its effects also depend on whether it is anticipated or unanticipated.

Unanticipated Inflation: Creditors Lose and Debtors Gain.
In most situations, unanticipated inflation benefits borrowers because the nominal interest rate they are being charged does not fully compensate creditors for the inflation that actually occurred. In other words, the lender did not anticipate inflation correctly. Whenever inflation rates are underestimated for the life of a loan, creditors lose and debtors gain. Periods of considerable unanticipated (higher than anticipated) inflation occurred in the late 1960s and all of the 1970s. During those years, creditors lost and debtors gained.

Protecting Against Inflation.
Banks attempt to protect themselves against inflation by raising nominal interest rates to reflect anticipated inflation. Adjustable-rate mortgages in fact do just that: The interest rate varies according to what happens to interest rates in the economy. Workers can protect themselves from inflation by obtaining **cost-of-living adjustments (COLAs),** which are automatic increases in wage rates to take account of increases in the price level.

To the extent that you hold non-interest-bearing cash, you will lose because of inflation. If you have put $100 in a mattress and the inflation rate is 10 percent for the year, you will have lost 10 percent of the purchasing power of that $100. If you have your funds in a non-interest-bearing checking account, you will suffer the same fate. Individuals attempt to reduce the cost of holding cash by putting it into interest-bearing accounts, a wide variety of which often pay nominal rates of interest that reflect anticipated inflation.

Cost-of-living adjustments (COLAs)
Clauses in contracts that allow for increases in specified nominal values to take account of changes in the cost of living.

The Resource Cost of Inflation.
Some economists believe that the main cost of inflation is the opportunity cost of resources used to protect against distortions that inflation introduces as firms attempt to plan for the long run. Individuals have to spend time and resources to figure out ways to adjust their behavior in case inflation is different from what it has been in the past. That may mean spending a longer time working out more complicated contracts for employment, for purchases of goods in the future, and for purchases of raw materials.

Inflation requires that price lists be changed. This is called the **repricing,** or **menu, cost of inflation.** The higher the rate of inflation, the higher the repricing cost of inflation, because prices must be changed more often within a given period of time.

Are the costs of inflation borne equally across all members of society?

Repricing, or menu, cost of inflation
The cost associated with recalculating prices and printing new price lists when there is inflation.

POLICY EXAMPLE

How Pervasive Is "Inflation Inequality" in the United States?

Rates of changes in price indexes provide an indication of the inflation experienced by the "average" household. But every household's spending undoubtedly departs from the average in some way. Recently, Federal Reserve Bank of New York economists Bart Hobijn and David Lagakos investigated just how much "inflation inequality" exists in the United States. They found evidence of substantial disparities in household-specific inflation rates, resulting mainly from differing levels of consumption of three categories of goods: education, health care, and gasoline. Households with children enrolled in college or with more elderly members purchasing greater amounts of health care tend to experience higher inflation than many other households. In addition, households whose members commute relatively long distances in automobiles naturally consume more gasoline, and the price of this commodity has risen faster than other prices in recent years.

Nevertheless, Hobijn and Lagakos found that a household that faces higher inflation than others typically does so only for a short time. Deviations of household-specific inflation from the inflation experienced by an "average" household do not last for more than a year. To the extent that inflation inequality exists, it is neither pervasive nor persistent. Hence, overall inflation measures do provide an indication of the inflation costs confronted by a typical household.

FOR CRITICAL ANALYSIS
If policymakers found that pervasive and persistent inflation inequality really existed, how might they alter a price index such as the CPI or the PCE Index to attach more importance to prices of items that contribute to such inequality? (Hint: Recall that the CPI and the PCE Index are weighted averages of all items' prices.)

QUICK QUIZ

Whenever **inflation** is _____ than anticipated, creditors lose and debtors gain. Whenever the rate of inflation is _____ than anticipated, creditors gain and debtors lose.

Holders of cash lose during periods of inflation because the _____ _____ of their cash depreciates at the rate of inflation.

Households and businesses spend resources in attempting to protect themselves against the prospect of inflation, thus imposing a _____ cost on the economy.

See page 183 for the answers. Review concepts from this section in MyEconLab.

CHANGING INFLATION AND UNEMPLOYMENT: BUSINESS FLUCTUATIONS

Business fluctuations
The ups and downs in business activity throughout the economy.

Expansion
A business fluctuation in which the pace of national economic activity is speeding up.

Contraction
A business fluctuation during which the pace of national economic activity is slowing down.

Some years unemployment goes up, and some years it goes down. Some years there is a lot of inflation, and other years there isn't. We have fluctuations in all aspects of our macroeconomy. The ups and downs in economywide economic activity are sometimes called **business fluctuations.** When business fluctuations are positive, they are called **expansions**—speedups in the pace of national economic activity. The opposite of an expansion is a **contraction,** which is a slowdown in the pace of national economic activity. The top of an expansion is usually called its *peak,* and the bottom of a contraction is usually called its *trough.* Business fluctuations used to be called *business cycles,* but that term no longer seems appropriate because *cycle* implies regular or automatic recurrence, and we have never had automatic recurrent fluctuations in general business and economic activity.

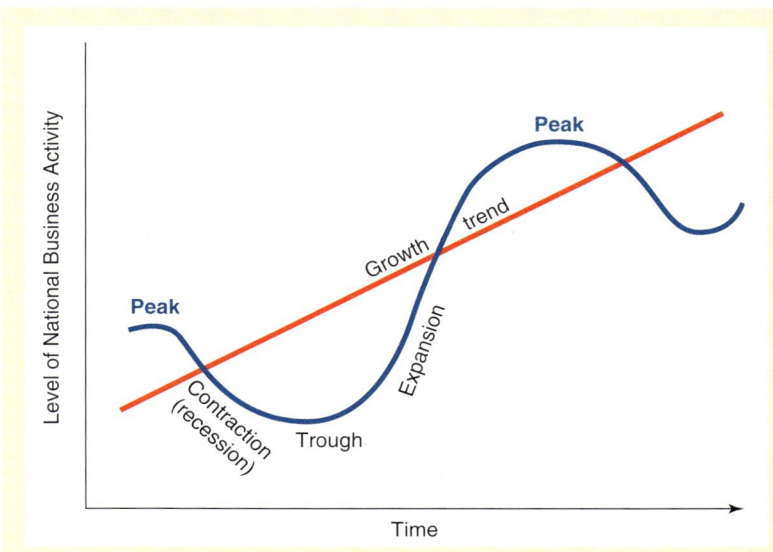

FIGURE 7-5
The Idealized Course of Business Fluctuations
A hypothetical business cycle would go from peak to trough and back again in a regular cycle.

What we have had are contractions and expansions that vary greatly in length. For example, the 10 post–World War II expansions have averaged 57 months, but three of those exceeded 90 months, and two lasted less than 25 months.

If the contractionary phase of business fluctuations becomes severe enough, we call it a **recession.** An extremely severe recession is called a **depression.** Typically, at the beginning of a recession, interest rates rise and as the recession gets worse, they fall. In addition, people's incomes start to fall, and the duration of unemployment increases so that the unemployment rate increases. In times of expansion, the opposite occurs.

In Figure 7-5, you see that typical business fluctuations occur around a growth trend in overall national business activity shown as a straight upward-sloping line. Starting out at a peak, the economy goes into a contraction (recession). Then an expansion starts that moves up to its peak, higher than the last one, and the sequence starts over again.

Recession
A period of time during which the rate of growth of business activity is consistently less than its long-term trend or is negative.

Depression
An extremely severe recession.

A Historical Picture of Business Activity in the United States

Figure 7-6 on the following page traces changes in U.S. business activity from 1880 to the present. Note that the long-term trend line is shown as horizontal, so all changes in business activity focus around that trend line. Major changes in business activity in the United States occurred during the Great Depression and World War II. Note that none of the actual business fluctuations that you see in Figure 7-6 exactly mirror the idealized course of a business fluctuation shown in Figure 7-5.

Go to www.econtoday.com/ch07 to learn about how economists at the National Bureau of Economic Research formally determine when a recession is under way.

Explaining Business Fluctuations: External Shocks

As you might imagine, because changes in national business activity affect everyone, economists for decades have attempted to understand and explain business fluctuations. For years, one of the most obvious explanations has been external events that tend to disrupt the economy. In many of the graphs in this chapter, you have seen that World War II was a critical point in this nation's economic history. A war is certainly an external shock—something that originates outside our economy.

FIGURE 7-6

National Business Activity, 1880 to the Present

Variations around the trend of U.S. business activity have been frequent since 1880.

Sources: *American Business Activity from 1790 to Today*, 67th ed., AmeriTrust Co., January 1996, plus author's projections.

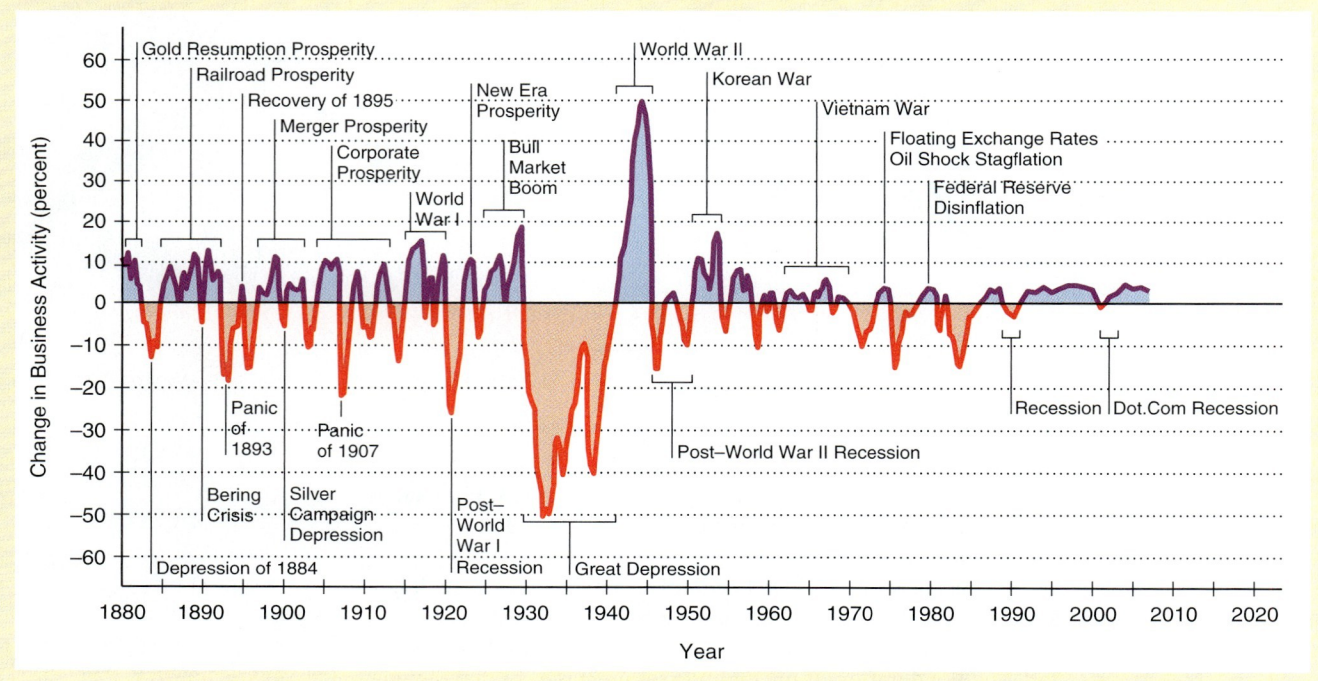

To try to help account for external shocks that may induce business fluctuations and thereby make fluctuations easier to predict, the U.S. Department of Commerce and private firms and organizations tabulate indexes (weighted averages) of **leading indicators.** These are events that economists have noticed typically occur *before* changes in business activity. For example, economic downturns often follow such events as a reduction in the average workweek, an increase in unemployment insurance claims, a decrease in the prices of raw materials, or a drop in the quantity of money in circulation.

To better understand the role of shocks in influencing business fluctuations, we need a theory of why national economic activity changes. The remainder of the macro chapters in this book develop the models that will help you understand the ups and downs of our business fluctuations.

Leading indicators
Events that have been found to occur before changes in business activity.

QUICK QUIZ

The ups and downs in economywide business activity are called _____ _____, which consist of **expansions** and **contractions** in overall business activity.

The lowest point of a contraction is called the _____; the highest point of an expansion is called the _____.

A _____ is a downturn in business activity for some length of time.

One possible explanation for business fluctuations relates to _____ _____, such as wars, dramatic increases in the prices of raw materials, and earthquakes, floods, and droughts.

See page 183 for the answers. Review concepts from this section in MyEconLab.

CASE STUDY: ECONOMICS FRONT AND CENTER

Looking to France for Answers

Moreau is a member of the parliament of an island nation that has strong historical and economic ties to France. He has been assigned to a committee that is developing legislative proposals for addressing the country's unemployment problem. The unemployment rate has exceeded 12 percent for several years, and recently it has been trending even higher.

One of Moreau's colleagues has suggested that parliament should consider passing a law similar to one that has been in force in France since the late 1990s. This law restricts each individual worker below the level of senior manager from being on the job more than an average of 35 hours per week. Moreau's colleague suggests that if the hours of people who have jobs are restricted, companies will have to hire additional workers. Therefore, the colleague argues, more people will become employed, and the unemployment rate will fall.

Moreau notes, however, that in 2005 the French government amended the law to allow some employees to exchange a modest amount of leisure time for overtime pay. This change was made after the original version of the law failed to bring about a decline in the French unemployment rate, which has remained in the neighborhood of 10 percent. Moreau concludes that because the French effort to reduce the unemployment rate by restricting time spent working failed, virtually identical legislation is unlikely to reduce the rate of unemployment in his own country.

CRITICAL ANALYSIS QUESTIONS

1. When faced with legal limits on how many hours current employees may work each week, in what ways, other than by hiring more workers, might employers respond?

2. If the French labor force remained unchanged and the unemployment rate did not change, what must have been true of the rate of employment in France since the 35-hour restriction on the workweek was put in place?

Issues and Applications

Wal-Mart, Product Quality, and the CPI

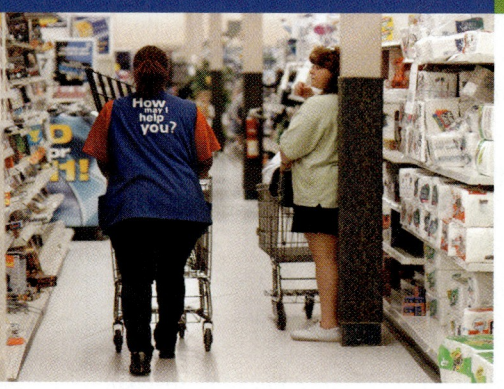

Concepts Applied
- Price Indexes
- Consumer Price Index
- Inflation

It is not unusual for Kroger, Albertsons, or Safeway to close down a grocery store in a community around the time that a Wal-Mart supercenter food outlet opens its doors, because Wal-Mart offers lower prices on most food items. In addition, it is not unusual for data collectors for the Bureau of Labor Statistics (BLS), which computes the Consumer Price Index, to stop by the Wal-Mart supercenter to check on prices of various items it sells. When statisticians receive the price data, however, they record the prices charged by a nearby Kroger, Albertsons, or Safeway store, instead of the often-lower prices actually observed at the Wal-Mart supercenter. Thus, as far as the BLS is concerned, the lower Wal-Mart prices must reflect a lower quality resulting from the sale of the items by Wal-Mart instead of a traditional grocer.

Quality Adjustment and the CPI

It has long been recognized that failure to adjust the CPI to reflect quality changes can introduce bias. For instance, when pocket calculators first appeared around 1970, a basic model selling for nearly $150 (in today's dollars, or $38 in 1970 dollars) performed four basic functions: addition, subtraction, multiplication, and division. Over time, of course, calculator prices declined. In addition, calculator producers began adding more functions. First, a square root key appeared. Then, "memory" buttons were added. Eventually, all manner of functions, keys, and buttons appeared on calculators. Consequently, nowadays a $150 outlay can obtain a calculator that will perform dozens of functions more than the four basic functions a 1970 calculator could perform. This implies, of course, that the quality-adjusted price of a $150 calculator is much lower today than it was in 1970.

In recent years, the BLS has sought to take into account the effects of quality changes by using statistical models to estimate how an item's price reflects its features. If a new model of a 27-inch television set appears at retail stores at the same $329.99 price as last year but with a better screen and other minor improvements, the BLS may determine that the quality-adjusted price has fallen to, say, $255.77. The BLS then uses this quality-adjusted price when calculating the CPI.

Does Wal-Mart Get Lost in CPI Calculations?

When tabulating the prices of grocery items sold by supercenter stores operated by Wal-Mart and Kmart, wholesalers such as Costco and Sam's Club, or mass merchants such as

Target, the BLS also makes a quality adjustment. In this instance, however, the BLS does not use sophisticated statistical models to value the features of Wal-Mart and other operators of supercenter stores compared with those of traditional grocers. Instead, the BLS uses what it calls a "linking procedure" that *assumes* that quality-adjusted prices of items sold at large supercenter stores must be the same as the prices of identical items sold at traditional supermarkets. Effectively, the BLS presumes that the experience of shopping at supercenters entails a quality *reduction,* which explains why supercenter operators such as Wal-Mart sell their products for less.

Jerry Hausman of the Massachusetts Institute of Technology has studied this BLS assumption and concluded that it has no basis in fact. Wal-Mart and other supercenters, he argues, sell products for less because their costs are lower and not necessarily because shoppers perceive that the quality is lower. Hausman finds that the failure to recognize supercenters' lower grocery prices as *truly* lower causes the BLS to overstate the annual rate of increase in home food prices by as much as 0.4 percentage point. Food is such an important product category in the CPI that, by Hausman's calculation, the annual CPI inflation rate may be only 85 percent as high as the BLS reports each year. Thus, in the case of supercenter grocery prices, BLS quality adjustments may result in an upward bias in the rate of CPI inflation.

Log in to **MyEconLab,** click on "Economic News," and test your understanding of the chapter by answering interactive questions that relate directly to this issue.

For Critical Analysis

1. Why might quality adjustment of the prices of electronic devices, computers, and information-technology products be particularly important for calculating a CPI that is suitable for year-to-year comparisons over the past three or four decades?

2. If there really were evidence that consumers view otherwise identical products purchased at Wal-Mart as being of lower quality, would it be appropriate to make an upward quality adjustment of those prices?

Web Resources

1. To learn about how the BLS computes quality-adjusted prices of audio electronic products, go to www.econtoday.com/ch07.

2. For a discussion of how the BLS performs quality adjustments when evaluating the prices of college textbooks, go to www.econtoday.com/ch07.

Research Project

Identify a general category of items other than electronic devices, computers, or information-technology equipment that you think has likely experienced a quality change in recent years. In your view, has the quality of this set of goods or services increased or decreased over time? Based on your answers to the previous questions, if the BLS were to quality-adjust the prices of these goods over the past several years, would the adjustments cause the values of the CPI in past years to be lower or higher than without the quality adjustments? In light of your answer, explain how making the quality adjustments you have suggested would alter the rate of CPI inflation in recent years.

Here is what you should know after reading this chapter. MyEconLab will help you identify what you know, and where to go when you need to practice.

WHAT YOU SHOULD KNOW		WHERE TO GO TO PRACTICE
How the U.S. Government Calculates the Official Unemployment Rate The total number of workers who are officially unemployed are noninstitutionalized people aged 16 or older who are willing and able to work and who are actively looking for work but have not found a job. To calculate the unemployment rate, the government determines what percentage this quantity is of the labor force, which consists of all noninstitutionalized people aged 16 years or older who either have jobs or are available for and actively seeking employment. Thus, the official unemployment rate does not include discouraged workers who have stopped looking for work because they are convinced that they will not find suitable employment; these individuals are not included in the labor force.	unemployment, 160 labor force, 160 stock, 162 flow, 162 job loser, 162 reentrant, 162 job leaver, 162 new entrant, 162 discouraged workers, 163 labor force participation rate, 163 **Key figure** Figure 7-3, 163	• **MyEconLab** Study Plan 7.1 • Audio introduction to Chapter 7 • Animated Figure 7-3
The Types of Unemployment Workers who are temporarily unemployed because they are searching for appropriate job offers are frictionally unemployed. The structurally unemployed lack the skills currently required by prospective employers. People unemployed due to business contractions are said to be cyclically unemployed. And certain workers can find themselves seasonally unemployed because of the seasonal patterns of occupations within specific industries. The natural unemployment rate is the seasonally adjusted rate of unemployment including only those who are frictionally and structurally unemployed during a given interval.	frictional unemployment, 164 structural unemployment, 165 cyclical unemployment, 165 seasonal unemployment, 165 full employment, 166 natural rate of unemployment, 166	• **MyEconLab** Study Plans 7.2 and 7.3 • Video: Major Types of Unemployment
How Price Indexes Are Calculated and Key Price Indexes To calculate any price index, economists multiply 100 times the ratio of the cost of a market basket of goods and services in the current year to the cost of the same market basket in a base year. The market basket used to compute the Consumer Price Index (CPI) is a weighted set of goods and services purchased by a typical consumer in urban areas. The Producer Price Index (PPI) is a weighted average of prices of goods sold by a typical firm. The GDP deflator measures changes in the overall level of prices of all goods produced in the economy during a given interval. The Personal Consumption Expenditure (PCE) Index is a statistical measure of average prices using weights from annual surveys of consumer spending.	inflation, 168 deflation, 168 purchasing power, 168 price index, 168 base year, 168 Consumer Price Index (CPI), 169 Producer Price Index (PPI), 169 GDP deflator, 169 Personal Consumption Expenditure (PCE) Index, 169 **Key figure** Figure 7-4, 171	• **MyEconLab** Study Plan 7.4 • Video: Measuring the Rate of Inflation • Video: Inflation and Interest Rates • Animated Figure 7-4

CHAPTER 7 The Macroeconomy: Unemployment, Inflation, and Deflation

WHAT YOU SHOULD KNOW		WHERE TO GO TO PRACTICE
Nominal Interest Rate versus Real Interest Rate The nominal interest rate is the market rate of interest applying to contracts expressed in current dollars. The real interest rate is net of inflation that borrowers and lenders anticipate will erode the value of nominal interest payments during the period that a loan is repaid. Hence the real interest rate equals the nominal interest rate minus the expected inflation rate.	anticipated inflation, 172 unanticipated inflation, 172 nominal rate of interest, 172 real rate of interest, 172	• MyEconLab Study Plan 7.5
Losers and Gainers from Inflation Creditors lose as a result of unanticipated inflation, or inflation that comes as a surprise after they have made a loan, because the real value of the interest payments they receive will turn out to be lower than they had expected. Borrowers gain when unanticipated inflation occurs, because the real value of their interest and principal payments declines. Key costs of inflation are the expenses that individuals and businesses incur to protect themselves against inflation, costs of altering business plans because of unexpected changes in prices, and menu costs arising from expenses incurred in repricing goods and services.	cost-of-living adjustments (COLAs), 173 repricing, or menu, cost of inflation, 173	• MyEconLab Study Plan 7.5
Key Features of Business Fluctuations Business fluctuations are increases and decreases in business activity. A positive fluctuation is an expansion, which is an upward movement in business activity from a trough, or low point, to a peak, or high point. A negative fluctuation is a contraction, which is a drop in the pace of business activity from a previous peak to a new trough.	business fluctuations, 174 expansion, 174 contraction, 174 recession, 175 depression, 175 leading indicators, 176 **Key figure** Figure 7-6, 176	• MyEconLab Study Plan 7.6 • Animated Figure 7-6

Log in to MyEconLab, take a chapter test, and get a personalized Study Plan that tells you which concepts you understand and which ones you need to review. From there, MyEconLab will give you further practice, tutorials, animations, videos, and guided solutions.

Log in to www.myeconlab.com

PROBLEMS

*Select problems, indicated by a blue oval, are assignable in **MyEconLab**.*
Answers to the odd-numbered problems appear at the back of the book.

7-1 Suppose that you are given the following information:

Total population	300.0 million
Adult, noninstitutionalized, nonmilitary population	200.0 million
Unemployment	7.5 million

a. If the labor force participation rate is 70 percent, what is the labor force?
b. How many workers are employed?
c. What is the unemployment rate?

7-2 Suppose that you are given the following information:

Labor force	206.2 million
Adults in the military	1.5 million
Nonadult population	48.0 million
Employed adults	196.2 million
Institutionalized adults	3.5 million
Nonmilitary, noninstitutionalized adults not in labor force	40.8 million

a. What is the total population?
b. How many people are unemployed, and what is the unemployment rate?
c. What is the labor force participation rate?

7-3 Suppose that the U.S. adult population is 200 million, the number employed is 152 million, and the number unemployed is 8 million.

a. What is the unemployment rate?
b. Suppose that there is a difference of 40 million between the adult population and the combined total of people who are employed and unemployed. How do we classify these 40 million people? Based on these figures, what is the U.S. labor force participation rate?

7-4 During the course of a year, the labor force consists of the same 1,000 people. Of these, 20 lack skills that employers desire and hence remain unemployed throughout the year. At the same time, every month during the year, 30 different people become unemployed, and 30 other different people who were unemployed find jobs. There is no seasonal employment.

a. What is the frictional unemployment rate?
b. What is the unemployment rate?
c. Suppose that a system of unemployment compensation is established. Each month, 30 new people (not including the 20 lacking required skills) continue to become unemployed, but each monthly group of newly unemployed now takes two months to find a job. After this change, what is the frictional unemployment rate?
d. After the change discussed in part (c), what is the unemployment rate?

7-5 Suppose that a nation has a labor force of 100 people. In January, Amy, Barbara, Carine, and Denise are unemployed; in February, those four find jobs, but Evan, Francesco, George, and Horatio become unemployed. Suppose further that every month, the previous four who were unemployed find jobs and four different people become unemployed. Throughout the year, however, the same three people—Ito, Jack, and Kelley—continually remain unemployed because their skills are a poor match with employers' requirements.

a. What is this nation's frictional unemployment rate?
b. What is its structural unemployment rate?
c. What is its unemployment rate?

7-6 In a country with a labor force of 200, a different group of 10 people becomes unemployed each month, but becomes employed once again a month later. No others outside these groups are unemployed.

a. What is this country's unemployment rate?
b. What is the average duration of unemployment?
c. Suppose that establishment of a system of unemployment compensation increases to two months the interval that it takes each group of job losers to become employed each month. Nevertheless, a different group of 10 people still becomes unemployed each month. Now what is the average duration of unemployment?
d. Following the change discussed in part (c), what is the country's unemployment rate?

7-7 A nation's frictional unemployment rate is 1 percent. Seasonal unemployment does not exist in this country. Its cyclical rate of unemployment is 3 percent, and its structural unemployment rate is 4 percent. What is this nation's overall rate of unemployment? What is its natural rate of unemployment?

7-8 In 2006, the cost of a market basket of goods was $2,000. In 2008, the cost of the same market basket of goods was $2,100. Use the price index formula to calculate the price index for 2008 if 2006 is the base year.

7-9 Consider the following price indexes: 90 in 2007, 100 in 2008, 110 in 2009, 121 in 2010, and 150 in 2011. Answer the following questions.

a. What is the base year?
b. What is the inflation rate from 2008 to 2009?
c. What is the inflation rate from 2009 to 2010?
d. If the cost of a market basket in 2008 is $2,000, what is the cost of the same basket of goods and services in 2007? In 2011?

7-10 The real interest rate is 4 percent, and the nominal interest rate is 6 percent. What is the anticipated rate of inflation?

7-11 Currently, the price index used to calculate the inflation rate is equal to 90. The general expectation throughout the economy is that next year its value will be 99. The current nominal interest rate is 12 percent. What is the real interest rate?

7-12 At present, the nominal interest rate is 7 percent, and the expected inflation rate is 5 percent. The current year is the base year for the price index used to calculate inflation.

a. What is the real interest rate?
b. What is the anticipated value of the price index next year?

7-13 Suppose that in 2011 there is a sudden, unanticipated burst of inflation. Consider the situations faced by the following individuals. Who gains and who loses?

a. A homeowner whose wages will keep pace with inflation in 2011 but whose monthly mortgage payments to a savings bank will remain fixed
b. An apartment landlord who has guaranteed to his tenants that their monthly rent payments during 2011 will be the same as they were during 2010
c. A banker who made an auto loan that the auto buyer will repay at a fixed rate of interest during 2011
d. A retired individual who earns a pension with fixed monthly payments from her past employer during 2011

7-14 Consider the diagram in the next column. The line represents the economy's growth trend, and the curve represents the economy's actual course of business fluctuations. For each part below, provide the letter label from the portion of the curve that corresponds to the associated term.

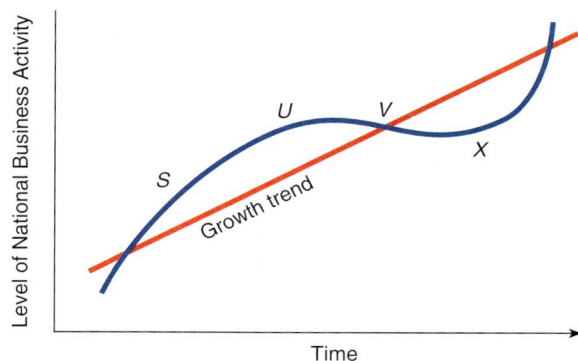

a. Contraction
b. Peak
c. Trough
d. Expansion
e. Recession

ECONOMICS ON THE NET

Looking at the Unemployment and Inflation Data This chapter reviewed key concepts relating to unemployment and inflation. In this application, you get a chance to examine U.S. unemployment and inflation data on your own.

Title: Bureau of Labor Statistics: Employment and Unemployment

Navigation: Use the link at www.econtoday.com/ch07 to visit the "Employment & Unemployment" page of the Bureau of Labor Statistics (BLS). Click on *Labor Force Statistics from the Current Population Survey*.

Application Perform the indicated operations, and answer the following questions.

1. Click checkmarks in the boxes for Civilian Labor Force, Employment Level, and Unemployment Level. Retrieve the data. Can you identify periods of sharp cyclical swings? Do they show up in data for the labor force, employment, or unemployment?

2. Are cyclical factors important?

For Group Study and Analysis Divide the class into groups, and assign a price index to each group. Ask each group to take a look at the index for All Years at the link to the BLS statistics on inflation at www.econtoday.com/ch07. Have each group identify periods during which their index accelerated or decelerated (or even fell). Do the indexes ever provide opposing implications about inflation and deflation?

ANSWERS TO QUICK QUIZZES

p. 164: (i) Unemployed . . . labor force; (ii) job losers . . . reentrants . . . job leavers . . . new entrants; (iii) increase; (iv) female
p. 167: (i) Frictional . . . Structural; (ii) natural
p. 172: (i) base; (ii) Consumer Price; (iii) GDP deflator; (iv) Personal Consumption Expenditure
p. 174: (i) greater . . . less; (ii) purchasing power; (iii) resource
p. 176: (i) business fluctuations; (ii) trough . . . peak; (iii) recession; (iv) external shocks

8 Measuring the Economy's Performance

Learning Objectives

After reading this chapter, you should be able to:

1. Describe the circular flow of income and output
2. Define gross domestic product (GDP)
3. Understand the limitations of using GDP as a measure of national welfare
4. Explain the expenditure approach to tabulating GDP
5. Explain the income approach to computing GDP
6. Distinguish between nominal GDP and real GDP

MyEconLab helps you master each objective and study more efficiently. See end of chapter for details.

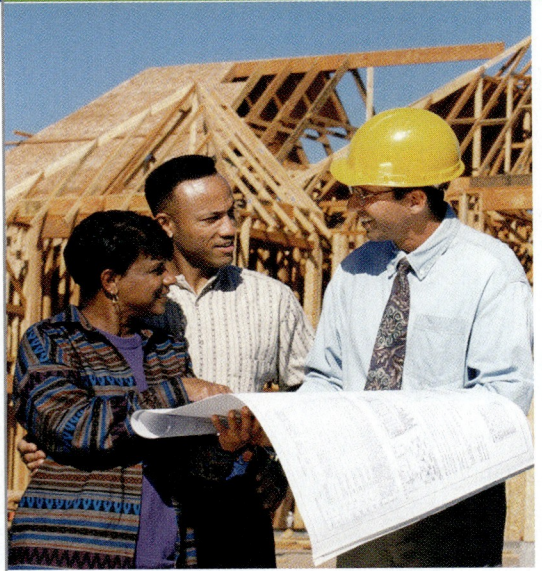

It is late in August, and more than 16 million students are preparing for their first day of fall semester classes at colleges and universities around the country. What economic forecasters and the financial news media are anticipating, however, is a news release by the U.S. government's Bureau of Economic Analysis (BEA). In July, the BEA released an advance estimate of the value of total production of new goods and services during the period from April 1 to June 30. This estimate had indicated that the nation's economic performance was slipping. Now rumors are swirling that the BEA is about to release a sharply altered revised estimate and that the revision will be in a downward direction.

How does the BEA attempt to gauge the U.S. economy's performance? You will find out in this chapter.

Did You Know That...

before the 2000s, the Bureau of Economic Analysis treated business expenses on computer software as "purchased inputs"? This meant that the BEA regarded business spending on software solely as an expense item, much like paper is an expense for newspaper publishers. Thus, business software was not explicitly included in *gross domestic product,* the government's key measure of overall economic activity.

Today, the BEA treats business spending on software as a final purchase that is part of national output. To make it possible to compare today's national output to the levels of years past, the BEA revised its measures of the inflation-adjusted value of national output for the 1980s and 1990s. It found that including business software as part of total national output made the recession of 1990–1991 appear much milder. When it had excluded business software expenditures, the reported decline in national output during that recession was 2.7 percent. After it included business spending on software and recalculated, the BEA found that there was a much smaller 1.8 percent decline in national output.

Clearly, it matters how the government conducts what has become known as **national income accounting** in an effort to measure the nation's overall economic performance. How this is done is the main focus of this chapter. But first we need to look at the flow of income within an economy, for it is the flow of goods and services from businesses to consumers and of payments from consumers to businesses that constitutes economic activity.

National income accounting
A measurement system used to estimate national income and its components; one approach to measuring an economy's aggregate performance.

THE SIMPLE CIRCULAR FLOW

The concept of a circular flow of income (ignoring taxes) involves two principles:

1. In every economic exchange, the seller receives exactly the same amount that the buyer spends.
2. Goods and services flow in one direction and money payments flow in the other.

In the simple economy shown in Figure 8-1 on the following page, there are only businesses and households. It is assumed that businesses sell their *entire* output *immediately* to households and that households spend their *entire* income *immediately* on consumer products. Households receive their income by selling the use of whatever factors of production they own, such as labor services.

Profits Explained

We have indicated in Figure 8-1 that profit is a cost of production. You might be under the impression that profits are not part of the cost of producing goods and services, but profits are indeed a part of this cost because entrepreneurs must be rewarded for providing their services or they won't provide them. Their reward, if any, is profit. The reward—the profit—is included in the cost of the factors of production. If there were no expectations of profit, entrepreneurs would not incur the risk associated with the organization of productive activities. That is why we consider profits a cost of doing business.

Total Income or Total Output

The arrow that goes from businesses to households at the bottom of Figure 8-1 is labeled "Total income." What would be a good definition of **total income?** If you answered "the total of all individuals' income," you would be right. But all income is actually a payment for something, whether it be wages paid for labor services, rent paid for the use of land, interest

Total income
The yearly amount earned by the nation's resources (factors of production). Total income therefore includes wages, rent, interest payments, and profits that are received by workers, landowners, capital owners, and entrepreneurs, respectively.

FIGURE 8-1
The Circular Flow of Income and Product

Businesses provide final goods and services to households (upper clockwise loop), who in turn pay for them (upper counterclockwise loop). Payments flow in a counterclockwise direction and can be thought of as a circular flow. The dollar value of output is identical to total income because profits are defined as being equal to total business receipts minus business outlays for wages, rents, and interest. Households provide factor services to businesses and receive income (lower loops).

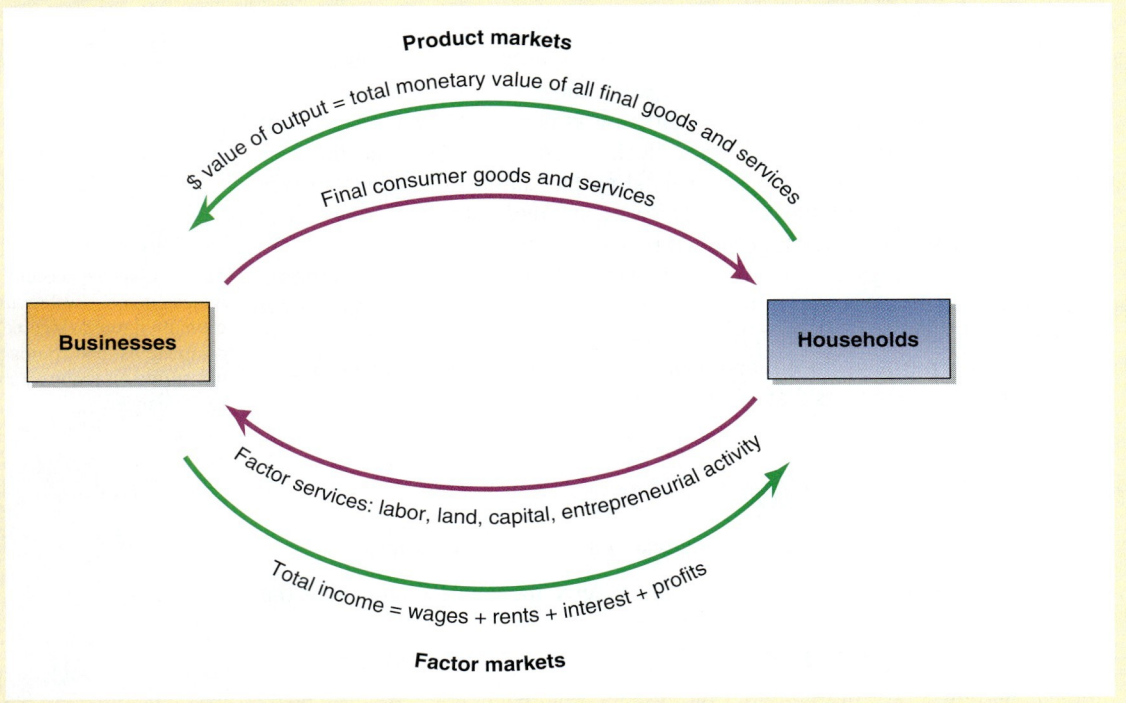

Final goods and services
Goods and services that are at their final stage of production and will not be transformed into yet other goods or services. For example, wheat is not ordinarily considered a final good because it is usually used to make a final good, bread.

paid for the use of capital, or profits paid to entrepreneurs. It is the amount paid to the resource suppliers. Therefore, total income is also defined as the annual *cost* of producing the entire output of **final goods and services.**

The arrow going from households to businesses at the top of the figure represents the dollar value of output in the economy. This is equal to the total monetary value of all final goods and services for this simple economy. In essence, it represents the total business receipts from the sale of all final goods and services produced by businesses and consumed by households. Business receipts are the opposite side of household expenditures. When households purchase goods and services, those payments become a *business receipt*. Every transaction, therefore, simultaneously involves an expenditure and a receipt.

Product Markets. Transactions in which households buy goods take place in the product markets—that's where households are the buyers and businesses are the sellers of consumer goods. *Product market* transactions are represented in the upper loops in Figure 8-1. Note that consumer goods and services flow to household demanders, while money flows in the opposite direction to business suppliers.

Factor Markets. *Factor market* transactions are represented by the lower loops in Figure 8-1. In the factor market, households are the sellers; they sell resources such as labor, land, capital, and entrepreneurial ability. Businesses are the buyers in factor markets; business expenditures represent receipts or, more simply, income for households. Also, in the lower loops of Figure 8-1, factor services flow from households to businesses, while the money paid for these services flows in the opposite direction from businesses to households. Observe also the flow of money (counterclockwise) from households to businesses and back again from businesses to households: It is an endless circular flow.

Why the Dollar Value of Total Output Must Equal Total Income

Total income represents the income received by households in payment for the production of goods and services. Why must total income be identical to the dollar value of total output? First, as Figure 8-1 shows, spending by one group is income to another. Second, it is a matter of simple accounting and the economic definition of profit as a cost of production. Profit is defined as what is *left over* from total business receipts after all other costs—wages, rents, interest—have been paid. If the dollar value of total output is $1,000 and the total of wages, rent, and interest for producing that output is $900, profit is $100. Profit is always the *residual* item that makes total income equal to the dollar value of total output.

> **QUICK QUIZ**
>
> In the circular flow model of income and output, households sell _____ services to businesses that pay for those services. The receipt of payments is total _____. Businesses sell goods and services to households that pay for them.
>
> The dollar value of total output is equal to the total monetary value of all _____ goods and services produced.
>
> The dollar value of final output must always equal total income; the variable that adjusts to make this so is known as _____.
>
> See page 212 for the answers. Review concepts from this section in MyEconLab.

NATIONAL INCOME ACCOUNTING

We have already mentioned that policymakers need information about the state of the national economy. Historical statistical records on the performance of the national economy aid economists in testing their theories about how the economy really works. National income accounting is therefore important. Let's start with the most commonly presented statistic on the national economy.

Gross Domestic Product (GDP)

Gross domestic product (GDP) represents the total market value of the nation's annual final product, or output, produced per year by factors of production located within national borders. We therefore formally define GDP as the total market value of all final goods and services produced in an economy during a year. We are referring here to the value of a *flow of production*. A nation produces at a certain rate, just as you receive income at a certain rate. Your income flow might be at a rate of $5,000 per year or $50,000 per year. Suppose

Gross domestic product (GDP)
The total market value of all final goods and services produced by factors of production located within a nation's borders.

you are told that someone earns $500. Would you consider this a good salary? There is no way to answer that question unless you know whether the person is earning $500 per month or per week or per day. Thus, you have to specify a time period for all flows. Income received is a flow. You must contrast this with, for example, your total accumulated savings, which are a stock measured at a point in time, not over time. Implicit in just about everything we deal with in this chapter is a time period—usually one year. All the measures of domestic product and income are specified as *rates* measured in dollars per year.

Stress on Final Output

Intermediate goods
Goods used up entirely in the production of final goods.

GDP does not count **intermediate goods** (goods used up entirely in the production of final goods) because to do so would be to count them twice. For example, even though grain that a farmer produces may be that farmer's final product, it is not the final product for the nation. It is sold to make bread. Bread is the final product.

Value added
The dollar value of an industry's sales minus the value of intermediate goods (for example, raw materials and parts) used in production.

We can use a numerical example to clarify this point further. Our example will involve determining the value added at each stage of production. **Value added** is the amount of dollar value contributed to a product at each stage of its production. In Table 8-1, we see the difference between total value of all sales and value added in the production of a donut. We also see that the sum of the values added is equal to the sale price to the final consumer. It is the

TABLE 8-1

Sales Value and Value Added at Each Stage of Donut Production

(1) Stage of Production	(2) Dollar Value of Sales	(3) Value Added
Stage 1: Fertilizer and seed	$.03	$.03
Stage 2: Growing	.06	.03
Stage 3: Milling	.12	.06
Stage 4: Baking	.30	.18
Stage 5: Retailing	.45	.15
Total dollar value of all sales $.96		Total value added $.45

Stage 1: A farmer purchases 3 cents' worth of fertilizer and seed, which are used as factors of production in growing wheat.

Stage 2: The farmer grows the wheat, harvests it, and sells it to a miller for 6 cents. Thus, we see that the farmer has added 3 cents' worth of value. Those 3 cents represent income over and above expenses incurred by the farmer.

Stage 3: The miller purchases the wheat for 6 cents and adds 6 cents as the value added; that is, there is 6 cents for the miller as income. The miller sells the ground wheat flour to a donut-baking company.

Stage 4: The donut-baking company buys the flour for 12 cents and adds 18 cents as the value added. It then sells the donut to the final retailer.

Stage 5: The donut retailer sells fresh hot donuts at 45 cents apiece, thus creating an additional value of 15 cents.

We see that the total value of transactions involved in the production of one donut was 96 cents, but the total value added was 45 cents, which is exactly equal to the retail price. The total value added is equal to the sum of all income payments.

45 cents that is used to measure GDP, not the 96 cents. If we used the 96 cents, we would be double counting from stages 2 through 5, for each intermediate good would be counted at least twice—once when it was produced and again when the good it was used in making was sold. Such double counting would grossly exaggerate GDP.

Exclusion of Financial Transactions, Transfer Payments, and Secondhand Goods

Remember that GDP is the measure of the dollar value of all final goods and services produced in one year. Many more transactions occur that have nothing to do with final goods and services produced. There are financial transactions, transfers of the ownership of preexisting goods, and other transactions that should not and do not get included in our measure of GDP.

Financial Transactions. There are three general categories of purely financial transactions: (1) the buying and selling of securities, (2) government transfer payments, and (3) private transfer payments.

Securities. When you purchase a share of existing stock in Microsoft Corporation, someone else has sold it to you. In essence, there was merely a *transfer* of ownership rights. You paid $100 to obtain the stock certificate. Someone else received the $100 and gave up the stock certificate. No producing activity was consummated at that time, unless a broker received a fee for performing the transaction, in which case only the fee is part of GDP. The $100 transaction is not included when we measure GDP.

Government Transfer Payments. Transfer payments are payments for which no productive services are concurrently provided in exchange. The most obvious government transfer payments are Social Security benefits, veterans' payments, and unemployment compensation. The recipients make no contribution to current production in return for such transfer payments (although they may have contributed in the past to be eligible to receive them). Government transfer payments are not included in GDP.

Go to www.econtoday.com/ch08 for the most up-to-date U.S. economic data at the Web site of the Bureau of Economic Analysis.

Private Transfer Payments. Are you receiving funds from your parents in order to attend school? Has a wealthy relative ever given you a gift of cash? If so, you have been the recipient of a private transfer payment. This is merely a transfer of funds from one individual to another. As such, it does not constitute productive activity and is not included in GDP.

Transfer of Secondhand Goods. If I sell you my two-year-old laptop computer, no current production is involved. I transfer to you the ownership of a computer that was produced years ago; in exchange, you transfer to me $350. The original purchase price of the computer was included in GDP in the year I purchased it. To include it again when I sell it to you would be counting the value of the computer a second time.

Other Excluded Transactions. Many other transactions are not included in GDP for practical reasons:

- Household production—housecleaning, child care, and other tasks performed by people in their *own* households and for which they are not paid through the marketplace
- Otherwise legal underground transactions—those that are legal but not reported and hence not taxed, such as paying housekeepers in cash that is not declared as income
- Illegal underground activities—these include prostitution, illegal gambling, and the sale of illicit drugs

Recognizing the Limitations of GDP

Like any statistical measure, gross domestic product is a concept that can be both well used and misused. Economists find it especially valuable as an overall indicator of a nation's economic performance. But it is important to realize that GDP has significant weaknesses. Because it includes only the value of goods and services traded in markets, it excludes *nonmarket* production, such as the household services of homemakers discussed earlier. This can cause some problems in comparing the GDP of an industrialized country with the GDP of a highly agrarian nation in which nonmarket production is relatively more important. It also causes problems if nations have different definitions of legal versus illegal activities. For instance, a nation with legalized gambling will count the value of gambling services, which has a reported market value as a legal activity. But in a country where gambling is illegal, individuals who provide such services will not report the market value of gambling activities, and so they will not be counted in that country's GDP. This can complicate comparing GDP in the nation where gambling is legal with GDP in the country that prohibits gambling.

Furthermore, although GDP is often used as a benchmark measure for standard-of-living calculations, it is not necessarily a good measure of the well-being of a nation. No measured figure of total national annual income can take account of changes in the degree of labor market discrimination, declines or improvements in personal safety, or the quantity or quality of leisure time. Measured GDP also says little about our environmental quality of life. As the now-defunct Soviet Union illustrated to the world, the large-scale production of such items as minerals, electricity, and irrigation for farming can have negative effects on the environment: deforestation from strip mining, air and soil pollution from particulate emissions or nuclear accidents at power plants, and erosion of the natural balance between water and salt in bodies of water such as the Aral Sea. Other nations, such as China and India, have also experienced greater pollution problems as their levels of GDP have increased. Hence it is important to recognize the following point:

> *GDP is a measure of the value of production in terms of market prices and an indicator of economic activity. It is not a measure of a nation's overall welfare.*

Nonetheless, GDP is a relatively accurate and useful measure to map *changes* in the economy's domestic economic activity. Understanding GDP is thus important for recognizing changes in economic activity over time.

ECONOMICS FRONT AND CENTER

To contemplate how failure to include illegal production in a nation's national income accounting can severely limit GDP's usefulness as a measure of welfare, read **Just How Poor Is Zimbabwe, Really?** on page 204.

QUICK QUIZ

_____ _____ _____ is the total market value of final goods and services produced in an economy during a one-year period by factors of production within the nation's borders. It represents the dollar value of the flow of production over a one-year period.

To avoid double counting, we look only at final goods and services produced or, equivalently, at _____ _____.

In measuring GDP, we must _____ (1) purely financial transactions, such as the buying and selling of securities; (2) government transfer payments and private transfer payments; and (3) the transfer of secondhand goods.

Many other transactions are excluded from measured _____, among them household services rendered by homemakers, underground economy transactions, and illegal economic activities, even though many of these result in the production of final goods and services.

GDP is a useful measure for tracking changes in the _____ _____ of overall economic activity over time, but it is not a measure of the well-being of a nation's residents because it fails to account for nonmarket transactions, the amount and quality of leisure time, environmental or safety issues, discrimination, and other factors that influence general welfare.

See page 212 for the answers. Review concepts from this section in MyEconLab.

TWO MAIN METHODS OF MEASURING GDP

The definition of GDP is the total value of all final goods and services produced during a year. How, exactly, do we go about actually computing this number?

The circular flow diagram presented in Figure 8-1 on page 186 gave us a shortcut method for calculating GDP. We can look at the *flow of expenditures,* which consists of consumption, investment, government purchases of goods and services, and net expenditures in the foreign sector (net exports). This is called the **expenditure approach** to measuring GDP, in which we add the dollar value of all final goods and services. We could also use the *flow of income,* looking at the income received by everybody producing goods and services. This is called the **income approach,** in which we add the income received by all factors of production.

Expenditure approach
Computing GDP by adding up the dollar value at current market prices of all final goods and services.

Income approach
Measuring GDP by adding up all components of national income, including wages, interest, rent, and profits.

Deriving GDP by the Expenditure Approach

To derive GDP using the expenditure approach, we must look at each of the separate components of expenditures and then add them together. These components are consumption expenditures, investment, government expenditures, and net exports.

Consumption Expenditures. How do we spend our income? As households or as individuals, we spend our income through consumption expenditure (*C*), which falls into three categories: **durable consumer goods, nondurable consumer goods,** and **services.** Durable goods are *arbitrarily* defined as items that last more than three years; they include automobiles, furniture, and household appliances. Nondurable goods are all the rest, such as food and gasoline. Services are intangible commodities: medical care, education, and the like.

Housing expenditures constitute a major proportion of anybody's annual expenditures. Rental payments on apartments are automatically included in consumption expenditure estimates. People who own their homes, however, do not make rental payments. Consequently, government statisticians estimate what is called the *implicit rental value* of existing owner-occupied homes. It is roughly equal to the amount of rent you would have to pay if you did not own the home but were renting it from someone else.

Durable consumer goods
Consumer goods that have a life span of more than three years.

Nondurable consumer goods
Consumer goods that are used up within three years.

Services
Mental or physical labor or help purchased by consumers. Examples are the assistance of physicians, lawyers, dentists, repair personnel, housecleaners, educators, retailers, and wholesalers; things purchased or used by consumers that do not have physical characteristics.

Gross Private Domestic Investment. We now turn our attention to **gross private domestic investment** (*I*) undertaken by businesses. When economists refer to investment, they are referring to additions to productive capacity. **Investment** may be thought of as an activity that uses resources today in such a way that they allow for greater production in the future and hence greater consumption in the future. When a business buys new equipment or puts up a new factory, it is investing; it is increasing its capacity to produce in the future.

In estimating gross private domestic investment, government statisticians also add consumer expenditures on *new* residential structures because new housing represents an addition to our future productive capacity in the sense that a new house can generate housing services in the future.

The layperson's notion of investment often relates to the purchase of stocks and bonds. For our purposes, such transactions simply represent the *transfer of ownership* of assets called stocks and bonds. Thus, you must keep in mind the fact that in economics, investment refers *only* to *additions* to productive capacity, not to transfers of assets.

Gross private domestic investment
The creation of capital goods, such as factories and machines, that can yield production and hence consumption in the future. Also included in this definition are changes in business inventories and repairs made to machines or buildings.

Investment
Any use of today's resources to expand tomorrow's production or consumption.

Fixed versus Inventory Investment. In our analysis, we will consider the basic components of investment. We have already mentioned the first one, which involves a firm's

Producer durables, or capital goods
Durable goods having an expected service life of more than three years that are used by businesses to produce other goods and services.

Fixed investment
Purchases by businesses of newly produced producer durables, or capital goods, such as production machinery and office equipment.

Inventory investment
Changes in the stocks of finished goods and goods in process, as well as changes in the raw materials that businesses keep on hand. Whenever inventories are decreasing, inventory investment is negative; whenever they are increasing, inventory investment is positive.

buying equipment or putting up a new factory. These are called **producer durables,** or **capital goods.** A producer durable, or a capital good, is simply a good that is purchased not to be consumed in its current form but to be used to make other goods and services. The purchase of equipment and factories—capital goods—is called **fixed investment.**

The other type of investment has to do with the change in inventories of raw materials and finished goods. Firms do not immediately sell off all their products to consumers. Some of this final product is usually held in inventory waiting to be sold. Firms hold inventories to meet future expected orders for their products. When a firm increases its inventories of finished products, it is engaging in **inventory investment.** Inventories consist of all finished goods on hand, goods in process, and raw materials.

The reason that we can think of a change in inventories as being a type of investment is that an increase in such inventories provides for future increased consumption possibilities. When inventory investment is zero, the firm is neither adding to nor subtracting from the total stock of goods or raw materials on hand. Thus, if the firm keeps the same amount of inventories throughout the year, inventory *investment* has been zero.

Government Expenditures. In addition to personal consumption expenditures, there are government purchases of goods and services (G). The government buys goods and services from private firms and pays wages and salaries to government employees. Generally, we value goods and services at the prices at which they are sold. But many government goods and services are not sold in the market. Therefore, we cannot use their market value when computing GDP. The value of these goods is considered equal to their *cost*. For example, the value of a newly built road is considered equal to its construction cost and is included in the GDP for the year it was built.

Net Exports (Foreign Expenditures). To get an accurate representation of gross domestic product, we must include the foreign sector. As U.S. residents, we purchase foreign goods called *imports*. The goods that foreign residents purchase from us are our *exports*. To determine the *net* expenditures from the foreign sector, we subtract the value of imports from the value of exports to get net exports (X) for a year:

$$\text{Net exports } (X) = \text{total exports} - \text{total imports}$$

To understand why we subtract imports rather than ignoring them altogether, recall that we want to estimate *domestic* output, so we have to subtract U.S. expenditures on the goods produced in other nations.

Presenting the Expenditure Approach

We have just defined the components of GDP using the expenditure approach. When we add them all together, we get a definition for GDP, which is as follows:

$$\text{GDP} = C + I + G + X$$

where
C = consumption expenditures
I = investment expenditures
G = government expenditures
X = net exports

The Historical Picture. To get an idea of the relationship among C, I, G, and X, look at Figure 8-2, which shows GDP, personal consumption expenditures, government

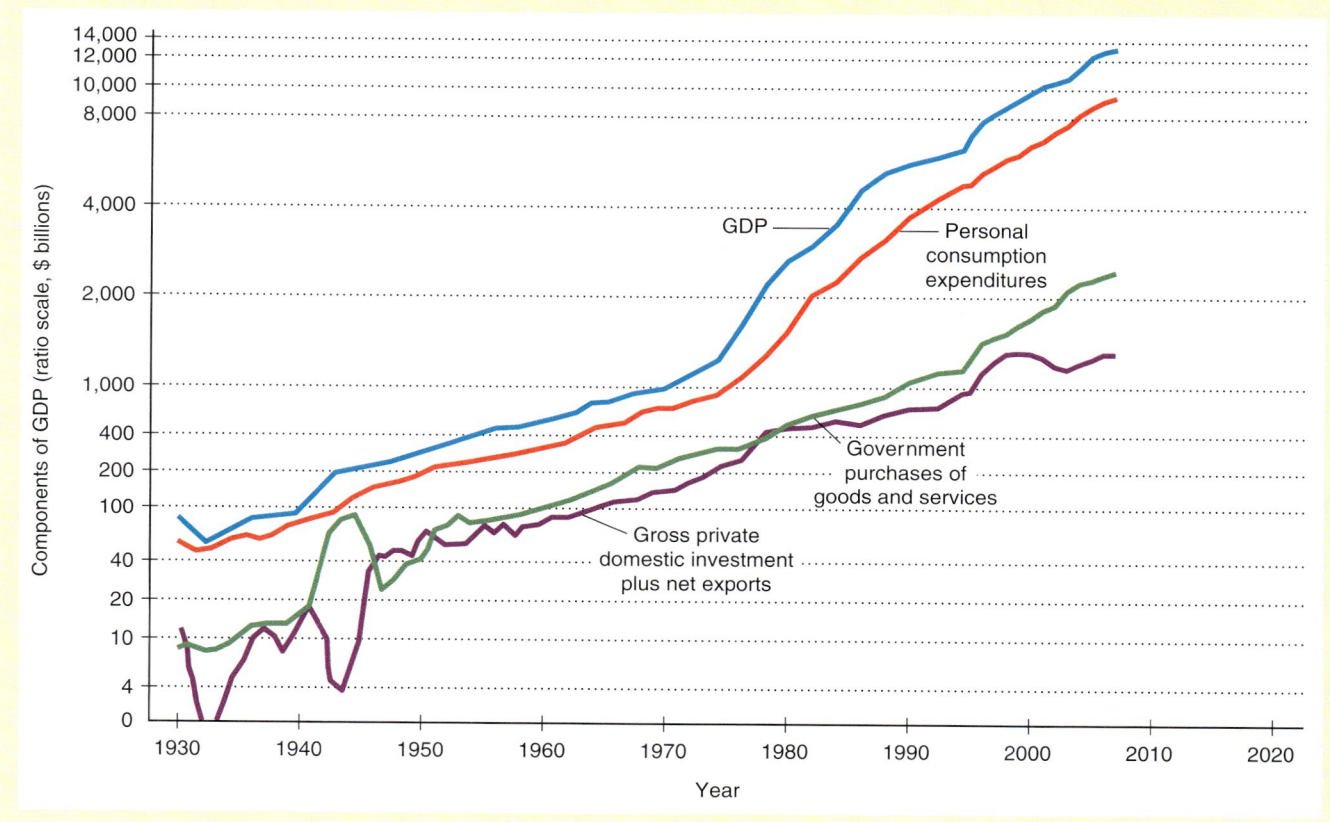

FIGURE 8-2

GDP and Its Components

Here we see a display of gross domestic product, personal consumption expenditures, government purchases, and gross private domestic investment plus net exports for the years since 1929. Note that the scale of the vertical axis changes as we move up the axis. During the Great Depression of the 1930s, gross private domestic investment *plus* net exports was negative because we were investing very little at that time. During the early 2000s, gross private domestic investment declined and then recovered slowly. Net exports also became increasingly negative. Hence, the sum of these two items has fallen off in recent years.

purchases, and gross private domestic investment plus net exports since 1929. When we add up the expenditures of the household, business, government, and foreign sectors, we get GDP.

Depreciation and Net Domestic Product. We have used the terms *gross domestic product* and *gross private domestic investment* without really indicating what *gross* means. The dictionary defines it as "without deductions," the opposite of *net*. Deductions for what? you might ask. The deductions are for something we call **depreciation**. In the course of a year, machines and structures wear out or are used up in the production of domestic product. For example, houses deteriorate as they are occupied, and machines need repairs or they will fall apart and stop working. Most capital, or durable, goods depreciate.

How fast do you think that personal computers depreciate?

Depreciation
Reduction in the value of capital goods over a one-year period due to physical wear and tear and also to obsolescence; also called *capital consumption allowance*.

> ## EXAMPLE
>
> ### Personal Computers Depreciate Rapidly
>
> To determine how fast personal computers (PCs) depreciate, Federal Reserve economists examined detailed information on the prices of new and used PCs. Their analysis focused on two key factors accounting for the decline in a computer's market value as it ages. The first is that the price of an existing PC per constant-quality unit changes as newer and better models are introduced. The second is that older PCs experience some wear and tear but, more importantly, they become unable to operate the latest software or lack the latest features, such as advanced DVD drives.
>
> After taking these factors into account, the economists found that the annual rate of depreciation for a typical PC is about 50 percent. That is, a PC loses about half of its remaining value each year. This means that you can anticipate that within five years after you purchase a PC, it will have depreciated 97 percent.
>
> **FOR CRITICAL ANALYSIS**
> *Why do you suppose that people often have trouble even giving away old personal computers?*

Net domestic product (NDP)
GDP minus depreciation.

An estimate of the amount that capital goods have depreciated during the year is subtracted from gross domestic product to arrive at a figure called **net domestic product (NDP)**, which we define as follows:

$$NDP = GDP - depreciation$$

Capital consumption allowance
Another name for depreciation, the amount that businesses would have to save in order to take care of the deterioration of machines and other equipment.

Depreciation is also called **capital consumption allowance** because it is the amount of the capital stock that has been consumed over a one-year period. In essence, it equals the amount a business would have to put aside to repair and replace deteriorating machines. Because we know that

$$GDP = C + I + G + X$$

we know that the formula for NDP is

$$NDP = C + I + G + X - depreciation$$

Alternatively, because net $I = I -$ depreciation,

$$NDP = C + net\ I + G + X$$

Net investment
Gross private domestic investment minus an estimate of the wear and tear on the existing capital stock. Net investment therefore measures the change in the capital stock over a one-year period.

Net investment measures *changes* in our capital stock over time and is positive nearly every year. Because depreciation does not vary greatly from year to year as a percentage of GDP, we get a similar picture of what is happening to our national economy by looking at either NDP or GDP data.

Net investment is an important variable to observe over time nonetheless. If everything else remains the same in an economy, changes in net investment can have dramatic consequences for future economic growth (a topic we cover in more detail in Chapter 9). Positive net investment by definition expands the productive capacity of our economy. This means that there is increased capital, which will generate even more income in the future. When net investment is zero, we are investing just enough to take account of depreciation. Our economy's productive capacity remains unchanged. Finally, when net investment is negative, we can expect negative economic growth prospects in the future. Negative net investment means that our productive capacity is actually declining—we are disinvesting. This actually occurred during the Great Depression.

> **QUICK QUIZ**
>
> The _____ approach to measuring GDP requires that we add up consumption expenditures, gross private investment, government purchases, and net exports. Consumption expenditures include consumer _____, consumer _____, and _____.
>
> Gross private domestic investment *excludes* transfers of asset ownership. It includes only additions to the productive _____ of a nation, repairs on existing capital goods, and changes in business _____.
>
> We value government expenditures at their cost because we usually do not have _____ prices at which to value government goods and services.
>
> To obtain **net domestic product (NDP)**, we subtract from GDP the year's _____ of the existing capital stock.
>
> See page 212 for the answers. Review concepts from this section in MyEconLab.

Deriving GDP by the Income Approach

If you go back to the circular flow diagram in Figure 8-1 on page 186, you see that product markets are at the top of the diagram and factor markets are at the bottom. We can calculate the value of the circular flow of income and product by looking at expenditures—which we just did—or by looking at total factor payments. Factor payments are called income. We calculate **gross domestic income (GDI)**, which we will see is identical to gross domestic product (GDP). Using the income approach, we have four categories of payments to individuals: wages, interest, rent, and profits.

1. *Wages.* The most important category is, of course, wages, including salaries and other forms of labor income, such as income in kind and incentive payments. We also count Social Security taxes (both the employees' and the employers' contributions).
2. *Interest.* Here interest payments do not equal the sum of all payments for the use of funds in a year. Instead, interest is expressed in *net* rather than in gross terms. The interest component of total income is only net interest received by households plus net interest paid to us by foreign residents. Net interest received by households is the difference between the interest they receive (from savings accounts, certificates of deposit, and the like) and the interest they pay (to banks for mortgages, credit cards, and other loans).
3. *Rent.* Rent is all income earned by individuals for the use of their real (nonmonetary) assets, such as farms, houses, and stores. As stated previously, we have to include here the implicit rental value of owner-occupied houses. Also included in this category are royalties received from copyrights, patents, and assets such as oil wells.
4. *Profits.* Our last category includes total gross corporate profits plus *proprietors' income*. Proprietors' income is income earned from the operation of unincorporated businesses, which include sole proprietorships, partnerships, and producers' cooperatives. It is unincorporated business profit.

All of the payments listed are *actual* factor payments made to owners of the factors of production. When we add them together, though, we do not yet have gross domestic income. We have to take account of two other components: **indirect business taxes,** such as sales and business property taxes, and depreciation, which we have already discussed.

Gross domestic income (GDI)
The sum of all income—wages, interest, rent, and profits—paid to the four factors of production.

Go to www.econtoday.com/ch08 to examine recent trends in U.S. GDP and its components.

Indirect business taxes
All business taxes except the tax on corporate profits. Indirect business taxes include sales and business property taxes.

Indirect Business Taxes. Indirect taxes are the (nonincome) taxes paid by consumers when they buy goods and services. When you buy a book, you pay the price of the book plus any state and local sales tax. The business is actually acting as the government's agent in collecting the sales tax, which it in turn passes on to the government. Such taxes therefore represent a business expense and are included in gross domestic income.

Depreciation. Just as we had to deduct depreciation to get from GDP to NDP, so we must *add* depreciation to go from net domestic income to gross domestic income. Depreciation can be thought of as the portion of the current year's GDP that is used to replace physical capital consumed in the process of production. Because somebody has paid for the replacement, depreciation must be added as a component of gross domestic income.

The last two components of GDP—indirect business taxes and depreciation—are called **nonincome expense items**.

Nonincome expense items
The total of indirect business taxes and depreciation.

Figure 8-3 shows a comparison between gross domestic product and gross domestic income for 2007. Whether you decide to use the expenditure approach or the income approach, you will come out with the same number. There are sometimes statistical discrepancies, but they are usually relatively small.

Is it possible to calculate GDP for the entire world?

INTERNATIONAL EXAMPLE

World GDP May Be Understated

To measure global GDP, economists commonly begin by converting the value of each nation's GDP into U.S. dollars. They do this by multiplying the nation's GDP by the exchange rate of the dollar for that nation's currency unit. Then the economists add up the dollar values of the GDPs of all nations to obtain a dollar value of global GDP. Using this method, current world GDP is less than $40 trillion per year, or just below 3.5 times U.S. GDP.

A problem with using exchange rates to convert other nations' GDPs into dollar values is that prices tend to be lower in less developed nations than in the United States and other developed countries. Thus, a U.S. dollar can often purchase more goods and services in those nations than it can in developed nations. When the calculation of global GDP is adjusted to take this fact into account, the U.S. dollar value of world GDP jumps to well over $50 trillion.

FOR CRITICAL ANALYSIS
How might understating GDP this year relative to last year bias estimates of the growth of the total output produced by an average resident of planet Earth this year?

QUICK QUIZ

To derive GDP using the income approach, we add up all factor payments, including _____, _____, _____, and _____.

To get an accurate measure of GDP using the income approach, we must also add _____ _____ _____ and _____ to those total factor payments.

See page 212 for the answers. Review concepts from this section in MyEconLab.

FIGURE 8-3

Gross Domestic Product and Gross Domestic Income, 2007 (in billions of 2007 dollars per year)

By using the two different methods of computing the output of the economy, we come up with gross domestic product and gross domestic income, which are by definition equal. One approach focuses on expenditures, or the flow of product; the other approach concentrates on income, or the flow of costs.

Sources: U.S. Department of Commerce and author's estimates.

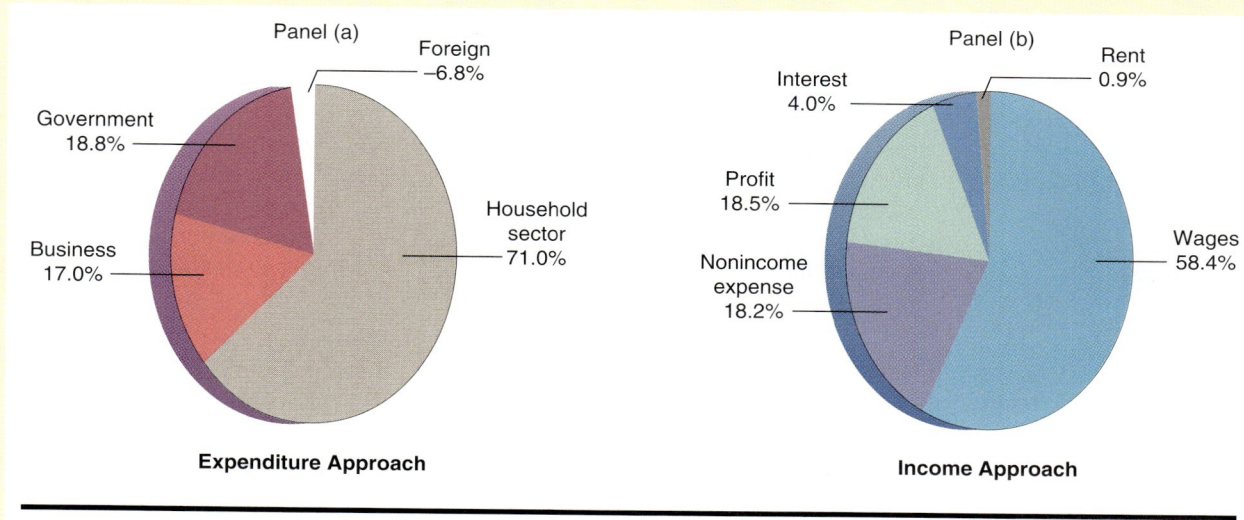

Panel (a) — Expenditure Approach
- Foreign −6.8%
- Government 18.8%
- Business 17.0%
- Household sector 71.0%

Panel (b) — Income Approach
- Rent 0.9%
- Interest 4.0%
- Profit 18.5%
- Nonincome expense 18.2%
- Wages 58.4%

Expenditure Point of View — Product Flow Expenditures by Different Sectors:		Income Point of View — Cost Flow Domestic Income (at Factor Cost):	
Household sector		*Wages*	
Personal consumption expenses	$9,957.6	All wages, salaries, and supplemental employee compensation	$8,190.4
Government sector		*Rent*	
Purchase of goods and services	2,636.7	All rental income of individuals plus implicit rent on owner-occupied dwellings	126.2
Business sector		*Interest*	
Gross private domestic investment (including depreciation)	2,384.2	Net interest paid by business	561.0
Foreign sector		*Profit*	
Net exports of goods and services	−953.7	Proprietorial income	1,182.0
		Corporate profits before taxes deducted	1,412.6
		Nonincome expense items	
		Indirect business taxes	637.6
		Depreciation	2,128.2
		Statistical discrepancy	−213.2
Gross domestic product	$14,024.8	Gross domestic income	$14,024.8

OTHER COMPONENTS OF NATIONAL INCOME ACCOUNTING

Gross domestic income or product does not really tell us how much income people have access to for spending purposes. To get to those kinds of data, we must make some adjustments, which we now do.

National Income (NI)

We know that net domestic product (NDP) is the total market value of goods and services available to consume and to add to the capital stock. NDP, however, includes indirect business taxes and transfers, which should not count as part of income earned by U.S. factors of production, but does not include various business incomes that should. We therefore subtract from NDP indirect taxes and transfers and add other business income adjustments. Because U.S. residents earn income abroad and foreign residents earn income in the United States, we also add net U.S. income earned abroad. The result is what we define as **national income (NI)**—income earned by all U.S. factors of production.

National income (NI)
The total of all factor payments to resource owners. It can be obtained from net domestic product (NDP) by subtracting indirect business taxes and transfers and adding net U.S. income earned abroad and other business income adjustments.

Personal Income (PI)

National income does not actually represent what is available to individuals to spend because some people obtain income for which they have provided no concurrent good or service and others earn income but do not receive it. In the former category are mainly recipients of transfer payments from the government, such as Social Security, welfare, and food stamps. These payments represent shifts of funds within the economy by way of the government, with no good or service concurrently rendered in exchange. For the other category, income earned but not received, the most obvious examples are corporate retained earnings that are plowed back into the business, contributions to social insurance, and corporate income taxes. When transfer payments are added and when income earned but not received is subtracted, we end up with **personal income (PI)**—income *received* by the factors of production prior to the payment of personal income taxes.

What did the computer software company Microsoft have to do with a large jump in personal income in late 2004?

Personal income (PI)
The amount of income that households actually receive before they pay personal income taxes.

E-COMMERCE EXAMPLE

Microsoft Single-Handedly Boosts U.S. Personal Income

In December 2004, U.S. personal income experienced an increase of 3.7 percent. This was the largest single-month increase since the U.S. government began calculating personal income back in 1959. This significant rise in personal income was caused by a $32 billion dividend payment by Microsoft to its 4.6 million shareholders. By itself, Microsoft's dividend payment boosted personal income growth for all of 2004 by more than 1 percentage point, from about 4 percent to more than 5 percent.

FOR CRITICAL ANALYSIS
What happened to 2004 gross domestic income as a result of Microsoft's dividend payment? (Hint: PI is part of GDI.)

Disposable Personal Income (DPI)

Everybody knows that you do not get to take home all your salary. To get **disposable personal income (DPI),** we subtract all personal income taxes from personal income. This is the income that individuals have left for consumption and saving.

Disposable personal income (DPI)
Personal income after personal income taxes have been paid.

TABLE 8-2
Going from GDP to Disposable Income, 2007

	Billions of Dollars
Gross domestic product (GDP)	14,024.8
Minus depreciation	−2,124.8
Net domestic product (NDP)	11,900.0
Minus indirect business taxes and transfers	−1,142.1
Plus other business income adjustments	1,259.8
Plus net U.S. income earned abroad	64.4
National income (NI)	12,082.1
Minus corporate taxes, Social Security contributions, corporate retained earnings	−1,769.1
Plus government transfer payments	+898.8
Personal income (PI)	11,211.8
Minus personal income tax and nontax payments	−1,068.6
Disposable personal income (DPI)	10,143.2

Sources: U.S. Department of Commerce and author's estimates.

Deriving the Components of GDP

Table 8-2 shows how to derive the various components of GDP. It explains how to go from gross domestic product to net domestic product to national income to personal income and then to disposable personal income. On the frontpapers of your book, you can see the historical record for GDP, NDP, NI, PI, and DPI for selected years since 1929.

We have completed our rundown of the different ways that GDP can be computed and of the different variants of national income and product. What we have not yet touched on is the difference between national income measured in this year's dollars and national income representing real goods and services.

QUICK QUIZ

To obtain _____ _____, we subtract indirect business taxes and transfers from net domestic product and add other business income adjustments and net U.S. income earned abroad.

To obtain _____ _____, we must add government transfer payments, such as Social Security benefits and food stamps. We must subtract income earned but not received by factor owners, such as corporate retained earnings, Social Security contributions, and corporate income taxes.

To obtain disposable personal income, we subtract all personal _____ _____ from personal income. Disposable personal income is income that individuals actually have for consumption or saving.

See page 212 for the answers. Review concepts from this section in MyEconLab.

DISTINGUISHING BETWEEN NOMINAL AND REAL VALUES

So far, we have shown how to measure *nominal* income and product. When we say "nominal," we are referring to income and product expressed in the current "face value" of today's dollar. Given the existence of inflation or deflation in the economy, we must also be able to distinguish between the **nominal values** that we will be looking at and the **real values** underlying them. Nominal values are expressed in current dollars. Real income involves our command over goods and services—purchasing power—and therefore depends on money income and a set of prices. Thus, real income refers to nominal income corrected for changes

Nominal values
The values of variables such as GDP and investment expressed in current dollars, also called *money values;* measurement in terms of the actual market prices at which goods and services are sold.

Real values
Measurement of economic values after adjustments have been made for changes in the average of prices between years.

in the weighted average of all prices. In other words, we must make an adjustment for changes in the price level. Consider an example. Nominal income *per person* in 1960 was only about $2,900 per year. In 2007, nominal income per person was about $44,000. Were people really that bad off in 1960? No, for nominal income in 1960 is expressed in 1960 prices, not in the prices of today. In today's dollars, the per-person income of 1960 would be closer to $14,500, or about 33 percent of today's income per person. This is a meaningful comparison between income in 1960 and income today. Next we will show how we can translate nominal measures of income into real measures by using an appropriate price index, such as the Consumer Price Index or the GDP deflator discussed in Chapter 7.

Correcting GDP for Price Changes

If a DVD movie costs $20 this year, 10 DVDs will have a market value of $200. If next year they cost $25 each, the same 10 DVDs will have a market value of $250. In this case, there is no increase in the total quantity of DVDs, but the market value will have increased by one-fourth. Apply this to every single good and service produced and sold in the United States, and you realize that changes in GDP, measured in *current* dollars, may not be a very useful indication of economic activity. If we are really interested in variations in the *real* output of the economy, we must correct GDP (and just about everything else we look at) for changes in the average of overall prices from year to year. Basically, we need to generate an index that approximates the changes in average prices and then divide that estimate into the value of output in current dollars to adjust the value of output to what is called **constant dollars,** or dollars corrected for general price level changes. This price-corrected GDP is called *real GDP.*

How much has correcting for price changes caused real GDP to differ from nominal GDP during the past few years?

Constant dollars
Dollars expressed in terms of real purchasing power using a particular year as the base or standard of comparison, in contrast to current dollars.

EXAMPLE

Correcting GDP for Price Index Changes, 1997–2007

Let's take a numerical example to see how we can adjust GDP for changes in the price index. We must pick an appropriate price index in order to adjust for these price level changes. We mentioned the Consumer Price Index, the Producer Price Index, and the GDP deflator in Chapter 7. Let's use the GDP deflator to adjust our figures. Table 8-3 gives 11 years of GDP figures. Nominal GDP figures are shown in column 2. The price index (GDP deflator) is in column 3, with base year of 2000, when the GDP deflator equals 100. Column 4 shows real (inflation-adjusted) GDP in 2000 dollars.

The formula for real GDP is

$$\text{Real GDP} = \frac{\text{nominal GDP}}{\text{price index}} \times 100$$

The step-by-step derivation of real (constant-dollar) GDP is as follows: The base year is 2000, so the price index for that year must equal 100. In 2000, nominal GDP was $9,817.0 billion, and so was real GDP expressed in 2000 dollars. In 2001, the price index increased to 102.399. Thus, to correct 2001's nominal GDP for inflation, we divide the price index, 102.399, into the nominal GDP figure of $10,128.0 billion and then multiply it by 100. The rounded result is $9,890.7 billion, which is 2001 GDP expressed in terms of the purchasing power of dollars in 2000. What about a situation when the price index is lower than in 2000? Look at 1997. Here the price index shown in column 3 is only 95.413. That means that in 1997, the average of all prices was about 95 percent of prices in 2000. To obtain 1997 GDP expressed in terms of 2000 purchasing power, we divide nominal GDP, $8,304.3 billion, by 95.413 and then multiply by 100. The rounded result is a larger number—$8,703.5 billion. Column 4 in Table 8-3 is a better measure of how the economy has performed than column 2, which shows nominal GDP changes.

FOR CRITICAL ANALYSIS
A few years ago, the base year for the GDP deflator was 1996. What does a change in the base year for the price index affect?

TABLE 8-3
Correcting GDP for Price Index Changes

To correct GDP for price index changes, we first have to pick a price index (the GDP deflator) with a specific year as its base. In our example, the base level is 2000 prices; the price index for that year is 100. To obtain 2000 constant-dollar GDP, we divide the price index into nominal GDP and multiply by 100. In other words, we divide column 3 into column 2 and multiply by 100. This gives us column 4, which (taking into account rounding of the deflator) is a measure of real GDP expressed in 2000 purchasing power.

(1) Year	(2) Nominal GDP (billions of dollars per year)	(3) Price Index (base year 2000 = 100)	(4) = [(2) ÷ (3)] × 100 Real GDP (billions of dollars per year, in constant 2000 dollars)
1997	8,304.3	95.413	8,703.5
1998	8,747.0	96.472	9,066.9
1999	9,268.4	97.868	9,470.3
2000	9,817.0	100.000	9,817.0
2001	10,128.0	102.399	9,890.7
2002	10,469.6	104.187	10,048.8
2003	10,971.2	106.305	10,320.6
2004	11,734.3	109.099	10,755.7
2005	12,487.1	112.145	11,134.8
2006	13,306.3	116.070	11,464.0
2007	14,024.8	119.088	11,776.8

Sources: U.S. Department of Commerce, Bureau of Economic Analysis, and author's estimates.

Plotting Nominal and Real GDP

Nominal GDP and real GDP since 1970 are plotted in Figure 8-4 on page 202. There is quite a big gap between the two GDP figures, reflecting the amount of inflation that has occurred. Note that the choice of a base year is arbitrary. We have chosen 2000 as the base year in our example. This happens to be the base year that is currently used by the government.

Per Capita Real GDP

Looking at changes in real GDP may be deceiving, particularly if the population size has changed significantly. If real GDP over a 10-year period went up 100 percent, you might jump to the conclusion that the real income of a typical person in the economy had increased by that amount. But what if during the same period the population increased by 200 percent? Then what would you say? Certainly, the amount of real GDP per person, or *per capita real GDP*, would have fallen, even though *total* real GDP had risen. To account not only for price changes but also for population changes, we must first deflate GDP and then divide by the total population, doing this for each year. If we were to look at certain less developed countries, we would find that in many cases, even though real GDP has risen over the past several decades, per capita real GDP has remained constant or fallen because the population has grown just as rapidly or even faster.

QUICK QUIZ

To correct **nominal GDP** for price changes, we first select a base year for our price index and assign it the number _____. Then we construct an index based on how a weighted average of prices has changed relative to that base year. For example, if in the next year a weighted average of the prices indicates that prices have increased by 10 percent, we would assign it the number _____. We then divide each year's price index, so constructed, into its respective nominal GDP figure (and multiply by 100).

We can divide the _____ into real GDP to obtain per capita real GDP.

See page 212 for the answers. Review concepts from this section in MyEconLab.

FIGURE 8-4

Nominal and Real GDP

Here we plot both nominal and real GDP. Real GDP is expressed in the purchasing power of 2000 dollars. The gap between the two represents price level changes.

Source: U.S. Department of Commerce.

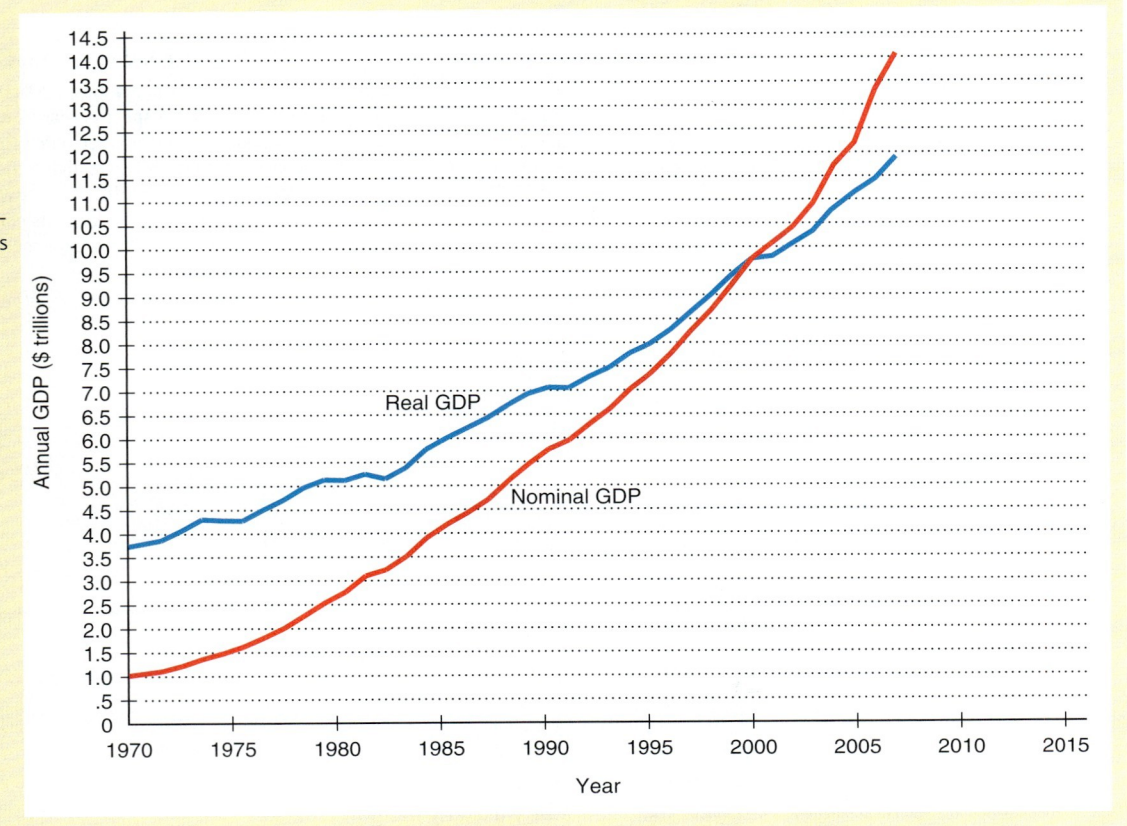

COMPARING GDP THROUGHOUT THE WORLD

It is relatively easy to compare the standard of living of a family in Los Angeles with that of one living in Boston. Both families get paid in dollars and can buy the same goods and services at Wal-Mart, McDonald's, and Costco. It is not so easy, however, to make a similar comparison between a family living in the United States and one in, say, Indonesia. The first problem concerns money. Indonesian residents get paid in rupiah, their national currency, and buy goods and services with those rupiah. How do we compare the average standard of living measured in rupiah with that measured in dollars?

Foreign Exchange Rates

In earlier chapters, you have encountered international examples that involved local currencies, but the dollar equivalent has always been given. The dollar equivalent is calculated by looking up the **foreign exchange rate** that is published daily in major newspapers throughout the world. If you know that you can exchange $1.25 per euro, the exchange rate is 1.25 to 1 (or otherwise stated, a dollar is worth 0.80 euros). So, if French incomes per capita are, say, 23,168.80 euros, that translates, at an exchange rate of $1.25 per euro, to $28,961. For years, statisticians calculated relative GDPs by simply adding up each country's GDP in its local currency and dividing by the respective dollar exchange rate.

Foreign exchange rate
The price of one currency in terms of another.

True Purchasing Power

The problem with simply using foreign exchange rates to convert other countries' GDPs and per capita GDPs into dollars is that not all goods and services are bought and sold in a world market. Restaurant food, housecleaning services, and home repairs do not get exchanged across countries. In countries that have very low wages, those kinds of services are much cheaper than foreign exchange rate computations would imply. Government statistics claiming that per capita income in some poor country is only $300 a year seem shocking. But such a statistic does not tell you the true standard of living of people in that country. Only by looking at what is called **purchasing power parity** can you determine other countries' true standards of living compared to ours.

Given that nations use different currencies, how can we compare nations' levels of real GDP per capita?

Purchasing power parity
Adjustment in exchange rate conversions that takes into account differences in the true cost of living across countries.

INTERNATIONAL EXAMPLE

Purchasing Power Parity Comparisons of World Incomes

A few years ago, the International Monetary Fund accepted the purchasing power parity approach as the correct one. It started presenting international statistics on each country's GDP relative to every other's based on purchasing power parity. The results were surprising. As you can see from Table 8-4, China's per capita GDP is higher based on purchasing power parity than when measured at market foreign exchange rates.

FOR CRITICAL ANALYSIS
What is the percentage increase in China's per capita GDP when one switches from foreign exchange rates to purchasing power parity?

Table 8-4
Comparing GDP Internationally

Country	Annual GDP Based on Purchasing Power Parity (billions of U.S. dollars)	Per Capita GDP Based on Purchasing Power Parity (U.S. dollars)	Per Capita GDP Based on Foreign Exchange Rates (U.S. dollars)
United States	11,693	39,820	41,440
Japan	3,809	29,810	37,050
China	7,634	5,890	1,500
Germany	2,324	28,170	30,690
France	1,779	29,460	30,370
Russia	1,392	9,680	3,400
Indonesia	757	3,480	1,140
Italy	1,613	28,020	26,280
United Kingdom	1,882	31,430	33,630
Brazil	1,460	7,940	3,220

Source: World Bank.

QUICK QUIZ

The foreign _____ _____ is the price of one currency in terms of another.

Statisticians often calculate relative GDP by adding up each country's GDP in its local currency and dividing by the dollar _____ _____.

Because not all goods and services are bought and sold in the world market, we must correct exchange rate conversions of other countries' GDP figures to take into account differences in the true _____ of _____ across countries.

See page 212 for the answers. Review concepts from this section in MyEconLab.

CASE STUDY: ECONOMICS FRONT AND CENTER

Just How Poor Is Zimbabwe, Really?

Drake is a World Bank employee. She has been sent to Zimbabwe to evaluate whether a recent dip in the nation's GDP indicates that the nation should receive more financial assistance than originally planned.

When Drake arrives in Harare, the nation's capital city, she is surprised by the amount of business activity that is clearly visible. Street vendors abound throughout the city. It is clear that they have many newly produced goods and services to sell, and it is also apparent that consumers are snapping them up on street corners everywhere.

After some study of government records, however, Drake finds that very few of the street vendors she has observed have official government approval to sell their wares. Nor does the government seek to track sales by these vendors, whose activities the government has deemed to be illegal.

In fact, so many businesses operate unofficially—and, hence, illegally—throughout Zimbabwe that an estimated 40 percent of the nation's actual production and sale of new final goods and services is not included in the nation's GDP statistics. Drake begins to wonder whether Zimbabwe's economy has really weakened as much as official data suggest—or whether it has truly weakened at all.

CRITICAL ANALYSIS QUESTIONS

1. *By what percentage would Zimbabwe's GDP increase if transactions that are currently unofficial and illegal were included in its national income accounts?*

2. *Even after taking inflation into account, why is Zimbabwe's officially reported GDP a relatively poor measure of the nation's overall welfare?*

Issues and Applications

The Art of Estimating GDP Often Requires Touch-Ups

In the month following every three-month, or quarterly, period, the U.S. government's Bureau of Economic Analysis (BEA) releases an "advance" estimate of GDP for that period. For instance, during the month of April, the BEA releases its advance estimate of GDP for the first quarter of the year. The BEA develops its advance estimate based on incomplete data from the quarter regarding growth in housing construction, sales of durable consumer goods such as automobiles, and changes in business inventories.

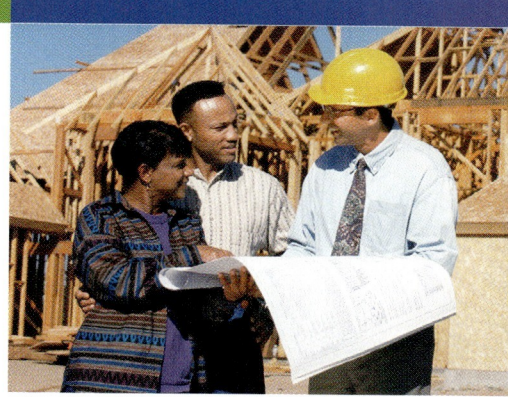

Concepts Applied
- Gross Domestic Product
- Durable Consumer Goods
- Inventory Investment

Trying to Paint a Moving Canvas

The advance quarterly GDP estimate receives considerable attention from the news media. Nevertheless, the BEA always updates its advance estimate at least twice. For instance, in May, the BEA releases a "preliminary" estimate revising the advance estimate of first-quarter GDP that it released in April. Typically, the BEA releases a "final" calculation of first-quarter GDP in June.

With each revision, the calculation of quarterly GDP undergoes changes, as the BEA receives additional data about factors that guided its initial, advance estimate of GDP. For instance, the BEA often discovers that business inventories actually rose or fell by more than initially estimated. These and other revisions together can sometimes produce significant changes in "final" GDP figures relative to the "advance" estimates.

How Different Is the Final Result?

Recently, the BEA took a careful look back at how far off its *final* estimates of quarterly GDP were from its *advance* estimates for the period from 1968 to 1998. Figure 8-5 on the following page shows how much difference these revisions made in GDP growth rates. As the figure shows, revisions in the 1980s and 1990s tended to be smaller than during the preceding years. During these more recent decades, however, upward revisions tended to be more common and also more pronounced than downward revisions.

How many dollars' worth of GDP are gained or lost in a typical BEA quarterly revision? The absolute difference between a final quarterly GDP figure and the advance estimate for that quarter is typically around $15 billion. It is not unusual, however, for some quarterly revisions to exceed twice that amount—or the equivalent, in dollar terms, of the entire *annual* GDP of the nation of Morocco.

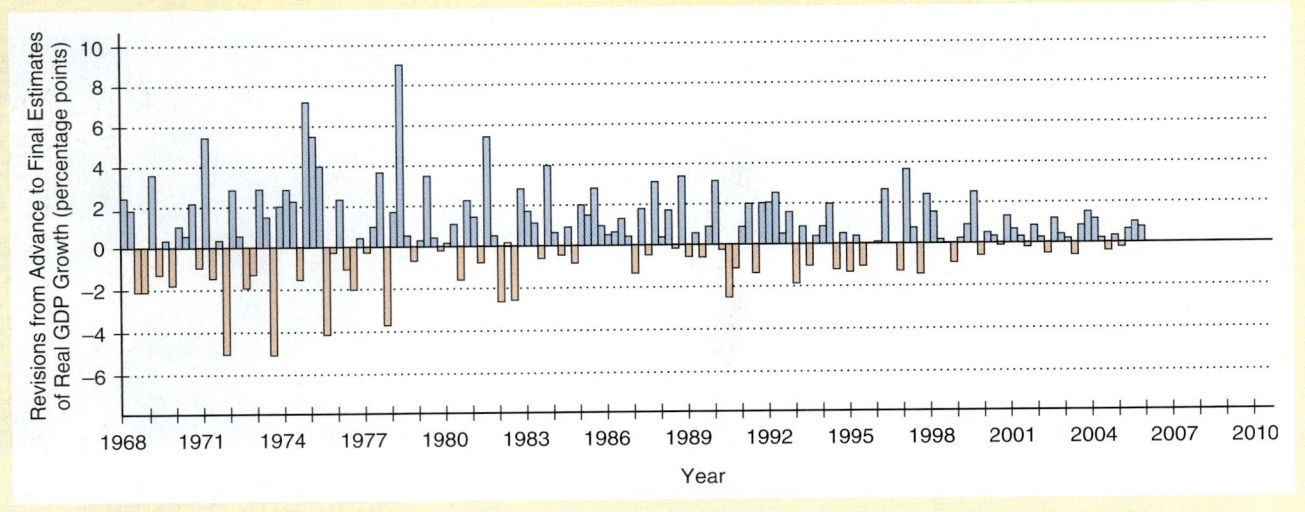

FIGURE 8-5

Effects of Revisions in GDP Estimates on Measured GDP Growth Rates

This figure shows the Bureau of Economic Analysis's (BEA's) revisions of its GDP estimates since the late 1960s. During the 1980s, 1990s, and 2000s, the BEA's revisions were generally smaller than in prior years. Upward revisions were larger and more frequent, however.

Source: Bureau of Economic Analysis.

Log in to **MyEconLab,** click on "Economic News," and test your understanding of the chapter by answering interactive questions that relate directly to this issue.

For Critical Analysis

1. Why do so many businesspeople pay close attention to the government's advance estimates of quarterly GDP?
2. Why do you suppose that the BEA sometimes revises even its "final" GDP reports?

Web Resources

1. For the BEA's latest GDP estimates, go to www.econtoday.com/ch08.
2. To review the key indicators of economic activity compiled by the BEA, go to www.econtoday.com/ch08.

Research Project

Put yourself in the place of a manager attempting to forecast business growth during upcoming quarters. In light of the historical record of revisions displayed in Figure 8-5, how much weight would you give to advance estimates of quarterly GDP for information on how fast the economy has been growing? Would you expect that the advance estimate will be more likely to be revised upward or downward?

Here is what you should know after reading this chapter. MyEconLab will help you identify what you know, and where to go when you need to practice.

WHAT YOU SHOULD KNOW		WHERE TO GO TO PRACTICE
The Circular Flow of Income and Output The circular flow of income and output captures two fundamental principles:\ (1) In every economic transaction, the seller receives exactly the same amount that the buyer spends; and (2) goods and services flow in one direction, and money payments flow in the other direction. In the circular flow, households ultimately purchase the nation's total output of final goods and services. They make these purchases using income—wages, rents, interest, and profits—earned from selling labor, land, capital, and entrepreneurial services. Hence the values of total income and total output must be the same in the circular flow.	national income accounting, 185 total income, 185 final goods and services, 186 **Key figure** Figure 8-1, 186	• MyEconLab Study Plan 8.1 • Audio introduction to Chapter 8 • Animated Figure 8-1
Gross Domestic Product (GDP) A nation's gross domestic product is the total market value of its final output of goods and services produced within a given year using factors of production located within the nation's borders. Because GDP measures the value of a flow of production during a year in terms of market prices, it is not a measure of a nation's wealth.	gross domestic product (GDP), 187 intermediate goods, 188 value added, 188	• MyEconLab Study Plan 8.2
The Limitations of Using GDP as a Measure of National Welfare Gross domestic product is a useful measure for tracking year-to-year changes in the value of a nation's overall economic activity in terms of market prices. But it excludes non-market transactions that may contribute to or detract from general welfare. It also fails to account for factors such as labor market discrimination, personal safety, environmental quality, and the amount and quality of leisure time available to a nation's residents. That is why GDP is not an accurate measure of national well-being.		• MyEconLab Study Plan 8.2 • Video: What GDP Excludes
The Expenditure Approach to Tabulating GDP To calculate GDP using the expenditure approach, we sum consumption spending, investment expenditures, government spending, and net export expenditures. Thus, we add up the total amount spent on newly produced goods and services during the year to obtain the dollar value of the output produced and purchased during the year.	expenditure approach, 191 income approach, 191 durable consumer goods, 191 nondurable consumer goods, 191 services, 191 gross private domestic investment, 191 investment, 191	• MyEconLab Study Plan 8.3 • Video: Investment and GDP • Animated Figure 8-2

WHAT YOU SHOULD KNOW		WHERE TO GO TO PRACTICE
The Expenditure Approach to Tabulating GDP (continued)	producer durables, or capital goods, 192 fixed investment, 192 inventory investment, 192 depreciation, 193 net domestic product (NDP), 194 capital consumption allowance, 194 net investment, 194 **Key figure** Figure 8-2, 193	
The Income Approach to Computing GDP To tabulate GDP using the income approach, we add total wages and salaries, rental income, interest income, profits, and nonincome expense items—indirect business taxes and depreciation—to obtain gross domestic income, which is equivalent to gross domestic product. Thus, the total value of all income earnings (equivalent to total factor costs) equals GDP.	gross domestic income (GDI), 195 indirect business taxes, 195 nonincome expense items, 196 national income (NI), 198 personal income (PI), 198 disposable personal income (DPI), 198	• **MyEconLab** Study Plans 8.3 and 8.4 • Video: Investment and GDP
Distinguishing Between Nominal GDP and Real GDP Nominal GDP is the value of newly produced output during the current year measured at current market prices. Real GDP adjusts the value of current output into constant dollars by correcting for changes in the overall level of prices from year to year. To calculate real GDP, we divide nominal GDP by the price index (the GDP deflator) and multiply by 100.	nominal values, 199 real values, 199 constant dollars, 200 foreign exchange rate, 202 purchasing power parity, 203 **Key figure** Figure 8-4, 202	• **MyEconLab** Study Plans 8.5 and 8.6 • Animated Figure 8-4

Log in to MyEconLab, take a chapter test, and get a personalized Study Plan that tells you which concepts you understand and which ones you need to review. From there, MyEconLab will give you futher practice, tutorials, animations, videos, and guided solutions.
Log in to www.myeconlab.com

PROBLEMS

Select problems, indicated by a blue oval ●, are assignable in *MyEconLab*. Answers to the odd-numbered problems appear at the back of the book.

8-1 Each year after a regular spring cleaning, Juanita spruces up her home a little by retexturing and repainting the walls of one room in her house. In a given year, she spends $25 on magazines to get ideas about wall textures and paint shades, $45 on newly produced texturing materials and tools, $35 on new paintbrushes and other painting equipment, and $175 on newly produced paint. Normally, she preps the walls, a service that a professional wall-texturing specialist would charge $200 to do, and applies two coats of paint, a service that a painter would charge $350 to do, on her own.

a. When she purchases her usual set of materials and does all the work on her home by herself in a given spring, how much does Juanita's annual spring texturing and painting activity contribute to GDP?
b. Suppose that Juanita hurt her back this year and is recovering from surgery. Her surgeon has instructed her not to do any texturing work, but he has given her the go-ahead to paint a room as long as she is cautious. Thus, she buys all the equipment required to both texture and paint a room. She hires someone else to do the texturing work but does the painting herself. How much would her spring painting activity add to GDP?
c. As a follow-up to part (b), suppose that as soon as Juanita bends down to dip her brush into the paint, she realizes that painting will be too hard on her back after all. She decides to hire someone else to do all the work using the materials she has already purchased. In this case, how much will her spring painting activity contribute to GDP?

8-2 Each year, Johan typically does all his own landscaping and yard work. He spends $200 per year on mulch for his flower beds, $225 per year on flowers and plants, $50 on fertilizer for his lawn, and $245 on gasoline and lawn mower maintenance. The lawn and garden store where he obtains his mulch and fertilizer charges other customers $500 for the service of spreading that much mulch in flower beds and $50 for the service of distributing fertilizer over a yard the size of Johan's. Paying a professional yard care service to mow his lawn would require an expenditure of $1,200 per year, but in that case Johan would not have to buy gasoline or maintain his own lawn mower.

a. In a normal year, how much does Johan's landscaping and yard work contribute to GDP?
b. Suppose that Johan has developed allergy problems this year and will have to reduce the amount of his yard work. He can wear a mask while running his lawn mower, so he will keep mowing his yard, but he will pay the lawn and garden center to spread mulch and distribute fertilizer. How much will all the work on Johan's yard contribute to GDP this year?
c. As a follow-up to part (b), at the end of the year, Johan realizes that his allergies are growing worse and that he will have to arrange for all his landscaping and yard work to be done by someone else next year. How much will he contribute to GDP next year?

8-3 Consider the following hypothetical data for the U.S. economy in 2012 (all amounts are in trillions of dollars).

Consumption	11.0
Indirect business taxes	.8
Depreciation	1.3
Government spending	2.8
Imports	2.7
Gross private domestic investment	3.0
Exports	2.5

a. Based on the data, what is GDP? NDP? NI?
b. Suppose that in 2013, exports fall to $2.3 trillion, imports rise to $2.85 trillion, and gross private domestic investment falls to $2.25 trillion. What will GDP be in 2013, assuming that other values do not change between 2012 and 2013?

8-4 Look back at Table 8-3 on page 201, which explains how to calculate real GDP in terms of 2000 constant dollars. Change the base year to 2006. Recalculate the price index, and then recalculate real GDP—that is, express column 4 of Table 8-3 in terms of 2006 dollars instead of 2000 dollars.

8-5 Consider the following hypothetical data for the U.S. economy in 2012 (in trillions of dollars), and assume that there are no statistical discrepancies or other adjustments.

Profit	2.8
Indirect business taxes and transfers	.8
Rent	.7
Interest	.8
Wages	8.2
Depreciation	1.3
Consumption	11.0
Exports	1.5
Government transfer payments	2.0
Personal income taxes and nontax payments	1.7
Imports	1.7
Corporate taxes and retained earnings	.5
Social Security contributions	2.0
Government spending	1.8

a. What is gross domestic income? GDP?
b. What is gross private domestic investment?
c. What is personal income? Personal disposable income?

8-6 Which of the following are production activities that are included in GDP? Which are not?

a. Mr. King performs the service of painting his own house instead of paying someone else to do it.
b. Mr. King paints houses for a living.
c. Mrs. King earns income from parents by taking baby photos in her home photography studio.
d. Mrs. King takes photos of planets and stars as part of her astronomy hobby.
e. E*Trade charges fees to process Internet orders for stock trades.
f. Mr. Ho spends $10,000 on shares of stock via an Internet trade order and pays a $10 brokerage fee.
g. Mrs. Ho receives a Social Security payment.
h. Ms. Chavez makes a $300 payment for an Internet-based course on stock trading.
i. Mr. Langham sells a used laptop computer to his neighbor.

8-7 Explain what happens to contributions to GDP in each of the following situations.

a. A woman who makes a living charging for investment advice on her Internet Web site marries one of her clients, to whom she now provides advice at no charge.
b. A tennis player wins two top professional tournaments as an unpaid amateur, meaning the tournament sponsor does not have to pay out his share of prize money.
c. A company that had been selling used firearms illegally finally gets around to obtaining an operating license and performing background checks as specified by law prior to each gun sale.

8-8 Explain what happens to the official measure of GDP in each of the following situations.

a. Air quality improves significantly throughout the United States, but there are no effects on aggregate production or on market prices of final goods and services.
b. The U.S. government spends considerably less on antipollution efforts this year than it did in recent years.
c. The quality of cancer treatments increases, so patients undergo fewer treatments, which hospitals continue to provide at the same price per treatment as before.

8-9 Which of the following activities of a computer manufacturer during the current year are included in this year's measure of GDP?

a. The manufacturer purchases a chip in June, uses it as a component in a computer in August, and sells the computer to a customer in November.
b. A retail outlet of the company sells a computer manufactured during the current year.
c. A marketing arm of the company receives fee income during the current year when a buyer of one of its computers elects to use the computer manufacturer as her Internet service provider.

8-10 Consider the following table for the economy of a nation whose residents produce five final goods.

	2007		2011	
Good	Price	Quantity	Price	Quantity
Shampoo	$ 2	15	$ 4	20
DVD drives	200	10	250	10
Books	40	5	50	4
Milk	3	10	4	3
Candy	1	40	2	20

Assuming a 2007 base year:
a. What is nominal GDP for 2007 and 2011?
b. What is real GDP for 2007 and 2011?

8-11 In the table for Problem 8-10, if 2007 is the base year, what is the price index for 2007? For 2011? (Round decimal fractions to the nearest tenth.)

8-12 Consider the following table for the economy of a nation whose residents produce four final goods.

	2009		2010	
Good	Price	Quantity	Price	Quantity
Computers	$1,000	10	$800	15
Bananas	6	3,000	11	1,000
Televisions	100	500	150	300
Cookies	1	10,000	2	10,000

Assuming a 2010 base year:
a. What is nominal GDP for 2009 and 2010?
b. What is real GDP for 2009 and 2010?

8-13 In the table for Problem 8-12, if 2010 is the base year, what is the price index for 2009? (Round decimal fractions to the nearest tenth.)

8-14 Suppose that early in a year, a hurricane hits a town in Florida and destroys a substantial number of homes. A portion of this stock of housing, which had a market value of $100 million (not including the market value of the land), was uninsured. The owners of the residences spent a total of $5 million during the rest of the year to pay salvage companies to help them save remaining belongings. A small percentage of uninsured owners had sufficient resources to spend a total of

$15 million during the year to pay construction companies to rebuild their homes. Some were able to devote their own time, the opportunity cost of which was valued at $3 million, to work on rebuilding their homes. The remaining people, however, chose to sell their land at its market value and abandon the remains of their houses. What was the combined effect of these transactions on GDP for this year? (Hint: Which transactions took place in the markets for *final* goods and services?) In what ways, if any, does the effect on GDP reflect a loss in welfare for these individuals?

8-15. Suppose that in 2011, geologists discover large reserves of oil under the tundra in Alaska. These reserves have a market value estimated at $50 billion at current oil prices. Oil companies spend $1 billion to hire workers and move and position equipment to begin exploratory pumping during that same year. In the process of loading some of the oil onto tankers at a port, one company accidentally spills some of the oil into a bay and by the end of the year pays $1 billion to other companies to clean it up. The oil spill kills thousands of birds, seals, and other wildlife. What was the combined effect of these events on GDP for this year? (Hint: Which transactions took place in the markets for *final* goods and services?) In what ways, if any, does the effect on GDP reflect a loss in national welfare?

8-16. Consider the following diagram, and answer the questions below.

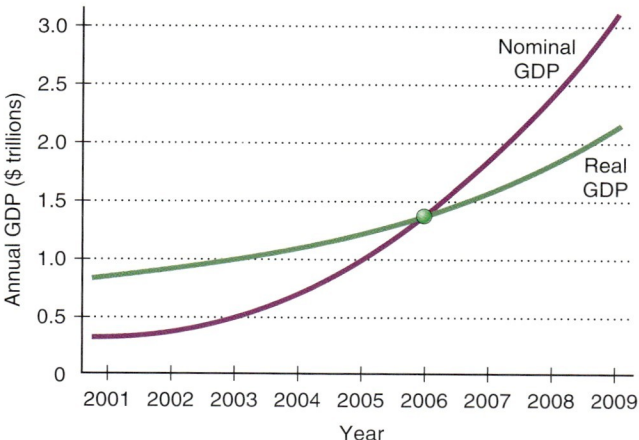

a. What is the base year? Explain.
b. Has this country experienced inflation or deflation since the base year? How can you tell?

ECONOMICS ON THE NET

Tracking the Components of Gross Domestic Product One way to keep tabs on the components of GDP is via the FRED database at the Web site of the Federal Reserve Bank of St. Louis.

Title: Gross Domestic Product and Components

Navigation: Use the link at **www.econtoday.com/ch08** to visit the home page of the Federal Reserve Bank of St. Louis. Click on *FRED*. Then click on *Gross Domestic Product and Components*.

Application

1. Click on *Gross Domestic Product*. Write down nominal GDP data for the past 10 quarters.

2. Back up to *Real Gross Domestic Product in Fixed 2000 Dollars*. Write down the amounts for the past 10 quarters. Use the formula on page 200 to calculate the price level for each quarter. Has the price level decreased or increased in recent quarters?

For Group Study and Analysis Divide the class into "consumption," "investment," "government sector," and "foreign sector" groups. Have each group evaluate the contribution of each category of spending to GDP and to its quarter-to-quarter volatility. Reconvene the class, and discuss the factors that appear to create the most variability in GDP.

ANSWERS TO QUICK QUIZZES

p. 187: (i) factor . . . income; (ii) final; (iii) profit
p. 190: (i) Gross domestic product; (ii) value added; (iii) exclude; (iv) GDP; (v) market value
p. 195: (i) expenditure . . . durables . . . nondurables . . . services; (ii) capacity . . . inventories; (iii) market; (iv) depreciation
p. 196: (i) wages . . . interest . . . rent . . . profits; (ii) indirect business taxes . . . depreciation
p. 199: (i) national income; (ii) personal income; (iii) income taxes
p. 201: (i) 100 . . . 110; (ii) population
p. 204: (i) exchange rate; (ii) exchange rate; (iii) cost . . . living

Global Economic Growth and Development

9

Learning Objectives

After reading this chapter, you should be able to:

1. Define economic growth
2. Recognize the importance of economic growth rates
3. Explain why productivity increases are crucial for maintaining economic growth
4. Describe the fundamental determinants of economic growth
5. Understand the basis of new growth theory
6. Discuss the fundamental factors that contribute to a nation's economic development

MyEconLab helps you master each objective and study more efficiently. See end of chapter for details.

About half of all U.S. engineers and computer scientists with Ph.D. degrees were born outside the United States. In addition, children of U.S. residents who were born abroad typically account for more than 60 percent of the top scores in the U.S. Math Olympiad and for almost half of the U.S. Physics Team. On the one hand, the ability of the United States to attract immigrant engineers and scientists and immigrants' children interested in pursuing careers in sciences has contributed to U.S. economic growth. On the other hand, the loss of well-trained emigrants and their children has had negative effects on economic growth in their nations of origin. In this chapter, you will learn why countries that attract and retain the world's brainiest and hardest-working people tend to experience the highest sustained rates of economic growth.

Did You Know That...

only one European nation, Luxembourg, has per capita real GDP—real GDP divided by the population—higher than the U.S. per capita real GDP? Luxembourg's per capita real GDP is nearly 50 percent greater than overall U.S. per capita real GDP, which puts its residents' incomes on a par with those of the U.S. states of Delaware and Connecticut. In Belgium, France, Germany, and Italy, however, per capita real GDP is only slightly higher than in the U.S. states of Arkansas and Montana, where per capita real GDP is less than 75 percent of the overall U.S. level. In fact, per capita real GDP in these four European nations is only about 14 percent higher than in West Virginia and Mississippi, the U.S. states with the lowest per capita real GDP.

A few decades ago, per capita real GDP in Arkansas, Montana, West Virginia, and Mississippi was far below the levels in Belgium, France, Germany, and Italy. Since then, per capita real GDP has grown more rapidly in the four U.S. states than in the four European nations. Thus, the four U.S. states have experienced a higher rate of *economic growth*, which is the topic of this chapter.

HOW DO WE DEFINE ECONOMIC GROWTH?

Recall from Chapter 2 that we can show economic growth graphically as an outward shift of a production possibilities curve, as is seen in Figure 9-1. If there is economic growth between 2009 and 2035, the production possibilities curve will shift outward toward the red curve. The distance that it shifts represents the amount of economic growth, defined as the increase in the productive capacity of a nation. Although it is possible to come up with a measure of a nation's increased productive capacity, it would not be easy. Therefore, we turn to a more readily obtainable definition of economic growth.

Most people have a general idea of what economic growth means. When a nation grows economically, its citizens must be better off in at least some ways, usually in terms of their material well-being. Typically, though, we do not measure the well-being of any nation solely in terms of its total output of real goods and services or in terms of real GDP without

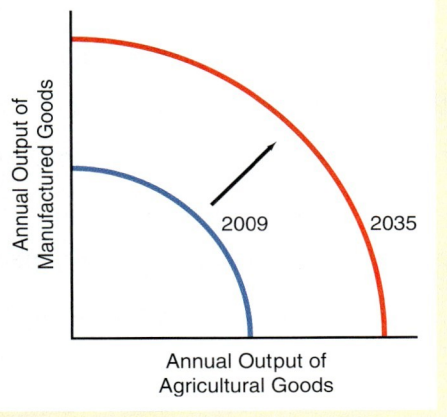

FIGURE 9-1

Economic Growth

If there is growth between 2009 and 2035, the production possibilities curve for the entire economy will shift outward from the blue line labeled 2009 to the red line labeled 2035. The distance that it shifts represents an increase in the productive capacity of the nation.

making some adjustments. After all, India has a real GDP more than 15 times as large as that of Denmark. The population in India, though, is about 200 times greater than that of Denmark. Consequently, we view India as a relatively poor country and Denmark as a relatively rich country. Thus, when we measure economic growth, we must adjust for population growth. Our formal definition becomes this: **Economic growth** occurs when there are increases in *per capita* real GDP, measured by the rate of change in per capita real GDP per year. Figure 9-2 presents the historical record of real GDP per person in the United States.

Economic growth
Increases in per capita real GDP measured by its rate of change per year.

Problems in Definition

Our definition of economic growth says nothing about the *distribution* of output and income. A nation might grow very rapidly in terms of increases in per capita real output, while its poor people remain poor or become even poorer. Therefore, in assessing the economic growth record of any nation, we must be careful to pinpoint which income groups have benefited the most from such growth. How much does economic growth differ across countries?

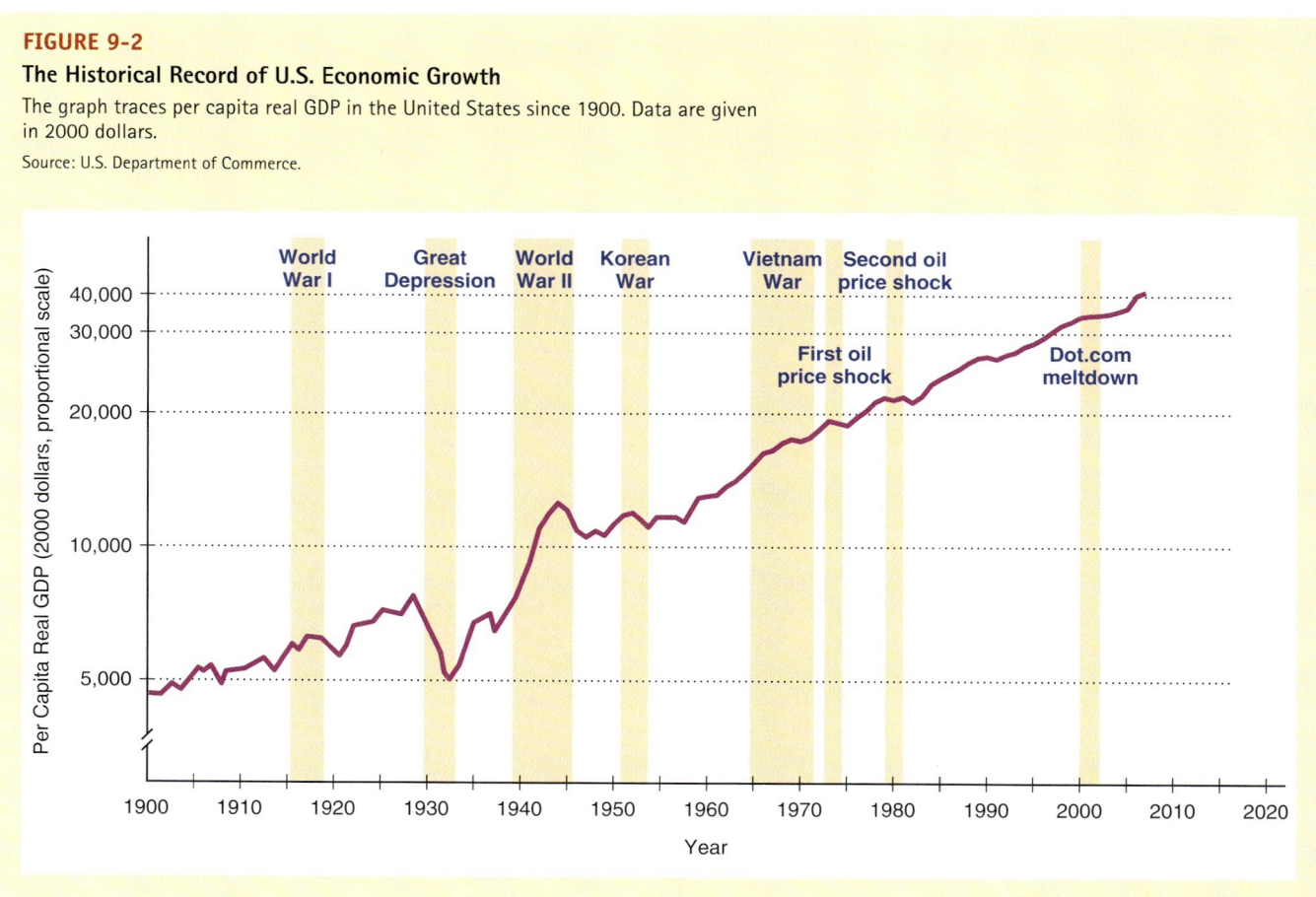

FIGURE 9-2

The Historical Record of U.S. Economic Growth

The graph traces per capita real GDP in the United States since 1900. Data are given in 2000 dollars.

Source: U.S. Department of Commerce.

INTERNATIONAL EXAMPLE

Growth Rates Around the World

Table 9-1 shows the average annual rate of growth of real GDP per person in selected countries for the period since 1990. Notice that during the time period under study the United States is positioned about midway in the pack. Thus, even though we are one of the world's richest countries, our rate of economic growth in recent decades has not been particularly high. The reason that U.S. per capita real GDP has remained higher than per capita real GDP in most other nations is that the United States has been able to sustain growth over many decades. This is something that most other countries have so far been unable to accomplish.

FOR CRITICAL ANALYSIS
"The largest change is from zero to one." Does this statement have anything to do with relative growth rates in poorer versus richer countries?

TABLE 9-1

Per Capita Real GDP Growth Rates in Various Countries

Country	Average Annual Rate of Growth of Real GDP Per Capita, 1990–2007 (%)
Brazil	2.4
France	2.5
Japan	3.1
Germany	3.1
Sweden	3.2
Canada	3.4
United States	3.8
Turkey	4.6
Indonesia	4.7
India	5.3
Malaysia	5.4
China	9.4

Sources: World Bank, International Monetary Fund, and authors' estimates.

Go to www.econtoday.com/ch09 to get the latest figures and estimates on economic growth throughout the world.

Real standards of living can go up without any positive economic growth. This can occur if individuals are, on average, enjoying more leisure by working fewer hours but producing as much as they did before. For example, if per capita real GDP in the United States remained at $40,000 a year for a decade, we could not automatically jump to the conclusion that U.S. residents were, on average, no better off. What if, during that same 10-year period, average hours worked fell from 37 per week to 33 per week? That would mean that during the 10 years under study, individuals in the labor force were "earning" 4 more hours of leisure a week. Actually, nothing so extreme has occurred in this country, but something similar has. Average hours worked per week fell steadily until the 1960s, when they leveled off. That means that during much of the history of this country, the increase in per capita real GDP *understated* the actual economic growth that we were experiencing because we were enjoying more and more leisure as time passed.

Is Economic Growth Bad?

Some commentators on our current economic situation believe that the definition of economic growth ignores its negative effects. Some psychologists even contend that economic growth makes us worse off. They say that the more we grow, the more "needs" are created so that we feel worse off as we become richer. Our expectations are rising faster than reality, so we presumably always suffer from a sense of disappointment. Also, the economist's measurement of economic growth does not take into account the spiritual and cultural aspects of the good life. As with all activities, both costs and benefits are associated with growth. You can see some of those listed in Table 9-2.

Any measure of economic growth that we use will be imperfect. Nonetheless, the measures that we do have allow us to make comparisons across countries and over time and, if used judiciously, can enable us to gain important insights. Per capita real GDP, used so often, is not always an accurate measure of economic well-being, but it is a serviceable measure of productive activity.

ECONOMICS FRONT AND CENTER

To contemplate whether economic growth has contributed to a drop in the number of U.S. manufacturing jobs, consider **The Congressman Wants to Know the Facts—Or Does He?** on page 232.

The Importance of Growth Rates

Notice in Table 9-1 that the growth rates in real per capita income for most countries differ very little—generally by only a few percentage points. You might want to know why such small differences in growth rates are important. What would it matter if we grew at 3 percent rather than at 4 percent per year?

It matters a lot—not for next year or the year after but for the more distant future. The power of *compounding* is impressive. Let's see what happens with three different annual rates of growth: 3 percent, 4 percent, and 5 percent. We start with $1 trillion per year of gross domestic product of the United States at some time in the past. We then compound this $1 trillion, or allow it to grow at these three different growth rates. The difference is huge. In 50 years, $1 trillion per year becomes $4.38 trillion per year if compounded at 3 percent per year. Just one percentage point more in the growth rate, 4 percent, results in a real GDP of $7.11 trillion per year in 50 years, almost double the previous amount. Two percentage points difference in the growth rate—5 percent per year—results in a real GDP of $11.5 trillion per year in 50 years, or nearly three times as much. Obviously, very small differences in annual growth rates result in great differences in economic growth. That is why nations are concerned if the growth rate falls even a little in absolute percentage terms.

Thus, when we talk about growth rates, we are talking about compounding. In Table 9-3 on the following page, we show how $1 compounded annually grows at different interest rates. We see in the 3 percent column that $1 in 50 years grows to $4.38. We merely multiplied $1 trillion times 4.38 to get the growth figure in our earlier example. In the 5 percent column, $1 grows to $11.50 after 50 years. Again, we multiplied $1 trillion times 11.50 to get the growth figure for 5 percent in the preceding example.

How must faster would Europe's economies have to grow for per capita real GDP to catch up with U.S. per capita real GDP?

TABLE 9-2
Costs and Benefits of Economic Growth

Benefits	Costs
Reduction in illiteracy	Environmental pollution
Reduction in poverty	Breakdown of the family
Improved health	Isolation and alienation
Longer lives	Urban congestion
Political stability	

TABLE 9-3
One Dollar Compounded Annually at Different Interest Rates

Here we show the value of a dollar at the end of a specified period during which it has been compounded annually at a specified interest rate. For example, if you took $1 today and invested it at 5 percent per year, it would yield $1.05 at the end of one year. At the end of 10 years, it would equal $1.63, and at the end of 50 years, it would equal $11.50.

Number of Years	Interest Rate						
	3%	4%	5%	6%	8%	10%	20%
1	1.03	1.04	1.05	1.06	1.08	1.10	1.20
2	1.06	1.08	1.10	1.12	1.17	1.21	1.44
3	1.09	1.12	1.16	1.19	1.26	1.33	1.73
4	1.13	1.17	1.22	1.26	1.36	1.46	2.07
5	1.16	1.22	1.28	1.34	1.47	1.61	2.49
6	1.19	1.27	1.34	1.41	1.59	1.77	2.99
7	1.23	1.32	1.41	1.50	1.71	1.94	3.58
8	1.27	1.37	1.48	1.59	1.85	2.14	4.30
9	1.30	1.42	1.55	1.68	2.00	2.35	5.16
10	1.34	1.48	1.63	1.79	2.16	2.59	6.19
20	1.81	2.19	2.65	3.20	4.66	6.72	38.30
30	2.43	3.24	4.32	5.74	10.00	17.40	237.00
40	3.26	4.80	7.04	10.30	21.70	45.30	1,470.00
50	4.38	7.11	11.50	18.40	46.90	117.00	9,100.00

INTERNATIONAL EXAMPLE

Europe Tries to Play Catch-Up

Per capita real GDP in the European Union (EU) is less than 75 percent of the U.S. level. As a consequence, the average U.S. resident is able to spend nearly $10,000 more on consumption per year than the average EU resident.

How much faster would EU nations' economies have to grow for real GDP per capita to catch up with the U.S. level? Suppose that U.S. per capita real GDP is frozen for the next couple of decades. At a sustained annual growth rate of 4 percent, EU per capita real GDP could reach equality with the U.S. level within seven years.

Of course, U.S. per capita real GDP is not frozen in time. In recent years, it has been growing at an annual rate of 3 to 4 percent per year. Thus, EU nations would have to achieve a sustained annual rate of economic growth of 5 to 10 percent for EU per capita real GDP to rise to the U.S. level within seven years. In fact, the rate of economic growth in the European Union in recent years has been closer to 1 percent. Consequently, the gap between U.S. per capita real GDP and EU per capita real GDP is actually more likely to *increase* during the coming years.

FOR CRITICAL ANALYSIS

If U.S. per capita real GDP were frozen and each EU nation grew at its current pace, per capita real GDP in Germany would take twice as long to reach the U.S. level as in Ireland. If both Germany and Ireland began near the EU average per capita real GDP, what would this imply about Ireland's rate of economic growth compared with the rate of economic growth in Germany?

QUICK QUIZ

Economic growth can be defined as the increase in _____ _____ real GDP, measured by its rate of change per year.

The _____ of economic growth are reductions in illiteracy, poverty, and illness and increases in life spans and political stability. The _____ of economic growth may include environmental pollution, alienation, and urban congestion.

Small percentage-point differences in growth rates lead to _____ differences in per capita real GDP over time. These differences can be seen by examining a compound interest table such as the one in Table 9-3.

See page 238 for the answers. Review concepts from this section in MyEconLab.

PRODUCTIVITY INCREASES: THE HEART OF ECONOMIC GROWTH

Let's say that you are required to type 10 term papers and homework assignments a year. You have a computer, but you do not know how to touch-type. You end up spending an average of two hours per typing job. The next summer, you buy a touch-typing tutorial to use on your computer and spend a few minutes a day improving your speed. The following term, you spend only one hour per typing assignment, thereby saving 10 hours a semester. You have become more productive. This concept of productivity summarizes your ability (and everyone else's) to produce the same output with fewer inputs. Thus, **labor productivity** is normally measured by dividing the total real domestic output (real GDP) by the number of workers or the number of labor hours. By definition, labor productivity increases whenever average output produced per worker during a specified time period increases.

Labor productivity
Total real domestic output (real GDP) divided by the number of workers (output per worker).

Has the official U.S. labor productivity measure been biased upward in recent years?

EXAMPLE

Is Official Labor Productivity Growth Overstated?

According to the primary measure of labor productivity utilized by the U.S. Bureau of Labor Statistics (BLS)—which features prominently in most media reports—U.S. labor productivity has increased by at least 21 percent since 2000. To obtain the data used to create its labor productivity measure, the BLS surveys businesses about their output of goods and services and the average weekly hours of full-time employees. When constructing its labor productivity measure, the BLS excludes government employees, self-employed people, managers, and part-time and temporary employees. Recent estimates indicate that including these forms of labor might reduce the growth in U.S. labor productivity since 2000 by as much as one-half, to an overall percentage increase as low as 11 percent.

FOR CRITICAL ANALYSIS
Why might the output of government workers be difficult to gauge for purposes of measuring labor productivity?

Clearly, there is a relationship between economic growth and increases in labor productivity. If you divide all resources into just capital and labor, economic growth can be defined simply as the cumulative contribution to per capita GDP growth of three components: the rate of growth of capital, the rate of growth of labor, and the rate of growth of capital and labor productivity. If everything else remains constant, improvements in labor productivity ultimately lead to economic growth and higher living standards.

Figure 9-3 on the following page displays estimates of the relative contributions of the growth of labor and capital and the growth of labor and capital productivity to economic growth in the United States, nations in South Asia, and Latin American countries. The growth of labor resources, through associated increases in labor force participation, has contributed to the expansion of output that has accounted for at least half of economic growth in all three regions. Total capital is the sum of physical capital, such as tools and machines, and human capital, which is the amount of knowledge acquired from research and education. Figure 9-3 shows the separate contributions of the growth of these forms of capital, which together have accounted for roughly a third of the growth rate of per capita incomes in the United States, South Asia, and Latin America. In these three parts of the world, growth in overall capital and labor productivity has contributed the remaining 7 to 18 percent.

Go to www.econtoday.com/ch09 for information about the latest trends in U.S. labor productivity.

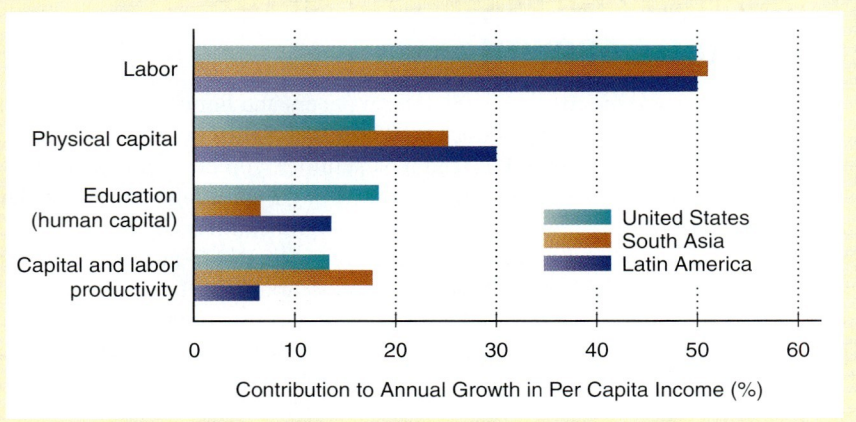

FIGURE 9-3

Factors Accounting for Economic Growth in Selected Regions

In the United States, South Asia, and Latin America, growth in labor resources, and in their participation in the process of production, is the main contributor to economic growth.

Source: International Monetary Fund.

SAVING: A FUNDAMENTAL DETERMINANT OF ECONOMIC GROWTH

Economic growth does not occur in a vacuum. It is not some predetermined fate of a nation. Rather, economic growth depends on certain fundamental factors. One of the most important factors that affects the rate of economic growth and hence long-term living standards is the rate of saving.

A basic proposition in economics is that if you want more tomorrow, you have to consume less today.

> *To have more consumption in the future, you have to consume less today and save the difference between your consumption and your income.*

On a national basis, this implies that higher saving rates eventually mean higher living standards in the long run, all other things held constant. Concern has been growing in the United States that we are not saving enough. Saving is important for economic growth because without saving, we cannot have investment. If there is no investment in our capital stock, there would be much less economic growth.

The relationship between the rate of saving and per capita real GDP is shown in Figure 9-4. Among the nations with the highest rates of saving are Saudi Arabia, Japan, and Germany.

QUICK QUIZ

Economic growth is numerically equal to the rate of growth of _____ plus the rate of growth of _____ plus the rate of growth in the productivity of _____ and of _____. Improvements in labor productivity, all other things being equal, lead to greater economic growth and higher living standards.

One fundamental determinant of the rate of growth is the rate of _____. To have more consumption in the future, we have to _____ rather than consume. In general, countries that have had higher rates of _____ have had higher rates of growth in real GDP.

See page 238 for the answers. Review concepts from this section in MyEconLab.

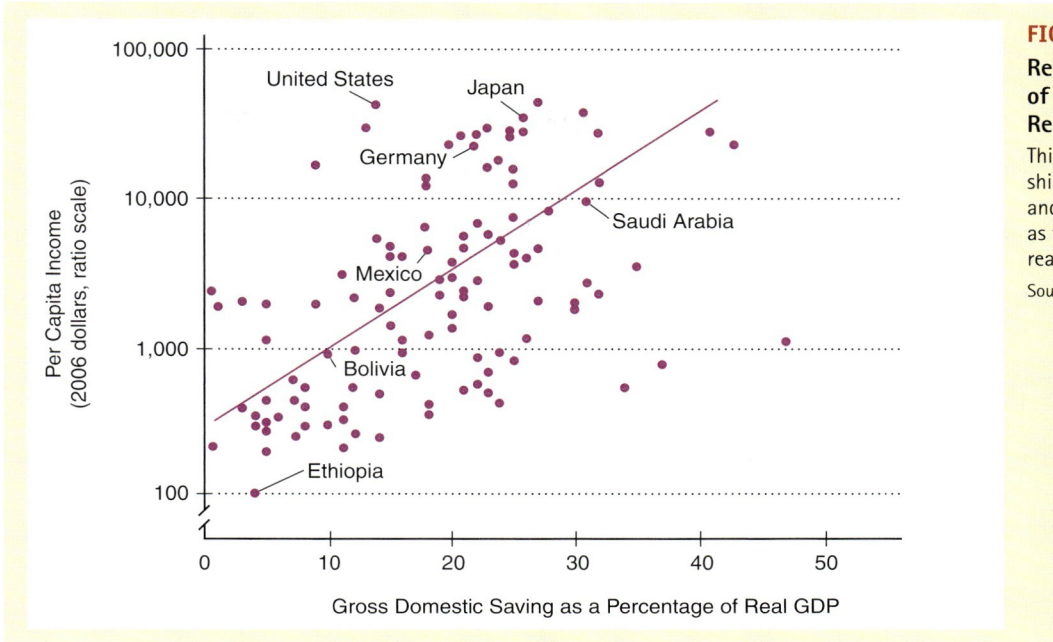

FIGURE 9-4
Relationship Between Rate of Saving and Per Capita Real GDP
This diagram shows the relationship between per capita real GDP and the rate of saving expressed as the average share of annual real GDP saved.
Source: World Bank.

NEW GROWTH THEORY AND THE DETERMINANTS OF GROWTH

A simple arithmetic definition of economic growth has already been given. The per capita growth rates of capital and labor plus the per capita growth rate of their productivity constitute the rate of economic growth. Economists have had good data on the growth of the physical capital stock in the United States as well as on the labor force. But when you add those two growth rates together, you still do not get the total economic growth rate in the United States. The difference has to be due to improvements in productivity. Economists typically labeled this "improvements in technology," and that was that. More recently, proponents of what is now called **new growth theory** argue that technology cannot simply be looked at as an outside factor without explanation. Technology must be understood in terms of what drives it. What are the forces that make productivity grow in the United States and elsewhere?

New growth theory
A theory of economic growth that examines the factors that determine why technology, research, innovation, and the like are undertaken and how they interact.

Growth in Technology

Consider some startling statistics about the growth in technology. Microprocessor speeds may increase from 4,000 megahertz to 10,000 megahertz by the year 2015. By that same year, the size of the thinnest circuit line within a transistor may decrease by 90 percent. The typical memory capacity (RAM) of computers will jump from 512 megabytes, or about eight times the equivalent text in the *Encyclopaedia Britannica,* to 128 gigabytes—a 250-fold increase. Predictions are that computers may become as powerful as the human brain by 2020.

How has the increased incorporation of digital technologies into cellphones helped speed the pace of economic growth in developing nations?

EXAMPLE

Putting in a Cellphone Call for Growth

In many nations, the cellphone is a key technology promoting economic growth. For instance, in the African nation of Zambia, becoming known as someone who carries cash has traditionally been an invitation to be robbed. Consequently, many consumers and businesses now use cellphone text messages to transmit payments to their banks. In this way, firms such as dry cleaners and restaurants can operate without cash that otherwise might attract criminals. The result has been less crime and greater economic growth.

Indeed, greater use of cellphones has contributed to economic growth in other nations around the globe besides Zambia. Current estimates indicate that an increase of 10 cellphones per 100 people boosts a typical developing nation's annual rate of economic growth by as much as half a percentage point. As a consequence, 25 years from now real per capita GDP will be almost 15 percent higher than it would have been in the absence of cellphones.

FOR CRITICAL ANALYSIS
Why do you suppose that when estimating the effects of cellphone use on economic growth, the effect of economic growth on cellphone use must be taken into account? (Hint: Economic growth pushes up incomes, which boosts purchases of cellphones.)

Technology: A Separate Factor of Production

We now recognize that technology must be viewed as a separate factor of production that is sensitive to rewards. Otherwise stated, one of the major foundations of new growth theory is this:

The greater the rewards, the more technological advances we will get.

Let's consider several aspects of technology here, the first one being research and development.

Research and Development

A certain amount of technological advance results from research and development (R&D) activities that have as their goal the development of specific new materials, new products, and new machines. How much spending a nation devotes to R&D can have an impact on its long-term economic growth. Part of how much a nation spends depends on what businesses decide is worth spending. That in turn depends on their expected rewards from successful R&D. If your company develops a new way to produce computer memory chips, how much will it be rewarded? The answer depends on whether others can freely copy the new technique.

Patents. To protect new techniques developed through R&D, we have a system of **patents,** in which the federal government gives the patent holder the exclusive right to make, use, and sell an invention for a period of 20 years. One can argue that this special position given to owners of patents increases expenditures on R&D and therefore adds to long-term economic growth. Figure 9-5 shows that U.S. patent grants fell during the 1970s, increased steadily after 1982, and then surged from 1995 until 2001.

Patent
A government protection that gives an inventor the exclusive right to make, use, or sell an invention for a limited period of time (currently, 20 years).

Positive Externalities and R&D. As we discussed in Chapter 5, positive externalities are benefits from an activity that are not enjoyed by the instigator of the activity. In the case of R&D spending, a certain amount of the benefits go to other companies that do not

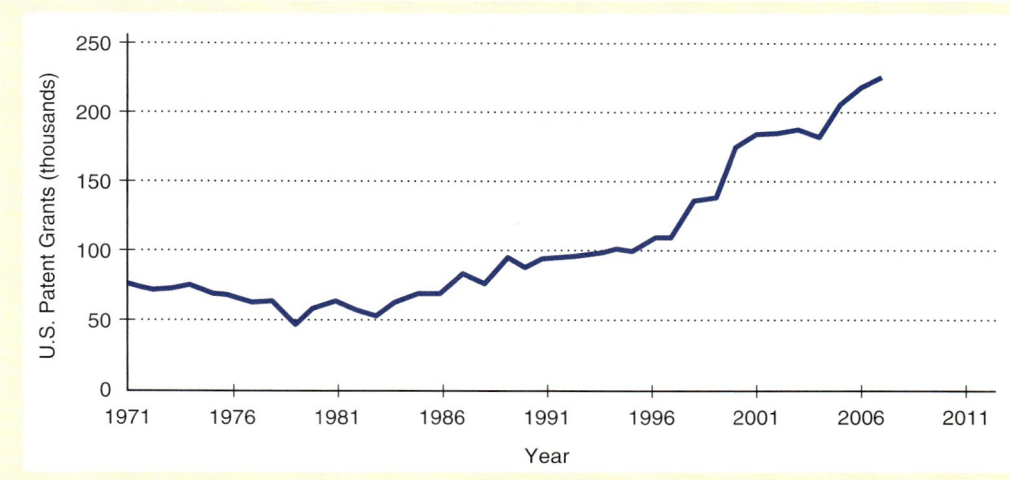

FIGURE 9-5
U.S. Patent Grants
The U.S. Patent and Trademark Office gradually began awarding more patent grants between the early 1980s and the mid-1990s. After 1995, the number of patents granted each year increased significantly until 2001.
Source: U.S. Patent and Trademark Office.

have to pay for them. In particular, according to economists David Coe of the International Monetary Fund and Elhanan Helpman of Tel Aviv University, about a quarter of the global productivity gains of R&D investment in the top seven industrialized countries goes to other nations. For every 1 percent rise in the stock of R&D in the United States alone, for example, productivity in the rest of the world increases by about 0.25 percent. One country's R&D expenditures benefit other countries because they are able to import capital goods—computers, telecommunications networks—from technologically advanced countries and then use them as inputs in making their own industries more efficient. In addition, countries that import high-tech goods are able to imitate the technology.

The Open Economy and Economic Growth

People who study economic growth today emphasize the importance of the openness of the economy. Free trade encourages a more rapid spread of technology and industrial ideas. Moreover, open economies may experience higher rates of economic growth because their own industries have access to a bigger market. When trade barriers are erected in the form of tariffs and the like, domestic industries become isolated from global technological progress. This occurred for many years in former communist countries and in many developing countries in Africa, Latin America, and elsewhere. Figure 9-6 on the following page shows the relationship between economic growth and openness as measured by the level of tariff barriers.

Innovation and Knowledge

We tend to think of technological progress as, say, the invention of the transistor. But invention means nothing by itself; **innovation** is required. Innovation involves the transformation of something new, such as an invention, into something that benefits the economy either by lowering production costs or by providing new goods and services. Indeed, the new growth theorists believe that real wealth creation comes from innovation and that invention is but a facet of innovation.

Historically, technologies have moved relatively slowly from invention to innovation to widespread use, and the dispersion of new technology remains for the most part slow and

Innovation
Transforming an invention into something that is useful to humans.

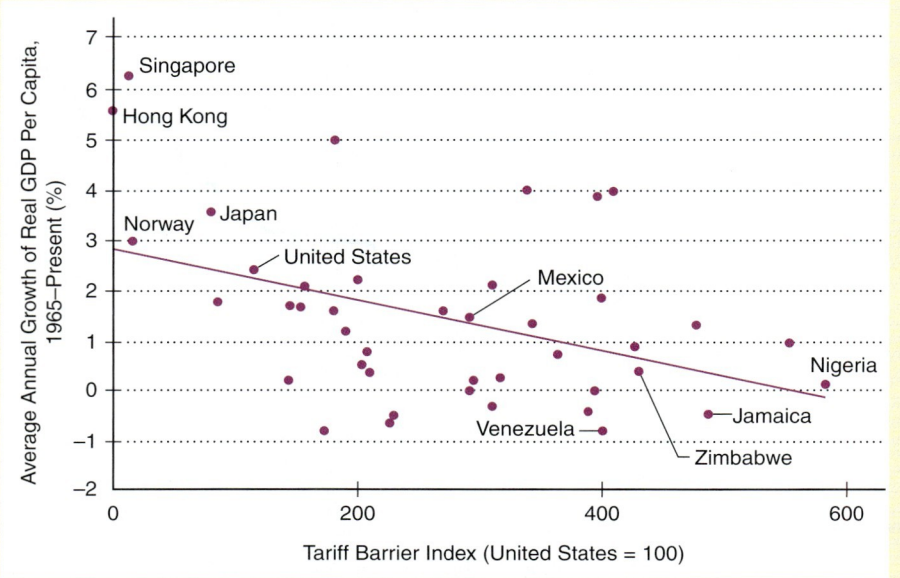

FIGURE 9-6

The Relationship Between Economic Growth and Tariff Barriers to International Trade

Nations with low tariff barriers are relatively open to international trade and have tended to have higher average annual rates of real GDP per capita growth since 1965.

Source: World Bank.

uncertain. The inventor of the transistor thought it might be used to make better hearing aids. At the time it was invented, the *New York Times*'s sole reference to it was in a small weekly column called "News of Radio." When the laser was invented, no one really knew what it could be used for. It was initially used to help in navigation, measurement, and chemical research. Today, it is used in the reproduction of music, printing, surgery, telecommunications, and optical data transmittal and storage. Tomorrow, who knows?

Figure 9-7 shows the process by which raw ideas turn into written ideas that are submitted for study in typical R&D laboratories. Businesses select a few of these for initial study and choose fewer still to evaluate in large research projects. Out of these full-scale research efforts, a few significant developments emerge and are launched as new products. If businesses are lucky, one or two of these product launches may ultimately pay off.

The Importance of Ideas and Knowledge

Economist Paul Romer has added at least one important factor that determines the rate of economic growth. He contends that production and manufacturing knowledge is just as important as the other determinants and perhaps even more so. He considers knowledge a factor of production that, like capital, has to be paid for by forgoing current consumption. Economies must therefore invest in knowledge just as they invest in machines. Because past investment in capital may make it more profitable to acquire more knowledge, there may be an investment-knowledge cycle in which investment spurs knowledge and knowledge spurs investment. A once-and-for-all increase in a country's rate of investment may permanently raise that country's growth rate. (According to traditional theory, a once-and-for-all increase in the rate of saving and therefore in the rate of investment simply leads to a new steady-state standard of living, not one that continues to increase.)

Another way of looking at knowledge is that it is a store of ideas. According to Romer, ideas are what drive economic growth. We have become, in fact, an idea economy. Consider

FIGURE 9-7
The Winnowing Process of Research and Development
Only a portion of new ideas are actually submitted for formal study, and just a fraction of these become subjects of research projects. Very few ideas actually lead to the development of new products.

Microsoft Corporation. A relatively small percentage of that company's labor force is involved in actually building products. Rather, a majority of Microsoft employees are attempting to discover new ideas that can be translated into computer code that can then be turned into products. The major conclusion that Romer and other new growth theorists draw is this:

Economic growth can continue as long as we keep coming up with new ideas.

The Importance of Human Capital

Knowledge, ideas, and productivity are all tied together. One of the threads is the quality of the labor force. Increases in the productivity of the labor force are a function of increases in human capital, the fourth factor of production discussed in Chapter 2. Recall that human capital consists of the knowledge and skills that people in the workforce acquire through education, on-the-job training, and self-teaching. To increase your own human capital, you have to invest by forgoing income-earning activities while you attend school. Society also has to invest in the form of libraries and teachers. According to the new growth theorists, human capital is at least as important as physical capital, particularly when trying to explain international differences in living standards.

It is therefore not surprising that one of the most effective ways that developing countries can become developed is by investing in secondary schooling.

One can argue that policy changes that increase human capital will lead to more technological improvements. One of the reasons that concerned citizens, policymakers, and politicians are looking for a change in the U.S. schooling system is that our educational system seems to be falling behind that of other countries. This lag is greatest in science and mathematics—precisely the areas required for developing better technology.

> **QUICK QUIZ**
>
> _____ _____ theory argues that the greater the rewards, the more rapid the pace of technology. And greater rewards spur research and development.
>
> The openness of a nation's economy to international _____ seems to correlate with its rate of economic growth.
>
> Invention and **innovation** are not the same thing. _____ are useless until _____ transforms them into things that people find valuable.
>
> According to _____ _____ theory, economic growth can continue as long as we keep coming up with new ideas.
>
> Increases in _____ capital can lead to greater rates of economic growth. These come about by increased education, on-the-job training, and self-teaching.
>
> See page 238 for the answers. Review concepts from this section in MyEconLab.

IMMIGRATION, PROPERTY RIGHTS, AND GROWTH

New theories of economic growth have also shed light on two additional factors that play important roles in influencing a nation's rate of growth of per capita real GDP: immigration and property rights.

Population and Immigration as They Affect Economic Growth

There are several ways to view population growth as it affects economic growth. On the one hand, population growth means an increase in the amount of labor, which is one major component of economic growth. On the other hand, population growth can be seen as a drain on the economy because for any given amount of GDP, more population means lower per capita GDP. According to MIT economist Michael Kremer, the first view is historically correct. His conclusion is that population growth drives technological progress, which then increases economic growth. The theory is simple: If there are 50 percent more people in the United States, there will be 50 percent more geniuses. And with 50 percent more people, the rewards for creativity are commensurately greater. Otherwise stated, the larger the potential market, the greater the incentive to become ingenious.

A larger market also provides an incentive for well-trained people to immigrate, which undoubtedly helps explain why the United States attracts a disproportionate number of top scientists from around the globe.

Does immigration help spur economic growth? Yes, according to the late economist Julian Simon, who pointed out that "every time our system allows in one more immigrant, on average, the economic welfare of American citizens goes up. . . . Additional immigrants, both the legal and the illegal, raise the standard of living of U.S. natives and have little or no negative impact on any occupational or income class." He further argued that immigrants do not displace natives from jobs but rather create jobs through their purchases and by starting new businesses. Immigrants' earning and spending simply expand the economy.

Property Rights and Entrepreneurship

If you were in a country where bank accounts and businesses were periodically expropriated by the government, how willing would you be to leave your financial assets in a savings account or to invest in a business? Certainly, you would be less willing than if such things never occurred. In general, the more securely private property rights are assigned, the more capital accumulation there will be. People will be willing to invest their savings in endeavors that will increase their wealth in future years. This requires that property rights in their wealth be sanctioned and enforced by the government. In fact, some economic historians have attempted to show that it was the development of well-defined private property rights and legal structures that allowed Western Europe to increase its growth rate after many centuries of stagnation. The ability and certainty with which they can reap the gains from investing also determine the extent to which business owners in other countries will invest capital in developing countries. The threat of loss of property rights that hangs over some developing nations probably stands in the way of foreign investments that would allow these nations to develop more rapidly.

When might property rights that apply to the space below a building be nearly as important as property rights associated with the land surface on which the building rests?

EXAMPLE

All That Stands in the Way of This Energy Source Is a City

Geologists call it the Barnett Shale formation. This geological formation is a massive wedge of blackish rock up to 400 feet thick, which contains 27 trillion cubic feet of natural gas. It also rests directly below Ft. Worth, Texas, a metropolitan area with 1.6 million residents. The owners of the mineral rights to lands containing the shale determine whether energy companies can drill for gas under residences, businesses, and government offices. Higher natural gas prices—and the corresponding higher royalty payments to the owners of mineral rights—have given many owners an incentive to accept the noise and clutter caused by drilling rigs. Consequently, nearly 100 rigs are drilling for natural gas in and around Ft. Worth. At one exclusive country club, for instance, a drill located off the club grounds chews its way diagonally down to 7,000 feet beneath the shoes of members as they play golf.

FOR CRITICAL ANALYSIS
Why is the rate of economic growth likely to be higher in a nation that has clearly established private rights to mineral resources?

The legal structure of a nation is closely tied to the degree with which its citizens use their own entrepreneurial skills. In Chapter 2, we identified entrepreneurship as the fifth factor of production. Entrepreneurs are the risk takers who seek out new ways to do things and create new products. To the extent that entrepreneurs are allowed to capture the rewards from their entrepreneurial activities, they will seek to engage in those activities. In countries where such rewards cannot be captured because of a lack of property rights, there will be less entrepreneurship. Typically, this results in fewer investments and a lower rate of growth. We shall examine the implications this has for policymakers in Chapter 18.

> **QUICK QUIZ**
>
> While some economists argue that population growth stifles _____ growth, others contend that the opposite is true. The latter economists consequently believe that immigration should be encouraged rather than discouraged.
>
> Well-defined and protected _____ rights are important for fostering entrepreneurship. In the absence of well-defined _____ rights, individuals have less incentive to take risks, and economic growth rates suffer.
>
> See page 238 for the answers. Review concepts from this section in MyEconLab.

ECONOMIC DEVELOPMENT

Development economics
The study of factors that contribute to the economic growth of a country.

How did developed countries travel paths of growth from extreme poverty to relative riches? That is the essential issue of **development economics,** which is the study of why some countries grow and develop and others do not and of policies that might help developing economies get richer. It is not enough simply to say that people in different countries are different and that is why some countries are rich and some countries are poor. Economists do not deny that different cultures have different work ethics, but they are unwilling to accept such a pat and fatalistic answer.

Look at any world map. About four-fifths of the countries you will see on the map are considered relatively poor. The goal of economists who study development is to help the more than 4 billion people today with low living standards join the more than 2 billion people who have at least moderately high living standards.

Putting World Poverty into Perspective

Most U.S. residents cannot even begin to understand the reality of poverty in the world today. At least one-half, if not two-thirds, of the world's population lives at subsistence level, with just enough to eat for survival. Indeed, the World Bank estimates that nearly 20 percent of the world's people live on less than $1 per day. The official poverty line in the United States is set above the average income of at least half the human beings on the planet. This is not to say that we should ignore domestic problems with the poor and homeless simply because they are living better than many people elsewhere in the world. Rather, it is necessary for us to maintain an appropriate perspective on what are considered problems for this country relative to what are considered problems elsewhere.

The Relationship Between Population Growth and Economic Development

The world's population is growing at the rate of about 2.3 people a second. That amounts to 198,720 a day or 72.5 million a year. Today, there are nearly 7 billion people on earth. By 2050, according to the United Nations, the world's population will be close to leveling off at around 9.1 billion. Panel (a) of Figure 9-8 shows which countries are growing the most. Panel (b) emphasizes an implication of panel (a), which is that virtually all the growth in population is occurring in developing nations. Many developed countries are expected to lose population over the next several decades.

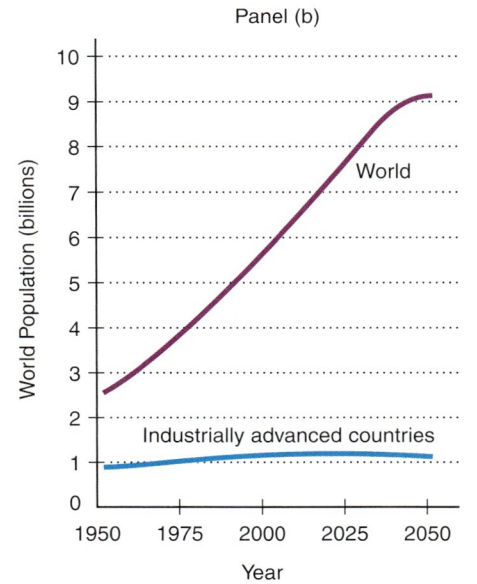

FIGURE 9-8
Expected Growth in World Population by 2050

Panel (a) displays the percentages of the world's population residing in the various continents and shows projected population growth for these continents and for selected nations. It indicates that Asia and Africa are expected to gain the most in population by the year 2050. Panel (b) indicates that population will increase in developing countries before beginning to level off around 2050, whereas industrially advanced nations will grow very little in population in the first half of this century.

Source: United Nations.

Ever since the Reverend Thomas Robert Malthus wrote *An Essay on the Principle of Population* in 1798, excessive population growth has been a concern. Modern-day Malthusians are able to generate great enthusiasm for the concept that population growth is bad. Over and over, media pundits and a number of scientists tell us that rapid population growth threatens economic development and the quality of life.

Malthus Was Proved Wrong. Malthus predicted that population would outstrip food supplies. This prediction has never been supported by the facts, according to economist Nicholas Eberstadt of the Harvard Center for Population Studies. As the world's population has grown, so has the world's food supply, measured by calories per person. Furthermore, the price of food, corrected for inflation, has been falling steadily for more than a century. That means that the supply of food has been expanding faster than the rise in demand caused by increased population.

Growth Leads to Smaller Families. Furthermore, economists have found that as nations become richer, average family size declines. Otherwise stated, the more economic development occurs, the slower the population growth rate becomes. This has certainly been true in Western Europe and in the former Soviet Union, where populations in some countries are actually declining. Predictions of birthrates in developing countries have often turned out to be overstated if those countries experience rapid economic growth. This was the case in Hong Kong, Mexico, Taiwan, and Chile. Recent research on population and economic development has revealed that social and economic modernization has been accompanied by a decline in childbearing significant enough that it might be called a fertility revolution. Modernization reduces infant mortality, which in turn reduces the incentive for couples to have many children to make sure that a certain number survive to adulthood. Modernization also lowers the demand for children for a variety of reasons, not the least being that couples in more developed countries do not need to rely on their children to take care of them in old age.

The Stages of Development: Agriculture to Industry to Services

If we analyze the development of modern rich nations, we find that they went through three stages. First is the agricultural stage, when most of the population is involved in agriculture. Then comes the manufacturing stage, when much of the population becomes involved in the industrialized sector of the economy. And finally there is a shift toward services. That is exactly what happened in the United States: The so-called tertiary, or service, sector of the economy continues to grow, whereas the manufacturing sector (and its share of employment) is declining in relative importance.

Of particular significance, however, is the requirement for early specialization in a nation's comparative advantage (see Chapter 2). The doctrine of comparative advantage is particularly appropriate for the developing countries of the world. If trading is allowed among nations, a country is best off if it produces what it has a comparative advantage in producing and imports the rest (for more details, see Chapter 33). This means that many developing countries should continue to specialize in agricultural production or in labor-intensive manufactured goods.

Keys to Economic Development

One theory of development states that for a country to develop, it must have a large natural resource base. This theory goes on to assert that much of the world is running out of natural resources, thereby limiting economic growth and development. Only the narrowest definition of a natural resource, however, could lead to such an opinion. In broader terms, a natural resource is something occurring in nature that we can use for our own purposes. As emphasized by new growth theory, natural resources therefore include human capital—education and experience. The natural resources that we could define several hundred years ago did not, for example, include hydroelectric power—no one knew that such a natural resource existed or how to bring it into existence.

Natural resources by themselves are not a prerequisite for or a guarantee of economic development, as demonstrated by Japan's extensive development despite a lack of domestic oil resources and by Brazil's slow pace of development in spite of a vast array of natural resources. Resources must be transformed into something usable for either investment or consumption.

Economists have found that four factors seem to be highly related to the pace of economic development:

1. *Establishing a system of property rights.* As noted earlier, if you were in a country where bank accounts and businesses were periodically expropriated by the government, you would be reluctant to leave some of your wealth in a savings account or to invest in a business. Expropriation of private property rarely takes place in developed countries. It has occurred in numerous developing countries, however. For example, private property was once nationalized in Chile and still is for the most part in Cuba. Economists have found that other things being equal, the more secure private property rights are, the more private capital accumulation and economic growth there will be.
2. *Developing an educated population.* Both theoretically and empirically, we know that a more educated workforce aids economic development because it allows individuals to build on the ideas of others. Thus, developing countries can advance more rapidly if they increase investments in education. Or, stated in the negative, economic development is difficult to sustain if a nation allows a sizable portion of its population to remain uneducated. Education allows impoverished young people to acquire skills that enable them to avoid poverty as adults.
3. *Letting "creative destruction" run its course.* The twentieth-century economist Joseph Schumpeter championed the concept of "creative destruction," through which new businesses ultimately create new jobs and economic growth after first destroying old jobs, old companies, and old industries. Such change is painful and costly, but it is necessary for economic advancement. Nowhere is this more important than in developing countries, where the principle is often ignored. Many governments in developing nations have had a history of supporting current companies and industries by discouraging new technologies and new companies from entering the marketplace. The process of creative destruction has not been allowed to work its magic in these countries.
4. *Limiting protectionism.* Open economies experience faster economic development than economies closed to international trade. Trade encourages individuals and businesses to discover ways to specialize so that they can become more productive and earn higher incomes. Increased productivity and subsequent increases in economic growth are the results. Thus, having fewer trade barriers promotes faster economic development.

Go to www.econtoday.com/ch09 to contemplate whether there may be a relationship between inequality and a nation's growth and to visit the home page of the World Bank's Thematic Group on Inequality, Poverty, and Socioeconomic Performance.

Go to www.econtoday.com/ch09 to link to a World Trade Organization explanation of how free trade promotes greater economic growth and higher employment.

QUICK QUIZ

Although many people believe that population growth hinders economic development, there is little evidence to support that notion. What is clear is that economic development tends to lead to a reduction in the rate of _____ growth.

Historically, there are three stages of economic development: the _____ stage, the _____ stage, and the _____-_____ stage, when a large part of the workforce is employed in providing services.

Although one theory of economic development holds that a sizable natural resource base is the key to a nation's development, this fails to account for the importance of the human element: The _____ _____ must be capable of using a country's natural resources.

Fundamental factors contributing to the pace of economic development are a well-defined system of _____ _____, training and _____, allowing new generations of companies and industries to _____ older generations, and promoting an open economy by allowing _____ _____.

See page 238 for the answers. Review concepts from this section in MyEconLab.

CASE STUDY: ECONOMICS FRONT AND CENTER

The Congressman Wants to Know the Facts—Or Does He?

Cameron recently graduated from college and has obtained a junior position on the staff of a member of the U.S. House of Representatives. The congressman has assigned Cameron the task of documenting how recent economic growth has resulted in a loss of manufacturing jobs to countries such as China and Japan. Cameron finds it easy to document that U.S. manufacturing employment has fallen in recent years. Since 1995, for instance, the number of U.S. workers employed in manufacturing has declined by about 12 percent.

What Cameron has also discovered, however, is that manufacturing employment has declined worldwide. All told, the number of manufacturing jobs in 20 of the world's largest economies has fallen by more than 22 million. Furthermore, Cameron has found that manufacturing employment has actually fallen by more than 15 percent in both China and Japan since 1995. Thus, the congressman's theory is unsupportable.

Cameron begins drafting a preliminary report for the congressman. In the introduction, he points out that economic growth typically increases total employment while changing the distribution of jobs. In the early twentieth century, buggy manufacturing jobs disappeared but were replaced by other manufacturing jobs. In the twenty-first century, he writes, manufacturing jobs are being replaced by service positions. Nevertheless, total employment is rising. He realizes that the congressman may not be happy with his report, but part of his job is to present the facts.

CRITICAL ANALYSIS QUESTIONS

1. Why might some people be able to justifiably conclude, at least in the near term, that economic growth harms their job prospects?

2. Even as the United States, China, and Japan have experienced decreases in manufacturing jobs since 1995, manufacturing employment in Spain and Canada has increased by more than 20 percent. Why do you think that increases in manufacturing jobs in these and a few other nations may have accompanied economic growth, even as most other countries lost manufacturing jobs? (Hint: Recall from Chapter 2 the concepts of specialization and gains from trade.)

Winners and Losers in the Brain-Drain Game

Issues and Applications

When a nation loses some of its best-educated workers, it experiences a *brain drain*. Nations that undergo brain drains experience an outflow of human capital and thereby lose a key productive resource. Of course, the movement of well-trained people to other countries generates a "brain gain" for these recipient nations.

Concepts Applied
- Economic Growth
- Immigration and Growth
- Human Capital

The Losers

Figure 9-9 on page 234 shows the countries of the world that experience the largest brain drains. Depicted in the figure are the percentages of college graduates who leave these nations to live and work in more industrialized nations.

It is not a coincidence that the nations that appear in Figure 9-9 are among those with the lowest per capita real GDP levels in the world. Because real GDP levels are low in these nations, incomes are low. As a consequence, job opportunities for well-trained people are few. Naturally, this gives highly skilled people incentives to move to other nations where they can find more challenging work and earn higher incomes. Industrialized nations, such as Canada and the United States, are typically the locations where such jobs are more readily available.

As you have learned in this chapter, however, the significant losses of college graduates depicted in Figure 9-9 represent huge outflows of human capital from these nations. These decreases in human capital damage the countries' prospects for economic growth. Stunted economic growth in turn causes incomes to remain low, thereby perpetuating a brain-drain cycle for these nations.

The Winners

Of course, the countries receiving immigrants from the nations in Figure 9-9 experience a "brain gain." Steady inflows of immigrants from these nations are a source of human capital that promotes economic growth in the recipient countries.

For instance, many highly skilled individuals from Jamaica and Haiti are among the nearly 240,000 people who now migrate to Canada each year. More than half of all new skilled jobs in Canada are filled by immigrants. Indeed, present estimates indicate that by 2011, immigrants are likely to provide *all* of the growth in Canada's *entire* labor force.

Canada is an extreme example of the countries, including the United States, that are winners in the world's brain-drain game. As described earlier, those nations that experience brain drains lose human capital, and this loss contributes to lower economic growth rates in those nations. For the foreseeable future, therefore, it appears likely that the losers will continue to lose, and the winners will continue to win.

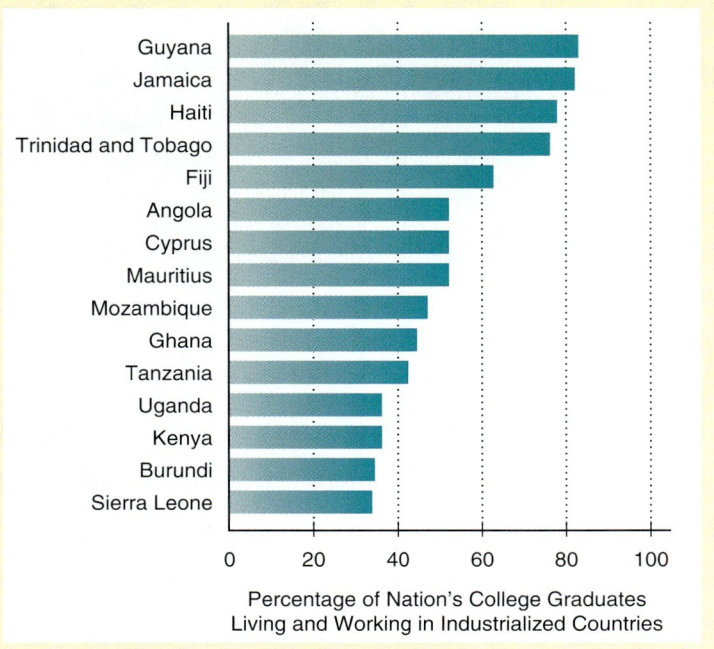

FIGURE 9-9
Nations with the Largest Percentage Emigrations of Skilled Workers

Countries with the largest proportionate brain drains to industrialized nations include nations with levels of per capita real GDP that are among the world's lowest.

Source: Organization for Economic Cooperation and Development.

Log in to **MyEconLab**, click on "Economic News," and test your understanding of the chapter by answering interactive questions that relate directly to this issue.

For Critical Analysis

1. What might nations with relatively low levels of per capita real GDP, such as those in Figure 9-9, do to try to slow the brain drains they are experiencing?
2. Why might some people in the nations currently experiencing "brain gains," such as some U.S. residents, favor policies aimed at restricting immigration of highly skilled workers from abroad? (Hint: Immigration of well-trained workers increases the supply of workers in U.S. markets for skilled labor. How does this affect the market wages earned by skilled workers in the United States?)

Web Resources

1. Read a detailed analysis of the brain-drain issue at **www.econtoday.com/ch09**.
2. For a discussion of Africa's brain-drain problems, go to **www.econtoday.com/ch09**.

Research Project

Suppose that you have been appointed to an international committee charged with working out a proposal for how developing nations can best break out of the vicious cycle in which the brain drain reduces growth and this lower growth, in turn, perpetuates the brain drain. Develop a list of policy approaches that might be implemented by the government of a developing nation to reduce its brain-drain problem without interfering with individual freedom or property rights. Why is the brain-drain problem so difficult for developing nations to solve?

CHAPTER 9 *Global Economic Growth and Development* **235**

Here is what you should know after reading this chapter. MyEconLab will help you identify what you know, and where to go when you need to practice.

WHAT YOU SHOULD KNOW		WHERE TO GO TO PRACTICE
Economic Growth The rate of economic growth is the annual rate of change in per capita real GDP. This measure of the growth of a nation's economy takes into account both its growth in overall production of goods and services and the growth of its population. It is an average measure that does not account for possible changes in the distribution of income or various welfare costs or benefits that may accompany growth of the economy.	economic growth, 215 **Key figures** Figure 9-1, 214 Figure 9-2, 215	• **MyEconLab** Study Plan 9.1 • Audio introduction to Chapter 9 • Animated Figures 9-1 and 9-2
Why Economic Growth Rates Are Important Over long intervals, relatively small differences in the rate of economic growth can accumulate to produce large disparities in per capita incomes. The reason is that like accumulations of interest, economic growth compounds over time. Thus, if a nation's rate of per capita real GDP growth rises by 3 percentage points per year, it has a level of per capita real GDP that is more than four times higher after 50 years, but a country with a per capita real GDP growth rate 4 percentage points higher per year ends up with per capita real GDP more than seven times higher.		• **MyEconLab** Study Plan 9.1 • Video: Growth Rates and Compound Interest
Why Productivity Increases Are Crucial for Maintaining Economic Growth For a nation with a relatively stable population and a steady rate of capital accumulation, productivity growth emerges as a fundamental factor influencing near-term changes in economic growth. Higher productivity growth unambiguously contributes to greater annual increases in a nation's per capita real GDP.	labor productivity, 219	• **MyEconLab** Study Plan 9.2
The Key Determinants of Economic Growth The fundamental factors contributing to economic growth are growth in a nation's pool of labor, growth of its capital stock, and growth in the productivity of its capital and labor. A key determinant of capital accumulation is a nation's saving rate. Higher saving rates contribute to greater investment and hence increased capital accumulation and economic growth.		• **MyEconLab** Study Plan 9.3 • Video: Saving and Economic Growth

236 PART II Introduction to Macroeconomics and Economic Growth

WHAT YOU SHOULD KNOW

New Growth Theory This is a relatively recent theory that examines why individuals and businesses conduct research into inventing and developing new technologies and how this process interacts with the rate of economic growth. This theory emphasizes how rewards to technological innovation contribute to higher economic growth rates. A key implication of the theory is that ideas and knowledge are crucial elements of the growth process.

new growth theory, 221
patent, 222
innovation, 223
Key figures
Figure 9-5, 223
Figure 9-6, 224

WHERE TO GO TO PRACTICE

- **MyEconLab** Study Plan 9.4
- Video: The Importance of Human Capital
- Animated Figures 9-5 and 9-6

Fundamental Factors That Contribute to a Nation's Economic Development The key characteristics shared by nations that succeed in attaining higher levels of economic development are protection of property rights, significant opportunities for their residents to obtain training and education, policies that permit new companies and industries to replace older ones, and the avoidance of protectionist barriers that hinder international trade.

development economics, 228
Key figure
Figure 9-8, 229

- **MyEconLab** Study Plans 9.5 and 9.6
- Animated Figure 9-8

Log in to MyEconLab, take a chapter test, and get a personalized Study Plan that tells you which concepts you understand and which ones you need to review. From there, MyEconLab will give you futher practice, tutorials, animations, videos, and guided solutions.

Log in to www.myeconlab.com

PROBLEMS

Select problems, indicated by a blue oval, are assignable in MyEconLab. Answers to the odd-numbered problems appear at the back of the book.

9-1 The graph shows a production possibilities curve for 2010 and two potential production possibilities curves for 2011, denoted 2011_A and 2011_B.

a. Which of the labeled points corresponds to maximum feasible 2010 production that is more likely to be associated with the curve denoted 2011_A?

b. Which of the labeled points corresponds to maximum feasible 2010 production that is more likely to be associated with the curve denoted 2011_B?

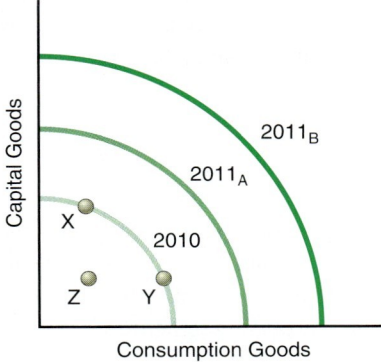

9-2 A nation's capital goods wear out over time, so a portion of its capital goods become unusable every year. Last year, its residents decided to produce no capital goods. It has experienced no growth in its population or in the amounts of other productive resources during the past year. In addition, the nation's technology and resource productivity have remained unchanged during the past year. Will the nation's economic growth rate for the current year be negative, zero, or positive?

9-3 In the situation described in Problem 9-2, suppose that educational improvements during the past year enable the people of this nation to repair all capital goods so that they continue to function as well as new. All other factors are unchanged, however. In light of this single change to the conditions faced in this nation, will the nation's economic growth rate for the current year be negative, zero, or positive?

9-4 Consider the following data. What is the per capita real GDP in each of these countries?

Country	Population (millions)	Real GDP ($ billions)
A	10	55
B	20	60
C	5	70

9-5 Suppose that during the next 10 years, real GDP triples and population doubles in each of the nations in Problem 9-4. What will per capita real GDP be in each country after 10 years have passed?

9-6 Consider the following table displaying annual growth rates for nations X, Y, and Z, each of which entered 2007 with real per capita GDP equal to $20,000:

	Annual Growth Rate (%)			
Country	2007	2008	2009	2010
X	7	1	3	4
Y	4	5	7	9
Z	5	4	3	2

a. Which nation most likely experienced a sizable earthquake in late 2007 that destroyed a significant portion of its stock of capital goods, but was followed by speedy investments in rebuilding the nation's capital stock? What is this nation's per capita real GDP at the end of 2010, rounded to the nearest dollar?

b. Which nation most likely adopted policies in 2007 that encouraged a gradual shift in production from capital goods to consumption goods? What is this nation's per capita real GDP at the end of 2010, rounded to the nearest dollar?

c. Which nation most likely adopted policies in 2007 that encouraged a gradual shift in production from consumption goods to capital goods? What is this nation's per capita real GDP at the end of 2010, rounded to the nearest dollar?

9-7 Per capita real GDP grows at a rate of 3 percent in country F and at a rate of 6 percent in country G. Both begin with equal levels of per capita real GDP. Use Table 9-3 on page 218 to determine how much higher per capita real GDP will be in country G after 20 years. How much higher will real GDP be in country G after 40 years?

9-8 Per capita real GDP in country L is three times as high as in country M. The economic growth rate in country M, however, is 8 percent, while country L's economy grows at a rate of 5 percent. Use Table 9-3 on page 218 to determine approximately how many years it will be before per capita real GDP in country M surpasses per capita real GDP in country L.

9-9 Per capita real GDP in country S is only half as great as per capita real GDP in country T. Country T's rate of economic growth is 4 percent. The government of country S, however, enacts policies that achieve a growth rate of 20 percent. Use Table 9-3 on page 218 to determine how long country S must maintain this growth rate before its per capita real GDP surpasses that of country T.

9-10 In 2008, a nation's population was 10 million. Its nominal GDP was $40 billion, and its price index was 100. In 2009, its population had increased to 12 million, its nominal GDP had risen to $57.6 billion, and its price index had increased to 120. What was this nation's economic growth rate during the year?

9-11 Between the start of 2008 and the start of 2009, a country's economic growth rate was 4 percent. Its population did not change during the year, nor did its price level. What was the rate of increase of the country's nominal GDP during this one-year interval?

9-12 In 2008, a nation's population was 10 million, its real GDP was $1.21 billion, and its GDP deflator had a value of 121. By 2009, its population had increased to

12 million, its real GDP had risen to $1.5 billion, and its GDP deflator had a value of 125. What was the percentage change in per capita real GDP between 2008 and 2009?

9-13 A nation's per capita real GDP was $2,000 in 2007, and the nation's population was 5 million in that year. Between 2007 and 2008, the inflation rate in this country was 5 percent, and the nation's annual rate of economic growth was 10 percent. Its population remained unchanged. What was per capita real GDP in 2008? What was the *level* of real GDP in 2008?

ECONOMICS ON THE NET

Multifactor Productivity and Its Growth Growth in productivity is a key factor determining a nation's overall economic growth.

Title: Bureau of Labor Statistics: Multifactor Productivity Trends

Navigation: Use the link at www.econtoday.com/ch09 to visit the multifactor productivity home page of the Bureau of Labor Statistics.

Application Read the summary, and answer the following questions.

1. What does multifactor productivity measure? Based on your reading of this chapter, how does multifactor productivity relate to the determination of economic growth?

2. Click on *Multifactor Productivity Trends in Manufacturing,* and then click on *Manufacturing Industries: Multifactor Productivity Trends.* According to these data, which industries have exhibited the greatest productivity growth in recent years?

For Group Study and Analysis Divide the class into three groups to examine multifactor productivity data for the private business sector, the private nonfarm business sector, and the manufacturing sector. Have each group identify periods when multifactor productivity growth was particularly fast or slow. Then compare notes. Does it appear to make a big difference which sector one looks at when evaluating periods of greatest and least growth in multifactor productivity?

ANSWERS TO QUICK QUIZZES

p. 218: (i) per capita; (ii) benefits . . . costs; (iii) large
p. 220: (i) capital . . . labor . . . capital . . . labor; (ii) saving . . . save . . . saving
p. 226: (i) New growth; (ii) trade; (iii) Inventions . . . innovation; (iv) new growth; (v) human
p. 228: (i) economic; (ii) property . . . property
p. 232: (i) population; (ii) agricultural . . . manufacturing . . . service-sector; (iii) labor force; (iv) property rights . . . education . . . replace . . . international trade

Real GDP and the Price Level in the Long Run

10

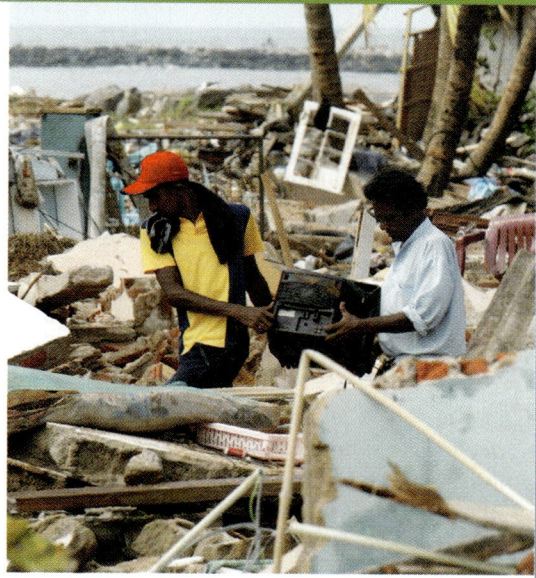

Shortly after a deadly tsunami hit the Indian Ocean region in December 2004, some media observers suggested that it might also deal a mortal blow to the economies of Indonesia, Malaysia, Sri Lanka, and Thailand. These observers speculated that reduced supplies of many items would push up prices sharply and cause inflation rates to spike across the region. They also worried that steep falloffs in tourism during the following years might push the economies of affected countries into a lengthy tailspin. In fact, inflation rates in most Southeast Asian nations hit by the tsunami rose only slightly in 2005, and during that year their levels of real GDP increased by at least 4 percent. In this chapter, you will learn how positive long-run real GDP and price level trends under way in these nations overwelmed the negative short-run economic effects of the devastating waves.

Learning Objectives

After reading this chapter, you should be able to:

1. Understand the concept of long-run aggregate supply
2. Describe the effect of economic growth on the long-run aggregate supply curve
3. Explain why the aggregate demand curve slopes downward and list key factors that cause this curve to shift
4. Discuss the meaning of long-run equilibrium for the economy as a whole
5. Evaluate why economic growth can cause deflation
6. Evaluate likely reasons for persistent inflation in recent decades

MyEconLab helps you master each objective and study more efficiently. See end of chapter for details.

Did You Know That . . .

several times between 1920 and 1929—the period known in the United States as the "Roaring Twenties"—the U.S. price level declined? Between 1920 and 1922, the price level fell at an average annual rate of 8.2 percent. From 1923 to 1926, the level of prices rose at an annual rate of about 1.4 percent. Then, from 1927 to 1929, the price level fell once more, at an average annual rate of decline equal to 1.1 percent. In the meantime, the average prices of shares of stock in U.S. corporations more than doubled, and real GDP increased.

Why did the United States experience periods of deflation even as the nation experienced economic growth during the 1920s? Why did sporadic periods of deflation continue even when economic growth turned negative in the 1930s, a time we now call the Great Depression? To answer these questions, you must learn about factors that influence the long-run stability of the price level.

OUTPUT GROWTH AND THE LONG-RUN AGGREGATE SUPPLY CURVE

In Chapter 2, we showed the derivation of the production possibilities curve. At any point in time, the economy can be inside or on the PPC but never outside it. Along the PPC, a country's resources are fully employed in the production of goods and services, and the sum total of the inflation-adjusted value of all final goods and services produced is the nation's real GDP. Economists refer to the total of all planned production for the entire economy as the **aggregate supply** of real output.

Aggregate supply
The total of all planned production for the economy.

The Long-Run Aggregate Supply Curve

Put yourself in a world in which nothing has been changing, year in and year out. The price level has not changed. Technology has not changed. The prices of inputs that firms must purchase have not changed. Labor productivity has not changed. All resources are fully employed, so the economy operates on its production possibilities curve, such as the one depicted in panel (a) of Figure 10-1. This is a world that is fully adjusted and in which people have all the information they are ever going to have about that world. The **long-run aggregate supply curve** (*LRAS*) in this world is some amount of real GDP—say, $12 trillion of real GDP—which is the value of the flow of production of final goods

Long-run aggregate supply curve
A vertical line representing the real output of goods and services after full adjustment has occurred. It can also be viewed as representing the real GDP of the economy under conditions of full employment—the full-employment level of real GDP.

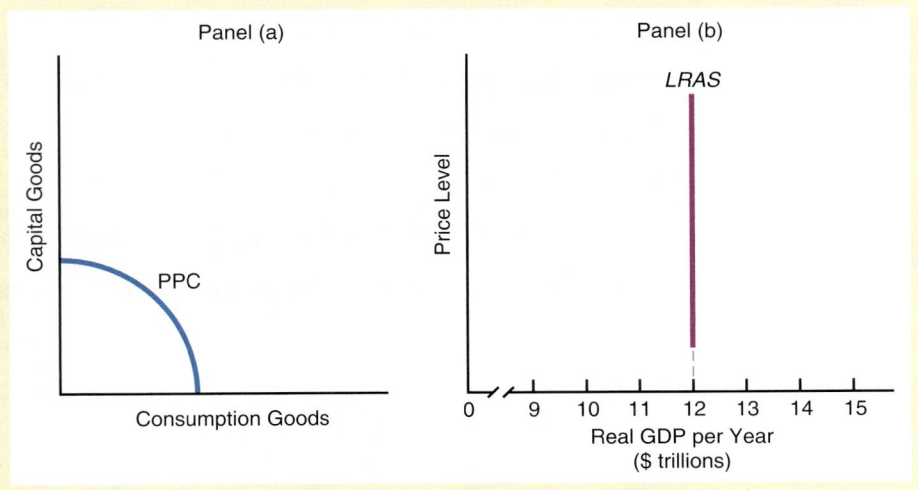

FIGURE 10-1

The Production Possibilities and the Economy's Long-Run Aggregate Supply Curve

At a point in time, a nation's base of resources and its technological capabilities define the position of its production possibilities curve, as shown in panel (a). This defines the real GDP that the nation can produce when resources are fully employed, which determines the position of the long-run aggregate supply curve (*LRAS*) displayed in panel (b). Because people have complete information and input prices adjust fully in the long run, the *LRAS* is vertical.

also that they know when it is going to occur and understand that its ultimate effect will be to push the price level from P_1 to P_3. Will workers wait until after the price level has increased to insist that their nominal wages go up? The rational expectations hypothesis says that they will not. Instead, they will go to employers and insist that their nominal wages move upward in step with the higher prices. From the workers' perspective, this is the only way to protect their real wages from declining due to the anticipated increase in the money supply.

The Policy Irrelevance Proposition.
As long as economic participants behave in this manner, when we draw the *SRAS* curve, we must be explicit about the nature of their expectations. This we have done in Figure 18-8. In the initial equilibrium, the short-run aggregate supply curve is labeled to show that the expected money supply (M_e) and the actual money supply (M_1) are equal ($M_e = M_1$). Similarly, when the money supply changes in a way that is anticipated by economic participants, the aggregate supply curve shifts to reflect this expected change in the money supply. The new short-run aggregate supply curve is labeled $M_e = M_2$) to reveal this. According to the rational expectations hypothesis, the short-run aggregate supply curve will shift upward *simultaneously* with the rise in aggregate demand. As a result, the economy will move directly from point *A* to point *C* in Figure 18-8 without passing through *B*: The *only* response to the rise in the money supply is a rise in the price level from P_1 to P_3; neither output nor unemployment changes at all. This conclusion—that fully anticipated monetary policy is irrelevant in determining the levels of real variables—is called the **policy irrelevance proposition:**

> Under the assumption of rational expectations on the part of decision makers in the economy, *anticipated* monetary policy cannot alter either the rate of unemployment or the level of real GDP. Regardless of the nature of the anticipated policy, the unemployment rate will equal the natural rate, and real GDP will be determined solely by the economy's long-run aggregate supply curve.

Policy irrelevance proposition
The conclusion that policy actions have no real effects in the short run if the policy actions are anticipated and none in the long run even if the policy actions are unanticipated.

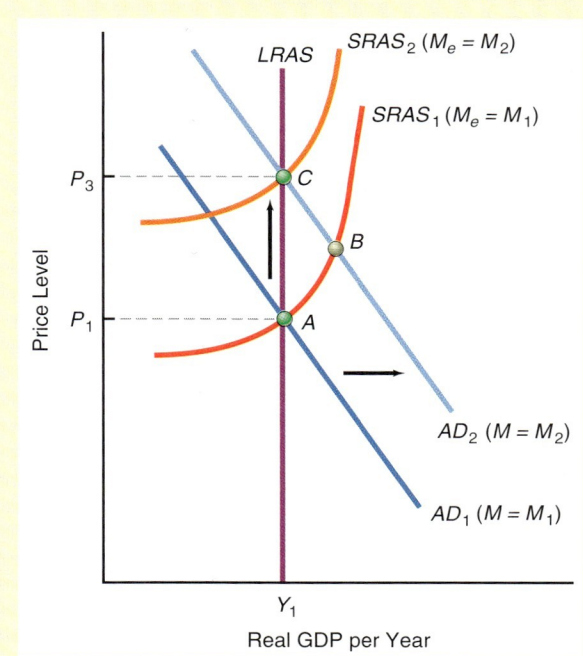

FIGURE 18-8

Effects of an Anticipated Rise in Aggregate Demand

When policy is fully anticipated, a rise in the money supply causes a rise in the price level from P_1 to P_3, with no change in real GDP.

What Must People Know? There are two important matters to keep in mind when considering this proposition. First, our discussion has assumed that economic participants know in advance exactly what the change in monetary policy is going to be and precisely when it is going to occur. In fact, the Federal Reserve does not announce exactly what the future course of monetary policy is going to be. Instead, the Fed tries to keep most of its plans secret, announcing only in general terms what policy actions are intended for the future.

It is tempting to conclude that because the Fed's intended policies are not freely available, they are not available at all. But such a conclusion would be wrong. Economic participants have great incentives to learn how to predict the future behavior of the monetary authorities, just as businesses try to forecast consumer behavior and college students do their best to forecast what their next economics exam will look like. Even if the economic participants are not perfect at forecasting the course of policy, they are likely to come a lot closer than they would in total ignorance. The policy irrelevance proposition really assumes only that *people don't persistently make the same mistakes in forecasting the future.*

What Happens If People Don't Know Everything? This brings us to our second point. Once we accept the fact that people are not perfect in their ability to predict the future, the possibility emerges that some policy actions will have systematic effects that look much like the movements A to B to C in Figure 18-7 on page 460. For example, just as other economic participants sometimes make mistakes, it is likely that the Federal Reserve sometimes makes mistakes—meaning that the money supply may change in ways that even the Fed does not predict. And even if the Fed always accomplished every policy action it intended, there is no guarantee that other economic participants would fully forecast those actions.

What happens if the Fed makes a mistake or if firms and workers misjudge the future course of policy? Matters will look much as they do in panel (a) of Figure 18-9, which shows the effects of an *unanticipated* increase in the money supply. Economic participants expect the money supply to be M_1, but the actual money supply turns out to be M_2. Because $M_2 > M_1$, aggregate demand shifts relative to aggregate supply. The result is a rise in real GDP in the short run from Y_1 to Y_2. Corresponding to this rise in real GDP will be an increase in employment and hence a fall in the unemployment rate. So, even under the rational expectations hypothesis, monetary policy *can* have an effect on real variables in the short run, but only if the policy is unsystematic and therefore unanticipated.

In the long run, this effect on real variables will disappear because people will figure out that the Fed either accidentally increased the money supply or intentionally increased it in a way that somehow fooled individuals. Either way, people's expectations will soon be revised so that the short-run aggregate supply curve will shift upward. As shown in panel (b) of Figure 18-9, real GDP will return to long-run levels, meaning that so will the employment and unemployment rates.

The Policy Dilemma

Perhaps the most striking and disturbing feature of the policy irrelevance proposition is that it seems to suggest that only mistakes can have real effects. If the Federal Reserve always does what it intends to do and if other economic participants always correctly anticipate the Fed's actions, monetary policy will affect only the price level and nominal input prices. It appears that only if the Fed makes a mistake in executing monetary policy or people err in anticipating that policy will changes in the money supply cause fluctuations in real GDP and employment. If this reasoning is correct, the Fed is effectively precluded from using monetary policy in any rational way to lower the unemployment rate or to raise the level of real GDP. This is because fully anticipated changes in the money supply will lead to exactly offsetting changes in prices and hence no real effects.

Many economists were disturbed at the prospect that if the economy happened to enter a recessionary period, policymakers would be powerless to push real GDP and unemploy-

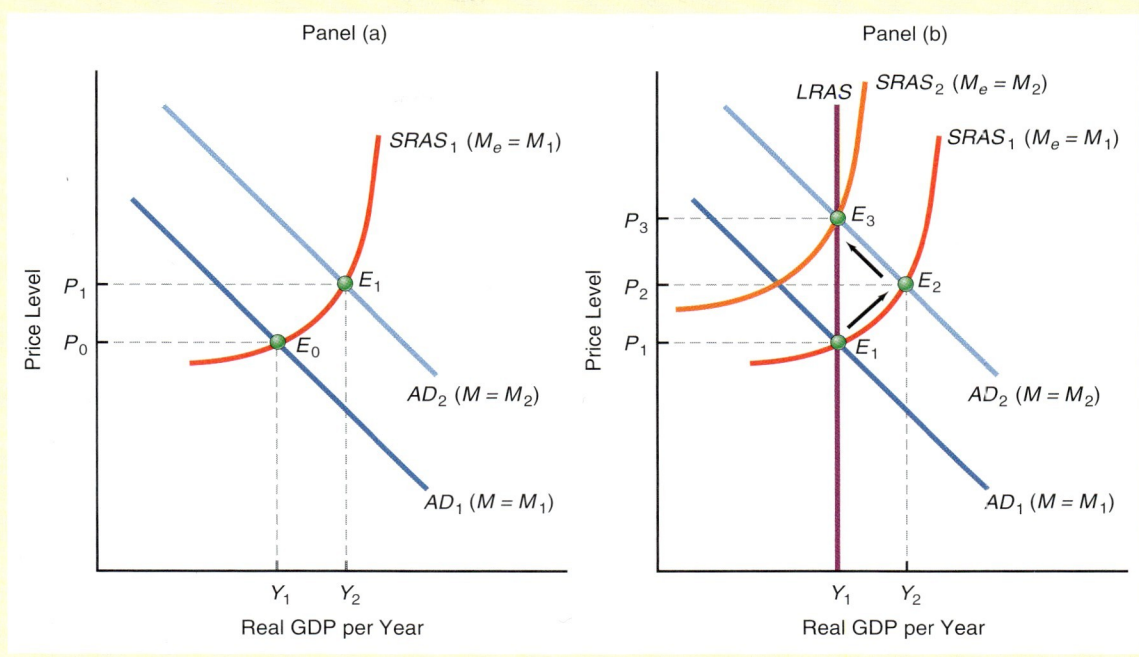

FIGURE 18-9
Effects of an Unanticipated Rise in Aggregate Demand
Even with rational expectations, an unanticipated change in demand can affect real GDP in the short run.

ment back to long-run levels. As a result, they asked, in light of the rational expectations hypothesis, is it *ever* possible for systematic policy to have predictable real effects on the economy? The answer has led to even more developments in the way we think about macroeconomics.

> **QUICK QUIZ**
>
> The _____ hypothesis assumes that individuals' forecasts incorporate all readily available information, including an understanding of government policy and its effects on the economy.
>
> If the **rational expectations hypothesis** is valid, there is pure competition, and all prices and wages are flexible, then the _____ proposition follows: Fully anticipated monetary policy actions cannot alter either the rate of unemployment or the level of real GDP.
>
> With rational expectations, flexible wages and prices, and pure competition, policies can alter real economic variables only if the policies are _____ and therefore _____; otherwise people learn and defeat the desired policy goals.
>
> See page 476 for the answers. Review concepts from this section in MyEconLab.

ANOTHER CHALLENGE TO POLICY ACTIVISM: REAL BUSINESS CYCLES

When confronted with the policy irrelevance proposition, many economists began to re-examine the first principles of macroeconomics with fully flexible wages and prices.

The Distinction Between Real and Monetary Shocks

Today, many economists argue that real, as opposed to purely monetary, forces might help explain aggregate economic fluctuations. An important stimulus for the idea that there are *real business cycles* was the economic turmoil of the 1970s. During that decade, world economies were staggered by two major disruptions to the supply of oil. The first occurred in 1973, and the second in 1979. In both episodes, members of the Organization of Petroleum Exporting Countries (OPEC) reduced the amount of oil they were willing to supply and raised the price at which they offered it for sale. Each time, the price level rose sharply in the United States, and real GDP declined. Thus, each episode involving these aggregate supply shocks (see Chapter 11) produced a period of "stagflation"—real economic stagnation combined with high inflation. Figure 18-10 illustrates the pattern of events.

We begin at point E_1 with the economy in both short- and long-run equilibrium, with the associated supply curves, $SRAS_1$ and $LRAS_1$. Initially, the level of real GDP is Y_1, and the price level is P_1. Because the economy is in long-run equilibrium, the unemployment rate must be at the natural rate.

A reduction in the supply of oil, as occurred in 1973 and 1979, causes the *SRAS* curve to shift to the left to $SRAS_2$ because fewer goods will be available for sale due to the reduced supplies. If the reduction in oil supplies is (or is believed to be) permanent, the *LRAS* shifts to the left also. This assumption is reflected in Figure 18-10, where $LRAS_2$ shows the new long-run aggregate supply curve associated with the lowered output of oil.

In the short run, two adjustments begin to occur simultaneously. First, the prices of oil and petroleum-based products begin to rise, so the overall price level rises to P_2. Second, the higher costs of production occasioned by the rise in oil prices induce firms to cut back production, so real GDP falls to Y_2 in the short run. The new temporary short-run equilibrium occurs at E_2, with a higher price level (P_2) and a lower level of real GDP (Y_2).

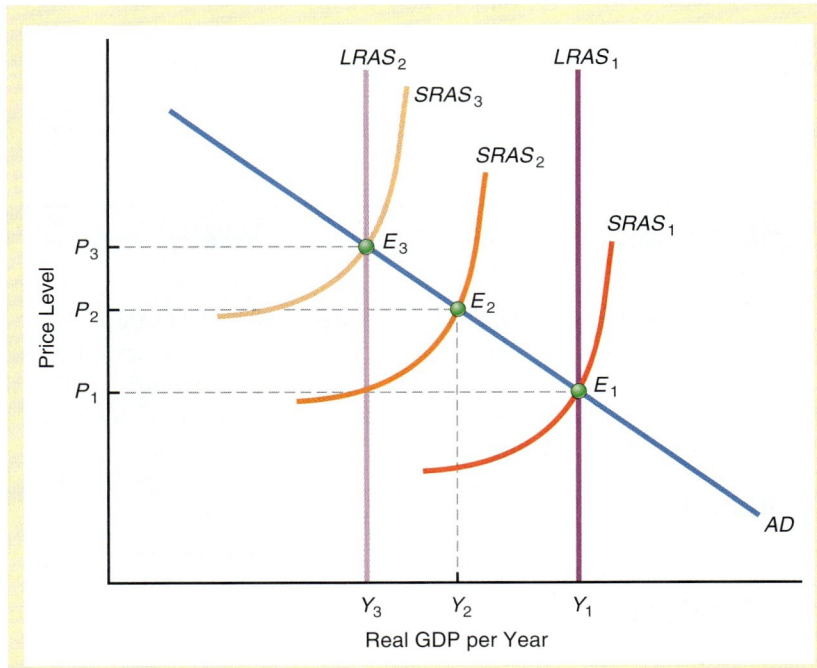

FIGURE 18-10

Effects of a Reduction in the Supply of Resources

The position of the *LRAS* depends on our endowments of all types of resources. Hence a permanent reduction in the supply of one of those resources, such as oil, causes a reduction—an inward shift—in the aggregate supply curve from $LRAS_1$ to $LRAS_2$. In addition, there is a rise in the equilibrium price level and a fall in the equilibrium rate of real GDP per year.

Impact on the Labor Market

If we were to focus on the labor market while this adjustment from E_1 to E_2 was taking place, we would find two developments occurring. The rise in the price level pushes the real wage rate downward, even as the scaled-back production plans of firms induce them to reduce the amount of labor inputs they are using. So not only does the real wage rate fall, but the level of employment declines as well. On both counts, workers are made worse off due to the reduction in the supply of oil.

This is not the full story, however. Owners of nonoil inputs (such as labor) who are willing to put up with reduced real payments in the short run simply will not tolerate them in the long run. Thus, for example, some workers who were willing to continue working at lower wages in the short run will eventually decide to retire, switch from full-time work to part-time employment, or drop out of the labor force altogether. In effect, there is a reduction in the supply of nonoil inputs, reflected in an upward shift in the SRAS curve from $SRAS_2$ to $SRAS_3$. This puts additional upward pressure on the price level and exerts a downward force on real GDP. The final long-run equilibrium thus occurs at point E_3, with the price level at P_3 and real GDP at Y_3. (In principle, because the oil supply shock has had no direct effect on labor markets, the natural rate of unemployment does not change when equilibrium moves from to E_1 to E_3.)

Generalizing the Theory

Naturally, the idea that the economy experiences real business cycles encompasses all types of real disturbances arising from aggregate supply shocks, such as sudden technological changes and shifts in the composition of the labor force. Moreover, a complete treatment of real shocks to the economy is typically much more complex than we have allowed for in our discussion. For example, an oil shock such as is shown in Figure 18-10 would likely also have effects on the real wealth of U.S. residents, causing a reduction in aggregate demand as well as aggregate supply. Nevertheless, our simple example still manages to capture the flavor of the real-business-cycle perspective, which indicates little role for policy activism to stabilize the economy.

The idea that aggregate supply shocks contribute to business cycles has improved our understanding of the economy's behavior, but economists agree that it alone is incapable of explaining all of the facets of business cycles that we observe. For example, it is difficult to imagine a real disturbance that could possibly account for the Great Depression in this country, when real GDP fell more than 30 percent and the unemployment rate rose to 25 percent. Moreover, the real-business-cycle approach continues to assume that all wages and prices are perfectly flexible and so fails to explain a great deal of the apparent rigidity of wages and prices throughout the economy.

MODERN APPROACHES TO RATIONALIZING ACTIVE POLICYMAKING

The policy irrelevance proposition and the idea that real shocks are primary causes of business cycles are major attacks on the desirability of trying to stabilize economic activity with activist policies. Both anti-activism suggestions arise from combining the rational expectations hypothesis with the assumptions of pure competition and flexible wages and prices. It should not be surprising, therefore, to learn that economists who see a role for activist policymaking do not believe that market clearing models of the economy can explain business cycles. They contend that the "sticky" wages and prices assumed by Keynes

Small Menu Costs and Sticky Prices

If prices do not respond to demand changes, two conditions must be true: someone must be consciously deciding not to change prices, and that decision must be in the decision maker's self-interest. One approach to explaining why many prices might be sticky in the short run supposes that much of the economy is characterized by imperfect competition (so firms are price searchers) and that it is costly for firms to change their prices in response to changes in demand. The costs associated with changing prices are called *menu costs*, and they include the costs of renegotiating contracts, printing price lists (such as menus), and informing customers of price changes.

Many such costs may not be very large, so economists call them **small menu costs**. Some of the costs of changing prices, however, such as those incurred in bringing together business managers from points around the nation or the world for meetings on price changes or renegotiating deals with customers, may be significant.

Firms in different industries have different cost structures. Such differences explain diverse small menu costs. Therefore, the extent to which firms hold their prices constant in the face of changes in demand for their products will vary across industries. Not all prices will be rigid. Nonetheless, some economists who promote policy activism argue that many—even most—firms' prices are sticky for relatively long time intervals. As a result, in the short run the aggregate level of prices could be very nearly rigid because of small menu costs. In recent years, these economists have produced a theory in which temporary rigidities in firms' price adjustments cause the short-run aggregate supply curve to be horizontal, as in the traditional Keynesian model.

Is there evidence of widespread price stickiness in the United States?

Small menu costs
Costs that deter firms from changing prices in response to demand changes—for example, the costs of renegotiating contracts or printing new price lists.

EXAMPLE

U.S. Price Stickiness—In the Eye of the Beholder?

Are prices sticky? One way to try to answer this question might be to examine prices in catalogs that firms distribute to potential customers. Indeed, some economists have concluded that failure of prices to change over time in catalogs is evidence of sticky prices. In many industries, however, firms often offer customers discounts from posted catalog prices. Thus, prices may be less sticky than implied by prices printed in catalogs and other price lists.

To address this problem, some new Keynesian economists have tried to *infer* how slowly prices adjust nationwide based on observed price level changes. Applying these methods to the rate of change in the U.S. GDP deflator or Consumer Price Index has indicated that, on average, prices change only about every 12 to 18 months. Nevertheless, when this approach is applied to industry-level Producer Price Indexes, significant variations in price adjustment times are revealed, as shown in Figure 18-11. The prices charged by some industries appear to take at least 12 months to change, but other prices change in nearly half that time.

Furthermore, studies of the prices that consumers pay for a broad array of consumption goods indicate even shorter intervals between price changes, often no longer than three or four months. Thus, although price stickiness seems to occur in some industries, prices of many goods appear to be relatively flexible.

(continued)

TABLE 10-1
Determinants of Aggregate Demand

Aggregate demand consists of the demand for domestically produced consumption goods, investment goods, government purchases, and net exports. Consequently, any change in total planned spending on any one of these components of real GDP will cause a change in aggregate demand. Some possibilities are listed here.

Changes That Cause an Increase in Aggregate Demand	Changes That Cause a Decrease in Aggregate Demand
An increase in the amount of money in circulation	A decrease in the amount of money in circulation
Increased security about jobs and future income	Decreased security about jobs and future income
Improvements in economic conditions in other countries	Declines in economic conditions in other countries
A reduction in real interest rates (nominal interest rates corrected for inflation) not due to price level changes	A rise in real interest rates (nominal interest rates corrected for inflation) not due to price level changes
Tax decreases	Tax increases
A drop in the foreign exchange value of the dollar	A rise in the foreign exchange value of the dollar

QUICK QUIZ

Aggregate demand is the total of all planned _____ in the economy, and **aggregate supply** is the total of all planned _____ in the economy. The aggregate demand curve shows the various quantities of total planned _____ on final goods and services at various price levels; it is downward sloping.

There are three reasons why the aggregate demand curve is downward sloping: the _____-_____ effect, the _____ _____ effect, and the _____ _____ effect.

The _____-_____ effect occurs because price level changes alter the real value of cash balances, thereby causing people to desire to spend more or less, depending on whether the price level decreases or increases.

The _____ _____ effect is caused by interest rate changes that mimic price level changes. At higher interest rates, people seek to buy _____ houses and cars, and at lower interest rates, they seek to buy _____.

The **open economy effect** occurs because of a shift away from expenditures on _____ goods and a shift toward expenditures on _____ goods when the domestic price level increases.

See page 260 for the answers. Review concepts from this section in MyEconLab.

LONG-RUN EQUILIBRIUM AND THE PRICE LEVEL

As noted in Chapter 3, equilibrium occurs where the demand and supply curves intersect. The same is true for the economy as a whole, as shown in Figure 10-5 on the next page: The equilibrium price level occurs at the point where the aggregate demand curve *(AD)* crosses the long-run aggregate supply curve *(LRAS)*. At this equilibrium price level of 120, the total of all planned real expenditures for the entire economy is equal to actual real GDP produced by firms after all adjustments have taken place. Thus, the equilibrium depicted in Figure 10-5 is the economy's *long-run equilibrium.*

The Long-Run Equilibrium Price Level

Note in Figure 10-5 that if the price level were to increase to 140, actual real GDP would exceed total planned real expenditures. Inventories of unsold goods would begin to accumulate, and firms would stand ready to offer more services than people wish to purchase. As a result, the price level would tend to fall.

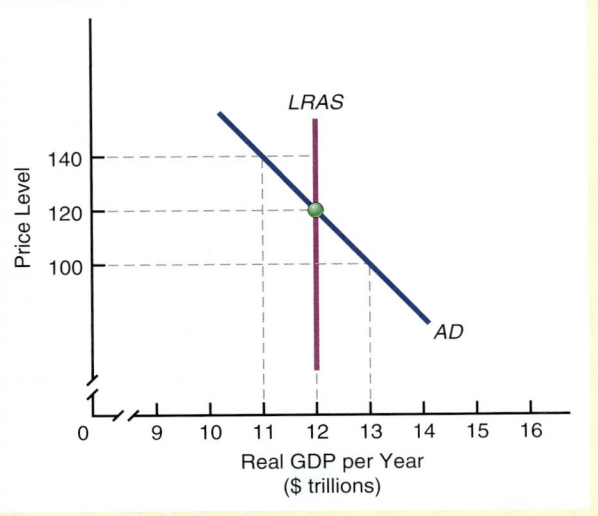

FIGURE 10-5

Long-Run Economywide Equilibrium

For the economy as a whole, long-run equilibrium occurs at the price level where the aggregate demand curve crosses the long-run aggregate supply curve. At this long-run equilibrium price level, which is 120 in the diagram, total planned real expenditures equal real GDP at full employment, which in our example is a real GDP of $12 trillion.

In contrast, if the price level were 100, then total planned real expenditures by individuals, businesses, and the government would exceed actual real GDP. Inventories of unsold goods would begin to be depleted. The price level would rise toward 120, and higher prices would encourage firms to expand production and replenish inventories of goods available for sale.

The Effects of Economic Growth on the Price Level

We now have a basic theory of how real GDP and the price level are determined in the long run when all of a nation's resources can change over time and all input prices can adjust fully to changes in the overall level of prices of goods and services that firms produce. Let's begin by evaluating the effects of economic growth on the nation's price level.

Economic Growth and Secular Deflation. Take a look at panel (a) of Figure 10-6, which shows what happens, other things being equal, when the *LRAS* shifts rightward over time. If the economy were to grow steadily during, say, a 10-year interval, the long-run aggregate supply schedule would shift to the right, from $LRAS_1$ to $LRAS_2$. In panel (a), this results in a downward movement along the aggregate demand schedule. The equilibrium price level falls, from 120 to 80.

Thus, if all factors that affect total planned real expenditures are unchanged, so that the aggregate demand curve does not noticeably move during the 10-year period of real GDP growth, the growing economy in the example would experience deflation. This is known as **secular deflation,** or a persistently declining price level resulting from economic growth in the presence of relatively unchanged aggregate demand.

Secular deflation
A persistent decline in prices resulting from economic growth in the presence of stable aggregate demand.

Secular Deflation in the United States. In the United States, between 1872 and 1894, the price of bricks fell by 50 percent, the price of sugar by 67 percent, the price of wheat by 69 percent, the price of nails by 70 percent, and the price of copper by nearly 75 percent. Founders of a late-nineteenth-century political movement called *populism* offered a proposal for ending deflation: They wanted the government to issue new money

FIGURE 10-6
Secular Deflation versus Long-Run Price Stability in a Growing Economy

Panel (a) illustrates what happens when economic growth occurs without a corresponding increase in aggregate demand. The result is a decline in the price level over time, known as *secular deflation*. Panel (b) shows that, in principle, secular deflation can be avoided if the aggregate demand curve shifts rightward at the same pace that the long-run aggregate supply curve shifts to the right.

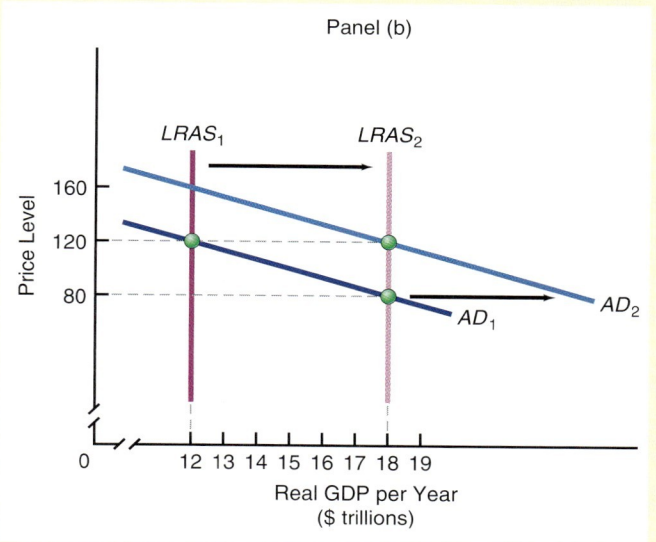

backed by silver. As noted in Table 10-1 on page 247, an increase in the quantity of money in circulation causes the aggregate demand curve to shift to the right. It is clear from panel (b) of Figure 10-6 that the increase in the quantity of money would indeed have pushed the price level back upward.

Nevertheless, money growth remained low for several more years. Not until the early twentieth century would the United States find a way to halt secular deflation, namely, by creating a central bank.

What major nation has experienced steady deflation in recent years?

Go to www.econtoday.com/ch10 to learn about how the price level has changed during recent years. Then click on "Gross Domestic Product and Components" (for GDP deflators) or "Consumer Price Indexes."

INTERNATIONAL EXAMPLE

Deflation Is the Norm in Japan

Since 1998, Japan's real GDP has increased in every year except 2002, when it briefly and very slightly declined. As long-run aggregate supply has steadily shifted rightward, the price level has gradually declined. Consequently, Japan has experienced deflation every year since 1998. During this period, Japan's price level has decreased at an average annual rate of just over 0.5 percent.

FOR CRITICAL ANALYSIS
If the Japanese government really wanted to end deflation, what policies might it consider adopting?

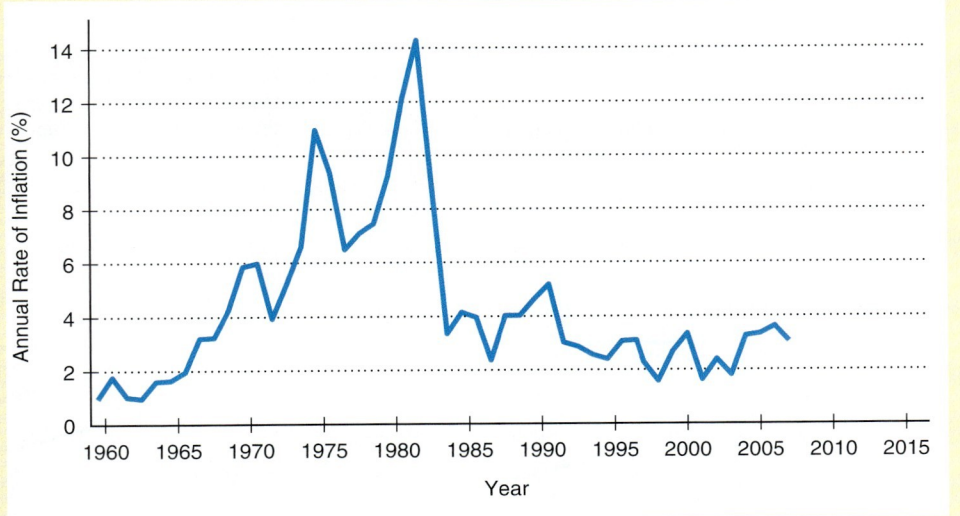

FIGURE 10-7

Inflation Rates in the United States

U.S. inflation rates rose considerably during the 1970s but declined to lower levels since the 1980s. Nevertheless, the United States has experienced inflation every year since 1959.

Sources: *Economic Report of the President; Economic Indicators,* various issues.

CAUSES OF INFLATION

Of course, so far during your lifetime, deflation has not been a problem in the United States. Instead, what you have experienced is inflation. Figure 10-7 shows annual U.S. inflation rates for the past few decades. Clearly, inflation rates have been variable. The other obvious fact, however, is that inflation rates have been consistently *positive*. The price level in the United States has *risen* almost every year. For today's United States, secular deflation has not been a big political issue. If anything, it is secular *inflation* that has plagued the nation.

Supply-Side Inflation?

What causes such persistent inflation? The model of aggregate demand and long-run aggregate supply provides two possible explanations for inflation. One potential rationale is depicted in panel (a) of Figure 10-8. This panel shows a rise in the price level caused by a *decline in long-run aggregate supply*. Hence one possible reason for persistent inflation would be continual reductions in economywide production.

Recall now the factors that would cause the aggregate supply schedule to shift leftward. One might be reductions in labor force participation, higher marginal tax rates on wages, or the provision of government benefits that give households incentives *not* to supply labor services to firms. Tax rates and government benefits have increased during recent decades, but so has the U.S. population. The significant overall rise in real GDP that has taken place during the past few decades tells us that population growth and productivity gains undoubtedly have dominated other factors. In fact, the aggregate supply schedule has actually shifted *rightward,* not leftward, over time. Consequently, this supply-side explanation for persistent inflation *cannot* be the correct explanation.

FIGURE 10-8

Explaining Persistent Inflation

As shown in panel (a), it is possible for a decline in long-run aggregate supply to cause a rise in the price level. Long-run aggregate supply *increases*, however, in a growing economy, so this cannot explain the observation of persistent U.S. inflation. Panel (b) provides the actual explanation of persistent inflation in the United States and most other nations today, which is that increases in aggregate demand push up the long-run equilibrium price level. Thus, it is possible to explain persistent inflation if the aggregate demand curve shifts rightward at a faster pace than the long-run aggregate supply curve.

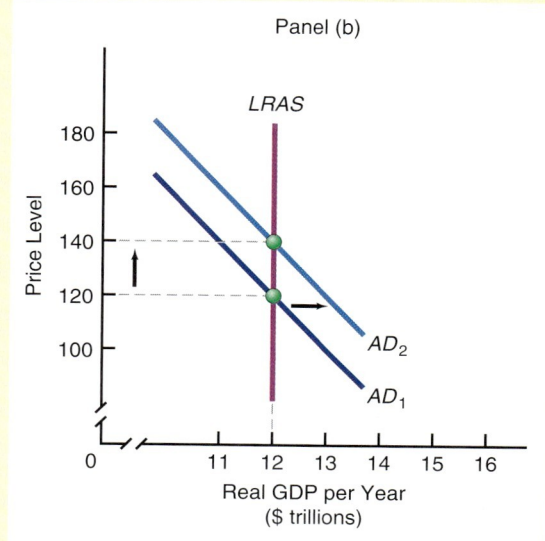

Demand-Side Inflation

This leaves only one other explanation for the persistent inflation that the United States has experienced in recent decades. This explanation is depicted in panel (b) of Figure 10-8. If aggregate demand increases for a given level of long-run aggregate supply, the price level must increase. The reason is that at an initial price level such as 120, people desire to purchase more goods and services than firms are willing and able to produce given currently available resources and technology. As a result, the rise in aggregate demand leads only to a general rise in the price level, such as the increase to a value of 140 depicted in the figure.

From a long-run perspective, we are left with only one possibility: Persistent inflation in a growing economy is possible only if the aggregate demand curve shifts rightward over time at a faster pace than the rightward progression of the long-run aggregate supply curve. Thus, in contrast to the experience of people who lived in the latter portion of the nineteenth century, when aggregate demand grew too slowly relative to aggregate supply to maintain price stability, your grandparents, parents, and you have lived in times when aggregate demand has grown too *speedily*. The result has been a continual upward drift in the price level, or long-term inflation.

Figure 10-9 on page 252 shows that U.S. real GDP has grown in most years since 1970. Nevertheless, this growth has been accompanied by higher prices every single year.

Why do you suppose that real GDP growth in China, which just a few years ago was accompanied by deflation, is now accompanied by inflation instead?

> **ECONOMICS FRONT AND CENTER**
>
> To contemplate demand-side versus supply-side factors that can affect inflation, read **Searching for Answers in Africa**, on page 253.

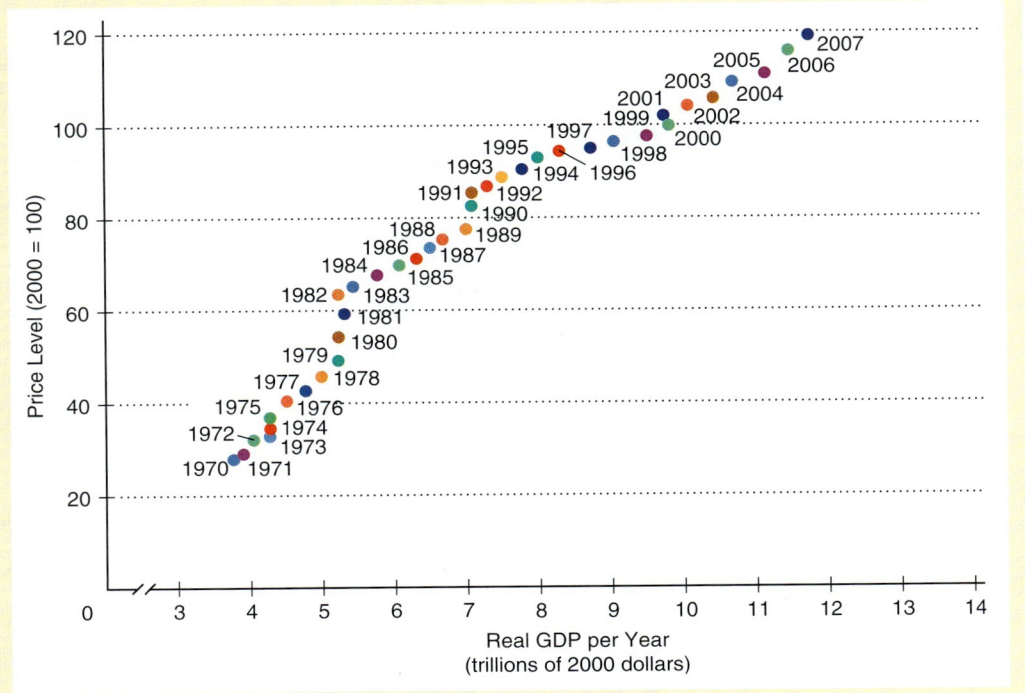

FIGURE 10-9

Real GDP and the Price Level in the United States, 1970 to the Present

This figure shows the points where aggregate demand and aggregate supply have intersected each year from 1970 to the present. The United States has experienced economic growth over this period, but not without inflation.

Sources: *Economic Report of the President; Economic Indicators*, various issues; author's estimates.

INTERNATIONAL POLICY EXAMPLE

The People's Bank of China Rediscovers How to Create Inflation

Long-run aggregate supply has been increasing rapidly in China. Real GDP has risen by at least 7 percent in every year since 1998. This helps to explain why, from 1998 to 2003, the price level in China *decreased* at an annual rate of 0.6 percent.

Since 2003, however, the price level in China has *increased* at an annual rate of close to 3 percent, while the pace of real GDP growth has continued at or above previous levels. What key factor changed after 2003 to cause China's economy to experience inflation instead of deflation? The answer is that since 2003, the quantity of money in circulation in China has increased by an annual average rate of about 15 percent, more than twice the average rate of growth in preceding years. This significant increase in money supply growth has caused aggregate demand to shift rightward at a faster pace than the annual rightward shifts in the long-run aggregate supply curve, thereby causing the price level to increase.

FOR CRITICAL ANALYSIS

What must have been true of the speed at which aggregate demand shifted rightward relative to rightward shifts in aggregate supply in China between 1998 and 2003?

QUICK QUIZ

When the economy is in long-run equilibrium, the price level adjusts to equate total planned real _____ by individuals, businesses, and the government with total planned _____ by firms.

Economic growth causes the long-run aggregate supply schedule to shift _____ over time. If the position of the aggregate demand curve does not change, the long-run equilibrium price level tends to _____, and there is **secular deflation**.

Because the U.S. economy has grown in recent decades, the persistent inflation during those years has been caused by the aggregate demand curve shifting _____ at a faster pace than the long-run aggregate supply curve.

See page 260 for the answers. Review concepts from this section in MyEconLab.

CASE STUDY — ECONOMICS FRONT AND CENTER

Searching for Answers in Africa

Slovo is the daughter of a couple who immigrated to the United States from a small African nation several years before her birth. She has a position as a staff economist at a U.S. Federal Reserve bank, but she has taken a leave from that position for a year so that she can study the central bank of her parents' home country. This African nation experienced relatively low economic growth between 1970 and 1989, and annual inflation rates were in the double digits during that period. In the 1990s, the average annual rate of growth of real GDP more than doubled, to about 5 percent per year, and the inflation rate dropped below 6 percent per year.

The nation's economic performance has come unglued during the 2000s, however. The country imports most of its energy resources, and energy prices have increased substantially. The rate of growth of government spending has doubled during the past three years, as has the growth rate of the money supply. Real GDP has increased at a rate of only about 0.5 percent per year since 2001, and the annual inflation rate has jumped to 12 percent.

Slovo will be meeting this morning with officials of the nation's government and central bank. She thinks about the policy recommendations she plans to make.

CRITICAL ANALYSIS QUESTIONS

1. *In this nation, what factors appear to account for the lower rate of real GDP growth during the 2000s?*
2. *What factors appear to explain the higher rates of inflation observed in this nation during the 2000s?*

Issues and Applications

Why the 2004 Tsunami Did Not Swamp Asian Economies

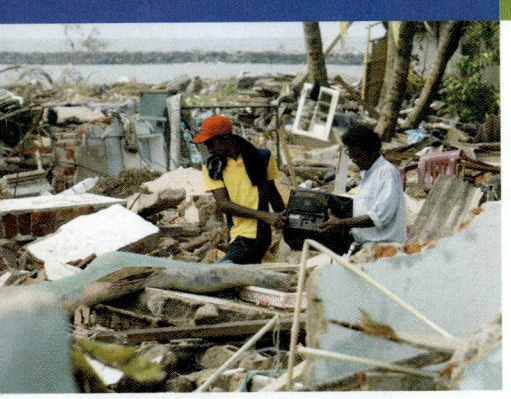

Concepts Applied
- Long-Run Aggregate Supply
- Aggregate Demand
- Long-Run Equilibrium

The estimated death toll of 240,000 resulting from the Indian Ocean earthquake and tsunami event of December 26, 2004, exceeded the tallies of all other earthquakes recorded since the year 1556, when a massive Chinese earthquake killed approximately 830,000 people. In spite of this huge human toll and the considerable property damage inflicted by the tsunami, however, most of the economies of the affected Southeast Asian nations were barely bumped from their long-run growth paths.

Dire Predictions for the Future

Why did some media observers suggest that the 2004 tsunami event might deal a lingering blow to the economies of the affected nations? These observers apparently felt that there would be a long-lasting negative effect on the nations' abilities to continue producing goods and services. This caused the observers to be concerned that long-run aggregate supply would decrease.

To be sure, in a nongrowing economy, reductions in productive capability caused by the tsunami damage could certainly have generated a reduction in aggregate supply. This is why the media observers suggested that the affected nations' price levels would jump, resulting in sudden inflation, and that real GDP would drop, leading to recession.

The Reality of the Long Run

In fact, as panel (a) of Table 10-2 shows, inflation rates in the major Southeast Asian nations most affected by the tsunami of late 2004 did increase in 2005. Only in Indonesia did inflation noticeably spike, however. In the other nations, where foreign tourism spending is typically 3 to 5 percent of aggregate planned expenditures, declines in aggregate demand generated by a tourism drop-off helped reduce price increases. In any event, all four nations' inflation rates quickly dropped back to levels consistent with longer-term trends.

Of the nations listed in Table 10-2, not a single country experienced a decline in real GDP during the years following the tsunami event. In fact, in 2005, real GDP grew at an annual rate of at least 5 percent in all four nations. Malaysia and Thailand experienced a slight falloff in real GDP growth during the year following the 2004 disaster. These slightly reduced growth rates perhaps reflected a tsunami effect on productive capabilities that tended to reduce the extent to which the aggregate supply curve shifted rightward. In Indonesia and Sri Lanka, however, real GDP growth actually *increased* in the year following the tsunami calamity. The pace of economic growth might have been even faster in these two nations in the absence of the tsunami event. Nevertheless, the event failed to depress the rate at which long-run aggregate supply increased in the two countries.

TABLE 10-2
Inflation Rates and Real GDP Growth Rates in Selected Southeast Asian Nations

(a) Inflation Rates				
	2004	2005	2006	2007
Indonesia	6.1	10.5	14.2	6.6
Malaysia	1.4	3.0	3.1	2.7
Sri Lanka	7.9	10.6	8.0	7.0
Thailand	2.8	4.5	3.6	2.2

(b) Real GDP Growth Rates				
	2004	2005	2006	2007
Indonesia	5.1	5.6	5.0	6.0
Malaysia	7.1	5.3	5.5	5.8
Sri Lanka	5.4	5.9	5.6	6.2
Thailand	6.2	4.4	5.0	5.4

Although Southeast Asian inflation rates rose in the year following the tsunami disaster that occurred at the end of 2004, rates of inflation quickly returned to levels closer to long-run trends. Real GDP growth rates dropped only very slightly in Malaysia and Thailand, and rates of growth of real GDP actually increased in Indonesia and Sri Lanka.

Source: International Monetary Fund, *World Economic Outlook*, various issues.

Log in to **MyEconLab**, click on "Economic News," and test your understanding of the chapter by answering interactive questions that relate directly to this issue.

For Critical Analysis

1. What are some possible reasons that the fast-growing nations listed in Table 10-2 may have recently experienced inflation instead of secular deflation?

2. Why do you suppose that the long-run negative macroeconomic effects of the tsunami disaster were greater in the very slow-growing African nation of Somalia than in the nations of Southeast Asia?

Web Resources

1. For a discussion of how the tsunami's limited economic impact had become clear even by early 2005, go to www.econtoday.com/ch10.

2. To learn why the macroeconomic effects of the tsunami event on the island nation of the Maldives were longer lasting, go to www.econtoday.com/ch10.

Research Project

Suppose that you have been appointed to advise the government of the Maldives, a country of nearly 1,200 islands, about the long-run macroeconomic effects of the 2004 tsunami disaster. The Maldives are surrounded by unusually clear water, and this has made them a tourist haven. Much of the islands' industry is oriented toward producing tourism-related goods and services. Because the islands of the Maldives are mostly flat, nearly the entire nation was affected by the tsunami. After the event, the landscape of many of the islands was littered with oil drums and other pollutants, and about 40 percent of tourism-oriented facilities were destroyed or heavily damaged. Why might the long-run negative consequences of the tsunami event have been more pronounced for the Maldives than for other Southeast Asian nations? What policy actions might the Maldives government undertake during the coming years to return to the long-run macroeconomic equilibrium that the nation had attained prior to the event?

WHAT YOU SHOULD KNOW

Long-Run Aggregate Supply
The long-run aggregate supply curve is vertical at the amount of real GDP that firms plan to produce when they have full information and when complete adjustment of input prices to any changes in output prices has taken place. This is the full-employment level of real GDP, or the economywide output level at which the natural rate of unemployment—the sum of frictional and structural unemployment as a percentage of the labor force—occurs.

aggregate supply, 240
long-run aggregate supply curve, 240
base-year dollars, 241
endowments, 241
Key figure
Figure 10-1, 240

WHERE TO GO TO PRACTICE
- **MyEconLab** Study Plan 10.1
- Audio introduction to Chapter 10
- Video: The Long-Run Aggregate Supply Curve
- Animated Figure 10-1

Economic Growth and the Long-Run Aggregate Supply Curve
Economic growth is an expansion of a country's production possibilities. Thus, the production possibilities curve shifts rightward when the economy grows, and so does the nation's long-run aggregate supply curve. In a growing economy, the changes in full-employment real GDP defined by the shifting long-run aggregate supply curve define the nation's long-run, or trend, growth path.

Key figures
Figure 10-2, 241
Figure 10-3, 242

- **MyEconLab** Study Plan 10.1
- Video: The Long-Run Aggregate Supply Curve
- Animated Figures 10-2 and 10-3

Why the Aggregate Demand Curve Slopes Downward and Factors That Cause It to Shift
A rise in the price level reduces the real value of cash balances in the hands of the public, which induces people to cut back on planned spending. This is the real-balance effect. In addition, higher interest rates typically accompany increases in the price level, and this interest rate effect induces people to cut back on borrowing and, consequently, spending. Finally, a rise in the price level at home causes domestic goods to be more expensive relative to foreign goods, so that there is a fall in exports and a rise in imports, both of which cause domestic planned expenditures to fall. These three factors together account for the downward slope of the aggregate demand curve. A shift in the aggregate demand curve results from a change in total planned real expenditures at any given price level and may be caused by a number of factors, including changes in security about jobs and future income, tax changes, variations in the quantity of money in circulation, changes in real interest rates, movements in exchange rates, and changes in economic conditions in other countries.

aggregate demand, 243
aggregate demand curve, 243
real-balance effect, 245
interest rate effect, 245
open economy effect, 246
Key figure
Figure 10-4, 244

- **MyEconLab** Study Plans 10.2 and 10.3
- Video: The Aggregate Demand Curve and What Happens When the Price Level Rises
- Video: Shifts in the Aggregate Demand Curve
- Animated Figure 10-4

WHAT YOU SHOULD KNOW		WHERE TO GO TO PRACTICE
Long-Run Equilibrium for the Economy In a long-run economywide equilibrium, the price level adjusts until total planned real expenditures equal actual real GDP. Thus, the long-run equilibrium price level is determined at the point where the aggregate demand curve intersects the long-run aggregate supply curve. If the price level is below its long-run equilibrium value, total planned real expenditures exceed actual real GDP, and the level of prices of goods and services will rise back toward the long-run equilibrium price level. In contrast, if the price level is above its long-run equilibrium value, actual real GDP is greater than total planned real expenditures, and the price level declines in the direction of the long-run equilibrium price level.	**Key figure** Figure 10-5, 248	• **MyEconLab** Study Plan 10.4 • Animated Figure 10-5
Why Economic Growth Can Cause Deflation If the aggregate demand curve is stationary during a period of economic growth, the long-run aggregate supply curve shifts rightward along the aggregate demand curve. The long-run equilibrium price level falls, so there is deflation. Historically, economic growth has in this way generated secular deflation, or relatively long periods of declining prices.	secular deflation, 248 **Key figure** Figure 10-6, 249	• **MyEconLab** Study Plan 10.4 • Animated Figure 10-6
Likely Reasons for Recent Persistent Inflation One event that can induce inflation is a decline in long-run aggregate supply, because this causes the long-run aggregate supply curve to shift leftward. In a growing economy, however, the long-run aggregate supply curve generally shifts rightward. This indicates that a much more likely cause of persistent inflation is a pace of aggregate demand growth that exceeds the pace at which long-run aggregate supply increases.	**Key figures** Figure 10-7, 250 Figure 10-8, 251	• **MyEconLab** Study Plan 10.5 • Animated Figures 10-7 and 10-8

Log in to MyEconLab, take a chapter test, and get a personalized Study Plan that tells you which concepts you understand and which ones you need to review. From there, MyEconLab will give you futher practice, tutorials, animations, videos, and guided solutions.

Log in to www.myeconlab.com

PROBLEMS

Select problems, indicated by a blue oval, are assignable in *MyEconLab*. Answers to the odd-numbered problems appear at the back of the book.

10-1 Many economists view the natural rate of unemployment as the level observed when real GDP is given by the position of the long-run aggregate supply curve. How can there be positive unemployment in this situation?

10-2 Suppose that the long-run aggregate supply curve is positioned at a real GDP level of $12 trillion in base-year dollars, and the long-run equilibrium price level (in index number form) is 115. What is the full-employment level of *nominal* GDP?

10-3 Continuing from Problem 10-2, suppose that the full-employment level of *nominal* GDP in the following year rises to $14.2 trillion. The long-run equilibrium price level, however, remains unchanged. By how much (in real dollars) has the long-run aggregate supply curve shifted to the right in the following year? By how much, if any, has the aggregate demand curve shifted to the right? (Hint: The equilibrium price level can stay the same only if *LRAS* and *AD* shift rightward by the same amount.)

10-4 Suppose that the position of a nation's long-run aggregate supply curve has not changed, but its long-run equilibrium price level has increased. Which of the following factors might account for this event?
a. A rise in the value of the domestic currency relative to other world currencies
b. An increase in the quantity of money in circulation
c. An increase in the labor force participation rate
d. A decrease in taxes
e. A rise in real incomes of countries that are key trading partners of this nation
f. Increased long-run economic growth

10-5 Suppose that during a given year, the quantity of U.S. real GDP that can be produced in the long run rises from $11.9 trillion to $12.0 trillion, measured in base-year dollars. During the year, no change occurs in the various factors that influence aggregate demand. What will happen to the U.S. long-run equilibrium price level during this particular year?

10-6 Assume that the position of a nation's aggregate demand curve has not changed, but the long-run equilibrium price level has declined. Other things being equal, which of the following factors might account for this event?

a. An increase in labor productivity
b. A decrease in the capital stock
c. A decrease in the quantity of money in circulation
d. The discovery of new mineral resources used to produce various goods
e. A technological improvement

10-7 Suppose that there is a sudden rise in the price level. What will happen to economywide planned spending on purchases of goods and services? Why?

10-8 Assume that the economy is in long-run equilibrium with complete information and that input prices adjust rapidly to changes in the prices of goods and services. If there is a sudden rise in the price level induced by an increase in aggregate demand, what happens to real GDP?

10-9 Consider the accompanying diagram when answering the questions that follow.

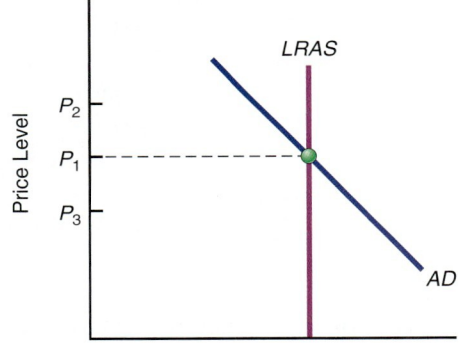

a. Suppose that the current price level is P_2. Explain why the price level will decline toward P_1.
b. Suppose that the current price level is P_3. Explain why the price level will rise toward P_1.

10-10 Explain whether each of the following events would cause a movement along or a shift in the position of the *LRAS* curve, other things being equal. In each case, explain the direction of the movement along the curve or shift in its position.

a. Last year, businesses invested in new capital equipment, so this year the nation's capital stock is higher than it was last year.

b. There has been an 8 percent increase in the quantity of money in circulation that has shifted the AD curve.
c. A hurricane of unprecedented strength has damaged oil rigs, factories, and ports all along the nation's coast.
d. Inflation has occurred during the past year as a result of rightward shifts of the AD curve.

10-11 Explain whether each of the following events would cause a movement along or a shift in the position of the AD curve, other things being equal. In each case, explain the direction of the movement along the curve or shift in its position.

a. Deflation has occurred during the past year.
b. Real GDP levels of all the nation's major trading partners have declined.
c. There has been a decline in the foreign exchange value of the nation's currency.
d. The price level has increased this year.

10-12 This year, a nation's long-run equilibrium real GDP and price level both increased. Which of the following combinations of factors might simultaneously account for *both* occurrences?

a. An isolated earthquake at the beginning of the year destroyed part of the nation's capital stock, and the nation's government significantly reduced its purchases of goods and services.
b. There was a minor technological improvement at the end of the previous year, and the quantity of money in circulation rose significantly during the year.
c. Labor productivity increased somewhat throughout the year, and consumers significantly increased their total planned purchases of goods and services.
d. The capital stock increased somewhat during the year, and the quantity of money in circulation declined considerably.

10-13 Explain how, if at all, each of the following events would affect equilibrium real GDP and the long-run equilibrium price level.

a. A reduction in the quantity of money in circulation

b. An income tax rebate (the return of previously paid taxes) from the government to households, which they can apply only to purchases of goods and services
c. A technological improvement
d. A decrease in the value of the home currency in terms of the currencies of other nations

10-14 For each question below, suppose that the economy *begins* at the long-run equilibrium point A. Identify which of the other points on the diagram—points B, C, D, or E—could represent a *new* long-run equilibrium

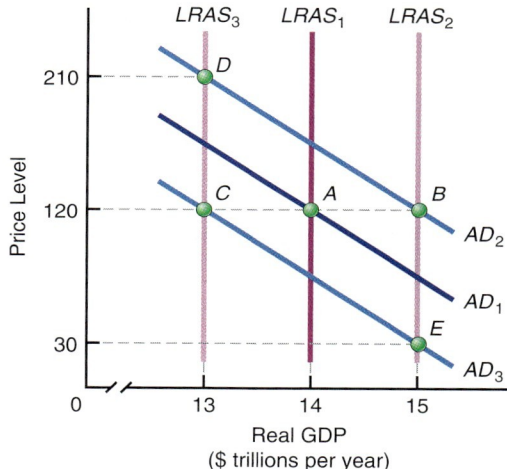

after the described events take place and move the economy away from point A.
a. Significant productivity improvements occur, and the quantity of money in circulation increases.
b. No new capital investment takes place, and a fraction of the existing capital stock depreciates and becomes unusable. At the same time, the government imposes a large tax increase on the nation's households.
c. More efficient techniques for producing goods and services are adopted throughout the economy at the same time that the government reduces its spending on goods and services.

ECONOMICS ON THE NET

Wages, Productivity, and Aggregate Supply How much firms pay their employees and the productivity of those employees influence firms' total planned production, so changes in these factors affect the position of the aggregate supply curve. This application gives you the opportunity to examine recent trends in measures of the overall wages and productivity of workers.

Title: Bureau of Labor Statistics: Economy at a Glance

Navigation: Use the link at www.econtoday.com/ch10 to visit the Bureau of Labor Statistics Web site.

Application Perform the indicated operations, and answer the following questions.

1. Click on *Employment Costs,* and then click on *Employee Cost Index.* What are the recent trends in wages and salaries and in benefits? In the long run, how should these trends be related to movements in the overall price level?

2. Back up to the home page, and click on *Productivity and Costs* and then on *PDF* next to "Economic News Releases: Productivity and Costs." How has labor productivity behaved recently? What does this imply for the long-run aggregate supply curve?

3. Back up to U.S. Economy at a Glance, and now click on *National Employment* and then on *PDF* next to "Economic News Releases: Employment Situation Summary." Does it appear that the U.S. economy is currently in a long-run growth equilibrium?

For Group Study and Analysis

1. Divide the class into aggregate demand and long-run aggregate supply groups. Have each group search the Internet for data on factors that influence its assigned curve. For which factors do data appear to be most readily available? For which factors are data more sparse or more subject to measurement problems?

2. The BLS home page displays a map of the United States. Assign regions of the nation to different groups, and have each group develop a short report about current and future prospects for economic growth within its assigned region. What similarities exist across regions? What regional differences are there?

ANSWERS TO QUICK QUIZZES

p. 243: (i) vertical; (ii) natural; (iii) rightward . . . increase
p. 247: (i) expenditures . . . production . . . spending; (ii) real-balance . . . interest rate . . . open economy; (iii) real-balance; (iv) interest rate . . . fewer . . . more; (v) domestic . . . foreign
p. 253: (i) expenditures . . . production; (ii) rightward . . . decline; (iii) rightward

Classical and Keynesian Macro Analyses

11

Between 1999 and 2007, the price of a barrel of crude oil increased from about $15 to more than $70. This led some in the media to compare this oil price increase to the price run-up from 1973 to 1981. Media observers tended to ignore two important points, however. One was that the oil price increase during the 2000s could not be compared directly with the price jump of the 1970s without adjusting for inflation. Second, they also failed to take note of the fact that U.S. producers rely less on oil to produce goods and services today than did producers in the 1970s. In this chapter, you will learn why these lapses caused many in the media to overestimate the effects of the oil price increase of the 2000s on U.S. real GDP and on the U.S. price level.

Learning Objectives

After reading this chapter, you should be able to:

1. Discuss the central assumptions of the classical model
2. Describe the short-run determination of equilibrium real GDP and the price level in the classical model
3. Explain circumstances under which the short-run aggregate supply curve may be either horizontal or upward sloping
4. Understand what factors cause shifts in the short-run and long-run aggregate supply curves
5. Evaluate the effects of aggregate demand and supply shocks on equilibrium real GDP in the short run
6. Determine the causes of short-run variations in the inflation rate

MyEconLab helps you master each objective and study more efficiently. See end of chapter for details.

Did You Know That...

the price of a bottle containing 6.5 ounces of Coca-Cola remained unchanged at 5 cents from 1886 to 1959? The prices of many other goods and services changed at least slightly during that 73-year period, and since then the prices of most items, including Coca-Cola, have generally moved in an upward direction. Nevertheless, prices of final goods and services have not always adjusted immediately in response to changes in aggregate demand. Consequently, one approach to understanding the determination of real GDP and the price level emphasizes *incomplete* adjustment in the prices of many goods and services. The simplest version of this approach was first developed by a twentieth-century economist named John Maynard Keynes (pronounced like *canes*). It assumes that in the short run, prices of most goods and services are nearly as rigid as the price of Coca-Cola from 1886 to 1959. Although the modern version of the Keynesian approach allows for greater flexibility of prices in the short run, incomplete price adjustment still remains a key feature of the modern Keynesian approach.

The Keynesian approach does not retain the long-run assumption, which you encountered in Chapter 10, of fully adjusting prices. Economists who preceded Keynes employed this assumption in creating an approach to understanding variations in real GDP and the price level that Keynes called the *classical model*. Like Keynes, we shall begin our study of variations in real GDP and the price level by considering the earlier, classical approach.

THE CLASSICAL MODEL

The classical model, which traces its origins to the 1770s, was the first systematic attempt to explain the determinants of the price level and the national levels of real GDP, employment, consumption, saving, and investment. Classical economists—Adam Smith, J. B. Say, David Ricardo, John Stuart Mill, Thomas Malthus, A. C. Pigou, and others—wrote from the 1770s to the 1930s. They assumed, among other things, that all wages and prices were flexible and that competitive markets existed throughout the economy.

Say's Law

Every time you produce something for which you receive income, you generate the income necessary to make expenditures on other goods and services. That means that an economy producing $12 trillion of real GDP, measured in base-year dollars, simultaneously produces the income with which these goods and services can be purchased. As an accounting identity, *actual* aggregate output always equals *actual* aggregate income. Classical economists took this accounting identity one step further by arguing that total national supply creates its own national demand. They asserted what has become known as **Say's law:**

> *Supply creates its own demand; hence it follows that* **desired** *expenditures will equal* **actual** *expenditures.*

What does Say's law really mean? It states that the very process of producing specific goods (supply) is proof that other goods are desired (demand). People produce more goods than they want for their own use only if they seek to trade them for other goods. Someone offers to supply something only because he or she has a demand for something else. The implication of this, according to Say, is that no general glut, or overproduction, is possible in a market economy. From this reasoning, it seems to follow that full employment of labor and other resources would be the normal state of affairs in such an economy.

Say's law
A dictum of economist J. B. Say that supply creates its own demand; producing goods and services generates the means and the willingness to purchase other goods and services.

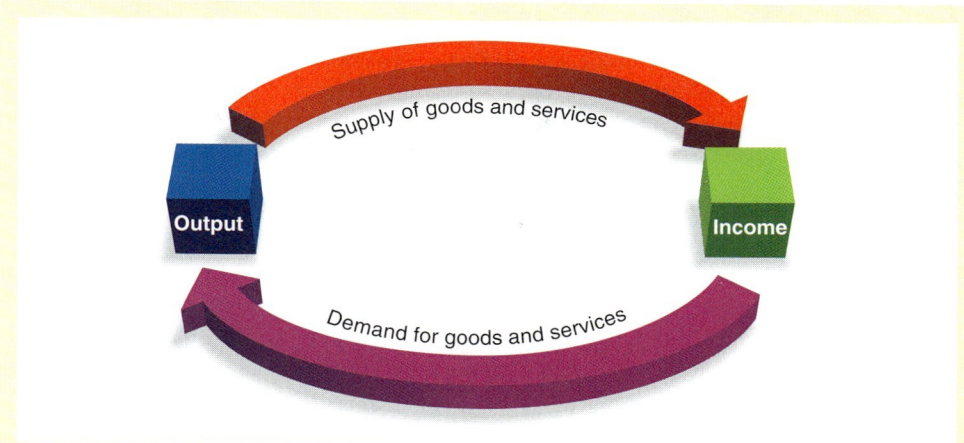

FIGURE 11-1
Say's Law and the Circular Flow
Here we show the circular flow of income and output. The very act of supplying a certain level of goods and services necessarily equals the level of goods and services demanded, in Say's simplified world.

Say acknowledged that an oversupply of some goods might occur in particular markets. He argued that such surpluses would simply cause prices to fall, thereby decreasing production as the economy adjusted. The opposite would occur in markets in which shortages temporarily appeared.

All this seems reasonable enough in a simple barter economy in which households produce most of the goods they want and trade for the rest. This is shown in Figure 11-1, where there is a simple circular flow. But what about a more sophisticated economy in which people work for others and money is used instead of barter? Can these complications create the possibility of unemployment? And does the fact that laborers receive money income, some of which can be saved, lead to unemployment? No, said the classical economists to these last two questions. They based their reasoning on a number of key assumptions.

Assumptions of the Classical Model

The classical model makes four major assumptions:

1. *Pure competition exists.* No single buyer or seller of a commodity or an input can affect its price.
2. *Wages and prices are flexible.* The assumption of pure competition leads to the notion that prices, wages, interest rates, and the like are free to move to whatever level supply and demand dictate (as the economy adjusts). Although no *individual* buyer can set a price, the community of buyers or sellers can cause prices to rise or to fall to an equilibrium level.
3. *People are motivated by self-interest.* Businesses want to maximize their profits, and households want to maximize their economic well-being.
4. *People cannot be fooled by money illusion.* Buyers and sellers react to changes in relative prices. That is to say, they do not suffer from **money illusion.** For example, workers will not be fooled into thinking that a doubling of wages makes them better off if the price level has also doubled during the same time period.

Money illusion
Reacting to changes in money prices rather than relative prices. If a worker whose wages double when the price level also doubles thinks he or she is better off, that worker is suffering from money illusion.

The classical economists concluded, after taking account of the four major assumptions, that the role of government in the economy should be minimal. If pure competition prevails, if all prices and wages are flexible, and if people are self-interested and do not experience money illusion, then any problems in the macroeconomy will be temporary. The market will correct itself.

Equilibrium in the Credit Market

When income is saved, it is not reflected in product demand. It is a type of *leakage* from the circular flow of income and output because saving withdraws funds from the income stream. Therefore, total planned consumption spending *can* fall short of total current real GDP. In such a situation, it does not appear that supply necessarily creates its own demand.

The Relationship Between Saving and Investment. The classical economists did not believe that the complicating factor of saving in the circular flow model of income and output was a problem. They contended that each dollar saved would be invested by businesses so that the leakage of saving would be matched by the injection of business investment. *Investment* here refers only to additions to the nation's capital stock. The classical economists believed that businesses as a group would intend to invest as much as households wanted to save.

The Equilibrium Interest Rate. Equilibrium between the saving plans of consumers and the investment plans of businesses comes about, in the classical economists' model, through the working of the credit market. In the credit market, the *price* of credit is the interest rate. At equilibrium, the price of credit—the interest rate—ensures that the amount of credit demanded equals the amount of credit supplied. Planned investment just equals planned saving, so there is no reason to be concerned about the leakage of saving. This is illustrated graphically in Figure 11-2.

Go to www.econtoday.com/ch11 to link to Federal Reserve data on U.S. interest rates.

In the figure, the vertical axis measures the rate of interest in percentage terms; on the horizontal axis are the amounts of desired saving and desired investment per unit time period. The desired saving curve is really a supply curve of saving. It shows that people wish to save more at higher interest rates than at lower interest rates.

In contrast, the higher the rate of interest, the less profitable it is to invest and the lower is the level of desired investment. Thus, the desired investment curve slopes downward. In this simplified model, the equilibrium rate of interest is 5 percent, and the equilibrium quantity of saving and investment is $2 trillion per year.

FIGURE 11-2
Equating Desired Saving and Investment in the Classical Model

The schedule showing planned investment is labeled "Desired investment." The supply of resources used for investment occurs when individuals do not consume but save instead. The desired saving curve is shown as an upward-sloping supply curve of saving. The equilibrating force here is, of course, the interest rate. At higher interest rates, people desire to save more. But at higher interest rates, businesses wish to engage in less investment because it is less profitable to invest. In this model, at an interest rate of 5 percent, planned investment just equals planned saving, which is $2 trillion per year.

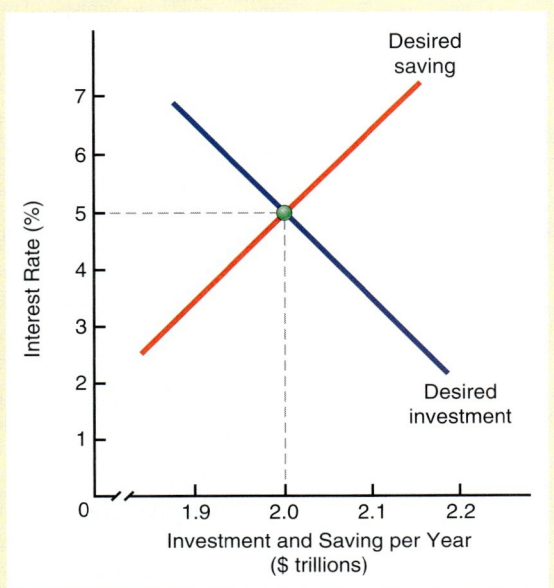

How do inflows of foreign saving affect the equilibrium interest rate in the United States?

INTERNATIONAL EXAMPLE

A Global Credit Market Awash in Saving

In the 1980s and 1990s, many of the world's governments lifted legal restrictions that had prevented their nations' residents from allocating their saving to purchases of foreign bonds and stocks. These legal changes have permitted people all over the world to seek to earn the highest possible returns by directing their saving beyond their nations' borders as well as close to home. Today, 15 percent of Japanese saving ultimately funds investment in other nations. An estimated $3 trillion of the accumulated savings of French residents goes to funding investment projects outside France.

Because rates of return in the United States have been higher than in many of the world's other locales, during the 2000s the U.S. credit market received substantial inflows of saving from abroad. The result has been a rightward shift in the U.S. saving supply curve. This foreign-fueled increase in the supply of saving has contributed to generally lower equilibrium U.S. interest rates in the 2000s, as compared with previous decades.

FOR CRITICAL ANALYSIS
Other things being equal, what would happen to U.S. interest rates if foreign residents suddenly decided to shift their saving to other nations, such as China?

Equilibrium in the Labor Market

Now consider the labor market. If an excess quantity of labor is supplied at a particular wage level, the wage level must be above equilibrium. By accepting lower wages, unemployed workers will quickly be put back to work. We show equilibrium in the labor market in Figure 11-3.

Go to www.econtoday.com/ch11 to find out the latest U.S. saving rate from the Bureau of Economic Analysis. Select "Personal saving as a percentage of disposable personal income."

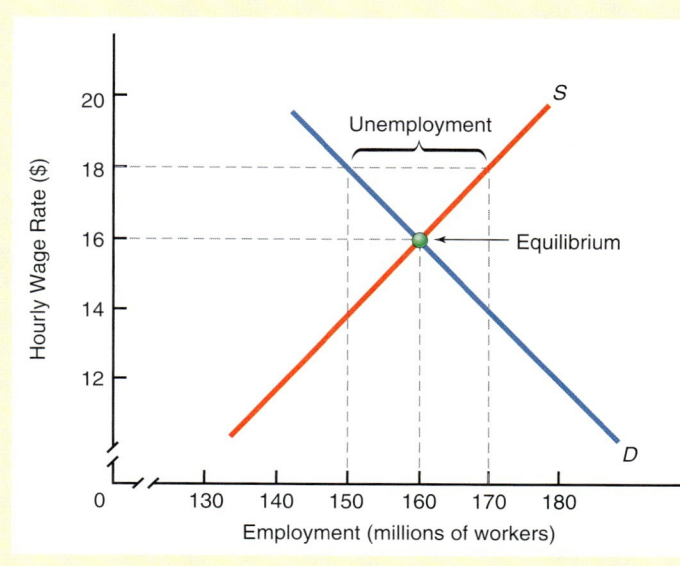

FIGURE 11-3
Equilibrium in the Labor Market
The demand for labor is downward sloping; at higher wage rates, firms will employ fewer workers. The supply of labor is upward sloping; at higher wage rates, more workers will work longer, and more people will be willing to work. The equilibrium wage rate is $16 with an equilibrium employment per year of 160 million workers.

TABLE 11-1
The Relationship Between Employment and Real GDP

Other things being equal, an increase in the quantity of labor input increases real GDP. In this example, if 160 million workers are employed, real GDP is $12 trillion in base-year dollars.

Labor Input per Year (millions of workers)	Real GDP per Year ($ trillions)
150	9
154	10
158	11
160	12
164	13
166	14

Assume that equilibrium exists at $16 per hour and 160 million workers employed. If the wage rate were $18 per hour, there would be unemployment—170 million workers would want to work, but businesses would want to hire only 150 million. In the classical model, this unemployment is eliminated rather rapidly by wage rates dropping back to $16 per hour, as seen in Figure 11-3 on the previous page.

The Relationship Between Employment and Real GDP.

Employment is not to be regarded simply as some isolated figure that government statisticians estimate. Rather, the level of employment in an economy determines its real GDP (output), other things held constant. A hypothetical relationship between input (number of employees) and the value of output (real GDP per year) is shown in Table 11-1. The row that has 160 million workers per year as the labor input is highlighted. That might be considered a hypothetical level of full employment, and it is related to a rate of real GDP, in base-year dollars, of $12 trillion per year.

Classical Theory, Vertical Aggregate Supply, and the Price Level

In the classical model, long-term unemployment is impossible. Say's law, coupled with flexible interest rates, prices, and wages, would always tend to keep workers fully employed so that the aggregate supply curve, as shown in Figure 11-4, is vertical at an amount of real GDP of $12 trillion, in base-year dollars. We have labeled the supply curve *LRAS*, which is the long-run aggregate supply curve introduced in Chapter 10. It was defined there as the quantity of output that would be produced in an economy with full information and full adjustment of wages and prices year in and year out. *LRAS* is therefore at the long-run rate of unemployment. In the classical model, this happens to be the *only* aggregate supply curve that exists. The classical economists made little distinction between the long run and the short run. Prices adjust so fast that the economy is essentially always on or quickly moving toward *LRAS*. Furthermore, because the labor market adjusts rapidly, real GDP is always at, or soon to be at, full employment. Full employment does not mean zero unemployment because there is always some frictional and structural unemployment (discussed in Chapter 7), even in the classical world. This is the natural rate of unemployment.

Effect of an Increase in Aggregate Demand in the Classical Model.

In this model, any change in aggregate demand will quickly cause a change in the price level. Consider starting at E_1, at price level 120, in Figure 11-4. If aggregate demand shifts to AD_2, the economy will tend toward point *A*, but because this is beyond full employment,

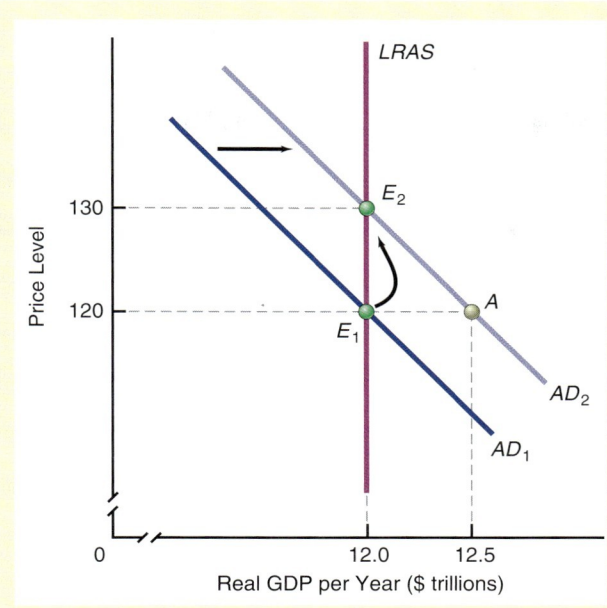

FIGURE 11-4

Classical Theory and Increases in Aggregate Demand

The classical theorists believed that Say's law, flexible interest rates, prices, and wages would always lead to full employment at real GDP of $12 trillion, in base-year dollars, along the vertical aggregate supply curve, *LRAS*. With aggregate demand AD_1 the price level is 120. An increase in aggregate demand shifts AD_1, to AD_2. At price level 120, the quantity of real GDP demanded per year would be $12.5 trillion at point *A* on AD_2. But $12.5 trillion in real GDP per year is greater than real GDP at full employment. Prices rise, and the economy quickly moves from E_1, to E_2, at the higher price level of 130.

prices will rise, and the economy will find itself back on the vertical *LRAS* at point E_2 at a higher price level, 130. The price level will increase as a result of the increase in *AD* because employers will end up bidding up wages for workers, as well as bidding up the prices of other inputs.

The level of real GDP per year clearly does not depend on the level of aggregate demand. Hence we say that in the classical model, the equilibrium level of real GDP per year is completely *supply determined*. Changes in aggregate demand affect only the price level, not real GDP.

Effect of a Decrease in Aggregate Demand in the Classical Model. The effect of a decrease in aggregate demand in the classical model is the converse of the analysis just presented for an increase in aggregate demand. You can simply reverse AD_2 and AD_1 in Figure 11-4. To help you see how this analysis works, consider the flowchart in Figure 11-5.

FIGURE 11-5

Effect of a Decrease in Aggregate Demand in the Classical Model

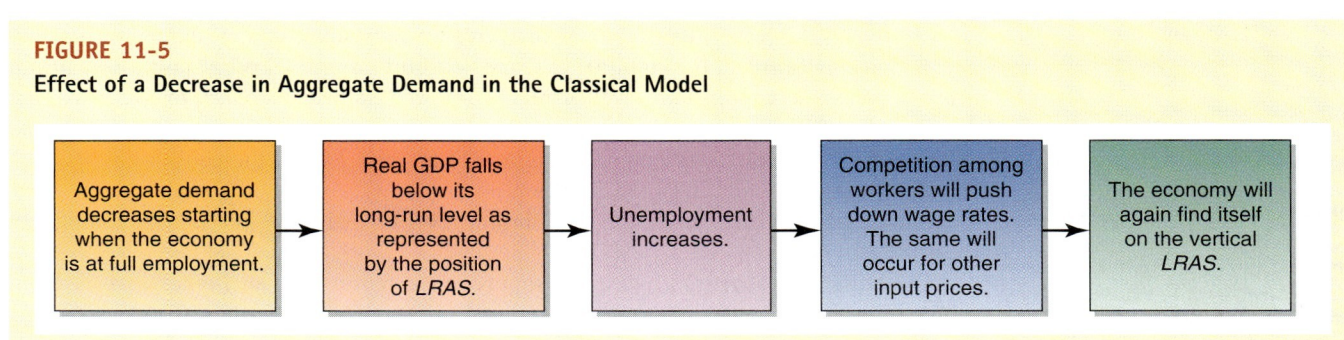

QUICK QUIZ

Say's law states that _____ creates its own _____ and therefore *desired* expenditures will equal *actual* expenditures.

The classical model assumes that (1) _____ _____ exists, (2) _____ and _____ are completely flexible, (3) individuals are motivated by _____-_____, and (4) they cannot be fooled by _____ _____.

When saving is introduced into the model, equilibrium occurs in the credit market through changes in the interest rate such that desired _____ equals desired _____ at the equilibrium rate of interest.

In the labor market, full employment occurs at a _____ _____ at which quantity demanded equals quantity supplied. That particular level of employment is associated with a full-employment value of real GDP per year.

In the classical model, because *LRAS* is _____, the equilibrium level of real GDP is supply determined. Any changes in aggregate demand simply change the _____ _____.

See page 286 for the answers. Review concepts from this section in MyEconLab.

KEYNESIAN ECONOMICS AND THE KEYNESIAN SHORT-RUN AGGREGATE SUPPLY CURVE

The classical economists' world was one of fully utilized resources. There would be no unused capacity and no unemployment. But then in the 1930s Europe and the United States entered a period of economic decline that seemingly could not be explained by the classical model. John Maynard Keynes developed an explanation that has since become known as the Keynesian model. Keynes and his followers argued that prices, especially the price of labor (wages), were inflexible downward due to the existence of unions and long-term contracts between businesses and workers. That meant that prices were "sticky." Keynes contended that in such a world, which has large amounts of excess capacity and unemployment, an increase in aggregate demand will not raise the price level, and a decrease in aggregate demand will not cause firms to lower prices.

This situation is depicted in Figure 11-6. For simplicity, Figure 11-6 does not show the point where the economy reaches capacity, and that is why the *short-run aggregate supply curve* (to be discussed further below) never starts to slope upward and is simply the horizontal line labeled *SRAS*. Moreover, we don't show *LRAS* in Figure 11-6 either. It would be a vertical line at the level of real GDP per year that is consistent with full employment. If we start out in equilibrium with aggregate demand at AD_1, the equilibrium level of real GDP per year, measured in base-year dollars, is $12 trillion at point E_1, and the equilibrium price level is 120. If there is a rise in aggregate demand, so that the aggregate demand curve shifts outward to the right to AD_2, the equilibrium price level at point E_2 will not change; only the equilibrium level of real GDP per year will increase, to $12.5 trillion. Conversely, if there is a fall in demand that shifts the aggregate demand curve to AD_3, the equilibrium price level will again remain at 120 at point E_3, but the equilibrium level of real GDP per year will fall to $11.5 trillion.

Under such circumstances, the equilibrium level of real GDP per year is completely *demand determined*.

The horizontal short-run aggregate supply curve represented in Figure 11-6 is often called the **Keynesian short-run aggregate supply curve.** According to Keynes, unions and long-term contracts are real-world factors that explain the inflexibility of *nominal*

Keynesian short-run aggregate supply curve
The horizontal portion of the aggregate supply curve in which there is excessive unemployment and unused capacity in the economy.

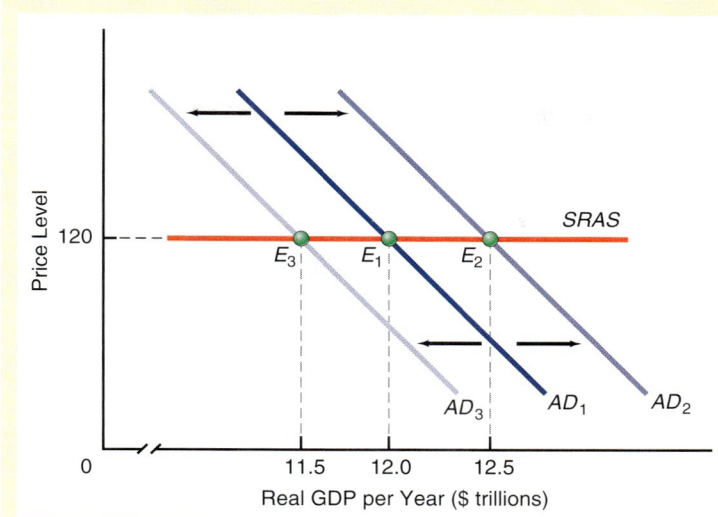

FIGURE 11-6

Demand-Determined Equilibrium Real GDP at Less Than Full Employment

Keynes assumed that prices will not fall when aggregate demand falls and that there is excess capacity, so prices will not rise when aggregate demand increases. Thus, the short-run aggregate supply curve is simply a horizontal line at the given price level, 120, represented by *SRAS*. An aggregate demand shock that increases aggregate demand to AD_2 will increase the equilibrium level of real GDP per year to $12.5 trillion. An aggregate demand shock that decreases aggregate demand to AD_3 will decrease the equilibrium level of real GDP to $11.5 trillion. The equilibrium price level will not change.

wage rates. Such stickiness of wages makes *involuntary* unemployment of labor a distinct possibility, because leftward movements along the Keynesian short-run aggregate supply curve reduce real production and, hence, employment. The classical assumption of ever-lasting full employment no longer holds.

A good example of a horizontal short-run aggregate supply curve can be seen by examining data from the 1930s. Look at Figure 11-7, where you see real GDP in billions of 2000 dollars on the horizontal axis and the price level index on the vertical axis. From the early days of recovery from the Great Depression to the outbreak of World War II, real GDP increased without much rise in the price level. During this period, the economy experienced neither supply constraints nor any dramatic changes in the price level. The most simplified Keynesian model in which prices do not change is essentially an immediate post-Depression model that fits the data very well during this period.

FIGURE 11-7

Real GDP and the Price Level, 1934–1940

Keynes suggested that in a depressed economy, increased aggregate spending can increase output without raising prices. The data for the United States' recovery from the Great Depression seem to bear this out. In such circumstances, real GDP is demand determined.

In a world in which inflation is a fact of life, how can modern macroeconomists rationalize working with theories in which the short-run aggregate supply curve is horizontal?

EXAMPLE

Bringing Keynesian Short-Run Aggregate Supply Back to Life

Even though the U.S. price level has increased during every quarterly (three-month) period since the late 1950s, a large group of economists calling themselves *New Keynesians* contend that the short-run aggregate supply curve is essentially flat. Though they recognize that some firms in the United States change their prices every day, these New Keynesian economists contend that price changes by U.S. producers are, on average, relatively infrequent.

Based on research into the manner in which inflation varies from quarter to quarter, studies by many of these economists have indicated that, on average, U.S. firms adjust their prices at most about once each year. Applying the same research technique to European data indicates that individual prices in most European nations adjust even less often. To New Keynesians, this means that the aggregate supply curve is horizontal in the short run, implying that variations in aggregate demand can exert significant near-term effects on real GDP without affecting the price level.

FOR CRITICAL ANALYSIS
If the short-run aggregate supply curve were really horizontal, how could the price level ever increase? (Hint: Over the longer term, the short-run aggregate supply curve can shift.)

OUTPUT DETERMINATION USING AGGREGATE DEMAND AND AGGREGATE SUPPLY: FIXED VERSUS CHANGING PRICE LEVELS IN THE SHORT RUN

The underlying assumption of the simplified Keynesian model is that the relevant range of the short-run aggregate supply schedule (*SRAS*) is horizontal, as depicted in panel (a) of Figure 11-8. There you see that short-run aggregate supply is fixed at price level 120. If aggregate demand is AD_1, then the equilibrium level of real GDP, in base-year dollars, is $12 trillion per year. If aggregate demand increases to AD_2, then the equilibrium level of real GDP increases to $13 trillion per year.

As discussed in Chapter 10, the price level has drifted upward during recent decades. Hence prices are not totally sticky. Modern Keynesian analysis recognizes that *some*—but not complete—price adjustment takes place in the short run. Panel (b) of Figure 11-8 displays a more general **short-run aggregate supply curve** (*SRAS*). This curve represents the relationship between the price level and real GDP with incomplete price adjustment and in the absence of complete information in the short run. Allowing for partial price adjustment implies that *SRAS* slopes upward, and its slope is steeper after it crosses long-run aggregate supply, *LRAS*. This is because higher and higher prices are required to induce firms to raise their production of goods and services to levels that temporarily exceed full-employment real GDP.

Short-run aggregate supply curve
The relationship between total planned economywide production and the price level in the short run, all other things held constant. If prices adjust incompletely in the short run, the curve is positively sloped.

With partial price adjustment in the short run, if aggregate demand is AD_1 then the equilibrium level of real GDP in panel (b) is also $12 trillion per year, at a price level of 120, too. An increase in aggregate demand to AD_2 such as occurred in panel (a) produces a different equilibrium, however. Equilibrium real GDP increases to $12.5 trillion per year, which is less than in panel (a) because an increase in the price level to 130 causes planned real spending to decline.

FIGURE 11-8
Real GDP Determination with Fixed versus Flexible Prices

In panel (a), the price level index is fixed at 120. An increase in aggregate demand from AD_1 to AD_2 moves the equilibrium level of real GDP from $12 trillion per year to $13 trillion per year in base-year dollars.

In panel (b), SRAS is upward sloping. The same shift in aggregate demand yields an equilibrium level of real GDP of only $12.5 trillion per year and a higher price level index at 130.

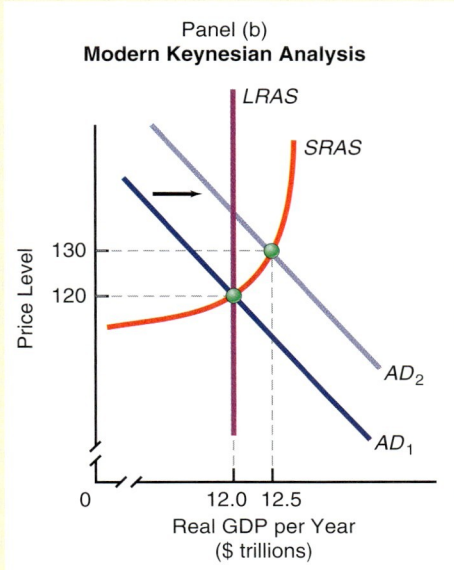

In the modern Keynesian short run, when the price level rises partially, real GDP can be expanded beyond the level consistent with its long-run growth path, discussed in Chapter 10, for a variety of reasons:

1. In the short run, most labor contracts implicitly or explicitly call for flexibility in hours of work at the given wage rate. Therefore, firms can use existing workers more intensively in a variety of ways: They can get workers to work harder, to work more hours per day, and to work more days per week. Workers can also be switched from *uncounted* production, such as maintenance, to *counted* production, which generates counted production of goods and services. The distinction between counted and uncounted is simply what is measured in the marketplace, particularly by government statisticians and accountants. If a worker cleans a machine, there is no measured output. But if that worker is put on the production line and helps increase the number of units produced each day, measured output will go up. That worker's production has then been counted.
2. Existing capital equipment can be used more intensively. Machines can be worked more hours per day. Some can be made to operate faster. Maintenance can be delayed.
3. Finally, if wage rates are held constant, a higher price level leads to increased profits from additional production, which induces firms to hire more workers. The duration of unemployment falls, and thus the unemployment rate falls. And people who were previously not in the labor force (homemakers and younger or older workers) can be induced to enter it.

All these adjustments cause real GDP to rise as the price level increases.

SHIFTS IN THE AGGREGATE SUPPLY CURVE

Just as non-price-level factors can cause a shift in the aggregate demand curve, there are non-price-level factors that can cause a shift in the aggregate supply curve. The analysis here is more complicated than the analysis for the non-price-level determinants for aggregate demand, for here we are dealing with both the short run and the long run—*SRAS* and *LRAS*. Still, anything other than the price level that affects the production of final goods and services will shift aggregate supply curves.

Shifts in Both Short- and Long-Run Aggregate Supply

There is a core class of events that cause a shift in both the short-run aggregate supply curve and the long-run aggregate supply curve. These include any change in our endowments of the factors of production. Any change in these factors of production—labor, capital, or technology—that influence economic growth will shift *SRAS* and *LRAS*. Look at Figure 11-9. Initially, the two curves are $SRAS_1$ and $LRAS_1$. Now consider a major discovery of mineral deposits in Idaho, in an area where no one thought deposits of mineral inputs existed. This shifts $LRAS_1$ to $LRAS_2$ at $12.5 trillion of real GDP, measured in base-year dollars. $SRAS_1$ also shifts outward horizontally to $SRAS_2$.

Shifts in *SRAS* Only

Some events, particularly those that are short-lived, will temporarily shift *SRAS* but not *LRAS*. One of the most obvious is a change in production input prices, particularly those caused by external events that are not expected to last forever. Consider a major hurricane that temporarily shuts down a significant portion of U.S. oil production, as happened after Hurricane Katrina. Oil is an important input in many production activities. The resulting drop in oil

ECONOMICS FRONT AND CENTER

To contemplate reasoning out how aggregate demand and aggregate supply respond to real-world events, consider **A Student Intern Is Put on the Spot**, on page 279.

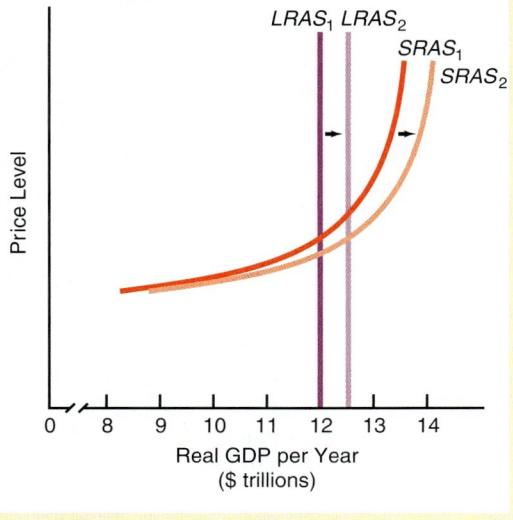

FIGURE 11-9

Shifts in Both Short- and Long-Run Aggregate Supply

Initially, the two supply curves are $SRAS_1$ and $LRAS_1$. Now consider a discovery of mineral deposits in Idaho in an area where no one thought such production inputs existed. This shifts $LRAS_1$ to $LRAS_2$ at $12.5 trillion of real GDP, in base-year dollars. $SRAS_1$ also shifts outward horizontally to $SRAS_2$.

CHAPTER 11 *Classical and Keynesian Macro Analyses* **273**

FIGURE 11-10

Shifts in *SRAS* Only

A temporary increase in an input price will shift the short-run aggregate supply curve from $SRAS_1$ to $SRAS_2$.

production will cause at least a temporary increase in the price of this input. You can see what happens in Figure 11-10. *LRAS* remains fixed, but $SRAS_1$ shifts to $SRAS_2$, reflecting the increase in input prices—the higher price of oil. This is because the rise in the costs of production at each level of real GDP per year requires a higher price level to cover those increased costs.

We summarize the possible determinants of aggregate supply in Table 11-2 on the next page. These determinants will cause a shift in the short-run or the long-run aggregate supply curve or both, depending on whether they are temporary or permanent.

QUICK QUIZ

If we assume that the economy is operating on a horizontal short-run aggregate supply curve, the equilibrium level of real GDP per year is completely _____ determined.

The horizontal short-run aggregate supply curve has been called the **Keynesian short-run aggregate supply curve** because Keynes believed that many prices, especially wages, would not be _____ even when aggregate demand decreased.

In modern Keynesian theory, the short-run **aggregate supply curve, *SRAS*,** shows the relationship between the price level and real GDP without full adjustment or full information. It is upward sloping because it allows for only _____ price adjustment in the short run.

Real GDP can be expanded in the short run because firms can use existing workers and capital equipment more _____. Also, in the short run, when input prices are fixed, a higher price level means _____ profits, which induces firms to hire more workers.

Any change in factors influencing long-run output, such as labor, capital, or technology, will shift both *SRAS* and *LRAS*. A temporary change in input prices, however, will shift only _____.

See page 286 for the answers. Review concepts from this section in MyEconLab.

TABLE 11-2
Determinants of Aggregate Supply

The determinants listed here can affect short-run or long-run aggregate supply (or both), depending on whether they are temporary or permanent.

Changes That Cause an Increase in Aggregate Supply	Changes That Cause a Decrease in Aggregate Supply
Discoveries of new raw materials	Depletion of raw materials
Increased competition	Decreased competition
A reduction in international trade barriers	An increase in international trade barriers
Fewer regulatory impediments to business	More regulatory impediments to business
An increase in the supply of labor	A decrease in labor supplied
Increased training and education	Decreased training and education
A decrease in marginal tax rates	An increase in marginal tax rates
A reduction in input prices	An increase in input prices

CONSEQUENCES OF CHANGES IN AGGREGATE DEMAND

We now have a basic model to apply when evaluating short-run adjustments of the equilibrium price level and equilibrium real GDP when there are shocks to the economy. Whenever there is a shift in the aggregate demand or supply curves, the equilibrium price level or real GDP level (or both) may change. These shifts are called **aggregate demand shocks** on the demand side and **aggregate supply shocks** on the supply side.

Aggregate demand shock
Any event that causes the aggregate demand curve to shift inward or outward.

Aggregate supply shock
Any event that causes the aggregate supply curve to shift inward or outward.

Effects When Aggregate Demand Falls While Aggregate Supply Is Stable

Now we can show what happens in the short run when aggregate supply remains stable but aggregate demand falls. The short-run outcome may be a recession and a rise in the unemployment rate. In Figure 11-11, you see that with AD_1, both long-run and short-run

FIGURE 11-11
The Short-Run Effects of Stable Aggregate Supply and a Decrease in Aggregate Demand: The Recessionary Gap

If the economy is at equilibrium at E_1, with price level 120 and real GDP per year of $12 trillion, a shift inward of the aggregate demand curve to AD_2 will lead to a new short-run equilibrium at E_2. The equilibrium price level will fall to 115, and the short-run equilibrium level of real GDP per year will fall to $11.8 trillion. There will be a recessionary gap of $200 billion.

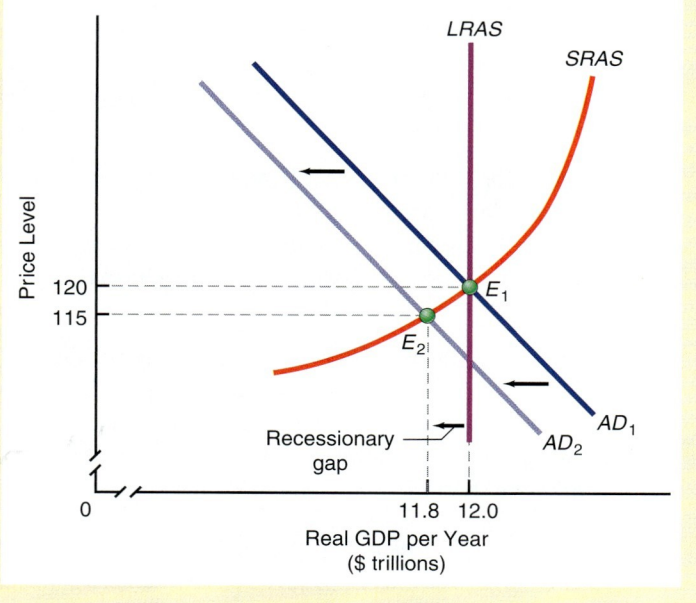

equilibrium are at $12 trillion (in base-year dollars) of real GDP per year (because *SRAS* and *LRAS* also intersect AD_1 at that level of real GDP). The long-run equilibrium price level is 120. A reduction in aggregate demand shifts the aggregate demand curve to AD_2. The new intersection with *SRAS* is at $11.8 trillion per year, which is less than the long-run equilibrium level of real GDP. The difference between $12 trillion and $11.8 trillion is called a **recessionary gap,** defined as the difference between the short-run equilibrium level of real GDP and real GDP if the economy were operating at full employment on its *LRAS*.

In effect, at E_2, the economy is in short-run equilibrium at less than full employment. With too many unemployed inputs, input prices will begin to fall. Eventually, *SRAS* will have to shift down. Where will it intersect AD_2?

Recessionary gap
The gap that exists whenever equilibrium real GDP per year is less than full-employment real GDP as shown by the position of the long-run aggregate supply curve.

Short-Run Effects When Aggregate Demand Increases

We can reverse the situation and have aggregate demand increase to AD_2, as is shown in Figure 11-12. The initial equilibrium conditions are exactly the same as in Figure 11-11. The move to AD_2 increases the short-run equilibrium from E_1 to E_2 such that the economy is operating at $12.2 trillion of real GDP per year, which exceeds *LRAS*. This is a condition of an overheated economy, typically called an **inflationary gap.**

At E_2 in Figure 11-12, the economy is at a short-run equilibrium that is beyond full employment. In the short run, more can be squeezed out of the economy than occurs in the long-run, full-information, full-adjustment situation. Firms will be operating beyond long-run capacity. Inputs will be working too hard. Input prices will begin to rise. That will eventually cause *SRAS* to shift upward. At what point on AD_2 in Figure 11-12 will the new *SRAS* stop shifting?

Inflationary gap
The gap that exists whenever equilibrium real GDP per year is greater than full-employment real GDP as shown by the position of the long-run aggregate supply curve.

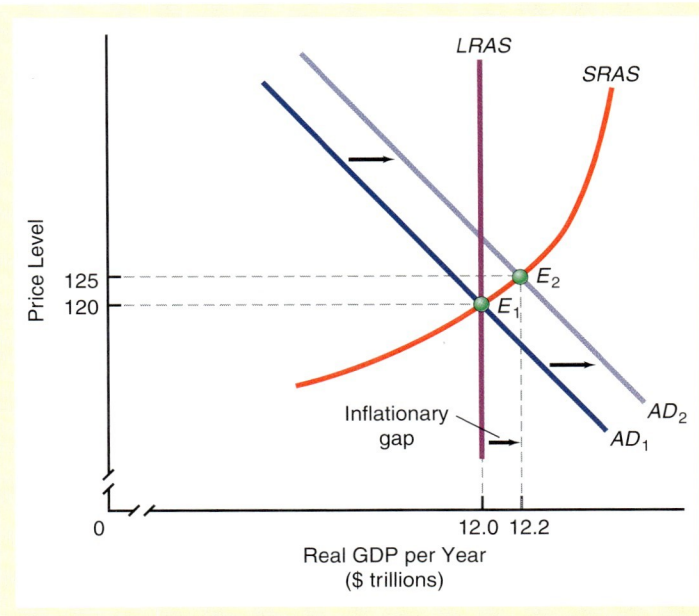

FIGURE 11-12

The Effects of Stable Aggregate Supply with an Increase in Aggregate Demand: The Inflationary Gap

The economy is at equilibrium at E_1. An increase in aggregate demand of AD_2 leads to a new short-run equilibrium at E_2 with the price level rising from 120 to 125 and equilibrium real GDP per year rising from $12 trillion to $12.2 trillion. The difference, $200 billion, is called the inflationary gap.

EXPLAINING SHORT-RUN VARIATIONS IN INFLATION

In Chapter 10, we noted that in a growing economy, the explanation for persistent inflation is that aggregate demand rises over time at a faster pace than the full-employment level of real GDP. Short-run variations in inflation, however, can arise as a result of both demand *and* supply factors.

Demand-Pull versus Cost-Push Inflation

Figure 11-12 on page 275 presents a demand-side theory explaining a short-run jump in prices, sometimes called *demand-pull inflation*. Whenever the general level of prices rises in the short run because of increases in aggregate demand, we say that the economy is experiencing **demand-pull inflation**—inflation caused by increases in aggregate demand.

Demand-pull inflation
Inflation caused by increases in aggregate demand not matched by increases in aggregate supply.

An alternative explanation for increases in the price level comes from the supply side. Look at Figure 11-13. The initial equilibrium conditions are the same as in Figure 11-12. Now, however, there is a decrease in the aggregate supply curve, from $SRAS_1$ to $SRAS_2$. Equilibrium shifts from E_1 to E_2. The price level increases from 120 to 125, while the equilibrium level of real GDP per year decreases from $12 trillion to $11.8 trillion. Such a decrease in aggregate supply causes what is called **cost-push inflation**.

Cost-push inflation
Inflation caused by decreases in short-run aggregate supply.

As the example of cost-push inflation shows, if the economy is initially in equilibrium on its *LRAS*, a decrease in *SRAS* will lead to a rise in the price level. Thus, any abrupt change in one of the factors that determine aggregate supply will alter the equilibrium level of real GDP and the equilibrium price level. If the economy is for some reason operating to the left of its *LRAS*, an increase in *SRAS* will lead to a simultaneous *increase* in the equilibrium level of real GDP per year and a *decrease* in the price level. You should be able to show this in a graph similar to Figure 11-13.

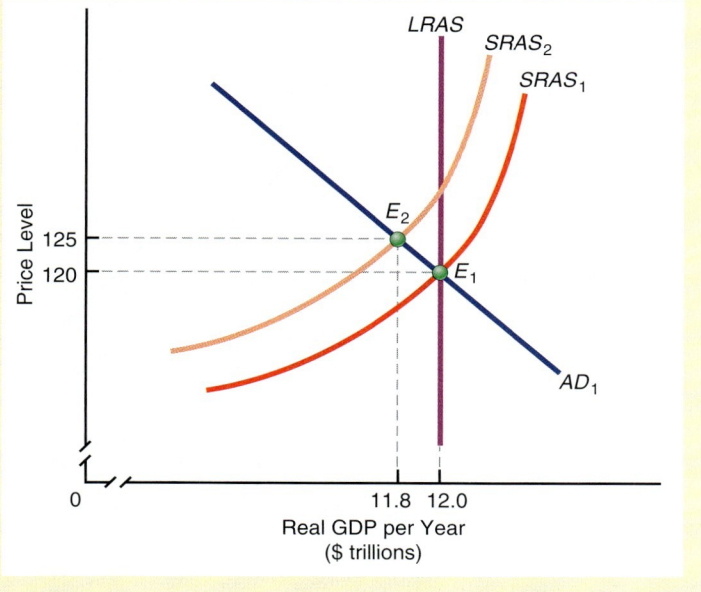

FIGURE 11-13
Cost-Push Inflation
If aggregate demand remains stable but $SRAS_1$ shifts to $SRAS_2$, equilibrium changes from E_1 to E_2. The price level rises from 120 to 125. If there are continual decreases in aggregate supply of this nature, the situation is called cost-push inflation.

In some situations, could government policymaking help to reduce the macroeconomic effects of supply shocks?

INTERNATIONAL POLICY EXAMPLE

Can Iran's Vicious Cycle of Supply Shocks Be Smoothed?

Iran, which is located at the boundary between two plates of the earth's crust, has experienced hundreds of earthquakes since 1990. Severe tremors in 1962, 1978, 1981, 1990, 1997, and 2003 caused the deaths of tens of thousands of people and destroyed thousands of buildings. The economic effects in each case were predictable: With fewer resources available for firms to produce goods and services at any given price level, the nation's aggregate supply curve shifted leftward. Thus, following each earthquake, Iran experienced both a sudden burst of inflation and a significant short-term dip in real GDP.

There is nothing that Iran can do about its location on the planet's surface. Nevertheless, economists agree that there is much that its government could do to limit its economy's exposure to aggregate supply shocks associated with the nation's recurring tremors. Following past Iranian disasters, homes, businesses, and factories damaged and destroyed by earthquakes have been rebuilt without regard to proven methods for building earthquake-resistant structures. The simple act of establishing and enforcing building codes would do much to protect Iran's physical and human capital from future earthquakes. This would prevent the nation's aggregate supply curve from shifting as far leftward following major earthquakes. Estimates indicate that enforcing modern building codes might reduce the inflationary and recessionary consequences of earthquake-induced aggregate supply shocks by more than 80 percent.

FOR CRITICAL ANALYSIS

How might the establishment and enforcement of building codes promote long-term Iranian growth as well as help shield the nation from recurring aggregate supply shocks? (Hint: The destruction of resources by earthquakes can affect the position of a nation's long-run aggregate supply curve.)

Aggregate Demand and Supply in an Open Economy

In many of the international examples in the early chapters of this book, we had to translate foreign currencies into dollars when the open economy was discussed. We used the exchange rate, or the dollar price of other currencies. In Chapter 10, you also learned that the open economy effect was one of the reasons why the aggregate demand curve slopes downward. When the domestic price level rises, U.S. residents want to buy cheaper-priced foreign goods. The opposite occurs when the U.S. domestic price level falls. Currently, the foreign sector of the U.S. economy constitutes over 14 percent of all economic activities.

How a Weaker Dollar Affects Aggregate Supply. Assume that the dollar becomes weaker in international foreign exchange markets. If last year the dollar could buy 130 *naira*, the Nigerian currency, but this year it now buys only 120 naira, the dollar has become weaker. To the extent that U.S. companies import raw and partially processed goods from Nigeria, a weaker dollar can lead to higher input prices. For instance, in a typical year, U.S. natural gas distributors purchase about 10,000 million (10 billion) cubic feet of natural gas from suppliers in Nigeria. Suppose that the price of Nigerian natural gas, quoted in Nigerian naira, is 0.910 naira per million cubic feet. At a rate of exchange of 130 naira per dollar, this means that the U.S. dollar price is $0.0070 per million cubic feet (0.910 naira divided by 130 naira per dollar equals $0.0070), so that 10 billion cubic feet of Nigerian natural gas imports cost U.S. distributors $70 million. If the U.S. dollar weakens against the Nigerian naira, so that a dollar purchases only 120 naira, then the U.S. dollar price rises to $0.0076 per million cubic feet (0.910 naira

Go to www.econtoday.com/ch11 for Federal Reserve Bank of New York data showing how the dollar's value is changing relative to other currencies.

divided by 120 naira per dollar equals $0.0076). As a consequence, the U.S. dollar price of 10 billion cubic feet of Nigerian natural gas imports increases to $76 million.

Thus, a general weakening of the dollar against the naira and other world currencies will lead to a shift inward to the left in the short-run aggregate supply curve as shown in panel (a) of Figure 11-14. In that simplified model, equilibrium real GDP would fall, and the price level would rise. Employment would also tend to decrease.

How a Weaker Dollar Affects Aggregate Demand. A weaker dollar has another effect that we must consider. Foreign residents will find that U.S.-made goods are now less expensive, expressed in their own currency. Suppose that as a result of the dollar's weakening, the dollar, which previously could buy 0.87 euros, can now buy only 0.80 euros. Before the dollar weakened, a U.S.-produced $10 compact disc cost a French person 8.7 euros at the exchange rate of 0.87 euro per $1. After the dollar weakens and the exchange rate changes to 0.80 euro per $1, that same $10 CD will cost 8 euros. Conversely, U.S. residents will find that the weaker dollar makes imported goods more expensive. The result for U.S. residents is more exports and fewer imports, or higher net exports (exports minus imports). If net exports rise, employment in export industries will rise: This is represented in panel (b) of Figure 11-14. After the dollar becomes weaker, the aggregate demand curve shifts outward from AD_1 to AD_2. The result is a tendency for equilibrium real GDP and the price level to rise and for unemployment to decrease.

The Net Effects on Inflation and Real GDP. We have learned, then, that a weaker dollar *simultaneously* leads to a decrease in *SRAS* and an increase in *AD*. In such situations, the equilibrium price level definitely rises. A weaker dollar results in inflation.

FIGURE 11-14
The Two Effects of a Weaker Dollar

When the dollar decreases in value in the international currency market, there are two effects. The first is higher prices for imported inputs, causing a shift inward to the left in the short-run aggregate supply schedule from $SRAS_1$ to $SRAS_2$ in panel (a). Equilibrium tends to move from E_1 to E_2 at a higher price level and a lower equilibrium real GDP per year. Second, a weaker dollar can also affect the aggregate demand curve because it will lead to more net exports and cause AD_1 to rise to AD_2 in panel (b). Due to this effect, equilibrium would move from E_1 to E_2 at a higher price level and a higher equilibrium real GDP per year. On balance, the price level rises, but real GDP may rise or fall.

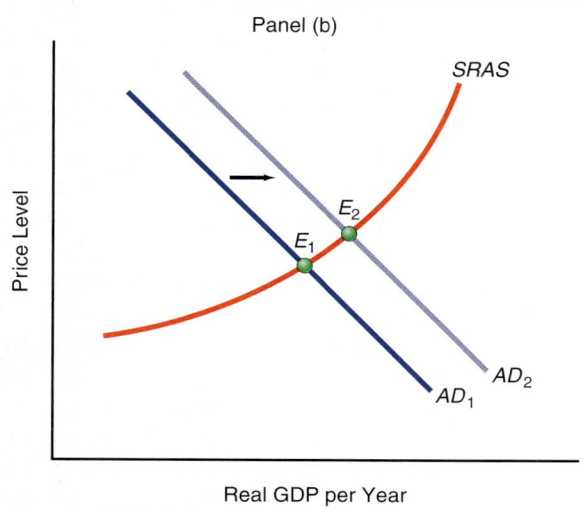

The effect of a weaker dollar on real GDP depends on which curve—*AD* or *SRAS*—shifts more. If the aggregate demand curve shifts more than the short-run aggregate supply curve, equilibrium real GDP will rise. Conversely, if the aggregate supply curve shifts more than the aggregate demand curve, equilibrium real GDP will fall.

You should be able to redo this entire analysis for a stronger dollar.

QUICK QUIZ

_____-run equilibrium occurs at the intersection of the aggregate demand curve, *AD*, and the short-run aggregate supply curve, *SRAS*. _____-run equilibrium occurs at the intersection of *AD* and the long-run aggregate supply curve, *LRAS*. Any unanticipated shifts in aggregate demand or supply are called aggregate demand _____ or aggregate supply _____.

When aggregate demand decreases while aggregate supply is stable, a _____ gap can occur, defined as the difference between the equilibrium level of real GDP and how much the economy could be producing if it were operating on its *LRAS*. An increase in aggregate demand leads to an _____ gap.

With stable aggregate supply, an abrupt outward shift in *AD* may lead to what is called _____-_____ inflation. With a stable aggregate demand, an abrupt shift inward in *SRAS* may lead to what is called _____-_____ inflation.

A _____ dollar will raise the cost of imported inputs, thereby causing *SRAS* to shift inward to the left. At the same time, a _____ dollar will also lead to higher net exports, causing the aggregate demand curve to shift outward. The equilibrium price level definitely rises, but the net effect on equilibrium real GDP depends on which shift is larger.

See page 286 for the answers. Review concepts from this section in MyEconLab.

CASE STUDY — ECONOMICS FRONT AND CENTER

A Student Intern Is Put on the Spot

Noland is a college student who has landed a summer internship with an economic forecasting firm. Noland's initial assignment is to spend his first few days reviewing data the firm has compiled about recent events in the U.S. economy.

Noland examines the facts. Federal income tax rates were cut earlier in the year, and government spending has increased during the past six months. The rate of growth in the quantity of money in circulation is nearly twice as high as it was last year. In addition, oil prices have shot up. A recent hurricane in southeastern Texas and a fire on the East Coast have shut down two of the nation's largest gasoline refineries, and these events have added to upward pressure on gasoline prices. Finally, the U.S. dollar has depreciated sharply relative to nearly all other world currencies.

On Friday morning, Noland's supervisor calls him to her office and asks what he thinks is likely to happen to the U.S. inflation rate and the rate of growth in U.S. real GDP during the next few months. She states that she does not expect precise forecasts, but she does want him to explain his reasoning. Noland takes a deep breath and prepares to answer her question.

CRITICAL ANALYSIS QUESTIONS

1. *What effects have the above events had on U.S. aggregate demand? On U.S. aggregate supply?*

2. *If you were in Noland's shoes, how would you answer his supervisor's question?*

Issues and Applications

Oil Prices Still Matter, but Not As Much As Before

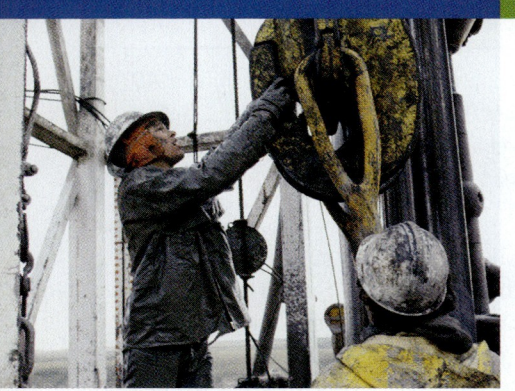

Concepts Applied
- Aggregate Supply Shock
- Short-Run Aggregate Supply Curve
- Cost-Push Inflation

As crude oil prices rose by as much as $60 per barrel during the years following 1999, many commentators in the media compared the oil price run-up and its possible macroeconomic effects to U.S. experiences in the 1970s. Some predicted that the resulting aggregate supply shock would generate both sharply lower—and possibly negative—real GDP growth and a potentially sharp spike in U.S. inflation.

In the end, of course, the media commentators got it wrong. Real GDP growth rates into the mid-2000s were respectable, and inflation rates remained close to levels experienced in the 1990s. Let's think about why commentators were so far off the mark.

Whoops!—Oil Prices Must Be Adjusted for Inflation

Of course, crude oil is a key factor of production. It is refined to produce gasoline and heating oils that are important sources of energy. In addition, processed oil is used to lubricate machinery, and it is an important ingredient in the production of many plastics and chemical products. Consequently, substantial increases in oil prices push up production costs for many businesses, resulting in less planned production of goods and services at any given price level. The result is a leftward shift in the short-run aggregate supply curve—an aggregate supply shock.

Many in the media made an important mistake, however. In comparing the oil price increase during the 2000s to the run-up in oil prices in the 1970s, they forgot to adjust oil prices for inflation. As panel (a) of Figure 11-15 indicates, this was an important oversight. Certainly, the nominal price of oil went higher in the 2000s than ever before. By as early as 2003 headlines trumpeted "Record High Oil Prices!" Once inflation is taken into account, however, it is clear that even as late as 2006 inflation-adjusted oil prices had not quite matched the peak reached in the late 1970s.

Reduced Sensitivity of Aggregate Supply to Oil Price Changes

Another important fact that many media commentators failed to recognize was that today's producers are less reliant on oil than producers were in the 1970s. To see this, take a look at panel (b) of Figure 11-15. As you can see, in the 1970s about 1.3 barrels of oil were required to produce $1,000 worth of real GDP, measured in 2006 dollars. Today, because items such as services and digital products are a larger share of real GDP than manufactured goods, only

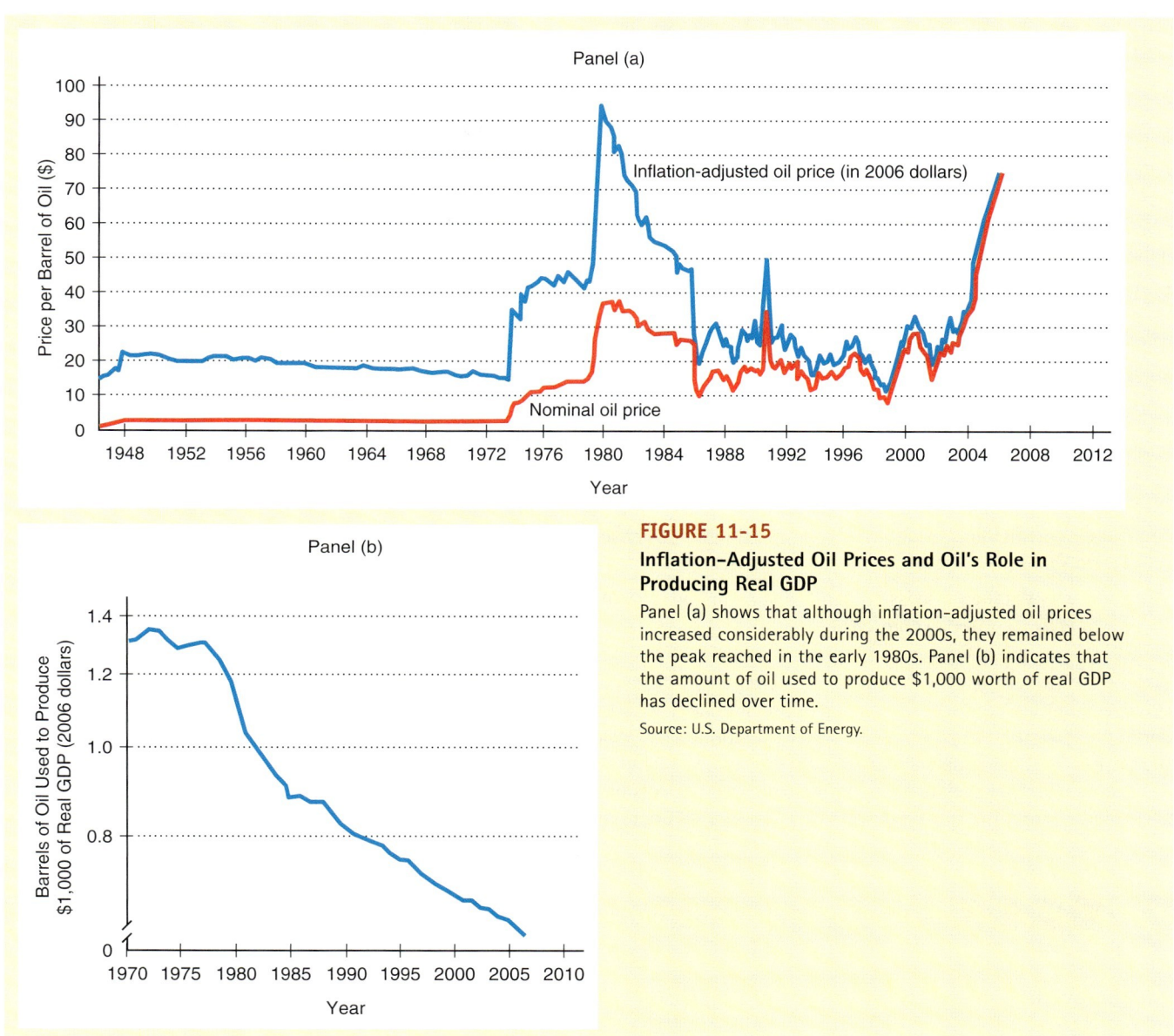

FIGURE 11-15

Inflation-Adjusted Oil Prices and Oil's Role in Producing Real GDP

Panel (a) shows that although inflation-adjusted oil prices increased considerably during the 2000s, they remained below the peak reached in the early 1980s. Panel (b) indicates that the amount of oil used to produce $1,000 worth of real GDP has declined over time.

Source: U.S. Department of Energy.

a little over 0.6 barrel of oil is required to produce the same amount of real GDP.

This drop in oil usage per unit of real GDP produced has had the effect of making U.S. aggregate supply less sensitive to oil price changes. A given increase in the inflation-adjusted price of oil during the 2000s reduces aggregate supply less than the same price increase did in the 1970s. As a consequence, oil-price-induced aggregate supply shocks are smaller today than they were back then.

Two Big Oversights Create a Significant Miscalculation

Thus, much of the media coverage of the effects of higher oil prices suffered from two problems. Commentators failed to adjust oil prices for inflation, and they did not take into account today's reduced reliance on oil as a factor of production.

This explains why predictions of economic doomsday in the mid-2000s did not come to pass. Undoubtedly, the oil price run-up that has occurred during the 2000s has tended to hinder the pace of increases in aggregate supply. The result has been lower real GDP growth and slightly higher inflation than the U.S. economy otherwise would have experienced. Nevertheless, the macroeconomic effects of the 2000s oil price increase have been much more muted than those of the truly significant jump in oil prices in the 1970s.

Log in to **MyEconLab**, click on "Economic News," and test your understanding of the chapter by answering interactive questions that relate directly to this issue.

For Critical Analysis

1. Would the comparison of the oil price increases of the 2000s with those of the 1970s be affected by choosing, say, 1975 as the base year for inflation adjustment? Why or why not?
2. In light of the reduced role of oil as a factor of production in the U.S. economy, would you expect an aggregate supply shock as large as in the 1970s if inflation-adjusted oil prices in the late 2000s really did climb as high as in the 1970s? Why or why not?

Web Resources

1. To see how nominal and inflation-adjusted oil prices have varied since the end of World War II, go to **www.econtoday.com/ch11**.
2. For a very detailed discussion about historical and current factors affecting oil prices, go to **www.econtoday.com/ch11**.

Research Project

When we consider the effects of oil price increases on the short-run aggregate supply curve, equilibrium real GDP, and the equilibrium price level, we usually engage in *ceteris paribus* reasoning. That is, we assume that everything else, including other factors affecting short-run aggregate supply and aggregate demand, is unchanged. Evaluate why this can be misleading when we seek to examine the real-world effects of aggregate supply shocks, particularly during the run-up of inflation-adjusted oil prices during the 2000s.

WHAT YOU SHOULD KNOW		WHERE TO GO TO PRACTICE
Central Assumptions of the Classical Model The classical model makes four fundamental assumptions: (1) pure competition prevails, so no individual buyer or seller of a good or service or of a factor of production can affect its price; (2) wages and prices are completely flexible; (3) people are motivated by self-interest; and (4) buyers and sellers do not experience money illusion, meaning that they respond only to changes in relative prices.	Say's law, 262 money illusion, 263	• **MyEconLab** Study Plan 11.1 • Audio introduction to Chapter 11 • Video: Say's Law
Short-Run Determination of Equilibrium Real GDP and the Price Level in the Classical Model Under the four assumptions of the classical model, the short-run aggregate supply curve is vertical at full-employment real GDP and thus corresponds to the long-run aggregate supply curve. So, even in the short run, real GDP cannot increase in the absence of changes in factors of production, such as labor, capital, and technology, which induce longer-term economic growth. Given the position of the classical aggregate supply curve, movements in the equilibrium price level are generated by variations in the position of the aggregate demand curve.	**Key figures** Figure 11-2, 264 Figure 11-3, 265 Figure 11-4, 267 Figure 11-5, 267	• **MyEconLab** Study Plan 11.1 • Audio introduction to Chapter 11 • Animated Figures 11-2, 11-3, 11-4, and 11-5
Circumstances Under Which the Short-Run Aggregate Supply Curve May Be Horizontal or Upward Sloping If product prices and wages and other input prices are "sticky," perhaps because of labor and other contracts, the short-run aggregate supply schedule can be horizontal over much of its range. This is the Keynesian short-run aggregate supply curve. More generally, however, to the extent that there is incomplete adjustment of prices in the short run, the short-run aggregate supply curve slopes upward.	Keynesian short-run aggregate supply curve, 268 short-run aggregate supply curve, 270 **Key figures** Figure 11-6, 269 Figure 11-8, 271	• **MyEconLab** Study Plans 11.2 and 11.3 • Video: The Short-Run Aggregate Supply Curve • Animated Figures 11-6 and 11-8
Factors That Induce Shifts in the Short-Run and Long-Run Aggregate Supply Curves The long-run aggregate supply curve shifts in response to changes in the availability of labor or capital or to changes in technology and productivity, and changes in these factors also cause the short-run aggregate supply curve to shift. Because output prices may adjust only partially to changing input prices in the short run, however, a widespread	**Key table** Table 11-2, 274 **Key figures** Figure 11-9, 272 Figure 11-10, 273	• **MyEconLab** Study Plan 11.4 • Animated Figures 11-9 and 11-10

284 PART III *Real GDP Determination and Fiscal Policy*

WHAT YOU SHOULD KNOW		WHERE TO GO TO PRACTICE
change in the prices of factors of production, such as an economywide change in wages, can cause a shift in the short-run aggregate supply curve without affecting the long-run aggregate supply curve.		
Effects of Aggregate Demand and Supply Shocks on Equilibrium Real GDP in the Short Run An aggregate demand shock that causes the aggregate demand curve to shift leftward pushes equilibrium real GDP below full-employment real GDP in the short run, so there is a recessionary gap. An aggregate demand shock that induces a rightward shift in the aggregate demand curve results in an inflationary gap in which short-run equilibrium real GDP exceeds full-employment real GDP.	aggregate demand shock, 274 aggregate supply shock, 274 recessionary gap, 275 inflationary gap, 275 **Key figures** Figure 11-11, 274 Figure 11-12, 275	• **MyEconLab** Study Plan 11-5 • Video: Shifts in the Short-Run Aggregate Supply Curve • Animated Figures 11-11 and 11-12
Causes of Short-Run Variations in the Inflation Rate In the short run, an upward movement in the price level can occur in the form of demand-pull inflation when the aggregate demand curve shifts rightward along an upward-sloping short-run aggregate supply curve. Cost-push inflation can arise in the short run when the short-run aggregate supply curve shifts leftward along the aggregate demand curve. A weakening of the dollar shifts the short-run aggregate supply curve leftward and the aggregate demand curve rightward, which causes inflation but has uncertain effects on real GDP.	demand-pull inflation, 276 cost-push inflation, 276 **Key figure** Figure 11-13, 276	• **MyEconLab** Study Plan 11.6 • Animated Figure 11-13

Log in to MyEconLab, take a chapter test, and get a personalized Study Plan that tells you which concepts you understand and which ones you need to review. From there, MyEconLab will give you further practice, tutorials, animations, videos, and guided solutions.

Log in to www.myeconlab.com

PROBLEMS

*Select problems, indicated by a blue oval, are assignable in **MyEconLab**.*
Answers to the odd-numbered problems appear at the back of the book.

11-1 Consider a country whose economic structure matches the assumptions of the classical model. After reading a recent best-seller documenting a growing population of low-income elderly people who were ill-prepared for retirement, most residents of this country decide to increase their saving at any given interest rate. Explain whether or how this could affect the following:

a. The current equilibrium interest rate
b. Current equilibrium real GDP
c. Current equilibrium employment
d. Current equilibrium investment
e. Future equilibrium real GDP

11-2 Consider a country with an economic structure consistent with the assumptions of the classical model.

Suppose that businesses in this nation suddenly anticipate higher future profitability from investments they undertake today. Explain whether or how this could affect the following:

a. The current equilibrium interest rate
b. Current equilibrium real GDP
c. Current equilibrium employment
d. Current equilibrium saving
e. Future equilibrium real GDP

11-3. "There is *absolutely no distinction* between the classical model and the model of long-run equilibrium discussed in Chapter 10." Is this statement true or false? Support your answer.

11-4. A nation in which the classical model applies experiences a decline in the quantity of money in circulation. Use an appropriate aggregate demand and aggregate supply diagram to explain what happens to equilibrium real GDP and to the equilibrium price level.

11-5. Suppose that the classical model is appropriate for a country that has suddenly experienced an influx of immigrants who possess a wide variety of employable skills and who have reputations for saving relatively large portions of their incomes, compared with native-born residents, at any given interest rate. Evaluate the effects of this event on the following:

a. Current equilibrium employment
b. Current equilibrium real GDP
c. The current equilibrium interest rate
d. Current equilibrium investment
e. Future equilibrium real GDP

11-6. Suppose that the Keynesian short-run aggregate supply curve is applicable for a nation's economy. Use appropriate diagrams to assist in answering the following questions:

a. What are two factors that can cause the nation's real GDP to increase in the short run?
b. What are two factors that can cause the nation's real GDP to increase in the long run?

11-7. What determines how much real GDP responds to changes in the price level along the short-run aggregate supply curve?

11-8. At a point along the short-run aggregate supply curve that is to the right of the point where it crosses the long-run aggregate supply curve, what must be true of the unemployment rate relative to the long-run, full-employment rate of unemployment? Why?

11-9. Suppose that the stock market crashes in an economy with an upward-sloping short-run aggregate supply curve, and consumer and business confidence plummets. What are the short-run effects on equilibrium real GDP and the equilibrium price level?

11-10. Suppose that there is a temporary, but significant, increase in oil prices in an economy with an upward-sloping *SRAS* curve. If the central bank wishes to prevent the equilibrium price level from changing in response to the oil price increase, should it increase or decrease the quantity of money in circulation? Why?

11-11. As in Problem 11-10, suppose that there is a temporary, but significant, increase in oil prices in an economy with an upward-sloping *SRAS* curve. In this case, however, suppose that the central bank wishes to prevent equilibrium real GDP from changing in response to the oil price increase. Should the central bank increase or decrease the quantity of money in circulation? Why?

11-12. Based on your answers to Problems 11-10 and 11-11, can a central bank stabilize *both* the price level *and* real GDP simultaneously in response to a short-lived but sudden rise in oil prices? Explain briefly.

11-13. For each question below, suppose that the economy *begins* at the short-run equilibrium point *A*. Identify which of the other points on the diagram—point *B*, *C*, *D*, or *E*—could represent a *new* short-run equilibrium after the described events take place and move the economy away from point *A*. Briefly explain your answers.

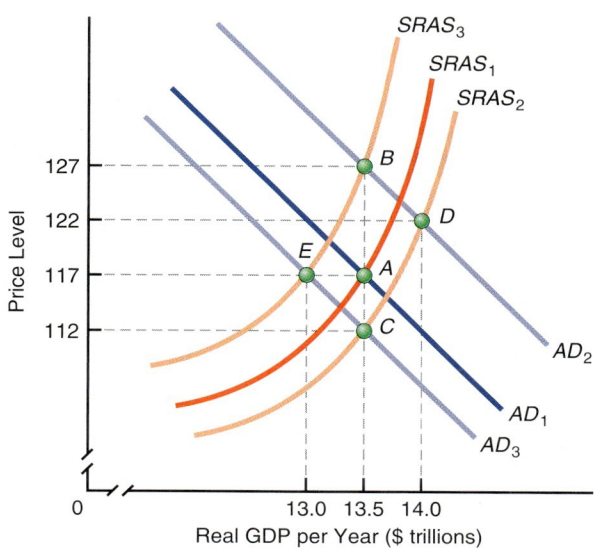

a. Most workers in this nation's economy are union members, and unions have successfully negotiated large wage boosts. At the same time, economic conditions suddenly worsen abroad, reducing real GDP and disposable income in other nations of the world.

b. A major hurricane has caused short-term halts in production at many firms and created major bottlenecks in the distribution of goods and services that had been produced prior to the storm. At the same time, the nation's central bank has significantly pushed up the rate of growth of the nation's money supply.

c. A strengthening of the value of this nation's currency in terms of other countries' currencies affects both the *SRAS* curve and the *AD* curve.

11-14 Consider an open economy in which the aggregate supply curve slopes upward in the short run. Firms in this nation do not import raw materials or any other productive inputs from abroad, but foreign residents purchase many of the nation's goods and services. What is the most likely short-run effect on this nation's economy if there is a significant downturn in economic activity in other nations around the world?

ECONOMICS ON THE NET

Money, the Price Level, and Real GDP The classical and Keynesian theories have differing predictions about how changes in the money supply should affect the price level and real GDP. Here you get to look at data on growth in the money supply, the price level, and real GDP.

Title: Federal Reserve Bank of St. Louis Monetary Trends

Navigation: Use the link at **www.econtoday.com/ch11** to visit the Federal Reserve Bank of St. Louis. Click on *Gross Domestic Product and M2*.

Application Read the article; then answer these questions.

1. Classical theory indicates that *ceteris paribus* changes in the price level should be closely related to changes in aggregate demand induced by variations in the quantity of money. Click on *Gross Domestic Product and M2*, and take a look at the charts labeled "Gross Domestic Product Price Index" and "M2." Are annual percentage changes in these variables closely related?

2. Keynesian theory predicts that, *ceteris paribus*, changes in GDP and the quantity of money should be directly related. Take a look at the charts labeled "Real Gross Domestic Product" and "M2." Are annual percentage changes in these variables closely related?

For Group Study and Analysis Both classical and Keynesian theories of relationships among real GDP, the price level, and the quantity of money hinge on specific assumptions. Have class groups search through the FRED database (accessible at **www.econtoday.com/ch11**) to evaluate factors that provide support for either theory's predictions. Which approach appears to receive greater support from recent data? Does this necessarily imply that this is the "true theory"? Why or why not?

ANSWERS TO QUICK QUIZZES

p. 268: (i) supply . . . demand; (ii) pure competition . . . wages and prices . . . self-interest . . . money illusion; (iii) saving . . . investment; (iv) wage rate; (v) vertical . . . price level
p. 273: (i) demand; (ii) reduced; (iii) partial; (iv) intensively . . . higher; (v) *SRAS*
p. 279: (i) Short . . . Long . . . shocks . . . shocks; (ii) recessionary . . . inflationary; (iii) demand-pull . . . cost-push; (iv) weaker . . . weaker

Consumption, Real GDP, and the Multiplier

12

Every three months, the federal government issues a report detailing the total income earned by all the individuals and families across the United States. This report also provides information about how these household units allocate their incomes. Naturally, they pay taxes, and they purchase various types of goods and services. A number of households also save a portion of their incomes during each three-month interval. Nevertheless, in recent years the federal government's regular report has contained a startling statistic: the measured rate at which U.S. households save out of their incomes has, on average, been very close to 0 percent.

Is the U.S. rate of saving really so low? How does the share of income that goes to saving matter for the U.S. economy? You will find out in this chapter.

Learning Objectives

After reading this chapter, you should be able to:

1. Distinguish between saving and savings and explain how saving and consumption are related
2. Explain the key determinants of consumption and saving in the Keynesian model
3. Identify the primary determinants of planned investment
4. Describe how equilibrium real GDP is established in the Keynesian model
5. Evaluate why autonomous changes in total planned expenditures have a multiplier effect on equilibrium real GDP
6. Understand the relationship between total planned expenditures and the aggregate demand curve

MyEconLab helps you master each objective and study more efficiently. See end of chapter for details.

Did You Know That...

at the end of the 1990s, some businesspeople, numerous media pundits, and even a few economists were speculating that the adoption of new information technologies might have made recessions obsolete? By early 2001, of course, it had become clear that recessions could not be relegated to the dustbin of history. Indeed, most economists blame a nearly 15 percent drop in information-technology investment between the middle of 2000 and the middle of 2001 for the last recession, which formally lasted from March 2001 until November 2001.

Instead of putting an end to recessions, variations in investment in new information technologies arguably have had a lot to do with fluctuations in real GDP during the present decade. John Maynard Keynes focused much of his research on how unanticipated changes in investment spending affect a nation's aggregate spending and real GDP. The key to determining the broader economic effects of investment fluctuations, Keynes reasoned, was to understand the relationship between how much people earn and their willingness to engage in personal consumption spending. Thus, Keynes argued that a prerequisite to understanding how investment affects a nation's economy is to understand the determinants of household consumption. In this chapter, you will learn how an understanding of consumption expenditures can assist you in evaluating the effects of variations in business investment on real GDP.

SOME SIMPLIFYING ASSUMPTIONS IN A KEYNESIAN MODEL

Continuing in the Keynesian tradition, we will assume that the short-run aggregate supply curve within the current range of real GDP is horizontal. That is, we assume that it is similar to Figure 11-6 on page 269. Thus, the equilibrium level of real GDP is demand determined. This is why Keynes wished to examine the elements of desired aggregate expenditures. Because of the Keynesian assumption of inflexible prices, inflation is not a concern. Hence real values are identical to nominal values.

To simplify the income determination model that follows, a number of assumptions are made:

1. Businesses pay no indirect taxes (for example, sales taxes).
2. Businesses distribute all of their profits to shareholders.
3. There is no depreciation (capital consumption allowance), so gross private domestic investment equals net investment.
4. The economy is closed—that is, there is no foreign trade.

Given all these simplifying assumptions, **real disposable income,** or after-tax income, will be equal to real GDP minus net taxes—taxes paid less transfer payments received.

Another Look at Definitions and Relationships

You can do only two things with a dollar of disposable income: consume it or save it. If you consume it, it is gone forever. If you save the entire dollar, however, you will be able to consume it (and perhaps more if it earns interest) at some future time. That is the distinction between **consumption** and **saving.** Consumption is the act of using income for the purchase of consumption goods. **Consumption goods** are goods purchased by households for immediate satisfaction. Consumption goods are such things as food and movies. By definition, whatever you do not consume you save and can consume at some time in the future.

Real disposable income
Real GDP minus net taxes, or after-tax real income.

Consumption
Spending on new goods and services out of a household's current income. Whatever is not consumed is saved. Consumption includes such things as buying food and going to a concert.

Saving
The act of not consuming all of one's current income. Whatever is not consumed out of spendable income is, by definition, saved. *Saving* is an action measured over time (a flow), whereas *savings* are a stock, an accumulation resulting from the act of saving in the past.

Consumption goods
Goods bought by households to use up, such as food and movies.

Stocks and Flows: The Difference Between Saving and Savings. It is important to distinguish between *saving* and *savings*. *Saving* is an action that occurs at a particular rate—for example, $10 per week or $520 per year. This rate is a flow. It is expressed per unit of time, usually a year. Implicitly, then, when we talk about saving, we talk about a *flow,* or rate, of saving. *Savings,* by contrast, is a *stock* concept, measured at a certain point or instant in time. Your current *savings* are the result of past *saving*. You may currently have *savings* of $2,000 that are the result of four years' *saving* at a rate of $500 per year. Consumption is also a flow concept. You consume from after-tax income at a certain rate per week, per month, or per year.

Relating Income to Saving and Consumption. A dollar of take-home income can be allocated either to consumption or to saving. Realizing this, we can see the relationship among saving, consumption, and disposable income from the following expression:

$$\text{Consumption} + \text{saving} \equiv \text{disposable income}$$

This is called an *accounting identity,* meaning that it has to hold true at every moment in time. (To indicate that the relationship is always true, we use the $\equiv$ symbol.)

From this relationship, we can derive the following definition of saving:

$$\text{Saving} \equiv \text{disposable income} - \text{consumption}$$

Hence, saving is the amount of disposable income that is not spent to purchase consumption goods.

Investment

Investment is also a flow concept. As noted in Chapter 8, *investment* as used in economics differs from the common use of the term. In common speech, it is often used to describe putting funds into the stock market or real estate. In economic analysis, investment is defined to include expenditures by firms on new machines and buildings—**capital goods**—that are expected to yield a future stream of income. This is called *fixed investment*. We also include changes in business inventories in our definition. This we call *inventory investment*.

Does it seem reasonable to you that in official government tabulations of consumption and investment spending, your educational expenses for college are treated just like your entertainment expenditures?

Investment
Spending by businesses on things such as machines and buildings, which can be used to produce goods and services in the future. The investment part of real GDP is the portion that will be used in the process of producing goods in the future.

Capital goods
Producer durables; nonconsumable goods that firms use to make other goods.

POLICY EXAMPLE

Spending on Human Capital: Investment or Consumption?

Economists define human capital as the accumulation of investments in training and education. From this perspective, educational expenses should be regarded as a form of investment spending. Nevertheless, in official U.S. government statistics, household spending on education is classified as a form of consumption spending.

This means that, according to the U.S. government, whenever aggregate investment in human capital increases, household consumption increases. Thus, when families forgo buying video games, purchasing movie tickets, or taking vacation trips to invest in education and training, their human capital investments are treated as simply an alternative form of consumption spending. Not surprisingly, many economists question whether classifying educational expenses as consumption spending is appropriate. At present, however, the government has no plans to alter its classification of educational spending.

(continued)

FOR CRITICAL ANALYSIS
Based on the U.S. government's current classification of educational spending, if disposable income is unchanged and households spend more on education, so that their total spending rises, what happens to the official measure of saving?

QUICK QUIZ

If we assume that we are operating on a _____ short-run aggregate supply curve, the equilibrium level of real GDP per year is completely demand determined.

_____ is a flow, something that occurs over time. It equals disposable income minus consumption. _____ is a stock. It is the accumulation resulting from saving.

_____ is also a flow. It includes expenditures on new machines, buildings, and equipment and changes in business inventories.

See page 316 for the answers. Review concepts from this section in MyEconLab.

DETERMINANTS OF PLANNED CONSUMPTION AND PLANNED SAVING

In the classical model discussed in Chapter 11, the supply of saving was determined by the rate of interest. Specifically, the higher the rate of interest, the more people wanted to save and therefore the less people wanted to consume.

In contrast, according to Keynes, the interest rate is *not* the most important determinant of an individual's real saving and consumption decisions. In his view, income, not the interest rate, is the main determinant of saving. Thus:

> *Keynes argued that real saving and consumption decisions depend primarily on a household's present real disposable income.*

The relationship between planned real consumption expenditures of households and their current level of real disposable income has been called the **consumption function.** It shows how much all households plan to consume per year at each level of real disposable income per year. Columns (1) and (2) of Table 12-1 illustrate a consumption function for a hypothetical household.

We see from Table 12-1 that as real disposable income rises, planned consumption also rises, but by a smaller amount, as Keynes suggested. Planned saving also increases with disposable income. Notice, however, that below an income of $30,000, the planned saving of this hypothetical household is actually negative. The further that income drops below that level, the more the household engages in **dissaving,** either by going into debt or by using up some of its existing wealth.

Graphing the Numbers

We now graph the consumption and saving relationships presented in Table 12-1. In the upper part of Figure 12-1 on page 292, the vertical axis measures the level of planned real consumption per year, and the horizontal axis measures the level of real disposable income per year. In the lower part of the figure, the horizontal axis is again real disposable income per year, but now the vertical axis is planned real saving per year. All of these are on a dollars-per-year basis, which emphasizes the point that we are measuring flows, not stocks.

Consumption function
The relationship between amount consumed and disposable income. A consumption function tells us how much people plan to consume at various levels of disposable income.

Dissaving
Negative saving; a situation in which spending exceeds income. Dissaving can occur when a household is able to borrow or use up existing assets.

TABLE 12-1
Real Consumption and Saving Schedules: A Hypothetical Case

Column 1 presents real disposable income from zero up to $60,000 per year; column 2 indicates planned consumption per year; column 3 presents planned saving per year. At levels of disposable income below $30,000, planned saving is negative. In column 4, we see the average propensity to consume, which is merely planned consumption divided by disposable income. Column 5 lists average propensity to save, which is planned saving divided by disposable income. Column 6 is the marginal propensity to consume, which shows the proportion of *additional* income that will be consumed. Finally, column 7 shows the proportion of *additional* income that will be saved, or the marginal propensity to save.

Combination	(1) Real Disposable Income per Year (Y_d)	(2) Planned Real Consumption per Year (C)	(3) Planned Real Saving per Year ($S \equiv Y_d - C$) (1) − (2)	(4) Average Propensity to Consume ($APC \equiv C/Y_d$) (2) ÷ (1)	(5) Average Propensity to Save ($APS \equiv S/Y_d$) (3) ÷ (1)	(6) Marginal Propensity to Consume ($MPC \equiv \Delta C/\Delta Y_d$)	(7) Marginal Propensity to Save ($MPS \equiv \Delta S/\Delta Y_d$)
A	$ 0	$ 6,000	$ −6,000	—	—	—	—
B	6,000	10,800	−4,800	1.8	−.8	.8	.2
C	12,000	15,600	−3,600	1.3	−.3	.8	.2
D	18,000	20,400	−2,400	1.133	−.133	.8	.2
E	24,000	25,200	−1,200	1.05	−.05	.8	.2
F	30,000	30,000	0	1.0	.0	.8	.2
G	36,000	34,800	1,200	.967	.033	.8	.2
H	42,000	39,600	2,400	.943	.057	.8	.2
I	48,000	44,400	3,600	.925	.075	.8	.2
J	54,000	49,200	4,800	.911	.089	.8	.2
K	60,000	54,000	6,000	.9	.1	.8	.2

As you can see, we have taken income-consumption and income-saving combinations A through K and plotted them. In the upper part of Figure 12-1 on the next page, the result is called the *consumption function*. In the lower part, the result is called the *saving function*. Mathematically, the saving function is the *complement* of the consumption function because consumption plus saving always equals disposable income. What is not consumed is, by definition, saved. The difference between actual disposable income and the planned rate of consumption per year *must* be the planned rate of saving per year.

How can we find the rate of saving or dissaving in the upper part of Figure 12-1? We draw a line that is equidistant from both the horizontal and the vertical axes. This line is 45 degrees from either axis and is often called the **45-degree reference line.** At every point on the 45-degree reference line, a vertical line drawn to the income axis is the same distance from the origin as a horizontal line drawn to the consumption axis. Thus, at point F, where the consumption function intersects the 45-degree line, real disposable income equals planned real consumption. Point F is sometimes called the *break-even income point* because there is neither positive nor negative real saving. This can be seen in the lower part of Figure 12-1 as well. The planned annual rate of real saving at a real disposable income level of $30,000 is indeed zero.

45-degree reference line
The line along which planned real expenditures equal real GDP per year.

Dissaving and Autonomous Consumption

To the left of point F in either part of Figure 12-1, this hypothetical family engages in dissaving, either by going into debt or by consuming existing assets. The rate of real saving

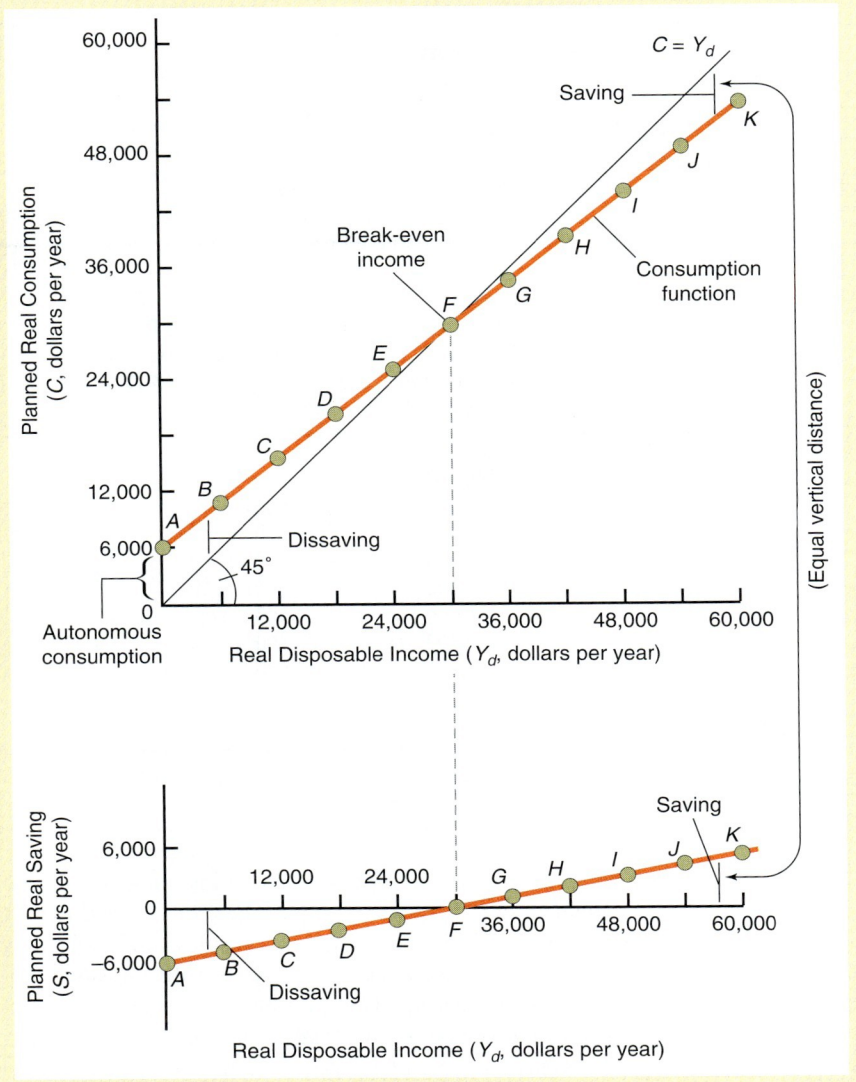

FIGURE 12-1

The Consumption and Saving Functions

If we plot the combinations of real disposable income and planned real consumption from columns 1 and 2 in Table 12-1 on the previous page, we get the consumption function.

At every point on the 45-degree line, a vertical line drawn to the income axis is the same distance from the origin as a horizontal line drawn to the consumption axis. Where the consumption function crosses the 45-degree line at F, we know that planned real consumption equals real disposable income and there is zero saving. The vertical distance between the 45-degree line and the consumption function measures the rate of real saving or dissaving at any given income level. If we plot the relationship between column 1—real disposable income—and column 3—planned real saving—from Table 12-1, we arrive at the saving function shown in the lower part of this diagram. It is the complement of the consumption function presented above it.

or dissaving in the upper part of the figure can be found by measuring the vertical distance between the 45-degree line and the consumption function. This simply tells us that if our hypothetical household sees its real disposable income fall to less than $30,000, it will not limit its consumption to this amount. It will instead go into debt or consume existing assets in some way to compensate for part of the lost income.

Now look at the point on the diagram where real disposable income is zero but planned consumption is $6,000. This amount of real planned consumption, which does not depend at all on actual real disposable income, is called **autonomous consumption**. The autonomous consumption of $6,000 is *independent* of disposable income. That means that no matter how low the level of real income of our hypothetical household falls, the household will always attempt to consume at least $6,000 per year. (We are, of course, assuming here that the household's real disposable income does not equal zero year in and year out.

Autonomous consumption
The part of consumption that is independent of (does not depend on) the level of disposable income. Changes in autonomous consumption shift the consumption function.

There is certainly a limit to how long our hypothetical household could finance autonomous consumption without any income.) That $6,000 of yearly consumption is determined by things other than the level of income. We don't need to specify what determines autonomous consumption; we merely state that it exists and that in our example it is $6,000 per year.

Just remember that the word *autonomous* means "existing independently." In our model, autonomous consumption exists independently of the hypothetical household's level of real disposable income. (Later we will review some of the determinants of consumption other than real disposable income.) There are many possible types of autonomous expenditures. Hypothetically, we can assume that investment is autonomous—independent of income. We can assume that government expenditures are autonomous. We will do just that at various times in our discussions to simplify our analysis of income determination.

Average Propensity to Consume and to Save

Let's now go back to Table 12-1 on page 291, and this time let's look at columns 4 and 5: **average propensity to consume (APC)** and **average propensity to save (APS)**. They are defined as follows:

$$APC \equiv \frac{\text{real consumption}}{\text{real disposable income}}$$

$$APS \equiv \frac{\text{real saving}}{\text{real disposable income}}$$

Notice from column 4 in Table 12-1 that for this hypothetical household, the average propensity to consume decreases as real disposable income increases. This decrease simply means that the fraction of the household's real disposable income going to consumption falls as income rises. The same behavior can be observed in column 5. The average propensity to save, which at first is negative, finally hits zero at an income level of $30,000 and then becomes positive. In this example, the APS reaches a value of 0.1 at income level $60,000. This means that the household saves 10 percent of a $60,000 income.

It's quite easy for you to figure out your own average propensity to consume or to save. Just divide the value of what you consumed by your total real disposable income for the year, and the result will be your personal APC at your current level of income. Also, divide your real saving during the year by your real disposable income to calculate your own APS.

Marginal Propensity to Consume and to Save

Now we go to the last two columns in Table 12-1: **marginal propensity to consume (MPC)** and **marginal propensity to save (MPS)**. The term *marginal* refers to a small incremental or decremental change (represented by the Greek letter delta, Δ, in Table 12-1). The marginal propensity to consume, then, is defined as

$$MPC \equiv \frac{\text{change in real consumption}}{\text{change in real disposable income}}$$

The marginal propensity to save is defined similarly as

$$MPS \equiv \frac{\text{change in real saving}}{\text{change in real disposable income}}$$

Average propensity to consume (APC)
Real consumption divided by real disposable income; for any given level of real income, the proportion of total real disposable income that is consumed.

Average propensity to save (APS)
Real saving divided by real disposable income; for any given level of real income, the proportion of total real disposable income that is saved.

Marginal propensity to consume (MPC)
The ratio of the change in consumption to the change in disposable income. A marginal propensity to consume of 0.8 tells us that an additional $100 in take-home pay will lead to an additional $80 consumed.

Marginal propensity to save (MPS)
The ratio of the change in saving to the change in disposable income. A marginal propensity to save of 0.2 indicates that out of an additional $100 in take-home pay, $20 will be saved. Whatever is not saved is consumed. The marginal propensity to save plus the marginal propensity to consume must always equal 1, by definition.

Marginal versus Average Propensities. What do MPC and MPS tell you? They tell you what percentage of a given increase or decrease in real income will go toward consumption and saving, respectively. The emphasis here is on the word *change*. The marginal propensity to consume indicates how much you will change your planned real consumption if there is a change in your real disposable income. If your marginal propensity to consume is 0.8, that does not mean that you consume 80 percent of *all* disposable income. The percentage of your total real disposable income that you consume is given by the average propensity to consume, or APC. As Table 12-1 on page 291 indicates, the APC is not equal to 0.8. Instead, an MPC of 0.8 means that you will consume 80 percent of any *increase* in your disposable income. Hence the MPC cannot be less than zero or greater than one. It follows that households increase their planned real consumption by more than zero and less than 100 percent of any increase in real disposable income that they receive.

Distinguishing the MPC from the APC. Consider a simple example in which we show the difference between the average propensity to consume and the marginal propensity to consume. Assume that your consumption behavior is exactly the same as our hypothetical household's behavior depicted in Table 12-1. You have an annual real disposable income of $54,000. Your planned consumption rate, then, from column 2 of Table 12-1 is $49,200. So your average propensity to consume is $49,200/$54,000 = 0.911. Now suppose that at the end of the year, your boss gives you an after-tax bonus of $6,000. What would you do with that additional $6,000 in real disposable income? According to the table, you would consume $4,800 of it and save $1,200. In that case, your *marginal* propensity to consume would be $4,800/$6,000 = 0.8 and your marginal propensity to save would be $1,200/$6,000 = 0.2. What would happen to your *average* propensity to consume? To find out, we add $4,800 to $49,200 of planned consumption, which gives us a new consumption rate of $54,000. The average propensity to consume is then $54,000 divided by the new higher salary of $60,000. Your APC drops from 0.911 to 0.9.

In contrast, your MPC remains, in our simplified example, 0.8 all the time. Look at column 6 in Table 12-1. The MPC is 0.8 at every level of income. (Therefore, the MPS is always equal to 0.2 at every level of income.) The constancy of MPC reflects the assumption that the amount that you are willing to consume out of additional income will remain the same in percentage terms no matter what level of real disposable income is your starting point.

Some Relationships

Consumption plus saving must equal income. Both your total real disposable income and the change in total real disposable income are either consumed or saved. The proportions of either measure must equal 1, or 100 percent. This allows us to make the following statements:

$$APC + APS \equiv 1 \; (= 100 \text{ percent of total income})$$

$$MPC + MPS \equiv 1 \; (= 100 \text{ percent of the } change \text{ in income})$$

The average propensities as well as the marginal propensities to consume and save must total 1, or 100 percent. Check the two statements by adding the figures in columns 4 and 5 for each level of real disposable income in Table 12-1. Do the same for columns 6 and 7.

Causes of Shifts in the Consumption Function

A change in any other relevant economic variable besides real disposable income will cause the consumption function to shift. The number of such nonincome determinants of the position of the consumption function is virtually unlimited. Real household **wealth** is one determinant of the position of the consumption function. An increase in the real wealth of the average household will cause the consumption function to shift upward. A decrease in real wealth will cause it to shift downward. So far we have been talking about the consumption function of an individual or a household. Now let's move on to the national economy.

Wealth
The stock of assets owned by a person, household, firm, or nation. For a household, wealth can consist of a house, cars, personal belongings, stocks, bonds, bank accounts, and cash.

QUICK QUIZ

The **consumption function** shows the relationship between planned rates of real consumption and real _____ per year. The saving function is the complement of the consumption function because real saving plus real _____ must equal real disposable income.

The _____ propensity to consume is equal to real consumption divided by real disposable income. The _____ propensity to save is equal to real saving divided by real disposable income.

The _____ propensity to consume is equal to the change in planned real consumption divided by the change in real disposable income. The _____ propensity to save is equal to the change in planned real saving divided by the change in real disposable income.

Any change in real disposable income will cause the planned rate of consumption to change; this is represented by a _____ _____ the consumption function. Any change in a nonincome determinant of consumption will cause a _____ _____ the consumption function.

See page 316 for the answers. Review concepts from this section in MyEconLab.

DETERMINANTS OF INVESTMENT

Investment, you will remember, consists of expenditures on new buildings and equipment and changes in business inventories. Historically, real gross private domestic investment in the United States has been extremely volatile over the years, relative to real consumption. If we were to look at net private domestic investment (investment after depreciation has been deducted), we would see that in the depths of the Great Depression and at the peak of the World War II effort, the figure was negative. In other words, we were eating away at our capital stock—we weren't even maintaining it by completely replacing depreciated equipment.

If we compare real investment expenditures historically with real consumption expenditures, we find that the latter are less variable over time than the former. Why is this so? One possible reason is that the real investment decisions of businesses are based on highly variable, subjective estimates of how the economic future looks.

The Planned Investment Function

Consider that at all times, businesses perceive an array of investment opportunities. These investment opportunities have rates of return ranging from zero to very high, with the number (or dollar value) of all such projects inversely related to the rate of return. Because a project is profitable only if its rate of return exceeds the opportunity cost of the investment—the rate of interest—it follows that as the interest rate falls, planned investment spending increases, and vice versa. Even if firms use retained earnings (internal financing) to fund an investment, the lower the market rate of interest, the smaller the *opportunity cost* of using those retained earnings. Thus, it does not matter in our analysis whether the firm must seek financing from external sources or can obtain such financing by using retained earnings. Whatever the method of financing, as the interest rate falls, more investment opportunities will be profitable, and planned investment will be higher.

It should be no surprise, therefore, that the investment function is represented as an inverse relationship between the rate of interest and the value of planned real investment. A hypothetical investment schedule is given in panel (a) of Figure 12-2 and plotted in panel (b). We see from this schedule that if, for example, the rate of interest is 5 percent, the dollar value of planned investment will be $2 trillion per year. Notice, by the way, that planned investment is also given on a per-year basis, showing that it represents a flow, not a stock. (The stock counterpart of investment is the stock of capital in the economy measured in inflation-adjusted dollars at a point in time.)

What Causes the Investment Function to Shift?

Because planned real investment is assumed to be a function of the rate of interest, any non-interest-rate variable that changes can have the potential of shifting the investment function. One of those variables is the expectations of businesses. If higher profits are expected, more machines and bigger plants will be planned for the future. More investment will be undertaken because of the expectation of higher profits. In this case, the investment

> **ECONOMICS FRONT AND CENTER**
>
> To think about the role of the interest rate in actual investment decisions, read **Considering an Investment in Internet Telephony**, on page 309.

Go to economic data provided by the Federal Reserve Bank of St. Louis via the link at **www.econtoday.com/ch12** to see how U.S. real private investment has varied in recent years.

FIGURE 12-2

Planned Real Investment

As shown in the hypothetical planned investment schedule in panel (a), the rate of planned real investment is inversely related to the rate of interest. If we plot the data pairs from panel (a), we obtain the investment function, *I*, in panel (b). It is negatively sloped.

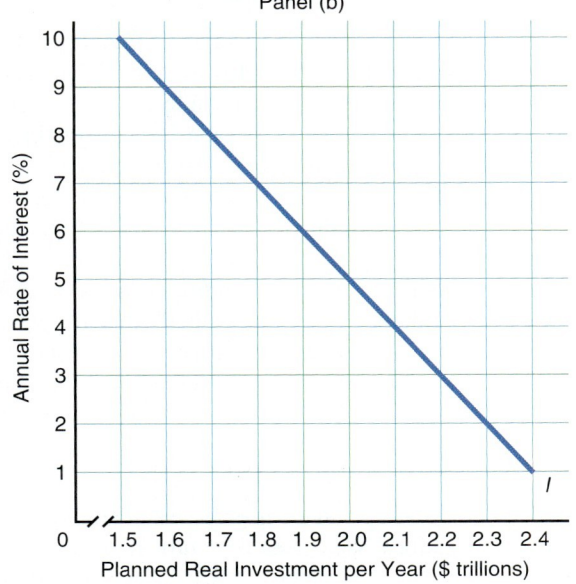

Panel (a)

Annual Rate of Interest (%)	Planned Real Investment per Year ($ trillions)
10	1.5
9	1.6
8	1.7
7	1.8
6	1.9
5	2.0
4	2.1
3	2.2
2	2.3
1	2.4

schedule, *I*, would shift outward to the right, meaning that more investment would be desired at all rates of interest. Any change in productive technology can potentially shift the investment function. A positive change in productive technology would stimulate demand for additional capital goods and shift *I* outward to the right. Changes in business taxes can also shift the investment schedule. If they increase, we predict a leftward shift in the planned investment function because higher taxes imply a lower (after-tax) rate of return.

In recent years, how have changes in business spending on information technology affected planned real investment in the United States?

EXAMPLE

Information-Technology Investment Continues to Lag

Business spending on information technology (IT) accounts for about 40 percent of U.S. investment expenditures. During the 1990s, IT investment drove an investment boom. Then, between 2000 and 2003, IT investment plunged, and so did total investment spending. Since 2003, other forms of investment have rebounded sharply. IT investment, however, has increased at a much slower pace.

Why is IT investment currently lagging behind other forms of business investment? One part of the answer is that during the 2001–2002 economic downturn, many firms learned how to use existing computing capital already on hand more efficiently. The mutual fund company Vanguard, for instance, created a new computer backup system by reconfiguring existing servers and computers to handle data more efficiently, thereby avoiding purchasing new devices.

Another reason IT investment is lagging is that more firms are using software with freely available computer code, such as Linux, rather than buying software from producers such as Microsoft. This has resulted in lower software expenditures, which are part of IT investment. Using open-source software has also enabled some firms to keep using older equipment instead of buying new devices that would require the latest proprietary software to operate. Consequently, using open-source software has also slowed the growth of IT equipment investment.

FOR CRITICAL ANALYSIS
In 2005, U.S. market interest rates rose, yet real investment expenditures increased. What must have happened to the U.S. investment schedule during 2005?

QUICK QUIZ

The planned investment schedule shows the relationship between real investment and the _____ _____; it slopes _____.

The non-interest-rate determinants of planned investment are _____, innovation and technological changes, and _____ _____.

Any change in the non-interest-rate determinants of planned investment will cause a _____ _____ the planned investment function so that at each and every rate of interest a different amount of planned investment will be made.

See page 316 for the answers. Review concepts from this section in MyEconLab.

DETERMINING EQUILIBRIUM REAL GDP

We are interested in determining the equilibrium level of real GDP per year. But when we examined the consumption function earlier in this chapter, it related planned real consumption expenditures to the level of real disposable income per year. We have already shown where adjustments must be made to GDP in order to get real disposable income (see Table 8-2 on page 199). Real disposable income turns out to be less than real GDP because real net taxes (real taxes minus real government transfer payments) are usually about 11 to 18 percent of GDP. A representative average is about 15 percent, so disposable income, on average, has in recent years been around 85 percent of GDP.

Consumption as a Function of Real GDP

To simplify our model, assume that real disposable income, Y_d, differs from real GDP by the same absolute amount every year. Therefore, we can relatively easily substitute real GDP for real disposable income in the consumption function.

We can now plot any consumption function on a diagram in which the horizontal axis is no longer real disposable income but rather real GDP, as in Figure 12-3. Notice that there is an autonomous part of real consumption that is so labeled. The difference between this graph and the graphs presented earlier in this chapter is the change in the horizontal axis from real disposable income to real GDP per year. For the rest of this chapter, assume that the MPC out of real GDP equals 0.8, suggesting that 20 percent of changes in real disposable income is saved: In other words, of an additional after-tax $100 earned, an additional $80 will be consumed.

The 45-Degree Reference Line

Like the earlier graphs, Figure 12-3 shows a 45-degree reference line. The 45-degree line bisects the quadrant into two equal spaces. Thus, along the 45-degree reference line, planned real consumption expenditures, C, equal real GDP per year, Y. One can see, then, that at any point where the consumption function intersects the 45-degree reference line, planned real consumption expenditures will be exactly equal to real GDP per year, or $C = Y$. Note that in this graph, because we are looking only at planned real consumption on the vertical axis, the 45-degree reference line is where planned real consumption, C, is always

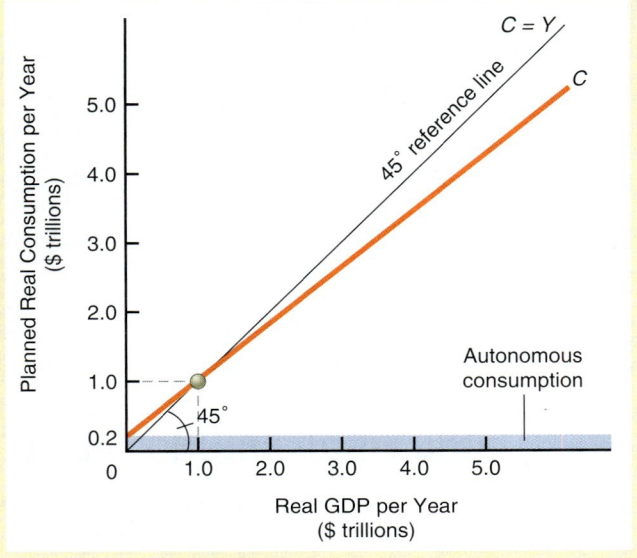

FIGURE 12-3

Consumption as a Function of Real GDP

This consumption function shows the rate of planned expenditures for each level of real GDP per year. In this example, there is an autonomous component of consumption equal to $0.2 trillion. Along the 45-degree reference line, planned real consumption expenditures per year, C, are identical to real GDP per year, Y. The consumption curve intersects the 45-degree reference line at a value of $1 trillion per year in base-year dollars.

equal to real GDP per year, Y. Later, when we add real investment, government spending, and net exports to the graph, the 45-degree reference line with respect to *all* planned real expenditures will be labeled as such on the vertical axis. In any event, consumption and real GDP are equal at $1 trillion per year. That is where the consumption curve, C, intersects the 45-degree reference line. At that GDP level, all real GDP is consumed.

Adding the Investment Function

Another component of private aggregate demand is, of course, investment spending, I. We have already looked at the planned investment function, which related real investment to the rate of interest. You see that as the downward-sloping curve in panel (a) of Figure 12-4. Recall from Figure 11-2 (on page 264) that the equilibrium rate of interest is determined at the intersection of the desired savings schedule, which is labeled S and is upward sloping. The equilibrium rate of interest is 5 percent, and the equilibrium rate of real investment is $2 trillion per year. The $2 trillion of real investment per year is *autonomous* with respect to real GDP—that is, it is independent of real GDP. In other words, given that we have a determinant investment level of $2 trillion at a 5 percent rate of interest, we can treat this level of real investment as constant, regardless of the level of GDP. This is shown in panel (b) of Figure 12-4. The vertical distance of real investment spending is $2 trillion. Businesses plan on investing a particular amount—$2 trillion per year—and will do so no matter what the level of real GDP.

How do we add this amount of real investment spending to our consumption function? We simply add a line above the C line that we drew in Figure 12-3 that is higher by the vertical distance equal to $2 trillion of autonomous real investment spending. This is shown by the arrow in panel (c) of Figure 12-4. Our new line, now labeled $C + I$, is called the *consumption plus investment line*. In our simple economy without real government

FIGURE 12-4

Combining Consumption and Investment

In panel (a), we show the determination of real investment in trillions of dollars per year. It occurs where the investment schedule intersects the saving schedule at an interest rate of 5 percent and is equal to $2 trillion per year. In panel (b), investment is a constant $2 trillion per year. When we add this amount to the consumption line, we obtain in panel (c) the $C + I$ line, which is vertically higher than the C line by exactly $2 trillion. Real GDP is equal to $C + I$ at $11 trillion per year where total planned real expenditures, $C + I$, are equal to actual real GDP, for this is where the $C + I$ line intersects the 45-degree reference line, on which $C + I$ is equal to Y at every point.

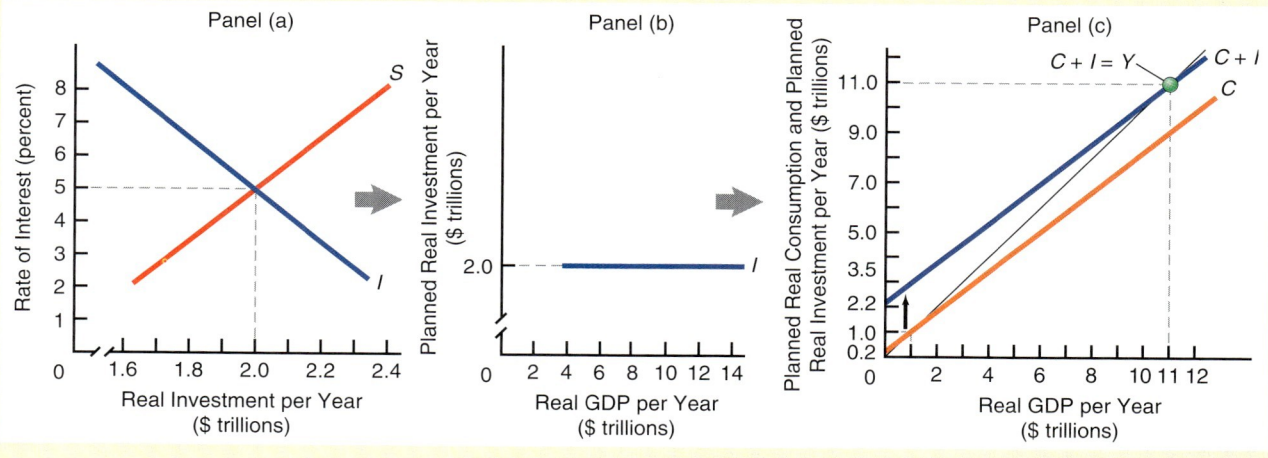

expenditures and net exports, the $C + I$ curve represents total planned real expenditures as they relate to different levels of real GDP per year. Because the 45-degree reference line shows all the points where planned real expenditures (now $C + I$) equal real GDP, we label it $C + I = Y$. Equilibrium Y equals $11 trillion per year. Equilibrium occurs when total planned real expenditures equal real GDP (given that any amount of production of goods and services in this model in the short run can occur without a change in the price level).

Saving and Investment: Planned versus Actual

Figure 12-5 shows the planned investment curve as a horizontal line at $2 trillion per year in base-year dollars. Real investment is completely autonomous in this simplified model—it does not depend on real GDP.

The planned saving curve is represented by S. Because in our model whatever is not consumed is, by definition, saved, the planned saving schedule is the complement of the planned consumption schedule, represented by the C line in Figure 12-3 (on page 298). For better exposition, we look at only a part of the saving and investment schedules—annual levels of real GDP between $9 trillion and $13 trillion.

Why does equilibrium have to occur at the intersection of the planned saving and planned investment schedules? If we are at E in Figure 12-5, planned saving equals planned investment. All anticipations are validated by reality. There is no tendency for businesses to alter the rate of production or the level of employment because they are neither increasing nor decreasing their inventories in an unplanned way.

Unplanned Increases in Business Inventories.
If real GDP is $13 trillion instead of $11 trillion, planned investment, as usual, is $2 trillion per year. It is exceeded, however, by planned saving, which is $2.4 trillion per year. This means that consumers will *actually* purchase fewer goods and services than businesses had *anticipated*. This will leave firms with unsold products, and their inventories will begin to rise above the levels they had planned.

FIGURE 12-5
Planned and Actual Rates of Saving and Investment
Only at the equilibrium level of real GDP of $11 trillion per year will planned saving equal actual saving, planned investment equal actual investment, and hence planned saving equal planned investment.

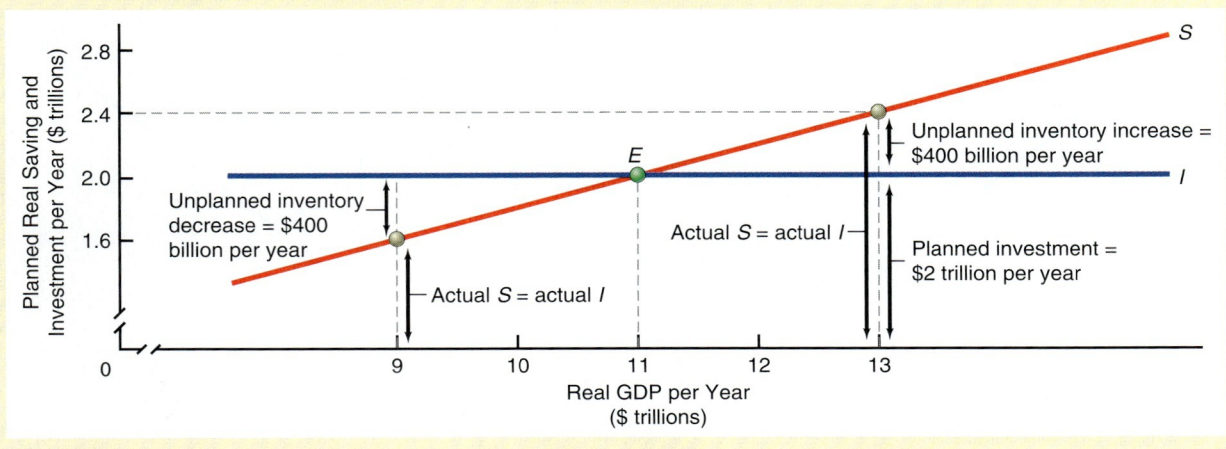

Unplanned business inventories will now rise at the rate of $400 billion per year, or $2.4 trillion in actual investment (including inventories) minus $2 trillion in planned investment by firms that had not anticipated an inventory buildup. But this situation cannot continue for long. Businesses will respond to the unplanned increase in inventories by cutting back production of goods and services and reducing employment, and we will move toward a lower level of real GDP.

Unplanned Decreases in Business Inventories. Conversely, if real GDP is $9 trillion per year, planned investment continues annually at $2 trillion, but planned saving is only $1.6 trillion. This means that households and businesses are purchasing more goods and services than businesses had planned. Businesses will find that they must draw down their inventories below the planned level by $400 billion (business inventories will fall now at the unplanned rate of $400 billion per year), bringing actual investment into equality with actual saving because the $400 billion decline in inventories is included in actual investment (thereby decreasing it).

Nevertheless, this situation cannot last forever either. In their attempt to increase inventories to the planned level, businesses will increase production of goods and services and increase employment. Consequently, real GDP will rise toward its equilibrium value of $11 trillion per year. Figure 12-5 demonstrates the necessary equality between actual saving and actual investment. Inventories adjust so that saving and investment, after the fact, are *always* equal in this simplified model. (Remember that changes in inventories count as part of investment.)

Every time the saving rate planned by households differs from the investment rate planned by businesses, there will be a shrinkage or an expansion in the circular flow of income and output (introduced in Chapter 8) in the form of unplanned inventory changes. Real GDP and employment will change until unplanned inventory changes are again zero—that is, until we have attained the equilibrium level of real GDP.

QUICK QUIZ

We assume that the consumption function has an _____ part that is independent of the level of real GDP per year. It is labeled "_____ consumption."

For simplicity, we assume that real investment is _____ with respect to real GDP and therefore unaffected by the level of real GDP per year.

The _____ level of real GDP can be found where planned saving equals planned investment.

Whenever planned saving exceeds planned investment, there will be unplanned inventory _____, and real GDP will fall as producers cut production of goods and services. Whenever planned saving is less than planned investment, there will be unplanned inventory _____, and real GDP will rise as producers increase production of goods and services.

See page 316 for the answers. Review concepts from this section in MyEconLab.

KEYNESIAN EQUILIBRIUM WITH GOVERNMENT AND THE FOREIGN SECTOR ADDED

To this point, we have ignored the role of government in our model. We have also left out the foreign sector of the economy. Let's think about what happens when we also consider these as elements of the model.

Government

To add real government spending, G, to our macroeconomic model, we assume that the level of resource-using government purchases of goods and services (federal, state, and local), *not* including transfer payments, is determined by the political process. In other words, G will be considered autonomous, just like real investment (and a certain component of real consumption). In the United States, resource-using government expenditures are around 20 percent of real GDP.

The other side of the coin, of course, is that there are real taxes, which are used to pay for much of government spending. We will simplify our model greatly by assuming that there is a constant **lump-sum tax** of $1.7 trillion a year to finance $1.7 trillion of government spending. This lump-sum tax will reduce disposable income by the same amount. We show this in Table 12-2 (column 2), where we give the numbers for a complete model.

Lump-sum tax
A tax that does not depend on income. An example is a $1,000 tax that every household must pay, irrespective of its economic situation.

The Foreign Sector

Go to www.econtoday.com/ch12 to find out from the U.S. Department of Agriculture how the North American Free Trade Agreement has affected U.S. agricultural imports and exports.

For years, the media have focused attention on the nation's foreign trade deficit. We have been buying merchandise and services from foreign residents—real imports—the value of which exceeds the value of the real exports we have been selling to them. The difference between real exports and real imports is *real net exports*, which we will label X in our graphs. The level of real exports depends on international economic conditions, especially in the countries that buy our products. Real imports depend on economic conditions here at home. For simplicity, assume that real imports exceed real exports (real net exports, X, is negative) and furthermore that the level of real net exports is autonomous—independent of

TABLE 12-2
The Determination of Equilibrium Real GDP with Government and Net Exports Added
Figures are trillions of dollars.

(1) Real GDP	(2) Real Taxes	(3) Real Disposable Income	(4) Planned Real Consumption	(5) Planned Real Saving	(6) Planned Real Investment	(7) Real Government Spending	(8) Real Net Exports (exports minus imports)	(9) Total Planned Real Expenditures (4)+(6)+(7)+(8)	(10) Unplanned Inventory Changes	(11) Direction of Change in Real GDP
6.0	1.7	4.3	4.3	0.0	2.0	1.7	−.8	7.2	−1.2	Increase
7.0	1.7	5.3	5.1	0.2	2.0	1.7	−.8	8.0	−1.0	Increase
8.0	1.7	6.3	5.9	0.4	2.0	1.7	−.8	8.8	−.8	Increase
9.0	1.7	7.3	6.7	0.6	2.0	1.7	−.8	9.6	−.6	Increase
10.0	1.7	8.3	7.5	0.8	2.0	1.7	−.8	10.4	−.4	Increase
11.0	1.7	9.3	8.3	1.0	2.0	1.7	−.8	11.2	−.2	Increase
12.0	1.7	10.3	9.1	1.2	2.0	1.7	−.8	12.0	0	Neither (equilibrium)
13.0	1.7	11.3	9.9	1.4	2.0	1.7	−.8	12.8	+.2	Decrease
14.0	1.7	12.3	10.7	1.6	2.0	1.7	−.8	13.6	+.4	Decrease

real national income. Assume a level of X of −$0.8 trillion per year, as shown in column 8 of Table 12-2.

Determining the Equilibrium Level of GDP per Year

We are now in a position to determine the equilibrium level of real GDP per year under the continuing assumptions that the price level is unchanging; that investment, government, and the foreign sector are autonomous; and that planned consumption expenditures are determined by the level of real GDP. As can be seen in Table 12-2, total planned real expenditures of $12 trillion per year equal real GDP of $12 trillion per year, and this is where we reach equilibrium.

Remember that equilibrium *always* occurs when total planned real expenditures equal real GDP (given that any amount of production of goods and services in this model in the short run can occur without a change in the price level).

Now look at Figure 12-6, which shows the equilibrium level of real GDP. There are two curves, one showing the consumption function, which is the exact duplicate of the one shown in Figure 12-3, and the other being the $C + I + G + X$ curve, which intersects the 45-degree reference line (representing equilibrium) at $12 trillion per year.

Whenever total planned real expenditures differ from real GDP, there are unplanned inventory changes. When total planned real expenditures are greater than real GDP, inventory levels drop in an unplanned manner. To get inventories back up, firms seek to expand their production of goods and services, which increases real GDP. Real GDP rises toward its equilibrium level. Whenever total planned real expenditures are less than real GDP, the opposite occurs. There are unplanned inventory increases, causing firms to cut back on their production of goods and services in an effort to push inventories back down to planned levels. The result is a drop in real GDP toward the equilibrium level.

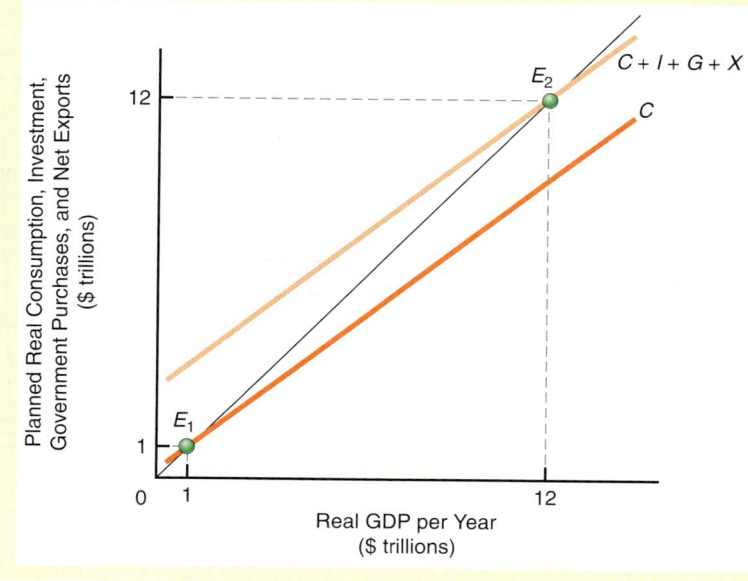

FIGURE 12-6
The Equilibrium Level of Real GDP
The consumption function, with no government and thus no taxes, is shown as C. When we add autonomous investment, government spending, and net exports, we obtain $C + I + G + X$. We move from E_1 to E_2. Equilibrium real GDP is $12 trillion per year.

QUICK QUIZ

When we add autonomous investment, I, and autonomous government spending, G, to the consumption function, we obtain the C + I + G curve, which represents total _____ _____ for a closed economy. In an open economy, we add the foreign sector, which consists of exports minus imports, or net exports, X. Total planned expenditures are thus represented by the C + I + G + X curve.

Equilibrium real GDP can be found by locating the intersection of the total planned real expenditures curve with the _____-_____ reference line. At that level of real GDP per year, planned real consumption plus planned real investment plus real government expenditures plus real net exports will equal real GDP.

Whenever total planned real expenditures exceed real GDP, there will be unplanned _____ in inventories; production of goods and services will increase, and a higher level of equilibrium real GDP will prevail. Whenever total planned real expenditures are less than real GDP, there will be unplanned _____ in inventories; production of goods and services will decrease, and equilibrium real GDP will decrease.

See page 316 for the answers. Review concepts from this section in MyEconLab.

THE MULTIPLIER

Look again at panel (c) of Figure 12-4 on page 299. Assume for the moment that the only real expenditures included in real GDP are real consumption expenditures. Where would the equilibrium level of real GDP be in this case? It would be where the consumption function (C) intersects the 45-degree reference line, which is at $1 trillion per year. Now we add the autonomous amount of planned real investment, $2 trillion, and then determine what the new equilibrium level of real GDP will be. It turns out to be $11 trillion per year. Adding $2 trillion per year of investment spending increased equilibrium real GDP by *five* times that amount, or by $10 trillion per year.

The Multiplier Effect

Multiplier
The ratio of the change in the equilibrium level of real GDP to the change in autonomous real expenditures; the number by which a change in autonomous real investment or autonomous real consumption, for example, is multiplied to get the change in equilibrium real GDP.

What is operating here is the multiplier effect of changes in autonomous spending. The **multiplier** is the number by which a permanent change in autonomous real investment or autonomous real consumption is multiplied to get the change in the equilibrium level of real GDP. Any permanent increases in autonomous real investment or in any autonomous component of consumption will cause an even larger increase in real GDP. Any permanent decreases in autonomous real spending will cause even larger decreases in real GDP per year. To understand why this multiple expansion (or contraction) in equilibrium real GDP occurs, let's look at a simple numerical example.

We'll use the same figures we used for the marginal propensity to consume and to save. MPC will equal 0.8, or $\frac{4}{5}$, and MPS will equal 0.2, or $\frac{1}{5}$. Now let's run an experiment and say that businesses decide to increase planned real investment permanently by $100 billion a year. We see in Table 12-3 that during what we'll call the first round in column 1, investment is increased by $100 billion; this also means an increase in real GDP of $100 billion, because the spending by one group represents income for another, shown in column 2. Column 3 gives the resultant increase in consumption by households that received this additional $100 billion in income. This is found by multiplying the MPC by the increase in real GDP. Because the MPC equals 0.8, real consumption expenditures during the first round will increase by $80 billion.

TABLE 12-3
The Multiplier Process

We trace the effects of a permanent $100 billion increase in autonomous real investment spending on real GDP. If we assume a marginal propensity to consume of 0.8, such an increase will eventually elicit a $500 billion increase in equilibrium real GDP per year.

Assumption: MPC = 0.8, or $\frac{4}{5}$

(1) Round	(2) Annual Increase in Real GDP ($ billions)	(3) Annual Increase in Planned Real Consumption ($ billions)	(4) Annual Increase in Planned Real Saving ($ billions)
1 ($100 billion per year increase in *I*)	100.00	80.000	20.000
2	80.00	64.000	16.000
3	64.00	51.200	12.800
4	51.20	40.960	10.240
5	40.96	32.768	8.192
.	.	.	.
.	.	.	.
.	.	.	.
All later rounds	163.84	131.072	32.768
Totals (*C* + *I* + *G*)	500.00	400.000	100.000

But that's not the end of the story. This additional household consumption is also spending, and it will provide $80 billion of additional income for other individuals. Thus, during the second round, we see an increase in real GDP of $80 billion. Now, out of this increased real GDP, what will be the resultant increase in consumption expenditures? It will be 0.8 times $80 billion, or $64 billion. We continue these induced expenditure rounds and find that an initial increase in autonomous investment expenditures of $100 billion will eventually cause the equilibrium level of real GDP to increase by $500 billion. A permanent $100 billion increase in autonomous real investment spending has induced an additional $400 billion increase in real consumption spending, for a total increase in real GDP of $500 billion. In other words, equilibrium real GDP will change by an amount equal to five times the change in real investment.

The Multiplier Formula

It turns out that the autonomous spending multiplier is equal to the reciprocal of the marginal propensity to save. In our example, the MPC was $\frac{4}{5}$; therefore, because MPC + MPS = 1, the MPS was equal to $\frac{1}{5}$. The reciprocal is 5. That was our multiplier. A $100 billion increase in real planned investment led to a $500 billion increase in the equilibrium level of real GDP. Our multiplier will always be the following:

$$\text{Multiplier} \equiv \frac{1}{1 - \text{MPC}} \equiv \frac{1}{\text{MPS}}$$

You can always figure out the multiplier if you know either the MPC or the MPS. Let's consider an example. If MPS = $\frac{1}{4}$,

$$\text{Multiplier} = \frac{1}{\frac{1}{4}} = 4$$

Because MPC + MPS = 1, it follows that MPS = 1 − MPC. Hence we can always figure out the multiplier if we are given the marginal propensity to consume. In this example, if the marginal propensity to consume is given as $\frac{3}{4}$,

$$\text{Multiplier} = \frac{1}{1 - \frac{3}{4}} = \frac{1}{\frac{1}{4}} = 4$$

By taking a few numerical examples, you can demonstrate to yourself an important property of the multiplier:

The smaller the marginal propensity to save, the larger the multiplier.

Otherwise stated:

The larger the marginal propensity to consume, the larger the multiplier.

Demonstrate this to yourself by computing the multiplier when the marginal propensity to save equals $\frac{3}{4}$, $\frac{1}{2}$, and $\frac{1}{4}$. What happens to the multiplier as the MPS gets smaller?

When you have the multiplier, the following formula will then give you the change in equilibrium real GDP due to a permanent change in autonomous spending:

$$\text{Change in equilibrium real GDP} = \text{multiplier} \times \text{change in autonomous spending}$$

The multiplier, as noted earlier, works for a permanent increase or a permanent decrease in autonomous spending. In our earlier example, if the autonomous component of consumption had fallen permanently by $100 billion, the reduction in equilibrium real GDP would have been $500 billion per year.

Significance of the Multiplier

Depending on the size of the multiplier, it is possible that a relatively small change in planned investment or in autonomous consumption can trigger a much larger change in equilibrium real GDP per year. In essence, the multiplier magnifies the fluctuations in equilibrium real GDP initiated by changes in autonomous spending.

As was just noted, the larger the marginal propensity to consume, the larger the multiplier. If the marginal propensity to consume is $\frac{1}{2}$, the multiplier is 2. In that case, a $1 billion decrease in (autonomous) real investment will elicit a $2 billion decrease in equilibrium real GDP per year. Conversely, if the marginal propensity to consume is $\frac{9}{10}$, the multiplier will be 10. That same $1 billion decrease in planned real investment expenditures with a multiplier of 10 will lead to a $10 billion decrease in equilibrium real GDP per year.

HOW A CHANGE IN REAL AUTONOMOUS SPENDING AFFECTS REAL GDP WHEN THE PRICE LEVEL CAN CHANGE

So far, our examination of how changes in real autonomous spending affect equilibrium real GDP has considered a situation in which the price level remains unchanged. Thus, our analysis has only indicated how much the aggregate demand curve shifts in response to a change in investment, government spending, net exports, or lump-sum taxes.

Of course, when we take into account the aggregate supply curve, we must also consider responses of the equilibrium price level to a multiplier-induced change in aggregate demand. We do so in Figure 12-7. The intersection of AD_1 and $SRAS$ is at a price level of

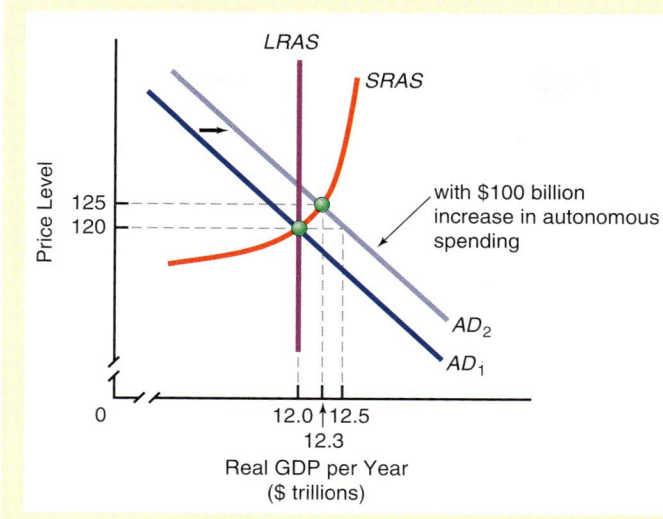

FIGURE 12-7

Effect of a Rise in Autonomous Spending on Equilibrium Real GDP

A $100 billion increase in autonomous spending (investment, government, or net exports), which moves AD_1 to AD_2. If the price index increases from 120 to 125, equilibrium real GDP goes up only to, say, $12.3 trillion per year instead of $12.5 trillion per year.

120 with equilibrium real GDP of $12 trillion per year. An increase in autonomous spending shifts the aggregate demand curve outward to the right to AD_2. If the price level remained at 120, the short-run equilibrium level of real GDP would increase to $12.5 trillion per year because, for the $100 billion increase in autonomous spending, the multiplier would be 5, as it was in Table 12-3.

The price level does not stay fixed, however, because ordinarily the *SRAS* curve is positively sloped. In this diagram, the new short-run equilibrium level of real GDP is hypothetically $12.3 trillion. Instead of the multiplier being 5, it is only 3. The ultimate effect on real GDP is smaller than the multiplier effect on nominal income because part of the additional income is used to pay higher prices. Not all is spent on additional goods and services, as is the case when the price level is fixed.

If the economy is at an equilibrium level of real GDP that is greater than *LRAS,* the implications for the eventual effect on real GDP are even more severe. Look again at Figure 12-7. The *SRAS* curve starts to slope upward more dramatically after $12 trillion of real GDP per year. Therefore, any increase in aggregate demand will lead to a proportionally greater increase in the price level and a smaller increase in equilibrium real GDP per year. The ultimate effect on real GDP of any increase in autonomous spending will be relatively small because most of the changes will be in the price level. Moreover, any increase in the short-run equilibrium level of real GDP will tend to be temporary because the economy is temporarily above *LRAS*—the strain on its productive capacity will raise the price level.

THE RELATIONSHIP BETWEEN AGGREGATE DEMAND AND THE $C + I + G + X$ CURVE

There is clearly a relationship between the aggregate demand curves that you studied in Chapters 10 and 11 and the $C + I + G + X$ curve developed in this chapter. After all, aggregate demand consists of consumption, investment, and government purchases, plus the foreign sector of our economy. There is a major difference, however, between the aggregate demand curve, *AD,* and the $C + I + G + X$ curve: The latter is drawn with the price level held constant, whereas the former is drawn, by definition, with the price level changing. To derive the aggregate demand curve from the $C + I + G + X$ curve, we must now allow the price level to change. Look at the upper part of Figure 12-8. Here we see the $C + I + G + X$ curve at a price level equal to 100, and at $12 trillion of real GDP per year, planned real expenditures exactly equal real GDP. This gives us point A in the lower graph, for it shows what real GDP would be at a price level of 100.

Now let's assume that in the upper graph, the price level increases to 125. What are the effects?

1. A higher price level can decrease the purchasing power of any cash that people hold (the real-balance effect). This is a decrease in real wealth, and it causes consumption expenditures, C, to fall, thereby putting downward pressure on the $C + I + G + X$ curve.
2. Because individuals attempt to borrow more to replenish their real cash balances, interest rates will rise, which will make it more costly for people to buy houses and cars (the interest rate effect). Higher interest rates make it less profitable, for example, to install new equipment and to erect new buildings. Therefore, the rise in the price level indirectly causes a reduction in total planned spending on goods and services.
3. In an open economy, our higher price level causes foreign spending on our goods to fall (the open economy effect). Simultaneously, it increases our demand for others' goods. If the foreign exchange price of the dollar stays constant for a while, there will be an increase in imports and a decrease in exports, thereby reducing the size of X, again putting downward pressure on the $C + I + G + X$ curve.

FIGURE 12-8

The Relationship Between AD and the $C + I + G + X$ Curve

In the upper graph, the $C + I + G + X$ curve at a price level equal to 100 intersects the 45-degree reference line at E_1 or $12 trillion of real GDP per year. That gives us point A (price level = 100; real GDP = $12 trillion) in the lower graph. When the price level increases to 125, the $C + I + G + X$ curve shifts downward, and the new level of real GDP at which planned real expenditures equal real GDP is at E_2 at $10 trillion per year. This gives us point B in the lower graph. Connecting points A and B, we obtain the aggregate demand curve.

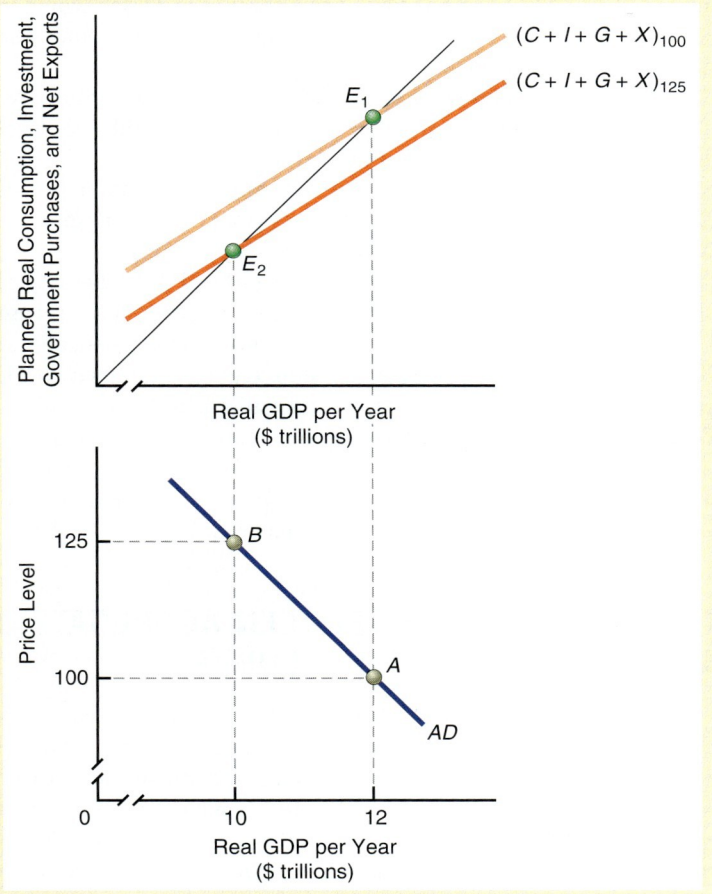

The result is that a new $C + I + G + X$ curve at a price level equal to 125 generates an equilibrium at E_2 at $10 trillion of real GDP per year. This gives us point B in the lower part of Figure 12-8. When we connect points A and B, we obtain the aggregate demand curve, AD.

QUICK QUIZ

Any change in autonomous spending shifts the expenditure curve and causes a _____ effect on equilibrium real GDP per year.

The **multiplier** is equal to the reciprocal of the _____ propensity to _____.

The smaller is the marginal propensity to _____, the larger is the **multiplier**. Otherwise stated, the larger is the marginal propensity to _____, the larger is the multiplier.

The $C + I + G + X$ curve is drawn with the price level held constant, whereas the AD curve allows the price level to _____. Each different price level generates a new $C + I + G + X$ curve.

See page 316 for the answers. Review concepts from this section in MyEconLab.

CASE STUDY — ECONOMICS FRONT AND CENTER

Considering an Investment in Internet Telephony

Sharma is the chief information officer (CIO) for a major department store chain. Managers and employees at various stores around the country contact each other by telephone every few minutes. Long-distance telephone rates have increased in recent years, and the retailer's top managers have asked Sharma to explore possible technological approaches to reducing the company's phone bills.

After considerable analysis by his staff, Sharma has found a potential long-term solution: an Internet telephone system. Sharma and his staff can link all the telephones throughout its chain using the firm's existing computer network. Special devices will convert voice signals into digital data that will then be transmitted through the network along with other computer traffic.

Sharma has put together a budget for the equipment required to install the proposed Internet phone system. Just a few minutes after he transmits the budget, Sharma learns that market interest rates increased that morning. He wonders if senior management will be as willing today as they would have been yesterday to approve the investment project he has proposed.

CRITICAL ANALYSIS QUESTIONS
1. What long-run return does Sharma's company stand to gain from a near-term investment in an Internet telephone system?
2. Why is Sharma justified in wondering if senior management might be less willing to invest in an Internet telephone system in light of the rise in market interest rates?

Issues and Applications

Is the U.S. Average Propensity to Save Really As Low As 0.01?

Concepts Applied
- Disposable Income
- Saving
- Average Propensity to Save

Most measures of U.S. saving have indicated a big drop-off in personal saving during the past 20 years. This has induced numerous politicians, businesspeople, Federal Reserve policymakers, and media analysts to engage in considerable hand-wringing about how the apparent lack of thrift might affect the U.S. economy. Some economists, however, question whether the saving *rate* really has fallen as much as official figures indicate.

The Personal Saving Rate

Government statisticians and the media often approximate the average propensity to save using the *personal saving rate*. To calculate the personal saving rate, government statisticians subtract household consumption from the government's measure of disposable personal income to obtain an official measure of personal saving. Then the statisticians divide this saving measure by the disposable personal income measure. This is, of course, how we compute the average propensity to save. Hence, the personal saving rate is an approximation of the APS for the United States.

The government's computation of the personal saving rate has yielded an approximate APS value close to 0.01 in recent years. Thus, according to the U.S. government, households in the United States on average save only 1 percent of their real disposable income.

Are Disposable Income and Saving Correctly Measured?

Some economists suggest that the government's calculation method seriously understates disposable income and saving. Disposable income, they contend, should include *changes* in the market values of household financial assets, which can be negative or positive. Counting positive changes in asset values as income would have increased the officially reported disposable income measure by as much as 10 percent.

In addition, these economists argue that saving should be measured as an addition to the stock of household savings instead of as a residual difference between disposable income and consumption. If saving were defined to equal *total* increases in the stock of household savings, including gains in the market values of household financial assets, then saving in recent years would have been much higher than reported. Indeed, according to some proposed measures of the personal saving rate that define disposable income and saving more broadly, the personal saving rate is actually closer to 0.20 than to 0.01.

Log in to **MyEconLab**, click on "Economic News," and test your understanding of the chapter by answering interactive questions that relate directly to this issue.

For Critical Analysis

1. If critics are correct that the economy's "actual" APS is really larger than the official APS, then how much smaller is the "actual" APC than the official APC?

2. Why do you suppose that the government calculates saving as a residual difference between disposable income and consumption instead of computing consumption as a residual difference between disposable income and saving? (Hint: Which do you think is likely to be easier to measure—total household expenditures on goods and services or total household saving?)

Web Resources

1. Take a look at the latest official figures on the personal saving rate at **www.econtoday.com/ch12**.

2. For a more detailed discussion of measurement problems associated with the government's saving rate measure, go to **www.econtoday.com/ch12**.

Research Project

Does the government's official personal saving rate assist in any way in determining how much a given change in total planned expenditures is likely to affect equilibrium real GDP? Under what condition could errors in official measures of disposable income and saving affect the calculation of how much a given change in total planned expenditures will affect equilibrium real GDP? (Hint: Given that the multiplier equals 1/MPS, how could measurement errors in disposable income and saving affect the measured value of the multiplier?)

WHAT YOU SHOULD KNOW		WHERE TO GO TO PRACTICE

The Difference Between Saving and Savings and the Relationship Between Saving and Consumption Saving is a flow over time, whereas savings is a stock of resources at a point in time. Thus, the portion of your disposable income that you do not consume during a week, a month, or a year is an addition to your stock of savings. By definition, saving during a year plus consumption during that year must equal total disposable (after-tax) income earned that year.

real disposable income, 288
consumption, 288
saving, 288
consumption goods, 288
investment, 289
capital goods, 289

- **MyEconLab** Study Plan 12.1
- Audio introduction to Chapter 12

Key Determinants of Consumption and Saving in the Keynesian Model In the classical model, the interest rate is the fundamental determinant of saving, but in the Keynesian model, the primary determinant is disposable income. The reason is that as real disposable income increases, so do real consumption expenditures. Because consumption and saving equal disposable income, this means that saving must also vary with changes in disposable income. Of course, factors other than disposable income can affect consumption and saving. The portion of consumption that is not related to disposable income is called autonomous consumption. The ratio of saving to disposable income is the average propensity to save (APS), and the ratio of consumption to disposable income is the average propensity to consume (APC). A change in saving divided by the corresponding change in disposable income is the marginal propensity to save (MPS), and a change in consumption divided by the corresponding change in disposable income is the marginal propensity to consume (MPC).

consumption function, 290
dissaving, 290
45-degree reference line, 291
autonomous consumption, 292
average propensity to consume (APC), 293
average propensity to save (APS), 293
marginal propensity to consume (MPC), 293
marginal propensity to save (MPS), 293
wealth, 295
Key figure
Figure 12-1, 292

- **MyEconLab** Study Plan 12.2
- Video: The Marginal Propensity to Consume
- Animated Figure 12-1

The Primary Determinants of Planned Investment An increase in the interest rate reduces the profitability of investment, so planned investment varies inversely with the interest rate. Hence the investment schedule slopes downward. Other factors that influence planned investment, such as business expectations, productive technology, or business taxes, can cause the investment schedule to shift. In the basic Keynesian model, changes in real GDP do not affect planned investment, meaning that investment is autonomous with respect to real GDP.

- **MyEconLab** Study Plan 12.3

WHAT YOU SHOULD KNOW		WHERE TO GO TO PRACTICE
How Equilibrium Real GDP Is Established in the Keynesian Model In equilibrium, total planned real consumption, investment, government, and net export expenditures equal real GDP, so $C + I + G + X = Y$. This occurs at the point where the $C + I + G + X$ curve crosses the 45-degree reference line. In a world without government spending and taxes, equilibrium also occurs when planned saving is equal to planned investment. Furthermore, at equilibrium real GDP, there is no tendency for business inventories to expand or contract.	lump-sum tax, 302 **Key figure** Figure 12-5, 300	• **MyEconLab** Study Plans 12.4 and 12.5 • Animated Figure 12-5
Why Autonomous Changes in Total Planned Real Expenditures Have a Multiplier Effect on Equilibrium Real GDP Any increase in autonomous expenditures, such as an increase in investment caused by a rise in business confidence, causes a direct rise in real GDP. The resulting increase in disposable income in turn stimulates increased consumption, and the amount of this increase is the marginal propensity to consume multiplied by the rise in disposable income that results. As consumption increases, however, so does real GDP, which induces a further increase in consumption spending. The ultimate expansion of real GDP is equal to the multiplier, $1/(1 - MPC)$ times the increase in autonomous expenditures. Because $MPS \equiv 1 - MPC$, the multiplier can also be written as $1/MPS$.	multiplier, 304 **Key table** Table 12-3, 305	• **MyEconLab** Study Plan 12.6 • Animated Table 12-3 • Video: The Multiplier
The Relationship Between Total Planned Expenditures and the Aggregate Demand Curve An increase in the price level decreases the purchasing power of cash holdings, which induces households and businesses to cut back on expenditures. In addition, as individuals and firms seek to borrow to replenish their cash balances, the interest rate tends to rise, which further discourages spending. Furthermore, a higher price level reduces exports as foreign residents cut back on purchases of domestically produced goods. These combined effects shift the $C + I + G + X$ curve downward following a rise in the price level, so that equilibrium real GDP falls. This yields the downward-sloping aggregate demand curve.	**Key figures** Figure 12-7, 307 Figure 12-8, 308	• **MyEconLab** Study Plans 12.7 and 12.8 • Animated Figures 12-7 and 12-8

Log in to MyEconLab, take a chapter test, and get a personalized Study Plan that tells you which concepts you understand and which ones you need to review. From there, MyEconLab will give you further practice, tutorials, animations, videos, and guided solutions.

Log in to www.myeconlab.com

PROBLEMS

Select problems, indicated by a blue oval, are assignable in MyEconLab.
Answers to the odd-numbered problems appear at the back of the book.

12-1 Examine the accompanying table.

Disposable Income	Saving	Consumption
$ 200	−$ 40	_____
400	0	_____
600	40	_____
800	80	_____
1,000	120	_____
1,200	160	_____

a. Complete the table.
b. Add two columns to the right of the table. Calculate the average propensity to save and the average propensity to consume at each level of disposable income. (Round to the nearest hundredth.)
c. Determine the marginal propensity to save and the marginal propensity to consume.

12-2 Classify each of the following as either a stock or a flow.

a. Myung Park earns $850 per week.
b. Time Warner purchases $100 million in new computer equipment this month.
c. Sally Schmidt has $1,000 in a savings account at a credit union.
d. XYZ, Inc., produces 200 units of output per week.
e. Giorgio Giannelli owns three private jets.
f. DaimlerChrysler's inventories decline by 750 autos per month.
g. Russia owes $25 billion to the International Monetary Fund.

12-3 Suppose that Apple is studying whether to undertake an investment of $100 million in new plants for manufacturing the newest version of the iPod and additional space to in-house developers of the latest generation of its iTunes music software. Apple's managers project an annual rate of return on this investment of 5.7 percent per year.

a. The current market interest rate is 5.1 percent per year. Will Apple undertake the investment?
b. Suddenly, there is an economic downturn. Although the market interest rate does not change, Apple changes the projected rate of return on the investment to only 4.8 percent per year. Will Apple now undertake the investment?

12-4 Consider the table at the end of this problem when answering the following questions. For this hypothetical economy, the marginal propensity to save is constant at all levels of real GDP, and investment spending is autonomous. There is no government.

a. Complete the table. What is the marginal propensity to save? What is the marginal propensity to consume?
b. Draw a graph of the consumption function. Then add the investment function to obtain $C + I$.
c. Under the graph of $C + I$, draw another graph showing the saving and investment curves. Note that the $C + I$ curve crosses the 45-degree reference line in the upper graph at the same level of real GDP where the saving and investment curves cross in the lower graph. (If not, redraw your graphs.) What is this level of real GDP?
d. What is the numerical value of the multiplier?
e. What is equilibrium real GDP without investment? What is the multiplier effect from the inclusion of investment?
f. What is the average propensity to consume at equilibrium real GDP?
g. If autonomous investment declines from $400 to $200, what happens to equilibrium real GDP?

Real GDP	Consumption	Saving	Investment
$ 2,000	$2,200	$_____	$400
4,000	4,000	_____	_____
6,000		_____	_____
8,000		_____	_____
10,000		_____	_____
12,000		_____	_____

12-5 Consider the table on the next page when answering the following questions. For this hypothetical economy, the marginal propensity to consume is constant at all levels of real GDP, and investment spending is autonomous. Equilibrium real GDP is equal to $8,000. There is no government.

Real GDP	Consumption	Saving	Investment
$ 2,000	$ 2,000	_____	_____
4,000	3,600	_____	_____
6,000	5,200	_____	_____
8,000	6,800	_____	_____
10,000	8,400	_____	_____
12,000	10,000	_____	_____

Real GDP (Y)	Average Propensity to Consume (APC)	Average Propensity to Save (APS)
$10,000	_____	_____
11,000	_____	_____
12,000	_____	_____
13,000	_____	_____
14,000	_____	_____
15,000	_____	_____

a. Complete the table. What is the marginal propensity to consume? What is the marginal propensity to save?
b. Draw a graph of the consumption function. Then add the investment function to obtain $C + I$.
c. Under the graph of $C + I$, draw another graph showing the saving and investment curves. Does the $C + I$ curve cross the 45-degree reference line in the upper graph at the same level of real GDP where the saving and investment curves cross in the lower graph, at the equilibrium real GDP of $8,000? (If not, redraw your graphs.)
d. What is the average propensity to save at equilibrium real GDP?
e. If autonomous consumption were to rise by $100, what would happen to equilibrium real GDP?

12-6 Calculate the multiplier for the following cases.
a. MPS = 0.25
b. MPC = $\frac{5}{6}$
c. MPS = 0.125
d. MPC = $\frac{6}{7}$
e. $C = \$200 + 0.9Y$

12-7 A nation's consumption function (expressed in millions of inflation-adjusted dollars) is $C = \$800 + 0.80Y$. There are no taxes in this nation.
a. What is the value of autonomous saving?
b. What is the marginal propensity to save in this economy?
c. What is the value of the multiplier?

12-8 Based on the information in Problem 12-7, complete the following table. (Round all decimal fractions to the nearest hundredth.)

12-9 Assume that the multiplier in a country is equal to 4 and that autonomous real consumption spending is $1 trillion. If current real GDP is $12 trillion, what is the current value of real consumption spending?

12-10 The multiplier in a country is equal to 5, and households pay no taxes. At the current equilibrium real GDP of $14 trillion, total real consumption spending by households is $12 trillion. What is real autonomous consumption in this country?

12-11 At an initial point on the aggregate demand curve, the price level is 125, and real GDP is $10 trillion. When the price level falls to a value of 120, total autonomous expenditures increase by $250 billion. The marginal propensity to consume is 0.75. What is the level of real GDP at the new point on the aggregate demand curve?

12-12 At an initial point on the aggregate demand curve, the price level is 100, and real GDP is $12 trillion. After the price level rises to 110, however, there is an upward movement along the aggregate demand curve, and real GDP declines to $11 trillion. If total autonomous spending declined by $200 billion in response to the increase in the price level, what is the marginal propensity to consume in this economy?

12-13 In an economy in which the multiplier has a value of 3, the price level has decreased from 115 to 110. As a consequence, there has been a movement along the aggregate demand curve from $12 trillion in real GDP to $12.9 trillion in real GDP.
a. What is the marginal propensity to save?
b. What was the amount of the change in autonomous expenditures generated by the decline in the price level?

12-14 Consider the accompanying diagram, which applies to a nation with no government spending, taxes, and net exports. Use the information in the diagram to answer the questions below, and explain your answers.

a. What is the marginal propensity to save?
b. What is the present level of planned investment spending for the present period?
c. What is the equilibrium level of real GDP for the present period?
d. What is the equilibrium level of saving for the present period?
e. If planned investment spending for the present period increases by $25 billion, what will be the resulting *change* in equilibrium real GDP? What will be the new equilibrium level of real GDP if other things, including the price level, remain unchanged?

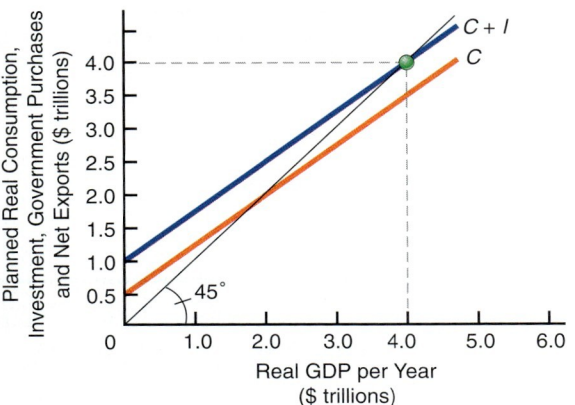

ECONOMICS ON THE NET

The Relationship Between Consumption and Real GDP
According to the basic consumption function we considered in this chapter, consumption rises at a fixed rate when both disposable income and real GDP increase. Your task here is to evaluate how reasonable this assumption is and to determine the relative extent to which variations in consumption appear to be related to variations in real GDP.

Title: Gross Domestic Product and Components

Navigation: Use the link at **www.econtoday.com/ch12** to visit the Federal Reserve Bank of St. Louis's Web page on *Gross Domestic Product and Components*.

Application

1. Scan down the alphabetical list, and click on *Personal Consumption Expenditure (Bil. of $; Q)*. Then click on "Download Data." Write down consumption expenditures for the past eight quarters. Now back up to *Gross Domestic Product and Components*, click on *Gross Domestic Product, 1 Decimal (Bil. $; Q)*, click on "Download Data," and write down GDP for the past eight quarters. Use these data to calculate implied values for the marginal propensity to consume, assuming that taxes do not vary with income. Is there any problem with this assumption?

2. Back up to *Gross Domestic Product and Components*. Now click on *Gross Domestic Product: Implicit Price Deflator*. Scan through the data since the mid-1960s. In what years did the largest variations in GDP take place? What component or components of GDP appear to have accounted for these large movements?

For Group Study and Analysis Assign groups to use the FRED database to try to determine the best measure of aggregate U.S. disposable income for the past eight quarters. Reconvene as a class, and discuss each group's approach to this issue.

ANSWERS TO QUICK QUIZZES

p. 290: (i) horizontal; (ii) Saving . . . Savings; (iii) Investment
p. 295: (i) disposable income . . . consumption; (ii) average . . . average; (iii) marginal . . . marginal; (iv) movement along . . . shift in
p. 297: (i) interest rate . . . downward; (ii) expectations . . . business taxes; (iii) shift in
p. 301: (i) autonomous . . . autonomous; (ii) autonomous; (iii) equilibrium; (iv) accumulation . . . depletion
p. 304: (i) planned expenditures; (ii) 45-degree; (iii) decreases . . . increases
p. 309: (i) multiplier; (ii) marginal . . . save; (iii) save . . . consume; (iv) change

The Keynesian Cross and the Multiplier — Appendix B

We can see the multiplier effect more clearly if we look at Figure B-1, in which we see only a small section of the graphs that we used in Chapter 12. We start with equilibrium real GDP of $11.5 trillion per year. This equilibrium occurs with total planned real expenditures represented by $C + I + G + X$. The $C + I + G + X$ curve intersects the 45-degree reference line at $11.5 trillion per year. Now we increase real investment, I, by $100 billion. This increase in investment shifts the entire $C + I + G + X$ curve vertically to $C + I' + G + X$. The vertical shift represents that $100 billion increase in autonomous investment. With the higher level of planned expenditures per year, we are no longer in equilibrium at E. Inventories are falling. Production of goods and services will increase as firms try to replenish their inventories. Eventually, real GDP will catch up with total planned expenditures. The new equilibrium level of real GDP is established at E' at the intersection of the new $C + I' + G + X$ curve and the 45-degree reference line, along which $C + I + G + X = Y$ (total planned expenditures equal real GDP). The new equilibrium level of real GDP is $12 trillion per year. Thus, the increase in equilibrium real GDP is equal to five times the permanent increase in planned investment spending.

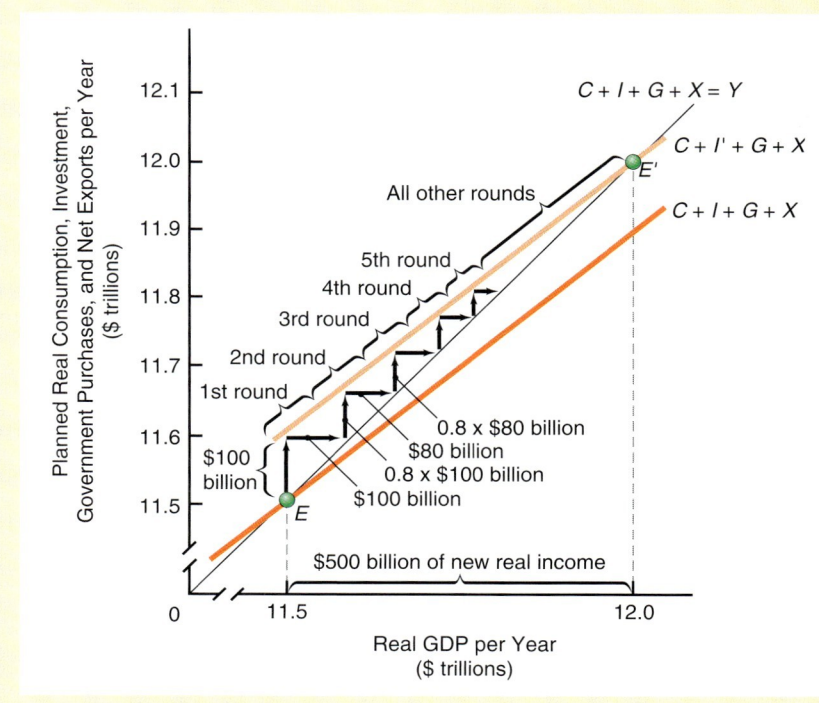

FIGURE B-1

Graphing the Multiplier

We can translate Table 12-3 on page 305 into graphic form by looking at each successive round of additional spending induced by an autonomous increase in planned investment of $100 billion. The total planned expenditures curve shifts from $C + I + G + X$, with its associated equilibrium level of real GDP of $11.5 trillion, to a new curve labeled $C + I' + G + X$. The new equilibrium level of real GDP is $12 trillion. Equilibrium is again established.

13 Fiscal Policy

Learning Objectives

After reading this chapter, you should be able to:

1. Use traditional Keynesian analysis to evaluate the effects of discretionary fiscal policies
2. Discuss ways in which indirect crowding out and direct expenditure offsets can reduce the effectiveness of fiscal policy actions
3. Explain why the Ricardian equivalence theorem calls into question the usefulness of tax changes
4. List and define fiscal policy time lags and explain why they complicate efforts to engage in fiscal "fine-tuning"
5. Describe how certain aspects of fiscal policy function as automatic stabilizers for the economy

MyEconLab helps you master each objective and study more efficiently. See end of chapter for details.

During the late 1990s, the government of Japan sought to boost the nation's total planned expenditures by increasing government spending and reducing taxes. In the early 2000s, it aimed to achieve additional increases in total planned spending through a series of tax cuts. By early 2004, however, the government had reversed course and launched plans to implement phased-in tax increases. Then, in the middle of 2005, the Japanese government began contemplating reversing itself once again and cutting taxes after all. Was the Japanese government simply fickle, or did it face deeper problems in trying to sort out its tax policies during the 2000s? In this chapter, you will learn about policy time lags, which contributed to the Japanese government's on-again, off-again tax policies.

Did You Know That...

the amount of government expenditures per U.S. resident per day, measured in 2006 dollars, has increased by more than 400 percent since 1948? In 1948, the combined daily spending per capita of U.S. state, local, and federal governments was about $6 (measured in 2006 dollars). Today, government expenditures per person per day exceed $30.

Since the early 2000s, total government spending has increased at a rate of about 8 percent per year, the largest annual rate of growth since the 1940s and 1950s. A relatively small portion of this increase in government spending was used to step up antiterrorism efforts and other forms of defense spending. Not all of this new defense spending really did much to aid national security. During 2004, for instance, the U.S. Department of Defense purchased 270,000 refundable commercial airline tickets worth $100 million that were never used and for which no refunds were requested.

The biggest government spending increases were in discretionary, nondefense expenditures, which rose by more than 25 percent. They included funding for such items as the Whaling Museum in New Bedford, Massachusetts; an indoor rain forest in Coralville, Iowa; and the National Cowgirl Museum and Hall of Fame in Ft. Worth, Texas. In addition, as you read this, Congress is considering plans to use government funds to construct a bridge in Alaska that is 80 feet higher than the Brooklyn Bridge and only 20 feet shorter than the Golden Gate Bridge. The proposed Alaska bridge would connect a village of 7,845 people to an island where 50 people reside.

In this chapter, you will learn about the consequences of higher government spending for equilibrium real GDP and the price level. You will also consider the macroeconomic effects of changes in the tax revenues used to fund most public spending.

DISCRETIONARY FISCAL POLICY

The making of deliberate, discretionary changes in government expenditures or taxes (or both) to achieve certain national economic goals is the realm of **fiscal policy.** Some national goals are high employment (low unemployment), price stability, economic growth, and improvement in the nation's international payments balance. Fiscal policy can be thought of as a deliberate attempt to cause the economy to move to full employment and price stability more quickly than it otherwise might.

Fiscal policy has typically been associated with the economic theories of John Maynard Keynes and what is now called *traditional* Keynesian analysis. Recall from Chapter 11 that Keynes's explanation of the Great Depression was that there was insufficient aggregate demand. Because he believed that wages and prices were "sticky downward," he argued that the classical economists' picture of an economy moving automatically and quickly toward full employment was inaccurate. To Keynes and his followers, government had to step in to increase aggregate demand. Expansionary fiscal policy initiated by the federal government was the way to ward off recessions and depressions.

Changes in Government Spending

In Chapter 11, we looked at the recessionary gap and the inflationary gap (see Figures 11-11 and 11-12 on pages 274 and 275). The recessionary gap was defined as the amount by which the current level of real GDP fell short of the economy's potential production if it were operating on its *LRAS* curve. The inflationary gap was defined as the amount by which the short-run equilibrium level of real GDP exceeds the long-run equilibrium level as given by *LRAS*. Let us examine fiscal policy first in the context of a recessionary gap.

> **Fiscal policy**
> The discretionary changing of government expenditures or taxes to achieve national economic goals, such as high employment with price stability.

FIGURE 13-1
Expansionary and Contractionary Fiscal Policy: Changes in Government Spending

If there is a recessionary gap and short-run equilibrium is at E_1, in panel (a), fiscal policy can presumably increase aggregate demand to AD_2. The new equilibrium is at E_2 at higher real GDP per year and a higher price level. In panel (b), the economy is at short-run equilibrium at E_1, which is at a higher real GDP than the LRAS. To reduce this inflationary gap, fiscal policy can be used to decrease aggregate demand from AD_1 to AD_2. Eventually, equilibrium will fall to E_2, which is on the LRAS.

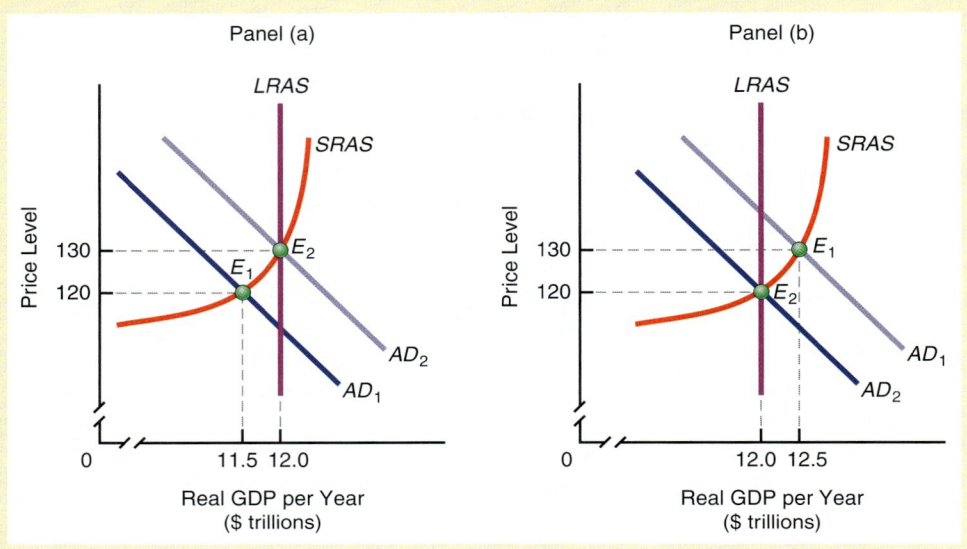

When There Is a Recessionary Gap.
The government, along with firms, individuals, and foreign residents, is one of the spending agents in the economy. When the government decides to spend more, all other things held constant, the dollar value of total spending must rise. Look at panel (a) of Figure 13-1. We begin by assuming that some negative shock in the near past has left the economy at point E_1, which is a short-run equilibrium in which AD_1 intersects SRAS at $11.5 trillion of real GDP per year. There is a recessionary gap of $500 billion of real GDP per year—the difference between LRAS (the economy's long-run potential) and the short-run equilibrium level of real GDP per year. When the government decides to spend more (expansionary fiscal policy), the aggregate demand curve shifts to the right to AD_2. Here we assume that the government knows exactly how much more to spend so that AD_2 intersects SRAS at $12 trillion, or at LRAS. Because of the upward-sloping SRAS, the price level rises from 120 to 130 as real GDP goes to $12 trillion per year.

When There Is an Inflationary Gap.
The entire process shown in panel (a) of Figure 13-1 can be reversed, as shown in panel (b). There, we assume that a recent shock has left the economy at point E_1, at which an inflationary gap exists at the intersection of SRAS and AD_1. Real GDP cannot be sustained at $12.5 trillion indefinitely, because this exceeds long-run aggregate supply, which in real terms is $12 trillion. If the government recognizes this and reduces its spending (pursues a contractionary fiscal policy), this action reduces aggregate demand from AD_1 to AD_2. Equilibrium will fall to E_2 on the LRAS, where real GDP per year is $12 trillion. The price level will fall from 130 to 120.

Changes in Taxes

The spending decisions of firms, individuals, and foreign residents depend on the taxes levied on them. Individuals in their role as consumers look to their disposable (after-tax) income when determining their desired rates of consumption. Firms look at their after-tax profits when deciding on the levels of investment to undertake. Foreign residents look at the tax-inclusive cost of goods when deciding whether to buy in the United States or elsewhere. Therefore, holding all other things constant, a rise in taxes causes a reduction in aggregate demand because it reduces consumption, investment, or net exports. What actually happens depends, of course, on the parties on whom the taxes are levied.

Why is a tax that was originally intended to be levied on only the highest-income households increasingly being paid by middle-income households?

POLICY EXAMPLE

A Millionaire Tax Morphs into a Tax on Middle-Income Workers

In 1969, after learning that 21 people with annual incomes exceeding $1 million (more than $4 million in today's dollars) had paid no income taxes, Congress created the *alternative minimum tax (AMT)*. It designed this tax to affect high-income taxpayers whose tax forms included numerous special deductions and credits, which were mechanisms that high-income people had used to avoid taxes in the 1960s.

Any individual taxpayers who have filled out the so-called long form for personal income tax must also complete a special worksheet to determine if they owe the AMT. If so, then instead of paying the income tax indicated by the regular tax form, they must pay the higher AMT.

When Congress created the AMT in 1969, it failed to take inflation into account. Over the intervening years, inflation has pushed up nominal incomes, so that nominal incomes that were "high" in 1969 are in the "middle" today. In addition, since then Congress has added numerous deductions and exemptions intended to benefit middle-income taxpayers. Both factors have had the effect of imposing the AMT on more middle-income taxpayers. At present, more than 4 million taxpayers must pay the AMT, but estimates indicate that by 2010 this number could rise to more than 30 million taxpayers.

FOR CRITICAL ANALYSIS
Other things being equal, how has the broader applicability of the higher AMT likely affected aggregate demand in the United States?

When the Current Short-Run Equilibrium Is to the Right of LRAS.
Assume that aggregate demand is AD_1 in panel (a) of Figure 13-2 on the following page. It intersects SRAS at E_1, which yields real GDP greater than LRAS. In this situation, an increase in taxes shifts the aggregate demand curve inward to the left. For argument's sake, assume that it intersects SRAS at E_2, or exactly where LRAS intersects AD_2. In this situation, the level of real GDP falls from $12.5 trillion per year to $12 trillion per year. The price level falls from 120 to 100.

When the Current Short-Run Equilibrium Is to the Left of LRAS.
Look at panel (b) in Figure 13-2. AD_1 intersects SRAS at E_1, with real GDP at $11.5 trillion, less than the LRAS of $12 trillion. In this situation, a decrease in taxes shifts the aggregate demand curve outward to the right. At AD_2, equilibrium is established at E_2, with the price level at 120 and equilibrium real GDP at $12 trillion per year.

FIGURE 13-2
Contractionary and Expansionary Fiscal Policy: Changes in Taxes

In panel (a), the economy is initially at E_1, where real GDP exceeds long-run equilibrium real GDP. Contractionary fiscal policy via a tax increase can move aggregate demand to AD_2 so that the new equilibrium is at E_2 at a lower price level. Real GDP is now consistent with *LRAS*, which eliminates the inflationary gap. In panel (b), with a recessionary gap (in this case of $500 billion), taxes are cut. AD_1 moves to AD_2. The economy moves from E_1 to E_2, and real GDP is now at $12 trillion per year, the long-run equilibrium level.

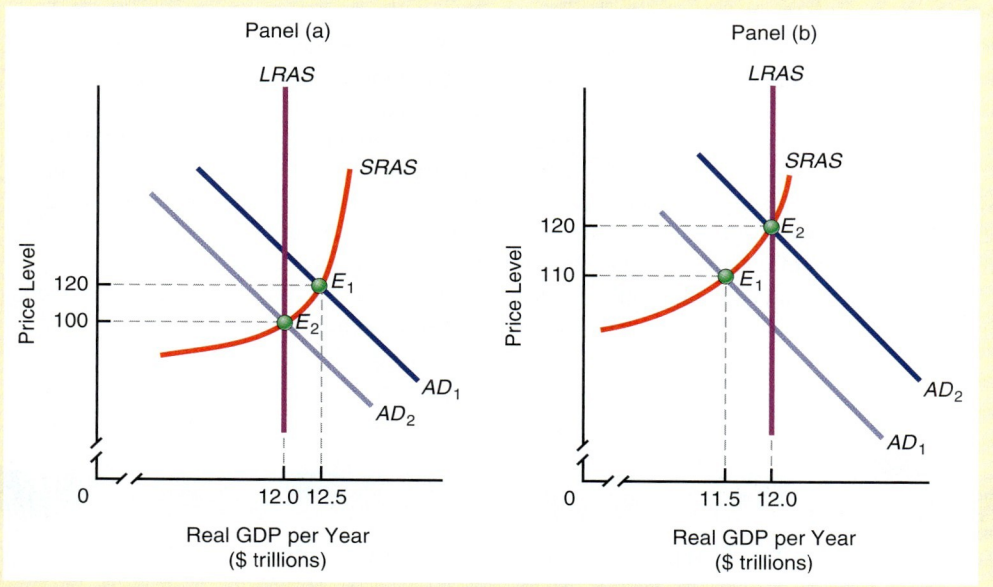

QUICK QUIZ

Fiscal policy is defined as making discretionary changes in government _____ or _____ to achieve such national goals as high employment or reduced inflation.

To address a situation in which there is a(n) _____ gap and the economy is operating at less than long-run aggregate supply (*LRAS*), the government can _____ its spending and thereby shift the aggregate demand curve to the right, causing real GDP per year to increase.

To address a situation in which there is a(n) _____ gap, the government can _____ its spending and cause the aggregate demand curve to shift to the left, which reduces the equilibrium level of real GDP per year.

Changes in taxes can have similar effects on the equilibrium rate of real GDP and the price level. A(n) _____ in taxes can lead to an increase in the equilibrium level of real GDP per year. In contrast, if there is an inflationary gap, a(n) _____ in taxes can decrease equilibrium real GDP.

See page 338 for the answers. Review concepts from this section in MyEconLab.

POSSIBLE OFFSETS TO FISCAL POLICY

Fiscal policy does not operate in a vacuum. Important questions have to be answered: If government expenditures increase, how are those expenditures financed, and by whom? If taxes are increased, what does the government do with the taxes? What will happen if individuals worry about increases in *future* taxes because the government is spending more today without raising current taxes? All of these questions involve *offsets* to the effects of fiscal policy. We will look at each of them and others in detail.

Indirect Crowding Out

Let's take the first example of fiscal policy in this chapter—an increase in government expenditures. If government expenditures rise and taxes are held constant, something has to give. Our government does not simply take goods and services when it wants them. It has to pay for them. When it pays for them and does not simultaneously collect the same amount in taxes, it must borrow. That means that an increase in government spending without raising taxes creates additional government borrowing from the private sector (or from foreign residents).

Induced Interest Rate Changes.
Holding everything else constant, if the government attempts to borrow more from the private sector to pay for its increased budget deficit, it is not going to have an easy time selling its bonds. If the bond market is in equilibrium, when the government tries to sell more bonds, it is going to have to offer a better deal in order to get rid of them. A better deal means offering a higher interest rate. This is the interest rate effect of expansionary fiscal policy financed by borrowing from the public. Consequently, when the federal government finances increased spending by additional borrowing, it will push interest rates up. When interest rates go up, it is less profitable for firms to finance new construction, equipment, and inventories. It is also more expensive for individuals to finance purchases of cars and homes.

Thus, a rise in government spending, holding taxes constant (that is, deficit spending), tends to crowd out private spending, dampening the positive effect of increased government spending on aggregate demand. This is called the **crowding-out effect.** In the extreme case, the crowding out may be complete, with the increased government spending having no net effect on aggregate demand. The final result is simply more government spending and less private investment and consumption. Figure 13-3 shows how the crowding-out effect occurs.

Crowding-out effect
The tendency of expansionary fiscal policy to cause a decrease in planned investment or planned consumption in the private sector; this decrease normally results from the rise in interest rates.

The Firm's Investment Decision.
To understand the interest rate effect better, consider a firm that is contemplating borrowing $100,000 to expand its business. Suppose that the interest rate is 5 percent. The interest payments on the debt will be 5 percent times $100,000, or $5,000 per year ($417 per month). A rise in the interest rate to 8 percent will push the payments to 8 percent of $100,000, or $8,000 per year ($667 per month). The extra $250 per month in interest expenses will discourage some firms from making the investment. Consumers face similar decisions when they purchase houses and

FIGURE 13-3
The Crowding-Out Effect, Step by Step

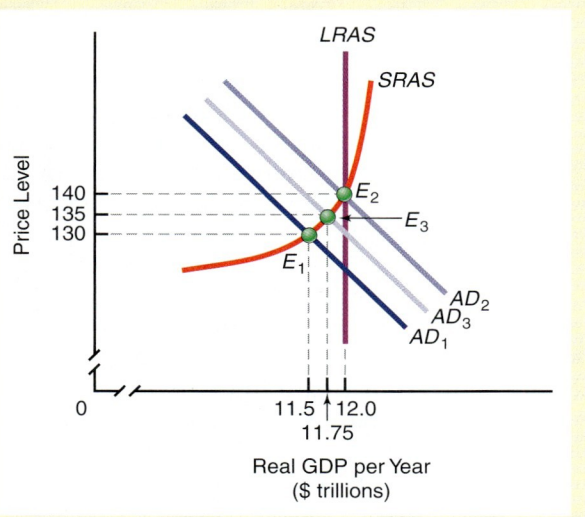

FIGURE 13-4

The Crowding-Out Effect

Expansionary fiscal policy that causes deficit financing initially shifts AD_1 to AD_2. Equilibrium initially moves toward E_2. But expansionary fiscal policy pushes up interest rates, thereby reducing interest-sensitive spending. This effect causes the aggregate demand curve to shift inward to AD_3, and the new short-run equilibrium is at E_3.

cars. An increase in the interest rate causes their monthly payments to go up, thereby discouraging some of them from purchasing cars and houses.

Graphical Analysis. You see in Figure 13-4 that the economy is in a situation in which, at point E_1, equilibrium real GDP is below the long-run level consistent with the position of the *LRAS* curve. But suppose that government expansionary fiscal policy in the form of increased government spending (without increasing current taxes) attempts to shift aggregate demand from AD_1 to AD_2. In the absence of the crowding-out effect, real GDP would increase to $12 trillion per year, and the price level would rise to 140 (point E_2). With the (partial) crowding-out effect, however, as investment and consumption decline, partly offsetting the rise in government spending, the aggregate demand curve shifts inward to the left to AD_3. The new equilibrium is now at E_3, with real GDP of $11.75 trillion per year at a price level of 135. In other words, crowding out dilutes the effect of expansionary fiscal policy, and a recessionary gap remains.

Planning for the Future: The Ricardian Equivalence Theorem

Economists have often implicitly assumed that people look at changes in taxes or changes in government spending only in the present. What if people actually think about the size of *future* tax payments? Does this have an effect on how they react to an increase in government spending with no current tax increases? Some economists believe that the answer is yes. What if people's horizons extend beyond this year? Don't we then have to take into account the effects of today's government policies on the future?

Consider an example. The government wants to reduce taxes by $100 billion today. Assume that government spending remains constant. Assume further that the government initially has a balanced budget. Thus, the only way for the government to pay for this $100 billion tax cut is to borrow $100 billion today. The public will owe $100 billion plus interest later. Realizing that a $100 billion tax cut today is mathematically equivalent to $100 billion plus interest later, people may wish to save the tax cut to meet future tax liabilities—payment of interest and repayment of debt.

Consequently, a tax cut may not affect total planned expenditures. A reduction in taxes without a reduction in government spending may therefore have no impact on aggregate demand.

Similarly, increased government spending without an increase in taxes may not have a large impact on aggregate demand. Suppose that an increase in government spending shifts the aggregate demand curve from AD_1 to AD_2 in Figure 13-4. If consumers partly compensate for a higher future tax liability by saving more, the aggregate demand curve shifts leftward, to a position such as AD_3. In the extreme case in which individuals fully take into account their increased tax liabilities, the aggregate demand curve shifts all the way back to AD_1, so that there is literally no effect on the economy. This is known as the **Ricardian equivalence theorem,** after the nineteenth-century economist David Ricardo, who first developed the argument publicly.

For economists who believe in the Ricardian equivalence theorem, it does not matter how government expenditures are financed—by taxes or by issuing debt. Is the theorem correct? Research indicates that Ricardian equivalence effects likely exist but has not provided much compelling evidence about their magnitudes.

Ricardian equivalence theorem
The proposition that an increase in the government budget deficit has no effect on aggregate demand.

Direct Expenditure Offsets

Government has a distinct comparative advantage over the private sector in certain activities such as diplomacy and national defense. Otherwise stated, certain resource-using activities in which the government engages do not compete with the private sector. In contrast, some of what government does, such as education, competes directly with the private sector. When government competes with the private sector, **direct expenditure offsets** to fiscal policy may occur. For example, if the government starts providing milk at no charge to students who are already purchasing milk, there is a direct expenditure offset. Households that do not wish to consume more milk at the same price spend less directly on milk, but government spends more.

Normally, the impact of an increase in government spending on aggregate demand is analyzed by implicitly assuming that government spending is *not* a substitute for private spending. This is clearly the case for a cruise missile. Whenever government spending is a substitute for private spending, however, a rise in government spending causes a direct reduction in private spending to offset it.

Direct expenditure offsets
Actions on the part of the private sector in spending income that offset government fiscal policy actions. Any increase in government spending in an area that competes with the private sector will have some direct expenditure offset.

The Extreme Case. In the extreme case, the direct expenditure offset is dollar for dollar, so we merely end up with a relabeling of spending from private to public. Assume that you have decided to spend $100 on groceries. Upon your arrival at the checkout counter, you find a U.S. Department of Agriculture official. She announces that she will pay for your groceries—but only the ones in the cart. Here increased government spending is $100. You leave the store in bliss. But just as you are deciding how to spend the $100, an Internal Revenue Service agent appears. He announces that as a result of the current budgetary crisis, your taxes are going to rise by $100. You have to pay right now. Increases in taxes have now been $100. We have a balanced-budget increase in government spending. In this scenario, *total* spending does not change. We simply end up with higher government spending, which directly offsets exactly an equal reduction in consumption. Aggregate demand and GDP are unchanged. Otherwise stated, if there is a full direct expenditure offset, the government spending multiplier is zero.

The Less Extreme Case. Much government spending has a private-sector substitute. When government expenditures increase, private spending tends to decline somewhat (but generally not dollar for dollar), thereby mitigating the upward impact on total aggregate demand. To the extent that there are some direct expenditure offsets to expansionary fiscal policy, predicted changes in aggregate demand will be lessened. Consequently, real GDP and the price level will be less affected.

Why does part of British government spending fail to generate much of an increase in aggregate demand within the United Kingdom?

INTERNATIONAL POLICY EXAMPLE

Britain Pays Up but Receives Little Economic Payoff

Nearly half of the spending side of the $100 billion budget of the European Union (EU) goes to farm subsidies, and about a third is spent on bridges and roads in the lowest-income EU nations. To fund these expenditures, the EU receives contributions from its member nations, including the United Kingdom. Each country's contribution to the EU budget is based on its real GDP as a share of the total real GDP of all 25 EU members.

Each member nation views its contribution as a portion of its own government spending. It is not always apparent, however, exactly what the British government purchases with its EU contribution. In relation to its real GDP, the United Kingdom is one of the smallest recipients of EU expenditures on farm subsidies or roads and bridges. Other things being equal, its net contribution to the EU budget would be 15 times larger than the net payment of France, even though France has a similar-sized economy, because France receives many more farm subsidies.

Because the United Kingdom would receive so little expenditure benefit from its contribution to the EU budget, since 1984 the EU has rebated a large portion of the British contribution back to the British government. Nevertheless, the United Kingdom still makes the third-highest *net* contribution to the EU budget, even though EU expenditures contribute so little to total planned spending in that nation.

FOR CRITICAL ANALYSIS
How do the taxes that British residents pay to fund their government's contribution to the EU budget affect aggregate demand in the United Kingdom?

The Supply-Side Effects of Changes in Taxes

We have talked about changing taxes and changing government spending, the traditional tools of fiscal policy. We have not really talked about the possibility of changing *marginal* tax rates. Recall from Chapter 6 that the marginal tax rate is the rate applied to the last, or highest, bracket of taxable income. In our federal tax system, higher marginal tax rates are applied as income rises. In that sense, the United States has a progressive federal individual income tax system. Expansionary fiscal policy could involve reducing marginal tax rates. Advocates of such changes argue that lower tax rates will lead to an increase in productivity because individuals will work harder and longer, save more, and invest more and that increased productivity will lead to more economic growth, which will lead to higher real GDP. The government, by applying lower marginal tax rates, will not necessarily lose tax revenues, for the lower marginal tax rates will be applied to a growing tax base because of economic growth—after all, tax revenues are the product of a tax rate times a tax base.

This relationship, which you may recall from the discussion of sales taxes in Chapter 6, is sometimes called the *Laffer curve,* named after economist Arthur Laffer, who explained the relationship to some journalists and politicians in 1974. It is reproduced in Figure 13-5. On the vertical axis are tax revenues, and on the horizontal axis is the marginal tax rate. As you can see, total tax revenues initially rise but then eventually fall as the tax rate continues to increase after reaching some unspecified tax-revenue-maximizing rate at the top of the curve.

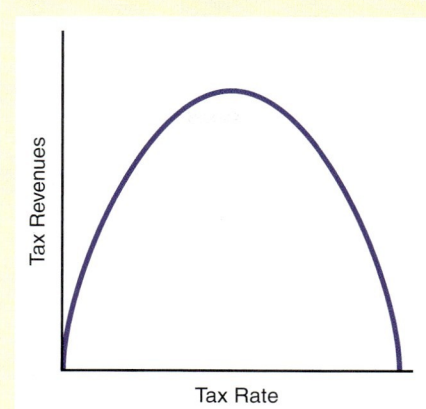

FIGURE 13-5
Laffer Curve
The Laffer curve indicates that tax revenues initially rise with a higher tax rate. Eventually, however, tax revenues decline as the tax rate increases.

People who support the notion that reducing taxes does not necessarily lead to reduced tax revenues are called supply-side economists. **Supply-side economics** involves changing the tax structure to create incentives to increase productivity. Due to a shift in the aggregate supply curve to the right, there can be greater real GDP without upward pressure on the price level.

Consider the supply-side effects of changes in marginal tax rates on labor. An increase in tax rates reduces the opportunity cost of leisure, thereby inducing individuals (at least on the margin) to reduce their work effort and to consume more leisure. But an increase in tax rates will also reduce spendable income, thereby shifting the demand curve for leisure inward to the left, which tends to increase work effort. The outcome of these two effects on the choice of leisure (and thus work) depends on which of them is stronger. Supply-side economists argue that at various times, the first effect has dominated: Increases in marginal tax rates have caused workers to work less, and decreases in marginal tax rates have caused workers to work more.

Is it possible that the U.S. economy was operating to the right of the top of the Laffer curve before the tax rate cuts of 2003?

Supply-side economics
The suggestion that creating incentives for individuals and firms to increase productivity will cause the aggregate supply curve to shift outward.

POLICY EXAMPLE

A Laffer Curve in the Mid-2000s?

In May 2003, at the urging of the administration of George W. Bush, Congress reduced the top tax rate on corporate dividends, from 39.6 percent to 15 percent, and the tax rate on capital gains, from 20 percent to 15 percent. In addition, Congress cut personal income tax rates slightly.

Many critics of the 2003 tax-rate cuts predicted that the federal government's tax revenues would plummet after the rates were cut. Nevertheless, by the middle of 2006, after three years of higher real GDP growth, total federal income tax receipts from corporations and individuals had increased by nearly 40 percent.

FOR CRITICAL ANALYSIS
Why do you suppose that it is difficult to determine exactly which factors are most responsible for increases or decreases in income tax revenues? (Hint: Income tax revenues depend on income, which in turn varies with equilibrium real GDP, which in turn changes with variations in aggregate demand and aggregate supply.)

QUICK QUIZ

Indirect crowding out occurs because of an interest rate effect in which the government's efforts to finance its deficit spending cause interest rates to _____, thereby crowding out private investment and spending, particularly on cars and houses. This is called the **crowding-out effect**.

_____ _____ _____ occur when government spending competes with the private sector and is increased. A direct crowding-out effect may occur.

A number of economists argue in favor of the _____ _____ theorem, which holds that an increase in the government budget deficit has no effect on aggregate demand because individuals anticipate that their future taxes will increase and therefore save more today to pay for them.

Changes in marginal tax rates may cause _____-_____ effects if a reduction in marginal tax rates induces enough additional work, saving, and investing. Government tax receipts can actually increase. This is called _____-_____ economics.

See page 338 for the answers. Review concepts from this section in MyEconLab.

DISCRETIONARY FISCAL POLICY IN PRACTICE: COPING WITH TIME LAGS

We can discuss fiscal policy in a relatively precise way. We draw graphs with aggregate demand and supply curves to show what we are doing. We could even in principle estimate the offsets that we just discussed. Even if we were able to measure all of these offsets exactly, however, would-be fiscal policymakers still face a problem: The conduct of fiscal policy involves a variety of time lags.

Policymakers must be concerned with time lags. Quite apart from the fact that it is difficult to measure economic variables, it takes time to collect and assimilate such data. Thus, policymakers must contend with the **recognition time lag,** the months that may elapse before national economic problems can be identified.

After an economic problem is recognized, a solution must be formulated; thus, there will be an **action time lag** between the recognition of a problem and the implementation of policy to solve it. For fiscal policy, the action time lag is particularly long. Such policy must be approved by Congress and is subject to political wrangling and infighting. The action time lag can easily last a year or two. Then it takes time to actually implement the policy. After Congress enacts fiscal policy legislation, it takes time to decide such matters as who gets new federal construction contracts.

Finally, there is the **effect time lag:** After fiscal policy is enacted, it takes time for the policy to affect the economy. To demonstrate the effects, economists need only shift curves on a chalkboard, a whiteboard, or a piece of paper, but in real time, such effects take quite a while to work their way through the economy.

Because the various fiscal policy time lags are long, a policy designed to combat a recession might not produce results until the economy is already out of that recession and perhaps experiencing inflation, in which case the fiscal policy would worsen the situation. Or a fiscal policy designed to eliminate inflation might not produce effects until the economy is in a recession; in that case, too, fiscal policy would make the economic problem worse rather than better.

Furthermore, because fiscal policy time lags tend to be *variable* (by anywhere from one to three years), policymakers have a difficult time fine-tuning the economy. Clearly, fiscal policy is more guesswork than science.

Recognition time lag
The time required to gather information about the current state of the economy.

Action time lag
The time between recognizing an economic problem and implementing policy to solve it. The action time lag is quite long for fiscal policy, which requires congressional approval.

Effect time lag
The time that elapses between the implementation of a policy and the results of that policy.

AUTOMATIC STABILIZERS

Not all changes in taxes (or in tax rates) or in government spending (including government transfers) constitute discretionary fiscal policy. There are several types of automatic (or nondiscretionary) fiscal policies. Such policies do not require new legislation on the part of Congress. Specific automatic fiscal policies—called **automatic,** or **built-in, stabilizers**—include the tax system itself, unemployment compensation, and income transfer payments.

Automatic, or built-in, stabilizers
Special provisions of certain federal programs that cause changes in desired aggregate expenditures without the action of Congress and the president. Examples are the federal progressive tax system and unemployment compensation.

The Tax System as an Automatic Stabilizer

You know that if you work less, you are paid less, and therefore you pay fewer taxes. The amount of taxes that our government collects falls automatically during a recession. Basically, incomes and profits fall when business activity slows down, and the government's take drops too. Some economists consider this an automatic tax cut, which therefore stimulates aggregate demand. It reduces the extent of any negative economic fluctuation.

The progressive nature of the federal personal and corporate income tax systems magnifies any automatic stabilization effect that might exist. If your hours of work are reduced because of a recession, you still pay some federal personal income taxes. But because of our progressive system, you may drop into a lower tax bracket, thereby paying a lower marginal tax rate. As a result, your disposable income falls by a smaller percentage than your before-tax income falls.

Unemployment Compensation and Income Transfer Payments

Like our tax system, unemployment compensation payments stabilize aggregate demand. Throughout the course of business fluctuations, unemployment compensation reduces *changes* in people's disposable income. When business activity drops, most laid-off workers automatically become eligible for unemployment compensation from their state governments. Their disposable income therefore remains positive, although at a lower level than when they were employed. During boom periods, there is less unemployment, and consequently fewer unemployment payments are made to the labor force. Less purchasing power is being added to the economy because fewer unemployment checks are paid out. In contrast, during recessions the opposite is true.

Income transfer payments act similarly as an automatic stabilizer. When a recession occurs, more people become eligible for income transfer payments. Therefore, those people do not experience so dramatic a drop in disposable income as they would have otherwise.

Stabilizing Impact

The key stabilizing impact of our tax system, unemployment compensation, and income transfer payments is their ability to mitigate changes in disposable income, consumption, and the equilibrium level of real GDP. If disposable income is prevented from falling as much as it otherwise would during a recession, the downturn will be moderated. In contrast, if disposable income is prevented from rising as rapidly as it otherwise would during a boom, the boom is less likely to get out of hand. The progressive income tax and unemployment compensation thus provide automatic stabilization to the economy. We present the argument graphically in Figure 13-6 on the following page.

FIGURE 13-6
Automatic Stabilizers

Here we assume that as real GDP rises, tax revenues rise and government transfers fall, other things remaining constant. Thus, as the economy expands from Y_f to Y_1, a budget surplus automatically arises; as the economy contracts from Y_f to Y_2, a budget deficit automatically arises. Such automatic changes tend to drive the economy back toward its full-employment real GDP.

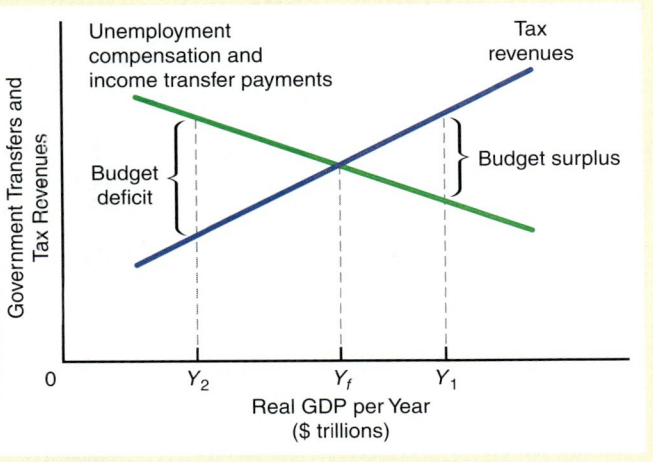

WHAT DO WE REALLY KNOW ABOUT FISCAL POLICY?

There are two ways of looking at fiscal policy. One prevails during normal times and the other during abnormal times.

Fiscal Policy During Normal Times

Go to www.econtoday.com/ch13 to learn about the current outlook for the budget of the U.S. government.

During normal times (without "excessive" unemployment, inflation, or problems in the national economy), we know that due to the recognition time lag and the modest size of any fiscal policy action that Congress will actually take, discretionary fiscal policy is probably not very effective. Congress ends up doing too little too late to help in a minor recession. Moreover, fiscal policy that generates repeated tax changes (as has happened) creates uncertainty, which may do more harm than good. To the extent that fiscal policy has any effect during normal times, it probably achieves this by way of automatic stabilizers rather than by way of discretionary policy.

Fiscal Policy During Abnormal Times

ECONOMICS FRONT AND CENTER

To think about the potential stabilizing role of government budget deficits and surpluses, take a look at **Budget Surplus or Bust!** on page 331.

During abnormal times, fiscal policy may be effective. Consider some classic examples: the Great Depression and war periods.

The Great Depression. When there is a catastrophic drop in real GDP, as there was during the Great Depression, fiscal policy may be able to stimulate aggregate demand. Because so many people have few assets left and thus are income-constrained during such periods, government spending is a way to get income into their hands—income that they are likely to spend immediately.

Wartime. Wars are in fact reserved for governments. War expenditures are not good substitutes for private expenditures—they have little or no direct expenditure offsets. Consequently, war spending as part of expansionary fiscal policy usually has noteworthy effects, such as occurred while we were waging World War II, when real GDP increased dramatically (though real per-capita personal income did not increase).

The "Soothing" Effect of Keynesian Fiscal Policy

One view of traditional Keynesian fiscal policy does not call for it to be used on a regular basis but nevertheless sees it as potentially useful. As you have learned in this chapter, many problems are associated with attempting to use fiscal policy. But if we should encounter a severe downturn, fiscal policy is available. Knowing this may reassure consumers and investors. Thus, the availability of fiscal policy may induce more buoyant and stable expectations of the future, thereby smoothing investment spending.

QUICK QUIZ

Time lags of various sorts reduce the effectiveness of fiscal policy. These include the _____ time lag, the _____ time lag, and the _____ time lag.

Two _____, or built-in, stabilizers are the progressive income tax and unemployment compensation.

Built-in stabilizers automatically tend to _____ changes in disposable income resulting from changes in overall business activity.

Although discretionary fiscal policy may not necessarily be a useful policy tool in normal times because of time lags, it may work well during _____ times, such as depressions and wartimes. In addition, the existence of fiscal policy may have a soothing effect on consumers and investors.

See page 338 for the answers. Review concepts from this section in MyEconLab.

CASE STUDY — ECONOMICS FRONT AND CENTER

Budget Surplus or Bust!

Hannity was reelected to her fifth term in the U.S. House of Representatives last year. Her main campaign promise was to use her authority as chair of one of the most powerful budget committees to push to remove red ink from the government's budget. Indeed, she pledged that she would press for the government to operate with budget surpluses by the end of this two-year term.

Her promise to eliminate the budget deficit has turned out to be easier to make than to keep, however. The government's tax revenues were already growing when Hannity made the pledge. They continued to increase during the first year of her latest term. Now, however, there are warning signs that the nation's economy may be on the verge of a recession. As Hannity calls her budget committee to order, she thinks back on her promise and contemplates how her constituents will react if she reneges by promoting policies likely to shift the government's budget back into deficit.

CRITICAL ANALYSIS QUESTIONS

1. Why might Hannity have cause to consider a budget deficit an appropriate policy to address the nation's potentially glum economic situation?

2. What types of government programs already in place might automatically help prevent a recession from occurring?

Issues and Applications

The Roller Coaster of Japanese Tax Policy

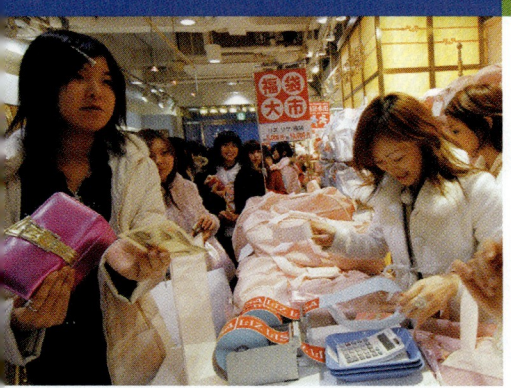

Concepts Applied
- Recognition Time Lag
- Action Time Lag
- Effect Time Lag

Between 2000 and 2002, the average rate of growth in total expenditures on goods and services in Japan was 0 percent. In an effort to boost aggregate demand amid a slumping economy, the Japanese government cut taxes.

As Figure 13-7 indicates, Japanese government spending also declined following 2000. Tax revenues fell at a faster pace, however, and for a few weeks near the end of 2004, the Japanese government was spending nearly twice as much as it was receiving in tax revenues. It was financing the rest of its spending by borrowing.

Recognition and Action Take Time

Originally, the Japanese government had planned to push taxes back up as soon as aggregate demand had begun to grow once again. Not until mid-2004, however, did the Japanese government recognize that total spending had increased by 0.6 percent in 2003, and by the end of 2004, the pace of spending growth had picked up more speed, to 1.7 percent. Real GDP growth, which had averaged only 0.4 percent between 2000 and 2002, had increased to 2.6 percent by 2004. Hence the period between 2003, when aggregate demand began to pick up in Japan, and 2004, when the Japanese government recognized that it had begun to increase, was a recognition lag.

In November 2004, the government began developing a plan to phase in a series of tax increases between 2005 and 2007. It did not begin implementing the first phase of the intended tax hikes until April 2005, however. Hence the action lag, the time before the initial tax hikes went into effect, was 5 months.

Will the Effect Lag End Before New Tax Cuts Are Considered?

In early 2005, the Japanese government waited for the effect lag to play out. During that period, it gradually phased in its first scheduled tax increase. As the rate of growth of total spending fell, new information about the economy began to arrive. Unexpectedly, the government learned that total planned expenditures had increased at an estimated rate of less than 1 percent during 2005. The tax increases slated to go into effect in 2006 and 2007 threatened to reduce aggregate demand even further.

During 2006, the Japanese government began rethinking its policy options once more. Some policymakers advocated scaling back or even eliminating the planned 2006 and 2007 tax hikes. These policymakers contended that recognition, action, and effect lags had caused the tax increase implemented earlier in 2005 to begin exerting its effects on the economy at the worst possible time. A few policymakers even began quietly suggesting rolling back the initial 2005 tax increase in hopes of giving a boost to the nation's total planned expenditures in 2006. Thus, the time-lag cycle began anew in Japan.

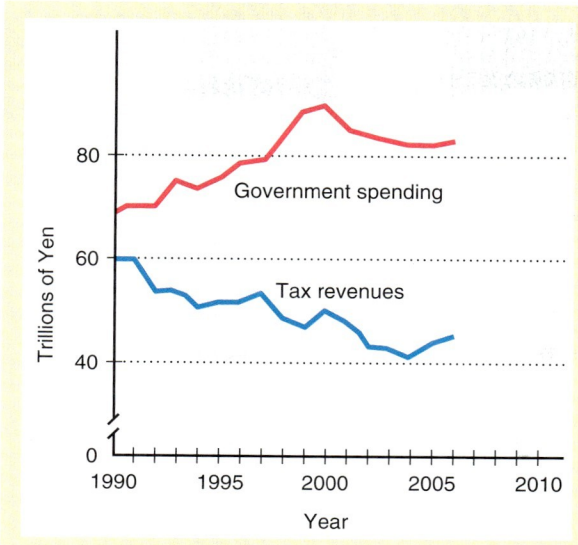

FIGURE 13-7

Government Spending and Tax Revenues in Japan

The Japanese government's expenditures increased by more than 30 percent between 1990 and 2000 before dropping off somewhat since. In the meantime, its tax revenues initially declined before rising slightly in 2005 and 2006.

Source: Japanese Ministry of Finance.

Log in to **MyEconLab**, click on "Economic News," and test your understanding of the chapter by answering interactive questions that relate directly to this issue.

For Critical Analysis

1. Taken together, do the time lags associated with fiscal policy appear to have combined lengths of months or years?
2. What factors are likely to make policy time lags faced by the Japanese government relatively lengthy?

Web Resources

1. For a summary of the phased-in Japanese tax increases that began in 2005, go to www.econtoday.com/ch13.
2. Track the latest developments in Japanese fiscal policy at www.econtoday.com/ch13.

Research Project

Take another look at Figure 13-7. What has happened to the Japanese government's budget deficit since 1990? Suppose that the Japanese government attempts to find a better way to determine appropriate tax policies. How might it better attune its fiscal policy to variations in the economy's performance so as to boost total planned spending during an economic downturn and reduce total planned spending during an upturn? (Hint: How might the Japanese government make its fiscal policies adjust more *automatically* to changes in economic activity?)

Here is what you should know after reading this chapter. MyEconLab will help you identify what you know, and where to go when you need to practice.

WHAT YOU SHOULD KNOW		WHERE TO GO TO PRACTICE
The Effects of Discretionary Fiscal Policies Using Traditional Keynesian Analysis In the Keynesian short-run framework of analysis, a deliberate increase in government spending or a reduction in taxes can raise aggregate demand. Thus, these fiscal policy actions can shift the aggregate demand curve outward and thereby close a recessionary gap in which current real GDP is less than the long-run level of real GDP. Likewise, an intentional reduction in government spending or a tax increase will reduce aggregate demand. These fiscal policy actions shift the aggregate demand curve inward and close an inflationary gap in which current real GDP exceeds the long-run level of real GDP.	fiscal policy, 319 **Key figures** Figure 13-1, 320 Figure 13-2, 322	• **MyEconLab** Study Plan 13.1 • Audio Introduction to Chapter 13 • Animated Figures 13-1 and 13-2
How Indirect Crowding Out and Direct Expenditure Offsets Can Reduce the Effectiveness of Fiscal Policy Actions Indirect crowding out occurs when the government engages in expansionary fiscal policy by increasing government spending or reducing taxes. When government spending exceeds tax revenues, the government must borrow by issuing bonds that compete with private bonds and thereby drive up market interest rates. This reduces, or crowds out, interest-sensitive private spending, thereby reducing the net effect of the fiscal expansion on aggregate demand. As a result, the aggregate demand curve shifts by a smaller amount than it would have in the absence of the crowding-out effect, and fiscal policy has a somewhat lessened net effect on equilibrium real GDP. Increased government spending may also substitute directly for private expenditures, and the resulting decline in private spending directly offsets the increase in total planned expenditures that the government had intended to bring about. This also mutes the net change in aggregate demand brought about by a fiscal policy action.	crowding-out effect, 323 direct expenditure offsets, 325 supply-side economics, 327 **Key figures** Figure 13-3, 323 Figure 13-4, 324 Figure 13-5, 327	• **MyEconLab** Study Plan 13.2 • Animated Figures 13-3, 13-4, and 13-5
The Ricardian Equivalence Theorem According to this proposition, when the government cuts taxes and borrows to finance the tax reduction, people realize that eventually the government will have to repay the loan. Thus, they anticipate that taxes will have to increase in the future. This induces them to save the proceeds of the tax cut to meet their future tax liabilities. Consequently, a tax cut fails to induce an increase in aggregate consumption spending. On net, therefore, if the Ricardian equivalence theorem is valid, a tax cut has no effect on total planned expenditures and aggregate demand.	Ricardian equivalence theorem, 325 **Key figure** Figure 13-4, 324	• **MyEconLab** Study Plan 13.2 • Animated Figure 13-4

CHAPTER 13 *Fiscal Policy* **335**

WHAT YOU SHOULD KNOW   **WHERE TO GO TO PRACTICE**

Fiscal Policy Time Lags and the Effectiveness of Fiscal "Fine-Tuning" Efforts to engage in fiscal policy actions intended to bring about carefully planned changes in aggregate demand are often complicated by policy time lags. One of these is the recognition time lag, which is the time required to collect information about the economy's current situation. Another is the action time lag, the period between recognition of a problem and implementation of a policy intended to address it. Finally, there is the effect time lag, which is the interval between the implementation of a policy and its having an effect on the economy. For fiscal policy, all of these lags can be lengthy and variable, often lasting one to three years. Hence fiscal "fine-tuning" may be a misnomer.

recognition time lag, 328
action time lag, 328
effect time lag, 328

- **MyEconLab** Study Plan 13.3
- Video: Time Lags

Automatic Stabilizers In our tax system, income taxes diminish automatically when economic activity drops, and unemployment compensation and income transfer payments increase. Thus, when there is a decline in real GDP, the automatic reduction in income tax collections and increases in unemployment compensation and income transfer payments tend to mute the reduction in total planned expenditures that would otherwise have resulted. The existence of these government programs thereby tends to stabilize the economy automatically in the face of variations in autonomous expenditures that induce fluctuations in economic activity.

automatic, or built-in, stabilizers, 329
Key figure
Figure 13-6, 330

- **MyEconLab** Study Plans 13.4 and 13.5
- Animated Figure 13-6

Log in to MyEconLab, take a chapter test, and get a personalized Study Plan that tells you which concepts you understand and which ones you need to review. From there, MyEconLab will give you further practice, tutorials, animations, videos, and guided solutions.
Log in to www.myeconlab.com

PROBLEMS

Select problems, indicated by a blue oval, are assignable in MyEconLab. Answers to the odd-numbered problems appear at the back of the book.

13-1. Suppose that Congress and the president decide that economic performance is weakening and that the government should "do something" about the situation. They make no tax changes but do enact new laws increasing government spending on a variety of programs.
   a. Prior to the congressional and presidential action, careful studies by government economists indicated that the direct multiplier effect of a rise in government expenditures on equilibrium real GDP is equal to 6. In the 12 months since the increase in government spending, however, it has become clear that the actual ultimate effect on real GDP will be less than half of that amount. What factors might account for this?
   b. Another year and a half elapses following passage of the government spending boost. The government has undertaken no additional policy actions, nor have there been any other events of significance. Nevertheless, by the end of the second year, real GDP has returned to its original level, and the price level has increased sharply. Provide a possible explanation for this outcome.

13-2. Suppose that Congress enacts a significant tax cut with the expectation that this action will stimulate aggregate demand and push up real GDP in the short run. In fact, however, neither real GDP nor the price level changes significantly as a result of the tax cut. What might account for this outcome?

13-3. Explain how time lags in discretionary fiscal policy-making could thwart the efforts of Congress and the president to stabilize real GDP in the face of an economic downturn. Is it possible that these time lags could actually cause discretionary fiscal policy to *destabilize* real GDP?

13-4. Determine whether each of the following is an example of a direct expenditure offset to fiscal policy.
   a. In an effort to help rejuvenate the nation's railroad system, a new government agency buys unused track, locomotives, and passenger and freight cars, many of which private companies would otherwise have purchased and put into regular use.
   b. The government increases its expenditures without raising taxes; to cover the resulting budget deficit, it issues more bonds, thereby pushing up the market interest rate and discouraging private planned investment spending.
   c. The government finances the construction of a classical music museum that otherwise never would have received private funding.

13-5. Determine whether each of the following is an example of indirect crowding out resulting from an expansionary fiscal policy action.
   a. The government provides a subsidy to help keep an existing firm operating, even though a group of investors otherwise would have provided a cash infusion that would have kept the company in business.
   b. The government reduces its taxes without decreasing its expenditures; to cover the resulting budget deficit, it issues more bonds, thereby pushing up the market interest rate and discouraging private planned investment spending.
   c. Government expenditures fund construction of a high-rise office building on a plot of land where a private company otherwise would have constructed an essentially identical building.

13-6. Under what circumstance might a tax reduction cause a long-run increase in real GDP and a long-run reduction in the price level?

13-7. Determine whether each of the following is an example of a discretionary fiscal policy action.
   a. A recession occurs, and government-funded unemployment compensation is paid to laid-off workers.
   b. Congress votes to fund a new jobs program designed to put unemployed workers to work.
   c. The Federal Reserve decides to reduce the quantity of money in circulation in an effort to slow inflation.
   d. Under powers authorized by an act of Congress, the president decides to authorize an emergency release of funds for spending programs intended to head off economic crises.

13-8. Determine whether each of the following is an example of an automatic fiscal stabilizer.
   a. A government agency arranges to make loans to businesses whenever an economic downturn begins.
   b. As the economy heats up, the resulting increase in equilibrium real GDP immediately results in higher income tax payments, which dampen consumption spending somewhat.

c. As the economy starts to recover from a recession and more people go back to work, government-funded unemployment compensation payments begin to decline.
d. To stem an overheated economy, the president, using special powers granted by Congress, authorizes emergency impoundment of funds that Congress had previously authorized for spending on government programs.

13-9 Consider the diagram below, in which the current short-run equilibrium is at point A, and answer the questions that follow.

a. What type of gap exists at point A?
b. If the marginal propensity to save equals 0.20, what change in government spending could eliminate the gap identified in part (a)? Explain.

13-10 Consider the diagram below, in which the current short-run equilibrium is at point A, and answer the questions that follow.

a. What type of gap exists at point A?
b. If the marginal propensity to consume equals 0.75, what change in government spending could eliminate the gap identified in part (a)? Explain.

13-11 Currently, a government's budget is balanced. The marginal propensity to consume is 0.80. The government has determined that each additional $10 billion in new government debt it issues to finance a budget deficit pushes up the market interest rate by 0.1 percentage point. It has also determined that every 0.1-percentage-point change in the market interest rate generates a change in planned investment expenditures equal to $2 billion. Finally, the government knows that to close a recessionary gap and take into account the resulting change in the price level, it must generate a net rightward shift in the aggregate demand curve equal to $200 billion. Assuming that there are no direct expenditure offsets to fiscal policy, how much should the government increase its expenditures? (Hint: How much private investment spending will each $10 billion increase in government spending crowd out?)

13-12 A government is currently operating with an annual budget deficit of $40 billion. The government has determined that every $10 billion reduction in the amount of bonds it issues each year would reduce the market interest rate by 0.1 percentage point. Furthermore, it has determined that every 0.1-percentage-point change in the market interest rate generates a change in planned investment expenditures in the opposite direction equal to $5 billion. The marginal propensity to consume is 0.75. Finally, the government knows that to eliminate an inflationary gap and take into account the resulting change in the price level, it must generate a net leftward shift in the aggregate demand curve equal to $40 billion. Assuming that there are no direct expenditure offsets to fiscal policy, how much should the government increase taxes? (Hint: How much new private investment spending is induced by each $10 billion decrease in government spending?)

13-13. Assume that the Ricardian equivalence theorem is not relevant. Explain why an income-tax-rate cut should affect short-run equilibrium real GDP.

13-14 Suppose that Congress enacts a lump-sum tax cut of $750 billion. The marginal propensity to consume is equal to 0.75. Assuming that Ricardian equivalence holds true, what is the effect on equilibrium real GDP? On saving?

ECONOMICS ON THE NET

Federal Government Spending and Taxation A quick way to keep up with the federal government's spending and taxation is by examining federal budget data at the White House Internet address.

Title: Historical Tables: Budget of the United States Government

Navigation: Use the link at www.econtoday.com/ch13 to visit the Office of Management and Budget. Select the most recent budget. Then click on *Historical Tables*.

Application After the document downloads, perform the indicated operations and answer the questions.

1. Go to section 2, "Composition of Federal Government Receipts." Take a look at Table 2.2, "Percentage Composition of Receipts by Source." Before World War II, what was the key source of revenues of the federal government? What has been the key revenue source since World War II?

2. Now scan down the document to Table 2.3, "Receipts by Source as Percentages of GDP." Have any government revenue sources declined as a percentage of GDP? Which ones have noticeably risen in recent years?

For Group Study and Analysis Split into four groups, and have each group examine section 3, "Federal Government Outlays by Function," and in particular Table 3.1, "Outlays by Superfunction and Function." Assign groups to the following functions: national defense, health, income security, and Social Security. Have each group prepare a brief report concerning recent and long-term trends in government spending on each function. Which functions have been capturing growing shares of government spending in recent years? Which have been receiving declining shares of total spending?

ANSWERS TO QUICK QUIZZES

p. 322: (i) expenditures . . . taxes; (ii) recessionary . . . increase; (iii) inflationary . . . decrease; (iv) decrease . . . increase
p. 328: (i) increase; (ii) Direct expenditure offsets; (iii) Ricardian equivalence; (iv) supply-side . . . supply-side
p. 331: (i) recognition . . . action . . . effect; (ii) automatic; (iii) moderate; (iv) abnormal

Fiscal Policy: A Keynesian Perspective — Appendix C

The traditional Keynesian approach to fiscal policy differs in three ways from that presented in Chapter 13. First, it emphasizes the underpinnings of the components of aggregate demand. Second, it assumes that government expenditures are not substitutes for private expenditures and that current taxes are the only taxes taken into account by consumers and firms. Third, the traditional Keynesian approach focuses on the short run and so assumes that as a first approximation, the price level is constant.

CHANGES IN GOVERNMENT SPENDING

Figure C-1 measures real GDP along the horizontal axis and total planned real expenditures (aggregate demand) along the vertical axis. The components of aggregate demand are real consumption (C), investment (I), government spending (G), and net exports (X). The height of the schedule labeled $C + I + G + X$ shows total planned real expenditures (aggregate demand) as a function of real GDP. This schedule slopes upward because consumption depends positively on real GDP. Everywhere along the 45-degree reference line, planned real spending equals real GDP. At the point Y^*, where the $C + I + G + X$ line intersects the 45-degree line, planned real spending is consistent with real GDP per year. At any income less than Y^*, spending exceeds real GDP, and so real GDP and thus real spending will tend to rise. At any level of real GDP greater than Y^*, planned spending is less than real GDP, and so real GDP and thus spending will tend to decline. Given the determinants of C, I, G, and X, total real spending (aggregate demand) will be Y^*.

The Keynesian approach assumes that changes in government spending cause no direct offsets in either consumption or investment spending because G is not a substitute for C, I, or X. Hence a rise in government spending from G to G' causes the $C + I + G + X$ line

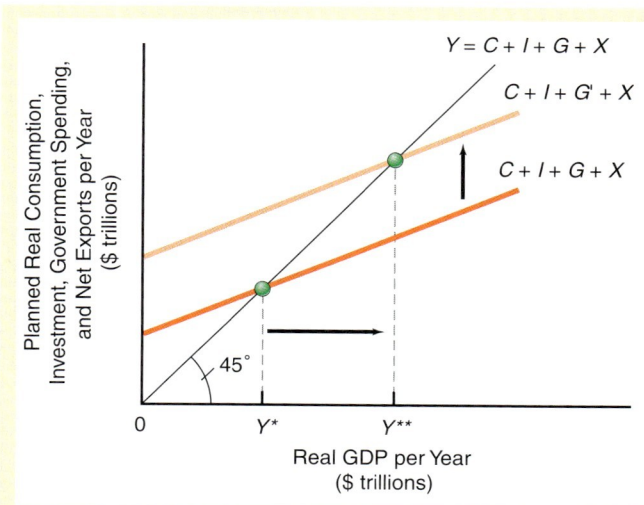

FIGURE C-1

The Impact of Higher Government Spending on Aggregate Demand

Government spending increases, causing $C + I + G + X$ to move to $C + I + G' + X$. Equilibrium real GDP per year increases to Y^{**}.

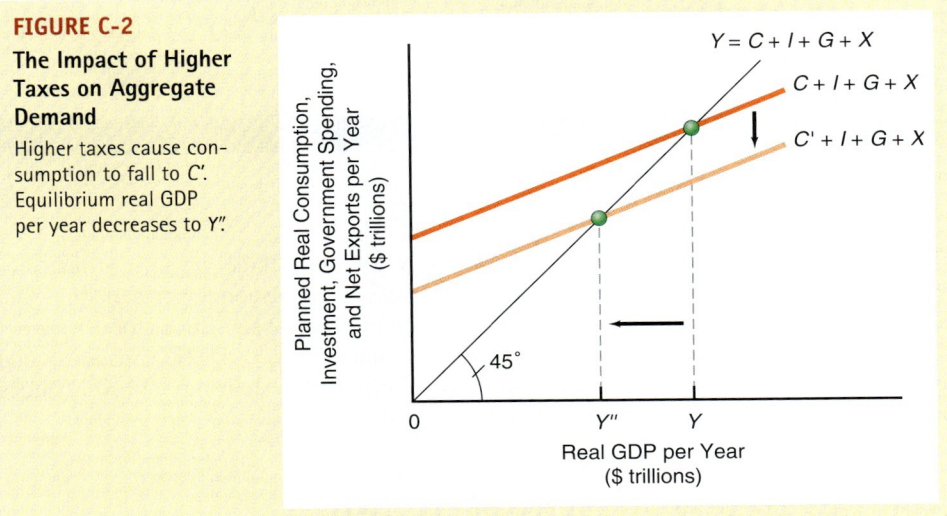

FIGURE C-2
The Impact of Higher Taxes on Aggregate Demand
Higher taxes cause consumption to fall to C'. Equilibrium real GDP per year decreases to Y''.

to shift upward by the full amount of the rise in government spending, yielding the line $C + I + G' + X$. The rise in real government spending causes real GDP to rise, which in turn causes consumption spending to rise, which further increases real GDP. Ultimately, aggregate demand rises to Y^{**}, where spending again equals real GDP. A key conclusion of the Keynesian analysis is that total spending rises by *more* than the original rise in government spending because consumption spending depends positively on real GDP.

CHANGES IN TAXES

According to the Keynesian approach, changes in current taxes affect aggregate demand by changing the amount of real disposable (after-tax) income available to consumers. A rise in taxes reduces disposable income and thus reduces real consumption; conversely, a tax cut raises disposable income and thus causes a rise in consumption spending. The effects of a tax increase are shown in Figure C-2. Higher taxes cause consumption spending to decline from C to C', causing total spending to shift downward to $C' + I + G + X$. In general, the decline in consumption will be less than the increase in taxes because people will also reduce their saving to help pay the higher taxes.

THE BALANCED-BUDGET MULTIPLIER

One interesting implication of the Keynesian approach concerns the impact of a balanced-budget change in government real spending. Suppose that the government increases spending by $1 billion and pays for it by raising current taxes by $1 billion. Such a policy is called a *balanced-budget increase in real spending*. Because the higher spending tends to push aggregate demand *up* by *more* than $1 billion while the higher taxes tend to push aggregate demand *down* by *less* than $1 billion, a most remarkable thing happens: A balanced-budget increase in G causes total spending to rise by *exactly* the amount of the rise in G—in this case, $1 billion. We say that the *balanced-budget multiplier* is equal to 1. Similarly, a balanced-budget reduction in government spending will cause total spending to fall by exactly the amount of the government spending cut.

THE FIXED PRICE LEVEL ASSUMPTION

The final key feature of the Keynesian approach is that it typically assumes that as a first approximation, the price level is fixed. Recall that nominal GDP equals the price level multiplied by real GDP. If the price level is fixed, an increase in government spending that causes nominal GDP to rise will show up exclusively as a rise in *real* GDP. This will in turn be accompanied by a decline in the unemployment rate because the additional real GDP can be produced only if additional factors of production, such as labor, are utilized.

PROBLEMS

Select problems, indicated by a blue oval ●, *are assignable in MyEconLab. Answers to the odd-numbered problems appear at the back of the book.*

C-1 Assume that equilibrium real GDP is $12.2 trillion and full-employment equilibrium (*FE*) is $12.55 trillion. The marginal propensity to save is $\frac{1}{7}$. Answer the questions using the data in the following graph.

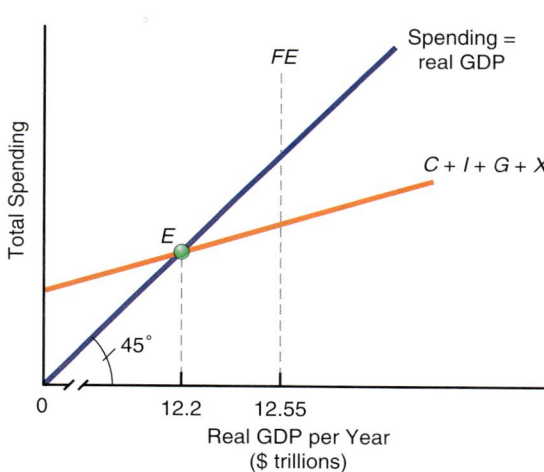

a. What is the marginal propensity to consume?
b. By how much must new investment or government spending increase to bring the economy up to full employment?
c. By how much must government cut personal taxes to stimulate the economy to the full-employment equilibrium?

C-2 Assume that MPC = $\frac{4}{5}$ when answering the following questions.

a. If government expenditures rise by $2 billion, by how much will the aggregate expenditure curve shift upward? By how much will equilibrium real GDP per year change?
b. If taxes increase by $2 billion, by how much will the aggregate expenditure curve shift downward? By how much will equilibrium real GDP per year change?

C-3 Assume that MPC = $\frac{4}{5}$ when answering the following questions.

a. If government expenditures rise by $1 billion, by how much will the aggregate expenditure curve shift upward?
b. If taxes rise by $1 billion, by how much will the aggregate expenditure curve shift downward?
c. If both taxes and government expenditures rise by $1 billion, by how much will the aggregate expenditure curve shift? What will happen to the equilibrium level of real GDP?
d. How does your response to the second question in part (c) change if MPC = $\frac{3}{4}$? If MPC = $\frac{1}{2}$?

14 Deficit Spending and the Public Debt

Learning Objectives

After reading this chapter, you should be able to:

1. Explain how federal government budget deficits occur
2. Define the public debt and understand alternative measures of the public debt
3. Evaluate circumstances under which the public debt could be a burden to future generations
4. Discuss why the federal budget deficit might be measured incorrectly
5. Analyze the macroeconomic effects of government budget deficits
6. Describe possible ways to reduce the government budget deficit

MyEconLab helps you master each objective and study more efficiently. See end of chapter for details.

In the early 1990s, when several European nations first decided to create the new currency called the euro, their governments agreed to abide by the terms of the *Stability and Growth Pact*. Under this treaty, each country agreed to limit any excess of government spending over tax collections to no more than 3 percent of its gross domestic product (GDP). Key proponents of the Stability and Growth Pact included the governments of Germany and France, which insisted on adopting an enforcement mechanism, including fines on governments that violated the pact. In nearly every year since 2000, however, the German and French governments have been among the most flagrant violators. In this chapter, you will learn why these governments have changed their tune about whether it is desirable for government spending to exceed taxes by more than 3 percent of GDP.

Did You Know That...

when the U.S. Treasury Department conducted an audit of federal government expenditures and revenues for a recent fiscal year, it found $24.5 billion in "unreconciled transactions"? The Treasury Department's auditors knew that during the year, a total of $24.5 billion (or $24,500,000,000) was spent by someone, somewhere, on something. The auditors could not, however, determine *who* spent the funds, *where* the funds were spent, or on *what* they were spent.

Ultimately, the auditors gave up trying to determine how the funds were spent. After all, $24.5 billion was only about 1 percent of the U.S. government's total spending, or just enough funds to finance the operations of the U.S. Department of Justice during the year. Nevertheless, as members of the media and some in Congress were quick to point out, this amount accounted for almost 7 percent of the government's *budget deficit*—expenditures in excess of tax revenues—during the year the auditors examined.

Every year since 2001, the U.S. government has spent more than it collected in taxes. The government anticipates continuing to spend more than it takes in until at least 2012. Should you be worried about this? The answer, as you will see in this chapter, is both yes and no. First, let's examine what the government actually does when it spends more than it receives.

PUBLIC DEFICITS AND DEBTS: FLOWS VERSUS STOCKS

A **government budget deficit** exists if the government spends more than it receives in taxes during a given period of time. The government has to finance this shortfall somehow. Barring any resort to money creation (the subject matter of Chapters 15, 16, and 17), the U.S. Treasury sells IOUs on behalf of the U.S. government, in the form of securities that are normally called bonds. In effect, the federal government asks U.S. and foreign households, businesses, and governments to lend funds to the government to cover its deficit. For example, if the federal government spends $100 billion more than it receives in revenues, the Treasury will raise that $100 billion by selling $100 billion of new Treasury bonds. Those who buy the Treasury bonds (lend funds to the U.S. government) will receive interest payments over the life of the bond. In return, the U.S. Treasury receives immediate purchasing power. In the process, it also adds to its indebtedness to bondholders.

Government budget deficit
An excess of government spending over government revenues during a given period of time.

Distinguishing Between Deficits and Debts

You have already learned about flows. GDP, for instance, is a flow because it is a dollar measure of the total amount of final goods and services produced within a given period of time, such as a year.

The federal deficit is also a flow. Suppose that the current federal deficit is $300 billion. This means that the federal government is currently spending at a rate of $300 billion *per year* more than it is collecting in taxes and other revenues.

Of course, governments do not always spend more each year than the revenues they receive. If a government spends an amount exactly equal to the revenues it collects during a given period, then during this interval the government operates with a **balanced budget**. If a government spends less than the revenues it receives during a given period, then during this interval it experiences a **government budget surplus**.

Balanced budget
A situation in which the government's spending is exactly equal to the total taxes and other revenues it collects during a given period of time.

Government budget surplus
An excess of government revenues over government spending during a given period of time.

The Public Debt

You have also learned about stocks, which are measured at a point in time. Stocks change between points in time as a result of flows. The amount of unemployment, for example, is a stock. It is the total number of people looking for work but unable to find it at a given point in time. Suppose that the stock of unemployed workers at the beginning of the month is 7.9 million and that at the end of the month the stock of unemployed workers has increased to 8.1 million. This means that during the month, assuming an unchanged labor force, there was a net flow of 0.2 million individuals away from the state of being employed into the state of being out of work but seeking employment.

Likewise, the total accumulated **public debt** is a stock measured at a given point in time, and it changes from one time to another as a result of government budget deficits or surpluses. For instance, on December 31, 2005, one measure of the public debt was $4.6 trillion. During 2006, the federal government operated at a deficit of nearly $0.26 trillion. As a consequence, on December 31, 2006, this measure of the public debt had increased to nearly $4.9 trillion.

Public debt
The total value of all outstanding federal government securities.

Go to www.econtoday.com/ch14 to learn more about the activities of the Congressional Budget Office, which reports to the legislative branch of the U.S. government about the current state of the federal government's spending and receipts.

GOVERNMENT FINANCE: SPENDING MORE THAN TAX COLLECTIONS

Following four consecutive years—1998 through 2001—of official budget surpluses, the federal government began to experience budget deficits once more beginning in 2002. Since then, government spending has increased considerably, and tax revenues have failed to keep pace. Consequently, the federal government has operated with a deficit each year since 2002, and most observers anticipate a steady flow of government red ink for the foreseeable future.

The Historical Record of Federal Budget Deficits

Figure 14-1 charts inflation-adjusted expenditures and revenues of the federal government since 1940. The *real* annual budget deficit is the arithmetic difference between real expenditures and real revenues during years in which the government's spending has exceeded its revenues. As you can see, there is nothing out of the ordinary about federal budget deficits. Indeed, the annual budget surpluses of the late 1990s and early 2000s were somewhat out of the ordinary. The 1998 budget surplus was the first since 1968, when the government briefly operated with a surplus. Before the 1998–2001 budget surpluses, the U.S. government had not experienced back-to-back annual surpluses since the 1950s.

Indeed, since 1940 the U.S. government has operated with an annual budget surplus for a total of only 13 years. In all other years, it has collected insufficient taxes and other revenues to fund its spending. Every year this has occurred, the federal government has borrowed to finance its additional expenditures.

Even though Figure 14-1 accounts for inflation, it does not give a clear picture of the size of the federal government's deficits or surpluses in relation to overall economic activity in the United States. Figure 14-2 provides a clearer view of the size of government deficits or surpluses relative to the size of the U.S. economy by expressing them as percentages of GDP. As you can see, the federal budget deficit reached a peak of nearly 6 percent of GDP in the early 1980s. It then fell back, increased once again during the late 1980s and early 1990s, and then declined steadily into the budget surplus years of 1998–2001. Since 2001, the government budget deficit has increased to as high as 3.5 percent of GDP before settling out at just above 2 percent of GDP.

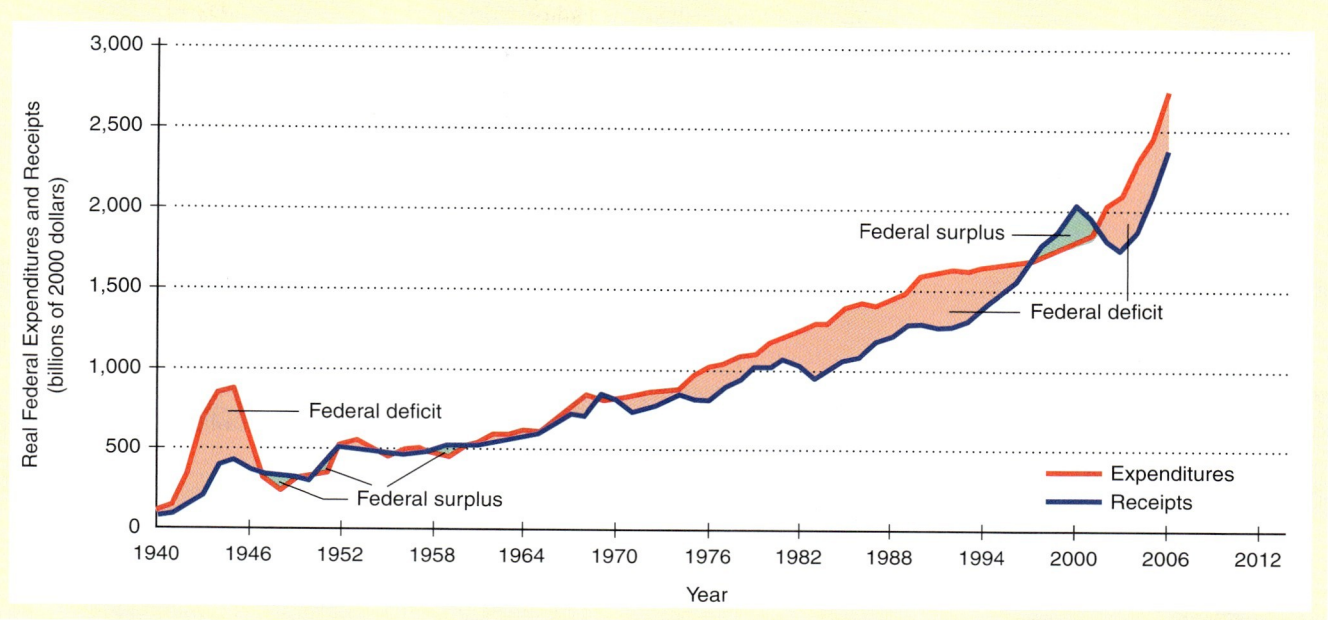

FIGURE 14-1
Federal Budget Deficits and Surpluses Since 1940
Federal budget deficits (expenditures in excess of receipts, in red) have been much more common than federal budget surpluses (receipts in excess of expenditures, in green).
Source: Office of Management and Budget.

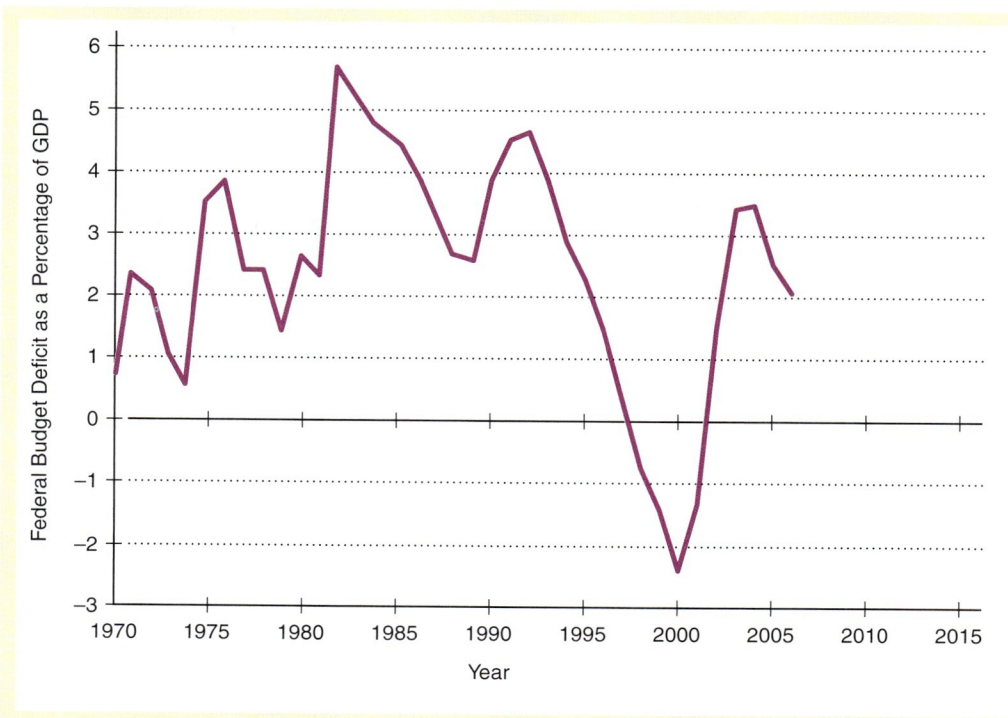

FIGURE 14-2
The Federal Budget Deficit Expressed as a Percentage of GDP

Beginning in 2000, the federal budget deficit rose as a share of GDP before declining in recent years. (Note that the negative values for the 1998–2001 period designate budget surpluses as a percentage of GDP during those years.)

Sources: *Economic Report of the President; Economic Indicators*, various issues.

The Resurgence of Federal Government Deficits

Why has the government's budget slipped from a surplus equal to nearly 2.5 percent of GDP into a deficit of about 2 percent of GDP? The simple answer is that since 2001 the government has spent more than it has collected in revenues. As noted in Chapter 13, government spending increased at a faster pace between 2002 and 2006 than in any other period of the same length since the end of World War II.

The more complex answer also considers government revenues. In 2001, Congress and the executive branch slightly reduced income tax rates, and in 2003 it also cut federal capital gains taxes and estate taxes. Because tax rates were reduced toward the end of a recession when real income growth was relatively low, government tax revenues were stagnant for a time. When economic activity began to expand into the mid-2000s, tax revenues started rising at a pace closer to the rapid rate of growth of government spending. Nevertheless, annual federal expenditures are continuing to exceed annual tax collections. As long as this situation persists, the U.S. government will operate with a budget deficit, just as it did so often during the previous six decades.

Why do the U.S. government's semiannual budget deficit projections almost always turn out to be off by tens of billions of dollars?

POLICY EXAMPLE

Explaining a $109 Billion Deficit Projection Turnaround

In late January 2005, the U.S. government projected that its budget deficit for the coming fiscal year would be $427 billion. In fact, the 2005 federal budget deficit turned out to be $318 billion.

Why was the government's initial 2005 deficit projection off by $109 billion? The answer is that the government seriously underestimated its 2005 tax revenues. At the beginning of 2005, the government assumed that its revenues would be about the same as in the previous year. In fact, federal tax revenues turned out to be more than 15 percent higher in 2005 than in 2004, because an unexpected upturn in economic growth caused taxable incomes, and hence income tax revenues, to be much higher than anticipated.

So, in January 2006, what did the government assume about its 2006 revenues when making its 2006 deficit projection? As usual, it assumed that tax revenues in 2006 would be about the same as in 2005, knowing full well that a few months later it probably would learn that it had underestimated the 2006 deficit by tens of billions of dollars—which is exactly what occurred.

FOR CRITICAL ANALYSIS
Why would successfully projecting future U.S. government budget deficits require correctly predicting the course of U.S. economic activity?

QUICK QUIZ

Whenever the federal government spends more than it receives during a given year, it operates with a _____ _____. If federal government spending exactly equals government revenues, then the government experiences a _____ _____. If the federal government collects more revenues than it spends, then it operates with a _____ _____.

The federal budget deficit is a flow, whereas accumulated budget deficits represent a _____, called the **public debt**.

The federal budget deficit expressed as a percentage of GDP hit its most recent peak of around 6 percent in the early 1980s. Between 1998 and 2001, the federal government experienced a budget _____, but since then its budget has once more been in _____. Currently, the budget _____ amounts to about 2 percent of GDP.

See page 364 for the answers. Review concepts from this section in MyEconLab.

EVALUATING THE RISING PUBLIC DEBT

All federal public debt, taken together, is called the **gross public debt.** We arrive at the **net public debt** when we subtract from the gross public debt the portion that is held by government agencies (in essence, what the federal government owes to itself). For instance, if the Social Security Administration holds U.S. Treasury bonds, the U.S. Treasury makes debt payments to another agency of the government. On net, therefore, the U.S. government owes these payments to itself.

The net public debt normally increases whenever the federal government experiences a budget deficit. That is, the net public debt increases when government outlays are greater than total government receipts.

Gross public debt
All federal government debt irrespective of who owns it.

Net public debt
Gross public debt minus all government interagency borrowing.

Accumulation of the Net Public Debt

Table 14-1 displays, for various years since 1940, real values, in base-year 2000 dollars, of the federal budget deficit, the total and per capita net public debt (the amount owed on the net public debt by a typical individual), and the net interest cost of the public debt in total and as a percentage of GDP. It shows that the level of the real net public debt and the real net public debt per capita grew following the early 1980s before declining in 2000. Thus, the real, inflation-adjusted amount that a typical individual owes to holders of the net public debt has varied over time.

ECONOMICS FRONT AND CENTER

To think further about the distinction between the gross public debt and the net public debt, take a look at **The Public Debt—Public Enemy Number One,** on page 358.

(1) Year	(2) Federal Budget Deficit (billions of 2000 dollars)	(3) Net Public Debt (billions of 2000 dollars)	(4) Per Capita Net Public Debt (2000 dollars)	(5) Net Interest Costs (billions of 2000 dollars)	(6) Net Interest as a Percentage of GDP
1940	36.1	395.4	2,992.6	8.3	0.90
1945	366.7	1,600.0	11,436.7	21.1	1.45
1950	15.7	1,106.1	7,262.6	24.2	1.68
1955	14.6	1,100.0	6,630.6	23.8	1.23
1960	1.4	1,113.6	6,162.9	32.4	1.37
1965	7.1	1,162.7	5,984.0	38.2	1.26
1970	10.2	1,036.0	5,051.3	52.4	1.47
1975	118.7	1,044.5	4,835.5	61.3	1.52
1980	136.7	1,313.5	5,815.7	97.2	1.92
1985	304.6	2,151.2	9,071.6	185.7	3.22
1990	271.3	2,953.9	11,815.7	215.2	3.23
1995	178.1	3,913.6	14,679.6	252.0	3.24
2000	−236.4	3,409.8	12,074.4	223.0	2.34
2003	353.1	3,681.7	12,651.7	154.4	1.34
2004	378.3	3,937.2	13,396.2	146.8	1.37
2005	283.8	4,094.7	13,803.7	153.4	1.38
2006	282.2	4,266.2	14,239.3	151.8	1.36
2007	287.2	4,433.9	14,652.5	149.5	1.34

Sources: U.S. Department of the Treasury; Office of Management and Budget. Note: Data for 2006 and 2007 are estimates.

TABLE 14-1
The Federal Deficit, Our Public Debt, and the Interest We Pay on It
Net public debt in column 3 is defined as total federal debt *excluding* all loans between federal government agencies. Per capita net public debt is obtained by dividing the net public debt by the population.

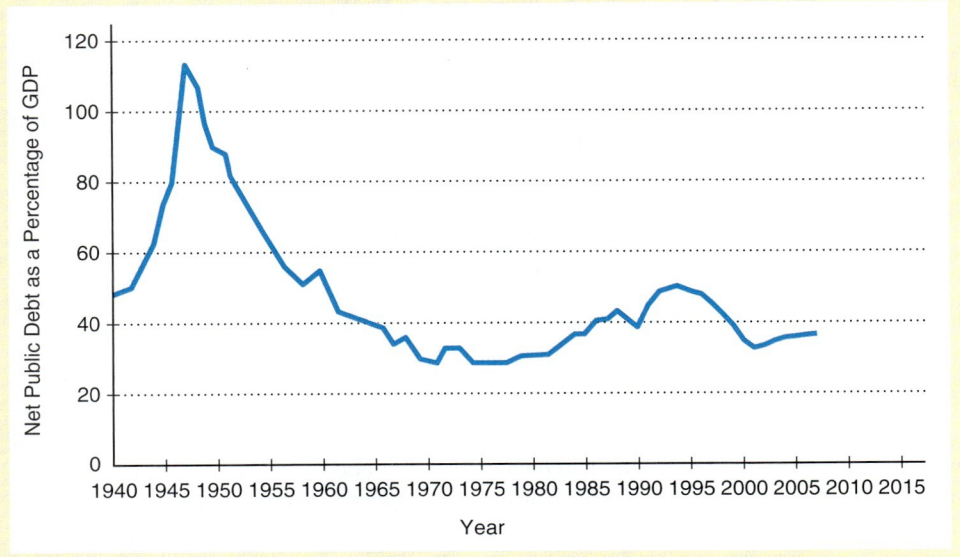

FIGURE 14-3

Net U.S. Public Debt as a Percentage of GDP

During World War II, the net public debt grew dramatically. After the war, it fell until the 1970s, started rising in the 1980s, declined once more in the 1990s, and recently has been increasing again.

Source: U.S. Department of the Treasury.

The net public debt levels reported in Table 14-1 do not provide a basis of comparison with the overall size of the U.S. economy. Figure 14-3 does this by displaying the net public debt as a percentage of GDP. We see that after World War II, this ratio fell steadily until the early 1970s (except for a small rise in the late 1950s) and then leveled off until the 1980s. After that, the ratio of the net public debt to GDP more or less continued to rise to around 50 percent of GDP, before dropping slightly in the late 1990s and early 2000s. With the reappearance of budget deficits since 2001, the ratio has been rising once again.

Annual Interest Payments on the Public Debt

Columns 5 and 6 of Table 14-1 on page 347 show an important consequence of the net public debt. This is the interest that the government must pay to those who hold the bonds it has issued to finance past budget deficits. Those interest payments started rising dramatically around 1975 and then declined in the 1990s and early 2000s. Government deficits have recently been higher than in the late 1990s and early 2000s, so interest payments expressed as a percentage of GDP might rise in the years to come.

If U.S. residents were the sole owners of the government's debts, the interest payments on the net public debt would go only to U.S. residents. In this situation, we would owe the debt to ourselves, with most people being taxed so that the government could pay interest to others (or to ourselves). During the 1970s, however, the share of the net public debt owned by foreign individuals, businesses, and governments started to rise, reaching 20 percent in 1978. From there it declined until the late 1980s, when it began to rise rapidly. Today, foreign residents, businesses, and governments hold nearly 50 percent of the net public debt. Thus, we do not owe the debt just to ourselves.

Burdens of the Public Debt

Do current budget deficits and the accumulating public debt create social burdens? One perspective on this question considers possible burdens on future generations. Another focuses on transfers from U.S. residents to residents of other nations.

How Today's Budget Deficits Might Burden Future Generations. If the federal government wishes to purchase goods and services valued at $100 billion, it can finance this expenditure either by raising taxes by $100 billion or by selling $100 billion in bonds. Many economists maintain that the second option, deficit spending, would lead to a higher level of national consumption and a lower level of national saving than the first option.

The reason, say these economists, is that if people are taxed, they will have to forgo private consumption now as society substitutes government goods for private goods. If the government does not raise taxes but instead sells bonds to finance the $100 billion in expenditures, the public's disposable income remains the same. Members of the public have merely shifted their allocations of assets to include $100 billion in additional government bonds. There are two possible circumstances that could cause people to treat government borrowing differently than they treat taxes. One is that people will fail to realize that their liabilities (in the form of higher future taxes due to increased interest payments on the public debt) have *also* increased by $100 billion. Another is that people will believe that they can consume the governmentally provided goods without forgoing any private consumption because the bill for the government goods will be paid by *future* taxpayers.

The Crowding-Out Effect. But if full employment exists, and society raises its present consumption by adding consumption of government-provided goods to the same quantity of privately provided goods, then something must be *crowded out*. In a closed economy, investment expenditures on capital goods must decline. As you learned in Chapter 13, the mechanism by which investment is crowded out is an increase in the interest rate. Deficit spending increases the total demand for credit but leaves the total supply of credit unaltered. The rise in interest rates causes a reduction in the growth of investment and capital formation, which in turn slows the growth of productivity and improvement in society's living standard.

This perspective suggests that deficit spending can impose a burden on future generations in two ways. First, unless the deficit spending is allocated to purchases that lead to long-term increases in real GDP, future generations will have to be taxed at a higher rate. That is, only by imposing higher taxes on future generations will the government be able to retire the higher public debt resulting from the present generation's consumption of governmentally provided goods. Second, the increased level of consumption by the present generation crowds out investment and reduces the growth of capital goods, leaving future generations with a smaller capital stock and thereby reducing their wealth.

Paying Off the Public Debt in the Future. Suppose that after 50 years of running deficits financed by selling bonds to U.S. residents, the public debt becomes so large that each adult person's implicit share of the net public debt liability is $50,000. Suppose further that the government chooses (or is forced) to pay off the debt at that time. Will that generation be burdened with our government's overspending? Assume that a large portion of the debt is owed to ourselves. It is true that every adult will have to come up with $50,000 in taxes to pay off the debt, but then the government will use these funds to pay off the bondholders. Sometimes the bondholders and taxpayers will be the same people. Thus, *some* people will be burdened because they owe $50,000 and own less than $50,000 in government bonds. Others, however, will receive more than $50,000 for the bonds they own. Nevertheless, as a generation within society, they will pay and receive about the same amount of funds.

Of course, there could be a burden on some low-income adults who will find it difficult or impossible to obtain $50,000 to pay off the tax liability. Still, nothing says that taxes to pay off the debt must be assessed equally. Indeed, it seems likely that a special tax would be levied, based on the ability to pay.

Our Debt to Foreign Residents. So far we have been assuming that we owe all of the public debt to ourselves. But, as we saw earlier, that is not the case. What about the nearly 50 percent owned by foreign residents?

It is true that if foreign residents buy U.S. government bonds, we do not owe that debt to ourselves. Thus, when debts held by foreign residents come due, future U.S. residents will be taxed to repay these debts plus accumulated interest. Portions of the incomes of future U.S. residents will then be transferred abroad. In this way, a potential burden on future generations may result.

But this transfer will not necessarily be a burden. Foreign residents will buy our government's debt if the real rate of return on the bonds it issues exceeds the real rate of return that investors can earn in another country. If they buy U.S. bonds voluntarily, they perceive a benefit in doing so.

It is important to realize that if the rate of return on projects that the government funds by operating with deficits exceeds the interest rate paid to foreign residents, both foreign residents and future U.S. residents will be better off. If funds obtained by selling bonds to foreign residents are expended on wasteful projects, however, a burden may well be placed on future generations.

We can apply the same reasoning to the problem of current investment and capital creation being crowded out by current deficits. If deficits lead to slower growth rates, future generations will be poorer. But if the government expenditures are really investments, and if the rate of return on such public investments exceeds the interest rate paid on the bonds, both present and future generations will be economically better off.

In which foreign countries do residents hold the most U.S. government debt?

INTERNATIONAL EXAMPLE

Where Are Most U.S. Treasury Securities Held Abroad?

More than $2 trillion in U.S. Treasury securities, or roughly half of the nearly $5 trillion in outstanding U.S. net public debt, is held outside the United States. Figure 14-4 shows the distribution of foreign holdings of U.S. Treasury securities. Japan accounts for more than one-third of all foreign holdings of the U.S. net public debt. Others with relatively large shares include China, the United Kingdom, foreign residents and companies with operations located in the nations of the Caribbean, and South Korea.

FOR CRITICAL ANALYSIS
Why might the fact that market interest rates in Japan have hovered very close to 0 percent during the 2000s help explain the relatively large holdings of U.S. Treasury securities by residents of that country?

FIGURE 14-4

The Distribution of Foreign Holdings of U.S. Treasury Securities

Japan accounts for the largest share of the nearly $2 trillion in U.S. Treasury securities held by foreign residents.

Source: U.S. Department of the Treasury.

*"Caribbean nations" includes the Bahamas, Bermuda, Cayman Islands, Netherlands Antilles, and Panama.

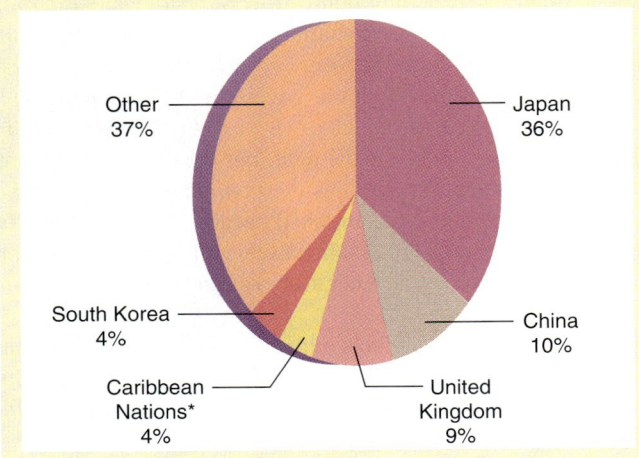

QUICK QUIZ

When we subtract the funds that government agencies borrow from each other from the _____ public debt, we obtain the _____ public debt.

The public debt may impose a burden on _____ generations if they have to be taxed at higher rates to pay for the _____ generation's increased consumption of governmentally provided goods. In addition, there may be a burden if the debt leads to crowding out of current investment, resulting in _____ capital formation and hence a _____ economic growth rate.

If foreign residents hold a significant part of our public debt, then we no longer "owe it to ourselves." If the rate of return on the borrowed funds is _____ than the interest to be paid to foreign residents, future generations can be made better off by government borrowing. Future generations will be worse off, however, if the opposite is true.

See page 364 for the answers. Review concepts from this section in MyEconLab.

FEDERAL BUDGET DEFICITS IN AN OPEN ECONOMY

Many economists believe that it is no accident that foreign residents hold such a large portion of the U.S. public debt. Their reasoning suggests that a U.S. trade deficit—a situation in which the value of U.S. imports of goods and services exceeds the value of its exports—will often accompany a government budget deficit.

Trade Deficits and Government Budget Deficits

Figure 14-5 on the following page shows U.S. trade deficits and surpluses compared to federal budget deficits and surpluses. In 1983, imports began to consistently exceed exports on an annual basis in the United States. At the same time, the federal budget deficit rose dramatically. When the federal budget officially moved into the surplus territory between 1998 and 2001, the U.S. trade deficit briefly eased very slightly. Since the early 2000s, however, both deficits have been increasing once more.

Thus, it appears that there is a relationship between trade deficits and government budget deficits: Larger trade deficits tend to accompany larger government budget deficits.

Why the Two Deficits Are Related

Intuitively, there is a reason why we would expect federal budget deficits to be associated with trade deficits. You might call this the unpleasant arithmetic of trade and budget deficits.

Suppose that, initially, the government's budget is balanced; government expenditures are matched by an equal amount of tax collections and other government revenues. Now assume that the federal government begins to experience a budget deficit; it increases its spending, collects fewer taxes, or both. Assume further that domestic consumption and domestic investment do not decrease relative to GDP. Where, then, do the funds come from to finance the government's budget deficit? A portion of these funds must come from abroad. That is to say, dollar holders abroad will have to purchase newly created government bonds.

Of course, foreign dollar holders will choose to hold the new government bonds only if there is an economic inducement to do so, such as an increase in U.S. interest rates.

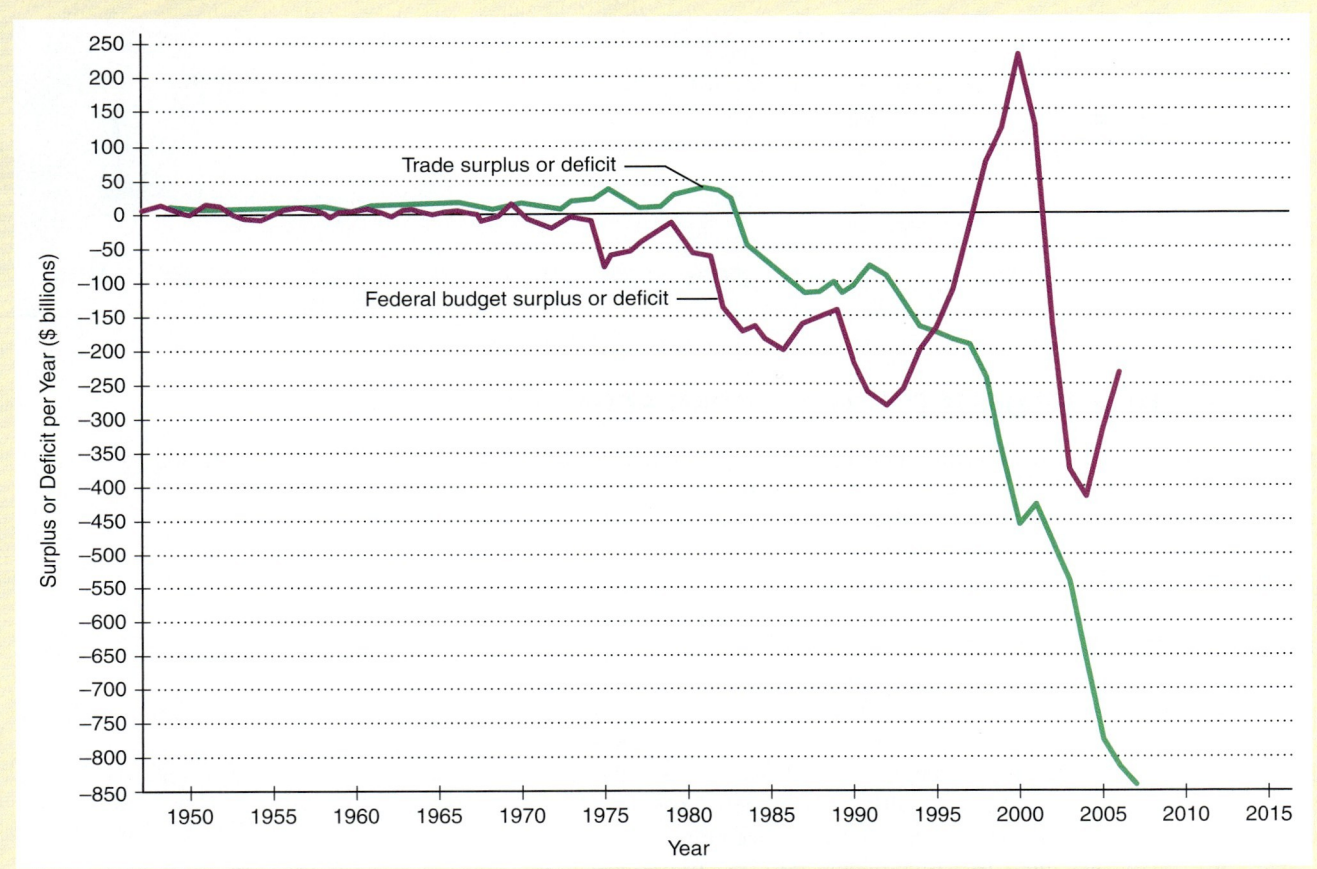

FIGURE 14-5

The Related U.S. Deficits

The United States exported more than it imported until 1983. Then it started experiencing large trade deficits, as shown in this diagram. The federal budget has been in deficit most years since the 1960s. The question is, has the federal budget deficit created the trade deficit?

Sources: *Economic Report of the President*; *Economic Indicators*, various issues; author's estimates.

Given that private domestic spending and other factors are unchanged, interest rates will indeed rise whenever there is an increase in deficits financed by increased borrowing.

When foreign dollar holders purchase the new U.S. government bonds, they will have fewer dollars to spend on our goods, that is, U.S. exports. Hence, when our nation's government operates with a budget deficit, we should expect to see foreign dollar holders spending more on U.S. government bonds and less on U.S.-produced goods and services. As a consequence of the U.S. government deficit, therefore, we should anticipate a decline in U.S. exports relative to U.S. imports, or a higher U.S. trade deficit.

GROWING U.S. GOVERNMENT DEFICITS: IMPLICATIONS FOR U.S. ECONOMIC PERFORMANCE

We have seen that one consequence of higher U.S. government budget deficits is higher international trade deficits. Higher budget deficits are also likely to have broader consequences for the economy. Reaching a consensus about these broader consequences, however, requires agreement about exactly how to measure deficits within the government's overall budget.

Which Government Deficit Is the "True" Deficit?

Assessing the implications of higher government deficits is complicated by the fact that the government may report distorted measures of its own budget. One problem is that the U.S. government has never adopted a particularly business-like approach to tracking its expenditures and receipts. Another is that even within its own accounting system, the government persists in choosing "official" measures that yield the lowest reported deficits and highest reported surpluses.

Capital Budgeting Theory.
The federal government has only one budget to guide its spending and taxing each fiscal year. It does not distinguish between current spending for upkeep of the grounds of the U.S. Capitol building, for example, and spending for a new aircraft carrier that will last for many years to come. In contrast, businesses, as well as state and local governments, have two budgets. One, called the *operating budget,* includes expenditures for current operations, such as salaries and interest payments. The other, called a *capital budget,* includes expenditures on investment items, such as machines, buildings, roads, and dams. Municipal governments, for example, may pay for items on the capital budget by long-term borrowing.

If the federal government used a capital budgeting system, we would see that a large portion of the more than $300 billion deficit estimated for fiscal year 2007 was being used to finance activities or assets yielding long-term returns. According to Office of Management and Budget (OMB) estimates for that year, investment-type outlays such as payments for military equipment and subsidies for research and development exceeded $165 billion.

For years, many economists have recommended that Congress create a capital budget and remove investment outlays from its operating budget. Opponents of such a change point out that it would allow the government to grow even faster than currently. After all, many new expenditures could be placed in the capital budget, thereby cutting the size of the operating budget deficit and reducing pressure on Congress to curtail the growth of federal government spending.

Pick a Deficit, Any Deficit.
Even using standard accounting techniques, the "official" U.S. government budget deficit can vary drastically, depending on what the government chooses to include or not include. Every year, the OMB makes predictions about the federal budget deficit. So does the Congressional Budget Office. The two budget agencies each produce several deficit estimates for each fiscal year. They give them names such as the "baseline deficit," the "policy deficit," or the "on-budget deficit."

There is also a deficit that is reduced by the amount of the Social Security surplus—for 2005 and 2006 combined a reduction on the order of $500 billion—even though Congress supposedly regards the Social Security surplus as a pool of funds set aside for future disbursement rather than a source of funds for current spending. We could go on, but the point is not to know the details of these various measures of "the government deficit," but rather to understand that no one number gives a complete picture of the total amount of the government budget deficit.

Public discourse might be simplified if everyone could agree on a single measure of the deficit, but the government's accounting system does not make it easy to determine which deficit figure is clearly "best." Thus, we should probably anticipate that for years to come, politicians and government officials will continue to bandy about whatever deficit figures best advance their own particular causes.

For more information about the role of the Office of Management and Budget in the government's budgeting process, go to **www.econtoday.com/ch14**.

The Macroeconomic Consequences of Budget Deficits

No matter how we choose to measure the federal government's deficit, everyone can agree that it has been rising in recent years. Let's consider, therefore, the broader effects of higher government budget deficits on the U.S. economy. When evaluating additional macroeconomic effects of government deficits, two important points must be kept well in mind. First, given the level of government expenditures, the main alternative to the deficit is higher taxes. Therefore, the effects of a deficit should be compared to the effects of higher taxes, not to zero. Second, it is important to distinguish between the effects of deficits when full employment exists and the effects when substantial unemployment exists.

Short-Run Macroeconomic Effects of Higher Budget Deficits. How do increased government budget deficits affect the economy in the short run? The answer depends on the initial state of the economy. Recall from Chapter 13 that higher government spending and lower taxes that generate budget deficits typically add to total planned expenditures, even after taking into account direct and indirect expenditure offsets. When there is a recessionary gap, the increase in aggregate demand can eliminate the recessionary gap and push the economy toward its full-employment real GDP level. In the presence of a short-run recessionary gap, therefore, government deficit spending can influence both real GDP and employment.

If the economy is at the full-employment level of real GDP, however, increased total planned expenditures and higher aggregate demand generated by a larger government budget deficit create an inflationary gap. Although greater deficit spending temporarily raises equilibrium real GDP above the full-employment level, the price level also increases.

Long-Run Macroeconomic Effects of Higher Budget Deficits. In a long-run macroeconomic equilibrium, the economy has fully adjusted to changes in all factors. These factors include changes in government spending and taxes and, consequently, the government budget deficit. Although increasing the government budget deficit raises aggregate demand, in the long run equilibrium real GDP remains at its full-employment level. Further increases in the government deficit via higher government expenditures or tax cuts can only be inflationary. They have no effect on equilibrium real GDP, which remains at the full-employment level in the long run.

The fact that long-run equilibrium real GDP is unaffected in the face of increased government deficits has an important implication:

> *In the long run, higher government budget deficits have no effect on equilibrium real GDP. Ultimately, therefore, government spending in excess of government receipts simply redistributes a larger share of real GDP to government-provided goods and services.*

Thus, if the government operates with higher deficits over an extended period, the ultimate result is a shrinkage in the share of privately provided goods and services. By continually spending more than it collects in taxes and other revenue sources, the government takes up a larger portion of economic activity.

How Could the Government Reduce All Its Red Ink?

There have been many suggestions about how to reduce the government deficit. One way to reduce the deficit is to increase tax collections.

QUICK QUIZ

Given constant shares of domestic consumption and domestic investment relative to GDP, funds to finance higher government budget deficits must come from abroad. To obtain the dollars required to purchase newly issued government bonds, foreign residents must sell _____ goods and services in the United States than U.S. residents sell abroad; thus, U.S. imports must _____ U.S. exports. For this reason, the federal budget deficit and the international trade _____ tend to be related.

Some people argue that the federal budget deficit is measured incorrectly because it lumps together spending on capital and spending on consumption. Establishing separate _____ and _____ budgets might, according to this view, promote more accurate measurement of federal finances.

Higher government deficits arise from increased government spending or tax cuts, which raise aggregate demand. Thus, larger government budget deficits can raise real GDP in a _____-gap situation. If the economy is already at the full-employment level of real GDP, however, higher government deficits can only temporarily push equilibrium real GDP _____ the full-employment level.

In the long run, higher government budget deficits cause the equilibrium price level to rise but fail to raise equilibrium real GDP above the full-employment level. Thus, the long-run effect of increased government deficits is simply a redistribution of real GDP from _____ provided goods and services to _____-provided goods and services.

See page 364 for the answers. Review concepts from this section in MyEconLab.

Increasing Taxes for Everyone. From an arithmetic point of view, a federal budget deficit can be wiped out by simply increasing the amount of taxes collected. Let's see what this would require. Projections for 2007 are instructive. The Office of Management and Budget estimated the 2007 federal budget deficit at about $230 billion. To have prevented this deficit from occurring by raising taxes, in 2007 the government would have had to collect at least $1,500 more in taxes from *every worker* in the United States. Needless to say, reality is such that we will never see annual federal budget deficits wiped out by simple tax increases.

Taxing the Rich. Some people suggest that the way to eliminate the deficit is to raise taxes on the rich. Data from the Internal Revenue Service (IRS) indicate that more than 84 percent of all federal income taxes are already being paid by the 25 percent of families earning the highest incomes in the United States. The entire lower 50 percent of families (those earning less than $60,000 per year) pay only slightly less than 4 percent of federal income taxes. At present, families whose incomes are in the top 5 percent pay nearly 57 percent of all federal income taxes each year. The richest 1 percent pay about 37 percent of all income taxes.

What does it mean to tax the rich more? If you talk about taxing "millionaires," you are referring to those who pay taxes on more than $1 million in income per year. There are fewer than 65,000 of them. Even if you were to double the taxes they currently pay, the reduction in the deficit would be relatively trivial. Changing marginal tax rates at the upper end will produce similarly unimpressive results. The IRS has determined that an increase in the top marginal tax rate from 35 percent to 45 percent would raise, at best, only about $30 billion in additional taxes. (This assumes that people do not figure out a way to avoid the higher tax rate.) Extra revenues of $30 billion per year represent less than 10 percent of the estimated 2007 federal budget deficit.

To what extent can high-income individuals avoid paying more taxes when the government raises their marginal income tax rates?

POLICY EXAMPLE

How Rich Taxpayers Avoid Part of a Tax-Rate Increase

Many who wish to raise taxes on the rich have proposed increasing the 35 percent marginal income tax rate faced by the highest-income taxpayers by 4.6 percentage points, to the 39.6 percent rate that applied during much of the 1990s. Proponents of this idea suggest that the government's tax collections would consequently increase by 4.6 percent of incomes within the highest bracket.

Just like everyone else, high-income individuals respond to incentives. Increasing the marginal tax rate for the highest-income bracket would induce more of the richest taxpayers to use *deferred-compensation plans.* These arrangements allow individuals to shift income earned in current years to future years, when tax rates might be lower. The U.S. government estimates that increasing the top-bracket tax rate from 35 percent to 39.6 percent would reduce total annual reported taxable income by at least 4 percent. Furthermore, it projects that such a tax-rate increase also would give the highest-income taxpayers a greater incentive to incorporate and pay lower corporate-profit tax rates. Thus, raising the income tax rate by 4.6 percentage points would result in government tax collections increasing by less than 4.6 percent of incomes in the highest bracket.

FOR CRITICAL ANALYSIS
Why would a $1 reduction in government spending do more to reduce the government budget deficit than imposing a higher tax rate on an additional $1 in income earned by an individual?

The reality is that the data do not support the notion that tax increases can reduce deficits. Although reducing a deficit in this way is possible arithmetically, politically just the opposite has occurred. When more tax revenues have been collected, Congress has usually responded by increasing government spending.

Reducing Expenditures. Reducing expenditures is another way to decrease the federal budget deficit. Figure 14-6 shows various components of government spending as a percentage of total expenditures. There you see that military spending as a share of total federal expenditures has risen slightly in recent years, though it remains much lower than in most previous years.

During the period from the conclusion of World War II until 1972, military spending was the most important aspect of the federal budget. Figure 14-6 shows that it no longer is, even taking into account the war on terrorism that began in late 2001. **Entitlements,** which are legislated federal government payments that anyone who qualifies is entitled to receive, are now the most important component of the federal budget. These include payments for Social Security and other income security programs and for Medicare and other health programs such as Medicaid. Entitlements are consequently often called **noncontrollable expenditures,** or nondiscretionary expenditures unrelated to national defense that automatically change without any direct action by Congress.

Entitlements
Guaranteed benefits under a government program such as Social Security, Medicare, or Medicaid.

Noncontrollable expenditures
Government spending that changes automatically without action by Congress.

Is It Time to Begin Whittling Away at Entitlements?
In 1960, spending on entitlements represented about 20 percent of the total federal budget. Today, entitlement expenditures make up more than half of total federal spending. Consider Social Security, Medicare, and Medicaid. In constant 2000 dollars, in 2007 Social Security, Medicare, and Medicaid represented about $1,250 billion of estimated federal expenditures, compared to

FIGURE 14-6

Components of Federal Expenditures as Percentages of Total Federal Spending

Although military spending as a percentage of total federal spending has risen and fallen with changing national defense concerns, national defense expenditures as a percentage of total spending have generally trended downward since the mid-1950s. Social Security and other income security programs and Medicare and other health programs now account for larger shares of total federal spending than any other programs.

Source: Office of Management and Budget.

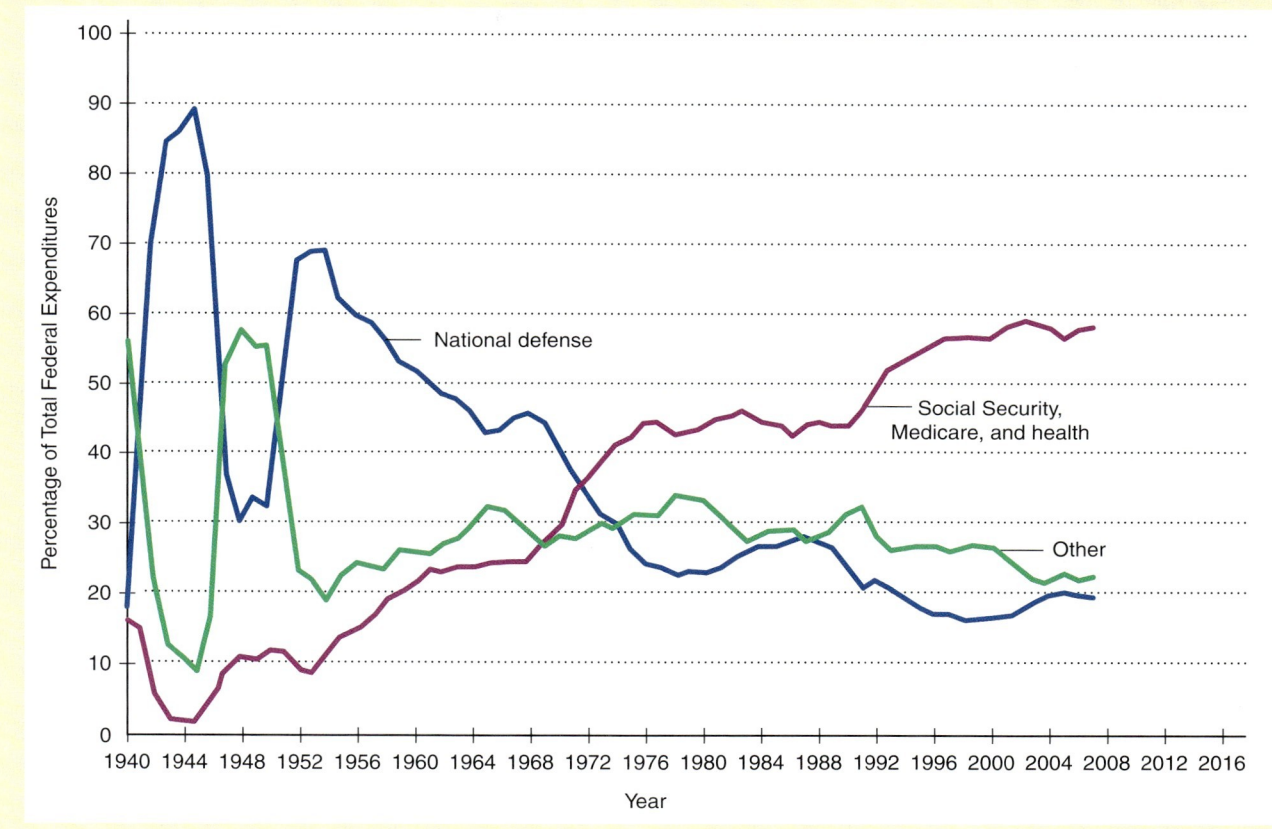

almost $1,200 billion of other spending by the federal government. (These exclude military and international payments and interest on the government debt.)

Entitlement payments for Social Security, Medicare, and Medicaid now exceed all other domestic spending. Entitlements are growing faster than any other part of the federal government budget. During the past two decades, real spending on entitlements (adjusted for inflation) grew between 7 and 8 percent per year, while the economy grew less than 3 percent per year. Social Security payments are growing in real terms at about 6 percent per year, but Medicare and Medicaid are growing at double-digit rates. The passage of Medicare prescription drug benefits in 2003 simply added to the already rapid growth of these health care entitlements.

Many people believe that entitlement programs are "necessary" federal expenditures. Interest on the public debt must be paid, but Congress can change just about every other federal expenditure labeled "necessary." The federal budget deficit is not expected to drop in the near future because entitlement programs are not likely to be eliminated. Governments have trouble cutting government benefit programs once they are established. This means that containing federal budget deficits is likely to prove to be a difficult task.

QUICK QUIZ

One way to reduce federal budget _____ is to increase taxes. Proposals to reduce deficits by raising taxes on the highest-income individuals will not appreciably reduce budget deficits, however.

Another way to decrease federal budget _____ is to cut back on government spending, particularly on _____, defined as benefits guaranteed under government programs such as Social Security and Medicare.

See page 364 for the answers. Review concepts from this section in MyEconLab.

CASE STUDY: ECONOMICS FRONT AND CENTER

The Public Debt—Public Enemy Number One

Senator Lampier, an influential member of the U.S. Senate, has declared that the rising U.S. public debt is imposing a burden on every citizen. His view, which he repeats in every media appearance, is that "the public debt is public enemy number one." His official Web site maintains daily updates on the magnitude of the gross public debt. Sometimes his staff assistants update the amount more than once per day.

In a recent appearance on a television news program, Senator Lampier blasted the U.S. Treasury for purchasing bonds that another government agency had issued last year to fund some of its expenditures. "Our nation's Treasury Department," he fumed, "should be concentrating on reducing the public debt, not on expanding that debt."

CRITICAL ANALYSIS QUESTIONS
1. Why might Senator Lampier's choice of a debt measure to report on his Web site be subject to legitimate criticism?
2. Is there a conceptual problem with Senator Lampier's concern about the Treasury's purchase of federal agency bonds?

Budget Deficit Rules Made to Be Broken?

Issues and Applications

Under the Stability and Growth Pact of the 25-nation European Union (EU), each EU member nation is supposed to satisfy two fiscal policy conditions. First, its net public debt as a percentage of GDP should be no higher than 60 percent. Second, the nation's annual government budget deficit is supposed to be no higher than 3 percent of its GDP.

All EU nations have satisfied the 60 percent constraint on net public debt as a proportion of GDP. In recent years, however, several EU countries have failed to satisfy the 3 percent limitation on the ratio of the budget deficit to GDP.

Concepts Applied
- Net Public Debt
- Government Budget Deficit
- Entitlements

The EU's Deficit Enforcement Procedure

If the EU's top policymaking agency, the European Commission, finds that a nation that uses the euro as its currency has breached the 3 percent deficit limit, it refers the matter to a group known as *Ecofin*. This group is the European Economic and Financial Affairs Council, which includes finance ministers and top budgetary officials of the EU nations.

Ecofin cannot rule that a nation's deficit is "excessive" if the country is in a "deep recession," defined as an annual decrease of more than 2 percent in GDP. The group has discretion to determine that a nation's deficit is "excessive" if its GDP has declined at an annual rate of at least 0.75 percent. If Ecofin does rule that a nation's deficit "excessively" exceeds the 3 percent limitation relative to GDP, then it can require the offending nation's government to hand over an amount of funds as high as 0.5 percent of its GDP. These funds would then be placed in a non-interest-bearing deposit. If the country's government fails to push the deficit-GDP ratio below 3 percent during the following two years, then the deposit becomes an unrecoverable fine.

Growing Entitlements Confront Stagnant Tax Revenues

Something that the authors of the EU's Stability and Growth Pact failed to foresee was that European economies might enter a period of very weak economic growth. Yet this is what happened in the 2000s, and slowed growth of real GDP caused taxable incomes in numerous European nations to increase at a snail's pace. As a consequence, governments' tax revenues fell flat even as public spending on various entitlements, such as old-age insurance programs and unemployment insurance, surged.

The combination of rising government spending and stalled tax revenues caused the German government to operate with budget deficits in excess of 3 percent of GDP for several consecutive years during the 2000s. By the mid-2000s, the governments of France, the Netherlands, Portugal, Italy, and Greece also were experiencing budget deficits exceeding the 3 percent limit.

359

Stretching the Rules in Hopes of Macroeconomic Payoffs

In principle, all six countries that violated the deficit limitation of the Stability and Growth Pact could have faced mandatory deposits and fines. In the end, however, Ecofin decided not to enforce the pact's rules. After the European Court of Justice determined that Ecofin had not properly enforced the treaty, EU heads of state negotiated formal changes to the Stability and Growth Pact. Under the revised treaty, Ecofin has broader discretionary authority *not* to enforce the 3 percent deficit-GDP limit. In effect, EU nations using the euro decided not to limit budget deficits after all.

Several of the governments that violated the 3 percent limit during the 2000s did so intentionally, in the hope that expansionary fiscal policies would boost aggregate demand and prevent recessions. Indeed, deficit spending may have helped raise aggregate demand and prevent short-run decreases in real GDP in Germany, France, and other nations that violated the Stability and Growth Pact's deficit limitations. Nevertheless, moribund economic growth continues throughout Europe. Stagnant tax revenues together with increased entitlement expenditures appear likely to fuel European government budget deficits for years to come.

Log in to MyEconLab, click on "Economic News," and test your understanding of the chapter by answering interactive questions that relate directly to this issue.

For Critical Analysis

1. Why do you suppose that some economists have questioned whether a fully enforced Stability and Growth Pact really would have provided much real GDP and employment stability for European economies?
2. Why might continued deficit spending in Germany, France, and other European nations have failed, so far, to help boost economic growth in the long run?

Web Resources

1. For background on the rationales for the Stability and Growth Pact, read the article available at www.econtoday.com/ch14.
2. To learn more about Ecofin's duties and responsibilities, go to www.econtoday.com/ch14.

Research Project

Apply the aggregate demand–aggregate supply framework to evaluate how instability in government spending and taxes—and, consequently, government budget deficits—can contribute to instability in real GDP. Why might your analysis help support the original aims of the Stability and Growth Pact? Now use the aggregate demand–aggregate supply model to explain how budget deficits or budget surpluses can, in principle, be used to help eliminate recessionary or inflationary gaps. How does this analysis weaken the case for the deficit limitations of the Stability and Growth Pact? On net, is there a clear-cut answer as to whether the pact's deficit limits make real GDP more stable?

WHAT YOU SHOULD KNOW

Federal Government Budget Deficits Whenever the flow of government expenditures exceeds the flow of government revenues during a period of time, a budget deficit occurs. If government expenditures are less than government revenues during a given interval, a budget surplus occurs. The government operates with a balanced budget during a specific period if its expenditures are equal to its revenues. The federal budget deficit expressed as a percentage of GDP most recently hit a peak of around 6 percent in the early 1980s. The federal government operated with a surplus between 1998 and 2001. The government budget went into deficit once more starting in 2002. The amount of the deficit is currently just above 2 percent of GDP.

government budget deficit, 343
balanced budget, 343
government budget surplus, 343
public debt, 344
Key figures
Figure 14-1, 345
Figure 14-2, 345

WHERE TO GO TO PRACTICE

- **MyEconLab** Study Plans 14.1 and 14.2
- Audio introduction to Chapter 14
- Animated Figures 14-1 and 14-2

The Public Debt The federal budget deficit is a flow, whereas accumulated budget deficits are a stock, called the public debt. The gross public debt is the stock of total government bonds, and the net public debt is the difference between the gross public debt and the amount of government agencies' holdings of government bonds. The net public debt as a share of GDP reached its peak right after World War II. In recent years, it has been running at around 40 percent of GDP.

gross public debt, 347
net public debt, 347
Key figure
Figure 14-3, 348

- **MyEconLab** Study Plan 14.3
- Animated Figure 14-3

How the Public Debt Might Prove a Burden to Future Generations If people are taxed, they must forgo private consumption as society substitutes government goods for private goods. Thus, if future generations must be taxed at higher rates to pay for the current generation's increased consumption of governmentally provided goods, future generations may experience a burden from the public debt. Also contributing to this potential burden is any current crowding out of investment as a consequence of additional debt accumulation, which can reduce capital formation and future economic growth. Furthermore, if capital invested by foreign residents who purchase some of the U.S. public debt has not been productively used, future generations will be worse off. If this capital is productive investment, however, future generations will be better off.

Key figure
Figure 14-5, 352

- **MyEconLab** Study Plans 14.3 and 14.4
- Animated Figure 14-5

WHAT YOU SHOULD KNOW

Why the Federal Budget Deficit Might Be Incorrectly Measured Some people contend that the federal budget deficit is measured incorrectly because it combines government capital and consumption expenditures. They argue that the federal government should have an operating budget and a capital budget.

- **MyEconLab** Study Plan 14.5

The Macroeconomic Effects of Government Budget Deficits Because higher government deficits are caused by increased government spending or tax cuts, they contribute to a rise in total planned expenditures and aggregate demand. If there is a short-run recessionary gap, higher government deficits can thereby push equilibrium real GDP toward the full-employment level. If the economy is already at the full-employment level of real GDP, however, then a higher deficit creates a short-run inflationary gap. In the long run, increased deficits only redistribute real GDP from privately provided goods and services to government-provided goods and services.

- **MyEconLab** Study Plan 14.5

Possible Ways to Reduce the Government Budget Deficit Suggested ways to reduce the deficit are to increase taxes, particularly on the rich, and to reduce expenditures, particularly on entitlements, defined as guaranteed benefits under government programs such as Social Security and Medicare.

entitlements, 356
noncontrollable
  expenditures, 356
Key figure
Figure 14-6, 357

- **MyEconLab** Study Plan 14.5
- Animated Figure 14-6

Log in to MyEconLab, take a chapter test, and get a personalized Study Plan that tells you which concepts you understand and which ones you need to review. From there, MyEconLab will give you further practice, tutorials, animations, videos, and guided solutions.

Log in to www.myeconlab.com

PROBLEMS

Select problems, indicated by a blue oval, are assignable in MyEconLab. Answers to the odd-numbered problems appear at the back of the book.

14-1 In 2009, government spending is $2.3 trillion, and taxes collected are $1.9 trillion. What is the federal government deficit in that year?

14-2 Suppose that the Office of Management and Budget provides the accompanying estimates of federal budget receipts, federal budget spending, and GDP, all expressed in billions of dollars. Calculate the implied estimates of the federal budget deficit as a percentage of GDP for each year.

Year	Federal Budget Receipts	Federal Budget Spending	GDP
2009	2,329.8	2,682.6	14,573.2
2010	2,392.4	2,741.6	15,316.0
2011	2,464.2	2,829.3	15,852.1
2012	2,513.5	2,900.1	16,454.4

14-3. It may be argued that the effects of a higher public debt are the same as the effects of a higher deficit. Why?

14-4. What happens to the net public debt if the federal government operates next year with a:
   a. budget deficit?
   b. balanced budget?
   c. budget surplus?

14-5. What is the relationship between the gross public debt and the net public debt?

14-6. Explain how each of the following will affect the net public debt, other things being equal.
   a. Previously, the government operated with a balanced budget, but recently there has been a sudden increase in federal tax collections.
   b. The federal government had been operating with a very small annual budget deficit until three successive hurricanes hit the Atlantic Coast, and now government spending has risen substantially.
   c. The General National Mortgage Association, a federal government agency that purchases certain types of home mortgages, buys U.S. Treasury bonds from another government agency.

14-7. Explain how each of the following will affect the net public debt, other things being equal.
   a. Until recently, the federal government has been operating with a very small annual budget surplus. Now Congress has eliminated several expenditure programs that it has decided wasted funds provided by taxpayers.
   b. Using funds raised from issuing bonds to another government agency, the U.S. Treasury decides to buy back bonds that it had issued three years ago to a different government agency.
   c. Previously, the government operated with a balanced budget, but there has been a drop in personal incomes and a corresponding decrease in individual income tax collections.

14-8. Explain in your own words why there is likely to be a relationship between federal budget deficits and U.S. international trade deficits.

14-9. Suppose that the share of U.S. GDP going to domestic consumption remains constant. Initially, the federal government was operating with a balanced budget, but this year it has increased its spending well above its collections of taxes and other sources of revenues. To fund its deficit spending, the government has issued bonds. So far, very few foreign residents have shown any interest in purchasing the bonds.

   a. What must happen to induce foreign residents to buy the bonds?
   b. If foreign residents desire to purchase the bonds, what is the most important source of dollars to buy them?

14-10. The Social Security surplus is a net sum of funds that Congress claims to "set aside" to help cover future payments of Social Security benefits. Why does including the Social Security surplus in a calculation of the government budget deficit reduce the reported size of the deficit?

14-11. Proponents of federal capital budgeting argue that whenever the government raises its spending by engaging in capital expenditures, such as spending on roads and dams, such spending should be recorded in a separate budget called the capital budget. By doing so, the federal government's budget deficit would be reduced by the amount of government capital spending. Would this alteration in the approach to measuring the government deficit actually change anything? Explain.

14-12. Suppose that the economy is experiencing the short-run equilibrium position depicted at point A in the diagram below. Then the government raises its spending and thereby runs a budget deficit in an effort to boost equilibrium real GDP to its long-run equilibrium level of $14 trillion (in base-year dollars). Explain the effects of an increase in the government deficit on equilibrium real GDP and the equilibrium price level. In addition, given that many taxes and government benefits vary with real GDP, discuss what change we might expect to see in the budget deficit as a result of the effects on equilibrium real GDP.

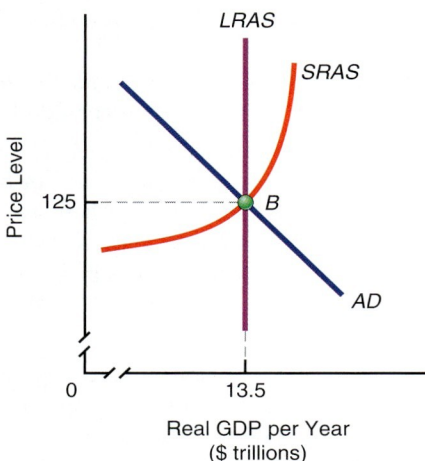

14-13 Suppose that the economy is experiencing the short-run equilibrium position depicted at point *B* in the diagram at the left. Explain the short-run effects of an increase in the government deficit on equilibrium real GDP and the equilibrium price level. What will be the long-run effects?

14-14. To reduce the size of the deficit (and reduce the growth of the net public debt), a politician suggests that "we should tax the rich." The politician makes a simple arithmetic calculation in which he applies the higher tax rate to the total income reported by "the rich" in a previous year. He says that this is how much the government could receive from increasing taxes on "the rich." What is the major fallacy in such calculations?

ECONOMICS ON THE NET

The Public Debt By examining the federal government's budget data, its current estimates of the public debt can be determined.

Title: Historical Tables: Budget of the United States Government

Navigation: Use the link at www.econontoday.com/ch14 to visit the Office of Management and Budget. Select the most recent budget. Then select *Historical Tables*.

Application After the document downloads, perform the indicated operations and answer the questions.

1. In the Table of Contents in the left-hand margin of the Historical Tables, click on Table 7.1, "Federal Debt at the End of the Year, 1940–2009." In light of the discussion in this chapter, which column shows the net public debt? What is the conceptual difference between the gross public debt and the net public debt? Last year, what was the dollar difference between these two amounts?

2. Table 7.1 includes estimates of the gross and net public debt over the next several years. Suppose that these estimates turn out to be accurate. Calculate how much the net public debt would increase on average each year. What are possible ways that the government could prevent these predicted increases from occurring?

For Group Study and Analysis Divide into two groups, and have each group take one side in answering the question, "Is the public debt a burden or a blessing?" Have each group develop rationales for supporting its position. Then reconvene the entire class, and discuss the relative merits of the alternative positions and rationales.

ANSWERS TO QUICK QUIZZES

p. 346: (i) budget deficit . . . balanced budget . . . budget surplus; (ii) stock; (iii) surplus . . . deficit . . . deficit
p. 351: (i) gross . . . net; (ii) future . . . current . . . less . . . lower; (iii) higher
p. 355: (i) more . . . exceed . . . deficit; (ii) operating . . . capital; (iii) recessionary . . . above; (iv) privately . . . government
p. 358: (i) deficits; (ii) deficits . . . entitlements

Money, Banking, and Central Banking

15

For decades, clearing checks has been a traditional function of the U.S. Federal Reserve System, our nation's central banking system that acts as a bank for private banks and for the government and that regulates the quantity of money in circulation. During the mid-2000s, however, the Federal Reserve began rapidly cutting back on the check-clearing capabilities of its banks and branches around the United States. Why is the Federal Reserve System clearing fewer checks? What is its role in our nation's financial system? In this chapter, you will learn the answers to these questions. First, however, you will learn more generally about money and banking in the United States and the rest of the world.

Learning Objectives

After reading this chapter, you should be able to:

1. Define the fundamental functions of money
2. Identify key properties that any good that functions as money must possess
3. Explain official definitions of the quantity of money in circulation
4. Understand why financial intermediaries such as banks exist
5. Describe the basic structure of the Federal Reserve System
6. Discuss the major functions of the Federal Reserve

MyEconLab helps you master each objective and study more efficiently. See end of chapter for details.

Did You Know That...

a Buddhist guru in Iowa recently issued his own paper currency? Four decades ago, the Maharishi Mahesh Yogi was best known as a guru to the 1960s rock-and-roll band called the Beatles. Today, he is the head of his own "nation," which he refers to as a "borderless state of mind" called the Global Country of World Peace. This "nation" has its own paper currency, the Raam Mudra (or simply, *raam*), which is available in one-, five-, and ten-raam denominations.

In Vedic City, Iowa, more than 3,000 members of the Global Country of World Peace are students at the Maharishi University of Management, which offers both an accredited MBA degree and a curriculum in a form of levitation known as "yogic flying." The official currency of the university is the raam. Backing the currency's value in the town is another item: $40,000 in U.S. dollars that the Maharishi has on deposit at Iowa State Bank and First National Bank of Fairfield, Iowa. Anyone in Vedic City who receives a raam-denominated payment from a Maharishi University student but would prefer to have dollars to spend elsewhere in the United States can trade 1 raam for $1 at either of these banks.

Coins, paper currency, and bank accounts from which people transmit debit-card and check payments are all included in the Federal Reserve's measure of the total amount of *money* that we can use to purchase goods and services. Money has been important to society for thousands of years. In the fourth century B.C., Aristotle claimed that everything had to "be accessed in money, for this enables men always to exchange their services, and so makes society possible." Money is indeed a part of our everyday existence. Nevertheless, we have to be careful when we talk about money. Often we hear a person say, "I wish I had more money," instead of "I wish I had more wealth," thereby confusing the concepts of money and wealth. Economists use the term **money** to mean anything that people generally accept in exchange for goods and services. Table 15-1 provides a list of some items that various civilizations have used as money. The best way to understand how these items served this purpose is to examine the functions of money.

Money
Any medium that is universally accepted in an economy both by sellers of goods and services as payment for those goods and services and by creditors as payment for debts.

THE FUNCTIONS OF MONEY

Money traditionally has four functions. The one that most people are familiar with is money's function as a *medium of exchange*. Money also serves as a *unit of accounting*, a *store of value* or *purchasing power*, and a *standard of deferred payment*. Anything that serves these four functions is money. Anything that could serve these four functions could be considered money.

TABLE 15-1

Types of Money

This is a partial list of things that have been used as money. Native Americans used *wampum*, beads made from shells. Fijians used whale teeth. The early colonists in North America used tobacco. And cigarettes were used in post–World War II Germany and in Poland during the breakdown of Communist rule in the late 1980s.

Iron	Boar tusk	Playing cards
Copper	Red woodpecker scalps	Leather
Brass	Feathers	Gold
Wine	Glass	Silver
Corn	Polished beads (wampum)	Knives
Salt	Rum	Pots
Horses	Molasses	Boats
Sheep	Tobacco	Pitch
Goats	Agricultural implements	Rice
Tortoise shells	Round stones with centers removed	Cows
Porpoise teeth	Crystal salt bars	Paper
Whale teeth	Snail shells	Cigarettes

Source: Roger LeRoy Miller and David D. VanHoose, *Money, Banking, and Financial Markets*, 3rd ed. (Cincinnati: South Western, 2007), p. 7.

Money as a Medium of Exchange

When we say that money serves as a **medium of exchange,** we mean that sellers will accept it as payment in market transactions. Without some generally accepted medium of exchange, we would have to resort to *barter*. In fact, before money was used, transactions took place by means of barter. **Barter** is simply a direct exchange of goods for goods. In a barter economy, the shoemaker who wants to obtain a dozen water glasses must seek out a glassmaker who at exactly the same time is interested in obtaining a pair of shoes. For this to occur, there has to be a high likelihood of a a *double coincidence of wants* for each specific item to be exchanged. If there isn't, the shoemaker must go through several trades in order to obtain the desired dozen glasses—perhaps first trading shoes for jewelry, then jewelry for some pots and pans, and then the pots and pans for the desired glasses.

Money facilitates exchange by reducing the transaction costs associated with means-of-payment uncertainty. That is, the existence of money means that individuals no longer have to hold a diverse collection of goods as an exchange inventory. As a medium of exchange, money allows individuals to specialize in producing those goods for which they have a comparative advantage and to receive money payments for their labor. Money payments can then be exchanged for the fruits of other people's labor. The use of money as a medium of exchange permits more specialization and the inherent economic efficiencies that come with it (and hence greater economic growth).

Medium of exchange
Any item that sellers will accept as payment.

Barter
The direct exchange of goods and services for other goods and services without the use of money.

Money as a Unit of Accounting

A **unit of accounting** is a way of placing a specific price on economic goods and services. It is the common denominator, the commonly recognized measure of value. The dollar is the unit of accounting in the United States. It is the yardstick that allows individuals easily to compare the relative value of goods and services. Accountants at the U.S. Department of Commerce use dollar prices to measure national income and domestic product, a business uses dollar prices to calculate profits and losses, and a typical household budgets regularly anticipated expenses using dollar prices as its unit of accounting.

Another way of describing money as a unit of accounting is to say that it serves as a *standard of value* that allows economic actors to compare the relative worth of various goods and services. This allows for comparison shopping, for example.

Unit of accounting
A measure by which prices are expressed; the common denominator of the price system; a central property of money.

Money as a Store of Value

One of the most important functions of money is that it serves as a **store of value** or purchasing power. The money you have today can be set aside to purchase things later on. In the meantime, money retains its nominal value, which you can apply to those future purchases. If you have $1,000 in your checking account, you can choose to spend it today on goods and services, spend it tomorrow, or spend it a month from now. In this way, money provides a way to transfer value (wealth) into the future.

Store of value
The ability to hold value over time; a necessary property of money.

Money as a Standard of Deferred Payment

The fourth function of the monetary unit is as a **standard of deferred payment.** This function involves the use of money both as a medium of exchange and as a unit of accounting. Debts are typically stated in terms of a unit of accounting; they are paid with a monetary medium of exchange. That is to say, a debt is specified in a dollar amount and paid in currency (or by check). A corporate bond, for example, has a face value—the

Standard of deferred payment
A property of an item that makes it desirable for use as a means of settling debts maturing in the future; an essential property of money.

dollar value stated on it, which is to be paid upon maturity. The periodic interest payments on that corporate bond are specified and paid in dollars, and when the bond comes due (at maturity), the corporation pays the face value in dollars to the holder of the bond.

How can vouchers purchased online function as money?

INTERNATIONAL EXAMPLE

Converting Dollars into African Vouchers on the Web

Many people who have immigrated to the United States from the African nations of Kenya and Uganda have been drawn to higher-wage jobs that they anticipate will provide higher incomes for themselves and for their families. In many cases, however, family members remain in Africa. If a Kenyan or Ugandan immigrant desires to convert hard-earned U.S. dollars into food products, visits to physicians, and other items for family members still living in Africa, one option is the Web site of Mama Mike's. This Nairobi-based service allows individuals to purchase vouchers online. Their family members in Africa are then notified that vouchers can be picked up in various locations in Kenya and Uganda and used to purchase goods and services at participating merchants throughout those African nations.

FOR CRITICAL ANALYSIS
In what ways do vouchers such as those issued through Mama Mike's service function as money?

LIQUIDITY

Liquidity
The degree to which an asset can be acquired or disposed of without much danger of any intervening loss in *nominal* value and with small transaction costs. Money is the most liquid asset.

Money is an asset—something of value—that accounts for part of personal wealth. Wealth in the form of money can be exchanged later for other assets, goods, or services. Although it is not the only form of wealth that can be exchanged for goods and services, it is the most widely and readily accepted one. This attribute of money is called **liquidity.** We say that an asset is *liquid* when it can easily be acquired or disposed of without high transaction costs and with relative certainty as to its value. Money is by definition the most liquid asset. Compare it, for example, with a share of stock listed on the New York Stock Exchange. To sell that stock, you may call a stockbroker, who will place the sell order for you. This generally must be done during normal business hours. You have to pay a commission to the broker or online service. Moreover, there is a distinct probability that you will get more or less for the stock than you originally paid for it. This is not the case with money. People can easily convert money to other asset forms. Therefore, most individuals hold at least a part of their wealth in the form of the most liquid of assets, money. You can see how assets rank in liquidity relative to one another in Figure 15-1.

FIGURE 15-1
Degrees of Liquidity
The most liquid asset is cash. Liquidity decreases as you move from right to left.

Antique furniture | Commercial office buildings | Old Masters paintings | Houses | Cars | Stocks and bonds | Certificates of deposit | Transactions deposits | Cash

Low Liquidity ←————————————————————————→ High Liquidity

When we hold money, however, we incur a cost for this advantage of liquidity. Because cash in your pocket and many checking or debit account balances do not earn interest, that price is the interest yield that could have been obtained had the asset been held in another form—for example, in the form of stocks and bonds.

The cost of holding money (its opportunity cost) is measured by the alternative interest yield obtainable by holding some other asset.

MONETARY STANDARDS, OR WHAT BACKS MONEY

In the past, many different monetary standards have existed. For example, commodity money, which is a physical good that may be valued for other uses it provides, has been used (see Table 15-1 on page 366). The main forms of commodity money were gold and silver. Today, though, most people throughout the world accept coins, paper currency, and balances held on deposit as **transactions deposits** (debitable and checkable accounts with banks and other financial institutions) in exchange for items sold, including labor services.

How has the Internet promoted the private use of gold-backed money?

Transactions deposits
Checkable and debitable account balances in commercial banks and other types of financial institutions, such as credit unions and mutual savings banks; any accounts in financial institutions from which you can easily transmit debit-card and check payments without many restrictions.

E-COMMERCE EXAMPLE

E-Gold-Backed E-Money

The Internet has served as a breeding ground for various forms of electronic money, known as e-money. One example is a throwback to the days of commodity money. This e-money, called "e-gold," is available at the Web site www.e-gold.com. At this site, an individual can open an account by purchasing e-gold that is fully backed by gold bars stored in repositories certified by the London Bullion Market Association. An account holder purchases an amount of e-gold based on the weight of actual gold backing the e-money. The site's online system allows an account holder to arrange to make a payment equal to, say, 20 troy ounces worth of e-gold to another authorized user located anywhere in the world. For those who prefer to keep track of their e-gold in dollars, euros, or six other national moneys, the system also automatically permits denomination of e-gold payments in these currencies as well. Hence, this e-gold-backed e-money effectively provides measures of the purchasing power, in terms of gold, of several major world currencies.

FOR CRITICAL ANALYSIS

How is e-gold's medium-of-exchange function somewhat limited?

The question remains, why are we willing to accept as payment something that has no intrinsic value? After all, you could not sell checks or debit cards to very many producers for use as a raw material in manufacturing. The reason is that payments in the modern world arise from a **fiduciary monetary system.** This means that the value of the payments rests on the public's confidence that such payments can be exchanged for goods and services. *Fiduciary* comes from the Latin *fiducia*, which means "trust" or "confidence." In our fiduciary monetary system, there is no legal requirement for money, in the form of currency or transactions deposits, to be convertible to a fixed quantity of gold, silver, or some other precious commodity. The bills are just pieces of paper. Coins have a value stamped on them that today is much greater than the market value of the metal in them. Nevertheless, currency and transactions deposits are money because of their acceptability and predictability of value.

Fiduciary monetary system
A system in which money is issued by the government and its value is based uniquely on the public's faith that the currency represents command over goods and services.

Acceptability

Transactions deposits and currency are money because they are accepted in exchange for goods and services. They are accepted because people have confidence that these items can later be exchanged for other goods and services. This confidence is based on the knowledge that such exchanges have occurred in the past without problems. Even during a period of inflation, we might still be inclined to accept money in exchange for goods and services because it is so useful. Barter is a costly and time-consuming alternative.

Realize that money is always socially defined. Acceptability is not something that you can necessarily predict. For example, the U.S. government has tried to circulate types of money, such as the $2 bill, that turned out to be socially unacceptable. How many $2 bills have you seen lately? The answer is probably none. No one wanted to make room for $2 bills in register tills or billfolds.

Predictability of Value

The purchasing power of the dollar (its real value) varies inversely with the price level. The more rapid the rate of increase of some price level index, such as the Consumer Price Index, the more rapid the decrease in the real value, or purchasing power, of a dollar. Money retains its usefulness even if its purchasing power is declining year in and year out, as in periods of inflation, if it still retains the characteristic of predictability of value. If you anticipate that the inflation rate is going to be around 3 percent during the next year, you know that any dollar you receive a year from now will have a purchasing power equal to 3 percent less than that same dollar today. Thus, you will not necessarily refuse to accept money in exchange simply because you know that its value will decline by the rate of inflation during the next year. You may, however, wish to be compensated for that *expected* decline in money's real value.

QUICK QUIZ

Money is defined by its functions, which are as a _____ of _____, _____ of _____, _____ of _____, and _____ of _____ _____.

Money is a highly _____ asset because it can be disposed of with low transaction costs and with relative certainty as to its value.

Modern nations have _____ monetary systems—national currencies are not convertible into a fixed quantity of a commodity such as gold or silver.

Money is accepted in exchange for goods and services because people have confidence that it can later be exchanged for other goods and services. In addition, money has _____ value.

See page 391 for the answers. Review concepts from this section in MyEconLab.

DEFINING MONEY

Money supply
The amount of money in circulation.

Money is important. Changes in the total **money supply**—the amount of money in circulation—and changes in the rate at which the money supply increases or decreases affect important economic variables (at least in the short run), such as the rate of inflation, interest rates, employment, and the level of real GDP. Although there is widespread agreement among economists that money is indeed important, they have struggled to reach agreement about how to define and measure it. There are two basic approaches: the **transactions approach,** which stresses the role of money as a medium of exchange, and the **liquidity approach,** which stresses the role of money as a temporary store of value.

The Transactions Approach to Measuring Money: M1

Using the transactions approach to measuring money, the money supply consists of currency, transactions deposits, and traveler's checks. One key designation of the money supply, including currency, transactions deposits, and traveler's checks not issued by banks, is **M1.** The various elements of M1 for a typical year are presented in panel (a) of Figure 15-2.

Currency. In the United States, currency includes coins minted by the U.S. Treasury and paper currency in the form of Federal Reserve notes issued by the Federal Reserve banks (to be discussed shortly). In other nations, currency also consists of coins and paper bills. The typical resident of another nation uses currency denominated in local money terms, but in many countries the U.S. dollar is the preferred currency for many transactions. For this reason, the bulk of U.S. currency "in circulation" actually does not circulate within the borders of the United States. Figure 15-3 on the next page displays the estimated value of U.S. currency in circulation elsewhere in the world. In any given year, at least two-thirds of the U.S. currency in existence circulates outside the United States!

> **Transactions approach**
> A method of measuring the money supply by looking at money as a medium of exchange.
>
> **Liquidity approach**
> A method of measuring the money supply by looking at money as a temporary store of value.
>
> **M1**
> The money supply, taken as the total value of currency plus transactions deposits plus traveler's checks not issued by banks.

FIGURE 15-2

Composition of the U.S. M1 and M2 Money Supply, 2007

Panel (a) shows estimates of the M1 money supply, of which the largest component (over 50 percent) is currency. M2 consists of M1 plus three other components, the most important of which is savings deposits at all depository institutions.

Sources: *Federal Reserve Bulletin; Economic Indicators,* various issues; author's estimates.

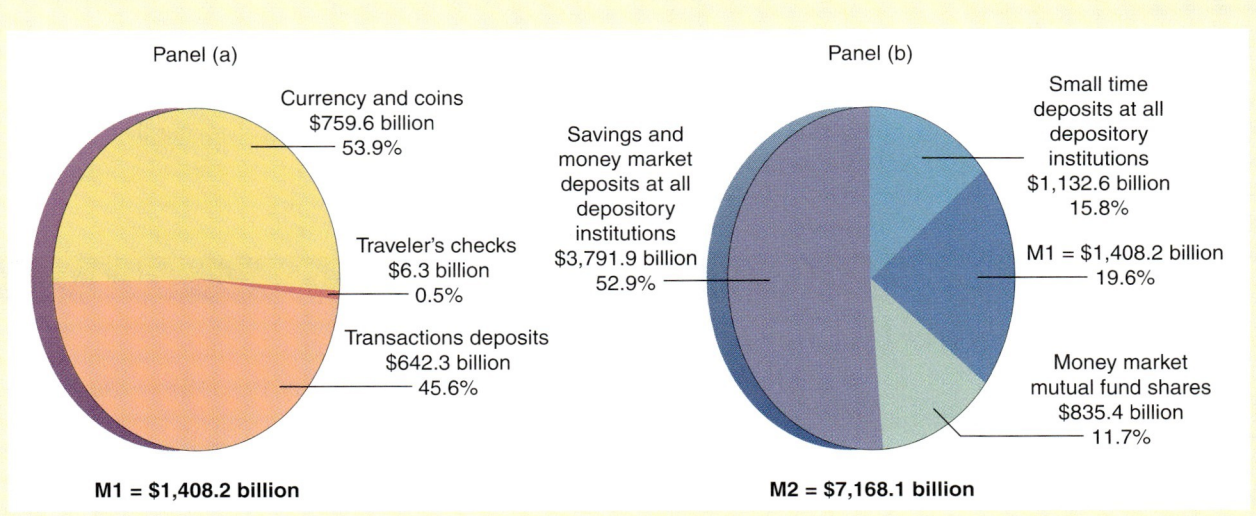

FIGURE 15-3
The Value of U.S. Currency in Circulation Outside the United States
The amount of U.S. dollars circulating beyond U.S. borders has grown steadily in recent years.
Sources: Board of Governors of the Federal Reserve System and author's estimates.

The United States is one of only a few nations that continues to issue a very small-denomination unit of currency—the dollar—in paper form. The norm in most other nations is to issue small denominations as coins instead of paper currency. For instance, when new European euro notes went into circulation in 2002, the smallest-denomination paper currency note was 5 euros, which was then worth roughly $5. The reason that most countries issue small currency denominations in the form of coins is that in the long run, coins are less costly than paper money to keep in circulation. A dollar bill normally wears out in about 18 months, but a coin typically lasts about 30 years. So, even though a dollar coin costs about 12 cents to produce, or more than three times the cost of producing a dollar bill, maintaining dollar coins in circulation over many years would be much less costly. Nevertheless, so far U.S. efforts to introduce dollar coins have not succeeded.

Why do you think that the fast-food retailer McDonald's is hoping that its customers will stop using cash to purchase soft drinks?

EXAMPLE

Why McDonald's Wants Your Card, Not Your Cash

Fast-food giant McDonald's has equipped virtually every restaurant to accept credit- and debit-card payments. Some restaurants have also begun offering radio frequency payment tags that allow customers to wave a card across a scanning device. Equipping each restaurant has entailed a one-time system installation cost of about $2,500 and a $100 monthly telecommunications expense. Processing a typical bank card transaction requires a McDonald's restaurant to pay a fee of nearly 2 percent of the transaction's dollar value.

(continued)

For years, McDonald's resisted accepting payment cards. The time customers spent providing verification signatures slowed lines and made it harder for restaurants to serve their fast food fast. Banks were also unwilling to process very small-denomination transactions, such as the purchase of a $1.25 soft drink. In recent years, however, banks have switched to debit-card systems that no longer require customer signatures and that process even the tiniest transactions.

McDonald's card-processing systems can complete a transaction in four to seven seconds, which is several seconds speedier than a cash exchange. This makes serving fast food even faster and, consequently, more cost-efficient for McDonald's restaurants.

FOR CRITICAL ANALYSIS
Why might McDonald's anticipate that promoting cashless payments could increase its overall profitability, even though the company incurred large costs for the equipment to process these payments?

Transactions Deposits. Individuals conduct most of their larger transactions with debit cards and checks. The convenience and safety of using debit cards and checks have made transactions deposits the most important component of the money supply. Debit and checking transactions are a means of transferring the ownership of deposits in financial institutions. Hence, transactions deposits are normally acceptable as a medium of exchange. The financial institutions that offer transactions deposits are numerous and include commercial banks and virtually all **thrift institutions**—savings banks, savings and loan associations (S&Ls), and credit unions.

Traveler's Checks. **Traveler's checks** are paid for by the purchaser at the time of transfer. The total quantity of traveler's checks outstanding issued by institutions other than banks is part of the M1 money supply. American Express, Cook's, and other institutions issue traveler's checks.

The Liquidity Approach to Measuring Money: M2

The liquidity approach to defining and measuring the U.S. money supply involves taking into account not only the most liquid assets that people use as money, which are already included in the definition of M1, but also other assets that are highly liquid—that is, assets that can be converted into money quickly without loss of nominal dollar value and without much cost. Any (non-M1) assets that come under this definition have been called **near moneys**. Thus, the liquidity approach to the definition of the money supply views money as a temporary store of value and so includes all of M1 *plus* several near moneys. Panel (b) of Figure 15-2 on page 371 shows the components of **M2**—money as a temporary store of value. We examine each of these components in turn.

Savings Deposits. Total **savings deposits** in all **depository institutions** (such as commercial banks, savings banks, savings and loan associations, and credit unions) are part of the M2 money supply. A savings deposit has no set maturity.

Since 1982, banks and thrift institutions have offered a popular form of savings deposit known as **money market deposit accounts (MMDAs)**. These deposits usually require a minimum balance and set limits on the number of monthly transactions (deposits and withdrawals by check).

Small-Denomination Time Deposits. A basic distinction has always been made between a transactions deposit, from which check or debit-card payments may be transmitted,

Thrift institutions
Financial institutions that receive most of their funds from the savings of the public; they include savings banks, savings and loan associations, and credit unions.

Traveler's checks
Financial instruments obtained from a bank or a nonbanking organization and signed during purchase that can be used as cash upon a second signature by the purchaser.

Near moneys
Assets that are almost money. They have a high degree of liquidity and thus can be easily converted into money without loss in value. Time deposits are an example.

M2
M1 plus (1) savings and small-denomination time deposits at all depository institutions, (2) balances in retail money market mutual funds, and (3) money market deposit accounts (MMDAs).

Savings deposits
Interest-earning funds that can be withdrawn at any time without payment of a penalty.

Depository institutions
Financial institutions that accept deposits from savers and lend funds from those deposits out at interest.

Money market deposit accounts (MMDAs)
Accounts issued by banks yielding a market rate of interest with a minimum balance requirement and a limit on transactions. They have no minimum maturity.

Time deposit
A deposit in a financial institution that requires notice of intent to withdraw or must be left for an agreed period. Withdrawal of funds prior to the end of the agreed period may result in a penalty.

Certificate of deposit (CD)
A time deposit with a fixed maturity date offered by banks and other financial institutions.

and a **time deposit,** which theoretically requires notice of withdrawal and on which the financial institution pays the depositor interest. The name indicates that there is an agreed period during which the funds must be left in the financial institution. If the deposit holder withdraws funds before the end of that period, the institution issuing the deposit may apply a penalty. Time deposits include savings certificates and small **certificates of deposit (CDs).** The owner of a savings certificate is given a receipt indicating the amount deposited, the interest rate to be paid, and the maturity date. A CD is an actual certificate that indicates the date of issue, its maturity date, and other relevant contractual matters.

The distinction between transactions deposits and time deposits has blurred over time, but it is still used in the official definition of the money supply. To be included in the M2 definition of the money supply, however, time deposits must be less than $100,000—hence the designation *small-denomination time deposits*. A variety of small-denomination time deposits are available from depository institutions, ranging in maturities from one month to 10 years.

Money Market Mutual Fund Balances.

Money market mutual funds
Funds obtained fron the public that investment companies hold in common and use to acquire short-maturity credit instruments, such as certificates of deposit and securities sold by the U.S. government.

Many individuals keep part of their assets in the form of shares in **money market mutual funds.** These retail mutual funds invest only in short-term credit instruments. The majority of these money market funds allow check-writing privileges, provided that the size of the check exceeds some minimum amount, usually $100. All money market mutual fund balances except those held by large institutions (which typically use them more like large time deposits) are included in M2.

M2 and Other Money Supply Definitions.

When all of these assets are added together, the result is M2, as shown in panel (b) of Figure 15-2 on page 371.

Economists and other researchers have come up with additional definitions of money. Some are simply broader than M2. Just remember that there is no best definition of the money supply. For different purposes and under varying institutional circumstances, different definitions are appropriate. The definition that seems to correlate best with economic activity on an economywide basis for most countries is probably M2, although some businesspeople and policymakers prefer a monetary aggregate known as *MZM*. The MZM aggregate is the so-called money-at-zero-maturity money stock. Obtaining MZM entails adding to M1 those deposits without set maturities, such as savings deposits, that are included in M2. MZM includes *all* money market funds, however, and it excludes all deposits with fixed maturities, such as small-denomination time deposits.

For Federal Reserve data concerning the latest trends in the monetary aggregates, go to www.econtoday.com/ch15 and click on "Money Stock Measures–H.6" under Money Stock and Reserve Balances.

QUICK QUIZ

The **money supply** can be defined in a variety of ways, depending on whether we use the transactions approach or the liquidity approach. Using the _____ approach, the money supply consists of currency, **transactions deposits,** and traveler's checks. This is called _____.

_____ deposits are any deposits in financial institutions from which the deposit owner can transfer funds using a debit card or checks.

When we add savings deposits, small-denomination time deposits (certificates of deposit), money market deposit accounts, and retail money market mutual fund balances to _____, we obtain the measure known as _____.

See page 391 for the answers. Review concepts from this section in MyEconLab.

FINANCIAL INTERMEDIATION AND BANKS

Most nations, including the United States, have a banking system that encompasses two types of institutions. One type consists of private banking institutions. These include commercial banks, which are privately owned profit-seeking institutions, and thrift institutions, such as savings banks, savings and loan associations, and credit unions. Thrift institutions may be profit-seeking institutions, or they may be *mutual* institutions that are owned by their depositors. The other type of institution is a **central bank,** which typically serves as a banker's bank and as a bank for the national treasury or finance ministry.

Central bank
A banker's bank, usually an official institution that also serves as a country's treasury's bank. Central banks normally regulate commercial banks.

Direct versus Indirect Financing

When individuals choose to hold some of their savings in new bonds issued by a corporation, their purchases of the bonds are in effect direct loans to the business. This is an example of *direct finance,* in which people lend funds directly to a business. Business financing is not always direct. Individuals might choose instead to hold a time deposit at a bank. The bank may then lend to the same company. In this way, the same people can provide *indirect finance* to a business. The bank makes this possible by *intermediating* the financing of the company.

Financial Intermediation

Banks and other financial institutions are all in the same business—transferring funds from savers to investors. This process is known as **financial intermediation,** and its participants, such as banks and savings institutions, are **financial intermediaries.** The process of financial intermediation is illustrated in Figure 15-4.

Financial intermediation
The process by which financial institutions accept savings from businesses, households, and governments and lend the savings to other businesses, households, and governments.

Financial intermediaries
Institutions that transfer funds between ultimate lenders (savers) and ultimate borrowers.

Asymmetric Information, Adverse Selection, and Moral Hazard.
Why might people wish to direct their funds through a bank instead of lending them directly to a business? One important reason is **asymmetric information**—the fact that the business may have better knowledge of its own current and future prospects than potential lenders do. For instance, the business may know that it intends to use borrowed funds for projects with a high risk of failure that would make repaying the loan difficult. This potential for

Asymmetric information
Information possessed by one party in a financial transaction but not by the other party.

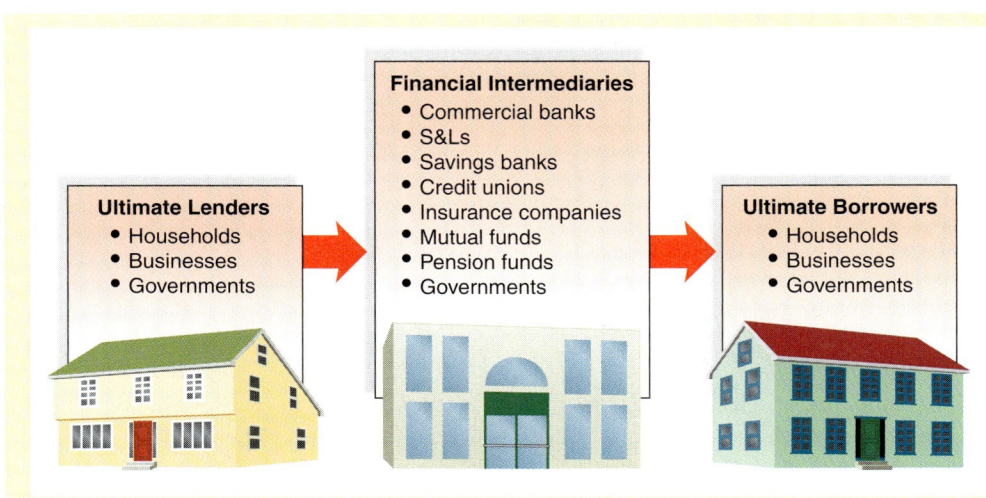

FIGURE 15-4

The Process of Financial Intermediation

The process of financial intermediation is depicted here. Note that ultimate lenders and ultimate borrowers are the same economic units—households, businesses, and governments—but not necessarily the same individuals. Whereas individual households can be net lenders or borrowers, households as an economic unit typically are net lenders. Specific businesses or governments similarly can be net lenders or borrowers; as economic units, both are net borrowers.

Adverse selection
The likelihood that individuals who seek to borrow may use the funds that they receive for high-risk projects.

Moral hazard
The possibility that a borrower might engage in riskier behavior after a loan has been obtained.

borrowers to use the borrowed funds in high-risk projects is known as **adverse selection.** Alternatively, a business that had intended to undertake low-risk projects may change management after receiving a loan, and the new managers may use the borrowed funds in riskier ways. The possibility that a borrower might engage in behavior that increases risk after borrowing funds is called **moral hazard.**

To minimize the possibility that a business might fail to repay a loan, people thinking about lending funds directly to the business must study the business carefully before making the loan, and they must continue to monitor its performance afterward. Alternatively, they can choose to avoid the trouble by holding deposits with financial intermediaries, which then specialize in evaluating the creditworthiness of business borrowers and in keeping tabs on their progress until loans are repaid. Thus, adverse selection and moral hazard both help explain why people use financial intermediaries.

ECONOMICS FRONT AND CENTER

For practice thinking through the difference between adverse selection and moral hazard, read **A Well-Intentioned Law Creates Problems in Japan,** on page 385.

Larger Scale and Lower Management Costs. Another important reason that financial intermediaries exist is that they make it possible for many people to pool their funds, thereby increasing the size, or *scale,* of the total amount of savings managed by an intermediary. This centralization of management reduces costs and risks below the levels savers would incur if all were to manage their savings alone. *Pension fund companies,* which are institutions that specialize in managing funds that individuals save for retirement, owe their existence largely to their abilities to provide such cost savings to individual savers. Likewise, *investment companies,* which are institutions that manage portfolios of financial instruments called mutual funds on behalf of shareholders, also exist largely because of cost savings from their greater scale of operations.

Why do you suppose that so many U.S. banks have offered a variety of incentives to encourage customers to use online banking services?

E-COMMERCE EXAMPLE

Why Banks Want Their Customers to Go Online

Have you noticed that banks have been trying to persuade their customers to bank online? The reason is that the banks themselves stand to gain. Some banks have reported that customers who use online banking cost about 15 percent less to serve than traditional customers. In addition, a typical online banking customer holds about 20 percent more funds on deposit and generates as much as 50 percent more revenues than a traditional customer.

Almost every household with Internet access has had the capability to undertake online banking transactions since the late 1990s. As late as 1998, however, fewer than 10 percent of households regularly engaged in online banking. In an effort to give more customers a greater incentive to click their way to online deposit transfers, bill payments, loan applications, and the like, during the 2000s banks have sharply reduced the fees they charge for Web access. A number of banks, such as Bank of America and J. P. Morgan Chase, have eliminated most online banking fees in an effort to induce their customers to move more transactions to the Internet. So far, these efforts have convinced about 35 percent of the nation's banking customers to use online banking services on a regular basis.

FOR CRITICAL ANALYSIS

How might a bank's profits increase even if it does not charge fees to those customers who utilize its online banking facilities?

Liabilities
Amounts owed; the legal claims against a business or household by nonowners.

Financial Institution Liabilities and Assets. Every financial intermediary has its own sources of funds, which are **liabilities** of that institution. When you place $100 in your transactions deposit at a bank, the bank creates a liability—it owes you $100—in exchange for the funds deposited. A commercial bank gets its funds from transactions

Financial Intermediary	Assets	Liabilities	
Commercial banks	Car loans and other consumer debt, business loans, government securities, home mortgages	Transactions deposits, savings deposits, various other time deposits, money market deposit accounts	**TABLE 15-2** **Financial Intermediaries and Their Assets and Liabilities**
Savings and loan associations and savings banks	Home mortgages, some consumer and business debt	Savings and loan shares, transactions deposits, various time deposits, money market deposit accounts	
Credit unions	Consumer debt, long-term mortgage loans	Credit union shares, transactions deposits	
Insurance companies	Mortgages, stocks, bonds, real estate	Insurance contracts, annuities, pension plans	
Pension and retirement funds	Stocks, bonds, mortgages, time deposits	Pension plans	
Money market mutual funds	Short-term credit instruments such as large-bank CDs, Treasury bills, and high-grade commercial paper	Fund shares with limited checking privileges	

and savings accounts; an insurance company gets its funds from insurance policy premiums.

Each financial intermediary has a different primary use of its **assets.** For example, a credit union usually makes small consumer loans, whereas a savings bank makes mainly mortgage loans. Table 15-2 lists the assets and liabilities of typical financial intermediaries. Be aware, though, that the distinctions between different types of financial institutions are becoming more and more blurred. As laws and regulations change, there will be less need to make any distinction. All may ultimately be treated simply as financial intermediaries.

Assets
Amounts owned; all items to which a business or household holds legal claim.

Payment Intermediaries

A commercial bank is an example of a type of financial intermediary that performs another important function. Together with savings and loan associations and credit unions, commercial banks operate as **payment intermediaries,** which are institutions that facilitate payments on behalf of holders of transactions deposits.

Payment intermediaries
Institutions that facilitate transfers of funds between depositors who hold transactions deposits with those institutions.

Transmitting Payments via Debit-Card Transactions.
In 2006, the dollar volume of payments transmitted using debit cards exceeded the value of checking transactions. To see how a debit-card transaction clears, take a look at Figure 15-5 on the following page. Suppose that Bank of America has provided a debit card to a college student named Jill Jones, who in turn uses the card to purchase $200 worth of clothing from Macy's, which has an account at Citibank. The debit-card transaction generates an electronic record, which Macy's transmits to Citibank.

The debit-card system automatically uses the electronic record to determine the bank that issued the debit card used to purchase the clothing. It transmits this information to Bank of America. Then Bank of America verifies that Jill Jones is an account holder, deducts $200 from her transactions deposit account, and transmits these funds electronically,

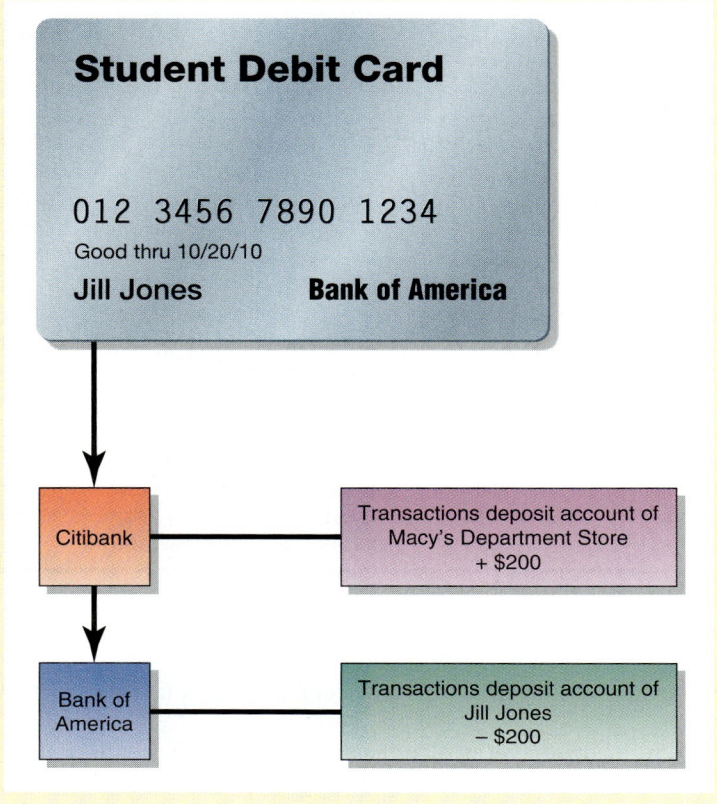

FIGURE 15-5

How a Debit-Card Transaction Clears

When a college student named Jill Jones uses a debit card issued by Bank of America to purchase clothing valued at $200 from Macy's, which has an account with Citibank, the debit-card transaction creates an electronic record that is transmitted to Citibank. The debit-card system forwards this record to Bank of America, which deducts $200 from Jill Jones's transactions deposit account. Then the debit-card system transmits the $200 payment to Citibank, which credits the $200 to Macy's account.

via the debit-card system, to Citibank. Finally, Citibank credits $200 to Macy's transactions deposit account, and payment for the clothing purchase is complete.

The Payoff from Payment Intermediation. Payment intermediation has traditionally been a key activity of banks. Until recently, however, the impact of this aspect of their operations on their bottom line has often been hard for economists to determine.

A Federal Reserve Bank of New York study recently attempted to determine banks' payoffs from providing payments-related services to their customers. This study of the income statements of the 25 largest U.S. banking companies revealed that revenues derived from debit-card and checking transfer services accounted for 28 percent of the banks' total earnings. Another 10 percent of the institutions' earnings were generated from processing payments for credit cards, stocks, and bonds. Thus, payment intermediation is a fundamental aspect of the banking business.

Financial Intermediation Across National Boundaries

Capital controls
Legal restrictions on the ability of a nation's residents to hold and trade assets denominated in foreign currencies.

International financial diversification
Financing investment projects in more than one country.

Some countries' governments restrict the financial intermediation process to within their national boundaries. They do so by imposing legal restraints called **capital controls** that bar certain flows of funds across their borders. Nevertheless, today many nations have reduced or even eliminated capital controls. This permits their residents to strive for **international financial diversification** by engaging in the direct or indirect financing of companies located in various nations.

TABLE 15-3
The World's Largest Banks
Historically, there usually are few U.S. banks among the world's top 10.

Bank	Country	Assets ($ billions)
Barclays PLC	United Kingdom	1,587
UBS AG	Switzerland	1,563
BNP Paribas	France	1,484
Royal Bank of Scotland	United Kingdom	1,300
Crédit Agricole	France	1,252
Deutsche Bank	Germany	1,170
Bank of America	United States	1,082
ABN Amro	Netherlands	1,039
Credit Suisse	Switzerland	1,016
J.P. Morgan Chase	United States	1,014

Source: *Banker's Almanac*, July 2006.

Because business conditions may be good in one country, as they were in the United States in the mid-2000s, at the same time that they are poor in another, such as Germany during the mid-2000s, people can limit their overall lending risks through international financial diversification. One way to do this is to hold a portion of one's savings with an investment company that offers a **world index fund.** This is a carefully designed set of globally issued bonds yielding returns that historically tend to move in offsetting directions. By holding world index funds, individuals can earn the average return on bonds from a number of nations while keeping overall risk of loss to a minimum.

Holding shares in a world index fund is an example of indirect finance across national borders through financial intermediaries. Banks located in various countries take part in the process of international financial intermediation by using some of the funds of depositors in their home nations to finance loans to companies based in other nations. Today, bank financing of U.S. business activities increasingly stems from loans by non-U.S. banks.

Indeed, as Table 15-3 indicates, the world's largest banks are not all based in the United States. Today, most of the largest banking institutions, sometimes called *megabanks,* are based in Europe. These megabanks typically take in deposits and lend throughout the world. Although they report their profits and pay taxes in their home nations, these megabanks are in all other ways international banking institutions.

World index fund
A portfolio of bonds issued in various nations whose individual yields generally move in offsetting directions, thereby reducing the overall risk of losses.

BANKING STRUCTURES THROUGHOUT THE WORLD

Multinational businesses have relationships with megabanks based in many nations. Individuals and companies increasingly retain the services of banks based outside their home countries. The business of banking varies from nation to nation, however. Each country has its own distinctive banking history, and this fact helps explain unique features of the world's banking systems.

A World of National Banking Structures

Countries' banking systems differ in a number of ways. In some nations, banks are the crucial component of the financial intermediation process, but in others, banking is only part of a varied financial system. In addition, some countries have only a few large banks, while others, such as the United States, have relatively large numbers of banks of various sizes. The legal environments regulating bank dealings with individual and business customers also differ considerably across nations.

To learn more from the Bank for International Settlements about worldwide banking developments, go to www.econtoday.com/ch15. Select "Annual Report."

The extent to which banks are the predominant means by which businesses finance their operations is a key way that national banking systems differ. For instance, in Britain, nearly 70 percent of funds raised by businesses typically stem from bank borrowings, and the proportions for Germany and Japan are on the order of 50 percent and 65 percent, respectively. By contrast, U.S. businesses normally raise less than 30 percent of their funds through bank loans.

The relative sizes of banks also differ from one country to another. The five largest banks in Belgium, Denmark, France, Italy, Luxembourg, Portugal, Spain, and the United Kingdom have over 60 percent of the deposits of their nations' residents. In Greece and the Netherlands, this figure is over 80 percent. In contrast, the top five U.S. banks account for less than 50 percent of the deposit holdings of U.S. residents. In Germany, Japan, and Britain, about three-fourths of total bank assets are held by the largest 10 banks. In the United States, this figure is about 60 percent.

Universal Banking

Universal banking
An environment in which banks face few or no restrictions on their powers to offer a full range of financial services and to own shares of stock in corporations.

Traditionally, another feature that has distinguished national banking systems has been the extent to which they have permitted **universal banking.** Under this form of banking, there are few, if any, limits on the ability of banks to offer a full range of financial services and to own shares of corporate stock.

In Germany, Britain, and other European nations, banks have had the right to sell insurance and to own stock for many years. Japanese banks face greater restrictions on their activities than European banks, but many Japanese banks have long had the authority to buy stocks. Until very recently, U.S. banks could not hold *any* shares of stock, even for brief periods, and were subject to limitations on their ability to offer insurance policies to their customers. This state of affairs changed, however, with passage of the Gramm-Leach-Bliley Act of 1999. This legislation authorized U.S. commercial banks to market insurance and to own stock. Consequently, national differences in banking powers are much narrower than they were just a few years ago.

QUICK QUIZ

_____ intermediaries, including depository institutions such as commercial banks and savings institutions, insurance companies, mutual funds, and pension funds, transfer funds from ultimate lenders (savers) to ultimate borrowers. Depository institutions also operate as _____ intermediaries that transfer funds on behalf of holders of transactions deposits.

Financial intermediaries specialize in tackling problems of _____ information. They address the _____ problem by carefully reviewing the creditworthiness of loan applicants, and they deal with the _____ _____ problem by monitoring borrowers after they receive loans. Many financial intermediaries also take advantage of cost reductions arising from the centralized management of funds pooled from the savings of many individuals.

In the absence of _____ _____ that inhibit flows of funds across national borders, many financial intermediaries also take advantage of overall risk reductions made possible by international financial _____. This has led to the development of megabanks, which operate in many countries.

See page 391 for the answers. Review concepts from this section in MyEconLab.

Central Banks and Their Roles

The first central bank, which began operations in 1668, was Sweden's Sveriges Riksbank (called the Risens Standers Bank until 1867). In 1694, the English Parliament established the most historically famous of central banks, the Bank of England. It authorized the Bank of England to issue currency notes redeemable in silver, and initially the Bank of

England's notes circulated alongside currency notes issued by the government and private finance companies. Until 1800, the Riksbank and the Bank of England were the only central banks. The number of central banks worldwide was less than 10 as late as 1873. The number expanded toward the end of the nineteenth century and again considerably during the second half of the twentieth century. Today, there are about 180 central banks.

The duties of central banks fall into three broad categories:

1. They perform banking functions for their nations' governments.
2. They provide financial services for private banks.
3. They conduct their nations' monetary policies.

The third is the area of central banking that receives the most media attention, even though most central banks devote the bulk of their resources to the other two tasks.

THE FEDERAL RESERVE SYSTEM

The Federal Reserve System, also known simply as **the Fed,** is the most important regulatory agency in the United States' monetary system and is usually considered the monetary authority. The Fed was established by the Federal Reserve Act, signed on December 13, 1913, by President Woodrow Wilson. The act was the outgrowth of recommendations from the National Monetary Commission, which had been authorized by the Aldridge-Vreeland Act of 1908. Basically, the commission had attempted to find a way to counter the periodic financial panics that had occurred in our country. Based on the commission's recommendations, which were developed after considerable study of the Bank of England and other central banks, Congress established the Federal Reserve System to aid and supervise banks and also to provide banking services for the U.S. Treasury.

The Fed
The Federal Reserve System; the central bank of the United States.

Organization of the Federal Reserve System

Figure 15-6 on the following page shows how the Federal Reserve System is organized. It is managed by the Board of Governors, composed of seven full-time members appointed by the U.S. president with the approval of the Senate. The chair of the Board of Governors is the leading official of the Board of Governors and of the Federal Reserve System. Since 2006, Ben Bernanke has held this position.

The 12 Federal Reserve district banks have a total of 25 branches. The boundaries of the 12 Federal Reserve districts and the cities in which Federal Reserve banks are located are shown in Figure 15-7 on page 383. The Federal Open Market Committee (FOMC) determines the future growth of the money supply and other important variables. This committee is composed of the members of the Board of Governors, the president of the New York Federal Reserve Bank, and presidents of four other Federal Reserve banks, rotated periodically. The chair of the Board of Governors also chairs the FOMC.

Depository Institutions

Depository institutions—all financial institutions that accept deposits—that comprise our monetary system consist of about 7,500 commercial banks, 1,300 savings and loan associations and savings banks, and 11,000 credit unions. All depository institutions may purchase services from the Federal Reserve System on an equal basis. Also, almost all depository institutions are required to keep a certain percentage of their deposits in reserve at the Federal Reserve district banks or as vault cash. This percentage depends on the bank's volume of business. (For further discussion, see Chapter 16.)

FIGURE 15-6

Organization of the Federal Reserve System

The 12 Federal Reserve district banks are headed by 12 separate presidents. The main authority of the Fed resides with the Board of Governors of the Federal Reserve System, whose seven members are appointed for 14-year terms by the president of the United States and confirmed by the Senate. Open market operations are carried out through the Federal Open Market Committee (FOMC), consisting of the seven members of the Board of Governors plus five presidents of the district banks (always including the president of the New York bank, with the others rotating).

Source: Board of Governors of the Federal Reserve System, *The Federal Reserve System: Purposes and Functions*, 7th ed. (Washington, D.C., 1984), p. 5.

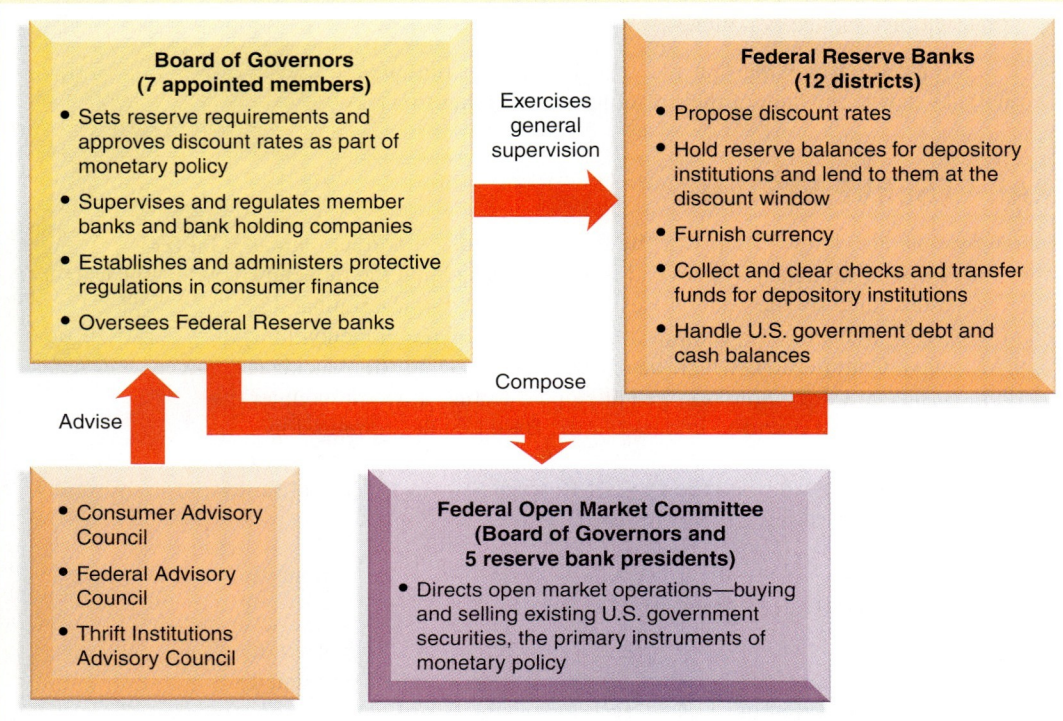

Functions of the Federal Reserve System

Here we present in detail what the Federal Reserve does.

1. ***The Fed supplies the economy with fiduciary currency.*** The Federal Reserve banks supply the economy with paper currency called Federal Reserve notes. For example, during holiday seasons, when very large numbers of currency transactions take place, more paper currency is desired. Commercial banks respond to the increased number and dollar amounts of depositors' currency withdrawals by turning to the Federal Reserve banks to replenish vault cash. Hence, the Federal Reserve banks must have on hand a sufficient amount of cash to accommodate the demands for paper currency at different times of the year. Note that even though all Federal Reserve notes are printed at the Bureau of Printing and Engraving in Washington, D.C., each note is assigned a code indicating which of the 12 Federal Reserve banks first

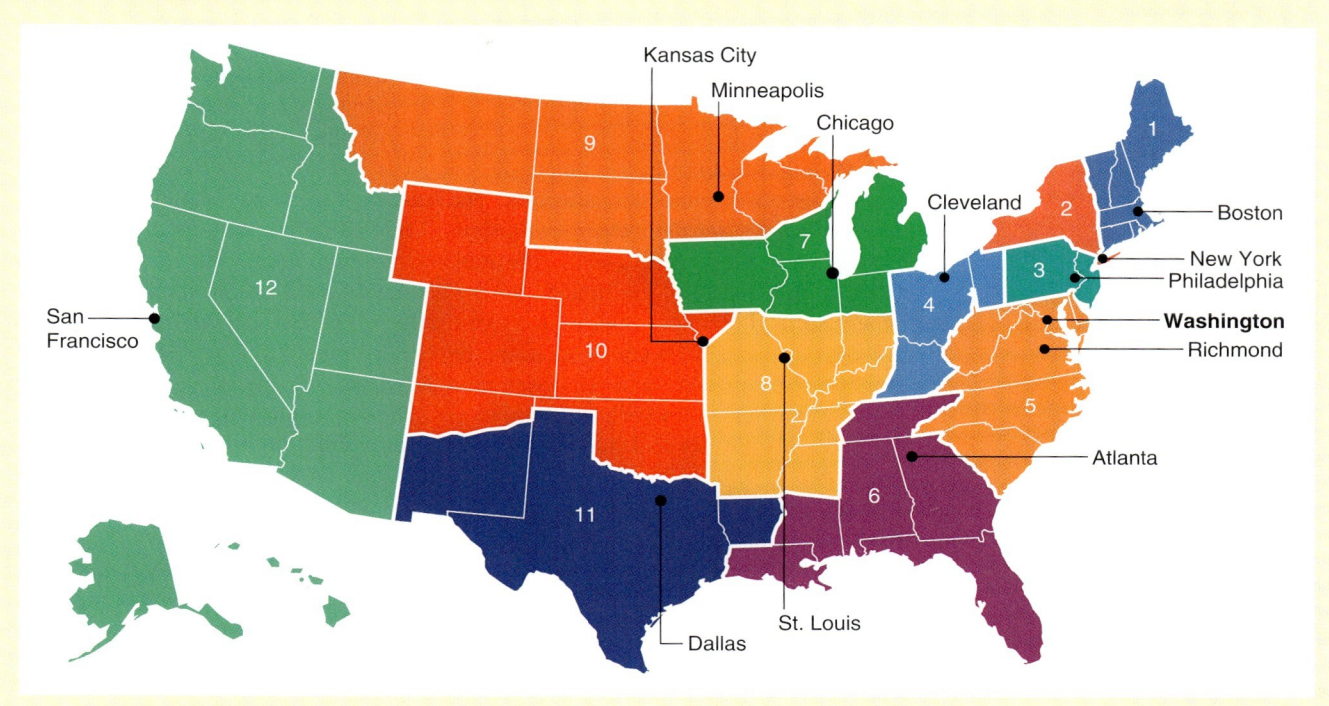

FIGURE 15-7

The Federal Reserve System

The Federal Reserve System is divided into 12 districts, each served by one of the Federal Reserve district banks, located in the cities indicated. The Board of Governors meets in Washington, D.C.

Source: Board of Governors of the Federal Reserve System.

introduced the note into circulation. Moreover, each of these notes is an obligation (liability) of the Federal Reserve System, *not* the U.S. Treasury.

2. ***The Fed provides payment-clearing systems.*** The Federal Reserve System has long operated systems for transmitting and clearing payments. Federal Reserve banks all offer check-clearing services to commercial banks, savings institutions, and credit unions.

In addition, the Federal Reserve System operates an electronic payments transfer system called *Fedwire,* which about 2,000 U.S. depository institutions use to process interbank payments. For instance, when a bank extends a loan to another institution, it typically transmits the payment using Fedwire. The other institution repays the loan the next day or a few days later by transmitting a payment on the same system. The average payment transfer on Fedwire exceeds $3 million, and the typical daily volume of all payments processed on this system is greater than $1 trillion.

The Fed charges fees to depository institutions to clear checks and transmit electronic payments, and its clearing operations compete with private clearinghouses. At present, the Fed clears a little less than one-third of all U.S. checks and transmits almost half of U.S. large-value electronic payments.

3. **The Fed holds depository institutions' reserves.** The 12 Federal Reserve district banks hold the reserves (other than vault cash) of depository institutions. As you will see in Chapter 16, depository institutions are required by law to keep a certain percentage of their transactions deposits as reserves. Even if they weren't required to do so by law, they would still wish to keep some reserves on which thay can draw funds as needed for expected and unexpected transactions.
4. **The Fed acts as the government's fiscal agent.** The Federal Reserve is the banker and fiscal agent for the federal government. The government, as we are all aware, collects large sums of funds through taxation. The government also spends and distributes equally large sums. Consequently, the U.S. Treasury has a transactions account with the Federal Reserve. Thus, the Fed acts as the government's banker, along with commercial banks that hold government deposits. The Fed also helps the government collect certain tax revenues and aids in the purchase and sale of government securities.
5. **The Fed supervises depository institutions.** The Fed (along with the Comptroller of the Currency, the Federal Deposit Insurance Corporation, the Office of Thrift Supervision in the Treasury Department, and the National Credit Union Administration) is a supervisor and regulator of depository institutions. The Fed and other regulators periodically and without warning examine depository institutions to see what kinds of loans have been made, what has been used as security for the loans, and who has received them. Whenever such an examination indicates that a bank is not conforming to current banking rules and standards, the Fed can require the bank to alter its banking practices.
6. **The Fed acts as the "lender of last resort."** From time to time, an individual bank that is otherwise in good financial condition can find itself temporarily low on cash and other liquid assets. Such an institution is said to be illiquid. A key justification for the formation of the Federal Reserve System was that the Fed would stand ready to prevent temporarily illiquid banks from failing by serving as the financial system's **lender of last resort.** In this capacity, the Fed stands ready to lend to any temporarily illiquid but otherwise financially healthy banking institution. In this way, the Fed seeks to prevent illiquidity at a few banks from leading to a general loss of depositors' confidence in the overall soundness of the banking system.
7. **The Fed regulates the money supply.** Perhaps the Fed's most important task is to regulate the nation's money supply. To understand how the Fed manages the money supply, we must examine more closely its reserve-holding function and the way in which depository institutions aid in expansion and contraction of the money supply. We will do this in Chapter 16.
8. **The Fed intervenes in foreign currency markets.** Sometimes the Fed attempts to keep the value of the dollar from changing. It does this by buying and selling U.S. dollars in foreign exchange markets. You will read more about this important topic in Chapter 34.

Lender of last resort
The Federal Reserve's role as an institution that is willing and able to lend to a temporarily illiquid bank that is otherwise in good financial condition to prevent the bank's illiquid position from leading to a general loss of confidence in that bank or in others.

QUICK QUIZ

A central bank is a banker's bank that typically acts as the _____ _____ for its nation's government as well. The central bank in the United States is the _____ _____ _____, which was established on December 13, 1913.

There are 12 Federal Reserve district banks, with 25 branches. The Federal Reserve System is managed by the _____ of _____ in Washington, D.C. The Fed interacts with virtually all depository institutions in the United States, most of which must keep a certain percentage of their transactions deposits on reserve with the Fed. The Fed serves as the chief regulatory agency for all depository institutions that have Federal Reserve System membership.

The functions of the Federal Reserve System are to supply fiduciary _____, provide payment-clearing services, hold depository institution _____, act as the government's fiscal agent, supervise depository institutions, act as the _____ of _____ _____, regulate the supply of money, and intervene in foreign currency markets.

See page 391 for the answers. Review concepts from this section in MyEconLab.

CASE STUDY — ECONOMICS FRONT AND CENTER

A Well-Intentioned Law Creates Problems in Japan

Tanaka is a sales manager at one of the most profitable Japanese life insurance companies. Her firm has done well even though returns that Japanese insurers have earned on their portfolios of stocks and bonds began deteriorating when market interest rates dropped close to 0 percent in the late 1990s and early 2000s. In recent years, the Japanese insurance industry has paid out a total of at least $5 billion more per year to policyholders than the firms earned in revenues. As a consequence, some firms failed in the early 2000s, and many are still struggling.

To stave off massive insurance failures, the Japanese parliament recently made it legal for troubled insurers to break insurance contracts that had guaranteed annual rates of return to policyholders. A number of insurers promptly responded by canceling promised interest payments to policyholders. Cutting interest expenses naturally helped keep these companies in business at the expense of their policyholders.

To the detriment of Tanaka's company, the actions of these competing companies have caused many young people to lose confidence in the Japanese life insurance industry and to seek alternative ways to save. Tanaka's sales force is looking to her for advice about how to convince prospective customers that their company has no intention of violating the terms of any policies that it issues. She thinks hard about what she might suggest.

CRITICAL ANALYSIS QUESTIONS

1. What type of asymmetric information problems does Tanaka's company face when considering whether to issue a policy to an individual or company that has applied for coverage?

2. Now that insurers that develop financial problems have the legal right to cancel promised interest payments, what asymmetric information problem do existing Japanese insurance policyholders face?

Issues and Applications

Check Clearing—A Rapidly Diminishing Fed Function

Concepts Applied
- The Fed
- Functions of the Federal Reserve System
- Payment Intermediary

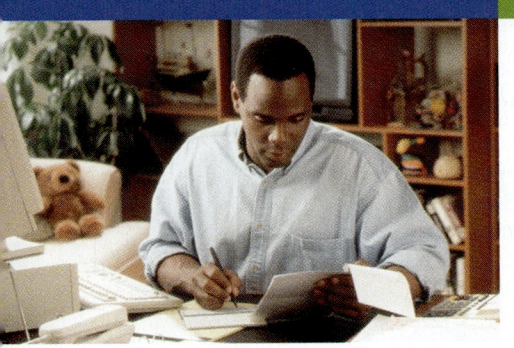

The volume of checks cleared by the Federal Reserve grew rapidly during the 1980s. By 1992, the Fed cleared an average of about 626 checks per second. Since then, the Fed's average check-clearing speed has dropped by 29 percent, to just over 440 checks per second. This drop has resulted from a decline in the demand for the Fed's check-clearing services.

Checks Fall Out of Favor

Figure 15-8 shows that since 1994, the number of checks cleared by the Fed has decreased by 1.3 percent per year on average. During this period, the dollar value of Fed-cleared checks has fallen at an average annual rate of 2.2 percent.

Two factors have contributed to the drop-off in the volume and value of checks. One is that in the early 1990s, the federal government initiated a significant effort to provide more transfer payments to recipients electronically. Today, all manner of government transfer payments, including Social Security, Medicare, Medicaid, and various supplemental income payments, are transmitted electronically instead of by check. The second factor accounting for the decreased use of checks has been a gradual shift toward electronic payments by households and businesses. Debit cards, Internet bill payments, and Web-based payment services such as PayPal have emerged as substitute means of payment, and check usage has declined further.

A Declining Business for the Fed

Back in the early 1990s, when check volumes and values were showing every sign of continuing to grow at a steady pace, the 12 Federal Reserve banks added check-processing centers at their various branch offices around the nation. By the late 1990s, there were a total of 45 Fed check-processing centers in the United States.

In the meantime, though, people had begun substituting electronic payments for checks at grocery stores, fast-food restaurants, and retail stores. As a result, as just described, the volume and value of checks processed by Federal Reserve banks began to drop off after 1994.

By 2003, it had become clear to Fed officials that the downward volume and value trends displayed in Figure 15-8 were unlikely to be reversed. Indeed, Federal Reserve banks were incurring losses by continuing to operate all their check-processing centers. Rapidly, the Fed banks began to close centers around the country. Today, Federal Reserve banks operate fewer than half as many check-processing centers as in 2003. For the Federal Reserve System, therefore, check clearing has definitely become a declining line of business.

FIGURE 15-8
The Volume and Value of Federal Reserve Check Clearings Since 1985

The number and value of checks cleared by the Federal Reserve System grew rapidly until the mid-1990s. Since then, however, Fed check clearings have steadily declined.

Source: Board of Governors of the Federal Reserve System.

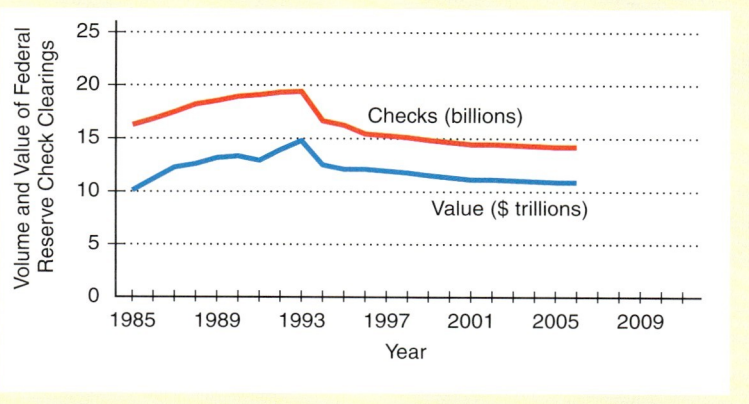

Log in to **MyEconLab**, click on "Economic News," and test your understanding of the chapter by answering interactive questions that relate directly to this issue.

For Critical Analysis

1. What would you anticipate has been happening to employment at Federal Reserve banks and branches since the mid-1990s?

2. The Fed has for years depended on machines that read magnetic ink on the checks, but recently it has begun scanning checks to electronic data. Why do you suppose people have been substituting in favor of paperless payment methods? (Hint: Which payment method do you think is likely to be cheaper to process and result in fewer errors?)

Web Resources

1. Learn more about the Fed's check-clearing operations at www.econtoday.com/ch15.
2. Learn how the Fed processes checks electronically, at www.econtoday.com/ch15.

Research Project

The Fed is not involved in the process of clearing debit-card transactions. In light of the gradual reduction in the Fed's involvement in check clearing, evaluate the Fed's future role as a U.S. payment intermediary. Will such a role still exist in future years?

Here is what you should know after reading this chapter. MyEconLab will help you identify what you know, and where to go when you need to practice.

WHAT YOU SHOULD KNOW

The Key Functions of Money Money has four functions. It is a medium of exchange, which means that people use money to make payments for goods, services, and financial assets. It is also a unit of accounting, meaning that prices are quoted in terms of money values. In addition, money is a store of value, so people can hold money for future use in exchange. Furthermore, money is a standard of deferred payment, enabling lenders to make loans and buyers to repay those loans with money.

money, 366
medium of exchange, 367
barter, 367
unit of accounting, 367
store of value, 367
standard of deferred payment, 367

WHERE TO GO TO PRACTICE

- **MyEconLab** Study Plan 15.1
- Audio introduction to Chapter 15
- Video: The Functions of Money

WHAT YOU SHOULD KNOW		WHERE TO GO TO PRACTICE
Important Properties of Goods That Serve as Money A good will successfully function as money only if people are widely willing to accept the good in exchange for other goods and services. People must have confidence that others will be willing to trade their goods and services for the good used as money. In addition, though people may continue to use money even if inflation erodes its real purchasing power, they will do so only if the value of money is relatively predictable.	liquidity, 368 transaction deposits, 369 fiduciary monetary system, 369 **Key figure** Figure 15-1, 368	• **MyEconLab** Study Plans 15.2 and 15.3 • Video: Monetary Standards, or What Backs Money • Animated Figure 15-1
Official Definitions of the Quantity of Money in Circulation The narrow definition of the quantity of money in circulation, called M1, focuses on money's role as a medium of exchange. It includes only currency, transactions deposits, and traveler's checks. A broader definition, called M2, stresses money's role as a temporary store of value. M2 is equal to M1 plus near-money assets such as savings deposits, small-denomination time deposits, money market deposit accounts, and noninstitutional holdings of money market mutual fund balances.	money supply, 370 transactions approach, 371 liquidity approach, 371 M1, 371 thrift institutions, 373 traveler's checks, 373 near moneys, 373 M2, 373 savings deposits, 373 depository institutions, 373 money market deposit accounts (MMDAs), 373 time deposit, 374 certificate of deposit (CD), 374 money market mutual funds, 374 **Key figure** Figure 15-3, 372	• **MyEconLab** Study Plan 15.4 • Animated Figure 15-3
Why Financial Intermediaries Such as Banks Exist Financial intermediaries help reduce problems stemming from the existence of asymmetric information in financial transactions. Asymmetric information can lead to adverse selection, in which uncreditworthy individuals and firms seek loans, and moral hazard problems, in which an individual or business that has been granted credit begins to engage in riskier practices. Financial intermediaries may also permit savers to benefit from economies of scale, which is the ability to reduce the costs and risks of managing funds by pooling funds and spreading costs and risks across many savers.	central bank, 375 financial intermediation, 375 financial intermediaries, 375 asymmetric information, 376 adverse selection, 376 moral hazard, 376 liabilities, 376 assets, 377 payment intermediaries, 377 capital controls, 378 international financial diversification, 378	• **MyEconLab** Study Plans 15.5 and 15.6 • Animated Figure 15-5

WHAT YOU SHOULD KNOW		WHERE TO GO TO PRACTICE
Why Financial Intermediaries Such as Banks Exist – Continued	world index fund, 379 universal banking, 380 **Key figure** Figure 15-5, 378	
The Basic Structure of the Federal Reserve System The central bank of the United States is the Federal Reserve System, which consists of 12 district banks with 25 branches. The governing body of the Federal Reserve System is the Board of Governors, which is based in Washington, D.C. Decisions about the quantity of money in circulation are made by the Federal Open Market Committee, which is composed of the Board of Governors and five Federal Reserve bank presidents.	The Fed, 381 **Key figure** Figure 15-6, 382	• **MyEconLab** Study Plan 15.7 • Animated Figure 15-6 • Video: The Federal Reserve System
Major Functions of the Federal Reserve The main functions of the Federal Reserve System are supplying the economy with fiduciary currency, providing systems for transmitting and clearing payments, holding depository institutions' reserves, acting as the government's fiscal agent, supervising banks, acting as a lender of last resort, regulating the money supply, and intervening in foreign exchange markets.	lender of last resort, 384	• **MyEconLab** Study Plan 15.7 • Animated Figure 15-7 • Video: The Federal Reserve System

Log in to MyEconLab, take a chapter test, and get a personalized Study Plan that tells you which concepts you understand and which ones you need to review. From there, MyEconLab will give you further practice, tutorials, animations, videos, and guided solutions.

Log in to www.myeconlab.com

PROBLEMS

*Select problems, indicated by a blue oval, are assignable in **MyEconLab**.*
Answers to the odd-numbered problems appear at the end of the book.

15-1 Until 1946, residents of the island of Yap used large doughnut-shaped stones as financial assets. Although prices of goods and services were not quoted in terms of the stones, the stones were often used in exchange for particularly large purchases, such as payments for livestock. To make the transaction, several individuals would place a large stick through a stone's center and carry it to its new owner. A stone was difficult for any one person to steal, so an owner typically would lean it against the side of his or her home as a sign to others of accumulated purchasing power that would hold value for later use in exchange. Loans would often be repaid using the stones. In what ways did these stones function as money?

15-2. During the late 1970s, prices quoted in terms of the Israeli currency, the shekel, rose so fast that grocery stores listed their prices in terms of the U.S. dollar and provided customers with dollar-shekel conversion tables that they updated daily. Although people continued to buy goods and services and make loans using shekels, many Israeli citizens converted shekels to dollars to avoid a reduction in their wealth due to inflation. In what way did the U.S. dollar function as money in Israel during this period?

15-3. During the 1945–1946 Hungarian hyperinflation, when the rate of inflation reached 41.9 *quadrillion* percent per month, the Hungarian government discovered that the real value of its tax receipts was falling dramatically. To keep real tax revenues more stable, it created a good called a "tax pengö," in which all bank deposits were denominated for purposes of taxation. Nevertheless, payments for goods and services were made only in terms of the regular Hungarian currency, whose value tended to fall rapidly even though the value of a tax pengö remained stable. Prices were also quoted only in terms of the regular currency. Lenders, however, began denominating loan payments in terms of tax pengös. In what ways did the tax pengö function as money in Hungary in 1945 and 1946?

15-4. Considering the following data (expressed in billions of U.S. dollars), calculate M1 and M2.

Currency	650
Savings deposits and money market deposit accounts	3,000
Small-denomination time deposits	1,600
Traveler's checks outside banks and thrifts	10
Total money market mutual funds	1,000
Institution-only money market mutual funds	200
Transactions deposits	940

15-5. Considering the following data (expressed in billions of U.S. dollars), calculate M1 and M2.

Transactions deposits	625
Savings deposits	1,900
Small-denomination time deposits	1,450
Money market deposit accounts	1,250
Noninstitution money market mutual funds	1,200
Traveler's checks outside banks and thrifts	25
Currency	800
Institution-only money market mutual funds	250

15-6. Identify whether each of the following items is counted in M1 only, M2 only, both M1 and M2, or neither:

a. A $1,000 balance in a transactions deposit at a mutual savings bank
b. A $100,000 certificate of deposit issued by a New York bank
c. A $10,000 time deposit an elderly widow holds at her credit union
d. A $50 traveler's check
e. A $50,000 money market deposit account balance

15-7. Identify whether each of the following amounts is counted in M1 only, M2 only, both M1 and M2, or neither:

a. $50 billion in U.S. Treasury bills
b. $15 billion in small-denomination time deposits
c. $5 billion in traveler's checks
d. $20 billion in money market deposit accounts

15-8. Indicate which of the following items are counted in M2 but not in M1.

a. A $20 Federal Reserve note
b. A $500 time deposit
c. A $50 traveler's check
d. A $25,000 money market deposit account

15-9. Match each of the rationales for financial intermediation listed below with at least one of the following financial intermediaries: insurance company, pension fund, savings bank. Explain your choices.

a. Adverse selection
b. Moral hazard
c. Lower management costs generated by larger scale

15-10. Match each of the rationales for financial intermediation listed below with at least one of the following financial intermediaries: commercial bank, money market mutual fund, stockbroker. Explain your choices.

a. Adverse selection
b. Moral hazard
c. Lower management costs generated by larger scale

15-11. Identify whether each of the following events poses an adverse selection problem or a moral hazard problem in financial markets.

a. A manager of a savings and loan association responds to reports of a likely increase in federal deposit insurance coverage. She directs loan officers to extend mortgage loans to less creditworthy borrowers.
b. A loan applicant does not mention that a legal judgment in his divorce case will require him to make alimony payments to his ex-wife.
c. An individual who was recently approved for a loan to start a new business decides to use some of the funds to take a Hawaiian vacation.

15-12. Identify whether each of the following events poses an adverse selection problem or a moral hazard problem in financial markets.

a. An individual with several children who has just learned that she has lung cancer applies for life insurance but fails to report this recent medical diagnosis.
b. A corporation that recently obtained a loan from several banks to finance installation of a new computer network instead directs some of the funds to executive bonuses.
c. A state-chartered financial institution exempt from laws requiring it to have federal deposit insurance decides to apply for deposit insurance after experiencing severe financial problems that may bankrupt the institution.

15-13. In what sense is currency a liability of the Federal Reserve System?

15-14. In what respects is the Fed like a private banking institution? In what respects is it more like a government agency?

15-15. Take a look at the map of the locations of the Federal Reserve districts and their headquarters in Figure 15-7 on page 383. Today, the U.S. population is centered just west of the Mississippi River—that is, about half of the population is either to the west or the east of a line running roughly just west of this river. Can you reconcile the current locations of Fed districts and banks with this fact? Why do you suppose the Fed has its current geographic structure?

ECONOMICS ON THE NET

What's Happened to the Money Supply? Deposits at banks and other financial institutions make up a portion of the U.S. money supply. This exercise gives you the chance to see how changes in these deposits influence the Fed's measures of money.

Title: FRED (Federal Reserve Economic Data)

Navigation: Go to www.econtoday.com/ch15 to visit the Web page of the Federal Reserve Bank of St. Louis.

Application

1. Select the data series for Demand Deposits at Commercial Banks (Bil. of $; M), either seasonally adjusted or not. Scan through the data. Do you notice any recent trend? (Hint: Compare the growth in the figures before 1993 with their growth after 1993.) In addition, take a look at the data series for currency and for other transactions deposits. Do you observe similar recent trends in these series?

2. Back up, and click on *M1 Money Stock (Bil. of $; M)*, again, either seasonally adjusted or not. Does it show any change in pattern beginning around 1993?

For Group Study and Analysis FRED contains considerable financial data series. Assign individual members or groups of the class the task of examining data on assets included in M1, M2, and MZM. Have each student or group look for big swings in the data. Then ask the groups to report to the class as a whole. When did clear changes occur in various categories of the monetary aggregates? Were there times when people appeared to shift funds from one aggregate to another? Are there any other noticeable patterns that may have had something to do with economic events during various periods?

ANSWERS TO QUICK QUIZZES

p. 370: (i) medium of exchange . . . unit of accounting . . . store of value . . . standard of deferred payment; (ii) liquid; (iii) fiduciary; (iv) predictable

p. 374: (i) transactions . . . M1; (ii) Transactions; (iii) M1 . . . M2

p. 380: (i) Financial . . . payment; (ii) asymmetric . . . adverse selection . . . moral hazard; (iii) capital controls . . . diversification

p. 385: (i) fiscal agent . . . Federal Reserve System; (ii) Board . . . Governors; (iii) currency . . . reserves . . . lender of last resort

16 Money Creation and Deposit Insurance

Learning Objectives

After reading this chapter, you should be able to:

1. Describe how the Federal Reserve assesses reserve requirements on banks and other depository institutions
2. Understand why the money supply is unaffected when someone deposits in a depository institution funds transferred from a transactions account at another depository institution
3. Explain why the money supply changes when someone deposits in a depository institution funds transferred from the Federal Reserve System
4. Determine the maximum potential extent to which the money supply will change following a Federal Reserve purchase or sale of government securities
5. Discuss the ways in which the Federal Reserve conducts monetary policy
6. Explain the essential features of federal deposit insurance

Smart cards are payment cards with embedded microchips that are capable of storing and processing security programming. Smart cards permit people to use *digital cash*, which consists of funds contained in software programs called digital algorithms. Smart cards' microchips can communicate with any device equipped with appropriate software. Such devices include automated teller machines and electronic cash registers, as well as any computer with sufficient memory and speed to operate the software, such as a personal computer. By the time you finish this chapter, you will know enough about how the U.S. money supply is created to understand how the use of smart cards and digital cash may affect the quantity of money in circulation in the United States.

 MyEconLab helps you master each objective and study more efficiently. See end of chapter for details.

Did You Know That...

even though the federal government currently insures deposits up to a limit of $100,000 per depositor per institution, it is still possible for individuals to obtain federal insurance for millions of dollars of deposits? They do so by spreading their funds across institutions.

The limit of $100,000 per depositor per institution was established in the 1980s. Since then, inflation has cut the purchasing-power value of this amount nearly in half. Thus, more individuals have had an incentive to spread their deposits across more than one institution in order to maintain federal insurance of their deposits.

For a private firm called Promontory Interfinancial Network, this increased incentive to hold federally insured deposit accounts in more than one institution has produced a business opportunity. Promontory breaks up customers' large deposits into amounts smaller than $100,000 and spreads those funds across a network of more than 600 banks that are members of the company's Certificate of Deposit Account Registry Service. Promontory arranges for its customers to be paid a single interest rate on all the funds they have on deposit at multiple institutions. It also provides customers with a consolidated bank statement and a single 1099 tax form for reporting their taxable interest earnings. Depositors utilizing Promontory's service can arrange for up to $10 million of their funds to receive federal deposit insurance coverage.

Why does the federal government insure much of the nation's funds held in deposit accounts at banks? The answer has to do with the fact that many deposit funds at banks are in transactions accounts from which people can order funds to be transferred via debit cards and checks. The widespread failure of banks would have a significant effect on the nation's money supply, thereby reducing total liquidity in the economy. A key objective of deposit insurance is to prevent such an event from occurring.

If you were to attend a luncheon of local bankers and ask the question, "Do you as bankers create money?" you would get a uniformly negative response. Bankers are certain that they do not create money. Indeed, *by itself*, no individual bank can create money. But through actions initiated by a central bank such as the Federal Reserve, depository institutions *together* do create money; they help determine the total deposits outstanding. In this chapter, we shall examine the money multiplier process, which explains how an injection of new money into the banking system leads to an eventual multiple expansion in the total money supply. We shall also consider an important institutional change that has had significant effects on the U.S. money supply. Then we shall examine federal deposit insurance and its role in the U.S. monetary and financial system.

LINKS BETWEEN CHANGES IN THE MONEY SUPPLY AND OTHER ECONOMIC VARIABLES

How fast the money supply grows or does not grow is important because no matter what model of the economy is used, theories link the money supply growth rate to business fluctuations. There is in fact a long-standing relationship between changes in the money supply and changes in both nominal GDP and real GDP. Some economists use this historical evidence to argue that money is an important determinant of the level of economic activity in the economy.

Money and Prices

Another key economic variable in our economy is the price level. As you learned in Chapter 10, both the quantity of money and the price level have risen since the 1950s, and one theory attributes changes in the rate of inflation to changes in the growth rate of money in

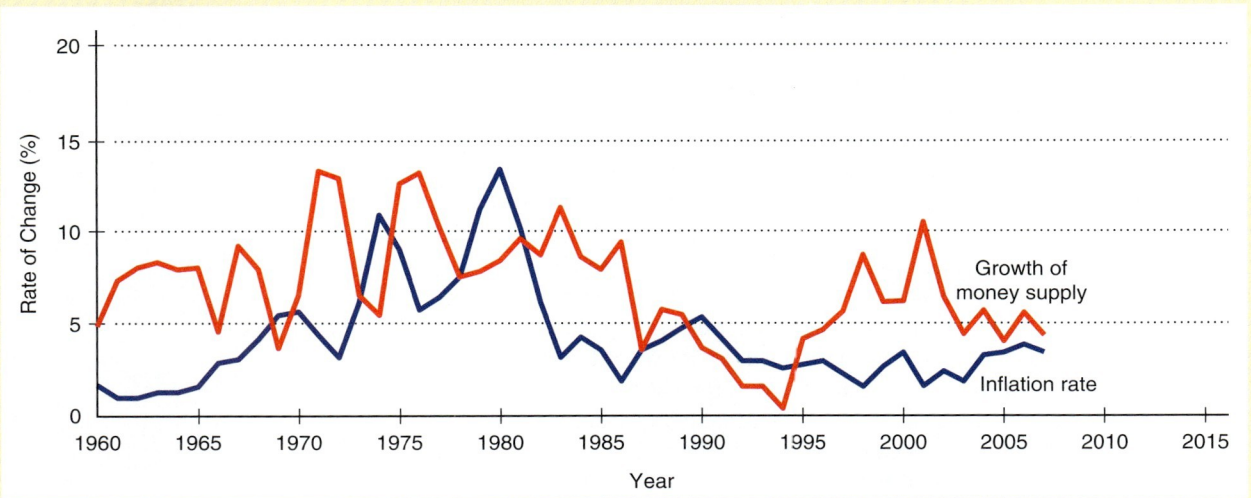

FIGURE 16-1

Money Supply Growth versus the Inflation Rate

These data plots indicate a loose correspondence between money supply growth (the rate of change in the M2 measure of money) and the inflation rate. Actually, closer inspection reveals a direct relationship between changes in the growth rate of money and changes in the inflation rate *in a later period*. This relationship seemed to hold well into the 1990s, when it became less strong.

Sources: *Economic Report of the President; Federal Reserve Bulletin; Economic Indicators,* various issues; author's estimates.

circulation. Figure 16-1 shows the relationship between the rate of growth of the money supply and the inflation rate. There seems to be a loose, long-run, direct relationship between growth in the money supply and the rate of inflation. Increases in the money supply growth rate seem to lead to increases in the inflation rate, after a time lag.

Banking and Money

As early as 1000 B.C., uncoined gold and silver were being used as money in Mesopotamia. Goldsmiths weighed and assessed the purity of those metals; later they started issuing paper notes indicating that the bearers held gold or silver of given weights and purity on deposit with the goldsmith. These notes could be transferred in exchange for goods and became the first paper currency. The gold and silver on deposit with the goldsmiths were the first bank deposits. Eventually, goldsmiths realized that inflows of gold and silver for deposit always exceeded the average amount of gold and silver withdrawn at any given time—often by a predictable ratio. These goldsmiths started making loans by issuing to borrowers paper notes that exceeded in value the amount of gold and silver they actually kept on hand. They charged interest on these loans. This constituted the earliest form of what is now called **fractional reserve banking.** We know that goldsmiths operated this way in Delphi, Didyma, and Olympia in Greece as early as the seventh century B.C. In Athens, fractional reserve banking was well developed by the sixth century B.C.

Fractional reserve banking
A system in which depository institutions hold reserves that are less than the amount of total deposits.

DEPOSITORY INSTITUTION RESERVES

In a fractional reserve banking system, banks do not keep sufficient reserves on hand to cover 100 percent of their depositors' accounts. And the reserves that are held by depository institutions in the United States are not kept in gold and silver, as they were with the early goldsmiths, but rather in the form of deposits on reserve with Federal Reserve district banks and in vault cash. Depository institutions are required by the Fed to maintain a specified percentage of certain customer deposits as **reserves.** There are three distinguishable types of reserves: legal, required, and excess.

> **Reserves**
> In the U.S. Federal Reserve System, deposits held by Federal Reserve district banks for depository institutions, plus depository institutions' vault cash.

Legal Reserves

For depository institutions, **legal reserves** constitute anything that the law permits them to claim as reserves. Today that consists only of deposits held at the Federal Reserve district bank plus vault cash. Government securities, for example, are not legal reserves, even though they can easily be turned into cash, should the need arise, to meet unusually large net withdrawals by customers. Economists refer to all legal reserves that banks hold with the Federal Reserve or keep in their vaults as their *total reserves*.

> **Legal reserves**
> Reserves that depository institutions are allowed by law to claim as reserves—for example, deposits held at Federal Reserve district banks and vault cash.

Required Reserves

Required reserves are the minimum amount of legal reserves that a depository institution (which, for simplicity, we shall assume to be a commercial bank) must have to "back" transactions deposits. They are expressed as a ratio of required reserves to total transactions deposits (banks need hold no reserves on nontransactions deposits). The **required reserve ratio** for almost all transactions deposits is 10 percent (except for about the first $50 million in deposits at any depository institution, which is subject to only a 3 percent requirement). The general formula is

$$\text{Required reserves} = \text{transactions deposits} \times \text{required reserve ratio}$$

Take a hypothetical example. If the required level of reserves is 10 percent and the bank has $1 billion in customer transactions deposits, it must hold at least $100 million as reserves. As we shall discuss later in this chapter, during the 1990s, banks discovered a novel way to reduce the amounts of reserves that they are required to hold.

> **Required reserves**
> The value of reserves that a depository institution must hold in the form of vault cash or deposits with the Fed.
>
> **Required reserve ratio**
> The percentage of total transactions deposits that the Fed requires depository institutions to hold in the form of vault cash or deposits with the Fed.

Excess Reserves

Depository institutions often hold reserves in excess of what is required by the Fed. This difference between actual (legal) reserves and required reserves is called **excess reserves.** (Excess reserves can be negative, but they rarely are. Negative excess reserves indicate that depository institutions do not have sufficient legal reserves to meet their required reserves. When this happens, they borrow from other depository institutions or from a Federal Reserve district bank, sell assets such as securities, or call in loans.) Excess reserves are an important potential determinant of the rate of growth of the money supply, for as we shall see, it is only to the extent that depository institutions have excess reserves that they can make new loans. Because reserves produce no income, profit-seeking financial institutions have an incentive to minimize excess reserves, disposing of them either to purchase income-producing securities or to make loans with which they earn income through interest payments received. In equation form, we can define excess reserves in this way:

$$\text{Excess reserves} = \text{legal reserves} - \text{required reserves}$$

In the analysis that follows, we examine the relationship between the level of reserves and the size of the money supply. This analysis implies that factors influencing the level of the reserves of the banking system as a whole will ultimately affect the size of the money

> **Excess reserves**
> The difference between legal reserves and required reserves.
>
> Go to www.econtoday.com/ch16 to see Federal Reserve reports on the current amounts of required and excess reserves at U.S. depository institutions.

supply, other things held constant. We show first that when someone deposits in one depository institution funds transmitted by debit card or check from an account at another depository institution, the two depository institutions involved are individually affected, but the overall money supply does not change. Then we show that when someone deposits in a depository institution funds transmitted from the Fed, a multiple expansion in the money supply results.

> **QUICK QUIZ**
>
> Ours is a **fractional reserve banking** system in which depository institutions must hold only a _____ of their deposits as reserves, either on deposit with a Federal Reserve district bank or as _____ cash.
>
> **Required reserves** are usually expressed as a _____, in percentage terms, of required reserves to total transactions deposits.
>
> See page 421 for the answers. Review concepts from this section in MyEconLab.

THE RELATIONSHIP BETWEEN LEGAL RESERVES AND TOTAL DEPOSITS

To show the relationship between reserves and bank deposits, we first analyze a single bank (existing alongside many others). A single bank is able to make new loans to its customers only to the extent that it has reserves above the level legally required to cover the new deposits. When an individual bank has no excess reserves, it cannot make loans.

How a Single Bank Reacts to an Increase in Reserves

To examine the **balance sheet** of a single bank after its reserves are increased, let's make the following assumptions:

1. The required reserve ratio is 10 percent for all transactions deposits.
2. Transactions deposits are the bank's only liabilities; reserves at a Federal Reserve district bank and loans are the bank's only assets. Loans are promises made by customers to repay some amount in the future; that is, they are customer IOUs and as such are assets to the bank.
3. An individual bank can lend as much as it is legally allowed.
4. Every time a loan is made to an individual (consumer or business), all the proceeds from the loan are put into a transactions deposit account; no cash (currency or coins) is withdrawn.
5. Depository institutions seek to keep zero excess reserves because reserves do not earn interest. (Depository institutions are operated to earn profits; we assume that all depository institutions wish to convert excess reserves that do not pay interest into interest-bearing loans.)
6. Depository institutions have zero **net worth.** (In reality, all depository institutions are required to have some positive owners' equity, or capital, which is another name for net worth. It is usually a small percentage of the institutions' total assets.)

Look at the simplified initial position of Typical Bank in Balance Sheet 16-1. Liabilities consist of $1 million in transactions deposits. Assets consist of $100,000 in reserves and $900,000 in loans to customers. Total assets of $1 million equal total liabilities of $1 million.

Balance sheet
A statement of the assets and liabilities of any business entity, including financial institutions and the Federal Reserve System. Assets are what is owned; liabilities are what is owed.

Net worth
The difference between assets and liabilities.

With a 10 percent reserve requirement and $1 million in transactions deposits, the bank has required reserves of $100,000 and therefore no excess reserves.

BALANCE SHEET 16-1
Typical Bank

Assets			Liabilities	
Total reserves		$100,000	Transactions deposits	$1,000,000
Required reserves	$100,000			
Excess reserves	0			
Loans		900,000		
Total		$1,000,000	Total	$1,000,000

Assume that a depositor deposits in Typical Bank a $100,000 debit-card payment drawn on a transactions account at another depository institution. Transactions deposits in Typical Bank immediately increase by $100,000, bringing the total to $1.1 million. After the debit-card transaction is finalized, total reserves of Typical Bank increase to $200,000. A $1.1 million total in transactions deposits means that required reserves will have to be 10 percent of $1.1 million, or $110,000. Typical Bank now has excess reserves equal to $200,000 minus $110,000, or $90,000. This is shown in Balance Sheet 16-2.

BALANCE SHEET 16-2
Typical Bank

Assets			Liabilities	
Total reserves		$200,000	Transactions deposits	$1,100,000
Required reserves	$110,000			
Excess reserves	90,000			
Loans		900,000		
Total		$1,100,000	Total	$1,100,000

Effect on Typical Bank's Balance Sheet. Look at excess reserves in Balance Sheet 16-2. Excess reserves were zero before the $100,000 deposit, and now they are $90,000—that's $90,000 worth of assets not earning any income. By assumption, Typical Bank will now lend out this entire $90,000 in excess reserves in order to obtain interest income. Loans will increase to $990,000. The borrowers who receive the new loans will not leave them on deposit in Typical Bank. After all, they borrow funds to spend them. As they spend them by making debit-card and check transfers that are deposited in other banks, actual reserves will fall to $110,000 (as required), and excess reserves will again become zero, as indicated in Balance Sheet 16-3.

BALANCE SHEET 16-3
Typical Bank

Assets			Liabilities	
Total reserves		$110,000	Transactions deposits	$1,100,000
Required reserves	$110,000			
Excess reserves	0			
Loans		990,000		
Total		$1,100,000	Total	$1,100,000

In this example, a person transmitted a $100,000 debit-card payment from an account at another bank. That $100,000 became part of the reserves of Typical Bank. Because that deposit immediately created excess reserves in Typical Bank, further loans were possible for Typical Bank. The excess reserves were lent out to earn interest. A bank will not lend more than its excess reserves because, by law, it must hold a certain amount of required reserves.

Effect on the Money Supply.

A look at the balance sheets for Typical Bank might give the impression that the money supply increased because of the new customer's $100,000 deposit. Remember, though, that the deposit resulted from a debit-card transfer from *another* bank. Therefore, the other bank suffered a *decline* in its transactions deposits and its reserves. While total assets and liabilities in Typical Bank have increased by $100,000, they have *decreased* in the other bank by $100,000. The total amount of money and credit in the economy is unaffected by the transfer of funds from one depository institution to another.

The thing to remember is that new reserves for the banking system as a whole are not created when debit-card or check payments transferred from one bank are deposited in another bank. The Federal Reserve System can, however, create new reserves; that is the subject of the next section.

Why do you suppose that many depositors who use debit cards are finding that signing a receipt may entail a reward from their bank, while keying in a personal identification number can incur a penalty?

EXAMPLE

Debiting with a PIN May Double-Debit Your Account

Depository institutions often allow depositors who use debit cards to choose whether to sign a receipt or punch in a personal identification number (PIN) to authorize a transfer. Under most agreements with retailers, depository institutions earn higher revenues from retailers when debit-card customers sign for their purchases. Retailers, in contrast, pay lower processing fees to depository institutions when customers enter PINs.

To give account holders an incentive to sign for their purchases, about 14 percent of depository institutions now charge a fee, ranging from as low as 10 cents to as much as $2, each time a debit-card user punches in a PIN. Some banks have even begun to offer rebates to depositors who sign debit-card payment authorizations instead of entering PINs.

FOR CRITICAL ANALYSIS

Why do you suppose that legal limits on a depositor's liability arising from fraudulent use of a stolen debit card give depository institutions an incentive to require debit-card users to authorize purchases with either signatures or PINs?

THE FED'S DIRECT EFFECT ON THE OVERALL LEVEL OF RESERVES

Now we shall examine the Fed's direct effect on the level of reserves, showing how a change in the level of reserves causes a multiple change in the total money supply. Consider the Federal Open Market Committee (FOMC), whose decisions essentially determine the level of reserves in the monetary system.

Federal Open Market Committee

Open market operations are FOMC-directed Fed purchases and sales of existing U.S. government securities in the open market, which is the private secondary U.S. securities market in which people exchange government securities that have not yet matured. If the FOMC decides that the Fed should buy or sell bonds, it instructs the New York Federal Reserve Bank's Trading Desk to do so.

Open market operations
The purchase and sale of existing U.S. government securities (such as bonds) in the open private market by the Federal Reserve System.

A Sample Transaction

Assume that the Trading Desk at the New York Fed has determined that to comply with the latest directive from the FOMC, it must purchase $100,000 worth of U.S. government securities. The Fed pays for these securities by electronically transferring $100,000 in newly created funds to the transactions deposit account that the selling bond dealer maintains at a bank. The bond dealer's bank now has $100,000 in new reserve assets and $100,000 in *new* transactions deposit liabilities.

Thus, the Fed has created $100,000 of reserves. The Fed can create reserves because it has the ability to add to the reserve accounts of depository institutions whenever it buys U.S. securities. When the Fed buys a U.S. government security in the open market, it initially expands total reserves by the amount of the purchase.

Using Balance Sheets. Consider the balance sheets of the Fed and of the depository institution receiving the electronic payment for the securities. Balance Sheet 16-4 shows the results for the Fed after the bond purchase and for the bank after the bond dealer's bank receives the Fed's funds transfer. The Fed's balance sheet (which here reflects only account changes) shows that after the purchase, the Fed's assets have increased by $100,000 in the form of U.S. government securities. Liabilities have also increased by $100,000 in the form of an increase in the reserve account of the bank. The balance sheet for the bank shows an increase in assets of $100,000 in the form of reserves with its Federal Reserve district bank. The bank also has an increase in its liabilities in the form of a $100,000 deposit in the transactions account of the bond dealer. This is an immediate $100,000 increase in the money supply because the dealer's deposit is not offset by a withdrawal from another bank.

The Fed		Bank	
Assets	Liabilities	Assets	Liabilities
+$100,000 U.S. government securities	+$100,000 depository institution's reserves	+$100,000 reserves	+$100,000 transactions deposit owned by bond dealer

BALANCE SHEET 16-4
Shown are balance sheets for the Fed and the bank when the Fed purchases a U.S. government security. Only changes in assets and liabilities are displayed.

Sale of a $100,000 U.S. Government Security by the Fed

The process is reversed when the account manager at the New York Fed Trading Desk sells a U.S. government security from the Fed's portfolio.

Sale of a Security by the Fed. When the individual or institution buying the security from the Fed transmits a $100,000 payment to the Fed, the Fed reduces the reserves and deposits of the security purchaser's bank. The $100,000 sale of the U.S. government security leads to a reduction in reserves in the banking system and a reduction in transactions deposits. Hence the money supply declines.

Using Balance Sheets Again. Balance Sheet 16-5 shows the results for the sale of a U.S. government security by the Fed. When the $100,000 payment transfer occurs, the Fed reduces by $100,000 the reserve account of the security purchaser's bank. The Fed's assets are also reduced by $100,000 because it no longer owns the U.S. government security. The bank's transactions deposit liabilities are reduced by $100,000 when that amount is deducted from the security purchaser's account, and the money supply is thereby reduced by that amount. The bank's assets are also reduced by $100,000 because the Fed has reduced its total reserves by that amount.

BALANCE SHEET 16-5
Balance sheets after the Fed has sold $100,000 of U.S. government securities, showing changes only in assets and liabilities

The Fed		Bank	
Assets	Liabilities	Assets	Liabilities
−$100,000 U.S. government securities	−$100,000 depository institution's reserves	−$100,000 reserves	−$100,000 transactions deposit balances

QUICK QUIZ

If funds are transferred from a transactions deposit account at one depository institution and deposited in another, there is _____ _____ in total deposits or in the total money supply. _____ additional reserves in the banking system have been created.

The Federal Reserve, through its Federal Open Market Committee (FOMC), can directly _____ depository institutions' reserves and the money supply by purchasing U.S. government securities from bond dealers in the open market; it can _____ depository institutions' reserves and the money supply by selling U.S. government securities to bond dealers in the open market.

See page 421 for the answers. Review concepts from this section in MyEconLab.

MONEY EXPANSION BY THE BANKING SYSTEM

Consider now the entire banking system. For practical purposes, we can look at all depository institutions taken as a whole. To understand how money is created, we must understand how depository institutions respond to Fed actions that increase reserves in the entire system.

Fed Purchases of U.S. Government Securities

Assume that the Fed purchases a $100,000 U.S. government security from a bond dealer. The Fed electronically transfers $100,000 to the bond dealer's transactions deposit account at Bank 1, which prior to this transaction is in the position depicted in Balance Sheet 16-6.

BALANCE SHEET 16-6
Bank 1

This shows Bank 1's original position before the Federal Reserve's purchase of a $100,000 U.S. government security.

Assets			Liabilities	
Total reserves		$100,000	Transactions deposits	$1,000,000
Required reserves	$100,000			
Excess reserves	0			
Loans		900,000		
Total		$1,000,000	Total	$1,000,000

Now look at the balance sheet for Bank 1 shown in Balance Sheet 16-7. Reserves have been increased by $100,000 to $200,000, and transactions deposits have also been increased by $100,000. Because required reserves on $1.1 million of transactions deposits are only $110,000, the depository institution has $90,000 in excess reserves.

BALANCE SHEET 16-7
Bank 1

Assets			Liabilities	
Total reserves		$200,000	Transactions deposits	$1,100,000
Required reserves	$110,000			
Excess reserves	90,000			
Loans		900,000		
Total		$1,100,000	Total	$1,100,000

Effect on the Money Supply. The purchase of a $100,000 U.S. government security by the Federal Reserve from the public (a bond dealer, for example) increases the money supply immediately by $100,000 because transactions deposits held by the public—the bond dealers are members of the public—are part of the money supply, and no other bank has lost deposits.

The process of money creation does not stop here. Look again at Balance Sheet 16-7. Bank 1 has excess reserves of $90,000. No other depository institution (or combination of depository institutions) has negative excess reserves of $90,000 as a result of the Fed's bond purchase. (Remember, the Fed simply *created* the reserves to pay for the bond purchase.)

Bank 1 will not wish to hold non-interest-bearing excess reserves. Assume that it will expand its loans by $90,000. This is shown in Balance Sheet 16-8.

BALANCE SHEET 16-8
Bank 1

Assets			Liabilities	
Total reserves		$110,000	Transactions deposits	$1,100,000
Required reserves	$110,000			
Excess reserves	0			
Loans		990,000		
Total		$1,100,000	Total	$1,100,000

The individual or business that has received the $90,000 loan will spend these funds, which will then be deposited in other banks. For the sake of simplicity, concentrate only on the balance sheet *changes* resulting from this new deposit, as shown in Balance Sheet 16-9.

BALANCE SHEET 16-9
Bank 2 (Changes Only)

Assets			Liabilities	
Total reserves		+$90,000	New transactions deposits	+$90,000
Required reserves	+$9,000			
Excess reserves	+$81,000			
Total		+$90,000	Total	+$90,000

For Bank 2, the $90,000 deposit becomes an increase in reserves as well as an increase in transactions deposits and hence the money supply. Because the reserve requirement is 10 percent, required reserves increase by $9,000, so Bank 2 will have excess reserves of $81,000. But, of course, excess reserves are not income producing, so by assumption Bank 2 will reduce them to zero by making a loan of $81,000 (which will earn interest income). This is shown in Balance Sheet 16-10.

BALANCE SHEET 16-10
Bank 2 (Changes Only)

Assets			Liabilities	
Total reserves		+$9,000	Transactions deposits	+$90,000
Required reserves	+$9,000			
Excess reserves	0			
Loans		+81,000		
Total		+$90,000	Total	+$90,000

Remember that in this example, the original $100,000 deposit was transmitted electronically by a Federal Reserve bank to the bond dealer's transactions deposit account. That $100,000 constituted an immediate increase in the money supply of $100,000. The deposit creation process (in addition to the original $100,000) occurs because of the fractional reserve banking system, coupled with the desire of depository institutions to maintain a minimum level of excess reserves. Under fractional reserve banking, banks must hold only a portion of new deposits as legal reserves, and in their quest to earn profits, they seek to transform excess reserves into holdings of loans and securities.

Continuation of the Deposit Creation Process. Look at Bank 3's simplified account in Balance Sheet 16-11, where again only *changes* in the assets and liabilities are shown. Assume that the firm borrowing $81,000 from Bank 2 spends these funds, which are deposited in Bank 3; transactions deposits and the money supply increase by $81,000. Legal reserves of Bank 3 rise by that amount when the payment transfer occurs.

BALANCE SHEET 16-11
Bank 3 (Changes Only)

Assets		Liabilities	
Total reserves	+$81,000	New transactions deposits	+$81,000
Required reserves +$8,100			
Excess reserves +$72,900			
Total	+$81,000	Total	+$81,000

Because the reserve requirement is 10 percent, required reserves rise by $8,100, and excess reserves therefore increase by $72,900. We assume that Bank 3 will want to lend all of those non-interest-earning assets (excess reserves). When it does, loans (and newly created transactions deposits) will increase by $72,900. This bank's legal reserves will fall to $8,100, and excess reserves become zero as debit-card or check payments are transferred from the new deposit. This is shown in Balance Sheet 16-12.

BALANCE SHEET 16-12
Bank 3 (Changes Only)

Assets		Liabilities	
Total reserves	+$8,100	New transactions deposits	+$81,000
Required reserves +$8,100			
Excess reserves 0			
Loans	+$72,900		
Total	+$81,000	Total	+$81,000

How are an increasing number of depository institutions clearing checks without ever physically handling them?

E-COMMERCE EXAMPLE

Remote Capture Speeds the Check-Clearing Process

Bank of America, Bank of New York, and Wachovia Corporation have recently joined a movement pioneered by Internet-based institutions, such as NetBank and E-Trade, to engage in *remote capture* of paper checks. With remote capture, a retailer electronically scans checks received from customers. The retailer then transmits a digital image to its bank, which automatically forwards the image either to the Fed or to a private clearinghouse for processing.

The traditional check-clearing process, which requires paper checks to be carried from businesses to a bank's branches and then on to the bank's check-clearing offices, typically takes at least one to three days to complete. Remote capture cuts the time to just an hour, thereby dramatically reducing the time required to complete transfers of funds between transactions accounts at depository institutions.

FOR CRITICAL ANALYSIS
It is technologically feasible for retailers to transmit check images directly to the Fed or a private clearinghouse. Why do retailers continue to use depository institutions as go-betweens in the check-clearing process?

TABLE 16-1
Maximum Money Creation with 10 Percent Required Reserves

This table shows the maximum new loans plus investments that banks can make, given the Fed's electronic transfer of $100,000 to a transactions deposit account at Bank 1. The required reserve ratio is 10 percent. We assume that all excess reserves in each bank are used for new loans or investments.

Bank	New Deposits	New Required Reserves	Maximum New Loans
1	$100,000 (from Fed)	$10,000	$90,000
2	90,000	9,000	81,000
3	81,000	8,100	72,900
4	72,900	7,290	65,610
.	.	.	.
.	.	.	.
.	.	.	.
All other banks	656,100	65,610	590,490
Totals	$1,000,000	$100,000	$900,000

Progression to Other Banks. This process continues to Banks 4, 5, 6, and so forth. Each bank obtains smaller and smaller increases in deposits because 10 percent of each deposit must be held in required reserves; therefore, each succeeding depository institution makes correspondingly smaller loans. Table 16-1 shows the new deposits, required reserves, and possible loans for the remaining depository institutions in the system.

Effect on Total Deposits. In this example, deposits (and the money supply) increased initially by the $100,000 that the Fed paid the bond dealer in exchange for a bond. Deposits (and the money supply) were further increased by a $90,000 deposit in Bank 2, and they were again increased by an $81,000 deposit in Bank 3. Eventually, total deposits and the money supply will increase by $1 million, as shown in Table 16-1. The $1 million consists of the original $100,000 created by the Fed, plus an extra $900,000 generated by deposit-creating bank loans. The deposit creation process is portrayed graphically in Figure 16-2.

Increase in Total Banking System Reserves

Even with fractional reserve banking, if there are zero excess reserves, deposits cannot expand unless total banking system reserves are increased. The original new deposit in Bank 1, in our example, was created by an electronic transfer from a Federal Reserve district bank. It therefore represented new reserves to the banking system. Had that transfer been from an existing account at Bank 3, in contrast, nothing would have happened to the total amount of transactions deposits; there would have been no change in the total money supply. To repeat: Funds transferred electronically or by check from accounts at banks within the system, without any expansion of overall reserves within the banking system, represent transfers of reserves and deposits among depository institutions that do not affect the money supply. *Only when additional new reserves and deposits are created by the Federal Reserve System does the money supply increase.*

You should be able to work through the foregoing example to show the reverse process when there is a decrease in reserves because the Fed sells a $100,000 U.S. government security. The result is a multiple contraction of deposits and, therefore, of the total money supply in circulation.

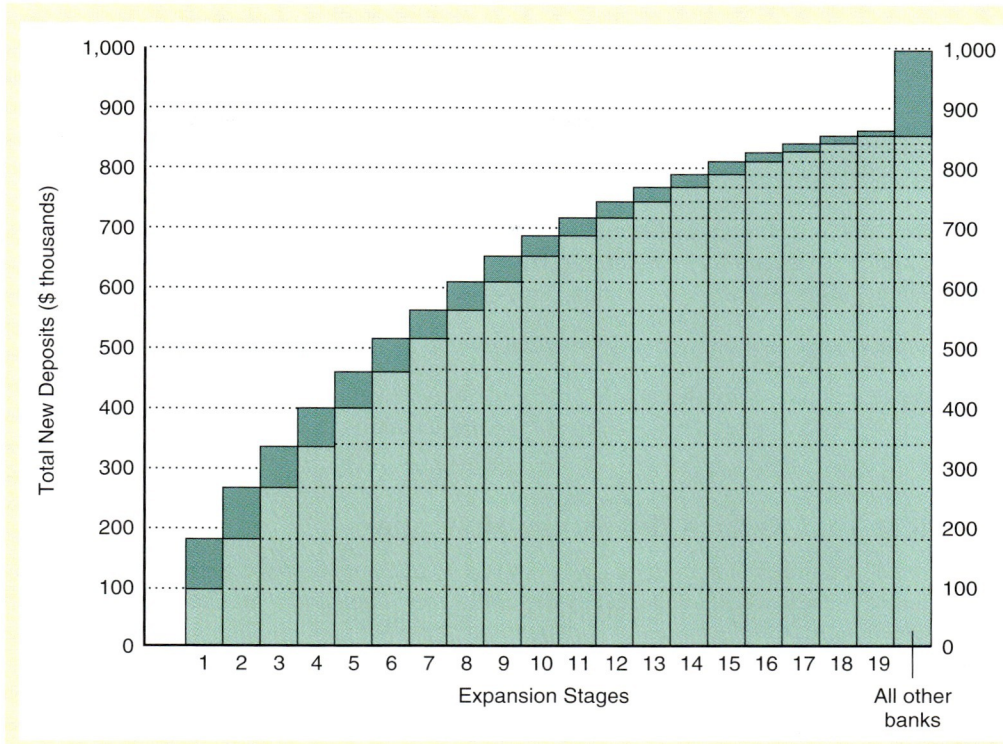

FIGURE 16-2
The Multiple Expansion in the Money Supply Due to $100,000 in New Reserves When the Required Reserve Ratio Is 10 Percent

The banks are all aligned in decreasing order of new deposits created. Bank 1 receives the $100,000 in new reserves and lends out $90,000. Bank 2 receives the $90,000 and lends out $81,000. The process continues through Banks 3 to 19 and then the rest of the banking system. Ultimately, assuming no leakages, the $100,000 of new reserves results in an increase in the money supply of $1 million, or 10 times the new reserves, because the required reserve ratio is 10 percent.

QUICK QUIZ

When the Fed _____ reserves through a purchase of U.S. government securities, the result is a multiple _____ of deposits and therefore of the supply of money.

When the Fed _____ the banking system's reserves by selling U.S. government securities, the result is a multiple _____ of deposits and therefore of the money supply.

See page 421 for the answers. Review concepts from this section in MyEconLab.

THE MONEY MULTIPLIER

In the example just given, a $100,000 increase in excess reserves generated by the Fed's purchase of a security yielded a $1 million increase in total deposits; deposits increased by a multiple of 10 times the initial $100,000 increase in overall reserves. Conversely, a $100,000 decrease in excess reserves generated by the Fed's sale of a security will yield a $1 million decrease in total deposits; they will decrease by a multiple of 10 times the initial $100,000 decrease in overall reserves.

We can now make a generalization about the extent to which the total money supply will change when the banking system's reserves are increased or decreased. The **money multiplier** gives the change in the money supply due to a change in reserves.

Money multiplier
A number that, when multiplied by a change in reserves in the banking system, yields the resulting change in the money supply.

Potential money multiplier
The reciprocal of the required reserve ratio, assuming no leakages into currency and no excess reserves. It is equal to 1 divided by the required reserve ratio.

If we assume that no excess reserves are kept and that all loan proceeds are deposited in depository institutions in the system, we obtain the **potential money multiplier**—the maximum possible value of the money multiplier when there is a reserve requirement. The following equation applies:

$$\text{Potential money multiplier} = \frac{1}{\text{required reserve ratio}}$$

That is, the maximum possible value of the money multiplier is equal to 1 divided by the required reserve ratio for transactions deposits. The *actual* change in the money supply—currency plus transactions account balances—will be equal to the following:

Actual change in money supply = actual money multiplier × change in total reserves

Now we examine why there is a difference between the potential money multiplier—1 divided by the required reserve ratio—and the actual money multiplier.

Forces That Reduce the Money Multiplier

We made a number of simplifying assumptions to come up with the potential money multiplier. In the real world, the actual money multiplier is considerably smaller. Two key factors account for this.

Leakages. The entire loan from one bank is not always deposited in another bank. At least two leakages can occur:

- *Currency drains.* When deposits increase, the public will want to hold more currency. Currency that is kept in a person's wallet remains outside the banking system and cannot be held by banks as reserves from which to make loans. The greater the amount of cash leakage, the smaller the actual money multiplier.
- *Excess reserves.* Depository institutions may wish to maintain excess reserves greater than zero. For example, a bank may wish to keep excess reserves so that it can make speedy loans when creditworthy borrowers seek funds. To the extent that banks want to keep positive excess reserves, the money multiplier will be smaller. The greater the excess reserves that banks maintain, the smaller the actual money multiplier.

Empirically, the currency drain is more significant than the effect of desired positive excess reserves.

Real-World Money Multipliers. The potential money multiplier is the reciprocal of the required reserve ratio. This potential is never attained for the system as a whole because of currency drains and excess reserves.

Each definition of the money supply, M1 or M2, will yield a different actual money multiplier. For several decades, the actual M1 multiplier has stayed in a range between 2.5 and 3.0. The actual M2 multiplier, however, has shown a trend upward, rising from 6.5 at the beginning of the 1960s to over 12 in the 2000s.

Other Ways That the Federal Reserve Can Change the Money Supply

As we have just seen, the Fed can change the money supply by directly changing reserves available to the banking system. It does this by engaging in open market operations. To repeat: The purchase of a U.S. government security by the Fed results in an increase in reserves and leads to a multiple expansion in the money supply. A sale of a U.S. government security by the Fed results in a decrease in reserves and leads to a multiple contraction in the money supply.

In principle, the Fed can change the money supply in two other ways, both of which will have multiplier effects similar to those outlined earlier.

Borrowed Reserves and the Discount Rate.

If a depository institution wants to increase its loans but has no excess reserves, it can borrow reserves. One place it can borrow reserves is from the Fed itself. The depository institution goes to the Federal Reserve and asks for a loan of a certain amount of reserves. The Fed charges these institutions for any reserves that it lends them. The interest rate that the Fed charges is the **discount rate,** and the borrowing is said to be done through the Fed's "discount window." Borrowing from the Fed increases reserves and thereby enhances the ability of the depository institution to engage in deposit creation, thus increasing the money supply.

Depository institutions actually do not often go to the Fed to borrow reserves. In years past, this was because the Fed would not lend them all they wanted to borrow. The Fed encouraged banks to tap an alternative source when they wanted to expand their reserves or when they needed reserves to meet a requirement. The primary source for banks to obtain funds is the **federal funds market.** The federal funds market is an interbank market in reserves, with one bank borrowing the excess reserves of another. The generic term *federal funds market* refers to the borrowing or lending of reserve funds that are usually repaid within the same 24-hour period.

Depository institutions that borrow in the federal funds market pay an interest rate called the **federal funds rate.** Because the federal funds rate is a ready measure of the price that banks must pay to raise funds, the Federal Reserve often uses it as a yardstick by which to measure the effects of its policies. Consequently, the federal funds rate is a closely watched indicator of the Fed's anticipated intentions.

For almost 80 years, the Fed tended to keep the discount rate unchanged for weeks at a time, and it typically set the discount rate slightly below the federal funds rate. Because this gave depository institutions an incentive to borrow from the Fed instead of from other banks in the federal funds market, the Fed established tough lending conditions. Often, when the Fed changed the discount rate, its objective was not necessarily to encourage or discourage depository institutions from borrowing from the Fed. Instead, altering the discount rate would signal to the banking system and financial markets that there had been a change in the Fed's monetary policy.

Today's Discount Rate Policy.

In 2003, the Fed altered the way it lends to depository institutions. It now sets the discount rate *above* the federal funds rate. This discourages depository institutions from seeking loans unless they face significant liquidity problems. Currently, the Fed keeps the discount rate 1 percentage point higher than the market-determined federal funds rate. If the market federal funds rate is 5 percent, therefore, the discount rate is 6 percent. If the federal funds rate increases to 5.5 percent, the Fed automatically raises the discount rate to 6.5 percent.

In principle, the Fed can continue to use the discount rate as an instrument of monetary policy by changing the amount by which the discount rate exceeds the federal funds rate. For instance, if the Fed reduced the differential from 1 percentage point to 0.5 percentage point, this would reduce depository institutions' disincentive from borrowing from the Fed. As Fed lending increased in response, borrowed reserves would rise, and total reserves in the banking system would increase. The Fed has indicated that it does not plan to conduct monetary policy in this way, however.

Discount rate
The interest rate that the Federal Reserve charges for reserves that it lends to depository institutions. It is sometimes referred to as the *rediscount rate* or, in Canada and England, as the *bank rate*.

Federal funds market
A private market (made up mostly of banks) in which banks can borrow reserves from other banks that want to lend them. Federal funds are usually lent for overnight use.

Federal funds rate
The interest rate that depository institutions pay to borrow reserves in the interbank federal funds market.

Reserve Requirement Changes. Another method by which the Fed can potentially alter the money supply is by changing the reserve requirements it imposes on all depository institutions. Earlier we assumed that reserve requirements were fixed. Actually, these requirements are set by the Fed within limits established by Congress. The Fed can vary reserve requirements within these broad limits.

What would a change in reserve requirements from 10 to 20 percent do (if there were no excess reserves and if we ignore currency leakages)? We have already seen that the potential money multiplier is the reciprocal of the required reserve ratio. If the required reserve ratio is 10 percent, then the potential money multiplier is the reciprocal of $\frac{1}{10}$, or 10 (assuming no leakages). If, for some reason, the Fed decided to increase reserve requirements to 20 percent, the potential money multiplier would equal the reciprocal of $\frac{1}{5}$, or 5. The potential money multiplier is therefore inversely related to the required reserve ratio. If the Fed decides to increase reserve requirements, the potential money multiplier will decrease. Therefore, with any given level of legal reserves already in existence, the money supply will contract.

In practice, open market operations allow the Federal Reserve to control the money supply much more precisely than changes in reserve requirements do, and they also allow the Fed to reverse itself quickly. In contrast, a small change in reserve requirements could, at least initially, result in a very large change in the money supply. Reserve requirement increases also impose costs on banks by restricting the portion of funds that they can lend, thereby inducing them to find legal ways to evade reserve requirements. That is why the Federal Reserve does not change reserve requirements very often.

> **ECONOMICS FRONT AND CENTER**
>
> To contemplate circumstances under which the Fed might not be able to use open market operations to conduct monetary policy, at least for a time, contemplate **A Job Enjoyed by No One at the Fed,** on page 415.

Sweep Accounts and the Decreased Relevance of Reserve Requirements

To many economists, reserve requirements are an outdated relic. They argue that reserve requirements might prove useful as a stabilizing tool if central banks really sought to achieve targets for the quantity of money in circulation, but they note that most central banks today pay little attention to variations in money growth. Hence, they contend, reserve requirements around the world should be reduced or even eliminated.

Table 16-2 shows that banks in many industrialized countries face lower required reserve ratios than they did a decade and a half ago. Relative to the required reserve ratios of other nations in the table, the official 10 percent ratio for transactions deposits in the United States stands out. This is misleading, however, because the *effective* U.S. required reserve ratio has been much lower than this since the mid-1990s.

The Great Reserve Requirement Loophole: Sweep Accounts. A key simplifying assumption in our example of the money creation process was that transactions deposits were the only bank liability that changes when total reserves change. Of course, banks also issue savings and time deposits. In addition, they offer *automatic transfer accounts.* In these accounts, which banks have offered since the 1970s, funds are automatically transferred from savings deposits to transactions deposits whenever the account holder makes a debit-card transaction or writes a check that would otherwise cause the balance of transactions deposits to become negative. Automatic transfer accounts thereby protect individuals and businesses from overdrawing their transactions deposit accounts.

Beginning in 1993, several U.S. banks discovered a way to use automatic transfer accounts to reduce their required reserves. The banks shift funds *out of* their customers' transactions deposit accounts, which are subject to reserve requirements, and *into* the customers' savings deposits—mainly money market deposit accounts—which are *not* subject

Required Reserve Ratio	1989	2007
Transactions Deposits		
Canada	10.0%	0%
European Monetary Union*	—	2.0
Japan	1.75	1.2
New Zealand	0	0
United Kingdom	0.45	0.35
United States	12.0	10.0
Nontransactions Deposits		
Canada	3.0	0
European Monetary Union*	—	2.0
Japan	2.5	1.3
New Zealand	0	0
United Kingdom	0.45	0.35
United States	3.0	0

TABLE 16-2

Required Reserve Ratios in Selected Nations

Several nations have reduced their required reserve ratios in recent years.

*The European Monetary Union was formed in 1999.
Sources: Gordon Sellon Jr. and Stuart Weiner, "Monetary Policy Without Reserve Requirements: Analytical Issues," Federal Reserve Bank of Kansas City *Economic Review* 81 (Fourth Quarter 1996), pp. 5–24; Bank for International Settlements, 2007.

to reserve requirements. Automatic transfer accounts with provisions permitting banks to shift funds from transactions deposits to savings deposits to avoid reserve requirements are called **sweep accounts.** Banks gave the accounts this name because they effectively use them to "sweep" funds from one deposit to another.

As panel (a) of Figure 16-3 shows, total funds in U.S. sweep accounts exempt from the 10 percent required reserve ratio have increased dramatically since 1995. Panel (b) indicates

Sweep account
A depository institution account that entails regular shifts of funds from transactions deposits that are subject to reserve requirements to savings deposits that are exempt from reserve requirements.

FIGURE 16-3

Sweep Accounts and Reserves of U.S. Depository Institutions at Federal Reserve Banks

Panel (a) depicts the growth of sweep accounts, which shift funds from transactions deposits subject to reserve requirements to savings deposits with no legal required reserve ratios. Panel (b) shows that sweep accounts induced an abrupt decline in reserve balances that depository institutions hold at Federal Reserve banks. Reserves have risen slightly and fallen again since (with a brief jump when the Fed made an emergency reserve injection after the 2001 terrorist attacks).

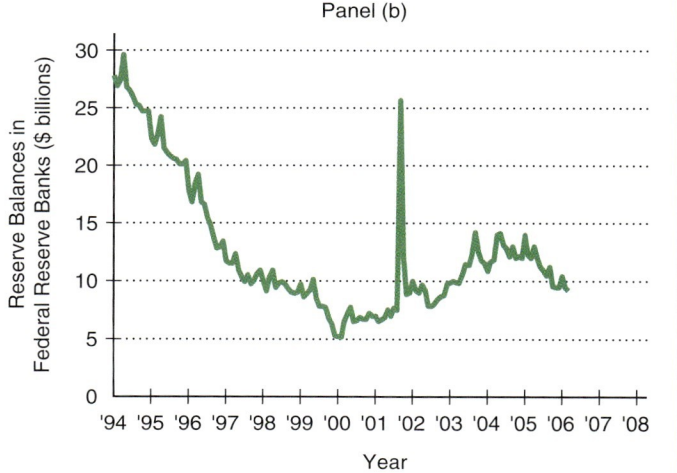

that the immediate result was a decline in the reserves that U.S. banks hold at Federal Reserve banks. Reserves have since risen but remain below previous levels.

Implications of Sweep Accounts for Measures of the Money Supply. Recall from Chapter 15 that there are two key measures of the U.S. money supply. One is M1, which consists of currency, transactions deposits, and traveler's checks. The other is M2, which is composed of M1 plus various other liquid assets, such as savings accounts, money market deposit accounts, and small-denomination time deposits.

Between 1984 and 1993, M2 grew at an annual rate of just under 5 percent, and M1 grew at an annual rate of just over 8 percent. Since 1993, the average annual rate of growth in M2 has remained close to 5 percent, but the average annual rate of growth of M1 has been close to 1 percent. The reason is the widespread use of sweep accounts since 1993. When depository institutions began using sweep accounts to shift funds from transactions deposits into savings accounts, the growth of the funds in transactions deposits abruptly halted. Since 1993, M1 has increased by only a few billion dollars. Growth in M2 has continued, however, because funds that depository institutions shift from transactions deposits to savings accounts are already included in M2.

Sweep accounts have therefore artificially changed the behavior of the M1 measure of the money supply. From the Fed's perspective, this has made M1 a less useful way to track total liquidity in the United States. It now relies on M2 as its key measure of the money supply.

> To learn more from the Federal Reserve Bank of St. Louis about the growth of sweep accounts, go to www.econtoday.com/ch16, and scan down the page to "Retail and Deposit Sweep Program."

QUICK QUIZ

The _____ money multiplier is equal to the reciprocal of the required reserve ratio. The _____ money multiplier is smaller than the _____ money multiplier because of currency drains and excess reserves held by banks.

The Fed can change the money supply through _____ _____, in which it buys and sells existing U.S. government securities. This is the key way in which the Fed conducts monetary policy.

In principle, the Fed can also conduct monetary policy by varying the _____ _____ to encourage changes in depository institutions' borrowings of reserves from the Fed. Starting in 2003, the Fed has automatically set the _____ _____ equal to the federal funds rate plus 1 percentage point.

Finally, the Fed can change the amount of deposits created from reserves by changing reserve requirements, but it has rarely done so. Furthermore, since the mid-1990s, U.S. depository institutions have used _____ _____ to shift funds from transactions deposits to savings deposits that are exempt from reserve requirements, thereby reducing the relevance of reserve requirements for monetary policy.

See page 421 for the answers. Review concepts from this section in MyEconLab.

FEDERAL DEPOSIT INSURANCE

When businesses fail, they create hardships for creditors, owners, and customers. But when a depository institution fails, an even greater hardship results, because many individuals and businesses depend on the safety and security of banks. Figure 16-4 indicates that during the 1920s, an average of about 600 banks failed each year. In the early 1930s, during the Great Depression, that average soared to nearly 3,000 failures each year.

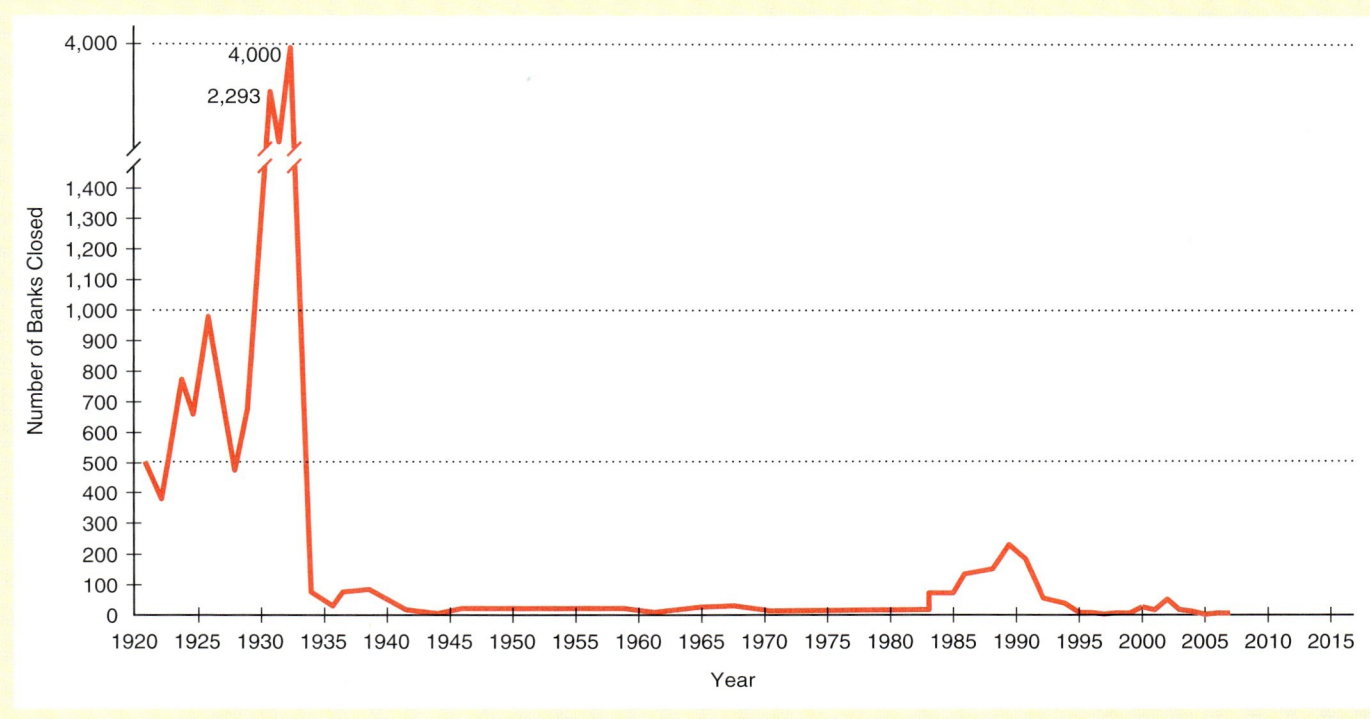

FIGURE 16-4

Bank Failures

During the Great Depression, a tremendous number of banks failed. Federal deposit insurance was created in 1933. Thereafter, bank failures were few until around 1984. Annual failures peaked at over 200 in 1989 and are now fewer than a dozen per year.

Source: Federal Deposit Insurance Corporation.

In 1933, at the height of such bank failures, the **Federal Deposit Insurance Corporation (FDIC)** was founded to insure the funds of depositors and remove the reason for ruinous runs on banks. In 1934, the Federal Savings and Loan Insurance Corporation (FSLIC) was established to insure deposits in savings and loan associations and mutual savings banks. In 1971, the National Credit Union Share Insurance Fund (NCUSIF) was created to insure deposits in credit unions. In 1989, the FSLIC was dissolved, and the Savings Association Insurance Fund (SAIF) was established, under FDIC supervision, to protect the deposits of those institutions.

As can be seen in Figure 16-4, bank failure rates dropped dramatically after passage of the early federal legislation. The long period from 1935 until the 1980s was relatively quiet. From World War II to 1984, fewer than nine banks failed per year. From 1985 until the beginning of 1993, however, 1,065 commercial banks failed—an average of nearly 120 bank failures per year, more than 10 times the average for the preceding 40 years! We will examine the reasons shortly. But first we need to understand how deposit insurance works.

Federal Deposit Insurance Corporation (FDIC)
A government agency that insures the deposits held in banks and most other depository institutions; all U.S. banks are insured this way.

The Rationale for Deposit Insurance

The FDIC, FSLIC (now SAIF), and NCUSIF were established to mitigate the primary cause of bank failures, **bank runs**—the simultaneous rush of depositors to convert their demand deposits or time deposits into currency.

Bank runs
Attempts by many of a bank's depositors to convert transactions and time deposits into currency out of fear that the bank's liabilities may exceed its assets.

Consider the following scenario. A bank begins to look shaky; its assets may not seem sufficient to cover its liabilities. If the bank has no deposit insurance, depositors in this bank (and any banks associated with it) will all want to withdraw their funds from the bank at the same time. Their concern is that this shaky bank will not have enough assets to return their deposits to them in the form of currency. Indeed, this is what happens in a bank failure when insurance doesn't exist. Just as when a regular business fails, the creditors of the bank may not all get paid, or if they do, they will get paid less than 100 percent of what they are owed. Depositors are creditors of a bank because their funds are on loan to the bank. As we have seen, in a fractional reserve banking system, banks do not hold 100 percent of their depositors' funds in the form of reserves. Consequently, all depositors cannot withdraw all their funds simultaneously. Hence the intent of the legislation enacted in the 1930s was to assure depositors that they could have their deposits converted into cash when they wished, no matter how serious the financial situation of the bank.

The FDIC (and later the FSLIC, NCUSIF, and SAIF) provided this assurance. Federal insurers charged premiums to depository institutions based on their total deposits, and these premiums went into funds that would reimburse depositors in the event of bank failures. By insuring deposits, the FDIC bolstered depositors' trust in the banking system and provided depositors with the incentive to leave their deposits with the bank, even in the face of widespread talk of bank failures. In 1933, it was sufficient for the FDIC to cover each account up to $2,500. The current maximum is $100,000 per depositor per institution.

To keep up with the latest issues in deposit insurance and banking with the assistance of the FDIC, go to www.econtoday.com/ch16.

How Deposit Insurance Causes Increased Risk Taking by Bank Managers

Until very recently, all insured depository institutions paid the same small fee for coverage. The fee that they paid was completely unrelated to how risky their assets were. A depository institution that made loans to companies such as Dell, Inc. and Microsoft Corporation paid the same deposit insurance premium as another depository institution that made loans (at higher interest rates) to the governments of developing countries that were teetering on the brink of financial collapse. Although deposit insurance premiums for a while were adjusted somewhat in response to the riskiness of a depository institution's assets, they never reflected all of the relative risk. Indeed, since the late 1990s, very few depository institutions have paid *any* deposit insurance premiums. This lack of correlation between risk and premiums can be considered a fundamental flaw in the deposit insurance scheme.

Because bank managers do not have to pay higher insurance premiums when they make riskier loans, they have an incentive to invest in more assets of higher yield, and therefore necessarily higher risk, than they would if there were no deposit insurance. The insurance premium rate is artificially low, permitting institution managers to obtain deposits at less than full cost (because depositors will accept a lower interest payment on insured deposits). Consequently, depository institution managers can increase their profits by using insured deposits to purchase higher-yield, higher-risk assets. The gains to risk taking accrue to the managers and stockholders of the depository institutions; the losses go to the deposit insurer (and, as we will see, ultimately to taxpayers).

To combat these flaws in the financial industry and in the deposit insurance system, a vast regulatory apparatus oversees depository institutions. The FDIC and other federal deposit insurance agencies possess regulatory powers to offset the risk-taking temptations to depository institution managers. Those powers include the ability to require higher capital investment; the ability to regulate, examine, and supervise bank affairs; and the ability to enforce regulatory decisions. Still higher capital requirements were imposed in the early 1990s and then adjusted somewhat beginning in 2000, but the basic flaws in the system remain.

Recently, the FDIC proposed insuring amounts held on stored-value cards. How may this proposal have contributed to efforts by depository institutions to expand the scope of federal deposit insurance?

POLICY EXAMPLE

Extending the Scope of FDIC Insurance with Stored-Value Cards

A few years ago, the Federal Deposit Insurance Corporation proposed extending insurance to funds on *stored-value cards* issued by commercial banks, savings institutions, and credit unions. Magnetically or digitally stored data on the cards indicate that the bearer of the card holds title to immediately spendable funds

In the mid-2000s, just as the FDIC was about to issue coverage to stored-value cards, some depository institutions announced preliminary plans to advertise new card products as "FDIC insured." Among these new products were payroll cards, which are stored-value cards that some employers use in place of old-fashioned paychecks to transmit wages to workers. Others included various bank-intermediated cards that retailers sell to customers to give away as gifts and that state governments issue for unemployment and public assistance payments.

Covering these new products could effectively extend federal deposit insurance to billions of dollars held on millions of cards issued through the nation's banking system. Consequently, the FDIC is currently reconsidering whether it will really extend federal insurance to stored-value cards issued by depository institutions.

FOR CRITICAL ANALYSIS

Would insuring bank-intermediated stored-value cards issued by retailers and governments "insure" these entities as well as depository institutions?

Deposit Insurance, Adverse Selection, and Moral Hazard

As a deposit insurer, the FDIC effectively acts as a government-run insurance company. This means that the FDIC's operations expose the federal government to the same kinds of asymmetric information problems that other financial intermediaries face.

Adverse Selection in Deposit Insurance.
One of these problems, as discussed in Chapter 15, is *adverse selection,* which arises when there is asymmetric information before a transaction takes place. Adverse selection is often a problem when insurance is involved because people or firms that are relatively poor risks are sometimes able to disguise that fact from insurers. It is instructive to examine the way this works with the deposit insurance provided by the FDIC. Deposit insurance shields depositors from the potential adverse effects of risky decisions and so makes depositors willing to accept riskier investment strategies by their banks. Clearly, this encourages more high-flying, risk-loving entrepreneurs to become managers of banks. Moreover, because depositors have so little incentive to monitor the activities of insured banks, it is also likely that the insurance actually encourages outright crooks—embezzlers and con artists—to enter the industry. The consequences for the FDIC—and for taxpayers—are larger losses.

Moral Hazard in Deposit Insurance. As you learned in Chapter 15, *moral hazard* arises as the result of information asymmetry after a transaction has occurred. Moral hazard is also an important phenomenon in the presence of insurance contracts, such as the deposit insurance provided by the FDIC. Insured depositors know that they will not suffer losses if their bank fails. Hence they have little incentive to monitor their bank's investment activities or to punish their bank by withdrawing their funds if the bank assumes too much risk. This means that insured banks have incentives to take on more risks than they otherwise would.

With those risks come higher losses for the FDIC and taxpayers, as the nation learned in the late 1980s when more than 1,500 savings and loan associations failed. In most cases, these failures occurred because managers of these thrift institutions undertook riskier actions than they otherwise would have in the absence of federal deposit insurance. The estimated taxpayer cost resulting from these thrift failures was about $200 billion.

Two major pieces of legislation were enacted to try to rein in some of the moral hazard risks exposed by this episode. One, the Financial Institutions Reform, Recovery, and Enforcement Act of 1989, provided the tax funds required to reimburse depositors and subjected weak institutions to tougher regulatory oversight. The other, the FDIC Improvement Act of 1991, toughened regulatory standards and required the FDIC to close weak depository institutions promptly, rather than letting their managers continue to roll the dice with taxpayers' dollars at stake.

A New Deposit Insurance Reform Effort

In February 2006, President George W. Bush signed into law the Federal Deposit Insurance Reform Act of 2005, which represents a new effort to reform the federal deposit insurance system. On the one hand, this law expanded the coverage of federal deposit insurance and hence potentially increased the system's moral hazard problems. The legislation increased deposit insurance coverage for Individual Retirement Accounts offered by banks and other depository institutions from $100,000 to $250,000. In addition, it authorized the FDIC to adjust, at five-year intervals beginning in 2010, the $100,000 limit on all other types of deposits to reflect inflation, as measured by the rate of change in the Personal Consumption Expenditures (PCE) Index.

On the other hand, the act provides the FDIC with improved tools for addressing moral hazard risks. The law combined the accumulated premium payments by banks and savings institutions into a single Deposit Insurance Fund (DIF), thereby formalizing identical treatment of all institutions covered by federal deposit insurance. In addition, the law changed a rule that prevented the FDIC from charging deposit insurance premiums if total accumulated premium funds exceed 1.25 percent of all deposits held at depository institutions. Now the FDIC can charge premiums if total DIF funds are less than 1.5 percent of all deposits. Furthermore, the legislation eliminated a limit on how often the FDIC could change deposit insurance premiums, so now the FDIC can also adjust deposit insurance premiums at any time. Finally, the law gave the FDIC more leeway to place institutions in any risk category it deems appropriate, irrespective of each institution's size.

Thus, the Federal Deposit Insurance Reform Act broadened the coverage of federal deposit insurance. At the same time, it expanded the discretion of the FDIC to combat the moral hazard risks that naturally arise from the existence of the deposit insurance system.

QUICK QUIZ

To limit the fallout from systemwide failures and bank runs, Congress created the _____ _____ _____ _____ in 1933. Since the advent of federal deposit insurance, there have been no true bank runs at federally insured banks.

Federal insurance of bank deposits insulates depositors from risks, so depositors are _____ concerned about riskier investment strategies by depository institutions. Thus, bank managers have an incentive to invest in _____ assets to make _____ rates of return.

On the one hand, the Federal Deposit Insurance Reform Act of 2005 expanded the _____ hazard risks associated with deposit insurance by increasing limits for insured retirement deposits and indexing limits for other deposits to inflation. On the other hand, the law granted the FDIC greater discretion to assess risk-based deposit insurance _____ intended to restrain _____ hazard risks.

See page 421 for the answers. Review concepts from this section in MyEconLab.

CASE STUDY

ECONOMICS FRONT AND CENTER

A Job Enjoyed by No One at the Fed

Edwards is a Fed economist who has drawn an assignment that he would have preferred to avoid. Together with other Fed employees, he is to develop an updated plan for policymaking in the event of a serious terrorist attack.

Among other things, the Fed's previous plan spelled out how responsibilities for policymaking would be distributed within the Federal Reserve System in the event of an attack on Washington, D.C. Nevertheless, the majority of the Fed's Board of Governors wants the new plan to provide more concrete guidelines for how the money supply would be influenced in the event of a major attack that halted trading of U.S. government securities for an extended period.

Edwards has been asked to draft the monetary policy portion of the report. He pauses as he prepares to lay out alternative ways that the Fed could conduct monetary policy if open market operations had to be halted for days or even weeks.

CRITICAL ANALYSIS QUESTIONS

1. *What would be the Fed's other options for conducting monetary policy if it were unable to conduct open market operations?*

2. *Based on your answer to Question 1, which alternative means of conducting policy do you think would be most feasible on a day-to-day basis?*

Issues and Applications

Smart Cards, Digital Cash, and the Money Supply

Concepts Applied
- Money Supply
- Open Market Operations
- Money Multiplier

The microchips embedded in smart cards give them a technical edge over debit cards with a magnetic stripe that are swiped through a card reader. In about 250 of every million transactions, stripe cards fail to process the transaction correctly. For smart cards, the failure rate is 80 percent lower, or less than 50 per million. This is one of the advantages of smart cards that have contributed to their growing use around the world.

How Smart Cards and Digital Cash Work

When a cardholder initiates a transaction with a retailer using a smart card, the chip in the retailer's electronic cash register confirms the authenticity of the smart card by examining a unique "digital signature" stored on the card's microchip. This digital signature is generated by software called a *cryptographic algorithm,* which is a secure program loaded onto the card's microchip.

The digital signature stored on the smart card guarantees to the retailer's electronic cash register that the smart card's chip is genuine and that it has not been tampered with by another party. The smart card's microchip can also contain other cryptographic algorithms, such as secure programs that effectively shout out, "I'm good money!" to any device capable of validating and transferring digital cash.

Where Smart Cards Have Caught On

At present, about 300 million smart cards are in use around the globe. Fewer than 15 million of them are in use in the United States, however. As Figure 16-5 indicates, more than 80 percent of all smart cards are utilized in Europe.

Most of the current growth in smart-card use is also occurring outside the United States. Smart-card distribution is rising, for instance, in Asia. It is also increasing rapidly in South America, where use of smart cards is helping banks cut down on fraudulent transactions.

Digital Cash and the Money Multiplier

Digital cash is a tiny portion of the U.S. money supply—so small that the Fed does not include digital cash in its measures of the quantity of money in circulation. Nevertheless, most observers agree that it is only a matter of time before smart cards and digital cash begin to catch on in the United States.

How would the use of smart cards and digital cash affect the U.S. deposit expansion process? Consider the effects of a Fed open market operation in a banking system in which smart cards and digital cash are widely used. Through the money multiplier process, a Fed open market purchase would generate a rise in deposits. People would shift a portion of funds from these deposits to digital cash stored on smart cards, much as they move funds from deposits to government-issued currency today. Unlike currency holdings, however, which together with bank reserves are determined by the Fed, the amount of privately issued digital cash would increase directly with the deposit expansion. This implies that the money supply would respond to the open market purchase by a larger amount, implying a larger money multiplier effect.

Smart cards would effectively reduce currency drain and thereby boost the actual multiplier to a higher value that is closer to the potential money multiplier. Thus, in a world in which people widely use digital cash instead of government currency, the money multiplier would be larger than its current value.

FIGURE 16-5
The Distribution of the World's Smart Cards
The bulk of the world's smart cards are currently held and utilized for payments in European countries.
Source: Bank for International Settlements.

Log in to MyEconLab, click on "Economic News," and test your understanding of the chapter by answering interactive questions that relate directly to this issue.

For Critical Analysis

1. How might U.S. banks' successes in protecting U.S. consumers from payment fraud have contributed to the slower rate of U.S. smart-card adoption?
2. What would happen to the U.S. money multiplier if digital cash completely replaced government currency? (Hint: Recall how the use of government currency affects the present money multiplier, and take into account the above discussion of how the use of digital cash will affect the money multiplier in the future.)

Web Resources

1. For more information about how digital cash works, go to www.econtoday.com/ch16.
2. To learn more about present mechanisms for using digital cash, go to a Web page with numerous links available at www.econtoday.com/ch16.

Research Project

Compare digital cash and smart cards to today's paper currency. A currency payment is anonymous and final, but it requires face-to-face transfers. Because smart cards use encrypted algorithms as "cash," they also are anonymous, and they can be utilized to complete face-to-face transactions. Unlike currency payments, however, digital cash payments can be made over long distances by using computers that can access the Internet. In light of these characterisitics and any others you can identify, what are the prospects for digital cash to emerge as a viable substitute for government-issued currency?

Here is what you should know after reading this chapter. MyEconLab will help you identify what you know, and where to go when you need to practice.

WHAT YOU SHOULD KNOW

WHERE TO GO TO PRACTICE

How the Federal Reserve Assesses Reserve Requirements The Federal Reserve establishes a required reserve ratio, which is currently 10 percent of nearly all transactions deposits at depository institutions. Legal reserves that depository institutions may hold to satisfy their reserve requirements include deposits they hold at Federal Reserve district banks and as cash in their vaults. Any legal reserves that a depository institution holds over and above its required reserves are called excess reserves.

fractional reserve banking, 394
reserves, 395
legal reserves, 395
required reserves, 395
required reserve ratio, 395
excess reserves, 395
Key figure
Figure 16-1, 394

- **MyEconLab** Study Plans 16.1 and 16.2
- Audio introduction to Chapter 16
- Animated Figure 16-1
- Video: Depository Institution Reserves

Why the Money Supply Does Not Change When Someone Deposits in a Depository Institution Funds Transferred from Another Depository Institution When an individual or a business deposits funds transferred from another depository institution, two things occur. First, the depository institution from which the funds were transferred experiences a reduction in its total deposits. Second, the depository institution that receives the deposit experiences an equal-sized increase in its total deposits. For the banking system as a whole, therefore, total deposits remain unchanged. Thus, the money supply is unaffected by the transaction.

balance sheet, 396
net worth, 396

- **MyEconLab** Study Plan 16.3

Why the Money Supply Does Change When Someone Deposits in a Depository Institution Funds Transferred from the Federal Reserve System When an individual or a business (typically a bond dealer) deposits funds transferred from the Federal Reserve System, the depository institution that receives the deposit experiences an equal-sized increase in its total deposits. Consequently, there is an immediate increase in total deposits in the banking system as a whole, and the money supply increases by the amount of the initial deposit. Furthermore, the depository institution that receives this deposit can lend any reserves in excess of required reserves, which will generate a rise in deposits at another bank. This process continues as each bank receiving a deposit has additional funds over and above required reserves that it can lend.

open market operations, 399
Key table
Table 16-1, 404
Key figure
Figure 16-2, 405

- **MyEconLab** Study Plans 16.4 and 16.5
- Animated Table 16-1
- Animated Figure 16-2

WHAT YOU SHOULD KNOW		WHERE TO GO TO PRACTICE
The Maximum Potential Change in the Money Supply Following a Federal Reserve Purchase or Sale of U.S. Government Securities When the Federal Reserve buys or sells securities, the maximum potential change in the money supply occurs when there are no leakages of currency or excess reserves during the process of money creation. The amount of the maximum potential change is equal to the amount of reserves that the Fed injects into or withdraws from the banking system times the reciprocal of the required reserve ratio.	money multiplier, 405 potential money multiplier, 406	• **MyEconLab** Study Plan 16.6
How the Fed Can and Does Influence the Money Supply In principle, the Fed can alter reserves and hence the money supply through open market operations, changing the discount rate and adjusting reserve requirements. When the Fed engages in open market operations, it buys or sells existing U.S. government securities, thereby injecting reserves into or withdrawing reserves from the banking system. Altering the discount rate relative to the federal funds rate can encourage changes in borrowed reserves. Since early 2003, however, the Fed has kept the discount rate 1 percentage point above the federal funds rate, which discourages borrowing from the Fed and limits the Fed's ability to use the discount rate as a separate policy tool. Varying reserve requirements can change the amount of deposits created from bank reserves. The Fed has rarely conducted monetary policy in this way, and reductions in required reserves resulting from depository institutions' use of sweep accounts have made reserve requirements less relevant to monetary policy. Thus, open market operations are the Fed's key tool of monetary policy.	discount rate, 407 federal funds market, 407 federal funds rate, 407 sweep account, 409 **Key figure** Figure 16-3, 409	• **MyEconLab** Study Plan 16.6 • Animated Figure 16-3
Features of Federal Deposit Insurance To help prevent runs on banks, the U.S. government in 1933 established the Federal Deposit Insurance Corporation (FDIC). This government agency provides deposit insurance by charging some depository institutions premiums based on the value of their deposits, and it places these funds in accounts for use in closing failed banks and reimbursing their depositors. One difficulty associated with providing deposit insurance is the problem of adverse selection because the availability of deposit insurance can potentially attract risk-taking individuals into the banking business. Another difficulty is the moral hazard problem. This problem arises when deposit insurance premiums fail to reflect the full extent of the risks taken on by depository institution managers and when depositors who know they are insured have little incentive to monitor the performance of the institutions that hold their deposit funds.	Federal Deposit Insurance Corporation (FDIC), 411 bank runs, 411	• **MyEconLab** Study Plan 16.7 • Video: Deposit Insurance and Risk Taking

PROBLEMS

Select problems, indicated by a blue oval, are assignable in MyEconLab. Answers to the odd-numbered problems appear at the back of the book.

16-1 Identify each of the following as a commercial bank asset or liability.
   a. An auto loan to an individual
   b. Funds borrowed from a credit union in the federal funds market
   c. A customer's savings deposit
   d. The bank's required reserves

16-2 A bank's total assets equal $1 billion. Its liabilities equal $1 billion. Transactions deposits equal $500 million, loans equal $700 million, and securities equal $250 million.
   a. If the bank's only other liabilities are savings deposits, what is the value of these savings deposits?
   b. If the bank's only other assets are vault cash and reserve deposits with a Federal Reserve bank, what is the total amount of these assets?

16-3 A bank's only liabilities are $15 million in transactions deposits. The bank currently meets its reserve requirement, and it holds no excess reserves. The required reserve ratio is 10 percent. Assuming that its only assets are legal reserves, loans, and securities, what is the value of loans and securities held by the bank?

16-4 Draw an empty bank balance sheet, with the heading "Assets" on the left and the heading "Liabilities" on the right. Then place the following items on the proper side of the balance sheet:
   a. Loans to a private company
   b. Borrowings from a Federal Reserve district bank
   c. Deposits with a Federal Reserve district bank
   d. U.S. Treasury bills
   e. Vault cash
   f. Loans to other banks in the federal funds market
   g. Transactions deposits

16-5. Suppose that the total liabilities of a depository institution are transactions deposits equal to $2 billion. It has $1.65 billion in loans and securities, and the required reserve ratio is 15 percent. Does this institution hold any excess reserves? If so, how much?

16-6 A bank has $120 million in total assets, which are composed of legal reserves, loans, and securities. Its only liabilities are $120 million in transactions deposits. The bank exactly satisfies its reserve requirement, and its total legal reserves equal $6 million. What is the required reserve ratio?

16-7 The Federal Reserve purchases $1 million in U.S. Treasury bonds from a bond dealer, and the dealer's bank credits the dealer's account. The required reserve ratio is 15 percent, and the bank typically lends any excess reserves immediately. Assuming that no currency leakage occurs, how much will the bank be able to lend to its customers following the Fed's purchase?

16-8 A depository institution holds $150 million in required reserves and $10 million in excess reserves. Its remaining assets include $440 million in loans and $150 million in securities. If the institution's only liabilities are transactions deposits, what is the required reserve ratio?

16-9 A bank has $260 million in total reserves, of which $10 million are excess reserves. The bank currently has $3.6 billion in loans, $1 billion in securities, and $140 million in other assets. The required reserve ratio for transactions deposits is 10 percent.
   a. What is this bank's total amount of liabilities and net worth?
   b. What additional amount of loans could this bank make to households and firms?
   c. What is the current quantity of transactions deposits at this bank?

16-10 A bank has issued $4 billion in transactions deposits and $2 billion in time deposits and other nontransactions deposits. Its other liabilities and net worth equal $1 billion. The bank has $100 million in total reserves. The only reserve requirement that this and all other banks must satisfy is a 2 percent ratio that applies to transactions deposits.

   a. What is the amount of the bank's total assets?
   b. What is the amount of the bank's excess reserves?
   c. What is the potential money multiplier for the banking system?

16-11 A bank has $16 billion in total assets, of which $200 million are its total reserves. Customers initially hold a total of $9 billion in their transactions deposit accounts with this bank, but it has automatically transformed $8 billion of this amount into money market deposit accounts through its sweep account arrangements with these customers. The required reserve ratio for transactions deposits is 20 percent. The bank faces no other reserve requirement.

   a. At present, does this bank meet its reserve requirement?
   b. How much in excess reserves can this bank currently use to make loans or purchase securities?
   c. What is the amount of this bank's contribution to the M1 measure of money?

16-12 Suppose that the value of the potential money multiplier is equal to 4. What is the required reserve ratio?

16-13. Why is it that you cannot induce any net multiple deposit expansion in the banking system by buying a U.S. government security, yet the Federal Reserve can do so?

16-14. Consider a world in which there is no currency and depository institutions issue only transactions deposits and desire to hold no excess reserves. The required reserve ratio is 20 percent. The central bank sells $1 billion in government securities. What ultimately happens to the money supply?

16-15 Assume a 1 percent required reserve ratio, zero excess reserves, and no currency leakages. What is the potential money multiplier? How will total deposits in the banking system ultimately change if the Federal Reserve purchases $5 million in U.S. government securities?

ECONOMICS ON THE NET

E-Checks and the Money Supply In this chapter, you learned about how monetary policy actions of the Federal Reserve induce changes in total deposits in the banking system. Now let's think about monetary policymaking in a world with online checking.

Title: What Is eCheck?

Navigation: Go directly to the eCheck home page **echeck.commerce.net/overview** via **www.econtoday.com/ch16,** and click on *What Is eCheck?*

Application Read the discussion, and then answer the following questions.

   1. Are e-checks substitutes for currency and coins, or are they substitutes for traditional paper checks? Does the answer to this question make a difference for how e-checks are likely to feature in the money multiplier process?

   2. Suppose that there is widespread adoption of e-check technology by consumers and businesses. Would this affect the basic money multiplier model that we developed in this chapter? If so, how? If not, why not?

For Group Study and Analysis Divide the class into groups. Have each group evaluate the likely effects of e-check adoption, as well as widespread adoption of other forms of electronic retail payment mechanisms, on the money multiplier. Meet again as a class, and discuss the channels by which adoption of electronic moneys will potentially affect the money multiplier.

ANSWERS TO QUICK QUIZZES

p. 396: (i) percentage . . . vault; (ii) ratio
p. 400: (i) no change . . . Zero; (ii) increase . . . decrease
p. 405: (i) increases . . . expansion; (ii) reduces . . . contraction
p. 410: (i) potential . . . actual . . . potential; (ii) open market operations; (iii) discount rate . . . discount rate; (iv) sweep accounts
p. 415: (i) Federal Deposit Insurance Corporation; (ii) less . . . riskier . . . higher; (iii) moral . . . premiums . . . moral

17 Domestic and International Dimensions of Monetary Policy

Learning Objectives

After reading this chapter, you should be able to:

1. Identify the key factors that influence the quantity of money that people desire to hold
2. Describe how the Federal Reserve's tools of monetary policy influence market interest rates
3. Evaluate how expansionary and contractionary monetary policy actions affect equilibrium real GDP and the price level in the short run
4. Understand the equation of exchange and its importance in the quantity theory of money and prices
5. Discuss the interest-rate-based transmission mechanism of monetary policy
6. Explain why the Federal Reserve cannot stabilize both the money supply and interest rates simultaneously

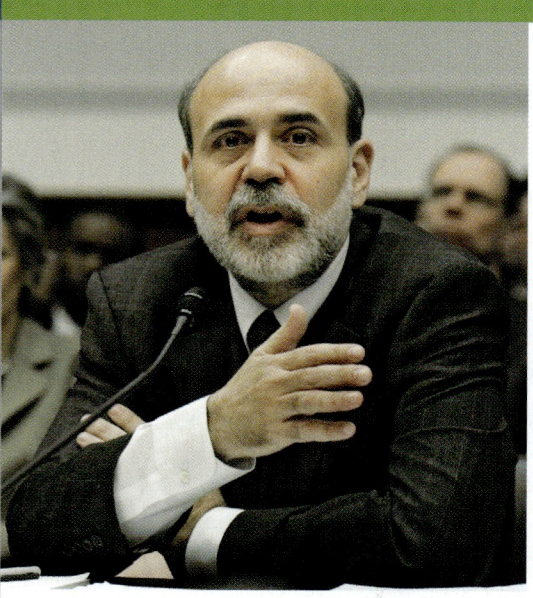

Between 2001 and 2004, the Fed's target for the *federal funds rate*, the interest rate at which depository institutions lend to one another, declined from above 6 percent to 1 percent. Then, starting in January 2004, the Fed's target rate began to increase steadily. During both periods, the Fed was searching for a "neutral federal funds rate." This is a rate at which the rate of growth of actual real GDP is just equal to the rate of growth of *potential real GDP*, which is the level of real GDP that the Fed estimates to be consistent with U.S. resource use at the maximum sustainable level. Why does the Federal Reserve use a federal funds rate target as its primary tool of monetary policy, and what are the implications of its choice? When you have completed this chapter, you will be able to answer this question.

 MyEconLab helps you master each objective and study more efficiently. See end of chapter for details.

CHAPTER 17 *Domestic and International Dimensions of Monetary Policy* **423**

> ### Did You Know That...
> the market prices of U.S. Treasury bonds sometimes change noticeably during televised congressional committee hearings featuring testimony by Ben Bernanke, chair of the Fed's Board of Governors? If Bernanke answers a congressperson's question in a way that indicates to listeners that interest rates are likely to increase in the future, bond prices often fall within a few minutes. If Bernanke provides a contradictory answer later in the same hearing and implies that interest rates may not rise after all, bond prices typically recover just as rapidly.
>
> What does Fed policymaking, which involves varying the supply of money or the rate at which it grows, have to do with market interest rates on bonds? Before we can address this question, you must first understand why money is special and what factors determine how much money people desire to hold.

WHAT'S SO SPECIAL ABOUT MONEY?

By definition, monetary policy has to do, in the main, with money. But what is so special about money? Money is the product of a "social contract" in which we all agree to do two things:

1. Express all prices in terms of a common unit of account, which in the United States we call the dollar
2. Use a specific medium of exchange for market transactions

These two features of money distinguish it from all other goods in the economy. As a practical matter, money is involved on one side of every nonbarter transaction in the economy—and trillions of them occur every year. What this means is that something that changes the amount of money in circulation will have some effect on many transactions and thus on elements of GDP. If something affects the number of snowmobiles in existence, probably only the snowmobile market will be altered. But something that affects the amount of money in existence is going to affect *all* markets.

Holding Money

All of us engage in a flow of transactions. We buy and sell things all of our lives. But because we use money—dollars—as our medium of exchange, all *flows* of nonbarter transactions involve a *stock* of money. We can restate this as follows:

To use money, one must hold money.

Given that everybody must hold money, we can now talk about the *demand* to hold it. People do not demand to hold money just to look at pictures of past leaders. They hold it to be able to use it to buy goods and services.

The Demand for Money: What People Wish to Hold

People have a certain motivation that causes them to want to hold **money balances.** Individuals and firms could try to do without non-interest-bearing money balances. But life is inconvenient without a ready supply of money balances. There is a demand for money by the public, motivated by several factors.

Money balances
Synonymous with money, money stock, money holdings.

The Transactions Demand. The main reason people hold money is that money can be used to purchase goods and services. People are paid at specific intervals (once a week, once a month, and so on), but they wish to make purchases more or less continuously. To free themselves from having to make expenditures on goods and services only on payday, people find it beneficial to hold money. The benefit they receive is convenience: They willingly forgo interest earnings in order to avoid the inconvenience and expense of cashing in nonmoney assets such as bonds every time they wish to make a purchase. Thus, people hold money to make regular, *expected* expenditures under the **transactions demand**. As nominal GDP rises, people will want to hold more money because they will be making more transactions.

Transactions demand
Holding money as a medium of exchange to make payments. The level varies directly with nominal GDP.

The Precautionary Demand.
The transactions demand involves money held to make *expected* expenditures. People also hold money for the **precautionary demand** to make *unexpected* purchases or to meet emergencies. When people hold money for the precautionary demand, they incur a cost in forgone interest earnings that they balance against the benefit that having cash on hand provides. The higher the rate of interest, the lower the money balances people wish to hold for the precautionary demand.

Precautionary demand
Holding money to meet unplanned expenditures and emergencies.

The Asset Demand.
Remember that one of the functions of money is to serve as a store of value. People can hold money balances as a store of value, or they can hold bonds or stocks or other interest-earning assets. The desire to hold money as a store of value leads to the **asset demand** for money. People choose to hold money rather than other assets for two reasons: its liquidity and the lack of risk.

Asset demand
Holding money as a store of value instead of other assets such as certificates of deposit, corporate bonds, and stocks.

The disadvantage of holding money balances as an asset, of course, is the interest earnings forgone. Each individual or business decides how much money to hold as an asset by looking at the opportunity cost of holding money. The higher the interest rate—which is the opportunity cost of holding money—the lower the money balances people will want to hold as assets. Conversely, the lower the interest rate offered on alternative assets, the higher the money balances people will want to hold as assets.

ECONOMICS FRONT AND CENTER

To contemplate how variations in the different factors motivating people to hold money can generate hard-to-predict changes in the overall demand for money, read **Predicting the Finicky U.S. Demand for Money**, on page 439.

The Demand for Money Curve

Assume for simplicity's sake that the amount of money demanded for transactions purposes is proportionate to income. That leaves the precautionary and asset demands for money, both determined by the opportunity cost of holding money. If we assume that the interest rate represents the cost of holding money balances, we can graph the relationship between the interest rate and the quantity of money demanded. In Figure 17-1, the demand

FIGURE 17-1

The Demand for Money Curve

If we use the interest rate as a proxy for the opportunity cost of holding money balances, the demand for money curve, M_d, is downward sloping, similar to other demand curves.

for money curve shows a familiar downward slope. The horizontal axis measures the quantity of money demanded, and the vertical axis is the interest rate. In this sense, the interest rate is the cost of holding money. At a higher interest rate, a lower quantity of money is demanded, and vice versa.

To see this, imagine two scenarios. In the first one, you can earn 20 percent a year if you put your cash into purchases of U.S. government securities. In the other scenario, you can earn 1 percent if you put your cash into purchases of U.S. government securities. If you have $1,000 average cash balances in a non-interest-bearing checking account, in the second scenario over a one-year period, your opportunity cost would be 1 percent of $1,000, or $10. In the first scenario, your opportunity cost would be 20 percent of $1,000, or $200. Under which scenario would you hold more cash instead of securities?

QUICK QUIZ

To use money, people must hold money. Therefore, they have a _____ for money balances.

The determinants of the demand for money balances are the _____ demand, the _____ demand, and the _____ demand.

Because holding money carries an _____ cost—the interest income forgone—the demand for money curve showing the relationship between the quantity of money balances demanded and the interest rate slopes _____.

See page 445 for the answers. Review concepts from this section in MyEconLab.

THE TOOLS OF MONETARY POLICY

The Fed seeks to alter consumption, investment, and aggregate demand as a whole by altering the rate of growth of the money supply. The Fed has three tools at its disposal as part of its policymaking action: open market operations, discount rate changes, and reserve requirement changes.

Open Market Operations

The Fed changes the amount of reserves in the system by its purchases and sales of government bonds issued by the U.S. Treasury. To understand how the Fed does this, you must first start out in an equilibrium in which all individuals, including the holders of bonds, are satisfied with the current situation. There is some equilibrium level of interest rate (and bond prices). Now, if the Fed wants to conduct open market operations, it must somehow induce individuals, businesses, and foreign residents to hold more or fewer U.S. Treasury bonds. The inducement must be in the form of making people better off. So, if the Fed wants to buy bonds, it is going to have to offer to buy them at a higher price than exists in the marketplace. If the Fed wants to sell bonds, it is going to have to offer them at a lower price than exists in the marketplace. Thus, an open market operation must cause a change in the price of bonds.

Go to www.econtoday.com/ch17 to learn about the Federal Reserve's current policy regarding open market operations. Scan down the page, and select the "Minutes" for the most recent date.

Graphing the Sale of Bonds. The Fed sells some of the bonds in its portfolio. This is shown in panel (a) of Figure 17-2 on the following page. Notice that the supply of bonds is shown here as a vertical line with respect to price. The demand for bonds is downward

FIGURE 17-2
Determining the Price of Bonds
In panel (a), the Fed offers more bonds for sale. The price drops from P_1 to P_2. In panel (b), the Fed purchases bonds. This is the equivalent of a reduction in the supply of bonds available for private investors to hold. The price of bonds must rise from P_1 to P_3 to clear the market.

sloping. If the Fed offers more bonds it owns for sale, the supply curve shifts from S_1 to S_2. People will not be willing to buy the extra bonds at the initial equilibrium bond price, P_1. They will be satisfied holding the additional bonds at the new equilibrium price, P_2.

The Fed's Purchase of Bonds. The opposite occurs when the Fed purchases bonds. You can view this purchase of bonds as a reduction in the stock of bonds available for private investors to hold. In panel (b) of Figure 17-2, the original supply curve is S_1. The new supply curve of outstanding bonds will end up being S_3 because of the Fed's purchases of bonds. To get people to give up these bonds, the Fed must offer them a more attractive price. The price will rise from to P_1 to P_3.

Relationship Between the Price of Existing Bonds and the Rate of Interest.
There is an inverse relationship between the price of existing bonds and the rate of interest. Assume that the average yield on bonds is 5 percent. You decide to purchase a bond. A local corporation agrees to sell you a bond that will pay you $50 a year forever. What is the price you are willing to pay for the bond? It is $1,000. Why? Because $50 divided by $1,000 equals 5 percent, which is as good as the best return you can earn elsewhere. You purchase the bond. The next year something happens in the economy, and you can now obtain bonds that have effective yields of 10 percent. (In other words, the prevailing interest rate in the economy is now 10 percent.) What will happen to the market price of the existing bond that you own, the one you purchased the year before? It will fall. If you try to sell the bond for $1,000, you will discover that no investors will buy it from you. Why should they when they can obtain the same $50-a-year yield from someone else by paying only $500? Indeed, unless you offer your bond for sale at a price of $500, no buyers will be forthcoming. Hence an increase in the prevailing interest rate in the economy has caused the market value of your existing bond to fall.

The important point to be understood is this:

The market price of existing bonds (and all fixed-income assets) is inversely related to the rate of interest prevailing in the economy.

Changes in the Difference Between the Discount Rate and the Federal Funds Rate

When the Fed was founded in 1913, the most important tool in its monetary policy kit was the discount rate, discussed in Chapter 16. The Fed originally relied on the discount rate to carry out monetary policy because it had no power over reserve requirements. More important, its initial portfolio of government bonds was practically nonexistent and hence insufficient to conduct a full range of open market operations. As the Fed has come increasingly to rely on open market operations, it has used the discount rate less frequently as a tool of monetary policy.

Recall that the discount rate is the interest rate the Fed charges depository institutions when they borrow reserves directly from the Fed. Since 2003, the Fed has kept the discount rate 1 percentage point above the market-determined federal funds rate. An increase in the discount rate relative to the federal funds rate would increase the cost of funds for depository institutions that seek loans from the Fed, in comparison to the cost of borrowing funds in the federal funds market. In principle, depository institutions that borrow from the Fed would pass on at least part of this increased cost to their borrowing customers by raising the interest rates they charge on loans.

Consequently, pushing up the discount rate relative to the federal funds rate could bring about a rise in market interest rates. Few depository institutions choose to borrow from the Fed at the higher discount rate, however, so this interest rate effect would likely be very small.

Changes in Reserve Requirements

Although the Fed rarely uses changes in reserve requirements as a form of monetary policy, it most recently did so in 1992, when it decreased reserve requirements on transactions deposits to 10 percent. In any event, here is how changes in reserve requirements can affect the economy.

If the Fed increases reserve requirements, banks must replenish their reserves by reducing their lending. To induce potential borrowers not to borrow so much, banks respond to an increase in reserve requirements by raising the interest rates they charge on the loans they offer. Conversely, when the Fed decreases reserve requirements, as it did in 1992, some depository institutions attempt to lend out their excess reserves. To induce customers to borrow more, depository institutions reduce interest rates.

Of course, as you learned in Chapter 16, depository institutions can use sweep accounts to reduce their effective reserve requirements. This institutional change has muted the effects that variations in reserve requirements can have on market interest rates.

QUICK QUIZ

Monetary policy can be conducted via _____ _____, _____ _____ changes, and _____ _____ changes undertaken by the Fed.

When the Fed sells bonds, it must offer them at a _____ price. When the Fed buys bonds, it must pay a _____ price.

There is a(n) _____ relationship between the prevailing rate of interest in the economy and the market price of existing bonds (and all fixed-income assets).

In principle, the Fed can conduct monetary policy by varying the discount rate relative to the _____ _____ rate or altering reserve requirements, but it rarely does so.

See page 445 for the answers. Review concepts from this section in MyEconLab.

EFFECTS OF AN INCREASE IN THE MONEY SUPPLY

To understand how monetary policy works in its simplest form, we are going to run an experiment in which you increase the money supply in a very direct way. Assume that the government has given you hundreds of millions of dollars in just-printed bills that you load into a helicopter. You then fly around the country, dropping the money out of the window. People pick it up and put it in their pockets. Some deposit the money in their transactions deposit accounts. The first thing that happens is that they have too much money—not in the sense that they want to throw it away but rather in relation to other things that they own. There are a variety of ways to dispose of this "new" money.

Direct Effect

The simplest thing that people can do when they have excess money balances is to go out and spend them on goods and services. Here they have a direct impact on aggregate demand. Aggregate demand rises because with an increase in the money supply, at any given price level people now want to purchase more output of real goods and services.

Indirect Effect

Not everybody will necessarily spend the newfound money on goods and services. Some people may wish to deposit some or all of those excess money balances in banks. The recipient banks now discover that they have higher reserves than they wish to hold. As you learned in Chapter 16, one thing that banks can do to get interest-earning assets is to lend out the excess reserves. But banks cannot induce people to borrow more funds than they were borrowing before unless the banks lower the interest rate that they charge on loans. This lower interest rate encourages people to take out those loans. Businesses will therefore engage in new investment with the funds loaned. Individuals will engage in more consumption of durable goods such as housing, autos, and home entertainment centers. Either way, the increased loans generate a rise in aggregate demand. More people will be involved in more spending—even those who did not pick up any of the money that was originally dropped out of your helicopter.

Graphing the Effects of an Expansionary Monetary Policy

Look at Figure 17-3. We start out in a situation in which the economy is operating at less than full employment. You see a recessionary gap in the figure, which is measured as the horizontal difference between the long-run aggregate supply curve, LRAS, and the current equilibrium. Short-run equilibrium is at E_1, with a price level of 120 and real GDP of $11.5 trillion. The LRAS curve is at $12 trillion. Assume now that the Fed increases the money supply. Because of the direct and indirect effects of this increase in the money supply, aggregate demand shifts outward to the right to AD_2. The new equilibrium is at an output rate of $12 trillion of real GDP per year and a price level of 125. Here expansionary monetary policy can move the economy toward its LRAS curve sooner than otherwise.

Graphing the Effects of Contractionary Monetary Policy

Assume that there is an inflationary gap as shown in Figure 17-4. There you see that the short-run aggregate supply curve, SRAS, intersects aggregate demand, AD_1, at E_1. This is to the right of the LRAS of real GDP per year of $12 trillion. Contractionary monetary policy can eliminate this inflationary gap. Because of both the direct and indirect effects of monetary policy, the aggregate demand curve shifts inward from AD_1 to AD_2. Equilibrium

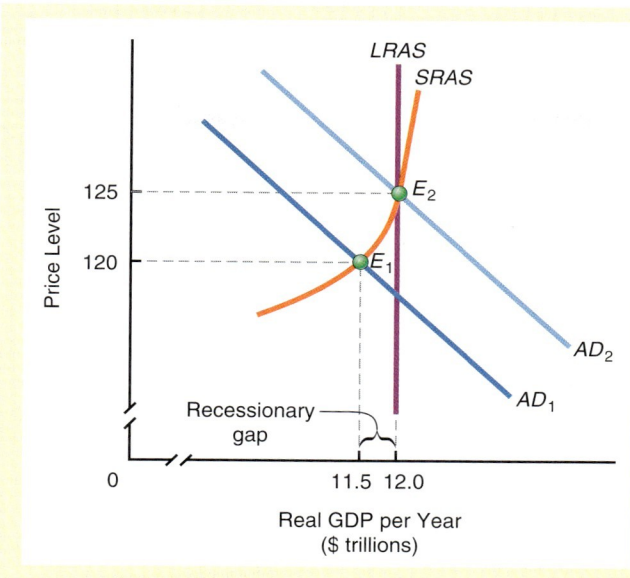

FIGURE 17-3

Expansionary Monetary Policy with Underutilized Resources

If we start out with equilibrium at E_1, expansionary monetary policy will shift AD_1 to AD_2. The new equilibrium will be at E_2.

is now at E_2, which is at a lower price level, 120. Equilibrium real GDP has now fallen from $12.5 trillion to $12 trillion.

Note that contractionary monetary policy involves a reduction in the money supply, with a consequent decline in the price level (deflation). In the real world, contractionary monetary policy normally involves reducing the *rate of growth* of the money supply, thereby reducing the rate of increase in the price level (inflation). Similarly, real-world expansionary monetary policy typically involves increasing the rate of growth of the money supply.

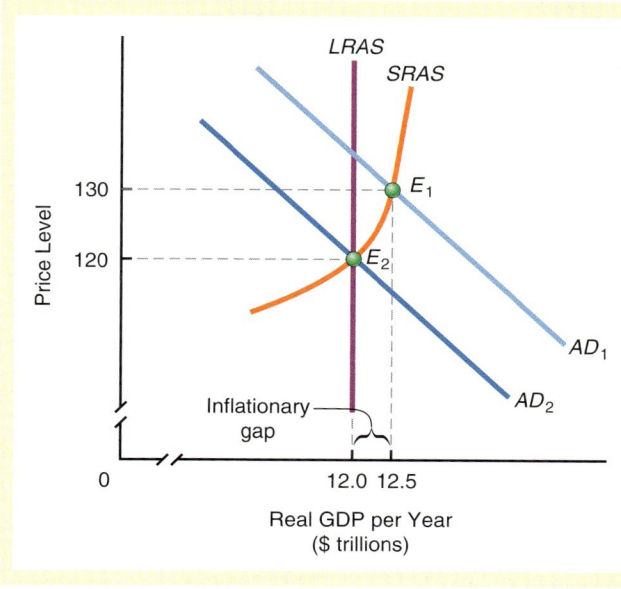

FIGURE 17-4

Contractionary Monetary Policy with Overutilized Resources

If we begin at short-run equilibrium at point E_1, contractionary monetary policy will shift the aggregate demand curve from AD_1 to AD_2. The new equilibrium will be at point E_2.

Why did efforts to reduce the rate of growth of the money supply recently fail to reduce real GDP growth and inflation in China?

INTERNATIONAL POLICY EXAMPLE

The People's Bank of China Learns About the Real Interest Rate

In 2004 and 2005, the People's Bank of China, the country's central bank, engaged in monetary policy actions that pushed up market interest rates for the first time in nine years. The objective of the interest rate increase was to try to reduce the growth of aggregate demand and thereby prevent inflation. Nevertheless, investment spending, which accounts for more than 40 percent of total planned expenditures in China, actually *increased*. As a consequence, total planned expenditures and aggregate demand *rose* in the mid-2000s.

What went wrong? The answer is that the People's Bank of China failed to take into account higher inflation expectations. Recall from Chapter 7 that the real interest rate equals the nominal interest rate minus the expected inflation rate. Even though the People's Bank of China pushed up the nominal interest rate, the expected inflation rate rose faster. Thus, on balance the real interest rate declined, which gave businesses an incentive to increase their investment spending. This is why aggregate demand and the price level continued to rise in the mid-2000s even though China's central bank pushed up nominal interest rates.

FOR CRITICAL ANALYSIS
Why do you think critics of the People's Bank of China argued that it should have acted more than once in nine years to push up nominal interest rates if it was serious about reducing the growth of aggregate demand?

QUICK QUIZ

The _____ effect of an increase in the money supply arises because people desire to spend more on real goods and services when they have excess money balances.

The _____ effect of an increase in the money supply works through a _____ in the interest rate, which encourages businesses to make new investments with the funds loaned to them. Individuals will also engage in more consumption (on consumer durables) because of _____ interest rates.

See page 445 for the answers. Review concepts from this section in MyEconLab.

Go to www.econtoday.com/ch17 for links to central banks around the globe, provided by the Bank for International Settlements.

OPEN ECONOMY TRANSMISSION OF MONETARY POLICY

So far we have discussed monetary policy in a closed economy. When we move to an open economy, with international trade and the international purchase and sale of all assets including dollars and other currencies, monetary policy becomes more complex. Consider first the effect of monetary policy on exports.

The Net Export Effect of Contractionary Monetary Policy

To see how a change in monetary policy can affect net exports, suppose that the Federal Reserve implements a contractionary policy that boosts the market interest rate. The higher U.S. interest rate, in turn, tends to attract foreign investment in U.S. financial assets, such as U.S. government securities.

If more residents of foreign countries decide that they want to purchase U.S. government securities or other U.S. assets, they first have to obtain U.S. dollars. As a consequence, the demand for dollars goes up in foreign exchange markets. The international price of the dollar therefore rises. This is called an *appreciation* of the dollar, and it tends to reduce net exports because it makes our exports more expensive in terms of foreign currency and imports cheaper in terms of dollars. Foreign residents demand fewer of our goods and services, and we demand more of theirs.

This reasoning implies that when contractionary monetary policy increases real, after-tax U.S. interest rates, there will be a negative net export effect because foreign residents will want more U.S. financial instruments. Hence they will demand additional dollars, thereby causing the international price of the dollar to rise. This makes our exports more expensive for the rest of the world, which then demands a smaller quantity of our exports. It also means that foreign goods and services are less expensive in the United States, so we therefore demand more imports. We come up this conclusion:

*Contractionary monetary policy causes interest rates to rise. Such a **rise** will induce international inflows of financial capital, thereby raising the international value of the dollar and making U.S. goods less attractive. The net export effect of contractionary monetary policy will be in the same direction as the monetary policy effect, thereby amplifying the effect of such policy.*

The Net Export Effect of Expansionary Monetary Policy

Now assume that the economy is experiencing a recession and the Federal Reserve wants to pursue an expansionary monetary policy. In so doing, it will cause interest rates to fall in the short run, as discussed earlier. Declining interest rates will cause financial capital to flow out of the United States. The demand for dollars will decrease, and their international price will go down. Foreign goods will now look more expensive to U.S. residents, and imports will fall. Foreign residents will desire more of our exports, and exports will rise. The result will be an increase in our international trade balance, that is, an increase in net exports. Again, the international consequences reinforce the domestic consequences of monetary policy.

Globalization of International Money Markets

On a broader level, the Fed's ability to control the rate of growth of the money supply may be hampered as U.S. money markets become less isolated. With the push of a computer button, billions of dollars can change hands halfway around the world. If the Fed reduces the growth of the money supply, individuals and firms in the United States can obtain dollars from other sources. People in the United States who want more liquidity can obtain their dollars from foreign residents. Indeed, as world markets become increasingly integrated, U.S. residents, who can already hold U.S. bank accounts denominated in foreign currencies, more regularly conduct transactions using other nations' currencies.

QUICK QUIZ

Monetary policy in an open economy has repercussions for net _____.

If contractionary monetary policy raises U.S. interest rates, there is a _____ net export effect because foreign residents will demand _____ U.S. financial instruments, thereby demanding _____ dollars and hence causing the international price of the dollar to rise. This makes our exports more expensive for the rest of the world.

When expansionary monetary policy causes interest rates to fall, foreign residents will want _____ U.S. financial instruments. The resulting _____ in the demand for dollars will reduce the dollar's value in foreign exchange markets, leading to a(n) _____ in net exports.

See page 445 for the answers. Review concepts from this section in MyEconLab.

MONETARY POLICY AND INFLATION

Most theories of inflation relate to the short run. The price index in the short run can fluctuate because of events such as oil price shocks, labor union strikes, or discoveries of large amounts of new natural resources. In the long run, however, empirical studies show a relatively stable relationship between excessive growth in the money supply and inflation.

Simple supply and demand analysis can explain why the price level rises when the money supply is increased. Suppose that there is a major oil discovery, and the supply of oil increases dramatically relative to the demand for oil. The relative price of oil will fall; now it will take more units of oil to exchange for specific quantities of nonoil products. Similarly, if the supply of money rises relative to the demand for money, more units of money are required to purchase specific quantities of goods and services. That is merely another way of stating that the price level increases or that the purchasing power of money declines. In fact, the classical economists referred to inflation as a situation in which more money is chasing the same quantity of goods and services.

The Equation of Exchange and the Quantity Theory

A simple way to show the relationship between changes in the quantity of money in circulation and the price level is through the **equation of exchange,** developed by Irving Fisher (note that " ≡ " refers to an identity or truism):

$$M_s V \equiv PY$$

where M_s = actual money balances held by the nonbanking public
V = **income velocity of money,** which is the number of times, on average per year, each monetary unit is spent on final goods and services
P = price level or price index
Y = real GDP per year

Equation of exchange
The formula indicating that the number of monetary units (M_s) times the number of times each unit is spent on final goods and services (V) is identical to the price level (P) times real GDP (Y).

Income velocity of money (V)
The number of times per year a dollar is spent on final goods and services; equal to nominal GDP divided by the money supply.

Consider a numerical example involving a one-commodity economy. Assume that in this economy, the total money supply, M_s, is $7.5 trillion; the quantity of output, Y, is $12 trillion (in base-year dollars); and the price level, P, is 1.25 (125 in index number terms). Using the equation of exchange,

$$M_s V \equiv PY$$
$$\$7.5 \text{ trillion} \times V \equiv 1.25 \times \$12 \text{ trillion}$$
$$\$7.5 \text{ trillion} \times V \equiv \$15 \text{ trillion}$$
$$V \equiv 2$$

Thus, each dollar is spent an average of two times a year.

The Equation of Exchange as an Identity. The equation of exchange must always be true—it is an *accounting identity*. The equation of exchange states that the total amount of funds spent on final output, $M_s V$, is equal to the total amount of funds *received* for final output, PY. Thus, a given flow of funds can be viewed from either the buyers' side or the producers' side. The value of goods purchased is equal to the value of goods sold.

If Y represents real GDP and P is the price level, PY equals the dollar value of national output of goods, and services, or *nominal* GDP. Thus,

$$M_s V \equiv PY \equiv \text{nominal GDP}$$

Quantity theory of money and prices
The hypothesis that changes in the money supply lead to equiproportional changes in the price level.

The Quantity Theory of Money and Prices. If we now make some assumptions about different variables in the equation of exchange, we come up with the simplified theory of why the price level changes, called the **quantity theory of money and prices.** If we

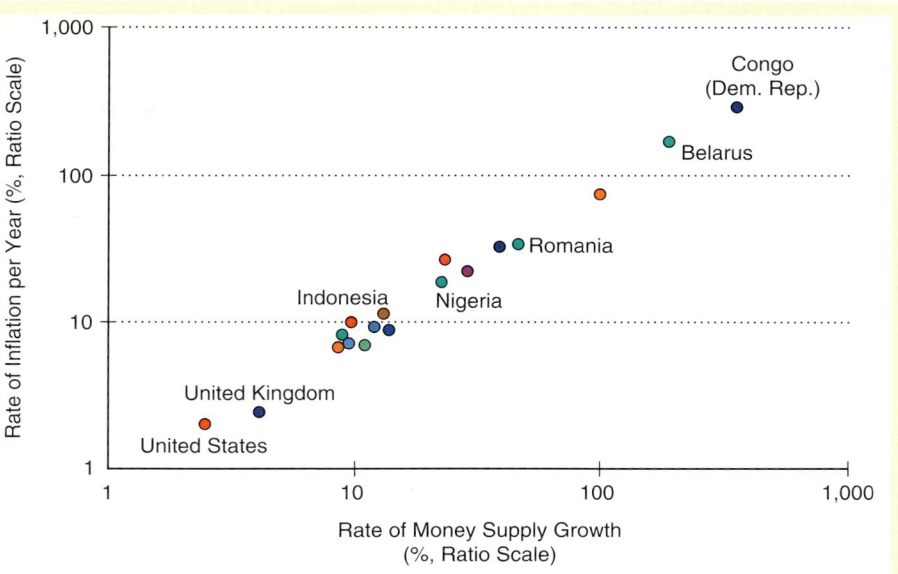

FIGURE 17-5
The Relationship Between Money Supply Growth Rates and Rates of Inflation

If we plot rates of inflation and rates of monetary growth for different countries, we come up with a scatter diagram that reveals an obvious direct relationship. If you were to draw a line through the "average" of the points in this figure, it would be upward sloping, showing that an increase in the rate of growth of the money supply leads to an increase in the rate of inflation.

Sources: International Monetary Fund and national central banks. Data are for latest available periods.

assume that the velocity of money, V, is constant and that real GDP, Y, is basically stable, the simple equation of exchange tells us that a change in the money supply can lead only to a equiproportional change in the price level. Continue with our numerical example. Y is $12 trillion. V equals 2. If the money supply increases by 20 percent, to $9 trillion, the only thing that can happen is that the price level, P, has to go up from 1.25 to 1.5. In other words, the price level must also increase by 20 percent. Otherwise the equation is no longer in balance.

Empirical Verification. There is considerable evidence of the empirical validity of the relationship between monetary growth and high rates of inflation. Figure 17-5 tracks the correspondence between money supply growth and the rates of inflation in various countries around the world.

Why do countries sometimes redefine their currency units to be a hundred, a thousand, or even a million times smaller?

INTERNATIONAL POLICY EXAMPLE

Zeroing Out Multiple Zeros

Until recently, inflation was so rampant in Turkey that individuals often held billions of *lire*, the Turkish currency, and banks routinely transmitted payments denominated in trillions or even quadrillions of lire. All these extra zeros complicated the task of Turkish accountants and statisticians, who commonly spent much of their time making sure they had the right number of digits in financial statements and data spreadsheets.

In at effort to end the complexities involved in keeping track of such large numbers of lire, on January 1, 2005, the Turkish government stripped six zeros from its currency.

Thus, instead of 1,800,000 lire being equal to 1 euro, only 1.8 lire were equal to 1 euro. This action made Turkey the fiftieth nation in recent years to slash excess zeros from its currency. Other examples include Romania, which cut four zeros from its currency, and Bulgaria and Afghanistan, each of which eliminated three zeros.

FOR CRITICAL ANALYSIS
What do you suppose happened to the prices of goods and services in Turkey, Romania, Bulgaria, and Afghanistan after each of these nations redefined its currency?

QUICK QUIZ

The _____ of _____ states that the expenditures by some people will equal income receipts by others, or $M_s V \equiv PY$ (money supply times velocity equals nominal GDP).

Viewed as an accounting identity, the equation of exchange is always _____, because the amount of funds _____ on final output of goods and services must equal the total amount of funds _____ for final output.

The quantity theory of money and prices states that a change in the _____ _____ will bring about an equiproportional change in the _____ _____.

See page 445 for the answers. Review concepts from this section in MyEconLab.

MONETARY POLICY IN ACTION: THE TRANSMISSION MECHANISM

At the start of this chapter, we talked about the direct and indirect effects of monetary policy. The direct effect is simply that an increase in the money supply causes people to have excess money balances. To get rid of these excess money balances, people increase their expenditures. The indirect effect, depicted in Figure 17-6 as the interest-rate-based money transmission mechanism, occurs because some people have decided to purchase interest-bearing assets with their excess money balances. This causes the price of such assets—bonds—to go up. Because of the inverse relationship between the price of existing bonds and the interest rate, the interest rate in the economy falls. This lower interest rate induces people and businesses to spend more than they otherwise would have spent.

An Interest-Rate-Based Transmission Mechanism

The indirect, interest-rate-based transmission mechanism can be seen explicitly in Figure 17-7. In panel (a), you see that an increase in the money supply reduces the interest rate. The economywide demand curve for money is labeled M_d in panel (a). At first, the money supply is at M_s, a vertical line determined by our central bank, the Federal Reserve System. The equilibrium interest rate is r_1. This occurs where the money supply curve intersects the money demand curve. Now assume that the Fed increases the money supply, say, via open market operations. This will shift the money supply curve outward to the right to M'_s. People find themselves with too much cash (liquidity). They buy bonds. When they buy bonds, they bid up the prices of bonds, thereby lowering the interest rate. The interest rate falls to r_2, where the new money supply curve M'_s intersects the money demand curve M_d. This reduction in the interest rate from r_1 to r_2 has an effect on planned investment, as can be seen in panel (b). Planned investment per year increases from I_1 to I_2. An increase in

FIGURE 17-6
The Interest-Rate-Based Money Transmission Mechanism

FIGURE 17-7
Adding Monetary Policy to the Aggregate Demand–Aggregate Supply Model

In panel (a), we show a demand for money function, M_d. It slopes downward to show that at lower rates of interest, a larger quantity of money will be demanded. The money supply is given initially as M_s, so the equilibrium rate of interest will be r_1. At this rate of interest, we see from the planned investment schedule given in panel (b) that the quantity of planned investment demanded per year will be I_1. After the shift in the money supply to M'_s, the resulting increase in investment from I_1 to I_2 shifts the aggregate demand curve in panel (c) outward from AD_1 to AD_2. Equilibrium moves from E_1 to E_2, at real GDP of $12 trillion per year.

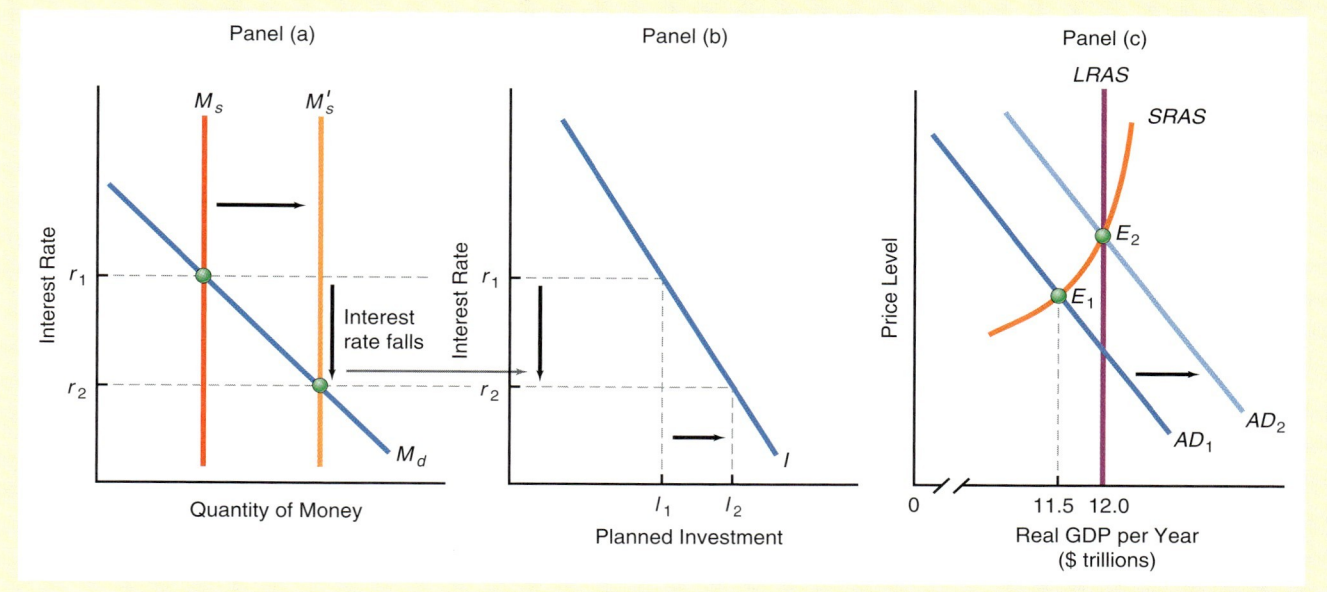

investment will increase aggregate demand, as shown in panel (c). Aggregate demand increases from AD_1 to AD_2. Equilibrium in the economy increases from real GDP per year of $11.5 trillion, which is not on the *LRAS*, to equilibrium real GDP per year of $12 trillion, which is on the *LRAS*.

FED TARGET CHOICE: INTEREST RATES OR MONEY SUPPLY?

It is not possible to stabilize the money supply and interest rates simultaneously. The Federal Reserve has often sought to achieve an *interest rate target*. There is a fundamental tension between targeting interest rates and controlling the money supply, however. Interest rate targets force the Fed to abandon control over the money supply; money stock growth targets force the Fed to allow interest rates to fluctuate.

The Interest Rate or the Money Supply?

Figure 17-8 on the following page shows the relationship between the total demand for money and the supply of money. Note that in the short run, when the demand for money is constant, short-run money supply changes leave the demand for money curve unaltered. In the short run, the Fed can choose either a particular interest rate (r_e or r_1) or a particular money supply (M_s or M'_s).

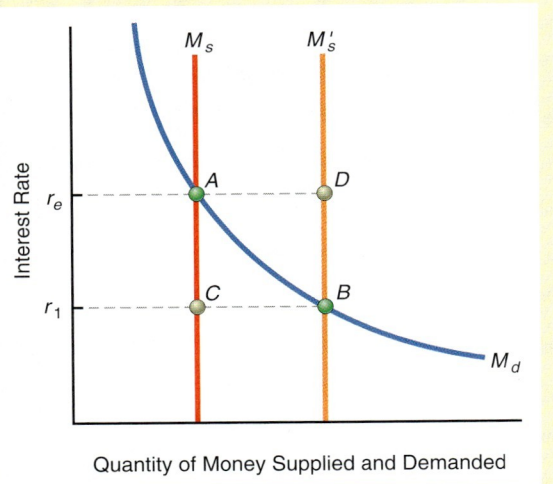

FIGURE 17-8

Choosing a Monetary Policy Target

The Fed, in the short run, can select an interest rate or a money supply target, but not both. It cannot, for example, choose r_e and M'_s. If it selects r_e, it must accept M_s. If it selects M'_s, it must allow the interest rate to fall to r_1. The Fed can obtain point A or B. It cannot get to point C or D. It must therefore choose one target or the other.

If the Fed wants interest rate r_e, it must select money supply M_s. If it desires a lower interest rate in the short run, it must increase the money supply. Thus, by targeting an interest rate, the Fed must relinquish control of the money supply. Conversely, if the Fed wants to target the money supply at, say, M'_s, it must allow the interest rate to fall to r_1.

Choosing a Policy Target

But which should the Fed target, interest rates or monetary aggregates? (And which interest rate or which money supply?) It is generally agreed that the answer depends on the source of instability in the economy. If the source of instability is variations in private or public spending, monetary aggregate (money supply) targets should be set and pursued because with a fixed interest rate, spending variations cause maximum volatility of real GDP. If the source of instability is an unstable demand for (or perhaps supply of) money, however, interest rate targets are preferred because the Fed's effort to keep the interest rate stable automatically offsets the effect of the money demand (or supply) change.

Go to www.econtoday.com/ch17 for Federal Reserve news events announcing its latest monetary policy actions.

THE WAY FED POLICY IS CURRENTLY IMPLEMENTED

No matter what the Fed is actually targeting, at present it announces an interest rate target. You should not be fooled, however. When the chair of the Fed states that the Fed is raising "the" interest rate from, say, 5.25 percent to 5.50 percent, he really means something else. In the first place, the interest rate referred to is the federal funds rate, or the rate at which banks can borrow excess reserves from other banks. In the second place, even if the Fed talks about changing interest rates, it can do so only by actively entering the market for federal government securities (usually Treasury bills). So, if the Fed wants to raise "the" interest rate, it essentially must engage in contractionary open market operations. That is to say, it must sell more Treasury securities than it buys, thereby reducing the money supply. This tends to boost the rate of interest. Conversely, when the Fed wants to decrease "the" rate of interest, it engages in expansionary open market operations, thereby increasing the money supply (or the rate of growth of the money supply).

Laying Out the Fed Policy Strategy

Open market operations are the key means by which the Fed pursues its announced objective for the federal funds rate. Every six to eight weeks, the voting members of the Federal Open Market Committee (FOMC)—the seven Fed board governors and five regional bank presidents—determine the Fed's general strategy of open market operations.

The FOMC outlines its strategy in a document called the **FOMC Directive.** This document lays out the FOMC's general economic objectives, establishes short-term federal funds rate objectives, and specifies target ranges for money supply growth. After each meeting, the FOMC issues a brief statement to the media, which then prints stories about the Fed's action or inaction and what it is likely to mean for the economy. Typically, these stories run under headlines such as "Fed Cuts Key Interest Rate," "Fed Acts to Push Up Interest Rates," or "Fed Decides to Leave Interest Rates Alone."

FOMC Directive
A document that summarizes the Federal Open Market Committee's general policy strategy, establishes near-term objectives for the federal funds rate, and specifies target ranges for money supply growth.

Open Market Operations and the Federal Funds Rate

The FOMC leaves the task of implementing the Directive to officials who manage an office at the Federal Reserve Bank of New York known as the **Trading Desk.** The media spend little time considering how the Fed's Trading Desk conducts its policies, taking it for granted that the Fed can implement the policy action that it has announced to the public.

The Trading Desk's open market operations typically are confined within a one-hour interval each weekday morning. If the Trading Desk purchases government securities during this interval, it increases the quantity of reserves available to depository institutions. As you learned in Chapter 16, depository institutions may use the portion of these reserves not held as required reserves to expand their securities holdings and increase their lending. Among the loans that a number of depository institutions extend are overnight loans to other depository institutions in the federal funds market. Hence depository institutions' receipts of new reserves via Fed open market purchases increase the supply of federal funds.

Other things being equal, an increase in the supply of federal funds at the currently prevailing federal funds rate results in an excess quantity of federal funds supplied at that rate. The market federal funds rate thereby falls until the quantity of federal funds supplied and demanded are once again equalized. In this way, open market purchases conducted by the Trading Desk induce a fall in the equilibrium federal funds rate.

Could the Fed determine its target for the market interest rate using a computer instead of relying on human officials?

Trading Desk
An office at the Federal Reserve Bank of New York charged with implementing monetary policy strategies developed by the Federal Open Market Committee.

Taylor rule
A suggested guideline for monetary policy, in the form of an equation determining the Fed's interest rate target based on an estimated long-run real interest rate, the present deviation of the actual inflation rate from the Fed's inflation objective, and the gap between actual real GDP and a measure of potential GDP.

POLICY EXAMPLE

Should the Fed Use a Computer to Set Its Interest Rate Target?

Must the Fed rely on people to make monetary policy decisions, or could a computer be used to perform this task in today's world of interest rate targeting? In the 1990s, John Taylor of Stanford University suggested a relatively simple equation that the Fed might use to determine the appropriate interest rate target. This equation entailed setting the interest rate target based on an estimated long-run real interest rate, the present deviation of the actual inflation rate from the Fed's inflation objective, and the gap between actual real GDP and a measure of potential GDP. Taylor and other economists applied his equation, which has become known as the **Taylor rule,** to actual Fed policy choices and found that it came very close to predicting the interest rate targets that the Fed has actually selected over time.

The Federal Reserve Bank of St. Louis now regularly tracks target levels for the federal funds rate predicted by a basic Taylor-rule equation. Figure 17-9 on the following page displays paths of both the actual federal funds rate (the bold line) and alternative Taylor-rule predictions under different assumptions about the Fed's inflation objective (thin lines consistent with goals of 0, 1, 2, 3, or 4 percent inflation).

(continued)

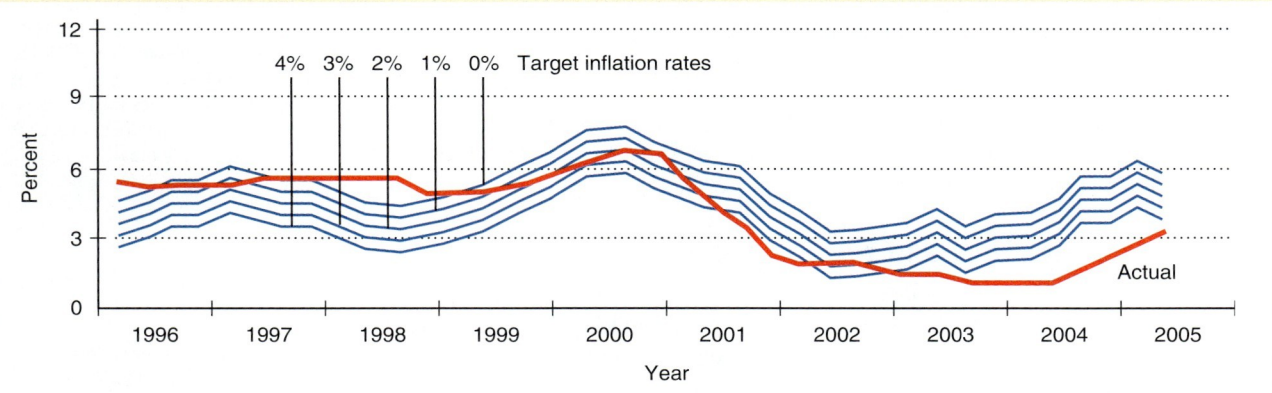

FIGURE 17-9
Actual Federal Funds Rates and Values Predicted by a Taylor Rule
This figure displays both the actual path of the federal funds rate since 1995 and the target paths specified by a Taylor-rule equation for alternative annual inflation objectives of 0, 1, 2, 3, and 4 percent.
Source: Federal Reserve Bank of St. Louis *Monetary Trends*, various issues.

When the actual federal funds rate is at a level consistent with a particular target inflation rate, then the Taylor rule predicts that Fed policymaking will tend to produce that inflation rate. For instance, in the middle of 2002 the actual federal funds rate was at a level that the Taylor rule indicated to be consistent with a 3 percent inflation target.

But if the actual federal funds rate is *below* the rate implied by a particular inflation target, then the Taylor rule implies that the Fed's policymaking is expansionary and will tend to push the actual inflation rate *above* target levels. Thus, during most of the 2003–2005 interval, the actual federal funds rate was below the level consistent with a 4 percent inflation rate. This implies that Fed policymaking was very expansionary during this period, sufficiently so as to be expected to yield a long-run inflation rate in excess of 4 percent per year.

Nevertheless, the actual federal funds rate has remained relatively close to the Taylor-rule predictions over time. To some economists, Figure 17-9 implies an alternative to having numerous Fed officials and economists devote untold hours of labor to deciding on a federal funds rate target. Instead, they suggest, a computer could be programmed to conduct the minimal open market operations required to vary the supply of reserves to the banking system as needed to attain a federal funds rate consistent with the Taylor rule.

FOR CRITICAL ANALYSIS
Why does the Taylor rule specify lower federal funds rates for higher Fed inflation objectives?

Maintaining a Federal Funds Rate Target

Now consider how the New York Fed's Trading Desk implements an FOMC Directive to raise the federal funds rate to a particular level and maintain the federal funds rate at this "targeted" level for the next several weeks. The day following receipt of the new Directive, officials of the Trading Desk sell government securities to reduce total reserves in the banking system and bring about a decrease in the supply of federal funds. Based on the current demand for federal funds, they sell an amount of government securities determined to be sufficient to push up the equilibrium federal funds rate to the level desired by the FOMC.

Keeping the Federal Funds Rate on Target.
To keep the market federal funds rate at this target level during the weeks that follow, Trading Desk officials react daily to changes in the market demand for and supply of federal funds. For instance, if the demand for federal funds by depository institutions decreases on a particular Tuesday, the equilibrium federal

funds rate will begin to fall. The Trading Desk officials will respond by selling even more government securities to generate a further decrease in the supply of federal funds.

If the market demand for federal funds increases on Wednesday, the equilibrium federal funds rate will start to rise. In response, Trading Desk officials will buy government securities to bring about an increase in the supply of federal funds, thereby pushing the equilibrium federal funds rate back down to the FOMC's target level.

The Fed Influences, but Does not "Set," the Federal Funds Rate. It is important to keep in mind that the Fed does not directly "set" the federal funds rate. Nevertheless, it can use open market operations to induce depository institutions to supply additional or fewer loans in the federal funds market.

Thus, the Fed can adjust total depository institution reserves, and hence the money supply, as required to keep the federal funds rate close to its specified target. And that is how the Fed and its chair (currently Ben Bernanke) change interest rates as reported in the media on numerous occasions.

QUICK QUIZ

According to the interest-rate-based monetary policy transmission mechanism, monetary policy operates through a change in _____ _____, which changes _____, causing a multiple change in the equilibrium level of real GDP per year.

The Fed can attempt to stabilize _____ _____ or the _____ _____, but not both.

The Fed's Federal Open Market Committee (FOMC) outlines the Fed's general monetary policy strategy in the FOMC _____, which it transmits to the Trading Desk of the Federal Reserve Bank of _____ _____ for implementation.

At present, the FOMC's policy strategy focuses on aiming for a target value of the _____ _____ rate, which the _____ _____ seeks to achieve via appropriate purchases or sales of U.S. government securities.

See page 445 for the answers. Review concepts from this section in MyEconLab.

CASE STUDY
ECONOMICS FRONT AND CENTER

Predicting the Finicky U.S. Demand for Money

Rogers is a staff economist with the Fed's Board of Governors. One of her duties is to try to estimate the aggregate demand for money in the United States. In recent months, this has proved to be a challenging task. Surges in the use of debit cards to buy groceries and other regular purchases have led to successive decreases in the average balances that people maintain in their transactions deposit accounts. Furthermore, the continuing growth in the use of credit cards has reduced the precautionary demand for money. The asset demand for money has been stable, and Rogers has determined that it is likely to remain stable for at least the next several months.

After considerable analysis, Rogers has determined that during the coming three-month period, the U.S. money demand curve is likely to shift leftward by about $100 billion at any given interest rate. She enters this forecast into the final draft of her report, which she knows will be consulted by the Federal Open Market Committee before it drafts the next Directive for transmittal to the Trading Desk at the Federal Reserve Bank of New York.

CRITICAL ANALYSIS QUESTIONS
1. Other things being equal, by approximately how much and in what direction should the Trading Desk aim to change the money supply if the next Directive keeps the Fed's interest rate target unchanged? (Hint: If the demand for money decreases, in what direction must the Fed adjust the money supply to prevent the market interest rate from changing?)

2. To generate the money supply change discussed in Question 1, should the Trading Desk conduct open market purchases or sales?

Issues and Applications

How the Fed Pursues "Neutral" Monetary Policymaking

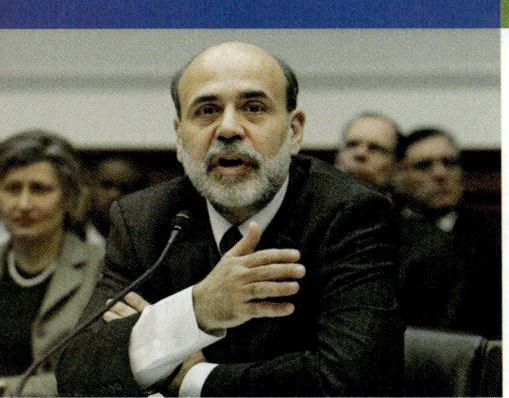

Concepts Applied
- Monetary Policy
- Trading Desk
- FOMC Directive

The key task that the Federal Reserve faces in its monetary policy procedure, in which the Trading Desk conducts open market operations to keep the federal funds rate at a target level, is determining the appropriate interest rate level to target. The Fed refers to this appropriate level of the federal funds rate as the *neutral federal funds rate*. At the neutral federal funds rate, the growth rate of real GDP tends neither to speed up nor to slow down in relation to the growth rate of potential real GDP, at which all the economy's resources are fully utilized.

Deviations of the Actual Federal Funds Rate from the Neutral Rate

Suppose that the Fed's policymaking arm, the Federal Open Market Committee (FOMC), has identified the neutral federal funds rate. If the actual market federal funds rate is below this neutral rate, real GDP starts to increase at a faster pace than potential GDP. As a consequence, aggregate demand begins rising too fast relative to aggregate supply, pushing up the price level at a faster pace and boosting inflation. To depress the aggregate demand growth and slow the rate of increase in the price level, the Trading Desk would conduct open market sales. This policy action would reduce the money supply and push the actual federal funds rate up to the neutral federal funds rate.

In contrast, if the actual value of the federal funds rate is above the neutral rate, actual real GDP begins to rise at a slower pace than potential GDP. The implied sluggish growth in aggregate demand relative to aggregate supply creates deflationary tendencies in the economy. In this case, the Fed would engage in open market purchases to increase the money supply and cause the actual federal funds rate to drop to the neutral value.

In theory, if the actual market federal funds rate exactly equals the neutral federal funds rate, then it is unnecessary for the Trading Desk to engage in either open market purchases or open market sales. The rate of growth of actual real GDP matches the rate of growth of potential GDP, and there are no longer any inflationary or deflationary pressures in the economy. This implies that the appropriate interest rate target for Fed policymaking is the neutral federal funds rate.

Easier Said Than Done

The policymakers on the FOMC face a fundamental problem in identifying the neutral federal funds rate, however: the value of the neutral federal funds rate varies over time.

A key reason that the neutral federal funds rate changes over time is that the rate of growth of potential real GDP is not constant. How fast potential real GDP rises from year to year depends on the speed at which the economy's long-run aggregate supply increases over time, which varies with productivity growth and the pace of technological improvements. Naturally, aggregate supply shocks can suddenly add to or subtract from the natural pace at which long-run aggregate supply rises, thereby causing potential real GDP to speed up or slow down unexpectedly.

Furthermore, factors that affect aggregate demand also change over time. Suppose, for instance, that desired investment spending suddenly rises or falls because of changes in firms' anticipations about future profitability. If so, then there will be a change in the rate of growth of actual real GDP relative to the growth rate of potential real GDP. The neutral federal funds rate will change.

Whenever the rate of growth of potential real GDP rises or falls or the manner in which interest rate changes affect aggregate demand changes, so does the value of the neutral federal funds rate. The FOMC, in turn, must respond by *changing* the target for the federal funds rate that it includes in the FOMC Directive transmitted to the Trading Desk. This explains why you so often see media reports speculating about whether the "Fed has decided to push interest rates up" or to "push interest rates down." The FOMC is always trying to aim at a moving interest rate target—a neutral federal funds rate that varies as economic conditions change.

Log in to **MyEconLab**, click on "Economic News" and test your understanding of the chapter by answering interactive questions that relate directly to this issue.

For Critical Analysis

1. If the neutral federal funds rate declines, perhaps because desired investment has suddenly fallen as businesspeople anticipate lower future returns on investment, how should the FOMC adjust its federal funds rate target?

2. Suppose that the rate of growth of actual real GDP initially is just equal to the rate of growth of potential real GDP, but then labor productivity suddenly falls, causing the rate of growth of potential real GDP to drop. Should the FOMC raise or lower its target for the federal funds rate? (Hint: After the aggregate supply shock occurs, does the economy begin to experience inflationary or deflationary pressures in the absence of a policy response by the Fed?)

Web Resources

1. For a summary of the FOMC's recent efforts to use open market operations to target the federal funds rate, go to www.econtoday.com/ch17.

2. Read more about how the FOMC seeks to identify the neutral federal funds rate at www.econtoday.com/ch17.

Research Project

Evaluate what happens to the money supply when the Fed's Trading Desk responds to an increase in the actual federal funds rate above the value that the FOMC has deemed to be neutral. What can you conclude about the extent to which the Fed "controls" the money supply when its monetary policy actions are focused on targeting the federal funds rate?

WHAT YOU SHOULD KNOW		WHERE TO GO TO PRACTICE
Key Factors That Influence the Quantity of Money That People Desire to Hold People generally make more transactions when nominal GDP rises, and they require more money to make these transactions. Consequently, they desire to hold more money when nominal GDP increases. People also hold money as a precaution against unexpected expenditures they may wish to make, and the interest rate is the opportunity cost of holding money for this purpose. In addition, money is a store of value that people may hold alongside bonds, stocks, and other interest-earning assets, and the opportunity cost of holding money as an asset is again the interest rate. Thus, the quantity of money demanded declines as the market interest rate increases.	money balances, 423 transactions demand, 424 precautionary demand, 424 asset demand, 424	• **MyEconLab** Study Plan 17.1 • Audio introduction to Chapter 17 • Video: Why People Wish to Hold Money
How the Federal Reserve's Monetary Policy Tools Influence Market Interest Rates An open market purchase of government securities, a reduction in the discount rate, or a decrease in the required reserve ratio are all ways that the Federal Reserve can bring about an increase in total reserves in the banking system and an increase in the money supply. The rise in reserve levels that banks have available to lend leads them to bid down interest rates on loans. Thus, market interest rates tend to fall in response to any of these changes in the Fed's tools of monetary policy.	**Key figure** Figure 17-2, 426	• **MyEconLab** Study Plan 17.2 • Animated Figure 17-2
How Expansionary and Contractionary Monetary Policies Affect Equilibrium Real GDP and the Price Level in the Short Run By pushing up the money supply and inducing a fall in market interest rates, an expansionary monetary policy action causes total planned expenditures to rise at any given price level. Hence the aggregate demand curve shifts rightward, which can eliminate a short-run recessionary gap in real GDP. In contrast, a contractionary monetary policy action reduces the money supply and causes an increase in market interest rates, thereby generating a fall in total planned expenditures at any given price level. This results in a leftward shift in the aggregate demand curve, which can eliminate a short-run inflationary gap in real GDP.	**Key figures** Figure 17-3, 429 Figure 17-4, 429	• **MyEconLab** Study Plans 17.3 and 17.4 • Animated Figures 17-3 and 17-4

WHAT YOU SHOULD KNOW

The Equation of Exchange and the Quantity Theory of Money and Prices The equation of exchange is a truism that states that the quantity of money in circulation times the average number of times a unit of money is used in exchange—the income velocity of money—must equal nominal GDP, or the price level times real GDP. According to the quantity theory of money and prices, we can regard the income velocity of money as constant and real GDP as relatively stable. Thus, a rise in the quantity of money must lead to a equiproportional increase in the price level.

equation of exchange, 432
income velocity of money (V), 432
quantity theory of money and prices, 432

WHERE TO GO TO PRACTICE

- **MyEconLab** Study Plan 17.5
- Video: The Quantity Theory of Money

The Interest-Rate-Based Transmission Mechanism of Monetary Policy The interest-rate-based approach to the monetary policy transmission mechanism operates through effects of monetary policy actions on market interest rates, which bring about changes in desired investment and thereby affect equilibrium real GDP via the multiplier effect.

Key figures
Figure 17-6, 434
Figure 17-7, 435

- **MyEconLab** Study Plan 17.6
- Animated Figures 17-6 and 17-7
- Video: The Monetary Rule

Why the Federal Reserve Cannot Stabilize the Money Supply and the Interest Rate Simultaneously To target the money supply, the Federal Reserve must be willing to let the market interest rate vary whenever the demand for money rises or falls. Consequently, stabilizing the money supply usually entails some degree of interest rate volatility. To target a market interest rate, however, the Federal Reserve must be willing to adjust the money supply as necessary when there are variations in the demand for money. Hence stabilizing the interest rate typically requires variations in the money supply. At present, this latter approach is specified by the policy Directive that the Fed's Federal Open Market Committee transmits to the Trading Desk, which implements policy by buying and selling securities.

FOMC Directive, 437
Trading Desk, 437
Taylor rule, 437

- **MyEconLab** Study Plans 17.7 and 17.8

Log in to MyEconLab, take a chapter test, and get a personalized Study Plan that tells you which concepts you understand and which ones you need to review. From there, MyEconLab will give you further practice, tutorials, animations, videos, and guided solutions.

Log in to www.myeconlab.com

PROBLEMS

*Select problems, indicated by a blue oval, are assignable in **MyEconLab**.
Answers to the odd-numbered problems appear at the back of the book.*

17-1 Let's denote the price of a nonmaturing bond (called a *consol*) as P_b. The equation that indicates this price is $P_b = I/r$, where I is the annual net income the bond generates and r is the nominal market interest rate.

a. Suppose that a bond promises the holder $500 per year forever. If the nominal market interest rate is 5 percent, what is the bond's current price?

b. What happens to the bond's price if the market interest rate rises to 10 percent?

17-2. Based on Problem 17-1, imagine that initially the market interest rate is 5 percent and at this interest rate you have decided to hold half of your financial wealth as bonds and half as holdings of non-interest-bearing money. You notice that the market interest rate is starting to rise, however, and you become convinced that it will ultimately rise to 10 percent.

a. In what direction do you expect the value of your bond holdings to go when the interest rate rises?

b. If you wish to prevent the value of your financial wealth from declining in the future, how should you adjust the way you split your wealth between bonds and money? What does this imply about the demand for money?

17-3. You learned in Chapter 11 that if there is an inflationary gap in the short run, then in the long run a new equilibrium arises when input prices and expectations adjust upward, causing the aggregate supply curve to shift upward and to the left and pushing equilibrium real GDP back to its long-run potential value. In this chapter, however, you learned that the Federal Reserve can eliminate an inflationary gap in the short run by undertaking a policy action that reduces aggregate demand.

a. Propose one monetary policy action that could eliminate an inflationary gap in the short run.

b. In what way might society gain if the Fed implements the policy you have proposed instead of simply permitting long-run adjustments to take place?

17-4. In addition, you learned in Chapter 11 that if there is a recessionary gap in the short run, then in the long run a new equilibrium arises when input prices and expectations adjust downward, causing the aggregate supply curve to shift downward and to the right and pushing equilibrium real GDP back to its long-run potential value. In this chapter, however, you learned that the Federal Reserve can eliminate a recessionary gap in the short run by undertaking a policy action that raises aggregate demand.

a. Propose a monetary policy action that could eliminate a recessionary gap in the short run but uses a different tool of monetary policy than the one you considered in Problem 17-3.

b. In what way might society gain if the Fed implements the policy you have proposed instead of simply permitting long-run adjustments to take place?

17-5. Explain why the net export effect of a contractionary monetary policy reinforces the usual impact that monetary policy has on equilibrium real GDP in the short run.

17-6. Suppose that, initially, the U.S. economy was in an aggregate demand–aggregate supply equilibrium at point A along the aggregate demand curve AD in the diagram below. Now, however, the value of the U.S. dollar has suddenly appreciated relative to foreign currencies. This appreciation happens to have no measurable effects on either the short-run or the long-run aggregate supply curve in the United States. It does, however, influence U.S. aggregate demand.

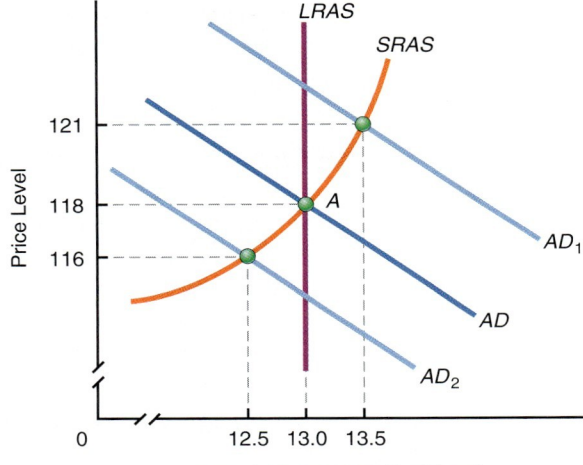

a. Explain in your own words how the dollar appreciation will affect U.S. net export expenditures.

b. Of the alternative aggregate demand curves depicted in the figure—AD_1 versus AD_2—which could represent the aggregate demand effect of the U.S. dollar's appreciation? What effects does the appreciation have on real GDP and the price level?

c. What policy action might the Federal Reserve take to prevent the dollar's appreciation from affecting equilibrium real GDP in the short run?

17-7. Use a diagram to illustrate how the Fed can reduce inflationary pressures by conducting open market sales of U.S. government securities.

17-8. Suppose that the quantity of money in circulation is fixed but the income velocity of money doubles. If real GDP remains at its long-run potential level, what happens to the equilibrium price level?

17-9. Suppose that following the events in Problem 17-8, the Fed cuts the money supply in half. How does the price level now compare with its value before the income velocity and the money supply changed?

17-10. Consider the following data: The money supply is $1 trillion, the price level equals 2, and real GDP is $5 trillion in base-year dollars. What is the income velocity of money?

17-11. Consider the data in Problem 17-10. Suppose that the money supply increases by $100 billion and real GDP and the income velocity remain unchanged.

   a. According to the quantity theory of money and prices, what is the new price level after the increase in the money supply?
   b. What is the percentage increase in the money supply?
   c. What is the percentage change in the price level?
   d. How do the percentage changes in the money supply and price level compare?

17-12. Assuming that the Fed judges inflation to be the most significant problem in the economy and that it wishes to employ all three of its policy instruments, what should the Fed do with its three policy tools?

17-13. Suppose that the Fed implements each of the policy changes you discussed in Problem 17-12. Now explain how the net export effect resulting from these monetary policy actions will reinforce their effects that operate through interest rate changes.

17-14. Suppose that the Federal Reserve wishes to keep the nominal interest rate at a target level of 4 percent. Draw a money supply and demand diagram in which the current equilibrium interest rate is 4 percent. Explain a specific policy action that the Fed, using one of its three tools of monetary policy, could take to keep the interest rate at its target level if the demand for money suddenly declines.

17-15. Imagine working at the Trading Desk at the New York Fed. Explain whether you would conduct open market purchases or sales in response to each of the following events. Justify your recommendation.

   a. The latest FOMC Directive calls for an increase in the target value of the federal funds rate.
   b. For a reason unrelated to monetary policy, the Fed's Board of Governors has decided to raise the differential between the discount rate and the federal funds rate. Nevertheless, the FOMC Directive calls for maintaining the present federal funds rate target.

ECONOMICS ON THE NET

The Fed's Policy Report to Congress Congress requires the Fed to make periodic reports on its recent activities. In this application, you will study recent reports to learn about what factors affect Fed decisions.

Title: Monetary Policy Report to the Congress

Navigation: Go to www.econtoday.com/ch17 to view the Federal Reserve's Monetary Policy Report to the Congress (formerly called the Humphrey-Hawkins Report).

Application Read the report; then answer the following questions.

1. According to the report, what economic events were most important in shaping recent monetary policy?
2. Based on the report, what are the Fed's current monetary policy goals?

For Group Study and Analysis Divide the class into "domestic" and "foreign" groups. Have each group read the past four monetary policy reports and then explain to the class how domestic and foreign factors, respectively, appear to have influenced recent Fed monetary policy decisions. Which of the two types of factors seem to have mattered most during the past year?

ANSWERS TO QUICK QUIZZES

p. 425: (i) demand; (ii) transactions ... precautionary ... asset; (iii) opportunity ... downward
p. 427: (i) open market operations ... discount rate ... reserve requirement; (ii) lower ... higher; (iii) inverse; (iv) federal funds
p. 430: (i) direct; (ii) indirect ... reduction ... lower
p. 431: (i) exports; (ii) negative ... more ... more; (iii) fewer ... decrease ... increase
p. 434: (i) equation ... exchange; (ii) true ... spent ... received; (iii) money supply ... price level
p. 439: (i) interest rates ... investment; (ii) interest rates ... money supply; (iii) Directive ... New York; (iv) federal funds ... Trading Desk

Appendix D: Monetary Policy: A Keynesian Perspective

According to the traditional Keynesian approach to monetary policy, changes in the money supply can affect the level of aggregate demand only through their effect on interest rates. Moreover, interest rate changes act on aggregate demand solely by changing the level of real planned investment spending. Finally, the traditional Keynesian approach argues that there are plausible circumstances under which monetary policy may have little or no effect on interest rates and thus on aggregate demand.

Figure D-1 measures real GDP along the horizontal axis and total planned expenditures (aggregate demand) along the vertical axis. The components of aggregate demand are real consumption (C), investment (I), government spending (G), and net exports (X). The height of the schedule labeled $C + I + G + X$ shows total real planned expenditures (aggregate demand) as a function of real GDP. This schedule slopes upward because consumption depends positively on real GDP. All along the line labeled $Y = C + I + G + X$, real planned spending equals real GDP. At point Y^*, where the $C + I + G + X$ line intersects this 45-degree reference line, real planned spending is consistent with real GDP. At any real GDP level less than Y^*, spending exceeds real GDP, so real GDP and thus spending will tend to rise. At any level of real GDP greater than Y^*, real planned spending is less than real GDP, so real GDP and thus spending will tend to decline. Given the determinants of C, I, G, and X, total spending (aggregate demand) will be Y^*.

INCREASING THE MONEY SUPPLY

According to the Keynesian approach, an increase in the money supply pushes interest rates down. This reduces the cost of borrowing and thus induces firms to increase the level of investment spending from I to I'. As a result, the $C + I + G + X$ line shifts upward in

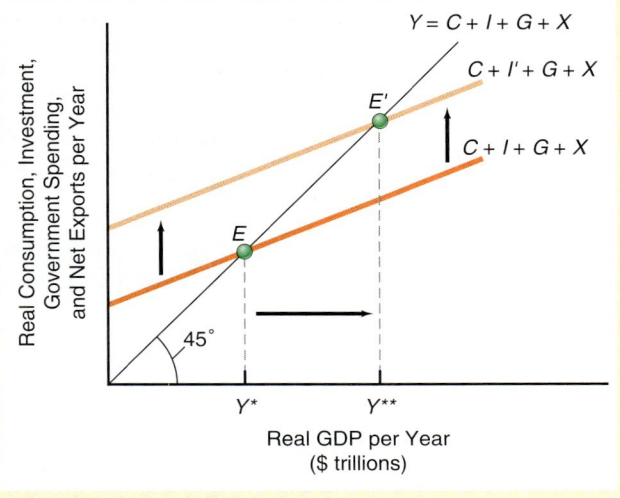

FIGURE D-1
An Increase in the Money Supply
An increase in the money supply increases real GDP by lowering interest rates and thus increasing investment from I to I'.

Figure D-1 by the full amount of the rise in investment spending, thus yielding the line $C + I' + G + X$. The rise in investment spending causes real GDP to rise, which in turn causes real consumption spending to rise, which further increases real GDP. Ultimately, aggregate demand rises to Y^{**}, where spending again equals real GDP. A key conclusion of the Keynesian analysis is that total spending rises by *more* than the original rise in investment spending because consumption spending depends positively on real GDP.

DECREASING THE MONEY SUPPLY

Not surprisingly, contractionary monetary policy works in exactly the reverse manner. A reduction in the money supply pushes interest rates up, which increases the cost of borrowing. Firms respond by reducing their investment spending, and this pushes real GDP downward. Consumers react to the lower real GDP by scaling back on their real consumption spending, which further depresses real GDP. Thus, the ultimate decline in real GDP is larger than the initial drop in investment spending. Indeed, because the change in real GDP is a multiple of the change in investment, Keynesians note that changes in investment spending (similar to changes in government spending) have a *multiplier* effect on the economy.

ARGUMENTS AGAINST MONETARY POLICY

It might be thought that this multiplier effect would make monetary policy a potent tool in the Keynesian arsenal, particularly when it comes to getting the economy out of a recession. In fact, however, many traditional Keynesians argue that monetary policy is likely to be relatively ineffective as a recession fighter. According to their line of reasoning, although monetary policy has the potential to reduce interest rates, changes in the money supply have little *actual* impact on interest rates. Instead, during recessions, people try to build up as much as they can in liquid assets to protect themselves from risks of unemployment and other losses of income. When the monetary authorities increase the money supply, individuals are willing to allow most of it to accumulate in their bank accounts. This desire for increased liquidity thus prevents interest rates from falling very much, which in turn means that there will be virtually no change in investment spending and thus little change in aggregate demand.

PROBLEMS

Select problems, indicated by a blue oval, are assignable in MyEconLab.
The answers to the odd-numbered problems appear at the back of the book.

D-1 Suppose that each 0.1-percentage-point decrease in the equilibrium interest rate induces a $10 billion increase in real planned investment spending by businesses. In addition, the investment multiplier is equal to 5, and the money multiplier is equal to 4. Furthermore, every $20 billion increase in the money supply brings about a 0.1-percentage-point reduction in the equilibrium interest rate. Use this information to answer the following questions under the assumption that all other things are equal.

a. How much must real planned investment increase if the Federal Reserve desires to bring about a $100 billion increase in equilibrium real GDP?

b. How much must the money supply change for the Fed to induce the change in real planned investment calculated in part a?

c. What dollar amount of open market operations must the Fed undertake to bring about the money supply change calculated in part b?

D-2 Suppose that each 0.1-percentage-point increase in the equilibrium interest rate induces a $5 billion decrease in real planned investment spending by businesses. In addition, the investment multiplier is equal to 4, and the money multiplier is equal to 3. Furthermore, every $9 billion decrease in the money supply brings about a 0.1-percentage-point increase in the equilibrium interest rate. Use this information to answer the following questions under the assumption that all other things are equal.

  a. How much must real planned investment decrease if the Federal Reserve desires to bring about an $80 billion decrease in equilibrium real GDP?
  b. How much must the money supply change for the Fed to induce the change in real planned investment calculated in part a?
  c. What dollar amount of open market operations must the Fed undertake to bring about the money supply change calculated in part b?

D-3 Assume that the following conditions exist:

  a. All banks are fully loaned up—there are no excess reserves, and desired excess reserves are always zero.
  b. The money multiplier is 3.
  c. The planned investment schedule is such that at a 6 percent rate of interest, investment is $1,200 billion; at 5 percent, investment is $1,225 billion.
  d. The investment multiplier is 3.
  e. The initial equilibrium level of real GDP is $12 trillion.
  f. The equilibrium rate of interest is 6 percent.

Now the Fed engages in expansionary monetary policy. It buys $1 billion worth of bonds, which increases the money supply, which in turn lowers the market rate of interest by 1 percentage point. Indicate by how much the money supply increased, and then trace out the numerical consequences of the associated reduction in interest rates on all the other variables mentioned.

D-4 Assume that the following conditions exist:

  a. All banks are fully loaned up—there are no excess reserves, and desired excess reserves are always zero.
  b. The money multiplier is 4.
  c. The planned investment schedule is such that at a 4 percent rate of interest, investment is $1,400 billion. At 5 percent, investment is $1,380 billion.
  d. The investment multiplier is 5.
  e. The initial equilibrium level of real GDP is $13 trillion.
  f. The equilibrium rate of interest is 4 percent.

Now the Fed engages in contractionary monetary policy. It sells $2 billion worth of bonds, which reduces the money supply, which in turn raises the market rate of interest by 1 percentage point. Indicate by how much the money supply decreased, and then trace out the numerical consequences of the associated increase in interest rates on all the other variables mentioned.

Stabilization in an Integrated World Economy

18

Among many economists and policymakers, the period since 1984 is known as the "Great Moderation." During this time, the quarterly (three-month) variability of U.S. real GDP has been more than 50 percent lower than was true from 1952 through 1983. Since the late 1990s, when this drop in the variability of real GDP growth became apparent, a number of U.S. policymakers have been figuratively patting themselves on the back. Surely, they have concluded, the reduction in volatility of real GDP has resulted from improved policymaking skills.

Can policymakers really contribute to greater macroeconomic stability? Even if they can do so in principle, are they really responsible for the so-called Great Moderation? This chapter will prepare you to contemplate these questions.

Learning Objectives

After reading this chapter, you should be able to:

1. Explain why the actual unemployment rate might depart from the natural rate of unemployment
2. Describe why there may be an inverse relationship between the inflation rate and the unemployment rate, reflected by the Phillips curve
3. Evaluate how expectations affect the actual relationship between the inflation rate and the unemployment rate
4. Understand the rational expectations hypothesis and its implications for economic policymaking
5. Identify the central features of the real-business-cycle challenge to active policymaking
6. Distinguish among alternative modern approaches to strengthening the case for active policymaking

MyEconLab helps you master each objective and study more efficiently. See end of chapter for details.

449

Did You Know That...

the average length of the 21 U.S. recessions that have occurred since the beginning of the twentieth century is about 15 months? In recent decades, the average recession has shortened. Between 1900 and 1945, a recession typically lasted 19 months. Since 1945, the average duration of a recession has fallen to approximately 9 months.

At the same time, business expansions have lengthened. Not including the most recent expansion, the 20 expansions since the start of the twentieth century have had an average length of 39 months. The average expansion between 1900 and 1945 lasted about 31 months. The average duration of an expansion since 1945 has been 50 months.

To some observers, shorter recessions and longer expansions have obviously resulted from improved monetary and fiscal policymaking. Others, however, are not so sure that policymakers really deserve much of the credit.

ACTIVE VERSUS PASSIVE POLICYMAKING

Central to the debate about whether policymakers deserve a collective pat on the back is whether the credit for a generally more stable U.S. economy should be given to **active (discretionary) policymaking.** This is the term for actions that monetary and fiscal policymakers undertake in reaction to or in anticipation of a change in economic performance. On the other side of the debate is the view that the best way to achieve economic stability is through **passive (nondiscretionary) policymaking,** in which there is no deliberate stabilization policy at all. Policymakers follow a rule and do not attempt to respond in a discretionary manner to actual or potential changes in economic activity. Recall from Chapter 13 that there are lags between the time when the national economy enters a recession or a boom and the time when that fact becomes known and acted on by policymakers. Proponents of passive policy argue strongly that such time lags often render short-term stabilization policy ineffective or, worse, procyclical.

Why might the Federal Reserve be more likely to become a more passive policymaker under chair Ben Bernanke?

Active (discretionary) policymaking
All actions on the part of monetary and fiscal policymakers that are undertaken in response to or in anticipation of some change in the overall economy.

Passive (nondiscretionary) policymaking
Policymaking that is carried out in response to a rule. It is therefore not in response to an actual or potential change in overall economic activity.

POLICY EXAMPLE

Will the Bernanke Fed Opt for Passivity via Inflation Targeting?

By appointing and confirming Ben Bernanke to be the chair of the Fed's Board of Governors, the president and Congress automatically raised a major policy issue for the Fed, because Bernanke has long been a proponent of *inflation targeting*. To understand how the Fed could go about targeting the rate of inflation, recall from Chapter 17 that the equation of exchange is $M_s V \equiv PY$. If the income velocity of money (V) and real GDP (Y) are predictable, then the Fed could aim to attain a specific percentage change in the price level (P)—that is, an inflation target—by ensuring that the money supply (M_s) grows at the appropriate rate. Under this policy, therefore, the Fed would passively adjust the money supply as appropriate to attain a single objective: a target rate of inflation. It would not actively engage in short-run money supply changes aimed at influencing real GDP.

Central banks in several nations, such as Canada, the United Kingdom, and New Zealand, target inflation rates in this manner. It remains to be seen whether under Bernanke the Fed will join this inflation-targeting club. Nevertheless, with Bernanke in charge, the idea is likely to get much more attention than it might have otherwise.

FOR CRITICAL ANALYSIS
Some economists have argued that the Fed should try to target the price level instead of the inflation rate. What would the rate of inflation be if the Fed always varied the money supply in a way that prevented the price level from changing?

To take a stand on this debate concerning active versus passive policymaking, you first need to know the potential trade-offs that policymakers believe they face. Then you need to see what the data actually show. The most important policy trade-off appears to be between price stability and unemployment. Before exploring that, however, we need to look at the economy's natural, or long-run, rate of unemployment.

THE NATURAL RATE OF UNEMPLOYMENT

Recall from Chapter 7 that there are different types of unemployment: frictional, cyclical, structural, and seasonal. *Frictional unemployment* arises because individuals take the time to search for the best job opportunities. Much unemployment is of this type, except when the economy is in a recession or a depression, when cyclical unemployment rises.

Note that we did not say that frictional unemployment was the *sole* form of unemployment during normal times. *Structural unemployment* is caused by a variety of "rigidities" throughout the economy. Structural unemployment results from factors such as these:

1. A mismatch of worker training and skills with requirements of employers
2. Government-imposed minimum wage laws, laws restricting entry into occupations, and welfare and unemployment insurance benefits that reduce incentives to work
3. Union activity that sets wages above the equilibrium level and also restricts the mobility of labor

Each of these factors reduces individuals' abilities or incentives to choose employment rather than unemployment.

Consider the effect of unemployment insurance benefits on the probability of an unemployed person's finding a job. When unemployment benefits run out, according to economists Lawrence Katz and Bruce Meyer, the probability of an unemployed person's finding a job doubles. The conclusion is that unemployed workers are more serious about finding a job when they are no longer receiving such benefits.

Frictional unemployment and structural unemployment both exist even when the economy is in long-run equilibrium—they are a natural consequence of costly information (the need to conduct a job search) and the existence of rigidities such as those noted. Because these two types of unemployment are a natural consequence of imperfect and costly information and rigidities, they are components of what economists call the **natural rate of unemployment.** As we discussed in Chapter 7, this is defined as the rate of unemployment that would exist in the long run after everyone in the economy fully adjusted to any changes that have occurred. Recall that real GDP tends to return to the level implied by the long-run aggregate supply curve (*LRAS*). Thus, whatever rate of unemployment the economy tends to return to in long-run equilibrium can be called the natural rate of unemployment.

How has the natural rate of unemployment changed over the years?

Natural rate of unemployment
The rate of unemployment that is estimated to prevail in long-run macroeconomic equilibrium, when all workers and employers have fully adjusted to any changes in the economy.

 EXAMPLE

The U.S. Natural Rate of Unemployment

In 1950, the unemployment rate was about 5 percent. In the mid-2000s, it was close to this level once again. These two nearly matching endpoints of unemployment rates prove nothing by themselves. But look at Figure 18-1 on the next page. There you see not only what has happened to the unemployment rate over that same time period but an estimate of the natural rate of unemployment. The line labeled "Natural rate of unemployment" is estimated by averaging unemployment rates from five years earlier to five years later at

(*continued*)

FIGURE 18-1
Estimated Natural Rate of Unemployment in the United States

As you can see in this figure, the actual rate of unemployment has varied widely in the United States in recent decades. If we estimate the natural rate of unemployment by averaging unemployment rates from five years earlier to five years later at each point in time, we get the line so labeled. It rose from the 1950s until the late 1980s and then gradually declined.

Sources: *Economic Report of the President; Economic Indicators*, various issues; author's estimates.

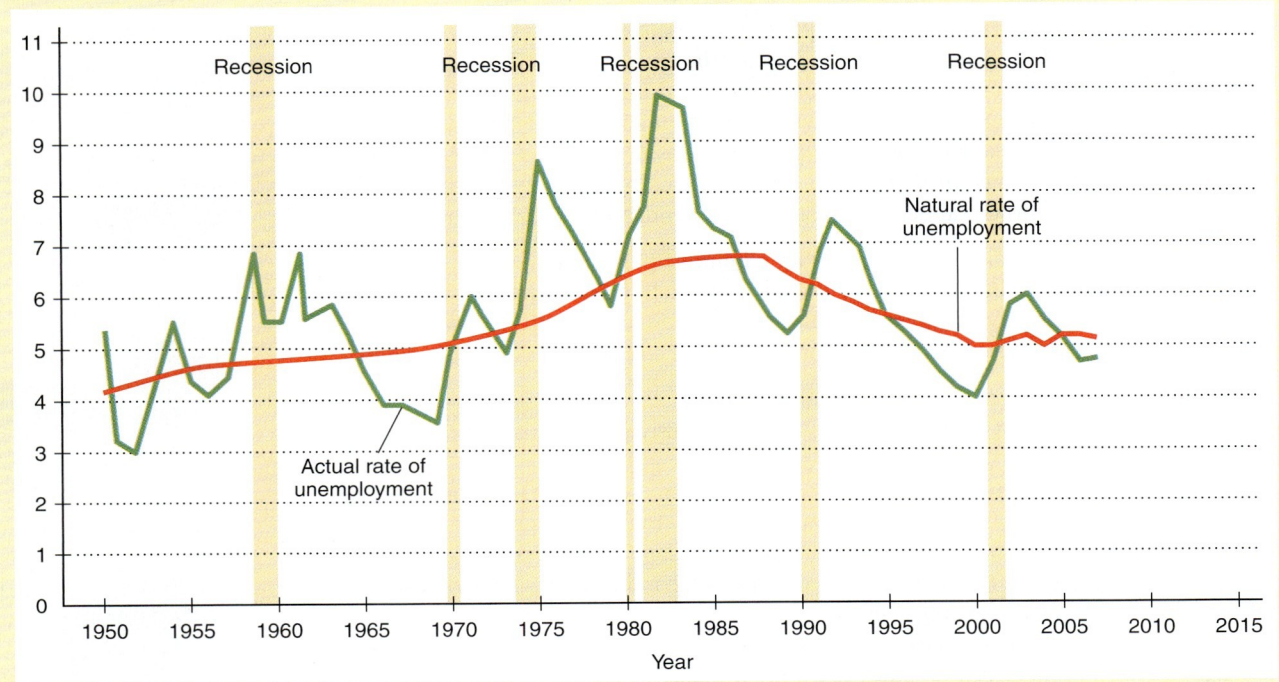

each point in time (except for the end period, which is estimated). This computation reveals that until the late 1980s, the natural rate of unemployment was rising. But since then, a generally downward trend has taken hold.

FOR CRITICAL ANALYSIS
Of the various factors that create structural unemployment, which ones do you think explained the gradual trend upward in the natural rate of unemployment from the late 1940s until the 1990s in the United States?

Departures from the Natural Rate of Unemployment

Even though the unemployment rate has a strong tendency to stay at and return to the natural rate, it is possible for other factors, such as changes in private spending or fiscal and monetary policy actions, to move the actual unemployment rate away from the natural rate, at least in the short run. Deviations of the actual unemployment rate from the natural rate are called *cyclical unemployment* because they are observed over the course of nationwide business fluctuations. During recessions, the overall unemployment rate exceeds the natural rate; cyclical unemployment is positive. During periods of economic booms, the overall unemployment rate can go below the natural rate; at such times, cyclical unemployment is negative.

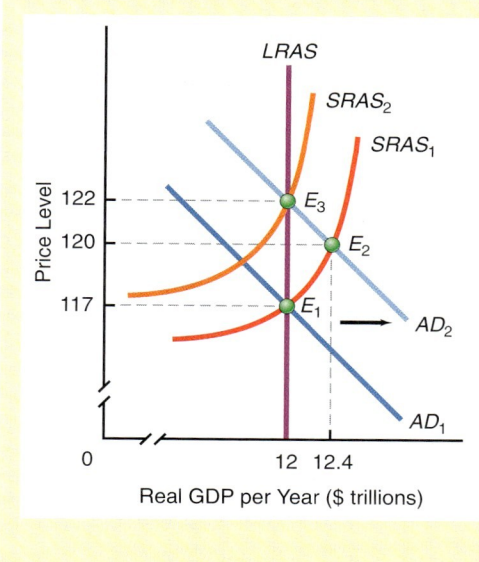

FIGURE 18-2
Impact of an Increase in Aggregate Demand on Real GDP and Unemployment

If the economy is operating at E_1, it is in both short-run and long-run equilibrium. Here the actual rate of unemployment is equal to the natural rate of unemployment. Subsequent to expansionary monetary or fiscal policy, the aggregate demand curve shifts outward to AD_2. The price level rises from 117 to 120; real GDP per year increases to $12.4 trillion in base-year dollars. The new short-run equilibrium is at E_2. The unemployment rate is now below the natural rate of unemployment. We are at a short-run equilibrium at E_2. In the long run, expectations of input owners are revised. The short-run aggregate supply curve shifts from $SRAS_1$ to $SRAS_2$ because of higher prices and higher resource costs. Real GDP returns to the LRAS level of $12 trillion per year. The price level increases to 122.

To see how departures from the natural rate of unemployment can occur, let's consider two examples. Referring to Figure 18-2, we begin in equilibrium at point E_1 with the associated price level 117 and real GDP per year of $12 trillion.

The Impact of Expansionary Policy. Now imagine that the government decides to use fiscal or monetary policy to stimulate the economy. Further suppose, for reasons that will soon become clear, that this policy surprises decision makers throughout the economy in the sense that they did not anticipate that the policy would occur.

As shown in Figure 18-2, the expansionary policy action causes the aggregate demand curve to shift from AD_1 to AD_2. The price level rises from 117 to 120. Real GDP, measured in base-year dollars, increases from $12 trillion to $12.4 trillion.

In the labor market, individuals find that conditions have improved markedly relative to what they expected. Firms seeking to expand output want to hire more workers. To accomplish this, they recruit more actively and possibly ask workers to work overtime, so individuals in the labor market find more job openings and more possible hours they can work. Consequently, as you learned in Chapter 7, the average duration of unemployment falls, and so does the unemployment rate.

The SRAS curve does not stay at $SRAS_1$ indefinitely, however. Input owners, such as workers and owners of capital and raw materials, revise their expectations. The short-run aggregate supply curve shifts to $SRAS_2$ as input prices rise. We find ourselves at a new equilibrium at E_3, which is on the LRAS. Long-run real GDP per year is $12 trillion again, but at a higher price level, 122. The unemployment rate returns to its original, natural level.

The Consequences of Contractionary Policy. Instead of expansionary policy, the government could have decided to engage in contractionary (or deflationary) policy. As shown in Figure 18-3 on the following page, the sequence of events would have been in the opposite direction of those in Figure 18-2.

Beginning from an initial equilibrium E_1, an unanticipated reduction in aggregate demand puts downward pressure on both prices and real GDP; the price level falls from 120 to 118, and real GDP declines from $12 trillion to $11.7 trillion. Fewer firms are hiring, and

FIGURE 18-3
Impact of a Decline in Aggregate Demand on Real GDP and Unemployment

Starting from equilibrium at E_1, a decline in aggregate demand to AD_2 leads to a lower price level, 118, and real GDP declines to $11.7 trillion. The unemployment rate will rise above the natural rate of unemployment. Equilibrium at E_2 is temporary, however. At the lower price level, the expectations of input owners are revised. $SRAS_1$ shifts to $SRAS_2$. The new long-run equilibrium is at E_3, with real GDP equal to $12 trillion and a price level of 116.

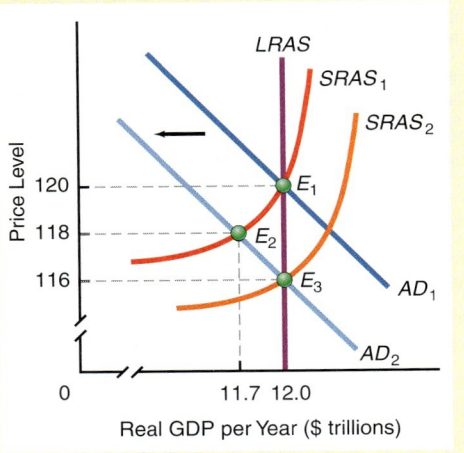

those that are hiring offer fewer overtime possibilities. Individuals looking for jobs find that it takes longer than predicted. As a result, unemployed individuals remain unemployed longer. The average duration of unemployment rises, and so does the rate of unemployment.

The equilibrium at E_2 is only a short-run situation, however. As input owners change their expectations about future prices, $SRAS_1$ shifts to $SRAS_2$, and input prices fall. The new long-run equilibrium is at E_3, which is on the long-run aggregate supply curve, $LRAS$. In the long run, the price level declines further, to 116, as real GDP returns to $12 trillion. Thus, in the long run the unemployment rate returns to its natural level.

The Phillips Curve: A Rationale for Active Policymaking?

Let's recap what we have just observed. In the short run, an *unexpected increase* in aggregate demand causes the price level to rise and the unemployment rate to fall. Conversely, in the short run, an *unexpected decrease* in aggregate demand causes the price level to fall and the unemployment rate to rise. Moreover, although not shown explicitly in either diagram, two additional points are true:

1. The greater the unexpected increase in aggregate demand, the greater the amount of inflation that results in the short run, and the lower the unemployment rate.
2. The greater the unexpected decrease in aggregate demand, the greater the deflation that results in the short run, and the higher the unemployment rate.

The Negative Short-Run Relationship Between Inflation and Unemployment.

Figure 18-4 summarizes these findings. The inflation rate (*not* the price level) is measured along the vertical axis, and the unemployment rate is measured along the horizontal axis. Point A shows an initial starting point, with the unemployment rate at the natural rate, U^*.

Note that as a matter of convenience, we are starting from an equilibrium in which the price level is stable (the inflation rate is zero). In the short run, unexpected increases in aggregate demand cause the price level to rise—the inflation rate becomes positive—and cause the unemployment rate to fall. Thus, the economy moves upward to the left from A to B.

Conversely, in the short run, unexpected decreases in aggregate demand cause the price level to fall and the unemployment rate to rise above the natural rate—the economy moves from point A to point C. If we look at both increases and decreases in aggregate demand,

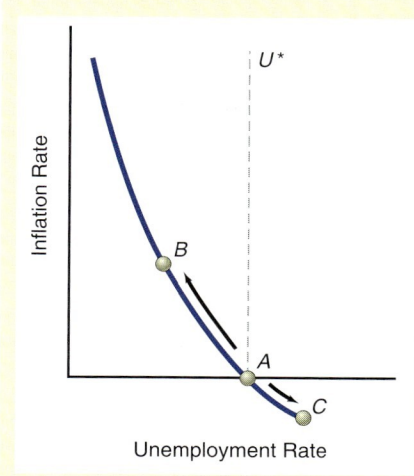

FIGURE 18-4

The Phillips Curve

Unanticipated changes in aggregate demand produce a negative relationship between the inflation rate and unemployment. U^* is the natural rate of unemployment.

we see that high inflation rates tend to be associated with low unemployment rates (as at B) and that low (or negative) inflation rates tend to be accompanied by high unemployment rates (as at C).

Is There a Trade-Off? The apparent negative relationship between the inflation rate and the unemployment rate shown in Figure 18-4 has come to be called the **Phillips curve,** after A. W. Phillips, who discovered that a similar relationship existed historically in Great Britain. Although Phillips presented his findings only as an empirical regularity, economists quickly came to view the relationship as representing a *trade-off* between inflation and unemployment. In particular, policymakers who favored active policymaking believed that they could *choose* alternative combinations of unemployment and inflation. Thus, it seemed that a government that disliked unemployment could select a point like B in Figure 18-4, with a positive inflation rate but a relatively low unemployment rate. Conversely, a government that feared inflation could choose a stable price level at A, but only at the expense of a higher associated unemployment rate. Indeed, the Phillips curve seemed to suggest that it was possible for discretionary policymakers to fine-tune the economy by selecting the policies that would produce the exact mix of unemployment and inflation that suited current government objectives. As it turned out, matters are not so simple.

Phillips curve
A curve showing the relationship between unemployment and changes in wages or prices. It was long thought to reflect a trade-off between unemployment and inflation.

The NAIRU. If one accepts that a trade-off exists between the rate of inflation and the rate of unemployment, then the notion of "noninflationary" rates of unemployment seems appropriate. In fact, some economists have proposed what they call the **nonaccelerating inflation rate of unemployment (NAIRU).** The NAIRU is the rate of unemployment that corresponds to a stable rate of inflation. When the unemployment rate is less than the NAIRU, the rate of inflation tends to increase. When the unemployment rate is more than the NAIRU, the rate of inflation tends to decrease. When the rate of unemployment is equal to the NAIRU, inflation continues at an unchanged rate. If the Phillips curve trade-off exists and if the NAIRU can be estimated, that estimate will define the potential short-run trade-off between the rate of unemployment and the rate of inflation.

Nonaccelerating inflation rate of unemployment (NAIRU)
The rate of unemployment below which the rate of inflation tends to rise and above which the rate of inflation tends to fall.

Distinguishing Between the Natural Unemployment Rate and the NAIRU.
The NAIRU is not always the same as the natural rate of unemployment. Recall that the natural rate of unemployment is the unemployment rate that is observed whenever all

cyclical factors have played themselves out. Thus, the natural unemployment rate applies to a long-run equilibrium in which any short-run adjustments have concluded. It depends on structural factors in the labor market and typically changes gradually over relatively lengthy intervals.

In contrast, the NAIRU is simply the rate of unemployment that is consistent at present with a steady rate of inflation. The unemployment rate consistent with a steady inflation rate can potentially change during the course of cyclical adjustments in the economy. Thus, the NAIRU typically varies by a relatively greater amount and relatively more frequently than the natural rate of unemployment.

The Importance of Expectations

The reduction in unemployment that takes place as the economy moves from A to B in Figure 18-4 occurs because the wage offers encountered by unemployed workers are unexpectedly high. As far as the workers are concerned, these higher *nominal* wages appear, at least initially, to be increases in *real* wages; it is this perception that induces them to reduce the duration of their job search. This is a sensible way for the workers to view the world if aggregate demand fluctuates up and down at random, with no systematic or predictable variation one way or another. But if activist policymakers attempt to exploit the apparent trade-off in the Phillips curve, according to economists who support passive policymaking, aggregate demand will no longer move up and down in an *unpredictable* way.

The Effects of an Unanticipated Policy.
Consider Figure 18-5, for example. If the Federal Reserve attempts to reduce the unemployment rate to U_1, it must increase the rate of growth of the money supply enough to produce an inflation rate (IR) of IR_1. If this is an unexpected one-shot action in which the rate of growth of the money supply is first increased and then held constant, the inflation rate will temporarily rise to IR_1, and the unemployment rate will temporarily fall to U_1. Proponents of passive policymaking contend that past experience with active policies indicates that after the money supply stops grow-

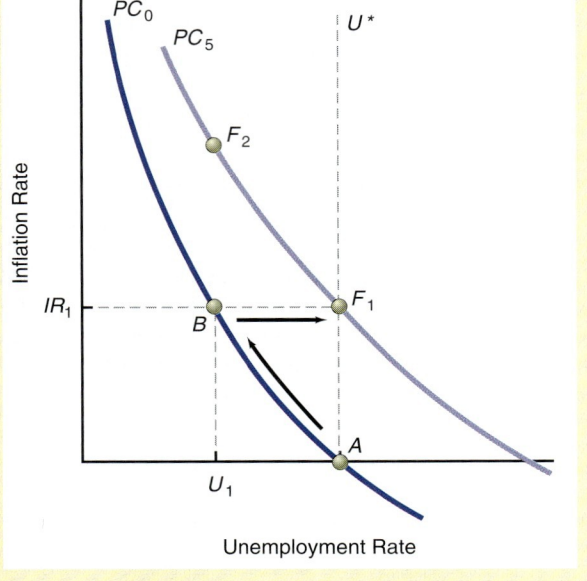

FIGURE 18-5

A Shift in the Phillips Curve

When there is a change in the expected inflation rate, the Phillips curve (*PC*) shifts to incorporate the new expectations. PC_0 shows expectations of zero inflation. PC_5 reflects a higher expected inflation rate, such as 5 percent.

ing, the inflation rate will soon return to zero and unemployment will return to U^*, its natural rate. Thus, an unexpected one-shot increase in money supply growth will cause a movement from point A to point B, and the economy will move on its own back to A.

Adjusting Expectations and a Shifting Phillips Curve.
Why do those advocating passive policymaking argue that variations in the unemployment rate from its natural rate typically are temporary? If activist authorities wish to prevent the unemployment rate from returning to U^*, they will conclude that the money supply must grow fast enough to keep the inflation rate up at IR_1. But if the Fed does this, argue those who favor passive policymaking, all of the economic participants in the economy—workers and job seekers included—will come to *expect* that inflation rate to continue. This, in turn, will change their expectations about wages. For example, suppose that IR_1 equals 5 percent per year. When the expected inflation rate was zero, a 5 percent rise in nominal wages meant a 5 percent expected rise in real wages, and this was sufficient to induce some individuals to take jobs rather than remain unemployed. It was this expectation of a rise in real wages that reduced search duration and caused the unemployment rate to drop from U^* to U_1. But if the expected inflation rate becomes 5 percent, a 5 percent rise in nominal wages means *no* rise in *real* wages. Once workers come to expect the higher inflation rate, rising nominal wages will no longer be sufficient to entice them out of unemployment. As a result, as the *expected* inflation rate moves up from 0 percent to 5 percent, the unemployment rate will move up also.

In terms of Figure 18-5, as authorities initially increase aggregate demand, the economy moves from point A to point B. If the authorities continue the stimulus in an effort to keep the unemployment rate down, workers' expectations will adjust, causing the unemployment rate to rise. In this second stage, the economy moves from B to point F_1: The unemployment rate returns to the natural rate, U^*, but the inflation rate is now IR_1 instead of zero. Once the adjustment of expectations has taken place, any further changes in policy will have to take place along a curve such as PC_5, say, a movement from F_1 to F_2. This new schedule is also a Phillips curve, differing from the first, PC_0, in that the actual inflation rate consistent with any given unemployment rate is higher because the expected inflation rate is higher.

To what extent do individuals and businesses take recent inflation into account when they make their predictions of future inflation?

To try out the "bit/ed" Web site's virtual economy and use the Phillips curve as a guide for policymaking in the United Kingdom, go to
www.econtoday.com/ch18.

INTERNATIONAL POLICY EXAMPLE

The Effects of Higher Inflation on Inflation Expectations

Three economists at the Federal Reserve Bank of St. Louis, Andrew Levin, Fabio Natalucci, and Jeremy Piger, have attempted to measure the effects of a short-lived increase in actual inflation on expectations of future inflation. They considered what would happen to U.S., Japanese, and Euro-area inflation expectations if the actual inflation rate rose by 1 percentage point for just three years.

Their estimates imply that, other things being equal, even five years after this short-lived increase in inflation occurred the public would expect the future annual inflation rate to be about a third of a percentage point higher. As much as ten years later, the expected annual inflation rate would still be one-fourth of a percentage point higher. Thus, the authors conclude that higher actual inflation has a significant holdover effect on long-term inflation expectations.

FOR CRITICAL ANALYSIS
The authors of this study also examined nations, such as Canada and the United Kingdom, in which central banks announce formal inflation targets. They concluded that in these nations a 1-percentage-point rise in actual inflation for three years would raise the expected future inflation rate by only 0.09 percentage point five years later and 0.01 percentage point ten years later. Why do you suppose that higher actual inflation has a smaller effect on inflation expectations when a central bank announces inflation targets?

The U.S. Experience with the Phillips Curve

In separate articles in 1968, Milton Friedman and E. S. Phelps published pioneering studies suggesting that the apparent trade-off suggested by the Phillips curve could not be exploited by activist policymakers. Friedman and Phelps both argued that any attempt to reduce unemployment by inflating the economy would soon be thwarted by economic participants' incorporating the new higher inflation rate into their expectations. The Friedman-Phelps research thus implies that for any given unemployment rate, *any* inflation rate is possible, depending on the actions of policymakers. As reflected in Figure 18-6, the propositions of Friedman and Phelps were to prove remarkably accurate.

When we examine U.S. unemployment and inflation data over the past half century, we see no clear relationship between them. Although there seemed to have been a Phillips curve trade-off between unemployment and inflation from the mid-1950s to the mid-1960s, apparently once people in the economy realized what was happening, they started revising their forecasts accordingly. So, as activist policymakers attempted to exploit the Phillips curve, the presumed trade-off between unemployment and inflation disappeared.

QUICK QUIZ

The **natural rate of unemployment** is the rate that exists in _____-run equilibrium, when workers' _____ are consistent with actual conditions.

Departures from the natural rate of unemployment can occur when individuals encounter unanticipated changes in fiscal or monetary policy. An unexpected _____ in aggregate demand will reduce unemployment below the natural rate, whereas an unanticipated _____ in aggregate demand will push unemployment above the natural rate.

The _____ curve exhibits a negative short-run relationship between the inflation rate and the unemployment rate that can be observed when there are *unanticipated* changes in aggregate _____.

_____ policymakers seek to take advantage of a proposed Phillips curve trade-off between inflation and unemployment.

See page 476 for the answers. Review concepts from this section in MyEconLab.

RATIONAL EXPECTATIONS AND THE POLICY IRRELEVANCE PROPOSITION

You already know that economists assume that economic participants act *as though* they were rational and calculating. We assume that firms rationally maximize profits when they choose today's rate of output and that consumers rationally maximize satisfaction when they choose how much of what goods to consume today. One of the pivotal features of current macro policy research is the assumption that economic participants think rationally about the future as well as the present. This relationship was developed by Robert Lucas, who won the Nobel Prize in 1995 for his work. In particular, there is widespread agreement among a growing group of macroeconomics researchers that the **rational expectations hypothesis** extends our understanding of the behavior of the macroeconomy. This hypothesis has two key elements:

Rational expectations hypothesis
A theory stating that people combine the effects of past policy changes on important economic variables with their own judgment about the future effects of current and future policy changes.

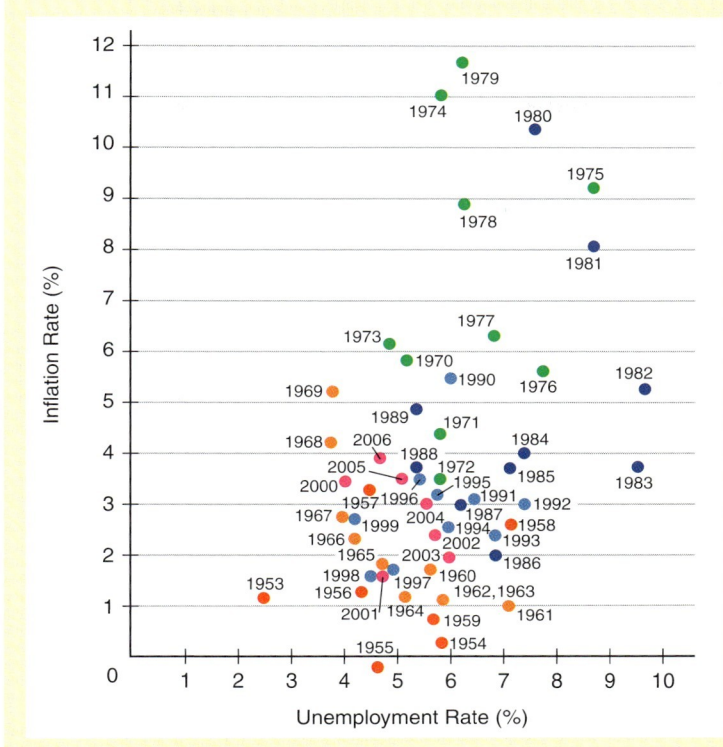

FIGURE 18-6

The Phillips Curve: Theory versus Data

If you plot points representing the rate of inflation and the rate of unemployment for the United States from 1953 to the present, there does not appear to be any Phillips curve trade-off between the two variables.

Sources: *Economic Report of the President; Economic Indicators,* various issues.

1. Individuals base their forecasts (expectations) about the future values of economic variables on all readily available past and current information.
2. These expectations incorporate individuals' understanding about how the economy operates, including the operation of monetary and fiscal policy.

In essence, the rational expectations hypothesis holds that Abraham Lincoln was correct when he said, "You may fool all the people some of the time; you can even fool some of the people all of the time; but you can't fool *all* of the people *all* the time."

Is there any way to observe whether people are successful at anticipating future values of economic variables such as the inflation rate?

EXAMPLE

Tracking Inflation Expectations

Each month, researchers at the University of Michigan survey 500 households about their expectations regarding future economic activity and prices. Beginning in late 2003 and into the spring of 2004, the average inflation expectation revealed by the survey increased from 1.8 percent to 3.2 percent. In fact, the inflation rate for the first quarter of 2004 turned out to be exactly 3.2 percent, or nearly double the inflation rate in the last quarter of 2003. The inflation expectations tracked by the monthly survey continued to closely match actual inflation throughout the mid-2000s.

FOR CRITICAL ANALYSIS

Does the rational expectations hypothesis necessarily imply that people's inflation expectations will always turn out to be as accurate as they appear to have been during the mid-2000s?

If we further assume that there is pure competition in all markets and that all prices and wages are flexible, we obtain what many call the *new classical* approach to evaluating the effects of maceconomic policies. To see how rational expectations operate in the new classical perspective, let's take a simple example of the economy's response to a change in monetary policy.

Flexible Wages and Prices, Rational Expectations, and Policy Irrelevance

Consider Figure 18-7, which shows the long-run aggregate supply curve (*LRAS*) for the economy, as well as the initial aggregate demand curve (AD_1) and the short-run aggregate supply curve ($SRAS_1$). The money supply is initially given by $M = M_1$, and the price level and real GDP are shown by P_1 and Y_1, respectively. Thus, point A represents the initial long-run equilibrium.

Suppose now that the money supply is unexpectedly increased to M_2, thereby causing the aggregate demand curve to shift outward to AD_2. Given the location of the short-run aggregate supply curve, this increase in aggregate demand will cause real GDP and the price level to rise to Y_2 and P_2, respectively. The new short-run equilibrium is at B. Because real GDP is *above* the long-run equilibrium level of Y_1, unemployment must be below long-run levels (the natural rate), and so workers will soon respond to the higher price level by demanding higher nominal wages. This will cause the short-run aggregate supply curve to shift upward vertically, moving the economy to the new long-run equilibrium at C. The price level thus continues its rise to P_3, even as real GDP declines back down to Y_1 (and unemployment returns to the natural rate). So, as we have seen before, even though an increase in the money supply can raise real GDP and lower unemployment in the short run, it has no effect on either variable in the long run.

The Response to Anticipated Policy.
Now let's look at this disturbance with the perspective given by the rational expectations hypothesis when wages and prices are flexible in a purely competitive environment. Suppose that workers (and other input owners) know ahead of time that this increase in the money supply is about to take place. Assume

FIGURE 18-7
Response to an Unanticipated Rise in Aggregate Demand

Unanticipated changes in aggregate demand have real effects. In this case, the rise in demand causes real GDP to rise from Y_1 to Y_2 in the short run. Initial equilibrium is at point A. At point B, the price level is higher, so workers seek higher wages. The resulting fall in short-run aggregate supply produces a long-run equilibrium at point C.

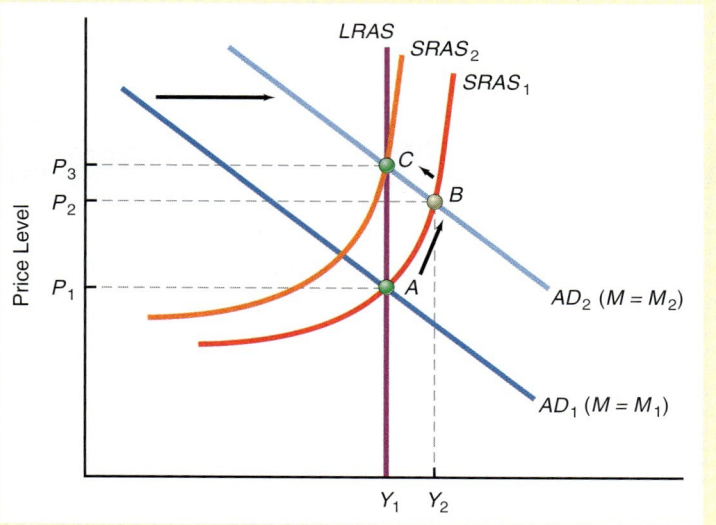

also that they know when it is going to occur and understand that its ultimate effect will be to push the price level from P_1 to P_3. Will workers wait until after the price level has increased to insist that their nominal wages go up? The rational expectations hypothesis says that they will not. Instead, they will go to employers and insist that their nominal wages move upward in step with the higher prices. From the workers' perspective, this is the only way to protect their real wages from declining due to the anticipated increase in the money supply.

The Policy Irrelevance Proposition.
As long as economic participants behave in this manner, when we draw the *SRAS* curve, we must be explicit about the nature of their expectations. This we have done in Figure 18-8. In the initial equilibrium, the short-run aggregate supply curve is labeled to show that the expected money supply (M_e) and the actual money supply (M_1) are equal ($M_e = M_1$). Similarly, when the money supply changes in a way that is anticipated by economic participants, the aggregate supply curve shifts to reflect this expected change in the money supply. The new short-run aggregate supply curve is labeled $M_e = M_2$) to reveal this. According to the rational expectations hypothesis, the short-run aggregate supply curve will shift upward *simultaneously* with the rise in aggregate demand. As a result, the economy will move directly from point *A* to point *C* in Figure 18-8 without passing through *B*: The *only* response to the rise in the money supply is a rise in the price level from P_1 to P_3; neither output nor unemployment changes at all. This conclusion—that fully anticipated monetary policy is irrelevant in determining the levels of real variables—is called the **policy irrelevance proposition:**

> *Under the assumption of rational expectations on the part of decision makers in the economy,* **anticipated** *monetary policy cannot alter either the rate of unemployment or the level of real GDP. Regardless of the nature of the anticipated policy, the unemployment rate will equal the natural rate, and real GDP will be determined solely by the economy's long-run aggregate supply curve.*

Policy irrelevance proposition
The conclusion that policy actions have no real effects in the short run if the policy actions are anticipated and none in the long run even if the policy actions are unanticipated.

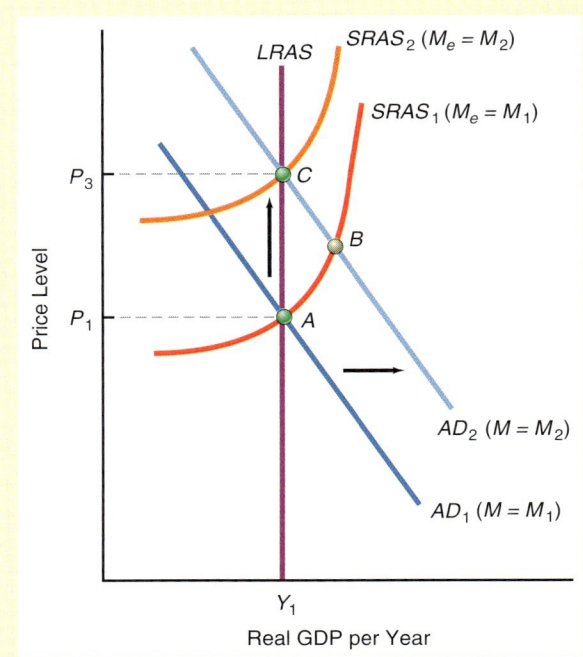

FIGURE 18-8

Effects of an Anticipated Rise in Aggregate Demand

When policy is fully anticipated, a rise in the money supply causes a rise in the price level from P_1 to P_3, with no change in real GDP.

What Must People Know?
There are two important matters to keep in mind when considering this proposition. First, our discussion has assumed that economic participants know in advance exactly what the change in monetary policy is going to be and precisely when it is going to occur. In fact, the Federal Reserve does not announce exactly what the future course of monetary policy is going to be. Instead, the Fed tries to keep most of its plans secret, announcing only in general terms what policy actions are intended for the future.

It is tempting to conclude that because the Fed's intended policies are not freely available, they are not available at all. But such a conclusion would be wrong. Economic participants have great incentives to learn how to predict the future behavior of the monetary authorities, just as businesses try to forecast consumer behavior and college students do their best to forecast what their next economics exam will look like. Even if the economic participants are not perfect at forecasting the course of policy, they are likely to come a lot closer than they would in total ignorance. The policy irrelevance proposition really assumes only that *people don't persistently make the same mistakes in forecasting the future.*

What Happens If People Don't Know Everything?
This brings us to our second point. Once we accept the fact that people are not perfect in their ability to predict the future, the possibility emerges that some policy actions will have systematic effects that look much like the movements A to B to C in Figure 18-7 on page 460. For example, just as other economic participants sometimes make mistakes, it is likely that the Federal Reserve sometimes makes mistakes—meaning that the money supply may change in ways that even the Fed does not predict. And even if the Fed always accomplished every policy action it intended, there is no guarantee that other economic participants would fully forecast those actions.

What happens if the Fed makes a mistake or if firms and workers misjudge the future course of policy? Matters will look much as they do in panel (a) of Figure 18-9, which shows the effects of an *unanticipated* increase in the money supply. Economic participants expect the money supply to be M_1, but the actual money supply turns out to be M_2. Because $M_2 > M_1$, aggregate demand shifts relative to aggregate supply. The result is a rise in real GDP in the short run from Y_1 to Y_2. Corresponding to this rise in real GDP will be an increase in employment and hence a fall in the unemployment rate. So, even under the rational expectations hypothesis, monetary policy *can* have an effect on real variables in the short run, but only if the policy is unsystematic and therefore unanticipated.

In the long run, this effect on real variables will disappear because people will figure out that the Fed either accidentally increased the money supply or intentionally increased it in a way that somehow fooled individuals. Either way, people's expectations will soon be revised so that the short-run aggregate supply curve will shift upward. As shown in panel (b) of Figure 18-9, real GDP will return to long-run levels, meaning that so will the employment and unemployment rates.

The Policy Dilemma
Perhaps the most striking and disturbing feature of the policy irrelevance proposition is that it seems to suggest that only mistakes can have real effects. If the Federal Reserve always does what it intends to do and if other economic participants always correctly anticipate the Fed's actions, monetary policy will affect only the price level and nominal input prices. It appears that only if the Fed makes a mistake in executing monetary policy or people err in anticipating that policy will changes in the money supply cause fluctuations in real GDP and employment. If this reasoning is correct, the Fed is effectively precluded from using monetary policy in any rational way to lower the unemployment rate or to raise the level of real GDP. This is because fully anticipated changes in the money supply will lead to exactly offsetting changes in prices and hence no real effects.

Many economists were disturbed at the prospect that if the economy happened to enter a recessionary period, policymakers would be powerless to push real GDP and unemploy-

FIGURE 18-9
Effects of an Unanticipated Rise in Aggregate Demand
Even with rational expectations, an unanticipated change in demand can affect real GDP in the short run.

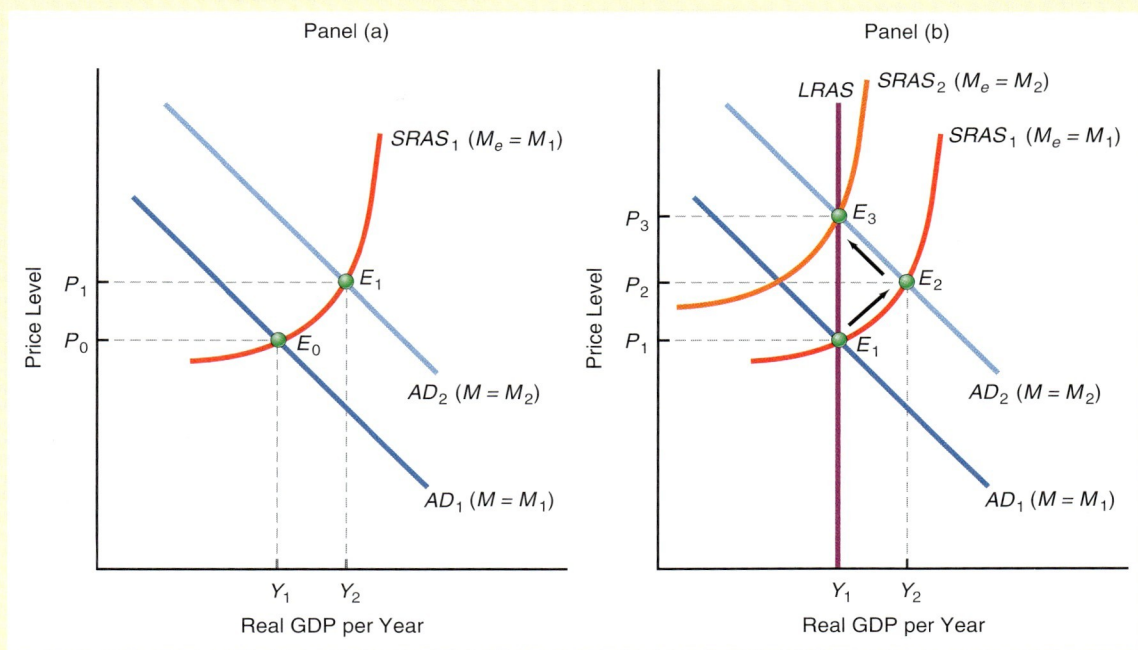

ment back to long-run levels. As a result, they asked, in light of the rational expectations hypothesis, is it *ever* possible for systematic policy to have predictable real effects on the economy? The answer has led to even more developments in the way we think about macroeconomics.

QUICK QUIZ

The _____ _____ hypothesis assumes that individuals' forecasts incorporate all readily available information, including an understanding of government policy and its effects on the economy.

If the **rational expectations hypothesis** is valid, there is pure competition, and all prices and wages are flexible, then the _____ _____ proposition follows: Fully anticipated monetary policy actions cannot alter either the rate of unemployment or the level of real GDP.

With rational expectations, flexible wages and prices, and pure competition, policies can alter real economic variables only if the policies are _____ and therefore _____; otherwise people learn and defeat the desired policy goals.

See page 476 for the answers. Review concepts from this section in MyEconLab.

ANOTHER CHALLENGE TO POLICY ACTIVISM: REAL BUSINESS CYCLES

When confronted with the policy irrelevance proposition, many economists began to reexamine the first principles of macroeconomics with fully flexible wages and prices.

The Distinction Between Real and Monetary Shocks

Today, many economists argue that real, as opposed to purely monetary, forces might help explain aggregate economic fluctuations. An important stimulus for the idea that there are *real business cycles* was the economic turmoil of the 1970s. During that decade, world economies were staggered by two major disruptions to the supply of oil. The first occurred in 1973, and the second in 1979. In both episodes, members of the Organization of Petroleum Exporting Countries (OPEC) reduced the amount of oil they were willing to supply and raised the price at which they offered it for sale. Each time, the price level rose sharply in the United States, and real GDP declined. Thus, each episode involving these aggregate supply shocks (see Chapter 11) produced a period of "stagflation"—real economic stagnation combined with high inflation. Figure 18-10 illustrates the pattern of events.

We begin at point E_1 with the economy in both short- and long-run equilibrium, with the associated supply curves, $SRAS_1$ and $LRAS_1$. Initially, the level of real GDP is Y_1, and the price level is P_1. Because the economy is in long-run equilibrium, the unemployment rate must be at the natural rate.

A reduction in the supply of oil, as occurred in 1973 and 1979, causes the $SRAS$ curve to shift to the left to $SRAS_2$ because fewer goods will be available for sale due to the reduced supplies. If the reduction in oil supplies is (or is believed to be) permanent, the $LRAS$ shifts to the left also. This assumption is reflected in Figure 18-10, where $LRAS_2$ shows the new long-run aggregate supply curve associated with the lowered output of oil.

In the short run, two adjustments begin to occur simultaneously. First, the prices of oil and petroleum-based products begin to rise, so the overall price level rises to P_2. Second, the higher costs of production occasioned by the rise in oil prices induce firms to cut back production, so real GDP falls to Y_2 in the short run. The new temporary short-run equilibrium occurs at E_2, with a higher price level (P_2) and a lower level of real GDP (Y_2).

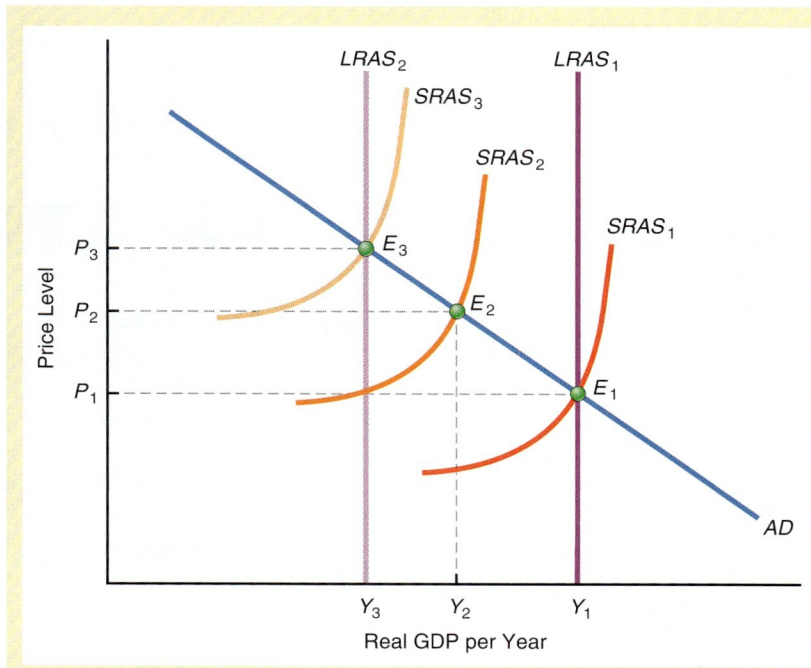

FIGURE 18-10

Effects of a Reduction in the Supply of Resources

The position of the *LRAS* depends on our endowments of all types of resources. Hence a permanent reduction in the supply of one of those resources, such as oil, causes a reduction—an inward shift—in the aggregate supply curve from $LRAS_1$ to $LRAS_2$. In addition, there is a rise in the equilibrium price level and a fall in the equilibrium rate of real GDP per year.

Impact on the Labor Market

If we were to focus on the labor market while this adjustment from E_1 to E_2 was taking place, we would find two developments occurring. The rise in the price level pushes the real wage rate downward, even as the scaled-back production plans of firms induce them to reduce the amount of labor inputs they are using. So not only does the real wage rate fall, but the level of employment declines as well. On both counts, workers are made worse off due to the reduction in the supply of oil.

This is not the full story, however. Owners of nonoil inputs (such as labor) who are willing to put up with reduced real payments in the short run simply will not tolerate them in the long run. Thus, for example, some workers who were willing to continue working at lower wages in the short run will eventually decide to retire, switch from full-time work to part-time employment, or drop out of the labor force altogether. In effect, there is a reduction in the supply of nonoil inputs, reflected in an upward shift in the *SRAS* curve from $SRAS_2$ to $SRAS_3$. This puts additional upward pressure on the price level and exerts a downward force on real GDP. The final long-run equilibrium thus occurs at point E_3, with the price level at P_3 and real GDP at Y_3. (In principle, because the oil supply shock has had no direct effect on labor markets, the natural rate of unemployment does not change when equilibrium moves from to E_1 to E_3.)

Generalizing the Theory

Naturally, the idea that the economy experiences real business cycles encompasses all types of real disturbances arising from aggregate supply shocks, such as sudden technological changes and shifts in the composition of the labor force. Moreover, a complete treatment of real shocks to the economy is typically much more complex than we have allowed for in our discussion. For example, an oil shock such as is shown in Figure 18-10 would likely also have effects on the real wealth of U.S. residents, causing a reduction in aggregate demand as well as aggregate supply. Nevertheless, our simple example still manages to capture the flavor of the real-business-cycle perspective, which indicates little role for policy activism to stabilize the economy.

The idea that aggregate supply shocks contribute to business cycles has improved our understanding of the economy's behavior, but economists agree that it alone is incapable of explaining all of the facets of business cycles that we observe. For example, it is difficult to imagine a real disturbance that could possibly account for the Great Depression in this country, when real GDP fell more than 30 percent and the unemployment rate rose to 25 percent. Moreover, the real-business-cycle approach continues to assume that all wages and prices are perfectly flexible and so fails to explain a great deal of the apparent rigidity of wages and prices throughout the economy.

MODERN APPROACHES TO RATIONALIZING ACTIVE POLICYMAKING

The policy irrelevance proposition and the idea that real shocks are primary causes of business cycles are major attacks on the desirability of trying to stabilize economic activity with activist policies. Both anti-activism suggestions arise from combining the rational expectations hypothesis with the assumptions of pure competition and flexible wages and prices. It should not be surprising, therefore, to learn that economists who see a role for activist policymaking do not believe that market clearing models of the economy can explain business cycles. They contend that the "sticky" wages and prices assumed by Keynes in his major work (see Chapter 11) remain important in today's economy. To explain how aggregate demand shocks and policies can influence a nation's real GDP and unemployment rate, these economists, who are sometimes called *new Keynesians*, have tried to refine the theory of aggregate supply.

Small Menu Costs and Sticky Prices

If prices do not respond to demand changes, two conditions must be true: someone must be consciously deciding not to change prices, and that decision must be in the decision maker's self-interest. One approach to explaining why many prices might be sticky in the short run supposes that much of the economy is characterized by imperfect competition (so firms are price searchers) and that it is costly for firms to change their prices in response to changes in demand. The costs associated with changing prices are called *menu costs,* and they include the costs of renegotiating contracts, printing price lists (such as menus), and informing customers of price changes.

Many such costs may not be very large, so economists call them **small menu costs.** Some of the costs of changing prices, however, such as those incurred in bringing together business managers from points around the nation or the world for meetings on price changes or renegotiating deals with customers, may be significant.

Firms in different industries have different cost structures. Such differences explain diverse small menu costs. Therefore, the extent to which firms hold their prices constant in the face of changes in demand for their products will vary across industries. Not all prices will be rigid. Nonetheless, some economists who promote policy activism argue that many—even most—firms' prices are sticky for relatively long time intervals. As a result, in the short run the aggregate level of prices could be very nearly rigid because of small menu costs. In recent years, these economists have produced a theory in which temporary rigidities in firms' price adjustments cause the short-run aggregate supply curve to be horizontal, as in the traditional Keynesian model.

Is there evidence of widespread price stickiness in the United States?

Small menu costs
Costs that deter firms from changing prices in response to demand changes—for example, the costs of renegotiating contracts or printing new price lists.

EXAMPLE

U.S. Price Stickiness—In the Eye of the Beholder?

Are prices sticky? One way to try to answer this question might be to examine prices in catalogs that firms distribute to potential customers. Indeed, some economists have concluded that failure of prices to change over time in catalogs is evidence of sticky prices. In many industries, however, firms often offer customers discounts from posted catalog prices. Thus, prices may be less sticky than implied by prices printed in catalogs and other price lists.

To address this problem, some new Keynesian economists have tried to *infer* how slowly prices adjust nationwide based on observed price level changes. Applying these methods to the rate of change in the U.S. GDP deflator or Consumer Price Index has indicated that, on average, prices change only about every 12 to 18 months. Nevertheless, when this approach is applied to industry-level Producer Price Indexes, significant variations in price adjustment times are revealed, as shown in Figure 18-11. The prices charged by some industries appear to take at least 12 months to change, but other prices change in nearly half that time.

Furthermore, studies of the prices that consumers pay for a broad array of consumption goods indicate even shorter intervals between price changes, often no longer than three or four months. Thus, although price stickiness seems to occur in some industries, prices of many goods appear to be relatively flexible.

(continued)

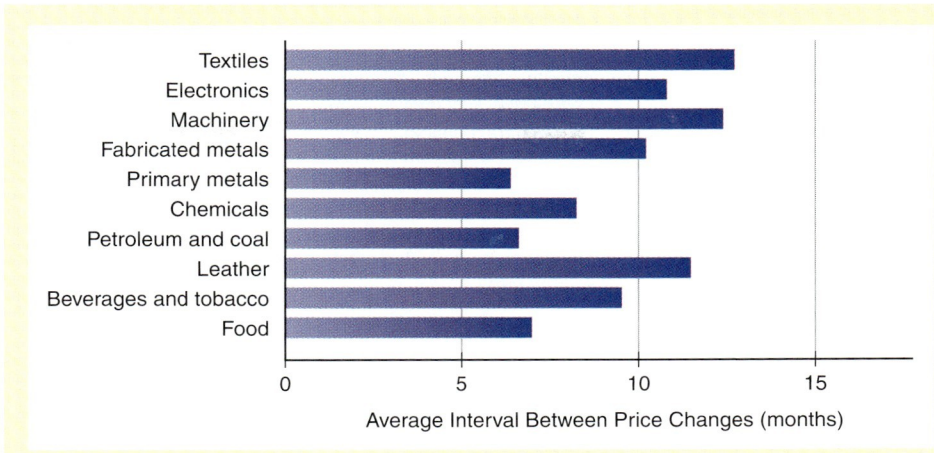

FIGURE 18-11
Estimated Intervals Between Price Changes in Selected Industries
Examination of Producer Price Indexes indicates that in some industries, inferred periods between price changes are 12 months or longer. In other industries, however, prices appear to adjust nearly twice as speedily.

Source: Carl Gwin and David VanHoose, "Disaggregate Evidence on U.S. Price Stickiness and Implications for Sticky-Price Macro Models," Baylor University, 2006.

FOR CRITICAL ANALYSIS
Why might the relative shares of real GDP produced by industries with differing degrees of price stickiness help in determining whether the idea of sticky prices has any macroeconomic relevance?

Real GDP and the Price Level in a Sticky-Price Economy

According to the new Keynesians, sticky prices strengthen the argument favoring active policymaking as a means of preventing substantial short-run swings in real GDP and, as a consequence, employment.

New Keynesian Inflation Dynamics. To see why the idea of price stickiness strengthens the case for active policymaking, consider panel (a) of Figure 18-12 on page 468. If a significant portion of all prices do not adjust rapidly, then in the short run the aggregate supply curve effectively is horizontal, as assumed in the traditional Keynesian theory discussed in Chapter 11. This means that a decline in aggregate demand, such as the shift from AD_1 to AD_2 shown in panel (a), will induce the largest possible decline in equilibrium real GDP, from $12 trillion to $11.7 trillion. When prices are sticky, economic contractions induced by aggregate demand shocks are as severe as they can be.

As panel (a) shows, in contrast to the traditional Keynesian theory, the new Keynesian sticky-price theory indicates that the economy will find its own way back to a long-run equilibrium. The theory presumes that small menu costs induce firms not to change their prices in the short run. In the long run, however, the profit gains to firms from reducing their prices to induce purchases of more goods and services cause them to cut their prices. Thus, in the long run, the price level declines in response to the decrease in aggregate demand. As firms reduce their prices, the horizontal aggregate supply curve shifts downward, from $SRAS_1$ to $SRAS_2$, and equilibrium real GDP returns to its former level, other things being equal.

Of course, an increase in aggregate demand would have effects opposite to those depicted in panel (a) of Figure 18-12. A rise in aggregate demand would cause real GDP to rise in the short run. In the long run, firms would gain sufficient profits from raising their prices to compensate for incurring menu costs, and the short-run aggregate supply curve would shift upward. Consequently, an economy with growing aggregate demand should exhibit so-called **new Keynesian inflation dynamics:** initial sluggish adjustment of the price level in response to aggregate demand increases followed by higher inflation later on.

New Keynesian inflation dynamics
In new Keynesian theory, the pattern of inflation exhibited by an economy with growing aggregate demand—initial sluggish adjustment of the price level in response to increased aggregate demand followed by higher inflation later.

FIGURE 18-12

Short- and Long-Run Adjustments in the New Keynesian Sticky-Price Theory

Panel (a) shows that when prices are sticky, the short-run aggregate supply curve is horizontal, here at a price level of 118. As a consequence, the short-run effect of a fall in aggregate demand from AD_1 to AD_2 generates the largest possible decline in real GDP, from $12 trillion at point E_1 to $11.7 trillion at point E_2. In the long run, producers perceive that they can increase their profits sufficiently by cutting prices and incurring the menu costs of doing so. The resulting decline in the price level implies a downward shift of the SRAS curve, so that the price level falls to 116 and real GDP returns to $12 trillion at point E_3. Panel (b) illustrates the argument for active policymaking based on the new Keynesian theory. Instead of waiting for long-run adjustments to occur, policymakers can engage in expansionary policies that shift the aggregate demand curve back to its original position, thereby shortening or even eliminating a recession.

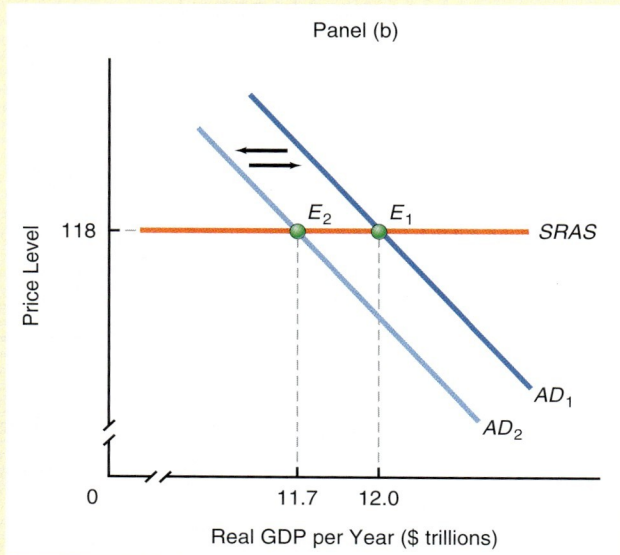

Why Active Policymaking Can Pay Off When Prices Are Sticky. To think about why the new Keynesian sticky-price theory supports the argument for active policymaking, let's return to the case of a decline in aggregate demand illustrated in panel (a) of Figure 18-12. Panel (b) shows the same decline in aggregate demand as in panel (a) and the resulting maximum contractionary effect on real GDP.

Monetary and fiscal policy actions that influence aggregate demand are as potent as possible when prices are sticky and short-run aggregate supply is horizontal. In principle, therefore, all that a policymaker confronted by the leftward shift in aggregate demand depicted in panel (a) must do is to conduct the appropriate policy to induce a rightward shift in the AD curve back to its previous position. Indeed, if the policymaker acts rapidly enough, the period of contraction experienced by the economy may be very brief. Active policymaking can thereby moderate or even eliminate recessions.

An Alternative New Keynesian Scenario: Bounded Rationality

Not all economists are convinced that prices adjust as sluggishly as presumed in the new Keynesian sticky-price analysis presented in Figure 18-12. Indeed, not even all new Keynesian economists are convinced that prices are really so sticky.

Recently, some new Keynesian theorists have proposed an alternative theory supporting active policymaking. This theory borrows from the *bounded rationality* assumption proposed by proponents of behavioral economics that was discussed in Chapter 1. Recall that under bounded rationality, people cannot examine every possible choice available to them, so they use simple rules of thumb to guide their decision making. According to the alternative new Keynesian sticky-price rationale for active policymaking, people in the economy cannot process all the information that confronts them, so they use rules of thumb to adjust wages and prices. While wages and prices do adjust, any adjustments are potentially very incomplete. Wages and prices are not fully flexible in the short run, but they are not completely rigid either.

Thus, a key prediction of this alternative theory is that bounded rationality causes prices to *adjust* particularly sluggishly to changes in aggregate demand. Instead of price stickiness, potentially very incomplete short-run adjustments of prices prevent real GDP from rapidly reaching its full-employment level, thereby providing a channel for active policymaking to have short-run stabilizing effects. Incomplete price adjustment alone, these other new Keynesians argue, provides sufficient rationale for policymakers to engage in active efforts aimed at dampening or even preventing cycles in real GDP and, as a result, employment.

SUMMING UP: ECONOMIC FACTORS FAVORING ACTIVE VERSUS PASSIVE POLICYMAKING

To many people who have never taken a principles of economics course, it seems apparent that the world's governments should engage in active policymaking aimed at achieving high and stable real GDP growth and a low and stable unemployment rate. As you have learned in this chapter, the advisability of policy activism is not so obvious.

Several factors are involved in assessing whether policy activism is really preferable to passive policymaking. Table 18-1 summarizes the issues involved in evaluating the case for active policymaking versus the case for passive policymaking.

> **ECONOMICS FRONT AND CENTER**
>
> To consider how economic theory might affect policymaking, read **A Federal Reserve Board Governor in Search of a Theory,** on page 470.

TABLE 18-1
Issues That Must Be Assessed in Determining the Desirability of Active versus Passive Policymaking
Economists who contend that active policymaking is justified argue that evidence on each issue listed in the first column supports conclusions listed in the second column. In contrast, economists who suggest that passive policymaking is appropriate argue that evidence regarding each issue in the first column leads to conclusions listed in the third column.

Issue	Support for Active Policymaking	Support for Passive Policymaking
Phillips curve inflation-unemployment trade-off	Stable in the short run; perhaps predictable in the long run	Varies with inflation expectations; at best fleeting in the short run and nonexistent in the long run
Aggregate demand shocks	Induce short-run and perhaps long-run effects on real GDP and unemployment	Have little or no short-run effects and certainly no long-run effects on real GDP and unemployment
Aggregate supply shocks	Can, along with aggregate demand shocks, influence real GDP and unemployment	Cause movements in real GDP and unemployment and hence explain most business cycles
Pure competition	Is not typical in most markets, where imperfect competition predominates	Is widespread in markets throughout the economy
Price flexibility	Is uncommon because factors such as small menu costs induce firms to change prices infrequently	Is common because firms adjust prices immediately when demand changes
Wage flexibility	Is uncommon because labor market adjustments occur relatively slowly	Is common because nominal wages adjust speedily to price changes, making real wages flexible

You may have heard about President Harry Truman's remark that he wished he could find a one-armed economist, so that he would not have to hear, "On the one hand . . . but on the other hand" quite so often. The current state of thinking on the relative desirability of active or passive policymaking may make you as frustrated as President Truman was in the early 1950s. On the one hand, most economists agree that active policymaking is unlikely to exert sizable long-run effects on any nation's economy. Most also agree that aggregate supply shocks contribute to business cycles. Consequently, there is general agreement that there are limits on the effectiveness of monetary and fiscal policies. On the other hand, a number of economists continue to argue that there is evidence indicating stickiness of prices and wages. They argue, therefore, that monetary and fiscal policy actions can offset, at least in the short run and perhaps even in the long run, the effects that aggregate demand shocks would otherwise have on real GDP and unemployment.

These diverging perspectives help explain why economists reach differing conclusions about the advisability of pursuing active or passive approaches to macroeconomic policymaking. Different interpretations of evidence on the issues summarized in Table 18-1 on the previous page will likely continue to divide economists for years to come.

QUICK QUIZ

Even if all prices and wages are perfectly flexible, aggregate _____ shocks such as sudden changes in technology or in the supplies of factors of production can cause national economic fluctuations. To the extent that these _____ _____ cycles predominate as sources of economic fluctuations, the case for active policymaking is weakened.

Some new Keynesian economists suggest that _____ _____ costs inhibit many firms from making speedy changes in their prices and that this price stickiness can make the short-run aggregate supply curve _____. Variations in aggregate demand have the largest possible effects on real GDP in the short run, so policies that influence aggregate demand also have the greatest capability to stabilize real GDP in the face of aggregate demand shocks.

Another new Keynesian approach suggests that _____ rationality prevents people from adjusting prices and wages fully in the short run. This creates a sufficient lack of short-run price and wage flexibility for discretionary policy actions to contribute to real GDP stability.

See page 476 for the answers. Review concepts from this section in MyEconLab.

CASE STUDY

ECONOMICS FRONT AND CENTER

A Federal Reserve Board Governor in Search of a Theory

Blake is an assistant to Governor Sloan, a member of the Federal Reserve's Board of Governors. Governor Sloan believes that the rest of the Board made a significant policy error in deciding to take a hands-off approach to a recent decline in planned investment spending. In Sloan's view, the Fed should respond more actively by substantially increasing money supply growth in an immediate effort either to prevent a recession or at least to reduce its severity.

Sloan has just assigned Blake the task of reviewing current academic theories and finding a theory providing support for the argument she plans to present next week in a speech at a New York bankers' convention. She wants a report from Blake in two days. Blake begins to review the arguments for and against active policymaking.

CRITICAL ANALYSIS QUESTIONS

1. Name an economic theory that Blake might suggest to Governor Sloan. Why do you think that this theory is appropriate?
2. Blake wants to be sure that Governor Sloan is aware of all potential shortcomings associated with the theory he will suggest to her. What are possible problems associated with the theory you proposed in Question 1?

Issues and Applications

Can Active Policymaking Take Credit for the "Great Moderation"?

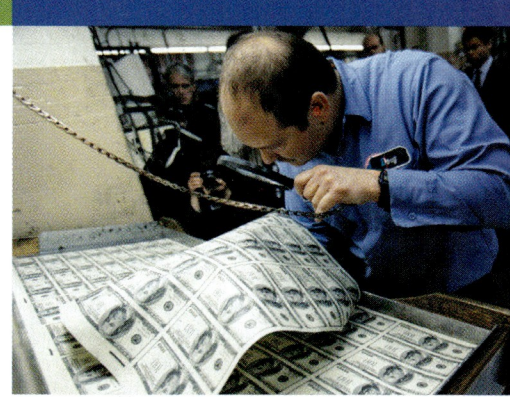

The "Great Moderation" is the period since 1984, when variability in real GDP growth dropped noticeably, as shown in Figure 18-13 on the following page. Between 1952 and 1983, a statistical measure of the variability of quarterly (three-month) rates of real GDP growth was equal to 4.7 percentage points. Since 1984, the value of this measure has fallen to 2.1 percentage points.

Concepts Applied
- Active Policymaking
- Policy Irrelevance Proposition
- Passive Policymaking

Improved Policymaking?

The significant drop in the variability of real GDP growth since 1984 first became apparent during the late 1990s. At that time, proponents of active policymaking jumped to what seemed to them a logical conclusion: Improved policymaking must have been responsible.

By the mid-2000s, however, most economists had ruled out this explanation. There is certainly some evidence that monetary and perhaps even fiscal policy actions may have slightly helped reduce the volatility of real GDP growth. Policy contributions to real GDP since the mid-1980s were simply too small, however, to have accounted for all of the observed reduction in real GDP variability.

A More Resilient Economy?

When it became apparent that slightly better policymaking could not really be responsible for the lower variability of real GDP growth, economists began to explore whether underlying changes in the economy might provide an explanation. They found little evidence that aggregate demand shocks exert smaller effects than in years past. As for aggregate supply shocks, reduced reliance of U.S. industry on fossil fuels has made U.S. aggregate supply less susceptible to shocks generated by higher energy prices. In addition, deregulation and increased competition in many product markets, plus reduced unionization of labor markets, also have contributed to speedier adjustments to aggregate supply shocks. Nevertheless, lessened effects of aggregate supply shocks were also insufficient to explain how the measured variability of quarterly real GDP growth rates could have declined by a factor exceeding one-half.

A Lucky Break?

This leaves only one factor that can best explain the greater stability that the U.S. economy has experienced since 1984: smaller-than-normal aggregate demand and aggregate supply shocks. Energy prices were more stable after 1983 than in previous years, and productivity growth was generally steady. In addition, aside from a drop-off in investment

471

FIGURE 18-13

Quarterly Real GDP Growth Rates Since 1952

The variability of the rate of growth over quarterly (three-month) intervals dropped noticeably beginning in 1984.

Source: Michelle Armesto and Jeremy Piger, "International Perspectives on the Great Moderation," *International Economic Trends*, Federal Reserve Bank of St. Louis, August 2005.

expenditures in 2001 and 2002, total planned spending was relatively stable.

This assessment yields a foreboding conclusion. Just because the incidence and severity of aggregate demand and supply shocks appear to have declined during the 1980s and 1990s does not mean the trend will continue. An analogy might be the frequency and intensity of U.S. hurricanes, which also happened to drop off during the 1980s and 1990s. Many climate scientists suggest that recent bouts with numerous, more powerful hurricanes during the 2000s indicate a return to times of more numerous hurricanes along the U.S. Atlantic and Gulf coasts. Aggregate supply and demand shocks could likewise return to historically observed levels of volatility and significance. To proponents of active policymaking, this means that policymakers should aim to learn how to do their jobs even better. To those who contend that the policy irrelevance proposition is valid, an alternative prescription is for policymakers to work now to design better passive policies, such as improved automatic stabilizers that you learned about in Chapter 13.

Log in to **MyEconLab**, click on "Economic News," and test your understanding of the chapter by answering interactive questions that relate directly to this issue.

For Critical Analysis

1. Does the fact that better policymaking cannot possibly eliminate all variability in real GDP growth imply that nothing can be gained from improved policymaking?

2. How might lower variability of aggregate demand and supply shocks help to explain the generally lower inflation and unemployment rates observed since 1984?

Web Resources

1. Read a discussion of the Great Moderation by Federal Reserve Board chair Ben Bernanke at **www.econtoday.com/ch18**.

2. For an evaluation of what monetary policymaking might be able to do to prolong the Great Moderation, go to **www.econtoday.com/ch18**.

Research Project

Evaluate how policymaking improvements and greater resilience of the economy to aggregate demand and supply shocks might help compensate for any increased volatility of such shocks in future years. According to the theories you studied in this chapter, how might better policymaking and speedier adjustments to shocks contribute to shortening recessions that might be caused by such shocks?

Here is what you should know after reading this chapter. MyEconLab will help you identify what you know, and where to go when you need to practice.

WHAT YOU SHOULD KNOW

WHERE TO GO TO PRACTICE

Why the Actual Unemployment Rate Might Depart from the Natural Rate of Unemployment According to the basic theory of aggregate demand and short- and long-run aggregate supply, an unexpected increase in aggregate demand can cause real GDP to rise in the short run, which results in a reduction in the unemployment rate. Consequently, for a time the actual unemployment rate can fall below the natural rate of unemployment. Likewise, an unanticipated reduction in aggregate demand can push down real GDP in the short run, thereby causing the actual unemployment rate to rise above the natural unemployment rate.

active (discretionary) policymaking, 450
passive (nondiscretionary) policymaking 450
natural rate of unemployment, 451
Key figures
Figure 18-1, 452
Figure 18-2, 453
Figure 18-3, 454

- **MyEconLab** Study Plans 18.1 and 18.2
- Audio Introduction to Chapter 18
- Animated Figures 18-1, 18-2, and 18-3
- Video: The Natural Rate of Unemployment

The Phillips Curve An unexpected increase in aggregate demand that causes a drop in the unemployment rate also induces a rise in the equilibrium price level and, consequently, inflation. Thus, the basic aggregate demand–aggregate supply model indicates that, other things being equal, there should be an inverse relationship between the inflation rate and the unemployment rate. This downward-sloping relationship is called the Phillips curve, and it implies that there may be a short-run trade-off between inflation and unemployment.

Phillips curve, 455
nonaccelerating inflation rate of unemployment (NAIRU), 455

- **MyEconLab** Study Plan 18.2

How Expectations Affect the Actual Relationship Between the Inflation Rate and the Unemployment Rate Theory predicts that there will be a Phillips curve relationship only when another important factor, expectations, is held unchanged. If people are able to anticipate policymakers' efforts to exploit the Phillips curve trade-off by engaging in inflationary policies to push down the unemployment rate, then basic theory also suggests that input prices such as nominal wages will adjust more rapidly to an increase in the price level. As a result, the Phillips curve will shift outward, and the economy will adjust more speedily toward the natural rate of unemployment. When plotted on a chart, therefore, the actual relationship between the inflation rate and the unemployment rate will not be a downward-sloping Phillips curve.

- **MyEconLab** Study Plan 18.3

WHAT YOU SHOULD KNOW		WHERE TO GO TO PRACTICE
Rational Expectations, Market Clearing, and Policy Ineffectiveness According to the rational expectations hypothesis, people form expectations of future economic variables such as inflation using all available past and current information and based on their understanding of how the economy functions. If pure competition prevails, wages and prices are flexible, and people form rational expectations, then only unanticipated policy actions can induce even short-run changes in real GDP. If people completely anticipate the actions of policymakers, wages and other input prices adjust immediately, so real GDP remains unaffected. A key implication of this expectations-based approach to macroeconomics is the policy irrelevance proposition, which states that the unemployment rate is unaffected by fully anticipated policy actions.	rational expectations hypothesis, 458 policy irrelevance proposition, 461 **Key figures** Figure 18-7, 460 Figure 18-8, 461	• **MyEconLab** Study Plan 18.3 • Animated Figures 18-7 and 18-8
The Real-Business-Cycle Challenge to Active Policymaking Even if pure competition prevails throughout the economy and prices and wages are flexible, technological changes and labor market shocks such as variations in the composition of the labor force can induce business fluctuations. To the extent that such aggregate supply shocks contribute to real business cycles, the case for active policymaking is weakened.		• **MyEconLab** Study Plan 18.4
Modern Approaches to Bolstering the Case for Active Policymaking New Keynesian approaches to understanding the sources of business fluctuations highlight wage and price stickiness. Firms that face costs of adjusting their prices may be slow to change prices in the face of variations in demand. Thus, the short-run aggregate supply curve is horizontal, and changes in aggregate demand have the largest possible effects on real GDP in the short run, which gives discretionary policies scope to offset aggregate demand shocks. Another new Keynesian approach suggests that people with bounded rationality who use rules of thumb to guide their decisions cannot fully adjust prices and wages fully in the short run. According to this alternative view, prices and wages are not fully sticky, but they are sufficiently inflexible in the short run that discretionary policy actions can stabilize real GDP.	small menu costs, 466 new Keynesian inflation dynamics, 467	• **MyEconLab** Study Plans 18.5 and 18.6 • Video: The New Keynesian Economics

Log in to MyEconLab, take a chapter test, and get a personalized Study Plan that tells you which concepts you understand and which ones you need to review. From there, MyEconLab will give you further practice, tutorials, animations, videos, and guided solutions.

Log in to www.myeconlab.com

PROBLEMS

Select problems, indicated by a blue oval ⬤, are assignable in MyEconLab.
Answers to the odd-numbered problems appear at the back of the book.

18-1. Suppose that the government altered the computation of the unemployment rate by including people in the military as part of the labor force.
  a. How would this affect the actual unemployment rate?
  b. How would such a change affect estimates of the natural rate of unemployment?
  c. If this computational change were made, would it in any way affect the logic of the short-run and long-run Phillips curve analysis and its implications for policymaking? Why might the government wish to make such a change?

18-2. When Alan Greenspan was nominated for his third term as chair of the Federal Reserve's Board of Governors, a few senators held up his confirmation. One of them explained their joint action to hinder his confirmation by saying, "Every time growth starts to go up, they [the Federal Reserve] push on the brakes, robbing working families and businesses of the benefits of faster growth." Evaluate this statement in the context of short-run and long-run perspectives on the Phillips curve.

18-3. Economists have not reached agreement on how lengthy the time horizon for "the long run" is in the context of Phillips curve analysis. Would you anticipate that this period is likely to have been shortened or extended by the advent of more sophisticated computer and communications technology? Explain your reasoning.

18-4. The natural rate of unemployment depends on factors that affect the behavior of both workers and firms. Make lists of possible factors affecting workers and firms that you believe are likely to influence the natural rate of unemployment.

18-5. What distinguishes the nonaccelerating inflation rate of unemployment (NAIRU) from the natural rate of unemployment? (Hint: Which is easier to quantify?)

18-6. When will the natural rate of unemployment and the NAIRU differ? When will they be the same?

18-7. Suppose that more unemployed people who are classified as part of frictional unemployment decide to stop looking for work and start their own businesses instead. What is likely to happen to each of the following, other things being equal?
  a. The natural unemployment rate
  b. The NAIRU
  c. The economy's Phillips curve

18-8. People called "Fed watchers" earn their living by trying to forecast what policies the Federal Reserve will implement within the next few weeks and months. Suppose that Fed watchers discover that the current group of Fed officials is following very systematic and predictable policies intended to reduce the unemployment rate. The Fed watchers then sell this information to firms, unions, and others in the private sector. If pure competition prevails, prices and wages are flexible, and people form rational expectations, are the Fed's policies likely to have their intended effects on the unemployment rate?

18-9. Suppose that economists were able to use U.S. economic data to demonstrate that the rational expectations hypothesis is true. Would this be sufficient to demonstrate the validity of the policy irrelevance proposition?

18-10. Evaluate the following statement: "In an important sense, the term *policy irrelevance proposition* is misleading because even if the rational expectations hypothesis is valid, economic policy actions can have significant effects on real GDP and the unemployment rate."

18-11. Consider the diagram below, which is drawn under the assumption that the new Keynesian sticky-price theory of aggregate supply applies. Assume that at present, the economy is in equilibrium at point A. Answer the following questions.

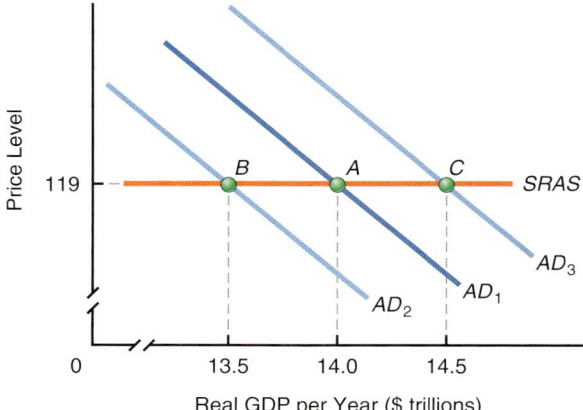

a. Suppose that there is a sudden increase in desired investment expenditures. Which of the alternative aggregate demand curves—AD_2 or AD_3—will apply after this event occurs? Other things being equal, what will happen to the equilibrium price level and to equilibrium real GDP in the *short run*? Explain.

b. Other things being equal, after the event and adjustments discussed in part a have taken place, what will happen to the equilibrium price level and to equilibrium real GDP in the *long run*? Explain.

18-12 Both the traditional Keynesian theory discussed in Chapter 11 and the new Keynesian theory considered in this chapter indicate that the short-run aggregate supply curve is horizontal.

a. In terms of their *short-run* implications for the price level and real GDP, is there any difference between the two approaches?

b. In terms of their *long-run* implications for the price level and real GDP, is there any difference between the two approaches?

18-13. The real-business-cycle approach attributes even short-run increases in real GDP largely to aggregate supply shocks. Rightward shifts in aggregate supply tend to push down the equilibrium price level. How, then, could the real-business-cycle perspective explain the low but persistent inflation that the United States has experienced in recent years?

18-14. Does the Federal Reserve have any role if real business cycles explain U.S. economic fluctuations? If so, what is that role?

18-15. Normally, when aggregate demand increases, firms find it more profitable to raise prices than to leave prices unchanged. The idea behind the small-menu-cost explanation for price stickiness is that firms will leave their prices unchanged if their profit gain from adjusting prices is less than menu costs they would incur if they change prices. If firms anticipate that a rise in demand is likely to last for a long time, does this make them more or less likely to adjust their prices when they face small menu costs? (Hint: Profits are a flow that firms earn from week to week and month to month, but small menu costs are a one-time expense.)

ECONOMICS ON THE NET

The Inflation-Unemployment Relationship According to the basic aggregate demand and aggregate supply model, the unemployment rate should be inversely related to changes in the inflation rate, other things being equal. This application allows you to take a direct look at unemployment and inflation data to judge for yourself whether the two variables appear to be related.

Title: Bureau of Labor Statistics: Economy at a Glance

Navigation: Go to www.econtoday.com/ch18 to visit the Bureau of Labor Statistics Economy at a Glance home page.

Application Perform the indicated operations, and then answer the following questions.

1. Click on the graph box next to *Consumer Price Index*. Take a look at the solid line showing inflation. How much has inflation varied in recent years? Compare this with previous years, especially the mid-1970s to mid-1980s.

2. Back up to *Economy at a Glance*, and now click on the graph box next to *Unemployment Rate*. During what recent years was the unemployment rate approaching and at its peak value? Do you note any appearance of an inverse relationship between the unemployment rate and the inflation rate?

For Group Study and Analysis Divide the class into groups, and have each group search through the *Economy at a Glance* site to develop an explanation for the key factors accounting for the recent behavior of the unemployment rate. Have each group report on its explanation. Is there any one factor that best explains the recent behavior of the unemployment rate?

ANSWERS TO QUICK QUIZZES

p. 458: (i) long . . . expectations; (ii) increase . . . decrease; (iii) Phillips . . . demand; (iv) Activist
p. 463: (i) rational expectations; (ii) policy irrelevance; (iii) unsystematic . . . unanticipated
p. 470: (i) supply . . . real business; (ii) small menu . . . horizontal; (iii) bounded

Policies and Prospects for Global Economic Growth

19

In Brazil, a nation endowed with a wealth of resources but saddled with one of the world's most complex legal systems, economic growth is at a standstill. Even though the act of physically constructing an apartment building usually requires only about 8 months in Brazil, the overall process of erecting an apartment building in that country usually takes 42 months. Builders have to devote all the extra time to obtaining legal permits from local and national government agencies. This is an expensive endeavor that drives the total construction cost for a typical apartment building up by 400 percent. In this chapter, you will learn why relatively complicated, slow-moving, and expensive legal systems are holding back economic growth in Brazil and other developing countries.

 MyEconLab helps you master each objective and study more efficiently. See end of chapter for details.

Learning Objectives

After reading this chapter, you should be able to:

1. Explain why population growth can have uncertain effects on economic growth
2. Understand why the existence of dead capital retards investment and economic growth in much of the developing world
3. Describe how government inefficiencies have contributed to the creation of relatively large quantities of dead capital in the world's developing nations
4. Discuss the sources of international investment funds for developing nations and identify obstacles to international investment in these nations
5. Identify the key functions of the World Bank and the International Monetary Fund
6. Explain the basis for recent criticisms of policymaking at the World Bank and the International Monetary Fund

> ### Did You Know That . . .
>
> in Haiti, registering a new company takes 203 days, which is at least 198 days longer than is required in the United States? Furthermore, to legally set up a business in Ethiopia, an entrepreneur must first deposit an amount equal to 18 times the average resident's annual income in an account that cannot be touched as long as the business is in operation. In Sierra Leone, the cost of officially establishing a business is 1,200 times the average resident's annual income. In the United States, in contrast, deposits are not required to set up businesses, and business registration fees are inconsequential.
>
> Businesses already in operation typically desire to buy and sell various types of property. In Nigeria, however, to record a sale of land, a business must complete 21 different procedures—a process that typically takes at least 39 weeks—and pay government fees equal to more than one-fourth the value of the property. In comparison, recording a land sale in the United States takes less than a day and typically costs less than 2 percent of the property's value.
>
> Naturally, the relatively high costs and long time lags associated with establishing businesses in Haiti, Ethiopia, and Sierra Leone discourage people from legally setting up firms in these countries. Likewise, the significant fees and delays associated with transferring properties discourage people from establishing rights to property ownership in Nigeria. The governments of many other countries also make it hard for people to legally operate businesses and own property.
>
> In the pages that follow, you will contemplate the prospects for economic growth in developing countries such as Haiti, Ethiopia, Sierra Leone, and Nigeria. You will learn about international institutions that the world's wealthier nations have established to promote global economic growth and about the policies of these institutions. You will also discover why prospects for economic growth remain bleak for many people around the globe, irrespective of the activities of these international institutions.

LABOR RESOURCES AND ECONOMIC GROWTH

You learned in Chapter 9 that the main determinants of economic growth are the growth of labor and capital resources and the rate of increase of labor and capital productivity. Human resources are abundant around the globe. Currently, the world's population increases by more than 75 million people each year. This population growth is not spread evenly over the earth's surface. Among the relatively wealthy nations of Europe, women bear an average of just over one child during their lifetimes. In the United States, a typical woman bears about 1.5 children. But in the generally poorer nations of Africa, women bear an average of six children.

Population growth does not necessarily translate into an increase in labor resources in a number of the poorest regions of the world. A number of people in poor nations do not join the labor force. Many who do so have trouble obtaining employment.

A common assumption is that high population growth in a less developed nation hinders the growth of its per capita GDP. Certainly, this is the presumption in China, where the government has imposed an absolute limit of one child per female resident. In fact, however, the relationship between population growth and economic growth is not really so clear-cut.

Basic Arithmetic of Population Growth and Economic Growth

Does a larger population raise or lower per capita real GDP? If a country has fixed borders and an unchanged level of aggregate real GDP, a higher population directly reduces per capita real GDP. After all, if there are more people, then dividing a constant amount of real GDP by a larger number of people reduces real GDP per capita.

This basic arithmetic works for growth rates too. We can express the growth rate of per capita real GDP in a nation as

$$\text{Rate of growth of per capita real GDP} = \text{rate of growth in real GDP} - \text{rate of growth of population}$$

Hence, if real GDP grows at a constant rate of 4 percent per year and the annual rate of population growth increases from 2 percent to 3 percent, the annual rate of growth of per capita real GDP will decline, from 2 percent to 1 percent.

How Population Growth Can Contribute to Economic Growth. The arithmetic of the relationship between economic growth and population growth can be misleading. Certainly, it is a mathematical fact that the rate of growth of per capita real GDP equals the difference between the rate of growth in real GDP and the rate of growth of the population. Economic analysis, however, indicates that population growth can affect the rate of growth of real GDP. Thus, these two growth rates are not necessarily independent.

Recall from Chapter 9 that a higher rate of labor force participation by a nation's population contributes to increased growth of real GDP. If population growth is also accompanied by growth in the rate of labor force participation, then population growth can contribute to real GDP growth. Even though population growth by itself tends to reduce the growth of per capita real GDP, greater labor force participation by an enlarged population can boost real GDP growth sufficiently to more than compensate for the increase in population. On balance, the rate of growth of per capita real GDP can thereby increase.

Consider a hypothetical example. Suppose that the flow of immigrants to a country increases, and many of the new immigrants are well-trained and highly productive individuals who desire to obtain employment. The basic arithmetic of economic growth indicates two effects of this increased flow of immigration. First, with the rate of real GDP growth initially unchanged, the resulting increase in population growth causes per capita real GDP growth to start to decline. Second, because so many of the new immigrants seek employment, the nation's overall labor force participation rate increases, which boosts the rate of growth of real GDP, because the new immigrants are highly productive workers. If the rate of real GDP growth generated by the higher inflow of immigrants is greater than the higher rate of population growth owing to increased immigration, then the rate of growth of per capita real GDP increases.

An increase in population via a higher birthrate obviously cannot immediately boost the rates of growth of labor resources and of real GDP, because years must pass before newborn individuals reach an age at which they are able to work. Nevertheless, over a period of years in which individuals mature and receive education that expands their human capital, it is still possible that increased population growth owing to a higher birthrate can also lead to a more rapid growth rate of total real GDP. This will occur directly as individuals enter the labor force when they reach working age. If higher population growth causes an eventual increase in labor force participation in conjunction with technological improvements or increased capital accumulation, there can be an additional stimulus to growth. In principle, therefore, it is possible for a higher rate of population growth to contribute to an overall rise in a nation's rate of growth of per capita real GDP.

Whether Population Growth Hinders or Contributes to Economic Growth Depends on Where You Live. On net, does an increased rate of population growth detract from or add to the rate of economic growth? Table 19-1 on the following page

TABLE 19-1			
Population Growth and Growth in Per Capita Real GDP in Selected Nations Since 1965	Country	Average Annual Population Growth Rate (%)	Average Annual Rate of Growth of Per Capita Real GDP (%)
	China	1.5	6.8
	Ghana	2.7	−1.0
	Hong Kong	2.1	5.5
	India	2.0	2.5
	Jordan	4.3	−0.4
	Niger	3.3	−2.9
	Pakistan	2.6	2.8
	Saudi Arabia	4.1	−3.0
	Sierra Leone	2.1	−1.4
	Singapore	2.1	6.2
	South Korea	1.4	7.2
	United States	1.0	1.4
	Zambia	3.0	−2.1

Source: World Bank.

indicates that the answer depends on which nation one considers. In some nations that have experienced relatively high average rates of population growth, such as China, Hong Kong (a province of China), Singapore, and, to a lesser extent, India and Pakistan, economic growth has accompanied population growth. In contrast, in nations such as Saudi Arabia, Niger, and Zambia, there has been a negative relationship between population growth and per capita real GDP growth. Other factors apparently must affect how population growth and economic growth ultimately interrelate.

The Role of Economic Freedom

A crucial factor influencing economic growth is the relative freedom of a nation's residents. Particularly important is the degree of **economic freedom**—the rights to own private property and to exchange goods, services, and financial assets with minimal government interference—available to the residents of a nation.

Approximately two-thirds of the world's people reside in about three dozen nations with governments unwilling to grant residents significant economic freedom. The economies of these nations, even though they have the majority of the world's population, produce only 13 percent of the world's total output. Several of these countries have experienced rates of economic growth at or above the 1.2 percent annual average for the world's nations during the past 30 years, but many are growing much more slowly. More than 30 of these countries have experienced negative rates of per capita income growth.

Only 17 nations, with 17 percent of the world's people, grant their residents high degrees of economic freedom. These nations, some of which have very high population densities, together account for 81 percent of total world output. All of the countries that grant considerable economic freedom have experienced positive rates of economic growth, and most are close to or above the world's average rate of economic growth.

Economic freedom
The rights to own private property and to exchange goods, services, and financial assets with minimal government interference.

Go to www.econtoday.com/ch19 to review the Heritage Foundation's evaluations of the degree of economic freedom in different nations.

The Role of Political Freedom

Interestingly, *political freedom*—the right to openly support and democratically select national leaders—appears to be less important than economic freedom in determining economic growth. Some countries that grant considerable economic freedom to their citizens have relatively strong restrictions on their residents' freedoms of speech and the press.

When nondemocratic countries have achieved high standards of living through consistent economic growth, they tend to become more democratic over time. This suggests that economic freedom tends to stimulate economic growth, which then leads to more political freedom.

Why do you suppose that per capita real GDP appears to be related to the extent to which the rule of law prevails?

INTERNATIONAL EXAMPLE

The Rule of Law and Per Capita Real GDP

Failure to abide by the rule of law makes the return on capital dependent more on whims of individuals than on laws. Property rights become less secure, which discourages individuals and businesses from investing and using property for productive purposes.

The growth-reducing effects of a breakdown in the rule of law should show up in the form of lower levels of per capita real GDP. Figure 19-1 shows the relationship between a measure of adherence to the rule of law and per capita real GDP for a number of countries. Clearly, less adherence to the rule of law is associated with lower levels of per capita real GDP.

FOR CRITICAL ANALYSIS
Even if Nigeria, a nation where the rule of law is relatively weak, found a way to enforce the rule of law and boost economic growth, why would its per capita real GDP take many years to close the gap with higher-income nations?

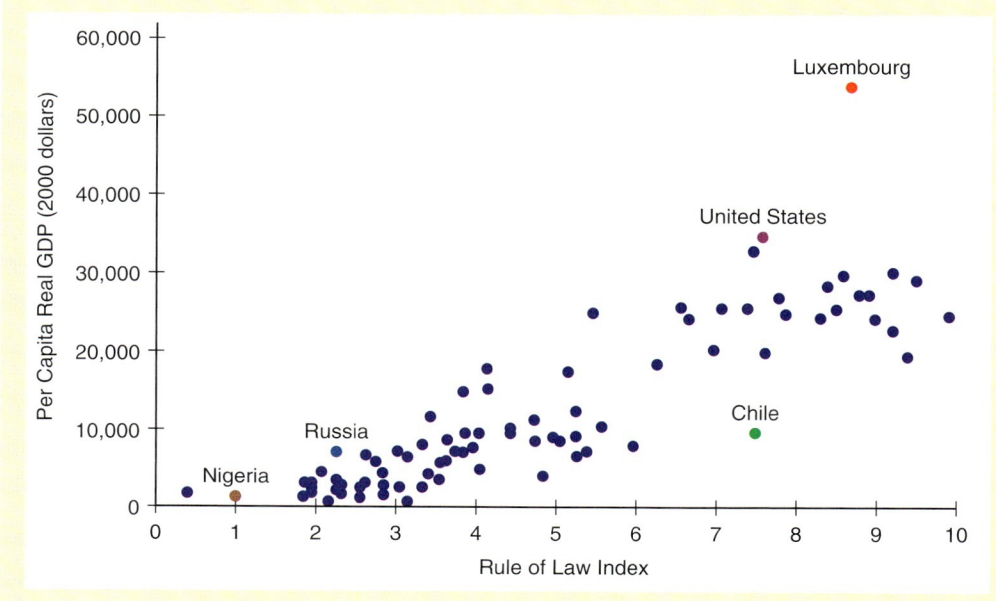

FIGURE 19-1

The Relationship Between Adherence to the Rule of Law and Per Capita Real GDP

Measured along the horizontal axis is a United Nations index of adherence to the rule of law. Less adherence to the rule of law is associated with a lower level of per capita real GDP.

Source: United Nations.

QUICK QUIZ

For a given rate of growth of aggregate real GDP, higher population growth tends to _____ the growth of per capita real GDP.

To the extent that increased population growth leads to greater _____ _____ participation that raises the growth of total real GDP, a higher population growth rate can potentially _____ the rate of growth in per capita real GDP.

In general, the extent of _____ freedom does not necessarily increase the rate of economic growth. A greater degree of _____ freedom, however, does have a positive effect on a nation's growth prospects.

See page 499 for the answers. Review concepts from this section in MyEconLab.

CAPITAL GOODS AND ECONOMIC GROWTH

A fundamental problem developing countries face is that a significant portion of their capital goods, or manufactured resources that may be used to produce other items in the future, is what economists call **dead capital,** a term coined by economist Hernando de Soto. This term describes a capital resource lacking clear title of ownership. Dead capital may actually be put to some productive purpose, but individuals and firms face difficulties in exchanging, insuring, and legally protecting their rights to this resource. Thus, dead capital is a resource that people cannot readily allocate to its *most efficient* use. As economists have dug deeper into the difficulties confronting residents of the world's poorest nations, they have found that dead capital is among the most significant impediments to growth of per capita incomes in these countries.

Dead capital
Any capital resource that lacks clear title of ownership.

Dead Capital and Inefficient Production

Physical structures used to house both business operations and labor resources are forms of capital goods. Current estimates indicate that unofficial, nontransferrable physical structures valued at more than $9 trillion are found in developing nations around the world. Because people in developing countries do not officially own this huge volume of capital goods, they cannot easily trade these resources. Thus, it is hard for many of the world's people to use capital goods in ways that will yield the largest feasible output of goods and services.

Consider, for instance, a hypothetical situation faced by an individual in Cairo, Egypt, a city in which an estimated 90 percent of all physical structures are unofficially owned. Suppose this person unofficially owns a run-down apartment building but has no official title of ownership for this structure. Also suppose that the building is better suited for use as a distribution center for a new import-export firm. The individual would like to sell or lease the structure to the new firm, but because he does not formally own the building, he is unable to do so. If the costs of obtaining formal title to the property are sufficiently high relative to the potential benefit—as they apparently are at present for about 9 out of every 10 Cairo businesses and households—this individual's capital resource will likely not be allocated to its highest-valued use.

This example illustrates a basic problem of dead capital. People who unofficially own capital goods are commonly constrained in their ability to use them efficiently. As a result, large quantities of capital goods throughout the developing world are inefficiently employed.

Dead Capital and Economic Growth

Recall from Chapter 2 that when we take into account production choices over time, any society faces a trade-off between consumption goods and capital goods. Whenever we make a choice to produce more consumption goods today, we incur an opportunity cost of fewer goods in the future. This means that when we make a choice to aim for more future economic growth to permit consumption of more goods in the future, we must allocate more resources to producing capital goods today. This entails incurring an opportunity cost today because society must allocate fewer resources to the current production of consumption goods.

This growth trade-off applies to any society, whether in a highly industrialized nation or a developing country. In a developing country, however, the inefficiencies of dead capital greatly reduce the rate of return on investment by individuals and firms. The resulting disincentives to invest in new capital goods can greatly hinder economic growth.

Government Inefficiencies, Investment, and Growth. A major factor contributing to the problem of dead capital in many developing nations is significant and often highly inefficient government regulation. Governments in many of the world's poorest nations place tremendous obstacles in the way of entrepreneurs interested in owning capital goods and directing them to profitable opportunities.

In addition to creating a problem with dead capital, overzealously administered government regulations that impede private resource allocation tend to reduce investment in new capital goods. If newly produced capital goods cannot be easily devoted to their most efficient uses, there is less incentive to invest. In a nation with a stifling government bureaucracy regulating the uses of capital goods, newly created capital will all too likely become dead capital.

Thus, government inefficiency can be a major barrier to economic growth. Figure 19-2 depicts the relationship between average growth of per capita incomes and index measures of governmental inefficiency for various nations. As you can see, the economies of countries

> **ECONOMICS FRONT AND CENTER**
>
> To think about how government inefficiencies can affect an actual business, contemplate **Trying to Start a Business in Kenya,** on page 492.

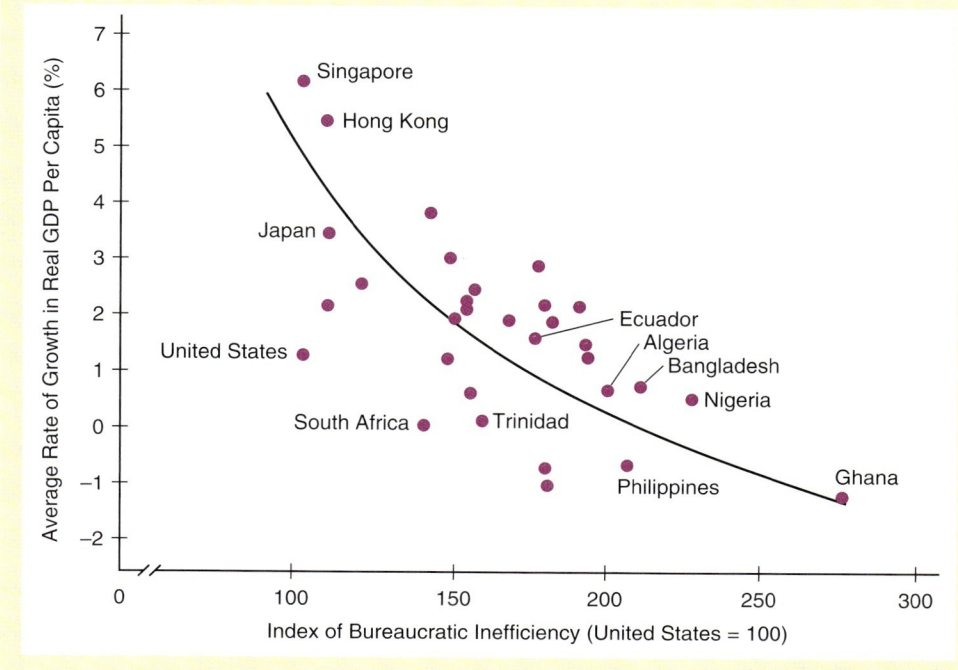

FIGURE 19-2

Bureaucratic Inefficiency and Economic Growth

Inefficiencies in government bureaucracies reduce the incentive to invest and thereby detract from economic growth.

Sources: International Monetary Fund; World Bank.

with less efficient governments tend to grow at relatively slower rates. The reason is that bureaucratic inefficiencies in these nations complicate efforts to direct capital goods to their most efficient uses.

QUICK QUIZ

Dead capital is a capital resource without clear title of _____. It is difficult for a buyer to trade, insure, or maintain a right to use dead capital.

The inability to put dead capital to its most efficient use contributes to _____ economic growth, particularly in _____ nations, where dead capital can be a relatively large portion of total capital goods.

Inefficient government _____ contribute to the dead capital problem, which reduces the incentive to invest in additional capital goods.

See page 499 for the answers. Review concepts from this section in MyEconLab.

PRIVATE INTERNATIONAL FINANCIAL FLOWS AS A SOURCE OF GLOBAL GROWTH

Given the large volume of inefficiently employed capital goods in developing nations, what can be done to promote greater global growth? One approach is to rely on private markets to find ways to direct capital goods toward their best uses in most nations. Another is to entrust the world's governments with the task of developing and implementing policies that enhance economic growth in developing nations. Let's begin by considering the market-based approach to promoting global growth.

Private Investment in Developing Nations

Each year since 1995, at least $150 billion in private funds have flowed to developing nations in the form of loans or purchases of bonds or stock. Of course, from year to year, international investors fail to renew loans to many developing nations and sell off quantities of bonds and stocks issued by these countries. When these international outflows of funds are taken into account, the *net* flows of funds to developing countries have averaged just over $100 billion per year since 1995. This is equivalent to more than one-tenth of the annual net investment that takes place within the United States.

Nearly all the funds that flow into developing countries do so to finance investment projects in those nations. Economists group these international flows of investment funds into three categories. One is loans from banks and other sources. The second is **portfolio investment,** or purchases of less than 10 percent of the shares of ownership in a company. The third is **foreign direct investment,** or the acquisition of sufficient stocks to obtain more than a 10 percent share of a firm's ownership.

Figure 19-3 displays percentages of each type of international investment financing provided to developing nations since the mid-1970s. As you can see, three decades ago, bank loans accounted for the bulk of international funding of investment in the world's less developed nations. Today, direct ownership shares in the form of portfolio investment and foreign direct investment account for most international investment financing.

Portfolio investment
The purchase of less than 10 percent of the shares of ownership in a company in another nation.

Foreign direct investment
The acquisition of more than 10 percent of the shares of ownership in a company in another nation.

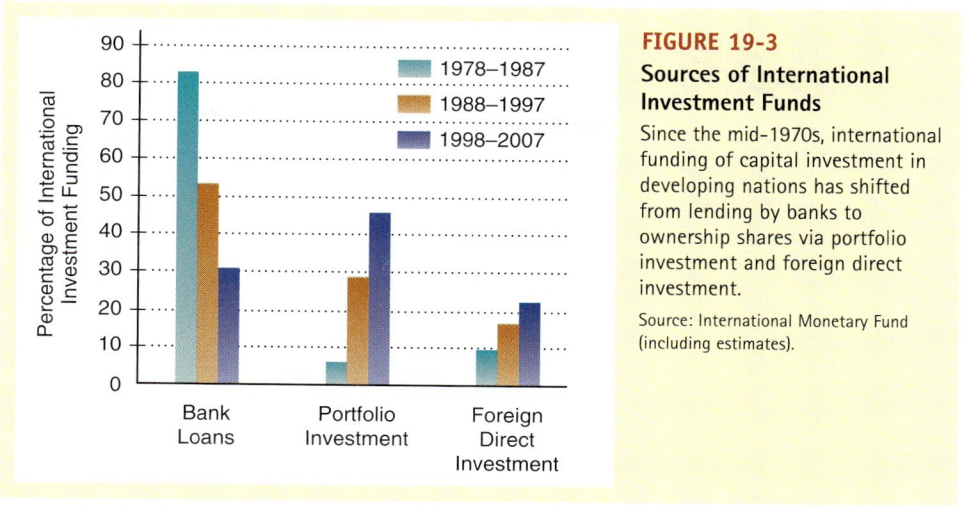

FIGURE 19-3

Sources of International Investment Funds

Since the mid-1970s, international funding of capital investment in developing nations has shifted from lending by banks to ownership shares via portfolio investment and foreign direct investment.

Source: International Monetary Fund (including estimates).

Obstacles to International Investment

There is an important difficulty with depending on international flows of funds to finance capital investment in developing nations. The markets for loans, bonds, and stocks in developing countries are particularly susceptible to problems relating to *asymmetric information* (see Chapter 15). International investors are well aware of the informational problems to which they are exposed in developing nations, so many stand ready to withdraw their financial support at a moment's notice.

Asymmetric Information as a Barrier to Financing Global Growth. Recall from Chapter 15 that asymmetric information in financial markets exists when institutions that make loans or investors who hold bonds or stocks have less information than those who seek to use the funds. *Adverse selection* problems arise when those who wish to obtain funds for the least worthy projects are among those who attempt to borrow or issue bonds or stocks. If banks and investors have trouble identifying these higher-risk individuals and firms, they may be less willing to channel funds to even creditworthy borrowers. Another asymmetric information problem is *moral hazard*. This is the potential for recipients of funds to engage in riskier behavior after receiving financing.

In light of the adverse selection problem, anyone thinking about funding a business endeavor in any locale must study the firm carefully before extending financial support. The potential for moral hazard requires a lender to a firm or someone who has purchased the firm's bonds or stock to continue to monitor the company's performance after providing financial support.

By definition, financial intermediation is still relatively undeveloped in less advanced regions of the world. Consequently, individuals interested in financing potentially profitable investments in developing nations typically cannot rely on financial intermediaries based in these countries. Asymmetric information problems may be so great in some developing nations that very few private lenders or investors will wish to direct their funds to worthy capital investment projects. In some countries, therefore, concerns about adverse selection and moral hazard can be a significant obstacle to economic growth.

To what countries do most residents of developing nations allocate the majority of their own foreign direct investment? See the next page.

For a link to an Asian Development Bank analysis of the effects of foreign direct investment on developing nations, go to
www.econtoday.com/ch19.

INTERNATIONAL EXAMPLE

Investing in the Usual Places

Worldwide, inflows of foreign direct investment have declined during the 2000s, from $1.4 trillion in 2000 to less than half that amount today. Residents of developing nations, however, have increased *their own* foreign direct investment in highly developed nations by 250 percent since 2000, to more than $50 billion. At present, more than two-thirds of the funds that residents of developing nations allocate to foreign direct investment go to the United States, Japan, and nations that are part of the European Monetary Union.

FOR CRITICAL ANALYSIS
Why do you think that residents of developing nations might prefer to allocate some of their investments to developed nations instead of investing at home or in other developing countries?

Incomplete Information and International Financial Crises. Those who are willing to contemplate making loans or buying bonds or stocks issued in developing nations must either do their own careful homework or follow the example of other lenders or investors whom they regard as better informed. Many relatively unsophisticated lenders and investors, such as relatively small banks and individual savers, rely on larger lenders and investors to evaluate risks in developing nations.

This has led some economists to suggest that a follow-the-leader mentality can influence international flows of funds. In extreme cases, they contend, the result can be an **international financial crisis.** This is a situation in which lenders rapidly withdraw loans made to residents of developing nations and investors sell off bonds and stocks issued by firms and governments in those countries. An international financial crisis occurred during the 1980s, for instance, following a severe drop in bank lending that affected many South American nations. Today, the growth prospects of a number of developing nations continue to be in doubt in the wake of international financial crises that took place in Southeast Asia, Central Asia, and Latin America in the late 1990s and early 2000s. This undoubtedly helps explain why there has been a decline in flows of private funds to developing countries in recent years.

International financial crisis
The rapid withdrawal of foreign investments and loans from a nation.

QUICK QUIZ

The three main categories of international flows of investment funds are loans by _____, _____ investment that involves purchasing less than 10 percent of the shares of ownership in a company, and _____ _____ investment that involves purchasing more than 10 percent of a company's ownership shares.

On net, an average of about $_____ billion in international investment funds flows to developing nations each year. In years past, bank loans were the source of most foreign funding of investment in developing countries, but recently _____ investment and _____ _____ investment have predominated.

Obstacles to private financing of capital accumulation and growth in developing nations include _____ _____ and _____ _____ problems caused by asymmetric information, which can restrain and sometimes destabilize private flows of funds.

See page 499 for the answers. Review concepts from this section in MyEconLab.

INTERNATIONAL INSTITUTIONS AND POLICIES FOR GLOBAL GROWTH

There has long been a recognition that adverse selection and moral hazard problems can both reduce international flows of private funds to developing nations and make these flows relatively variable. Since 1945, the world's governments have taken an active role in supplementing private markets. Two international institutions, the World Bank and the International Monetary Fund, have been at the center of government-directed efforts to attain higher rates of global economic growth.

The World Bank

The **World Bank** specializes in extending relatively long-term loans for capital investment projects that otherwise might not receive private financial support. When the World Bank was first formed in 1945, it provided assistance in the post–World War II rebuilding period. In the 1960s, the World Bank broadened its mission by widening its scope to encompass global antipoverty efforts.

Today, the World Bank makes loans solely to about 100 developing nations containing roughly half the world's population. Governments and firms in these countries typically seek loans from the World Bank to finance specific projects, such as improved irrigation systems, road improvements, and better hospitals.

The World Bank is actually composed of five separate institutions: the International Development Association, the International Bank for Reconstruction and Development, the International Finance Corporation, the Multinational Investment Guarantee Agency, and the International Center for Settlement of Investment Disputes. These World Bank organizations each have between 137 and 182 member nations, and on their behalf, the approximately 10,000 people employed by World Bank institutions coordinate the funding of investment activities undertaken by various governments and private firms in developing nations. Figure 19-4 displays the current regional distribution of nearly $20 billion in World Bank lending. Governments of the world's wealthiest countries provide most of the funds that the World Bank lends each year, although the World Bank also raises some of its funds in private financial markets.

World Bank
A multinational agency that specializes in making loans to about 100 developing nations in an effort to promote their long-term development and growth.

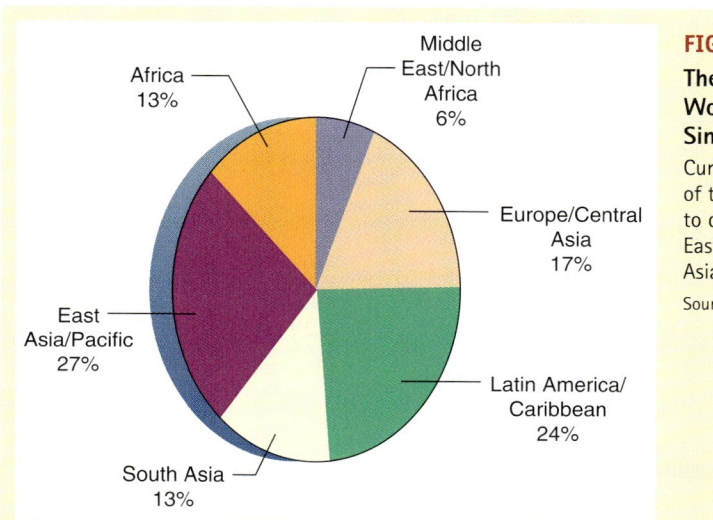

FIGURE 19-4

The Distribution of World Bank Lending Since 1990

Currently, about 40 percent of the World Bank's loans go to developing nations in the East Asia/Pacific and South Asia regions.

Source: World Bank.

The International Monetary Fund

International Monetary Fund (IMF)
A multinational organization that aims to promote world economic growth through more financial stability.

Quota subscription
A nation's account with the International Monetary Fund, denominated in special drawing rights.

The **International Monetary Fund (IMF)** is an international organization that aims to promote global economic growth by fostering financial stability. At present, the IMF has more than 180 member nations.

When a country joins the IMF, it deposits funds to an account called its **quota subscription.** These funds are measured in terms of an international unit of accounting called *special drawing rights* (*SDRs*), which have a value based on a weighted average of a basket of four key currencies: the euro, the pound sterling, the yen, and the dollar. At present, one SDR is equivalent to just under $1.50.

Special drawing rights form a pool of funds from which the IMF can draw to lend to members. Figure 19-5 displays current quota subscriptions for selected IMF member nations.

The IMF sets each nation's quota subscription based on the country's national income. The quota subscription determines how much a member can borrow from the IMF under the organization's standard credit arrangements. It also determines the member's share of voting power within the IMF. The U.S. quota subscription is just over 17 percent of the total funds provided by all member nations, so the U.S. government has an IMF voting share equal to that percentage.

The IMF assists developing nations primarily by making loans to their governments. Originally, the IMF's primary function was to provide so-called stand-by arrangements and short-term credits, and it continues to offer these forms of assistance.

After the 1970s, however, nations' demands for short-term credit declined, and the IMF adapted by expanding its other lending programs. It now provides certain types of credit directly to poor and heavily indebted countries, either as long-term loans intended to support growth-promoting projects or as short- or long-term assistance aimed at helping countries experiencing problems in repaying existing debts. Under these funding programs, the IMF seeks to assist any qualifying member experiencing an unusual fluctuation in exports or imports, a loss of confidence in its own financial system, or spillover effects from financial problems originating elsewhere.

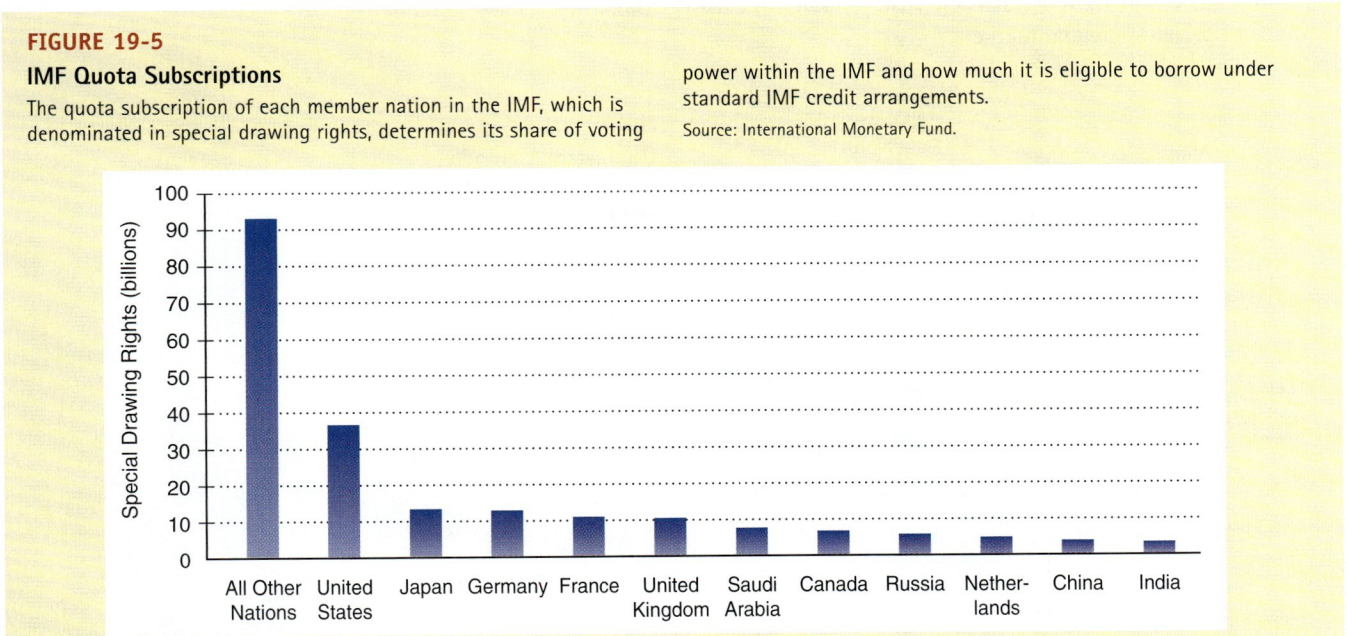

FIGURE 19-5

IMF Quota Subscriptions

The quota subscription of each member nation in the IMF, which is denominated in special drawing rights, determines its share of voting power within the IMF and how much it is eligible to borrow under standard IMF credit arrangements.

Source: International Monetary Fund.

The World Bank and the IMF: Part of the Solution or Part of the Problem?

Among the World Bank's client nations, meager economic growth in recent decades shows up in numerous ways. The average resident in a nation receiving World Bank assistance lives on less than $2 per day. Hundreds of millions of people in nations receiving its financial support will never attend school, and about 40,000 people in these countries die of preventable diseases every day. Thus, there is an enormous range of areas where World Bank funds might be put to use.

The International Monetary Fund also continues to deal with an ongoing string of major international financial crisis situations. Countries most notably involved in such crises have included Mexico in 1995; Thailand, Indonesia, Malaysia, and South Korea in 1997; Russia in 1998; Brazil in 1999 and 2000; Turkey in 2001; and Argentina in 2001 and 2002.

Naturally, officials of both organizations conclude that world economic growth would have been even lower and financial instability even greater if the institutions did not exist. In recent years, however, economists have increasingly questioned World Bank and IMF policymaking.

Does the World Bank Really Have a Mission Anymore?

In some nations, particularly in Africa, attracting private investment has proved difficult. Consequently, the World Bank has been a key source of credit for these nations. Nevertheless, as Figure 19-4 on page 487 indicates, only about 13 percent of lending by the World Bank since 1990 has been directed to African countries.

The World Bank's official mission is to make loans to developing nations that fund projects incapable of attracting private financing from investors at home or abroad. Nevertheless, the World Bank makes many of its loans to nations that have little trouble attracting private funds, such as rapidly growing Asian countries. Critics of such loans argue that they often interfere with the private market for capital goods and encourage the kind of inefficient investment that contributed to Asia's economic woes in the late 1990s and to Argentina's financial collapse in the early 2000s.

Some observers also contend that a number of countries that receive World Bank funds are inappropriate recipients of development assistance. For instance, China has reserves of currencies of other nations exceeding $400 billion, and its residents are net *lenders* of funds to other nations of the world. Nevertheless, the Chinese government and Chinese companies annually borrow between $2 billion and $3 billion from the World Bank.

Asymmetric Information and the World Bank and IMF.

Like any other lenders, the World Bank and IMF encounter adverse selection and moral hazard problems. In an effort to address these problems, both institutions impose conditions that borrowers must meet to receive funds.

Officials of these organizations do not publicly announce all terms of lending agreements, however, so it is largely up to the organizations to monitor whether borrower nations are wisely using funds donated by other countries. In addition, the World Bank and IMF tend to place very imprecise initial conditions on the loans they extend. They typically toughen conditions only after a borrowing nation has violated the original arrangement. By giving nations that are most likely to try to take advantage of vague conditions a greater incentive to seek funding, this policy worsens the adverse selection problem the World Bank and IMF face.

Some policymakers, economists, and other observers contend that the policies of the World Bank and the IMF have contributed to international financial crises. They argue that when the World Bank and the IMF provide subsidized credit for industries and governments, private lenders and investors anticipate that these two institutions will back up nations' debts. Thus, private lenders and investors may lower their standards and make loans to, and buy bonds and stocks from, less creditworthy borrowers. Furthermore, if governments know that they can apply for World Bank and IMF assistance in the event of widespread financial failures, they have little incentive to rein in risky business practices.

Rethinking Long-Term Development Lending.

Since the early 1990s, one of the main themes of development economics has been the reform of market processes in developing nations. Markets work better at promoting growth when a developing nation has more effective institutions, such as basic property rights, well-run legal systems, and uncorrupt government agencies.

Hence, there is considerable agreement that a top priority of the World Bank and the IMF should be to identify ways to put basic market foundations into place by guaranteeing property and contract rights. This requires constructing legal systems that can credibly enforce laws protecting these rights. Another key requirement is simplifying the processes for putting capital goods to work in developing countries.

A fundamental issue is what, if anything, international organizations such as the World Bank and the IMF can do to promote pro-growth institutional improvements in developing nations. From one standpoint, there may be little that the World Bank and the IMF can accomplish. After all, the forms of national legal institutions are largely political matters for the nations' leaders to decide. Nevertheless, a number of economists have suggested that the World Bank and the IMF should adopt strict policies against countries with institutional structures that fail to promote individual property rights, law enforcement, and anti-corruption efforts. This would, they argue, give countries an incentive to shape up their institutional structures.

Other economists, in contrast, advocate direct financial assistance to governments attempting to implement such institutional reforms. Funds put to such use, they argue, could compensate those who lose power as a result of reform efforts, when shifting to a more capitalist system takes away a ruling group's dictatorial powers to control national resources. Such financial assistance could also help fund investments required to make reforms work. Those proposing this more active role for international lenders contend that the result could be much larger long-term returns for borrowing and lending nations alike. They argue that the overall return would be much greater than the sum of piecemeal payoffs from such projects as dams, power plants, and bridges.

How might "catastrophe bonds" help assist residents of poor nations suffering from droughts?

INTERNATIONAL POLICY EXAMPLE

Using Catastrophe Bonds to Aid Drought-Stricken Nations

First, the rains come to a halt. Then the harvest fails. Next, people begin going hungry. After a while, television cameras arrive. Donors in high-income nations, moved by pictures of malnourished children, send funds or lobby national governments and multinational agencies to provide assistance. But the assistance begins to flow only when people start to die. All too often, this scenario plays out over and over in poorer regions of the world subject to unpredictable weather changes that generate sudden droughts.

The World Food Program (WFP), an agency of the United Nations, is poised to implement a program that will rely on *catastrophe bonds* to help when droughts take place. The WFP will issue annual bonds to private investors, who will receive back both their principal and interest paid at above-market rates in years when rainfall in specific nations is above drought levels. In years when rainfall suddenly drops below drought levels, however, holders of catastrophe bonds will lose both their principal and interest. The WFP will then direct those funds to provide immediate assistance to all affected countries.

FOR CRITICAL ANALYSIS

In principle, could catastrophe bonds or even famine insurance policies for nations adversely affected by droughts replace other forms of aid and lending, such as World Bank and other assistance programs?

CHAPTER 19 Policies and Prospects for Global Economic Growth

Alternative Institutional Structures for Limiting Financial Crises. There are also different views on the appropriate role for the International Monetary Fund in anticipating and reacting to international financial crises. In recent years, economists have advanced a wide variety of proposals. Many of these proposals share common features, such as more frequent and in-depth releases of information both by the IMF and by countries that borrow from this institution. Nearly all economists also recommend improved financial and accounting standards for those receiving funds from multinational lenders, as well as other changes that might help reduce moral hazard problems in IMF lending.

Nevertheless, many of the proposals for change diverge sharply. The IMF and its supporters have proposed maintaining its current structure but working harder to develop so-called early warning systems of financial crises so that aid can be provided to head off crises before they develop. Some economists have proposed establishing an international system of rules restricting capital outflows that might threaten international fianancial stability.

Other economists call for more dramatic changes. For instance, one proposal suggests creating a board composed of finance ministers of member nations directly in charge of day-to-day management of the IMF. Another suggests providing government incentives, in the form of tax breaks and subsidies, for increased private-sector lending that would supplement or even replace loans now made by the IMF.

To learn about the International Monetary Fund's view on its role in international financial crises, go to www.econtoday.com/ch19.

Time to Replace the World Bank and the IMF? A few economists have called for completely eliminating both the World Bank and the IMF. Even economists who think these institutions should disappear, however, disagree on what should replace them. On the one hand, a proposal calls for reducing the current scope of government involvement in multinational lending by replacing the World Bank and the IMF with a single institution that would make only short-term loans to countries experiencing temporary financial difficulties. On the other hand, another proposal suggests broadening the roles of governments by developing a "global central bank" that would engage in open market operations using funds raised from new international taxes and other government funds.

So far, few proposals for altering the international financial architecture have led to actual change. The IMF has adopted some minor changes in its procedures for collecting and releasing information, and it has stiffened some of the financial and accounting standards that borrowers must follow to obtain credit. Naturally, the member nations of the IMF would have to agree to the adoption of more dramatic proposals for change. To date there has been little movement in this direction. Undoubtedly, consideration of proposals for an altered international financial structure will continue to generate global debate in the years to come.

QUICK QUIZ

The **World Bank** is an umbrella institution for _____ international organizations, each of which has more than 130 member nations, which coordinate _____-term loans to governments and private firms in developing nations.

The **International Monetary Fund** is an organization with more than 180 member nations. It coordinates mainly _____-term and some longer-term financial assistance to developing nations in an effort to _____ international flows of funds.

In principle, the World Bank's role is to provide loans to developing countries where _____ _____ problems deter private investment. But in recent years, the World Bank has provided funds to countries and companies that could have obtained financing from private investors.

Like other lenders, the World Bank and the IMF confront _____ _____ and _____ _____ problems. Some observers worry that failure to deal with these problems has actually contributed to a string of international financial crises. Recently, there have been suggestions that both institutions should impose tougher preconditions on borrowers, such as requiring internal reforms that promote domestic investment.

See page 499 for the answers. Review concepts from this section in MyEconLab.

CASE STUDY: ECONOMICS FRONT AND CENTER

Trying to Start a Business in Kenya

Pillay is frustrated. She has developed a plan for a new wireless phone company in Kenya and has received financial support from a U.S. firm interested in establishing a presence in her nation. Nevertheless, after seven months and visits to nine government agencies, she still lacks official approval even to open the doors of her now fully equipped office in Nairobi.

Pillay just completed her ninth agency visit a few minutes ago. There, she learned that no action had been taken on her documents requesting to sell phone services because a government bureaucrat felt that the headings on the new company's proposed invoices should be in a different typeface. Now she must have new invoices printed before the official will sign her form. During their discussion, Pillay learned that the official is about to leave on a one-month vacation. Thus, she knows there is not a moment to lose, because this single bureaucrat is the only official in Nairobi who is authorized to act on her application.

Pillay recently read that Kenya's ranking as an attractive location for investment has slipped relative to other African nations. She thinks she has a good idea why the country's relative position has been declining.

CRITICAL ANALYSIS QUESTIONS

1. *How can bureaucratic inefficiencies that make regulations difficult to discern and follow and that impede adherence to the rule of law slow the pace of a nation's economic growth?*

2. *What is true of all the capital equipment located in Pillay's as-yet-unopened Nairobi office?*

Issues and Applications

Bogging Down Business in Brazil

Brazil's legal system, which is based on a 245-article constitution that is among the world's lengthiest and includes a labor law containing 922 articles, is perhaps the most complicated in the Western Hemisphere. This helps explain why the average time required for a firm to resolve a legal dispute is 81 weeks, which is 36 weeks longer than in the United States. Laying off a worker requires a Brazilian business to incur an expense equivalent to paying the worker for 165 weeks, whereas a U.S. firm normally faces a layoff expense no greater than 8 weeks' worth of wage payments to the employee.

Concepts Applied
- Foreign Direct Investment
- International Monetary Fund
- World Bank

Losing Ground with Private Investors

In spite of the legal quagmires faced by companies trying to do business in Brazil, since the mid-1990s the nation has attracted more than $200 billion in foreign direct investment. Nevertheless, by the early 2000s nearly half of all individuals and firms that had funneled funds to Brazil discovered that the higher costs of doing business amid a labyrinth of legal hurdles had made their investments unprofitable.

Since 2000, international investors have been more hesitant to allocate funds to Brazilian business projects. As a consequence, annual inflows of foreign direct investment to Brazil have dropped to an average of $12 billion, or less than half the average annual inflow in the late 1990s.

The World Bank Steps In

For years, Brazil's government has been the recipient of long-term loans from the World Bank. Cyclical waves of financial breakdowns and crises have also led the nation's government to seek shorter-term loans from the International Monetary Fund from time to time, mainly to allow the government to repay its World Bank loans.

Recently, the World Bank has sought to break this cycle by granting loans aimed at promoting Brazilian business formation. The World Bank has committed to providing the Brazilian government with more than $500 million in so-called *competitiveness loans*. The government is directing a portion of these loans to reforming business-registration requirements, which have been known to slow approval of a firm's formation if its invoices have margins a few millimeters off from approved dimensions.

A Help or Hindrance to Brazilian Economic Progress?

Nevertheless, most observers agree that Brazil, which within a decade has dropped from the world's eighth largest economy to its fifteenth largest, will fail to experience significant economic growth if it does not reform its legal system. A country where bankruptcy filings require 10 years to adjudicate and the number of labor lawsuits faced by most firms exceeds the number of employed workers, critics contend, should not receive World Bank support.

Indeed, some critics of the World Bank's competitiveness loans worry that the willingness of the World Bank to step in after private investors have backed out reduces the incentive for Brazil's government to engage in legal reform. The end result of World Bank credits and IMF bailouts, they worry, may be a perpetuation of Brazil's legal labyrinth.

Log in to MyEconLab, click on "Economic News," and test your understanding of the chapter by answering interactive questions that relate directly to this issue.

For Critical Analysis

1. During the time that it takes for entrepreneurs legally to register a business with the Brazilian government, the entrepreneurs cannot legally utilize their capital investment to seek profits, nor can they sell their capital investment. Within this period, what is true of their capital?
2. Recently, a Brazilian court clerk made a mathematical error that translated into a *$56 trillion* (more than four and a half times U.S. GDP in that year) legal judgment against a German airline. The Brazilian legal system took seven years to correct the mistake. Why might such legal inefficiencies detract from Brazil's growth prospects?

Web Resources

1. To learn more about Brazil's complicated legal system, go to www.econtoday.com/ch19.
2. For a review of labor law issues that foreign investors must consider when buying shares in firms in Brazil, go to www.econtoday.com/ch19.

Research Project

Suppose that you are a co-owner of a business that is considering opening a production facility in one of three countries: the Czech Republic, China, or Brazil. After some research, you learn that registering a business in the Czech Republic and China takes about 40 days, but doing so in Brazil takes 152 days. In China and the Czech Republic, a typical court case, which businesses commonly face in any country, takes between 250 and 300 days, whereas 566 days are required in Brazil. The cost of firing a worker in the Czech Republic and China is less than half the cost of terminating a worker in Brazil. In light of these facts and any others you are able to uncover in your own research into Brazil's legal climate for business, evaluate how the legal climate provides economic disincentives to invest in Brazil.

Here is what you should know after reading this chapter. MyEconLab will help you identify what you know, and where to go when you need to practice.

WHAT YOU SHOULD KNOW **WHERE TO GO TO PRACTICE**

Effects of Population Growth and Personal Freedoms on Economic Growth Increased population growth has contradictory effects on economic growth. On the one hand, for a

WHAT YOU SHOULD KNOW		WHERE TO GO TO PRACTICE
given growth rate of real GDP, increased population growth tends to reduce growth of per capita real GDP. On the other hand, if increased population growth is accompanied by higher labor productivity, the growth rate of real GDP can increase. The net effect can be an increase in the growth rate of per capita GDP. Greater political freedoms do not necessarily contribute to higher rates of economic growth, but there is evidence of a positive relationship between the extent of economic freedom and the rate of growth of per capita real GDP.	economic freedom, 480 **Key figure** Figure 19-1, 481	• **MyEconLab** Study Plan 19.1 • Audio introduction to Chapter 19 • Animated Figure 19-1
Why Dead Capital Deters Investment and Slows Economic Growth Relatively few people in less developed countries establish legal ownership of capital goods. These unofficially owned resources are known as dead capital. Inability to trade, insure, and enforce rights to dead capital make it difficult for unofficial owners to use these resources most efficiently. As a result, in many developing nations, there is a disincentive to accumulate capital, which tends to limit their economic growth prospects.	dead capital, 482	• **MyEconLab** Study Plan 19.2
Government Inefficiencies and Dead Capital in Developing Nations In many developing nations, government regulations and red tape impose very high costs on those who officially register capital ownership. The dead capital problem that these government inefficiencies create reduces investment and growth. This helps explain why there is a negative relationship between measures of government inefficiency and economic growth.	dead capital, 482 **Key figure** Figure 19-2, 483	• **MyEconLab** Study Plan 19.2 • Animated Figure 19-2

Sources of International Investment Funds and Obstacles to Investing in Developing Nations International flows of funds to developing nations can potentially do much to promote global economic growth. There are three basic categories of these flows of funds: (1) bank loans, (2) portfolio investment, or purchases of less than 10 percent of the shares of ownership in a company, and (3) foreign direct investment, or purchases of more than 10 percent of the shares of ownership in a company. Problems relating to asymmetric information, such as adverse selection and moral hazard problems, are likely to be particularly acute in developing nations. Thus, asymmetric information problems present obstacles to international flows of funds to developing nations.	portfolio investment, 484
	foreign direct
	  investment, 484
	international financial
	  crisis, 486
	Key figure
	  Figure 19-3, 485
		• **MyEconLab** Study Plan 19.3
		• Animated Figure 19-3

The Functions of the World Bank and the International Monetary Fund Adverse selection and moral hazard problems faced by private investors can both limit and		

WHAT YOU SHOULD KNOW

destabilize international flows of funds to developing countries. The World Bank's function is to finance capital investment in countries that have trouble attracting funds from private individuals and firms. A fundamental duty of the International Monetary Fund is to stabilize international financial flows by extending loans to countries caught up in international financial crises.

World Bank, 487
International Monetary Fund (IMF), 488
quota subscription, 488
Key figure
Figure 19-5, 488

WHERE TO GO TO PRACTICE

- **MyEconLab** Study Plan 19.4
- Animated Figure 19-5

The Basis for Recent Criticisms of World Bank and IMF Policymaking Even though the World Bank's fundamental role is to make loans to developing countries that receive little private investment financing, recently it has extended credit to companies and governments that could have obtained funds in private loan markets. Critics also contend that the World Bank and the IMF have failed to deal effectively with the adverse selection and moral hazard problems they face. These critics suggest that the World Bank and the IMF should place more stringent conditions on access to credit, including requiring government borrowers to implement reforms that give domestic residents more incentive to invest.

World Bank, 487
International Monetary Fund (IMF), 488

- **MyEconLab** Study Plan 19.4

Log in to MyEconLab, take a chapter test, and get a personalized Study Plan that tells you which concepts you understand and which ones you need to review. From there, MyEconLab will give you further practice, tutorials, animations, videos, and guided solutions.

Log in to www.myeconlab.com

PROBLEMS

Select problems, indicated by a blue oval, are assignable in MyEconLab.
Answers to the odd-numbered problems appear at the back of the book.

19-1 A country's real GDP is growing at an annual rate of 3.1 percent, and the current rate of growth of per capita real GDP is 0.3 percent. What is the population growth rate in this nation?

19-2 The annual rate of growth of real GDP in a developing nation is 0.3 percent. Initially, the country's population was stable from year to year. Recently, however, a significant increase in the nation's birthrate has raised the annual rate of population growth to 0.5 percent.

a. What was the rate of growth of per capita real GDP before the increase in population growth?

b. If the rate of growth of real GDP remains unchanged, what is the new rate of growth of per capita real GDP following the increase in the birthrate?

19-3 During the 1990s, the average rate of growth of per capita real GDP in a developing country was 0.1 percent per year. Its average annual rate of population growth was 2.2 percent.

a. What was the average annual rate of growth of real GDP in this nation during the 1990s?

b. So far in the 2000s, a steady inflow of immigrants has caused the average annual rate of population growth to rise to 2.7 percent. If we assume that the average annual rate of growth of real GDP has remained unchanged, what has the average annual rate of per capita real GDP growth been during the 2000s?

c. Suppose that in fact a number of immigrants have found employment and contributed to a 0.8-percentage-point increase in the average annual rate of growth of the nation's real GDP. Given this additional information, what has been the net average rate of growth of per capita real GDP during the 2000s?

19-4 A developing country has determined that each additional $1 billion of investment in capital goods adds 0.01 percentage point to its long-run average annual rate of growth of per capita real GDP.

a. Domestic entrepreneurs recently began to seek official approval to open a range of businesses employing capital resources valued at $20 billion. If the entrepreneurs undertake these investments, by what fraction of a percentage point will the nation's long-run average annual rate of growth of per capita real GDP increase, other things being equal?

b. After weeks of effort trying to complete the first of 15 stages of bureaucratic red tape necessary to obtain authorization to start their businesses, a number of entrepreneurs decide to drop their investment plans completely, and the amount of official investment that actually takes place turns out to be $10 billion. Other things being equal, by what fraction of a percentage point will this decision reduce the nation's long-run average annual rate of growth of per capita real GDP from what it would have been if investment had been $20 billion?

19-5 Consider the estimates that the World Bank has assembled for the following nations:

Country	Legal Steps Required to Start a Business	Days Required to Start a Business	Cost of Starting a Business as a Percentage of Per Capita GDP
Angola	14	146	838%
Bosnia-Herzegovina	12	59	52%
Morocco	11	36	19%
Togo	14	63	281%
Uruguay	10	27	47%

Rank the nations in order starting with the one you would expect to have the highest rate of economic growth, other things being equal. Explain your reasoning.

19-6 The World Bank has also constructed index measures of the flexibility available to firms in hiring and firing workers. The higher the index number for the nation in the following table, the greater the degree of government regulation of the hiring and firing processes.

Country	Hiring Flexibility Index	Firing Flexibility Index
Brazil	78	68
Germany	63	45
Ireland	48	30
Mexico	81	70
Singapore	33	1
Yemen	33	28

Rank the nations in order starting with the one you would expect to have the highest rate of economic growth, other things being equal. Explain your reasoning.

19-7 Suppose that every $500 billion of dead capital reduces the average rate of growth in worldwide per capita real GDP by 0.1 percentage point. If there is $10 trillion in dead capital in the world, by how many percentage points does the existence of dead capital reduce average worldwide growth of per capita real GDP?

19-8 Assume that each $1 billion in investment in capital goods generates 0.3 percentage point of the average percentage rate of growth of per capita real GDP, given the nation's labor resources. Firms have been investing exactly $6 billion in capital goods each year, so the annual average rate of growth of per capita real GDP has been 1.8 percent. Now a government that fails to consistently adhere to the rule of law has come to power, and firms must make $100 million in bribe payments to gain official approval for every $1 billion in investment in capital goods. In response, companies cut back their total investment spending to $4 billion per year. If other things are equal and companies maintain this rate of investment, what will be the nation's new average annual rate of growth of per capita real GDP?

19-9 During the past year, several large banks extended $200 million in loans to the government and several firms in a developing nation. International investors also purchased $150 million in bonds and $350 million in stocks issued by domestic firms. Of the stocks that foreign investors purchased, $100 million were shares that amounted to less than a 10 percent interest in domestic firms. This was the first year this nation had ever permitted inflows of funds from abroad.

a. Based on the investment category definitions discussed in this chapter, what was the amount of portfolio investment in this nation during the past year?
b. What was the amount of foreign direct investment in this nation during the past year?

19-10 Last year, $100 million in outstanding bank loans to a developing nation's government were not renewed, and the developing nation's government paid off $50 million in maturing government bonds that had been held by foreign residents. During that year, however, a new group of banks participated in a $125 million loan to help finance a major government construction project in the capital city. Domestic firms also issued $50 million in bonds and $75 million in stocks to foreign investors. All of the stocks issued gave the foreign investors more than 10 percent shares of the domestic firms.

a. What was gross foreign investment in this nation last year?
b. What was net foreign investment in this nation last year?

19-11 Identify which of the following situations currently faced by international investors are examples of adverse selection and which are examples of moral hazard.

a. Among the governments of several developing countries that are attempting to issue new bonds this year, it is certain that a few will fail to collect taxes to repay the bonds when they mature. It is difficult, however, for investors considering buying government bonds to predict which governments will experience this problem.
b. Foreign investors are contemplating purchasing stock in a company that, unknown to them, may have failed to properly establish legal ownership over a crucial capital resource.
c. Companies in a less developed nation have already issued bonds to finance the purchase of new capital goods. After receiving the funds from the bond issue, however, the company's managers pay themselves large bonuses instead.
d. When the government of a developing nation received a bank loan three years ago, it ultimately repaid the loan but had to reschedule its payments after officials misused the funds for unworthy projects. Now the government, which still has many of the same officials, is trying to raise funds by issuing bonds to foreign investors, who must decide whether or not to purchase them.

19-12 Identify which of the following situations currently faced by the World Bank or the International Monetary Fund are examples of adverse selection and which are examples of moral hazard.

a. The World Bank has extended loans to the government of a developing country to finance construction of a canal with a certain future flow of earnings. Now, however, the government has decided to redirect those funds to build a casino that may or may not generate sufficient profits to allow the government to repay the loan.
b. The IMF is considering extending loans to several nations that failed to fully repay loans they received from the IMF during the past decade but now claim to be better credit risks. The IMF is not sure which of these nations are unlikely to fully repay new loans.
c. The IMF recently extended a loan to a government directed by democratically elected officials that would permit the nation to adjust to an abrupt reduction in private flows of funds from abroad. A coup has just occurred, however, in response to newly discovered corruption within the government's elected leadership. The new military dictator has announced tentative plans to disburse some of the funds in equal shares to all citizens.

19-13 For each of the following situations, explain which of the policy issues discussed in this chapter is associated with the stance the institution has taken.

a. The World Bank offers to make a loan to a company in an impoverished nation at a lower interest rate than the company had been about to agree to pay to borrow the same amount from a group of private banks.
b. The World Bank makes a loan to a company in a developing nation that has not yet received formal approval to operate there, even though the government approval process typically takes 15 months.
c. The IMF extends a loan to a developing nation's government, with no preconditions, to enable the government to make already overdue payments on a loan it had previously received from the World Bank.

19-14 For each of the following situations, explain which of the policy issues discussed in this chapter is associated with the stance the institution has taken.

a. The IMF extends a long-term loan to a nation's government to help it maintain publicly supported production of goods and services that the government otherwise would have turned over to private companies.

b. The World Bank makes a loan to companies in an impoverished nation in which government officials typically demand bribes equal to 50 percent of companies' profits before allowing them to engage in any new investment projects.

c. The IMF offers to make a loan to banks in a country in which the government's rulers commonly require banks to extend credit to finance high-risk investment projects headed by the rulers' friends and relatives.

19-15. Answer the following questions concerning proposals to reform long-term development lending programs currently offered by the IMF and World Bank.

a. Why might the World Bank face moral hazard problems if it were to offer to provide funds to governments that promise to allocate the funds to major institutional reforms aimed at enhancing economic growth?

b. How does the IMF face an adverse selection problem if it is considering making loans to governments in which the ruling parties have already shown predispositions to try to "buy" votes by creating expensive public programs in advance of elections? How might following an announced rule in which the IMF cuts off future loans to governments that engage in such activities reduce this problem and promote increased economic growth in nations that do receive IMF loans?

ECONOMICS ON THE NET

The International Monetary Fund The purpose of this exercise is to evaluate the IMF's role in promoting global economic growth.

Title: International Monetary Fund

Navigation: Go to the home page of the IMF on the Web at www.econtoday.com/ch19, and click on *About the IMF* in the left-hand column.

Application Read each entry, and then answer the question.

1. Click on the link at the top-middle of the Web page titled *Purposes of the IMF*. Which of these purposes are most directly related to promoting a higher rate of global economic growth? Are any related more indirectly to this goal?

2. Back up to *About the IMF*, and click on *Surveillance*. Based on this discussion, what type of asymmetric information problem does IMF surveillance attempt to address?

3. Back up to *About the IMF*, and click on *Financial Assistance*. Which IMF lending "facilities" appear to be aimed at maintaining stability of international flows of funds? Which appear to be longer-term loans similar to those extended by the World Bank?

For Group Study and Analysis The section titled *How Does the IMF Lend?* discusses interest rate terms applied to different groups of nations. What are the likely rationales for charging some nations lower interest rates than others? Are there any potential problems with this policy? (Hint: Consider the adverse selection and moral hazard problems faced by the IMF.)

ANSWERS TO QUICK QUIZZES

p. 482: (i) reduce; (ii) labor force . . . increase; (iii) political . . . economic
p. 484: (i) ownership; (ii) lower . . . developing; (iii) bureaucracies
p. 486: (i) banks . . . portfolio . . . foreign direct; (ii) 100 . . . portfolio . . . foreign direct; (iii) adverse selection . . . moral hazard
p. 491: (i) five . . . long; (ii) short . . . stabilize; (iii) asymmetric information; (iv) adverse selection . . . moral hazard

20 Consumer Choice

Learning Objectives

After reading this chapter, you should be able to:

1. Distinguish between total utility and marginal utility
2. Discuss why marginal utility at first rises but ultimately tends to decline as a person consumes more of a good or service
3. Explain why an individual's optimal choice of how much to consume of each good or service entails equalizing the marginal utility per dollar spent across all goods and services
4. Describe the substitution effect of a price change on the quantity demanded of a good or service
5. Understand how the real-income effect of a price change affects the quantity demanded of a good or service
6. Evaluate why the price of diamonds is so much higher than the price of water even though people cannot survive long without water

Passenger traffic at San Francisco International Airport has fallen by more than 15 percent since 2002, while about 30 percent more passengers have flown out of the nearby Oakland International Airport since that year. During the same period, passenger volumes at the Cleveland Hopkins International Airport have fallen by about 10 percent, but the volume of passengers served by Ohio's Akron-Canton Airport has risen by nearly 50 percent. These are just two examples of shifts in air travel away from facilities located in larger metropolitan areas to airports in smaller cities. In this chapter, you will learn about the theory of consumer choice, which helps to explain why this shift in air travel has taken place.

 MyEconLab helps you master each objective and study more efficiently. See end of chapter for details.

CHAPTER 20 Consumer Choice

Did You Know That...

during a typical year, manufacturers of consumer products introduce more than 30,000 new items, or more than twice as many as they did 20 years ago? Although most producers retire old products as they introduce new items, on net the variety of products available to consumers has increased. Hence there has been a proliferation of choices at U.S. grocery stores, which now stock an average of 40,000 items. Consumers today can choose among 16 flavors of frozen waffles; dozens of varieties of toothpaste; garbage bags with twist, drawstring, or handle ties; and wide varieties of other products.

In Chapter 3, you learned that a determinant of the quantity demanded of any particular item is the price of that item. The law of demand implies that at a lower overall price, there will be a higher quantity demanded. Understanding the derivation of the law of demand is useful because it allows us to examine the relevant variables, such as price, income, and tastes, in such a way as to make better sense of the world and even perhaps generate predictions about it. One way of deriving the law of demand involves an analysis of the logic of consumer choice in a world of limited resources. In this chapter, therefore, we discuss what is called *utility analysis*.

UTILITY THEORY

When you buy something, you do so because of the satisfaction you expect to receive from having and using that good. For everything that you like to have, the more you have of it, the higher the level of total satisfaction you receive. Another term that can be used for satisfaction is **utility**, or want-satisfying power. This property is common to all goods that are desired. The concept of utility is purely subjective, however. There is no way that you or I can measure the amount of utility that a consumer might be able to obtain from a particular good, for utility does not imply "useful" or "utilitarian" or "practical." For this reason, there can be no accurate scientific assessment of the utility that someone might receive by consuming a fast-food dinner or a movie relative to the utility that another person might receive from that same good or service.

The utility that individuals receive from consuming a good depends on their tastes and preferences. These tastes and preferences are normally assumed to be given and stable for a particular individual. An individual's tastes determine how much utility that individual derives from consuming a good, and this in turn determines how that individual allocates his or her income to purchases of that good. But we cannot explain why tastes are different between individuals. For example, we cannot explain why some people like yogurt but others do not.

We can analyze in terms of utility the way consumers decide what to buy, just as physicists have analyzed some of their problems in terms of what they call force. No physicist has ever seen a unit of force, and no economist has ever seen a unit of utility. In both cases, however, these concepts have proved useful for analysis.

Throughout this chapter, we will be discussing **utility analysis,** which is the analysis of consumer decision making based on utility maximization—that is, making choices with the aim of attaining the highest feasible satisfaction.

Utility
The want-satisfying power of a good or service.

Utility analysis
The analysis of consumer decision making based on utility maximization.

Utility and Utils

Economists once believed that utility could be measured. In fact, there is a philosophical school of thought based on utility theory called *utilitarianism,* developed by the English philosopher Jeremy Bentham (1748–1832). Bentham held that society should seek the

Util
A representative unit by which utility is measured.

greatest happiness for the greatest number. He sought to apply an arithmetic formula for measuring happiness. He and his followers developed the notion of measurable utility and invented the **util** to measure it. For the moment, we will also assume that we can measure satisfaction using this representative unit. Our assumption will allow us to quantify the way we examine consumer behavior. Thus, the first chocolate bar that you eat might yield you 4 utils of satisfaction; the first peanut cluster, 6 utils; and so on. Today, no one really believes that we can actually measure utils, but the ideas forthcoming from such analysis will prove useful in understanding how consumers choose among alternatives.

Total and Marginal Utility

Consider the satisfaction, or utility, that you receive each time that you download and listen to digital music albums. To make the example straightforward, let's say that there are hundreds of downloadable music albums to choose from each year and that each of them is of the same quality. Let's say that you normally download and listen to one music album per week. You could, of course, download two, or three, or four per week. Presumably, each time you download and listen to another music album per week, you will get additional satisfaction, or utility. The question, though, that we must ask is, given that you are already downloading and listening to one album per week, will the next one downloaded and listened to during that week give you the same amount of additional utility?

Marginal utility
The change in total utility due to a one-unit change in the quantity of a good or service consumed.

That additional, or incremental, utility is called **marginal utility**, where *marginal* means "incremental" or "additional." (Marginal changes also refer to decreases, in which cases we talk about *decremental* changes.) The concept of marginality is important in economics because people make decisions by comparing additional (marginal) benefits with additional (marginal) costs.

Applying Marginal Analysis to Utility

The example in Figure 20-1 will clarify the distinction between total utility and marginal utility. The table in panel (a) shows the total utility and the marginal utility of downloading and listening to digital music albums each week. Marginal utility is the difference between total utility derived from one level of consumption and total utility derived from another level of consumption within a given time interval. A simple formula for marginal utility is this:

$$\text{Marginal utility} = \frac{\text{change in total utility}}{\text{change in number of units consumed}}$$

In our example, when a person has already downloaded and listened to two music albums in one week and then downloads and listens to another, total utility increases from 16 utils to 19. Therefore, the marginal utility (of downloading and listening to one more album of Internet music after already having downloaded and listened to two in one week) is equal to 3 utils.

GRAPHICAL ANALYSIS

We can transfer the information in panel (a) onto a graph, as we do in panels (b) and (c) of Figure 20-1. Total utility, which is represented in column 2 of panel (a), is transferred to panel (b).

FIGURE 20-1

Total and Marginal Utility of Downloading and Listening to Digital Music Albums

If we were able to assign specific values to the utility derived from downloading and listening to digital music albums each week, we could obtain a marginal utility schedule similar in pattern to the one shown in panel (a). In column 1 is the number of music albums downloaded and listened to per week; in column 2, the total utility derived from each quantity; and in column 3, the marginal utility derived from each additional quantity, which is defined as the change in total utility due to a change of one unit of listening to downloaded albums per week. Total utility from panel (a) is plotted in panel (b). Marginal utility is plotted in panel (c), where you see that it reaches zero where total utility hits its maximum at between 4 and 5 units.

Panel (a)

(1) Number of Music Albums Downloaded and Listened to per Week	(2) Total Utility (utils per week)	(3) Marginal Utility (utils per week)
0	0	
1	10	10 (10 − 0)
2	16	6 (16 − 10)
3	19	3 (19 − 16)
4	20	1 (20 − 19)
5	20	0 (20 − 20)
6	18	−2 (18 − 20)

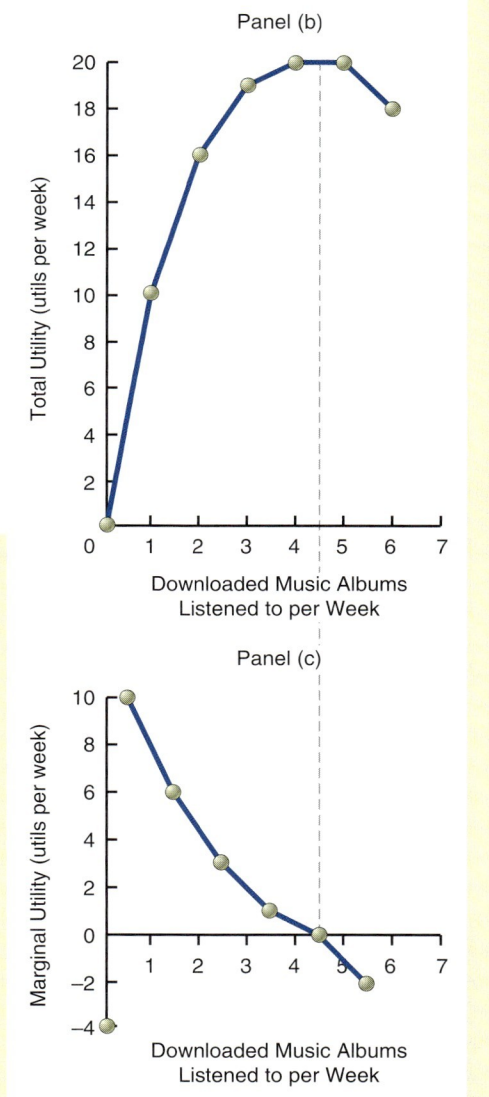

Total utility continues to rise until four digital music albums are downloaded and listened to per week. This measure of utility remains at 20 utils through the fifth album, and at the sixth album per week it falls to 18 utils; we assume that at some quantity consumed per unit time period, boredom with consuming more digital music albums begins to set in. Thus, at some quantity consumed, the additional utility from consuming an additional album begins to fall, so total utility first rises and then declines in panel (b).

Marginal Utility

If you look carefully at panels (b) and (c) of Figure 20-1, the notion of marginal utility becomes clear. In economics, the term *marginal* always refers to a *change* in the total. The marginal utility of listening to three downloaded digital music albums per week instead of two albums per week is the increment in total utility and is equal to 3 utils per week. All of the points in panel (c) are taken from column 3 of the table in panel (a). Notice that marginal utility falls throughout the graph. A special point occurs after four albums are downloaded and listened to per week because the total utility curve in panel (b) is unchanged after the consumption of the fourth album. That means that the consumer receives no additional (marginal) utility from downloading and listening to the fifth album. This is shown in panel (c) as *zero* marginal utility. After that point, marginal utility becomes negative.

In our example, when marginal utility becomes negative, it means that the consumer is tired of downloading and listening to digital music albums and would require some form of compensation to listen to any more. When marginal utility is negative, an additional unit consumed actually lowers total utility by becoming a nuisance. Rarely does a consumer face a situation of negative marginal utility. Whenever this point is reached, goods in effect become "bads." Consuming more units actually causes total utility to *fall* so that marginal utility is negative. A rational consumer will stop consuming at the point at which marginal utility becomes negative, even if the good is available at a price of zero.

How much compensation would be required to make up for "bads" that people sometimes experience?

EXAMPLE

The High Cost of Certain Sources of Negative Marginal Utility

Conventional wisdom says that it is impossible to put a price tag on happiness. Nevertheless, economists have recently attempted to use surveys of how happy people say they are to determine how much people would have to be compensated for "bads" that yield negative marginal utility. To do this, the economists take into account additional factors, such as people's incomes. Results obtained from one set of happiness surveys appear in Figure 20-2. They indicate that classic "bads" encountered by some people during their lives yield sufficiently negative marginal utility that significant dollar amounts are required to compensate a typical individual to incur such "bads."

FOR CRITICAL ANALYSIS
Why do economists usually attempt to attach dollar values to economic goods and "bads" instead of trying to explicitly measure levels of satisfaction or dissatisfaction associated with the items?

FIGURE 20-2
Compensation for Economic "Bads" That Yield Negative Marginal Utility

Estimates derived from happiness surveys indicate that being widowed or divorced or failing to find a job or to marry are economic "bads" that would require significant annual compensation for associated negative marginal utilities.

Source: David Blanchflower and Andrew Oswald, "Well-Being over Time in Britain and the U.S.A.," National Bureau of Economic Research Working Paper No. 7487, January 2000.

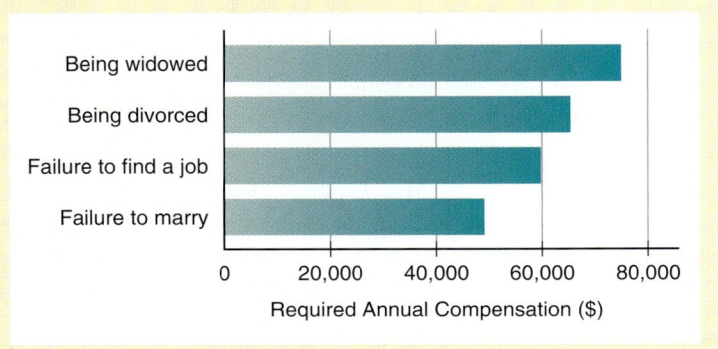

> **QUICK QUIZ**
>
> _____ is defined as want-satisfying power; it is a power common to all desired goods and services.
>
> We arbitrarily measure **utility** in units called _____.
>
> It is important to distinguish between **total utility** and **marginal utility**. _____ utility is the total satisfaction derived from the consumption of a given quantity of a good or service. _____ utility is the *change* in total utility due to a one-unit change in the consumption of the good or service.
>
> See page 519 for the answers. Review concepts from this section in MyEconLab.

DIMINISHING MARGINAL UTILITY

Notice that in panel (c) of Figure 20-1 on page 503, marginal utility is continuously declining. This property has been named the principle of **diminishing marginal utility**. There is no way that we can prove diminishing marginal utility; nonetheless, economists and others have for years believed strongly in the notion. Diminishing marginal utility has even been called a law. This supposed law concerns a psychological, or subjective, utility that you receive as you consume more and more of a particular good. Stated formally, the law is as follows:

Diminishing marginal utility
The principle that as more of any good or service is consumed, its extra benefit declines. Otherwise stated, increases in total utility from the consumption of a good or service become smaller and smaller as more is consumed during a given time period.

> *As an individual consumes more of a particular commodity, the total level of utility, or satisfaction, derived from that consumption usually increases. Eventually, however, the rate at which it increases diminishes as more is consumed.*

Take a hungry individual at a dinner table. The first serving is greatly appreciated, and the individual derives a substantial amount of utility from it. The second serving does not have quite as much pleasurable impact as the first one, and the third serving is likely to be even less satisfying. This individual experiences diminishing marginal utility of food until he or she stops eating, and this is true for most people. All-you-can-eat restaurants count on this fact; a second helping of ribs may provide some marginal utility, but the third helping would have only a little or even negative marginal utility.

Consider for a moment the opposite possibility—increasing marginal utility. Under such a situation, the marginal utility after consuming, say, one hamburger would increase. The second hamburger would be more valuable to you, and the third would be even more valuable yet. If increasing marginal utility existed, each of us would consume only one good or service! Rather than observing that "variety is the spice of life," we would see that monotony in consumption was preferred. We do not observe this, and therefore we have great confidence in the concept of diminishing marginal utility.

Can diminishing marginal utility explain why newspaper vending machines rarely prevent people from taking more than the one current issue they have paid to purchase?

EXAMPLE

Newspaper Vending Machines versus Candy Vending Machines

Have you ever noticed that newspaper vending machines nearly everywhere in the United States allow you to put in the correct change, lift up the door, and—if you were willing to violate the law—take as many newspapers as you want? Contrast this type of vending machine with candy machines.

(continued)

They are completely locked at all times. You must designate the candy that you wish, normally by using some type of keypad. The candy then drops down so that you can retrieve it but cannot grab any other candy.

The difference between these two types of vending machines is explained by diminishing marginal utility. Newspaper companies dispense newspapers from coin-operated boxes that allow dishonest people to take more copies than they pay for. What would a dishonest person do with more than one copy of a newspaper, however? The marginal utility of a second newspaper is normally zero. The benefit of storing excessive newspapers is usually nil because yesterday's news has no value. But the same analysis does not hold for candy. The marginal utility of a second candy bar is certainly less than the first, but it is normally not zero. Moreover, one can store candy for relatively long periods of time at relatively low cost. Consequently, food vending machine companies have to worry about dishonest users of their equipment and must make that equipment more theftproof than newspaper companies do.

FOR CRITICAL ANALYSIS
Can you think of a circumstance under which a substantial number of newspaper purchasers might be inclined to take more than one newspaper out of a vending machine?

OPTIMIZING CONSUMPTION CHOICES

Every consumer has a limited income. Choices must be made. When a consumer has made all of his or her choices about what to buy and in what quantities, and when the total level of satisfaction, or utility, from that set of choices is as great as it can be, we say that the consumer has *optimized*. When the consumer has attained an optimum consumption set of goods and services, we say that he or she has reached **consumer optimum.**

Consumer optimum
A choice of a set of goods and services that maximizes the level of satisfaction for each consumer, subject to limited income.

A Two-Good Example

Consider a simple two-good example. The consumer has to choose between spending income on downloads of digital music albums at $5 per download and on purchasing sandwiches at $3 each. Let's say that when the consumer has spent all income on music album downloads and sandwiches, the last dollar spent on a sandwich yields 3 utils of utility but the last dollar spent on downloading music albums yields 10 utils. Wouldn't this consumer increase total utility if some dollars were taken away from consumption of sandwiches and allocated to music album downloads? The answer is yes. More dollars spent downloading music albums will reduce marginal utility per last dollar spent, whereas fewer dollars spent on consumption of sandwiches will increase marginal utility per last dollar spent. The loss in utility from spending fewer dollars purchasing fewer sandwiches is more than made up by spending additional dollars on more album downloads. As a consequence, total utility increases. The consumer optimum—where total utility is maximized—occurs when the satisfaction per last dollar spent on both sandwiches and music album downloads per week is equal for the two goods. Thus, the amount of goods consumed depends on the prices of the goods, the income of the consumer, and the marginal utility derived from the amounts of each good consumed.

Table 20-1 presents information on utility derived from consuming various quantities of music album downloads and sandwiches. Columns 4 and 8 show the marginal utility per dollar spent on music downloads and sandwiches, respectively. If the prices of both goods are zero, individuals will consume each as long as their respective marginal utility is positive (at least five units of each and probably much more). It is also true that a consumer with infinite income will continue consuming goods until the marginal utility of each is equal to zero. When the price is zero or the consumer's income is infinite, there is no effective constraint on consumption.

TABLE 20-1
Total and Marginal Utility from Consuming Music Album Downloads and Sandwiches on an Income of $26

(1) Music Album Downloads per Period	(2) Total Utility of Music Album Downloads per Period (utils)	(3) Marginal Utility (utils) MU_d	(4) Marginal Utility per Dollar Spent (MU_d/P_d) (price = $5)	(5) Sandwiches per Period	(6) Total Utility of Sandwiches per Period (utils)	(7) Marginal Utility (utils) MU_s	(8) Marginal Utility per Dollar Spent (MU_s/P_s) (price = $3)
0	0	—	—	0	0	—	—
1	50.0	50.0	10.0	1	25	25	8.3
2	95.0	45.0	9.0	2	47	22	7.3
3	135.0	40.0	8.0	3	65	18	6.0
4	171.5	36.5	7.3	4	80	15	5.0
5	200.0	28.5	5.7	5	89	9	3.0

A Two-Good Consumer Optimum

Consumer optimum is attained when the marginal utility of the last dollar spent on each good yields the same utility and income is completely exhausted. In the situation in Table 20-1, the individual's income is $26. From columns 4 and 8 of Table 20-1, equal marginal utilities per dollar spent occur at the consumption level of four music album downloads and two sandwiches (the marginal utility per dollar spent equals 7.3). Notice that the marginal utility per dollar spent for both goods is also (approximately) equal at the consumption level of three music album downloads and one sandwich, but here total income is not completely exhausted. Likewise, the marginal utility per dollar spent is (approximately) equal at five music album downloads and three sandwiches, but the expenditures necessary for that level of consumption ($34) exceed the individual's income.

Table 20-2 on the next page shows the steps taken to arrive at consumer optimum. The first download of a music album from the Internet would yield a marginal utility per dollar of 10 (50 units of utility divided by $5 per music album download), while the first sandwich would yield a marginal utility of only 8.3 per dollar (25 units of utility divided by $3 per sandwich). Because it yields the higher marginal utility per dollar, the music album is downloaded. This leaves $21 of income. The second download of a music album yields a higher marginal utility per dollar (9, versus 8.3 for sandwiches), so it is also purchased, leaving an unspent income of $16. At the third purchase, the first sandwich now yields a higher marginal utility per dollar than the next download of a music album (8.3 versus 8), so the first sandwich is purchased. This leaves income of $13 to spend. The process continues until all income is exhausted and the marginal utility per dollar spent is equal for both goods.

To restate, consumer optimum requires the following:

A consumer's money income should be allocated so that the last dollar spent on each good purchased yields the same amount of marginal utility (when all income is spent), because this rule yields the largest possible total utility.

TABLE 20-2
Steps to Consumer Optimum

In each purchase situation described here, the consumer always purchases the good with the higher marginal utility per dollar spent (MU/P). For example, at the time of the third purchase, the marginal utility per last dollar spent on downloads of music albums is 8, but it is 8.3 for sandwiches, and $16 of income remains, so the next purchase will be a sandwich. Here $P_d = \$5$, $P_s = \$3$, MU_d is the marginal utility of consumption of music album downloads, and MU_s is the marginal utility of consumption of sandwiches.

	Choices					
	Music Album Downloads		Sandwiches			
Purchase	Unit	MU_d/P_d	Unit	MU_s/P_s	Buying Decision	Remaining Income
1	First	10.0	First	8.3	First music album download	$26 − $5 = $21
2	Second	9.0	First	8.3	Second music album download	$21 − $5 = $16
3	Third	8.0	First	8.3	First sandwich	$16 − $3 = $13
4	Third	8.0	Second	7.3	Third music album download	$13 − $5 = $8
5	Fourth	7.3	Second	7.3	Fourth music album download and Second sandwich	$8 − $5 = $3 $3 − $3 = $0

A Little Math

We can state the rule of consumer optimum in algebraic terms by examining the ratio of marginal utilities and prices of individual products. The rule simply states that a consumer maximizes personal satisfaction when allocating money income in such a way that the last dollars spent on good A, good B, good C, and so on, yield equal amounts of marginal utility. Marginal utility (MU) from good A is indicated by "MU of good A." For good B, it is "MU of good B." Our algebraic formulation of this rule, therefore, becomes

$$\frac{MU \text{ of good A}}{\text{Price of good A}} = \frac{MU \text{ of good B}}{\text{price of good B}} = \cdots = \frac{MU \text{ of good Z}}{\text{price of good Z}}$$

The letters A, B, . . . , Z indicate the various goods and services that the consumer might purchase.

We know, then, that the marginal utility of good A divided by the price of good A must equal the marginal utility of any other good divided by its price in order for the consumer to maximize utility. Note, though, that the application of the rule of equal marginal utility per dollar spent does not necessarily describe an explicit or conscious act on the part of consumers. Rather, this is a *model* of consumer optimum.

ECONOMICS FRONT AND CENTER

To think about how consideration of the consumer optimum can influence retailing managers, read **An Open Secret for Success in the "Dollar-Store" Business**, on page 513.

HOW A PRICE CHANGE AFFECTS CONSUMER OPTIMUM

Consumption decisions are summarized in the law of demand, which states that the amount purchased is inversely related to price. We can now see why by using utility analysis.

A Consumer's Response to a Price Change

When a consumer has optimally allocated all her income to purchases, the marginal utility per dollar spent at current prices of goods and services is the same for each good or service she buys. No consumer will, when optimizing, buy 10 units of a good per unit of time

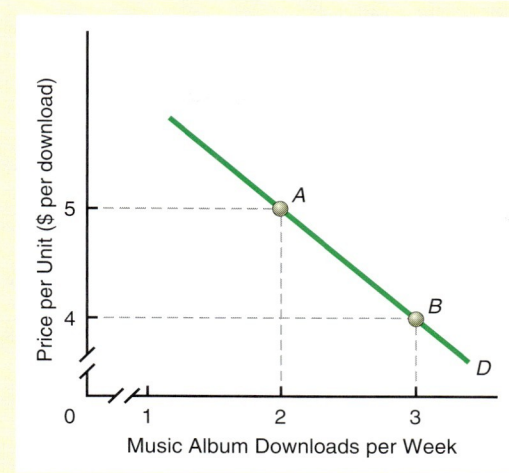

FIGURE 20-3
Digital Music Download Prices and Marginal Utility
When consumers respond to a reduction in music download prices from $5 per download to $4 per download by increasing consumption, marginal utility falls. The movement from point A to point B thereby reduces marginal utility to bring about the equalization of the marginal utility per dollar spent across all purchases.

when the marginal utility per dollar spent on the tenth unit of that good is less than the marginal utility per dollar spent on some other item.

If we start out at a consumer optimum and then observe a good's price decrease, we can predict that consumers will respond to the price decrease by consuming more of that good. This is because before the price change, the marginal utility per dollar spent on each good or service consumed was the same. Now, when a specific good's price is lower, it is possible to consume more of that good while continuing to equalize the marginal utility per dollar spent on that good with the marginal utility per dollar spent on other goods and services. If the law of diminishing marginal utility holds, then the purchase and consumption of additional units of the lower-priced good will cause the marginal utility from consuming the good to fall. Eventually, it will fall to the point at which the marginal utility per dollar spent on the good is once again equal to the marginal utility per dollar spent on other goods and services. At this point, the consumer will stop buying additional units of the lower-priced good.

A hypothetical demand curve for music downloads per week for a typical consumer is presented in Figure 20-3. Suppose that at point A, at which the price per music download is $5, the marginal utility of the last music album downloaded per week is MU_A. At point B, at which the price is $4 per music download per week, the marginal utility is represented by MU_B. Because of the law of diminishing marginal utility—with the consumption of more downloaded digital music, the marginal utility of the last unit of these additional music downloads is lower—MU_B must be less than MU_A. What has happened is that at a lower price, the number of music album downloads per week increased from two to three; marginal utility must have fallen. At a higher consumption rate, the marginal utility falls in response to the rise in downloadable music consumption so that the marginal utility per dollar spent is equalized across all purchases.

The Substitution Effect

What is happening as the price of music downloads falls is that consumers are substituting the now relatively cheaper music downloads for other goods and services, such as restaurant meals and live concerts. We call this the **substitution effect** of a change in the price of a good because it occurs when consumers substitute relatively cheaper goods for relatively more expensive ones.

We assume that people desire a variety of goods and pursue a variety of goals. That means that few, if any, goods are irreplaceable in meeting demand. We are generally able

Substitution effect
The tendency of people to substitute cheaper commodities for more expensive commodities.

Principle of substitution
The principle that consumers and producers shift away from goods and resources that become priced relatively higher in favor of goods and resources that are now priced relatively lower.

to substitute one product for another to satisfy demand. This is commonly referred to as the **principle of substitution.**

An Example. Let's assume now that there are several goods, not exactly the same, and perhaps even very different from one another, but all contributing to consumers' total utility. If the relative price of one particular good falls, we will most likely substitute in favor of the lower-priced good and against the other similar goods that we might have been purchasing. Conversely, if the price of that good rises relative to the price of the other similar goods, we will substitute in favor of them and not buy as much of the now higher-priced good. An example is the growth in purchases of personal computers since the late 1980s. As the relative price of computers has plummeted, people have substituted away from other, now relatively more expensive goods in favor of purchasing additional computers to use in their homes.

Purchasing power
The value of money for buying goods and services. If your money income stays the same but the price of one good that you are buying goes up, your effective purchasing power falls, and vice versa.

Purchasing Power and Real Income. If the price of some item that you purchase goes down while your money income and all other prices stay the same, your ability to purchase goods goes up. That is to say, your effective **purchasing power** has increased, even though your money income has stayed the same. If you purchase 20 gallons of gas a week at $3 per gallon, your total outlay for gas is $60. If the price goes down by 50 percent, to $1.50 cents a gallon, you would have to spend only $30 a week to purchase the same number of gallons of gas. If your money income and the prices of other goods remain the same, it would be possible for you to continue purchasing 20 gallons of gas a week *and* to purchase more of other goods. You will feel richer and will indeed probably purchase more of a number of goods, including perhaps even more gasoline.

The converse will also be true. When the price of one good you are purchasing goes up, without any other change in prices or income, the purchasing power of your income will drop. You will have to reduce your purchases of either the now higher-priced good or other goods (or a combination).

Real-income effect
The change in people's purchasing power that occurs when, other things being constant, the price of one good that they purchase changes. When that price goes up, real income, or purchasing power, falls, and when that price goes down, real income increases.

In general, this **real-income effect** is usually quite small. After all, unless we consider broad categories, such as housing or food, a change in the price of one particular item that we purchase will have a relatively small effect on our total purchasing power. Thus, we expect that the substitution effect will be more important than the real-income effect in causing us to purchase more of goods that have become cheaper and less of goods that have become more expensive.

THE DEMAND CURVE REVISITED

Linking the "law" of diminishing marginal utility and the rule of equal marginal utilities per dollar gives us a negative relationship between the quantity demanded of a good or service and its price. As the relative price of digital music downloads goes up, for example, the quantity demanded will fall; and as the relative price of music downloads goes down, the quantity demanded will rise. Figure 20-3 on page 509 showed this demand curve for music downloads. As the price of music downloads falls, the consumer can maximize total utility only by purchasing more digital music, and vice versa. In other words, the relationship between price and quantity desired is simply a downward-sloping demand curve. Note, though, that this downward-sloping demand curve (the law of demand) is derived under the assumption of constant tastes and incomes. You must remember that we are keeping these important determining variables constant when we look at the relationship between price and quantity demanded.

How might improving the likelihood that apparel items will fit allow retailers to boost consumers' purchases of their clothing lines?

E-COMMERCE EXAMPLE

Have You Got My Size?

The U.S. government has determined that the average person today is about an inch taller and 24 pounds heavier than a typical individual was in the 1950s. Nevertheless, many people still desire to fit into the chicest new clothing styles. To help people avoid overly tight fits, retailers must be able to recommend appropriate clothing sizes. The problem is that providing these recommendations for all types of apparel can require measuring and recording as many as 38 different body dimensions—a time-consuming ordeal with a standard tape measure.

A business called Intellifit manufactures and sells a $50,000 device that can record the positions of 200,000 body points. A person steps into a cylinder that is eight feet in diameter. An embedded scanner uses millimeter radio waves to provide accurate measurements within 10 seconds. Retailers using Intellifit's scanners can use these data to provide customers with printouts of brands, styles, and sizes likely to fit best. Their objective is to push up prospective customers' marginal utility at any given price of an apparel item, thereby boosting sales.

FOR CRITICAL ANALYSIS
If marginal utility increases at each possible quantity consumed at a given price, does this cause a change in quantity demanded (a movement along the demand curve) or a change in demand (a shift in the demand curve)?

Marginal Utility, Total Utility, and the Diamond-Water Paradox

Even though water is essential to life and diamonds are not, water is cheap and diamonds are expensive. The economist Adam Smith in 1776 called this the "diamond-water paradox." The paradox is easily understood when we make the distinction between total utility and marginal utility. The total utility of water greatly exceeds the total utility derived from diamonds. What determines the price, though, is what happens on the margin. We have relatively few diamonds, so the marginal utility of the last diamond consumed is relatively high. The opposite is true for water. Total utility does not determine what people are willing to pay for a unit of a particular commodity; marginal utility does. Look at the situation graphically in Figure 20-4. We show the demand curve for diamonds, labeled $D_{diamonds}$. The demand curve for water is labeled D_{water}. We plot quantity in terms of kilograms per

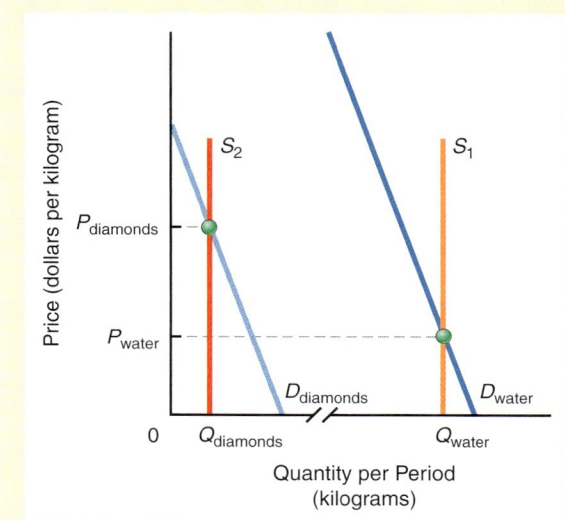

FIGURE 20-4

The Diamond–Water Paradox

We pick kilograms as a common unit of measurement for both water and diamonds. To demonstrate that the demand for and supply of water are immense, we have put a break in the horizontal quantity axis. Although the demand for water is much greater than the demand for diamonds, the marginal valuation of water is given by the marginal value placed on the *last* unit of water consumed. To find that, we must know the supply of water, which is given as S_1. At that supply, the price of water is P_{water}. But the supply for diamonds is given by S_2. At that supply, the price of diamonds is $P_{diamonds}$. The total valuation that consumers place on water is tremendous relative to the total valuation consumers place on diamonds. What is important for price determination, however, is the marginal valuation, or the marginal utility received.

unit time period on the horizontal axis. On the vertical axis, we plot price in dollars per kilogram. We use kilograms as our common unit of measurement for water and for diamonds. We could just as well have used gallons, acre-feet, or liters.

Notice that the demand for water is many, many times the demand for diamonds (even though we really can't show this in the diagram). We draw the supply curve of water as S_1 at a quantity of Q_{water}. The supply curve for diamonds is given as S_2 at quantity $Q_{diamonds}$. At the intersection of the supply curve of water with the demand curve of water, the price per kilogram is P_{water}. The intersection of the supply curve of diamonds with the demand curve of diamonds is at $P_{diamonds}$. Notice that $P_{diamonds}$ exceeds P_{water}. Diamonds sell at a higher price than water.

BEHAVIORAL ECONOMICS AND CONSUMER CHOICE THEORY

Utility analysis has long been appealing to economists because it makes clear predictions about how individuals will adjust their consumption of different goods and services based on the prices of those items and their incomes. Traditionally, another attraction of utility analysis to many economists has been its reliance on the assumption that consumers behave *rationally*, or that they do not intentionally make decisions that would leave them worse off. As we discussed in Chapter 1, proponents of behavioral economics have doubts about the rationality assumption, which causes them to question the utility-based theory of consumer choice.

Does Behavioral Economics Better Predict Consumer Choices?

Advocates of behavioral economics question whether utility theory is supported by the facts, which they argue are better explained by applying the assumption of bounded rationality. Recall from Chapter 1 that this assumption states that human limitations prevent people from examining every possible choice available to them and thereby thwart their efforts to effectively pursue long-term personal interests.

As evidence favoring the bounded rationality assumption, proponents of behavioral economics point to real-world examples that they claim violate rationality-based utility theory. For instance, economists have found that when purchasing electric appliances such as refrigerators, people sometimes buy the lowest-priced, energy-inefficient models even though the price savings often fail to compensate for higher future energy costs. There is also evidence that people who live in earthquake- or flood-prone regions commonly fail to purchase sufficient insurance against these events. In addition, experiments have shown that when people are placed in situations in which strong emotions come into play, they may be willing to pay different amounts for items than they would pay in calmer settings.

These and other observed behaviors, behavioral economists suggest, indicate that consumers do not behave as if they are rational. If the rationality assumption does not apply to actual behavior, they argue, it follows that utility-based consumer choice theory cannot, either.

Consumer Choice Theory Remains Alive and Well

In spite of the doubts expressed by proponents of behavioral economics, most economists continue to apply the assumption that people behave *as if* they act rationally with an aim to maximize utility. These economists continue to utilize utility theory because of a fundamental strength of this approach: it yields clear-cut predictions regarding consumer choices.

In contrast, if the rationality assumption is rejected, any number of possible human behaviors might be considered. To proponents of behavioral economics, ambiguities about actual outcomes make the bounded rationality approach to consumer choice more realistic than utility-based consumer choice theory. Nevertheless, a major drawback is that no clearly testable predictions emerge from the many alternative behaviors that people might exhibit if they fail to behave *as if* they are rational.

Certainly, arguments among economists about the "reasonableness" of rational consumers maximizing utility are likely to continue. So far, however, the use of utility-based consumer choice theory has allowed economists to make a wide array of predictions about how consumers respond to changes in prices, incomes, and other factors. By and large, these key predictions continue to be supported by the actual choices that consumers make.

QUICK QUIZ

The principle of **diminishing marginal utility** tells us that each successive marginal unit of a good consumed adds _____ extra utility.

The consumer maximizes total utility by _____ the marginal utility of the last dollar spent on one good with the marginal utility per last dollar spent on all other goods. That is the state of consumer _____.

To remain in **consumer optimum**, a price decrease requires a(n) _____ in consumption; a price increase requires a(n) _____ in consumption.

Each change in price has a substitution effect and a real-income effect. When the price of a good _____, the consumer substitutes in favor of that relatively cheaper good. When price _____, the consumer's real purchasing power increases, causing the consumer to purchase more of most goods. Assuming that the principle of diminishing marginal utility holds, the demand curve must slope downward.

See page 519 for the answers. Review concepts from this section in MyEconLab.

CASE STUDY

ECONOMICS FRONT AND CENTER

An Open Secret for Success in the "Dollar-Store" Business

Hanover has been hired as president and chief executive officer of Just a Buck, a retail chain that sells all items for $1 apiece. The board of directors has charged her with managing a nationwide expansion of the chain, which will bring it into direct competition with other so-called dollar-store companies, including Dollar General, Dollar Tree, and Family Dollar. The board's expectations are high because the industry's annual revenues have been climbing toward $20 billion. Some members of the board are hopeful that in some regions Just a Buck will be able to compete with other discount retailers, such as Wal-Mart.

Hanover realizes that the key to success at Just a Buck will be to manage the company from the perspective of a consumer who is choosing among the products sold by competing discount retailers. Hanover has vowed that she will concentrate on maximizing customers' satisfaction from visits to Just a Buck stores. Toward that end, she has already developed a remodeling plan for the company's older outlets. She has spent most of her time, however, reviewing the firm's product offerings. Hanover's economics training taught her that the marginal utility per dollar spent is equalized at a consumer optimum. Thus, she has decided that her main objective must be to offer an array of the highest-quality products possible. She closes the door of her office so that she can concentrate on reviewing the company's list of potential shampoo suppliers, in the hope of identifying two that will offer the highest-quality products at very low prices.

CRITICAL ANALYSIS QUESTIONS

1. In light of the fact that dollar stores sell each item at $1 apiece, why does it make sense for Hanover to emphasize the utility that consumers will stand to gain from shopping at Just a Buck outlets?

2. Are products sold by Just a Buck more likely to be closer substitutes for those offered for sale by Dollar General or by Wal-Mart?

Issues and Applications

The Upside of Taking Off from a Less Convenient Airport

Concepts Applied
- Principle of Substitution
- Consumer Optimum
- Substitution Effect

According to the principle of substitution, people shift away from consuming items that become priced relatively higher in favor of items that are now priced relatively lower. In recent years, the principle of substitution has applied to the services offered by several major airports. Many consumers of air travel are choosing to drive for some distance before they depart to their ultimate destinations by plane.

Weighing Relative Marginal Utilities and Prices

Table 20-3 lists several airports in major cities and alternative, secondary airports to which residents of the larger metropolitan areas might consider driving in order to take different airline flights to their final destinations. Some alternative airports are more distant than others, but in all cases people considering using secondary airports typically must navigate their way through busy traffic.

Traditionally, the time and trouble associated with driving to a more distant airport have kept the marginal utility per dollar spent on using facilities closer to home well above the marginal utility per dollar associated with traveling to an alternative airport. For instance, suppose that airfares available to a resident of Boston were very nearly the same from either the Boston airport or the Manchester, New Hampshire airport. In the past, a resident of the Boston metropolitan area would almost always choose to use Boston's facilities. The utility per dollar spent making the next trip from Manchester's airport was too low for the latter airport to be among the set of choices consistent with a consumer optimum.

Opting to Avoid Hassles That Reduce Marginal Utility

Since the early 2000s, however, two factors affecting the consumer optimum for air travel have changed. First, travelers departing from busy metropolitan airports now face much longer lines at tightened security checkpoints. In some large-city airports, the slow pace of security screening during peak travel periods can create lines stretching more than a hundred yards. The associated waiting time can be up to an hour. To catch a flight, therefore, people must leave as much as an hour earlier than before—which for several of the large cities listed in Table 20-3 is about the amount of time it would take to drive to an alternative airport with shorter security lines. Thus, the typical metropolitan resident's marginal utility per dollar spent taking the next flight from the closest airport is now lower than it was in the past. This factor alone has resulted in more-distant departure locations factoring into many passengers' range of choices for a consumer optimum.

TABLE 20-3
Selected Substitute Airport Pairs in the United States

Alternatives to several major metropolitan airports are close enough for residents of those cities to reach by automobile. Factors affecting the marginal utility derived from departing from large-city airports and the relative prices of metropolitan versus smaller-city airports have induced an increasing number of travelers to substitute air travel from the latter for the former.

Source: U.S. Department of Transportation.

Major-City Airport	Substitute Airport	Distance Between Airports (miles)
Boston, Massachusetts	Manchester, New Hampshire	45
Cincinnati, Ohio	Dayton, Ohio	64
Charlotte, North Carolina	Greensboro, North Carolina	82
Cleveland, Ohio	Akron-Canton, Ohio	36
Detroit, Michigan	Toledo, Ohio	49
Los Angeles, California	Long Beach, California	18
Philadelphia, Pennsylvania	Baltimore, Maryland	90
Richmond, Virginia	Norfolk, Virginia	75
San Francisco, California	Oakland, California	11

Responding to Price Changes

For a number of metropolitan air travelers, however, relative price changes that have occurred during the 2000s have also altered the marginal utility per dollar spent on airport facilities in alternative locations. Ticket prices charged by airlines that tend to serve the largest metropolitan airports have increased. So have parking and ground transportation fees at those airports. Thus, there has been an increase in the total price of flying out of most major-city airports, which has further reduced a metropolitan resident's marginal utility per dollar spent on flying out of the closest facility.

Simultaneously, budget airlines such as JetBlue and Southwest have begun offering more flights at smaller-city locations, where parking and ground transportation fees are also much lower. Consequently, the total price that a resident of a major city must pay to fly from an alternative airport has decreased, raising the marginal utility per dollar spent on a flight from a more distant facility.

The result has been exactly the outcome predicted by consumer choice theory. Consistent with the substitution effect, a higher total price of flying out of the nearest airport and a lower total price of departing from a more distant airport have induced many air travelers to spend some time driving before they fly.

Log in to MyEconLab, click on "Economic News," and test your understanding of the chapter by answering interactive questions that relate directly to this issue.

For Critical Analysis

1. What factors can cause an item to lie entirely outside the bundle of goods and services that together comprise a consumer optimum? (Hint: What would cause a person to purchase a zero quantity?)
2. Until recently, why did more distant airports lie outside the bundle of items consumed by dwellers of large U.S. cities?

Web Resources

1. To obtain the Transportation Security Administration's estimates of the security wait times on various days of the week and at various times of the day at U.S. airports, use the link at www.econtoday.com/ch20.
2. To learn about how the Oakland, California airport has fostered policies aimed at reducing the marginal utility per dollar spent on its facilities, go to www.econtoday.com/ch20.

516 PART V Dimensions of Microeconomics

Identify the two facilities closest to your location that are served by airlines flying large passenger jets. Use a search engine such as Google or Yahoo to find the Web sites of these airlines, and price tickets to an airport elsewhere in the United States. In addition, use a search engine to link to the Web sites of the alternative departure airports you identified. Holding a consumer's income constant, what factors are likely to determine which airport the consumer chooses as a point of departure?

Research Project

Here is what you should know after reading this chapter. MyEconLab will help you identify what you know, and where to go when you need to practice.

WHAT YOU SHOULD KNOW		WHERE TO GO TO PRACTICE
Total Utility versus Marginal Utility Total utility is the total satisfaction that an individual derives from consuming a given amount of a good or service during a given period. Marginal utility is the additional satisfaction that a person gains by consuming an additional unit of the good or service.	utility, 501 utility analysis, 501 util, 502 marginal utility, 502 **Key figure** Figure 20-1, 503	• **MyEconLab** Study Plans 20.1 and 20.2 • Audio introduction to Chapter 20 • Animated Figure 20-1
The Law of Diminishing Marginal Utility For at least the first unit of consumption of a good or service, a person's total utility increases with increased consumption. Eventually, however, the rate at which an individual's utility rises with greater consumption tends to fall. Thus, marginal utility ultimately declines as the person consumes more and more of the good or service.	diminishing marginal utility, 505	• **MyEconLab** Study Plan 20.3
The Consumer Optimum An individual optimally allocates available income to consumption of all goods and services when the marginal utility per dollar spent on the last unit consumed of each good is equalized. Thus, a consumer optimum occurs when (1) the ratio of the marginal utility derived from an item to the price of that item is equal across all goods and services that the person consumes and (2) when the person spends all available income.	consumer optimum, 506	• **MyEconLab** Study Plan 20.4 • Video: Optimizing Consumption Choices
The Substitution Effect of a Price Change One effect of a change in the price of a good or service is that the price change induces people to substitute among goods. For example, if the price of a good rises, the individual will tend to consume some other good that has become relatively less expensive as a result. In addition, the individual will tend to reduce consumption of the good whose price increased.	substitution effect, 509 principle of substitution, 510 **Key figure** Figure 20-3, 509	• **MyEconLab** Study Plan 20.5 • Animated Figure 20-3

WHAT YOU SHOULD KNOW		WHERE TO GO TO PRACTICE
The Real-Income Effect of a Price Change Another effect of a price change is that it affects the purchasing power of an individual's available income. For instance, if the price of a good increases, a person must reduce purchases of either the now higher-priced good or other goods (or a combination of both of these responses). Normally, we anticipate that the real-income effect is smaller than the substitution effect, so that when the price of a good or service increases, people will purchase more of goods or services that have lower relative prices as a result.	purchasing power, 510 real-income effect, 510 **Key figure** Figure 20-3, 509	• **MyEconLab** Study Plan 20.5 • Animated Figure 20-3
Why the Price of Diamonds Exceeds the Price of Water Even Though People Cannot Long Survive Without Water The reason for this price difference is that marginal utility, not total utility, determines how much people are willing to pay for any particular good. Because there are relatively few diamonds, the number of diamonds consumed by a typical individual is relatively small, which means that the marginal utility derived from consuming a diamond is relatively high. By contrast, water is abundant, so people consume relatively large volumes of water, and the marginal utility for the last unit of water consumed is relatively low. It follows that at a consumer optimum, in which the marginal utility per dollar spent is equalized for diamonds and water, people are willing to pay a much higher price for diamonds.	**Key figure** Figure 20-4, 511	• **MyEconLab** Study Plan 20.6 • Animated Figure 20-4

Log in to MyEconLab, take a chapter test, and get a personalized Study Plan that tells you which concepts you understand and which ones you need to review. From there, MyEconLab will give you further practice, tutorials, animations, videos, and guided solutions.

Log in to www.myeconlab.com

PROBLEMS

Select problems, indicated by a blue oval, are assignable in MyEconLab.
Answers to the odd-numbered problems appear at the back of the book.

20-1 The campus pizzeria sells a single pizza for $12. If you order a second pizza, however, the pizzeria charges a price of only $5 for the additional pizza. Explain how an understanding of marginal utility helps to explain the pizzeria's pizza pricing.

20-2. As an individual consumes more units of an item, the person eventually experiences diminishing marginal utility. This means that to increase marginal utility, the person must often consume less of an item. Explain the logic of this behavior using the example in Problem 20-1.

20-3 Where possible, complete the missing cells in the table.

Number of Cheese-burgers	Total Utility of Cheese-burgers	Marginal Utility of Cheese-burgers	Bags of French Fries	Total Utility of French Fries	Marginal Utility of French Fries
0	0	—	0	0	—
1	20	—	1	—	10
2	36	—	2	—	8
3	—	12	3	—	2
4	—	8	4	21	—
5	—	4	5	21	—

20-4 From the data in Problem 20-3, if the price of a cheeseburger is $2, the price of a bag of french fries is $1, and you have $6 to spend (and you spend all of it), what is the utility-maximizing combination of cheeseburgers and french fries?

20-5 Return to Problem 20-4. Suppose that the price of cheeseburgers falls to $1. Determine the new utility-maximizing combination of cheeseburgers and french fries.

20-6 Suppose that you observe that total utility rises as more of an item is consumed. What can you say for certain about marginal utility? Can you say for sure that it is rising or falling or that it is positive or negative?

20-7 After monitoring your daily consumption patterns, you determine that your daily consumption of soft drinks is 3 and your daily consumption of tacos is 4 when the prices per unit are 50 cents and $1, respectively. Explain what happens to your consumption bundle, the marginal utility of soft drinks, and the marginal utility of tacos when the price of soft drinks rises to 75 cents.

20-8. At a consumer optimum, for all goods purchased, marginal utility per dollar spent is equalized. A high school student is deciding between attending Western State University and Eastern State University. The student cannot attend both universities simultaneously. Both are fine universities, but the reputation of Western is slightly higher, as is the tuition. Use the rule of consumer optimum to explain how the student will go about deciding which university to attend.

20-9 Consider the movements that take place from one point to the next (A to B to C and so on) along the total utility curve below as the individual successively increases consumption by one more unit, and answer the questions that follow.

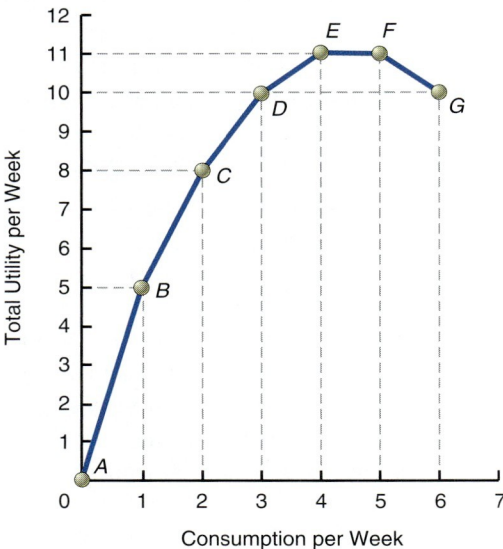

a. Which one-unit increase in consumption from one point to the next along the total utility curve generates the highest marginal utility?
b. Which one-unit increase in consumption from one point to the next along the total utility curve generates zero marginal utility?
c. Which one-unit increase in consumption from one point to the next along the total utility curve generates negative marginal utility?

20-10 Draw a marginal utility curve corresponding to the total utility curve depicted in Problem 20-9.

20-11 Refer to the following table. If the price of a fudge bar is $2, the price of a Popsicle is $1, and a student has $9 to spend on these two items, what quantity of each item will she purchase at a consumer optimum?

Quantity of Fudge Bars per Week	Marginal Utility	Quantity of Popsicles per Week	Marginal Utility
1	1,200	1	1,700
2	1,000	2	1,400
3	800	3	1,100
4	600	4	800
5	400	5	500
6	100	6	200

20-12 Refer to the following table, and assume that each week this consumer buys only hot dogs and tickets to baseball games. The price of a hot dog is $2, and the price of a baseball game is $60. If the consumer's income is $128 per week, what quantity of each item will he purchase each week at a consumer optimum?

Quantity of Hot Dogs per Week	Total Utility	Quantity of Baseball Games per Week	Total Utility
1	40	1	400
2	60	2	700
3	76	3	850
4	86	4	950
5	91	5	1,000
6	93	6	1,025

20-13 In Problem 20-12, if the consumer's income rises to $190 per week, what new quantities characterize the new consumer optimum?

20-14 At a consumer optimum involving goods A and B, the marginal utility of good A is twice the marginal utility of good B. The price of good B is $3.50. What is the price of good A?

20-15 At a consumer optimum involving goods X and Y, the marginal utility of good X equals 3 utils. The price of good Y is three times the price of good X. What is the marginal utility of good Y?

ECONOMICS ON THE NET

Book Prices and Consumer Optimum This application helps you see how a consumer optimum can be attained when one engages in Internet shopping.

Title: Amazon.com Web site

Navigation: Go to www.econtoday.com/ch20 to start at Amazon.com's home page. Click on the *Books* tab.

Application

1. At the top of the page, find the list of the top books in the Amazon.com "Top Sellers" section. Click on the number one book. Record the price of the book. Then locate the Search window. Type in "Roger LeRoy Miller." Scroll down until you find your class text listed. Record the price.

2. Suppose you are an individual who has purchased both the number one book and your class text through Amazon.com. Describe how economic analysis would explain this choice.

3. Using the prices you recorded for the two books, write an equation that relates the prices and your marginal utilities of the two books. Use this equation to explain verbally how you might quantify the magnitude of your marginal utility for the number one book relative to your marginal utility for your class text.

For Group Study and Analysis Discuss what changes might occur if the price of the number one book were lowered but the student remains enrolled in this course. Discuss what changes might take place regarding the consumer optimum if the student were not enrolled in this course.

ANSWERS TO QUICK QUIZZES

p. 505: (i) Utility; (ii) utils; (iii) Total . . . Marginal
p. 513: (i) less; (ii) equating . . . optimum; (iii) increase . . . decrease; (iv) falls . . . falls

Appendix E: More Advanced Consumer Choice Theory

It is possible to analyze consumer choice verbally, as we did for the most part in Chapter 20. The theory of diminishing marginal utility can be fairly well accepted on intuitive grounds and by introspection. If we want to be more formal and perhaps more elegant in our theorizing, however, we can translate our discussion into a graphical analysis with what we call *indifference curves* and the *budget constraint*. Here we discuss these terms and their relationship and demonstrate consumer equilibrium in geometric form.

ON BEING INDIFFERENT

What does it mean to be indifferent? It usually means that you don't care one way or the other about something—you are equally disposed to either of two alternatives. With this interpretation in mind, we will turn to two choices, playing golf and consuming restaurant meals. In panel (a) of Figure E-1, we show several combinations of golf outings and restaurant meals per week that a representative consumer considers equally satisfactory. That is to say, for each combination, A, B, C, and D, this consumer will have exactly the same level of total utility.

FIGURE E-1

Combinations That Yield Equal Levels of Satisfaction

A, B, C, and D represent combinations of golf outings and restaurant meals per week that give an equal level of satisfaction to this consumer. In other words, the consumer is indifferent among these four combinations.

Panel (a)

Combination	Golf Outings per Week	Restaurant Meals per Week
A	1	7
B	2	4
C	3	2
D	4	1

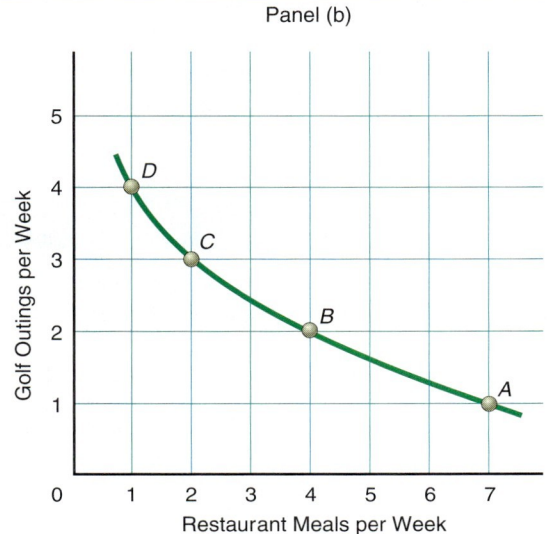

The simple numerical example that we have used happens to concern golf outings and the consumption of restaurant meals (both of which we assume this consumer enjoys) per week. This example is used to illustrate general features of indifference curves and related analytical tools that are necessary for deriving the demand curve. Obviously, we could have used any two commodities. Just remember that we are using a *specific* example to illustrate a *general* analysis.

We plot these combinations graphically in panel (b) of Figure E-1, with restaurant meals per week on the horizontal axis and golf outings per week on the vertical axis. These are our consumer's indifference combinations—the consumer finds each combination as acceptable as the others. These combinations lie along a smooth curve that is known as the consumer's **indifference curve**. Along the indifference curve, every combination of the two goods in question yields the same level of satisfaction. Every point along the indifference curve is equally desirable to the consumer. For example, four golf outings per week and one restaurant meal per week will give our representative consumer exactly the same total satisfaction as two golf outings per week and four restaurant meals per week.

Indifference curve
A curve composed of a set of consumption alternatives, each of which yields the same total amount of satisfaction.

PROPERTIES OF INDIFFERENCE CURVES

Indifference curves have special properties relating to their slope and shape.

Downward Slope

The indifference curve shown in panel (b) of Figure E-1 slopes downward; that is, it has a negative slope. Now consider Figure E-2. Here we show two points, *A* and *B*. Point *A* represents four golf outings per week and two restaurant meals per week. Point *B* represents five golf outings per week and six restaurant meals per week. Clearly, *B* is always preferred to *A* for a consumer who enjoys both restaurant meals and golf outings, because *B* represents more of everything. If *B* is always preferred to *A*, it is impossible for points *A* and *B* to be on the same indifference curve because the definition of the indifference curve is a set of combinations of two goods that are preferred equally.

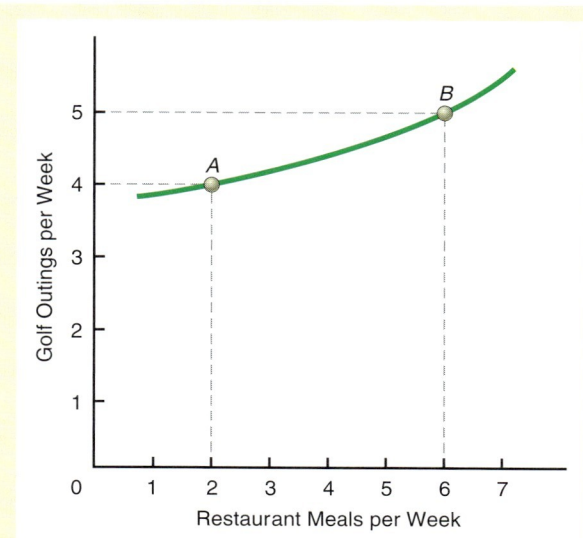

FIGURE E-2
Indifference Curves: Impossibility of an Upward Slope

Point *B* represents a consumption of more golf outings per week and more restaurant meals per week than point *A*. *B* is always preferred to *A*. Therefore, *A* and *B* cannot be on the same *positively* sloped indifference curve. An indifference curve shows *equally preferred* combinations of the two goods.

Curvature

The indifference curve that we have drawn in panel (b) of Figure E-1 on page 520 is special. Notice that it is curved. Why didn't we just draw a straight line, as we have usually done for a demand curve?

Imagining a Straight-Line Indifference Curve. To find out why we don't posit straight-line indifference curves, consider the implications. We show such a straight-line indifference curve in Figure E-3. Start at point A. The consumer has no restaurant meals and five golf outings per week. Now the consumer wishes to go to point B. She is willing to give up only one golf outing in order to get one restaurant meal. Now let's assume that the consumer is at point C, playing golf once a week and consuming four restaurant meals per week. If the consumer wants to go to point D, she is again willing to give up one golf outing in order to get one more restaurant meal per week.

In other words, no matter how many times the consumer plays golf, she is willing to give up one golf outing to get one restaurant meal per week—which does not seem plausible. Doesn't it make sense to hypothesize that the more times the consumer plays golf each week, the less she will value an *additional* golf outing that week? Presumably, when the consumer has five golf outings and no restaurant meals per week, she should be willing to give up *more than* one golf outing in order to get one restaurant meal. Therefore, a straight-line indifference curve as shown in Figure E-3 no longer seems plausible.

Convexity of the Indifference Curve. In mathematical jargon, an indifference curve is convex with respect to the origin. Let's look at this in panel (a) of Figure E-1 on page 520. Starting with combination A, the consumer has one golf outing but seven restaurant meals per week. To remain indifferent, the consumer would have to be willing to give up three restaurant meals to obtain one more golf outing (as shown in combination B). To go from combination C to combination D, however, notice that the consumer would have to be willing to give up only one restaurant meal for an additional golf outing per week. The quantity of the substitute considered acceptable changes as the rate of consumption of the original item changes.

Consequently, the indifference curve in panel (b) of Figure E-1 will be convex when viewed from the origin.

FIGURE E-3
Implications of a Straight-Line Indifference Curve

This straight-line indifference curve indicates that the consumer will always be willing to give up the same number of golf outings to get one more restaurant meal per week. For example, the consumer at point A plays golf five times and consumes no restaurant meals per week. She is willing to give up one golf outing in order to get one restaurant meal per week. At point C, however, the consumer has only one golf outing and four restaurant meals per week. Because of the straight-line indifference curve, this consumer is willing to give up the last golf outing in order to get one more restaurant meal per week, even though she already has four.

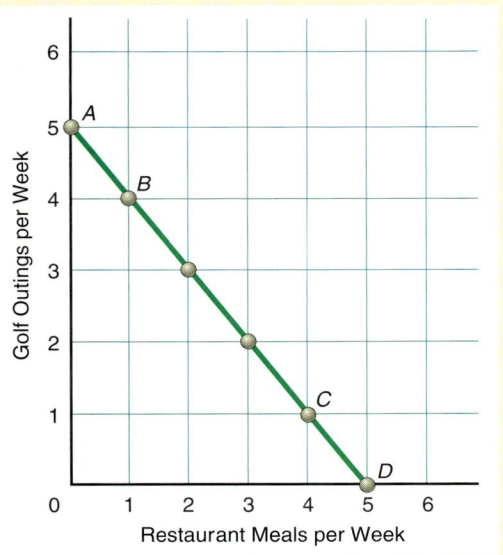

THE MARGINAL RATE OF SUBSTITUTION

Instead of using marginal utility, we can talk in terms of the *marginal rate of substitution* between restaurant meals and golf outings per week. We can formally define the consumer's marginal rate of substitution as follows:

> *The marginal rate of substitution is equal to the change in the quantity of one good that just offsets a one-unit change in the consumption of another good, such that total satisfaction remains constant.*

We can see numerically what happens to the marginal rate of substitution in our example if we rearrange panel (a) of Figure E-1 on page 520 into Table E-1. Here we show restaurant meals in the second column and golf outings in the third. Now we ask the question, what change in the number of golf outings per week will just compensate for a three-unit change in the consumption of restaurant meals per week and leave the consumer's total utility constant? The movement from *A* to *B* increases the number of weekly golf outings by one. Here the marginal rate of substitution is 3:1—a three-unit decrease in restaurant meals requires an increase of one golf outing to leave the consumer's total utility unaltered. Thus, the consumer values the three restaurant meals as the equivalent of one golf outing. We do this for the rest of the table and find that as restaurant meals decrease further, the marginal rate of substitution goes from 3:1 to 2:1 to 1:1. The marginal rate of substitution of restaurant meals for golf outings per week falls as the consumer plays more golf. That is, the consumer values successive golf outings less and less in terms of restaurant meals. The first golf outing is valued at three restaurant meals; the last (fourth) golf outing is valued at only one restaurant meal. The fact that the marginal rate of substitution falls is sometimes called the *law of substitution*.

In geometric language, the slope of the consumer's indifference curve (actually, the negative of the slope of the indifference curve) measures the consumer's marginal rate of substitution.

THE INDIFFERENCE MAP

Let's now consider the possibility of having both more golf outings *and* more restaurant meals per week. When we do this, we can no longer stay on the same indifference curve that we drew in Figure E-1. That indifference curve was drawn for equally satisfying combinations of golf outings and restaurant meals per week. If the individual can now obtain

TABLE E-1

Calculating the Marginal Rate of Substitution

As we move from combination *A* to combination *B*, we are still on the same indifference curve. To stay on that curve, the number of restaurant meals decreases by three and the number of golf outings increases by one. The marginal rate of substitution is 3:1. A three-unit decrease in restaurant meals requires an increase in one golf outing to leave the consumer's total utility unaltered.

(1) Combination	(2) Restaurant Meals per Week	(3) Golf Outings per Week	(4) Marginal Rate of Substitution of Restaurant Meals for Golf Outings
A	7	1	3:1
B	4	2	2:1
C	2	3	1:1
D	1	4	

FIGURE E-4
A Set of Indifference Curves
An infinite number of indifference curves can be drawn. We show three possible ones. Realize that a higher indifference curve represents the possibility of higher rates of consumption of both goods. Hence a higher indifference curve is preferred to a lower one because more is preferred to less. Look at points A and B. Point B represents more golf outings than point A; therefore, bundles on indifference curve I_2 have to be preferred over bundles on I_1 because the number of restaurant meals per week is the same at points A and B.

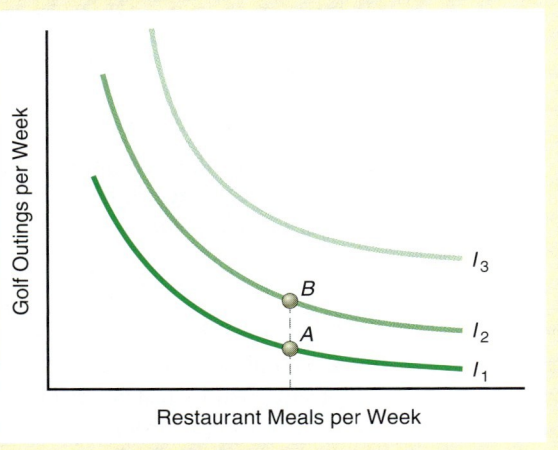

more of both, a new indifference curve will have to be drawn, above and to the right of the one shown in panel (b) of Figure E-1. Alternatively, if the individual faces the possibility of having less of both golf outings and restaurant meals per week, an indifference curve will have to be drawn below and to the left of the one in panel (b) of Figure E-1 on page 520. We can map out a whole set of indifference curves corresponding to these possibilities.

Figure E-4 shows three possible indifference curves. Indifference curves that are higher than others necessarily imply that for every given quantity of one good, more of the other good can be obtained on a higher indifference curve. Looked at another way, if one goes from curve I_1 to I_2, it is possible to consume the same number of restaurant meals *and* be able to play more golf each week. This is shown as a movement from point A to point B in Figure E-4. We could do it the other way. When we move from a lower to a higher indifference curve, it is possible to play the same amount of golf *and* to consume more restaurant meals each week. Thus, the higher an indifference curve is for a consumer, the greater that consumer's total level of satisfaction.

THE BUDGET CONSTRAINT

Budget constraint
All of the possible combinations of goods that can be purchased (at fixed prices) with a specific budget.

Our problem here is to find out how to maximize consumer satisfaction. To do so, we must consult not only our *preferences*—given by indifference curves—but also our *market opportunities*, which are given by our available income and prices, called our **budget constraint**. We might want more of everything, but for any given budget constraint, we have to make choices, or trade-offs, among possible goods. Everyone has a budget constraint; that is, everyone faces a limited consumption potential. How do we show this graphically? We must find the prices of the goods in question and determine the maximum consumption of each allowed by our budget. For example, let's assume that there is a $10 fee for each golf outing and that a restaurant meal costs $20. Let's also assume that our representative consumer has a total budget of $60 per week. What is the maximum number of golf outings the consumer can make? Six. And the maximum number of restaurant meals per week she can consume? Three. So now, as shown in Figure E-5, we have two points on our budget line, which is sometimes called the *consumption possibilities curve*. These anchor points of the budget line are obtained by dividing money income by the price of each product. The first point is at b on the vertical axis; the second, at b' on the horizontal axis. The budget line is linear because prices are constant.

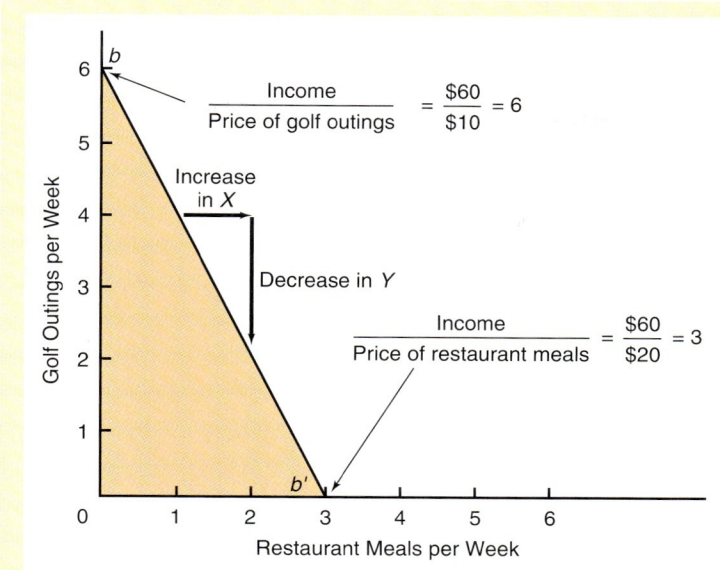

FIGURE E-5
The Budget Constraint

The line bb' represents this individual's budget constraint. Assuming that golf outings cost $10 each, restaurant meals cost $20 each, and the individual has a budget of $60 per week, a maximum of six golf outings or three restaurant meals can be bought each week. These two extreme points are connected to form the budget constraint. All combinations within the colored area and on the budget constraint line are feasible.

Any combination along line bb' is possible; in fact, any combination in the colored area is possible. We will assume, however, that the individual consumer completely uses up the available budget, and we will consider as possible only those points along bb'.

Slope of the Budget Constraint

The budget constraint is a line that slopes downward from left to right. The slope of that line has a special meaning. Look carefully at the budget line in Figure E-5. Remember from our discussion of graphs in Appendix A that we measure a negative slope by the ratio of the decrease in Y over the run in X. In this case, Y is golf outings per week and X is restaurant meals per week. In Figure E-5, the decrease in Y is −2 golf outings per week (a drop from 4 to 2) for an increase in X of one restaurant meal per week (an increase from 1 to 2); therefore, the slope of the budget constraint is −2/1 or −2. This slope of the budget constraint represents the rate of exchange between golf outings and restaurant meals.

Now we are ready to determine how the consumer achieves the optimum consumption rate.

CONSUMER OPTIMUM REVISITED

Consumers will try to attain the highest level of total utility possible, given their budget constraints. How can this be shown graphically? We draw a set of indifference curves similar to those in Figure E-4, and we bring in reality—the budget constraint bb'. Both are drawn in Figure E-6 on the following page. Because a higher level of total satisfaction is represented by a higher indifference curve, we know that the consumer will strive to be on the highest indifference curve possible. The consumer cannot get to indifference curve I_3, however, because the budget will be exhausted before any combination of golf outings and restaurant meals represented on indifference curve I_3 is attained. This consumer can maximize total utility, subject to the budget constraint, only by being at point E on indifference

Go to www.econtoday.com/ch20 for a numerical example illustrating the consumer optimum.

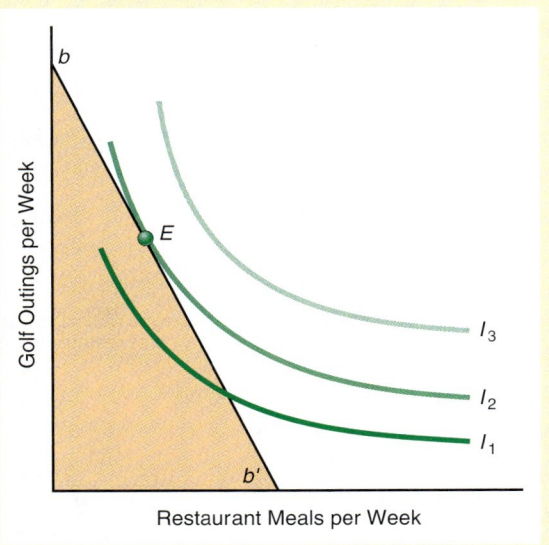

FIGURE E-6

Consumer Optimum

A consumer reaches an optimum when he or she ends up on the highest indifference curve possible, given a limited budget. This occurs at the tangency between an indifference curve and the budget constraint. In this diagram, the tangency is at E.

curve I_2 because here the consumer's income is just being exhausted. Mathematically, point E is called the *tangency point* of the curve I_2 to the straight line bb'.

Consumer optimum is achieved when the marginal rate of substitution (which is subjective) is just equal to the feasible, or realistic, rate of exchange between golf outings and restaurant meals. This realistic rate is the ratio of the two prices of the goods involved. It is represented by the absolute value of the slope of the budget constraint (i.e., ignoring the negative signs). At point E, the point of tangency between indifference curve I_2 and budget constraint bb', the rate at which the consumer wishes to substitute golf outings for restaurant meals (the numerical value of the slope of the indifference curve) is just equal to the rate at which the consumer *can* substitute golf outings for restaurant meals (the slope of the budget line).

To learn about the effects of changes of income and prices and to work with problems on advanced consumer choice theory, go to www.econtoday.com/ch20.

Demand and Supply Elasticity

21

The market prices of various illicit drugs have declined considerably during the past two decades. Since the mid-1970s, the inflation-adjusted price of cocaine has fallen by almost 90 percent, and the inflation-adjusted price of heroin has decreased by more than 80 percent. The market price of methamphetamine, commonly known by such names as "meth," "speed," "ice," or "crystal," has declined by almost 50 percent. Should these relatively substantial decreases in the prices of illicit drugs motivate concerns that consumption of these drugs may have risen dramatically as a result? In this chapter, you will find that the answer to this question depends on how responsive quantities demanded are to decreases in the market prices of these illicit drugs.

Learning Objectives

After reading this chapter, you should be able to:

1. Express and calculate price elasticity of demand
2. Understand the relationship between the price elasticity of demand and total revenues
3. Discuss the factors that determine the price elasticity of demand
4. Describe the cross price elasticity of demand and how it may be used to indicate whether two goods are substitutes or complements
5. Explain the income elasticity of demand
6. Classify supply elasticities and explain how the length of time for adjustment affects the price elasticity of supply

MyEconLab helps you master each objective and study more efficiently. See end of chapter for details.

Did You Know That...

a fall in the price of beer helps explain why nearly one-third of the nearly 15 million U.S. college students are involved in some kind of campus violence each year? The law of demand indicates that a decline in the price of beer increases consumption of beer. In turn, students who drink greater amounts of beer are more likely to have arguments and fights, to commit sexual assaults, and to get into altercations with college officials and police. Economists have found that a 10 percent reduction in the price of beer is associated with an increase in incidents of campus violence of just over 3.5 percent. Since the early 1990s, the inflation-adjusted price of beer has declined by more than 10 percent, which helps explain why more than half a million additional instances of U.S. campus violence now occur each year.

College officials aren't alone in having to worry about how individuals respond to lower prices. Businesses must constantly take into account consumer response to changing prices. If Dell reduces its prices by 10 percent, will consumers respond by buying so many more computers that the company's revenues will rise? At the other end of the spectrum, can Rolls Royce dealers "get away" with a 2 percent increase in prices? That is, will Rolls Royce purchasers respond so little to the relatively small increase in price that the total revenues received for Rolls Royce sales will not fall and may actually rise? The only way to answer these questions is to know how responsive consumers in the real world will be to changes in prices. Economists have a special name for quantity responsiveness—*elasticity*, which is the subject of this chapter.

PRICE ELASTICITY

To begin to understand what elasticity is all about, just keep in mind that it means "responsiveness." Here we are concerned with the price elasticity of demand. We wish to know the extent to which a change in the price of, say, petroleum products will cause the quantity demanded to change, other things held constant. We want to determine the percentage change in quantity demanded in response to a percentage change in price.

Price Elasticity of Demand

Price elasticity of demand (E_p)
The responsiveness of the quantity demanded of a commodity to changes in its price; defined as the percentage change in quantity demanded divided by the percentage change in price.

We will formally define the **price elasticity of demand,** which we will label E_p, as follows:

$$E_p = \frac{\text{percentage change in quantity demanded}}{\text{percentage change in price}}$$

What will price elasticity of demand tell us? It will tell us the *relative* amount by which the quantity demanded will change in response to a change in the price of a particular good.

Consider an example in which a 10 percent rise in the price of oil leads to a reduction in quantity demanded of only 1 percent. Putting these numbers into the formula, we find that the price elasticity of demand for oil in this case equals the percentage change in quantity demanded divided by the percentage change in price, or

$$E_p = \frac{-1\%}{+10\%} = -0.1$$

An elasticity of -0.1 means that a 1 percent *increase* in the price would lead to a mere 0.1 percent *decrease* in the quantity demanded. If you were now told, in contrast, that the price elasticity of demand for oil was -1, you would know that a 1 percent increase in the price of oil would lead to a 1 percent decrease in the quantity demanded.

Relative Quantities Only. Notice that in our elasticity formula, we talk about *percentage* changes in quantity demanded divided by *percentage* changes in price. We focus on relative amounts of price changes, because percentage changes are independent of the units chosen. This means that it doesn't matter if we measure price changes in terms of cents, dollars, or hundreds of dollars. It also doesn't matter whether we measure quantity changes in ounces, grams, or pounds.

Always Negative. The law of demand states that quantity demanded is *inversely* related to the relative price. An *increase* in the price of a good leads to a *decrease* in the quantity demanded. If a *decrease* in the relative price of a good should occur, the quantity demanded would *increase* by a certain percentage. The point is that price elasticity of demand will always be negative. By convention, however, *we will ignore the minus sign in our discussion from this point on.*

Basically, the greater the *absolute* price elasticity of demand (disregarding the sign), the greater the demand responsiveness to relative price changes—a small change in price has a great impact on quantity demanded. Conversely, the smaller the absolute price elasticity of demand, the smaller the demand responsiveness to relative price changes—a large change in price has little effect on quantity demanded.

Go to www.econtoday.com/ch21 for additional review of the price elasticity of demand.

QUICK QUIZ

Elasticity is a measure of the price _____ of the quantity demanded and the quantity supplied.

The **price elasticity of demand** is equal to the percentage change in _____ _____ divided by the percentage change in _____.

Price elasticity of demand is calculated in terms of _____ changes in quantity demanded and in price.

Thus, it is expressed as a unitless, dimensionless number that is _____ of units of measurement.

The law of demand states that quantity demanded and price are _____ related. Therefore, the price elasticity of demand is always _____, because an increase in price will lead to a decrease in quantity demanded and a decrease in price will lead to an increase in quantity demanded. By convention, we ignore the negative sign in discussions of the price elasticity of demand.

See page 551 for the answers. Review concepts from this section in MyEconLab.

Calculating Elasticity

To calculate the price elasticity of demand, we must compute percentage changes in quantity demanded and in price. For the percentage change in quantity demanded, we might divide the change in the quantity demanded by the original quantity demanded:

$$\frac{\text{Change in quantity demanded}}{\text{Original quantity demanded}}$$

To find the percentage change in price, we might divide the change in price by the original price:

$$\frac{\text{Change in price}}{\text{Original price}}$$

There is an arithmetic problem, though, when we calculate percentage changes in this manner. The percentage change, say, from 2 to 3—50 percent—is not the same as the percentage change from 3 to 2—$33\frac{1}{3}$ percent. In other words, it makes a difference where you start. One way out of this dilemma is simply to use average values.

To compute the price elasticity of demand, we take the average of the two prices and the two quantities over the range we are considering and compare the change with these averages. Thus, the formula for computing the price elasticity of demand is as follows:

$$E_p = \frac{\text{change in quantity}}{\text{sum of quantities}/2} \div \frac{\text{change in price}}{\text{sum of prices}/2}$$

We can rewrite this more simply if we do two things: (1) We can let Q_1 and Q_2 equal the two different quantities demanded before and after the price change and let P_1 and P_2 equal the two different prices. (2) Because we will be dividing a percentage by a percentage, we simply use the ratio, or the decimal form, of the percentages. Therefore,

$$E_p = \frac{\Delta Q}{(Q_1 + Q_2)/2} \div \frac{\Delta P}{(P_1 + P_2)/2}$$

where the Greek letter Δ (delta) stands for "change in."

How can we use actual price changes and associated changes in the quantity of gasoline demanded to calculate the price elasticity of demand for gasoline using this formula?

EXAMPLE

The Price Elasticity of Demand for Gasoline

During the week following the Gulf Coast devastation wrought by Hurricane Katrina in September 2005, the nationwide price of gasoline rose from $2.61 to $3.07. The total quantity of gasoline consumed in the United States declined from 9.42 million barrels to 9.04 million barrels.

We can calculate the price elasticity of the demand for gasoline by U.S. consumers using the formula presented earlier (under the assumption, of course, that all other things, such as bus fares, were constant):

$$E_p = \frac{\text{change in } Q}{\text{sum of quantities}/2} \div \frac{\text{change in } P}{\text{sum of prices}/2}$$

$$= \frac{9.42 \text{ million} - 9.04 \text{ million}}{(9.42 \text{ million} + 9.04 \text{ million})/2} \div \frac{\$3.07 - \$2.61}{(\$3.07 + \$2.61)/2}$$

$$= \frac{0.38 \text{ million}}{18.46 \text{ million}/2} \div \frac{\$0.46}{\$5.68/2} = 0.25.$$

The price elasticity of 0.25 means that a 1 percent increase in price generated a 0.25 percent decrease in the quantity of gasoline demanded.

FOR CRITICAL ANALYSIS
Would the estimated price elasticity of demand for gasoline have been different if we had not used the average-values formula? How?

Elastic demand
A demand relationship in which a given percentage change in price will result in a larger percentage change in quantity demanded. Total expenditures and price changes are inversely related in the elastic region of the demand curve.

PRICE ELASTICITY RANGES

We have names for the varying ranges of price elasticities, depending on whether a 1 percent change in price elicits more or less than a 1 percent change in the quantity demanded.

- We say that a good has an **elastic demand** whenever the price elasticity of demand is greater than 1. A 1 percent change in price causes a greater than 1 percent change in the quantity demanded.

- In a situation of **unit elasticity of demand,** a 1 percent change in price causes exactly a 1 percent change in the quantity demanded.
- In a situation of **inelastic demand,** a 1 percent change in price causes a change of less than 1 percent in the quantity demanded.

When we say that a commodity's demand is elastic, we are indicating that consumers are relatively responsive to changes in price. When we say that a commodity's demand is inelastic, we are indicating that its consumers are relatively unresponsive to price changes. When economists say that demand is inelastic, it very rarely means that quantity demanded is *totally* unresponsive to price changes. Remember, the law of demand implies that there will be some responsiveness in quantity demanded to a price change. The question is how much. That's what elasticity attempts to determine.

Unit elasticity of demand
A demand relationship in which the quantity demanded changes exactly in proportion to the change in price. Total expenditures are invariant to price changes in the unit-elastic region of the demand curve.

Inelastic demand
A demand relationship in which a given percentage change in price will result in a less than proportionate percentage change in the quantity demanded. Total expenditures and price are directly related in the inelastic region of the demand curve.

Extreme Elasticities

There are two extremes in price elasticities of demand. One extreme represents total unresponsiveness of quantity demanded to price changes, which is referred to as **perfectly inelastic demand,** or zero elasticity. The other represents total responsiveness, which is referred to as infinitely or **perfectly elastic demand.**

We show perfect inelasticity in panel (a) of Figure 21-1. Notice that the quantity demanded per year is 8 million units, no matter what the price. Hence, for any price change, the quantity demanded will remain the same, and thus the change in the quantity demanded will be zero. Look back at our formula for computing elasticity. If the change in the quantity demanded is zero, the numerator is also zero, and a nonzero number divided into zero results in a value of zero too. This is true at any point along the demand curve. Hence there is perfect inelasticity.

At the opposite extreme is the situation depicted in panel (b) of Figure 21-1. Here we show that at a price of 30 cents, an unlimited quantity will be demanded. At a price that is only slightly above 30 cents, no quantity will be demanded. There is perfect, or infinite, responsiveness at each point along this curve, and hence we call the demand schedule in panel (b) perfectly elastic.

Perfectly inelastic demand
A demand that exhibits zero responsiveness to price changes; no matter what the price is, the quantity demanded remains the same.

Perfectly elastic demand
A demand that has the characteristic that even the slightest increase in price will lead to zero quantity demanded.

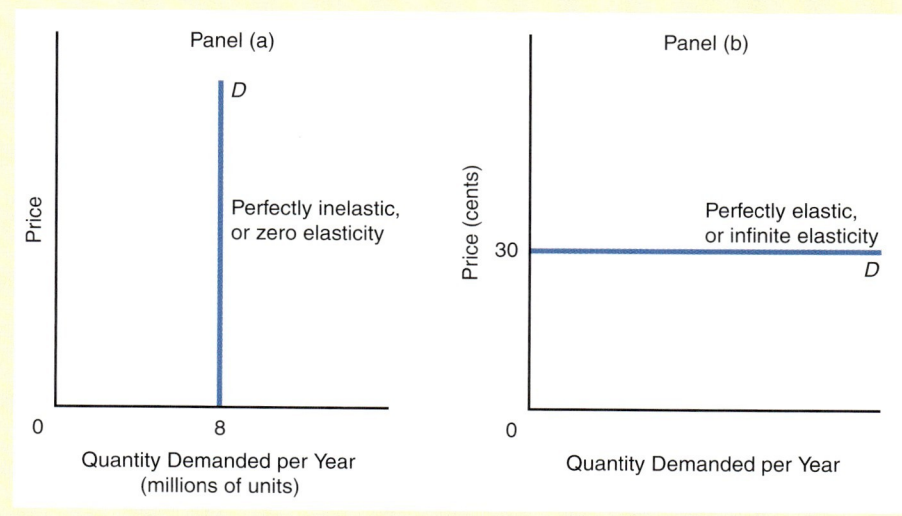

FIGURE 21-1

Extreme Price Elasticities

In panel (a), we show infinite price unresponsiveness. The demand curve is vertical at the quantity of 8 million units per year. This means that the price elasticity of demand is zero. In panel (b), we show complete price responsiveness. At a price of 30 cents, in this example, consumers will demand an unlimited quantity of the particular good in question. This is a case of infinite price elasticity of demand.

QUICK QUIZ

One extreme elasticity occurs when a demand curve is vertical. It has _____ price elasticity of demand. It is completely _____.

Another extreme elasticity occurs when a demand curve is horizontal. It has completely _____ demand. Its price elasticity of demand is _____.

See page 551 for the answers. Review concepts from this section in MyEconLab.

ELASTICITY AND TOTAL REVENUES

Suppose that you are in charge of the pricing decision for a cellular telephone service company. How would you know when it is better to raise or not to raise prices? The answer depends in part on the effect of your pricing decision on total revenues, or the total receipts of your company. (The rest of the equation is, of course, your cost structure, a subject we examine in Chapter 23.) It is commonly thought that the way to increase total receipts is to increase price per unit. But is it possible that a rise in price per unit could lead to a decrease in total revenues? The answer to this question depends on the price elasticity of demand.

How does elasticity affect who pays cigarette taxes?

POLICY EXAMPLE

Who Pays Higher Cigarette Taxes?

State governments impose cigarette taxes, which are assessed as a flat amount per pack sold. These taxes are paid by sellers of cigarettes from the revenues they earn from their total sales. Thus, to receive the same effective price for selling a given quantity, a cigarette seller would have to receive a price that is higher by exactly the amount of the tax. As shown in panel (a) of Figure 21-2, this means that imposing a cigarette tax shifts the supply curve upward by the amount of the tax. Sellers supply a given quantity of cigarettes at a price that is higher by the amount of the tax that they will transmit to the government.

Who *truly* pays the tax depends on the price elasticity of demand, however. Take a look at panel (b) of Figure 21-2, which illustrates what would happen to the market price in the case of perfectly inelastic demand for cigarettes. In this instance, the market price rises by the full amount that the supply curve shifts upward. This amount, of course, is the amount of the tax. Consequently, if cigarette consumers were to have a perfectly inelastic demand for cigarettes, they would effectively pay the entire tax in the form of higher prices. Panel (c) illustrates the opposite case, in which the demand for cigarettes happens to be perfectly elastic. In this situation, the market price is unresponsive to a tax-induced shift in the supply curve, so sellers must pay all the tax.

Realistically, the price elasticity of demand for cigarettes is relatively low—most cigarette price elasticity estimates indicate values of 0.2 to 0.4. Thus, the burden of cigarette taxes falls mainly on cigarette consumers.

FOR CRITICAL ANALYSIS
Based on the information in this example, if excise taxes on cigarettes increase by 10 percent, by what range of percentages may desired cigarette purchases decline?

(continued)

FIGURE 21-2
Price Elasticity and a Cigarette Tax

Placing a per-pack tax on cigarettes causes the supply curve to shift upward by the amount of the tax, as illustrated in panel (a), in order for sellers to receive the same effective price for any given quantity of cigarettes they sell. If the demand for cigarettes were perfectly inelastic, as depicted in panel (b), imposing the tax would cause the market price of cigarettes to rise by the amount of the tax, so that cigarette consumers would effectively pay all the tax. Conversely, if the demand for cigarettes were perfectly elastic, as shown in panel (c), the market price would not change, and sellers would pay all the tax. The quantity demanded would fall to Q_2.

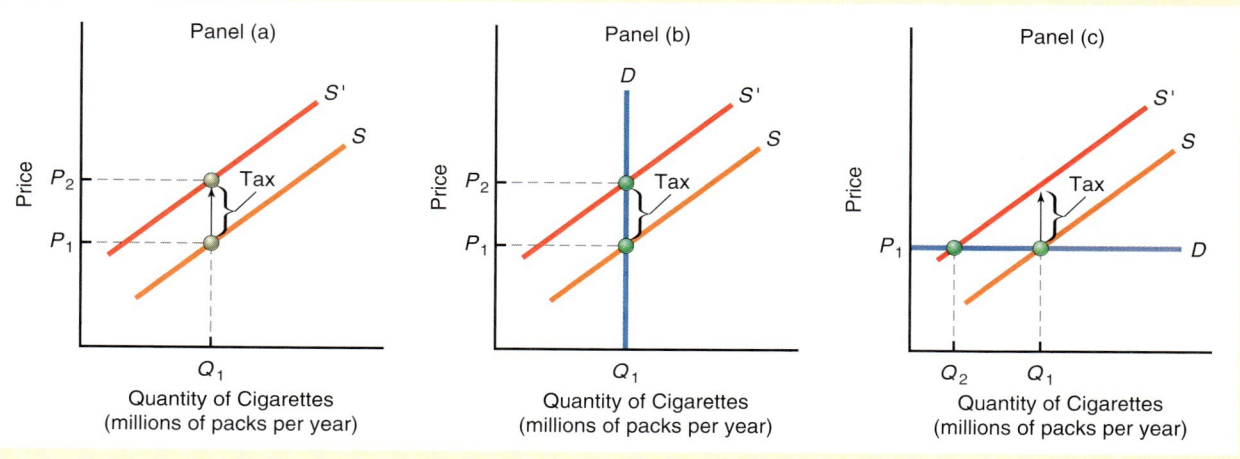

Let's look at Figure 21-3 on the following page. In panel (a), column 1 shows the price of cellular telephone service in cents per minute, and column 2 represents billions of minutes per year. In column 3, we multiply column 1 times column 2 to derive total revenue because total revenue is always equal to the number of units (quantity) sold times the price per unit. In column 4, we calculate values of elasticity. Notice what happens to total revenues throughout the schedule. They rise steadily as the price rises from 1 cent to 5 cents per minute; but when the price rises further to 6 cents per minute, total revenues remain constant at $3 billion. At prices per minute higher than 6 cents, total revenues fall as price increases. Indeed, if prices are above 6 cents per minute, total revenues can be increased only by *reducing* prices, not by raising them.

Labeling Elasticity

The relationship between price and quantity on the demand schedule is given in columns 1 and 2 of panel (a) in Figure 21-3. In panel (b), the demand curve, D, representing that schedule is drawn. In panel (c), the total revenue curve representing the data in column 3 is drawn. Notice first the level of these curves at small quantities. The demand curve is at a maximum height, but total revenue is zero, which makes sense according to this demand schedule—at a price of 11 cents per minute and above, no units will be purchased, and therefore total revenue will be zero. As price is lowered, we travel down the demand curve, and total revenues increase until price is 6 cents per minute, remain constant from 6 cents to 5 cents per minute, and then fall at lower unit prices. Corresponding to those three sections, demand is elastic, unit-elastic, and inelastic. Hence we have three relationships among the three types of price elasticity and total revenues.

Go to www.econtoday.com/ch21 to participate in an Economics Interactive Tutorial at the University of South Carolina that provides further practice with elasticity.

FIGURE 21-3

The Relationship Between Price Elasticity of Demand and Total Revenues for Cellular Phone Service

In panel (a), we show the elastic, unit-elastic, and inelastic sections of the demand schedule according to whether a reduction in price increases total revenues, causes them to remain constant, or causes them to decrease, respectively. In panel (b), we show these regions graphically on the demand curve. In panel (c), we show them on the total revenue curve.

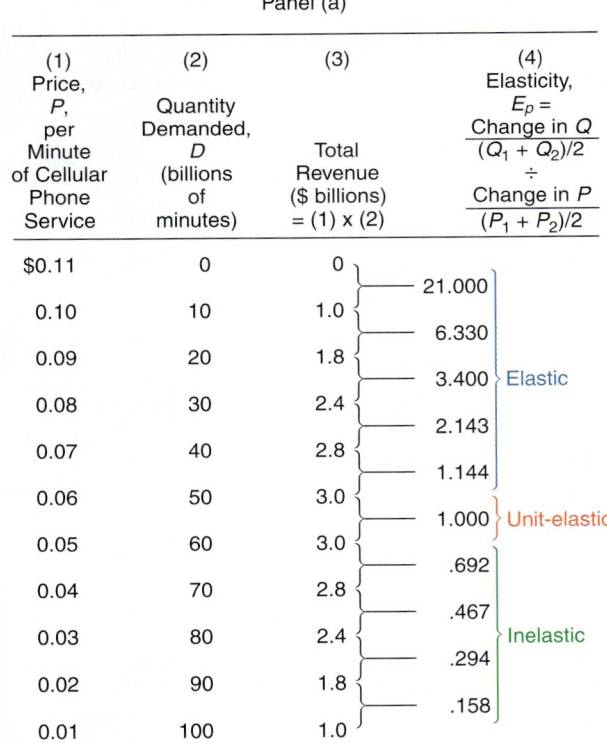

- *Elastic demand.* A negative relationship exists between changes in price and changes in total revenues. That is to say, if price is lowered, total revenues will rise when the firm faces demand that is elastic, and if it raises price, total revenues will fall. Consider another example. If the price of Diet Coke were raised by 25 percent and the price of all other soft drinks remained constant, the quantity demanded of Diet Coke would proba-

bly fall dramatically. The decrease in quantity demanded due to the increase in the price of Diet Coke would lead in this example to a reduction in the total revenues of the Coca-Cola Company. Therefore, if demand is elastic, price and total revenues will move in *opposite* directions.
- **Unit-elastic demand.** Changes in price do not change total revenues. When the firm is facing demand that is unit-elastic, if it increases price, total revenues will not change; if it decreases price, total revenues will not change either.
- **Inelastic demand.** A positive relationship exists between changes in price and total revenues. When the firm is facing demand that is inelastic, if it raises price, total revenues will go up; if it lowers price, total revenues will fall. Consider another example. You have just invented a cure for the common cold that has been approved by the Food and Drug Administration for sale to the public. You are not sure what price you should charge, so you start out with a price of $1 per pill. You sell 20 million pills at that price over a year. The next year, you decide to raise the price by 25 percent, to $1.25. The number of pills you sell drops to 18 million per year. The price increase of 25 percent has led to a 10 percent decrease in quantity demanded. Your total revenues, however, will rise to $22.5 million because of the price increase. We therefore conclude that if demand is inelastic, price and total revenues move in the *same* direction.

Graphic Presentaion. The elastic, unit-elastic, and inelastic areas of the demand curve are shown in Figure 21-3. For prices from 11 cents per minute of cellular phone time to 6 cents per minute, as price decreases, total revenues rise from zero to $3 billion. Demand is elastic. When price changes from 6 cents to 5 cents, however, total revenues remain constant at $3 billion; demand is unit-elastic. Finally, when price falls from 5 cents to 1 cent, total revenues decrease from $3 billion to $1 billion; demand is inelastic. In panels (b) and (c) of Figure 21-3, we have labeled the sections of the demand curve accordingly, and we have also shown how total revenues first rise, then remain constant, and finally fall.

The Elasticity-Revenue Relationship. The relationship between price elasticity of demand and total revenues brings together some important microeconomic concepts. Total revenues, as we have noted, are the product of price per unit times number of units sold. The law of demand states that along a given demand curve, price and quantity changes will move in opposite directions: One increases as the other decreases. Consequently, what happens to the product of price times quantity depends on which of the opposing changes exerts a greater force on total revenues. But this is just what price elasticity of demand is designed to measure—responsiveness of quantity demanded to a change in price. The relationship between price elasticity of demand and total revenues is summarized in Table 21-1.

ECONOMICS FRONT AND CENTER

To consider pricing issues that pet food manufacturers face in light of different price elasticities of demand for different food formulas, read **Total Revenues and the Price Elasticity of Demand for Dog Food**, on page 545.

TABLE 21-1

Relationship Between Price Elasticity of Demand and Total Revenues

Price Elasticity of Demand (E_p)		Effect of Price Change on Total Revenues (TR)	
		Price Decrease	Price Increase
Inelastic	($E_p < 1$)	TR ↓	TR ↑
Unit-elastic	($E_p = 1$)	No change in TR	No change in TR
Elastic	($E_p > 1$)	TR ↑	TR ↓

QUICK QUIZ

Price elasticity of demand is related to total _____ (and total consumer _____).

When demand is *elastic*, the change in price elicits a change in total revenues in the _____ direction from the price change.

When demand is *unit-elastic*, a change in price elicits _____ change in total revenues (or in total consumer expenditures).

When demand is *inelastic*, a change in price elicits a change in total revenues (and in consumer expenditures) in the _____ direction as the price change.

See page 551 for the answers. Review concepts from this section in MyEconLab.

DETERMINANTS OF THE PRICE ELASTICITY OF DEMAND

We have learned how to calculate the price elasticity of demand. We know that theoretically it ranges numerically from zero—completely inelastic—to infinity—completely elastic. What we would like to do now is come up with a list of the determinants of the price elasticity of demand. The price elasticity of demand for a particular commodity at any price depends, at a minimum, on the following factors:

- The existence, number, and quality of substitutes
- The percentage of a consumer's total budget devoted to purchases of that commodity
- The length of time allowed for adjustment to changes in the price of the commodity

Existence of Substitutes

The closer the substitutes for a particular commodity and the more substitutes there are, the greater will be its price elasticity of demand. At the limit, if there is a perfect substitute, the elasticity of demand for the commodity will be infinity. Thus, even the slightest increase in the commodity's price will cause a dramatic reduction in the quantity demanded: Quantity demanded will fall to zero.

Keep in mind that we are really talking about two goods that the consumer believes are exactly alike and equally desirable, like dollar bills whose only difference is their serial numbers. When we talk about less extreme examples, we can speak only in terms of the number and the similarity of substitutes that are available.

Thus, we will find that the more narrowly we define a good, the closer and greater will be the number of substitutes available. For example, the demand for Diet Coke may be highly elastic because consumers can switch to Diet Pepsi. The demand for diet drinks in general, however, is relatively less elastic because there are fewer substitutes.

Share of Budget

We know that the greater the share of a person's total budget that is spent on a commodity, the greater that person's price elasticity of demand is for that commodity. A key reason that the demand for pepper is very inelastic is because individuals spend so little on it relative to their total budgets. In contrast, the demand for items such as transportation and housing is far more elastic because they occupy a large part of people's budgets—changes in their prices cannot easily be ignored without sacrificing a lot of other alternative goods that could be purchased.

Consider a numerical example. A household spends $40,000 a year. It purchases $4 of pepper per year and $4,000 of transportation services. Now consider the spending power of this family when the price of pepper and the price of transportation both double. If the household buys the same amount of pepper, it will now spend $8. It will thus have to reduce other expenditures by $4. This $4 represents only 0.01 percent of the entire household budget. By contrast, a doubling of transportation costs requires that the family spend $8,000, or $4,000 more on transportation, if it is to purchase the same quantity. That increased expenditure on transportation of $4,000 represents 10 percent of total expenditures that must be switched from other purchases. We would therefore predict that the household will react differently to the doubling of the price of pepper than it will for a doubling of transportation prices. It will reduce its transportation purchases by a proportionately greater amount.

Time for Adjustment

When the price of a commodity changes and that price change persists, more people will learn about it. Further, consumers will be better able to revise their consumption patterns the longer the time period they have to do so. And in fact, the longer the time they do take, the less costly it will be for them to engage in this revision of consumption patterns. Consider a price decrease. The longer the price decrease persists, the greater will be the number of new uses that consumers will discover for the particular commodity, and the greater will be the number of new users of that particular commodity.

It is possible to make a very strong statement about the relationship between the price elasticity of demand and the time allowed for adjustment:

The longer any price change persists, the greater the elasticity of demand, other things held constant. Elasticity of demand is greater in the long run than in the short run.

Short-Run versus Long-Run Adjustments. Let's consider an example. Suppose that the price of electricity goes up 50 percent. How do you adjust in the short run? You can turn the lights off more often, you can stop using your personal computer as much as you usually do, and so on. Otherwise it's very difficult to cut back on your consumption of electricity.

In the long run, though, you can devise methods to reduce your consumption. Instead of using only electric heaters, the next time you have a house built you will install solar panels. You will purchase fluorescent bulbs because they use less electricity. The more time you have to think about it, the more ways you will find to cut your electricity consumption.

Demand Elasticity in the Short Run and in the Long Run. We would expect, therefore, that the short-run demand curve for electricity would be relatively less elastic (in the price range around P_e), as demonstrated by D_1 in Figure 21-4 on the following page. However, the long-run demand curve will exhibit more elasticity (in the neighborhood of P_e), as demonstrated by D_3. Indeed, we can think of an entire family of demand curves such as those depicted in the figure. The short-run demand curve is for the period when there is little time for adjustment. As more time is allowed, the demand curve goes first to D_2 and then all the way to D_3. Thus, in the neighborhood of P_e, elasticity differs for each of these curves. It is greater for the less steep curves (but slope alone does not measure elasticity for the entire curve).

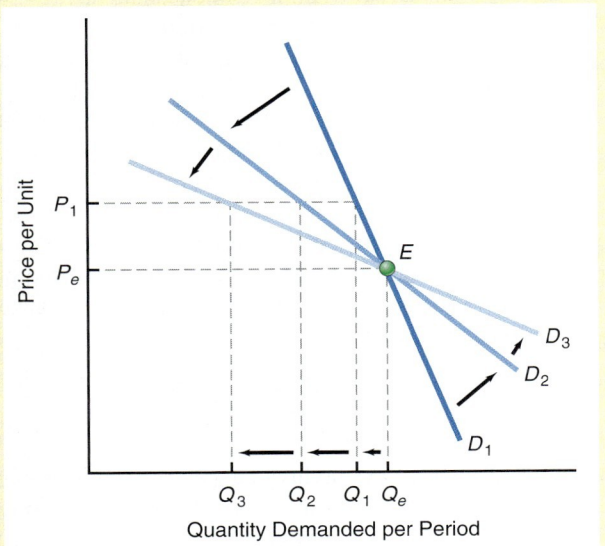

FIGURE 21-4

Short-Run and Long-Run Price Elasticity of Demand

Consider a situation in which the market price is P_e and the quantity demanded is Q_e. Then there is a price increase to P_1. In the short run, as evidenced by the demand curve D_1, we move from equilibrium quantity demanded, Q_e, to Q_1. After more time is allowed for adjustment, the demand curve rotates at original price P_e to D_2. Quantity demanded falls again, now to Q_2. After even more time is allowed for adjustment, the demand curve rotates at price P_e to D_3. At the higher price P_1 in the long run, the quantity demanded falls all the way to Q_3.

How to Define the Short Run and the Long Run. We've mentioned the short run and the long run. Is the short run one week, two weeks, one month, two months? Is the long run three years, four years, five years? The answer is that there is no single answer. What we mean by the long run is the period of time necessary for consumers to make a full adjustment to a given price change, all other things held constant. In the case of the demand for electricity, the long run will be however long it takes consumers to switch over to cheaper sources of heating, to buy houses that are more energy-efficient, to purchase appliances that are more energy-efficient, and so on. The long-run elasticity of demand for electricity therefore relates to a period of at least several years. The short run—by default—is any period less than the long run.

EXAMPLE

What Do Real-World Price Elasticities of Demand Look Like?

In Table 21-2, we present demand elasticities for selected goods. None of them is zero, and the largest is 4.6. Remember that even though we are leaving off the negative sign, there is an inverse relationship between price and quantity demanded, and the minus sign is understood. Also remember that these elasticities represent averages over given price ranges. Choosing different price ranges could yield different elasticity estimates for these goods.

Economists have consistently found that estimated price elasticities of demand are greater in the long run than in the short run, as seen in Table 21-2. There you see that all available estimates indicate that the long-run price elasticity of demand for vacation air travel is 2.7, whereas the estimate for the short run is 1.1. Throughout the table, you see that all estimates of long-run price elasticities of demand exceed their short-run counterparts.

FOR CRITICAL ANALYSIS

Explain the intuitive reasoning behind the difference between long-run and short-run price elasticity of demand.

(continued)

TABLE 21-2
Price Elasticities of Demand for Selected Goods

Here are estimated demand elasticities for selected goods. All of them are negative, although we omit the minus sign. We have given some estimates of the long-run price elasticities of demand. The long run is associated with the time necessary for consumers to adjust fully to any given price change. (Note: "N.A." indicates that no estimate is available.)

Category	Estimated Elasticity Short Run	Estimated Elasticity Long Run
Air travel (business)	0.4	1.2
Air travel (vacation)	1.1	2.7
Beef	0.6	N.A.
Cheese	0.3	N.A.
Electricity	0.1	1.7
Fresh tomatoes	4.6	N.A.
Gasoline	0.2	0.5
Hospital services	0.1	0.7
Intercity bus service	0.6	2.2
Physician services	0.1	0.6
Private education	1.1	1.9
Restaurant meals	2.3	N.A.
Tires	0.9	1.2

CROSS PRICE ELASTICITY OF DEMAND

In Chapter 3, we discussed the effect of a change in the price of one good on the demand for a related good. We defined substitutes and complements in terms of whether a reduction in the price of one caused a decrease or an increase, respectively, in the demand for the other. If the price of compact discs is held constant, the number of CDs purchased (at any price) will certainly be influenced by the price of a close substitute such as Internet digital music downloads. If the price of computer printers is held constant, the amount of computer printers demanded (at any price) will certainly be affected by changes in the price of computers. (These goods are complements.)

Measuring the Cross Price Elasticity of Demand

What we now need to do is come up with a numerical measure of the price responsiveness of demand to the prices of related goods. This is called the **cross price elasticity of demand (E_{xy})**, which is defined as the percentage change in the demand for one good (a shift in the demand curve) divided by the percentage change in the price of the related good. In equation form, the cross price elasticity of demand between good X and good Y is

$$E_{xy} = \frac{\text{percentage change in demand for good X}}{\text{percentage change in price of good Y}}$$

Alternatively, the cross price elasticity of demand between good Y and good X would use the percentage change in the demand for good Y as the numerator and the percentage change in the price of good X as the denominator.

Cross price elasticity of demand (E_{xy}) The percentage change in the demand for one good (holding its price constant) divided by the percentage change in the price of a related good.

Substitutes and Complements

When two goods are substitutes, the cross price elasticity of demand will be positive. For example, when the price of rewritable DVD drives goes up, the demand for flash memory drives will rise in response as consumers shift away from the now relatively more expensive rewritable DVD drives to flash memory drives. A producer of flash memory drives could benefit from a numerical estimate of the cross price elasticity of demand between rewritable DVD drives and flash memory drives. For example, if the price of rewritable DVD drives went up by 10 percent and the producer of flash memory drives knew that the cross price elasticity of demand was 1, the flash drive producer could estimate that the demand for flash memory drives would also go up by 10 percent at any given price. Plans for increasing production of flash memory drives could then be made.

When two related goods are complements, the cross price elasticity of demand will be negative (and we will *not* disregard the minus sign). For example, when the price of personal computers declines, the demand for computer printers will rise. This is because as prices of computers decrease, the number of printers purchased at any given price of printers will naturally increase, because computers and printers are often used together. Any manufacturer of computer printers must take this into account in making production plans.

If goods are completely unrelated, their cross price elasticity of demand will, by definition, be zero.

What does evidence about the cross price elasticity of demand for wireless and wired phone services tell us about the extent to which people view these telecommunications services as substitutes?

EXAMPLE

Do People Substitute Wireless Phone Services for Wired Services?

If people regard cellphones as a form of communication that they use mainly on the go while viewing traditional land-wired phone service as a means of communication from their homes, then the two types of services are not substitutes. In contrast, if people respond to higher prices of land-wired phone service by consuming more wireless phone services instead—and perhaps using only wireless services—then they are substitute services.

Recently, two economists, Allan Ingraham and J. Gregory Sidak, estimated that the cross price elasticity of demand between wireless and wired phone services is about 0.02.

This estimate implies that a 10 percent increase in the price of land-wired phone services induces a 0.2 percent increase in the quantity of wireless phone services demanded. The two types of phone services are substitutes, but the degree of substitution is very slight.

FOR CRITICAL ANALYSIS
As younger U.S. residents, who tend to use cellphones more than land-line phones, gradually replace their elders, what is likely to happen to the cross price elasticity of demand for the two types of telecommunications services?

INCOME ELASTICITY OF DEMAND

In Chapter 3, we discussed the determinants of demand. One of those determinants was income. We can apply our understanding of elasticity to the relationship between changes in income and changes in demand.

Measuring the Income Elasticity of Demand

Income elasticity of demand (E_i)
The percentage change in demand for any good, holding its price constant, divided by the percentage change in income; the responsiveness of demand to changes in income, holding the good's relative price constant.

We measure the responsiveness of quantity purchased to income changes by the **income elasticity of demand (E_i)**:

$$E_i = \frac{\text{percentage change in demand}}{\text{percentage change in income}}$$

holding relative price constant.

Period	Number of DVDs Demanded per Month	Income per Month
1	6	$4,000
2	8	6,000

TABLE 21-3
How Income Affects Quantity of DVDs Demanded

Income elasticity of demand refers to a *horizontal shift* in the demand curve in response to changes in income, whereas price elasticity of demand refers to a *movement along* the curve in response to price changes. Thus, income elasticity of demand is calculated at a given price, and price elasticity of demand is calculated at a given income.

Calculating the Income Elasticity of Demand

To get the same income elasticity of demand over the same range of values regardless of the direction of change (increase or decrease), we can use the same formula that we used in computing the price elasticity of demand. When doing so, we have

$$E_i = \frac{\text{change in quantity}}{\text{sum of quanties}/2} \div \frac{\text{change in income}}{\text{sum of incomes}/2}$$

A simple example will demonstrate how income elasticity of demand can be computed. Table 21-3 gives the relevant data. The product in question is prerecorded DVDs. We assume that the price of DVDs remains constant relative to other prices. In period 1, six DVDs per month are purchased. Income per month is $4,000. In period 2, monthly income increases to $6,000, and the number of DVDs demanded per month increases to eight. We can apply the following calculation:

$$E_i = \frac{2/[(6+8)/2]}{\$2,000/[(\$4,000+\$6,000)/2]} = \frac{2/7}{2/5} = 0.71$$

Hence measured income elasticity of demand for DVDs for the individual represented in this example is 0.71.

What can we infer from the fact that the income elasticity of demand for lamb is negative?

EXAMPLE

Good News for Sheep, but Bad News for the U.S. Lamb Industry

The U.S. Department of Agriculture estimates income elasticities of demand for a wide variety of farm products. Among these are meat products, such as beef, which has an estimated income elasticity of demand of 0.34. Thus, when U.S. consumers' incomes increase by 10 percent, their consumption of beef rises by 3.4 percent.

In contrast, the estimated income elasticity of demand for lamb is about −0.54, so a 10 percent increase in income induces U.S. consumers to *reduce* their consumption of lamb by 5.4 percent. The fact that an income increase generates a decline in purchases of lamb means that lamb is an *inferior good*. Other things being equal, the demand for lamb declines as consumers' incomes rise. This helps explain why, as inflation-adjusted U.S. per capita real income has steadily risen since the early 1970s, annual U.S. per capita consumption of lamb has declined from 3 pounds per person to only about 1 pound per person.

FOR CRITICAL ANALYSIS
Assuming that U.S. residents' incomes keep rising, what does the negative income elasticity of demand for lamb suggest about the likely long-term success of efforts by the U.S. government to spend $5 million each year promoting lamb consumption?

You have just been introduced to three types of elasticities. All three elasticities are important in influencing the consumption of most goods. Reasonably accurate estimates of these elasticities can go a long way toward making accurate forecasts of demand for goods or services.

> **QUICK QUIZ**
>
> Some determinants of price elasticity of demand are (1) the existence, number, and quality of _____; (2) the _____ of the total budget spent on the good in question; and (3) the length of time allowed for _____ to a change in prices.
>
> _____ price elasticity of demand measures one good's demand responsiveness to another's price changes.
>
> For substitutes, it is _____; for complements, it is _____.
>
> **Income elasticity of demand** tells you by what percentage _____ will change for a particular percentage change in _____.
>
> See page 551 for the answers. Review concepts from this section in MyEconLab.

PRICE ELASTICITY OF SUPPLY

Price elasticity of supply (E_s)
The responsiveness of the quantity supplied of a commodity to a change in its price; the percentage change in quantity supplied divided by the percentage change in price.

The **price elasticity of supply (E_s)** is defined similarly to the price elasticity of demand. Supply elasticities are generally positive; this is because at higher prices, larger quantities will generally be forthcoming from suppliers. The definition of the price elasticity of supply is as follows:

$$E_s = \frac{\text{percentage change in quantity supplied}}{\text{percentage change in price}}$$

Classifying Supply Elasticities

Just as with demand, there are different ranges of supply elasticities. They are similar in definition to the ranges of demand elasticities.

If a 1 percent increase in price elicits a greater than 1 percent increase in the quantity supplied, we say that at the particular price in question on the supply schedule, *supply is elastic*. The most extreme elastic supply is called **perfectly elastic supply**—the slightest reduction in price will cause quantity supplied to fall to zero.

Perfectly elastic supply
A supply characterized by a reduction in quantity supplied to zero when there is the slightest decrease in price.

Perfectly inelastic supply
A supply for which quantity supplied remains constant, no matter what happens to price.

If, conversely, a 1 percent increase in price elicits a less than 1 percent increase in the quantity supplied, we refer to that as an *inelastic supply*. The most extreme inelastic supply is called **perfectly inelastic supply**—no matter what the price, the quantity supplied remains the same.

If the percentage change in the quantity supplied is just equal to the percentage change in the price, we call this *unit-elastic supply*.

Figure 21-5 shows two supply schedules, S and S'. You can tell at a glance, even without reading the labels, which one is perfectly elastic and which one is perfectly inelastic. As you might expect, most supply schedules exhibit elasticities that are somewhere between zero and infinity.

FIGURE 21-5
The Extremes in Supply Curves
Here we have drawn two extremes of supply schedules: S is a perfectly elastic supply curve; S' is a perfectly inelastic one. In the former, an unlimited quantity will be supplied at price P_1. In the latter, no matter what the price, the quantity supplied will be Q_1. An example of S' might be the supply curve for fresh (unfrozen) fish on the morning the boats come in.

Price Elasticity of Supply and Length of Time for Adjustment

We pointed out earlier that the longer the time period allowed for adjustment, the greater the price elasticity of demand. It turns out that the same proposition applies to supply. The longer the time for adjustment, the more elastic the supply curve. Consider why this is true:

1. The longer the time allowed for adjustment, the more resources can flow into (or out of) an industry through expansion (or contraction) of existing firms. As an example, suppose that there is a long-lasting, significant increase in the demand for gasoline. The result is a sustained rise in the market price of gasoline. Initially, gasoline refiners will not be able to expand their production with the operating refining equipment available to them. Over time, however, some refining companies might be able to recondition old equipment that had fallen into disuse. They can also place orders for construction of new gasoline-refining equipment, and once the equipment arrives, they can also put it into place to expand their gasoline production. Given sufficient time, therefore, existing gasoline refiners can eventually respond to higher gasoline prices by adding new refining operations.

2. The longer the time allowed for adjustment, the entry (or exit) of firms increases (or decreases) production in an industry. Consider what happens if the price of gasoline remains higher than before as a result of a sustained rise in gasoline demand. Even as existing refiners add to their capability to produce gasoline by retooling old equipment, purchasing new equipment, and adding new refining facilities, additional businesses may seek to earn profits at the now-higher gasoline prices. Over time, the entry of new gasoline-refining companies adds to the productive capabilities of the entire refining industry, and the quantity of gasoline supplied increases.

We therefore talk about short-run and long-run price elasticities of supply. The short run is defined as the time period during which full adjustment has not yet taken place. The long run is the time period during which firms have been able to adjust fully to the change in price.

What do current estimates of the short-run and long-run price elasticities of supply of crude oil tell us about the global oil industry's likely adjustments in response to recent increases in oil prices?

INTERNATIONAL EXAMPLE

Low Short- and Long-Run Price Elasticities of Oil Supply

Economists at the Organization for Economic Cooperation and Development (OECD) estimate the short-run price elasticity of supply of crude oil to be in the range of 0.04 to 0.07. This range of estimates implies that, in the short run, a 10 percent increase in the price of crude oil induces an increase in the quantity supplied of only about 0.4 to 0.7 percent. This explains why world oil production failed to rise significantly during the run-up in oil prices in the mid-2000s.

In the long run, the quantity of oil supplied by global producers is likely to be more responsive to an increase in price. Nevertheless, the rise in oil prices in the 2000s has taken place following a long period of restrained long-term investment by the oil industry. Oil companies replaced aging drilling rigs and offshore oil exploration equipment at a slower pace during the late 1990s and early 2000s than they had in previous years. Companies also pared their staffs of exploration engineers, who must obtain many years of training to become qualified petroleum engineers. Worldwide, the number of trained petroleum engineers is almost 50 percent lower today than in the 1980s.

With a smaller number of top-quality drilling rigs and platforms and fewer trained engineers, oil companies confront significant challenges in responding to price increases by ramping up their productive capabilities. Recent OECD estimates indicate that the long-run price elasticity of global oil supply may not be much higher than 1.0. Thus, for years to come, each percentage increase in the world price of crude oil is likely to generate roughly an equal percentage increase in the quantity of oil supplied.

FOR CRITICAL ANALYSIS
What would happen to the long-run price elasticity of supply if a technological breakthrough enabled today's trained petroleum engineers to find and pump larger volumes of oil with fewer oil rigs?

A Graphic Presentation. We can show a whole set of supply curves similar to the ones we generated for demand. As Figure 21-6 shows, when nothing can be done in the immediate run, the supply curve is vertical, S_1. As more time is allowed for adjustment, the supply curve rotates to S_2 and then to S_3, becoming more elastic as it rotates.

QUICK QUIZ

Price elasticity of supply is calculated by dividing the percentage change in _____ _____ by the percentage change in _____.

Usually, price elasticities of supply are _____—higher prices yield _____ quantities supplied.

Long-run supply curves are _____ elastic than short-run supply curves because the _____ the time allowed, the more resources can flow into or out of an industry when price changes.

See page 551 for the answers. Review concepts from this section in MyEconLab.

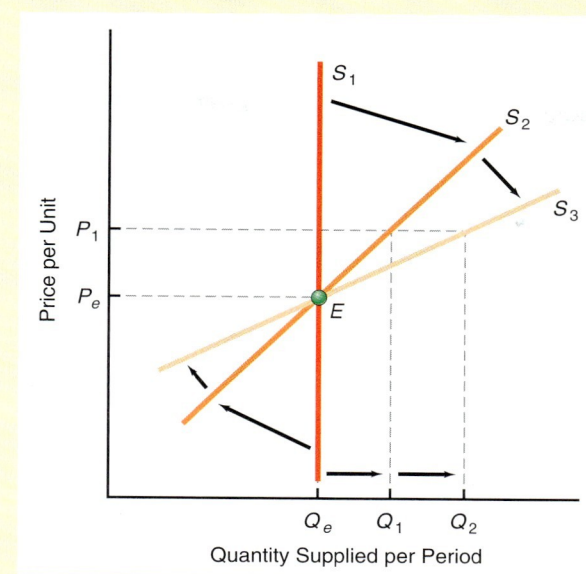

FIGURE 21-6
Short-Run and Long-Run Price Elasticity of Supply
Consider a situation in which the price is P_e and the quantity supplied is Q_e. In the immediate run, we hypothesize a vertical supply curve, S_1. With the price increase to P_1, therefore, there will be no change in the short run in quantity supplied; it will remain at Q_e. Given some time for adjustment, the supply curve will rotate to S_2. The new amount supplied will increase to Q_1. The long-run supply curve is shown by S_3. The amount supplied again increases to Q_2.

CASE STUDY
ECONOMICS FRONT AND CENTER

Total Revenues and the Price Elasticity of Demand for Dog Food

Mayer has been appointed to a product-pricing unit for a pet food company. His first assignment is to review the company's dog food prices and recommend price adjustments intended to raise the company's total revenues. After spending a few days studying conditions in the market for dog food, Mayer has determined that the company should change the prices of most of its brands.

As Mayer studies a recent research report prepared by the marketing staff, he records the following estimated price elasticities of demand for the company's various "formulas" of dog food: puppy formula: 0.58; small breed formula: 1.31; large breed formula: 1.18; overweight formula: 0.82; sensitive skin formula: 0.39; older dog formula: 0.95; sensitive stomach formula: 0.28. It is clear, he concludes, that price changes for most of the company's brands will boost its revenues. Now Mayer prepares to compose a report making specific recommendations.

CRITICAL ANALYSIS QUESTIONS
1. For which dog food formulas is demand inelastic? For which dog food formulas is demand elastic?
2. For which dog food formulas will price increases push up revenues? For which will price reductions increase revenues? Are price changes unlikely to have much of an effect on total revenues for any of the dog food formulas?

Issues and Applications

The Price Elasticity of Demand for Illicit Drugs

Concepts Applied
- Price Elasticity of Demand
- Inelastic Demand
- Elastic Demand

Economists have faced a number of challenges in trying to measure the price elasticity of demand for illicit drugs such as cocaine, heroin, and methamphetamine. The most obvious challenge is that possession and use of these drugs are illegal in the United States, so price and quantity information is typically gleaned from people who have been arrested or received hospital treatment.

Another challenge is that two types of price elasticities are of interest to policymakers. The price elasticity of most interest is the price elasticity of demand for illicit drugs: the responsiveness of quantity consumed to a change in price. The second elasticity, which helps determine the price elasticity of demand, is commonly called the *price elasticity of participation:* the responsiveness of the number of people using an illicit drug for the first time to a change in the price of that drug.

Price Elasticities of Demand for Illicit Drugs

Table 21-4 provides ranges of recent estimates of price elasticities of demand for cocaine, heroin, and methamphetamine. Generally speaking, economists are unable to provide many estimates of short-run versus long-run price elasticities of demand for illicit drugs. In cases in which they have attempted to do so, the estimated long-run elasticities are typically not significantly larger than the short-run elasticities.

The ranges of estimates overlap somewhat for all three drugs. Nevertheless, the lower ends of the ranges for cocaine and heroin—0.08 and 0.07, respectively—are noticeably smaller values than the lower end of the range for methamphetamine, 0.80. In addition, the upper ends of the ranges of estimates for cocaine and heroin—0.80 and 0.60, respectively—are much lower than the 2.50 value at the upper end of the range for methamphetamine. Most economists who study the issue of illicit drugs agree that these estimates indicate that the demand for cocaine and heroin is probably inelastic, whereas the demand for methamphetamine is more likely to be elastic.

The Price Elasticity of Participation in Drug Use

Economists have derived the estimates of price elasticities of demand reported in Table 21-4 from information about

TABLE 21-4
Estimated Price Elasticities of Demand for Selected Illicit Drugs

The ranges of estimates of the price elasticity of demand for cocaine and heroin generally encompass lower values than the elasticity range for methamphetamine.

Drug	Range of Estimated Price Elasticities of Demand
Cocaine	0.08–0.80
Heroin	0.07–0.60
Methamphetamine	0.80–2.50

Source: U.S. Department of Health and Human Services.

prices paid by and quantities of drugs consumed by people who were already drug users. To estimate price elasticities of participation in drug use, economists attempt to gauge the responsiveness of people's first experiments with illicit drugs to observed price changes.

Ranges of estimates of price elasticities of participation in drug use tend to be slightly higher than the ranges reported in Table 21-4. This fact provides some evidence that people contemplating their first use of an illicit drug are more responsive to price changes than those who have already used the drug before.

Implications of Price Decreases for Drug Use

The inflation-adjusted prices of cocaine, heroin, and methamphetamine have declined considerably in recent years. Based on the ranges of estimates reported in Table 21-4, we would, other things being equal, anticipate observing the largest proportionate quantity response in consumption of methamphetamine.

There is considerable evidence that this is exactly what has occurred. Participation in the use and continued consumption of cocaine and heroin has increased only slightly since the mid-1990s, in spite of (inflation-adjusted) price decreases exceeding 30 percent. In contrast, roughly the same proportionate price reduction has induced a surge in methamphetamine participation and use. In 1996, an estimated 5 million people had ever tried methamphetamine. Today, this figure is close to 13 million. In addition, estimates indicate that the number of regular methamphetamine users nearly doubled during the same period.

Log in to **MyEconLab,** click on "Economic News," and test your understanding of the chapter by answering interactive questions that relate directly to this issue.

For Critical Analysis

1. Why do you suppose that some economists interpret the elasticity estimates in Table 21-4 as evidence that cocaine and heroin could be somewhat more addictive than methamphetamine?
2. Based on the ranges of elasticity estimates reported in Table 21-4, dealers of which illicit drugs would be more likely to experience revenue increases if the market prices of those drugs were to increase?

Web Resources

1. For basic facts about methamphetamine prices, go to www.econtoday.com/ch21.
2. Learn more about the sale and use of illicit drugs in the United States at www.econtoday.com/ch21.

Research Project

Critics of enforcement of antidrug laws contend that the primary effect of such laws is to restrict supply and drive up prices. According to these critics, people end up consuming about the same amount of illicit drugs whether or not such laws are in effect. Based on the ranges of elasticity estimates reported in Table 21-4, to which drug(s) might this argument most readily apply? Does Table 21-4 provide any evidence against applying this argument to any other drug(s)?

Here is what you should know after reading this chapter. MyEconLab will help you identify what you know, and where to go when you need to practice.

WHAT YOU SHOULD KNOW		WHERE TO GO TO PRACTICE
Expressing and Calculating the Price Elasticity of Demand The price elasticity of demand is the responsiveness of the quantity demanded of a good to a change in the price of the good. It is the percentage change in quantity demanded divided by the percentage change in price. To calculate the price elasticity of demand for relatively small changes in price, the percentage change in quantity demanded is equal to the change in the quantity resulting from a price change divided by the average of the initial and final quantities, and the percentage change in price is equal to the price change divided by the average of the initial and final prices.	price elasticity of demand (E_p), 528	• **MyEconLab** Study Plan 21.1 • Audio introduction to Chapter 21
The Relationship Between the Price Elasticity of Demand and Total Revenues Demand is elastic when the price elasticity of demand exceeds 1, and over the elastic range of a demand curve, an increase in price reduces total revenues. Demand is inelastic when the price elasticity of demand is less than 1, and over this range of a demand curve, an increase in price raises total revenues. Finally, demand is unit-elastic when the price elasticity of demand equals 1, and over this range of a demand curve, an increase in price does not affect total revenues.	elastic demand, 530 unit elasticity of demand, 531 inelastic demand, 531 perfectly inelastic demand, 531 perfectly elastic demand, 531 **Key figures** Figure 21-1, 531 Figure 21-2, 533 Figure 21-3, 534	• **MyEconLab** Study Plans 21.2 and 21.3 • Animated Figures 21-1, 21-2, and 21-3
Factors That Determine the Price Elasticity of Demand Three factors affect the price elasticity of demand. If there are more close substitutes for a good, the price elasticity of demand increases. The price elasticity of demand for a good also tends to be higher when a larger portion of a person's budget is spent on the good. In addition, if people have a longer period of time to adjust to a price change and change their consumption patterns, the price elasticity of demand tends to be higher.		• **MyEconLab** Study Plan 21.4 • Video: The Determinants of the Price Elasticity of Demand
The Cross Price Elasticity of Demand and Using It to Determine Whether Two Goods Are Substitutes or Complements The cross price elasticity of demand for a good is the percentage change in the demand for that good divided by the percentage change in the price of a related good. If two goods are substitutes in consumption, an increase in the	cross price elasticity of demand (E_{xy}), 539	• **MyEconLab** Study Plan 21.5 • Video: Cross Price Elasticity of Demand

WHAT YOU SHOULD KNOW		WHERE TO GO TO PRACTICE
price of one of the goods induces an increase in the demand for the other good, so that the cross price elasticity of demand is positive. In contrast, if two goods are complements in consumption, an increase in the price of one of the goods brings about a decrease in the demand for the other good, so that the cross price elasticity of demand is negative.		
The Income Elasticity of Demand The income elasticity of demand for any good is the responsiveness of the demand for the good to a change in income, holding the good's relative price unchanged. It is equal to the percentage change in demand for the good divided by the percentage change in income.	income elasticity of demand (E_i), 540	• **MyEconLab** Study Plan 21.6 • Video: Income Elasticity of Demand
Classifying Supply Elasticities and How the Length of Time for Adjustment Affects the Price Elasticity of Supply The price elasticity of supply is equal to the percentage change in quantity supplied divided by the percentage change in price. If the price elasticity of supply is greater than 1, supply is elastic, and if the price elasticity of supply is less than 1, supply is inelastic. Supply is unit-elastic if the price elasticity of supply equals 1. Supply is more likely to be elastic when sellers have more time to adjust to price changes. One reason for this is that the more time sellers have to adjust, the more resources can flow into (or out of) an industry via expansion (or contraction) of firms. Another reason is that the longer the time allowed for adjustment, the entry (or exit) of firms increases (or decreases) production in response to a price increase (or decrease).	price elasticity of supply (E_s), 542 perfectly elastic supply, 542 perfectly inelastic supply, 542 **Key figure** Figure 21-6, 545	• **MyEconLab** Study Plan 21.7 • Animated Figure 21-6

Log in to MyEconLab, take a chapter test, and get a personalized Study Plan that tells you which concepts you understand and which ones you need to review. From there, MyEconLab will give you further practice, tutorials, animations, videos, and guided solutions.

Log in to www.myeconlab.com

PROBLEMS

*Select problems, indicated by a blue oval, are assignable in **MyEconLab**. Answers to the odd-numbered problems appear at the back of the book.*

21-1 A student organization finds that when it prices shirts emblazoned with the college logo at $10, the organization sells 150 per week. When the price is reduced to $9, the organization sells 200 per week. Based on this information, calculate the price elasticity of demand for logo-emblazoned shirts.

21-2 Table 21-2 on page 539 indicates that the short-run price elasticity of demand for tires is 0.9. If an increase in the price of petroleum (used in producing tires) causes the market prices of tires to rise from $50 to $60, by what percentage would you expect the quantity of tires demanded to change?

21-3 The diagram below depicts the demand curve for "miniburgers" purchased from Joe's Campus Grill. Use the information in this diagram to answer the questions that follow.

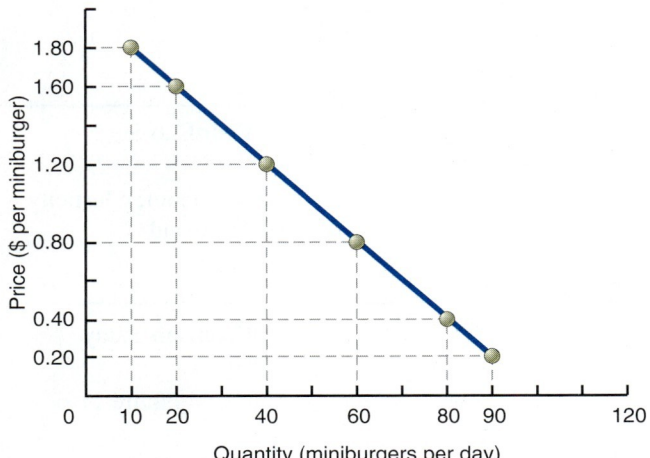

a. What is the price elasticity of demand along the range of the demand curve between a price of $0.20 per miniburger and a price of $0.40 per miniburger? Is demand elastic or inelastic over this range?

b. What is the price elasticity of demand along the range of the demand curve between a price of $0.80 per miniburger and a price of $1.20 per miniburger? Is demand elastic or inelastic over this range?

c. What is the price elasticity of demand along the range of the demand curve between a price of $1.60 per miniburger and a price of $1.80 per miniburger? Is demand elastic or inelastic over this range?

21-4 In a local market, the monthly price of Internet access service decreases from $20 to $10, and the total quantity of monthly accounts across all Internet access providers increases from 100,000 to 200,000. What is the price elasticity of demand? Is demand elastic, unit-elastic, or inelastic?

21-5 At a price of $17.50 to play 18 holes on a golf course, 120 consumers pay to play a game of golf each day. Increasing the price to $22.50 causes the number of consumers to decline to 80. What is the price elasticity of demand? Is demand elastic, unit-elastic, or inelastic?

21-6 It is very difficult to find goods with perfectly elastic or perfectly inelastic demand. We can, however, find goods that lie near these extremes. Characterize demands for the following goods as being near perfectly elastic or near perfectly inelastic.

a. Corn grown and harvested by a small farmer in Iowa
b. Heroin for a drug addict
c. Water for a desert hiker
d. One of several optional textbooks in a pass-fail course.

21-7 A craftsman who makes guitars by hand finds that when he prices his guitars at $800, his annual revenue is $64,000. When he prices his guitars at $700, his annual revenue is $63,000. Over this range of guitar prices, does the craftsman face elastic, unit-elastic, or inelastic demand?

21-8 Suppose that over a range of prices, the price elasticity of demand varies from 15.0 to 2.5. Over another range of prices, the price elasticity of demand varies from 1.5 to 0.75. What can you say about total revenue and the total revenue curve over these two ranges of the demand curve as price falls?

21-9 Based on the information provided alone, characterize the demands for the following goods as being more elastic or more inelastic.

a. A 45-cent box of salt that you buy once a year
b. A type of high-powered ski boat that you can rent from any one of a number of rental agencies
c. A specific brand of bottled water
d. Automobile insurance in a state that requires autos to be insured but has few insurance companies
e. A 75-cent guitar pick for the lead guitarist of a major rock band

21-10 The value of cross price elasticity of demand between goods X and Y is 1.25, while the cross price elasticity of demand between goods X and Z is −2.0. Characterize X and Y and X and Z as substitutes or complements.

21-11 Suppose that the cross price elasticity of demand between eggs and bacon is −0.5. What would you expect to happen to sales of bacon if the price of eggs rises by 10 percent?

21-12 Assume that the income elasticity of demand for hot dogs is −1.25 and that the income elasticity of demand for lobster is 1.25. Explain why the measure for hot dogs is negative while that for lobster is positive. Based on this information alone, are these normal or inferior goods? (Hint: You may want to refer to the discussion of normal and inferior goods in Chapter 3.)

21-13 At a price of $25,000, producers of midsized automobiles are willing to manufacture and sell 75,000 cars per month. At a price of $35,000, they are willing to produce and sell 125,000 a month. Using the same type of calculation method used to compute the price elasticity of demand, what is the price elasticity of supply? Is supply elastic, unit-elastic, or inelastic?

21-14 The price elasticity of supply of a basic commodity that a nation imports from producers in other countries is 2. What would you expect to happen to the volume of imports if the price of this commodity rises by 10 percent?

21-15 A 20 percent increase in the price of skis induces ski manufacturers to increase production of skis by 10 percent in the short run. In the long run, other things being equal, the 20 percent price increase generates a production increase of 40 percent. What is the short-run price elasticity of supply? What is the long-run price elasticity of supply?

21-16 An increase in the market price of men's haircuts, from $15 per haircut to $25 per haircut, initially causes a local barbershop to have its employees work overtime to increase the number of daily haircuts provided from 35 to 45. When the $25 market price remains unchanged for several weeks and all other things remain equal as well, the barbershop hires additional employees and provides 65 haircuts per day. What is the short-run price elasticity of supply? What is the long-run price elasticity of supply?

ECONOMICS ON THE NET

Price Elasticity and Consumption of Illegal Drugs Making the use of certain drugs illegal drives up their market prices, so the price elasticity of demand is a key factor affecting the use of illegal drugs. This application applies concepts from this chapter to analyze how price elasticity of demand affects drug consumption.

Title: The Demand for Illicit Drugs

Navigation: Go to www.econtoday.com/ch21, and follow the link to the summary of this paper published by the National Bureau of Economic Research.

Application Read the summary of the results of this study of price elasticities of participation in use of illegal drugs, and answer the following questions.

1. Based on the results of the study, is the demand for cocaine more or less price elastic than the demand for heroin? For which drug, therefore, will quantity demanded fall by a greater percentage in response to a proportionate increase in price?

2. The study finds that decriminalizing currently illegal drugs would bring about sizable increases both in overall consumption of heroin and cocaine and in the price elasticity of demand for both drugs. Why do you suppose that the price elasticity of demand would rise? (Hint: At present, users of cocaine and heroin are restricted to only a few illegal sources of the drugs, but if the drugs could legally be produced and sold, there would be many more suppliers providing a variety of different types of both drugs.)

For Group Study and Analysis Discuss ways that government officials might use information about the price elasticities of demand for illicit drugs to assist in developing policies intended to reduce the use of these drugs. Which of these proposed policies might prove most effective? Why?

ANSWERS TO QUICK QUIZZES

p. 529: (i) responsiveness; (ii) quantity demanded . . . price; (iii) percentage . . . independent; (iv) inversely . . . negative
p. 532: (i) zero . . . inelastic; (ii) elastic . . . infinite
p. 536: (i) revenues . . . expenditures; (ii) opposite; (iii) zero; (iv) same
p. 542: (i) substitutes . . . share . . . adjustment; (ii) Cross . . . positive . . . negative; (iii) demand . . . income
p. 544: (i) quantity supplied . . . price; (ii) positive . . . larger; (iii) more . . . longer

22 Rents, Profits, and the Financial Environment of Business

Learning Objectives

After reading this chapter, you should be able to:

1. Understand the concept of economic rent
2. Distinguish among the main organizational forms of business and explain the chief advantages and disadvantages of each
3. Explain the difference between accounting profits and economic profits
4. Discuss how the interest rate performs a key role in allocating resources
5. Calculate the present discounted value of a payment to be received at a future date
6. Identify the three main sources of corporate funds and differentiate between stocks and bonds

MyEconLab helps you master each objective and study more efficiently. See end of chapter for details.

Before the New York Stock Exchange (NYSE) became a public company in 2006, people owned "seats," which were rights to buy and sell stocks on the exchange. The market price of an NYSE seat fluctuated between $1.7 million and $2.1 million between 2000 and 2002. Then, aside from a brief recovery in early 2003, the market price of an NYSE seat dropped considerably, bottoming out at $975,000 in January 2005. By August 2005, however, the price of an NYSE seat had jumped to $3 million. To understand the factors that accounted for these gyrations in the price of a seat on the NYSE, you will have to study two topics: the NYSE and a concept known as *discounted present value*. Both of these topics are subjects covered in this chapter.

CHAPTER 22 Rents, Profits, and the Financial Environment of Business

Did You Know That...

at present, there are almost 800,000 *nonprofit organizations*—groups that pursue various objectives without aiming to earn profits—in the United States? This is more than twice the number of nonprofit organizations that existed in 1990. Some of these organizations are dedicated to social causes, such as environmental protection or saving species from extinction. Others, such as nonprofit hospitals, provide medical services to communities. Several are dedicated to civic improvement. Many nonprofit organizations, such as clubs, exist simply to provide entertainment or other benefits to their members.

The number of nonprofit organizations pales when compared with the nearly 28 million profit-seeking businesses in the United States. How do we measure the profits that owners of businesses strive to earn? How are business firms organized, and how do they finance their activities? In this chapter, you will learn the answers to these questions. First, however, you must learn about the important function of economic rent.

ECONOMIC RENT

When you hear the term *rent*, you are accustomed to having it mean the payment made to property owners for the use of land or dwellings. The term *rent* has a different meaning in economics. **Economic rent** is payment to the owner of a resource in excess of its *opportunity cost*—that is, the minimum payment that would be necessary to call forth production of that amount of the resource.

Economic rent
A payment for the use of any resource over and above its opportunity cost.

Determining Land Rent

Economists originally used the term *rent* to designate payment for the use of land. What was thought to be important about land was that its supply is completely inelastic. That is, the supply curve for land was thought to be a vertical line, so that no matter what the prevailing market price for land, the quantity supplied would remain the same.

The concept of economic rent is associated with the British economist David Ricardo (1772–1823). Here is how Ricardo analyzed economic rent for land. He first simplified his model by assuming that all land is equally productive. Then Ricardo assumed that the quantity of land in a country is *fixed* so that land's opportunity cost is equal to zero. Graphically, then, in terms of supply and demand, we draw the supply curve for land vertically (zero price elasticity). In Figure 22-1 on the following page, the supply curve for land is represented by S. If the demand curve is D_1, it intersects the supply curve, S, at price P_1. The entire amount of revenues obtained, $P_1 \times Q_1$, is labeled "Economic rent." If the demand for land increases to D_2, the equilibrium price will rise to P_2. Additions to economic rent are labeled "More economic rent." Notice that the quantity of land remains insensitive to the change in price. Another way of stating this is that the supply curve is perfectly inelastic.

Economic Rent to Labor

Land and natural resources are not the only factors of production to which the analysis of economic rent can be applied. In fact, the analysis is probably more often applicable to labor. Here is a list of people who provide different labor services, some of whom probably receive large amounts of economic rent:

- Professional sports superstars
- Rock stars

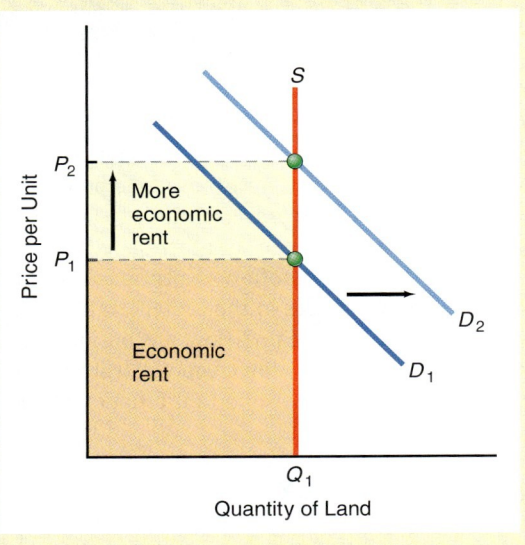

FIGURE 22-1

Economic Rent

If indeed the supply curve of land were completely price-inelastic in the long run, it would be depicted by S. The opportunity cost of land is zero, so the same quantity of land is forthcoming at any price. Thus, at the quantity in existence, Q_1, any and all revenues are economic rent. If demand is D_1, the price will be P_1; if demand is D_2, price will rise to P_2. Economic rent would be $P_1 \times Q_1$, and $P_2 \times Q_1$, respectively.

- Movie stars
- World-class models
- Successful inventors and innovators
- World-famous opera stars

> **ECONOMICS FRONT AND CENTER**
>
> To think about why the potential to earn significant economic rents is not limited to *living* celebrities, contemplate **Earning Economic Rents from Beyond the Grave,** on page 570.

Just apply the definition of economic rent to the phenomenal earnings that these people make. They would undoubtedly work for considerably less than they earn. Therefore, much of their earnings constitutes economic rent (but not all, as we shall see). Economic rent occurs because specific resources cannot be replicated exactly. No one can duplicate today's most highly paid entertainment figures, and therefore they receive economic rent.

Economic Rent and the Allocation of Resources

If a highly paid movie star would make the same number of movies at half his or her current annual earnings, does that mean that 50 percent of his or her income is inappropriate? To evaluate the question, consider first why the superstar gets such a high income. The answer can be found in Figure 22-1. Substitute *entertainment activities of the superstars* for the word *land*. The high "price" received by the superstar is due to the demand for his or her services. If Reese Witherspoon announces that she will work for a million dollars per movie and do two movies a year, how is she going to know which production company values her services the most highly? Witherspoon and other movie stars let the market decide where their resources should be used. In this sense, we can say the following:

Economic rent allocates resources to their highest-valued use.

Otherwise stated, economic rent directs resources to the people who can use them most efficiently.

How much do top performers earn?

EXAMPLE

Do Entertainment Superstars Make Super Economic Rents?

Superstars certainly do well financially. Table 22-1 shows the earnings of selected individuals in the entertainment industry as estimated by *Forbes* magazine. Earnings are totaled for a two-year period. How much of these earnings can be called economic rent? The question is not easy to answer, because an entertainment newcomer would almost certainly work for much less than he or she earns, implying that the newcomer is making high economic rent. The same cannot necessarily be said for entertainers who have been raking in millions for years. They probably have very high accumulated wealth and also a more jaded outlook about their work. It is therefore not clear how much they would work if they were not offered those huge sums of money.

FOR CRITICAL ANALYSIS
Even if some superstar entertainers would work for less, what forces cause them to make so much income anyway?

TABLE 22-1
Superstar Earnings

Name	Occupation	Two-Year Earnings
Steven Spielberg	Director, producer, studio owner	$200,000,000
George Lucas	Director, producer, studio owner	185,000,000
Oprah Winfrey	Talk show host and owner, author	180,000,000
Rolling Stones	Rock group	66,500,000
Will Smith	Actor	60,000,000
Paul McCartney	Rock singer	59,000,000
David Copperfield	Magician	55,000,000
Tom Hanks	Actor	55,000,000
Eddie Murphy	Actor	45,000,000
Jim Carrey	Actor	40,000,000

Source: *Forbes*, 2006.

QUICK QUIZ

Economic rent is defined as payment for a factor of production that is completely _____ in supply.

Economic rent _____ resources to their _____-valued use.

See page 577 for the answers. Review concepts from this section in MyEconLab.

FIRMS AND PROFITS

Firms or businesses, like individuals, seek to earn the highest possible returns. We define a **firm** as follows:

A firm is an organization that brings together factors of production—labor, land, physical capital, human capital, and entrepreneurial skill—to produce a product or service that it hopes can be sold at a profit.

Firm
A business organization that employs resources to produce goods or services for profit. A firm normally owns and operates at least one "plant" or facility in order to produce.

A typical firm will have an organizational structure consisting of an entrepreneur, managers, and workers. The entrepreneur is the person who takes the risks, mainly of losing his or her personal wealth. In compensation, the entrepreneur will get any profits that are made. Recall from Chapter 2 that entrepreneurs take the initiative in combining land, labor, and capital to produce a good or a service. Entrepreneurs are the ones who innovate in the form of new production and new products. The entrepreneur also decides whom to hire to manage the firm. Some economists maintain that the true quality of an entrepreneur becomes evident with his or her selection of managers.

Managers, in turn, decide who should be hired and fired and how the business should be operated on a day-to-day basis. The workers ultimately use the other inputs to produce the products or services that are being sold by the firm. Workers and managers are paid contractual wages. They receive a specified amount of income for a specified time period. Entrepreneurs are not paid contractual wages. They receive no reward specified in advance. The entrepreneurs make profits if there are any, for profits accrue to those who are willing to take risks. (Because the entrepreneur gets only what is left over after all expenses are paid, he or she is often referred to as a *residual claimant*. The entrepreneur lays claim to the residual—whatever is left.)

The Legal Organization of Firms

We all know that firms differ from one another. Some sell frozen yogurt, others make automobiles; some advertise, some do not; some have annual sales of a few thousand dollars, others have sales in the billions of dollars. The list of differences is probably endless. Yet for all this diversity, the basic organization of *all* firms can be thought of in terms of a few simple structures, the most important of which are the proprietorship, the partnership, and the corporation.

Proprietorship.
A business owned by one individual who makes the business decisions, receives all the profits, and is legally responsible for the debts of the firm.

Proprietorship. The most common form of business organization is the **proprietorship**. As shown in Table 22-2, close to 72 percent of all firms in the United States are proprietorships. Each is owned by a single individual who makes the business decisions, receives all the profits, and is legally responsible for all the debts of the firm. Although proprietorships are numerous, they are generally rather small businesses, with annual sales averaging not much more than $58,000. For this reason, even though there are nearly 19 million proprietorships in the United States, they account for less than 5 percent of all business revenues.

Advantages of Proprietorships. Proprietorships offer several advantages as a form of business organization. First, they are *easy to form and to dissolve*. In the simplest case, all one must do to start a business is to start working; to dissolve the firm, one simply stops working. Second, *all decision-making power resides with the sole proprietor.* No partners,

TABLE 22-2
Forms of Business Organization

Type of Firm	Percentage of U.S. Firms	Average Size (annual sales in dollars)	Percentage of Total Business Revenues
Proprietorship	71.6	58,000	4.6
Partnership	8.5	1,190,000	11.8
Corporation	19.9	3,579,000	83.6

Sources: U.S. Bureau of the Census; *2006 Statistical Abstract.*

shareholders, or board of directors need be consulted. The third advantage is that its *profit is taxed only once*. All profit is treated by law as the net income of the proprietor and as such is subject only to personal income taxation.

Disadvantages of Proprietorships. The most important disadvantage of a proprietorship is that the proprietor faces **unlimited liability** *for the debts of the firm*. This means that the owner is personally responsible for all of the firm's debts. The second disadvantage is that many lenders are reluctant to lend large sums to a proprietorship. Consequently, a proprietorship may have a *limited ability to raise funds,* to expand the business or even simply to help it survive bad times. The third disadvantage of proprietorships is that they normally *end with the death of the proprietor,* which creates added uncertainty for prospective lenders or employees.

Partnership. The second important form of business organization is the **partnership**. As shown in Table 22-2, partnerships are far less numerous than proprietorships but tend to be larger businesses—about 20 times greater on average. A partnership differs from a proprietorship chiefly in that there are two or more co-owners, called partners. They share the responsibilities of operating the firm and its profits, and they are *each* legally responsible for *all* of the debts incurred by the firm. In this sense, a partnership may be viewed as a proprietorship with more than one owner.

Advantages of Partnerships. The first advantage of a partnership is that it is *easy to form*. In fact, it is almost as easy to form as a proprietorship. Second, partnerships, like proprietorships, often help *reduce the costs of monitoring job performance*. This is particularly true when interpersonal skills are important for successful performance and in lines of business in which, even after the fact, it is difficult to measure performance objectively. Thus, attorneys and physicians often organize themselves as partnerships. A third advantage of the partnership is that it *permits more effective specialization* in occupations in which, for legal or other reasons, the multiple talents required for success are unlikely to be uniform across individuals. Finally, the income of the partnership is treated as personal income and thus is *subject only to personal taxation*.

Disadvantages of Partnerships. Partnerships also have their disadvantages. First, the *partners each have unlimited liability*. Thus, the personal assets of *each* partner are at risk due to debts incurred on behalf of the partnership by *any* of the partners. Second, *decision making is generally more costly* in a partnership than in a proprietorship; more people are involved in making decisions, and they may have differences of opinion that must be resolved before action is possible. Finally, *dissolution of the partnership* often occurs when a partner dies or voluntarily withdraws or when one or more partners wish to remove someone from the partnership. This creates potential uncertainty for creditors and employees.

Corporation. A **corporation** is a legal entity that may conduct business in its own name just as an individual does. The owners of a corporation are called *shareholders* because they own shares of the profits earned by the firm. By law, shareholders enjoy **limited liability,** meaning that if the corporation incurs debts that it cannot pay, the shareholders' personal property is shielded from claims by the firm's creditors. As shown in Table 22-2, corporations are far less numerous than proprietorships, but because of their large size, they are responsible for more than 83 percent of all business revenues in the United States.

Advantages of Corporations. Perhaps the greatest advantage of corporations is that their owners (the shareholders) enjoy *limited liability*. The liability of shareholders is limited to

Unlimited liability
A legal concept whereby the personal assets of the owner of a firm can be seized to pay off the firm's debts.

Partnership
A business owned by two or more joint owners, or partners, who share the responsibilities and the profits of the firm and are individually liable for all the debts of the partnership.

Corporation
A legal entity that may conduct business in its own name just as an individual does; the owners of a corporation, called shareholders, own shares of the firm's profits and enjoy the protection of limited liability.

Limited liability
A legal concept in which the responsibility, or liability, of the owners of a corporation is limited to the value of the shares in the firm that they own.

the value of their shares. The second advantage is that, legally, the corporation *continues to exist* even if one or more owners cease to be owners. A third advantage of the corporation stems from the first two: Corporations are well positioned to *raise large sums of financial capital.* People are able to buy ownership shares or lend funds to the corporation knowing that their liability is limited to the amount of funds they invest and confident that the corporation's existence does not depend on the life of any one of the firm's owners.

Disadvantages of Corporations.

The chief disadvantage of the corporation is that corporate income is subject to *double taxation.* The profits of the corporation are subject first to corporate taxation. Then, if any of the after-tax profits are distributed to shareholders as **dividends,** such payments are treated as personal income to the shareholders and subject to personal taxation, although the dividends may be taxed at lower rates than other personal income. Despite the lower tax rates on dividends, owners of corporations generally pay higher taxes on corporate income than on other forms of income because the corporate income is also taxed at the corporate level.

A second disadvantage of the corporation is that corporations are potentially subject to problems associated with the *separation of ownership and control.* The owners and managers of a corporation are typically different persons and may have different incentives. The problems that can result are discussed later in the chapter.

Dividends
Portion of a corporation's profits paid to its owners (shareholders).

The Profits of a Firm

Most people think of a firm's profit as the difference between the amount of revenues the firm takes in and the amount it spends for wages, materials, and so on. In a bookkeeping sense, the following formula could be used:

$$\text{Accounting profit} = \text{total revenues} - \text{explicit costs}$$

where **explicit costs** are expenses that must actually be paid out by the firm. This definition of profit is known as **accounting profit.** It is appropriate when used by accountants to determine a firm's taxable income. Economists are more interested in how firm managers react not just to changes in explicit costs but also to changes in **implicit costs,** defined as expenses that business managers do not have to pay out of pocket but are costs to the firm nonetheless because they represent an opportunity cost. They do not involve any direct cash outlay by the firm and must therefore be measured by the *opportunity cost principle.* That is to say, they are measured by what the resources (land, capital) currently used in producing a particular good or service could earn in other uses. Economists use the full opportunity cost of all resources (including both explicit and implicit costs) as the figure to subtract from revenues to obtain a definition of profit. Therefore, another definition of implicit cost is the opportunity cost of using factors that a producer does not buy or hire but already owns.

Explicit costs
Costs that business managers must take account of because they must be paid; examples are wages, taxes, and rent.

Accounting profit
Total revenues minus total explicit costs.

Implicit costs
Expenses that managers do not have to pay out of pocket and hence do not normally explicitly calculate, such as the opportunity cost of factors of production that are owned; examples are owner-provided capital and owner-provided labor.

Opportunity Cost of Capital

Firms enter or remain in an industry if they earn, at minimum, a **normal rate of return.** People will not invest their wealth in a business unless they obtain a positive normal (competitive) rate of return—that is, unless their invested wealth pays off. Any business wishing to attract capital must expect to pay at least the same rate of return on that capital as all other businesses (of similar risk) are willing to pay. Put another way, when a firm requires the use of a resource in producing a particular product, it must bid against alternative users of that resource. Thus, the firm must offer a price that is at least as much as other potential

Normal rate of return
The amount that must be paid to an investor to induce investment in a business; also known as the *opportunity cost of capital.*

users are offering to pay. For example, if individuals can invest their wealth in almost any publishing firm and get a rate of return of 10 percent per year, each firm in the publishing industry must *expect* to pay 10 percent as the normal rate of return to present and future investors. This 10 percent is a *cost to the firm,* the **opportunity cost of capital.** The opportunity cost of capital is the amount of income, or yield, that could have been earned by investing in the next-best alternative. Capital will not stay in firms or industries in which the expected rate of return falls below its opportunity cost—that is, what could be earned elsewhere. If a firm owns some capital equipment, it can either use it or lease it and earn a return. If the firm uses the equipment for production, part of the cost of using that equipment is the forgone revenue that the firm could have earned had it leased out that equipment.

Opportunity cost of capital
The normal rate of return, or the available return on the next-best alternative investment. Economists consider this a cost of production, and it is included in our cost examples.

Opportunity Cost of Owner-Provided Labor and Capital

Single-owner proprietorships often grossly exaggerate their profit rates because they understate the opportunity cost of the labor that the proprietor provides to the business. Here we are referring to the opportunity cost of labor. For example, you may know people who run a small grocery store. These people will sit down at the end of the year and figure out what their "profits" are. They will add up all their sales and subtract what they had to pay to other workers, what they had to pay to their suppliers, what they had to pay in taxes, and so on. The end result they will call "profit." They normally will not, however, have figured into their costs the salary that they could have made if they had worked for somebody else in a similar type of job. By working for themselves, they become residual claimants—they receive what is left after all explicit costs have been accounted for. Part of the costs, however, should include the salary the owner-operator could have received working for someone else.

Consider a simple example of a skilled auto mechanic working 14 hours a day at his own service station, six days a week. Compare this situation to how much he could earn working 84 hours a week as a trucking company mechanic. This self-employed auto mechanic might have an opportunity cost of about $25 an hour. For his 84-hour week in his own service station, he is forfeiting $2,100. Unless his service station shows accounting profits of more than that per week, he is incurring losses in an economic sense.

Another way of looking at the opportunity cost of running a business is that opportunity cost consists of all explicit and implicit costs. Accountants only take account of explicit costs. Therefore, accounting profit ends up being the residual after only explicit costs are subtracted from total revenues.

This same analysis can apply to owner-provided capital, such as land or buildings. The fact that the owner owns the building or the land with which he or she operates a business does not mean that it is "free." Rather, use of the building and land still has an opportunity cost—the value of the next-best alternative use for those assets.

Go to **www.econtoday.com/ch22** for a link to Internal Revenue Service reports on U.S. annual revenues and expenses of proprietorships, partnerships, and corporations based on tax returns. Click on recent quarters and choose relevant reports.

Accounting Profits versus Economic Profits

The term *profits* in economics means the income that entrepreneurs earn, over and above all costs including their own opportunity cost of time, plus the opportunity cost of the capital they have invested in their business. Profits can be regarded as total revenues minus total costs—which is how accountants think of them—but we must now include *all* costs. Our definition of **economic profits** will be the following:

Economic profits
Total revenues minus total opportunity costs of all inputs used, or the total of all implicit and explicit costs.

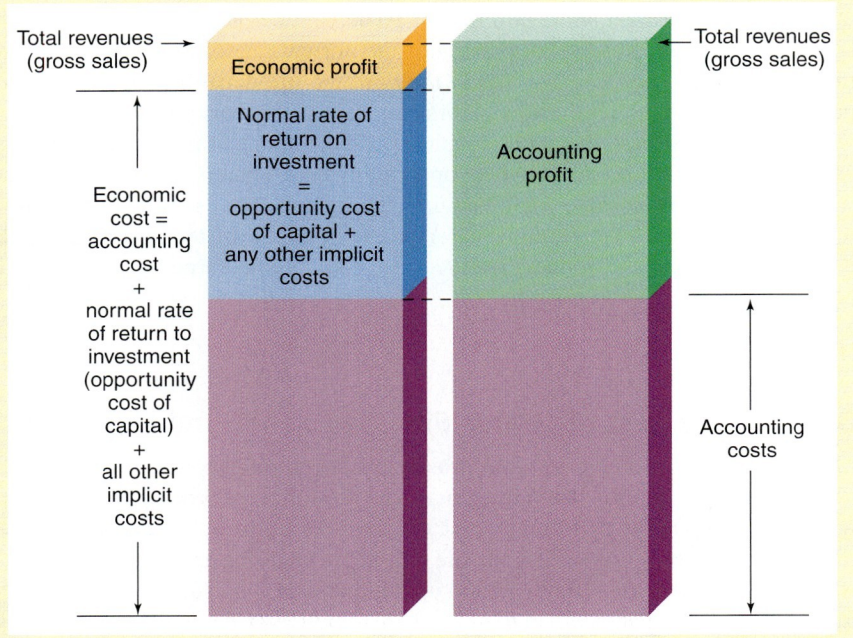

FIGURE 22-2
Simplified View of Economic and Accounting Profit
We see on the right column that accounting profit is the difference between total revenues and total explicit accounting costs. Conversely, we see on the left column that economic profit is equal to total revenues minus economic costs. Economic costs equal explicit accounting costs plus all implicit costs, including a normal rate of return on invested capital.

$$\text{Economic profits} = \text{total revenues} - \text{total opportunity cost of all inputs used}$$

or

$$\text{Economic profits} = \text{total revenues} - (\text{explicit} + \text{implicit costs})$$

Remember that implicit costs include a normal rate of return on invested capital. We show this relationship in Figure 22-2.

The Goal of the Firm: Profit Maximization

When we examined the theory of consumer demand, utility (or satisfaction) maximization by the individual provided the basis for the analysis. In the theory of the firm and production, *profit maximization* is the underlying hypothesis of our predictive theory. The goal of the firm is to maximize economic profits, and the firm is expected to try to make the positive difference between total revenues and total costs as large as it can.

Our justification for assuming profit maximization by firms is similar to our assumption concerning utility maximization by individuals (see Chapter 20). To obtain labor, capital, and other resources required to produce commodities, firms must first obtain financing from investors. In general, investors are indifferent about the details of how a firm uses the funds they provide. They are most interested in the earnings on these funds and the risk of obtaining lower returns or losing the funds they have invested. Firms that can provide relatively higher risk-corrected returns will therefore have an advantage in obtaining the financing needed to continue or expand production. Over time, we would expect a policy of profit maximization to become the dominant mode of behavior for firms that survive.

QUICK QUIZ

_____ are the most common form of business organization, comprising close to 72 percent of all firms. Each is owned by a single individual who makes all business decisions, receives all the profits, and has _____ liability for the firm's debts.

_____ are much like proprietorships, except that two or more individuals, or partners, share the decisions and the profits of the firm. In addition, each partner has _____ liability for the debts of the firm.

Corporations are responsible for the largest share of business revenues. The owners, called _____, share in the firm's profits but normally have little responsibility for the firm's day-to-day operations. They enjoy _____ liability for the debts of the firm.

Accounting profits differ from **economic profits**, which are defined as total revenues minus total costs, where costs include the full _____ cost of all of the factors of production plus all other implicit costs.

The full opportunity cost of capital invested in a business is generally not included as a cost when accounting profits are calculated. Thus, accounting profits often are _____ than economic profits. We assume throughout that the goal of the firm is to _____ economic profits.

See page 577 for the answers. Review concepts from this section in MyEconLab.

INTEREST

Interest is the price paid by debtors to creditors for the use of loanable funds. Often businesses go to credit markets to obtain so-called **financial capital** in order to invest in physical capital and rights to patents and trademarks from which they hope to make a satisfactory return. In other words, in our complicated society, the production of capital goods is often facilitated by the existence of credit markets. These are markets in which borrowing and lending take place.

Financial capital
Funds used to purchase physical capital goods, such as buildings and equipment, and patents and trademarks.

Interest and Credit

When you obtain credit, you actually obtain funds to have command over resources today. We can say, then, that **interest** is the payment for current rather than future command over resources. Thus, interest is the payment for obtaining credit. If you borrow $100 from me, you have command over $100 worth of goods and services today. I no longer have that command. You promise to pay me back $100 plus interest at some future date. The interest that you pay is usually expressed as a percentage of the total loan, calculated on an annual basis. If at the end of one year you pay me back $105, the annual interest rate is $5 ÷ $100, or 5 percent. When you go out into the marketplace to obtain credit, you will find that the interest rate charged differs greatly. A loan to buy a house (a mortgage) may cost you 6 to 8 percent in annual interest. An installment loan to buy an automobile may cost you 7 to 9 percent in annual interest. The federal government, when it wishes to obtain credit (issue U.S. Treasury securities), may have to pay only 2 to 6 percent in annual interest. Variations in the rate of annual interest that must be paid for credit depend on the following factors.

Interest
The payment for current rather than future command over resources; the cost of obtaining credit.

1. *Length of loan.* In many (but not all) cases, the longer the loan will be outstanding, other things being equal, the greater will be the interest rate charged.
2. *Risk.* The greater the risk of nonrepayment of the loan, other things being equal, the greater the interest rate charged. Risk is assessed on the basis of the creditworthiness of the borrower and whether the borrower provides collateral for the loan. Collateral

Go to www.econtoday.com/ch22 for Federal Reserve data on U.S. interest rates.

consists of any asset that will automatically become the property of the lender should the borrower fail to comply with the loan agreement.

3. *Handling charges.* It takes resources to set up a loan. Papers have to be filled out and filed, credit references have to be checked, collateral has to be examined, and so on. The larger the amount of the loan, the smaller the handling (or administrative) charges as a percentage of the total loan. Therefore, we would predict that, other things being equal, the larger the loan, the lower the interest rate.

Why would issuers of credit cards offer a card promising "zero interest for life"?

EXAMPLE

No Interest for the Life of the Loan, but with Strings Attached

Recently, Discover and J.P. Morgan Chase offered to issue credit cards to selected consumers with a commitment to charge "zero interest for life" on amounts transferred to their credit cards. The zero interest rate applied only to transfers of existing balances on the credit cards of other issuers. In addition, only consumers that the credit-card issuers judged to be highly creditworthy received the offers, and only balances these consumers agreed to transfer to Discover or J.P. Morgan Chase were charged a zero percent rate. Furthermore, consumers who accepted the offer had to agree to unusually high penalties in the event of late payments.

Why did Discover and J.P. Morgan Chase offer the zero-interest commitment? They wished to attract creditworthy customers who tend to borrow significant amounts using their credit cards and who thereby would be attracted by the zero-interest guarantee. Discover and J.P. Morgan Chase anticipated that these customers would *add* to balances on new credit-card accounts. The card issuers were careful to notify new customers attracted by "zero interest for life" that any *additions* to credit-card balances would be subject to *positive* interest rates.

FOR CRITICAL ANALYSIS
Why didn't Discover and J.P. Morgan Chase offer credit cards with "zero interest for life" to all their customers?

Real versus Nominal Interest Rates

Nominal rate of interest
The market rate of interest expressed in today's dollars.

We have been assuming that there is no inflation. In a world of inflation—a persistent rise in an average of all prices—the **nominal rate of interest** will be higher than it would be in a world with no inflation. Nominal, or market, rates of interest rise to take account of the anticipated rate of inflation. If, for example, no inflation is expected, the nominal rate of interest might be 5 percent for home mortgages. If the rate of inflation goes to 4 percent a year and stays there, everybody will anticipate that inflation rate. The nominal rate of interest will rise to about 9 percent to take account of the anticipated rate of inflation. If the interest rate did not rise to 9 percent, the principal plus interest earned at 5 percent would be worth less in the future because inflation would have eroded its purchasing power. We can therefore say that the nominal, or market, rate of interest is approximately equal to the real rate of interest plus the anticipated rate of inflation, or

$$i_n = i_r + \text{anticipated rate of inflation}$$

Real rate of interest
The nominal rate of interest minus the anticipated rate of inflation.

where i_n equals the nominal rate of interest and i_r equals the real rate of interest. In short, you can expect to see high nominal rates of interest in periods of high inflation rates. The **real rate of interest** may not necessarily be high, though. We must first correct the nominal rate of interest for the anticipated rate of inflation before determining whether the real interest rate is in fact higher than normal.

The Allocative Role of Interest

In Chapter 4, we talked about the price system and the role that prices play in the allocation of resources. Interest is a price that allocates loanable funds (credit) to consumers and to businesses. Within the business sector, interest allocates funds to different firms and therefore to different investment projects. Investment, or capital, projects with rates of return higher than the market rate of interest in the credit market will be undertaken, given an unrestricted market for loanable funds. For example, if the expected rate of return on the purchase of a new factory or of intellectual property—patents or copyrights—in some industry is 10 percent and funds can be acquired for 6 percent, the investment project will proceed. If, however, that same project had an expected rate of return of only 4 percent, it would not be undertaken. In sum, the interest rate allocates funds to industries whose investments yield the highest (risk-adjusted) returns—where resources will be the most productive.

It is important to realize that the interest rate performs the function of allocating financial capital and that this ultimately allocates real physical capital to various firms for investment projects.

After contemplating market interest rates, how did the computer hardware firm Dell and the software company Microsoft recently choose to reallocate significant accumulations of funds?

E-COMMERCE EXAMPLE

Two Firms Find Different Uses for Big Loads of Cash

Two of the world's most successful companies in the area of computing and electronic commerce are Dell and Microsoft. Dell generates an annual inflow of funds exceeding $5 billion. When Dell recently compared the market rate of interest with the rate of return it could earn from plowing this flow of cash back into producing more computers, the firm found a better use for the funds. Dell got into the lending business. The company began offering credit to customers who borrow to finance their computer purchases, because the interest return it earns from its lending activities exceeds the rate of return from producing even more computers.

For years, Microsoft generated even more funds than Dell, and by 2004 it had accumulated $75 billion. Microsoft spent months trying to find ways to allocate all these funds to high-return investments. In the end, however, Microsoft decided that it could not find projects that would yield a higher return than its owners could earn elsewhere. Consequently, in 2004 the company embarked on a plan to return most of the funds to its owners, beginning with a onetime $32 billion dividend and continuing with higher regular dividend payments through at least 2008.

Thus, at Dell, consideration of the prevailing interest rate induced a reallocation of capital away from manufacturing and into lending instead. At Microsoft, the same consideration led to a reallocation away from producing computer software.

FOR CRITICAL ANALYSIS
What might Microsoft have done differently if there had been opportunities to earn higher rates of return on investments related to new types of software?

Interest Rates and Present Value

Businesses make investments in which they often incur large costs today but don't make any profits until some time in the future. Somehow they have to be able to compare their investment cost today with a stream of future profits. How can they relate present cost to future benefits?

Interest rates are used to link the present with the future. After all, if you have to pay $105 at the end of the year when you borrow $100, that 5 percent interest rate gives you

Go to www.econtoday.com/ch22 to utilize an MFM Communication Software, Inc. manual providing additional review of present value.

a measure of the premium on the earlier availability of goods and services. If you want to have things today, you have to pay the 5 percent interest rate in order to have current purchasing power.

The question could be put this way: What is the present value (the value today) of $105 that you could receive one year from now? That depends on the market rate of interest, or the rate of interest that you could earn in some appropriate savings institution, such as in a savings account. To make the arithmetic simple, let's assume that the rate of interest is 5 percent. Now you can figure out the **present value** of $105 to be received one year from now. You figure it out by asking the question, What sum must I put aside today at the market interest rate of 5 percent to receive $105 one year from now? Mathematically, we represent this equation as

Present value
The value of a future amount expressed in today's dollars; the most that someone would pay today to receive a certain sum at some point in the future.

$$(1 + 0.05)PV_1 = \$105$$

where PV_1 is the sum that you must set aside now.

Let's solve this simple equation to obtain PV_1:

$$PV_1 = \frac{\$105}{1.05} = \$100$$

That is, $100 will accumulate to $105 at the end of one year with a market rate of interest of 5 percent. Thus, the present value of $105 one year from now, using a rate of interest of 5 percent, is $100. The formula for present value of any sums to be received one year from now thus becomes

$$PV_1 = \frac{FV_1}{1 + i}$$

where

PV_1 = present value of a sum one year hence
FV_1 = future sum paid or received one year hence
i = market rate of interest

Present Values for More Distant Periods. The present-value formula for figuring out today's worth of dollars to be received at a future date can now be determined. How much would have to be put in the same savings account today to have $105 two years from now if the account pays a rate of 5 percent per year compounded annually?

After one year, the sum that would have to be set aside, which we will call PV_2, would have grown to $PV_2 \times 1.05$. This amount during the second year would increase to $PV_2 \times 1.05 \times 1.05$, or $PV_2 \times (1.05)^2$. To find the PV_2 that would grow to $105 over two years, let

$$PV_2 \times (1.05)^2 = \$105$$

and solve for PV_2:

$$PV_2 = \frac{\$105}{(1.05)^2} = \$95.24$$

Thus, the present value of $105 to be paid or received two years hence, discounted at an interest rate of 5 percent per year compounded annually, is equal to $95.24. In other words, $95.24 put into a savings account yielding 5 percent per year compounded interest would accumulate to $105 in two years.

TABLE 22-3
Present Value of a Future Dollar

This table shows how much a dollar received at the end of a certain number of years in the future is worth today. For example, at 5 percent a year, a dollar to be received 20 years in the future is worth 37.7 cents; if received in 50 years, it isn't even worth a dime today. To find out how much $10,000 would be worth a certain number of years from now, just multiply the figures in the table by 10,000. For example, $10,000 received at the end of 10 years discounted at a 5 percent rate of interest would have a present value of $6,140.

Discounted Present Values of $1

Year	3%	5%	8%	10%	20%
1	.971	.952	.926	.909	.833
2	.943	.907	.857	.826	.694
3	.915	.864	.794	.751	.578
4	.889	.823	.735	.683	.482
5	.863	.784	.681	.620	.402
6	.838	.746	.630	.564	.335
7	.813	.711	.583	.513	.279
8	.789	.677	.540	.466	.233
9	.766	.645	.500	.424	.194
10	.744	.614	.463	.385	.162
15	.642	.481	.315	.239	.0649
20	.554	.377	.215	.148	.0261
25	.478	.295	.146	.0923	.0105
30	.412	.231	.0994	.0573	.00421
40	.307	.142	.0460	.0221	.000680
50	.228	.087	.0213	.00852	.000109

The General Formula for Discounting. The general formula for **discounting** becomes

$$PV_t = \frac{FV_t}{(1 + i)^t}$$

where *t* refers to the number of periods in the future the money is to be paid or received.

Table 22-3 gives the present value of $1 to be received in future years at various interest rates. The interest rate used to derive the present value is called the **rate of discount**.

Each individual has his or her own *personal rate of discount,* which is the annual rate at which the individual discounts values to be received in future years. People with relatively low personal rates of discount are more willing to save funds today, because they subjectively perceive a higher present value on future interest payments. Those with relatively high personal rates of discount are more likely to borrow, because they perceive a lower present value on future interest payments. The market interest rate, therefore, lies between the upper and lower ranges of personal rates of discount.

Discounting
The method by which the present value of a future sum or a future stream of sums is obtained.

Rate of discount
The rate of interest used to discount future sums back to present value.

QUICK QUIZ

Interest is the price of obtaining credit. In the credit market, the rate of interest paid depends on the _____ of the loan, the _____, and the handling charges, among other things.

Nominal interest rates include a factor to take account of the _____ rate of inflation. Therefore, during periods of high _____ inflation, nominal interest rates will be relatively high.

Payments received or costs incurred in the future are worth less than those received or incurred today. The _____ _____ of any future sum is lower the further it occurs in the future and the greater the discount rate used.

See page 577 for the answers. Review concepts from this section in MyEconLab.

CORPORATE FINANCING METHODS

When the Dutch East India Company was founded in 1602, it raised financial capital by selling shares of its expected future profits to investors. The investors thus became the owners of the company, and their ownership shares eventually became known as "shares of stock," or simply *stocks*. The company also issued notes of indebtedness, which involved borrowing funds in return for interest paid on the funds, plus eventual repayment of the principal amount borrowed. In modern parlance, these notes of indebtedness are called *bonds*. As the company prospered over time, some of its revenues were used to pay lenders the interest and principal owed them; of the profits that remained, some were paid to shareholders in the form of dividends, and some were retained by the company for reinvestment in further enterprises. The methods of financing used by the Dutch East India Company four centuries ago—stocks, bonds, and reinvestment—remain the principal methods of financing for today's corporations.

Stocks

Share of stock
A legal claim to a share of a corporation's future profits. If it is *common stock*, it incorporates certain voting rights regarding major policy decisions of the corporation. If it is *preferred stock*, its owners are accorded preferential treatment in the payment of dividends but do not have any voting rights.

A **share of stock** in a corporation is simply a legal claim to a share of the corporation's future profits. If there are 100,000 shares of stock in a company and you own 1,000 of them, you own the right to 1 percent of that company's future profits. If the stock you own is *common stock*, you also have the right to vote on major policy decisions affecting the company, such as the selection of the corporation's board of directors. Your 1,000 shares would entitle you to cast 1 percent of the votes on such issues.

If the stock you own is *preferred stock*, you own a share of the future profits of the corporation but do *not* have regular voting rights. You do, however, get something in return for giving up your voting rights: preferential treatment in the payment of dividends. Specifically, the owners of preferred stock generally must receive at least a certain amount of dividends in each period before the owners of common stock can receive *any* dividends.

Bonds

Bond
A legal claim against a firm, usually entitling the owner of the bond to receive a fixed annual coupon payment, plus a lump-sum payment at the bond's maturity date. Bonds are issued in return for funds lent to the firm.

A **bond** is a legal claim against a firm, entitling the owner of the bond to receive a fixed annual *coupon* payment, plus a lump-sum payment at the maturity date of the bond. Bonds are issued in return for funds lent to the firm; the coupon payments represent interest on the amount borrowed by the firm, and the lump-sum payment at maturity of the bond generally equals the amount originally borrowed by the firm.

Bonds are *not* claims on the future profits of the firm; legally, bondholders must be paid whether the firm prospers or not. To help ensure this, bondholders generally receive their coupon payments each year, along with any principal that is due, before *any* shareholders can receive dividend payments.

Reinvestment

Reinvestment
Profits (or depreciation reserves) used to purchase new capital equipment.

Reinvestment takes place when the firm uses some of its profits to purchase new capital equipment rather than paying the profits out as dividends to shareholders. Although sales of stock are an important source of financing for new firms, reinvestment and borrowing are the primary means of financing for existing firms. Indeed, reinvestment by established firms is such an important source of financing that it dominates the other two sources of corporate finance, amounting to roughly 75 percent of new financial capital for corporations in recent years. Also, small businesses, which are the source of much current growth, often cannot rely on the stock market to raise investment funds.

THE MARKETS FOR STOCKS AND BONDS

Economists often refer to the "market for wheat" or the "market for labor," but these are concepts rather than actual places. For **securities** (stocks and bonds), however, there really are markets—centralized, physical locations where exchange takes place. The most prestigious of these markets are the New York Stock Exchange (NYSE) and the New York Bond Exchange, both located in New York City. More than 2,500 stocks are traded on the NYSE, which is sometimes called the "Big Board." Numerous other stock and bond markets, or exchanges, exist throughout the United States and in various financial capitals of the world, such as London and Tokyo.

Securities
Stocks and bonds.

Although the exact process by which exchanges are conducted in these markets varies slightly from one to another, the process used on the NYSE is representative of the principles involved. Essentially, brokers attempt to earn commissions from volumes of shares traded, while dealers attempt to profit from "buying low and selling high."

Even though the NYSE is traditionally the most prestigious of U.S. stock exchanges, it is no longer the largest. Since the mid-2000s, this title has belonged to the National Association of Securities Dealers Automated Quotations (Nasdaq), which began in 1971 as a tiny electronic network linking about 100 securities firms. Today, the Nasdaq market links about 500 dealers, and Nasdaq is home to nearly 5,500 stocks, including those of such companies as Microsoft, Intel, and Cisco.

Why do you suppose that China is hoping that establishing its own version of the U.S. Nasdaq exchange may serve as a catalyst for further economic development?

INTERNATIONAL EXAMPLE

Aiming to Duplicate Nasdaq's Successes in China

Publicly traded stocks of the largest companies in China are exchanged on the Shanghai Stock Exchange. Smaller firms, including new start-up companies, have traditionally relied on bank loans to finance their operations. Nevertheless, banks are reluctant to lend to new firms without a proven track record. Consequently, smaller Chinese firms have difficulty obtaining funds to expand their operations.

In hopes of broadening the sources of funds available to smaller firms, China's State Council recently approved a plan by the Shenzhen Stock Exchange to mimic the operations of the U.S. Nasdaq system. Managers of the Shenzhen Stock Exchange hope that adopting this plan will enable the exchange to attract shares of new companies specializing in information technologies. Their objective is to offer a Nasdaq-style electronic trading network through which traders will be able to exchange shares of future new Chinese versions of Microsoft or Intel—which in turn will blossom and contribute to the nation's development.

FOR CRITICAL ANALYSIS

How might the fact that average stock prices on both the Shanghai and Shenzhen exchanges have fallen by more than 30 percent since 2000 have contributed to the financing problems faced by smaller Chinese firms?

The Theory of Efficient Markets

At any point in time, there are tens of thousands, even millions, of persons looking for any bit of information that will enable them to forecast correctly the future prices of stocks. Responding to any information that seems useful, these people try to buy low and sell high. The result is that all publicly available information that might be used to forecast stock prices gets taken into account by those with access to the information and the knowledge and ability to learn from it, leaving no forecastable profit opportunities. And because so

Random walk theory
The theory that there are no predictable trends in securities prices that can be used to "get rich quick."

many people are involved in this process, it occurs quite swiftly. Indeed, there is some evidence that *all* information entering the market is fully incorporated into stock prices within less than a minute of its arrival. One view is that any information about specific stocks will prove to have little value by the time it reaches you.

Consequently, stock prices tend to drift upward following a *random walk,* which is to say that the best forecast of tomorrow's price is today's price plus the effect of any upward drift. This is called the **random walk theory.** Although large values of the random component of stock price changes are less likely than small values, nothing else about the magnitude or direction of a stock price change can be predicted. Indeed, the random component of stock prices exhibits behavior much like what would occur if you rolled two dice and subtracted 7 from the resulting total. On average, the dice will show a total of 7, so after you subtract 7, the average result will be zero. It is true that rolling a 12 or a 2 (resulting in a total of +5 or −5) is less likely than rolling an 8 or a 6 (yielding a total of +1 or −1). Nevertheless, positive and negative totals are equally likely, and the expected total is zero.

How might "program trading" contribute to efficiency in U.S. stock markets?

E-COMMERCE EXAMPLE

"Program Trading" Takes Center Stage in U.S. Stock Markets

In recent years, the use of sophisticated information technologies in U.S. stock markets has fueled significant growth of *program trading*, which entails the use of computers to buy and sell baskets of 15 or more stocks simultaneously. Traders engaging in program trading use computer software to monitor stock prices. The software generates "buy" and "sell" signals whenever opportunities for profits arise. In a typical week of trading on the NYSE, program trading accounts for about 60 percent of all exchanges of corporate stocks.

FOR CRITICAL ANALYSIS
In what way could program trading make stock markets more efficient?

Inside Information

Inside information
Information that is not available to the general public about what is happening in a corporation.

Go to www.econtoday.com/ch22 to explore how the U.S. Securities and Exchange Commission seeks to prevent the use of inside information.

Isn't there any way to "beat the market"? The answer is yes—but normally only if you have **inside information** that is not available to the public. Suppose that your best friend is in charge of new product development at the world's largest software firm, Microsoft Corporation. Your friend tells you that the company's smartest programmer has just come up with major new software that millions of computer users will want to buy. No one but your friend and the programmer—and now you—is aware of this. You could indeed make a killing using this information by purchasing shares of Microsoft and then selling them (at a higher price) as soon as the new product is publicly announced. There is one problem: Stock trading based on inside information such as this is illegal, punishable by substantial fines and even imprisonment. So, unless you happen to have a stronger-than-average desire for a long vacation in a federal prison, you might be better off investing in Microsoft after the new program is publicly announced.

It is, of course, possible for people to influence stock or bond prices through the accidental release of inside information. For instance, when the U.S. Treasury decided it would discontinue issuing 30-year bonds, it chose to announce its decision on October 31, 2001. Treasury officials told the media that the information of the bond's demise would be public as of 10 AM. Nevertheless, as a courtesy officials informed reporters in advance in an impromptu 9 AM meeting so that the reporters would have some time to write stories to release at that time. Officials failed to check the credentials of everyone who attended the meeting, however, and one of those individuals was a financial consultant who did not understand that this early news of the bond's end was "embargoed" until 10 AM. After the news conference ended just before 9:30 AM, the consultant called some of his clients and told them of the media announcement. Within a very few minutes, word of the Treasury's plans had spread widely. Ten minutes before the Treasury's formal announcement, 30-year bond prices rose in response to higher demand for existing bonds.

What can we learn from stock quotes available from the financial media?

EXAMPLE

How to Read the Financial Press: Stock Prices

Table 22-4, reproduced from the *Wall Street Journal*, contains information about the stocks of four companies. Across the top of the financial page are a series of column headings. Under the heading "STOCK (DIV)," we find the name of the company—in the second row, for example, is Hewlett-Packard Corporation, identified by the stock name in the third column, HewlettPk. The two columns to the left of the company's name show the highest and lowest prices at which shares of that company's stock traded during the past 52 weeks.

The last two columns of information for each firm summarize the behavior of the firm's stock price on the latest trading day. On this particular day, the last (or closing) price at which Hewlett-Packard Corporation stock traded was $32.37 per share. The net change in the price was +0.26 which means that it *closed* the day at a price about $0.26 per share above the price at which it closed the day before.

Immediately after the company's name in the "STOCK (DIV)" column is the annual dividend (in dollars and cents) that the company has paid over the preceding year on each share of its stock. In Hewlett-Packard's case, this amounts to $0.32 a share. If the dividend is divided by the closing price of the stock ($0.32 ÷ $32.37), the result is 1.0 percent, which is shown in the yield percentage ("YLD %") column in Hewlett-Packard's stock price listing. In a sense, the company is paying interest on the stock at a rate of about 1.0 percent. At first glance, this seems like a relatively low

TABLE 22-4
Reading Stock Quotes

52-WEEK HI	52-WEEK LO	STOCK (DIV)	YLD %	PE	VOL 100s	CLOSE	NET CHG
30.23	24.48	Hewitt	...	20	4039	25.49	0.19
34.52	22.38	HewlettPk .32	1.0	29	123048	32.37	0.26
24.91	14.40	Hexcel	...	12	11159	20	−0.32
13.55	9.78	HighIndHspty .64	5.3	48	2709	12.03	0.13

The summary of stock market information presented on the financial pages and Web sites of many newspapers reveals the following:

52-WEEK HI/LO: The highest and lowest prices, in dollars per share, of the stock during the previous 52 weeks
STOCK: The name of the company (frequently abbreviated)
DIV: Dividend paid, in dollars per share
YLD %: Yield in percent per year; the dividend divided by the price of the stock
PE: Price-earnings ratio; the price of the stock divided by the earnings (profits) per share of the company
VOL 100s: Number of shares traded during the day, in hundreds of shares
CLOSE: Last price at which the stock traded that day
NET CHG: Net change in the stock's price from the previous day's closing price

(continued)

amount; after all, at the time this issue of the *Wall Street Journal* was printed, ordinary checking accounts were paying about this much. The reason people tolerate this seemingly low yield on Hewlett-Packard's stock (or any other firm's stock) is that they expect that the price of the stock will rise over time, yielding capital gains.

The column heading "PE" stands for *price-earnings ratio*. To obtain the entries for this column, the firm's total earnings (profits) for the year are divided by the number of the firm's shares in existence to give the earnings per share. When the price of the stock is divided by the earnings per share, the result is the price-earnings ratio.

The column to the right of the PE ratio shows the total *volume* of the shares of the stock traded that day, measured in hundreds of shares.

FOR CRITICAL ANALYSIS
Is there necessarily any relationship between the net change in a stock's price and how many shares have been sold on a particular day?

QUICK QUIZ

The three primary sources of corporate funds are _____, _____, and _____ of profits.

A share of **stock** is a share of _____ providing a legal claim to a corporation's future profits. A _____ is a legal claim entitling the owner to a fixed annual coupon payment and to a lump-sum payment on the date it matures.

Many economists believe that asset markets, especially the stock market, are _____, meaning that one cannot make a higher-than-normal rate of return without having inside information (information that the general public does not possess). Stock prices normally drift upward following a _____ _____, meaning that you cannot predict changes in future stock prices based on information about stock price behavior in the past.

See page 577 for the answers. Review concepts from this section in MyEconLab.

CASE STUDY

ECONOMICS FRONT AND CENTER

Earning Economic Rents from Beyond the Grave

Ferraro has made a living as an agent for actors, singers, and supermodels. Recently, however, some of her top clients have been involved in scandals that have harmed their careers and the profitability of her firm. Consequently, at present Ferraro is on the lookout for new clients.

While sitting in the waiting room of her physician prior to a checkup, Ferraro flips through a magazine. She happens to glance at an article about the top earning dead celebrities. The leading dead celebrity earner, she learns, is Elvis Presley, who from beyond the grave continues to generate more than $30 million in sales, of which a portion is transmitted each year to the heirs to his estate. There are several other celebrities who have passed from this world but whose works continue to generate millions of dollars in earnings each year. Examples include Charles Schulz, author of the *Peanuts* comic strip; John Lennon and George Harrison, both former Beatles; Dale Earnhardt, the racecar driver; and Theodor "Dr. Seuss" Geisel and J. R. R. Tolkien, both renowned best-selling authors.

Ferraro grabs her cellphone and punches in her attorney's phone number. She wants him to identify the heirs to the estate of a top actor who recently passed away. Ferraro has no doubt that at least one of the actor's heirs could use the services of a top agent such as herself.

CRITICAL ANALYSIS QUESTIONS
1. *What is true of the price elasticity of supply for the products of a deceased celebrity entertainer or author?*
2. *Why can the heirs of deceased top celebrities continue to earn significant amounts from sales of the late celebrities' past works?*

Issues and Applications

Downs and Ups in Seats on the New York Stock Exchange

As you learned in this chapter, the New York Stock Exchange (NYSE) is an important component of the U.S. system of markets for stocks and bonds. The securities traded on the NYSE are corporate stocks.

Before the NYSE's 2006 reorganization, the right to execute purchases and sales of stocks, known as a membership *seat*, was also an asset that could be bought or sold. The market price of this particular asset fluctuated considerably in the run-up to the NYSE's restructuring, as shown in Figure 22-3 on the following page. The market price of an NYSE seat declined by 63 percent between late 2002 and the beginning of 2005, but then the price increased to an all-time high in December 2005. Why did the price of an NYSE seat go through such extreme variations in the early and middle part of the 2000s?

Concepts Applied
- Markets for Stocks and Bonds
- Securities
- Discounted Present Value

The Key Determinant of a Seat's Price

The main factor influencing the price of any asset, whether a security or a pre-2006 seat on the NYSE, is the discounted present value of anticipated future returns from ownership of the asset. For instance, in the case of a five-year bond that is supposed to yield a specified annual payoff, the maximum price that a person will probably be willing to pay is the sum of the discounted present values of the returns that will be obtained in each year. In reality, in light of transaction costs and risks of default or other loss of return, most people will offer less than this price, unless they are speculating that the asset's price will rise in the future.

Likewise, the maximum amount that an individual would likely have been willing to pay for a seat on the NYSE was the sum of the discounted present values of annual returns that the person anticipated receiving for all years of expected ownership of the seat. For instance, suppose that at some point, given the current market interest rate, anticipated future returns from ownership of an NYSE seat increased. Then the sum of discounted present values of future returns also increased, and the market price of the seat rose. Conversely, if expected future returns from owning a seat declined, then so did the sum of discounted present values of future returns and the probable market price of the seat.

Explaining Variations in an NYSE Seat's Price in the 2000s

Because only owners of NYSE seats could trade stocks on the NYSE before 2006, the main source of returns from seat ownership were fees that owners receive from engaging in stock trades. Thus, during periods in which NYSE trading volumes declined and were expected to remain subdued, expected returns from seat ownership fell. Consequently, given market interest rates, so did the sum of the discounted present values of anticipated future returns from seat ownership, and the market price of a seat fell. During the 2000–2001 recession, for

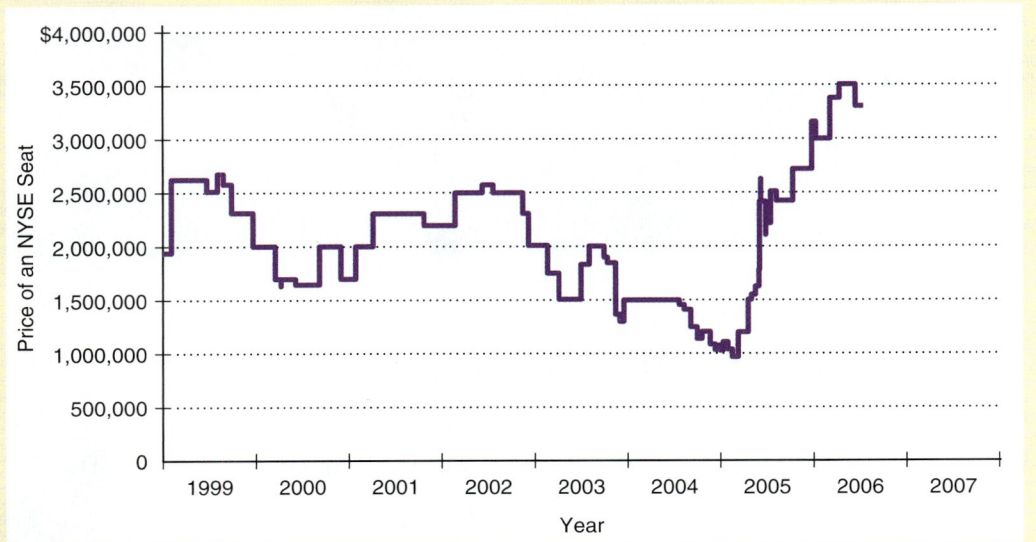

FIGURE 22-3

The Price of a Seat on the New York Stock Exchange Since 1999

A seat on the NYSE lost more than half its market value between late 2002 and the beginning of 2005. Then the market price of a seat rose considerably during 2005.

Source: Securities and Exchange Commission.

instance, NYSE trading volume fell. Uncertainty about when the volume of trades might recover accounted for the dip in the market price of a seat during this period.

The big overall decline in the price of a seat between late 2002 and the beginning of 2005 took place during an economic expansion. Nevertheless, during this period the NYSE began introducing more facilities for investors to trade stocks electronically and bypass the services of floor brokers. This development reduced the sum of anticipated future returns to seat ownership, and the price of a seat accordingly declined.

So why did the price of an NYSE seat recover so rapidly in 2005? When the NYSE reorganized as a publicly held company in 2006, it converted seats to shares of stock. Thus, the owners of the 1,366 seats suddenly had ownership shares in the entire NYSE, including the value of *all* future earnings, whether derived from floor trades *or* electronic trades. This immediately pushed up the sum of discounted present values of anticipated future returns from owning a seat and, consequently, future shares of NYSE stock. As a result, the market price of an NYSE seat increased.

Log in to **MyEconLab,** click on "Economic News," and test your understanding of the chapter by answering interactive questions that relate directly to this issue.

For Critical Analysis

1. In what sense did an NYSE seat effectively become a share of stock ownership as soon as the NYSE restructuring was announced in the spring of 2005? (Hint: Why were people willing to pay a much higher price for an NYSE seat during the following months?)
2. How might rising market interest rates during 2005 have affected the price of an NYSE seat?

Web Resources

1. To learn more about the NYSE, use the link available at www.econtoday.com/ch22.
2. For additional discussion of factors explaining the rise in the price of a seat on the NYSE, go to www.econtoday.com/ch22.

Research Project

Evaluate the following statement: "Gyrations in the price of a seat on the New York Stock Exchange during the 2000s are evidence against the idea that financial markets, including the stock market, efficiently take into account all relevant information."

Here is what you should know after reading this chapter. MyEconLab will help you identify what you know, and where to go when you need to practice.

WHAT YOU SHOULD KNOW		WHERE TO GO TO PRACTICE
Economic Rent and Resource Allocation Owners of a resource in fixed supply, meaning that the resource supply curve is perfectly inelastic, are paid economic rent. Originally, this term was used to refer to payment for the use of land or any other natural resource that is considered to be in fixed supply. More generally, however, economic rent is a payment for use of any resource that exceeds the opportunity cost of the resource. People who provide labor services that are difficult for others to provide, such as sports superstars, movie stars, and the like, typically receive earnings well in excess of the earnings that would otherwise have been sufficient to induce them to provide their services. Nevertheless, the economic rents that they earn reflect the maximum market valuation of their value, so economic rent allocates resources to their highest-valued use.	economic rent, 553 **Key figure** Figure 22-1, 554	• **MyEconLab** Study Plan 22.1 • Audio introduction to Chapter 22 • Animated Figure 22-1 • Video: Economic Rent and the Allocation of Resources
The Main Organizational Forms of Business and the Chief Advantages and Disadvantages of Each The primary organizational forms businesses take are the proprietorship, the partnership, and the corporation. The proprietorship is owned by a single person, the proprietor, who makes the business decisions, is entitled to all the profits, and is subject to unlimited liability—that is, is personally responsible for all debts incurred by the firm. The partnership differs from the proprietorship chiefly in that there are two or more owners, called partners. They share the responsibility for decision making, share the firm's profits, and individually bear unlimited liability for the firm's debts. The net income, or profits, of both proprietorships and partnerships is subject only to personal income taxes. Both types of firms legally cease to exist when the proprietor or a partner gives up ownership or dies. The corporation differs from proprietorships and partnerships in three important dimensions. Owners of corporations enjoy limited liability; that is, their responsibility for the debts of the corporation is limited to the value of their ownership shares. In addition, the income from corporations is subject to double taxation—corporate taxation when income is earned by the corporation and personal taxation when after-tax profits are paid as dividends to the owners. Finally, corporations do not legally cease to exist due to a change of ownership or the death of an owner.	firm, 555 proprietorship, 556 unlimited liability, 557 partnership, 557 corporation, 557 limited liability, 557 dividends, 558	• **MyEconLab** Study Plan 22.2 • Video: The Goal of the Firm Is Profit Maximization

WHAT YOU SHOULD KNOW | WHERE TO GO TO PRACTICE

Accounting Profits versus Economic Profits A firm's accounting profits equal its total revenues minus its total explicit costs, which are expenses directly paid out by the firm. Economic profits equal accounting profits minus implicit costs, which are expenses that managers do not have to pay out of pocket, such as the opportunity cost of factors of production dedicated to the firm's production process. Owners of a firm seek to maximize the firm's economic profits to ensure that they earn at least a normal rate of return, meaning that the firm's total revenues at least cover explicit costs and implicit opportunity costs.

explicit costs, 558
accounting profit, 558
implicit costs, 558
normal rate of return, 558
opportunity cost of capital, 559
economic profits, 559
Key figure
Figure 22-2, 560

- **MyEconLab** Study Plan 22.2
- Animated Figure 22-2
- Video: The Goal of the Firm Is Profit Maximization

Interest Rates Interest is a payment for the ability to use resources today instead of in the future. Factors that influence interest rates are the length of the term of a loan, the loan's risk, and handling charges. The nominal interest rate includes a factor that takes into account the anticipated inflation rate. Therefore, during periods of high anticipated inflation, current market (nominal) interest rates are high. Comparing the market interest rate with the rate of return on prospective capital investment projects enables owners of funds to determine the highest-valued uses of the funds. Thus, the interest rate allocates funds to industries whose investments yield the highest (risk-adjusted) returns, thereby ensuring that available resources will be put to their most productive uses.

financial capital, 561
interest, 561
nominal rate of interest, 562
real rate of interest, 562

- **MyEconLab** Study Plan 22.3
- Video: Interest Rates and Present Value

Calculating the Present Discounted Value of a Payment to Be Received at a Future Date The present value of a future payment is the value of the future amount expressed in today's dollars, and it is equal to the most that someone would pay today to receive that amount in the future. The method by which the present value of a future sum is calculated is called *discounting*. This method implies that the present value of a sum to be received a year from now is equal to the future amount divided by 1 plus the appropriate rate of interest, which is called the *rate of discount*.

present value, 564
discounting, 565
rate of discount, 565

- **MyEconLab** Study Plan 22.3
- Video: Interest Rates and Present Value

The Three Main Sources of Corporate Funds The main sources of financial capital for corporations are stocks, bonds, and reinvestment of profits. Stocks are ownership shares, promising a share of profits, sold to investors. Common stocks also embody voting rights regarding the major decisions of the firm; preferred stocks typically have no voting rights but enjoy priority status in the payment of dividends. Bonds are notes of indebtedness, issued in return for the loan of money. They typically prom-

share of stock, 566
bond, 566
reinvestment, 566
securities, 567
random walk theory, 568
inside information, 568

- **MyEconLab** Study Plans 22.4 and 22.5
- Video: The Theory of Efficient Markets and Inside Information

ise to pay interest in the form of annual coupon payments, plus repayment of the original principal amount upon maturity. Bondholders are generally promised payment before any payment of dividends to shareholders, and for this reason bonds are less risky than stocks. Reinvestment involves the purchase of assets by the firm, using retained profits or depreciation reserves it has set aside for this purpose. No new stocks or bonds are issued in the course of reinvestment, although the firm's value is fully reflected in the price of existing shares of stock.

Log in to MyEconLab, take a chapter test, and get a personalized Study Plan that tells you which concepts you understand and which ones you need to review. From there, MyEconLab will give you further practice, tutorials, animations, videos, and guided solutions.

Log in to www.myeconlab.com

PROBLEMS

Select problems, indicated by a blue oval, are assignable in MyEconLab. Answers to the odd-numbered problems appear at the back of the book.

22-1 Which of the following would you expect to have a high level of economic rent, and which would you expect to have a low level of economic rent? Explain why for each.
  a. Bob has a highly specialized medical skill that is in great demand.
  b. Sally has never attended school. She is 25 years old and is an internationally known supermodel.
  c. Tim is a high school teacher and sells insurance part time.

22-2. Though he has retired as a professional football receiver, Jerry Rice still earns a sizable annual income from endorsements. Explain why, in economic terms, his level of economic rent is so high.

22-3. Former professional basketball star Michael Jordan once left basketball to play baseball. As a result, his annual dollar income dropped from the millions to the thousands. Eventually, Jordan quit baseball and returned to basketball. What role did economic rents likely play in influencing his decision?

22-4. A British pharmaceutical company spent several years and considerable funds on the development of a treatment for HIV patients. Now, with the protection afforded by patent rights, the company has the potential to reap enormous gains. The government, in response, has threatened to tax away any rents the company may earn. Is this an advisable policy? Why or why not? (Hint: Contrast the short-run and long-run effects of taxing away the economic rents.)

22-5. Write a brief explanation of the differences between a sole proprietorship, a partnership, and a corporation. In addition, list one advantage and one disadvantage of a proprietorship, a partnership, and a corporation.

22-6 After graduation, you face a choice. One option is to work for a multinational consulting firm and earn a starting salary (benefits included) of $40,000. The other option is to use $5,000 in savings to start your own consulting firm. You could earn an interest return of 5 percent on your savings. You choose to start your own consulting firm. At the end of the first year, you add up all of your expenses and revenues. Your total includes $12,000 in rent, $1,000 in office supplies, $20,000 for office staff, and $4,000 in telephone expenses. What are your total explicit costs and total implicit costs?

22-7 Suppose, as in Problem 22-6, that you have now operated your consulting firm for a year. At the end of the first year, your total revenues are $77,250. Based on the information in Problem 22-6, what is the accounting profit, and what is your economic profit?

22-8 An individual leaves a college faculty, where she was earning $40,000 a year, to begin a new venture. She invests her savings of $10,000, which were earning 10 percent annually. She then spends $20,000 renting office equipment, hires two students at $30,000 a year each, rents office space for $12,000, and has other variable expenses of $40,000. At the end of the year, her revenues are $200,000. What are her accounting profit and her economic profit for the year?

22-9 Classify the following items as either financial capital or physical capital.
  a. A computer server owned by an information-processing company
  b. $100,000 set aside in an account to purchase a computer server
  c. Funds raised through a bond offer to expand plant and equipment
  d. A warehouse owned by a shipping company

22-10. Explain the difference between the dividends of a corporation and the profits of a proprietorship or partnership, particularly in their tax treatment.

22-11 The owner of WebCity is trying to decide whether to remain a proprietorship or to incorporate. Suppose that the corporate tax rate on profits is 20 percent and the personal income tax rate is 30 percent. For simplicity, assume that all corporate profits (after corporate taxes are paid) are distributed as dividends in the year they are earned and that such dividends are subject to tax at the personal income tax rate.
  a. If the owner of WebCity expects to earn $100,000 in before-tax profits this year, regardless of whether the firm is a proprietorship or a corporation, which method of organization should be chosen?
  b. What is the dollar value of the after-tax advantage of the form of organization determined in part (a)?
  c. Suppose that the corporate form of organization has cost advantages that will raise before-tax profits by $50,000. Should the owner of WebCity incorporate?
  d. By how much will after-tax profits change due to incorporation?
  e. Suppose that tax policy is changed to completely exempt from personal taxation the first $40,000 per year in dividends. Would this change in policy affect the decision made in part (a)?
  f. How can you explain the fact that even though corporate profits are subject to double taxation, most business in the United States is conducted by corporations rather than by proprietorships or partnerships?

22-12 Explain how the following events would likely affect the relevant interest rate.

  a. A major bond-rating agency has improved the risk rating of a developing nation.
  b. To regulate and protect the public, the government has passed legislation that requires a considerable increase in the reporting paperwork when a bank makes a loan.

22-13 Suppose that the interest rate in Japan is only 2 percent, while the comparable rate in the United States is 4 percent. Japan's rate of inflation is 0.5 percent, while the U.S. inflation rate is 3 percent. Which economy has the higher real interest rate?

22-14 You expect to receive a payment of $104 one year from now.
  a. Your discount rate is 4 percent. What is the present value of the payment to be received?
  b. Suppose that your discount rate rises to 5 percent. What is the present value of the payment to be received?

22-15 Outline the differences between common stock and preferred stock.

22-16. Explain the basic differences between a share of stock and a bond.

22-17. Suppose that one of your classmates informs you that he has developed a method of forecasting stock market returns based on past trends. With a monetary investment by you, he claims that the two of you could profit handsomely from this forecasting method. How should you respond to your classmate?

22-18 Suppose that you are trying to decide whether to spend $1,000 on stocks issued by WildWeb or on bonds issued by the same company. There is a 50 percent chance that the value of the stock will rise to $2,200 at the end of the year and a 50 percent chance that the stock will be worthless at the end of the year. The bonds promise an interest rate of 20 percent per year, and it is certain that the bonds and interest will be repaid at the end of the year.
  a. Assuming that your time horizon is exactly one year, will you choose the stocks or the bonds?
  b. By how much is your expected end-of-year wealth reduced if you make the wrong choice?
  c. Suppose the odds of success improve for WildWeb: Now there is a 60 percent chance that the value of the stock will be $2,200 at year's end and only a 40 percent chance that it will be worthless. Should you now choose the stocks or the bonds?
  d. By how much did your expected end-of-year wealth rise as a result of the improved outlook for WildWeb?

ECONOMICS ON THE NET

How the New York Stock Exchange Operates This application gives you the chance to learn about how the New York Stock Exchange functions.

Title: The New York Stock Exchange: Market Quality

Navigation: Follow the link at **www.econtoday.com/ch22** to visit the New York Stock Exchange. In the left margin in the pop-up menu next to "About NYSE Group." click on *Education*. Along the top, select the tab named *Educational Materials*. Under "Related Information" near the bottom of the page, click on *Other NYSE Publications*. Then, under "Market Information," click on *NYSE Market Quality*.

Application Perform the following operations, and answer the associated questions.

1. Next to "Overview," click on *Best Price,* and read the article. Why might companies contemplating issuing stock value the relatively low costs of trading shares on the New York Stock Exchange?

2. Back up, and, next to "Overview," click on *Speed/Certainty*. Read this article. Why might people who buy and sell stocks value the relatively faster speeds of trade execution that the NYSE has achieved in recent years?

For Group Study and Analysis Divide the class into groups, and have each group examine and discuss the information located under the headings *Liquidity* and *Volatility*. Ask each group to evaluate the trade-offs that buyers and sellers of stocks face when considering price, trading costs, liquidity, and volatility. Then go through these as a class, and discuss which of these factors is likely to be most important in influencing issuers and traders of stocks.

ANSWERS TO QUICK QUIZZES

p. 555: (i) inelastic; (ii) allocates . . . highest
p. 561: (i) Proprietorships . . . unlimited; (ii) Partnerships . . . unlimited; (iii) shareholders . . . limited; (iv) opportunity; (v) greater . . . maximize
p. 565: (i) length . . . risk; (ii) anticipated . . . anticipated; (iii) present value
p. 570: (i) stocks . . . bonds . . . reinvestment; (ii) ownership . . . bond; (iii) efficient . . . random walk

23 The Firm: Cost and Output Determination

Learning Objectives

After reading this chapter, you should be able to:

1. Discuss the difference between the short run and the long run from the perspective of a firm
2. Understand why the marginal physical product of labor eventually declines as more units of labor are employed
3. Explain the short-run cost curves a typical firm faces
4. Describe the long-run cost curves a typical firm faces
5. Identify situations of economies and diseconomies of scale and define a firm's minimum efficient scale

MyEconLab helps you master each objective and study more efficiently. See end of chapter for details.

In a typical year, publishers of hardcover books have workers cut the spines from about 4 million unsold and unread books. Each day, the workers load steady flows of the spineless books into recycling machines the size of a large trash dumpster. The machines chew up the books into bales of paper, some of which will find its way into books that once again will be unsold. Most likely, the unread pages of more than a third of these future books will also be fed into the machines and recycled once more. Why do publishers print so many books each year and then destroy them? How does doing this affect their costs of doing business? By the time you have completed this chapter, you will be able to analyze these questions.

Did You Know That . . .

within an hour after a typical modern laptop computer has booted up, at least one spot on its chassis reaches a temperature of 130 degrees Fahrenheit, or about 22 degrees above the human pain threshold? The shrinkage of computer microprocessors allows them to operate much faster, which enables computations at far greater speeds on smaller computing devices, including thinner, lighter laptop computers. Nevertheless, the heat generated by speedier computing devices does not simply expose human users to pain. It also threatens to drive up costs faced by computer producers. The tremendous heat created by faster microprocessors shortens the average time before computer components fail, which exposes computer manufacturers to higher costs of providing warranty services. Thus, the overall costs of producing and selling the computers increase.

Computer producers are taking heart from recent developments in *nanotechnology*, the science of building structures using individual atoms and molecules. Nanotechnology is aiding the development of materials with better thermal conductivity, which helps reduce temperatures, and with greater durability, which enables components to withstand heat for longer periods. Nanotechnology-enabled improvements may help computer manufacturers lengthen the time that components last in today's high-temperature computers, thereby reducing their costs.

Clearly, production technologies and the costs that producers face are related. By the time you have finished this chapter, you will have a full understanding of the nature of this relationship between production technologies and costs.

SHORT RUN VERSUS LONG RUN

In Chapter 21, we discussed short-run and long-run price elasticities of supply and demand. As you will recall, for consumers, the long run means the time period during which all adjustments to a change in price can be made, and anything shorter than that is considered the short run. For suppliers, the long run is the time in which all adjustments can be made, and anything shorter than that is the short run.

Now that we are discussing firms only, we will maintain a similar distinction between the short and the long run, but we will be more specific. In the theory of the firm, the **short run** is defined as any time period that is so short that there is at least one input, such as current **plant size,** that the firm cannot alter. In other words, during the short run, a firm makes do with whatever big machines and factory size it already has, no matter how much more it wants to produce because of increased demand for its product. We consider the plant and heavy equipment, the size or amount of which cannot be varied in the short run, as fixed resources. In agriculture and in some other businesses, land may be a fixed resource.

There are, of course, variable resources that the firm can alter when it wants to change its rate of production. These are called *variable inputs* or *variable factors of production*. Typically, the variable inputs of a firm are its labor and its purchases of raw materials. In the short run, in response to changes in demand, the firm can, by definition, change only the amounts of its variable inputs.

The **long run** can now be considered the period of time in which *all* inputs can be varied. Specifically, in the long run, the firm can alter its plant size. How long is the long run? That depends on each individual industry. For Wendy's or McDonald's, the long run may be four or five months, because that is the time it takes to add new franchises. For a steel company, the long run may be several years, because that's how long it takes to plan and build a new plant. An electric utility might need over a decade to build a new plant, as another example.

Short run
The time period during which at least one input, such as plant size, cannot be changed.

Plant size
The physical size of the factories that a firm owns and operates to produce its output. Plant size can be defined by square footage, maximum physical capacity, and other physical measures.

Long run
The time period during which all factors of production can be varied.

Short run and *long run* in our discussion are terms that apply to planning decisions made by managers. Managers routinely take account of both the short-run and the long-run consequences of their behavior. While always making decisions about what to do today, tomorrow, and next week—the short-run as it were—they keep an eye on the long-run net benefits of all short-run actions. As an individual, you have long-run plans, such as going to graduate school or on vacation, and you make a series of short-run decisions with these long-run plans in mind.

THE RELATIONSHIP BETWEEN OUTPUT AND INPUTS

A firm takes numerous inputs, combines them using a technological production process, and ends up with an output. There are, of course, a great many factors of production, or inputs. Keeping the quantity of land fixed, we classify production inputs into two broad categories—labor and capital. The relationship between output and these two inputs is as follows:

$$\text{Output per time period} = \text{some function of capital and labor inputs}$$

In simple math, the production relationship can be written $Q = f(K, L)$, where Q = output per time period, K = capital, and L = labor.

We have used the word *production* but have not defined it. **Production** is any process by which resources are transformed into goods or services. Production includes not only making things but also transporting them, retailing, repackaging them, and so on. Notice that the production relationship tells nothing about the worth or value of the inputs or the output.

Production
Any activity that results in the conversion of resources into products that can be used in consumption.

The Production Function: A Numerical Example

The relationship between maximum physical output and the quantity of capital and labor used in the production process is sometimes called the **production function**. The production function is a technological relationship between inputs and output.

Production function
The relationship between inputs and maximum physical output. A production function is a technological, not an economic, relationship.

Properties of the Production Function. The production function specifies the maximum possible output that can be produced with a given amount of inputs. It also specifies the minimum amount of inputs necessary to produce a given level of output. Firms that are inefficient or wasteful in their use of capital and labor will obtain less output than the production function in theory will show. No firm can obtain more output than the production function shows, however. The production function also depends on the technology available to the firm. It follows that an improvement in technology that allows the firm to produce more output with the same amount of inputs (or the same output with fewer inputs) results in a new production function.

How has holographic technology allowed product designers to use fewer labor resources to create more models of new product ideas?

E-COMMERCE EXAMPLE

Put Away the Clay and Turn On the Holographic Camera

Traditionally, manufacturers and builders have relied on clay models to create three-dimensional images of what products on the drawing board might look like once they were constructed. Increasingly, however, they are making use of holograms, or three-dimensional photographs. A typical holographic model

(continued)

of a car design contains 2 trillion characters of data on a three-dimensional image file containing 500,000 photos recorded from different perspectives. Each individual photo is encoded on a laser, focused through a spherical lens, and burned onto a section of plastic a millimeter across. Once a company has integrated a holographic camera system into its existing computer network, creating holographic images of product designs takes only a fraction of the time that sculptors require to make clay models. Consequently, product developers using holographic techniques can now create more designs while utilizing fewer labor resources.

FOR CRITICAL ANALYSIS
Why do technological improvements often reduce labor requirements for specific tasks, thereby allowing more labor to be utilized for other purposes?

Panel (a) of Figure 23-1 on the next page shows a production function relating maximum output in column 2 to the quantity of labor in column 1. Zero workers per week produce no output. Five workers per week of input produce a total output of 50 computer printers per week. (Ignore for the moment the rest of that panel.) Panel (b) of Figure 23-1 displays production function. It relates to the short run, because plant size is fixed, and it applies to a single firm.

Total Physical Product. Panel (b) shows a total physical product curve, or the maximum feasible output when we add successive equal-sized units of labor while holding all other inputs constant. The graph of the production function in panel (b) is not a straight line. It peaks at seven workers per week and then starts to go down.

Average and Marginal Physical Product

To understand the shape of the total physical product curve, let's examine columns 3 and 4 of panel (a) of Figure 23-1—that is, average and marginal physical product. **Average physical product** is the total product divided by the number of worker-weeks. You can see in column 3 of panel (a) of Figure 23-1 that the average physical product of labor first rises and then steadily falls after two workers are hired.

Marginal means "additional," so the **marginal physical product** of labor is the *change* in total product that occurs when a worker is added to a production process. (The term *physical* here emphasizes the fact that we are measuring in terms of material quantities of goods or tangible amounts of services, not in dollar terms.) The marginal physical product of labor therefore refers to the *change in output caused by a one-unit change in the labor input* as shown in column 4 of panel (a) of Figure 23-1. (Marginal physical product is also referred to as *marginal product*.)

Average physical product
Total product divided by the variable input.

Marginal physical product
The physical output that is due to the addition of one more unit of a variable factor of production; the change in total product occurring when a variable input is increased and all other inputs are held constant; also called *marginal product*.

DIMINISHING MARGINAL PRODUCT

Note that in Figure 23-1, after the first worker is employed, marginal product declines. The concept of diminishing marginal product applies to many situations. If you put a seat belt across your lap, a certain amount of safety is obtained. If you add another seat belt over your shoulder, some additional safety is obtained, but less than when the first belt was secured. When you add a third seat belt over the other shoulder, the amount of *additional* safety obtained is even smaller.

FIGURE 23-1

The Production Function and Marginal Product: A Hypothetical Case

Marginal product is the addition to the total product that results when one additional worker is hired. Thus, in panel (a), the marginal product of the fourth worker is eight computer printers. With four workers, 44 printers are produced, but with three workers, only 36 are produced; the difference is 8. In panel (b), we plot the numbers from columns 1 and 2 of panel (a). In panel (c), we plot the numbers from columns 1 and 4 of panel (a). When we go from 0 to 1, marginal product is 10. When we go from one worker to two workers, marginal product increases to 16. After two workers, marginal product declines, but it is still positive. Total product (output) reaches its peak at seven workers, so after seven workers, marginal product is negative. When we move from seven to eight workers, marginal product becomes −1 printer.

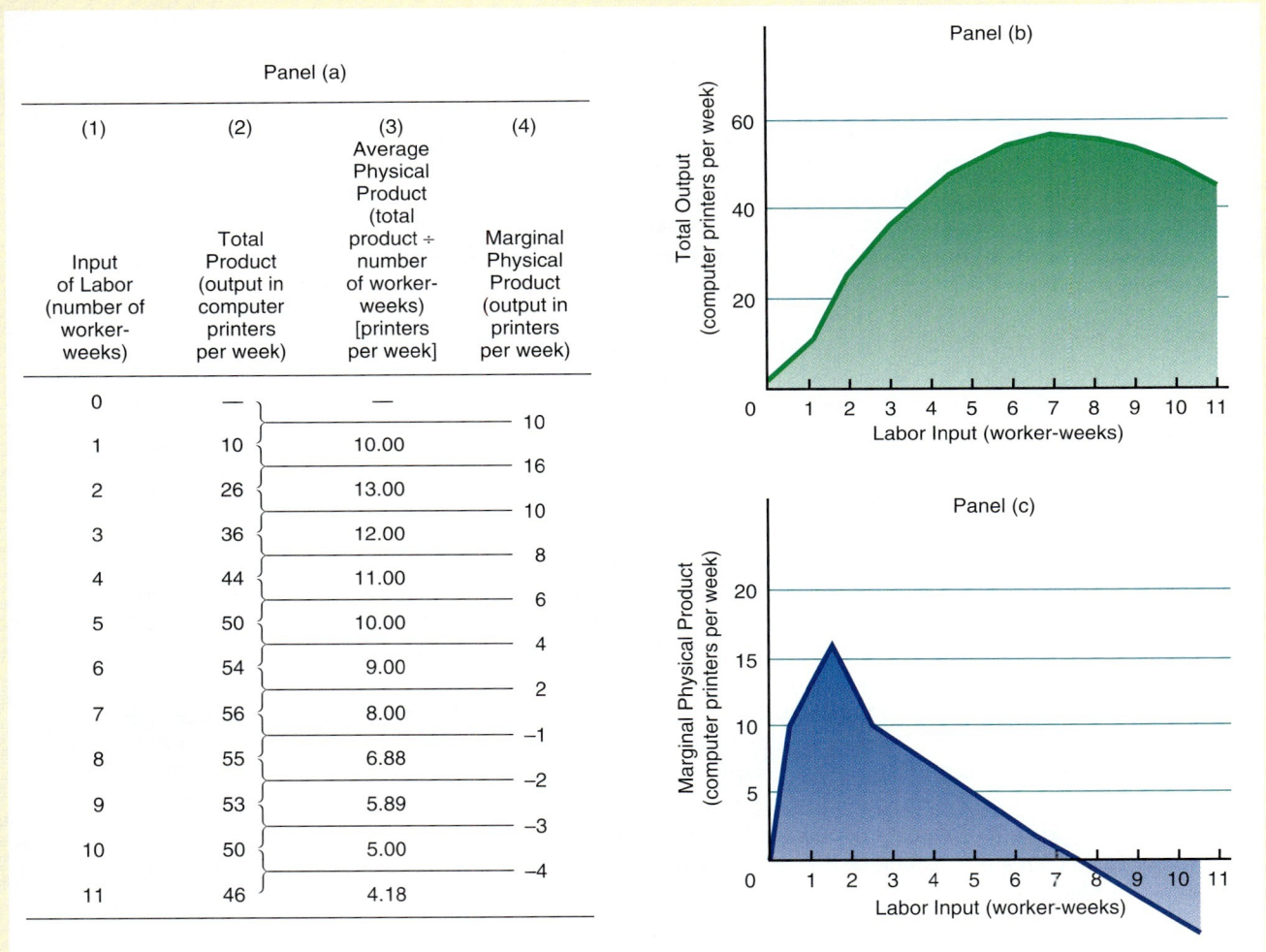

(1) Input of Labor (number of worker-weeks)	(2) Total Product (output in computer printers per week)	(3) Average Physical Product (total product ÷ number of worker-weeks) [printers per week]	(4) Marginal Physical Product (output in printers per week)
0	—	—	
1	10	10.00	10
2	26	13.00	16
3	36	12.00	10
4	44	11.00	8
5	50	10.00	6
6	54	9.00	4
7	56	8.00	2
8	55	6.88	−1
9	53	5.89	−2
10	50	5.00	−3
11	46	4.18	−4

Measuring Diminishing Marginal Product

How do we measure diminishing marginal product? First, we limit the analysis to only one variable factor of production (or input)—let's say the factor is labor. Every other factor of production, such as machines, must be held constant. Only in this way can we calculate the marginal product from using more workers and know when we reach the point of diminishing marginal product.

Specialization and Marginal Product. The marginal productivity of labor may increase rapidly at the very beginning. A firm starts with no workers, only machines. The firm then hires one worker, who finds it difficult to get the work started. But when the firm hires more workers, each is able to *specialize* in performing different tasks, and the marginal product of those additional workers may actually be greater than the marginal product of the previous few workers.

Diminishing Marginal Product. Beyond some point, however, diminishing marginal product must set in—*not* because new workers are less qualified but because each worker has, on average, fewer machines with which to work (remember, all other inputs are fixed). In fact, eventually the firm's plant will become so crowded that workers will start to get in each other's way. At that point, marginal physical product becomes negative, and total production declines.

Using these ideas, we can define the **law of diminishing marginal product:**

As successive equal increases in a variable factor of production are added to fixed factors of production, there will be a point beyond which the extra, or marginal, product that can be attributed to each additional unit of the variable factor of production will decline.

Law of diminishing marginal product
The observation that after some point, successive equal-sized increases in a variable factor of production, such as labor, added to fixed factors of production, will result in smaller increases in output.

Note that the law of diminishing marginal product is a statement about the *physical* relationships between inputs and outputs that we have observed in many firms. If the law of diminishing marginal product were not a fairly accurate statement about the world, what would stop firms from hiring additional workers forever?

An Example of the Law of Diminishing Marginal Product

Production of computer printers provides an example of the law of diminishing marginal product. With a fixed amount of factory space, assembly equipment, and quality-control diagnostic software, the addition of more workers eventually yields successively smaller increases in output. After a while, when all the assembly equipment and quality-control diagnostic software are being used, additional workers will have to start assembling and troubleshooting quality problems manually. They obviously won't be as productive as the first workers who had access to other productive inputs. The marginal physical product of an additional worker, given a specified amount of capital, must eventually be less than that for the previous workers.

Graphing the Marginal Product of Labor. A hypothetical set of numbers illustrating the law of diminishing marginal product is presented in panel (a) of Figure 23-1 on the previous page. The numbers are presented graphically in panel (c). Marginal productivity (returns from adding more workers) first increases, then decreases, and finally becomes negative.

When one worker is hired, total output goes from 0 to 10. Thus, marginal physical product is 10 computer printers per week. When the second worker is hired, total product goes from 10 to 26 printers per week. Marginal physical product therefore increases to 16 printers per week. When a third worker is hired, total product again increases, from 26 to 36 printers per week. This represents a marginal physical product of only 10 printers per week. Therefore, the point of diminishing marginal product occurs after two workers are hired.

The Point of Saturation. Notice that after seven workers per week, marginal physical product becomes negative. That means that the hiring of an eighth worker would reduce total product. Sometimes this is called the *point of saturation,* indicating that given the amount of fixed inputs, there is no further positive use for more of the variable input. We have entered the region of negative marginal product.

> ## QUICK QUIZ
>
> The technological relationship between output and inputs is called the _____ function. It relates _____ per time period to several inputs, such as capital and labor.
>
> After some rate of output, the firm generally experiences diminishing marginal _____.
>
> The law of diminishing marginal product states that if all factors of production are held constant except one, equal increments in that one variable factor will eventually yield _____ increments in _____.
>
> See page 604 for the answers. Review concepts from this section in MyEconLab.

SHORT-RUN COSTS TO THE FIRM

You will see that costs are the extension of the production ideas just presented. Let's consider the costs the firm faces in the short run. To make this example simple, assume that there are only two factors of production, capital and labor. Our definition of the short run will be the time during which capital is fixed but labor is variable.

In the short run, a firm incurs certain types of costs. We label all costs incurred **total costs.** Then we break total costs down into total fixed costs and total variable costs, which we will explain shortly. Therefore,

Total costs
The sum of total fixed costs and total variable costs.

Total costs (TC) = total fixed costs (TFC) + total variable costs (TVC)

Remember that these total costs include both explicit and implicit costs, including the normal rate of return on investment.

After we have looked at the elements of total costs, we will find out how to compute average and marginal costs.

Total Fixed Costs

Let's look at an ongoing business such as Dell, Inc. The decision makers in that corporate giant can look around and see big machines, thousands of parts, huge buildings, and a multitude of other components of plant and equipment that have already been bought and are in place. Dell has to take into account expenses to replace some worn-out equipment, no matter how many computers it produces. The payments on the loans taken out to buy the equipment will all be exactly the same. The opportunity costs of any land that Dell owns will all be exactly the same. In the short run, these costs are more or less the same for Dell no matter how many computers it produces.

We also have to point out that the opportunity cost (or normal rate of return) of capital must be included along with other costs. Remember that we are dealing in the short run, during which capital is fixed. If investors in Dell have already put $100 million into a factory addition, the opportunity cost of that capital invested is now, in essence, a *fixed cost.* Why? Because in the short run, nothing can be done about that cost; the investment has already been made. This leads us to a very straightforward definition of fixed costs:

All costs that do not vary—that is, all costs that do not depend on the rate of production—are called **fixed costs.**

Let's now take as an example the fixed costs incurred by a producer of 64-megabyte flash memory pen drives, the smallest and typically the lowest-price portable memory drives for personal computers. This firm's total fixed costs will usually include the cost of the rent on its equipment and the insurance it has to pay. We see in panel (a) of Figure 23-2 on the following page that total fixed costs per day are $10. In panel (b), these total fixed costs are represented by the horizontal line at $10 per day. They are invariant to changes in the daily output of these flash memory drives—no matter how many are produced, fixed costs will remain at $10 per day.

Fixed costs
Costs that do not vary with output. Fixed costs typically include such things as rent on a building. These costs are fixed for a certain period of time (in the long run, though, they are variable).

Total Variable Costs

Total **variable costs** are costs whose magnitude varies with the rate of production. Wages are an obvious variable cost. The more the firm produces, the more labor it has to hire; therefore, the more wages it has to pay. Parts are another variable cost. To manufacture flash memory pen drives, for example, microchips must be bought. The more flash drives that are made, the greater the number of chips that must be bought. A portion of the rate of depreciation (wear and tear) on machines that are used in the assembly process can also be considered a variable cost if depreciation depends partly on how long and how intensively the machines are used. Total variable costs are given in column 3 in panel (a) of Figure 23-2 on the next page. These are translated into the total variable cost curve in panel (b). Notice that the total variable cost curve lies below the total cost curve by the vertical distance of $10. This vertical distance represents, of course, total fixed costs.

Variable costs
Costs that vary with the rate of production. They include wages paid to workers and purchases of materials.

Short-Run Average Cost Curves

In panel (b) of Figure 23-2, we see total costs, total variable costs, and total fixed costs. Now we want to look at average cost. With the average cost concept, we are measuring cost per unit of output. It is a matter of simple arithmetic to figure the averages of these three cost concepts. We can define them as follows:

$$\text{Average total costs (ATC)} = \frac{\text{total costs (TC)}}{\text{output }(Q)}$$

$$\text{Average variable costs (AVC)} = \frac{\text{total variable costs (TVC)}}{\text{output }(Q)}$$

$$\text{Average fixed costs (AFC)} = \frac{\text{total fixed costs (TFC)}}{\text{output }(Q)}$$

The arithmetic is done in columns 5, 6, and 7 in panel (a) of Figure 23-2. The numerical results are translated into a graphical format in panel (c). Because total costs (TC) equal variable costs (TVC) plus fixed costs (TFC), the difference between average total costs (ATC) and average variable costs (AVC) will always be identical to average fixed costs (AFC). That means that average total costs and average variable costs move together as output expands.

Now let's see what we can observe about the three average cost curves in Figure 23-2.

Average Fixed Costs (AFC). **Average fixed costs** continue to fall throughout the output range. In fact, if we were to continue panel (c) of Figure 23-2 farther to the right, we would find that average fixed costs would get closer and closer to the horizontal axis. That

Average fixed costs
Total fixed costs divided by the number of units produced.

FIGURE 23-2
Cost of Production: An Example

In panel (a), the derivations of columns 4 through 9 are given in parentheses in each column heading. For example, column 6, average variable costs, is derived by dividing column 3, total variable costs, by column 1, total output per day. Note that marginal cost (MC) in panel (c) intersects average variable costs (AVC) at the latter's minimum point. Also, MC intersects average total costs (ATC) at that latter's minimum point. It is a little more difficult to see that MC equals AVC and ATC at their respective minimum points in panel (a) because we are using discrete one-unit changes. You can see, though, that the marginal cost of going from 4 units per day to 5 units per day is $2 and increases to $3 when we move to 6 units per day. Somewhere between it equals AVC of $2.60, which is in fact the minimum average variable cost. The same analysis holds for ATC, which hits minimum at 7 units per day at $4.28 per unit. MC goes from $4 to $5 and just equals ATC somewhere in between.

Panel (a)

(1) Total Output (Q/day)	(2) Total Fixed Costs (TFC)	(3) Total Variable Costs (TVC)	(4) Total Costs (TC) (4) = (2) + (3)	(5) Average Fixed Costs (AFC) (5) = (2) ÷ (1)	(6) Average Variable Costs (AVC) (6) = (3) ÷ (1)	(7) Average Total Costs (ATC) (7) = (4) ÷ (1)	(8) Total Costs (TC) (4)	(9) Marginal Cost (MC) $(9) = \frac{\text{Change in (8)}}{\text{Change in (1)}}$
0	$10	$ 0	$10	—	—	—	$10	
1	10	5	15	$10.00	$5.00	$15.00	15	$5
2	10	8	18	5.00	4.00	9.00	18	3
3	10	10	20	3.33	3.33	6.67	20	2
4	10	11	21	2.50	2.75	5.25	21	1
5	10	13	23	2.00	2.60	4.60	23	2
6	10	16	26	1.67	2.67	4.33	26	3
7	10	20	30	1.43	2.86	4.28	30	4
8	10	25	35	1.25	3.12	4.38	35	5
9	10	31	41	1.11	3.44	4.56	41	6
10	10	38	48	1.00	3.80	4.80	48	7
11	10	46	56	.91	4.18	5.09	56	8

is because total fixed costs remain constant. As we divide this fixed number by a larger and larger number of units of output, the resulting AFC becomes smaller and smaller. In business, this is called "spreading the overhead."

Average Variable Costs (AVC). We assume a particular form of the curve for **average variable costs.** The form that it takes is U-shaped: First it falls; then it starts to rise. It is possible for the AVC curve to take other shapes in the long run.

Average variable costs
Total variable costs divided by the number of units produced.

Average Total Costs (ATC). This curve has a shape similar to that of the AVC curve. Nevertheless, it falls even more dramatically in the beginning and rises more slowly after it has reached a minimum point. It falls and then rises because **average total costs** are the summation of the AFC curve and the AVC curve. Thus, when AFC and AVC are both falling, ATC must fall too. At some point, however, AVC starts to increase while AFC continues to fall. Once the increase in the AVC curve outweighs the decrease in the AFC curve, the ATC curve will start to increase and will develop a U shape, just like the AVC curve.

Average total costs
Total costs divided by the number of units produced; sometimes called *average per-unit total costs.*

Marginal Cost

We have stated repeatedly that the basis of decisions is always on the margin—movement in economics is always determined at the margin. This dictum also holds true within the firm. Firms, according to the analysis we use to predict their behavior, are very concerned with their **marginal costs.** Because the term *marginal* means "additional" or "incremental" (or "decremental," too) here, *marginal costs* refer to costs that result from a one-unit change in the production rate. For example, if the production of 10 flash memory pen drives per day costs a firm $48 and the production of 11 of these flash drives costs it $56 per day, the marginal cost of producing 11 rather than 10 flash memory pen drives per day is $8.

Marginal costs
The change in total costs due to a one-unit change in production rate.

Marginal costs can be measured by using the formula

$$\text{Marginal cost} = \frac{\text{change in total cost}}{\text{change in output}}$$

We show the marginal costs of production of flash memory pen drives per day in column 9 of panel (a) in Figure 23-2 on the previous page, computed according to the formula just given. In our example, we have changed output by one unit every time, so the denominator in that particular formula always equals one.

This marginal cost schedule is shown graphically in panel (c) of Figure 23-2. Just like average variable costs and average total costs, marginal costs first fall and then rise. The U shape of the marginal cost curve is a result of increasing and then diminishing marginal product. At lower levels of output, the marginal cost curve declines. The reasoning is that as marginal physical product increases with each addition of output, the marginal cost of this last unit of output must fall. Conversely, when diminishing marginal product sets in, marginal physical product decreases (and eventually becomes negative); it follows that the marginal cost must rise when the marginal product begins its decline. These relationships are clearly reflected in the geometry of panels (b) and (c) of Figure 23-2.

In summary:

As long as marginal physical product rises, marginal cost will fall, and when marginal physical product starts to fall (after reaching the point of diminishing marginal product), marginal cost will begin to rise.

How are the odd-looking fins appearing on passenger jets around the world helping to reduce airlines' marginal costs? See the next page.

EXAMPLE

Reducing the Marginal Cost of Air Transport with "Winglets"

Long wings on some species of birds, such as eagles, provide the birds with more lift than those with shorter wings. Nevertheless, birds with long wings must labor harder to overcome a drag from air currents swirling off the tips of their wings. Airlines encounter the same advantages and disadvantages when they employ jetliners with long wings. The greater lift experienced by planes with long wings helps them take off, but overcoming the added drag from swirling air requires additional fuel for more heavily taxed engines.

For years, aircraft engineers sought to find a way to mimic *winglets*, or upturned feathers on the wingtips of large birds that help reduce the drag the air currents place on their wings. After years of experimentation, engineers created winglets by making jetliners' wings slightly longer and curving them upward at the ends. Since the early 2000s, most new planes ordered by airlines have included winglets, which provide fuel savings for every mile that a plane is in the air. Some airlines are in the process of adding winglets to their existing fleets of planes.

FOR CRITICAL ANALYSIS

How has airlines' use of winglets affected their total cost curves?

The Relationship Between Average and Marginal Costs

Let us now examine the relationship between average costs and marginal costs. There is always a definite relationship between averages and marginals. Consider the example of 10 football players with an average weight of 200 pounds. An eleventh player is added. His weight is 250 pounds. That represents the marginal weight. What happens now to the average weight of the team? It must increase. That is, when the marginal player weighs more than the average, the average must increase. Likewise, if the marginal player weighs less than 200 pounds, the average weight will decrease.

Average Variable Costs and Marginal Costs. There is a similar relationship between average variable costs and marginal costs. When marginal costs are less than average costs, the latter must fall. Conversely, when marginal costs are greater than average costs, the latter must rise. When you think about it, the relationship makes sense. The only way average variable costs can fall is if the extra cost of the marginal unit produced is less than the average variable cost of all the preceding units. For example, if the average variable cost for two units of production is $4.00 a unit, the only way for the average variable cost of three units to be less than that of two units is for the variable costs attributable to the last unit—the marginal cost—to be less than the average of the past units. In this particular case, if average variable cost falls to $3.33 a unit, total variable cost for the three units would be three times $3.33, or almost exactly $10.00. Total variable cost for two units is two times $4.00 (average variable cost), or $8.00. The marginal cost is therefore $10.00 minus $8.00, or $2.00, which is less than the average variable cost of $3.33.

A similar type of computation can be carried out for rising average variable costs. The only way average variable costs can rise is if the average variable cost of additional units is more than that for units already produced. But the incremental cost is the marginal cost. In this particular case, the marginal costs have to be higher than the average variable costs.

Average Total Costs and Marginal Costs. There is also a relationship between marginal costs and average total costs. Remember that average total cost is equal to total costs divided by the number of units produced. Also remember that marginal cost does not include any fixed costs. Fixed costs are, by definition, fixed and cannot influence marginal costs. Our example can therefore be repeated substituting *average total costs* for *average variable costs*.

These rising and falling relationships can be seen in panel (c) of Figure 23-2 on page 586, where MC intersects AVC and ATC at their respective minimum points.

Minimum Cost Points

At what rate of output of flash memory pen drives per day does our representative firm experience the minimum average total costs? Column 7 in panel (a) of Figure 23-2 shows that the minimum average total cost is $4.28, which occurs at an output rate of seven of these flash drives per day. We can also find this minimum cost by finding the point in panel (c) of Figure 23-2 where the marginal cost curve intersects the average total cost curve. This should not be surprising. When marginal cost is below average total cost, average total cost falls. When marginal cost is above average total cost, average total cost rises. At the point where average total cost is neither falling nor rising, marginal cost must then be equal to average total cost. When we represent this graphically, the marginal cost curve will intersect the average total cost curve at the latter's minimum.

The same analysis applies to the intersection of the marginal cost curve and the average variable cost curve. When are average variable costs at a minimum? According to panel (a) of Figure 23-2, average variable costs are at a minimum of $2.60 at an output rate of five flash memory pen drives per day. This is where the marginal cost curve intersects the average variable cost curve in panel (c) of Figure 23-2.

How can guard dogs equipped with biosensors help reduce some firms' costs?

E-COMMERCE EXAMPLE

High-Tech Canines Help Reduce Theft Costs

Every time a thief steals items from a warehouse, the thief's actions drive up a company's costs. This is why many warehouses have long relied on a traditional impediment to theft: guard dogs. The barking of guard dogs, though, only helps deter theft if a human being is around to hear it and respond to stop the theft from occurring. To increase the likelihood that the guard dogs will prevent thefts, a growing number of security firms are using biosensors that monitor the dogs' heartbeats, the pace of their movements, and the levels of their barks. If a guard dog excitedly yaps at a squirrel, the monitoring systems are programmed to ignore the dog's action. If the dog becomes alarmed and snarls at an intruder, however, the systems transmit alerts by cellphone or via wireless Internet connections. A security command center then dispatches human security personnel who can prevent a theft from occurring and thereby keep firms' costs from rising.

FOR CRITICAL ANALYSIS

Is a regular monthly payment that a firm makes to a company providing security services at the firm's warehouses a fixed or a variable cost?

QUICK QUIZ

Total costs equal total _____ costs plus total _____ costs.

Fixed costs are those that do not vary with the rate of production; variable costs are those that do vary with the rate of production.

_____ total costs equal total costs divided by output (_____ = TC/Q).

Average _____ costs equal total variable costs divided by output (_____ = TVC/Q).

Average _____ costs equal total fixed costs divided by output (_____ = TFC/Q).

_____ cost equals the change in _____ cost divided by the change in output (_____ = Δ_____/ΔQ, where the Greek letter Δ, delta, means "change in").

The marginal cost curve intersects the _____ point of the average total cost curve and the _____ point of the average variable cost curve.

See page 604 for the answers. Review concepts from this section in MyEconLab.

THE RELATIONSHIP BETWEEN DIMINISHING MARGINAL PRODUCT AND COST CURVES

There is a unique relationship between output and the shape of the various cost curves we have drawn. Let's consider specifically the relationship between marginal cost and the example of diminishing marginal physical product in panel (a) of Figure 23-3. It turns out that if wage rates are constant, the shape of the marginal cost curve in panel (d) of Figure 23-3 is both a reflection of and a consequence of the law of diminishing marginal product.

Marginal Cost and Marginal Physical Product

Let's assume that each unit of labor can be purchased at a constant price. Further assume that labor is the only variable input. We see that as more workers are hired, marginal physical product first rises and then falls. Thus, the marginal cost of each extra unit of output will first fall as long as marginal physical product is rising, and then it will rise as long as marginal physical product is falling. Recall that marginal cost is defined as

$$MC = \frac{\text{change in total cost}}{\text{change in output}}$$

Because the price of labor is assumed to be constant, the change in total cost depends solely on the unchanged price of labor, W. The change in output is simply the marginal physical product (MPP) of the one-unit increase in labor. Therefore, we see that

$$\text{Marginal cost} = \frac{W}{\text{MPP}}$$

This means that initially, when marginal physical product is increasing, marginal cost falls (we are dividing W by increasingly larger numbers), and later, when marginal product is falling, marginal cost must increase (we are dividing W by smaller numbers). So, as marginal physical product increases, marginal cost decreases, and as marginal physical product decreases, marginal cost must increase. Thus, when marginal physical product reaches its maximum, marginal cost necessarily reaches its minimum.

Panel (a)

(1) Labor Input	(2) Total Product (number of Internet access accounts serviced)	(3) Average Physical Product (accounts per technician) (3) = (2) ÷ (1)	(4) Marginal Physical Product	(5) Average Variable Cost (5) = W ($1,000) ÷ (3)	(6) Marginal Cost (6) = W ($1,000) ÷ (4)
0	0	—	—	—	—
1	50	50	50	$20.00	$20.00
2	110	55	60	18.18	16.67
3	180	60	70	16.67	14.29
4	240	60	60	16.67	16.67
5	290	58	50	17.24	20.00
6	330	55	40	18.18	25.00
7	360	51	30	19.61	33.33

FIGURE 23-3

The Relationship Between Output and Costs

As the number of skilled technicians increases, the total number of Internet access accounts serviced each month rises, as shown in panels (a) and (b). In panel (c), marginal physical product (MPP) first rises and then falls. Average physical product (APP) follows. The near mirror image of panel (c) is shown in panel (d), in which MC and AVC first fall and then rise.

An Illustration

To illustrate this, let's return to Figure 23-1 on page 582 and consider specifically panel (a). Assume that a skilled printer-assembly worker is paid $1,000 a week. When we go from zero labor input to one unit, output increases by 10 computer printers. Each of those 10 printers has a marginal cost of $100. Now the second unit of labor is hired, and this individual costs $1,000 per week. Output increases by 16. Thus, the marginal cost is $1,000 ÷ 16 = $62.50. We continue the experiment. We see that the next unit of labor yields only 10 additional computer printers, so marginal cost starts to rise again back to $100. The following unit of labor increases marginal physical product by only 8, so marginal cost becomes $1,000 ÷ 8 = $125.

All of the foregoing can be restated in relatively straightforward terms:

Firms' short-run cost curves are a reflection of the law of diminishing marginal product. Given any constant price of the variable input, marginal costs decline as long as the marginal physical product of the variable resource is rising. At the point at which marginal product begins to diminish, marginal costs begin to rise as the marginal physical product of the variable input begins to decline.

The result is a marginal cost curve that slopes down, hits a minimum, and then slopes up.

Average Costs and Average Physical Product

Of course, the average total cost curve and average variable cost curve are affected. They will have their familiar U shape in the short run. Again, to see this, recall that

$$\text{AVC} = \frac{\text{total variable costs}}{\text{total output}}$$

As we move from zero labor input to one unit in panel (a) of Figure 23-1 on page 582, output increases from zero to 10 computer printers. The total variable costs are the price per worker, W ($1,000), times the number of workers (1). Because the average product of one worker (column 3) is 10, we can write the total product, 10, as the average product, 10, times the number of workers, 1. Thus, we see that

$$\text{AVC} = \frac{\$1,000 \times 1}{10 \times 1} = \frac{\$1,000}{10} = \frac{W}{\text{AP}}$$

From column 3 in panel (a) of Figure 23-1, we see that the average product increases, reaches a maximum, and then declines. Because AVC = W/AP, average variable cost decreases as average product increases and increases as average product decreases. AVC reaches its minimum when average product reaches its maximum. Furthermore, because ATC = AVC + AFC, the average total cost curve inherits the relationship between the average variable cost and diminishing returns.

To illustrate, consider an Internet service provider that employs skilled technicians to provide access services within a given geographic area. Panel (a) of Figure 23-3 on the previous page presents in column 2 the total number of Internet access accounts serviced as the number of technicians increases. Notice that the total product first increases at an increasing rate and later increases at a decreasing rate. This is reflected in column 4, which shows that the marginal physical product increases at first and then falls. The average physical product too first rises and then falls. The marginal and average physical products are graphed in panel (c) of Figure 23-3.

Our immediate interest here is the average variable and marginal costs. Because we can define average variable cost as $1,000/AP (assuming that the wage paid is constant at

$1,000), as the average product rises from 50 to 55 to 60 Internet access accounts, the average variable cost falls from $20.00 to $18.18 to $16.67. Conversely, as average product falls from 60 to 51, average variable cost rises from $16.67 to $19.61. Likewise, because marginal cost can also be defined as W/MPP, we see that as marginal physical product rises from 50 to 70, marginal cost falls from $20.00 to $14.29. As marginal physical product falls to 30, marginal cost rises to $33.33. These relationships are also expressed in panels (b), (c), and (d) of Figure 23-3.

LONG-RUN COST CURVES

The long run is defined as a time period during which full adjustment can be made to any change in the economic environment. Thus, in the long run, *all* factors of production are variable. Long-run curves are sometimes called *planning curves,* and the long run is sometimes called the **planning horizon.** We start our analysis of long-run cost curves by considering a single firm contemplating the construction of a single plant. The firm has three alternative plant sizes from which to choose on the planning horizon. Each particular plant size generates its own short-run average total cost curve. Now that we are talking about the difference between long-run and short-run cost curves, we will label all short-run curves with an S and long-run curves with an L; short-run average (total) costs will be labeled SAC; and long-run average cost curves will be labeled LAC.

Panel (a) of Figure 23-4 shows short-run average cost curves for three successively larger plants. Which is the optimal size to build, if we can only choose among these three?

Planning horizon
The long run, during which all inputs are variable.

FIGURE 23-4
Preferable Plant Size and the Long-Run Average Cost Curve

If the anticipated permanent rate of output per unit time period is Q_1, the optimal plant to build is the one corresponding to SAC_1 in panel (a) because average cost is lower. However, if the permanent rate of output increases to Q_2, it will be more profitable to have a plant size corresponding to SAC_2. Unit costs fall to C_3.

If we draw all the possible short-run average cost curves that correspond to different plant sizes and then draw the envelope (a curve tangent to each member of a set of curves) to these various curves, SAC_1–SAC_8, we obtain the long-run average cost curve, or the planning curve, as shown in panel (b).

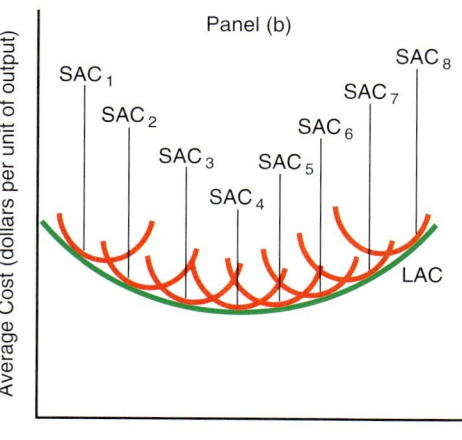

That depends on the anticipated normal, sustained rate of output per time period. Assume for a moment that the anticipated normal, sustained rate is Q_1. If a plant of size 1 is built, average cost will be C_1. If a plant of size 2 is built, we see on SAC_2 that average cost will be C_2, which is greater than C_1. Thus, if the anticipated rate of output is Q_1, the appropriate plant size is the one from which SAC_1 was derived.

However, if the anticipated permanent rate of output per time period increases from Q_1 to Q_2 and a plant of size 1 is selected, average cost will be C_4. If a plant of size 2 is chosen, average cost will be C_3, which is clearly less than C_4.

In choosing the appropriate plant size for a single-plant firm during the planning horizon, the firm will pick the size whose short-run average cost curve generates an average cost that is lowest for the expected rate of output.

Long-Run Average Cost Curve

If we now assume that the entrepreneur faces an infinite number of choices of plant sizes in the long run, we can conceive of an infinite number of SAC curves similar to the three in panel (a) of Figure 23-4 on the previous page. We are not able, of course, to draw an infinite number, but we have drawn quite a few in panel (b) of Figure 23-4. We then draw the "envelope" to all these various short-run average cost curves. The resulting envelope is the **long-run average cost curve.** This long-run average cost curve is sometimes called the **planning curve,** for it represents the various average costs attainable at the planning stage of the firm's decision making. It represents the locus (path) of points giving the least unit cost of producing any given rate of output. Note that the LAC curve is *not* tangent to each individual SAC curve at the latter's minimum points, except at the minimum point of the LAC curve. Then and only then are minimum long-run average costs equal to minimum short-run average costs.

Long-run average cost curve
The locus of points representing the minimum unit cost of producing any given rate of output, given current technology and resource prices.

Planning curve
The long-run average cost curve.

WHY THE LONG-RUN AVERAGE COST CURVE IS U-SHAPED

Notice that the long-run average cost curve, LAC, in panel (b) of Figure 23-4 on the previous page is U-shaped, similar to the U shape of the short-run average cost curve developed earlier in this chapter. The reason behind the U shape of the two curves is not the same, however. The short-run average cost curve is U-shaped because of the law of diminishing marginal product. But the law cannot apply to the long run, because in the long run, all factors of production are variable; there is no point of diminishing marginal product because there is no fixed factor of production.

Why, then, do we see the U shape in the long-run average cost curve? The reasoning has to do with economies of scale, constant returns to scale, and diseconomies of scale. When the firm is experiencing **economies of scale,** the long-run average cost curve slopes downward—an increase in scale and production leads to a fall in unit costs. When the firm is experiencing **constant returns to scale,** the long-run average cost curve is at its minimum point, such that an increase in scale and production does not change unit costs. When the firm is experiencing **diseconomies of scale,** the long-run average cost curve slopes upward—an increase in scale and production increases unit costs. These three sections of the long-run average cost curve are broken up into panels (a), (b), and (c) in Figure 23-5.

Economies of scale
Decreases in long-run average costs resulting from increases in output.

Constant returns to scale
No change in long-run average costs when output increases.

Diseconomies of scale
Increases in long-run average costs that occur as output increases.

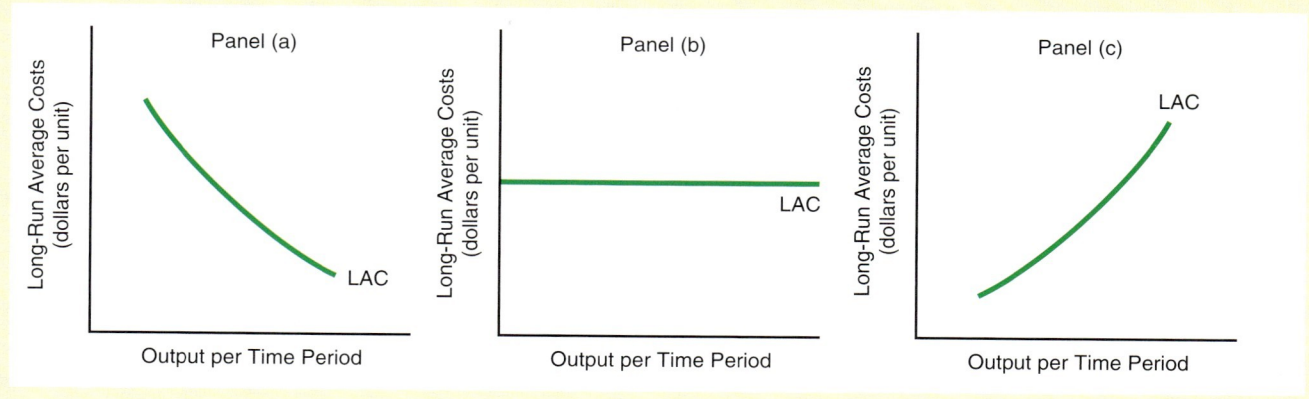

FIGURE 23-5

Economies of Scale, Constant Returns to Scale, and Diseconomies of Scale Shown with Long-Run Average Cost Curve

The long-run average cost curve will fall when there are economies of scale, as shown in panel (a). It will be constant (flat) when the firm is experiencing constant returns to scale, as shown in panel (b). It will rise when the firm is experiencing diseconomies of scale, as shown in panel (c).

Reasons for Economies of Scale

We shall examine three of the many reasons why a firm might be expected to experience economies of scale: specialization, the dimensional factor, and improved productive equipment.

Specialization. As a firm's scale of operation increases, the opportunities for specialization in the use of resource inputs also increase. This is sometimes called *increased division of tasks* or *operations*. Gains from such division of labor or increased specialization are well known. When we consider managerial staffs, we also find that larger enterprises may be able to put together more highly specialized staffs.

Dimensional Factor. Large-scale firms often require proportionately less input per unit of output simply because certain inputs do not have to be physically doubled in order to double the output. Consider the cost of storing oil. The cost of storage is related to the cost of steel that goes into building the storage container; however, the amount of steel required goes up less than in proportion to the volume (storage capacity) of the container (because the volume of a container increases more than proportionately with its surface area).

Improved Productive Equipment. The larger the scale of the enterprise, the more the firm is able to take advantage of larger-volume (output capacity) types of machinery. Small-scale operations may not be able profitably to use large-volume machines that can be more efficient per unit of output. Also, smaller firms often cannot use technologically more advanced machinery because they are unable to spread out the high cost of such sophisticated equipment over a large output.

For any of these reasons, the firm may experience economies of scale, which means that equal percentage increases in output result in a decrease in average cost. Thus, output can double, but total costs will less than double; hence average cost falls. Note that the factors listed for causing economies of scale are all *internal* to the firm; they do not depend on what other firms are doing or what is happening in the economy.

Why a Firm Might Experience Diseconomies of Scale

One of the basic reasons that a firm can expect to run into diseconomies of scale is that there are limits to the efficient functioning of management. This is so because larger levels of output imply successively larger *plant* size, which in turn implies successively larger *firm* size. Thus, as the level of output increases, more people must be hired, and the firm gets bigger. As this happens, however, the support, supervisory, and administrative staff and the general paperwork of the firm all increase. As the layers of supervision grow, the costs of information and communication grow more than proportionately; hence the average unit cost will start to increase.

Some observers of corporate giants claim that many of them have been experiencing some diseconomies of scale. Witness the difficulties that firms such as Hewlett-Packard and General Motors have experienced in the 2000s. Some analysts say that the profitability declines they encountered were at least partly a function of their size relative to their smaller, more flexible competitors, who could make decisions more quickly and then take advantage of changing market conditions more rapidly. In the case of Hewlett-Packard, a 2001 merger with the world's then-largest computer maker Compaq produced an even larger manufacturer of computers and peripheral devices. Within a couple of years following this merger, however, the combined company's profit rate dropped off. Initially, Hewlett-Packard adapted very slowly to changes in the personal computer market, which caused it to lose ground in the marketplace to competitors such as Dell.

How did the Federal Reserve System, which in addition to conducting monetary policy provides payment services to private banks, reduce its long-run average cost?

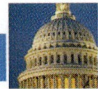

POLICY EXAMPLE

Economies of Scale in Payment Processing

Automated clearing houses (ACHs) process both private payments, such as automatic payroll deposits to wage earners' bank accounts, and public payments, such as direct deposits of Social Security stipends. The 12 regional banks operated by the Federal Reserve provide ACH services to banks around the United States. Since 2000, the annual volume of payments transmitted by the Federal Reserve's ACH system has increased from 3.8 billion to more than 6 billion. At the same time, the average cost of transmitting a payment has declined from more than 1.6 cents to about 1 cent.

FOR CRITICAL ANALYSIS
Why do you suppose that, aside from the Federal Reserve, there are only a handful of large firms operating ACH systems in the United States, instead of a large number of smaller ACH companies?

MINIMUM EFFICIENT SCALE

Economists and statisticians have obtained actual data on the relationship between changes in all inputs and changes in average cost. It turns out that for many industries, the long-run average cost curve does not resemble that shown in panel (b) of Figure 23-4 on page 593. Rather, it more closely resembles Figure 23-6. What you can observe there is a small portion of declining long-run average costs (economies of scale) and then a wide range of outputs over which the firm experiences relatively constant economies of scale.

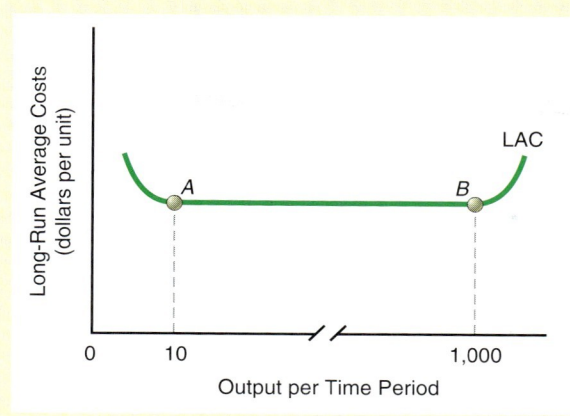

FIGURE 23-6

Minimum Efficient Scale

This long-run average cost curve reaches a minimum point at A. After that point, long-run average costs remain horizontal, or constant, and then rise at some later rate of output. Point A is called the minimum efficient scale for the firm because that is the point at which it reaches minimum costs. It is the lowest rate of output at which average long-run costs are minimized. At point B, diseconomies of scale arise, so long-run average cost begins to increase with further increases in output.

At the output rate when economies of scale end and constant economies of scale start, the **minimum efficient scale (MES)** for the firm is encountered. It occurs at point A. The minimum efficient scale is defined as the lowest rate of output at which long-run average costs are minimized. In any industry with a long-run average cost curve similar to the one in Figure 23-6, larger firms will have no cost-saving advantage over smaller firms as long as the smaller firms have at least obtained the minimum efficient scale at point A.

How did one company increase its scale by building its relatively small products in a larger number of downsized factories?

Minimum efficient scale (MES)
The lowest rate of output per unit time at which long-run average costs for a particular firm are at a minimum.

EXAMPLE

A Company Thinks Smaller to Boost Its Minimum Efficient Scale

While some companies produce large, high-powered engines that propel jet fighters or massive ocean tankers, another firm, Briggs & Stratton Corporation, concentrates on building small motors that power lawn mowers and speedboats. During the 2000s, smaller has become the name of the game for this company in another respect. In the 1990s, the company produced most of its engines in a massive facility outside Milwaukee containing 2 million square feet of floor space. Today, however, it has dispersed its production among six smaller plants, each of which utilizes more automated equipment and employs fewer workers than during the 1990s. Downsizing its plants enabled the company to increase its overall scale of operations, from an output rate of 8 million engines per year to more than 10 million engines per year. The result of this output increase has been lower long-run average total cost, which has helped to boost the company's annual profitability by more than 30 percent.

FOR CRITICAL ANALYSIS
Why does a firm that attains relatively large minimum efficient scale not necessarily have to operate facilities that individually produce output at a large scale?

ECONOMICS FRONT AND CENTER

To think about why attaining the minimum efficient scale matters to a business, read **I've Been Working on the Railroad—But Inefficiently, So Far**, on page 598.

Among its uses, the minimum efficient scale gives us a rough measure of the degree of competition in an industry. If the MES is small relative to industry demand, the extent of competition in that industry is likely to be high because there is room for many efficiently sized plants. Conversely, when the MES is large relative to industry demand, the degree of competition is likely to be small because there is room for a relatively small number of efficiently sized plants or firms. Looked at another way, if it takes a very large scale of plant to obtain minimum long-run average cost, the output of just a few of these very large firms can fully satisfy total market demand. This means that there isn't room for a large number of smaller plants if maximum efficiency is to be obtained in the industry.

QUICK QUIZ

The _____ run is often called the **planning horizon**. The _____-run average cost curve is the planning curve. It is found by drawing a curve tangent to one point on a series of _____-run average cost curves, each corresponding to a different plant size.

The firm can experience **economies of scale**, **diseconomies of scale**, or **constant returns** to scale, all according to whether the long-run average cost curve slopes _____, slopes _____, or is _____. Economies of scale refer to what happens to average cost when all factors of production are increased.

We observe economies of scale for a number of reasons, including specialization, improved productive equipment, and the _____ factor, because large-scale firms require proportionately less input per unit of output. The firm may experience _____ of scale primarily because of limits to the efficient functioning of management.

The **minimum efficient scale** occurs at the _____ rate of output at which long-run average costs are _____.

See page 604 for the answers. Review concepts from this section in MyEconLab.

CASE STUDY — ECONOMICS FRONT AND CENTER

I've Been Working on the Railroad—But Inefficiently, So Far

Taylor is a regional manager for Western Southern Railroad, once a stand-alone firm but now a division of a rail transport company with tracks sprawled all across the nation. Unfortunately for him, the parent company is having trouble efficiently transporting merchandise along its rail network. Today, Taylor has been fielding calls from irate customers who are falling behind on production because they lack inputs that should have arrived days or weeks ago. He can only reply that the trains are moving as fast as they possibly can, which is in fact the truth.

During a letup from his hectic day, Taylor reviews the situation that has been thrust on Western Southern. The parent company's tracks are so clogged that entire trains have been stuck for days. Empty cars cannot be moved past fully loaded trains that are moving slowly along tracks, making it difficult to pick up additional shipments as promised. Keeping disgruntled locomotive engineers on the job is requiring salary increases that are driving up labor costs.

A key rationale for the parent company's purchase of Western Southern was to help break this bottleneck. Taylor studies a computer tracking system that displays the position of every train throughout the combined rail network. A separate window on the computer screen displays revenues and costs during the present month and the past three years. Average cost per mile of track declined following the Western Southern acquisition, but it is clear that the parent company's rail network is still too small to provide its current rate of freight transport services at the minimum feasible average cost. Taylor wonders what regional rail firm might be next on the parent company's list of possible acquisition targets.

CRITICAL ANALYSIS QUESTIONS

1. *Is Western Southern's parent company experiencing economies of scale, constant returns to scale, or diseconomies of scale at this time?*

2. *How might the parent company of Western Southern attain its minimum efficient scale without acquiring other rail firms?*

Issues and Applications

Book Publishers Search for a Lower-Cost Business Model

Hachette Book Group, a major U.S. publisher of hardcover books, operates two large warehouses. One is called the "happy" warehouse, because it is filled with newly printed books awaiting distribution to retail booksellers across the nation. The other is dubbed the "sad" warehouse. This is where unsold books, which not much more than a year earlier had been stored in the "happy" warehouse, are initially placed after being returned by those same retailers.

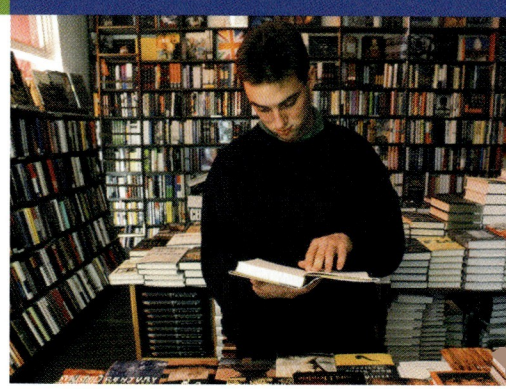

Concepts Applied
- Fixed Costs
- Total Costs
- Marginal Costs

In Publishing, Destruction Is an Element of Production

Other publishers have their own names for these two types of warehouses, but the functions of the warehouses are similar to those operated by Hachette Book Group. There is a 34 percent chance that any book that leaves a publisher's "happy" warehouse will find its way back to the "sad" warehouse.

During the life span of a book that finds its way from the "happy" warehouse to the "sad" warehouse, the publisher incurs the cost of printing the book, transporting it to the "happy" warehouse, and shipping it to a bookseller. Then the company incurs the cost of receiving the book for temporary storage at the "sad" warehouse, where workers will feed its pages into machines to be transformed into bales of recycled paper.

For years, the production process at U.S. book publishers has involved this annual cycle of printing and distributing millions of books that the publishers know will never be sold. The process of shipping and destroying books generates costs that publishers have long taken into account.

The Cost Consequences of Book "Overproduction"

Why are publishers willing to engage in an activity that outside observers might perceive to be wasteful "overproduction" of books? The answer to this question has two parts. First, once the fixed costs of copy editing, typesetting, and printing the first copy of a book have been incurred, the marginal cost of printing each additional copy is relatively low—essentially the costs of paper, printing, and binding for each book. The total cost of producing each additional book, therefore, rises very slowly after the first book has been produced. That is, once a publisher has incurred the fixed costs of printing a book, the marginal cost of printing another book is relatively small.

Second, publishers also regard at least some of the cost of producing more books than they will sell to be a marketing expense. Stacks of copies of a new book attract much more attention from potential buyers at bookstores than just a few copies on a shelf. Unless a publisher produces lots of copies, booksellers cannot create catchy displays that cause people to notice the book.

We cannot forget about distribution expenses, however. Publishers must pay considerable sums to distribute books to towns and cities hundreds and thousands of miles distant from the locales where the books are printed. In recent years, these distribution expenses have been increasing, which has given publishers an incentive to consider cutting back on the number of books printed.

Log in to **MyEconLab**, click on "Economic News," and test your understanding of the chapter by answering interactive questions that relate directly to this issue.

For Critical Analysis

1. At the second unit of output for a book publisher, which is higher—average fixed cost or average variable cost?
2. Are publishers that wish to substantially reduce their annual total costs more likely to publish the same number of titles each year but print fewer copies of each book or to publish fewer titles each year while printing as many copies per title? (Hint: Would a publisher's total costs fall very much if it printed just one fewer copy of every book it publishes?)

Web Resources

1. To learn about why some book authors might conclude that they benefit from publishers' book return programs, go to www.econtoday.com/ch23.
2. For a discussion of various potential inefficiencies in the book publishing industry, go to www.econtoday.com/ch23.

Research Project

Place yourself in the following situation: You work for a division of a textbook publisher that manages the company's economics textbooks. Senior managers have instructed you to find a way to reduce your division's total costs by 30 percent. Currently, your division handles three economics principles textbooks that are purchased by thousands of students every year and 25 textbooks in specialized areas of advanced economics, each of which is purchased by a few hundred students per year. If your only objective is to reduce total costs as requested by senior management, would you recommend that your division stop publishing one or more principles books, one or more specialized books, or a mix of the two responses? Explain your reasoning.

Here is what you should know after reading this chapter. MyEconLab will help you identify what you know, and where to go when you need to practice.

WHAT YOU SHOULD KNOW		WHERE TO GO TO PRACTICE
The Short Run versus the Long Run from a Firm's Perspective The short run for a firm is a period during which at least one input, such as plant size, cannot be altered. Inputs that cannot be changed in the short run are fixed inputs, whereas factors of production that may be adjusted in the short run are variable inputs. The long run is a period in which a firm may vary all factors of production.	short run, 579 plant size, 579 long run, 579	• **MyEconLab** Study Plan 23.1 • Audio introduction to Chapter 23
The Law of Diminishing Marginal Product The production function is the relationship between inputs and the maximum physical output, or total product, that a firm can produce. Typically, a firm's marginal physical product—the physical output resulting from the addition of one more unit of a variable factor of production—increases with the first few units of the variable factor of production that it employs. Eventually, however, as the firm adds more and more units of the variable input, the marginal physical product begins to decline. This is the law of diminishing marginal product.	production, 580 production function, 580 average physical product, 581 marginal physical product, 581 law of diminishing marginal product, 583 **Key figure** Figure 23-1, 582	• **MyEconLab** Study Plans 23.2 and 23.3 • Animated Figure 23-1
A Firm's Short-Run Cost Curves The expenses for a firm's fixed inputs are its fixed costs, and the expenses for its variable inputs are variable costs. The total costs of a firm are the sum of its fixed costs and variable costs. Dividing fixed costs by various possible output levels traces out the firm's average fixed cost curve, which slopes downward because dividing fixed costs by a larger total product yields a lower average fixed cost. Average variable cost equals total variable cost divided by total product, and average total cost equals total cost divided by total product. For the latter two, doing these computations at various possible output levels yields U-shaped curves. Finally, marginal cost is the change in total cost resulting from a one-unit change in production. A firm's marginal costs typically decline as the firm produces the first few units of output, but at the point where marginal product begins to diminish, the marginal cost curve begins to slope upward. The marginal cost curve also intersects the minimum points of the average variable cost curve and average total cost curve.	total costs, 584 fixed costs, 585 variable costs, 585 average fixed costs, 585 average variable costs, 587 average total costs, 587 marginal costs, 587 **Key figure** Figure 23-2, 586	• **MyEconLab** Study Plans 23.4 and 23.5 • Animated Figure 23-2 • Video: Short-Run Costs to the Firm

WHAT YOU SHOULD KNOW

WHERE TO GO TO PRACTICE

A Firm's Long-Run Cost Curves Over a firm's long-run, or planning, horizon, it can choose all factors of production, including plant size. Thus, it can choose a long-run scale of production along a long-run average cost curve. The long-run average cost curve, which for most firms is U-shaped, is traced out by the short-run average cost curves corresponding to various plant sizes.

planning horizon, 593
long-run average cost curve, 594
planning curve, 594
Key figures
Figure 23-3, 591
Figure 23-4, 593

- **MyEconLab** Study Plans 23.6 and 23.7
- Animated Figures 23-2 and 23-4

Economies and Diseconomies of Scale and a Firm's Minimum Efficient Scale Along the downward-sloping range of a firm's long-run average cost curve, the firm experiences economies of scale, meaning that its long-run production costs decline as it increases its plant size and thereby raises its output scale. In contrast, along the upward-sloping portion of the long-run average cost curve, the firm encounters diseconomies of scale, so that its long-run costs of production rise as it increases its output scale. The minimum point of the long-run average cost curve occurs at the firm's minimum efficient scale, which is the lowest rate of output at which the firm can achieve minimum long-run average cost.

economies of scale, 594
constant returns to scale, 594
diseconomies of scale, 594
minimum efficient scale (MES), 597
Key figures
Figure 23-5, 595
Figure 23-6, 597

- **MyEconLab** Study Plans 23.7 and 23.8
- Animated Figures 23-5 and 23-6
- Video: Reasons for Economies of Scale

Log in to MyEconLab, take a chapter test, and get a personalized Study Plan that tells you which concepts you understand and which ones you need to review. From there, MyEconLab will give you further practice, tutorials, animations, videos, and guided solutions.

Log in to www.myeconlab.com

PROBLEMS

Select problems, indicated by a blue oval, are assignable in MyEconLab.
Answers to odd-numbered problems appear at the back of the book.

23-1. The academic calendar for a university is August 15 through May 15. A professor commits to a contract that binds her to a teaching position at this university for this period. Based on this information, explain the short run and long run that the professor faces.

23-2. The short-run production function for a manufacturer of flash memory drives is shown at the right. Based on this information, calculate the average physical product at each quantity of labor.

Input of Labor (workers per week)	Total Output of Flash Memory Drives
0	0
1	25
2	60
3	85
4	105
5	115
6	120

23-3 Using the information provided in Problem 23-2, calculate the marginal physical product of labor at each quantity of labor.

23-4 For the manufacturer of flash memory drives in Problems 23-2 and 23-3, at what point does marginal product begin to diminish?

23-5 At the end of the year, a firm produced 10,000 laptop computers. Its total costs were $5 million, and its fixed costs were $2 million. What are the average variable costs of this firm?

23-6 The cost structure of a manufacturer of microchips is described in the following table. The firm's fixed costs equal $10 per day. Calculate the average variable cost, average fixed cost, and average total cost at each output level.

Output (microchips per day)	Total Cost of Output ($ thousands)
0	10
25	60
50	95
75	150
100	220
125	325
150	465

23-7 The diagram below displays short-run cost curves for a facility that produces liquid crystal display (LCD) screens for cellphones:

a. What are the daily total fixed costs of producing LCD screens?
b. What are the total variable costs of producing 100 LCD screens per day?
c. What are the total costs of producing 100 LCD screens per day?
d. What is the marginal cost of producing the hundredth LCD screen? (Hint: To answer this question, you must first determine the total costs—or, alternatively, the total variable costs—of producing 99 LCD screens.)

23-8 A watch manufacturer finds that at 1,000 units of output, its marginal costs are below average total costs. If it produces an additional watch, will its average total costs rise, fall, or stay the same?

23-9 At its current short-run level of production, a firm's average variable costs equal $20 per unit, and its average fixed costs equal $30 per unit. Its total costs at this production level equal $2,500.

a. What is the firm's current output level?
b. What are its total variable costs at this output level?
c. What are its total fixed costs?

23-10 In the short run, a firm's total costs of producing the hundredth unit of output equal $10,000. If it produces one more unit, its total costs will increase to $10,150.

a. What is the marginal cost of the 101st unit of output?
b. What is the firm's average total cost of producing 100 units?
c. What is the firm's average total cost of producing 101 units?

23-11 Suppose that a firm's only variable input is labor, and the constant hourly wage rate is $20 per hour. The last unit of labor hired enabled the firm to increase its hourly production from 250 units to 251 units. What was the marginal cost of the 251st unit of output?

23-12 Suppose that a firm's only variable input is labor. The firm increases the number of employees from four to five, thereby causing weekly output to rise by two units and total costs to increase from $3,000 per week to $3,300 per week.

a. What is the marginal physical product of the fifth worker?
b. What is the weekly wage rate earned by the fifth worker?

23-13 Suppose that a company currently employs 1,000 workers and produces 1 million units of output per month. Labor is its only variable input, and the company pays each worker the same monthly wage. The company's current total variable costs equal $2 million.

a. What are average variable costs at this firm's current output level?
b. What is the average physical product of labor?
c. What monthly wage does the firm pay each worker?

23-14 A manufacturing firm with a single plant is contemplating changing its plant size. It must choose from among seven alternative plant sizes. In the table, plant size A is the smallest it might build, and size G is the largest. Currently, the firm's plant size is B.

Plant Size	Average Total Cost ($)
A (smallest)	4,250
B	3,600
C	3,100
D	3,100
E	3,100
F	3,250
G (largest)	4,100

a. At plant site B, is this firm currently experiencing economies of scale or diseconomies of scale?
b. What is the firm's minimum efficient scale?

23-15 An electricity-generating company confronts the following long-run average total costs associated with alternative plant sizes. It is currently operating at plant size G.

Plant Size	Average Total Cost ($)
A (smallest)	2,000
B	1,800
C	1,600
D	1,550
E	1,500
F	1,500
G (largest)	1,500

a. What is this firm's minimum efficient scale?
b. If damage caused by a powerful hurricane generates a reduction in the firm's plant size from its current size to B, would there be a leftward or rightward movement along the firm's long-run average total cost curve?

ECONOMICS ON THE NET

Industry-Level Capital Expenditures In this chapter, you learned about the explicit and implicit costs that firms incur in the process of producing goods and services. This Internet application gives you an opportunity to consider one type of cost—expenditures on capital goods.

Title: U.S. Census Bureau's Annual Capital Expenditures Survey

Navigation: Follow the link at www.econtoday.com/ch23, and select *PDF and Spreadsheet.* Then click on the PDF for the most recent *Annual Capital Expenditures Survey.*

Application Read the Introduction in the report, and then answer the following questions:

1. What types of business expenditures does the Census Bureau include in this report?
2. Are the inputs that generate these business expenditures more likely to be inputs that firms can vary in the short run or in the long run?
3. Which inputs account for the largest portion of firms' capital expenditures? Why do you suppose this is so?

For Group Discussion and Analysis Review reports for the past several years. Do capital expenditures vary from year to year? What factors might account for such variations? Are there noticeable differences in capital expenditures from industry to industry?

ANSWERS TO QUICK QUIZZES

p. 584: (i) production . . . output; (ii) product; (iii) decreasing . . . output
p. 590: (i) fixed . . . variable; (ii) Average . . . ATC; (iii) variable . . . AVC; (iv) fixed . . . AFC; (v) Marginal . . . total . . . MC . . . TC; (vi) minimum . . . minimum
p. 598: (i) long . . . long . . . short; (ii) downward . . . upward . . . horizontal; (iii) dimensional . . . diseconomies; (iv) lowest . . . minimized

Perfect Competition 24

Not long ago, firms that provided digital photo printing services, such as discount department stores and pharmacies, charged as much as 50 cents per printed photo. Today, many consumers pay little more than a dime to have a digital photo printed. Some consumers continue to use the printing services of discount retailers and drugstores. Others, however, have their photos printed at booths, or *kiosks*, most of which did not exist a few years ago but now have sprouted up in numerous locations in towns and cities across the land. Why has the range of choices among providers of digital photo printing services expanded so much during the 2000s? How has this expansion contributed to the decline in the price of printed digital photos? In this chapter, you will learn the answers to these questions.

Learning Objectives

After reading this chapter, you should be able to:

1. Identify the characteristics of a perfectly competitive market structure
2. Discuss the process by which a perfectly competitive firm decides how much output to produce
3. Understand how the short-run supply curve for a perfectly competitive firm is determined
4. Explain how the equilibrium price is determined in a perfectly competitive market
5. Describe what factors induce firms to enter or exit a perfectly competitive industry
6. Distinguish among constant-, increasing-, and decreasing-cost industries based on the shape of the long-run industry supply curve

MyEconLab helps you master each objective and study more efficiently. See end of chapter for details.

605

Did You Know That...

market clearing prices of bus trips between major cities in the northeastern United States have been dropping rapidly? This price decrease cannot be explained either by technological improvements in bus service by firms such as Greyhound, Trailways, or Peter Pan, or by a large decrease in the demand for intercity transport in that part of the country. The main explanation is that other firms have been offering to provide bus transport at lower prices. During the mid-2000s, bus companies with names such as Kristine Travel, Lucky Star Lines, Eastern Travel, and Dragon Lines began busing people between northeastern cities at fares less than half those charged by Greyhound and other traditional firms. Within just a few months, Greyhound and other previously existing bus services had lowered their prices to match those of their new competitors.

In common speech, *competition* simply means "rivalry." In the extreme, perfectly competitive situations, individual buyers and sellers cannot affect the market price—it is determined by the market forces of demand and supply. In addition, economic profits that perfectly competitive firms may earn for a time ultimately disappear as other firms respond by entering the industry. In this chapter, we examine these and other implications of the theory of perfect competition.

CHARACTERISTICS OF A PERFECTLY COMPETITIVE MARKET STRUCTURE

Perfect competition
A market structure in which the decisions of *individual* buyers and sellers have no effect on market price.

Perfectly competitive firm
A firm that is such a small part of the total *industry* that it cannot affect the price of the product it sells.

Price taker
A perfectly competitive firm that must take the price of its product as given because the firm cannot influence its price.

We are interested in studying how a firm acting within a perfectly competitive market structure makes decisions about how much to produce. In a situation of **perfect competition,** each firm is such a small part of the total industry that it cannot affect the price of the product in question. That means that each **perfectly competitive firm** in the industry is a **price taker**—the firm takes price as a given, something determined *outside* the individual firm.

This definition of a competitive firm is obviously idealized, for in one sense the individual firm *has* to set prices. How can we ever have a situation in which firms regard prices as set by forces outside their control? The answer is that even though every firm sets its own prices, a firm in a perfectly competitive situation will find that it will eventually have no customers at all if it sets its price above the competitive price. The best example is in agriculture. Although the individual farmer can set any price for a bushel of wheat, if that price doesn't coincide with the market price of a bushel of similar-quality wheat, no one will purchase the wheat at a higher price; nor would the farmer be inclined to reduce revenues by selling below the market price.

Let's examine why a firm in a perfectly competitive industry is a price taker.

1. *There is a large number of buyers and sellers.* When this is the case, the quantity demanded by one buyer or the quantity supplied by one seller is negligible relative to the market quantity. No one buyer or seller has any influence on price.
2. *The product sold by the firms in the industry is homogeneous.* The product sold by each firm in the industry is a perfect substitute for the product sold by every other firm. Buyers are able to choose from a large number of sellers of a product that the buyers regard as being the same.
3. *Both buyers and sellers have equal access to information.* Consumers are able to find out about lower prices charged by competing firms. Firms are able to find out about cost-saving innovations that can lower production costs and prices, and they are able to learn about profitable opportunities in other industries.

4. *Any firm can enter or leave the industry without serious impediments.* Firms in a competitive industry are not hampered in their ability to get resources or reallocate resources. They move labor and capital in pursuit of profit-making opportunities to whatever business venture gives them their highest expected rate of return on their investment.

How did a group of Wisconsin monks take advantage of a lack of impediments to entry to go into the business of selling remanufactured printer ink cartridges?

E-COMMERCE EXAMPLE

A Monastery Takes Advantage of Unhindered Entry

For centuries, monks residing in Catholic monasteries have supported themselves with their own labor by engaging in such pursuits as making wine, baking breads, and transcribing and translating documents. Recently, monks at a western Wisconsin monastery using laser printers to create documents wondered why replacement ink cartridges were so expensive. When they discovered that they could purchase generic printing supplies, remanufacture printer ink cartridges, and offer them for sale on the Internet, a new business called Lasermonk.com was born. During 2002, Lasermonk.com's first year in operation, the business brought in $2,000 to help finance the monastery's operations. By the mid-2000s, the business was earning more than $3 million per year, which the monastery uses to fund activities ranging from computer classes for orphans to food programs for homeless children.

FOR CRITICAL ANALYSIS
Was Lasermonk.com's entry into the market for remanufactured printing cartridges entirely "free"?

THE DEMAND CURVE OF THE PERFECT COMPETITOR

When we discussed substitutes in Chapter 21, we pointed out that the more substitutes there are and the more similar they are to the commodity in question, the greater is the price elasticity of demand. Here we assume that the perfectly competitive firm is producing a homogeneous commodity that has perfect substitutes. That means that if the individual firm raises its price one penny, it will lose all of its business. This, then, is how we characterize the demand schedule for a perfectly competitive firm: It is the going market price as determined by the forces of market supply and market demand—that is, where the market demand curve intersects the market supply curve. The demand curve for the product of an individual firm in a perfectly competitive industry is perfectly elastic at the going market price. Remember that with a perfectly elastic demand curve, any increase in price leads to zero quantity demanded.

We show the market demand and supply curves in panel (a) of Figure 24-1 on the following page. Their intersection occurs at the price of $5. The commodity in question is flash memory pen drives. Assume for the purposes of this exposition that all of these flash drives are perfect substitutes for all others. At the going market price of $5 apiece, a hypothetical individual demand curve for a producer of flash drives who sells a very, very small part of total industry production is shown in panel (b). At the market price, this firm can sell all the output it wants. At the market price of $5 each, which is where the demand curve for the individual producer lies, consumer demand for the flash drives of that one producer is perfectly elastic. This can be seen by noting that if the firm raises its price, consumers, who are assumed to know that this supplier is charging more than other producers, will buy elsewhere, and the producer in question will have no sales at all. Thus,

FIGURE 24-1
The Demand Curve for a Producer of Flash Memory Pen Drives

At $5—where market demand, D, and market supply, S, intersect—the individual firm faces a perfectly elastic demand curve, d. If it raises its price even one penny, it will sell no flash drives at all. Notice the difference in the quantities of flash drives represented on the horizontal axis of panels (a) and (b).

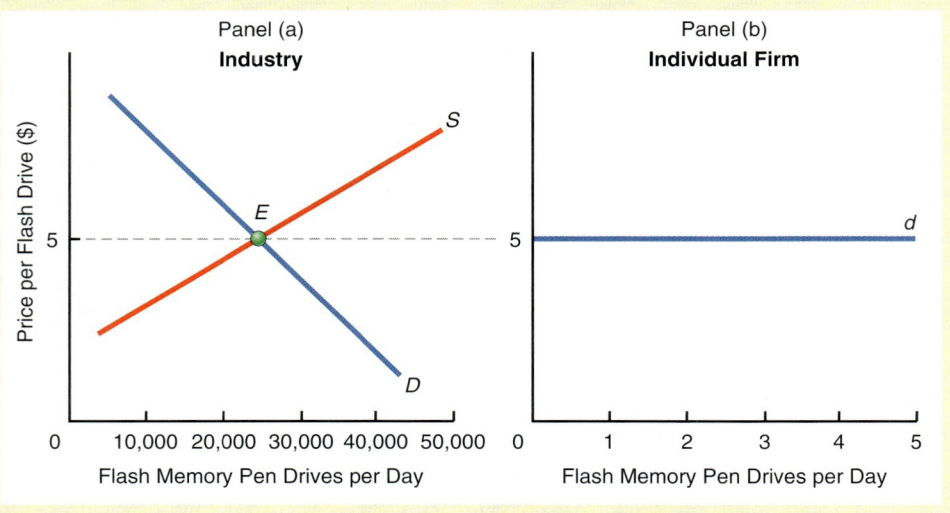

the demand curve for that producer is perfectly elastic. We label the individual producer's demand curve d, whereas the *market* demand curve is always labeled D.

HOW MUCH SHOULD THE PERFECT COMPETITOR PRODUCE?

As we have shown, a perfect competitor has to accept the price of the product as a given. If the firm raises its price, it sells nothing; if it lowers its price, it earns lower revenues per unit sold than it otherwise could. The firm has one decision left: How much should it produce? We will apply our model of the firm to this question to come up with an answer. We'll use the *profit-maximization model,* which assumes that firms attempt to maximize their total profits—the positive difference between total revenues and total costs. This also means that firms seek to minimize any losses that arise in times when total revenues may be less than total costs.

Total Revenues

Total revenues
The price per unit times the total quantity sold.

Every firm has to consider its *total revenues*. **Total revenues** are defined as the quantity sold multiplied by the price per unit. (They are the same as total receipts from the sale of output.) The perfect competitor must take the price as a given.

Look at Figure 24-2. The information in panel (a) comes from panel (a) of Figure 23-2 on page 586, but we have added some essential columns for our analysis. Column 3 is the market price, P, of $5 per flash drive. Column 4 shows the total revenues, or TR, as equal to the market price, P, times the total output per day, or Q. Thus, $TR = PQ$.

For the perfect competitor, price is also equal to average revenue (AR) because

$$AR = \frac{TR}{Q} = \frac{PQ}{Q} = P$$

Panel (a)

(1) Total Output and Sales per Day (Q)	(2) Total Costs (TC)	(3) Market Price (P)	(4) Total Revenues (TR) (4) = (3) × (1)	(5) Total Profit (TR − TC) (5) = (4) − (2)	(6) Average Total Cost (ATC) (6) = (2) ÷ (1)	(7) Average Variable Cost (AVC)	(8) Marginal Cost (MC) (8) = Change in (2) / Change in (1)	(9) Marginal Revenue (MR) (9) = Change in (4) / Change in (1)
0	$10	$5	$ 0	−$10	—	—		
							$5	$5
1	15	5	5	−10	$15.00	$5.00		
							3	5
2	18	5	10	−8	9.00	4.00		
							2	5
3	20	5	15	−5	6.67	3.33		
							1	5
4	21	5	20	−1	5.25	2.75		
							2	5
5	23	5	25	2	4.60	2.60		
							3	5
6	26	5	30	4	4.33	2.67		
							4	5
7	30	5	35	5	4.28	2.86		
							5	5
8	35	5	40	5	4.38	3.12		
							6	5
9	41	5	45	4	4.56	3.44		
							7	5
10	48	5	50	2	4.80	3.80		
							8	5
11	56	5	55	−1	5.09	4.18		

FIGURE 24-2
Profit Maximization

Profit maximization occurs where marginal revenue equals marginal cost. Panel (a) indicates that this point occurs at a rate of sales of between seven and eight flash memory pen drives per day. In panel (b), we find maximum profits where total revenues exceed total costs by the largest amount. This occurs at a rate of production and sales per day of seven or eight flash drives. In panel (c), the marginal cost curve, MC, intersects the marginal revenue curve at a rate of output and sales of somewhere between seven and eight flash drives per day.

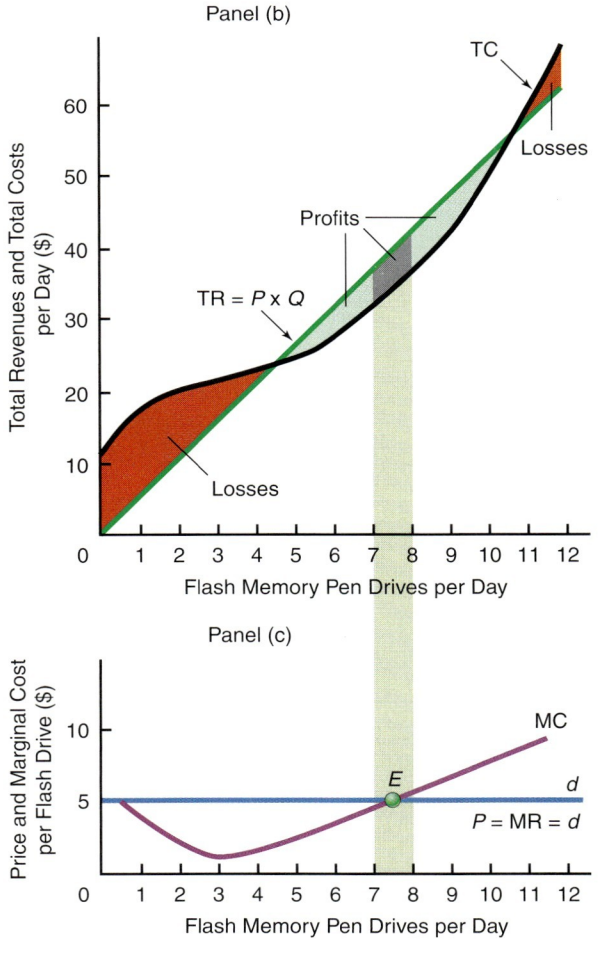

where Q stands for quantity. If we assume that all units sell for the same price, it becomes apparent that another name for the demand curve is the *average revenue curve* (this is true regardless of the type of market structure under consideration).

We are assuming that the market supply and demand schedules intersect at a price of $5 and that this price holds for all the firm's production. We are also assuming that because our maker of flash memory pen drives is a small part of the market, it can sell all that it produces at that price. Thus, panel (b) of Figure 24-2 on the previous page shows the total revenue curve as a straight green line. For every additional flash memory pen drive sold, total revenue increases by $5.

Comparing Total Costs with Total Revenues

Total costs are given in column 2 of panel (a) of Figure 24-2 and plotted in panel (b). Remember, the firm's costs always include a normal rate of return on investment. So, whenever we refer to total costs, we are talking not about accounting costs but about economic costs. When the total cost curve is above the total revenue curve, the firm is experiencing losses. When it is below the total revenue curve, the firm is making profits.

By comparing total costs with total revenues, we can figure out the number of flash memory pen drives the individual competitive firm should produce per day. Our analysis rests on the assumption that the firm will attempt to maximize total profits. In panel (a) of Figure 24-2, we see that total profits reach a maximum at a production rate of either seven or eight of these flash drives per day. We can see this graphically in panel (b) of the figure. The firm will maximize profits where the total revenue curve lies above the total cost curve by the greatest amount. That occurs at a rate of output and sales of either seven or eight flash memory pen drives per day; this rate is called the **profit-maximizing rate of production.** (If output were continuously divisible or we were dealing with extremely large numbers of flash drives, we would get a unique profit-maximizing output.)

We can also find the profit-maximizing rate of production for the individual competitive firm by looking at marginal revenues and marginal costs.

Profit-maximizing rate of production
The rate of production that maximizes total profits, or the difference between total revenues and total costs; also, the rate of production at which marginal revenue equals marginal cost.

USING MARGINAL ANALYSIS TO DETERMINE THE PROFIT-MAXIMIZING RATE OF PRODUCTION

It is possible—indeed, preferred—to use marginal analysis to determine the profit-maximizing rate of production. We end up with the same results derived in a different manner, one that focuses more on where decisions are really made—on the margin. Managers examine changes in costs and relate them to changes in revenues. In fact, whether the question is how much more or less to produce, how many more workers to hire or fire, or how much more to study or not study, we compare changes in costs with changes in benefits, where change is occurring at the margin.

Marginal Revenue

Marginal revenue represents the change in total revenues attributable to changing production of an item by one unit. Hence a more formal definition of marginal revenue is

Marginal revenue
The change in total revenues resulting from a change in output (and sale) of one unit of the product in question.

$$\text{Marginal revenue} = \frac{\text{change in total revenues}}{\text{change in output}}$$

In a perfectly competitive market, the marginal revenue curve is exactly equivalent to the price line, which is the individual firm's demand curve. Each time the firm produces and sells one more unit, total revenues rise by an amount equal to the (constant) market price of the good. Thus, in Figure 24-1 on page 608, the demand curve, d, for the individual producer is at a price of $5—the price line is coincident with the demand curve. But so is the marginal revenue curve, for marginal revenue in this case also equals $5.

The marginal revenue curve for our competitive producer of flash memory pen drives is shown as a line at $5 in panel (c) of Figure 24-2 on page 609. Notice again that the marginal revenue curve is the price line, which is the firm's demand, or average revenue, curve, d.

When Are Profits Maximized?

Now we add the marginal cost curve, MC, taken from column 8 in panel (a) of Figure 24-2. As shown in panel (c) of that figure, because of the law of diminishing marginal product, the marginal cost curve first falls and then starts to rise, eventually intersecting the marginal revenue curve and then rising above it. Notice that the numbers for both the marginal cost schedule, column 8 in panel (a), and the marginal revenue schedule, column 9 in panel (a), are printed *between* the rows on which the quantities appear. This indicates that we are looking at a *change* between one rate of output and the next rate of output.

Equalizing Marginal Revenue and Marginal Cost.
In panel (c) of Figure 24-2 on page 609, the marginal cost curve intersects the marginal revenue curve somewhere between seven and eight flash memory pen drives per day. The firm has an incentive to produce and sell until the amount of the additional revenue received from selling one more flash drive just equals the additional costs incurred for producing and selling that flash drive. This is how the firm maximizes profit. Whenever marginal cost is less than marginal revenue, the firm will always make more profit by increasing production.

Now consider the possibility of producing at an output rate of 10 flash memory pen drives per day. The marginal cost curve at that output rate is higher than the marginal revenue (or d) curve. The firm would be spending more to produce that additional output than it would be receiving in revenues; it would be foolish to continue producing at this rate.

The Profit-Maximizing Output Rate.
But how much should the firm produce? It should produce at point E in panel (c) of Figure 24-2, where the marginal cost curve intersects the marginal revenue curve from below. The firm should continue production until the cost of increasing output by one more unit is just equal to the revenues obtainable from that extra unit. This is a fundamental rule in economics:

> *Profit maximization occurs at the rate of output at which marginal revenue equals marginal cost.*

For a perfectly competitive firm, this rate of output is at the intersection of the demand schedule, d, and the marginal cost curve, MC. When MR exceeds MC, each additional unit of output adds more to total revenues than to total costs, so the additional unit should be produced. When MC is greater than MR, each unit produced adds more to total cost than to total revenues, so this unit should not be produced. Therefore, profit maximization occurs when MC equals MR. In our particular example, our profit-maximizing, perfectly competitive producer of flash memory pen drives will produce at a rate of either seven or eight flash drives a day. (If we were dealing with a very large rate of output, we would come up with an exact profit-maximizing rate.)

QUICK QUIZ

Four fundamental characteristics of the market in **perfect competition** are (1) a _____ number of buyers and sellers, (2) a _____ product, (3) good information in the hands of both buyers and sellers, and (4) _____ exit from and entry into the industry by other firms.

A perfectly competitive firm is a **price taker**. It has _____ control over price and consequently has to take price as a given, but it can sell _____ that it wants at the going market price.

The demand curve for a perfect competitor is perfectly elastic at the going market price. The demand curve is also the perfect competitor's _____ revenue curve because _____ revenue is defined as the change in total revenue due to a one-unit change in output.

Profit is maximized at the rate of output at which the positive difference between total revenues and total costs is the greatest. This is the same level of output at which marginal _____ equals marginal _____. The perfectly competitive firm produces at an output rate at which marginal cost equals the _____ per unit of output, because MR is always equal to P.

See page 636 for the answers. Review concepts from this section in MyEconLab.

SHORT-RUN PROFITS

To find what our competitive individual producer of flash memory pen drives is making in terms of profits in the short run, we have to add the average total cost curve to panel (c) of Figure 24-2 on page 609. We take the information from column 6 in panel (a) and add it to panel (c) to get Figure 24-3. Again the profit-maximizing rate of output is between seven

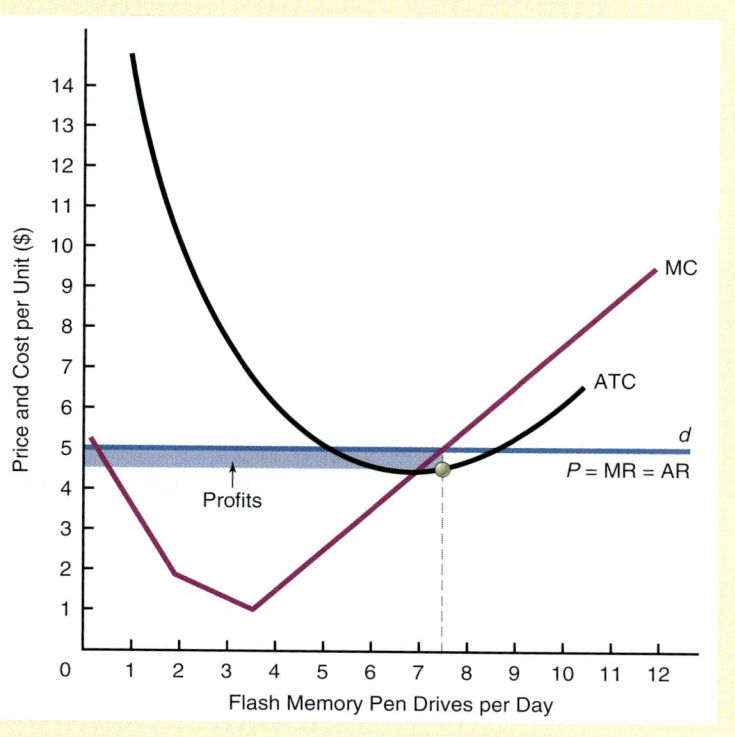

FIGURE 24-3

Measuring Total Profits

Profits are represented by the shaded area. The height of the profit rectangle is given by the difference between average total costs and price ($5), where price is also equal to average revenue. This is found by the vertical difference between the ATC curve and the price, or average revenue, line d, at the profit-maximizing rate of output of between seven and eight flash drives per day.

and eight flash drives per day. If we have production and sales of seven flash drives per day, total revenues will be $35 a day. Total costs will be $30 a day, leaving a profit of $5 a day. If the rate of output and sales is eight flash drives per day, total revenues will be $40 and total costs will be $35, again leaving a profit of $5 a day.

A Graphical Depiction of Maximum Profits

In Figure 24-3, the lower boundary of the rectangle labeled "Profits" is determined by the intersection of the profit-maximizing quantity line represented by vertical dashes and the average total cost curve. Why? Because the ATC curve gives us the cost per unit, whereas the price ($5), represented by d, gives us the revenue per unit, or average revenue. The difference is profit per unit.

Thus, the height of the rectangular box representing profits equals profit per unit, and the length equals the amount of units produced. When we multiply these two quantities, we get total profits. Note, as pointed out earlier, that we are talking about *economic profits* because a normal rate of return on investment is included in the average total cost curve, ATC.

A Graphical Depiction of Minimum Losses

It is also certainly possible for the competitive firm to make short-run losses. We give an example in Figure 24-4, where we show the firm's demand curve shifting from d_1 to d_2. The going market price has fallen from $5 to $3 per flash memory pen drive because of changes in market supply or demand conditions (or both). The firm will do the best it can by producing where marginal revenue equals marginal cost.

We see in Figure 24-4 that the marginal revenue (d_2) curve is intersected (from below) by the marginal cost curve at an output rate of about $5\frac{1}{2}$ flash drives per day. The firm is clearly not making profits because average total costs at that output rate are greater than the price of $3 per flash drive. The losses are shown in the shaded area. By producing

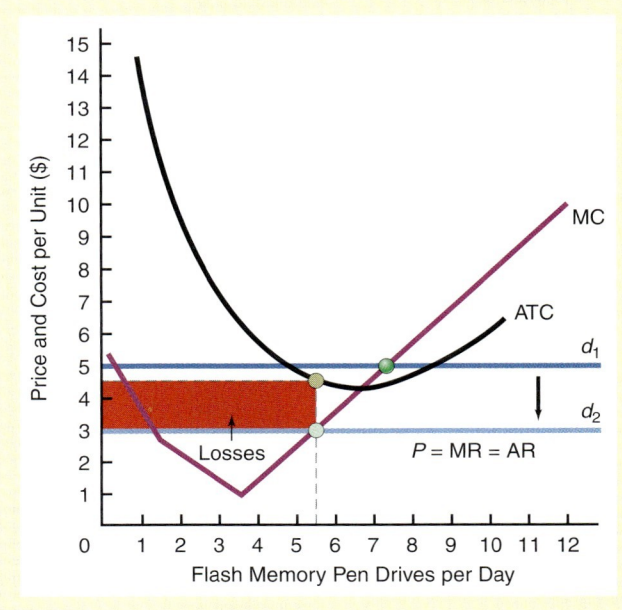

FIGURE 24-4

Minimization of Short-Run Losses

In situations in which average total costs exceed price, which in turn is greater than or equal to average variable cost, profit maximization is equivalent to loss minimization. This again occurs where marginal cost equals marginal revenue. Losses are shown in the shaded area.

where marginal revenue equals marginal cost, however, the firm is minimizing its losses; that is, losses would be greater at any other output.

THE SHORT-RUN BREAK-EVEN PRICE AND THE SHORT-RUN SHUTDOWN PRICE

In Figure 24-4, the firm is sustaining economic losses. Will it go out of business? In the long run it will, but in the short run the firm will not necessarily go out of business. As long as the loss from staying in business is less than the loss from shutting down, the firm will continue to produce. A firm *goes out of business* when the owners sell its assets to someone else. A firm temporarily *shuts down* when it stops producing, but it still is in business.

Now how can a firm that is sustaining economic losses in the short run tell whether it is still worthwhile *not* to shut down? The firm must compare the cost of producing (while incurring losses) with the cost it incurs if it ceases production. The cost of staying in production in the short run is given by the total *variable* cost. Looking at the problem on a per-unit basis, as long as average variable cost (AVC) is covered by average revenues (price), the firm is better off continuing to produce. If average variable costs are exceeded even a little bit by the price of the product, staying in production produces some revenues in excess of variable costs that can be applied toward covering fixed costs.

A simple example will demonstrate this situation. Suppose that the price of some product is $8, and average total costs equal $9 at an output of 100. In this example, we assume that average total costs are broken up into average variable costs of $7 and average fixed costs of $2. Total revenues, then, equal $8 × 100, or $800, and total costs equal $9 × 100, or $900. Total losses therefore equal $100. However, this does not mean that the firm will shut down. After all, if it does shut down, it still has fixed costs to pay. And in this case, because average fixed costs equal $2 at an output of 100, the fixed costs are $200. Thus, the firm has losses of $100 if it continues to produce, but it has losses of $200 (the fixed costs) if it shuts down. The logic is fairly straightforward:

As long as the price per unit sold exceeds the average variable cost per unit produced, the earnings of the firm's owners will be higher if it continues to produce in the short run than if it shuts down.

Calculating the Short-Run Break-Even Price

Look at demand curve d_1 in Figure 24-5. It just touches the minimum point of the average total cost curve, which, as you will remember, is exactly where the marginal cost curve intersects the average total cost curve. At that price, which is about $4.30, the firm will be making exactly zero short-run *economic* profits. That price is called the **short-run break-even price**, and point E_1 therefore occurs at the short-run break-even price for a competitive firm. It is the point at which marginal revenue, marginal cost, and average total cost are all equal (that is, at which $P = MC$ and $P = ATC$). The break-even price is the one that yields zero short-run *economic* profits or losses.

Short-run break-even price
The price at which a firm's total revenues equal its total costs. At the break-even price, the firm is just making a normal rate of return on its capital investment. (It is covering its explicit and implicit costs.)

Calculating the Short-Run Shutdown Price

To calculate the firm's shutdown price, we must introduce the average variable cost (AVC) to our graph. In Figure 24-5, we have plotted the AVC values from column 7 in panel (a) of Figure 24-2 on page 609. For the moment, consider two possible demand curves, d_1 and d_2, which are also the firm's respective marginal revenue curves. If demand is d_1, the firm

FIGURE 24-5
Short-Run Shutdown and Break-Even Prices

We can find the short-run break-even price and the short-run shutdown price by comparing price with average total costs and average variable costs. If the demand curve is d_1, profit maximization occurs at output E_1, where MC equals marginal revenue (the d_1 curve). Because the ATC curve includes all relevant opportunity costs, point E_1 is the break-even point, and zero economic profits are being made. The firm is earning a normal rate of return. If the demand curve falls to d_2, profit maximization (loss minimization) occurs at the intersection of MC and MR (the d_2 curve), or E_2. Below this price, it does not pay for the firm to continue in operation because its average variable costs are not covered by the price of the product.

will produce at E_1, where that curve intersects the marginal cost curve. If demand falls to d_2, the firm will produce at E_2. The special feature of the hypothetical demand curve, d_2, is that it just touches the average variable cost curve at the latter's minimum point, which is also where the marginal cost curve intersects it. This price is the **short-run shutdown price.** Why? Below this price, the firm would be paying out more in variable costs than it is receiving in revenues from the sale of its product. Each unit it sold would generate losses. Clearly, the way to avoid incurring these losses, if price falls below the shutdown point, is in fact to shut down operations.

The intersection of the price line, the marginal cost curve, and the average variable cost curve is labeled E_2. The resulting short-run shutdown price is valid only for the short run because, of course, in the long run the firm will not stay in business at a yield less than a normal rate of return (zero economic profits).

Why did South African gold-mining firms temporarily shut down some of their mines during the mid-2000s?

Short-run shutdown price
The price that covers average variable costs. It occurs just below the intersection of the marginal cost curve and the average variable cost curve.

INTERNATIONAL EXAMPLE

In South Africa, Gold Does Not Glitter Unless the Price Is Right

Between late 2004 and late 2005, the price South African gold-mining firms received for the gold they produced declined by more than 20 percent. Most South African gold mines are very deep, which makes the average variable cost of extracting gold, mainly wages paid to miners specially trained to work in mines up to two miles underground, relatively high. Consequently, when the price received by South African gold-mining companies dropped, the firms responded by shutting down some of their deepest mines.

FOR CRITICAL ANALYSIS
Why do you suppose that companies in other parts of the world, where gold near the surface can be extracted at relatively low average variable cost via "open pit mining," kept their gold mines open following the drop in the world price of gold?

> **ECONOMICS FRONT AND CENTER**
>
> For practice distinguishing between the short-run shutdown price and the short-run break-even price, take a look at **Confronting Lower Crop Prices**, on page 626.

The Meaning of Zero Economic Profits

The fact that we labeled point E_1 in Figure 24-5 on the previous page the break-even point may have disturbed you. At point E_1, price is just equal to average total cost. If this is the case, why would a firm continue to produce if it were making no profits whatsoever? If we again make the distinction between accounting profits and economic profits, you will realize that at that price, the firm has zero economic profits but positive accounting profits. Recall that accounting profits are total revenues minus total explicit costs. But such accounting ignores the reward offered to investors—the opportunity cost of capital—plus all other implicit costs.

In economic analysis, the average total cost curve includes the full opportunity cost of capital. Indeed, the average total cost curve includes the opportunity cost of *all* factors of production used in the production process. At the short-run break-even price, economic profits are, by definition, zero. Accounting profits at that price are not, however, equal to zero; they are positive. Consider an example. A baseball bat manufacturer sells bats at some price. The owners of the firm have supplied all the funds in the business. They have not borrowed from anyone else, and they explicitly pay the full opportunity cost to all factors of production, including any managerial labor that they themselves contribute to the business. Their salaries show up as a cost in the books and are equal to what they could have earned in the next-best alternative occupation. At the end of the year, the owners find that after they subtract all explicit costs from total revenues, they have earned $100,000. Let's say that their investment was $1 million. Thus, the rate of return on that investment is 10 percent per year. We will assume that this turns out to be equal to the market rate of return.

This $100,000, or 10 percent rate of return, is actually, then, a competitive, or normal, rate of return on invested capital in all industries with similar risks. If the owners had made only $50,000, or 5 percent on their investment, they would have been able to make higher profits by leaving the industry. The 10 percent rate of return is the opportunity cost of capital. Accountants show it as a profit; economists call it a cost. We include that cost in the average total cost curve, similar to the one shown in Figure 24-5. At the short-run break-even price, average total cost, including this opportunity cost of capital, will just equal that price. The firm will be making zero economic profits but a 10 percent *accounting profit*.

THE SUPPLY CURVE FOR A PERFECTLY COMPETITIVE INDUSTRY

The logic of the short-run break-even price and the short-run shutdown price makes clear that a perfectly competitive firm's output rate varies directly with the price it receives for producing and selling its product. As you learned in Chapter 3, the relationship between a product's price and the quantity produced and offered for sale is a supply curve. Let's now examine the supply curve for a perfectly competitive industry.

The Perfect Competitor's Short-Run Supply Curve

What does the supply curve for the individual firm look like? Actually, we have been looking at it all along. We know that when the price of flash drives is $5, the firm will supply seven or eight of them per day. If the price falls to $3, the firm will supply five or six flash drives per day. And if the price falls below $3, the firm will shut down. Hence, in

FIGURE 24-6
The Individual Firm's Short-Run Supply Curve
The individual firm's short-run supply curve is the portion of its marginal cost curve at and above the minimum point on the average variable cost curve.

Figure 24-6, the firm's supply curve is the marginal cost curve above the short-run shutdown point. This is shown as the solid part of the marginal cost curve.

By definition, then, a firm's short-run supply curve in a competitive industry is its marginal cost curve at and above the point of intersection with the average variable cost curve.

The Short-Run Industry Supply Curve

In Chapter 3, we indicated that the market supply curve was the summation of individual supply curves. At the beginning of this chapter, we drew a market supply curve in Figure 24-1 on page 608. Now we want to derive more precisely a market, or industry, supply curve to reflect individual producer behavior in that industry. First we must ask, What is an industry? It is merely a collection of firms producing a particular product. Therefore, we have a way to figure out the total supply curve of any industry: As discussed in Chapter 3, we add the quantities that each firm will supply at every possible price. In other words, we sum the individual supply curves of all the competitive firms *horizontally*. The individual supply curves, as we just saw, are simply the marginal cost curves of each firm.

Consider doing this for a hypothetical world in which there are only two producers of flash memory pen drives in the industry, firm A and firm B. These two firms' marginal cost curves are given in panels (a) and (b) of Figure 24-7 on the following page. The marginal cost curves for the two separate firms are presented as MC_A in panel (a) and MC_B in panel (b). Those two marginal cost curves are drawn only for prices above the minimum average variable cost for each respective firm. Hence we are not including any of the marginal cost curves below minimum average variable cost. In panel (a), for firm A, at a price of $6 per unit, the quantity supplied would be 7 units. At a price of $10 per unit, the quantity supplied would be 12 units. In panel (b), we see the two different quantities that would be supplied by firm B corresponding to those two prices. Now, at a price of $6, we add horizontally the quantities 7 and 10 to obtain 17 units. This gives us one point, *F*, for our short-run **industry supply curve**, *S*. We obtain the other point, *G*, by doing the same horizontal adding of quantities at a price of $10 per unit. When we connect all points such as *F* and

Industry supply curve
The locus of points showing the minimum prices at which given quantities will be forthcoming; also called the *market supply curve*.

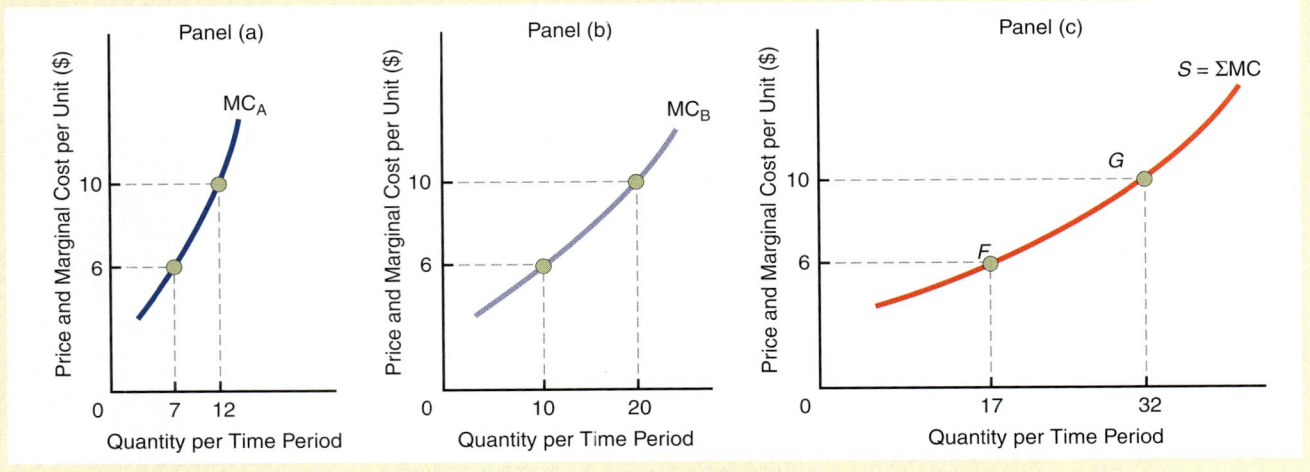

FIGURE 24-7

Deriving the Industry Supply Curve

Marginal cost curves at and above minimum average variable cost are presented in panels (a) and (b) for firms A and B. We horizontally sum the two quantities supplied, 7 units by firm A and 10 units by firm B, at a price of $6. This gives us point F in panel (c). We do the same thing for the quantities supplied at a price of $10. This gives us point G. When we connect those points, we have the industry supply curve, S, which is the horizontal summation—represented by the Greek letter sigma (Σ)—of the firms' marginal cost curves above their respective minimum average variable costs.

G, we obtain the industry supply curve S, which is also marked ΣMC (where the capital Greek sigma, Σ, is the symbol for summation), indicating that it is the horizontal summation of the marginal cost curves (at and above the respective minimum average variable cost of each firm). Because the law of diminishing marginal product makes marginal cost curves rise, the short-run supply curve of a perfectly competitive industry must be upward sloping.

Factors That Influence the Industry Supply Curve

As you have just seen, the industry supply curve is the horizontal summation of all of the individual firms' marginal cost curves at and above their respective minimum average variable cost points. This means that anything that affects the marginal cost curves of the firm will influence the industry supply curve. Therefore, the individual factors that will influence the supply schedule in a competitive industry can be summarized as the factors that cause the variable costs of production to change. These are factors that affect the individual marginal cost curves, such as changes in the individual firm's productivity, in factor costs (such as wages paid to labor and prices of raw materials), in per-unit taxes, and in anything else that would influence the individual firm's marginal cost curve.

All of these are *ceteris paribus* conditions of supply (see page 66). Because they affect the position of the marginal cost curve for the individual firm, they affect the position of the industry supply curve. A change in any of these will shift the firms' marginal cost curves and thus shift the industry supply curve.

QUICK QUIZ

Short-run average profits or losses are determined by comparing _____ total costs with _____ (average revenue) at the **profit-maximizing rate of output**. In the short run, the perfectly competitive firm can make economic profits or economic losses.

The perfectly competitive firm's short-run _____-_____ price equals the firm's minimum average total cost, which is at the point at which the _____ cost curve intersects the average total cost curve.

The perfectly competitive firm's short-run _____ price equals the firm's minimum average variable cost, which is at the point at which the _____ cost curve intersects the average variable cost curve. Shutdown will occur if price falls below average variable cost.

The firm will continue production at a price that exceeds average variable costs because revenues exceed total _____ costs of producing.

At the short-run break-even price, the firm is making _____ economic profits, which means that it is just making a _____ rate of return for industries with similar risks.

The firm's short-run supply curve is the portion of its marginal cost curve at and above its minimum average _____ cost. The industry short-run supply curve is a horizontal _____ of the individual firms' marginal cost curves at and above their respective minimum average _____ costs.

See page 636 for the answers. Review concepts from this section in MyEconLab.

PRICE DETERMINATION UNDER PERFECT COMPETITION

How is the market, or "going," price established in a competitive market? This price is established by the interaction of all the suppliers (firms) and all the demanders (consumers).

The Market Clearing Price

The market demand schedule, D, in panel (a) of Figure 24-8 on the following page represents the demand schedule for the entire industry, and the supply schedule, S, represents the supply schedule for the entire industry. The market clearing price, P_e, is established by the forces of supply and demand at the intersection of D and the short-run industry supply curve, S. Even though each individual firm has no control or effect on the price of its product in a competitive industry, the interaction of *all* the producers and buyers determines the price at which the product will be sold.

We say that the price P_e and the quantity Q_e in panel (a) of Figure 24-8 constitute the competitive solution to the resource allocation problem in that particular industry. It is the equilibrium at which quantity demanded equals quantity supplied, and both suppliers and demanders are doing as well as they can. The resulting individual firm demand curve, d, is shown in panel (b) of Figure 24-8 at the price P_e.

Market Equilibrium and the Individual Firm

In a purely competitive industry, the individual producer takes price as a given and chooses the output level that maximizes profits. (This is also the equilibrium level of output from the producer's standpoint.) We see in panel (b) of Figure 24-8 that this is at q_e. If the producer's average costs are given by AC_1, the short-run break-even price arises at q_e

FIGURE 24-8
Industry Demand and Supply Curves and the Individual Firm Demand Curve

The industry demand curve is represented by D in panel (a). The short-run industry supply curve is S and is equal to ΣMC. The intersection of the demand and supply curves at E determines the equilibrium or market clearing price at P_e. The demand curve faced by the individual firm in panel (b) is perfectly elastic at the market clearing price determined in panel (a). If the producer has a marginal cost curve MC, its profit-maximizing output level is at q_e. For AC_1, economic profits are zero; for AC_2, profits are negative; and for AC_3, profits are positive.

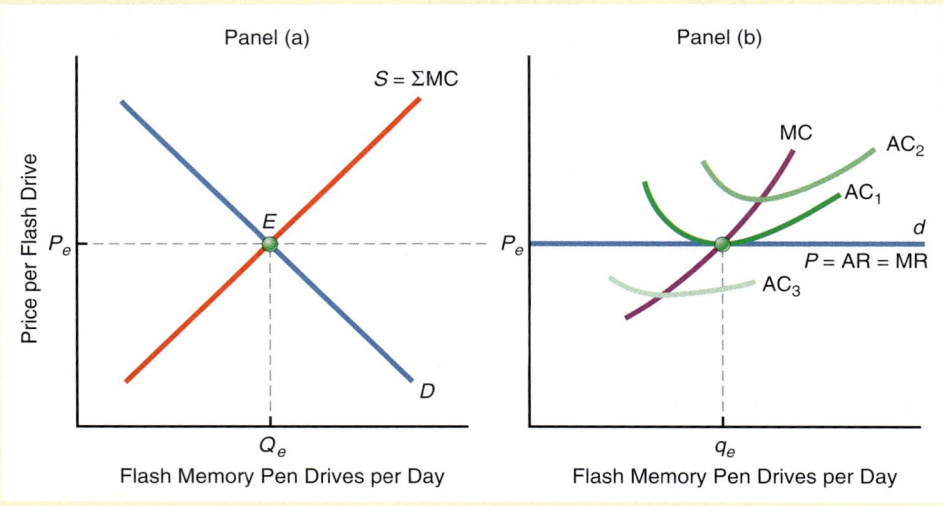

(see Figure 24-5 on page 615). If its average costs are given by AC_2, then at q_e, AC exceeds price (average revenue), and the firm is incurring losses. Alternatively, if average costs are given by AC_3, the firm will be making economic profits at q_e. In the former case, we would expect, over time, that some firms will cease production (exit the industry), causing supply to shift inward, whereas in the latter case, we would expect new firms to enter the industry to take advantage of the economic profits, thereby causing supply to shift outward. We now turn to these long-run considerations.

THE LONG-RUN INDUSTRY SITUATION: EXIT AND ENTRY

In the long run in a competitive situation, firms will be making zero economic profits. We surmise, therefore, that in the long run a perfectly competitive firm's price (marginal and average revenue) curve will just touch its average total cost curve. How does this occur? It is through an adjustment process that depends on economic profits and losses.

Exit and Entry of Firms

Look back at Figure 24-3 on page 612 and Figure 24-4 on page 613. The existence of either profits or losses is a signal to owners of capital both inside and outside the industry. If the industry is characterized by firms showing economic profits as represented in Figure 24-3, this will signal owners of capital elsewhere in the economy that they, too, should enter this industry. If, by contrast, there are firms in the industry suffering economic losses as represented in Figure 24-4, this signals resource owners outside the industry to stay out. It also signals resource owners within the industry not to reinvest and if possible to leave the industry. It is in this sense that we say that profits direct resources to their highest-valued use. In the long run, capital will flow into industries in which profitability is highest and will flow out of industries in which profitability is lowest.

Allocation of Capital and Market Signals.
The price system therefore allocates capital according to the relative expected rates of return on alternative investments. Entry restrictions will thereby hinder economic efficiency by not allowing resources to flow to their highest-valued use. Similarly, exit restrictions (such as laws that require firms to give advance notice of closings) will act to trap resources (temporarily) in sectors in which their value is below that in alternative uses. Such laws will also inhibit the ability of firms to respond to changes in the domestic and international marketplaces.

Not every industry presents an immediate source of opportunity for every firm. In a brief period of time, it may be impossible for a firm that produces tractors to switch to the production of computers, even if there are very large profits to be made. Over the long run, however, we would expect to see such a change. In a market economy, investors supply firms in the more profitable industry with more investment funds, which they take from firms in less profitable industries. (Also, positive economic profits induce existing firms to use internal investment funds for expansion.) Consequently, resources useful in the production of more profitable goods, such as labor, will be bid away from lower-valued opportunities. Investors and other suppliers of resources respond to market **signals** about their highest-valued opportunities.

Signals
Compact ways of conveying to economic decision makers information needed to make decisions. An effective signal not only conveys information but also provides the incentive to react appropriately. Economic profits and economic losses are such signals.

Tendency Toward Equilibrium.
Market adjustment to changes in demand will occur regardless of the wishes of the managers of firms in less profitable markets. They can either attempt to adjust their product line to respond to the new demands, be replaced by managers who are more responsive to new conditions, or see their firms go bankrupt as they find themselves unable to replace worn-out plant and equipment.

In addition, when we say that in a competitive long-run equilibrium situation firms will be making zero economic profits, we must realize that at a particular point in time it would be pure coincidence for a firm to be making *exactly* zero economic profits. Real-world information is not as precise as the curves we use to simplify our analysis. Things change all the time in a dynamic world, and firms, even in a very competitive situation, may for many reasons not be making exactly zero economic profits. We say that there is a *tendency* toward that equilibrium position, but firms are adjusting all the time to changes in their cost curves and in their individual demand curves.

Long-Run Industry Supply Curves

In panel (a) of Figure 24-8, we drew the summation of all of the portions of the individual firms' marginal cost curves at and above each firm's respective minimum average variable costs as the upward-sloping supply curve of the entire industry. We should be aware, however, that a relatively inelastic supply curve may be appropriate only in the short run. After all, one of the prerequisites of a competitive industry is free entry.

Remember that our definition of the long run is a period of time in which all adjustments can be made. The **long-run industry supply curve** is a supply curve showing the relationship between quantities supplied by the entire industry at different prices after firms have been allowed to either enter or leave the industry, depending on whether there have been positive or negative economic profits. Also, the long-run industry supply curve is drawn under the assumption that firms are identical and that entry and exit have been

Long-run industry supply curve
A market supply curve showing the relationship between prices and quantities after firms have been allowed the time to enter into or exit from an industry, depending on whether there have been positive or negative economic profits.

completed. This means that along the long-run industry supply curve, firms in the industry earn zero economic profits.

The long-run industry supply curve can take one of three shapes, depending on whether input prices stay constant, increase, or decrease as the number of firms in the industry changes. In Chapter 23, we assumed that input prices remained constant to the firm regardless of the firm's rate of output. When we look at the entire industry, however, when all firms are expanding and new firms are entering, they may simultaneously bid up input prices.

Constant-Cost Industries. In principle, there are industries that use such a small percentage of the total supply of inputs required for industrywide production that firms can enter the industry without bidding up input prices. In such a situation, we are dealing with a **constant-cost industry.** Its long-run industry supply curve is therefore horizontal and is represented by S_L in panel (a) of Figure 24-9.

We can work through the case in which constant costs prevail. We start out in panel (a) with demand curve D_1 and supply curve S_1. The equilibrium price is P_1. Market demand shifts rightward to D_2. In the short run, the equilibrium price rises to P_2. This generates positive economic profits for existing firms in the industry. Such economic profits induce capital to flow into the industry. The existing firms expand or new firms enter (or both). The short-run supply curve shifts outward to S_2. The new intersection with the new demand curve is at E_3. The new equilibrium price is again P_1. The long-run supply curve is obtained by connecting the intersections of the corresponding pairs of demand and supply curves, E_1 and E_3. Labeled S_L, it is horizontal; its slope is zero. In a constant-cost industry, long-run supply is perfectly elastic. Any shift in demand is eventually met by just enough entry or exit of suppliers that the long-run price is constant at P_1.

Constant-cost industry
An industry whose total output can be increased without an increase in long-run per-unit costs; its long-run supply curve is horizontal.

FIGURE 24-9
Constant-Cost, Increasing-Cost, and Decreasing-Cost Industries

In panel (a), we show a situation in which the demand curve shifts from D_1 to D_2. Price increases from P_1 to P_2. In time, the short-run supply curve shifts outward because positive profits are being earned, and the equilibrium shifts from E_2 to E_3. The market clearing price is again P_1. If we connect points such as E_1 and E_3, we come up with the long-run supply curve S_L. This is a constant-cost industry. In panel (b), costs are increasing for the industry, and therefore the long-run supply curve, S_L', slopes upward and long-run prices rise from P_1 to P_2. In panel (c), costs are decreasing for the industry as it expands, and therefore the long-run supply curve, S_L'', slopes downward such that long-run prices decline from P_1 to P_2.

Retail trade is often given as an example of such an industry because output can be expanded or contracted without affecting input prices. Banking is another example.

Increasing-Cost Industries. In an **increasing-cost industry,** expansion by existing firms and the addition of new firms cause the price of inputs specialized to that industry to be bid up. As costs of production rise, the ATC curve and the firms' MC curves shift upward, causing short-run supply curves (each firm's marginal cost curve) to shift upward. Hence, industry supply shifts out by less than in a constant-cost industry. The result is a long-run industry supply curve that slopes upward, as represented by S'_L in panel (b) of Figure 24-9. Examples are residential construction and coal mining—both use specialized inputs that cannot be obtained in ever-increasing quantities without causing their prices to rise.

Increasing-cost industry
An industry in which an increase in industry output is accompanied by an increase in long-run per-unit costs, such that the long-run industry supply curve slopes upward.

Decreasing-Cost Industries. An expansion in the number of firms in an industry can lead to a reduction in input costs and a downward shift in the ATC and MC curves. When this occurs, the long-run industry supply curve will slope downward. An example, S''_L, is given in panel (c) of Figure 24-9. This is a **decreasing-cost industry.**

Based on this discussion, what evidence would support a conclusion that the firms that manufacture electronic transistors operate within a decreasing-cost industry?

Decreasing-cost industry
An industry in which an increase in output leads to a reduction in long-run per-unit costs, such that the long-run industry supply curve slopes downward.

EXAMPLE

Decreasing Costs and the Market for Transistors

Figure 24-10 shows that the world's output of transistors, the main components of microprocessors used in computers, has exploded, from just over 1 billion in the late 1960s to more than 1 quintillion (a million trillions) today. During this same period, the average price of a transistor has plummeted, from about $1 to less than $0.00002, or two one-thousandths of a cent. Thus, the transistor industry is an example of a decreasing-cost industry.

FOR CRITICAL ANALYSIS
How does the decrease in transistor prices help to explain why average (constant-quality) computer prices have declined by 99 percent since the 1960s?

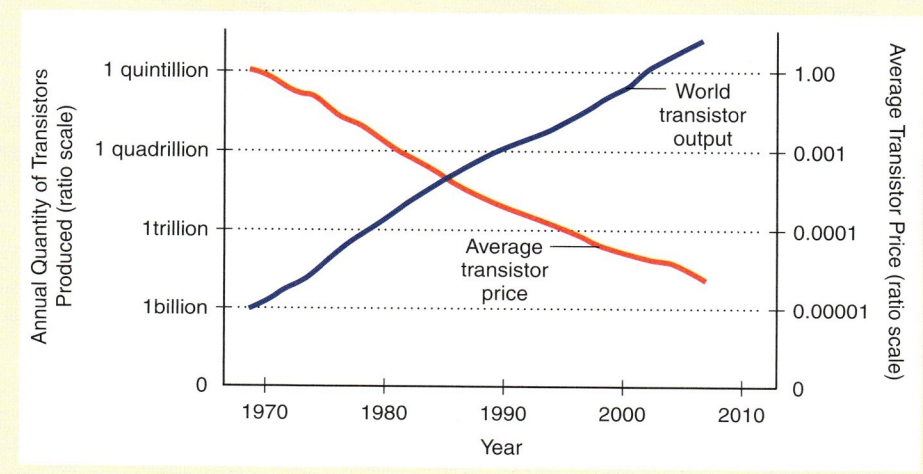

FIGURE 24-10

World Transistor Production and Prices Since 1968

As global output of transistors has increased, the average market price of transistors has decreased.

Source: Organization for Economic Cooperation and Development.

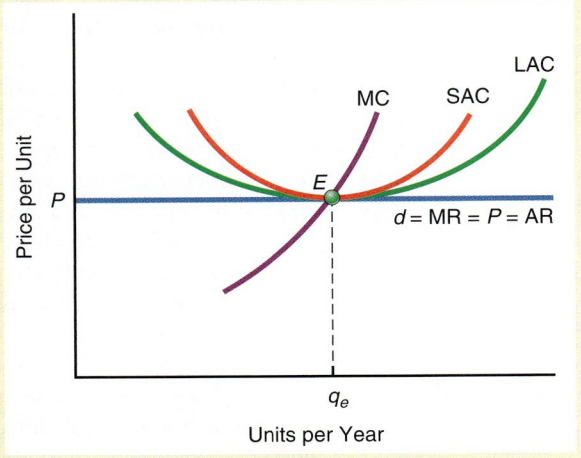

FIGURE 24-11

Long-Run Firm Competitive Equilibrium

In the long run, the firm operates where price, marginal revenue, marginal cost, short-run minimum average cost, and long-run minimum average cost are all equal. This occurs at point E.

LONG-RUN EQUILIBRIUM

In the long run, the firm can change the scale of its plant, adjusting its plant size in such a way that it has no further incentive to change. It will do so until profits are maximized.

The Firm's Long-Run Situation

Figure 24-11 shows the long-run equilibrium of the perfectly competitive firm. Given a price of P and a marginal cost curve, MC, the firm produces at output q_e. Because profits must be zero in the long run, the firm's short-run average costs (SAC) must equal P at q_e, which occurs at minimum SAC. In addition, because we are in long-run equilibrium, any economies of scale must be exhausted, so we are on the minimum point of the long-run average cost curve (LAC). In other words, the long-run equilibrium position is where "everything is equal," which is at point E in Figure 24-11. There, *price* equals *marginal revenue* equals *marginal cost* equals *average cost* (minimum, short-run, and long-run).

Perfect Competition and Minimum Average Total Cost

Look again at Figure 24-11. In long-run equilibrium, the perfectly competitive firm finds itself producing at output rate q_e. At that rate of output, the price is just equal to the minimum long-run average cost as well as the minimum short-run average cost. In this sense, perfect competition results in the production of goods and services using the least costly combination of resources. This is an important attribute of a perfectly competitive long-run equilibrium, particularly when we wish to compare the market structure of perfect competition with other market structures that are less than perfectly competitive. We will examine these other market structures in later chapters.

COMPETITIVE PRICING: MARGINAL COST PRICING

In a perfectly competitive industry, each firm produces where its marginal cost curve intersects its marginal revenue curve from below. Thus, perfectly competitive firms always sell their goods at a price that just equals marginal cost. This represents an optimal pricing situation because the price that consumers pay reflects the opportunity cost to society of producing the good. Recall that marginal cost is the amount that a firm must spend to purchase the additional resources needed to expand output by one unit. Given competitive markets, the amount paid for a resource will be the same in all of its alternative uses. Thus, MC reflects relative resource input use; that is, if the MC of good 1 is twice the MC of good 2, one more unit of good 1 requires twice the resource input of one more unit of good 2. Because price equals marginal cost under perfect competition, the consumer, in determining her or his allocation of income on purchases on the basis of relative prices, is actually allocating income on the basis of relative resource input use.

Marginal Cost Pricing

The competitive firm produces up to the point at which the market price just equals the marginal cost. Herein lies the element of the optimal nature of a competitive solution. It is called **marginal cost pricing.** The competitive firm sells its product at a price that just equals the cost to society—the opportunity cost—for that is what the marginal cost curve represents. (But note here that it is the self-interest of firm owners that causes price to equal the marginal cost to society.) In other words, the marginal benefit to consumers, given by the price that they are willing to pay for the last unit of the good purchased, just equals the marginal cost to society of producing the last unit. (If the marginal benefit exceeds the marginal cost, that is, if $P > MC$, too little is being produced in that people value additional units more than the cost to society of producing them; if $P < MC$, the opposite is true.)

Marginal cost pricing
A system of pricing in which the price charged is equal to the opportunity cost to society of producing one more unit of the good or service in question. The opportunity cost is the marginal cost to society.

When an individual pays a price equal to the marginal cost of production, the cost to the user of that product is equal to the sacrifice or cost to society of producing that quantity of that good as opposed to more of some other good. (We are assuming that all marginal social costs are accounted for.) The competitive solution, then, is called *efficient,* in the economic sense of the word. Economic efficiency means that it is impossible to increase the output of any good without lowering the *value* of the total output produced in the economy. No juggling of resources, such as labor and capital, will result in an output that is higher in total value than the value of all of the goods and services already being produced. In an efficient situation, it is impossible to make one person better off without making someone else worse off. All resources are used in the most advantageous way possible, and society therefore enjoys an efficient allocation of productive resources. All goods and services are sold at their opportunity cost, and marginal cost pricing prevails throughout.

How do you suppose that competition from abroad has helped to push price closer to marginal cost for Japanese retail goods?

INTERNATIONAL EXAMPLE

Pressuring Japanese Retailers to Equalize Price and Average Total Cost

Since the late 1990s, discount retailers based outside Japan, such as Wal-Mart and Costco from the United States and Carrefour from France, have entered the Japanese discount-store industry. To be able to reduce their prices to the levels charged by these companies, Japanese retailers have had to become more cost-efficient. This has required Japanese retailers to downsize traditionally complex and expensive distribution networks. By establishing direct links to manufacturers, they have also reduced their reliance on intermediaries in the distribution chain. Now Japanese retailers are selling their products at the same prices as their U.S. and French competitors—and operating at very close to the same average total cost. In this way, the entry of the foreign firms has induced retailers in Japan to identify and employ the least costly combinations of resources.

FOR CRITICAL ANALYSIS
Would U.S. companies have as much incentive to minimize long-run average total cost if non-U.S. firms were prevented from selling their products in this country?

Market Failure

Market failure
A situation in which an unrestrained market operation leads to either too few or too many resources going to a specific economic activity.

Although perfect competition does offer many desirable results, situations arise when perfectly competitive markets cannot efficiently allocate resources. Either too many or too few resources are used in the production of a good or service. These situations are instances of **market failure.** Externalities arising from failures to fully assign property rights and public goods are examples. For reasons discussed in later chapters, perfectly competitive markets cannot efficiently allocate resources in these situations, and alternative allocation mechanisms are called for. In some cases, alternative market structures or government intervention *may* improve the economic outcome.

QUICK QUIZ

The perfectly competitive price is determined by the _____ of the market demand curve and the market supply curve; the market supply curve is equal to the horizontal summation of the portions of the individual marginal cost curves above their respective minimum average _____ costs.

In the long run, perfectly competitive firms make _____ economic profits because of entry and exit whenever there are industrywide economic profits or losses.

A constant-cost industry has a _____ long-run supply curve. An increasing-cost industry has a(n) _____-sloping long-run supply curve. A decreasing-cost industry has a(n) _____-sloping long-run supply curve.

In the long run, a perfectly competitive firm produces to the point at which price, marginal revenue, marginal cost, short-run minimum average cost, and long-run minimum average cost are all _____.

Perfectly competitive pricing is essentially _____ _____ pricing. Therefore, the perfectly competitive solution is called efficient because _____ _____ represents the social opportunity cost of producing one more unit of the good.

See page 636 for the answers. Review concepts from this section in MyEconLab.

CASE STUDY — ECONOMICS FRONT AND CENTER

Confronting Lower Crop Prices

Conway owns a large farming operation in northeastern Indiana. His main crops are soybeans and corn. In recent years, Conway's business has expanded beyond his own farm to encompass lands owned by aging neighbors, with whom he has arranged to farm the land and share proceeds from crop sales. The weather during the past three years has been perfect for raising soybeans and corn, and Conway's operations have produced ever-larger harvests.

Spring planting season is on the horizon, and Conway reviews his business performance. In spite of his expanded operations and increased production, he is barely keeping his head above water financially. Soybean and corn crops worldwide are near record levels, and the market clearing prices of both products are currently very low. Conway's wife, who is an executive assistant at a nearby factory, has recently suggested that he might be able to earn a higher annual income and work fewer hours per year if he stopped farming and took a job at the plant.

Conway does not think it is time to give up farming, but he is sure of one thing: Unless soybean and corn prices rise soon, he will have to tell about half of the men and women he usually hires to help with spring planting that he will not be able to use them this year. He thinks that his earnings will be sufficient to justify raising crops on his own property this year, but he will have to stop farming his neighbors' lands.

CRITICAL ANALYSIS QUESTIONS

1. *What cost curve is determining Conway's short-run decision regarding his production plans for this year?*

2. *Along the cost curve discussed in your answer to Question 1, is Conway currently closer to operating below his short-run break-even price or below his short-run shutdown price?*

The Big Rush to Provide Digital Snaps in a Snap

Issues and Applications

The photography industry brings in about $85 billion in revenues each year. Since 2000, the majority of those revenues have been earned from the sale of digital cameras and related digital photography products and services. During the mid-2000s, a rapidly growing part of the digital photography business has been the market for digital photo printing services.

Concepts Applied
- Perfect Competition
- Industry Supply Curve
- Decreasing-Cost Industry

The Short Run—Expanding Economic Profits

Early entrants in the market for digital photo printing services were retailers who for years had provided developing and printing services for old-style photography that utilized film instead of digital imaging technologies. As old-style film cameras began to fall out of favor, discount retailers such as Wal-Mart and pharmacies such as Walgreens began offering digital photo printing services.

Panel (a) of Figure 24-12 on page 628 depicts the short-run adjustments that occurred as the demand for digital photo developing services increased. In panel (a), the rise in demand for these services during the early 2000s, from D_1 to D_2, induced a rightward movement up and along the industry supply curve. As the equilibrium price rose, the quantity supplied by service providers increased. Furthermore, existing service providers began to earn positive economic profits.

The Long Run—Massive Entry and Declining Prices

Of course, positive economic profits acted as a market signal to other potential entrants. Entrepreneurs quickly determined that the only impediment to entry into the business of printing digital photos was the few thousand dollars required to purchase a small booth, called a *kiosk* in the industry, and photo-printing machines. By 2004, entrepreneurs had opened kiosks in such diverse locales as shopping malls, hospitals, and college campuses. Within a few more months, large corporations, including Sony, Eastman Kodak, Fuji Photo Film, and Kinko's outlets owned by FedEx, began opening digital photo printing kiosks as well. Today, kiosks can be found on cruise ships, in restaurants, inside baseball and football stadiums, and at racetracks.

Panel (b) of Figure 24-12 illustrates the long-run adjustment that has taken place as a result of the explosion of entries into the market for digital photo printing services. The supply of digital photo printing services has shifted rightward, from S_1 to S_2, which has generated a significant increase in the quantity of services provided. Panel (b) also shows another result of the burst of new entries into the market: The equilibrium price charged to print a typical digital photo has declined. Thus, the long-run supply curve for these services, S_L, slopes downward. The digital photo printing services industry appears to be a decreasing-cost industry.

FIGURE 24-12

Short-Run and Long-Run Adjustments in the Digital Photo Printing Industry

Panel (a) shows that when the demand for digital photo printing services increased in the early 2000s, the market clearing price rose from about 15 cents per photo at point E_1 to about 19 cents per photo at point E_2. The equilibrium quantity of services also increased. Panel (b) displays the long-run adjustments that took place during the mid-2000s as numerous firms entered the industry, causing market supply to increase. The equilibrium quantity of digital photo printing services continued to rise, but the market clearing price declined, from 19 cents per photo at point E_2 to about 12 cents per photo at point E_3. Hence, the long-run supply curve in this industry sloped downward, indicating that this is a decreasing-cost industry.

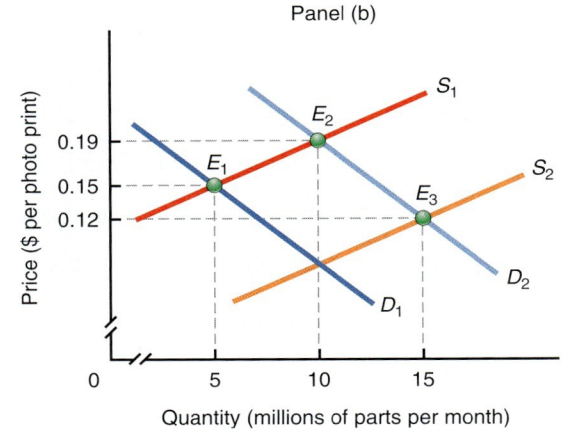

Log in to MyEconLab, click on "Economic News," and test your understanding of the chapter by answering interactive questions that relate directly to this issue.

For Critical Analysis

1. Why do you suppose that even Hewlett-Packard, the leading maker of home printers for digital photos, began opening photo-printing kiosks in 2005?

2. In the long run, what appears to have happened to the ATC and MC curves of firms that provide digital photo printing services?

Web Resources

1. To see an assessment of the profit opportunities available to entrepreneurs contemplating opening digital photo printing kiosks in the mid-2000s, go to www.econtoday.com/ch24.

2. For a pessimistic forecast indicating that the recent expansion of the digital photo printing industry could eventually be reversed, go to www.econtoday.com/ch24.

Research Project

Suppose that a technological advance enabled Hewlett-Packard and other printer manufacturers to sell home printers that could produce prints of digital photos at sharply lower prices. What short-run and long-run adjustments would then take place in the digital photo printing industry?

CHAPTER 24 *Perfect Competition* **629**

Here is what you should know after reading this chapter. MyEconLab will help you identify what you know, and where to go when you need to practice.

WHAT YOU SHOULD KNOW		WHERE TO GO TO PRACTICE
The Characteristics of a Perfectly Competitive Market Structure A perfectly competitive industry has four fundamental characteristics: (1) there is a large number of buyers and sellers, (2) firms in the industry produce and sell a homogeneous product, (3) information is equally accessible to both buyers and sellers, and (4) there are insignificant barriers to industry entry or exit. These characteristics imply that each firm in a perfectly competitive industry is a price taker, meaning that the firm takes the market price as given and outside its control.	perfect competition, 606 perfectly competitive firm, 606 price taker, 606	• **MyEconLab** Study Plan 24.1 • Audio introduction to Chapter 24
How a Perfectly Competitive Firm Decides How Much to Produce Because a perfectly competitive firm sells the amount that it wishes at the market price, the additional revenue it earns from selling an additional unit of output is the market price. Thus, the firm's marginal revenue equals the market price, and its marginal revenue curve is the firm's own perfectly elastic demand curve. The firm maximizes economic profits when marginal cost equals marginal revenue, as long as the market price is not below the short-run shutdown price, where the marginal cost curve crosses the average variable cost curve.	total revenues, 608 profit-maximizing rate of production, 610 marginal revenue, 610 **Key figures** Figure 24-1, 608 Figure 24-2, 609	• **MyEconLab** Study Plans 24.2 and 24.3 • Animated Figures 24-1 and 24-2
The Short-Run Supply Curve of a Perfectly Competitive Firm If the market price is below the short-run shutdown price, the firm's total revenues fail to cover its variable costs. Then the firm would be better off halting production, thereby minimizing its economic loss in the short run. If the market price is above the short-run shutdown price, however, the firm produces the rate of output where marginal revenue, the market price, equals marginal cost. Thus, the range of the firm's marginal cost curve above the short-run shutdown price gives combinations of market prices and production choices of the perfectly competitive firm. This range of the firm's marginal cost curve is therefore the firm's short-run supply curve.	short-run break-even price, 614 short-run shutdown price, 615 industry supply curve, 617 **Key figures** Figure 24-3, 612 Figure 24-4, 613 Figure 24-5, 615 Figure 24-6, 617	• **MyEconLab** Study Plans 24.4, 24.5, 24.6, and 24.7 • Animated Figures 24-3, 24-4, 24-5, and 24-6 • Video: The Short-Run Shutdown Price • Video: The Meaning of Zero Economic Profits
The Equilibrium Price in a Perfectly Competitive Market The short-run supply curve for a perfectly competitive industry is obtained by summing the quantities supplied at each price by all firms in the industry. At the equilibrium market price, the total amount of output supplied by all firms is equal to the total amount of output demanded by all buyers.		• **MyEconLab** Study Plan 24.8

WHAT YOU SHOULD KNOW		WHERE TO GO TO PRACTICE
Incentives to Enter or Exit a Perfectly Competitive Industry In the short run, a perfectly competitive firm will continue to produce output as long as the market price exceeds the short-run shutdown price. This is so even if the market price is below the short-run break-even point where the marginal cost curve crosses the firm's average total cost curve. Even though the firm earns an economic loss, it minimizes the amount of the loss by continuing to produce in the short run. In the long run, however, an economic loss is a signal that the firm is not engaged in the highest-value activity available to its owners, and continued economic losses in the long run will induce exit from the industry.	signals, 621	• **MyEconLab** Study Plan 24.9
The Long-Run Industry Supply Curve and Constant-, Increasing-, and Decreasing-Cost Industries The long-run industry supply curve in a perfectly competitive industry shows the relationship between prices and quantities after firms have the opportunity to enter or leave the industry in response to economic profits or losses. In a constant-cost industry, total output can increase without a rise in long-run per-unit production costs, so the long-run industry supply curve is horizontal. In an increasing-cost industry, however, per-unit costs increase with a rise in industry output, so the long-run industry supply curve slopes upward. In contrast, in a decreasing-cost industry per-unit costs decline as industry output increases, and the long-run industry supply curve slopes downward.	long-run industry supply curve, 621 constant-cost industry, 622 increasing-cost industry, 623 decreasing-cost industry, 623 marginal cost pricing, 625 market failure, 626 **Key figure** Figure 24-9, 622	• **MyEconLab** Study Plans 24.10 and 24.11 • Animated Figure 24-9

Log in to MyEconLab, take a chapter test, and get a personalized Study Plan that tells you which concepts you understand and which ones you need to review. From there, MyEconLab will give you further practice, tutorials, animations, videos, and guided solutions.

Log in to www.myeconlab.com

PROBLEMS

Select problems, indicated by a blue oval, are assignable in MyEconLab.
Answers to the odd-numbered problems appear at the back of the book.

24-1 Explain why each of the following examples is *not* a perfectly competitive industry.

  a. Even though one firm produces a large portion of the industry's total output, there are many firms in the industry, and their products are indistinguishable. Firms can easily exit and enter the industry.

  b. There are many buyers and sellers in the industry. Consumers have equal information about the prices of firms' products, which differ slightly in quality from firm to firm.

  c. Many taxicabs compete in a city. The city's government requires all taxicabs to provide identical service. Taxicabs are virtually identical, and all drivers must wear a designated uniform. The government also limits the number of taxicab companies that can operate within the city's boundaries.

24-2 Consider the market for DVD movie rentals, which is perfectly competitive. The market supply curve slopes upward, the market demand curve slopes downward, and the equilibrium rental price equals

$3.50. Consider each of the following events, and discuss the effects they will have on the market clearing price and on the demand curve faced by the individual rental store.

a. People's tastes change in favor of going to see more movies at cinemas with their friends and family members.
b. National DVD-rental chains open a number of new stores in this market.
c. There is a significant increase in the price of downloading movies on the Internet.

24-3 Consider the diagram below, which applies to a perfectly competitive firm, which at present faces a market clearing price of $20 per unit and produces 10,000 units of output per week.

a. What is the firm's current average revenue per unit?
b. What are the present economic profits of this firm? Is the firm maximizing economic profits? Explain.
c. If the market clearing price drops to $12.50 per unit, should this firm continue to produce in the short run if it wishes to maximize its economic profits (or minimize its economic losses)? Explain.
d. If the market clearing price drops to $7.50 per unit, should this firm continue to produce in the short run if it wishes to maximize its economic profits (or minimize its economic losses)? Explain.

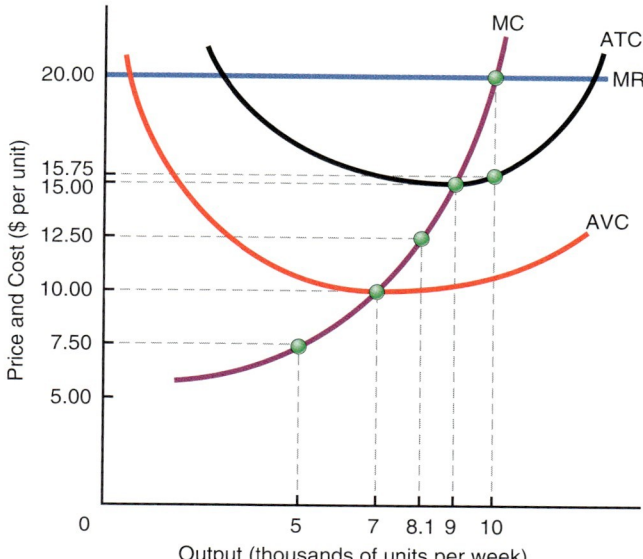

24-4 The following table represents the hourly output and cost structure for a local pizza shop. The market is perfectly competitive, and the market price of a pizza in the area is $10. Total costs include all implicit opportunity costs.

a. Calculate the total revenue and total economic profit for this pizza shop at each rate of output.
b. Assuming that the pizza shop always produces and sells at least one pizza per hour, does this appear to be a situation of short-run or long-run equilibrium?

Total Hourly Output and Sales of Pizzas	Total Hourly Cost ($)
0	5
1	9
2	11
3	12
4	14
5	18
6	24
7	32
8	42
9	54
10	68

24-5 Using the information provided in Problem 24-4, calculate the pizza shop's marginal cost and marginal revenue at each rate of output. Based on marginal analysis, what is the profit-maximizing rate of output for the pizza shop?

24-6 Based on the information in Problems 24-4 and 24-5 and your answers to them, draw a diagram depicting the short-run marginal revenue and marginal cost curves for this pizza shop, and illustrate the determination of its profit-maximizing output rate.

24-7 Consider the information provided in Problem 24-4. Suppose the market price drops to only $5 per pizza. In the short run, should this pizza shop continue to make pizzas, or will it maximize its economic profits (that is, minimize its economic loss) by shutting down?

24-8 Yesterday, a perfectly competitive producer of construction bricks manufactured and sold 10,000 bricks per week at a market price that was just equal to the minimum average variable cost of producing each brick. Today, all the firm's costs are the same, but the market price of bricks has declined.

a. Assuming that this firm has positive fixed costs, did the firm earn economic profits, economic losses, or zero economic profits yesterday?
b. To maximize economic profits today, how many bricks should this firm produce today?

24-9. Suppose that a perfectly competitive firm faces a market price of $5 per unit, and at this price the upward-sloping portion of the firm's marginal cost curve crosses its marginal revenue curve at an output level of 1,500 units. If the firm produces 1,500 units, its average variable costs equal $5.50 per unit, and its average fixed costs equal 50 cents per unit. What is the firm's profit-maximizing (or loss-minimizing) output level? What is the amount of its economic profits (or losses) at this output level?

24-10. Suppose that the price of a service sold in a perfectly competitive market is $25 per unit. For a firm in this market, the output level corresponding to a marginal cost of $25 per unit is 2,000 units. Average variable costs at this output level equal $15 per unit, and average fixed costs equal $5 per unit. What is the firm's profit-maximizing (or loss-minimizing) output level? What is the amount of its economic profits (or losses) at this output level?

24-11. Suppose that a firm in a perfectly competitive industry finds that at its current output rate, marginal revenue exceeds the minimum average total cost of producing any feasible rate of output. Furthermore, the firm is producing an output rate at which marginal cost is less than the average total cost at that rate of output. Is the firm maximizing its economic profits? Why or why not?

24-12. A perfectly competitive industry is initially in a short-run equilibrium in which all firms are earning zero economic profits but in which firms are operating below their minimum efficient scale. Explain the long-run adjustments that will take place for the industry to attain long-run equilibrium with firms operating at their minimum efficient scale.

24-13. Two years ago, a large number of firms entered a market in which existing firms had been earning positive economic profits. By the end of last year, the typical firm in this industry had begun earning negative economic profits. No other events occurred in this market during the past two years.
   a. Explain the adjustment process that occurred last year.
   b. Predict what adjustments will take place in this market beginning this year, other things being equal.

ECONOMICS ON THE NET

The Cost Structure of the Movie Theater Business A key idea in this chapter is that competition among firms in an industry can influence the long-run cost structure within the industry. Here you get a chance to apply this concept to a multinational company that owns movie theaters.

Title: AMC International

Navigation: Follow the link at www.econtoday.com/ch24 to visit American Multi-Cinema's home page.

Application Answer the following questions.

1. Click on *Investor Resources*. What is the average number of screens in an AMC theater? How many theaters does AMC own and manage?

2. Click on *Locations Worldwide,* and use the map to select the theater in Toyohashi City, Japan. This is the largest megaplex theater in Japan. How many screens does the megaplex have?

3. Based on the average number of screens at an AMC theater and the number of screens at the Japanese facility, what can you conclude about the cost structure of this industry? Illustrate the long-run average cost curve for this industry.

For Group Discussion and Analysis Is the Japanese facility the largest multiplex? What do you think constrains the size of a multiplex in Japan? How does the location of AMC's headquarters affect the cost structure of the firm? Is it easier for AMC to have fewer facilities that are larger in size than to have many smaller facilities?

ANSWERS TO QUICK QUIZZES

p. 612: (i) large . . . homogeneous . . . unrestrained; (ii) no . . . all; (iii) marginal . . . marginal; (iv) revenue . . . cost . . . price

p. 619: (i) average . . . price; (ii) break-even . . . marginal; (iii) shutdown . . . marginal; (iv) variable; (v) zero . . . normal; (vi) variable . . . summation . . . variable

p. 626: (i) intersection . . . variable; (ii) zero; (iii) horizontal . . . upward . . . downward; (iv) equal; (v) marginal cost . . . marginal cost

Monopoly

25

The Ambassador Bridge spans the river separating Detroit, Michigan, from Windsor, Ontario. It is about 50 feet wide and less than a mile long. Unless drivers of cars and trucks want to take the time and trouble to drive two hours out of their way, they must pass over this bridge to travel between the two cities. To make this crossing, they must pay fees to the private company that owns the bridge. Clearly, this is a firm that owns a resource with few close substitutes. How does a firm in this situation, known as a *monopoly*, determine the price to charge for its product—in the case of the Ambassador Bridge, the toll the owner charges users? In this chapter, you will learn the answer to this question.

Learning Objectives

After reading this chapter, you should be able to:

1. Identify situations that can give rise to monopoly
2. Describe the demand and marginal revenue conditions a monopolist faces
3. Discuss how a monopolist determines how much output to produce and what price to charge
4. Evaluate the profits earned by a monopolist
5. Understand price discrimination
6. Explain the social cost of monopolies

MyEconLab helps you master each objective and study more efficiently. See end of chapter for details.

Did You Know That...

after the U.S. Supreme Court struck down state laws preventing wine purchases via mail or the Internet, New York's state government proposed a new law limiting direct shipments of wine to no more than two cases per month? Officially, the New York government stated that the proposed law was intended to "help New York wineries." Most observers agreed, however, that the main objective was to limit the extent to which out-of-state alcohol distributors could compete with New York distributors.

In this chapter, you will learn how restricting the sale of an item such as wine to a limited set of providers can push up the item's price. By coordinating their actions, the providers can search for the price that maximizes their combined profits. This creates a situation called *monopoly*.

DEFINITION OF A MONOPOLIST

The word *monopoly* probably brings to mind notions of a business that gouges the consumer, sells faulty products, and gets unconscionably rich in the process. But if we are to succeed in analyzing and predicting the behavior of imperfectly competitive firms, we will have to be more objective in our definition. Although most monopolies in the United States are relatively large, our definition will be equally applicable to small businesses: A **monopolist** is the *single supplier* of a good or service for which there is no close substitute.

In a monopoly market structure, the firm (the monopolist) and the industry are one and the same. Occasionally, there may be a problem in identifying an industry and therefore determining if a monopoly exists. For example, should we think of aluminum and steel as separate industries, or should we define the industry in terms of basic metals? Our answer depends on the extent to which aluminum and steel can be substituted in the production of a wide range of products.

As we shall see in this chapter, a seller prefers to have a monopoly than to face competitors. In general, we think of monopoly prices as being higher than prices under perfect competition and of monopoly profits as being higher than profits under perfect competition (which are, in the long run, merely equivalent to a normal rate of return). How does a firm obtain a monopoly in an industry? Basically, there must be *barriers to entry* that enable firms to receive monopoly profits in the long run. Barriers to entry are restrictions on who can start a business or who can stay in a business.

Monopolist
The single supplier of a good or service for which there is no close substitute. The monopolist therefore constitutes its entire industry.

BARRIERS TO ENTRY

For any amount of monopoly power to continue to exist in the long run, the market must be closed to entry in some way. Either legal means or certain aspects of the industry's technical or cost structure may prevent entry. We will discuss several of the barriers to entry that have allowed firms to reap monopoly profits in the long run (even if they are not pure monopolists in the technical sense).

Ownership of Resources Without Close Substitutes

Preventing a newcomer from entering an industry is often difficult. Indeed, some economists contend that no monopoly acting without government support has been able to prevent entry into the industry unless that monopoly has had the control of some essential natural resource. Consider the possibility of one firm's owning the entire supply of a raw material input that is essential to the production of a particular commodity. The exclusive ownership of such a vital resource serves as a barrier to entry until an alternative source of the raw material input is found or an alternative technology not requiring the raw material in question is developed. A good example of control over a vital input is the Aluminum Company of America (Alcoa), a firm that prior to World War II owned most world stocks of bauxite, the essential raw material in the production of aluminum. Such a situation is rare, though, and is ordinarily temporary.

What country is the location of most of the world's production of tungsten, a chemical element used as a factor of production for various hardened metals?

INTERNATIONAL EXAMPLE

Looking for Lots of Tungsten? The Choices Are Limited

Tungsten is a chemical element that has the highest melting point and the greatest tensile strength of all metals. Its corrosion resistance is so strong that it can be attacked only slightly by most mineral acids. Combining tungsten in small quantities with steel creates a very hard metal. All of these attributes make tungsten useful for electrical, heating, and welding applications and as a component in rifle bullets, military armor, and missiles and rockets. The metal also has more mundane uses, including as an input in the production of fluorescent lights, furnaces, and jewelry.

More than 85 percent of the world's output of tungsten is mined in China. Furthermore, Chinese companies mine tungsten under oversight by the nation's government, which in recent years has taken steps aimed at preventing foreign firms from acquiring rights to join tungsten-mining efforts in that country.

FOR CRITICAL ANALYSIS
How might the fact that tungsten prices have more than doubled since early 2005 encourage more producers to locate and extract more tungsten in other nations besides China?

Economies of Scale

Sometimes it is not profitable for more than one firm to exist in an industry. This is so if one firm would have to produce such a large quantity in order to realize lower unit costs that there would not be sufficient demand to warrant a second producer of the same product. Such a situation may arise because of a phenomenon we discussed in Chapter 23, economies of scale. When economies of scale exist, total costs increase less than proportionately to the increase in output. That is, proportional increases in output yield proportionately smaller increases in total costs, and per-unit costs drop. When economies of scale exist, larger firms (with larger output) have an advantage in that they have lower costs that enable them to charge lower prices and thereby drive smaller firms out of business.

When economies of scale occur over a wide range of outputs, a **natural monopoly** may develop. A natural monopoly is the first firm to take advantage of persistent declining long-run average costs as scale increases. The natural monopolist is able to underprice its competitors and eventually force all of them out of the market.

Figure 25-1 on the following page shows a downward-sloping long-run average cost curve (LAC). Recall that when average costs are falling, marginal costs are less than average costs. Thus, when the long-run average cost curve (LAC) slopes downward, the long-run marginal cost curve (LMC) will be below the LAC.

In our example, long-run average costs are falling over such a large range of production rates that we would expect only one firm to survive in such an industry. That firm would be the natural monopolist. It would be the first one to take advantage of the decreasing

> **ECONOMICS FRONT AND CENTER**
>
> To think about how different types of entry barriers can prove important at different times in a real-world industry, see **Entry Barriers in the Diamond Industry: Cracking or Crystallizing?** on page 652.

Natural monopoly
A monopoly that arises from the peculiar production characteristics in an industry. It usually arises when there are large economies of scale relative to the industry's demand such that one firm can produce at a lower average cost than can be achieved by multiple firms.

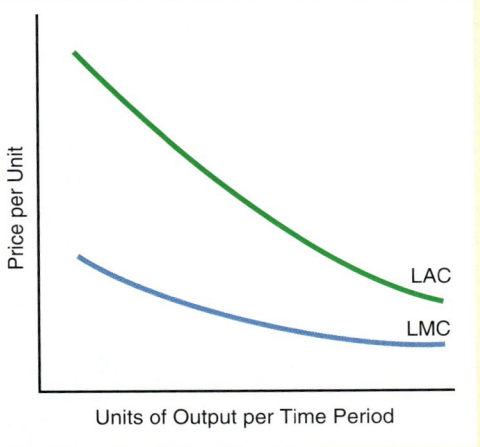

FIGURE 25-1

The Cost Curves That Might Lead to a Natural Monopoly

Whenever long-run marginal costs (LMC) are less than long-run average costs (LAC), then long-run average costs will be falling. A natural monopoly might arise when this situation exists over most output rates. The first firm to establish low-unit-cost capacity would be able to take advantage of declining average total cost. This firm would drive out all rivals by charging a lower price than the others could sustain at their higher average costs.

average costs; that is, it would construct the large-scale facilities first. As its average costs fell, it would lower prices and get an ever-larger share of the market. Once that firm had driven all other firms out of the industry, it would set its price to maximize profits.

Legal or Governmental Restrictions

Governments and legislatures can also erect barriers to entry. These include licenses, franchises, patents, tariffs, and specific regulations that tend to limit entry.

What do you think happened when third- and fifth-grade boys recently tried to sell lemonade without a license in a Massachusetts city?

EXAMPLE

Go Away, Kids, You Bother Me!

In Salem, Massachusetts, two boys, aged 9 and 11, recently opened a lemonade stand to earn a little extra cash. Within days, however, police had shut down their business. What was their offense? A nearby street vendor had filed a complaint, contending that the boys were adversely affecting his business by operating a vending business without paying a fee in excess of $2,000 to obtain a government license. The boys were able to reopen their stand only after agreeing to act as "subcontractors" under the complaining vendor's license and to share some of their roughly $200 in earnings from lemonade sales with that vendor.

FOR CRITICAL ANALYSIS
Why do street vendors in Salem, Massachusetts, have an incentive to report to the police all others—including grade school children—who try to sell drinks and snacks without a license?

Licenses, Franchises, and Certificates of Convenience. It is illegal to enter many industries without a government license, or a "certificate of convenience and public necessity." For example, in some states you cannot form an electrical utility to compete with the electrical utility already operating in your area. You would first have to obtain a certificate of convenience and public necessity from the appropriate authority, which is usually the state's public utility commission. Yet public utility commissions in these states rarely, if ever, issue a certificate to a group of investors who want to compete directly in the same geographic area as an existing electrical utility. Hence, entry into the industry in a particular geographic area is prohibited, and long-run monopoly profits could conceivably be earned by the electrical utility already serving the area.

To enter interstate (and also many intrastate) markets for pipelines, television and radio broadcasting, and transmission of natural gas, to cite a few such industries, it is often necessary to obtain similar permits. Because these franchises or licenses are restricted, long-run monopoly profits might be earned by the firms already in the industry.

Why do you suppose that pharmaceutical prices are rising in Malaysia, even though total costs of producing pills and capsules have not increased?

INTERNATIONAL POLICY EXAMPLE

Malaysia's Drug-Labeling Monopoly

The Malaysian government requires all sellers of drugs and other medical products sold in that country to affix holographic labels providing information about how to use the products safely. To obtain the labels, however, sellers of these items have only one choice. They must buy the labels from a company called Mediharta, which is the only label manufacturer that Malaysia's Registrar of Companies has approved to produce holographic labels in that nation. In this way, the Malaysian government has created a drug-labeling monopoly.

FOR CRITICAL ANALYSIS

Why do you suppose that sellers of wine, beer, and cigarettes in Malaysia raised the prices they charged consumers for these products after the government granted a monopoly on labels it required to be affixed to these items prior to sale?

Patents. A patent is issued to an inventor to provide protection from having the invention copied or stolen for a period of 20 years. Suppose that engineers working for Ford Motor Company discover a way to build an engine that requires half the parts of a regular engine and weighs only half as much. If Ford is successful in obtaining a patent on this discovery, it can (in principle) prevent others from copying it. The patent holder has a monopoly. It is the patent holder's responsibility to defend the patent, however. That means that Ford—like other patent owners—must expend resources to prevent others from imitating its invention. If the costs of enforcing a particular patent are greater than the benefits, though, the patent may not bestow any monopoly profits on its owner. The policing costs would be just too high.

Go to www.econtoday.com/ch25 to learn more about patents and trademarks from the U.S. Patent and Trademark Office and to learn all about copyrights from the U.S. Copyright Office.

Tariffs. **Tariffs** are special taxes that are imposed on certain imported goods. Tariffs make imports more expensive relative to their domestic counterparts, encouraging consumers to switch to the relatively cheaper domestically made products. If the tariffs are high enough, domestic producers gain monopoly advantage as the sole suppliers. Many countries have tried this protectionist strategy by using high tariffs to shut out foreign competitors.

Tariffs
Taxes on imported goods.

Regulations. Throughout the twentieth century and to the present, government regulation of the U.S. economy has increased, especially along the dimensions of safety and quality. For example, pharmaceutical quality-control regulations enforced by the Food and Drug Administration may require that each pharmaceutical company install a $200 million computerized testing system that requires elaborate monitoring and maintenance.

Presumably, this large fixed cost can be spread over a greater number of units of output by larger firms than by smaller firms, thereby putting the smaller firms at a competitive disadvantage. It will also deter entry to the extent that the scale of operation of a potential entrant must be sufficiently large to cover the average fixed costs of the required equipment. We examine regulation in more detail in Chapter 28.

Cartels

Cartel
An association of producers in an industry that agree to set common prices and output quotas to prevent competition.

Go to www.econtoday.com/ch25 to find out from WTRG Economics how effective the Organization of Petroleum Exporting Countries has been in acting as an oil market cartel.

"Being the only game in town" is preferable because such a monopoly position normally allows the monopolist to charge higher prices and make greater profits. Not surprisingly, manufacturers and sellers have frequently attempted to form an organization (which often is international) that acts as one. This is called a **cartel.** Cartels are an attempt by their members to earn higher-than-competitive profits. They set common prices and output quotas for their members. The key to the success of a cartel is keeping one member from competing against other members by expanding production and thereby lowering price.

Does it surprise you that cartels have even existed in university systems?

INTERNATIONAL EXAMPLE

Germany's Economics Cartel Breaks Down

Did you ever wonder how your economics professor became qualified to teach your course? If the professor earned a U.S. Ph.D., he or she completed challenging courses and passed difficult examinations. The professor also had to finish the toughest requirement of all: writing an approved dissertation.

In Germany, the Verein für Socialpolitik, the national economics association, long required people who wished to teach economics in German universities to write not just one, but *two* Ph.D. dissertations. Even after earning a Ph.D., however, an economist had to serve indefinitely under the tutelage of a *chaired professor*. A small group of chaired professors together had exclusive control over who could eventually advance into chaired positions. Naturally, agreeing to perpetuate this quota system for economics professors was a key qualification for advancement.

In recent years, however, many aspiring German economists have been pursuing their training in other countries. Rather than work as apprentices to chaired professors in Germany, Ph.D. holders now spend part of each year abroad, where they further develop their skills on their own and often become better qualified than people with chaired professorships. To improve the quality of teaching and research, German universities have been creating positions for many of these professors, over the objections of the existing group of chaired professors.

FOR CRITICAL ANALYSIS
What is likely to happen to the average salary of a chaired German economics professor as universities create additional economics professor positions?

QUICK QUIZ

A **monopolist** is the single seller of a product or good for which there is no _____ substitute.

To maintain a monopoly, there must be barriers to entry. Barriers to entry include _____ of resources without close substitutes; economies of _____; legally required licenses, franchises, and certificates of convenience; patents; tariffs; and safety and quality regulations.

See page 657 for the answers. Review concepts from this section in MyEconLab.

THE DEMAND CURVE A MONOPOLIST FACES

A *pure monopolist* is the sole supplier of *one* product, good, or service. A pure monopolist faces a demand curve that is the demand curve for the entire market for that good.

> *The monopolist faces the industry demand curve because the monopolist is the entire industry.*

Because the monopolist faces the industry demand curve, which is by definition downward sloping, its choice regarding how much to produce is not the same as for a perfect competitor. When a monopolist changes output, it does not automatically receive the same price per unit that it did before the change.

Profits to Be Made from Increasing Production

How do firms benefit from changing production rates? What happens to price in each case? Let's first review the situation among perfect competitors.

Marginal Revenue for the Perfect Competitor.

Recall that a perfectly competitive firm faces a perfectly elastic demand curve. That is because the perfectly competitive firm is such a small part of the market that it cannot influence the price of its product. It is a *price taker*. If the forces of supply and demand establish that the price per constant-quality pair of shoes is $50, the individual firm can sell all the pairs of shoes it wants to produce at $50 per pair. The average revenue is $50, the price is $50, and the marginal revenue is also $50.

Let us again define marginal revenue:

> *Marginal revenue equals the change in total revenue due to a one-unit change in the quantity produced and sold.*

In the case of a perfectly competitive industry, each time a single firm changes production by one unit, total revenue changes by the going price, and price is always the same. Marginal revenue never changes; it always equals price, or average revenue. Average revenue was defined as total revenue divided by quantity demanded, or

$$\text{Average revenue} = \frac{TR}{Q} = \frac{PQ}{Q} = P$$

Hence marginal revenue, average revenue, and price are all the same for the price-taking firm.

Marginal Revenue for the Monopolist.

What about a monopoly firm? We begin by considering a situation in which a monopolist charges every buyer the same price for each unit of its product. Because a monopoly is the entire industry, the monopoly firm's demand curve is the market demand curve. The market demand curve slopes downward, just like the other demand curves that we have seen. Therefore, to sell more of a particular product, given the industry demand curve, the monopoly firm must lower the price. Thus, the monopoly firm moves *down* the demand curve. If all buyers are to be charged the same price, the monopoly must lower the price on *all* units sold in order to sell more. It cannot lower the price on just the *last* unit sold in any given time period in order to sell a larger quantity.

Put yourself in the shoes of a monopoly ferryboat owner. You have a government-bestowed franchise, and no one can compete with you. Your ferryboat goes between two islands. If you are charging $1 per crossing, a certain quantity of your services will be demanded. Let's say that you are ferrying 100 people a day each way at that price. If you

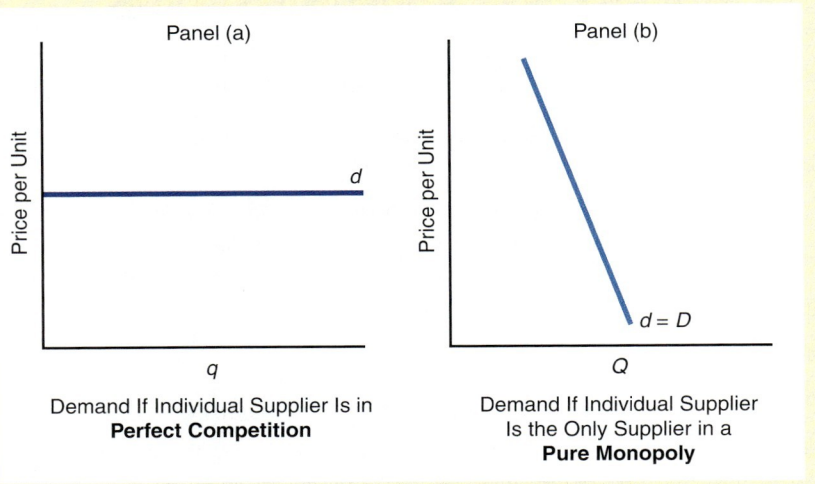

FIGURE 25-2

Demand Curves for the Perfect Competitor and the Monopolist

The perfect competitor in panel (a) faces a perfectly elastic demand curve, d. The monopolist in panel (b) faces the entire industry demand curve, which slopes downward.

decide that you would like to ferry more individuals, you must lower your price to all individuals—you must move *down* the existing demand curve for ferrying services. To calculate the marginal revenue of your change in price, you must first calculate the total revenues you received at $1 per passenger per crossing and then calculate the total revenues you would receive at, say, 90 cents per passenger per crossing.

Perfect Competition versus Monopoly. It is sometimes useful to compare monopoly markets with perfectly competitive markets. The monopolist is constrained by the demand curve for its product, just as a perfectly competitive firm is constrained by its demand. The key difference is the nature of the demand curve each type of firm faces. We see this in Figure 25-2, which compares the demand curves of the perfect competitor and the monopolist.

Here we see the fundamental difference between the monopolist and the perfect competitor. The perfect competitor doesn't have to worry about lowering price to sell more. In a purely competitive situation, the perfectly competitive firm accounts for such a small part of the market that it can sell its entire output, whatever that may be, at the same price. The monopolist cannot. The more the monopolist wants to sell, the lower the price it has to charge on the last unit (and on *all* units put on the market for sale). To sell the last unit, the monopolist has to lower the price because it is facing a downward-sloping demand curve, and the only way to move down the demand curve is to lower the price on all units. Consequently, the extra revenues the monopolist receives from selling one more unit are going to be smaller than the extra revenues received from selling the next-to-last unit.

The Monopolist's Marginal Revenue: Less Than Price

An essential point is that for the monopolist, marginal revenue is always less than price. To understand why, look at Figure 25-3, which shows a unit increase in output sold due to a reduction in the price of a commodity from P_1 to P_2. After all, the only way that the firm can sell more output, given a downward-sloping demand curve, is to reduce the price. Price P_2 is the price received for the last unit. Thus, if previous units sell at the price P_1, the price P_2 times the last unit sold represents revenues received from the last unit sold. That is equal to the vertical column (area A). Area A is one unit wide by P_2 high.

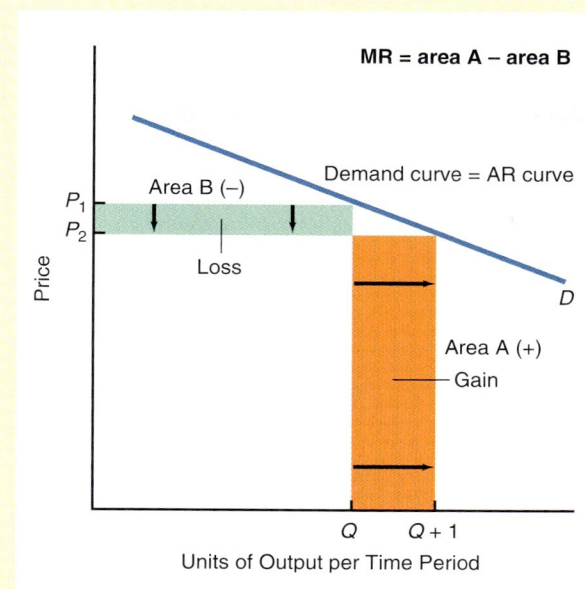

FIGURE 25-3
Marginal Revenue: Always Less Than Price
The price received for the last unit sold is equal to P_2. The revenues received from selling this last unit are equal to P_2 times one unit, or the area of the vertical column. However, if a single price is being charged for all units, total revenues do not go up by the amount of the area represented by that column. The price had to be reduced on all the previous Q units that were being sold at price P_1. Thus, we must subtract area B—the rectangle between P_1 and P_2 from the vertical axis to Q—from area A in order to derive marginal revenue. Marginal revenue is therefore always less than price.

But price times the last unit sold is *not* the addition to *total* revenues received from selling that last unit. Why? Because price had to be reduced on all previous units sold (Q) in order to sell the larger quantity $Q + 1$. The reduction in price is represented by the vertical distance from P_1 to P_2 on the vertical axis. We must therefore subtract area B from area A to come up with the *change* in total revenues due to a one-unit increase in sales. Clearly, the change in total revenues—that is, marginal revenue—must be less than price because marginal revenue is always the difference between areas A and B in Figure 25-3. For example, if the initial price is $8 and quantity demanded is 3, to increase quantity to 4 units, it is necessary to decrease price to $7, not just for the fourth unit, but on all three previous units as well. Thus, at a price of $7, marginal revenue is $7 − $3 = $4 because there is a $1 per unit price reduction on three previous units. Hence marginal revenue, $4, is less than price, $7.

ELASTICITY AND MONOPOLY

The monopolist faces a downward-sloping demand curve (its average revenue curve). That means that it cannot charge just *any* price with no changes in quantity (a common misconception) because, depending on the price charged, a different quantity will be demanded.

Earlier we defined a monopolist as the single seller of a well-defined good or service with no *close* substitute. This does not mean, however, that the demand curve for a monopoly is vertical or exhibits zero price elasticity of demand. (Indeed, as we shall see, the profit-maximizing monopolist will never operate in a price range in which demand is inelastic.) After all, consumers have limited incomes and unlimited wants. The downward slope of a monopolist's demand curve occurs because individuals compare the marginal satisfaction they will receive to the cost of the commodity to be purchased. Take the example of telephone service. Even if miraculously there were absolutely no substitutes whatsoever for telephone service, the market demand curve would still slope downward. At lower prices, people will add more phones and separate lines for different family members.

Furthermore, the demand curve for telephone service slopes downward because there are at least several *imperfect* substitutes, such as letters, e-mail, in-person conversations, and Internet telephony. Thus, even though we defined a monopolist as a single seller of a commodity with no *close* substitutes, we can talk about the range of *imperfect* substitutes. The more such imperfect substitutes there are, and the better these substitutes are, the more elastic will be the monopolist's demand curve, all other things held constant.

How have government officials operating airport security systems found ways to help finance these systems by taking into account the price elasticity of demand?

E-COMMERCE EXAMPLE

The Airport Security Monopoly and Demand Elasticity

In 2001, following the September terrorist attacks, federal law made the U.S. Department of Transportation the monopoly provider of security at all U.S. airports. The department toughened security precautions, which greatly slowed the process of passing through the labyrinth of airport security systems.

Recently, the Department of Transportation realized that it could profit from the fact that frequent fliers in a hurry to catch flights have a relatively low price elasticity of demand for speedy security screening. Under a new program in use at some of the busiest U.S. airports, travelers who pay an annual fee of $79.95 can register to receive a special card. Card ownership provides access to reserved parking and a special skycap service that picks up luggage at hotels for routing through security. Travelers holding these cards can use them at these airports to enter special security lanes, where they receive speedy fingerprint and iris scans. After computers verify that these scans match those provided when the travelers obtained their cards, security personnel usher the cardholders to their flights.

FOR CRITICAL ANALYSIS
Why do operators of theme parks, such as Universal Studios in Florida, profit from selling low-priced tickets to people willing to wait in long lines to attractions and higher-priced tickets to people desiring to jump ahead of lines?

QUICK QUIZ

The monopolist estimates its marginal revenue curve, where marginal revenue is defined as the _____ in _____ revenues due to a one-unit change in quantity sold.

For the perfect competitor, price equals _____ revenue equals average revenue. For the monopolist, _____ revenue is always less than price because price must be reduced on all units to sell more.

The price _____ of demand for the monopolist depends on the number and similarity of substitutes. The more numerous and more similar the substitutes, the greater the price _____ of demand of the monopolist's demand curve.

See page 657 for the answers. Review concepts from this section in MyEconLab.

COSTS AND MONOPOLY PROFIT MAXIMIZATION

To find out the rate of output at which the perfect competitor would maximize profits, we had to add cost data. We will do the same thing now for the monopolist. We assume that profit maximization is the goal of the pure monopolist, just as it is for the perfect competitor. The perfect competitor, however, has only to decide on the profit-maximizing rate of output because price is given. The perfect competitor is a price taker. For the pure monopolist, we must seek a profit-maximizing *price-output combination* because the monopolist is a **price searcher.** We can determine this profit-maximizing price-output combination with either of two equivalent approaches—by looking at total revenues and total costs or by looking at marginal revenues and marginal costs. We shall examine both approaches.

Price searcher
A firm that must determine the price-output combination that maximizes profit because it faces a downward-sloping demand curve.

The Total Revenues–Total Costs Approach

Suppose that the government of a small town located in a remote desert area grants a single satellite television company the right to offer services within its jurisdiction. It enforces rules that prevent other cable companies and other firms from offering television services. We show demand (daily rate of output and price per unit), revenues, costs, and other data in panel (a) of Figure 25-4 on the next page. In column 3, we see total revenues for this TV service monopolist, and in column 4, we see total costs. We can transfer these two columns to panel (b). The fundamental difference between the total revenue and total cost diagram in panel (b) and the one we showed for a perfect competitor in Chapter 24 is that the total revenue line is no longer straight. Rather, it curves. For any given demand curve, in order to sell more, the monopolist must lower the price. Thus, the basic difference between a monopolist and a perfect competitor has to do with the demand curve for the two types of firms. The monopolist faces a downward-sloping demand curve.

Profit maximization involves maximizing the positive difference between total revenues and total costs. This occurs at an output rate of between 9 and 10 units per day.

The Marginal Revenue–Marginal Cost Approach

Profit maximization will also occur where marginal revenue equals marginal cost. This is as true for a monopolist as it is for a perfect competitor (but the monopolist will charge a price in excess of marginal revenue). When we transfer marginal cost and marginal revenue information from columns 6 and 7 in panel (a) of Figure 25-4 to panel (c), we see that marginal revenue equals marginal cost at a daily quantity of satellite TV services of between 9 and 10 units. Profit maximization occurs at the same output as in panel (b).

Why Produce Where Marginal Revenue Equals Marginal Cost?
If the monopolist goes past the point where marginal revenue equals marginal cost, marginal cost will exceed marginal revenue. That is, the incremental cost of producing any more units will exceed the incremental revenue. It just would not be worthwhile, as was true also in perfect competition. Furthermore, just as in the case of perfect competition, if the monopolist produces less than that, it is also not making maximum profits. Look at output rate Q_1 in Figure 25-5 on page 645. Here the monopolist's marginal revenue is at A, but marginal cost is at B. Marginal revenue exceeds marginal cost on the last unit sold; the profit for that *particular* unit, Q_1, is equal to the vertical difference between A and B, or the difference between marginal revenue and marginal cost. The monopolist would be foolish to stop at output rate Q_1 because if output is expanded, marginal revenue will still exceed marginal cost, and therefore total profits will rise. In fact, the profit-maximizing monopolist will continue to expand output and sales until marginal revenue equals marginal cost, which is at output rate Q_m. The monopolist won't produce at rate Q_2 because here, as we see, marginal costs are C and marginal revenues are F. The difference between C and F represents the *reduction* in total profits from producing that additional unit. Total profits will rise as the monopolist reduces its rate of output back toward Q_m.

FIGURE 25-4
Monopoly Costs, Revenues, and Profits

In panel (a), we give demand (daily satellite television services and price), revenues, costs, and other relevant data. As shown in panel (b), the satellite TV monopolist maximizes profits where the positive difference between TR and TC is greatest. This is at an output rate of between 9 and 10 units per day. Put another way, profit maximization occurs where marginal revenue equals marginal cost, as shown in panel (c). This is at the same daily service rate of between 9 and 10 units. (The MC curve must cut the MR curve from below.)

Panel (a)

(1) Output (units)	(2) Price per Unit	(3) Total Revenues (TR) (3) = (2) × (1)	(4) Total Costs (TC)	(5) Total Profit (5) = (3) − (4)	(6) Marginal Cost (MC)	(7) Marginal Revenue (MR)
0	$8.00	$ .00	$10.00	−$10.00		
					$4.00	$7.80
1	7.80	7.80	14.00	−6.20		
					3.50	7.40
2	7.60	15.20	17.50	−2.30		
					3.25	7.00
3	7.40	22.20	20.75	1.45		
					3.05	6.60
4	7.20	28.80	23.80	5.00		
					2.90	6.20
5	7.00	35.00	26.70	8.30		
					2.80	5.80
6	6.80	40.80	29.50	11.30		
					2.75	5.40
7	6.60	46.20	32.25	13.95		
					2.85	5.00
8	6.40	51.20	35.10	16.10		
					3.20	4.60
9	6.20	55.80	38.30	17.50		
					4.40	4.20
10	6.00	60.00	42.70	17.30		
					6.00	3.80
11	5.80	63.80	48.70	15.10		
					9.00	3.40
12	5.60	67.20	57.70	9.50		

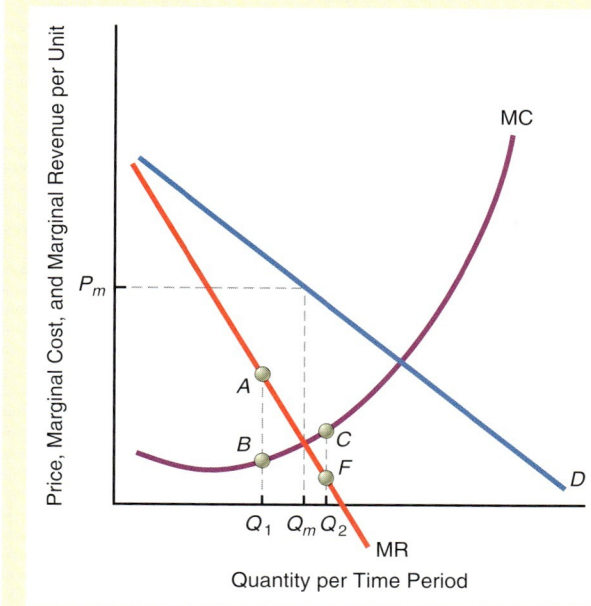

FIGURE 25-5

Maximizing Profits

The profit-maximizing production rate is Q_m, and the profit-maximizing price is P_m. The monopolist would be unwise to produce at the rate Q_1 because here marginal revenue would be $Q_1 A$, and marginal cost would be $Q_1 B$. Marginal revenue would exceed marginal cost. The firm will keep producing until the point Q_m, where marginal revenue just equals marginal cost. It would be foolish to produce at the rate Q_2, for here marginal cost exceeds marginal revenue. It would behoove the monopolist to cut production back to Q_m.

What Price to Charge for Output?

How does the monopolist set prices? We know the quantity is set at the point at which marginal revenue equals marginal cost. The monopolist then finds out how much can be charged—how much the market will bear—for that particular quantity, Q_m, in Figure 25-5.

The Monopoly Price.
We know that the demand curve is defined as showing the *maximum* price for which a given quantity can be sold. That means that our monopolist knows that to sell Q_m, it can charge only P_m because that is the price at which that specific quantity, Q_m, is demanded. This price is found by drawing a vertical line from the quantity, Q_m, to the market demand curve. Where that line hits the market demand curve, the price is determined. We find that price by drawing a horizontal line from the demand curve over to the price axis; that gives us the profit-maximizing price, P_m.

In our detailed numerical example, at a profit-maximizing quantity of satellite TV services of between 9 and 10 units in Figure 25-4, the firm can charge a maximum price of about $6 and still sell all the satellite TV services it provides, all at the same price.

The basic procedure for finding the profit-maximizing short-run price-quantity combination for the monopolist is first to determine the profit-maximizing rate of output, by either the total revenue–total cost method or the marginal revenue–marginal cost method, and then to determine by use of the demand curve, D, the maximum price that can be charged to sell that output.

Real-World Informational Limitations.
Don't get the impression that just because we are able to draw an exact demand curve in Figures 25-4 and 25-5, real-world monopolists have such perfect information. The process of price searching by a less-than-perfect competitor is just that—a process. A monopolist can only estimate the actual demand curve and therefore can only make an educated guess when it sets its profit-maximizing price. This is not a problem for the perfect competitor because price is given already by the

intersection of market demand and market supply. The monopolist, in contrast, reaches the profit-maximizing output-price combination by trial and error.

How does the city of Shanghai, China, determine the prices of the very limited stock of auto license plates that it issues?

INTERNATIONAL POLICY EXAMPLE

Forcing People to Reveal How Much They Are Willing to Pay

Shanghai is a bustling city of more than 16 million people that is growing rapidly. Nevertheless, the city government strictly limits the number of available auto license plates according to a mathematical formula that takes into account the number of recently scrapped cars and recent auto sales. In a typical year, this means that only 6,000 license plates will be available for purchase, even though at least 20,000 people would like to obtain plates. To determine how much people are willing to pay for the restricted number of plates, the government conducts an auction. Those willing to pay the most for a license plate—often amounts exceeding the equivalent of $4,000—obtain the right to drive. In this way, Shanghai's government seeks to obtain economic profits from its control over license plates.

FOR CRITICAL ANALYSIS
Why do you suppose that many Chinese cities require drivers to relinquish their license plates after a certain time period so that the government can auction the plates off once again?

CALCULATING MONOPOLY PROFIT

We have talked about the monopolist's profit. We have yet to indicate how much profit the monopolist makes.

The Graphical Depiction of Monopoly Profits

We have actually shown total profits in column 5 of panel (a) in Figure 25-4 on page 644. We can also find total profits by adding an average total cost curve to panel (c) of that figure. We do that in Figure 25-6. When we add the average total cost curve, we find that the profit that a monopolist makes is equal to the shaded area—or total revenues ($P \times Q$) minus total costs ($ATC \times Q$). Given the demand curve and a uniform pricing system (that is, all units sold at the same price), there is no way for a monopolist to make greater profits than those shown by the shaded area. The monopolist is maximizing profits where marginal cost equals marginal revenue. If the monopolist produces less than that, it will be forfeiting some profits. If the monopolist produces more than that, it will also be forfeiting some profits.

The same is true of a perfect competitor. The perfect competitor produces where marginal revenues equal marginal costs because it produces at the point where the marginal cost curve intersects the perfectly elastic firm demand curve. The perfectly elastic firm demand curve represents the marginal revenue curve for the pure competitor, because the same average revenues are obtained on all the units sold. Perfect competitors maximize profits at $MR = MC$, as do pure monopolists. But the last perfect competitor remaining in the market in the long run makes no true economic profits. Instead, it earns a normal, competitive rate of return.

FIGURE 25-6

Monopoly Profit

We find monopoly profit by subtracting total costs from total revenues at a quantity of satellite TV services of between 9 and 10 units, labeled Q_m, which is the profit-maximizing rate of output for the satellite TV monopolist. The profit-maximizing price is therefore about $6 and is labeled P_m. Monopoly profit is given by the shaded area, which is equal to total revenues ($P \times Q$) minus total costs (ATC $\times Q$). This diagram is similar to panel (c) of Figure 25-4 on page 644, with the short-run average total cost curve (ATC) added.

In Chapter 24, we talked about companies experiencing short-run economic profits because they had, for example, invented something new. Competition, though, gradually eroded those higher-than-normal profits. The fact that a firm experiences higher-than-normal profits today does not mean that it will have a monopoly forever. Try as companies may, keeping competitors away is never easy.

No Guarantee of Profits

The term *monopoly* conjures up the notion of a greedy firm ripping off the public and making exorbitant profits. The mere existence of a monopoly, however, does not guarantee high profits. Numerous monopolies have gone bankrupt. Figure 25-7 on the next page shows the monopolist's demand curve as *D* and the resultant marginal revenue curve as MR. It does not matter at what rate of output this particular monopolist operates; total costs cannot be covered. Look at the position of the average total cost curve. It lies everywhere above *D* (the average revenue curve). Thus, there is no price-output combination that will allow the monopolist even to cover costs, much less earn profits. This monopolist will, in the short run, suffer economic losses as shown by the shaded area. The graph in Figure 25-7, which applies to many inventions, depicts a situation of resulting monopoly. The owner of a patented invention or discovery has a pure legal monopoly, but the demand and cost curves are such that production is not profitable. Every year at inventors' conventions, one can see many inventions that have never been put into production because they were deemed "uneconomic" by potential producers and users.

FIGURE 25-7

Monopolies: Not Always Profitable

Some monopolists face the situation shown here. The average total cost curve, ATC, is everywhere above the average revenue, or demand, curve, D. In the short run, the monopolist will produce where MC = MR at point A. Output Q_m will be sold at price P_m, but average total cost per unit is C_1. Losses are the shaded rectangle. Eventually, the monopolist will go out of business.

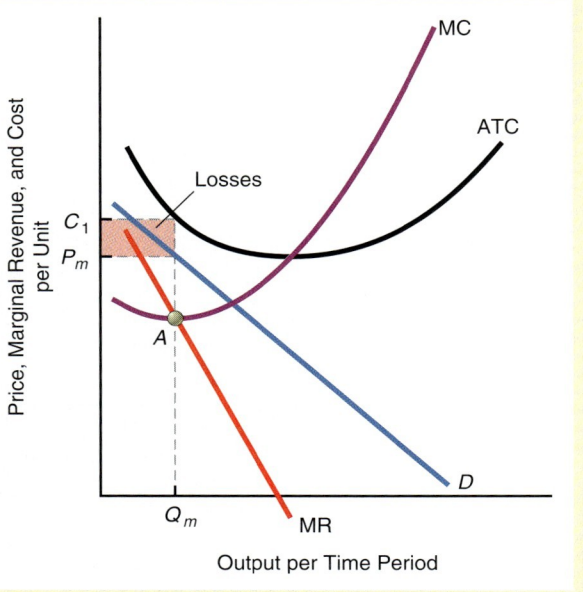

QUICK QUIZ

The basic difference between a monopolist and a perfect competitor is that a monopolist faces a(n) _____-sloping demand curve, and therefore marginal revenue is _____ than price.

The monopolist must choose the profit-maximizing price-output combination—the output at which _____ revenue equals _____ cost and the highest price possible as given by the _____ curve for that particular output rate.

Monopoly profits are found by looking at average _____ costs compared to price per unit. This difference multiplied by _____ sold at that price determines monopoly profit.

A monopolist does not necessarily earn a profit. If the average _____ cost curve lies entirely _____ the demand curve for a monopoly, no production rate will be profitable.

See page 657 for the answers. Review concepts from this section in MyEconLab.

ON MAKING HIGHER PROFITS: PRICE DISCRIMINATION

In a perfectly competitive market, each buyer is charged the same price for every unit of the particular commodity (corrected for differential transportation charges). Because the product is homogeneous and we also assume full knowledge on the part of the buyers, a difference in price cannot exist. Any seller of the product who tried to charge a price higher than the going market price would find that no one would purchase it from that seller.

In this chapter, we have assumed until now that the monopolist charged all consumers the same price for all units. A monopolist, however, may be able to charge different people different prices or different unit prices for successive units sought by a given buyer. When there is no cost difference, such strategies are called **price discrimination.** A firm will engage in price discrimination whenever feasible to increase profits. A price-discriminating firm is able to charge some customers more than other customers.

Price discrimination
Selling a given product at more than one price, with the price difference being unrelated to differences in marginal cost.

It must be made clear at the outset that charging different prices to different people or for different units to reflect differences in the cost of service does not amount to price discrimination. This is **price differentiation:** differences in price that reflect differences in marginal cost.

We can also say that a uniform price does not necessarily indicate an absence of price discrimination. Charging all customers the same price when production costs vary by customer is actually a case of price discrimination.

Price differentiation
Establishing different prices for similar products to reflect differences in marginal cost in providing those commodities to different groups of buyers.

Necessary Conditions for Price Discrimination

Three conditions are necessary for price discrimination to exist:

1. The firm must face a downward-sloping demand curve.
2. The firm must be able to readily (and cheaply) identify buyers or groups of buyers with predictably different elasticities of demand.
3. The firm must be able to prevent resale of the product or service.

Has it ever occurred to you that most of the other students seated in your college classroom pay different overall tuition rates than you do because your college and others use financial aid packages to engage in price discrimination?

EXAMPLE

Why Students Pay Different Prices to Attend College

Out-of-pocket tuition rates for any two college students can differ by considerable amounts, even if the students happen to major in the same subjects and enroll in many of the same courses. The reason is that colleges offer students diverse financial aid packages depending on their "financial need."

To document their "need" for financial aid, students must provide detailed information about family income and wealth. This information, of course, helps the college determine the prices that different families are most likely to be willing and able to pay, so that it can engage in price discrimination. Figure 25-8 shows how this collegiate price-discrimination process works. Colleges charge the price P_7, which is the college's official posted "tuition rate," to students with families judged to be most willing and able to pay

FIGURE 25-8
Toward Perfect Price Discrimination in College Tuition Rates

Students that a college determines to be "neediest" and least able to pay the full tuition price, P_7, receive a financial aid package equal to $P_7 - P_1$. These students effectively pay only the price P_1. The college groups the remaining students into categories on the basis of their willingness and ability to pay a higher price, and each group receives a progressively smaller financial aid package. Those students who are willing and able to pay the full price, P_7, receive no financial aid from the college.

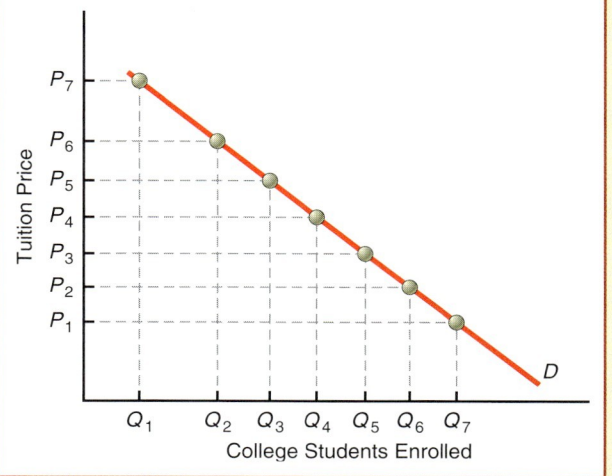

(continued)

the highest price. Students whose families have the lowest levels of income and wealth are judged to be willing and able to pay a much lower price, such as P_1. To charge these students this lower tuition rate, the college provides them with a financial aid package that reduces the price they pay by the difference between P_7, the full tuition price, and P_1. In this way, the actual price paid by these "neediest" students is only P_1.

Likewise, the college groups other, somewhat less "needy" students into a slightly higher income-and-wealth category and determines that they are likely to be willing to pay a somewhat higher price, P_2. Hence it grants them a smaller financial aid package, equal to $P_7 - P_2$, so that the students actually pay the price P_2. The college continues this process for other groups, thereby engaging in price discrimination in its tuition charges.

FOR CRITICAL ANALYSIS
Does the educational product supplied by colleges satisfy all three conditions necessary for price discrimination?

THE SOCIAL COST OF MONOPOLIES

Let's run a little experiment. We will start with a purely competitive industry with numerous firms, each one unable to affect the price of its product. The supply curve of the industry is equal to the horizontal sum of the marginal cost curves of the individual producers above their respective minimum average variable costs. In panel (a) of Figure 25-9, we show the market demand curve and the market supply curve in a perfectly competitive

FIGURE 25-9

The Effects of Monopolizing an Industry
In panel (a), we show a perfectly competitive situation in which equilibrium is established at the intersection of D and S at point E. The equilibrium price is P_e and the equilibrium quantity is Q_e. Each individual perfectly competitive producer faces a demand curve that is perfectly elastic at the market clearing price, P_e. What happens if the industry is suddenly monopolized? We assume that the costs stay the same; the only thing that changes is that the monopolist now faces the entire downward-sloping demand curve. In panel (b), we draw the marginal revenue curve. Marginal cost is S because that is the horizontal summation of all the individual marginal cost curves. The monopolist therefore produces at Q_m and charges price P_m. This price P_m in panel (b) is higher than P_e in panel (a), and Q_m is less than Q_e.

situation. The perfectly competitive price in equilibrium is equal to P_e, and the equilibrium quantity at that price is equal to Q_e. Each individual perfect competitor faces a demand curve (not shown) that is coincident with the price line P_e. No individual supplier faces the market demand curve, D.

Comparing Monopoly with Perfect Competition

Now let's assume that a monopolist comes in and buys up every single perfect competitor in the industry. In so doing, we'll assume that monopolization does not affect any of the marginal cost curves or demand. We can therefore redraw D and S in panel (b) of Figure 25-9, exactly the same as in panel (a).

How does this monopolist decide how much to charge and how much to produce? If the monopolist is profit maximizing, it is going to look at the marginal revenue curve and produce at the output where marginal revenue equals marginal cost. But what is the marginal cost curve in panel (b) of Figure 25-9? It is merely S, because we said that S was equal to the horizontal summation of the portions of the individual marginal cost curves above each firm's respective minimum average variable cost. The monopolist therefore produces quantity Q_m, and sells it at price P_m. Notice that Q_m is less than Q_e and that P_m is greater than P_e. A monopolist therefore produces a smaller quantity and sells it at a higher price. This is the reason usually given when economists criticize monopolists. Monopolists raise the price and restrict production, compared to a perfectly competitive situation. For a monopolist's product, consumers pay a price that exceeds the marginal cost of production. Resources are misallocated in such a situation—too few resources are being used in the monopolist's industry, and too many are used elsewhere. (See Appendix F.)

Implications of Higher Monopoly Prices

Notice from Figure 25-9 that by setting MR = MC, the monopolist produces at a rate of output where $P >$ MC (compare P_m to MC_m). The marginal cost of a commodity (MC) represents what society had to give up in order to obtain the last unit produced. Price, by contrast, represents what buyers are willing to pay to acquire that last unit. Thus, the price of a good represents society's valuation of the last unit produced. The monopoly outcome of $P >$ MC means that the value to society of the last unit produced is greater than its cost (MC); hence not enough of the good is being produced. As we have pointed out before, these differences between monopoly and perfect competition arise not because of differences in costs but rather because of differences in the demand curves the individual firms face. The monopolist faces a downward-sloping demand curve. The individual perfect competitor faces a perfectly elastic demand curve.

Before we leave the topic of the cost to society of monopolies, we must repeat that our analysis is based on a heroic assumption. That assumption is that the monopolization of the perfectly competitive industry does not change the cost structure. If monopolization results in higher marginal cost, the net cost of monopoly to society is even greater.

Conversely, if monopolization results in cost savings, the net cost of monopoly to society is less than we infer from our analysis. Indeed, we could have presented a hypothetical example in which monopolization led to such a dramatic reduction in cost that society actually benefited. Such a situation is a possibility in industries in which economies of scale exist for a very great range of outputs.

QUICK QUIZ

Three conditions are necessary for price discrimination: (1) The firm must face a(n) _____-sloping demand curve, (2) the firm must be able to identify buyers with predictably different price _____ of demand, and (3) _____ of the product or service must be preventable.

Price _____ should not be confused with price _____, which occurs when differences in price reflect differences in marginal cost.

Monopoly tends to result in a _____ quantity being sold, because the price is _____ than it would be in an ideal perfectly competitive industry in which the cost curves were essentially the same as the monopolist's.

See page 657 for the answers. Review concepts from this section in MyEconLab.

CASE STUDY: ECONOMICS FRONT AND CENTER

Entry Barriers in the Diamond Industry: Cracking or Crystallizing?

Olmonsky operates a Russian diamond mining and distributing company based in St. Petersburg. For years, she labored in the shadow of the De Beers Diamond Cartel, the world's primary supplier of so-called true-gem diamonds. Even though the world knows that De Beers diamonds come from South Africa, Namibia, and Botswana, the cartel went to great lengths to keep secret the exact locations from which it obtained its best diamonds. The cartel also etched onto the surface of every diamond an identifying serial number, invisible to the human eye but detectable by special instruments, so that it could track each diamond until it was ultimately sold at the cartel price. To ensure that it could charge the price consistent with maximum monopoly profits, the cartel often restricted sales of true-gem diamonds.

Now, however, Olmonsky has her own source of high-quality, true-gem diamonds in the Ural Mountains. Hers is not the only firm offering true-gem diamonds to buyers around the world. Other firms in Russia, as well as companies based in Canada and Australia, are now competing with De Beers, whose share of world diamond production has dropped from 80 percent in the late 1990s to just above 40 percent today.

Nevertheless, the Russian government has recently reached an agreement with De Beers to require all legally licensed producers of true-gem diamonds in Russia to market their output through the De Beers distribution system. This will push the share of true-gem diamond sales that go through the De Beers network up to 55 percent. It will also force Olmonsky to deal with the cartel she has long sought to break.

CRITICAL ANALYSIS QUESTIONS

1. *In years past, what was the main global barrier to entry into the true-gem diamond industry?*

2. *In Russia, what is now the main barrier to entry into the true-gem diamond industry? (Hint: What entity is now determining how firms distribute their diamonds?)*

Issues and Applications

For This Monopoly, Location Is the Key

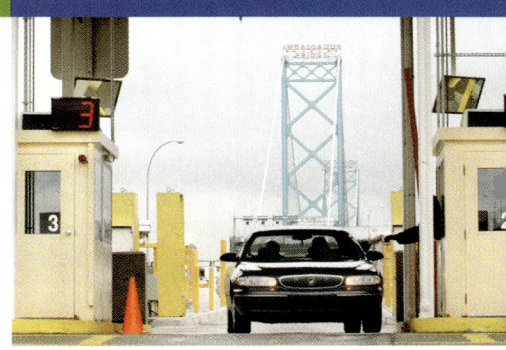

The border between the lower 48 U.S. states and Canada stretches for 5,500 miles. Nevertheless, 40 percent of all U.S. truck shipments to points north cross at a single location between Detroit, Michigan, and Windsor, Ontario. This location is the Ambassador Bridge, which spans the Detroit River. The bridge is 47 feet wide and almost a mile long. It is also the primary asset of private companies that in turn are owned by a firm called Cen Tra, which earns considerable profits as a monopolist.

Concepts Applied
- Monopolist
- Ownership of a Resource Without Close Substitutes
- Price Searcher

A Resource with *Literally* Few *Close* Substitutes

The Ambassador Bridge faces little competition for traffic because the closest bridge linking the Detroit and Windsor manufacturing centers is more than two hours out of the way for truck traffic.

In 1929, a private company built the Ambassador Bridge at the single best crossing point along the Detroit River. Development along the riverfront since its construction has hindered efforts to build additional bridges or tunnels in the vicinity. Consequently, Cen Tra owns a resource for which there are few close substitutes at this time.

Price Searches That Have Boosted Profits

Price searching for the profit-maximizing toll rates by Cen Tra since the 1980s has resulted in cumulative, inflation-adjusted increases of 25 percent in toll rates for the 3.3 million trucks that cross the bridge each year. Inflation-adjusted toll charges for automobiles have increased by almost 150 percent during the period.

Estimates indicate that the bridge generates total revenues in excess of $60 million per year and that its market value is in excess of half a billion dollars.

Log in to MyEconLab, click on "Economic News," and test your understanding of the chapter by answering interactive questions that relate directly to this issue.

For Critical Analysis

1. Other things being equal, what will happen to the profit-maximizing toll rates for trucks and autos traversing the Ambassador Bridge if the demand for cross-border traffic increases during the next few years?
2. Toughened security requirements at all U.S.-Canadian border crossings have required Cen Tra to spend more on security each week. How has this likely affected the fees it charges cars and trucks to cross the Ambassador Bridge? Why?

653

654 PART VI *Market Structure, Resource Allocation, and Regulation*

Web Resources

1. To learn about how a private company came to own the Ambassador Bridge, go to www.econtoday.com/ch25.
2. To consider the status of the Ambassador Bridge today, its home page is available at www.econtoday.com/ch25.

Research Project

Recently, a formal proposal was filed to construct a new tunnel connecting Detroit and Windsor under the Detroit River. Explain what is most likely to happen to each of the following at the Ambassador Bridge: demand for truck and auto passage, profit-maximizing price, total revenues, and maximum profits.

Here is what you should know after reading this chapter. MyEconLab will help you identify what you know, and where to go when you need to practice.

WHAT YOU SHOULD KNOW		WHERE TO GO TO PRACTICE
Why Monopoly Can Occur Monopoly, a situation in which a single firm produces and sells a good or service that has no close substitute, can occur when there are significant barriers to market entry by other firms. Examples of barriers to entry include (1) ownership of important resources for which there are no close substitutes, (2) economies of scale for ever-larger ranges of output, or natural monopoly conditions, (3) legal or governmental restrictions, and (4) associations of producers called cartels that work together to stifle competition.	monopolist, 634 natural monopoly, 635 tariffs, 637 cartel, 638	• **MyEconLab** Study Plans 25.1 and 25.2 • Audio introduction to Chapter 25 • Video: Barriers to Entry
Demand and Marginal Revenue Conditions a Monopolist Faces Because a monopolist constitutes the entire industry, it faces the entire market demand curve. When it reduces the price of its product, it is able to sell more units at the new price, which pushes up its revenues, but it also sells other units at this lower price, which pushes its revenues down somewhat. For this reason, the monopolist's marginal revenue at any given quantity is less than the price at which it sells that quantity of output. Hence the monopolist's marginal revenue curve slopes downward and lies below the demand curve it faces.	**Key figure** Figure 25-3, 641	• **MyEconLab** Study Plans 25.3 and 25.4 • Video: The Demand Curve Facing a Monopoly Is Not Vertical • Animated Figure 25-3
How a Monopolist Determines How Much Output to Produce and What Price to Charge A monopolist is a price searcher, meaning that it seeks to charge the price consistent with the production level that maximizes its economic profits. It maximizes its profits by producing to the point at which marginal revenue equals marginal cost. The monopolist then charges the maximum price for this amount of output, which is the price that consumers are willing to pay for that quantity of output.	price searcher, 643 **Key figure** Figure 25-4, 644	• **MyEconLab** Study Plan 25.5 • Animated Figure 25-4

WHAT YOU SHOULD KNOW		WHERE TO GO TO PRACTICE
A Monopolist's Profits The amount of profit earned by a monopolist is equal to the difference between the price it charges and its average production cost times the amount of output it produces and sells. At the profit-maximizing output rate, the monopolist's price is at the point on the demand curve corresponding to this output rate, and its average total cost of producing this output rate is at the corresponding point on the monopolist's average total cost curve. A monopolist commonly earns positive economic profits, but situations can arise in which average total cost exceeds the profit-maximizing price, yielding negative profits.	**Key figures** Figure 25-6, 647 Figure 25-7, 648	• **MyEconLab** Study Plan 25.6 • Animated Figures 25-6 and 25-7
Price Discrimination If a monopolist engages in price discrimination, it sells its product at more than one price, with the price difference being unrelated to differences in production costs. To be able to engage successfully in price discrimination, a monopolist must be able to identify and separate buyers with different price elasticities of demand. This allows the monopolist to sell some of its output at higher prices to consumers with less elastic demand. Even then, however, the monopolist must be able to prevent resale of its product by those with more elastic demand to those with less elastic demand.	price discrimination, 648 price differentiation, 649	• **MyEconLab** Study Plan 25.7 • Video: Price Discrimination
Social Cost of Monopolies Because a monopoly is a price searcher, it is able to charge the highest price that people are willing to pay for the amount of output it produces. This price exceeds the marginal cost of producing the output. In addition, if the monopolist's marginal cost curve corresponds to the sum of the marginal cost curves for the number of firms that would exist if the industry were perfectly competitive instead, then the monopolist produces and sells less output than perfectly competitive firms would have produced and sold.	**Key figure** Figure 25-9, 650	• **MyEconLab** Study Plan 25.8 • Animated Figure 25-9

Log in to MyEconLab, take a chapter test, and get a personalized Study Plan that tells you which concepts you understand and which ones you need to review. From there, MyEconLab will give you futher practice, tutorials, animations, videos, and guided solutions.

Log in to www.myeconlab.com

PROBLEMS

Select problems, indicated by a blue oval ●, are assignable in MyEconLab. Answers to the odd-numbered problems appear at the back of the book.

25-1 Suppose that it is the year 2038. Exclusive ownership of a resource found to be required for the production of fusion power has given a firm monopoly power in the provision of this good. What is true of the relationship between the price of this resource and the marginal revenue the firm receives?

25-2. Consider the resource owner and seller discussed in Problem 25-1. Discuss what would have been true of the price elasticity of demand if this firm had been a perfectly competitive seller of this resource. Contrast this with the price elasticity of demand for this firm in its actual role as monopoly provider. Explain why the price elasticities in the two situations are different.

25-3 The following table depicts the daily output, price, and costs of a monopoly dry cleaner located near the campus of a remote college town.

   a. Compute revenues and profits at each output rate.
   b. What is the profit-maximizing rate of output?

Output (suits cleaned)	Price per Suit ($)	Total Costs ($)
0	8.00	3.00
1	7.50	6.00
2	7.00	8.50
3	6.50	10.50
4	6.00	11.50
5	5.50	13.50
6	5.00	16.00
7	4.50	19.00
8	4.00	24.00

25-4 Given the information in Problem 25-3, calculate the dry cleaner's marginal revenue and marginal cost at each output level. Based on marginal analysis, what is the profit-maximizing level of output?

25-5. A manager of a monopoly firm notices that the firm is producing output at a rate at which average total cost is falling but is not at its minimum feasible point. The manager argues that surely the firm must not be maximizing its economic profits. Is this argument correct?

25-6 Use the graph to answer the following questions.

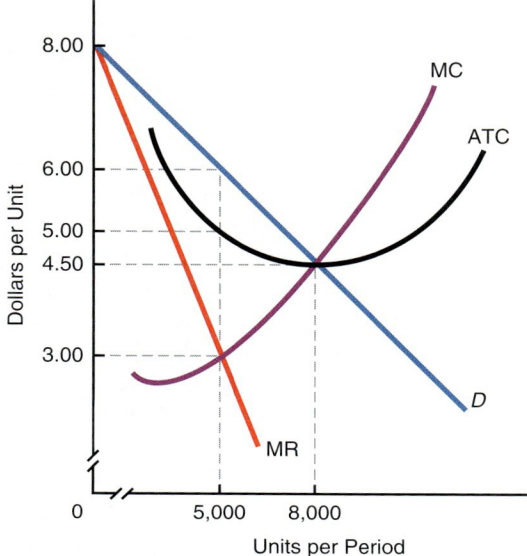

   a. What is the monopolist's profit-maximizing output?
   b. At the profit-maximizing output rate, what are average total cost and average revenue?
   c. At the profit-maximizing output rate, what are the monopolist's total cost and total revenue?
   d. What is the maximum profit?

25-7. Using the diagram for Problem 25-6, suppose that the marginal cost and average total cost curves also illustrate the horizontal summation of the firms in a perfectly competitive industry in the long run. What would the equilibrium price and output be if the market were perfectly competitive? Explain the economic cost to society of allowing a monopoly to exist.

25-8 The marginal revenue curve of a monopoly crosses its marginal cost curve at $30 per unit, and an output of 2 million units. The price that consumers are willing to pay for this output is $40 per unit. If it produces this output, the firm's average total cost is $43 per unit, and its average fixed cost is $8 per unit. What is the profit-maximizing (loss-minimizing) output? What are the firm's economic profits (or economic losses)?

25-9 Consider the revenue and cost conditions for a monopolist that are depicted in the figure below.

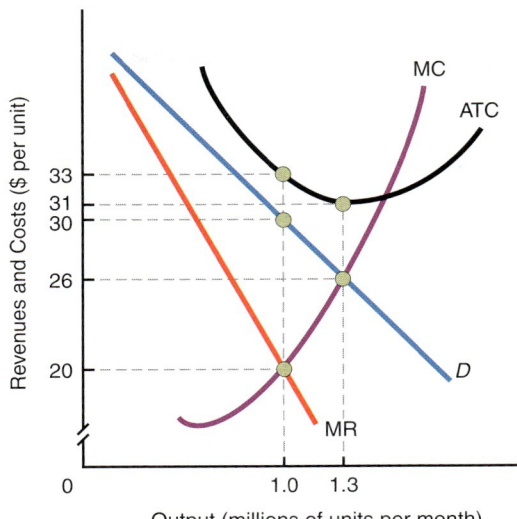

a. What is this producer's profit-maximizing (or loss-minimizing) output?
b. What are the firm's economic profits (or losses)?

25-10 For each of the following examples, explain how and why a monopoly would try to price discriminate.

a. Air transport for businesspeople and tourists
b. Serving food on weekdays to businesspeople and retired people. (Hint: Which group has more flexibility during a weekday to adjust to a price change and, hence, a higher price elasticity of demand?)
c. A theater that shows the same movie to large families and to individuals and couples. (Hint: For which set of people will the overall expense of a movie be a larger part of their budget, so that demand is more elastic?)

25-11 A monopolist's revenues vary directly with price. Is it maximizing its economic profits? Why or why not? (Hint: Recall that the relationship between revenues and price depends on price elasticity of demand.)

25-12. A new competitor enters the industry and competes with a second firm, which had been a monopolist. The second firm finds that although demand is not perfectly elastic, it is now relatively more elastic. What will happen to the second firm's marginal revenue curve and to its profit-maximizing price?

25-13 A monopolist's marginal cost curve has shifted upward. What is likely to happen to the monopolist's price, output rate, and economic profits?

25-14 Demand has fallen. What is likely to happen to the monopolist's price, output rate, and economic profits?

ECONOMICS ON THE NET

Patents, Trademarks, and Intellectual Property This Internet application explores a firm's view on legal protections.

Title: Intellectual Property

Navigation: Follow the link at www.econtoday.com/ch25 to the GlaxoSmithKline Web site. Select *Investors,* then *Reports.* View the PDF of Annual Report 2005. Scroll down to Intellectual Property (page 25).

Application Read the statement and table; then answer the following questions.

1. What are the differences between patents, trademarks, and registered designs and copyrights?

2. What are GlaxoSmithKline's intellectual property goals? Do patents or trademarks seem to be more important?

For Group Discussion and Analysis In 1969, GlaxoSmithKline developed Ventolin, a treatment for asthma symptoms. Though the patent and trademark have long expired, the company still retains over a third of the market in this treatment. Explain, in economic terms, the source of GlaxoSmithKline's strength in this area. Discuss whether patents and trademarks are beneficial for the development and discovery of new treatments.

ANSWERS TO QUICK QUIZZES

p. 638: (i) close; (ii) ownership . . . scale
p. 642: (i) change . . . total; (ii) marginal . . . marginal; (iii) elasticity . . . elasticity
p. 648: (i) downward . . . less; (ii) marginal . . . marginal . . . demand; (iii) total . . . quantity; (iv) total . . . above
p. 652: (i) downward . . . elasticities . . . resale; (ii) discrimination . . . differentiation; (iii) lower . . . higher

Appendix F

Consumer Surplus and Losses Resulting from Monopoly

You have learned that a monopolist produces fewer units than would otherwise be produced in a perfectly competitive market and that it sells these units at a higher price. It seems that consumers surely must be worse off under monopoly than they would be under perfect competition. This appendix shows that, in fact, consumers are harmed by the existence of a monopoly in a market that otherwise could be perfectly competitive.

CONSUMER SURPLUS

Let's first examine how economists measure the benefits that consumers gain from engaging in market transactions. Consider Figure F-1, which displays a market demand curve, D. We assume that at the present time consumers face a per-unit price of this item given by P_A. Thus, the quantity demanded of this particular product is equal to Q_A at point A on the demand curve.

Typically, we visualize the market demand curve indicating the quantities that all consumers are willing to purchase at each possible price. In addition, however, the demand curve tells us the price that consumers are willing to pay for a unit of output at various possible quantities. For instance, if consumers were to buy Q_1 units of this good, they would be willing to pay a price equal to P_1 for the last unit purchased. If they only have to pay the price P_A for each unit they buy, however, consumers gain an amount equal to $P_1 - P_A$ for the last of the Q_1 units purchased. This benefit to consumers equals the vertical distance between the demand curve and the level of the market clearing price. Economists call this vertical distance a *surplus* value to consumers from being able to consume the last of the Q_1 units at the lower, market clearing price.

Likewise, if consumers were to purchase Q_2 units of this good, they would be willing to pay a price equal to P_2 for the last unit. Nevertheless, because they only have to pay the

FIGURE F-1
Consumer Surplus

If the per-unit price is P_A, then at point A on the demand curve D, consumers desire to purchase Q_A units. To purchase Q_1 units of this item, consumers would have been willing to pay the price P_1 for the last unit purchased but only have to pay the per-unit price P_A, so they gain a surplus equal to $P_1 - P_A$ for the last of the Q_1 units purchased. Likewise, to buy Q_2 units, consumers would have been willing to pay P_2 for the last unit purchased but only have to pay P_A, so they gain the surplus $P_2 - P_A$ for the last of the Q_2 units purchased. Summing these and all other surpluses consumers receive from purchasing all Q_A units at the price P_A yields the total consumer surplus at this price.

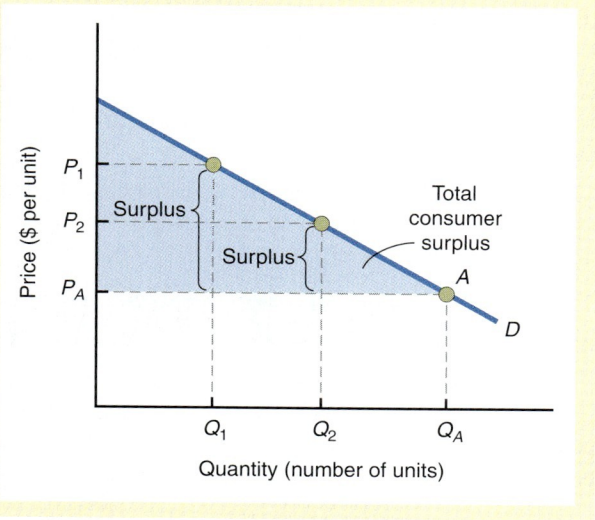

price P_A for each unit purchased, consumers gain an amount equal to $P_2 - P_A$. Hence, this is the surplus value associated with the last of the Q_2 units that consumers buy.

Of course, when they pay the same per-unit price P_A for every unit of this product that they purchase at point A, consumers obtain Q_A units. Thus, consumers gain surplus values—vertical distances between the demand curve and the level of the market clearing price—for each unit consumed, up to the total of Q_A units. Graphically, this is equivalent to the *entire* blue-shaded *area under the demand curve* but above the market clearing price. This entire area equals the total **consumer surplus,** which is the difference between the total amount that consumers *would have been willing to pay* for an item and the total amount that they *actually pay*.

Consumer surplus
The total difference between the total amount that consumers would have been willing to pay for a good or service and the total amount that they actually pay.

CONSUMER SURPLUS IN A PERFECTLY COMPETITIVE MARKET

Now let's consider the determination of consumer surplus in a perfectly competitive market. Take a look at the market diagram depicted in Figure F-2. In the figure, we assume that all firms producing in this market incur no fixed costs. We also assume that each firm faces the same marginal cost that does not vary with its output. These assumptions imply that the marginal cost curve is horizontal and that marginal cost is the same as average total cost at any level of output. Thus, if many perfectly competitive firms operate in this market, the horizontal summation of all firms' marginal cost curves, which is the market supply curve, is this same horizontal curve, labeled MC = ATC.

Under perfect competition, the point at which this market supply curve crosses the market demand curve, D, determines the equilibrium quantity, Q_{pc}, and the market clearing price, P_{pc}. Thus, in a perfectly competitive market, consumers obtain Q_{pc} units at the same per-unit price of P_{pc}. Consumers gain surplus values—vertical distances between the demand curve and the level of the market clearing price—for each unit consumed, up to the total of Q_{pc} units. This totals to the entire cross-hatched area under the demand curve above the market clearing price. Consumer surplus is the difference between the total amount that consumers would have been willing to pay and the total amount that they actually pay, given the market clearing price that prevails in the perfectly competitive market.

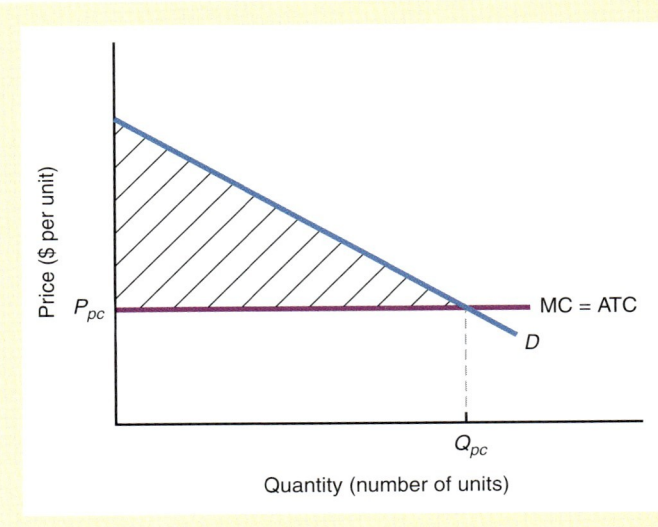

FIGURE F-2
Consumer Surplus in a Perfectly Competitive Market
If all firms in this market incur no fixed costs and face the same, constant marginal costs, then the marginal cost curve, MC, and the average total cost curve, ATC, are equivalent and horizontal. Under perfect competition, the horizontal summation of all firms' marginal cost curves is this same horizontal curve, which is the market supply curve, so the market clearing price is P_{pc}, and the equilibrium quantity is Q_{pc}. The total consumer surplus in a perfectly competitive market is the cross-hatched area.

FIGURE F-3
Losses Generated by Monopoly

If firms are able to form a cartel and act as a single monopoly, then the monopolist will produce only Q_m units at the point at which marginal revenue equals marginal cost and charge the price P_m. Economic profits, $Q_m \times (P_m - ATC)$, equal the yellow-shaded rectangular area, which is a portion of the competitive level of consumer surplus (the original cross-hatched area) transferred to the monopolist. Consumers can now purchase Q_m units of output at a per-unit price, P_m, below the prices they otherwise would have been willing to pay, so the blue-shaded triangular area above this monopoly-profit rectangle is remaining consumer surplus. The green-shaded triangular area is lost consumer surplus that results from the monopoly producing Q_m units instead of the Q_{pc} units that would have been produced under perfect competition. This is called a *deadweight loss* because it is a portion of the competitive level of consumer surplus that no one in society can obtain under monopoly.

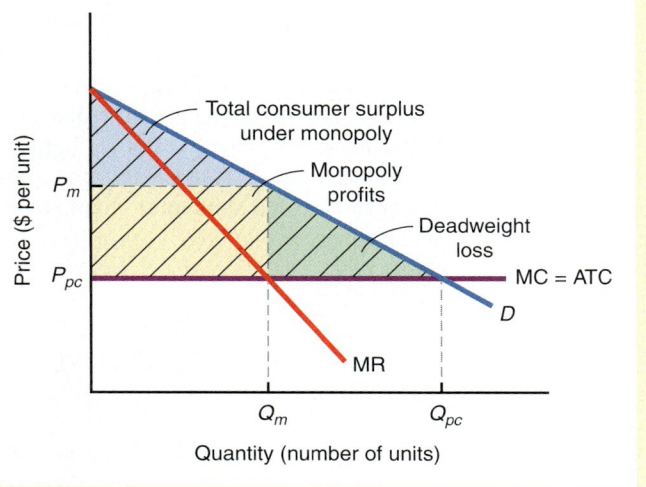

HOW SOCIETY LOSES FROM MONOPOLY

Now let's think about what happens if a monopoly situation arises in this market, perhaps because a government licenses a cartel arrangement by all the producers. These producers respond by acting as a single monopoly firm, which searches for the profit-maximizing quantity and price.

In this altered situation, which is depicted in Figure F-3, the new monopolist (which we assume is unable to engage in price discrimination—see page 648) will produce to the point at which marginal revenue equals marginal cost. This rate of output is Q_m units. The demand curve indicates that consumers are willing to pay a price equal to P_m for this quantity of output. Consequently, as you learned in this chapter, the monopolist will produce fewer units of output than the quantity, Q_{pc}, that firms would have produced in a perfectly competitive market. The monopolist also charges a higher price than the market clearing price, P_{pc}, that would have prevailed under perfect competition.

Recall that the monopolist's maximized economic profits equal its output times the difference between price and average total cost, or the yellow-shaded rectangular area equal to $Q_m \times (P_m - ATC)$. By setting its price at P_m, therefore, the monopolist is able to transfer this portion of the competitive level of consumer surplus to itself in the form of monopoly profits. Consumers are still able to purchase Q_m units of output at a per-unit price, P_m, below the prices they would otherwise have been willing to pay. Hence the blue-shaded triangular area above this monopoly-profit rectangle is consumer surplus that remains in the new monopoly situation.

Once the monopoly is formed, what happens to the green-shaded portion of the competitive consumer surplus? The answer is that this portion of consumer surplus is lost to society. The monopolist's failure to produce the additional $Q_{pc} - Q_m$ units of output that would have been forthcoming in a perfectly competitive market eliminates this portion of the original consumer surplus. This lost consumer surplus resulting from monopoly production and pricing is called a **deadweight loss** because it is a portion of the competitive level of consumer surplus that no one in society can obtain in a monopoly situation.

Thus, as a result of monopoly, consumers are worse off in two ways. First, the monopoly profits that result constitute a transfer of a portion of consumer surplus away from consumers to the monopolist. Second, the failure of the monopoly to produce as many units as would have been produced under perfect competition eliminates consumer surplus that otherwise would have been a benefit to consumers. No one in society, not even the monopoly, can obtain this deadweight loss.

Deadweight loss
The portion of consumer surplus that no one in society is able to obtain in a situation of monopoly.

Monopolistic Competition

26

The typical consumers of "toy trains" are not children. They are middle-aged adults who are always on the lookout for particularly realistic-looking model locomotives, cabooses, or tank cars to add to their collections. Each producer of model railroad products knows this and does its best to differentiate its products from those of other sellers. Recently, however, real-world rail transport companies have pushed up the cost of product differentiation by requiring model train producers to pay licensing fees to print the railroads' names and logos on model railroad products. How are such fees likely to affect the prices and outputs of model train producers? To be able to answer this question, you must first learn about the market structure in which model train producers interact, known as *monopolistic competition*.

Learning Objectives

After reading this chapter, you should be able to:

1. Discuss the key characteristics of a monopolistically competitive industry
2. Contrast the output and pricing decisions of monopolistically competitive firms with those of perfectly competitive firms
3. Explain why brand names and advertising are important features of monopolistically competitive industries
4. Describe the fundamental properties of information products and evaluate how the prices of these products are determined under monopolistic competition

MyEconLab helps you master each objective and study more efficiently. See end of chapter for details.

Did You Know That...

since 2004, annual spending on new building construction at U.S. colleges and universities has exceeded $14 billion per year? A portion of this spending has funded new science laboratories and classroom space. Most of the expenditures, however, have financed student centers with various amenities that individual universities hope will help their schools stand out from the pack when high school students contemplate which college to attend. Lavish and spacious new student centers, built at costs exceeding $50 million, often include food courts, restaurants, sports bars, convenience stores, and recreation centers. Across the land, colleges and universities are using these facilities as recruiting tools. One college advertises a nightclub in its newly constructed student center, while another boasts more than 50 videogames in its new sports bar. The marketing brochure for one university's student center even advertises theme park attractions, such as a helicopter simulator.

Advertising did not show up in our analysis of perfect competition. Nevertheless, it plays a large role in industries that cannot be described as perfectly competitive but cannot be described as pure monopolies, either. A combination of consumers' preferences for variety and competition among producers has led to similar but *differentiated* products in the marketplace. This situation has been described as *monopolistic competition*, the subject of this chapter.

MONOPOLISTIC COMPETITION

In the 1920s and 1930s, economists became increasingly aware that there were many industries for which both the perfectly competitive model and the pure monopoly model did not apply and did not seem to yield very accurate predictions. Theoretical and empirical research was instituted to develop some sort of middle ground. Two separately developed models of **monopolistic competition** resulted. At Harvard, Edward Chamberlin published *Theory of Monopolistic Competition* in 1933. The same year, Britain's Joan Robinson published *The Economics of Imperfect Competition*. In this chapter, we will outline the theory as presented by Chamberlin.

Monopolistic competition
A market situation in which a large number of firms produce similar but not identical products. Entry into the industry is relatively easy.

Chamberlin defined monopolistic competition as a market structure in which a relatively large number of producers offer similar but differentiated products. Monopolistic competition therefore has the following features:

1. Significant numbers of sellers in a highly competitive market
2. Differentiated products
3. Sales promotion and advertising
4. Easy entry of new firms in the long run

Even a cursory look at the U.S. economy leads to the conclusion that monopolistic competition is an important form of market structure in the United States. Indeed, that is true of all developed economies.

Number of Firms

In a perfectly competitive industry, there is an extremely large number of firms; in pure monopoly, there is only one. In monopolistic competition, there is a large number of firms, but not as many as in perfect competition. This fact has several important implications for a monopolistically competitive industry.

1. *Small share of market.* With so many firms, each firm has a relatively small share of the total market.

2. *Lack of collusion.* With so many firms, it is very difficult for all of them to get together to collude—to cooperate in setting a pure monopoly price (and output). Collusive pricing in a monopolistically competitive industry is virtually impossible. Also, barriers to entry are minor, and the flow of new firms into the industry makes collusive agreements less likely. The large number of firms makes the monitoring and detection of cheating very costly and extremely difficult. This difficulty is compounded by differentiated products and high rates of innovation; collusive agreements are easier for a homogeneous product than for heterogeneous ones.
3. *Independence.* Because there are so many firms, each one acts independently of the others. No firm attempts to take into account the reaction of all of its rival firms—that would be impossible with so many rivals. Thus, an individual producer does not try to take into account possible reactions of rivals to its own output and price changes.

Follow the link at www.econtoday.com/ch26 to *Wall Street Journal* articles about real-world examples of monopolistic competition.

Product Differentiation

Perhaps the most important feature of the monopolistically competitive market is **product differentiation.** We can say that each individual manufacturer of a product has an absolute monopoly over its own product, which is slightly differentiated from other similar products. This means that the firm has some control over the price it charges. Unlike the perfectly competitive firm, it faces a downward-sloping demand curve.

Consider the abundance of brand names for toothpaste, soap, gasoline, vitamins, shampoo, and most other consumer goods and a great many services. We are not obliged to buy just one type of television set, just one type of jeans, or just one type of footwear. We can usually choose from a number of similar but differentiated products. The greater a firm's success at product differentiation, the greater the firm's pricing options.

Why do cranberry producers seek to differentiate this fruit from others?

Product differentiation
The distinguishing of products by brand name, color, and other minor attributes. Product differentiation occurs in other than perfectly competitive markets in which products are, in theory, homogeneous, such as wheat or corn.

EXAMPLE

What Else Besides a Tart Taste Do Cranberries Have to Offer?

Only three fruits are native to North America: Concord grapes, blueberries, and cranberries. The last of these was dubbed the "crane berry" by European settlers because of the pointy pink blossoms that reminded them of a bird called the sandhill crane. Native Americans, however, used a descriptive name based on a word that summed up the fruit's flavor: "bitter." To broaden the appeal of cranberries, producers have spent years developing milder-tasting versions of the fruit. Indeed, some varieties of cranberries now taste more like oranges, cherries, or raspberries than the cranberries originally grown by Native Americans.

Making cranberries taste more like other fruits and berries presented cranberry producers with the problem of how to differentiate their product. Recent cranberry ads have emphasized a feature reflected in another Native American name for the fruit based on a word meaning "noisy," namely the fruit's unique "crunchiness" when chewed. Producers have also promoted the healthful properties of cranberry juice, which kills bacteria and helps to prevent infections. Thus, even though cranberries' flavors are now more similar to the flavors of other fruits and berries, sellers emphasize the distinctive experience associated with eating the fruit and its curative properties.

FOR CRITICAL ANALYSIS

In contrast to other fruits and juices that spoil within days, cranberries and their juices last on shelves for months, making them the lowest-cost fruits and juices to distribute and sell. Why does this give sellers of cranberries and cranberry juice an added incentive to differentiate their products from other fruits and berries?

Each separate differentiated product has numerous similar substitutes. This clearly has an impact on the price elasticity of demand for the individual firm. Recall that one determinant of price elasticity of demand is the availability of substitutes: The greater the number and closeness of substitutes available, other things being equal, the greater the price elasticity of demand. If the consumer has a vast array of alternatives that are just about as good as the product under study, a relatively small increase in the price of that product will lead many consumers to switch to one of the many close substitutes. Thus, the ability of a firm to raise the price above the price of *close* substitutes is very small. Even though the demand curve slopes downward, it is highly elastic compared to a monopolist's demand curve. In the extreme case, with perfect competition, the substitutes are perfect because we are dealing with only one particular undifferentiated product. In that case, the individual firm has a perfectly elastic demand curve.

Sales Promotion and Advertising

Monopolistic competition differs from perfect competition in that no individual firm in a perfectly competitive market will advertise. A perfectly competitive firm, by definition, can sell all that it wants to sell at the going market price anyway. Why, then, would it spend even one penny on advertising? Furthermore, by definition, the perfect competitor is selling a product that is identical to the product that all other firms in the industry are selling. Any advertisement that induces consumers to buy more of that product will, in effect, be helping all the competitors too. A perfect competitor therefore cannot be expected to incur any advertising costs (except when all firms in an industry collectively agree to advertise to urge the public to buy more beef or drink more milk).

The monopolistic competitor, however, has at least *some* monopoly power. Because consumers regard the monopolistic competitor's product as distinguishable from the products of the other firms, the firm can search for the price consumers are willing to pay for its differentiated product. Advertising, therefore, may result in increased profits. Advertising is used to increase demand and to differentiate one's product. How much advertising should be undertaken? It should be carried to the point at which the additional revenue from one more dollar of advertising just equals that one dollar of additional cost.

Ease of Entry

For any current monopolistic competitor, potential competition is always lurking in the background. The easier—that is, the less costly—entry is, the more a current monopolistic competitor must worry about losing business.

A good example of a monopolistic competitive industry is the computer software industry. Many small firms provide different programs for many applications. The fixed capital costs required to enter this industry are small; all you need are skilled programmers. In addition, there are few legal restrictions. The firms in this industry also engage in extensive advertising in over 150 computer publications.

Are easy entries sometimes followed speedily by easy exits?

EXAMPLE

Half the Calories, but a Tiny Fraction of the Revenues

In response to the low-carbohydrate diet craze that began in the late 1990s and lasted through the mid-2000s, new "low-carb" soft drinks, such as Pepsi-Cola's Pepsi Edge brand and Coca-Cola's C2 brand, appeared beginning in the spring of 2004. All these and other soft-drink companies had to do to introduce new low-carb diet drinks was to utilize different formula mixes

(continued)

in existing factories and slightly alter existing advertising campaigns. At Coca-Cola, for instance, a key advertising vehicle was in fact a *vehicle:* The soft-drink company had already arranged for several Nascar race drivers to drive "Coke" cars in races, so the company simply switched these to "C2" cars.

Pepsi Edge, Pepsi-Cola's eleventh attempt to introduce diet brands alongside its long-running Diet Pepsi brand, never caught on with consumers. By the end of 2005, the company had already quietly, and with relative ease, exited the low-carb soft-drink market. Indeed, all firms that have entered this market have found it difficult to generate sustained demand for their products. Revenues from sales of C2 have been so low that industry observers anticipate that Coca-Cola may exit the low-carb market as well.

FOR CRITICAL ANALYSIS
In addition to the fact that the soft-drink industry has more than 100 competing producers, what other characteristics of this industry make it a good example of a monopolistically competitive industry?

QUICK QUIZ

In a **monopolistically competitive** industry, a relatively _____ number of firms interact in a _____ competitive market.

Because monopolistically competitive firms sell _____ products, sales promotion and advertising are common features of a monopolistically competitive industry.

There is _____ entry (or exit) of new firms in a monopolistically competitive industry.

See page 681 for the answers. Review concepts from this section in MyEconLab.

PRICE AND OUTPUT FOR THE MONOPOLISTIC COMPETITOR

Now that we are aware of the assumptions underlying the monopolistic competition model, we can analyze the price and output behavior of each firm in a monopolistically competitive industry. We assume in the analysis that follows that the desired product type and quality have been chosen. We further assume that the budget and the type of promotional activity have already been chosen and do not change.

The Individual Firm's Demand and Cost Curves

Because the individual firm is not a perfect competitor, its demand curve slopes downward, as in all three panels of Figure 26-1 on the following page. Hence it faces a marginal revenue curve that is also downward sloping and below the demand curve. To find the profit-maximizing rate of output and the profit-maximizing price, we go to the output where the marginal cost (MC) curve intersects the marginal revenue (MR) curve from below. That gives us the profit-maximizing output rate. Then we draw a vertical line up to the demand curve. That gives us the price that can be charged to sell exactly that quantity produced. This is what we have done in Figure 26-1. In each panel, a marginal cost curve intersects the marginal revenue curve at A. The profit-maximizing rate of output is q, and the profit-maximizing price is P.

FIGURE 26-1

Short-Run and Long-Run Equilibrium with Monopolistic Competition

In panel (a), the typical monopolistic competitor is shown making economic profits. In this situation, there would be entry into the industry, forcing the demand curve for the individual monopolistic competitor leftward. Eventually, firms would find themselves in the situation depicted in panel (c), where zero *economic* profits are being made. In panel (b), the typical firm is in a monopolistically competitive industry making economic losses. In this situation, firms would leave the industry. Each remaining firm's demand curve would shift outward to the right. Eventually, the typical firm would find itself in the situation depicted in panel (c).

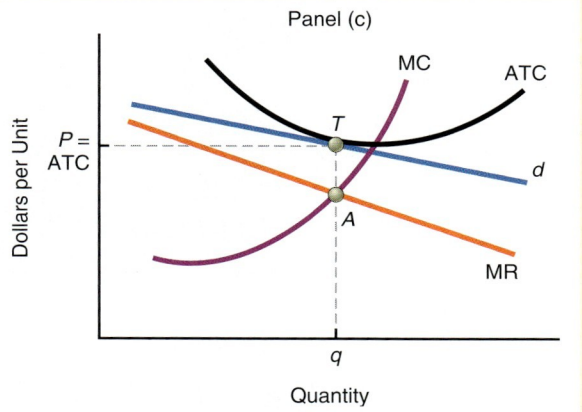

Short-Run Equilibrium

In the short run, it is possible for a monopolistic competitor to make economic profits—profits over and above the normal rate of return or beyond what is necessary to keep that firm in that industry. We show such a situation in panel (a) of Figure 26-1. The average total cost (ATC) curve is drawn below the demand curve, d, at the profit-maximizing rate of output, q. Economic profits are shown by the shaded rectangle in that panel.

Losses in the short run are clearly also possible. They are presented in panel (b) of Figure 26-1. Here the average total cost curve lies everywhere above the individual firm's demand curve, d. The losses are marked as the shaded rectangle.

Just as with any market structure or any firm, in the short run it is possible to observe either economic profits or economic losses. In either case, the price does not equal marginal cost but rather is above it. Therefore, there may be some misallocation of resources, a topic that we will discuss later in this chapter.

The Long Run: Zero Economic Profits

The long run is where the similarity between perfect competition and monopolistic competition becomes more obvious. In the long run, because so many firms produce substitutes for the product in question, any economic profits will disappear with competition. They will be reduced to zero either through entry by new firms seeing a chance to make a higher rate of return than elsewhere or by changes in product quality and advertising outlays by existing firms in the industry. (Profitable products will be imitated by other firms.) As for economic losses in the short run, they will disappear in the long run because the firms that suffer them will leave the industry. They will go into another business where the expected rate of return is at least normal. Panels (a) and (b) of Figure 26-1 therefore represent only short-run situations for a monopolistically competitive firm. In the long run, the individual firm's demand curve *d* will just touch the average total cost curve at the particular price that is profit maximizing for that particular firm. This is shown in panel (c) of Figure 26-1.

A word of warning: This is an idealized, long-run equilibrium situation for each firm in the industry. It does not mean that even in the long run we will observe every single firm in a monopolistically competitive industry making *exactly* zero economic profits or *just* a normal rate of return. We live in a dynamic world. All we are saying is that if this model is correct, the rate of return will *tend toward* normal—economic profits will *tend toward* zero.

COMPARING PERFECT COMPETITION WITH MONOPOLISTIC COMPETITION

If both the monopolistic competitor and the perfect competitor make zero economic profits in the long run, how are they different? The answer lies in the fact that the demand curve for the individual perfect competitor is perfectly elastic. Such is not the case for the individual monopolistic competitor; its demand curve is less than perfectly elastic. This firm has some control over price. Price elasticity of demand is not infinite.

We see the two situations in Figure 26-2 on the next page. Both panels show average total costs just touching the respective demand curves at the particular price at which the firm is selling the product. Notice, however, that the perfect competitor's average total costs are at a minimum. This is not the case with the monopolistic competitor. The equilibrium rate of output is to the left of the minimum point on the average total cost curve where price is greater than marginal cost. The monopolistic competitor cannot expand output to the point of minimum costs without lowering price, and then marginal cost would exceed marginal revenue. A monopolistic competitor at profit maximization charges a price that exceeds marginal cost. In this respect it is similar to the monopolist.

It has consequently been argued that monopolistic competition involves *waste* because minimum average total costs are not achieved and price exceeds marginal cost. There are too many firms, each with excess capacity, producing too little output. According to critics of monopolistic competition, society's resources are being wasted.

Chamberlin had an answer to this criticism. He contended that the difference between the average cost of production for a monopolistically competitive firm in an open market and the minimum average total cost represented what he called the cost of producing "differentness." Chamberlin did not consider this difference in cost between perfect competition and monopolistic competition a waste. In fact, he argued that it is rational for consumers to have a taste for differentiation; consumers willingly accept the resultant increased production costs in return for more choice and variety of output.

FIGURE 26-2
Comparison of the Perfect Competitor with the Monopolistic Competitor

In panel (a), the perfectly competitive firm has zero economic profits in the long run. The price is set equal to marginal cost, and the price is P_1. The firm's demand curve is just tangent to the minimum point on its average total cost curve. With the monopolistically competitive firm in panel (b), there are also zero economic profits in the long run. The price is greater than marginal cost. The monopolistically competitive firm does not find itself at the minimum point on its average total cost curve. It is operating at a rate of output to the left of the minimum point on the ATC curve.

QUICK QUIZ

In the _____ run, it is possible for monopolistically competitive firms to make economic profits or economic losses.

In the _____ run, monopolistically competitive firms will make _____ economic profits—that is, they will make a _____ rate of return.

Because the monopolistic competitor faces a downward-sloping demand curve, it does not produce at the minimum point on its average _____ cost curve. Hence we say that a monopolistic competitor has higher average _____ costs per unit than a perfect competitor would have.

Chamberlin argued that the difference between the _____ _____ cost of production for a monopolistically competitive firm and the _____ average total cost at which a perfectly competitive firm would produce is the cost of producing "differentness."

See page 681 for the answers. Review concepts from this section in MyEconLab.

BRAND NAMES AND ADVERTISING

Because "differentness" has value to consumers, monopolistically competitive firms regard their brand names as valuable. Firms use trademarks—words, symbols, and logos—to distinguish their product brands from goods or services sold by other firms. Consumers associate these trademarks with the firms' products. Thus, companies regard their brands as valuable private (intellectual) property, and they engage in advertising to maintain the differentiation of their products from those of other firms.

Brand	Market Value ($ billions)
Coca-Cola	67.5
Microsoft	59.9
International Business Machines (IBM)	53.4
General Electric (GE)	47.0
Intel	35.6
Nokia	26.5
Disney	26.4
McDonald's	26.0
Toyota	24.8
Marlboro	21.2

Source: Interbrand Annual Survey, 2006.

TABLE 26-1

Values of the Top Ten Brands

The market value of a company is equal to the number of shares of stock ownership issued by the company times the market price of each share. To a large extent, the company's value reflects the value of its brand.

Brand Names and Trademarks

A firm's ongoing sales generate current profits and, as long as the firm is viable, the prospect of future profits. A company's value in the marketplace, or its purchase value, depends largely on its current profitability and perceptions of its future profitability.

Table 26-1 gives the market values of the world's most valuable product brands. Each valuation depends on the market prices of shares of stock in a company times the number of shares traded. Brand names, symbols, and logos relate to consumers' perceptions of product differentiation and hence to the market values of firms. Companies protect their trademarks from misuse by registering them with the U.S. Patent and Trademark Office. Once its trademark application is approved, a company has the right to seek legal damages if someone makes unauthorized use of its brand name, spreads false rumors about the company, or engages in other activities that can reduce the value of its brand.

Advertising

To help ensure that consumers differentiate their product brands from those of other firms, monopolistically competitive firms commonly engage in advertising. Advertising comes in various forms, and the nature of advertising can depend considerably on the types of products that firms wish to distinguish from competing brands.

Methods of Advertising. Figure 26-3 on the following page shows the current distribution of advertising expenses among the various advertising media. Today, as in the past, firms primarily rely on two approaches to advertising their products. One is **direct marketing,** in which firms engage in personalized advertising using postal mailings, phone calls, and e-mail messages (excluding so-called banner and pop-up ads on Web sites). The other is **mass marketing,** in which firms aim advertising messages at as many consumers as possible via media such as television, newspapers, radio, and magazines.

A third advertising method is called **interactive marketing.** This advertising approach allows a consumer to respond directly to an advertising message; often the consumer is able to search for more detailed information and place an order as part of the response. Sales booths and some types of Internet advertising, such as banner ads with links to sellers' Web pages, are forms of interactive marketing.

Direct marketing
Advertising targeted at specific consumers, typically in the form of postal mailings, telephone calls, or e-mail messages.

Mass marketing
Advertising intended to reach as many consumers as possible, typically through television, newspaper, radio, or magazine ads.

Interactive marketing
Advertising that permits a consumer to follow up directly by searching for more information and placing direct product orders.

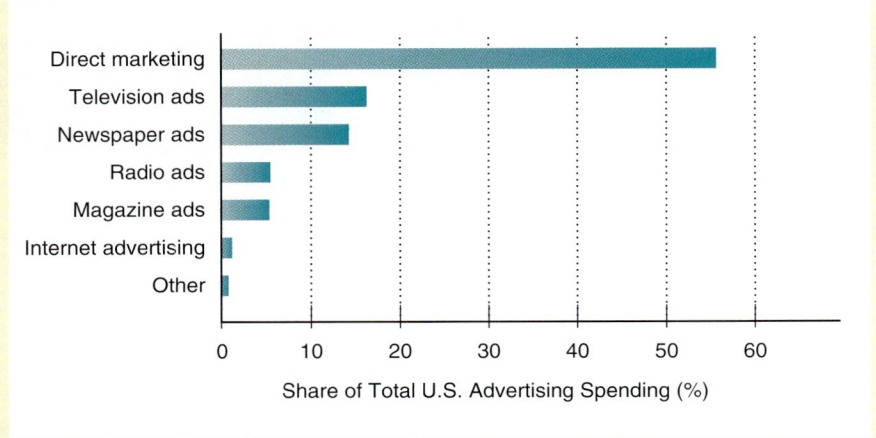

FIGURE 26-3

Distribution of U.S. Advertising Expenses

Direct marketing accounts for more than half of advertising expenses in the United States.

Sources: *Advertising Today*; *Direct Marketing Today*; and Internet Advertising Bureau.

Informational versus Persuasive Advertising. Some ads provide considerable information about products, while others seem designed mainly to attract a consumer's attention. The qualities and characteristics of a product determine how the firm should advertise that product. Some types of products, known as **search goods,** possess qualities that are relatively easy for consumers to assess in advance of their purchase. Clothing and music are common examples of items that have features that a consumer may assess, or perhaps even sample, before purchasing. Other products, known as **experience goods,** are products that people must actually consume before they can determine their qualities. Soft drinks, restaurant meals, and haircutting services are examples of experience goods. A third category of products, called **credence goods,** includes goods and services with qualities that might be difficult for consumers lacking expertise to assess without assistance. Products such as pharmaceuticals and services such as health care and legal advice are examples of credence goods.

The forms of advertising that firms use to market a search good are likely to be considerably different from those employed in marketing an experience good. If the item is a search good, a firm is more likely to use **informational advertising** that emphasizes the features of its product. An audio or video ad for the latest CD by a rock group is likely to include snippets of songs that are featured on the CD, which helps potential buyers assess the quality of the music. In contrast, if the product is an experience good, a firm is more likely to engage in **persuasive advertising** intended to induce a consumer to try the product and, as a consequence, discover a previously unknown taste for it. For example, a soft-drink ad is likely to depict happy people drinking the clearly identified product during breaks from enjoyable outdoor activities on a hot day. If a product is a credence good, producers commonly use a mix of informational and persuasive advertising. For instance, an ad for a pharmaceutical product commonly provides both detailed information about the product's curative properties and side effects and suggestions to consumers to ask physicians to help them assess the drug.

Search good
A product with characteristics that enable an individual to evaluate the product's quality in advance of a purchase.

Experience good
A product that an individual must consume before the product's quality can be established.

Credence good
A product with qualities that consumers lack the expertise to assess without assistance.

Informational advertising
Advertising that emphasizes transmitting knowledge about the features of a product.

Persuasive advertising
Advertising that is intended to induce a consumer to purchase a particular product and discover a previously unknown taste for the item.

ECONOMICS FRONT AND CENTER

Contemplate the issues that producers face when trying to determine appropriate methods and forms of advertising by reading **Trying to Generate a Surging Demand for Surge Protectors,** on page 675.

Advertising as Signaling Behavior. Recall from Chapter 24 that *signals* are compact gestures or actions that convey information. For example, high profits in an industry are signals that resources should flow to that industry. Individual companies can explicitly engage in signaling behavior. A firm can do so by establishing brand names or trademarks and then promoting them heavily. This is a signal to prospective consumers that this is a company that plans to stay in business. Before the modern age of advertising, U.S. banks needed a way to signal their soundness. To do this, they constructed large, imposing bank buildings using marble and granite. Stone communicated permanence. The effect was to give bank customers confidence that they were not doing business with fly-by-night operations.

When Toyota advertises its brand name heavily, it incurs substantial costs. The only way it can recoup those costs is by selling many Toyota vehicles over a long period of time. Heavy advertising in the company's brand name thereby signals to car buyers that Toyota intends to stay in business a long time and wants to develop a loyal customer base—because loyal customers are repeat customers.

> ### QUICK QUIZ
>
> _____ such as words, symbols, and logos distinguish firms' products from those of other firms. Firms seek to differentiate their brands through advertising, via _____ marketing, _____ marketing, or _____ marketing.
>
> A firm is more likely to use _____ advertising that emphasizes the features of its product if the item is a **search good** with features that consumers can assess in advance.
>
> A firm is more likely to use _____ advertising to affect consumers' tastes and preferences if it sells an **experience good.** This is an item that people must actually consume before they can determine its qualities.
>
> A firm that sells a _____ good, which is an item possessing qualities that consumers lack the expertise to fully assess, typically uses a combination of informational and persuasive advertising.
>
> See page 681 for the answers. Review concepts from this section in MyEconLab.

INFORMATION PRODUCTS AND MONOPOLISTIC COMPETITION

A number of industries sell **information products,** which entail relatively high fixed costs associated with the use of knowledge and other information-intensive inputs as key factors of production. Once the first unit has been produced, however, it is possible to produce additional units at a relatively low per-unit cost. Most information products can be put into digital form. Good examples are computer games, computer operating systems, digital music and videos, educational and training software, electronic books and encyclopedias, and office productivity software.

Information product
An item that is produced using information-intensive inputs at a relatively high fixed cost but distributed for sale at a relatively low marginal cost.

Special Cost Characteristics of Information Products

Creating the first copy of an information product often entails incurring a relatively sizable up-front cost. Once the first copy is created, however, making additional copies can be very inexpensive. For instance, a firm that sells a computer game can simply make properly formatted copies of the original digital file of the game on a CD. Alternatively, the firm might make the game available for consumers to download, at a price, via the Internet.

Costs of Producing Information Products.
To think about the cost conditions faced by the seller of an information product, consider the production and sale of a computer game. The company that creates a computer game must devote many hours of labor to developing and editing its content. Each hour of labor and each unit of other resources devoted to performing this task entail an opportunity cost. The sum of all these up-front costs constitutes a relatively sizable *fixed cost* that the company must incur to generate the first copy of the computer game.

Once the company has developed the computer game in a form that is readable by personal computers, the marginal cost of making and distributing additional copies is very low. In the case of a computer game, it is simply a matter of incurring a minuscule cost to place the required files on a CD or on the company's Web site.

Cost Curves for an Information Product.
Suppose that a manufacturer decides to produce and sell a computer game. Creating the first copy of the game requires incurring a total fixed cost equal to $250,000. The marginal cost that the company incurs to place the computer game on a CD or in downloadable format is a constant amount equal to $2.50 per computer game.

Figure 26-4 displays the firm's cost curves for this information product. By definition, average fixed cost is total fixed cost divided by the quantity produced and sold. Hence the average fixed cost of the first computer game is $250,000. But if the company sells 5,000 copies, the average fixed cost drops to $50 per game. If the total quantity sold is 50,000, average fixed cost declines to $5 per game. The average fixed cost (AFC) curve slopes downward over the entire range of possible quantities of computer games.

Average variable cost equals total variable cost divided by the number of units of a product that a firm sells. If this company sells only one copy, then the total variable cost it incurs is the per-unit cost of $2.50, and this is also the average variable cost of producing one unit. Because the per-unit cost of producing the computer game is a constant $2.50, producing two games entails a total variable cost of $5.00, and the average variable cost of producing two games is $5.00 ÷ 2 = $2.50. Thus, as shown in Figure 26-4, the average variable cost of producing and selling this computer game is always equal to the constant marginal cost of $2.50 per game that the company incurs. The average variable cost (AVC) curve is the same as the marginal cost (MC) curve, which for this company is the horizontal line depicted in Figure 26-4.

Short-Run Economies of Operation.
By definition, average total cost equals the sum of average fixed cost and average variable cost. The average total cost (ATC) curve for this computer game company slopes downward over its entire range.

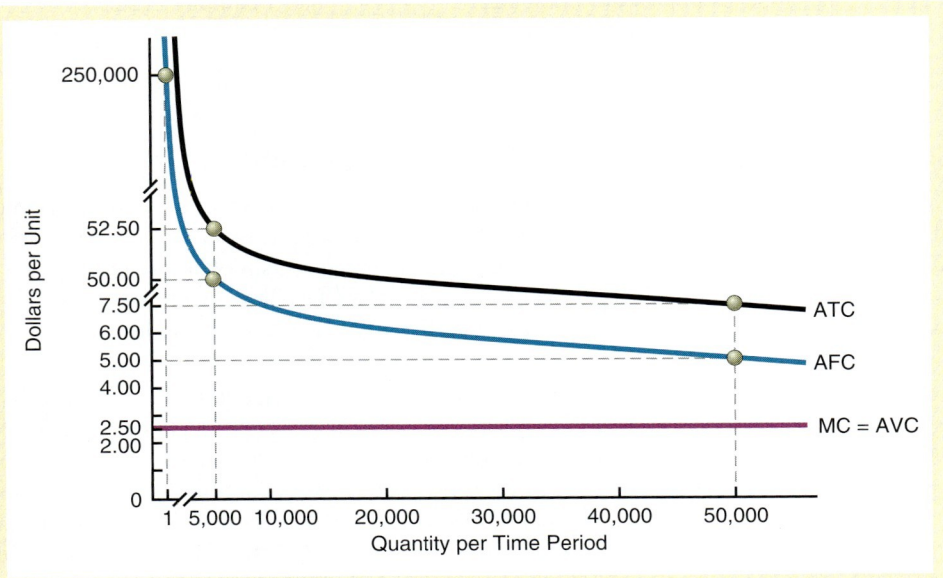

FIGURE 26-4

Cost Curves for a Producer of an Information Product

The total fixed cost of producing a computer game is $250,000. If the producer sells 5,000 copies, average fixed cost falls to $50 per copy. If quantity sold rises to 50,000, average fixed cost decreases to $5 per copy. Thus, the producer's average fixed cost (AFC) curve slopes downward. If the per-unit cost of producing each copy of the game is $2.50, then both the marginal cost (MC) and average variable cost (AVC) curves are horizontal at $2.50 per copy. Adding the AFC and AVC curves yields the ATC curve. Because the ATC curve slopes downward, the producer of this information product experiences short-run economies of operation.

Recall from Chapter 23 that along the downward-sloping range of an individual firm's *long-run* average cost curve, the firm experiences *economies of scale*. For the producer of an information product such as a computer game, the *short-run* average total cost curve slopes downward. Consequently, sellers of information products typically experience **short-run economies of operation.** The average total cost of producing and selling an information product declines as more units of the product are sold. Short-run economies of operation are a distinguishing characteristic of information products that sets them apart from most other goods and services.

Short-run economies of operation
A distinguishing characteristic of an information product arising from declining short-run average total cost as more units of the product are sold.

Monopolistic Competition and Information Products

In the example depicted in Figure 26-4, the information product is a computer game. There are numerous computer games among which consumers can choose. Hence there are many products that are close substitutes in the market for computer games. Yet no two computer games are exactly the same. This means that the particular computer game product sold by the company in our example is distinguishable from other competing products.

For the sake of argument, therefore, let's suppose that this company participates in a monopolistically competitive market for this computer game. Panels (a) and (b) of Figure 26-5 on the following page display a possible demand curve for the computer game manufactured and sold by this particular company.

Marginal Cost Pricing and Information Products.

What if the company making this particular computer game were to behave *as if* it were a perfectly competitive firm by setting the price of its product equal to marginal cost? Panel (a) of Figure 26-5 provides the answer to this question. If the company sets the price of the computer game equal to marginal cost, it will charge only $2.50 per game it sells. Naturally, a larger number of people desire to purchase computer games at this price, and given the demand curve in the figure, the company could sell 20,000 copies of this game.

The company would face a problem, however. At a price of $2.50 per computer game, it would earn $50,000 in revenues on sales of 20,000 copies. The average fixed cost of 20,000 copies equals $250,000/20,000, or $12.50 per computer game. Adding this to the constant $2.50 average variable cost implies an average total cost of selling 20,000 copies of $15 per game. Under marginal cost pricing, therefore, the company would earn an average loss of $12.50 (price − average total cost = $2.50 − $15.00 = −$12.50) per computer game for all 20,000 copies sold. The company's total economic loss from selling 20,000 computer games at a price equal to marginal cost would amount to $250,000. Hence the company would fail to recoup the $250,000 total fixed cost of producing the computer game. If the company had planned to set its price equal to the computer game's marginal production cost, it would never have sought to produce the computer game in the first place!

The failure of marginal cost pricing to allow firms selling information products to cover the fixed costs of producing those products is intrinsic to the nature of such products. In the presence of short-run economies of operation in producing information products, marginal cost pricing is simply not feasible in the marketplace.

Recall that marginal cost pricing is associated with perfect competition. An important implication of this example is that markets for information products cannot function as perfectly competitive markets. Imperfect competition is the rule, not the exception, in the market for information products.

The Case in Which Price Equals Average Total Cost.

Panel (b) of Figure 26-5 illustrates how the price of the computer game is ultimately determined in a monopolisti-

FIGURE 26-5
The Infeasibility of Marginal Cost Pricing of an Information Product

In panel (a), if the firm with the average total cost and marginal cost curves shown in Figure 26-4 sets the price of the computer game equal to its constant marginal cost of $2.50 per copy, then consumers will purchase 20,000 copies. This yields $50,000 in revenues. The firm's average total cost of 20,000 games is $15 per copy, so its total cost of selling that number of copies is $15 × 20,000 = $300,000. Marginal cost pricing thereby entails a $250,000 loss, which is the total fixed cost of producing the computer game. Panel (b) illustrates how the price of the game is ultimately determined under monopolistic competition. Setting a price of $27.50 per game induces consumers to buy 10,000 copies, and the average total cost of producing this number of copies is also $27.50. Consequently, total revenues equal $275,000, which just covers the sum of the $250,000 in total fixed costs and $25,000 (the 10,000 copies times the constant $2.50 average variable cost) in total variable costs. The firm earns zero economic profits.

cally competitive market. After all entry or exit from the market has occurred, the price of the computer game will equal the producer's average cost of production, including all implicit opportunity costs. The price charged for the game generates total revenues sufficient to cover all explicit and implicit costs and therefore is consistent with earning a normal return on invested capital.

Given the demand curve depicted in Figure 26-5, at a price of $27.50 per computer game, consumers are willing to purchase 10,000 copies. The company's average total cost of offering 10,000 copies for sale is also equal to $27.50 per computer game. Consequently, the price of each copy equals the average total cost of producing the game.

At a price of $27.50 per computer game, the company's revenues from selling 10,000 copies equal $275,000. This amount of revenues is just sufficient to cover the company's total fixed cost (including the opportunity cost of capital) of $250,000 and the $25,000 total variable cost it incurs in producing 10,000 copies at an average variable cost of $2.50 per game. Thus, the company earns zero economic profits.

Long-Run Equilibrium for an Information Product Industry. When the price of an information product equals average total cost, sellers charge the minimum price required to cover their production costs, including the relatively high initial costs they must incur to develop their products in the first place. Consumers thereby pay the lowest price necessary to induce sellers to provide the item.

The situation illustrated in panel (b) of Figure 26-5 corresponds to a long-run equilibrium for this particular firm in a monopolistically competitive market for computer games.

If this and other companies face a situation such as the diagram depicts, there is no incentive for additional companies to enter or leave the computer game industry. Consequently, the product price naturally tends to adjust to equality with average total cost as a monopolistically competitive industry composed of sellers of information products moves toward long-run equilibrium.

QUICK QUIZ

Firms that sell **information products** experience relatively _____ fixed costs, but once they have produced the first unit, they can sell additional units at a relatively _____ per-unit cost. Consequently, the manufacturer of an information product experiences short-run _____ of _____.

If a firm sets the price of an information product equal to marginal cost, it earns only sufficient revenues to cover its _____ costs. Engaging in marginal cost pricing, therefore, fails to cover the relatively high fixed costs of making an information product.

In a long-run equilibrium outcome under monopolistic competition, the price of an information product equals _____ _____ cost. The seller's total revenues exactly cover _____ costs, including the opportunity cost of capital.

See page 681 for the answers. Review concepts from this section in MyEconLab.

CASE STUDY

ECONOMICS FRONT AND CENTER

Trying to Generate a Surging Demand for Surge Protectors

Li is a mid-level executive at a company that sells battery-run backup surge protectors for use with personal computers, printers, copiers, and other office equipment. His firm faces competition from a large number of other producers, each of which sells a similar product. Some differentiate their battery-run backup protective devices by including software that, in the event of a power failure, automatically shuts down a computer before the battery loses its charge. Some offer special, long-life batteries. Others include guarantees to pay for repair of products damaged by a power surge.

Li has been charged with allocating the company's advertising budget to a single advertising approach judged most likely to boost the company's revenues and profits. Li has broken his task down to accomplishing two specific goals: (1) raise the demand for the brand, and (2) generate a reduction in the price elasticity of demand for the brand. He also realizes that he must choose not only the method of advertising—direct, mass, or interactive—but also the form of advertising—informational or persuasive. He begins to systematically explore his options.

CRITICAL ANALYSIS QUESTIONS

1. *Is the product of Li's company a search good, an experience good, or a credence good? Support your answer.*

2. *Based on your answer to the first question, what method and form of advertising should Li choose? Explain your reasoning.*

Issues and Applications

Paying for the Right to Produce Realistic Model Trains

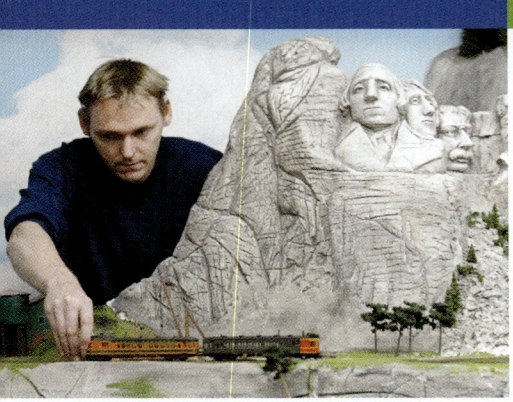

Concepts Applied
- Monopolistic Competition
- Product Differentiation
- Trademarks

A good example of a monopolistically competitive industry is the model electric train industry. There are numerous competing model electric train manufacturers in operation today, including Lionel, MTH, Atlas, Williams, Weaver, Life-Like, Bachmann, Athearn, and dozens of others. Each company's line of model locomotives and *rolling stock*—passenger cars and freight cars—includes both scale models of real-world counterparts and whimsical representations of items that "might have been."

To differentiate their model locomotives and rolling stock from those offered by competitors, sellers have long strived to produce distinctively designed and decorated products. Toward this end, model railroad firms commonly paint the names, symbols, and distinctive color schemes of present and past railroad companies on the plastic bodies of the model train items that they manufacture and sell. In accord with a long tradition in the model railroading business, they engaged in this practice without any concern about violating trademarks of modern or historical real-world rail lines. Recently, this tradition came to an abrupt end.

A Toy Hobby Meets Trademark Protection

When most people think of model electric trains, they have visions of young children awakening on Christmas morning to find a new toy train traversing tracks laid around a Christmas tree. In fact, most consumers of model train products are hobbyists aged 40 and older. To appeal to these hobbyists attempting to re-create small-scale representations of modern or historical rail lines in their homes, model train manufacturers strive to make their scale reproductions of railroad items look as realistic as possible. Creating these reproductions entails engaging in exacting efforts to duplicate as nearly as possible the logos and paint schemes used by present and past rail companies. To make more whimsical products, such as imagined Santa Fe and B&O locomotives that never actually existed, look more realistic nonetheless, producers commonly paint the classic Santa Fe and B&O logos onto such items.

In 2003, however, the nation's largest and oldest operator of *real* railroads, Union Pacific, announced that it planned to charge a licensing fee for each use of its name and logo on train models. It also specified fees for use of railroad trademarks that had been merged into the Union Pacific Company over the years, such as Southern Pacific, Western Pacific, Chicago & North Western, and Denver & Rio Grande.

In Model Railroading, Product Differentiation Now Has a Price

Model railroad firms initially resisted Union Pacific's demands, but by 2006 all had agreed to pay trademark licensing fees. Out-of-court settlements that Union Pacific reached with model train firms during the mid-2000s were not public, but industry experts estimate that most firms agreed to pay a licensing fee of about $1 per item.

Thus, each model railroad firm must now pay just a bit more to differentiate its products. Furthermore, an actual railroad company has found a way to earn revenues from rail models that electricity powers along small tracks as well as from the diesel-powered trains that it operates on life-sized tracks.

Log in to **MyEconLab**, click on "Economic News," and test your understanding of the chapter by answering interactive questions that relate directly to this issue.

For Critical Analysis

1. Why might today's owners of the remnants of now-defunct firms, such as the Cotton Belt Railroad that ceased operations in 1930, actively seek to protect the value of old trademarks?

2. Why might the difference between actual and minimum average total costs of producing exact scale replicas of railroad locomotives be regarded as an amount that hobbyists are willing to pay for greater variety?

Web Resources

1. For links to Web sites of the numerous competitors in the model train industry, go to www.econtoday.com/ch26.

2. Learn about the structure of Union Pacific's model train licensing program at www.econtoday.com/ch26.

Research Project

Evaluate how a $1-per-item licensing fee affects the cost curves faced by a typical monopolistically competitive producer of model locomotives. What are the implications of such a fee for the profit-maximizing quantity of model locomotives the firm sells and the price the firm charges for each locomotive?

Here is what you should know after reading this chapter. MyEconLab will help you identify what you know, and where to go when you need to practice.

WHAT YOU SHOULD KNOW		WHERE TO GO TO PRACTICE
The Key Characteristics of a Monopolistically Competitive Industry A monopolistically competitive industry consists of a large number of firms that sell differentiated products that are close substitutes. Firms can easily enter or exit a monopolistically competitive industry. Because monopolistically competitive firms can increase their profits if they can successfully distinguish their products from those of their rivals, they have an incentive to engage in sales promotions and advertising.	monopolistic competition, 662 product differentiation, 663	• **MyEconLab** Study Plan 26.1 • Audio introduction to Chapter 26 • Video: Characteristics of Monopolistic Competition
Contrasting the Output and Pricing Decisions of Monopolistically Competitive Firms with Those of Perfectly Competitive Firms In the short run, a monopolistically competitive firm produces output to the point where marginal revenue equals marginal cost. The price it charges for this output, which is the maximum price that people are willing to pay as determined by the demand for its product, can exceed both marginal cost and average total cost in the short run, and the resulting economic profits can induce new firms to enter the industry. As they do, existing firms in the industry experience declines in the demand for their products and reduce their prices to the point at which price equals average total cost. In the long run, therefore, monopolistically competitive firms, like perfectly competitive firms, earn zero economic profits. In contrast to perfectly competitive firms, however, price still exceeds marginal cost in the long-run equilibrium for monopolistically competitive firms.	**Key figures** Figure 26-1, 666 Figure 26-2, 668	• **MyEconLab** Study Plans 26.2 and 26.3 • Animated Figures 26-1 and 26-2
Why Brand Names and Advertising Are Important Features of Monopolistically Competitive Industries Monopolistically competitive firms attempt to boost the demand for their products through product differentiation. They use words, symbols, and logos (trademarks) to distinguish their products from substitute items produced by other firms in the industry. In addition, they engage in advertising, in the form of direct marketing, mass marketing, or interactive marketing. If the product is a search good with features that consumers can evaluate prior to purchase, the seller is more likely to use advertising to transmit information about product features. If the firm is selling an experience good, which has features that are apparent only when consumed, it is more likely to engage in persuasive advertising intended to cause consumers to discover unknown tastes. If the product is a credence good with characteristics that consumers cannot readily assess unaided, then the firm often uses a mix of informational and persuasive advertising.	direct marketing, 669 mass marketing, 669 interactive marketing, 669 search good, 670 experience good, 670 credence good, 670 informational advertising, 670 persuasive advertising, 670	• **MyEconLab** Study Plan 26.4

WHAT YOU SHOULD KNOW

Properties of Information Products and Determining Their Prices Providing an information product entails incurring relatively high fixed costs but a relatively low per-unit cost for additional units of output. Hence the average total cost curve for a firm that sells an information product slopes downward, meaning that the firm experiences economies of operation in the short run. Under marginal cost pricing, the producer of an information product earns only sufficient revenues to cover its variable costs, so it incurs economic losses equal to its total fixed costs. In a long-run monopolistically competitive equilibrium, price adjusts to equality with average total cost. The firm earns sufficient revenues to cover total costs, including the opportunity cost of capital.

information product, 671
short-run economies of operation, 673
Key figures
Figure 26-4, 672
Figure 26-5, 674

WHERE TO GO TO PRACTICE

- **MyEconLab** Study Plan 26.5
- Animated Figures 26-4 and 26-5

Log in to MyEconLab, take a chapter test, and get a personalized Study Plan that tells you which concepts you understand and which ones you need to review. From there, MyEconLab will give you further practice, tutorials, animations, videos, and guided solutions.

Log in to www.myeconlab.com

PROBLEMS

Select problems, indicated by a blue oval, are assignable in MyEconLab. Answers to the odd-numbered problems appear at the back of the book.

26-1 Explain why the following are examples of monopolistic competition.

    a. There are a number of fast-food restaurants in town, and they compete fiercely. Some restaurants cook their hamburgers over open flames. Others fry their hamburgers. In addition, some serve broiled fish sandwiches, while others serve fried fish sandwiches. A few serve ice cream cones for dessert, while others offer frozen ice cream pies.

    b. There is a vast number of colleges and universities across the country. Each competes for top students. All offer similar courses and programs, but some have better programs in business, while others have stronger programs in the arts and humanities. Still others are academically stronger in the sciences.

26-2 Consider the diagram at the right depicting the revenue and cost conditions faced by a monopolistically competitive firm.

a. What are the total revenues, total costs, and economic profits experienced by this firm?
b. Is this firm more likely in short- or long-run equilibrium? Explain.

26-3 The following table depicts the prices and total costs a local used-book store faces. The bookstore competes with a number of similar stores, but it capitalizes on its location and the word-of-mouth reputation of the coffee it serves to its customers. Calculate the store's total revenue, total profit, marginal revenue, and marginal cost at each level of output, beginning with the first unit. Based on marginal analysis, what is the approximate profit-maximizing level of output for this business?

Output	Price per Book ($)	Total Costs ($)
0	6.00	2.00
1	5.75	5.25
2	5.50	7.50
3	5.25	9.60
4	5.00	12.10
5	4.75	15.80
6	4.50	20.00
7	4.00	24.75

26-4 Calculate total average costs for the bookstore in Problem 26-3. Illustrate the store's short-run equilibrium by plotting demand, marginal revenue, average total costs, and marginal costs. What is its total profit?

26-5 Suppose that after long-run adjustments take place in the used-book market, the business in Problem 26-3 ends up producing 4 units of output. What are the market price and economic profits of this monopolistic competitor in the long run?

26-6 Classify each of the following as an example of direct, interactive, and/or mass marketing.
a. The sales force of a pharmaceutical company visits physicians' offices to promote new medications and to answer physicians' questions about treatment options and possible side effects.
b. A mortgage company targets a list of specific low-risk borrowers for a barrage of e-mail messages touting its low interest rates and fees.
c. An online bookseller pays fees to an Internet search engine to post banner ads relating to each search topic chosen by someone conducting a search; in part this helps promote the bookseller's brand, but clicking on the banner ad also directs the person to a Web page displaying books on the topic that are available for purchase.
d. A national rental car chain runs advertisements on all of the nation's major television networks.

26-7 Classify each of the following as an example of direct, interactive, and/or mass marketing.
a. A cosmetics firm pays for full-page display ads in a number of top women's magazines.
b. A magazine distributor mails a fold-out flyer advertising its products to the addresses of all individuals it has identified as possibly interested in magazine subscriptions.
c. An online gambling operation arranges for pop-up ads to appear on the computer screen every time a person uses a media player to listen to digital music or play video files, and clicking on the ads directs an individual to its Web gambling site.
d. A car dealership places advertisements in newspapers throughout the region where potential customers reside.

26-8 Categorize each of the following as an experience good, a search good, or a credence good or service, and justify your answer.
a. A heavy-duty filing cabinet
b. A restaurant meal
c. A wool overcoat
d. Psychotherapy

26-9 Categorize each of the following as an experience good, a search good, or a credence good or service, and justify your answer.
a. Services of a carpet cleaning company
b. A new cancer treatment
c. Athletic socks
d. A silk necktie

26-10. In what ways do credence goods share certain characteristics of both experience goods and search goods? How do credence goods differ from both experience goods and search goods? Explain your answers.

26-11. In light of your answer to Problem 26-10, explain why advertising of credence goods commonly contains both informational and persuasive elements.

26-12 Is each of the following items more likely to be the subject of an informational or a persuasive advertisement? Why?
a. An office copying machine
b. An automobile loan
c. A deodorant
d. A soft drink

26-13 Discuss the special characteristics of an information product, and explain the implications for a producer's short-run average and marginal cost curves.

26-14 Explain why having a price equal to marginal cost is not feasible for the producer of an information product.

26-15 The producer of a downloadable antivirus software program spends exactly $2,850,000 producing the first copy and incurring various costs required to make the software "user-friendly." The firm can produce and distribute additional copies at a per-unit cost of $1. If the company sold as many copies as consumers wished to purchase at a price of $1 per copy, it would sell 300,000 copies. If the company maximizes its economic profits in the short run, it sells 100,000 copies at a price of $35. Finally, the company earns zero economic profits when it sells 150,000 copies.

   a. What are the firm's economic profits (or losses) if it sells 300,000 copies of the antivirus software program at a $1 price per copy?

   b. What are the maximum economic profits that the firm can earn in the short run?

   c. What is marginal revenue when the firm maximizes its short-run economic profits?

   d. In the long run, after entry of competing firms, what amount of economic profits will this firm earn?

26-16 A firm that sells e-books—books in digital form downloadable from the Internet—sells all e-books relating to do-it-yourself topics (home plumbing, gardening, and so on) at the same price. At present, the company can earn a maximum annual profit of $25,000 when it sells 10,000 copies within a year's time. The firm incurs a 50-cent expense each time a consumer downloads a copy, but the company must spend $100,000 per year developing new editions of the e-books. The company has determined that it would earn zero economic profits if price were equal to average total cost, and in this case it could sell 20,000 copies. Under marginal cost pricing, it could sell 100,000 copies.

   a. In the short run, what is the profit-maximizing price of e-books relating to do-it-yourself topics?

   b. At the profit-maximizing quantity, what is the average total cost of producing e-books?

ECONOMICS ON THE NET

Legal Services on the Internet A number of legal firms now offer services on the Internet, and in this application you contemplate features of the market for Web-based legal services.

Title: Nolo.com—Law for All

Navigation: Link to the Nolo.com site via www.econtoday.com/ch26.

Application Answer the following questions.

1. In what respects does the market for legal services, such as those provided online by Nolo.com, have the characteristics of a monopolistically competitive industry?

2. How can providers of legal services differentiate their products? How does Nolo.com attempt to do this?

For Group Discussion and Analysis Assign groups to search the Web for at least three additional online legal firms and compare the services these firms offer. Reconvene the entire class and discuss whether it is reasonable to classify the market for online legal services as monopolistically competitive.

ANSWERS TO QUICK QUIZZES

p. 665: (i) large . . . highly; (ii) differentiated; (iii) easy
p. 668: (i) short; (ii) long . . . zero . . . normal; (iii) total . . . total; (iv) average total . . . minimum
p. 671: (i) Trademarks . . . direct . . . mass . . . interactive; (ii) informational; (iii) persuasive; (iv) credence
p. 675: (i) high . . . low . . . economies . . . operation; (ii) variable; (iii) average total . . . total

27 Oligopoly and Strategic Behavior

Learning Objectives

After reading this chapter, you should be able to:

1. Outline the fundamental characteristics of oligopoly
2. Understand how to apply game theory to evaluate the pricing strategies of oligopolistic firms
3. Explain the kinked demand theory of oligopolistic price rigidity
4. Describe theories of how firms may deter market entry by potential rivals
5. Illustrate why network effects and market feedback can explain why some industries are oligopolies

MyEconLab helps you master each objective and study more efficiently. See end of chapter for details.

About 10,000 years ago, when the world's population was no larger than 10 million people, there were about 12,000 languages in use. Today, a world population exceeding 6.5 billion people uses fewer than 7,000 languages. Of these, close to 3,000 languages are little used, and if current trends continue, another 2,000 or so languages may be gone by the end of this century. Why did the number of languages decrease by 40 percent during the past 100 centuries even as global population exploded? A concept known as *network effects* helps provide the answer to this question. The application of this concept to markets can also help to explain why the number of firms in certain industries tends to shrink to a relatively small number, a situation that economists call *oligopoly*.

Did You Know That . . .

only two private companies, AccuWeather, which began operations in 1971, and the Weather Channel, which was launched in 1982, provide weather forecasts on a nationwide basis? AccuWeather's staff of more than 100 meteorologists provides forecasts for more than 200 companies, state and local governments, 45 television stations, 200 radio stations, 850 newspapers, and 600 Web sites. Nevertheless, AccuWeather's revenues of about $100 million per year are less than half as large as those earned by the Weather Channel, which reaches more than 20 million people daily by television and 25 million unique daily Web site visitors.

The weather-forecasting industry is not the only industry with identifiably predominant firms. In the microprocessor-chip and defense industries, for instance, the top five firms account for more than 80 percent of all sales. Similarly, the top three publishers of college textbooks generate well over 70 percent of all textbook sales. In this chapter, you will learn about the special characteristics of industries composed of a few firms.

OLIGOPOLY

An important market structure that we have yet to discuss involves a situation in which a few large firms comprise essentially an entire industry. They are not perfectly competitive in the sense that we have used the term. They are not even monopolistically competitive. And because there are several of them, a pure monopoly does not exist. We call such a situation an **oligopoly,** which consists of a small number of *interdependent* sellers. Each firm in the industry knows that other firms will react to its changes in prices, quantities, and qualities. An oligopoly market structure can exist for either a homogeneous or a differentiated product.

Oligopoly
A market structure in which there are very few sellers. Each seller knows that the other sellers will react to its changes in prices, quantities, and qualities.

Characteristics of Oligopoly

Oligopoly is characterized by a small number of interdependent firms that constitute the entire market.

Small Number of Firms. How many is "a small number of firms"? More than two but less than a hundred? The question is not easy to answer. Basically, though, oligopoly exists when the top few firms in the industry account for an overwhelming percentage of total industry output.

Oligopolies usually involve three to five big companies that produce the bulk of industry output. Between World War II and the 1970s, three firms—General Motors, Chrysler, and Ford—produced and sold nearly all the output of the U.S. automobile industry. Among manufacturers of chewing gum and coin-operated amusement games, four large firms produce and sell essentially the entire output of each industry.

Interdependence. All markets and all firms are, in a sense, interdependent. But only when a few large firms produce most of the output in an industry does the question of **strategic dependence** of one on the others' actions arise. In this situation, when any one firm changes its output, its product price, or the quality of its product, other firms notice the effects of its decisions. The firms must recognize that they are interdependent and that any action on the part of one firm with respect to output, price, quality, or product differentiation will cause a reaction on the part of other firms. A model of such mutual interdependence is difficult to build, but examples of such behavior are not hard to find in the real world. Oligopolists in the cigarette industry, for example, are constantly reacting to each other.

Strategic dependence
A situation in which one firm's actions with respect to price, quality, advertising, and related changes may be strategically countered by the reactions of one or more other firms in the industry. Such dependence can exist only when there are a limited number of major firms in an industry.

Recall that in the model of perfect competition, each firm ignores the behavior of other firms because each firm is able to sell all that it wants at the going market price. At the other extreme, the pure monopolist does not have to worry about the reaction of current rivals because there are none. In an oligopolistic market structure, the managers of firms are like generals in a war: *They must attempt to predict the reaction of rival firms.* It is a strategic game.

Why Oligopoly Occurs

Follow the link at www.econtoday.com/ch27 to *Wall Street Journal* articles about real-world examples involving oligopoly.

Why are some industries composed chiefly of a few large firms? What causes an industry that might otherwise be competitive to tend toward oligopoly? We can provide some partial answers here.

Economies of Scale.
Perhaps the most common reason that has been offered for the existence of oligopoly is economies of scale. Recall that economies of scale exist when a doubling of output results in less than a doubling of total costs. When economies of scale exist, the firm's long-run average total cost curve will slope downward as the firm produces more and more output. Average total cost can be reduced by continuing to expand the scale of operation. Smaller firms in such a situation will have average total costs greater than those incurred by large firms. Little by little, they will go out of business or be absorbed into larger firms.

Barriers to Entry.
It is possible that certain barriers to entry have prevented more competition in oligopolistic industries. They include legal barriers, such as patents, and control and ownership of critical supplies. Indeed, we can find periods in the past when firms were able not only to erect a barrier to entry but also to keep it in place year after year. In principle, the chemical, electronics, and aluminum industries have been at one time or another either monopolistic or oligopolistic because of the ownership of patents and the control of strategic inputs by specific firms.

How did a government barrier recently fail to prevent a new firm from joining the U.S. overnight delivery oligopoly?

EXAMPLE

DHL Flies Over a Barrier in the Overnight Delivery Industry

At present, three firms earn 90 percent of total revenues in the overnight package delivery industry: UPS (51 percent), FedEx (28 percent), and the U.S. Postal Service (11 percent). To transport packages over long distances in less than 24 hours requires jet aircraft. When German-owned DHL tried to break into the U.S. market by using its own airline, Astar, to move packages, UPS and FedEx launched an effort to halt its plans. The two companies claimed that the plan violated U.S. government rules regarding the operation of airlines within the United States.

After years of legal battles over whether at least 75 percent of Astar's stock was owned by U.S. citizens and whether its president and two-thirds of its board exerted "actual control" over the airline, DHL won the right to enter the U.S. market. The company proceeded to splash a new yellow-and-red color scheme across 20,000 uniforms, 467 service centers, 16,000 drop boxes, 17,000 delivery trucks, and more than 275 million envelopes, packages, and airbills. Today, DHL earns 9 percent of total revenues in the overnight package delivery industry.

FOR CRITICAL ANALYSIS
How would the entry of additional firms into the overnight package delivery industry complicate efforts by UPS, FedEx, and the U.S. Postal Service to predict the reactions of rival firms in the industry?

Oligopoly by Merger. Another reason that oligopolistic market structures may sometimes develop is that firms merge. A merger is the joining of two or more firms under single ownership or control. The merged firm naturally becomes larger, enjoys greater economies of scale as output increases, and may ultimately have a greater ability to influence the market price for the industry's output.

There are two key types of mergers, vertical and horizontal. A **vertical merger** occurs when one firm merges with either a firm from which it purchases an input or a firm to which it sells its output. Vertical mergers occur, for example, when a coal-using electrical utility purchases a coal-mining firm or when a shoe manufacturer purchases retail shoe outlets.

Obviously, vertical mergers cannot create oligopoly as we have defined it. But that can indeed occur via a **horizontal merger,** which involves firms selling a similar product. If two shoe manufacturing firms merge, that is a horizontal merger. If a group of firms, all producing steel, merge into one, that is also a horizontal merger.

So far we have been talking about oligopoly in a theoretical manner. Now it is time to look at the actual oligopolies in the United States.

Vertical merger
The joining of a firm with another to which it sells an output or from which it buys an input.

Horizontal merger
The joining of firms that are producing or selling a similar product.

Measuring Industry Concentration

As we have stated, oligopoly is a market structure in which a few interdependent firms produce a large part of total output in an industry. This has been called *industry concentration*. Before we show the concentration statistics in the United States, let's determine how industry concentration can be measured.

Concentration Ratio. The most popular way to compute industry concentration is to determine the percentage of total sales or production accounted for by the top four or top eight firms in an industry. This gives the four- or eight-firm **concentration ratio,** also known as the *industry concentration ratio*. An example of an industry with 25 firms is given in Table 27-1. We can see in that table that the four largest firms account for almost 90 percent of total output in the hypothetical industry. This is an example of an oligopoly because a few firms will recognize the interdependence of their output, pricing, and quality decisions.

Concentration ratio
The percentage of all sales contributed by the leading four or leading eight firms in an industry; sometimes called the *industry concentration ratio*.

U.S. Concentration Ratios. Table 27-2 on the following page shows the four-firm *domestic* concentration ratios for various industries. Is there any way that we can show or determine which industries to classify as oligopolistic? There is no definite answer. If we arbitrarily picked a four-firm concentration ratio of 75 percent, we could infer that tobacco products and breakfast cereals were oligopolistic. But we would always be dealing with an arbitrary definition.

TABLE 27-1
Computing the Four–Firm Concentration Ratio

Firm	Annual Sales ($ millions)	
1	150	
2	100	= 400, Total number of firms in industry = 25
3	80	
4	70	
5 through 25	50	
Total	450	

Four-firm concentration ratio = 400/450 = 88.9%

TABLE 27-2
Four-Firm Domestic Concentration Ratios for Selected U.S. Industries

Industry	Share of Value of Total Domestic Shipments Accounted for by the Top Four Firms (%)
Tobacco products	99
Breakfast cereals	83
Household vacuum cleaners	69
Primary aluminum	59
Soft drinks	47
Computers	45
Printing and publishing	34
Commercial banking	29.5

Source: U.S. Bureau of the Census.

How concentrated is the computer printer industry?

E-COMMERCE EXAMPLE

Market Concentration in the Computer Printer Industry

Although various software developments make it easier to work with electronic files than with physical documents, most people still find themselves using computer printers to transform a considerable amount of digital information into print. To do so, they utilize computer printers and ink cartridges. The industry from which they obtain these items generated $50 billion in revenues in a recent year. Hewlett-Packard earned $24 billion of those revenues, Lexmark earned $9.7 billion, Dell earned $6.9 billion, and Epson earned $5.2 billion. These figures imply that Hewlett-Packard's market share was 48.0 percent, Lexmark's was 19.4 percent, Dell's was 13.8 percent, and Epson's was 10.4 percent, and the four-firm concentration ratio for the computer printer industry was 91.6 percent. Thus, the computer printer industry is very concentrated.

FOR CRITICAL ANALYSIS
In light of the fact that Canon earned $3.7 billion in revenues from selling computer printers and ink cartridges during this particular year, what was the five-firm concentration ratio in the computer printer industry?

Oligopoly, Efficiency, and Resource Allocation

Although oligopoly is not the dominant form of market structure in the United States, oligopolistic industries do exist. To the extent that oligopolists have *market power*—the ability to *individually* affect the *market* price for the industry's output—they lead to resource misallocations, just as monopolies do. Oligopolists charge prices that exceed marginal cost. But what about oligopolies that occur because of economies of scale? Consumers might actually end up paying lower prices than if the industry were composed of numerous smaller firms.

All in all, there is no definite evidence of serious resource misallocation in the United States because of oligopolies. In any event, *the more U.S. firms face competition from the rest of the world, the less any current oligopoly will be able to exercise market power.*

QUICK QUIZ

An **oligopoly** is a market situation in which there is a _____ number of _____ sellers.

Oligopoly may result from _____ of scale, barriers to entry, and _____.

_____ mergers involve the merging of one firm with either the supplier of an input or the purchaser of its output.

_____ mergers involve the joining of firms selling a similar product.

Industry concentration can be measured by the combined _____ of total _____ accounted for by the top four or top eight firms in the industry.

See page 704 for the answers. Review concepts from this section in MyEconLab.

STRATEGIC BEHAVIOR AND GAME THEORY

At this point, we would like to be able to show oligopoly price and output determination in the way we showed it for perfect competition, pure monopoly, and monopolistic competition, but we cannot. Whenever there are relatively few firms competing in an industry, each can and does react to the price, quantity, quality, and product innovations that the others undertake. In other words, each oligopolist has a **reaction function.** Oligopolistic competitors are interdependent. Consequently, the decision makers in such firms must employ strategies. And we must be able to model their strategic behavior if we wish to predict how prices and outputs are determined in oligopolistic market structures. In general, we can think of reactions of other firms to one firm's actions as part of a *game* that is played by all firms in the industry. Economists have developed **game theory** models to describe firms' rational interactions. Game theory is the analytical framework in which two or more individuals, companies, or nations compete for certain payoffs that depend on the strategy that the others employ. Poker is such a game situation because it involves a strategy of reacting to the actions of others.

Some Basic Notions About Game Theory

Games can be either cooperative or noncooperative. If firms get together to collude or form a cartel, that is considered a **cooperative game.** Whenever it is too costly for firms to negotiate such collusive agreements and to enforce them, they are in a **noncooperative game** situation. Most strategic behavior in the marketplace is best described as a noncooperative game.

What do economic experiments reveal about whether people tend to be cooperative or noncooperative?

Reaction function
The manner in which one oligopolist reacts to a change in price, output, or quality made by another oligopolist in the industry.

Game theory
A way of describing the various possible outcomes in any situation involving two or more interacting individuals when those individuals are aware of the interactive nature of their situation and plan accordingly. The plans made by these individuals are known as *game strategies*.

Cooperative game
A game in which the players explicitly cooperate to make themselves better off. As applied to firms, it involves companies colluding in order to make higher than perfectly competitive rates of return.

Noncooperative game
A game in which the players neither negotiate nor cooperate in any way. As applied to firms in an industry, this is the common situation in which there are relatively few firms and each has some ability to change price.

EXAMPLE

Using Experiments to Find Cooperative Players

Some years back, economic researchers experimented with pigeons and rats. Today, experimental economics has moved well beyond animals. Researchers try to replicate complex market processes, often by using computer networks to conduct experiments with college student subjects who presumably can mimic typical human responses much better than pigeons and rats can. The students are usually offered opportunities to earn differential dollar returns from their experimental interactions, depending on the choices that they make.

Among other things, experimental economists have sought to use experiments to determine whether people have a natural

(*continued*)

tendency to engage in cooperative or noncooperative behavior. Typically, experiments aimed at revealing whether or not people cooperate have found that about 15 to 20 percent of experimental subjects engage in cooperative behavior and that 15 to 20 percent do not. The remaining 60 to 70 percent of experimental subjects are *reciprocators*: They choose to cooperate with people who reveal by their actions that they will cooperate but choose not to cooperate with those who reveal that they will not.

FOR CRITICAL ANALYSIS
Why might the unwillingness of only a few firms to cooperate in a real-world industry result in all firms choosing not to cooperate?

Zero-sum game
A game in which any gains within the group are exactly offset by equal losses by the end of the game.

Negative-sum game
A game in which players as a group lose at the end of the game.

Positive-sum game
A game in which players as a group are better off at the end of the game.

Strategy
Any rule that is used to make a choice, such as "Always pick heads."

Dominant strategies
Strategies that always yield the highest benefit. Regardless of what other players do, a dominant strategy will yield the most benefit for the player using it.

Games can be classified by whether the payoffs are negative, zero, or positive. In a **zero-sum game,** one player's losses are offset by another player's gains. If two retailers have an absolutely fixed total number of customers, for example, the customers that one retailer wins over are exactly equal to the customers that the other retailer loses. In a **negative-sum game,** players as a group lose at the end of the game (although one perhaps by more than the other, and it's possible for one or more players to win). In a **positive-sum game,** players as a group end up better off. Some economists describe all voluntary exchanges as positive-sum games. After an exchange, both the buyer and the seller are better off than they were prior to the exchange.

Strategies in Noncooperative Games. Players, such as decision makers in oligopolistic firms, have to devise a **strategy,** which is defined as a rule used to make a choice. The goal of the decision maker is to devise a strategy that is more successful than alternative strategies. Whenever a firm's decision makers can come up with certain strategies that are generally successful no matter what actions competitors take, these are called **dominant strategies.** The dominant strategy always yields the unique best action for the decision maker no matter what action the other "players" undertake. Relatively few business decision makers over a long period of time have successfully devised dominant strategies. We know this by observation: Few firms in oligopolistic industries have maintained relatively high profits consistently over time.

How can a real-world situation faced by two captured bank robbers help to illustrate basic principles of game theory?

 EXAMPLE

The Prisoners' Dilemma

A real-world example of game theory occurs when two people involved in a bank robbery are caught. What should they do when questioned by police? The result has been called the **prisoners' dilemma.** The two suspects, Sam and Carol, are interrogated separately (they cannot communicate with each other) and are given various alternatives. The interrogator indicates to Sam and Carol the following:

1. If both confess to the bank robbery, they will both go to prison for five years.
2. If neither confesses, they will each be given a sentence of two years on a lesser charge.
3. If one prisoner turns state's evidence and confesses, that prisoner goes free and the other one, who did not confess, will serve 10 years on bank robbery charges.

You can see the prisoners' alternatives in the **payoff matrix** in Figure 27-1. The two possibilities for each prisoner are "confess" and "don't confess." There are four possibilities:

1. Both confess.
2. Neither confesses.
3. Sam confesses (turns state's evidence) but Carol doesn't.
4. Carol confesses (turns state's evidence) but Sam doesn't.

(continued)

In Figure 27-1, all of Sam's possible outcomes are shown on the upper half of each rectangle, and all of Carol's possible outcomes are shown on the lower half.

By looking at the payoff matrix, you can see that if Carol confesses, Sam's best strategy is to confess also—he'll get only 5 years instead of 10. Conversely, if Sam confesses, Carol's best strategy is also to confess—she'll get 5 years instead of 10. Now let's say that Sam is being interrogated and Carol doesn't confess. Sam's best strategy is still to confess, because then he goes free instead of serving two years. Conversely, if Carol is being interrogated, her best strategy is still to confess even if Sam hasn't. She'll go free instead of serving 10 years. To confess is a dominant strategy for Sam. To confess is also a dominant strategy for Carol. The situation is exactly symmetrical. So this is the prisoners' dilemma. The prisoners know that both of them will be better off if neither confesses. Yet it is in each individual prisoner's interest to confess, even though the *collective* outcome of each prisoner's pursuit of his or her own interest is inferior for both.

FOR CRITICAL ANALYSIS
Can you apply the prisoners' dilemma to the firms in a two-firm industry that agree to share market sales equally? (Hint: Think about the payoff to cheating on the market-sharing agreement.)

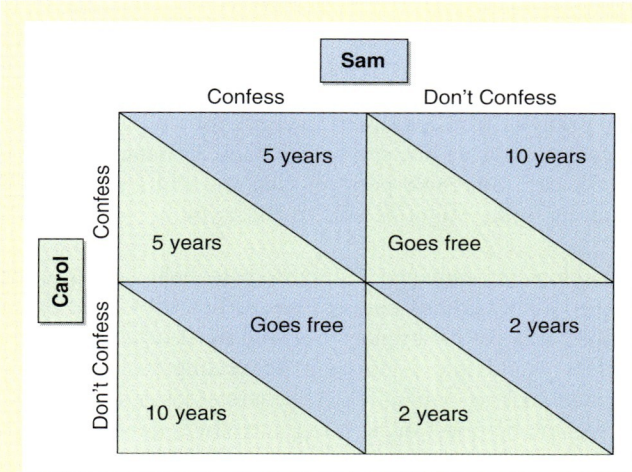

FIGURE 27-1
The Prisoners' Dilemma Payoff Matrix
Regardless of what the other prisoner does, each prisoner is better off if he or she confesses. So confessing is the dominant strategy, and each ends up behind bars for five years.

Prisoners' dilemma
A famous strategic game in which two prisoners have a choice between confessing and not confessing to a crime. If neither confesses, they serve a minimum sentence. If both confess, they serve a longer sentence. If one confesses and the other doesn't, the one who confesses goes free. The dominant strategy is always to confess.

Payoff matrix
A matrix of outcomes, or consequences, of the strategies available to the players in a game.

Applying Game Theory to Pricing Strategies

We can apply game strategy to two firms—oligopolists—that have to decide on their pricing strategy. Each can choose either a high or a low price. Their payoff matrix is shown in Figure 27-2 on the following page. If they both choose a high price, each will make $6 million, but if they both choose a low price, each will make only $4 million. If one sets a high price and the other a low one, the low-priced firm will make $8 million, but the high-priced firm will make only $2 million. As in the prisoners' dilemma, in the absence of collusion, they will end up choosing low prices.

Opportunistic Behavior

In the prisoners' dilemma, it is clear that cooperative behavior—both parties standing firm without admitting to anything—leads to the best outcome for both players. But each prisoner (player) stands to gain by cheating. Such action is called **opportunistic behavior.** Our daily economic activities involve the equivalent of the prisoners' dilemma all the time.

Opportunistic behavior
Actions that focus solely on short-run gains because long-run benefits of cooperation are perceived to be smaller.

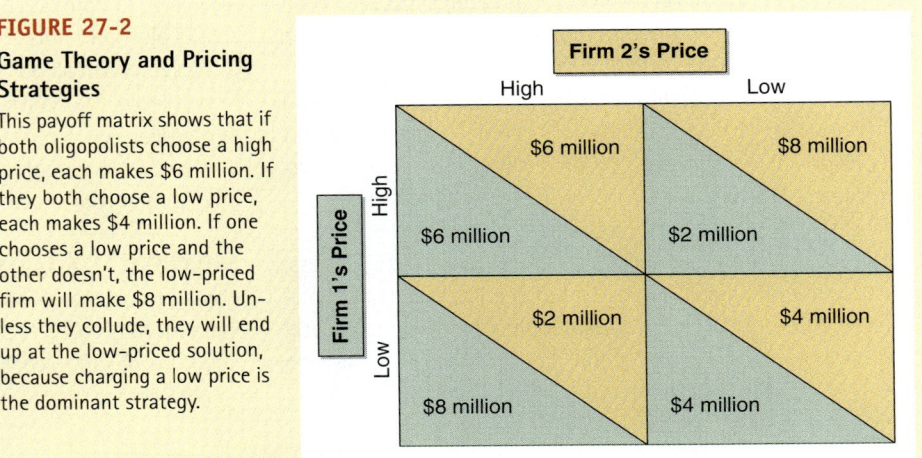

FIGURE 27-2
Game Theory and Pricing Strategies
This payoff matrix shows that if both oligopolists choose a high price, each makes $6 million. If they both choose a low price, each makes $4 million. If one chooses a low price and the other doesn't, the low-priced firm will make $8 million. Unless they collude, they will end up at the low-priced solution, because charging a low price is the dominant strategy.

We could engage in opportunistic behavior. You could write a check for a purchase knowing that it is going to bounce because you have just closed that bank account. When you agree to perform a specific task for pay, you could perform your work in a substandard way. When you go to buy an item, the seller might be able to cheat you by selling you a defective item.

In short, if all of us—sellers and buyers—engaged in opportunistic behavior all of the time, we would constantly be acting in a world of noncooperative behavior. That is not the world in which most of us live, however. Why not? Because most of us engage in *repeat transactions*. Manufacturers would like us to keep purchasing their products. Sellers would like us to keep coming back to their stores. As sellers of labor services, we all would like to keep our jobs, get promotions, or be hired away by another firm at a higher wage rate. Therefore, we engage in **tit-for-tat strategic behavior.** A consumer using a tit-for-tat strategy may, for instance, continue to purchase items from a firm each period as long as the firm provides products of the same quality and abides by any guarantees. If the firm fails in any period to provide high-quality products and honor its product guarantees, the consumer purchases items elsewhere.

Tit-for-tat strategic behavior
In game theory, cooperation that continues as long as the other players continue to cooperate.

PRICE RIGIDITY AND THE KINKED DEMAND CURVE

Let's hypothesize that the decision makers in an oligopolistic firm assume that rivals will react in the following way: They will match all price decreases (in order not to be undersold) but not price increases (because they want to capture more business). There is no collusion. The implications of this reaction function are rigid prices and a kinked demand curve for each firm.

Nature of the Kinked Demand Curve

In Figure 27-3, we draw a kinked demand curve, which is implicit in the assumption that oligopolists match price decreases but not price increases. We start off in panel (a) at a given price of P_0 and assume that the quantity demanded at this price for this individual oligopolist is q_0. The price P_0 is usually the stable market price. If the oligopolist assumes that rivals will not react by matching a change in the price of its own product, it faces demand

FIGURE 27-3

The Kinked Demand Curve

If the oligopolist assumes that rivals will not match price changes, it faces demand curve d_1d_1 and marginal revenue curve MR_1. If it assumes that rivals will match price changes, it faces demand curve d_2d_2 and marginal revenue curve MR_2. If the oligopolist believes that rivals will not react to price increases but will react to price decreases, at prices above P_0, it faces demand curve d_1d_1, and at prices below P_0, it faces the other demand curve, d_2d_2. The overall demand curve will therefore have a kink at price P_0, as is seen in panel (b). The MR curve will have a vertical break, as shown by the dashed line in panel (b).

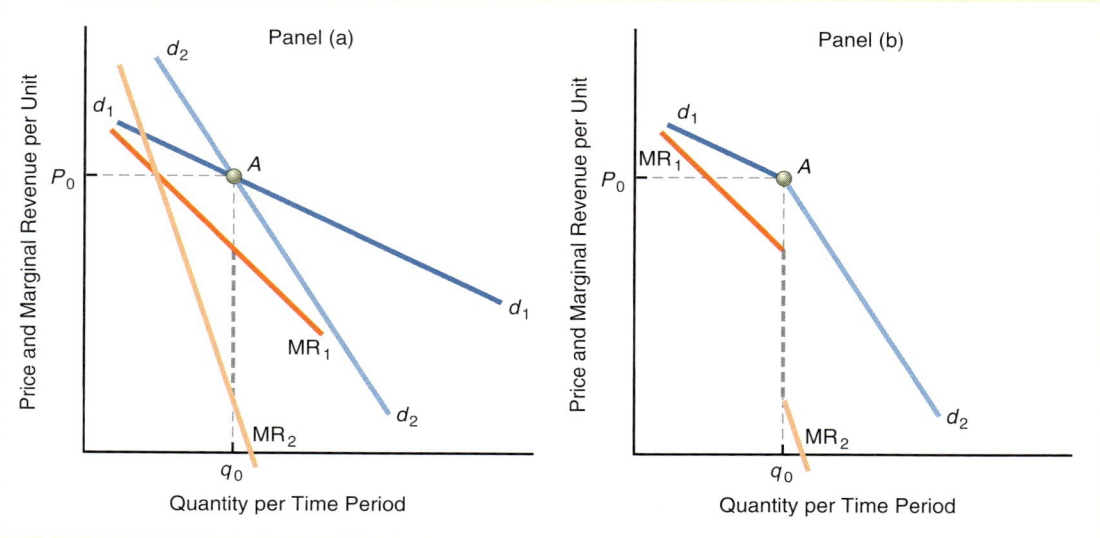

curve d_1d_1 with marginal revenue curve MR_1. Conversely, if it assumes that rivals will react to a change in the price of its product by matching the price change, it faces demand curve d_2d_2 with marginal revenue curve MR_2. More than likely, the oligopolist firm will assume that if it lowers price, rivals will react by matching that reduction to avoid losing their respective shares of the market.

The oligopolist that initially lowers its price will not greatly increase its quantity demanded. So, when it lowers its price, it believes that it will face demand curve d_2d_2. But if it increases price above P_0, rivals will probably not follow suit. Thus, a higher price than P_0 will cause quantity demanded to decrease rapidly. The demand schedule to the left of and above point A will be relatively elastic, as represented by d_1d_1. At prices above P_0, the relevant demand curve is d_1d_1, whereas below price P_0, the relevant demand curve will be d_2d_2. Consequently, at point A there will be a *kink* in the resulting demand curve. This is shown in panel (b) of Figure 27-3, where the demand curve is labeled d_1d_2. The resulting marginal revenue curve is labeled MR_1MR_2. It has a discontinuous portion, or gap, represented by the boldfaced dashed vertical lines in both panels.

Price Rigidity

The kinked demand curve analysis may help explain why price changes might be infrequent in an oligopolistic industry without collusion. Each oligopolist can see only harm in a price change: If price is increased, the oligopolist will lose many of its customers to rivals that do not raise their prices. That is to say, the oligopolist moves up from point A along demand curve d_1 in panel (b) of Figure 27-3. However, if an oligopolist lowers its price, given that rivals will lower their prices too, its sales will not increase very much. Moving down from point A in panel (b) of Figure 27-3 on the previous page, we see that the demand curve is relatively inelastic. If the elasticity is less than 1, total revenues will fall rather than rise with the lowering of price. Given that the production of a larger output will increase total costs, the oligopolist's profits will fall. The lowering of price by the oligopolist might start a *price war* in which its rival firms will charge an even lower price.

A Break in the Marginal Revenue Curve. The theoretical reason for price inflexibility under the kinked demand curve model has to do with the discontinuous portion of the marginal revenue curve shown in panel (b) of Figure 27-3, which we reproduce in Figure 27-4. Assume that marginal cost is represented by MC. The profit-maximizing rate of output is q_0, which can be sold at a price of P_0. Now assume that the marginal cost curve shifts upward to MC'. What will happen to the profit-maximizing rate of output? Nothing. Both quantity and price will remain the same for this oligopolist.

A Theory of Price Rigidity. Remember that the profit-maximizing rate of output is where marginal revenue equals marginal cost. The shift in the marginal cost curve to MC' does not change the profit-maximizing rate of output in Figure 27-4 because MC' still cuts the marginal revenue curve in the latter's discontinuous portion. Thus, the equality between marginal revenue and marginal cost still holds at output rate q_0 even when the marginal cost curve shifts upward.

What will happen when marginal costs fall to MC″? Nothing. This oligopolist will continue to produce at a rate of output q_0 and charge a price of P_0. Whenever the marginal cost curve cuts the discontinuous portion of the marginal revenue curve, fluctuations (within limits) in marginal cost will not affect output or price because the profit-maximizing condition MR = MC will hold. The result is that even when firms in an oligopolistic industry such as this experience increases or decreases in costs, their prices do not change as long as MC cuts MR in the discontinuous portion. Hence prices are seen to be rigid in oligopolistic industries if oligopolists react the way we assume they do in this model.

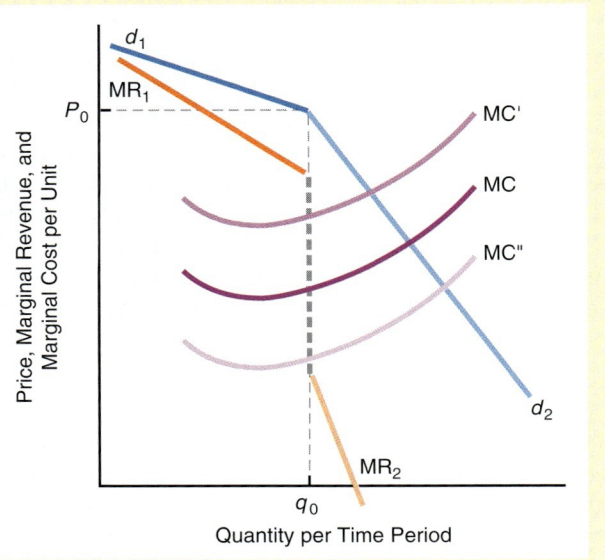

FIGURE 27-4

Changes in Cost May Not Alter the Profit-Maximizing Price and Output

As long as the marginal cost curve intersects the marginal revenue curve in the latter's discontinuous portion, the profit-maximizing price P_0 (and output q_0) will remain unchanged even with changes in MC. (The firm's rate of profit will change, however.)

Criticisms of the Kinked Demand Curve

One of the criticisms directed against the kinked demand curve is that we have no idea how the existing price, P_0, came to be. If every oligopolistic firm faced a kinked demand curve, it would not pay for the firm to change prices. The problem is that the kinked demand curve does not show us how demand and supply originally determine the going price of an oligopolist's product.

As far as the evidence goes, it is not encouraging. Oligopoly prices do not appear to be as rigid, particularly in the upward direction, as the kinked demand curve theory implies. During the 1970s and early 1980s, when prices in the economy were rising overall, oligopolistic producers increased their prices frequently. Evidence of price changes during the Great Depression showed that oligopolies changed prices much more frequently than monopolies.

QUICK QUIZ

Each oligopolist has a _____ function because oligopolistic competitors are interdependent. They must therefore engage in _____ behavior. One way to model this behavior is to use **game theory**.

Games can be either **cooperative** or **noncooperative**. A cartel is cooperative. When a cartel breaks down and its members start cheating, the industry becomes a noncooperative game. In a _____-sum game, one player's losses are exactly offset by another player's gains. In a _____-sum game, all players collectively lose, perhaps one player more than the others. In a _____-sum game, the players as a group end up better off.

Decision makers in oligopolistic firms must devise a strategy. A _____ strategy is one that is generally successful no matter what actions competitors take.

The _____ _____ curve oligopoly model predicts that major shifts in marginal cost will not cause any change in industry price.

See page 704 for the answers. Review concepts from this section in MyEconLab.

STRATEGIC BEHAVIOR WITH IMPLICIT COLLUSION: A MODEL OF PRICE LEADERSHIP

What if oligopolists do not collude to raise prices and share markets but do so implicitly? There are no formal cartel arrangements and no formal meetings. Nonetheless, there is *tacit collusion*. One example of this is the model of **price leadership**.

The Theory of Price Leadership

In the theory of price leadership, the basic assumption is that the leading firm, usually the biggest, sets the price and allows other firms to sell all they can at that price. The dominant firm then sells the rest. The leading firm always makes the first move in a price leadership model.

By definition, price leadership requires that one firm be the leader. Because of laws against collusion, firms in an industry cannot communicate this directly. That is why it is often natural for the largest firm to become the price leader. In the automobile industry during the period of General Motors' market leadership (until the 1980s), that company

Price leadership
A practice in many oligopolistic industries in which the largest firm publishes its price list ahead of its competitors, who then match those announced prices. Also called *parallel pricing*.

was traditionally the price leader. At various times in the breakfast food industry, Kellogg was the price leader. Some observers have argued that Harvard University was once the price leader among Ivy League schools. In the banking industry, various leading banks have been price leaders in announcing changes in the prime rate, the interest rate charged on loans offered to the best credit risks. One day a large New York–based bank, such as J. P. Morgan Chase, would announce an increase or decrease in its prime rate. Within five or six hours, all other banks would announce the same change in their prime rate.

Price Wars

Price leadership may not always work. If the price leader ends up much better off than the firms that follow, the followers may in fact not set prices according to those set by the leading firm. The result may be a **price war.** The leading firm lowers its prices a little bit, but the other firms lower theirs even more. Price wars have occurred in many industries. Supermarkets within a given locale often engage in price wars, especially during holiday periods. One may offer turkeys at so much per pound on Wednesday; competing stores cut their price on turkeys on Thursday, so the first store cuts its price even more on Friday.

Price war
A pricing campaign designed to capture additional market share by repeatedly cutting prices.

DETERRING ENTRY INTO AN INDUSTRY

ECONOMICS FRONT AND CENTER
To consider issues a firm may confront if it attempts to deter entry into its industry, read **A No-Frills Airline Contemplates Adding Some Frills**, on page 698.

Some economists believe that all decision making by existing firms in a stable industry involves some type of game playing. An important part of game playing does not have to do with how existing competitors might react to a decision by others. Rather, it has to do with how *potential* competitors might react. Strategic decision making requires that existing firms in an industry come up with strategies to deter entrance into that industry. One important way is, of course, to get a local, state, or federal government to restrict entry. Adopting certain pricing and investment strategies may also deter entry.

Increasing Entry Costs

Entry deterrence strategy
Any strategy undertaken by firms in an industry, either individually or together, with the intent or effect of raising the cost of entry into the industry by a new firm.

One **entry deterrence strategy** is to raise the cost of entry by a new firm. The threat of a price war is one technique. To be able to sustain a long price war, existing firms might invest in excess capacity so that they can expand output if necessary. When existing firms invest in excess capacity, they are signaling potential competitors that they will engage in a price war.

Another way that existing domestic firms can raise the entry cost of foreign firms is by getting the U.S. government to pass stringent environmental or health and safety standards. These typically raise costs more for foreign producers, often in developing countries, than for domestic producers.

Limit-Pricing Strategies

Limit-pricing model
A model that hypothesizes that a group of colluding sellers will set the highest common price that they believe they can charge without new firms seeking to enter that industry in search of relatively high profits.

Sometimes existing firms will make it clear to potential competitors that the existing firms would not change their output rate if new firms were to enter the industry. Instead, the existing firms would simply lower the market price (moving down their demand curves) enough to sell the same quantity as they currently do. This new price would be below the level at which an entering firm could earn a normal profit, and that prospect effectively discourages entry. This is called the **limit-pricing model.**

Raising Customers' Switching Costs

If an existing firm can make it more costly for customers to switch from its product or service to a competitor's, the existing firm can deter entry. Existing firms can raise customers' switching costs in a host of ways. Makers of computer equipment have in the past altered their operating systems and software products so that they would not operate on new competitors' computers. Any customer wanting to change from one computer system to another faced a high switching cost.

Why is high-definition television (HDTV) programming still so hard to obtain?

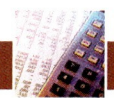

EXAMPLE

Switching Costs Keep the HDTV Market on a Dim Setting

Imagine purchasing and setting up a new HDTV, only to discover that the set-top box the cable company provided does not include a separate tuner that enables the device to receive high-definition television signals. You find that you will have to buy this device, which you discover is difficult to locate in your part of the country. Finally, after you set up the high-definition tuner, you discover that you accidentally purchased an HDTV that does not show high-definition programming.

Consumers are not the only ones who face switching costs in the market for HDTVs. Indeed, the complications that consumers face in purchasing and using HDTVs arise in part from the fact that producers have also been struggling with switching costs of their own. HDTV appeared before high-definition technologies had been fully developed. Consequently, many manufacturers of HDTVs and cable and satellite HDTV set-top boxes did not incorporate high-definition capabilities into their products. Only recently have most manufacturers incurred the costs of redesigning their products to include HDTV and high-definition capabilities simultaneously.

Thus, substantial switching costs have slowed sales in the market for HDTVs. At present, sales of HDTVs account for only slightly more than 10 percent of total television sales.

FOR CRITICAL ANALYSIS

Why is the fact that every cable and satellite television provider has its own technologies for TV signal receivers, remote controls, and other devices for use with new interactive TV programs likely to initially slow sales of this programming?

QUICK QUIZ

One type of strategic behavior involving implicit collusion is price _____. The dominant firm is assumed to set the price and then allows other firms to sell all that they want to sell at that price. Whatever is left over is sold by the dominant firm. The dominant firm always makes the first move in a price leadership model. If the nondominant firms decide to compete, they may start a price _____.

One strategic decision may be to attempt to raise the cost of _____ of _____ firms into an industry. The threat of a **price war** is one technique. Another is to lobby the federal government to pass stringent environmental or health and safety standards in an attempt to keep out foreign competition.

In a _____-pricing model, existing firms limit prices to a level above perfectly competitive prices before entry of new firms but are willing to reduce prices.

Another way for a firm to raise the cost to new firms is to make it more costly for customers to _____ from its product or service to the product of a _____ firm.

See page 704 for the answers. Review concepts from this section in MyEconLab.

NETWORK EFFECTS

A common source of switching costs is a shared understanding among consumers about how to use a product. Such a shared understanding can sometimes generate **network effects,** or situations in which a consumer's willingness to use an item depends on how many others use it. Commonplace examples are telephones and fax machines. Ownership of a phone or fax machine is not particularly useful if no one else has one, but once a number of people own a phone or fax machine, the benefits that others gain from consuming these devices increases.

In like manner, people who commonly work on joint projects within a network of fellow employees, consultants, or clients naturally find it useful to share computer files. Trading digital files is an easier process if all use common word processing and office productivity software. The benefit that each person receives from using word processing and office productivity software increases when others also use the same software.

Network effect
A situation in which a consumer's willingness to purchase a good or service is influenced by how many others also buy or have bought the item.

Network Effects and Market Feedback

On the one hand, industries in which firms produce goods or services subject to network effects can experience sudden surges in growth. On the other hand, the fortunes of such industries can also undergo significant and sometimes sudden reversals.

Positive Market Feedback. When network effects are an important characteristic of an industry's product, an industry can experience **positive market feedback.** This is the potential for a network effect to arise when an industry's product catches on with consumers. Increased use of the product by some consumers then induces other consumers to purchase the product as well.

Positive market feedback
A tendency for a good or service to come into favor with additional consumers because other consumers have chosen to buy the item.

Positive market feedback can affect the prospects of an entire industry. The market for Internet service provider (ISP) servers is an example. The growth of this industry has roughly paralleled the rapid growth of Internet servers worldwide. Undoubtedly, positive market feedback resulting from network effects associated with Internet communications and interactions resulted in additional people desiring to obtain access to the Internet.

How has Apple blended digital applications, Internet access, portability, and a physical product to capture positive market feedback effects in two markets?

E-COMMERCE EXAMPLE

Jumping on the "i" Bandwagon

In 2001, Apple introduced iTunes. Among other things, this digital music service allows users to organize music playlists, record compact discs, copy files to a digital audio player, and purchase music on the Internet through Apple's music store. A key feature that helped iTunes catch on with consumers is its ability to store audio data in a binary format, which allows iTunes to adapt to numerous alternative digital music formats. Apple also intentially constructed the iTunes service so that software developers can easily write applications that access its music formats.

Simultaneously, Apple also developed the iPod portable digital music player, which naturally plays iTunes digital music files. By the mid-2000s, both the iTunes service and the iPod had caught on with consumers of digital music. Positive market feedback had boosted Apple's market share in the music download industry to 70 percent and its market share in the portable digital music player industry to 60 percent.

FOR CRITICAL ANALYSIS
What aspects of the digital music business create network effects and the potential for positive market feedback?

Negative Market Feedback. Network effects can also result in **negative market feedback,** in which a speedy downward spiral of product sales occurs for a product subject to network effects. If a sufficient number of consumers cut back on their use of the product, others are induced to reduce their consumption as well, and the product can rapidly become a "has-been."

> **Negative market feedback**
> A tendency for a good or service to fall out of favor with more consumers because other consumers have stopped purchasing the item.

An example of an industry that has experienced negative market feedback of late is the telecommunications industry. Traditional telecommunications firms such as AT&T, WorldCom, and Sprint experienced positive market feedback during the late 1980s and early 1990s as cellphones and fax machines proliferated and individuals and firms began making long-distance phone calls from cellphones or via fax machines. Since the mid-1990s, as more people have acquired Internet access via cable and satellite Internet service providers, e-mail communications and e-mail document attachments have supplanted large volumes of phone and fax communications. For the telecommunications industry, the greater use of e-mail and e-mail attachments by some individuals induced others to follow suit. This resulted in negative market feedback that reduced the overall demand for traditional long-distance phone services.

Network Effects and Industry Concentration

In some industries, a few firms can potentially reap most of the benefits of positive market feedback. Suppose that firms in an industry sell differentiated products that are subject to network effects. If the products of two or three firms catch on, these firms will capture the bulk of the sales due to industry network effects.

A good example is the market for online auction services. An individual is more likely to use the services of an auction site if there is a significant likelihood that many other potential buyers or sellers also trade items at that site. Hence there is a network effect present in the online auction industry, in which eBay, Amazon, and Yahoo account for more than 80 percent of total sales. eBay in particular has experienced positive market feedback, and its share of sales of online auction services has increased to more than 50 percent.

Consequently, in an industry that produces and sells products subject to network effects, a small number of firms may be able to secure the bulk of the payoffs resulting from positive market feedback. In such an industry, oligopoly is likely to emerge as the prevailing market structure.

QUICK QUIZ

_____ effects exist when a consumer's demand for an item depends in part on how many other consumers also use the product.

_____ market feedback arises if consumption of a product by a sufficient number of individuals induces others to purchase it. _____ market feedback can take place if a falloff in usage of a product by some consumers causes others to stop purchasing the item.

In an industry with differentiated products subject to **network effects,** an oligopoly may arise if a few firms can reap most of the sales _____ resulting from _____ market feedback.

See page 704 for the answers. Review concepts from this section in MyEconLab.

COMPARING MARKET STRUCTURES

Now that we have looked at perfect competition, pure monopoly, monopolistic competition, and oligopoly, we are in a position to compare the attributes of these four different market structures. We do this in summary form in Table 27-3 on the next page, in which we compare the number of sellers, their ability to set price, and the degree of product differentiation and also give some examples of each of the four market structures.

TABLE 27-3
Comparing Market Structures

Market Structure	Number of Sellers	Unrestricted Entry and Exit	Ability to Set Price	Long-Run Economic Profits Possible	Product Differentiation	Nonprice Competition	Examples
Perfect competition	Numerous	Yes	None	No	None	None	Agriculture, roofing nails
Monopolistic competition	Many	Yes	Some	No	Considerable	Yes	Toothpaste, toilet paper, soap, retail trade
Oligopoly	Few	Partial	Some	Yes	Frequent	Yes	Recorded music, college textbooks
Pure monopoly	One	No (for entry)	Considerable	Yes	None (product is unique)	Yes	Some electric companies, some local telephone companies

CASE STUDY — ECONOMICS FRONT AND CENTER

A No-Frills Airline Contemplates Adding Some Frills

Dirkson works for a budget airline. For several years now, its key advantage over most other airlines has been that its labor costs are lower, and it has offered no-nonsense, no-frills, low-cost air transportation to its passengers. Lately, traditional airline competitors such as US Airways, United, Delta, and Northwest have significantly scaled back their operations. The departures of these airlines from several markets have strengthened the position of Dirkson's airline. On the majority of its routes, Dirkson's company now faces only a few competitors. Furthermore, as more travelers have begun purchasing tickets from her airline, it has experienced a positive market feedback effect: If the airline fills more planes, it can profitably offer more flights, which in turn attracts more passengers. Now the airline has found itself transformed from a "fringe competitor" to a major player in the industry.

In spite of the continuing rise in airline fuel prices, several entrepreneurs have openly discussed trying to start new airlines to compete in some of the markets served by Dirkson's company. Today, Dirkson is reviewing a two-part proposal that her subordinates have offered for discouraging entry into the airline's markets: (1) keep ticket prices unchanged but offer free meals and other frills, thereby making new entrants feel that they can compete only if they also incur higher costs; and (2) buy more planes to create additional flying capacity that can be directed to any routes that a new entrant might try to serve.

Dirkson sits back in her chair and thinks about these ideas. Should her firm, she wonders, really consider abandoning its traditional "no-frills" approach to providing air service in an effort to discourage entry by potential competitors?

CRITICAL ANALYSIS QUESTIONS

1. What is the general term for the sort of strategy that Dirkson's subordinates have proposed?
2. Why might profit-maximizing owners of shares in Dirkson's airline have reason to disapprove of the proposed strategy in the short run? Why might they potentially approve of the strategy in the long run?

The Network Economics of Languages

Issues and Applications

Today, the world's people regularly speak about 6,800 languages. More than half of these are utilized by only a handful of people—perhaps a few thousand people per language. As you read these English words, hundreds of languages are on the verge of extinction, and linguists classify nearly 3,000 languages as "endangered."

Learning to speak and write a language requires the allocation of scarce resources, such as income and time. Thus, although no industry produces languages, economic analysis can be applied to the use of language. In particular, the concept of network effects can help us to understand why the number of languages in regular use has been declining rapidly even as the world's population has grown.

Concepts Applied
- Network Effects
- Positive Market Feedback
- Negative Market Feedback

Network Effects and Language

An individual typically has to put considerable time and effort into learning a language. Consequently, most people will go to the trouble to do so only if they are likely to have the opportunity to communicate with numerous other individuals who have also learned that language.

Recall that a network effect arises when an individual's willingness to utilize a good or service is influenced by how many others also use it. This is, of course, the situation confronted by any individual seeking to determine what language to learn and use as a primary or secondary form of spoken or written communication. The use of language, therefore, is a classic situation in which network effects apply.

The Roles of Positive and Negative Market Feedback

Why have thousands of languages died out in recent centuries? To answer this question, we must recognize that network effects can generate both positive and negative market feedback.

A key incentive to make an investment in learning to speak and write any language is the anticipation of earning a relatively high rate of return on that investment. Languages that allow a person to communicate with larger numbers of potential business partners and customers are more likely to yield a higher rate of return. Naturally, such languages are likely to be those utilized in nations or cultures with large populations, which helps explain why, as shown in Figure 27-5 on the next page, Chinese, Spanish, Hindi, Arabic, and Bengali are among the world's ten most-used languages. The fact that English now accounts for two-thirds of all the information on the Internet undoubtedly is contributing positive market feedback that lies behind its growing use.

Over the years, as more people have invested in learning languages they anticipate will yield higher rates of return, many allowed their native languages to fall into disuse. Eventually, more people stopped teaching the languages of their youth to their children. The result, for thousands of languages,

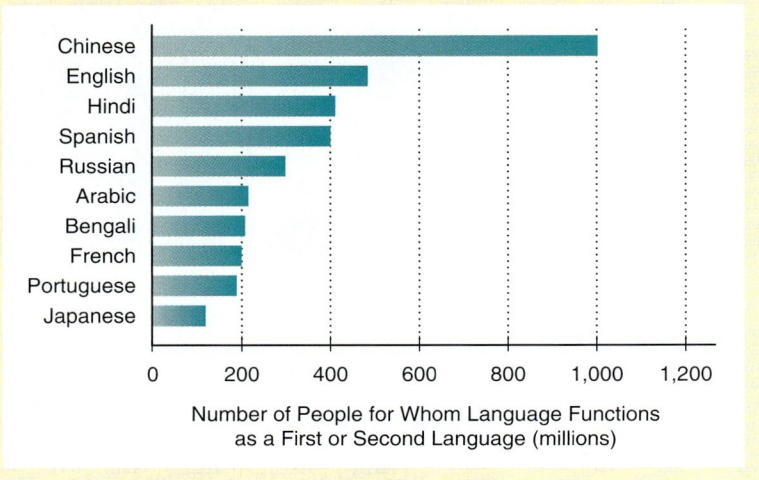

FIGURE 27-5

The Top Ten Languages Used as First or Second Languages

About 3.5 billion people, or more than half of the world's population, use these ten languages as first or second languages.

Source: United Nations Educational, Scientific, and Cultural Organization.

has been negative market feedback. Young people in various lands increasingly have found that they have an incentive to communicate through only one language. As a consequence, the languages their ancestors utilized have fallen out of favor—which in turn has reduced the incentive for people to learn and use them regularly. Even as network effects boost the growing use of a few of the world's languages, these effects are leading many more down a path to extinction.

Log in to MyEconLab, click on "Economic News," and test your understanding of the chapter by answering interactive questions that relate directly to this issue.

For Critical Analysis

1. What products in widespread use today possess certain features analogous to those of spoken and written forms of communication?
2. In what ways are information technologies utilizing telecommunications subject to network effects similar to those experienced by languages?

Web Resources

1. For a list of languages still in use but in danger of becoming extinct, go to www.econtoday.com/ch27.
2. For a list of languages that have recently become extinct, go to www.econtoday.com/ch27.

Research Project

Languages such as Latin, the official language of the Roman Empire, were once in widespread use but now are read mainly by scholars and rarely spoken. Make a list of characteristics that extinct languages and defunct products, such as 8-track stereo tapes and $5\frac{1}{4}$-inch computer floppy disks, have in common. In addition, make a list of features that languages that are becoming more widely used, such as English, share with products that you perceive have "caught on" in recent years. How do characteristics of languages and of certain products make them susceptible both to sudden utilization growth spurts and to a falling out of favor that can lead to extinction?

CHAPTER 27 *Oligopoly and Strategic Behavior* **701**

Here is what you should know after reading this chapter. MyEconLab will help you identify what you know, and where to go when you need to practice.

WHAT YOU SHOULD KNOW | **WHERE TO GO TO PRACTICE**

The Fundamental Characteristics of Oligopoly

Economies of scale, certain barriers to entry, and horizontal mergers among firms that sell similar products can result in an oligopoly, a situation in which a few firms produce the bulk of an industry's total output. To measure the extent to which a few firms account for an industry's production and sales, economists calculate concentration ratios, which are the percentages of total sales or total production by the top handful of firms in an industry. Strategic dependence is an important characteristic of oligopoly. One firm's decisions concerning price, product quality, or advertising can bring about responses by other firms. Thus, one firm's choices can affect the prices charged by other firms in the industry.

oligopoly, 683
strategic dependence, 683
vertical merger, 685
horizontal merger, 685
concentration ratio, 685

- **MyEconLab** Study Plan 27.1
- Audio introduction to Chapter 27

Applying Game Theory to Evaluate the Pricing Strategies of Oligopolistic Firms

Game theory is the analytical framework that economists apply to evaluate how two or more individuals, companies, or nations compete for payoffs that depend on the strategies that others employ. When firms get together to collude or form a cartel, they participate in cooperative games, but when they cannot work together, they engage in noncooperative games. One important type of game often applied to oligopoly situations is the prisoners' dilemma, in which the inability to cooperate in determining prices of their products can cause firms to choose lower prices than they otherwise would prefer.

reaction function, 687
game theory, 687
cooperative game, 687
noncooperative game, 687
zero-sum game, 688
negative-sum game, 688
positive-sum game, 688
strategy, 688
dominant strategies, 688
prisoners' dilemma, 689
payoff matrix, 689
opportunistic behavior, 689
tit-for-tat strategic behavior, 690
Key figures
Figure 27-1, 689
Figure 27-2, 690

- **MyEconLab** Study Plan 27.2
- Video: Opportunistic Behavior
- Animated Figures 27-1 and 27-2

The Kinked Demand Theory of Oligopolistic Price Rigidity

If an oligopolistic firm believes that no other firms selling similar products will raise their prices in response to an increase in the price of its product, it perceives the demand curve for its product to be relatively elastic at prices above the price it currently charges. At the same time, if the firm believes that all other firms would respond to a cut in the price of its product by

Key figures
Figure 27-3, 691
Figures 27-4, 692

- **MyEconLab** Study Plan 27.3
- Animated Figures 27-3 and 27-4

WHAT YOU SHOULD KNOW		WHERE TO GO TO PRACTICE
reducing the prices of their products, it views the demand for its product as relatively inelastic at prices below the current price. Hence, in this situation, the firm perceives the demand for its product to be kinked, which means that its marginal revenue curve has a break at the current price. Therefore, changes in the firm's marginal cost will not necessarily induce the firm to change its production and pricing decisions, so price rigidity may result.		
How Firms May Deter Market Entry by Potential Rivals To strategically deter market entry by potential competitors, firms in an industry may seek to raise the entry costs that such potential rivals would face. For example, existing firms may invest in excess productive capacity to signal that they could outlast other firms in sustained price wars, or they might engage in lobbying efforts to forestall competition from potential foreign entrants into domestic markets. Existing firms may also engage in limit pricing, signaling to potential entrants that the entry of new rivals would cause them to reduce prices so low that entering the market is no longer economically attractive. Existing firms may also develop ways to make it difficult for current customers to switch to products produced by new entrants.	price leadership, 693 price war, 694 entry deterrence strategy, 694 limit-pricing model, 694	• **MyEconLab** Study Plans 27.4 and 27.5 • Video: Price War
Why Network Effects and Market Feedback Encourage Oligopoly Network effects arise when a consumer's demand for a good or service is affected by how many other consumers also use the item. There is positive market feedback when enough people consume a product to induce others to purchase it as well. Negative market feedback occurs when decreased purchases of a good or service by some consumers give others an incentive to stop buying the item. Oligopoly can develop in an industry with differentiated products subject to network effects because a few firms may be able to capture most of the growth in demand induced by positive market feedback.	network effect, 696 positive market feedback, 696 negative market feedback, 697 **Key table** Table 27-3, 698	• **MyEconLab** Study Plans 27.6 and 27.7 • Animated Table 27-3

Log in to MyEconLab, take a chapter test, and get a personalized Study Plan that tells you which concepts you understand and which ones you need to review. From there, MyEconLab will give you further practice, tutorials, animations, videos, and guided solutions.

Log in to www.myeconlab.com

PROBLEMS

Select problems, indicated by a blue oval 🔵*, are assignable in* **MyEconLab**.
Answers to the odd-numbered problems appear at the back of the book.

27-1 Suppose that the distribution of sales within an industry is as shown in the table.

  a. What is the four-firm concentration ratio for this industry?
  b. What is the eight-firm concentration ratio for this industry?

Firm	Share of Total Market Sales
A	15%
B	14
C	12
D	11
E	10
F	10
G	8
H	7
All others	13
Total	100%

27-2 Suppose that the distribution of sales within an industry is as follows:

Firm	Share of Total Market Sales
A	25%
B	24
C	13
D	11
E	7
F	7
G	5
H	5
I	3
Total	100%

  a. What is the four-firm concentration ratio for this industry?
  b. What is the eight-firm concentration ratio for this industry?

27-3 Characterize each of the following as a positive-sum game, a zero-sum game, or a negative-sum game.

  a. Office workers contribute $10 each to a pool of funds, and whoever best predicts the winners in a professional sports playoff wins the entire sum.
  b. After three years of fighting with large losses of human lives and matériel, neither nation involved in a war is any closer to its objective than it was before the war began.
  c. Two collectors who previously owned incomplete and nearly worthless sets of trading cards exchange several cards, and as a result both end up with completed sets with significant market value.

27-4 Characterize each of the following as a positive-sum game, a zero-sum game, or a negative-sum game.

  a. You play a card game in your dorm room with three other students. Each player brings $5 to the game to bet on the outcome, winner take all.
  b. Two nations exchange goods in a mutually beneficial transaction.
  c. A thousand people buy $1 lottery tickets with a single payoff of $800.

27-5. Last weekend, Bob attended the university football game. At the opening kickoff, the crowd stood up. Bob therefore had to stand up as well to see the game. For the crowd (not the football team), explain the outcomes of a cooperative game and a noncooperative game. Explain what Bob's "tit-for-tat strategic behavior" would be.

27-6 One of the three shops on campus that sell university logo clothing has found that if it sells a sweatshirt for $30 or more, the other two shops keep their prices constant and the store loses revenues. If, however, the shop reduces its price below $30, the other stores react by lowering their prices. What kind of market structure does this store face? If the store's marginal costs fluctuate up and down very slightly, how should the store adjust its prices?

27-7. At the beginning of each semester, the university cafeteria posts the prices of its sandwiches. Business students note that as soon as the university posts these prices, the area delis adjust their prices accordingly. The business students argue that this is price collusion and that the university should be prosecuted for collusion. Are the students necessarily correct?

27-8 Consider two strategically dependent firms in an oligopolistic industry, Firm A and Firm B. Firm A knows that if it offers extended warranties on its products but Firm B does not, it will earn $6 million in profits, and Firm B will earn $2 million. Likewise, Firm B knows that if it offers extended warranties but

Firm A does not, it will earn $6 million in profits, and Firm A will earn $2 million. The two firms know that if they both offer extended warranties on their products, each will earn $3 million in profits. Finally, the two firms know that if neither offers extended warranties, each will earn $5 million in profits.

a. Set up a payoff matrix that fits the situation faced by these two firms.

b. What is the dominant strategy in this situation? Explain.

27-9. Consider the diagram below, which applies to a firm in an oligopolistic industry.

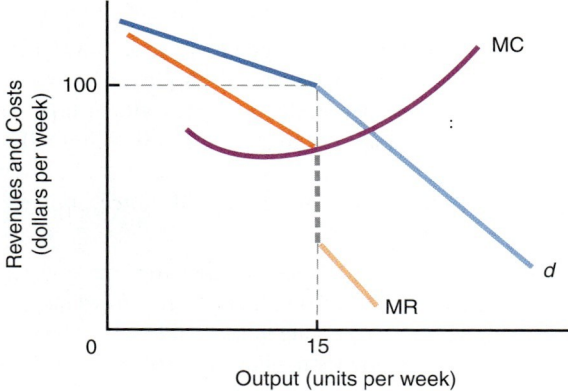

a. Explain the shape of the demand curve faced by this oligopolistic firm.

b. If consumers are willing to pay a slightly higher price for this firm's product at any given quantity, so that there is a small upward shift in demand, will this firm necessarily change its price? Explain.

27-10. Explain why network effects can cause the demand for a product *either* to expand *or* to contract relative to what it would be if there were no network effects.

27-11. List three products that you think are subject to network effects. For each product, indicate whether, in your view, all or just a few firms within the industry that produces each product experience market feedback effects. In your view, are any market feedback effects in these industries currently positive or negative?

ECONOMICS ON THE NET

Current Concentration Ratios in U.S. Manufacturing Industries
As you learned in this chapter, economists sometimes use concentration ratios to evaluate whether industries are oligopolies. In this application, you will make your own determination using the most recent data available.

Title: Concentration Ratios in Manufacturing

Navigation: Follow the link at www.econtoday.com/ch27 to get to the U.S. Census Bureau's report on Concentration Ratios in Manufacturing.

Application Answer the following questions.

1. Select the report for the most recent year. Find the four-firm concentration ratios for the following industries: fluid milk (311511), women's and girls' cut & sew dresses (315233), envelopes (322232), electronic computers (334111).

2. Which industries are characterized by a high level of competition? Which industries are characterized by a low level of competition? Which industries qualify as oligopolies?

3. Name some of the firms that operate in the industries that qualify as oligopolies.

For Group Study and Analysis Discuss whether the four-firm concentration ratio is a good measure of competition. Consider some of the firms you named in item 3. Do you consider these firms to be "competitive" in their pricing and output decisions? Consider the four-firm concentration ratio for ready-mix concrete (327320). Do you think that on a local basis, this industry is competitive? Why or why not?

ANSWERS TO QUICK QUIZZES

p. 687: (i) small . . . interdependent; (ii) economies . . . mergers; (iii) Vertical; (iv) Horizontal; (v) percentage . . . sales
p. 693: (i) reaction . . . strategic; (ii) zero . . . negative . . . positive; (iii) dominant; (iv) kinked demand
p. 695: (i) leadership . . . war; (ii) entry . . . new; (iii) limit; (iv) switch . . . competing
p. 697: (i) Network; (ii) Positive . . . Negative; (iii) gains . . . positive

Regulation and Antitrust Policy in a Globalized Economy

28

In 1997, the U.S. government ruled out a proposed merger between the granddaddy of all telephone companies, American Telephone & Telegraph (AT&T), and Texas-based SBC, a regional phone-service provider. Such a combination, one government official stated, would cause an "unthinkable" reduction in the degree of competition in the telecommunications industry. Only eight years later, the government changed its tune and permitted AT&T and SBC to merge their operations. Why was this merger "unthinkable" in 1997 but entirely permissible in 2005? To understand this shift in the government's view of the social desirability of a telecommunications merger, you will have to learn more about *antitrust policy*, which is one of the key topics of this chapter.

Learning Objectives

After reading this chapter, you should be able to:

1. Distinguish between economic regulation and social regulation
2. Recognize the practical difficulties in regulating the prices charged by natural monopolies
3. Explain the main rationales for regulation of industries that are not inherently monopolistic
4. Identify alternative theories aimed at explaining the behavior of regulators
5. Understand the foundations of antitrust laws and regulations
6. Discuss basic issues in enforcing antitrust laws.

MyEconLab helps you master each objective and study more efficiently. See end of chapter for details.

> **Did You Know That...**
>
> the twenty-five member nations of the European Union (EU) are in a transition toward a "regulatory regime" known as REACH—an acronym that stands for "registration, evaluation, authorization, and restriction of chemicals"? Once this 1,700-page body of regulations goes into effect, it will apply to more than 30,000 different chemical substances. Before any given chemical can be manufactured, purchased, and used within EU countries, its manufacturer will have to subject it to a prescribed range of tests. Results of these tests will then be reported to the agencies of all EU nations responsible for registering allowed chemicals. Any chemical that either fails certain evaluative tests or is not fully tested will not be authorized for manufacture or purchase. Already, many European companies are contemplating withdrawing a wide variety of chemicals from the market. In most cases, the firms are considering this action not because they believe the chemicals are dangerous but because the costs of testing and registering the chemicals will exceed the revenues they will lose from halting sales.
>
> Firms in Europe, the United States, and many other countries are highly regulated. Consequently, how regulations and other forms of government oversight *should act* to promote greater economic efficiency and how they *actually act* are important topics for understanding how every economy works. Nevertheless, before you can begin your study of the economic effects of regulation, it is important to understand the various ways in which the government oversees the activities of U.S. businesses.

FORMS OF INDUSTRY REGULATION

The U.S. government began regulating social and economic activity early in the nation's history. The amount of government regulation began increasing in the twentieth century and has grown considerably since 1970. Figure 28-1 displays two common measures of regulation in the United States. Panel (a) shows regulatory spending by federal agencies (in 2005 dollars), which has generally trended upward since 1970. Panel (b) depicts the number of pages in the *Federal Register,* a government publication that lists all new regulatory rules. According to this measure, the scope of new federal regulations increased sharply during the 1970s, dropped off in the 1980s, and has generally increased since then.

There are two basic types of government regulation. One is *economic regulation* of natural monopolies and of specific nonmonopolistic industries. For instance, some state commissions regulate the prices and quality of services provided by electric power companies, which are considered natural monopolies that experience lower long-run average costs as their output increases. Financial services industries and interstate transportation industries are examples of nonmonopolistic industries that are subjected to considerable government regulation. The other form of government regulation is *social regulation,* which covers all industries. Examples include various occupational, health, and safety rules that federal and state governments impose on most businesses.

Economic Regulation

Initially, most economic regulation in the United States was aimed at controlling prices in industries considered to be natural monopolies. Over time, federal and state governments have also sought to influence the characteristics of products or processes of firms in a variety of industries without inherently monopolistic features.

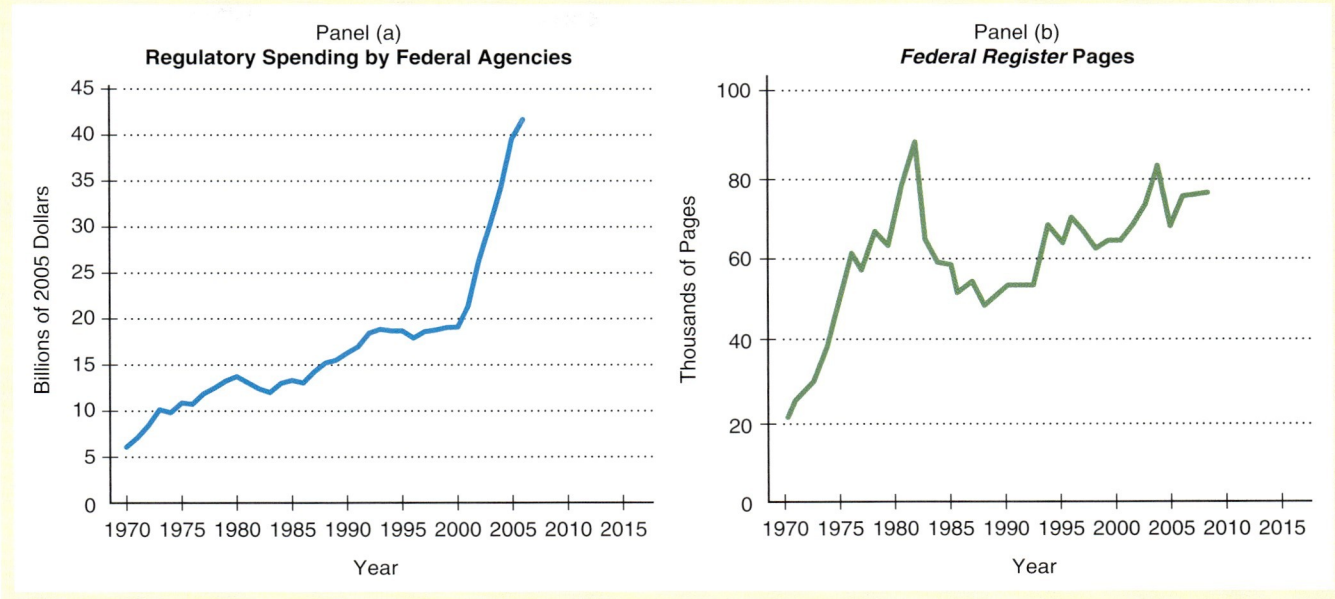

FIGURE 28-1
Regulation on the Rise
Panel (a) shows that federal government regulatory spending is now more than $40 billion per year. State and local spending is not shown. As panel (b) shows, the number of pages in the *Federal Register* per year rose from 1990 to 2000, dropped off somewhat, and then began to rise once more.
Sources: Institute for University Studies; *Federal Register*, various issues.

Regulation of Natural Monopolies. The regulation of natural monopolies has tended to emphasize restrictions on product prices. Various public utility commissions throughout the United States regulate the rates (prices) of electrical utility companies and some telephone operating companies. This *rate regulation*, as it is usually called, has been aimed at preventing such industries from earning monopoly profits.

Regulation of Nonmonopolistic Industries. The prices charged by firms in many other industries that do not have steadily declining long-run average costs, such as financial services industries, have also been subjected to regulations. Every state in the United States, for instance, has a government agency devoted to regulating the prices that insurance companies charge.

More broadly, government regulations establish rules pertaining to production, product (or service) features, and entry and exit within a number of specific nonmonopolistic industries. The federal government is heavily involved, for instance, in regulating the securities, banking, transportation, and communications industries. The Securities and Exchange Commission regulates securities markets. The Federal Reserve, Office of the Comptroller of the Currency, and Federal Deposit Insurance Corporation regulate commercial banks. The Office of Thrift Supervision regulates savings banks, and the National Credit Union Administration supervises credit unions. The Federal Aviation Administration supervises the airline industry, and the Federal Motor Carrier Safety Administration regulates the trucking industry. The Federal Communications Commission has oversight powers relating to broadcasting and telephone and communications services.

TABLE 28-1
Federal Agencies Engaged in Social Regulation

Agency	Jurisdiction	Date Formed	Major Regulatory Functions
Federal Trade Commission (FTC)	Product markets	1914	Responsible for preventing businesses from engaging in misleading advertising, unfair trade practices, and monopolistic actions, as well as for protecting consumer rights.
Food and Drug Administration (FDA)	Food and pharmaceuticals	1938	Regulates the quality and safety of foods, health and medical products, pharmaceuticals, cosmetics, and animal feed.
Equal Employment Opportunity Commission (EEOC)	Labor markets	1964	Investigates complaints of discrimination based on race, religion, gender, or age in hiring, promotion, firing, wages, testing, and all other conditions of employment.
Environmental Protection Agency (EPA)	Environment	1970	Develops and enforces environmental standards for air, water, waste, and noise.
Occupational Safety and Health Administration (OSHA)	Health and safety	1970	Regulates workplace safety and health conditions.
Consumer Product Safety Commission (CPSC)	Consumer product safety	1972	Responsible for protecting consumers from products posing fire, electrical, chemical, or mechanical hazards or dangers to children.

Social Regulation

In contrast to economic regulation, which covers only particular industries, social regulation applies to all firms in the economy. In principle, the aim of social regulation is a better quality of life through improved products, a less polluted environment, and better working conditions. Since the 1970s, an increasing array of government resources has been directed toward regulating product safety, advertising, and environmental effects. Table 28-1 lists some major federal agencies involved in these broad regulatory activities.

The essential objectives of social regulation are to protect people from incompetent or unscrupulous producers. The *potential* benefits of more social regulations are many. For example, the water supply in some cities is known to be contaminated with cancer-causing chemicals, and air pollution contributes to many illnesses. Society would clearly benefit from cleaning up these pollutants. As we shall discuss, however, broad social regulations also entail costs that we all pay, and not just as taxpayers who fund the regulatory activities of agencies such as those listed in Table 28-1.

QUICK QUIZ

_____ regulation applies to specific industries, whereas _____ regulation applies to businesses throughout the economy.

Governments commonly regulate the prices and quality of services provided by electric, gas, and other utilities, which traditionally have been considered _____ monopolies.

Governments also single out various nonmonopolistic industries, such as the financial and transportation industries, for special forms of _____ regulation.

Among the common forms of _____ regulation covering all industries are the occupational, health, and safety rules that federal and state governments impose on producers.

See page 731 for the answers. Review concepts from this section in MyEconLab.

REGULATING NATURAL MONOPOLIES

At one time, much government regulation of business aimed to solve the so-called monopoly problem. Of particular concern was implementing appropriate regulations for natural monopolies.

The Theory of Natural Monopoly Regulation

Recall from Chapter 25 that a natural monopoly arises whenever a single firm can produce all of an industry's output at a lower per-unit cost than other firms attempting to produce less than total industry output. In a natural monopoly, therefore, economies of large-scale production exist, leading to a single-firm industry.

The Unregulated Natural Monopoly. Like any other firm, an unregulated natural monopolist will produce to the point at which marginal revenue equals marginal cost. Panel (a) of Figure 28-2 depicts a situation in which a monopolist faces the market demand curve, D, and the marginal revenue curve, MR. The monopolist searches along the demand curve for the profit-maximizing price and quantity. The profit-maximizing quantity is at point A,

FIGURE 28-2

Profit Maximization and Regulation Through Marginal Cost Pricing

The profit-maximizing natural monopolist here would produce at the point in panel (a) where marginal costs equal marginal revenue—that is, at point A, which gives the quantity of production Q_m. The price charged would be P_m at point F, which is the price consumers would be willing to pay for the quantity produced. If a regulatory commission attempted to regulate natural monopolies so that price equaled long-run marginal cost, the commission would make the monopolist set production at the point where the marginal cost curve intersects the demand schedule. This is shown in panel (b). The quantity produced would be Q_1, and the price would be P_1. Average costs at Q_1 are equal to AC_1, however. Losses would ensue, equal to the shaded area. It would be self-defeating for a regulatory commission to force a natural monopolist to produce at an output rate at which $MC = P$ without subsidizing some of its costs because losses would eventually drive the natural monopolist out of business.

at which the marginal revenue curve crosses the long-run marginal cost curve, LMC, and the unregulated monopolist maximizes profits by producing the quantity Q_m. Consumers are willing and able to pay the price P_m for this quantity at point F. This price is above marginal cost, so it leads to a socially inefficient allocation of resources by restricting production to a rate below that at which price equals marginal cost.

The Impracticality of Marginal Cost Pricing.
What would happen if the government were to require the monopolist in Figure 28-2 on the previous page to produce to the point at which price equals marginal cost, which is point B in panel (b)? Then it would produce a larger output rate, Q_1. Consumers, however, would pay only the price P_1 for this quantity, which would be less than the average cost of producing this output rate, AC_1. Consequently, requiring the monopolist to engage in marginal cost pricing would yield a loss for the firm equal to the shaded rectangular area in panel (b). The profit-maximizing monopolist would go out of business rather than face such regulation.

Average Cost Pricing.
Regulators cannot practically force a natural monopolist to engage in marginal cost pricing. Thus, regulation of natural monopolies has often taken the form of allowing the firm to set price at the point at which LAC intersects the demand curve. In panel (b) of Figure 28-2, this is point C. In this situation, the regulator forces the firm to engage in *average cost pricing,* with average cost including what the regulators deem a "fair" rate of return on investment. For instance, a regulator might impose **cost-of-service regulation,** which requires a natural monopoly to charge only prices that reflect the actual average cost of providing products to consumers. Alternatively, although in a similar vein, a regulator might use **rate-of-return regulation,** which allows firms to set prices that ensure a normal return on investment.

Cost-of-service regulation
Regulation that allows prices to reflect only the actual average cost of production and no monopoly profits.

Rate-of-return regulation
Regulation that seeks to keep the rate of return in an industry at a competitive level by not allowing prices that would produce economic profits.

Natural Monopolies No More?

For years, the electricity, natural gas, and telecommunications industries have been subjected to regulations intended to induce firms in these industries to engage in average cost pricing. Traditionally, a feature common to all three industries has been that they utilize large networks of wires or pipelines to transmit their products to consumers. Federal, state, and local governments concluded that the average costs of providing electricity, natural gas, and telecommunications declined as the output rates of firms in these industries increased. Consequently, governments treated these industries as natural monopolies and established regulatory commissions to subject the industries to forms of cost-of-service and rate-of-return regulation.

Electricity and Natural Gas: Separating Production from Delivery.
Today, 15 different companies provide electricity to homes, office buildings, and factories in Houston. Eight different firms compete to sell electricity in New York City, and six companies provide electricity in Philadelphia. Similarly, various producers of natural gas vie to market their product in a number of cities across the country. In nearly half of the U.S. states, there is active competition in the production of electricity and natural gas.

What circumstances led to this transformation? The answer is that regulators of electricity and natural gas companies figured out that the function of *producing* electricity or natural gas did not necessarily have to be combined with the *delivery* of the product. Until the mid-1980s, producers of natural gas and electricity had exclusive ownership of the pipeline and wire networks that provided energy for homes, office buildings, and factories. Since then, various regulators have gradually implemented policies that have separated production of electricity and natural gas from the distribution of these items to consumers.

Thus, in a growing number of U.S. locales, multiple producers now pay to use wire and pipeline networks to get their products to buyers. Economies of scale still exist in these distribution networks, and regulatory commissions impose cost-of-service or rate-of-return regulations on the network owners. Individual producers of electricity and natural gas openly compete, however, in the markets for the products that consumers actually utilize in their homes and businesses. The market clearing rates that consumers pay to consume electricity and natural gas reflect both the costs of producing these items and the transportation costs that producers pay to deliver them via regulated distribution networks.

Telecommunications Services Meet the Internet. As the production and sale of electricity and natural gas began to become more competitive undertakings, regulators started to apply the same principles to telecommunications services. In the 1980s, the Federal Communications Commission (FCC) required AT&T to open its existing phone networks to competing providers of long-distance phone services. Gradually, during the 1990s and early 2000s, federal, state, and local regulators applied the same principles to local telecommunications services. Today, many U.S. cities and towns are served by two or more competing producers of wired phone services.

At the same time, other forces reshaped the cost structure of the telecommunications industry. First, during the 1990s, significant technological advances drastically reduced the costs of providing wireless telecommunications. Most individuals and businesses regarded cellphone services as imperfect substitutes for wire-based telecommunications. Nevertheless, the growing use of cellphones slowed growth in the demand for services delivered over traditional wire networks.

Second, during the 2000s, Internet phone service became more widely available. Most cable television companies that provide Internet access now offer Web-based telephone services as well. Many other companies also offer Web phone services for purchase by anyone who already has access to the Internet.

What lessons about cellular telecommunications have Irish regulators learned from the U.S. experience?

INTERNATIONAL POLICY EXAMPLE

Time to Break Up the Irish Cellphone Duopoly?

Since the mid-1990s, two companies, Vodafone and mmO2, have accounted for more than 95 percent of all sales of cellphone services in Ireland. Effectively, therefore, these two firms constitute a cellphone *duopoly*—the term economists use for a market with only two producers. The firms' ability to search for the profit-maximizing price enables them to receive 50 percent more revenues per customer than is received by firms in other nations with more competitive cellphone markets.

Ireland's telecommunications regulators recently decided to follow the U.S. example by proposing that Vodafone and mmO2 open their exclusive cellular-service networks to competitors. Under the proposal, the Irish regulators would regulate the fees charged for use of these networks to ensure a "fair" rate of return to the owners of the two companies. Naturally, the two companies initially balked at giving up their duopoly arrangement. Nevertheless, it now appears likely that new entrants will eventually end the Irish cellphone duopoly.

FOR CRITICAL ANALYSIS
What key barrier to entry has enabled the Irish cellphone duopoly to survive for a decade?

Are Natural Monopolies Relics of the Past? Clearly, the scope of the government's role as regulator of natural monopolies has decreased with the unraveling of conditions that previously created this market structure. In many U.S. electricity and natural gas markets, government agencies now apply traditional cost-of-service or rate-of-return regulations primarily to wire and pipeline owners. Otherwise, the government's main role in many regional markets is to serve as a "traffic cop," enforcing property rights and rules governing the regulated networks that serve competing electricity and natural gas producers.

In telecommunications, any natural monopoly rationale for a governmental regulator role is rapidly dissipating as more and more households and businesses substitute cellular and Web-based phone services for wired phone services. Since 2000, consumers have stopped using 28 million land phone lines. At present, phone signals stop flowing on an additional 4 percent of existing lines each year. Telecommunications has become a technology-driven, competitive free-for-all. This industry is now far from a natural monopoly.

Just how much competition exists in the market for Internet phone services?

E-COMMERCE EXAMPLE

Vying to Offer VOIP

The technical term for Internet telephony is Voice Over Internet Protocol (VOIP), in which sounds are transformed into digital packets of information and transmitted across the Internet much like e-mails. The digital information is then transformed back into sound when received by the recipient's Web-connected phone service.

Initially, the main adopters of VOIP were businesses that chose to use it for internal phone communications while retaining traditional wired lines for external telecommunications services. Nevertheless, during the early 2000s, VOIP began to catch on for international calls, and today almost 25 percent of phone calls across national borders are completed using the Internet.

By the mid-2000s, technological improvements enabled cable and DSL providers of broadband Internet service to roll out VOIP as an option for virtually all of their residential customers.

Today, all manner of companies have entered the market for VOIP services. Recently, America Online and eBay have joined the ranks of companies with names such as CallWave, Net2Phone, and VoiceGlo, which along with many other firms hope to profit from entering the VOIP market.

FOR CRITICAL ANALYSIS
Why is a single VOIP provider unlikely to emerge as a natural monopolist?

QUICK QUIZ

A **natural monopoly** arises when one firm can produce all of an industry's output at a _____ per-unit cost than other firms. A profit-maximizing natural monopolist produces to the point at which marginal _____ equals long-run marginal _____ and charges the price that people are willing to pay for the quantity produced.

Because a natural monopolist that is required to set price equal to long-run marginal cost will sustain long-run losses and shut down, regulators typically allow natural monopolists to charge prices that just cover _____ costs. Traditionally, regulators have done this through **cost-of-service regulation,** in which prices are based on actual production costs, or **rate-of-return regulation,** in which prices are set to yield a rate of return consistent with _____ economic profits.

Technological and regulatory innovations have made the concept of natural monopoly less relevant. In the electricity, natural gas, and telecommunications industries, production increasingly is accomplished by numerous competing firms that _____ their products through regulated _____.

See page 731 for the answers. Review concepts from this section in MyEconLab.

REGULATING NONMONOPOLISTIC INDUSTRIES

Traditionally, a fundamental purpose of governments has been to provide a coordinated system of safeguarding the interests of their citizens. Not surprisingly, protecting consumer interests is the main rationale offered for governmental regulatory functions.

Rationales for Consumer Protection in Nonmonopolistic Industries

The Latin phrase *caveat emptor,* or "let the buyer beware," was once the operative principle in most consumer dealings with businesses. The phrase embodies the idea that the buyer alone is ultimately responsible for assessing a producer and the quality of the items it sells before agreeing to purchase the firm's product. Today, various federal agencies require companies to meet specific minimal standards in their dealings with consumers. For instance, a few years ago, the U.S. Federal Trade Commission assessed monetary penalties on Toys "Я" Us and KB Toys because they failed to ship goods sold on their Web sites in time for a pre-Christmas delivery. Such a government action would have been unheard of a few decades ago.

In some industries, federal agencies dictate the rules of the game for firms' interactions with consumers. The Federal Aviation Administration (FAA), for example, oversees virtually every aspect of the delivery of services by airline companies. The FAA regulates the process by which tickets for flights are sold and distributed, oversees all flight operations, and even establishes rules governing the procedures for returning luggage after flights are concluded.

Reasons for Government-Orchestrated Consumer Protection.
Two rationales are commonly advanced for heavy government involvement in overseeing and supervising nonmonopolistic industries. One, which you encountered in Chapter 5, is the possibility of *market failures*. For example, the presence of negative externalities such as pollution may induce governments to regulate industries that create such externalities.

The second common rationale is *asymmetric information*. In the context of many producer-consumer interactions, this term refers to situations in which a producer has information about a product that the consumer lacks. For instance, administrators of your college or university may know that another school in your vicinity offers better-quality degree programs in certain fields. If so, it would not be in your college or university's interest to transmit this information to applicants who are interested in pursuing degrees in those fields.

For certain products, asymmetric information problems can pose special difficulties for consumers trying to assess product quality in advance of purchase. In unregulated financial markets, for example, individuals contemplating buying a company's stock, a municipality's bond, or a bank's certificate of deposit might struggle to assess the associated risks of financial loss. If the air transportation industry were unregulated, a person might have trouble determining if one airline's planes were considerably less safe than those of competing airlines. In an unregulated market for pharmaceuticals, parents might worry about whether one company's childhood-asthma medication could have more dangerous side effects than medications sold by other firms.

Asymmetric Information and Product Quality.
In extreme cases, asymmetric information can create situations in which most of the available products are of low quality. A commonly cited example is the market for used automobiles. Current owners of cars that *appear* to be in good condition know the autos' service records. Some owners know

that their cars have been well maintained and really do run great. Others, however, have not kept their autos in good repair and thus are aware that they will be susceptible to greater-than-normal mechanical or electrical problems.

Suppose that in your local used-car market, half of all used cars offered for sale are high-quality autos. The other half are low-quality cars, commonly called "lemons," that are likely to break down within a few months or perhaps even weeks. In addition, suppose that a consumer is willing to pay $20,000 for a particular car model if it is in excellent condition but is willing to pay only $10,000 if it is a lemon. Finally, suppose that people who own truly high-quality used cars are only willing to sell at a price of at least $20,000, but people who own lemons are willing to sell at any price at or above $10,000.

Because there is a 50–50 chance that a given car up for sale is of either quality, the average amount that a prospective buyer is willing to pay equals $(\frac{1}{2} \times \$20,000) + (\frac{1}{2} \times \$10,000) = \$15,000$. Owners of low-quality used cars are willing to sell them at this price, but owners of high-quality used cars are not. In this example, only lemons will be traded in the used-car market because most owners of cars in excellent condition will not sell their cars at a price that prospective buyers are willing to pay.

Lemons problem
The potential for asymmetric information to bring about a general decline in product quality in an industry.

The Lemons Problem. Economists refer to the possibility that asymmetric information can lead to a general reduction in product quality in an industry as the **lemons problem.** This problem does not apply only to the used-car industry. In principle, any product with qualities that are difficult for consumers to fully assess is susceptible to the same problem. *Credence goods,* which as you learned in Chapter 26 are items such as pharmaceuticals, health care, and professional services, also may be particularly vulnerable to the lemons problem.

Market Solutions to the Lemons Problem. Firms offering truly high-quality products for sale can address the lemons problem in a variety of ways. They can offer product guarantees and warranties. In addition, to help consumers separate high-quality producers from incompetent or unscrupulous competitors, the high-quality producers may work together to establish industry standards.

In some cases, firms in an industry may even seek external product certification. They may, for example, solicit scientific reports supporting proposed industry standards and bearing witness that products of certain firms in the industry meet those standards. To legitimize a product-certification process, firms may hire outside companies or groups to issue such reports.

Implementing Consumer Protection Regulation

Governments offering asymmetric information and lemons problems as rationales for regulation presumably have concluded that private market solutions such as warranties, industry standards, and product certification are insufficient. To address asymmetric information problems, governments may offer legal remedies to consumers or enforce licensing requirements in an effort to provide minimum product standards. In some cases, governments go well beyond simple licensing requirements by establishing a regulatory apparatus for overseeing all aspects of an industry's operations.

Go to www.econtoday.com/ch28 to see how the Federal Trade Commission imposes regulations intended to protect consumers.

Liability Laws and Government Licensing. Sometimes liability laws, which specify penalties for product failures, provide consumers with protections similar to guarantees and warranties. When the Federal Trade Commission (FTC) charged Toys "Я" Us and KB Toys with failing to meet pre-Christmas delivery dates for Internet toy orders, it operated under a mail-order statute Congress passed in the early 1970s. The mail-order law effectively made the toy companies' delivery guarantees legally enforceable. Although the FTC applied the law in this particular case, any consumer could have filed suit for damages under the terms of the statute.

Federal and state governments also get involved in consumer protection by issuing licenses granting only qualifying firms the legal right to produce and sell certain products. For instance, in an effort to ensure that bodies of deceased individuals are handled with care and dignity, governments of nearly half of the states give the right to sell caskets only to people who have a mortuary or funeral director's license.

Although government licensing may successfully limit the sale of low-quality goods, licensing requirements also often limit the number of providers. As you learned in Chapter 25, this can ease efforts by established firms to search for the profit-maximizing price, thereby enabling them to act as monopolists. In addition, if governments rely on the expertise of established firms for assistance in drafting licensing requirements, these firms may have strong incentives to recommend low standards for themselves but high standards for prospective entrants.

Direct Economic and Social Regulation. In some instances, governments determine that liability laws and licensing requirements are insufficient to protect the interests of consumers. A government may decide that lemons problems in banking are so severe that without an extensive banking regulatory apparatus, consumers will lose confidence in banks, and bank runs may ensue. It may rely on similar rationales to establish economic regulation of other financial services industries. Eventually, it may apply consumer protection rationales to justify the economic regulation of other industries such as trucking or air transportation.

The government may establish an oversight authority to make certain that consumers are protected from incompetent producers of foods and pharmaceuticals. Eventually, the government may determine that a host of other products should meet government consumer protection standards. It may also decide that the people who produce the products also require government agencies to ensure workplace safety. In this way, social regulation emerges, as it has in the United States and most other developed nations.

QUICK QUIZ

Governments tend to regulate industries in which they think market _____ and _____ information problems are most severe.

A common justification for government regulation is to protect consumers from adverse effects of _____ information.

To address the _____ problem, or the potential for _____-quality products to predominate when asymmetric information is widespread, governments often supplement private firms' guarantees, warranties, and certification standards with liability laws and licensing requirements.

See page 731 for the answers. Review concepts from this section in MyEconLab.

INCENTIVES AND COSTS OF REGULATION

Abiding by government regulations is a costly undertaking for firms. Consequently, businesses engage in a number of activities intended to avoid the true intent of regulations or to bring about changes in the regulations that government agencies establish.

Creative Response and Feedback Effects: Results of Regulation

Sometimes firms respond to a regulation in a way that conforms to the letter of the law but undermines its spirit. When they do so, they engage in **creative response** to regulations.

Creative response
Behavior on the part of a firm that allows it to comply with the letter of the law but violate the spirit, significantly lessening the law's effects.

Consider state laws requiring male-female pay equity: The wages of women must be on a par with those paid to males who are performing the same tasks. Employers that pay the same wages to both males and females are clearly not in violation of the law. Yet wages are only one component of total employee compensation. Another component is fringe benefits, such as on-the-job training. Because on-the-job training is difficult to observe from outside the firm, employers could offer less on-the-job training to women and still not be in technical violation of pay-equity laws. This unobservable difference would mean that males were able to acquire skills that could raise their future income even though males and females were receiving the same current wages, in compliance with the law.

One type of creative response has been labeled a *feedback effect*. Individuals' behaviors may change after a regulation has been put into effect. If regulation requires fluoridated water, then parents know that their children's teeth have significant protection against tooth decay. Consequently, the feedback effect is that parents become less concerned about how many sweets their children eat.

How has a government regulation intended to reduce automobiles' contributions to urban air pollution generated a socially costly feedback effect?

POLICY EXAMPLE

How Dare You Get Ahead of Me in That HOV Lane!

To give people an incentive to carpool and thereby release less auto exhaust into the air, the federal government uses regulatory inducements and rules to encourage construction of high-occupancy-vehicle (HOV) lanes along highways in major cities. Typically, vehicles containing at least two or more passengers can use HOV lanes, and under normal conditions, they can travel faster than vehicles in non-HOV lanes. Since 1990, total stretches of HOV lanes nationwide have increased from about 600 miles to more than 2,500 miles.

There is growing evidence, however, that adding more HOV lanes to combat air pollution has had an unintended—and sometimes deadly—feedback effect. HOV lanes often run directly alongside other highway traffic so that drivers of vehicles in HOV lanes can merge into the regular highway to exit the highway. To merge safely from an HOV lane into a non-HOV lane, the driver of the merging vehicle often must slow down, while drivers of vehicles in the non-HOV lane yield to the merging vehicle. All too often, drivers of vehicles merging from an HOV lane drive faster than traffic conditions warrant. Furthermore, postaccident interviews indicate that drivers in non-HOV lanes often resent the fact that vehicles using HOV lanes can move at a faster pace. Acting on this resentment, they stubbornly refuse to yield to traffic merging from HOV lanes. The result is a regulatory feedback effect: higher accident rates along highways with HOV lanes. In many cities, accident rates along roadways with HOV lanes are more than two times higher than accident rates on comparable stretches without HOV lanes.

FOR CRITICAL ANALYSIS
Why do you suppose that the federal government is now contemplating new regulations requiring long stretches of concrete buffers to separate HOV lanes from regular highway traffic?

Explaining Regulators' Behavior

Those charged with enforcing government regulations operate outside the market, so their decisions are determined by nonmarket processes. A number of theories have emerged to describe the behavior of regulators. These theories explain how regulation can harm consumers by generating higher prices and fewer product choices while benefiting producers by reducing competitive forces and allowing higher profits. Two of the best-known theories of regulatory behavior are the *capture hypothesis* and the *share-the-gains, share-the-pains theory*.

The Capture Hypothesis.
Regulators often end up becoming champions of the firms they are charged with regulating. According to the **capture hypothesis,** regardless of why a regulatory agency was originally established, eventually special interests of the industry it regulates will capture it. After all, the people who know the most about a regulated industry are the people already in the industry. Thus, people who have been in the industry and have allegiances and friendships with others in the industry will most likely be asked to regulate the industry.

According to the capture hypothesis, individual consumers of a regulated industry's products and individual taxpayers who finance a regulatory agency have interests too diverse to be greatly concerned with the industry's actions. In contrast, special interests of the industry are well organized and well defined. These interests also have more to offer political entrepreneurs within a regulatory agency, such as future employment with one of the regulated firms. Therefore, regulators have a strong incentive to support the position of a well-organized special-interest group within the regulated industry.

Capture hypothesis
A theory of regulatory behavior that predicts that regulators will eventually be captured by special interests of the industry being regulated.

"Share the Gains, Share the Pains."
The **share-the-gains, share-the-pains theory** offers a somewhat different view of regulators' behavior. This theory focuses on the specific aims of regulators. It proposes that a regulator's main objective is simply to keep his or her job as a regulator. To do so, the regulator must obtain the approval of both the legislators who originally established and continue to oversee the regulatory agency and the regulated industry. The regulator must also take into account the views of the industry's customers.

In contrast to the capture hypothesis, which holds that regulators must take into account only industry special interests, the share-the-gains, share-the-pains theory contends that regulators must worry about legislators and consumers as well. After all, if industry customers who are hurt by improper regulation complain to legislators, the regulators might lose their jobs. Whereas the capture theory predicts that regulators will quickly allow electric utilities to raise their rates in the face of higher fuel costs, the share-the-gains, share-the-pains theory predicts a slower, more measured regulatory response. Ultimately, regulators will permit an increase in utility rates, but the allowed adjustment will not be as speedy or complete as predicted by the capture hypothesis. The regulatory agency is not completely captured by the industry; it also has to consider the views of consumers and legislators.

Share-the-gains, share-the-pains theory
A theory of regulatory behavior that holds that regulators must take account of the demands of three groups: legislators, who established and oversee the regulatory agency; firms in the regulated industry; and consumers of the regulated industry's products.

ECONOMICS FRONT AND CENTER

To think about how alternative theories of regulator behavior might apply, take a look at **Balancing Auto Safety and Fuel Economy Is a High-Wire Act**, on page 724.

The Benefits and Costs of Regulation
As noted earlier, regulation offers many *potential* benefits. *Actual* benefits, however, are difficult to measure. Putting a dollar value on safer products, a cleaner environment, and better working conditions is a difficult proposition. Furthermore, the benefits of most regulations accrue to society over a long time.

The Direct Costs of Regulation to Taxpayers.
Measuring the costs of regulation is also a challenging undertaking. After all, about 4,500 new federal regulations are issued each year. One cost, though, is certain: U.S. taxpayers pay more than $40 billion per year to staff regulatory agencies with more than 190,000 employees and to fund their various activities. Figure 28-3 on the next page displays the distribution of total federal government outlays for economic and social regulation of various areas of the economy.

FIGURE 28-3
The Distribution of Federal Regulatory Spending

This figure shows the areas of the economy to which more than $40 billion of taxpayer-provided funds are distributed to finance economic and social regulation.

Source: Office of Management and Budget.

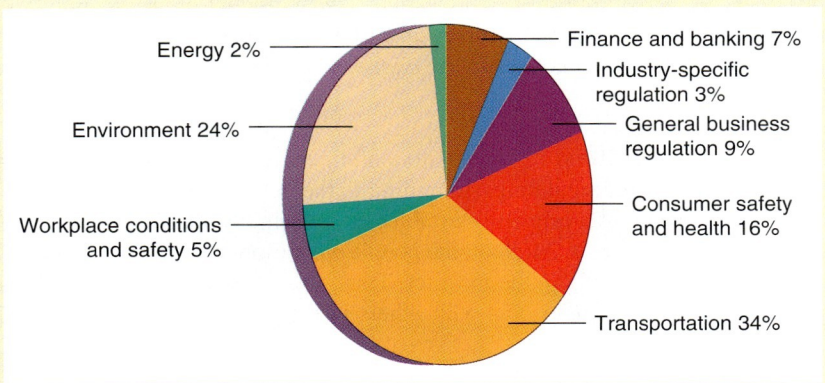

The *total* cost of regulation is much higher than just the explicit government outlays to fund the administration of various regulations, however. After all, businesses must expend resources complying with regulations, developing creative responses to regulations, and funding special-interest lobbying efforts directed at legislators and regulatory officials. Sometimes companies find that it is impossible to comply with one regulation without violating another, and determining how to avoid the resulting legal entanglements can entail significant expenditures.

The Total Social Cost of Regulation. According to the Office of Management and Budget, annual expenditures that U.S. businesses must make solely to comply with regulations issued by various federal agencies amount to between $500 billion and $600 billion per year. Nevertheless, this estimate encompasses only explicit costs of satisfying regulatory demands placed on businesses. It ignores relevant opportunity costs. After all, owners, managers, and employees of companies could be doing other things with their time and resources than complying with regulations. Economists estimate that the opportunity costs of complying with federal regulations may be as high as $270 billion per year.

All told, therefore, the total social cost associated with satisfying federal regulations in the United States is probably between $800 billion and $900 billion per year. This figure, of course, applies only to federal regulations. It does not include the explicit and implicit opportunity costs associated with regulations issued by 50 different state governments and thousands of municipalities. Undoubtedly, the annual cost of regulation throughout the United States exceeds $1 trillion per year.

QUICK QUIZ

The **capture hypothesis** holds that regulatory agencies will eventually be captured by industry special interests because _____ individually are not greatly influenced by regulation, whereas regulated _____ are directly affected.

According to the **share-the-gains, share-the-pains theory** of regulation, regulators must take into account the interests of three groups: the _____, _____, and _____.

Regulation has benefits that are difficult to quantify in dollars. The costs of regulation include direct _____ expenditures on regulatory agencies and _____ explicit and implicit opportunity costs of complying.

See page 731 for the answers. Review concepts from this section in MyEconLab.

ANTITRUST POLICY

An expressed aim of the U.S. government is to foster competition. To this end, Congress has made numerous attempts to legislate against business practices it has perceived to be anticompetitive. This is the general idea behind antitrust legislation. If the courts can prevent collusion among sellers of a product, there will be no restriction of output, and monopoly prices will not result. Instead, the perfectly competitive solution to the price-quantity problem will emerge: The competitive output will prevail in each industry, producers will earn zero economic profits in the long run, and the price of each item will equal its marginal social opportunity cost.

Antitrust Policy in the United States

Congress has enacted four key antitrust laws, which Table 28-2 summarizes. The most important of these is the original U.S. antitrust law, called the Sherman Act.

The Sherman Antitrust Act of 1890. The Sherman Antitrust Act, which was passed in 1890, was the first attempt by the federal government to control the growth of monopoly in the United States. The most important provisions of that act are as follows:

Section 1: Every contract, combination in the form of a trust or otherwise, or conspiracy, in restraint of trade or commerce among the several states, or with foreign nations, is hereby declared to be illegal.

TABLE 28-2
Key U.S. Antitrust Laws

Sherman Antitrust Act of 1890	Forbids any contract, combination, or conspiracy to restrain trade or commerce within the United States or across U.S. borders. Holds any person who attempts to monopolize trade or commerce criminally liable.
Clayton Act of 1914	Prohibits specific business practices deemed to restrain trade or commerce. Bans discrimination in prices charged to various purchasers when price differences are not due to actual differences in selling or transportation costs. Also forbids a company from selling goods on the condition that the purchaser must deal exclusively with that company. In addition, prevents corporations from holding stock in other companies when this may lessen competition.
Federal Trade Commission Act of 1914 (and 1938 Amendment)	Outlaws business practices that reduce the extent of competition, such as alleged cutthroat pricing intended to drive rivals from the marketplace. Also established the Federal Trade Commission and empowered it to issue cease and desist orders in situations where it determines "unfair methods of competition in commerce" exist. The 1938 amendment added deceptive business practices to the list of illegal acts.
Robinson–Patman Act of 1936	Bans selected discriminatory price cuts by chain stores that allegedly drive smaller competitors from the marketplace. In addition, forbids price discrimination through special concessions in the form of price or quantity discounts, free advertising, or promotional allowances granted to one buyer but not to others, if these actions substantially reduce competition.

Section 2: Every person who shall monopolize, or attempt to monopolize, or combine or conspire with any other person or persons to monopolize any part of the trade or commerce . . . shall be guilty of a misdemeanor [now a felony].

Notice how vague this act really is. No definition is given for the terms *restraint of trade* or *monopolize*. Despite this vagueness, however, the act was used to prosecute the infamous Standard Oil Trust of New Jersey. This company was charged with and convicted of violations of Sections 1 and 2 of the Sherman Antitrust Act in 1906. At the time it controlled more than 80 percent of the nation's oil-refining capacity. In addressing the company's legal appeal, the U.S. Supreme Court ruled that Standard Oil's predominance in the oil market created "a *prima facie* presumption of intent and purpose to control and maintain dominancy . . . not as a result from normal methods of industrial development, but by means of combinations." Here the word *combination* meant entering into associations and preferential arrangements with the intent of restraining competition. The Supreme Court forced Standard Oil of New Jersey to break up into many smaller companies that would have no choice but to compete.

The Sherman Act applies today just as it did more than a century ago. In June 2001, the federal Court of Appeals for the District of Columbia determined that Microsoft Corporation had violated the Sherman Act. The court ruled that Microsoft had engaged in anticompetitive conduct in an effort to monopolize the market for operating systems for personal computers. Initially, the U.S. Justice Department proposed a Standard Oil–style remedy: splitting Microsoft into several companies. Ultimately, however, Microsoft reached a settlement that kept the company intact but required it to alter many of its business practices.

Other Important Antitrust Legislation. Table 28-2 on the previous page lists three other important antitrust laws. In 1914, Congress passed the Clayton Act to clarify some of the vague provisions of the Sherman Act by identifying specific business practices that were to be legally prohibited.

Congress also passed the Federal Trade Commission Act in 1914. In addition to establishing the Federal Trade Commission to investigate unfair trade practices, this law enumerated certain business practices that, according to Congress, involved overly aggressive competition. A 1938 amendment to this law expressly prohibited "unfair or deceptive acts or practices in commerce" and empowered the FTC to regulate advertising and marketing practices by U.S. firms.

The Robinson-Patman Act of 1936 amended the Clayton Act by singling out specific business practices, such as selected price cuts, aimed at driving smaller competitors out of business. The act is often referred to as the "Chain Store Act" because it was intended to protect *independent* retailers and wholesalers from "unfair competition" by chain stores.

Exemptions from Antitrust Laws. Numerous laws exempt the following industries and business practices from antitrust legislation:

- Labor unions
- Public utilities—electric, gas, and telephone companies
- Professional baseball
- Cooperative activities among U.S. exporters
- Hospitals
- Public transit and water systems
- Suppliers of military equipment
- Joint publishing arrangements in a single city by two or more newspapers

Thus, not all U.S. businesses are subject to antitrust laws.

International Discord in Antitrust Policy

What, if anything, should U.S. antitrust authorities do if AT&T decides that it wishes to merge with British Telecommunications or if Germany's Deutsche Telecom wants to acquire Sprint Nextel? What, if anything, should they do if Time Warner, the largest U.S. entertainment company, attempts to merge with London-based EMI, one of the world's largest recorded-music companies? These are not just rhetorical questions, as U.S. and European antitrust authorities learned in the early 2000s when these issues actually surfaced. Growing international linkages among markets for many goods and services have increasingly made antitrust policy a global undertaking.

The international dimensions of antitrust pose a problem for U.S. antitrust authorities in the Department of Justice and the Federal Trade Commission. In the United States, the overriding goal of antitrust policies has traditionally been protecting the interests of consumers. This is also a formal objective of antitrust efforts of European Union (EU) antitrust authorities. In the EU, however, policymakers are also required to reject any business combination that "creates or strengthens a dominant position as a result of which effective competition would be significantly impeded."

This additional clause is creating tension between U.S. and EU policymaking. In the United States, increasing dominance of a market by a single firm arouses the concern of antitrust authorities. Nevertheless, U.S. authorities typically will remain passive if they determine that the larger market dominance arises from factors such as exceptional management and greater cost efficiencies that ultimately benefit consumers by reducing prices. In contrast, under EU rules antitrust authorities are obliged to block *any* business combination that increases the dominance of any producer. They must do so irrespective of what factors might have caused the business's preeminence in the marketplace.

QUICK QUIZ

The first national antitrust law was the _____ Antitrust Act of 1890, which made illegal every contract and combination in restraint of trade; it remains the single most important antitrust law in the United States.

The _____ Act of 1914 made illegal various specific business practices, such as price discrimination.

The _____ _____ _____ Act of 1914 and its 1938 amendment established the Federal Trade Commission and prohibited "unfair or deceptive acts or practices in commerce."

The _____-_____ Act of 1936 aimed to prevent large producers from driving out small competitors by means of selective discriminatory price cuts.

See page 731 for the answers. Review concepts from this section in MyEconLab.

ANTITRUST ENFORCEMENT

How are antitrust laws enforced? In the United States, most enforcement continues to be based on the Sherman Act. The Supreme Court has defined the offense of **monopolization** as involving the following elements: "(1) the possession of monopoly power in the relevant market and (2) the willful acquisition or maintenance of that power, as distinguished from growth or development as a consequence of a superior product, business acumen, or historical accident."

Monopolization
The possession of monopoly power in the relevant market and the willful acquisition or maintenance of that power, as distinguished from growth or development as a consequence of a superior product, business acumen, or historical accident.

Monopoly Power and the Relevant Market

The Sherman Act does not define monopoly. Monopoly need not be a single entity. Also, monopoly is not a function of size alone. For example a "mom and pop" grocery store located in an isolated town can function as a monopolist.

It is difficult to define and measure market power precisely. As a workable proxy, courts often look to the firm's percentage share of the "relevant market." This is the so-called **market share test.** A firm is generally considered to have monopoly power if its share of the relevant market is 70 percent or more. This is only a rule of thumb, however, not an absolute dictum. In some cases, a smaller share may be held to constitute monopoly power.

What well-known U.S. firm captures more than 70 percent of total revenues in several different markets?

Market share test
The percentage of a market that a particular firm supplies; used as the primary measure of monopoly power.

E-COMMERCE EXAMPLE

Microsoft's Market Shares

In the market for personal computer (PC) software, one company stands almost alone. Microsoft Corporation's market share in the market for operating software for PCs exceeds 95 percent. Microsoft's market share in the office-productivity software market stands at about 94 percent, and its market share in the Web-browsing software market is just over 95 percent. In the market for operating software for computer servers, Microsoft faces increasingly tough competition from Linux. As a result, Microsoft's share of revenues in this market is "only" 85 percent. Thus, by the standard rule of thumb for gauging monopoly power, Microsoft possesses this power in four different software markets.

FOR CRITICAL ANALYSIS
Why might it be argued that Microsoft is not necessarily a computer software monopoly under the Sherman Act? (Hint: Recall the second of the two criteria that the U.S. Supreme Court has specified in defining the offense of monopolization.)

The relevant market consists of two elements: a relevant *product* market and a relevant *geographic* market. What should the relevant product market include? It must include all items produced by different firms that have identical attributes, such as sugar. Yet products that are not identical may sometimes be substituted for one another. Coffee may be substituted for tea, for example. In defining the relevant product market, the key issue is the degree to which products are interchangeable. If one product is sufficiently substitutable for another, then the two products are considered to be part of the same product market.

The second component of the relevant market is the geographic boundaries of the market. For items that are sold nationwide, the geographic boundaries of the market encompass the entire United States. If a producer and its competitors sell in only a limited area (one in which customers have no access to other sources of the product), the geographic market is limited to that area. A national firm may thus compete in several distinct areas and have monopoly power in one area but not in another.

Product Packaging and Antitrust Enforcement

A particular problem in U.S. antitrust enforcement is determining whether a firm has engaged in "willful acquisition or maintenance" of market power. Unfortunately, actions that appear to some observers to be good business look like antitrust violations to others. To illustrate why quandaries can arise in antitrust enforcement, let's consider two examples: *versioning* and *bundling*.

Product Versioning. A firm engages in product **versioning** when it sells an item in slightly altered forms to different groups of consumers. A typical method of versioning is to remove certain features from an item and offer what remains as a somewhat stripped-down version of the product at a different price.

Versioning
Selling a product in slightly altered forms to different groups of consumers.

Consider an office-productivity software program, such as Adobe Acrobat or Microsoft Word. Firms selling such programs typically offer both a "professional" version containing a full range of features and a "standard" version providing only basic functions. One perspective on this practice regards it as a form of price discrimination, or selling essentially the same product at different prices to different consumers. People who desire to use the full range of features in Adobe Acrobat or Microsoft Word are likely to be computing professionals. Compared to most other consumers, their demand for the full-featured version of an office-productivity software program is likely to be less elastic. In principle, therefore, Adobe and Microsoft can earn higher profits by offering "professional" versions at higher prices and selling a "standard" version at a lower price.

Price discrimination—charging varying prices to different consumers when the price differences are not a result of different production or transportation costs—is illegal under the Clayton Act of 1914. Are Adobe, Microsoft, and other companies engaging in illegal price discrimination? Another perspective on versioning indicates that they are not. According to this point of view, consumers regard "professional" and "standard" versions of software packages as imperfect substitutes. Consequently, each version is a distinctive product sold in a unique market. If so, versioning increases overall consumer satisfaction because consumers who are not computing professionals are able to utilize certain features of software products at a lower price. So far, antitrust authorities in the United States and elsewhere have been inclined toward this view of the economic effects of versioning, rather than perceiving it as a form of price discrimination.

Product Bundling. Antitrust authorities have been less tolerant of another form of product packaging, known as **bundling,** which involves the joint sale of two or more products as a set. Antitrust authorities usually are not concerned if a firm allows consumers to purchase the products either individually or as a set. They are more likely to investigate a firm's business practices, however, when it allows consumers to purchase one product only when it is bundled with another. Antitrust officials often view this form of bundling as a method of price discrimination known as **tie-in sales,** in which a firm requires consumers who wish to buy one of its products to purchase another item the firm sells as well.

Bundling
Offering two or more products for sale as a set.

Tie-in sales
Purchases of one product that are permitted by the seller only if the consumer buys another good or service from the same firm.

To understand their reasoning, consider a situation in which one group of consumers is willing to pay $500 for a computer operating system but only $100 for an Internet-browsing program. A second group of consumers is willing to pay only $250 for the same computer operating system but is willing to pay $350 for the same Internet-browsing program. If the same company that sells both types of software offers the operating system at a price above $250, then only consumers in the first group will buy this software. Likewise, if it sells the Internet-browsing program at a price above $100, then only the second group of consumers will purchase that program.

But if the firm sells both products as a bundled set, it can charge $600 and generate sales of both software products to both groups. One interpretation is that the first group pays $500 for the operating system, but for the second group, the operating system's price is $250. At the same time, the first group has paid $100 for the Internet-browsing program, while the second group perceives the price of the program to be $350. Effectively, bundling enables the software company to engage in price discrimination by charging different prices to different groups.

Antitrust enforcers in the Justice Department applied this interpretation in their prosecution of Microsoft, which for years had bundled its Internet-browsing program, Internet

Explorer, together with its Windows operating system. Enforcement officials added another twist by contending that Microsoft also had monopoly power in the market for computer operating systems. By bundling the two products, they argued, Microsoft had sought both to price-discriminate and to extend its monopoly power to the market for Internet-browsing software. The remedy that the courts imposed was for Microsoft to alter some of its business practices. As part of this legal remedy, Microsoft was required to unbundle its Windows and Internet Explorer products.

QUICK QUIZ

As part of the enforcement of antitrust laws, officials at the U.S. Department of Justice and the Federal Trade Commission often apply _____ _____ tests to determine if a few firms account for most of industry _____.

Antitrust enforcers must decide whether producers seek to monopolize the relevant market, which involves determining both the relevant _____ market and the relevant _____ market.

Antitrust authorities generally have not considered product _____, or offering different versions of essentially the same product for sale at different prices, to be illegal price discrimination. Both U.S. and European authorities have, however, raised antitrust concerns about product _____, which they view as a method of engaging in **tie-in sales** that require consumers to purchase one product in order to obtain another.

See page 731 for the answers. Review concepts from this section in MyEconLab.

CASE STUDY — ECONOMICS FRONT AND CENTER

Balancing Auto Safety and Fuel Economy Is a High-Wire Act

Sherman, a top official with the National Highway Transportation Safety Administration (NHTSA), tugs nervously at his collar as his conference call with U.S. auto industry executives becomes increasingly more heated. At issue is the latest in a series of NHTSA reports indicating that new technologies have made smaller, more fuel-efficient cars much safer than they used to be. This new finding is an about-face from many years of agency research indicating that smaller cars were much less safe than heavier, gas-guzzling vehicles. In years past, the NHTSA had published reports suggesting that reducing a vehicle's weight by as little as 100 pounds could generate a significant increase in traffic fatalities.

Sherman is not surprised to learn that the auto industry is unhappy with the NHTSA's altered stance on small-car safety. After all, U.S. producers rely on sales of fuel-*in*efficient sport utility vehicles (SUVs) to generate most of their revenues. In addition to government safety regulations, auto producers also face fuel economy standards requiring them to achieve an average level of fuel efficiency across their auto fleets. In years past, automakers were able to convince Congress and the U.S. Transportation Department not to toughen fuel economy rules further, arguing that this would require making smaller, less safe automobiles. The NHTSA's recent research conclusions about small-car safety have weakened that argument.

Sherman is in a difficult position. Consumer groups are lobbying Congress to toughen fuel economy standards for automakers, and members of Congress are responding by pressuring Sherman to keep pushing research on small-car safety. At the same time, auto executives are now threatening to go to the president and ask for Sherman to be replaced. When he took his current job, Sherman, a Michigan native, had hoped it might someday help him land a position with one of the automakers in Detroit, close to his extended family. Now he wonders if he will simply be able to ride out this controversy and keep his job in Washington.

CRITICAL ANALYSIS QUESTIONS

1. *Is Sherman's agency involved in economic or social regulation?*
2. *What theory (or theories) of regulator behavior might be applied in trying to understand the situation that Sherman confronts?*

Issues and Applications

Identifying the Relevant Telecommunications Market

Concepts Applied
- Antitrust Policy
- Relevant Market
- Market Share Test

In 1997, two telecommunications companies, AT&T and SBC, the "Southwestern Bell" phone company that had separated from AT&T 13 years earlier, held preliminary talks about merging their companies again. The head of the Federal Communications Commission (FCC), the U.S. regulator charged with regulating U.S. telecommunications industries, quickly scotched the initiative. Before a Washington luncheon crowd of 100 people, including several representatives of the financial media, the FCC chief described the idea as "unthinkable." Such a merger, he suggested, would squelch the competition that breaking off SBC and other regional companies from AT&T had been intended to foster. Antitrust authorities at the U.S. Justice Department and the Federal Trade Commission also quietly raised concerns about the proposed combination.

Nevertheless, eight years later the two companies merged after all, and neither the FCC nor the U.S. antitrust authorities raised objections to the combination. Furthermore, the combined company, which kept the name AT&T, followed up by proposing a merger with BellSouth, another company that had separated from the old AT&T years before. What had happened? The answer is that the relevant market for SBC, AT&T, and other telecommunications companies had expanded considerably during those eight years.

Telephony, Television, Internet—All One Telecommunications Market?

A lot happened in the telecommunications industry between 1997 and 2005. Even as companies such as SBC and BellSouth began to branch out and compete with the initial providers of cellular phone services, they began to face competition in traditional phone services. Cable television companies, such as Comcast and Time Warner, discovered low-cost methods of providing regular phone services, which they could transmit through cables alongside television programming signals.

Furthermore, cable providers also began offering broadband Internet access services. These cable services also competed directly with dial-up and digital-subscriber-line (DSL) services offered by telephone companies.

Hence, by the mid-2000s, AT&T, SBC, and BellSouth were not just competing with each other in the market for telephone services. They were also in direct competition with cable companies that provided these and other telecommunications services, including broadband Internet access. Along all three dimensions—telephone services, television service, and Internet access services—telephone and cable companies were trying to sell their products to the same sets of customers.

An Example: The Market for Broadband Access Services

To see how widened competition across telecommunications affected regulators' view of the relevant market for antitrust policy, let's focus exclusively on the broadband Internet access services that telephone and cable companies provide. Take a look at Table 28-3. The left-hand column lists shares of total revenues from broadband access services provided via DSL by phone companies. The implied four-firm concentration ratio if these telephone companies were regarded as a single "DSL-access industry" would be 85.5 percent. The middle column lists market shares for cable companies that provide broadband Internet access. If these companies were treated as a single "cable-access industry," the four-firm concentration ratio for this industry would be 76.2 percent.

Realistically, DSL and cable broadband Internet access services are very close substitutes—so close that DSL and cable providers compete directly for the same customers. The right-hand column provides market shares if both types of providers are considered part of the same industry. The four-firm concentration ratio under this widened perspective of the relevant market for broadband Internet access services drops to 61.9 percent.

In 1997, the FCC and antitrust regulators perceived that telephone companies and cable companies competed in separate markets. By 2005, these regulators recognized that the environment had changed. Telephone and cable companies all competed with one another in a variety of markets, including a single market for broadband Internet access services. Consequently, in 2005 regulators raised no objections to a re-merger between SBC and AT&T.

TABLE 28-3

Shares of Industry Sales in Alternative Markets for Broadband Internet Access

This table provides the most recent market share figures available for DSL and cable providers of broadband Internet access. These figures imply that if DSL access and cable access are viewed as different services, the four-firm concentration ratios for separate broadband DSL and broadband cable "industries" are 85.5 percent and 76.2 percent, respectively.

Source: Federal Communications Commission.

Broadband DSL	Market Share	Broadband Cable	Market Share	Total Broadband	Market Share
AT&T	37.2%	Comcast	34.6%	Comcast	21.5%
Verizon	26.3	Time Warner	19.3	AT&T	18.1
BellSouth	14.7	Cox	12.9	Time Warner	13.0
Qwest	7.3	Charter	9.4	Verizon	9.3
Sprint Nextel	3.6	Cablevision	6.9	Cox	8.1
Covad	3.6	Adelphia	6.4	Charter	6.6
Others	7.3	Others	10.5	Others	23.4
DSL Four-Firm Concentration Ratio	85.5%	Cable Four-Firm Concentration Ratio	76.2%	Combined Four-Firm Concentration Ratio	61.9%

Log in to **MyEconLab**, click on "Economic News," and test your understanding of the chapter by answering interactive questions that relate directly to this issue.

For Critical Analysis

1. Why does broadening the definition of the relevant market to encompass more firms automatically reduce the four-firm concentration ratio?
2. When SBC and AT&T merged in 2005, AT&T was not among the top four firms in either the DSL broadband market or the overall broadband market. What happened to the four-firm concentration ratios in both markets as a result of the 2005 merger?

Web Resources

1. To read a recent review of competition issues in the U.S. market for broadband Internet access services, go to **www.econtoday.com/ch28**.
2. For a review of the experiences of various countries with competition in markets for broadband Internet access services, go to **www.econtoday.com/ch28**.

Research Project

Recall from Chapter 21 that a positive cross-price elasticity of demand—a percentage increase in the price of one item causes a positive percentage increase in the quantity demanded of another—indicates that two items are substitutes. Evaluate how telecommunications regulators use this fact to help determine the relevant market in telecommunications. Why might using the cross-price elasticity of demand pose some judgmental problems for regulators charged with enforcing antitrust laws within relevant markets?

Here is what you should know after reading this chapter. MyEconLab will help you identify what you know, and where to go when you need to practice.

WHAT YOU SHOULD KNOW		WHERE TO GO TO PRACTICE
Government Regulation of Business There are two basic forms of government regulation of business: economic regulation and social regulation. Economic regulation applies to specific industries; it includes the regulation of prices charged by natural monopolies and the regulation of certain activities of specific nonmonopolistic industries. Social regulations affect nearly all businesses and encompass a broad range of objectives concerning such issues as product safety, environmental quality, and working conditions.	**Key figure** Figure 28-1, 707	• **MyEconLab** Study Plan 28.1 • Audio introduction to Chapter 28 • Animated Figure 28-1
Practical Difficulties in Regulating the Prices Charged by Natural Monopolies To try to ensure that a monopolist charges a price consistent with marginal cost, a government regulator might contemplate requiring the firm to set price equal to marginal cost at the point where the demand curve crosses the		

WHAT YOU SHOULD KNOW		WHERE TO GO TO PRACTICE

marginal cost curve. In the case of a natural monopoly, however, long-run marginal cost is typically less than long-run average total cost, so requiring marginal cost pricing forces the firm to incur an economic loss. Hence, regulators normally aim for a natural monopoly to charge a price equal to average total cost so that the firm earns zero economic profits. At one time, regulators viewed the electricity, natural gas, and telecommunications industries as natural monopolies because their products flowed through networks subject to significant economies of scale. In recent years, uncoupling production of these items from their distribution has enabled regulators to promote competition in these industries. In the telecommunications industry, technological advances have further eroded the relevance of treating the industry as a natural monopoly.

cost-of-service regulation, 710
rate-of-return regulation, 710
Key figure
Figure 28-2, 709

- **MyEconLab** Study Plan 28.2
- Animated Figure 28-2

Rationales for Regulating Nonmonopolistic Industries
The two most common rationales for regulation of nonmonopolistic industries relate to addressing market failures and protecting consumers from problems arising from information asymmetries they face in some markets. Asymmetric information can also create a lemons problem, which occurs when uncertainty about product quality leads to markets containing mostly low-quality items. Governments may seek to reduce the lemons problem by establishing liability laws and business licensing requirements.

lemons problem, 714

- **MyEconLab** Study Plan 28.3

Regulators' Incentives and the Costs of Regulation
The capture theory of regulator behavior predicts that because people with expertise about a regulated industry are most likely to be selected to regulate the industry, these regulators will eventually find themselves supporting the positions of the firms that they regulate. An alternative view, called the share-the-gains, share-the-pains theory, predicts that a regulator takes into account the preferences of legislators and consumers as well as those of the regulated firms themselves. Thus, a regulator tries to satisfy all constituencies, at least in part. The costs of regulation are easier to quantify in dollar terms than the benefits. These costs include both the direct costs to taxpayers of funding regulatory agencies and the explicit and implicit opportunity costs that businesses must incur to comply with regulations.

creative response, 716
capture hypothesis, 717
share-the-gains, share-the-pains theory, 717
Key figure
Figure 28-3, 718

- **MyEconLab** Study Plan 28.4
- Animated Figure 28-3
- Video: Creative Response and Feedback Effects: Results of Regulation

Foundations of Antitrust
There are four key antitrust laws. The Sherman Act of 1890 forbids attempts to monopolize an industry. The Clayton Act of 1914 clarified antitrust law by prohibiting specific types of business practices that Congress determined were aimed at restraining trade. In addition, the Federal Trade Commission Act of 1914, as amended in 1938, seeks to prohibit deceptive business practices and to prevent "cutthroat

WHAT YOU SHOULD KNOW		WHERE TO GO TO PRACTICE
pricing," which Congress felt could unfairly eliminate too many competitors. Finally, the Robinson-Patman Act of 1936 outlawed price cuts that Congress had determined to be discriminatory and predatory.		• **MyEconLab** Study Plan 28.5 • Video: Antitrust Laws
Issues in Enforcing Antitrust Laws Antitrust laws are vague, so enforcement of the laws is based on court interpretations of their meaning. The Supreme Court has defined monopolization as possessing or seeking monopoly pricing power in the "relevant market." Authorities charged with enforcing antitrust laws use a market share test, which involves determining the percentage of market production or sales supplied by a firm. A key issue in applying the market share test is defining the relevant market. In recent years, antitrust officials have raised questions about whether product packaging, either in the form of different versions or as bundled sets, is a type of price discrimination. There are alternative views about whether firms truly use product versioning to practice price discrimination, so this business practice has not attracted much antitrust attention. U.S. antitrust authorities have, however, charged that product bundling is a means of engaging in tie-in sales, in which a firm price-discriminates by requiring consumers to purchase one product before being able to buy another item.	monopolization, 721 market share test, 722 versioning, 723 bundling, 723 tie-in sales, 723	• **MyEconLab** Study Plan 28.6 • Video: Theory of Contestable Markets

Log in to MyEconLab, take a chapter test, and get a personalized Study Plan that tells you which concepts you understand and which ones you need to review. From there, MyEconLab will give you further practice, tutorials, animations, videos, and guided solutions.

Log in to www.myeconlab.com

PROBLEMS

Select problems, indicated by a blue oval ⬬ *, are assignable in **MyEconLab**.*
Answers to the odd-numbered problems appear at the back of the book.

28-1. Local cable television companies are sometimes granted monopoly rights to service a particular territory of a metropolitan area. The companies typically pay special taxes and licensing fees to local municipalities. Why might a municipality give monopoly rights to a cable company?

28-2. A local cable company, the sole provider of cable television service, is regulated by the municipal government. The owner of the company claims that she is normally opposed to regulation by government, but asserts that regulation is necessary because local residents would not want a large number of different cables crisscrossing the city. Why do you think the owner is defending regulation by the city?

28-3. The table on the next page depicts the cost and demand structure a natural monopoly faces. Calculate total revenues, marginal revenue, and marginal cost at each output level. If this firm were allowed to operate as a monopolist, what would be the quantity produced and the price charged by the firm? What would be the amount of monopoly profit?

Quantity	Price ($)	Long-Run Total Cost ($)
0	100	0
1	95	92
2	90	177
3	85	255
4	80	331
5	75	406
6	70	480

28-4 If regulators required the firm in Problem 28-3 to practice marginal cost pricing, what quantity would it produce, and what price would it charge? What is the firm's profit under this regulatory framework?

28-5 If regulators required the firm in Problem 28-3 to practice average cost pricing, what quantity would it produce, and what price would it charge? What is the firm's profit under this regulatory framework?

28-6. As noted in the chapter, separating the *production* of electricity from its *delivery* has led to considerable deregulation of producers.

  a. Briefly explain which of these two aspects of the sale of electricity remains susceptible to natural monopoly problems.

  b. Suppose that the potential natural monopoly problem you identified in part a actually arises. Why is marginal cost pricing not a feasible solution? What makes average cost pricing a feasible solution?

  c. Discuss two approaches that a regulator could use to try to implement an average-cost-pricing solution to the problem identified in part a.

28-7. Are lemons problems likely to be more common in some industries and less common in others? Based on your answer to this question, should government regulatory activities designed to reduce the scope of lemons problems take the form of economic regulation or social regulation? Take a stand, and support your reasoning.

28-8. Research into genetically modified crops has led to significant productivity gains for countries such as the United States that employ these techniques. Countries such as the European Union member nations, however, have imposed controls on the import of these products, citing concern for public health. Is the European Union's regulation of genetically modified crops social regulation or economic regulation?

28-9. Using the example in Problem 28-8, do you think this is more likely an example of the capture hypothesis or the share-the-gains, share-the-pains theory? Why?

28-10. Suppose that a business has developed a very high-quality product and operates more efficiently in producing that product than any other potential competitor. As a consequence, at present it is the only seller of this product, for which there are few close substitutes. Is this firm in violation of U.S. antitrust laws? Explain.

28-11 Consider the following fictitious sales data (in thousands of dollars) for books sold both over the Internet and in physical retail establishments. Firms have numbers instead of names, and Firm 1 generates book sales only over the Internet. Antitrust authorities judge that a single firm possesses "monopoly power" if its share of sales in the relevant market exceeds 70 percent.

Internet Book Sales		Book Sales in Physical Stores		Combined Book Sales	
Firm	Sales	Firm	Sales	Firm	Sales
1	$ 750	2	$4,200	2	$ 4,250
2	50	3	2,000	3	2,050
3	50	4	1,950	4	2,000
4	50	5	450	1	750
5	50	6	400	5	500
6	50			6	450
Total	$1,000		$9,000		$10,000

  a. Suppose that the antitrust authorities determine that bookselling in physical retail stores and Internet bookselling are individually separate relevant markets. Does any single firm have monopoly power, as defined by the antitrust authorities?

  b. Suppose that in fact there is really only a single book industry, in which firms compete both in physical retail stores and via the Internet. According to the antitrust authorities' measure of monopoly power, is there actually cause for concern?

28-12. In recent years, the Internet auction firm eBay has sought to make its auction technology the favorite of software programmers, and it has begun licensing its technology to other Web sites. The company's managers have publicly stated that their goal is for eBay's auction system to become the dominant "operating system" of all auction applications on the Internet. Are there any potential antitrust issues related to the company's efforts?

28-13. Recently, the U.S. Justice Department initiated an antitrust investigation of Homestore.com, a Web site containing the listings of thousands of real estate agents in the United States. In cities and even in local communities, there is considerable rivalry among realtors. Nevertheless, nearly all belong to the National Association of Realtors, which is the majority owner of Homestore.com. In 2000, Homestore.com purchased a rival site, Move.com, which left the Microsoft Network's Homeadvisor.com as its only remaining key rival. Why do you suppose the Justice Department became concerned about the activities of Homestore.com? What factors are likely to affect its decision about whether Homestore.com has violated any antitrust laws?

28-14 A package delivery company provides both overnight and second-day delivery services. It charges almost twice as much to deliver an overnight package to any world location as it does to deliver the same package to the same location in two days. Often, second-day packages arrive at company warehouses in destination cities by the next day, but drivers intentionally do not deliver these packages until the following day. What is this business practice called? Briefly summarize alternative perspectives concerning whether this activity should or should not be viewed as a form of price discrimination.

28-15 A firm that sells both Internet-security software and computer antivirus software will sell the antivirus software as a stand-alone product. It will only sell the Internet-security software to consumers in a combined package that also includes the antivirus software. What is this business practice called? Briefly explain why an antitrust authority might view this practice as a form of price discrimination.

ECONOMICS ON THE NET

Guidelines for U.S. Antitrust Merger Enforcement How does the U.S. government apply antitrust laws to mergers? This application gives you the opportunity to learn about the standards applied by the Antitrust Division of the U.S. Department of Justice when it evaluates a proposed merger.

Title: U.S. Department of Justice Antitrust Merger Enforcement Guidelines

Navigation: Go to www.econtoday.com/ch28 to access the home page of the Antitrust Division of the U.S. Department of Justice. Click on *Public Documents* and then on *Merger Enforcement*.

Application Answer the following questions.

1. Click on *Horizontal Merger Guidelines*. In section 1, click on *Overview*, and read this section. What factors do U.S. antitrust authorities consider when evaluating the potential for a horizontal merger to "enhance market power"—that is, to place the combination in a monopoly situation?

2. Back up to the page titled *Merger Enforcement Guidelines*, and click on *Non-Horizontal Merger Guidelines*. Read the guidelines. In what situations will the antitrust authorities most likely question a nonhorizontal merger?

For Group Study and Analysis Have three groups of students from the class examine sections 1, 2, and 3 of the Horizontal Merger Guidelines discussed in item 1. After each group reports on all the factors that the antitrust authorities consider when evaluating a horizontal merger, discuss why large teams of lawyers and many economic consultants are typically involved when the Antitrust Division of the Department of Justice alleges that a proposed merger would be "anticompetitive."

ANSWERS TO QUICK QUIZZES

p. 708: (i) Economic . . . social; (ii) natural . . . economic; (iii) social
p. 712: (i) lower . . . revenue . . . cost; (ii) average . . . zero; (iii) deliver . . . networks
p. 715: (i) failures . . . asymmetric; (ii) asymmetric; (iii) lemons . . . low
p. 718: (i) consumers . . . firms; (ii) industry . . . legislators . . . consumers; (iii) government . . . firms'
p. 721: (i) Sherman; (ii) Clayton; (iii) Federal Trade Commission; (iv) Robinson-Patman
p. 724: (i) market share . . . sales; (ii) product . . . geographic; (iii) versioning . . . bundling

29 The Labor Market: Demand, Supply, and Outsourcing

Learning Objectives

After reading this chapter, you should be able to:

1. Understand why a firm's marginal revenue product curve is its labor demand curve
2. Explain in what sense the demand for labor is a "derived" demand
3. Identify the key factors influencing the elasticity of demand for inputs
4. Describe how equilibrium wage rates are determined for perfectly competitive firms
5. Explain what labor outsourcing is and how it is ultimately likely to affect U.S. workers' earnings and employment prospects
6. Contrast the demand for labor and wage determination by a product market monopolist with outcomes that would arise under perfect competition

Technovate and 24/7 Customer sound as though they might be the names of U.S. firms, but in fact both companies are based in India. Like a growing number of Indian companies, Technovate and 24/7 Customer specialize in offering low-cost labor services to U.S. firms that provide call centers for customer-service questions. When a consumer of a U.S. firm's product, such as a laptop computer, punches in an assistance number, the call is automatically routed to technically trained, English-speaking support workers in India. Many U.S. politicians assert that these and other Indian companies are "stealing" U.S. jobs and thereby reducing U.S. employment. Before you can evaluate the legitimacy of this claim, you must learn about labor demand and labor supply.

 MyEconLab helps you master each objective and study more efficiently. See end of chapter for details.

Did You Know That . . .

the largest migration in human history is now taking place in China? Throughout the nation, an estimated 115 million young men and women—more than three times the entire number of Europeans who emigrated to the United States during the twentieth century—have migrated from rural villages to cities. These young people are moving to work in factories, restaurants, hair salons, and construction sites located hundreds of miles from where they grew up. During the nation's Lunar New Year holiday, most of these workers travel back home to visit their families. As a consequence, passenger trains typically transport more than 140 million people between various points along China's rail system between late January and mid-February each year.

These youthful workers from small towns and farming communities around China provide labor inputs that firms in the nation's cities use to produce goods and services. The demand for inputs by these firms or by any other businesses we might consider can be studied in different market situations, just as the demand for a firm's product can be examined in different market situations. Our analysis will always end with the same conclusion: A firm will hire employees up to the point beyond which it isn't profitable to hire any more. It will hire employees to the point at which the marginal benefit of hiring a worker will just equal the marginal cost. Indeed, in every profit-maximizing situation, it is most profitable to carry out an activity up to the point at which the marginal benefit equals the marginal cost. Remembering that guideline will help you in analyzing decision making at the firm level, which is where we will begin our discussion of the demand for labor.

LABOR DEMAND FOR A PERFECTLY COMPETITIVE FIRM

We will start our analysis under the assumption that the market for input factors is perfectly competitive. We will further assume that the output market is perfectly competitive. This provides a benchmark against which to compare other situations in which labor markets or product markets are not perfectly competitive.

Competition in the Product Market

Let's take as our example a firm that sells handheld, touch-screen electronic organizers and is in competition with many companies selling the same kind of product. Assume that the laborers hired by this manufacturing firm do not need any special skills. This firm sells electronic organizers in a perfectly competitive market. It also buys labor (its variable input) in a perfectly competitive market. A firm that hires labor under perfectly competitive conditions hires only a minuscule proportion of all the workers who are potentially available to the firm. By "potentially available," we mean all the workers in a given geographic area who possess the skills demanded by our perfect competitor. In such a market, it is always possible for the individual firm to hire extra workers without having to offer a higher wage. Thus, the supply of labor to the firm is perfectly elastic at the going wage rate established by the forces of supply and demand in the entire labor market. The firm is a *price taker* in the labor market.

Marginal Physical Product

Look at panel (a) of Figure 29-1 on the following page. In column 1, we show the number of workers per week that the firm can employ. In column 2, we show total physical product (TPP) per week, the total *physical* production of touch-screen electronic organizers that

FIGURE 29-1

Marginal Revenue Product

In panel (a), column 4 shows marginal revenue product (MRP), which is the additional revenue the firm receives for the sale of that additional output. Marginal revenue product is simply the revenue the additional worker brings in—the combination of that worker's contribution to production and the revenue that that production will bring to the firm. For this perfectly competitive firm, marginal revenue is equal to the price of the product, or $10 per unit. At a weekly wage of $830, the profit-maximizing employer will pay for only 12 workers because then the marginal revenue product is just equal to the wage rate or weekly salary.

Panel (a)

(1) Labor Input (workers per week)	(2) Total Physical Product (TPP) (electronic organizers per week)	(3) Marginal Physical Product (MPP) (electronic organizers per week)	(4) Marginal Revenue (MR = P = $10) × MPP = Marginal Revenue Product (MRP) ($ per additional worker)	(5) Wage Rate ($ per week) = Marginal Factor Cost (MFC) = Change in Total Costs ÷ Change in Labor
6	882			
		118	$1,180	$830
7	1,000			
		111	1,110	830
8	1,111			
		104	1,040	830
9	1,215			
		97	970	830
10	1,312			
		90	900	830
11	1,402			
		83	830	830
12	1,485			
		76	760	830
13	1,561			

In panel (b), we find the number of workers the firm will want to hire by observing the wage rate that is established by the forces of supply and demand in the entire labor market. We show that this employer is hiring labor in a perfectly competitive labor market and therefore faces a perfectly elastic supply curve represented by s at $830 per week. As in other situations, we have a supply and demand model; in this example, the demand curve is represented by MRP, and the supply curve is s. Profit maximization occurs at their intersection.

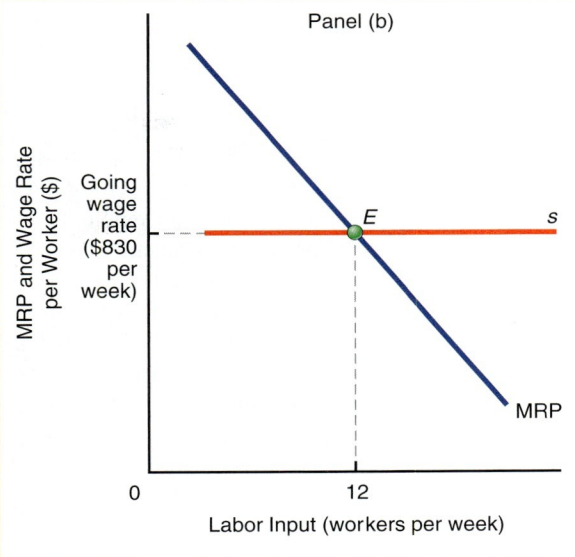

different quantities of the labor input (in combination with a fixed amount of other inputs) will generate in a week's time. In column 3, we show the additional output gained when the company adds workers to its existing manufacturing facility. This column, the **marginal physical product (MPP) of labor,** represents the extra (additional) output attributed to employing additional units of the variable input factor. If this firm employs seven workers rather than six, the MPP is 118. The law of diminishing marginal product predicts that additional units of a variable factor will, after some point, cause the MPP to decline, other things held constant.

We are assuming that all other nonlabor factors of production are held constant. So, if our manufacturing firm wants to add one more worker to its production line, it has to crowd all the existing workers a little closer together because it does not increase its capital stock (the production equipment). Therefore, as we add more workers, each one has a smaller and smaller fraction of the available capital stock with which to work. If one worker uses one machine, adding another worker usually won't double the output because the machine can run only so fast and for so many hours per day. In other words, MPP declines because of the law of diminishing marginal product (see Chapter 23).

Marginal physical product (MPP) of labor
The change in output resulting from the addition of one more worker. The MPP of the worker equals the change in total output accounted for by hiring the worker, holding all other factors of production constant.

Marginal Revenue Product

We now need to translate into a dollar value the physical product that results from hiring an additional worker. This is done by multiplying the marginal physical product by the marginal revenue of the firm. Because this firm sells touch-screen electronic organizers in a perfectly competitive market, marginal revenue is equal to the price of the product. If employing seven workers rather than six yields an MPP of 118 and the marginal revenue is $10 per electronic organizer, the **marginal revenue product (MRP)** is $1,180 (118 × $10). The MRP is shown in column 4 of panel (a) of Figure 29-1. *The marginal revenue product represents the incremental worker's contribution to the firm's total revenues.*

When a firm operates in a perfectly competitive product market, the marginal physical product times the product price is also sometimes referred to as the *value of marginal product (VMP).* Because price and marginal revenue are the same for a perfectly competitive firm, the VMP is also the MRP for such a firm.

In column 5 of panel (a) of Figure 29-1, we show the wage rate, or *marginal factor cost,* of each worker. The marginal cost of workers is the extra cost incurred in employing an additional unit of that factor of production. We call that cost the **marginal factor cost (MFC).** Otherwise stated,

Marginal revenue product (MRP)
The marginal physical product (MPP) times marginal revenue (MR). The MRP gives the additional revenue obtained from a one-unit change in labor input.

$$\text{Marginal factor cost} = \frac{\text{change in total cost}}{\text{change in amount of resource used}}$$

Because each worker is paid the same competitively determined wage of $830 per week, the MFC is the same for all workers. And because the firm is buying labor in a perfectly competitive labor market, the wage rate of $830 per week really represents the supply curve of labor to the firm. That supply curve is perfectly elastic because the firm can purchase all labor at the same wage rate, considering that it is a minuscule part of the entire labor-purchasing market. (Recall the definition of perfect competition.) We show this perfectly elastic supply curve as *s* in panel (b) of Figure 29-1.

Marginal factor cost (MFC)
The cost of using an additional unit of an input. For example, if a firm can hire all the workers it wants at the going wage rate, the marginal factor cost of labor is the wage rate.

General Rule for Hiring. Virtually every optimizing rule in economics involves comparing marginal benefits with marginal cost. Because the benefit from added workers is extra output and consequently more revenues, the general rule for the hiring decision of a firm is this:

> ***The firm hires workers up to the point at which the additional cost associated with hiring the last worker is equal to the additional revenue generated by hiring that worker.***

In a perfectly competitive market, this is the point at which the wage rate just equals the marginal revenue product. If the firm were to hire more workers, the additional wages would not be covered by additional increases in total revenue. If the firm were to hire fewer workers, it would be forfeiting the contributions that those workers otherwise could make to total profits.

Therefore, referring to columns 4 and 5 in panel (a) of Figure 29-1 on page 734, we see that this firm would certainly employ at least seven workers because the MRP is $1,180 while the MFC is only $830. The firm would continue to add workers up to the point at which MFC = MRP because as workers are added, those additional workers contribute more to revenue than to cost.

The MRP Curve: Demand for Labor. We can also use panel (b) of Figure 29-1 to find how many workers our firm should hire. First, we draw a line at the going wage rate, which is determined by demand and supply in the labor market. The line is labeled s to indicate that it is the supply curve of labor for the *individual* firm purchasing labor in a perfectly competitive labor market. That firm can purchase all the labor it wants of equal quality at $830 per worker. This perfectly elastic supply curve, s, intersects the marginal revenue product curve at 12 workers per week. At the intersection, E, the wage rate is equal to the marginal revenue product. The firm maximizes profits where its demand curve for labor, which turns out to be its MRP curve, intersects the firm's supply curve for labor, shown as s. The firm in our example would not hire the thirteenth worker, who will add only $760 to revenue but $830 to cost. If the price of labor should fall to, say, $760 per worker per week, it would become profitable for the firm to hire an additional worker; the quantity of labor demanded increases as the wage decreases.

Derived Demand for Labor

We have identified an individual firm's demand for labor curve, which shows the quantity of labor that the firm will wish to hire at each wage rate, as its MRP curve. Under conditions of perfect competition in both product and labor markets, MRP is determined by multiplying MPP times the product's price. This suggests that the demand for labor is a **derived demand.** Factors of production are rented or purchased not because they give any intrinsic satisfaction to the firms' owners but because they can be used to manufacture output that is expected to be sold at a profit.

We know that an increase in the market demand for a given product raises the product's price (all other things held constant), which in turn increases the marginal revenue product, or demand for the resource. Figure 29-2 illustrates the effective role played by changes in product demand in a perfectly competitive product market. The MRP curve shifts whenever there is a change in the price of the final product that the workers are producing. Suppose, for example, that the market price of touch-screen electronic organizers declines. In that case, the MRP curve will shift to the left from MRP_0 to MRP_1. We know that $MRP \equiv MPP \times MR$. If marginal revenue (here the output price) falls, so does the demand for labor. At the same going wage rate, the firm will hire fewer workers. This is because at various levels of labor use, the marginal revenue product of labor is now lower. At

Derived demand
Input factor demand derived from demand for the final product being produced.

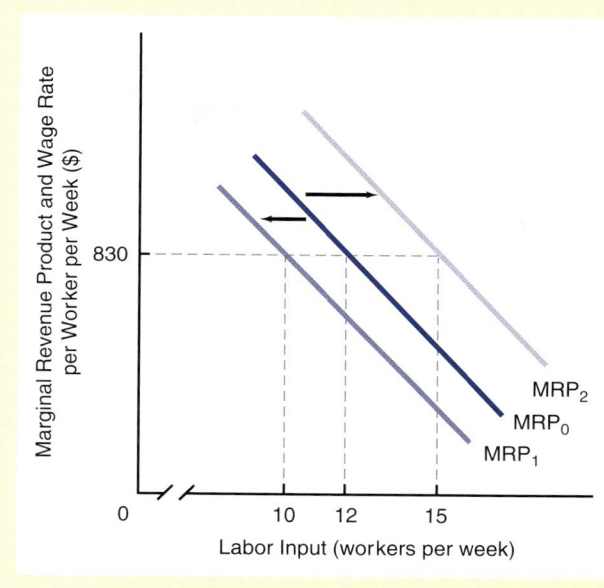

FIGURE 29-2

Demand for Labor, a Derived Demand

The demand for labor is derived from the demand for the final product being produced. Therefore, the marginal revenue product curve will shift whenever the price of the product changes. If we start with the marginal revenue product curve MRP_0 at the going wage rate of $830 per week, 12 workers will be hired. If the price of touch-screen electronic organizers goes down, the marginal product curve will shift to MRP_1, and the number of workers hired will fall, in this case to 10. If the price of electronic organizers goes up, the marginal revenue product curve will shift to MRP_2, and the number of workers hired will increase, in this case to 15.

the initial equilibrium, therefore, the price of labor (here the MFC) becomes greater than MRP. Thus, the firm would reduce the number of workers hired. Conversely, if the marginal revenue (output price) rises, the demand for labor will also rise, and the firm will want to hire more workers at each and every possible wage rate.

We just pointed out that $MRP \equiv MPP \times MR$. Clearly, then, a change in marginal productivity, or in the marginal physical product of labor, will shift the MRP curve. If the marginal productivity of labor decreases, the MRP curve, or demand curve, for labor will shift inward to the left. Again, this is because at every quantity of labor used, the MRP will be lower. A lower quantity of labor will be demanded at every possible wage rate.

QUICK QUIZ

The change in total _____ due to a one-unit change in one variable _____, holding all other _____ constant, is called the **marginal physical product (MPP)**. When we multiply marginal physical product times _____ _____, we obtain the **marginal revenue product (MRP)**.

A firm will hire workers up to the point at which the additional cost of hiring one more worker is equal to the additional revenue generated. For the individual firm, therefore, its MRP of labor curve is also its _____ _____ labor curve.

The demand for labor is a _____ demand, _____ from the demand for final output. Therefore, a change in the price of the final output will cause a _____ in the MRP curve (which is also the firm's demand for labor curve).

See page 758 for the answers. Review concepts from this section in MyEconLab.

THE MARKET DEMAND FOR LABOR

The downward-sloping portion of each individual firm's marginal revenue product curve is also its demand curve for the one variable factor of production—in our example, labor. When we go to the entire market for a particular type of labor in a particular industry, we will also find that the quantity of labor demanded will vary inversely as the wage rate changes.

Constructing the Market Labor Demand Curve

Given that the market demand curve for labor is made up of the individual firms' downward-sloping demand curves for labor, we can safely infer that the market demand curve for labor will look like D in panel (b) of Figure 29-3: It will slope downward. That market demand curve for labor in the electronic organizer industry shows the quantities of labor demanded by all of the firms in the industry at various wage rates.

Nevertheless, the market demand curve for labor is *not* a simple horizontal summation of the labor demand curves of all individual firms. Remember that the demand for labor is a derived demand. Even if we hold labor productivity constant, the demand for labor still depends on both the wage rate and the price of the final output.

For instance, suppose that we start at a wage rate of $20 per hour and employment level 10 in panel (a) of Figure 29-3. If we sum all such employment levels—point a in panel (a)—across 200 firms, we get a market quantity demanded of 2,000, or point A in panel (b), at the wage rate of $20. A decrease in the wage rate to $10 per hour would induce individual firms' employment levels to increase toward a quantity demanded of 22 *if price did not change*.

As all 200 firms simultaneously increase employment, total industry output also increases at the present price. Indeed, this would occur at *any* price, meaning that the industry product supply curve will shift rightward, and the market clearing price of the product must fall. The fall in the output price in turn causes a downward shift of each firm's MRP curve (d_0) to MRP_1 (d_1) in panel (a). Thus, each firm's employment of labor increases to

FIGURE 29-3
Derivation of the Market Demand Curve for Labor
The market demand curve for labor is not simply the horizontal summation of each individual firm's demand curve for labor. If wage rates fall from $20 to $10, all 200 firms will increase employment and therefore output, causing the price of the product to fall. This causes the marginal revenue product curve of each firm to shift inward, from d_0 to d_1 in panel (a). The resulting market demand curve, D, in panel (b) is therefore less elastic around prices from $10 to $20 than it would be if the output price remained constant.

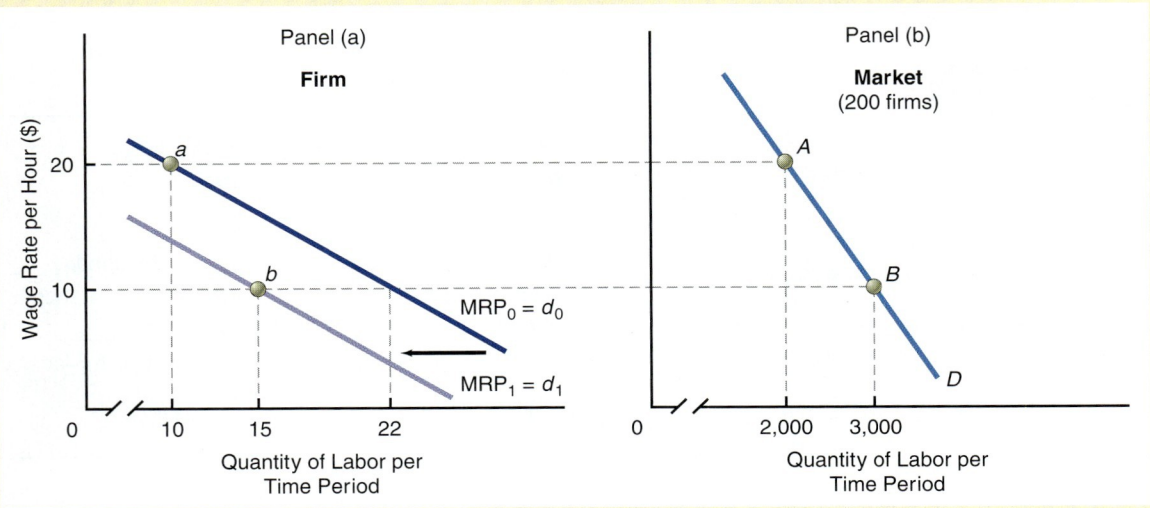

15 rather than to 22 at the wage rate of $10 per hour. A summation of all such 200 employment levels gives us 3,000—point B—in panel (b).

Determinants of Demand Elasticity for Inputs

Just as we were able to discuss the price elasticity of demand for different commodities in Chapter 21, we can discuss the price elasticity of demand for inputs. The price elasticity of demand for labor is defined in a manner similar to the price elasticity of demand for goods: the percentage change in quantity demanded divided by the percentage change in the price of labor. When the *numerical* (or absolute) value of this ratio is less than 1, demand is inelastic; when it is 1, demand is unit-elastic; and when it is greater than 1, demand is elastic.

There are four principal determinants of the price elasticity of demand for an input. The price elasticity of demand for a variable input will be greater:

1. The greater the price elasticity of demand for the final product
2. The easier it is to employ substitute inputs in production
3. The larger the proportion of total costs accounted for by the particular variable input
4. The longer the time period available for adjustment

Final Product Price Elasticity. An individual radish farmer faces an extremely elastic demand for radishes, given the existence of many competing radish growers. If the farmer's laborers tried to obtain a significant wage increase, the farmer couldn't pass on the resultant higher costs to radish buyers. So any wage increase would lead to a large reduction in the quantity of labor demanded by the individual radish farmer.

Ease of Substitution. Clearly, the easier it is for producers to switch to using another factor of production, the more responsive those producers will be to an increase in an input's price. If plastic can easily substitute for aluminum in the production of, say, car bumpers, then a rise in the price of aluminum will cause automakers to greatly reduce their quantity of aluminum demanded.

Portion of Total Cost. When a particular input's costs account for a very large share of total costs, any increase in that input's price will affect total costs relatively more. If labor costs are 80 percent of total costs, companies will cut back on employment more aggressively than if labor costs are only 8 percent of total costs, for any given wage increase.

Adjustment Period. Finally, over longer periods, firms have more time to figure out ways to economize on the use of inputs whose prices have gone up. Furthermore, over time, technological change will allow for easier substitution in favor of relatively cheaper inputs and against inputs whose prices went up. At first, a pay raise obtained by a strong telephone industry union may not result in many layoffs, but over time, the telephone companies will use new technology to replace many of the now more expensive workers.

QUICK QUIZ

Because the demand for labor is a derived demand that depends on both the _____ rate and the _____ of final output, the market demand curve for labor is not a simple horizontal summation of the labor demand curves of all individual firms. The market demand curve for labor does slope _____, however.

Input price elasticity of demand depends on the final product's _____ of demand, the ease of substituting other _____, the relative importance of the input's cost in total _____, and the time available for _____.

See page 758 for the answers. Review concepts from this section in MyEconLab.

WAGE DETERMINATION IN A PERFECTLY COMPETITIVE LABOR MARKET

Having developed the demand curve for labor (and all other variable inputs) in a particular industry, let's turn to the labor supply curve. By adding supply to the analysis, we can determine the equilibrium wage rate that workers earn in an industry. We can think in terms of a supply curve for labor that slopes upward in a particular industry. At higher wage rates, more workers will want to enter that particular industry. The individual firm, however, does not face the entire *market* supply curve. Rather, in a perfectly competitive case, the individual firm is such a small part of the market that it can hire all the workers that it wants at the going wage rate. We say, therefore, that the industry faces an upward-sloping supply curve but that the individual *firm* faces a perfectly elastic supply curve for labor.

Labor Market Equilibrium

The demand curve for labor in the electronic organizer industry is D in Figure 29-4, and the supply curve of labor is S. The equilibrium wage rate of $830 a week is established at the intersection of the two curves. The quantity of workers both supplied and demanded at that rate is Q_1. If for some reason the wage rate fell to $800 a week, in our hypothetical example, there would be an excess number of workers demanded at that wage rate. Conversely, if the wage rate rose to $900 a week, there would be an excess quantity of workers supplied at that wage rate. In either case, competition would quickly force the wage back to the equilibrium level.

We have just found the equilibrium wage rate for the entire electronic organizer industry. The individual firm must take that equilibrium wage rate as given in the perfectly competitive model used here because the individual firm is a very small part of the total demand for labor. Thus, each firm purchasing labor in a perfectly competitive market can purchase all of the input it wants at the going market price.

How has the market clearing wage paid to professionally qualified mining workers responded to an increased global demand for commodities that can be unearthed with their skills?

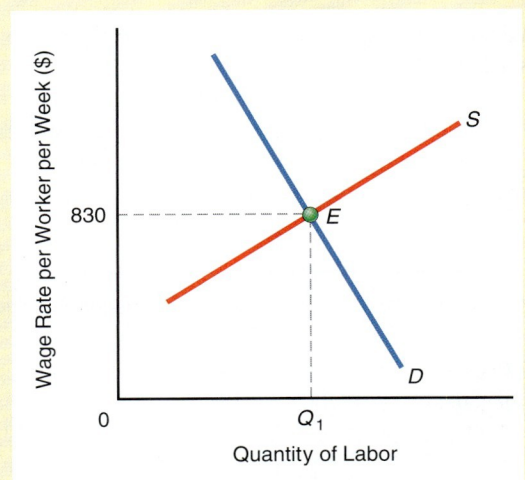

FIGURE 29-4

The Equilibrium Wage Rate and the Electronic Organizer Industry

The industry demand curve for labor is D. We put in a hypothetical upward-sloping labor supply curve for the electronic organizer industry, S. The intersection is at point E, giving an equilibrium wage rate of $830 per week and an equilibrium quantity of labor demanded of Q_1. At a wage above $830 per week, there will be an excess quantity of workers supplied. At a wage below $830 per week, there will be an excess quantity of workers demanded.

INTERNATIONAL EXAMPLE

A Global Shortage Hits the Market for Mining Workers

As manufacturing industries in nations such as India and China have rapidly grown during the 2000s, the global demand for mined commodities used as manufacturing inputs, such as aluminum, copper, zinc, and nickel, has soared. Commodity prices have increased around the world, which has raised the marginal revenue product of a key input in producing these and other mined commodities: mine workers. Increased worldwide demand for individuals trained to engage in the sometimes dangerous occupation of mining has pushed the quantity of qualified mining labor demanded above the quantity of qualified mining labor supplied. In nations such as Australia and Brazil, managers of mining companies commonly try to hire away other firms' workers in parking lots as they get in and out of their cars. Not surprisingly, the key inducement the managers offer in their efforts to convince miners to switch jobs is the promise of higher wages.

FOR CRITICAL ANALYSIS
In some parts of the world, mining companies have established special schools to train people in the art of safe commodities mining. What effect is the establishment of such training centers likely to have in the market for qualified mining labor?

Shifts in the Market Demand for and the Supply of Labor

Just as we discussed shifts in the supply curve and the demand curve for various products in Chapter 3, we can discuss the effects of shifts in supply and demand in labor markets.

Reasons for Labor Demand Curve Shifts.
Many factors can cause the demand curve for labor to shift. We have already discussed a number of them. Clearly, because the demand for labor or any other variable input is a derived demand, the labor demand curve will shift if there is a shift in the demand for the final product. There are two other important determinants of the position of the demand curve for labor: changes in labor's productivity and changes in the price of related factors of production (substitutes and complements).

1. *Changes in the demand for the final product.* The demand for labor or any other variable input is derived from the demand for the final product. The marginal revenue product is equal to marginal physical product times marginal revenue. Therefore, any change in the price of the final product will change MRP. This happened when we derived the market demand for labor. The rule of thumb is as follows:

   A change in the demand for the final product that labor (or any other variable input) is producing will shift the market demand curve for labor in the same direction.

2. *Changes in labor productivity.* The second part of the MRP equation is MPP, which relates to labor productivity. We can surmise, then, that, other things being equal:

   A change in labor productivity will shift the market labor demand curve in the same direction.

   Labor productivity can increase because labor has more capital or land to work with, because of technological improvements, or because labor's quality has improved. Such considerations explain why the real standard of living of workers in the United States is higher than in most other countries. U.S. workers generally work with a larger capital stock, have more natural resources, are in better physical condition, and are better trained than workers in many countries. Hence the demand for labor in the United States is, other things held constant, greater.

3. *Change in the price of related factors.* Labor is not the only resource that firms use. Some resources are substitutes and some are complements. If we hold output constant, we have the following general rule:

> *A change in the price of a substitute input will cause the demand for labor (or any other input) to change in the same direction.*

Thus, if the price of an input for which labor can substitute as a factor of production increases, the demand for labor rises. For instance, if the price of ditch-digging equipment increases, the demand for workers who can use shovels to dig ditches increases.

In general, an increase in the price of an input generates a rise in demand for any substitute input. Why do you suppose that the demand for and market price of uranium, a key input in producing energy with nuclear reactors, have increased significantly during the 2000s?

EXAMPLE

Choosing the Nuclear Option

When the price of oil used to heat homes and power electrical generators rose during the 2000s, many energy-producing companies began substituting away from oil in favor of nuclear power as an energy source. The key input that nuclear power plants use in producing energy is processed uranium. Thus, the demand for uranium has increased throughout the 2000s. As the demand for this input has increased, so has its market clearing price, which has more than doubled since 2000, from $10 per pound to about $22 per pound today.

FOR CRITICAL ANALYSIS
What do you suppose happened to the demand for natural gas, another substitute input used to produce energy, as the price of oil rose during the 2000s?

Suppose that a particular type of capital equipment and labor are complementary. In general, we predict the following:

> *A change in the price of a complementary input will cause the demand for labor to change in the opposite direction.*

If the cost of machines goes up but they must be used with labor, fewer machines will be purchased and therefore fewer workers will be used.

Naturally, an increase in the number of firms employing labor also results in an increase in the market demand for labor and thereby pushes up the market clearing wage rate. Why do you suppose that market clearing wages in Indonesia increased substantially during the months following the tsunami disaster of December 26, 2004?

INTERNATIONAL EXAMPLE

How Tsunami Relief Efforts Boosted Indonesian Wages

Following the tsunami disaster that struck Indian Ocean nations in December 2004, the Red Cross and other relief agencies from all over the world established offices throughout the region. For several months, the agencies hired local workers to help with the massive cleanup efforts, to assist in providing medical services to survivors, and to aid in various other relief efforts. This generated a rise in the demand for labor throughout Indonesia, and the market clearing wage rate rose to nearly twice the average wage that workers had earned prior to the tsunami event.

FOR CRITICAL ANALYSIS
What do you think happened to the wages that Indonesian firms paid their workers after many relief organizations completed their work in late 2005 and 2006?

Determinants of the Supply of Labor. Labor supply curves may shift in a particular industry for a number of reasons. For example, if wage rates for factory workers in the digital camera industry remain constant while wages for factory workers in the computer industry go up dramatically, the supply curve of factory workers in the digital camera industry will shift inward to the left as these workers move to the computer industry.

Changes in working conditions in an industry can also affect its labor supply curve. If employers in the digital camera industry discover a new production technique that makes working conditions much more pleasant, the supply curve of labor to the digital camera industry will shift outward to the right.

Job flexibility also determines the position of the labor supply curve. For example, when an industry allows workers more flexibility, such as the ability to work at home via computer, the workers are likely to provide more hours of labor. That is to say, their supply curve will shift outward to the right. Some industries in which firms offer *job sharing*, particularly to people raising families, have found that the supply curve of labor has shifted outward to the right.

QUICK QUIZ

The individual perfectly competitive firm faces a perfectly _____ labor supply curve—it can hire all the labor it wants at the going market wage rate. The industry supply curve of labor slopes _____.

By plotting an industrywide supply curve for labor and an industrywide demand curve for labor on the same graph, we obtain the _____ wage rate in the industry.

The labor demand curve can shift because the _____ for the final product shifts, labor _____ changes, or the price of a related (_____ or _____) factor of production changes.

See page 758 for the answers. Review concepts from this section in MyEconLab.

LABOR OUTSOURCING, WAGES, AND EMPLOYMENT

In addition to making it easier for people to work at home, computer technology has made it possible for them to provide labor services to companies located in another country. Some companies based in Canada regularly transmit financial records—often via e-mail and the Internet—to U.S. accountants so that they can process payrolls and compile income statements. Meanwhile, some U.S. manufacturers of personal computers and peripheral devices arrange for customers' calls for assistance to be directed to call centers in India, where English-speaking technical-support specialists help the customers with their problems.

A firm that employs labor located outside the country in which it is based engages in labor **outsourcing.** Canadian companies that hire U.S. accountants outsource accounting services to the United States. U.S. computer manufacturers that employ Indian call-center staff outsource technical-support services to India. How does outsourcing affect employment and wages in the United States? Who loses and who gains from outsourcing? Let's consider each of these questions in turn.

Outsourcing
A firm's employment of labor outside the country in which the firm is located.

Wage and Employment Effects of Outsourcing

Equilibrium wages and levels of employment in U.S. labor markets are determined by the demands for and supplies of labor in those markets. As you have learned, one of the determinants of the market demand for labor is the price of a substitute input. Availability of a lower-priced substitute, you also learned, causes the demand for labor to fall.

Thus, the *immediate* economic effects of labor outsourcing are straightforward. When a home industry's firms can obtain *foreign* labor services that are a close substitute for *home* labor services, the demand for labor services provided by home workers will decrease. What this economic reasoning ultimately implies for U.S. labor markets, however, depends on whether we view the United States as the "home" country or the "foreign" country.

U.S. Labor Market Effects of Outsourcing by U.S. Firms.

To begin, let's view the United States as the home country. Suppose that initially all U.S. firms employ only workers located in the United States. Then developments in computer, communications, and transportation technologies enable an increasing number of U.S. firms to regard the labor of foreign workers as a close substitute for labor provided by U.S. workers. Take a look at Figure 29-5. Panel (a) depicts demand and supply curves in the U.S. market for workers who handle calls for technical support for U.S. manufacturers of personal computers. Suppose that before technological change makes foreign labor substitutable for U.S. labor, point E_1 is the initial equilibrium. At this point, the market wage rate in this U.S. labor market is $19 per hour.

Now suppose that improvements in communications technologies enable U.S. personal computer manufacturers to consider foreign labor as a substitute input for U.S. labor. Panel (b) displays demand and supply curves in a market for substitutable labor services in India. At the initial equilibrium point E_1, the wage rate denominated in U.S. dollars is $8 per hour. Firms in this U.S. industry will respond to the lower price of substitute labor in India by increasing their demand for labor services in that country and reducing their demand for U.S. labor. Thus, in panel (b), the market demand for the substitute labor services available in India rises. The market wage in India rises to $13 per

FIGURE 29-5
Outsourcing of U.S. Computer Technical-Support Services

Initially, the market wage for U.S. workers providing technical support for customers of U.S. computer manufacturers is $19 per hour at point E_1 in panel (a), while the market wage for Indian workers who provide the same service is $8 per hour in panel (b). Then, improvements in communications technologies enable U.S. firms to substitute away from U.S. workers to Indian workers. The market demand for U.S. labor decreases in panel (a), generating a new equilibrium at point E_2 at a lower U.S. market wage and employment level. The market demand for Indian labor increases in panel (b), bringing about higher wages and employment at point E_2.

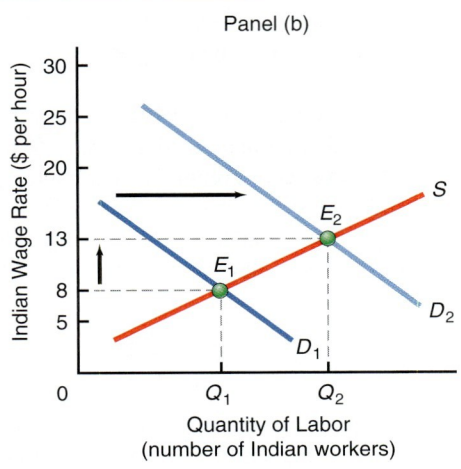

hour, at point E_2, and Indian employment increases. In panel (a), the market demand for U.S. labor services decreases. At the new equilibrium point E_2, the U.S. market wage has fallen to $16 per hour, and equilibrium employment has decreased.

Consequently, when U.S. firms are the home firms engaging in labor outsourcing, the effects are lower wages and decreased employment in the relevant U.S. labor markets. In those nations where workers providing the outsourced labor reside, the effects are higher wages and increased employment.

What are examples of labor services that U.S. firms now regularly outsource abroad?

INTERNATIONAL EXAMPLE

The Widening Expanse of Labor Outsourcing

Outsourcing has now become a fundamental aspect of operating many businesses in the United States. U.S. airlines such as JetBlue Airways, U.S. Airways, and Northwest Airlines now regularly fly significant portions of their fleets of aircraft to nations such as El Salvador, Singapore, and Hong Kong for servicing and maintenance. U.S. automakers General Motors and Ford Motor Company outsource basic auto design work to Germany and Sweden. Many U.S. firms, such as DuPont, obtain a variety of services relating to U.S. legal matters from lawyers based in India. Recently, a growing number of U.S. law firms have even begun retaining the services of Indian workers who specialize in developing searchable legal databases. The list goes on and on. Engaging in labor outsourcing has become part of doing business across U.S. industries.

FOR CRITICAL ANALYSIS
How does labor outsourcing by U.S. firms help to fuel the demand for U.S. export products? (Hint: How does outsourcing by U.S. firms affect foreign workers' wage incomes, which they can use to buy items from other nations, including the United States?)

U.S. Labor Market Effects of Outsourcing by Foreign Firms. U.S. firms are not the only companies that engage in outsourcing. Consider the Canadian companies that hire U.S. accountants to calculate their payrolls and maintain their financial records. Figure 29-6 on the following page shows the effects in the Canadian and U.S. markets for labor services provided by accountants before and after *Canadian* outsourcing of accountants' labor. At point E_1 in panel (a), before any outsourcing takes place, the initial market wage for qualified accountants in Canada is $29 per hour. In panel (b), the market wage for similarly qualified U.S. accountants is $21 per hour.

After e-mail and Internet access allow companies in Canada to transfer financial data electronically, the services of U.S. accountants become available as a less expensive substitute for those provided by Canadian accountants. When Canadian firms respond by seeking to hire U.S. accountants, the demand for U.S. accountants' labor services rises in panel (b). This causes the market wage earned by U.S. accountants to increase to $23 per hour. Canadian firms substitute away from the services of Canadian accountants, so in panel (a) the demand for the labor of accountants in Canada declines. Canadian accountants' wages decline to $26 per hour.

In contrast to the situation in which U.S. firms are the home firms engaging in labor outsourcing, when foreign firms outsource by hiring workers in the United States, wages and employment levels rise in the affected U.S. markets. In the nations where the firms engaging in outsourcing are located, the effects are lower wages and decreased employment.

Gauging the Net Effects of Outsourcing on the U.S. Economy

In the example depicted in Figure 29-5, the market wage and employment level for U.S. technical-support workers declined as a result of outsourcing by U.S. firms. In contrast, in

FIGURE 29-6
Outsourcing of Accounting Services by Canadian Firms

Suppose that the market wage for accounting services in Canada is initially $29 per hour, at point E_1 in panel (a), but in the United States accountants earn just $21 per hour at point E_1 in panel (b). Then, access to e-mail and Internet communications enables Canadian firms to substitute labor services provided by U.S. accountants for the services of Canadian accountants. The market demand for the services of Canadian accountants decreases in panel (a), and at point E_2 fewer Canadian accountants are employed at a lower market wage. The market demand for U.S. accounting services increases in panel (b). This generates higher wages and employment for U.S. accountants at point E_2.

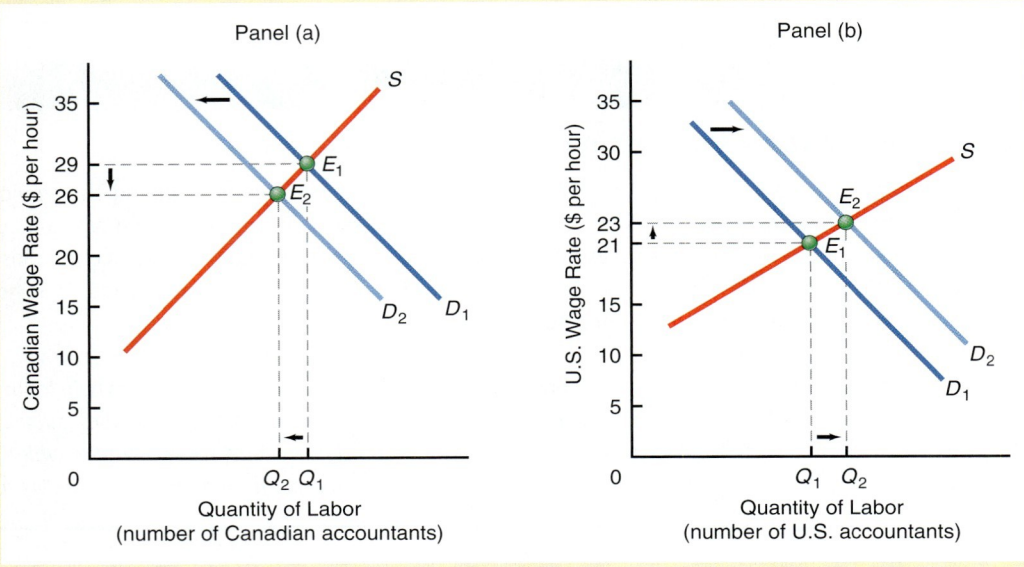

To read a Heritage Foundation lecture about the net effects of outsourcing on U.S. jobs, use the link at www.econtoday.com/ch29.

the example shown in Figure 29-6, U.S. accountants earned higher wages and experienced increased employment as a result of outsourcing by Canadian firms. Together, these examples illustrate a fundamental conclusion concerning the short-run effects of global labor outsourcing in U.S. labor markets:

> *Labor outsourcing by U.S. firms tends to reduce U.S. wages and employment. Whenever foreign firms engage in labor outsourcing in the United States, however, U.S. wages and employment increase.*

Consequently, the immediate effects of increased worldwide labor outsourcing are lower wages and employment in some U.S. labor markets and higher wages and employment in others. In this narrow sense, some U.S. workers "lose" from outsourcing while others "gain," just as some Canadian workers "lose" while some Indian workers "gain."

Short-Run versus Long-Run Effects of Outsourcing.
Even in the best of times workers in labor markets experience short-run ups and downs in wages and jobs. In the United States, after all, about 4 million jobs come and go every month.

To be sure, in the near term certain groups of U.S. workers, at least for a time, earn lower pay or experience reduced employment opportunities as a result of labor outsourcing. Nevertheless, what really matters when gauging the overall effects of increased global outsourcing of labor is the *long-term* effects on the *overall* levels of wages and employment. If the ultimate effects of outsourcing are higher wages and increased employment levels across all U.S. labor markets, then U.S. workers ultimately benefit from outsourcing. So do workers in India, Canada, and other countries.

The Long-Term Benefits of Outsourcing for the U.S. Economy. As you will learn in Chapter 33, computer companies' labor outsourcing to India constitutes a form of U.S. spending on imports. Many of the dollars that U.S. firms spend to purchase Indian labor services, however, ultimately flow back into the United States. A number of Indian workers use their higher wages to buy more U.S. export products. Some invest some of their earnings in U.S. companies.

Increased labor outsourcing is part of a broader trend toward increased international trade of goods and services. Engaging in international trade allows residents of a nation to specialize in producing the goods and services that they can produce most efficiently. The resource saving that results expands the ability of a nation's residents to produce more goods and services than they could have produced in the absence of trade. This generates higher incomes, which the nation's residents can use to consume more items as well. On net, therefore, outsourcing makes consumers in the United States and other countries better off.

Benefits of Outsourcing for U.S. Workers. What are the net effects of outsourcing on the well-being of U.S. workers? As you have already seen, the immediate effects are mixed. Initially, some workers gain, and some workers lose.

Nevertheless, in the long run most workers must also be better off. After all, if outsourcing allows U.S. firms to operate more efficiently, then those firms can allocate their resource savings to the production of more goods and services. Furthermore, because outsourcing contributes to higher incomes, consumers will buy these goods and services. Thus, the expanded production and consumption possibilities made possible by outsourcing and other forms of international trade generate higher total revenues across U.S. firms.

As you learned earlier, the demand for labor is a derived demand determined by each worker's marginal revenue product. In the long run, outsourcing helps boost the overall value of the marginal revenue product in industries throughout the U.S. economy. Consequently, the ultimate long-run effect of outsourcing is an increase in the demand for labor in most industries. Increased labor demand, in turn, pushes up wages and boosts employment. Labor economists have concluded that labor outsourcing has probably created many more jobs in the United States than it has destroyed.

International labor outsourcing is also known as "labor offshoring." What U.S. firm has found a way to literally engage in "offshore" outsourcing activities?

> **ECONOMICS FRONT AND CENTER**
>
> To contemplate how efforts to keep U.S. firms from hiring foreign workers for certain tasks might backfire in the long run, read **Efforts to Protect Maine Logging Jobs May Destroy Them,** on page 752.

E-COMMERCE EXAMPLE

Outsourcing Computer Programming Very Close to the Border

A U.S. company called SeaCode recently arranged to install hundreds of workers from nations such as India and Russia on a cruise ship off the coast of El Segundo, California, just outside the three-mile limit of U.S. territorial waters. SeaCode classifies these workers as "seamen," the legal term for anyone who works on a sea vessel. In reality, however, most of them are computer programmers that SeaCode hires to write software for U.S. businesses. In this way, people from abroad who cannot obtain immigration visas can earn roughly $1,800 per month. In their off hours, they eat, dine, and sleep in the ship's cabins, play shuffleboard and engage in other activities on deck, and take water taxis to shore to sightsee.

FOR CRITICAL ANALYSIS

If someday a fleet of cruise ships filled with foreign programmers employed by U.S. firms were anchored off the California coast, what would be the effect on the demand for U.S. programmers?

QUICK QUIZ

Advances in telecommunications and computer networking are making foreign labor more easily _____ for home labor, and home firms' _____ of foreign labor for home labor is known as labor **outsourcing**.

In the short run, outsourcing by U.S. firms _____ the demand for labor, market wages, and equilibrium employment in U.S. labor markets. Outsourcing by foreign firms that hire U.S. labor _____ the demand for labor, market wages, and equilibrium employment in U.S. labor markets. The net short-run effects on U.S. wages and employment are mixed.

In the long run, outsourcing enables U.S. firms to operate more efficiently, which allows resources to be redirected to other revenue-generating activities that bring about overall _____ in U.S. wages and employment.

See page 758 for the answers. Review concepts from this section in MyEconLab.

MONOPOLY IN THE PRODUCT MARKET

So far we've considered only perfectly competitive markets, both in selling the final product and in buying factors of production. We will continue our assumption that the firm purchases its factors of production in a perfectly competitive factor market. Now, however, we will assume that the firm sells its product in an *imperfectly* competitive output market. In other words, we are considering the output market structures of monopoly, oligopoly, and monopolistic competition. In all such cases, the firm, be it a monopolist, an oligopolist, or a monopolistic competitor, faces a downward-sloping demand curve for its product.

Throughout the rest of this chapter, we will simply refer to a monopoly situation for ease of analysis. The analysis holds for all industry structures that are less than perfectly competitive. In any event, the fact that our firm now faces a downward-sloping demand curve for its product means that if it wants to sell more of its product (at a uniform price), it has to lower the price, *not just on the last unit, but on all preceding units*. The *marginal revenue* received from selling an additional unit is continuously falling (and is less than price) as the firm attempts to sell more and more. This is certainly different from our earlier discussions in this chapter in which the firm could sell all it wanted at a constant price. Why? Because the firm we discussed until now was a perfect competitor.

Constructing the Monopolist's Input Demand Curve

In reconstructing our demand schedule for an input, we must account for the facts that (1) the marginal *physical* product falls because of the law of diminishing marginal product as more workers are added and (2) the price (and marginal revenue) received for the product sold also falls as more is produced and sold. That is, for the monopolist, we have to account for both the diminishing marginal physical product and the diminishing marginal revenue. Marginal revenue is always less than price for the monopolist. The marginal revenue curve is always below the downward-sloping product demand curve.

Marginal Revenue Product for a Perfectly Competitive Firm.
Marginal revenue for the perfect competitor is equal to the price of the product because all units can be sold at the going market price. In our example involving the production of handheld, touchscreen electronic organizers, we assumed that the perfect competitor could sell all it wanted at $10 per unit. A one-unit change in sales always led to a $10 change in total revenues. Hence marginal revenue was always equal to $10 for that perfect competitor. Multiplying this unchanging marginal revenue by the marginal physical product of labor then yielded the perfectly competitive firm's marginal revenue product.

Marginal Revenue Product for a Monopoly Firm. The monopolist, however, cannot simply calculate marginal revenue by looking at the price of the product. To sell the additional output from an additional unit of input, the monopolist has to cut prices on all previous units of output. As output is increasing, then, marginal revenue is falling. The underlying concept is, of course, the same for both the perfect competitor and the monopolist. We are asking exactly the same question in both cases: When an additional worker is hired, what is the benefit? In either case, the benefit is obviously the change in total revenues due to the one-unit change in the variable input, labor. In our discussion of the perfect competitor, we were able simply to look at the marginal physical product and multiply it by the *constant* per-unit price of the product because the price of the product never changed (for the perfect competitor, $P = MR$).

A single monopolist ends up hiring fewer workers than would all of the perfectly competitive firms added together. To see this, we must consider the marginal revenue product for the monopolist, which varies with each one-unit change in the monopolist's labor input. This is what we do in panel (a) of Figure 29-7 on the following page, where column 5, "Marginal Revenue Product," gives the monopolist a quantitative notion of how additional workers and additional production generate additional revenues. The marginal revenue product curve for this monopolist has been plotted in panel (b) of the figure. To emphasize the lower elasticity of the monopolist's MRP curve (MRP_m) around the wage rate $830, the labor demand curve for a perfectly competitive industry (labeled D) has been plotted on the same graph in Figure 29-7. Recall that this curve is not simply the sum of the marginal revenue product curves of all perfectly competitive firms, because when competitive firms together increase employment, their output expands and the product price declines. Nevertheless, at any given wage rate, the quantity of labor demanded by the monopoly is still less than the quantity of labor demanded by a perfectly competitive industry.

Why does MRP_m represent the monopolist's input demand curve? As always, our profit-maximizing monopolist will continue to hire labor as long as additional profits result. Profits are made as long as the additional cost of more workers is outweighed by the additional revenues made from selling the output of those workers. When the wage rate equals these additional revenues, the monopolist stops hiring. That is, the firm stops hiring when the wage rate is equal to the marginal revenue product because additional workers would add more to cost than to revenue.

Why the Monopolist Hires Fewer Workers

Because we have used the same numbers as in Figure 29-1 on page 734, we can see that the monopolist hires fewer workers per week than firms in a perfect competitive market would. That is to say, if we could magically change the electronic organizer industry in our example from one in which there is perfect competition in the output market to one in which there is monopoly in the output market, the amount of employment would fall. Why? Because the monopolist must take account of the declining product price that must be charged in order to sell a larger number of touch-screen electronic organizers. Remember that every firm hires up to the point at which marginal benefit equals marginal cost. The marginal benefit to the monopolist of hiring an additional worker is not simply the additional output times the price of the product. Rather, the monopolist faces a reduction in the price charged on *all* units sold in order to be able to sell more.

So the monopolist ends up hiring fewer workers than all of the perfect competitors taken together, assuming that all other factors remain the same for the two hypothetical examples. But this should not come as a surprise. In considering product markets, by implication we saw that a monopolized electronic organizer industry would produce less output than a competitive one. Therefore, the monopolized industry would hire fewer workers.

FIGURE 29-7

A Monopolist's Marginal Revenue Product

The monopolist hires just enough workers to make marginal revenue product equal to the going wage rate. If the going wage rate is $830 per week, as shown by the labor supply curve, s, in panel (b), the monopolist would want to hire approximately 10 workers per week. That is the profit-maximizing amount of labor. The labor demand curve for a perfectly competitive industry from Figure 29-4 on page 740 is also plotted (D). The monopolist's MRP curve will always be less elastic around the going wage rate than it would be if marginal revenue were constant.

Panel (a)

(1) Labor Input (workers per week)	(2) Marginal Physical Product (MPP) (electronic organizers per week)	(3) Price of Product (P)	(4) Marginal Revenue (MR)	(5) Marginal Revenue Product (MRP_m) = (2) × (4)
8	111	$11.60	$9.40	$1,043.40
9	104	11.40	9.00	936.00
10	97	11.20	8.60	834.20
11	90	11.00	8.20	738.00
12	83	10.80	7.80	647.40
13	76	10.60	7.40	562.40

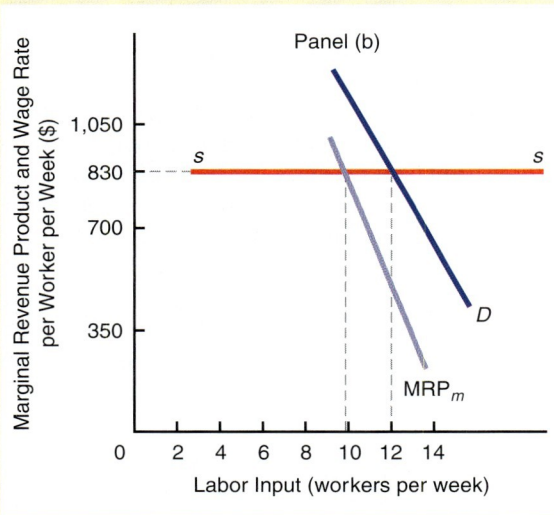

THE UTILIZATION OF OTHER FACTORS OF PRODUCTION

The analysis in this chapter has been given in terms of the demand for the variable input labor. The same analysis holds for any other variable factor input. We could have talked about the demand for fertilizer or the demand for the services of tractors by a farmer instead of the demand for labor and reached the same conclusions. The entrepreneur will hire or buy any variable input up to the point at which its price equals the marginal revenue product.

A further question remains: How much of each variable factor should the firm utilize when all the variable factors are combined to produce the product? We can answer this question by looking at either the profit-maximizing side of the question or the cost-minimizing side.

Profit Maximization Revisited

If a firm wants to maximize profits, how much of each factor should be hired (or bought)? As we just saw, the firm will never utilize a factor of production unless the marginal benefit from hiring that factor is at least equal to the marginal cost. What is the marginal benefit? As we have pointed out several times, the marginal benefit is the change in total revenues due to a one-unit change in utilization of the variable input. What is the marginal cost? In the case of a firm buying in a perfectly competitive market, it is the price of the variable factor—the wage rate if we are referring to labor.

The profit-maximizing combination of resources for the firm will be where, in a perfectly competitive market structure,

$$\text{MRP of labor} = \text{price of labor (wage rates)}$$
$$\text{MRP of capital} = \text{price of capital (cost per unit of service)}$$
$$\text{MRP of land} = \text{price of land (rental rate per unit)}$$

To attain maximum profits, the marginal revenue product of each of a firm's resources must be exactly equal to its price. If the MRP of labor is $20 and its price is only $15, the firm will expand its employment of labor.

Cost Minimization and Factor Utilization

From the cost minimization point of view, how can the firm minimize its total costs for a given output? Assume that you are an entrepreneur attempting to minimize costs. Consider a hypothetical situation in which if you spend $1 more on labor, you would get 20 more units of output, but if you spend $1 more on machines, you would get only 10 more units of output. What would you want to do in such a situation? You would wish to hire more workers or sell off some of your machines, for you are not getting as much output per *last* dollar spent on machines as you are per *last* dollar spent on labor. You would want to employ factors of production so that the marginal products per last dollar spent on each are equal. Thus, the least-cost, or cost minimization, rule will be as follows:

To minimize total costs for a particular rate of production, the firm will hire factors of production up to the point at which the marginal physical product per last dollar spent on each factor of production is equalized.

That is,

$$\frac{\text{MPP of labor}}{\text{price of labor (wage rate)}} = \frac{\text{MPP of capital}}{\text{price of capital (cost per unit of service)}} = \frac{\text{MPP of land}}{\text{price of land (rental rate per unit)}}$$

All we are saying here is that the profit-maximizing firm will always utilize *all* resources in such combinations that cost will be minimized for any given output rate. This is commonly called the *least-cost combination of resources*. There is an exact match between the profit-maximizing combination of resources and the least-cost combination of resources. In other words, either rule can be used to yield the same cost-minimizing rate of utilization of each variable resource.

QUICK QUIZ

When a firm sells its output in a monopoly market, marginal revenue is _____ than price.

Just as the MRP is the perfectly competitive firm's input demand curve, the MRP is also the _____ input demand curve.

The profit-maximizing combination of factors will occur when each factor is used up to the point at which its MRP is equal to its unit _____.

To minimize total costs for a given output, the profit-maximizing firm will hire each factor of production up to the point at which the marginal _____ product per last dollar spent on each factor is equal to the marginal _____ product per last dollar spent on each of the other factors of production.

See page 758 for the answers. Review concepts from this section in MyEconLab.

CASE STUDY

ECONOMICS FRONT AND CENTER

Efforts to Protect Maine Logging Jobs May Destroy Them

Albertson is at his wit's end. Throughout the year, his Maine logging company regularly employs 25 to 30 Canadian loggers under the terms of short-term U.S. visas granting Canadians the right to work temporarily in the United States. Taken together, all Maine logging operations employ about 800 Canadians to supplement their U.S. workforce. The Canadian workers assist about 1,500 U.S. workers, including about 50 employed at Albertson's firm, in the toughest, dirtiest jobs in logging. They fell and strip trees and drag them to the firm's wood yards. There workers who are almost all Maine residents use cranes to load the logs onto trucks, which transport the logs to sawmills, where they are cut into lumber or used for wood pulp.

All told, the operations of Albertson's company and other logging firms provide employment for at least 25,000 U.S. residents. But the jobs of many U.S. workers are now in jeopardy because of recent efforts by the U.S. government to toughen visa standards and enforcement. In part, the stiffer regulations are aimed at protecting U.S. residents from terrorist threats, but they also serve to protect U.S. logging workers from Canadian competition.

The problem that Albertson is facing is that as the visas of his Canadian workers expire, he is having trouble finding either Canadian workers with visas or U.S. workers to do the toughest, dirtiest logging jobs. To induce U.S. workers to take these jobs, he must offer higher wages, and these wage increases are squeezing his profits. Albertson suspects that soon he and other Maine logging companies may have no choice but to lay off some of their employees who operate cranes, drive trucks, and run sawmills here in the United States.

CRITICAL ANALYSIS QUESTIONS

1. *Do U.S. visa restrictions affect labor demand or labor supply in the market for logging workers? Explain.*

2. *If Albertson and other logging operators are able to convince many licensed truck drivers to fell and strip trees instead, what is likely to happen to the market clearing wage earned by truck drivers?*

Now Indian Outsourcing Specialists Are Also Outsourcing

Issues and Applications

Providing outsourcing services to U.S. companies has become a big business for many Indian firms. Indeed, a growing number of Indian companies have found that they have taken on more than they can handle, which in turn has induced them to outsource outside India.

Concepts Applied • Outsourcing • Marginal Revenue Product • Labor Demand

An Outsourcing Specialist Chooses to Outsource

Worldwide declines in telecommunications prices have reduced the price of a complementary input in U.S. firms' production of technical-support services: English-speaking workers who can provide call-center support to their customers. Heavily populated India has traditional ties with the United Kingdom, so a number of Indian residents speak English. A portion of these have sufficient technical training to provide technical support that meets U.S. companies' customer-service standards. Consequently, thousands of Indian workers now staff technical-support centers of U.S. producers of computers and peripheral devices.

Consider, for instance, India's Bharti Tele-Ventures. This company has prospered from hiring English-speaking Indian residents to provide call-center support for U.S. firms. As Bharti Tele-Ventures expanded its outsourcing operations, however, its customer billing, internal company communications, and worker payroll systems became too complicated for the company's management staff to handle. Its chief officers, therefore, decided to look abroad for assistance in handling its billing, e-mail, and payroll operations. Recently, the Indian company hired the U.S. firm International Business Machines to manage most of these aspects of its business.

Indian Outsourcing Firms Increasingly Look Abroad for Talent

Other Indian call-center firms have so increased the scale of their operations that they are having difficulties finding a sufficient number of qualified, English-speaking support personnel. New Delhi–based Technovate, for instance, now supplements its Indian staff with college-aged workers hired from Germany, Norway, and Sweden. It has even hired a few U.S. workers. The firm helps reimburse the costs these individuals incur to move to India for a year and pays them annual wages between $5,000 and $8,000. Although such pay is only about 25 percent of the wages that young Europeans could earn in their home countries, it is a significant salary in India, where prices of many goods and services are much lower than in Europe.

Other Indian firms face problems recruiting Indian workers with sufficient experience in supervising technical-support workers at their call centers. The Bangalore company 24/7 Customer now regularly recruits U.S. residents to serve as mid-level supervisors at its call centers. Many of these individuals continue to maintain their residences in the United States while "commuting" to India for long stretches of time. Some Indian firms, including Tata Consultancy Services, Infosys Technologies, Ltd., and Wipro Technologies, Ltd., have recently recruited some of their senior executives from the United States.

For India, Outsourcing Has Become a Two-Way Street

Thus, on the one hand Indian firms specializing in providing outsourcing services to U.S. firms have contributed to near-term reductions in employment in some U.S. labor markets. On the other hand, they have increased employment in other U.S. labor markets as they have begun to outsource some of their own jobs.

One thing is certain. In the long run, the two-way street of labor outsourcing between the United States and India is boosting overall incomes in both nations.

Log in to MyEconLab, click on "Economic News," and test your understanding of the chapter by answering interactive questions that relate directly to this issue.

For Critical Analysis

1. How are the demands for labor in *U.S.* markets for call-center workers, business software specialists, and supervisory workers affected by the operations of Indian companies such as Bharti Tele-Ventures and 24/7 Customer?
2. What are the effects of the operations of firms such as Bharti Tele-Ventures and 24/7 Customer on the demands for labor in *India's* markets for call-center workers, business software specialists, and supervisory workers?

Web Resources

1. For more information about the areas in which Technovate specializes in global outsourcing, go to www.econtoday.com/ch29.
2. Learn more about the outsourcing services offered by 24/7 Customer at www.econtoday.com/ch29.

Research Project

Before Indian outsourcing specialists began outsourcing as well, what was the short-run effect of their activities on labor markets in the United States? What have been the longer-run effects in U.S. labor markets as Indian firms have also begun outsourcing? How do these conclusions square with the discussion of labor outsourcing in this chapter?

Here is what you should know after reading this chapter. MyEconLab will help you identify what you know, and where to go when you need to practice.

WHAT YOU SHOULD KNOW		WHERE TO GO TO PRACTICE
Why a Firm's Marginal Revenue Product Curve Is Its Labor Demand Curve The marginal revenue product of labor equals marginal revenue times the marginal physical product of labor. Because of the law of diminishing marginal product, for a perfectly competitive producer the marginal revenue product curve slopes downward. To maximize profits, a firm hires labor to the point where the marginal factor cost of labor—the addition to total input costs resulting from employing an additional unit of labor—equals the marginal revenue product. For firms that hire	marginal physical product (MPP) of labor, 735 marginal revenue product (MRP), 735 marginal factor cost (MFC), 735 **Key figure** Figure 29-1, 734	• **MyEconLab** Study Plan 29.1 • Audio introduction to Chapter 29 • Animated Figure 29-1

WHAT YOU SHOULD KNOW		WHERE TO GO TO PRACTICE
labor in competitive labor markets, the market wage rate is the marginal factor cost of labor, so profit maximization requires hiring labor to the point where the wage rate equals marginal revenue product, which is a point on the marginal revenue product schedule. Thus, the marginal revenue product curve gives combinations of wage rates and desired employment of labor for a firm, which means that it is the firm's labor demand curve.		
The Demand for Labor as a Derived Demand For firms that are perfect competitors in their product markets, marginal revenue equals the market price of their output, so the marginal revenue product of labor equals the product price times the marginal physical product of labor. As conditions in the product market vary and cause the market price at which firms sell their output to change, their marginal revenue product curves shift. Hence the demand for labor by perfectly competitive firms is derived from the demand for the final products these firms produce.	derived demand, 736	• **MyEconLab** Study Plan 29.2
Key Factors Affecting the Elasticity of Demand for Inputs The price elasticity of demand for an input, such as labor, is equal to the percentage change in the quantity of the input demanded divided by the percentage change in the price of the input, such as the wage rate. The price elasticity of demand for a particular input is relatively high when any one of the following is true: (1) the price elasticity of demand for the final product is relatively high; (2) it is relatively easy to substitute other inputs in the production process; (3) the proportion of total costs accounted for by the input is relatively large; or (4) the firm has a longer time period to adjust to the change in the input's price.	**Key figure** Figure 29-3, 738	• **MyEconLab** Study Plan 29.2 • Animated Figure 29-3 • Video: Determinants of Demand Elasticity for Inputs
How Equilibrium Wage Rates at Perfectly Competitive Firms Are Determined For perfectly competitive firms, the market labor demand curve is the sum of the individual labor demand curves for all firms, which in turn are the firms' marginal revenue product curves. At the equilibrium wage rate, the quantity of labor demanded by all firms is equal to the quantity of labor supplied by all workers in the marketplace. At this wage rate, each firm looks to its own labor demand curve to determine how much labor to employ.	**Key figure** Figure 29-4, 740	• **MyEconLab** Study Plan 29.3 • Animated Figure 29-4 • Video: Shifts in the Market Demand for Labor
U.S. Wage and Employment Effects of Labor Outsourcing Technological changes are increasingly making foreign labor more readily available as a cheaper substitute for home labor for firms that engage in labor outsourcing. The immediate, short-run effects on wages and employment in U.S. labor markets are mixed. Outsourcing by U.S. firms reduces the demand for labor in affected U.S. labor markets and thereby pushes down wages and employment. Outsourcing by foreign firms that hire U.S. labor, however, raises the demand for labor in related U.S.	outsourcing, 743 **Key figures** Figure 29-5, 744 Figure 29-6, 746	• **MyEconLab** Study Plan 29.4 • Animated Figures 29-5 and 29-6

PART VII Labor Resources and the Environment

WHAT YOU SHOULD KNOW

labor markets, which boosts wages and employment in those labor markets. In the long run, outsourcing allows U.S. firms to operate more efficiently. The resulting resource savings effectively increase U.S. production and consumption possibilities, thereby raising revenues of U.S. firms. This induces an overall rise in U.S. labor demand and a general increase in U.S. wages and employment.

Contrasting the Demand for Labor and Wage Determination Under Monopoly with Outcomes Under Perfect Competition If a firm that is a monopolist in its product market competes with firms of other industries for labor in a competitive labor market, it takes the market wage rate as given. Its labor demand curve, however, lies to the left of the labor demand curve for the industry that would have arisen if the industry included a number of perfectly competitive firms. The reason is that marginal revenue is less than price for a monopolist, so the marginal revenue product of the monopolist is lower than under competition. Thus, at the competitively determined wage rate, a monopolized industry employs fewer workers than the industry otherwise would if it were perfectly competitive.

WHERE TO GO TO PRACTICE

Key figure
Figure 29-7, 750

- MyEconLab Study Plans 29.5 and 29.6
- Animated Figure 29-7

Log in to MyEconLab, take a chapter test, and get a personalized Study Plan that tells you which concepts you understand and which ones you need to review. From there, MyEconLab will give you further practice, tutorials, animations, videos, and guided solutions.

Log in to www.myeconlab.com

PROBLEMS

Select problems, indicated by a blue oval, are assignable in MyEconLab.
Answers to the odd-numbered problems appear at the back of the book.

29-1. The following table depicts the output of a firm that manufactures computer printers. The printers sell for $100 each.

Labor Input (workers per week)	Total Physical Output (printers per week)
10	200
11	218
12	234
13	248
14	260
15	270
16	278

Calculate the marginal physical product and marginal revenue product at each input level above 10 units.

29-2. Suppose that the firm in Problem 29-1 has chosen to hire 15 workers. What is the maximum wage the firm would be willing to pay?

29-3. The weekly wage paid by computer printer manufacturers in a perfectly competitive market is $1,200. Using the information provided in the table that accompanies Problem 29-1, how many workers will the profit-maximizing employer hire?

29-4. Suppose that there is an increase in the demand for personal computer systems. Explain the likely effects on marginal revenue product, marginal factor cost, and the number of workers hired by the firm in Problem 29-1.

29-5. Explain what happens to the elasticity of demand for labor in a given industry after each of the following events.

a. A new manufacturing technique makes capital easier to substitute for labor.
b. There is an increase in the number of substitutes for the final product that labor produces.
c. After a drop in the prices of capital inputs, labor accounts for a larger portion of a firm's factor costs.

29-6. Explain how the following events would affect the demand for labor.

a. A new education program administered by the company increases labor's marginal product.
b. The firm completes a new plant with a larger workspace and new machinery.

29-7. The following table depicts the product market and labor market an MP3 player manufacturer faces.

Labor Input (workers per day)	Total Physical Product	Product Price ($)
10	100	50
11	109	49
12	116	48
13	121	47
14	124	46
15	125	45

Calculate the firm's marginal physical product, total revenue, and marginal revenue product at each input level above 10 units.

29-8. The firm in Problem 29-7 competes in a perfectly competitive labor market, and the market wage it faces is $100. How many workers will the profit-maximizing employer hire?

29-9. A firm hires labor in a perfectly competitive labor market. Its current profit-maximizing hourly output is 100 units, which the firm sells at a price of $5 per unit. The marginal physical product of the last unit of labor employed is 5 units per hour. The firm pays each worker an hourly wage of $15.

a. What marginal revenue does the firm earn from sale of the output produced by the last worker employed?
b. Does this firm sell its output in a perfectly competitive market?

29-10. Top and mid-level managers of Japanese firms with U.S. offices and plants must travel to the United States several times each month. Most Japanese firms previously employed their own travel staffs to arrange these trips, but increasingly they have been outsourcing this work to U.S. travel agents. Suppose this trend becomes widespread. Use the diagrams below to explain what will happen to wages and employment of Japanese and U.S. workers who provide travel services.

29-11. Explain why the short-term effects of outsourcing on U.S. wages and employment tend to be more ambiguous than the long-term effects.

29-12. A profit-maximizing monopolist hires workers in a perfectly competitive labor market. Employing the last worker increased the firm's total weekly output from 110 units to 111 units and caused the firm's weekly revenues to rise from $25,000 to $25,750. What is the current prevailing weekly wage rate in the labor market?

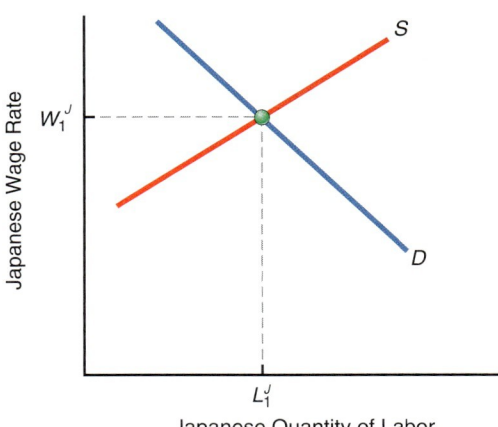

29-13. A monopoly firm hires workers in a perfectly competitive labor market in which the market wage rate is $20 per day. If the firm maximizes profit, and if the marginal revenue from the last unit of output produced by the last worker hired equals $10, what is the marginal physical product of that worker?

29-14. The current market wage rate is $10, the rental rate of land is $1,000 per unit, and the rental rate of capital is $500. Production managers at a firm find that under their current allocation of factors of production, the marginal revenue product of labor is 100, the marginal revenue product of land is $10,000, and the marginal revenue product of capital is $4,000. Is the firm maximizing profit? Why or why not?

29-15. The current wage rate is $10, and the rental rate of capital is $500. A firm's marginal physical product of labor is 200, and its marginal physical product of capital is 20,000. Is the firm maximizing profits for the given cost outlay? Why or why not?

ECONOMICS ON THE NET

Current Trends in U.S. Labor Markets The Federal Reserve's "Beige Book," which summarizes regional economic conditions around the United States, provides a wealth of information about the current status of U.S. labor markets. This Internet application helps you assess developments in employment and wages in the United States.

Title: The Beige Book—Summary

Navigation: Go to www.econtoday.com/ch29 to access the home page of the Federal Reserve's Board of Governors. Click on *Monetary Policy,* and then click on *Beige Book*. Then select the report for the most recent period.

Application Read the section entitled "Labor Markets" and answer the following questions.

1. Has overall employment been rising or falling during the most recent year? Based on what you learned in this chapter, what factors might account for this pattern? Does the Beige Book summary bear our any of these explanations for changes in U.S. employment?

2. Have U.S. workers' wages been rising or falling during the most recent year?

For Group Study and Analysis The left-hand margin of the Beige Book site lists the reports of the 12 Federal Reserve districts. Divide the class into two groups, and have each group develop brief summaries of the main conclusions of one district's report concerning employment and wages within that district. Reconvene and compare the reports. Are there pronounced regional differences?

ANSWERS TO QUICK QUIZZES

p. 737: (i) output . . . input . . . inputs . . . marginal revenue; (ii) demand for; (iii) derived . . . derived . . . shift
p. 739: (i) wage . . . price . . . downward; (ii) elasticity . . . inputs . . . costs . . . adjustment
p. 743: (i) elastic . . . upward; (ii) equilibrium; (iii) demand . . . productivity . . . substitute . . . complementary
p. 748: (i) substitutable . . . substitution; (ii) reduces . . . increases; (iii) increases
p. 752: (i) less; (ii) monopolist's; (iii) price; (iv) physical . . . physical

Unions and Labor Market Monopoly Power

30

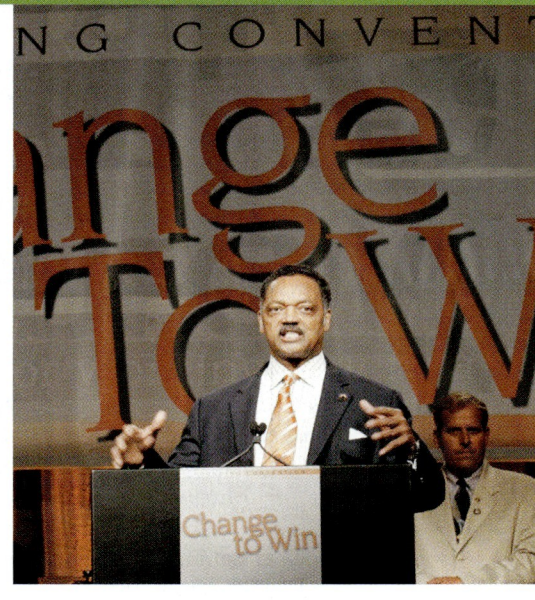

For five decades, about 85 percent of workers who were members of U.S. labor unions were united under a single banner: the flag of the American Federation of Labor–Congress of Industrial Organizations, or AFL-CIO. In 2005, however, this grand union of labor unions began to unravel. Seven of the largest U.S. labor unions disassociated from the AFL-CIO and formed their own, independently operated umbrella labor organization. What are labor unions? What are the objectives of unions, and what strategies do they utilize to pursue their goals? Why have the aims of some unions recently clashed with those of others? In this chapter, you will learn what you must know to be able to answer these questions.

Learning Objectives

After reading this chapter, you should be able to:

1. Outline the essential history of the labor union movement
2. Discuss the current status of labor unions
3. Describe the basic economic goals and strategies of labor unions
4. Evaluate the potential effects of labor unions on wages and productivity
5. Explain how a monopsonist determines how much labor to employ and what wage rate to pay
6. Compare wage and employment decisions by a monopsonistic firm with the choices made by firms in industries with alternative market structures

MyEconLab helps you master each objective and study more efficiently. See end of chapter for details.

Labor unions
Worker organizations that seek to secure economic improvements for their members; they also seek to improve the safety, health, and other benefits (such as job security) of their members.

> ### Did You Know That . . .
>
> half of the members of U.S. **labor unions**—organizations that seek to secure economic improvements for their members—reside in only six states (California, Illinois, Michigan, New York, Ohio, and Pennsylvania)? These states are homes to a large majority of the private-sector workers who belong to unions. Even within these states, however, the only area experiencing *growth* in union membership during the past four decades is the public sector. In the early 1960s, only about 10 percent of all government employees in the United States belonged to unions. Now nearly 40 percent of government workers are union members, and 46 percent of *all* U.S. union members work in the public sector.
>
> Clearly, the labor landscape is shifting in the United States. Traditionally, one rationale for forming a union was that members might be able to earn more than they would in a competitive labor market by obtaining a type of monopoly power. Because the entire supply of a particular group of workers is controlled by a single source when a union bargains as a single entity with management, a certain monopoly element enters into the determination of employment. We can no longer talk about a perfectly competitive labor supply situation. Later in the chapter, we will examine the converse—a single employer who is the sole employer of a particular group of workers.

INDUSTRIALIZATION AND LABOR UNIONS

In most parts of the world, labor movements began with local **craft unions.** These were groups of workers in individual trades, such as shoemaking, printing, or baking. Beginning around the middle of the eighteenth century, new technologies permitted reductions in unit production costs through the formation of larger-scale enterprises that hired dozens or more workers. By the late 1790s, workers in some British craft unions began trying to convince employers to engage in **collective bargaining,** in which business management negotiates with representatives of all union members about wages and hours of work.

In 1799 and 1800, the British Parliament passed laws called the Combination Acts aimed at prohibiting the formation of unions. In 1825, Parliament enacted a replacement Combination Act allowing unions to exist and to engage in limited collective bargaining. Unions on the European continent managed to convince most governments throughout Europe to enact similar laws during the first half of the nineteenth century.

Craft unions
Labor unions composed of workers who engage in a particular trade or skill, such as baking, carpentry, or plumbing.

Collective bargaining
Negotiation between the management of a company or of a group of companies and the management of a union or a group of unions for the purpose of reaching a mutually agreeable contract that sets wages, fringe benefits, and working conditions for all employees in all the unions involved.

Unions in the United States

The development of unions in the United States lagged several decades behind events in Europe. In the years between the Civil War and the Great Depression (1861–1930s), the Knights of Labor, an organized group of both skilled and unskilled workers, pushed for an eight-hour workday and equal pay for women and men. In 1886, a dissident group from the Knights of Labor formed the American Federation of Labor (AFL) under the leadership of Samuel Gompers. During World War I, union membership increased to more than 5 million. But after the war, the government decided to stop protecting labor's right to organize. Membership began to fall.

The Formation of Industrial Unions. The Great Depression was a landmark event in U.S. labor history. Franklin Roosevelt's National Industrial Recovery Act of 1933 gave labor the federal right to bargain collectively, but that act was declared unconstitutional. The 1935 National Labor Relations Act (NLRA), otherwise known as the Wagner Act, took its place. The NLRA guaranteed workers the right to form unions, to engage in collective bargaining, and to be members in any union.

In 1938, the Congress of Industrial Organizations (CIO) was formed by John L. Lewis, the president of the United Mine Workers. Prior to the formation of the CIO, most labor organizations were craft unions. The CIO was composed of **industrial unions,** which drew their membership from an entire industry such as steel or automobiles. In 1955, the CIO and the AFL merged because the leaders of both associations thought a merger would help organized labor grow faster.

Industrial unions
Labor unions that consist of workers from a particular industry, such as automobile manufacturing or steel manufacturing.

Congressional Control over Labor Unions. Since the Great Depression, Congress has occasionally altered the relationship between labor and management through significant legislation. One of the most important pieces of legislation was the Taft-Hartley Act of 1947 (the Labor Management Relations Act). In general, the Taft-Hartley Act outlawed certain labor practices of unions, such as imposing make-work rules and forcing unwilling workers to join a particular union. Among other things, it allowed individual states to pass their own **right-to-work laws.** A right-to-work law makes it illegal for union membership to be a requirement for continued employment in any establishment.

More specifically, the Taft-Hartley Act made a **closed shop** illegal; a closed shop requires union membership before employment can be obtained. A **union shop,** however, is legal; a union shop does not require membership as a prerequisite for employment, but it can, and usually does, require that workers join the union after a specified amount of time on the job. (Even a union shop is illegal in states with right-to-work laws.)

Jurisdictional disputes, sympathy strikes, and secondary boycotts were also made illegal by the Taft-Hartley Act. A **jurisdictional dispute** involves two or more unions fighting (and striking) over which should have control in a particular jurisdiction. For example, should carpenters working for a steel manufacturer be members of the steelworkers' union or the carpenters' union? A **sympathy strike** occurs when one union strikes in sympathy with another union's cause or strike. For example, if the retail clerks' union in an area is striking grocery stores, Teamsters union members may refuse to deliver products to those stores in sympathy with the retail clerks' demands for higher wages or better working conditions. A **secondary boycott** is the boycotting of a company that deals with a struck company. For example, if union workers strike a baking company, the boycotting of grocery stores that continue to sell that company's products is a secondary boycott. A secondary boycott brings pressure on third parties to force them to stop dealing with an employer who is being struck.

Perhaps the most famous aspect of the Taft-Hartley Act is its provision allowing the president to obtain a court injunction that will stop a strike for an 80-day cooling-off period if the strike is expected to imperil the nation's safety or health.

Right-to-work laws
Laws that make it illegal to require union membership as a condition of continuing employment in a particular firm.

Closed shop
A business enterprise in which employees must belong to the union before they can be hired and must remain in the union after they are hired.

Union shop
A business enterprise that may hire nonunion members, conditional on their joining the union by some specified date after employment begins.

Jurisdictional dispute
A disagreement involving two or more unions over which should have control of a particular jurisdiction, such as a particular craft or skill or a particular firm or industry.

Sympathy strike
A work stoppage by a union in sympathy with another union's strike or cause.

Secondary boycott
A refusal to deal with companies or purchase products sold by companies that are dealing with a company being struck.

Go to www.econtoday.com/ch30 to link to the Legal Information Institute's review of all the key U.S. labor laws.

The Current Status of Labor Unions

Every country has its own rules governing unions and the circumstances under which they can engage in work actions such as strikes. Furthermore, union-organizing efforts have been more successful in some nations than in others. These international differences complicate efforts to compare the status of unions in various nations. Nevertheless, it is possible to assess how widespread union membership is in different countries and to evaluate overall trends in the extent of unionization.

Worldwide Trends in Unionization. Figure 30-1 on the following page shows union membership as a share of total employment for a diverse set of nations. As the figure indicates, rates of unionization vary considerably from country to country. More than 70 percent of workers belong to unions in Finland and Sweden, while fewer than 10 percent of workers in India and South Korea are union members.

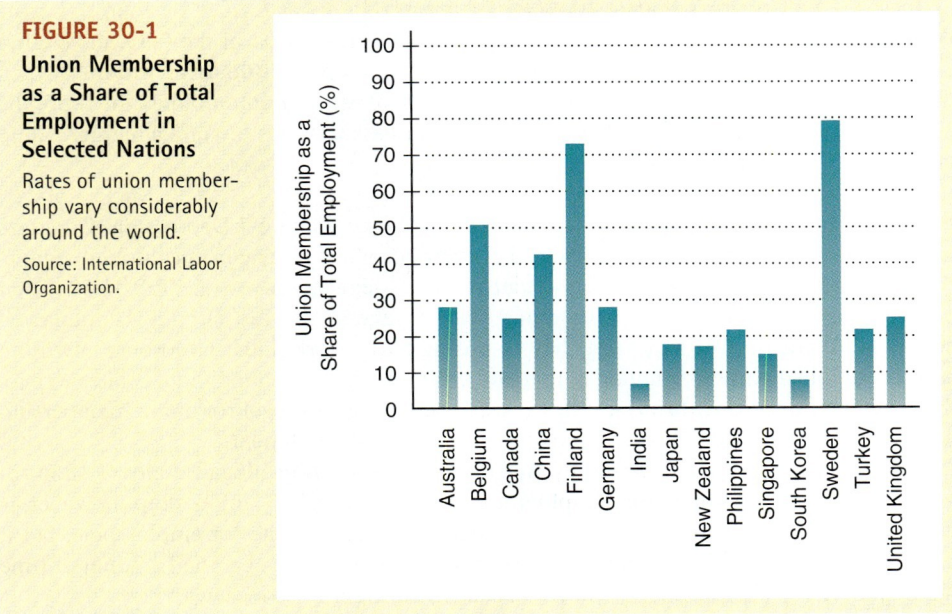

FIGURE 30-1
Union Membership as a Share of Total Employment in Selected Nations
Rates of union membership vary considerably around the world.
Source: International Labor Organization.

In nearly all these countries, the percentages of workers who are union members have been declining steadily during the past several years. Since the 1970s, union membership rates have dropped in every country depicted in Figure 30-1 with the exception of Finland, where the rate of unionization has risen slightly. In all other countries, union membership rates have dropped by at least 5 percentage points since the 1970s. In Australia, union membership as a share of total employment has fallen by more than 25 percentage points.

U.S. Unionization Trends. Figure 30-2 shows that union membership has also been declining in the United States since the 1970s. At present, only slightly more than 12 percent of U.S. workers are union members. If we remove labor unions in the public sector—federal, state, and local government workers—only about 9 percent of workers in the private sector belong to unions.

A large part of the explanation for the decline in union membership has to do with the shift away from manufacturing. In 1948, workers in goods-producing industries, transportation, and utilities, which traditionally have been among the most heavily unionized industries, constituted more than half of private nonagricultural employment. Today, that fraction is about one-fifth. Manufacturing jobs account for less than 15 percent of all employment in the United States.

The relative decline in manufacturing employment helps explain why most of the largest U.S. unions now draw their members primarily from workers in service industries and governments. As you can see in Table 30-1, five of the ten largest unions now represent workers in these areas. The remaining five largest unions represent the goods-producing industries, transportation, and utilities that once dominated the U.S. union movement.

Although the trend away from manufacturing is the main reason for the decline in unionism, the deregulation of certain industries, such as airlines and trucking, has also contributed, as has increased global competition. In addition, immigration has weakened the power of unions. Much of the unskilled and typically nonunionized work in the United States is done by foreign-born workers, and immigrant workers who are undocumented cannot legally join a union.

FIGURE 30-2
Decline in Union Membership

Numerically, union membership in the United States has increased dramatically since the 1930s, but as a percentage of the labor force, union membership peaked around 1960 and has been falling ever since. Most recently, the absolute number of union members has also diminished.

Sources: L. Davis et al., *American Economic Growth* (New York: HarperCollins, 1972), p. 220; U.S. Department of Labor, Bureau of Labor Statistics.

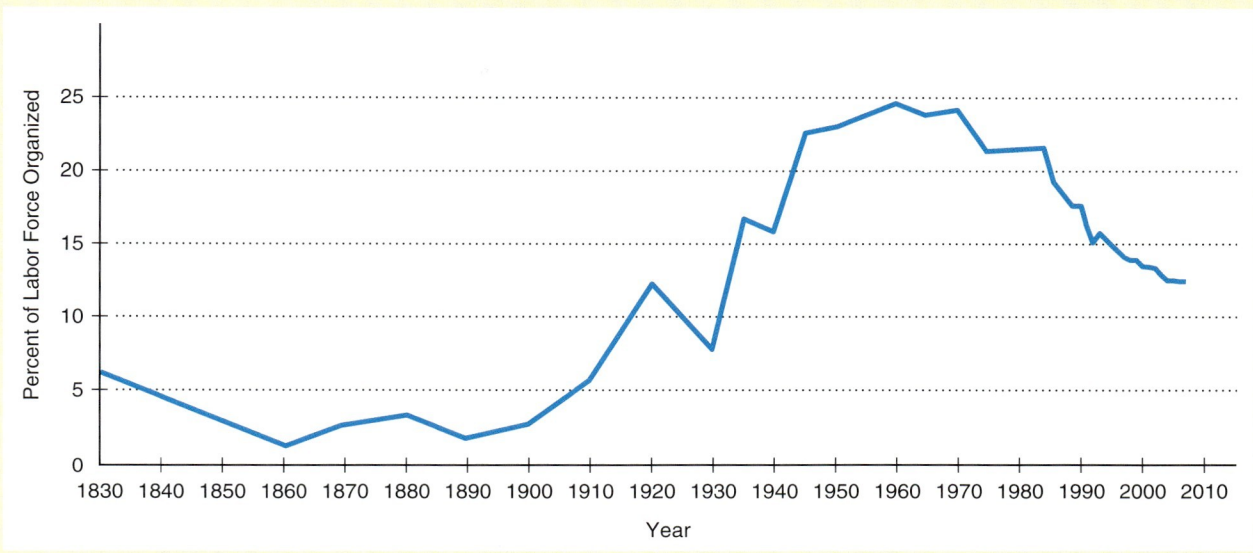

TABLE 30-1
The Ten Largest Unions in the United States

Half of the top ten U.S. unions have members who work in service and government occupations.

Union	Industry	Members
National Education Association	Education	2,752,000
International Brotherhood of Teamsters	Trucking, delivery	1,397,000
United Food and Commercial Workers International Union	Food and grocery services	1,391,000
Service Employees International Union	Health care, public, and janitorial services	1,380,000
American Federation of State, County, and Municipal Employees	Government services	1,310,000
Laborers' International Union of North America	Construction, utilities	794,000
American Federation of Teachers	Education	742,000
International Association of Machinists and Aerospace Workers	Machine and aerospace	720,000
International Brotherhood of Electrical Workers	Electrical	719,000
International Union, United Automobile, Aerospace, and Agricultural Implement Workers of America	Auto, aerospace, and agricultural implements	700,000

Source: U.S. Department of Labor.

QUICK QUIZ

The _____ _____ of _____, composed of **craft unions**, was formed in 1886 under the leadership of Samuel Gompers. Membership increased until after World War I, when the government temporarily stopped protecting labor's right to organize.

During the Great Depression, legislation was passed that allowed for **collective bargaining**. The _____ _____ _____ Act of 1935 guaranteed workers the right to form unions. The Congress of Industrial Organizations (CIO), composed of _____ unions, was formed during the Great Depression. The AFL and the CIO merged in 1955.

Rates of union membership vary considerably across countries. In the United States, union membership as a percentage of the labor force peaked at nearly _____ percent in 1960 and has declined since then to only slightly more than _____ percent.

See page 782 for the answers. Review concepts from this section in MyEconLab.

UNION GOALS AND STRATEGIES

Through collective bargaining, unions establish the wages below which no individual worker can legally offer his or her services. Each year, union representatives and management negotiate collective bargaining contracts covering wages as well as working conditions and fringe benefits for about 6 million workers. If approved by the members, a union labor contract sets wage rates, maximum workdays, working conditions, fringe benefits, and other matters, usually for the next two or three years.

Strike: The Ultimate Bargaining Tool

Whenever union-management negotiations break down, union negotiators may turn to their ultimate bargaining tool, the threat or the reality of a strike. Strikes make headlines, but a strike occurs in less than 2 percent of all labor-management disputes before the contract is signed. In the other 98 percent, contracts are signed without much public fanfare.

The purpose of a strike is to impose costs on recalcitrant management to force it to accept the union's proposed contract terms. Strikes disrupt production and interfere with a company's or an industry's ability to sell goods and services. The strike works both ways, though, because workers receive no wages while on strike (though they may be partly compensated out of union strike funds). Striking union workers may also be eligible to draw state unemployment benefits.

The impact of a strike is closely related to the ability of striking unions to prevent nonstriking (and perhaps nonunion) employees from continuing to work for the targeted company or industry. Therefore, steps are usually taken to prevent others from working for the employer. **Strikebreakers** can effectively destroy whatever bargaining power rests behind a strike. Numerous methods have been used to prevent strikebreakers from breaking strikes. Violence has been known to erupt, almost always in connection with union attempts to prevent strikebreaking.

In recent years, companies have had less incentive to hire strikebreakers, because work stoppages have become much less common. From 1945 until 1990, on average more than 200 union strikes took place in the United States each year. Since 1990, however, the average has been closer to 25 strikes per year.

Strikebreakers
Temporary or permanent workers hired by a company to replace union members who are striking.

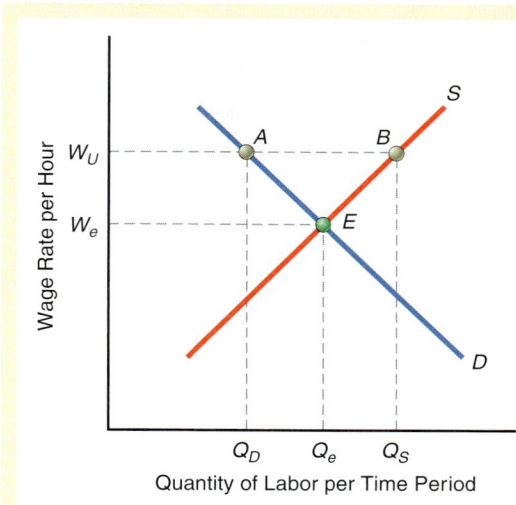

FIGURE 30-3

Unions Must Ration Jobs

If the union succeeds in obtaining wage rate W_U, the quantity of labor demanded will be Q_D, but the quantity of labor supplied will be Q_S. The union must ration a limited number of jobs to a greater number of workers; the surplus of labor is equivalent to a shortage of jobs at that wage rate.

Union Goals with Direct Wage Setting

We have already pointed out that one of the goals of unions is to set minimum wages. The effects of setting a wage rate higher than a competitive market clearing wage rate can be seen in Figure 30-3. We have a perfectly competitive market for labor. The market demand curve is D, and the market supply curve is S. The market clearing wage rate is W_e. The equilibrium quantity of labor is Q_e. If the union establishes by collective bargaining a minimum wage rate that exceeds W_e, an excess quantity of labor will be supplied (assuming no change in the labor demand schedule). If the minimum wage established by union collective bargaining is W_U, the quantity supplied will be Q_S. The quantity demanded will be Q_D. The difference is the excess quantity supplied, or surplus. Hence the following point becomes clear:

> *One of the major roles of a union that establishes a wage rate above the market clearing wage rate is to ration available jobs among the excess number of workers who wish to work in unionized industries.*

Note also that the surplus of labor is equivalent to a shortage of jobs at wage rates above equilibrium.

To ration jobs, the union may use a seniority system, lengthen the apprenticeship period to discourage potential members from joining, or institute other rationing methods. This has the effect of shifting the supply of labor curve to the left in order to support the higher wage, W_U.

There is a trade-off here that any union's leadership must face: Higher wages inevitably mean a reduction in total employment—a smaller number of positions. When facing higher wages, management may replace part of the workforce with machinery. In addition, at higher wages, more workers will seek to enter the industry.

Did you know that most employees of the Federal Deposit Insurance Corporation (FDIC), which insures deposits at commercial banks and savings institutions and regulates many state-chartered banks, are unionized? See the next page.

POLICY EXAMPLE

Higher FDIC Wages for Some Means Fewer FDIC Jobs for Others

Employees of the FDIC are represented by the National Treasury Employees Union (NTEU), which also has members in the U.S. Treasury Department and various other government agencies. Over the years, the NTEU has won significant wage increases for its members, including workers at the FDIC. These pay boosts have been good news for many of these employees but have created problems for others. During the 2000s, the agency's earnings, derived primarily from insurance premiums paid by banks and savings institutions, failed to keep pace with NTEU-bargained pay increases. In the mid-2000s, the FDIC's available operating funds actually decreased. To continue operating within its means, the agency began laying off hundreds of workers. Those FDIC employees who held onto their jobs continued to earn the higher wages that the NTEU had won for its employed members, but those who were laid off earned no wages at all from the FDIC.

FOR CRITICAL ANALYSIS

How might a proposed government plan to expand the scope of federal deposit insurance and require banks and savings institutions to pay more deposit insurance premiums affect employment at the FDIC?

If we view unions as monopoly sellers of a service, we can identify three different types of goals that they may pursue: ensuring employment for all members of the union, maximizing aggregate income of workers, and maximizing wage rates for some workers.

Employing All Members in the Union. Assume that the union has Q_1 workers. If it faces a labor demand curve such as D in Figure 30-4, the only way it can "sell" all of those workers' services is to accept a wage rate of W_1. This is similar to any other market. The demand curve tells the maximum price that can be charged to sell any particular quantity of a good or service. Here the service happens to be labor.

Maximizing Member Income. If the union is interested in maximizing the gross income of its members, it will normally want a smaller membership than Q_1—namely, Q_2

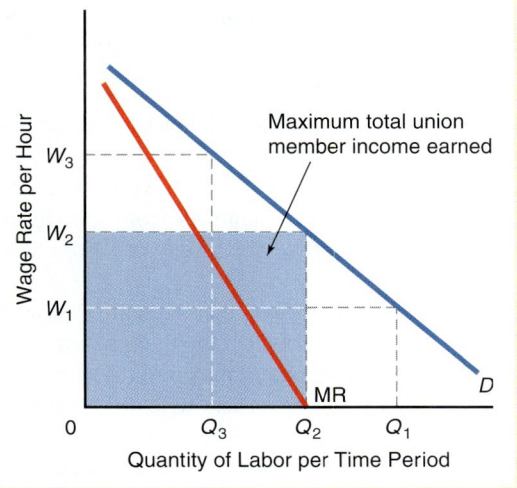

FIGURE 30-4

What Do Unions Maximize?

Assume that the union wants to employ all its Q_1 members. It will attempt to get wage rate W_1. If the union wants to maximize total wage receipts (income) of members who have jobs in this industry, it will do so at wage rate W_2, where the elasticity of the demand for labor is equal to 1. (The shaded area represents the maximum total income that the union would earn at W_2.) If the union wants to maximize the wage rate for a given number of workers, say, Q_3, it will set the wage rate at W_3.

workers, all employed and paid a wage rate of W_2. The aggregate income to all members of the union is represented by the wages of only the ones who work. Total income earned by union members is maximized where the price elasticity of demand is numerically equal to 1. That occurs where marginal revenue equals zero. In Figure 30-4, marginal revenue equals zero at a quantity of labor Q_2. So we know that if the union obtains a wage rate equal to W_2, and therefore Q_2 workers are demanded, the total income to the union membership will be maximized. In other words, $Q_2 \times W_2$ (the shaded area) will be greater than any other combination of wage rates and quantities of union workers demanded. It is, for example, greater than $Q_1 \times W_1$. Note that in this situation, if the union started out with Q_1 members, there would be $Q_1 - Q_2$ members out of *union* work at the wage rate W_2. (Those out of union work either remain unemployed or go to other industries. Such actions have a depressing effect on wages in nonunion industries due to the increase in supply of workers there.)

Maximizing Wage Rates for Certain Workers. Assume that the union wants to maximize the wage rates for some of its workers—perhaps those with the most seniority. If it wants to maximize the wage rate for a given quantity of workers, Q_3, it will seek to obtain a wage rate of W_3. This will require deciding which workers should be unemployed and which workers should work and for how long each week or each year they should be employed.

When faced with a choice between wage cuts for some workers at auto factories or no plants and no jobs, what do you suppose the United Auto Workers (UAW) decided to do?

EXAMPLE

To Save Members' Jobs, the UAW Agrees to a Two-Tier Pay Scale

Many of DaimlerChrysler's Jeep vehicles are assembled in two plants located in Toledo, Ohio. In an effort to reduce the costs associated with paying all workers at those plants the same hourly wages, DaimlerChrysler began shifting some pre-assembly work out of those plants. It would, for instance, buy pre-assembled seat components from other companies instead of having unionized workers do the work in Toledo. DaimlerChrysler even contemplated purchasing all pre-assembled components from other firms and closing one of the Toledo plants.

To preserve union jobs, the United Auto Workers agreed to adopt a two-tier wage system at the Toledo Jeep plants. DaimlerChrysler now pays workers who specialize in final vehicle assembly tasks, such as placing motors into vehicle frames, more than $26 per hour (plus benefits). In contrast, DaimlerChrysler employees working in the same factories who are assigned to pre-assembly operations receive only $15 per hour (plus benefits).

FOR CRITICAL ANALYSIS
In the situation described above, why might a two-tier union pay system have attained higher overall income for UAW members than setting a wage aimed at maximizing income for people employed in the Toledo Jeep plants? (Hint: How much income would have been earned by workers who would have lost their jobs if DaimlerChrysler had closed one of its Jeep plants?)

Union Strategies to Raise Wages Indirectly

One way or another, unions seek above-market wages for some or all of their members. Sometimes unions try to achieve this goal without making wage increases direct features of contract negotiations.

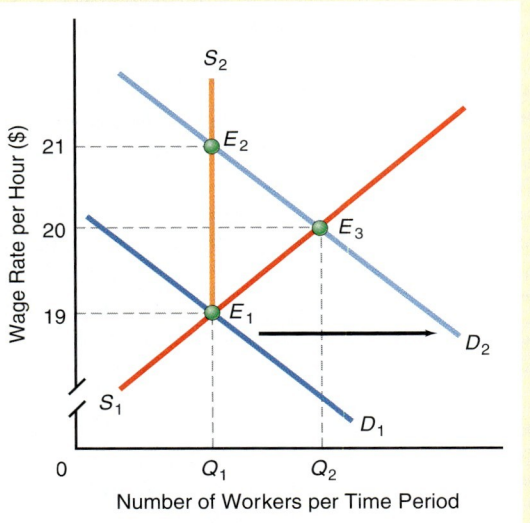

FIGURE 30-5

Restricting Supply over Time

When the union was formed, it didn't affect wage rates or employment, which remained at $19 and Q_1 (the equilibrium wage rate and quantity at point E_1). However, as demand increased—that is, as the demand schedule shifted outward from D_1 to D_2—the union restricted membership to its original level of Q_1. The new supply curve is $S_1 S_2$, which intersects D_2 at E_2, or at a wage rate of $21. Without the union, equilibrium would be at E_3, with a wage rate of $20 and employment of Q_2.

Limiting Entry over Time. One way to raise wage rates without specifically setting wages is for unions to limit the size of their membership to the size of their employed workforce at the time the union was first organized. No workers are put out of work when the union is formed. Over time, as the demand for labor in the industry increases, the union prevents any net increase in membership, so larger wage increases are obtained than would otherwise be the case. We see this in Figure 30-5. In this example, union members freeze entry into their union, thereby obtaining a wage rate of $21 per hour instead of allowing a wage rate of $20 per hour with no restriction on labor supply.

Altering the Demand for Union Labor. Another way that unions can increase wages is to shift the demand curve for labor outward to the right. This approach has the advantage of increasing both wage rates and the employment level. The demand for union labor can be increased by increasing worker productivity, increasing the demand for union-made goods, and decreasing the demand for non-union-made goods.

> **ECONOMICS FRONT AND CENTER**
>
> To learn about how a growing number of psychologists in the state of New York are hoping that a union affiliation will help boost the demand for their labor, read **A Psychologist Contemplates Union "Affiliation,"** on page 776.

1. *Increasing worker productivity.* Supporters of unions have argued that unions provide a good system of industrial jurisprudence. The presence of unions may induce workers to feel that they are working in fair and just circumstances. If so, they work harder, increasing labor productivity. Productivity is also increased when unions resolve differences and reduce conflicts between workers and management, thereby providing a more peaceful administrative environment.
2. *Increasing demand for union-made goods.* Because the demand for labor is a derived demand, a rise in the demand for products produced by union labor will increase the demand for union labor itself. One way that unions attempt to increase the demand for goods produced by union labor is by advertising "Look for the union label."
3. *Decreasing the demand for non-union-made goods.* When the demand for goods that are competing with (or are substitutes for) union-made goods is reduced, consumers shift to union-made goods, increasing the demand. The campaigns of various unions against imports are a good example. The United Auto Workers support restrictions on imported cars as strongly as the Textile Workers Unions support restrictions on imported textile

goods. The result is greater demand for goods "made in the USA," which in turn presumably increases the demand for U.S. union (and nonunion) labor.

ECONOMIC EFFECTS OF LABOR UNIONS

Figure 30-6 displays the percentages of workers who are union members in the most heavily unionized occupations. Do union members in these and other occupations earn higher wages? Are they more or less productive than nonunionized workers in their industries? What are the broader economic effects of unionization? Let's consider each of these questions in turn.

Unions and Wages

You have learned that unions are able to raise the wages of their members if they can successfully limit the supply of labor in a particular industry. Unions are also able to raise wages if they can induce increases in the demand for union labor.

Economists have extensively studied the differences between union wages and nonunion wages. They have found that the average *hourly* wage earned by a typical union worker is about $2.25 higher than the hourly wage earned by a typical worker who is not a union member. Adjusted for inflation, this union-nonunion hourly wage differential is only about half as large as it was two decades ago, however.

Comparisons of the *annual* earnings of union and nonunion workers indicate that in recent years, unions have not succeeded in raising the annual incomes of their members. In 1985, workers who belonged to unions earned nearly 7 percent more per year than nonunion workers, even though union workers worked fewer hours per week. Today, a

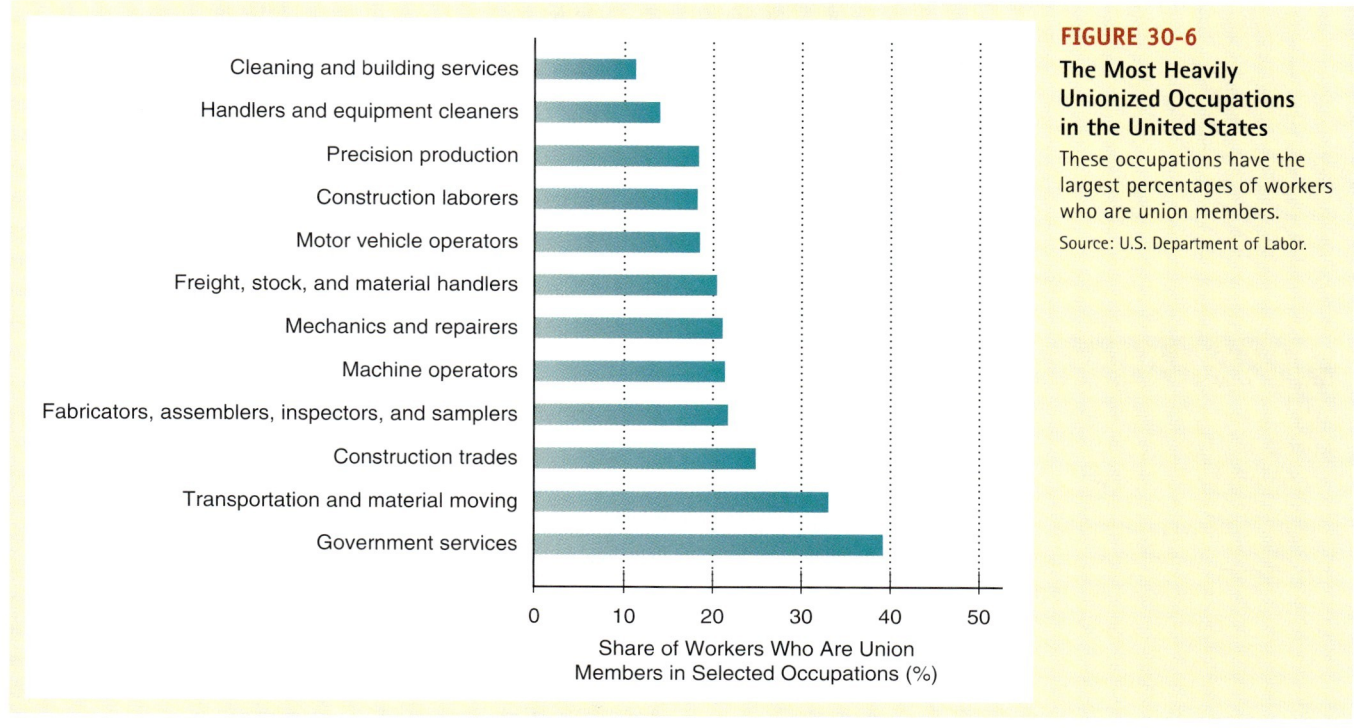

FIGURE 30-6

The Most Heavily Unionized Occupations in the United States

These occupations have the largest percentages of workers who are union members.

Source: U.S. Department of Labor.

typical nonunion employee still works slightly longer each week, but the average nonunion worker also has a higher annual income than the average union worker.

Even the $2.25 hourly wage differential already mentioned is somewhat misleading because it is an average across *all* U.S. workers. In the private sector, union workers earn only about 4 percent more than nonunion workers, or a little less than 60 cents per hour. The hourly wage gain for government workers is nearly six times higher at about $3.55 per hour. A state government employee who belongs to a union currently earns an hourly wage more than 20 percent higher than a state government worker who is not a union member.

Unions and Labor Productivity

A traditional view of union behavior is that unions decrease productivity by artificially shifting the demand curve for union labor outward through excessive staffing and make-work requirements. For example, some economists have traditionally argued that unions tend to bargain for excessive use of workers, as when an airline union requires an engineer on all flights. This is called **featherbedding.** Many painters' unions, for example, resisted the use of paint sprayers and required that their members use only brushes. They even specified the maximum width of the brush. Moreover, whenever a union strikes, productivity drops, and this reduction in productivity in one sector of the economy can spill over into other sectors.

Featherbedding
Any practice that forces employers to use more labor than they would otherwise or to use existing labor in an inefficient manner.

Economic Benefits and Costs of Labor Unions

As should be clear by now, there are two opposing views of unions. One sees them as monopolies whose main effect is to raise the wage rate of high-seniority members at the expense of low-seniority members (and nonunion workers). The other contends that unions can increase labor productivity by promoting safer working conditions and generally better work environments and that they contribute to workforce stability by providing arbitration and grievance procedures.

Critics point out that the positive view of unionism overlooks the fact that many of the benefits that unions provide do not require that unions engage in restrictive labor practices, such as the closed shop. Unions could still do positive things for workers without restricting the labor market.

Consequently, a key issue that economists seek to assess when judging the social costs of unions is the extent to which their existence has a negative effect on employment growth. Most evidence indicates that while unions do significantly reduce employment in some of the most heavily unionized occupations, the overall effects on U.S. employment are modest. On the whole, therefore, the social costs of unions in the United States are probably relatively low.

QUICK QUIZ

When unions set wage rates _____ market clearing prices, they face the problem of _____ a restricted number of jobs to workers who desire to earn the higher wages.

Unions may pursue any one of three goals: (1) to employ _____ union members, (2) to maximize total _____ of the union's members, or (3) to _____ wages for certain, usually high-seniority, workers.

Unions can increase the wage rate of members by engaging in practices that shift the union labor supply curve _____ or shift the demand curve for union labor _____ (or both).

Some economists believe that unions can increase _____ by promoting safer working conditions and generally better work environments.

See page 782 for the answers. Review concepts from this section in MyEconLab.

MONOPSONY: A BUYER'S MONOPOLY

Let's assume that a firm is a perfect competitor in the product market. The firm cannot alter the price of the product it sells, and it faces a perfectly elastic demand curve for its product. We also assume that the firm is the only buyer of a particular input. Although this situation may not occur often, it is useful to consider. Let's think in terms of a factory town, like those dominated by textile mills or those in the mining industry. One company not only hires the workers but also owns the businesses in the community, owns the apartments that workers live in, and hires the clerks, waiters, and all other personnel. This buyer of labor is called a **monopsonist,** the only buyer in the market.

Monopsonist
The only buyer in a market.

What does this situation mean to a monopsonist in terms of the costs of hiring extra workers? It means that if the monopsonist wants to hire more workers, it has to offer higher wages. Our monopsonist firm cannot hire all the labor it wants at the going wage rate. Instead, it faces an upward-sloping supply curve. If it wants to hire more workers, it has to raise wage rates, including the wages of all its current workers (assuming a non-wage-discriminating monopsonist). It therefore has to take account of these increased costs when deciding how many more workers to hire.

How has the Canadian government created a monopsony in the market for wheat to be exported abroad?

INTERNATIONAL POLICY EXAMPLE

The Canadian Wheat Export Monopsony

In Canada, wheat farmers can grow as much wheat as they wish. The only catch is that wheat farmers can sell their wheat to only one organization, called the Canadian Wheat Board (CWB). In theory, the idea behind making the CWB the only legally sanctioned buyer and seller of Canadian wheat is to give the CWB monopoly power in the world wheat market. In actuality, the CWB provides less than 20 percent of world wheat exports, so it has no monopoly power. As the only authorized purchaser of wheat, however, the CWB does function as a government-created monopsony. The CWB faces the entire supply curve for Canadian wheat crops. Hence, when it alters the price it pays for wheat, the price received by all Canadian wheat farmers changes. Many wheat farmers are pressing for the CWB to be dismantled. They believe that they could earn higher revenues if they were able to sell wheat on their own.

FOR CRITICAL ANALYSIS
If the CWB wishes to obtain more wheat to export abroad, why must it pay a higher price for wheat?

Marginal Factor Cost

The monopsonist faces an upward-sloping supply curve of the input in question because as the only buyer, it faces the entire market supply curve. Each time the monopsonist buyer of labor, for example, wishes to hire more workers, it must raise wage rates. Thus, the marginal cost of another unit of labor is rising. In fact, the marginal cost of increasing its workforce will always be greater than the wage rate. This is because the monopsonist must pay the same wage rate to everyone in order to obtain another unit of labor; thus, the higher wage rate has to be offered not only to the last worker but also to *all* its other workers. We call the additional cost to the monopsonist of hiring one more worker the marginal factor cost (MFC).

The marginal factor cost of hiring the last worker is therefore that worker's wages plus the increase in the wages of all other existing workers. As we pointed out in Chapter 29, marginal factor cost is equal to the change in total variable costs due to a one-unit change in the one variable factor of production—in this case, labor. In Chapter 29, marginal factor cost was simply the competitive wage rate because the employer could hire all workers at the same wage rate.

Derivation of a Marginal Factor Cost Curve

Panel (a) of Figure 30-7 shows the quantity of labor purchased, the wage rate per hour, the total cost of the quantity of labor supplied per hour, and the marginal factor cost per hour for the additional labor bought.

FIGURE 30-7

Derivation of a Marginal Factor Cost Curve

The supply curve, S, in panel (b) is taken from columns 1 and 2 of panel (a). The marginal factor cost curve (MFC) is taken from columns 1 and 4. It is the increase in the total wage bill resulting from a one-unit increase in labor input.

Panel (a)

(1) Quantity of Labor Supplied to Management	(2) Required Hourly Wage Rate	(3) Total Wage Bill (3) = (1) × (2)	(4) Marginal Factor Cost (MFC) = Change in (3) / Change in (1)
0	—	—	
1	$12	$12	$12
2	14	28	16
3	16	48	20
4	18	72	24
5	20	100	28
6	22	132	32

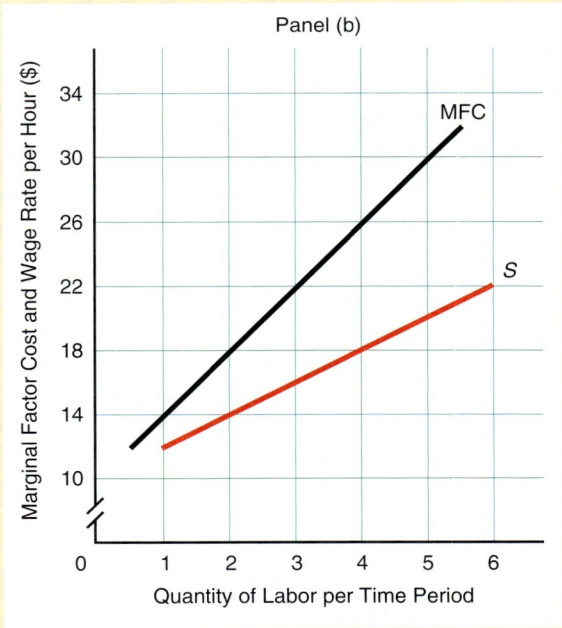

We translate the columns from panel (a) to the graph in panel (b) of the figure. We show the supply curve as S, which is taken from columns 1 and 2. (Note that this is the same as the *average* factor cost curve; hence you can view Figure 30-7 as showing the relationship between average factor cost and marginal factor cost.) The marginal factor cost curve (MFC) is taken from columns 1 and 4. The MFC curve must be above the supply curve whenever the supply curve is upward sloping. If the supply curve is upward sloping, the firm must pay a higher wage rate in order to attract a larger amount of labor. This higher wage rate must be paid to all workers; thus, the increase in total costs due to an increase in the labor input will exceed the wage rate. (Recall from Chapter 29 that in a perfectly competitive input market, the supply curve facing the firm is perfectly elastic and the marginal factor cost curve is identical to the supply curve.)

Employment and Wages Under Monopsony

To determine the number of workers that a monopsonist desires to hire, we compare the marginal benefit to the marginal cost of each hiring decision. The marginal cost is the marginal factor cost (MFC) curve, and the marginal benefit is the marginal revenue product (MRP) curve. In Figure 30-8, we assume competition in the output market and monopsony in the input market. A monopsonist finds its profit-maximizing quantity of labor demanded at A, where the marginal revenue product is just equal to the marginal factor cost. The monopsonist will therefore desire to hire exactly Q_m workers.

The Input Price Paid by a Monopsony.

How much is the firm going to pay these workers? The monopsonist sets the wage rate so that it will get exactly the quantity, Q_m, supplied to it by its "captive" labor force. We find that wage rate is W_m. There is no reason to pay the workers any more than W_m because at that wage rate, the firm can get exactly the quantity it wants. The actual quantity used is determined by the intersection of the marginal factor cost curve and the marginal revenue product curve for labor—that is, at the point at which the marginal revenue from expanding employment just equals the marginal cost of doing so (point A in Figure 30-8).

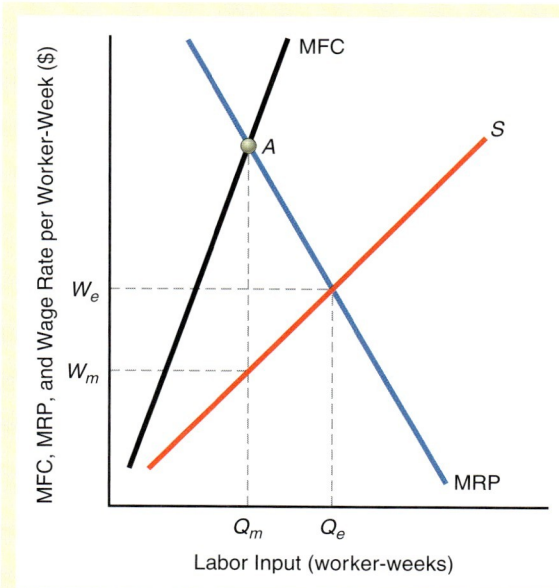

FIGURE 30-8
Wage and Employment Determination for a Monopsonist

The monopsonist firm looks at a marginal cost curve, MFC, that slopes upward and is above its labor supply curve, S. The marginal benefit of hiring additional workers is given by the firm's MRP curve (its demand-for-labor curve). The intersection of MFC with MRP, at point A, determines the number of workers hired. The firm hires Q_m workers but has to pay them only W_m in order to attract them. Compare this with the perfectly competitive solution, in which the wage rate would have to be W_e and the quantity of labor would be Q_e.

Monopsonistic exploitation
Paying a price for the variable input that is less than its marginal revenue product; the difference between marginal revenue product and the wage rate.

Notice that the profit-maximizing wage rate paid to workers (W_m) is lower than the marginal revenue product. That is to say, workers are paid a wage that is less than their contribution to the monopsonist's revenues. This is sometimes referred to as **monopsonistic exploitation** of labor. The monopsonist is able to do this because each individual worker has little power in bargaining for a higher wage.

You learned in Chapter 4 that in a perfectly competitive labor market, establishing a minimum wage rate above the market clearing wage rate causes employers to reduce the quantity of labor demanded, resulting in a decline in employment. What happens if a minimum wage rate is established above the wage rate that a *monopsony* would otherwise pay its workers?

POLICY EXAMPLE

Can Minimum Wage Laws Ever Boost Employment?

How does a monopsony respond to a minimum wage law that sets a wage floor above the wage rate it otherwise would pay its workers? Figure 30-9 provides the answer to this question. In the figure, the entire upward-sloping curve labeled S is the labor supply curve in the absence of a minimum wage. Given the associated MFC curve and the firm's MRP curve, Q_m is the quantity of labor hired by a monopsony in the absence of a minimum wage law. The profit-maximizing wage rate is W_m. If the government establishes a minimum wage equal to W_{min}, however, then the supply of labor to the firm becomes horizontal at the minimum wage and includes only the upward-sloping portion of the curve S above this legal minimum. In addition, the wage rate W_{min} becomes the monopsonist's marginal factor cost along the horizontal portion of this new labor supply curve, because when the firm hires one more unit of labor, it must pay each unit of labor the same wage rate, W_{min}.

To maximize its economic profits under the minimum wage, the monopsony equalizes the minimum wage rate with marginal revenue product and hires Q_{min} units of labor. This quantity exceeds the amount of labor, Q_m, that the monopsony would have hired in the absence of the minimum wage law. Thus, establishing a minimum wage can generate a rise in employment at a monopsony firm.

FOR CRITICAL ANALYSIS
If a government establishes a minimum wage law covering all firms within its jurisdiction, including firms operating in both perfectly competitive and monopsonistic labor markets, will overall employment necessarily increase?

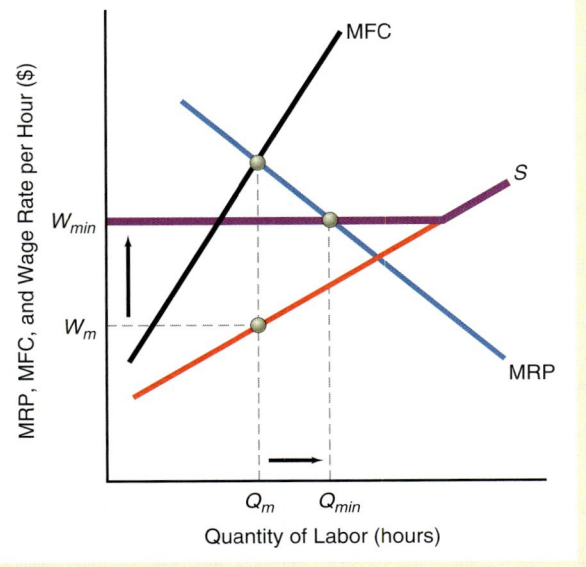

FIGURE 30-9
A Monopsony's Response to a Minimum Wage
In the absence of a minimum wage law, a monopsony faces the upward-sloping labor supply curve, S, and the marginal factor cost curve, MFC. To maximize its profits, the monopsony hires Q_m units of labor, at which MFC is equal to MRP, and it pays the wage rate W_m. Once the minimum wage rate, W_{min}, is established, the supply of labor becomes horizontal at the minimum wage and includes only the upward-sloping portion of the labor supply curve above this legal minimum. Because the monopsony must pay the same wage rate W_{min} for each unit of labor along this horizontal portion of the new labor supply curve, its marginal factor cost is also equal to the minimum wage rate, W_{min}. Thus, the monopsony hires Q_{min} units of labor. Employment at the monopsony firm increases.

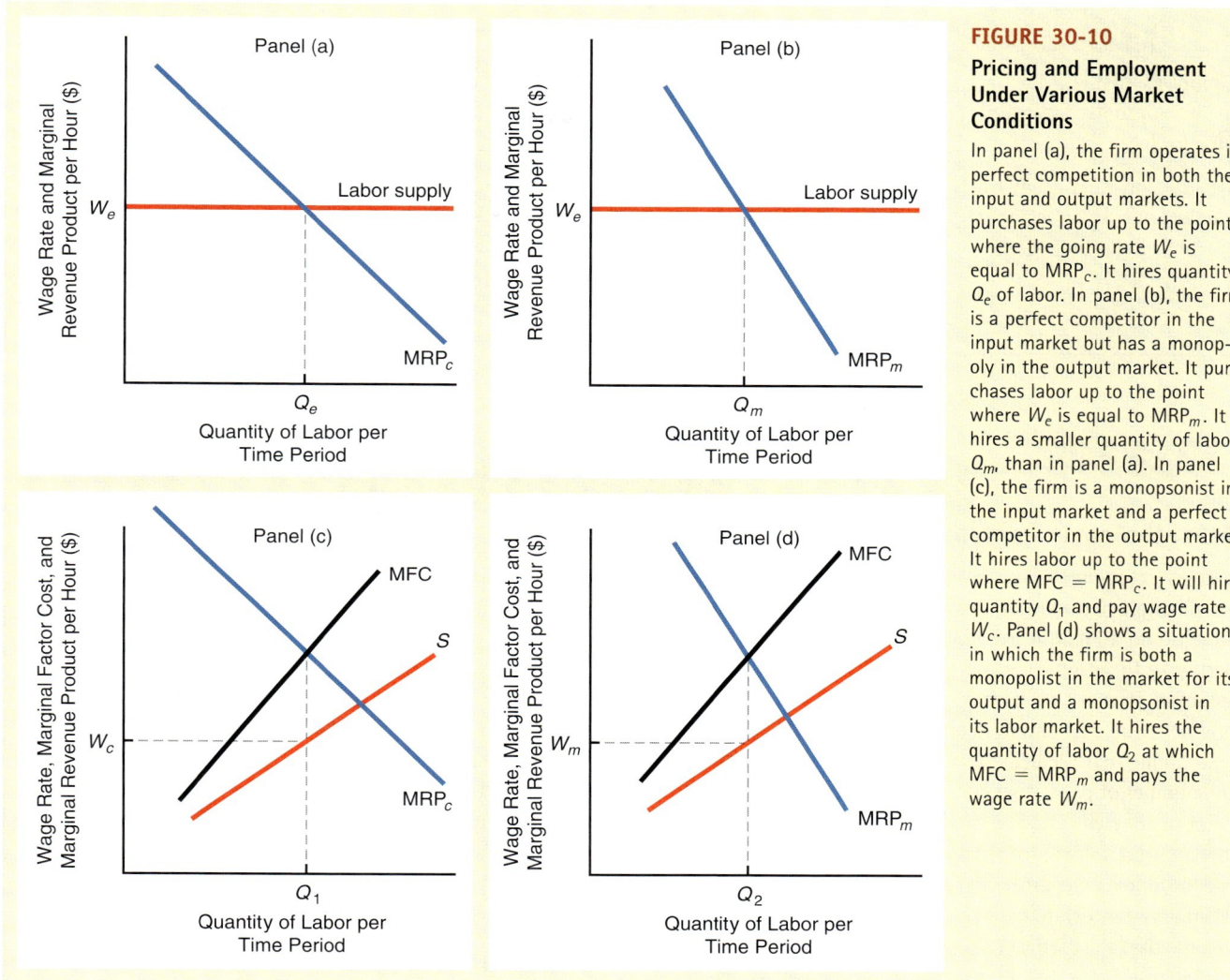

FIGURE 30-10

Pricing and Employment Under Various Market Conditions

In panel (a), the firm operates in perfect competition in both the input and output markets. It purchases labor up to the point where the going rate W_e is equal to MRP_c. It hires quantity Q_e of labor. In panel (b), the firm is a perfect competitor in the input market but has a monopoly in the output market. It purchases labor up to the point where W_e is equal to MRP_m. It hires a smaller quantity of labor, Q_m, than in panel (a). In panel (c), the firm is a monopsonist in the input market and a perfect competitor in the output market. It hires labor up to the point where $MFC = MRP_c$. It will hire quantity Q_1 and pay wage rate W_c. Panel (d) shows a situation in which the firm is both a monopolist in the market for its output and a monopsonist in its labor market. It hires the quantity of labor Q_2 at which $MFC = MRP_m$ and pays the wage rate W_m.

Bilateral Monopoly. The organization of workers into a union normally creates a monopoly supplier of labor, which gives the union some power to bargain for higher wages. What happens when a monopsonist meets a monopolist? This situation is called **bilateral monopoly,** defined as a market structure in which a single buyer faces a single seller. An example of bilateral monopoly is a county education employer facing a single teachers' union in that labor market. Another example is a players' union facing an organized group of team owners, as has occurred in professional baseball and football. To analyze bilateral monopoly, we would have to look at the interaction of both sides, buyer and seller. The price outcome turns out to be indeterminate.

We have studied the pricing of labor in various situations, including perfect competition in both the output and input markets and monopoly in both the output and input markets. Figure 30-10 shows four possible situations graphically.

Bilateral monopoly
A market structure consisting of a monopolist and a monopsonist.

QUICK QUIZ

A monopsonist is the _____ _____ in a market. The monopsonist faces a(n) _____ -sloping supply curve of labor.

Because the monopsonist faces a(n) _____ -sloping supply curve of labor, the marginal factor cost of increasing the labor input by one unit is _____ than the wage rate. Thus, the marginal factor cost curve always lies _____ the supply curve.

A monopsonist will hire workers up to the point at which marginal _____ cost equals marginal _____ product. Then the monopsonist will find the lowest necessary wage to attract that number of workers, as indicated by the supply curve.

See page 782 for the answers. Review concepts from this section in MyEconLab.

CASE STUDY — ECONOMICS FRONT AND CENTER

A Psychologist Contemplates Union "Affiliation"

Jones is contemplating an action that she never imagined would enter her mind back when she was a graduate student working on a Ph.D. in psychology. Her youthful goal, after all, had been to set up a private practice in New York City, not to establish formal ties with a union. She has established her practice, but she now has grown weary of battling against restrictions that Medicaid and private insurers have placed on the number of patient sessions, even as the insurers reduce the amount they will pay for each session. To prevent her annual income from falling, Jones has been doing consulting work for the local police department. As a consequence, she now works 70 hours per week to earn the same inflation-adjusted annual income that she used to earn working 45 to 50 hours per week.

Because Jones, like 80 percent of psychologists, has a private practice, she is legally considered an independent contractor. Under antitrust laws, therefore, she and other psychologists are prohibited from forming a union. Nevertheless, Jones has discovered that more than 3,000 New York psychologists have legally established an "affiliation" with the American Federation of Teachers (AFT), a union of teachers and professors. This union, she has learned, is actively lobbying state and federal governments on behalf of psychologists, seeking to maintain funding for state-funded psychological services and to expand Medicaid coverage of such services.

Jones has attended a meeting at which an AFT organizer promised that the union will pay all new psychologist members' union dues for the first year, provide them with long-term health care insurance, and offer them discounts on life insurance and financial counseling. She is still on the fence, however, about whether to become an affiliated member of the AFT. She is concerned that affiliation will not pay off for her unless the union enrolls many more New York psychologists than the 25 percent who have now chosen AFT affiliation.

CRITICAL ANALYSIS QUESTIONS

1. *What do you suppose that the AFT hopes to gain from offering the first year's union dues free to psychologists who opt to affiliate with the union?*

2. *Do you agree with Jones that affiliation with the AFT is unlikely to have clear-cut benefits for her unless most other New York psychologists also opt for AFT affiliation? Why or why not?*

Issues and Applications

Big Labor Breaks Up

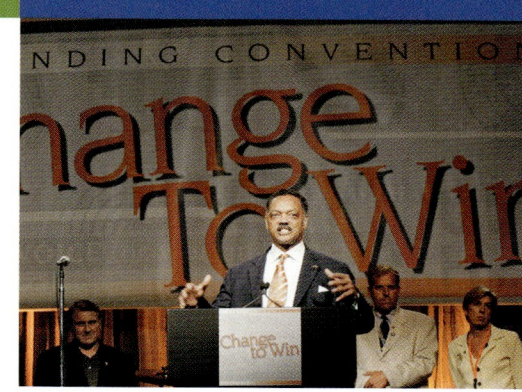

For five decades, the AFL-CIO, with membership that included nearly 85 percent of all unionized workers in the United States, was the overarching umbrella organization of the U.S. union movement. For most people, the AFL-CIO was the public face of collective bargaining in the United States. Since 2005, however, the AFL-CIO has had to face competition from a new union organization.

Concepts Applied
- Collective Bargaining
- Union Goals and Strategies
- Industrial Unions

A Gradual Splintering of Goals and Strategies

Beginning in the early 2000s, seven unions within the AFL-CIO began advocating for changes in its goals and strategies. The unions were the International Brotherhood of Teamsters, the Laborers International Union of North America, the Service Employees International Union, the United Food and Commercial Workers International Union, the United Brotherhood of Carpenters and Joiners of America, the United Farm Workers of America, and Unite Here.

In the view of these unions, the AFL-CIO was stuck in a rut. Some of its largest member unions are industrial unions, such as the United Steelworkers of America, the United Auto Workers, and the United Mine Workers, whose members work in shrinking industries. As revenues in those industries continued to decline in the 2000s, most of these older industrial unions were struggling to maintain existing wages and benefits. Many were simply trying to retain employment and wage agreements for their senior members and put little emphasis on recruiting new junior members. These industrial unions had also begun avoiding boycotts and strikes, which they feared might harm their employers and cost their members jobs. These unions favored allocating the AFL-CIO's resources toward political activities aimed at electing legislators who might pass new laws protecting existing union jobs.

In contrast, the unions advocating change had members in industries that were expanding their presence in the U.S. economy, such as transportation and delivery services, health care, public services, construction, restaurants, and hotels. Because these unions still had the opportunity to grow, they wanted the AFL-CIO to redirect its resources toward efforts aimed at promoting an expansion of U.S. union membership. They were also more interested in advocating boycotts against companies viewed as anti-union, such as Wal-Mart, and strikes against industries trying to slow the growth of union membership, such as the hotel industry.

The Big Breakup

Despite years of discussion and then months of intensive negotiations, the seven rebel unions could not reach an agreement with the other unions in the AFL-CIO about common goals and

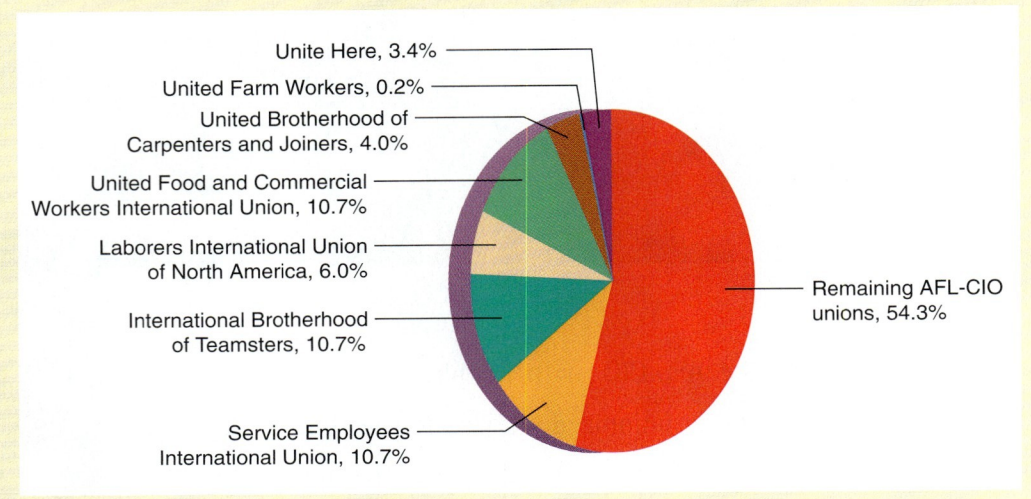

FIGURE 30-11

Membership Shares for Unions in the Change to Win Federation versus Unions Remaining in the AFL-CIO

In 2005, seven unions with more than 45 percent of the total membership of the AFL-CIO split off from that organization.

Source: U.S. Department of Labor.

strategies. Accordingly, they withdrew and established a new labor organization, called the Change to Win Federation.

Figure 30-11 depicts the extent to which this breakup split the U.S. union movement. The unions that remained in the AFL-CIO still have a majority of the old organization's membership—but only barely. Because the Change to Win Federation's members are employed by firms in growing industries, it is probably only a matter of time until this new labor organization becomes larger than the AFL-CIO. Certainly, that is the objective of this new union organization.

Log in to **MyEconLab**, click on "Economic News," and test your understanding of the chapter by answering interactive questions that relate directly to this issue.

For Critical Analysis

1. Which of the three basic union goals—employing all members in the union, maximizing member income, or maximizing wage rates for certain workers—appears to be the main objective of unions remaining in the AFL-CIO?

2. Which of the three basic union goals appears to be the main objective of unions that have organized the new Change to Win Federation?

Web Resources

1. To learn more about the Change to Win Federation, go to www.econtoday.com/ch30.

2. To find out about some of the goals for the future of today's union organizers, go to www.econtoday.com/ch30.

Research Project

Evaluate the stance taken by unions that founded the Change to Win Federation versus that of the unions that remained in the AFL-CIO. Were the two groups' goals truly incompatible? Why or why not?

CHAPTER 30 Unions and Labor Market Monopoly Power

Here is what you should know after reading this chapter. MyEconLab will help you identify what you know, and where to go when you need to practice.

WHAT YOU SHOULD KNOW		WHERE TO GO TO PRACTICE
Labor Unions The first labor unions were craft unions, representing workers in specific trades. In the United States, the American Federation of Labor (AFL) emerged in the late nineteenth century. In 1935, the National Labor Relations Act (or Wagner Act) granted workers the right to form unions and bargain collectively. Industrial unions, which represent workers of specific industries formed the Congress of Industrial Organizations (CIO) in 1938, and in 1955 a merger formed the current AFL-CIO. The Taft-Hartley Act of 1947 placed limitations on unions' rights to organize, strike, and boycott.	labor unions, 760 craft unions, 760 collective bargaining, 760 industrial unions, 761 right-to-work laws, 761 closed shop, 761 union shop, 761 jurisdictional dispute, 761 sympathy strike, 761 secondary boycott, 761	• **MyEconLab** Study Plan 30.1 • Audio introduction to Chapter 30
The Current Status of Labor Unions In some nations, more than half of all workers belong to unions, but in the United States, only about one in eight workers is a union member. A key reason for the decline in U.S. union membership rates is undoubtedly the relative decline in manufacturing jobs as a share of total employment. In addition, in less skilled occupations that would otherwise be attractive to union organizers, many workers are undocumented and foreign-born (i.e., illegal immigrants). Greater domestic and global competition has probably also had a part in bringing about a decline in unions in the United States.		• **MyEconLab** Study Plan 30.1
Basic Goals and Strategies of Labor Unions A key goal of most unions is to achieve higher wages. Often this entails bargaining for wages above competitive levels, which produces surplus labor. Thus, a major task of many unions is to ration available jobs among the excess number of individuals who desire to work at the wages established by collective bargaining agreements. One strategy that unions often use to address this trade-off between wages and the number of jobs is to maximize the total income of members. If the focus of union objectives is the well-being of current members only, the union may bargain for limits on entry of new workers and seek to maximize the wages of current union members only. Another way for unions to try to push up wages is to try to increase worker productivity and lobby consumers to increase their demands for union-produced goods and reduce their demands for goods produced by nonunionized industries.	strikebreakers, 764 **Key figures** Figure 30-3, 765 Figure 30-4, 766 Figure 30-5, 768	• **MyEconLab** Study Plan 30.2 • Video: Union Goals • Animated Figures 30-3, 30-4, and 30-5
Effects of Labor Unions on Wages and Productivity Economists have found that hourly wages of unionized workers are typically higher than those of workers who are not union members. On average, union hourly wages are about $2.25 higher than wages of nonunionized workers. Because unionized employees		

WHAT YOU SHOULD KNOW		WHERE TO GO TO PRACTICE
typically work fewer hours per year, however, their average annual earnings are lower than those of nonunionized employees. It is less clear how unions affect worker productivity. On the one hand, some collective bargaining rules specifying how jobs are performed appear to reduce productivity. On the other hand, unionization promotes generally better work environments, which may enhance productivity.	featherbedding, 770	• **MyEconLab** Study Plan 30.3 • Video: The Benefits of Labor Unions
How a Monopsonist Determines How Much Labor to Employ and What Wage Rate to Pay A monopsony is the only firm that buys a particular input, such as labor, in a specific market. For a monopsonist in a labor market, paying a higher wage to attract an additional unit of labor increases its total factor costs for all other labor employed. For this reason, the marginal factor cost of labor is always higher than the wage rate, so the marginal factor cost schedule lies above the labor supply schedule. The labor market monopsonist employs labor to the point at which the marginal factor cost of labor equals the marginal revenue product of labor. It then pays the workers it hires the wage at which they are willing to work, as determined by the labor supply curve, which lies below the marginal factor cost curve. As a result, the monopsonist pays workers a wage that is less than their marginal revenue product.	monopsonist, 771 monopsonistic exploitation, 774 bilateral monopoly, 775 **Key figures** Figure 30-7, 772 Figure 30-8, 773 Figure 30-9, 774	• **MyEconLab** Study Plan 30.4 • Video: The Buyer's Monopoly—Monopsony • Animated Figures 30-7, 30-8, and 30-9
Comparing a Monopsonist's Wage and Employment Decisions with Choices by Firms in Industries with Other Market Structures Firms that are perfect competitors or monopolies in their product markets but hire workers in perfectly competitive labor markets take the wage rate as market determined, meaning that their individual actions are unable to influence the market wage rate. A product market monopolist tends to employ fewer workers than would be employed if the monopolist's industry were perfectly competitive, but the product market monopolist nonetheless cannot affect the market wage rate. In contrast, a monopsonist is the only employer of labor, so it searches for the wage rate that maximizes its profit. This wage rate is less than the marginal revenue product of labor. In a situation in which a firm is both a product market monopolist and a labor market monopsonist, the firm's demand for labor is also lower than it would be if the firm's product market were competitive, and hence the firm hires fewer workers as well.	**Key figure** Figure 30-10, 775	• **MyEconLab** Study Plan 30.4 • Animated Figure 30-10

Log in to MyEconLab, take a chapter test, and get a personalized Study Plan that tells you which concepts you understand and which ones you need to review. From there, MyEconLab will give you further practice, tutorials, animations, videos, and guided solutions.

Log in to www.myeconlab.com

PROBLEMS

*Select problems, indicated by a blue oval, are assignable in MyEconLab.
Answers to the odd-numbered problems appear at the back of the book.*

30-1. Discuss three aspects of collective bargaining that society might deem desirable.

30-2. Give three reasons why a government might seek to limit the power of a union.

30-3. What effect do strikebreakers have on the collective bargaining power of a union or other collective bargaining arrangement?

30-4. Suppose that the objective of a union is to maximize the total dues paid to the union by its membership. Explain the union strategy, in terms of the wage level and employment level, under the following two scenarios.

  a. Union dues are a percentage of total earnings of the union membership.

  b. Union dues are paid as a flat amount per union member employed.

30-5. Explain why, in economic terms, the total income of union membership is maximized when marginal revenue is zero. (Hint: How much more revenue is forthcoming when marginal revenue is equal to zero?)

30-6. Explain the impact of each of the following events on the market for union labor.

  a. Union-produced TV and radio commercials convince consumers to buy domestically manufactured clothing instead of imported clothing.

  b. The union sponsors periodic training programs that instruct union laborers about the most efficient use of machinery and tools.

30-7. Why are unions in industries in which inputs such as machines are poor substitutes for labor more likely to be able to bargain for wages higher than market levels?

30-8. How is it possible for the average annual earnings of nonunionized workers to exceed those of unionized workers even though unionized workers' hourly wages are more than $2 higher?

30-9. In the short run, a tool manufacturer has a fixed amount of capital. Labor is a variable input. The cost and output structure that the firm faces is depicted in the following table:

Labor Supplied	Total Physical Product	Hourly Wage Rate ($)
10	100	5
11	109	6
12	116	7
13	121	8
14	124	9
15	125	10

Derive, at each level of labor supplied, the firm's total wage costs and marginal factor cost.

30-10. Suppose that for the firm in Problem 30-9, the goods market is perfectly competitive. The market price of the product the firm produces is $4 at each quantity supplied by the firm. What is the amount of labor that this profit-maximizing firm will hire, and what wage rate will it pay?

30-11. A firm finds that the price of its product changes with the rate of output. In addition, the wage it pays its workers varies with the amount of labor it employs. The price and wage structure that the firm faces is depicted in the following table.

Labor Supplied	Total Physical Product	Hourly Wage Rate ($)	Product Price ($)
10	100	5	3.11
11	109	6	3.00
12	116	7	2.95
13	121	8	2.92
14	124	9	2.90
15	125	10	2.89

This firm maximizes profits. How many units of labor will it hire? What wage will it pay?

30-12. What is the amount of monopsonistic exploitation that takes place at the firm examined in Problem 30-11?

30-13. A profit-maximizing clothing producer in a remote area is the only employer of people in that area. It sells its clothing in a perfectly competitive market.

The firm pays each worker the same weekly wage rate. The last worker hired raised the firm's total weekly wage expenses from $105,600 to $106,480. What is the marginal revenue product of the last worker hired by this firm if it is maximizing profits?

30-14. A single firm is the only employer in a labor market. The marginal revenue product, labor supply, and marginal factor cost curves that it faces are displayed in the diagram at the right. Use this information to answer the following questions.

    a. How many units of labor will this firm employ in order to maximize its economic profits?
    b. What hourly wage rate will this firm pay its workers?
    c. What is the total amount of wage payments that this firm will make to its workers each hour?

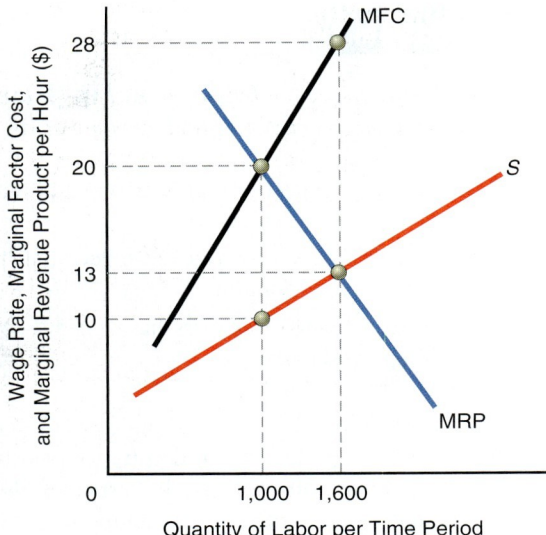

ECONOMICS ON THE NET

Evaluating Union Goals As discussed in this chapter, unions can pursue any of a number of goals. The AFL-CIO's home page provides links to the Web sites of several unions, and reviewing these sites can help you determine the objectives these unions have selected.

Title: American Federation of Labor–Congress of Industrial Organizations

Navigation: Go to www.econtoday.com/ch30 to visit the AFL-CIO's home page.

Application Perform the indicated operations, and answer the following questions.

1. Click on *About Us*, and then click on *Mission Statement*. Does the AFL-CIO claim to represent the interests of all workers or just workers in specific firms or industries? Can you discern what broad wage and employment strategy the AFL-CIO pursues?

2. Click on *Unions of the AFL-CIO*. Explore two or three of these Web sites. Do these unions appear to represent the interests of all workers or just workers in specific firms or industries? What general wage and employment strategies do these unions appear to pursue?

For Group Study and Analysis Divide up all the unions affiliated with the AFL-CIO among groups, and have each group explore the Web sites listed under *Unions of the AFL-CIO* at the AFL-CIO Web site. Have each group report on the wage and employment strategies that appear to prevail for the unions it examined.

ANSWERS TO QUICK QUIZZES

p. 764: (i) American Federation . . . Labor; (ii) National Labor Relations . . . industrial; (iii) 25 . . . 12
p. 770: (i) above . . . rationing; (ii) all . . . income . . . maximize; (iii) inward . . . outward; (iv) productivity
p. 776: (i) only buyer . . . upward; (ii) upward . . . greater . . . above; (iii) factor . . . revenue

Income, Poverty, and Health Care

31

In the early 1980s, only about 5 percent of U.S. individuals with incomes among the lowest 20 percent of income earners during the 1960s were still within that lowest-income group 20 years later. In contrast, in the 2000s about 30 percent of people who were among the lowest 20 percent of income earners back in the early 1980s were still earning incomes ranked among the lowest. Some economists interpret this as evidence that there is less "income mobility"—that is, less upward and downward movement of people's incomes relative to incomes earned by others—than there used to be. Other economists are not convinced that this is necessarily true. To understand the disagreement on this issue, you must learn more about the *distribution of income*, which is a key topic of this chapter.

Learning Objectives

After reading this chapter, you should be able to:

1. Describe how to use a Lorenz curve to represent a nation's income distribution
2. Identify the key determinants of income differences across individuals
3. Discuss theories of desired income distribution
4. Distinguish among alternative approaches to measuring and addressing poverty
5. Recognize the major reasons for rising health care costs
6. Describe alternative approaches to paying for health care

MyEconLab helps you master each objective and study more efficiently. See end of chapter for details.

Did You Know That...

one of every 125 U.S. residents is a "millionaire"? Thus, 0.8 percent of U.S. residents possess financial wealth—not including ownership of a home (or homes)—exceeding $1 million. These roughly 2.4 million U.S. millionaires account for about a third of all the millionaires in the world.

About 30,000 U.S. millionaires possess personal wealth exceeding $30 million. These ultrarich individuals typically earn annual incomes that place them at one end of the U.S. **distribution of income,** which is the way that income is allocated among the population. At the other end are the 37 million U.S. residents who, according to the U.S. government, live in a state of poverty.

What determines the distribution of income? Economists have devised various theories to explain income distribution. We will present some of these theories in this chapter. We will also present some of the more obvious institutional reasons why income is not distributed equally in the United States. In addition, we will examine what might be done about health care problems confronting individuals in all income groups.

Distribution of income
The way income is allocated among the population.

INCOME

Income provides each of us with the means of consuming and saving. Income can be the result of a payment for labor services or a payment for ownership of one of the other factors of production besides labor—land, physical capital, or entrepreneurship. In addition, individuals obtain spendable income from gifts and government transfers. (Some individuals also obtain income by stealing, but we will not treat this matter here.) Right now, let us examine how money income is distributed across classes of income earners within the United States.

Measuring Income Distribution: The Lorenz Curve

We can represent the distribution of money income graphically with what is known as the **Lorenz curve,** named after a U.S.-born statistician, Max Otto Lorenz, who proposed it in 1905. The Lorenz curve shows what portion of total money income is accounted for by different proportions of the nation's households. Look at Figure 31-1. On the horizontal axis, we measure the *cumulative* percentage of households, lowest-income households first. Starting at the left corner, there are zero households; at the right corner, we have 100 percent of households; and in the middle, we have 50 percent of households. The vertical axis represents the cumulative percentage of money income. The 45-degree line represents complete equality: 50 percent of the households obtain 50 percent of total income, 60 percent of the households obtain 60 percent of total income, and so on. Of course, in no real-world situation is there such complete equality of income; no actual Lorenz curve would be a straight line. Rather, it would be some curved line, like the one labeled "Actual money income distribution" in Figure 31-1. For example, the bottom 50 percent of households in the United States receive about 28 percent of total money income.

Lorenz curve
A geometric representation of the distribution of income. A Lorenz curve that is perfectly straight represents complete income equality. The more bowed a Lorenz curve, the more unequally income is distributed.

In Figure 31-2, we again show the actual money income distribution Lorenz curve, and we also compare it to the distribution of money income in 1929. Since that year, the Lorenz curve has generally become less bowed; that is, it has moved closer to the line of complete equality.

Criticisms of the Lorenz Curve.
In recent years, economists have placed less and less emphasis on the shape of the Lorenz curve as an indication of the degree of income

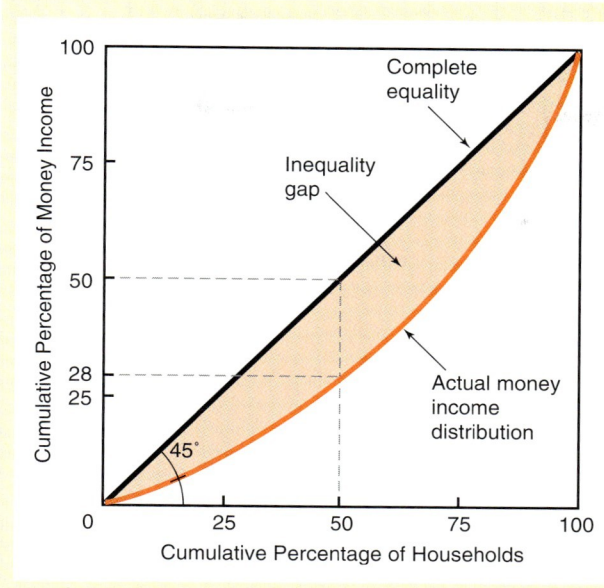

FIGURE 31-1

The Lorenz Curve

The horizontal axis measures the cumulative percentage of households, with lowest-income households first, from 0 to 100 percent. The vertical axis measures the cumulative percentage of money income from 0 to 100. A straight line at a 45-degree angle cuts the box in half and represents a line of complete income equality, along which 25 percent of the families get 25 percent of the money income, 50 percent get 50 percent, and so on. The observed Lorenz curve, showing actual money income distribution, is not a straight line but rather a curved line as shown. The difference between complete money income equality and the Lorenz curve is the inequality gap.

inequality in a country. There are five basic reasons why the Lorenz curve has been criticized:

1. The Lorenz curve is typically presented in terms of the distribution of *money* income only. It does not include **income in kind,** such as government-provided food stamps, education, or housing aid, and goods or services produced and consumed in the home or on the farm.

Income in kind
Income received in the form of goods and services, such as housing or medical care; to be contrasted with money income, which is simply income in dollars, or general purchasing power, that can be used to buy *any* goods and services.

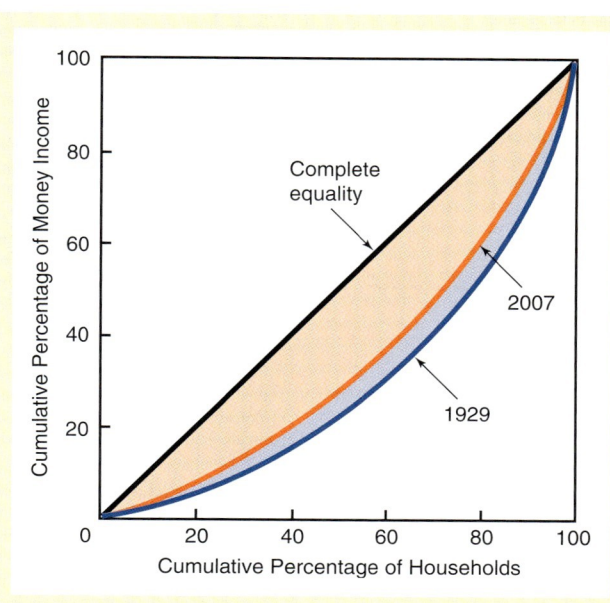

FIGURE 31-2

Lorenz Curves of Income Distribution, 1929 and 2007

Since 1929, the Lorenz curve has moved inward toward the straight line of perfect income equality.

Source: U.S. Department of Commerce.

2. The Lorenz curve does not account for differences in the size of households or the number of wage earners they contain.
3. It does not account for age differences. Even if all families in the United States had exactly the same *lifetime* incomes, chances are that young families would have modest incomes, middle-aged families would have relatively high incomes, and retired families would have low incomes. Because the Lorenz curve is drawn at a moment in time, it can never tell us anything about the inequality of *lifetime* income.
4. The Lorenz curve ordinarily reflects money income *before* taxes.
5. It does not measure unreported income from the underground economy, a substantial source of income for some individuals.

Income Distribution in the United States

Go to www.econtoday/ch31 to view the U.S. Census Bureau's most recent data on the U.S. income distribution. Click on the most recent year next to "Money Income in the United States."

We could talk about the percentage of income earners within specific income classes—those earning between $20,001 and $30,000 per year, those earning between $30,001 and $40,000 per year, and so on. The problem with this type of analysis is that we live in a growing economy. Income, with exceptions, is going up all the time. If we wish to compare the relative shares of total income going to different income classes, we cannot look at specific amounts of money income. Instead, we talk about a distribution of income over five groups. Then we can talk about how much the bottom fifth (or quintile) makes compared with the top fifth, and so on.

In Table 31-1, we see the percentage share of income for households before direct taxes. The table groups households according to whether they are in the lowest 20 percent of the income distribution, the second lowest 20 percent, and so on. We see that in 2007, the lowest 20 percent had an estimated combined money income of 3.6 percent of the total money income of the entire population. This is a little less than the lowest 20 percent had at the end of World War II. Accordingly, some have concluded that the distribution of money income has changed only slightly. *Money* income, however, understates *total* income for individuals who receive in-kind transfers from the government in the form of food stamps, public housing, education, and so on. In particular, since World War II, the share of *total* income—money income plus in-kind benefits—going to the bottom 20 percent of households has more than doubled.

When evaluating the distribution of income, why do economists focus on *total* income earned by households instead of looking only at the wages and salaries they earn?

TABLE 31-1
Percentage Share of Money Income for Households Before Direct Taxes

Income Group	2007	1975	1960	1947
Lowest fifth	3.6	4.4	4.8	5.1
Second fifth	8.5	10.5	12.2	11.8
Third fifth	14.5	17.1	17.8	16.7
Fourth fifth	23.0	24.8	24.0	23.2
Highest fifth	50.4	43.2	41.3	43.3

Note: Figures may not sum to 100 percent due to rounding.
Sources: U.S. Bureau of the Census; author's estimates.

EXAMPLE

Why It Is Misleading to Examine Only Wages and Salaries

At the end of the 1960s, total wages and salaries accounted for close to 60 percent of income received from all sources in the United States. Since then, as shown in Figure 31-3, the share of total U.S. national income accounted for by wages has generally trended downward. Today, only about 52 percent of national income is derived from wages and salaries.

Some media pundits and politicians have claimed that the decline in the percentage of national income going to wages and salaries paid to households is evidence that laborers are receiving a smaller share of U.S. national income. As you can see in Figure 31-3, however, the *total compensation* received by workers, which includes employer-paid health insurance and pension benefits, has remained close to 70 percent of U.S. national income since the 1940s.

Effectively, U.S. workers have exchanged some of their wage and salary payments for other (usually nontaxable) benefits. Their total compensation relative to national income has not really declined. This illustrates why it is so important to include all income receipts when measuring the distribution of income.

FOR CRITICAL ANALYSIS

If the percentage of the population made up of workers who receive wages and salaries has remained the same since the 1960s, has a Lorenz curve based only on U.S. income from wages and salaries necessarily become more bowed over time?

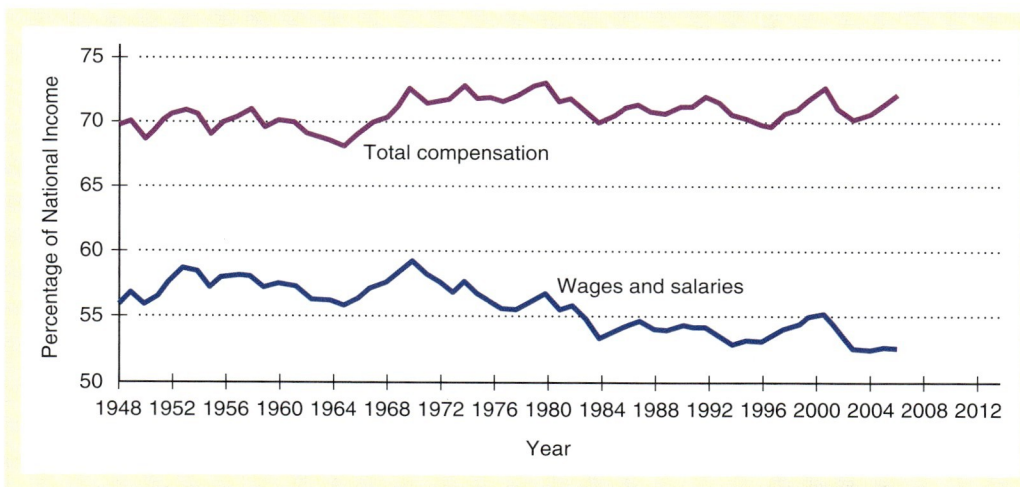

FIGURE 31-3

Wages and Salaries and Total Labor Compensation as Percentages of U.S. National Income

The share of U.S. national income accounted for by wages and salaries has trended downward since the late 1960s. Total labor compensation as a percentage of national income has remained close to 70 percent, however.

Source: Federal Reserve Bank of St. Louis.

The Distribution of Wealth

When referring to the distribution of income, we must realize that income—a flow—can be viewed as a return on wealth (both human and nonhuman)—a stock. A discussion of the distribution of income is not necessarily the same thing as a discussion of the distribution of wealth, however. A complete concept of wealth would include not only tangible objects, such as buildings, machinery, land, cars, and houses—nonhuman wealth—but also people who have skills, knowledge, initiative, talents, and so on—human wealth. The total of human and nonhuman wealth in the United States makes up our nation's capital stock. (Note that the terms *wealth* and *capital* are sometimes used only with reference to

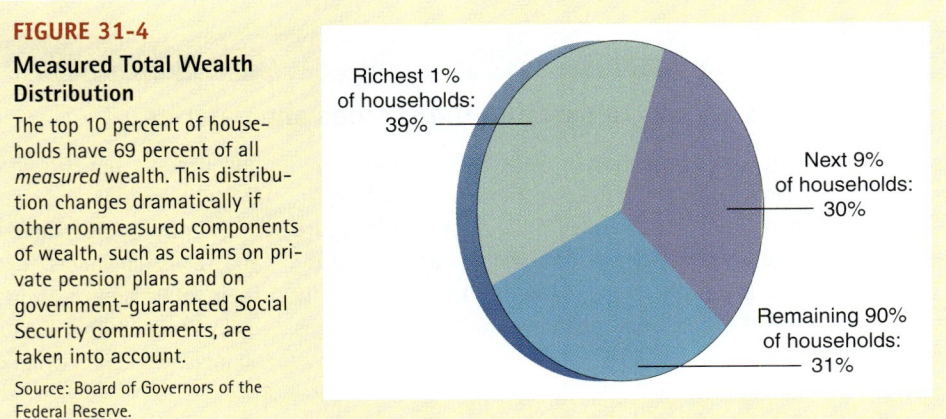

FIGURE 31-4
Measured Total Wealth Distribution

The top 10 percent of households have 69 percent of all *measured* wealth. This distribution changes dramatically if other nonmeasured components of wealth, such as claims on private pension plans and on government-guaranteed Social Security commitments, are taken into account.

Source: Board of Governors of the Federal Reserve.

nonhuman wealth.) The capital stock consists of anything that can generate utility to individuals in the future. A fresh ripe tomato is not part of our capital stock. It has to be eaten before it turns rotten and becomes worthless. Once it has been eaten, it can no longer generate satisfaction.

Figure 31-4 shows that the richest 10 percent of U.S. households hold more than two-thirds of all measured wealth. The problem with those data, gathered by the Federal Reserve System, is that they do not include many important assets. One of these is workers' claims on private pension plans, which equal at least $6 trillion. If you add the value of these pensions, household wealth increases by almost 25 percent and reveals that the majority of U.S. households are middle-wealth households (popularly known as the *middle class*). Another asset excluded from the data is anticipated claims on the Social Security system, which tend to comprise a larger share of the wealth of lower-income individuals. Expected claims on the Social Security system are also unevenly distributed across the population because some groups of people, such as African American men, have lower life expectancies than other groups.

QUICK QUIZ

The **Lorenz curve** graphically represents the distribution of _____. If it is a straight line, there is complete _____ of income. The more it is bowed, the more _____ income is distributed.

The distribution of wealth is not the same as the distribution of income. Wealth includes _____ such as houses, stocks, and bonds. Although the apparent distribution of wealth seems to be _____ concentrated at the top than income, the data used are not very accurate, and most summary statistics fail to take account of workers' claims on private and public pensions, which are substantial.

See page 812 for the answers. Review concepts from this section in MyEconLab.

DETERMINANTS OF INCOME DIFFERENCES

We know that there are income differences—that is not in dispute. A more important question is why these differences in income occur, for if we know why income differences occur, perhaps we can change public policy, particularly with respect to helping people in the lowest income classes climb the income ladder. What is more, if we know the reasons for income differences, we can ascertain whether any of these determinants have changed over time. We will look at four determinants of income differences: age, marginal productivity, inheritance, and discrimination.

Age

Age turns out to be a determinant of income because with age come, usually, more education, more training, and more experience. It is not surprising that within every class of income earners, there seem to be regular cycles of earning behavior. Most individuals earn more when they are middle-aged than when they are younger or older. We call this the **age-earnings cycle**.

The Age-Earnings Cycle.
Every occupation has its own age-earnings cycle, and every individual will probably experience some variation from the average. Nonetheless, we can characterize the typical age-earnings cycle graphically in Figure 31-5. Here we see that at age 18, earnings from wages are relatively low. Earnings gradually rise until they peak at about age 50. Then they fall until retirement, when they become zero (that is, currently earned wages become zero, although retirement payments may then commence). The reason for such a regular cycle in earnings is fairly straightforward.

When individuals start working at a young age, they typically have no work-related experience. Their ability to produce is less than that of more seasoned workers—their productivity is lower. As they become older, they obtain more training and accumulate more experience. Their productivity rises, and they are therefore paid more. They also generally start to work longer hours. As the age of 50 approaches, the productivity of individual workers usually peaks. So do the number of hours per week that are worked. After this peak in the age-earnings cycle, the effects of aging—decreases in stamina, strength, reaction time, and the like—usually outweigh any increases in training or experience. Also, hours worked usually start to fall for older people. Finally, as a person reaches retirement, both productivity and hours worked diminish rather drastically.

Note that general increases in overall productivity for the entire workforce will result in an upward shift in the typical age-earnings profile depicted in Figure 31-5. Thus, even at the end of the age-earnings cycle, when just about to retire, the worker would receive a relatively high wage compared with the starting wage 45 years earlier. The wage would be

Age-earnings cycle
The regular earnings profile of an individual throughout his or her lifetime. The age-earnings cycle usually starts with a low income, builds gradually to a peak at around age 50, and then gradually curves down until it approaches zero at retirement.

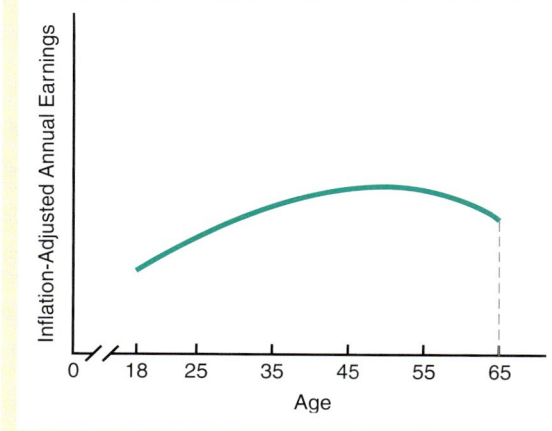

FIGURE 31-5

Typical Age-Earnings Profile

Within every class of income earners there is usually a typical age-earnings profile. Earnings from wages are lowest when starting work at age 18, reach their peak at around age 50, and then taper off until retirement around age 65, when they become zero for most people. The rise in earnings up to age 50 is usually due to increased experience, longer working hours, and better training and schooling. (We abstract from economywide productivity changes that would shift the entire curve upward.)

higher due to factors that contribute to rising real wages for everyone, regardless of the stage in the age-earnings cycle.

Now we have some idea why specific individuals earn different incomes at different times in their lives, but we have yet to explain why different people are paid different amounts for their labor. One way to explain this is to recall the marginal productivity theory developed in Chapter 29.

Marginal Productivity

When trying to determine how many workers a firm would hire, we had to construct a marginal revenue product curve. We found that as more workers were hired, the marginal revenue product fell due to diminishing marginal product. If the forces of demand and supply established a certain wage rate, workers would be hired until their marginal physical product times marginal revenue (which equals the market price under perfect competition) was equal to the going wage rate. Then the hiring would stop. This analysis suggests what workers can expect to be paid in the labor market: They can each expect to be paid their marginal revenue product (assuming that there are low-cost information flows and that the labor and product markets are competitive).

In a perfectly competitive situation, with mobility of labor resources (at least on the margin), workers who are being paid less than their marginal revenue product will be bid away to better employment opportunities. Either they will seek better employment themselves, or other employers will offer them a higher wage rate. This process will continue until each worker is being paid his or her marginal revenue product.

Determinants of Marginal Productivity.
If we accept marginal revenue product theory, we have a way to find out how people can earn higher incomes. If they can increase their marginal physical product, they can expect to be paid more. Some of the determinants of marginal physical product are talent, experience, and training. Most of these are means by which marginal physical product can be increased. Let's examine them in greater detail.

Talent. Talent is the easiest factor to explain, but it is difficult to acquire if you don't have it. Innate abilities and attributes can be very strong, if not overwhelming, determinants of a person's potential productivity. Strength, coordination, and mental alertness are facets of nonacquired human capital and thus have some bearing on the ability to earn income. Someone who is tall and agile has a better chance of being a basketball player than someone who is short and unathletic. A person born with a superior talent for abstract thinking has a better chance of earning a relatively high income as a mathematician or a physicist than someone who is not born with that capability.

Experience. Additional experience at particular tasks is another way to increase productivity. Experience can be linked to the well-known *learning curve* that applies when the same task is done over and over. The worker repeating a task becomes more efficient: The worker can do the same task in less time or in the same amount of time but better. Take an example of a person going to work on an automobile assembly line. At first she is able to fasten only three bolts every two minutes. Then the worker becomes more adept and can fasten four bolts in the same time plus insert a rubber guard on the bumper. After a few more weeks, another task can be added. Experience allows this individual to improve her productivity. The more effectively people learn to do something, the more quickly they can do it and the more efficient they are.

Hence we would expect experience to lead to higher productivity. And we would expect people with more experience to be paid more than those with less experience. More experience, however, does not guarantee a higher wage rate. The *demand* for a person's services must also exist. Spending a long time to become a first-rate archer in modern society would probably add very little to a person's income. Experience has value only if the output is demanded by society.

Training. Training is similar to experience but is more formal. Much of a person's increased productivity is due to on-the-job training. Many companies have training programs for new workers.

Investment in Human Capital. Investment in human capital is just like investment in anything else. If you invest in yourself by going to college, rather than going to work after high school and earning more current income, you will presumably be rewarded in the future with a higher income or a more interesting job (or both). This is exactly the motivation that underlies the decision of many college-bound students to obtain a formal higher education. Undoubtedly, some students would go to school even if the rate of return on formal education were zero or negative. But we do expect that the higher the rate of return on investing in ourselves, the more such investment there will be. U.S. Labor Department data demonstrate conclusively that, on average, high school graduates make more than grade school graduates and that college graduates make more than high school graduates. The estimated annual income of a full-time worker with four years of college in the mid-2000s was about $56,000. That person's high school counterpart was estimated to earn a little less than $34,000, so the "college premium" was just over 65 percent. Generally, the rate of return on investment in human capital is on a par with the rate of return on investment in other areas.

To determine the rate of return on an investment in a college education, we first have to figure out the marginal cost of going to school. A major cost is not what you have to pay for books, fees, and tuition but rather the income you forgo. *A key cost of education is the income forgone—the opportunity cost of not working.* In addition, the direct expenses of college must be paid for. Not all students forgo all income during their college years. Many work part time. Taking account of those who work part time and those who are supported by tuition grants and other scholarships, the average rate of return on going to college ranges between 6 and 10 percent per year.

For a discussion of how the Organization for Economic Cooperation and Development seeks to measure investments in human capital, go to www.econtoday.com/ch31.

Inheritance

It is not unusual to inherit cash, jewelry, stocks, bonds, homes, or other real estate. Yet only about 10 percent of income inequality in the United States can be traced to differences in inherited wealth. If for some reason the government confiscated all property that had been inherited, the immediate result would be only a modest change in the distribution of income in the United States. In any event, at both federal and state levels substantial inheritance taxes have been levied on the estates of relatively wealthy deceased Americans (although there are some legally valid ways to avoid certain estate taxes).

How many U.S. millionaires have inherited their fortunes?

EXAMPLE

More of the "Self-Made" Rise to the Top

In years past, most U.S. residents owning more than $1 million in financial wealth inherited the bulk of their fortunes. Most of today's millionaires, however, amassed the vast majority of their wealth on their own. At present, only about 20 percent of U.S. millionaires inherited most of their wealth from parents or other relatives.

FOR CRITICAL ANALYSIS
How has it been possible for the distribution of wealth displayed in Figure 31-4 on page 788 to remain about the same over the years even as a number of households originally outside the richest 1 percent earned new fortunes and broke into that classification?

Discrimination

Economic discrimination occurs whenever workers with the same marginal revenue product receive unequal pay due to some noneconomic factor such as their race, gender, or age. It is possible—and indeed quite obvious—that discrimination affects the distribution of income. Certain groups in our society are not paid wages at rates comparable to those received by other groups, even when we correct for productivity. Differences in income remain between whites and nonwhites and between men and women. For example, the median income of black families is about 65 percent that of white families. The median wage rate of women is about 70 percent that of men. Some people argue that all of these differences are due to discrimination against nonwhites and against women.

We cannot simply accept *any* differences in income as due to discrimination, though. What we need to do is discover why differences in income between groups exist and then determine if factors other than discrimination in the labor market can explain them. The unexplained part of income differences can rightfully be considered the result of discrimination.

Among female college graduates, who would you guess earns the most on average: a white woman, an Asian American woman, or an African American woman?

EXAMPLE

Do Employers Favor Minority Female Graduates?

White female college graduates in the United States earn an average of about $38,000 per year. This compares with average annual earnings of just over $41,000 for African American female college graduates and about $44,000 for Asian American female college graduates. Does this necessarily mean that employers that hire women with college degrees discriminate against those who are white? The answer is, not necessarily. A number of factors may account for the lower average earnings of white female graduates. For instance, there is evidence that African American and Asian American women with college degrees are more likely to hold multiple jobs, to work in excess of 40 hours per week, and to return to work sooner after having a child. Thus, minority women with college degrees may earn higher average incomes because they typically spend more time at work each year.

FOR CRITICAL ANALYSIS
What nondiscriminatory factors might help to explain why white males with college degrees earn more than $66,000 per year on average, or 65 percent more than the average of about $40,000 earned annually by a female graduate?

Access to Education. African Americans and other minorities have faced discrimination in the acquisition of human capital. The amount and quality of schooling offered black U.S. residents has generally been inferior to that offered whites. As a result, among other things, African Americans and certain other minority groups, such as Hispanics, suffer from reduced investment in human capital. Even when this difference in human capital is taken into account, however, there still appears to be an income differential that cannot be explained.

The unexplained income differential between whites and blacks is often attributed to discrimination in the labor market. Because no better explanation is offered, we will infer that discrimination in the labor market does indeed exist.

The Doctrine of Comparable Worth. Discrimination against women can occur because of barriers to entry in higher-paying occupations and because of discrimination in the acquisition of human capital, just as has occurred for African Americans. Consider the distribution of the highest-paying and lowest-paying occupations. The lowest-paying jobs are dominated by females, both white and nonwhite. For example, the proportion of women in secretarial, clerical, janitorial, and food service jobs ranges from 70 percent (food service) to 97 percent (secretarial). Proponents of the **comparable-worth doctrine** argue that female secretaries, janitors, and food service workers should be making salaries comparable to those of male truck drivers or construction workers, assuming that the levels of skill and responsibility in these jobs are comparable. These advocates also believe that a comparable-worth policy would benefit the economy overall. They contend that adjusting the wages of workers in female-dominated jobs upward would help to create more efficient and less discriminatory labor markets.

Comparable-worth doctrine
The belief that women should receive the same wages as men if the levels of skill and responsibility in their jobs are equivalent.

THEORIES OF DESIRED INCOME DISTRIBUTION

We have talked about the factors affecting the distribution of income, but we have not yet mentioned the normative issue of how income *ought* to be distributed. This, of course, requires a value judgment. We are talking about the problem of economic justice. We can never completely resolve this problem because there are always going to be conflicting values. It is impossible to give all people what each thinks is just. Nonetheless, two particular normative standards for the distribution of income have been popular with economists. These are income distribution based on productivity and income distribution based on equality.

Productivity

The *productivity standard* for the distribution of income can be stated simply as "To each according to what he or she produces." This is also called the *contributive standard* because it is based on the principle of rewarding according to the contribution to society's total output. It is also sometimes referred to as the *merit standard* and is one of the oldest concepts of justice. People are rewarded according to merit, and merit is judged by one's ability to produce what is considered useful by society.

Just as any standard is a value judgment, however, so is the productivity standard. It is rooted in the capitalist ethic and has been attacked vigorously by some economists and philosophers, including Karl Marx (1818–1883), who felt that people should be rewarded according to need and not according to productivity.

We measure a person's productive contribution in a capitalist system by the market value of that person's output. We have already referred to this as the marginal revenue product theory of wage determination.

Do not immediately jump to the conclusion that in a world of income distribution determined by productivity, society will necessarily allow the aged, the infirm, and the disabled to die of starvation because they are unproductive. In the United States today, the productivity standard is mixed with a standard based on people's "needs" so that the aged, the disabled, the involuntarily unemployed, the very young, and other unproductive (in the market sense of the word) members of the economy are provided for through private and public transfers.

Equality

The *egalitarian principle* of income distribution is simply "To each exactly the same." Everyone would have exactly the same amount of income. This criterion of income distribution has been debated as far back as biblical times. This system of income distribution has been considered equitable, meaning that presumably everybody is dealt with fairly and equally. There are problems, however, with an income distribution that is completely equal.

Some jobs are more unpleasant or more dangerous than others. Should the people undertaking these jobs be paid exactly the same as everyone else? Indeed, under an equal distribution of income, what incentive would there be for individuals to take risky, hazardous, or unpleasant jobs at all? What about overtime? Who would be willing to work overtime without additional pay? There is another problem: If everyone earned the same income, what incentive would there be for individuals to invest in their own human capital—a costly and time-consuming process?

Just consider the incentive structure within a corporation. Within corporations, much of the differential between, say, the pay of the CEO and the pay of all of the vice presidents is meant to create competition among the vice presidents for the CEO's job. The result is higher productivity. If all incomes were the same, much of this competition would disappear, and productivity would fall.

There is some evidence that differences in income lead to higher rates of economic growth. Future generations are therefore made better off. Elimination of income differences may reduce the rate of economic growth and cause future generations to be poorer than they otherwise might have been.

QUICK QUIZ

Most people follow an _____-_____ cycle in which they earn relatively small incomes when they first start working, increase their incomes until about age 50, and then slowly experience a decrease in their real incomes as they approach retirement.

If we accept the marginal _____ product theory of wages, workers can expect to be paid their marginal _____ product.

Marginal physical productivity depends on _____, _____, _____, and _____.

Going to school and receiving on-the-job training can be considered an investment in _____ capital. A key cost of education is the _____ cost of not working.

_____ is most easily observed in various groups' access to high-paying jobs and to quality education. Minorities and women are disproportionately underrepresented in high-paying jobs. Also, minorities sometimes do not receive access to higher education of the same quality offered to majority-group members.

Proponents of the _____-_____ doctrine contend that disparate jobs can be compared by examining efforts, skill, and training and that wages should be paid on the basis of this _____ _____.

Two normative standards for income distribution are income distribution based on _____ and income distribution based on _____.

See page 812 for the answers. Review concepts from this section in MyEconLab.

POVERTY AND ATTEMPTS TO ELIMINATE IT

Throughout the history of the world, mass poverty has been accepted as inevitable. This nation and others, particularly in the Western world, however, have sustained enough economic growth in the past several hundred years so that *mass* poverty can no longer be said to be a problem for these fortunate countries. As a matter of fact, the residual of poverty in the United States strikes us as bizarre, an anomaly. How can there still be so much poverty in a nation of such abundance? Having talked about the determinants of the distribution of income, we now have at least some ideas of why some people are destined to remain low-income earners throughout their lives.

Income can be transferred from the relatively well-to-do to the relatively poor by various methods, and as a nation we have been using them for a long time. Today, we have a vast array of welfare programs set up for the purpose of redistributing income. As we know, however, these programs have not been entirely successful. Are there alternatives to our current welfare system? Is there a better method of helping the poor? Before we answer these questions, let's look at the concept of poverty in more detail and at the characteristics of the poor. Panel (a) of Figure 31-6 shows that the total number of people that the government has classified as poor fell steadily from 1959 to 1969, then leveled off until the recession of 1981–1982. The number then rose dramatically, fell back during the late 1980s, rose again after the recession in the early 1990s, fell once again thereafter, and then rose in the early 2000s before leveling off in recent years.

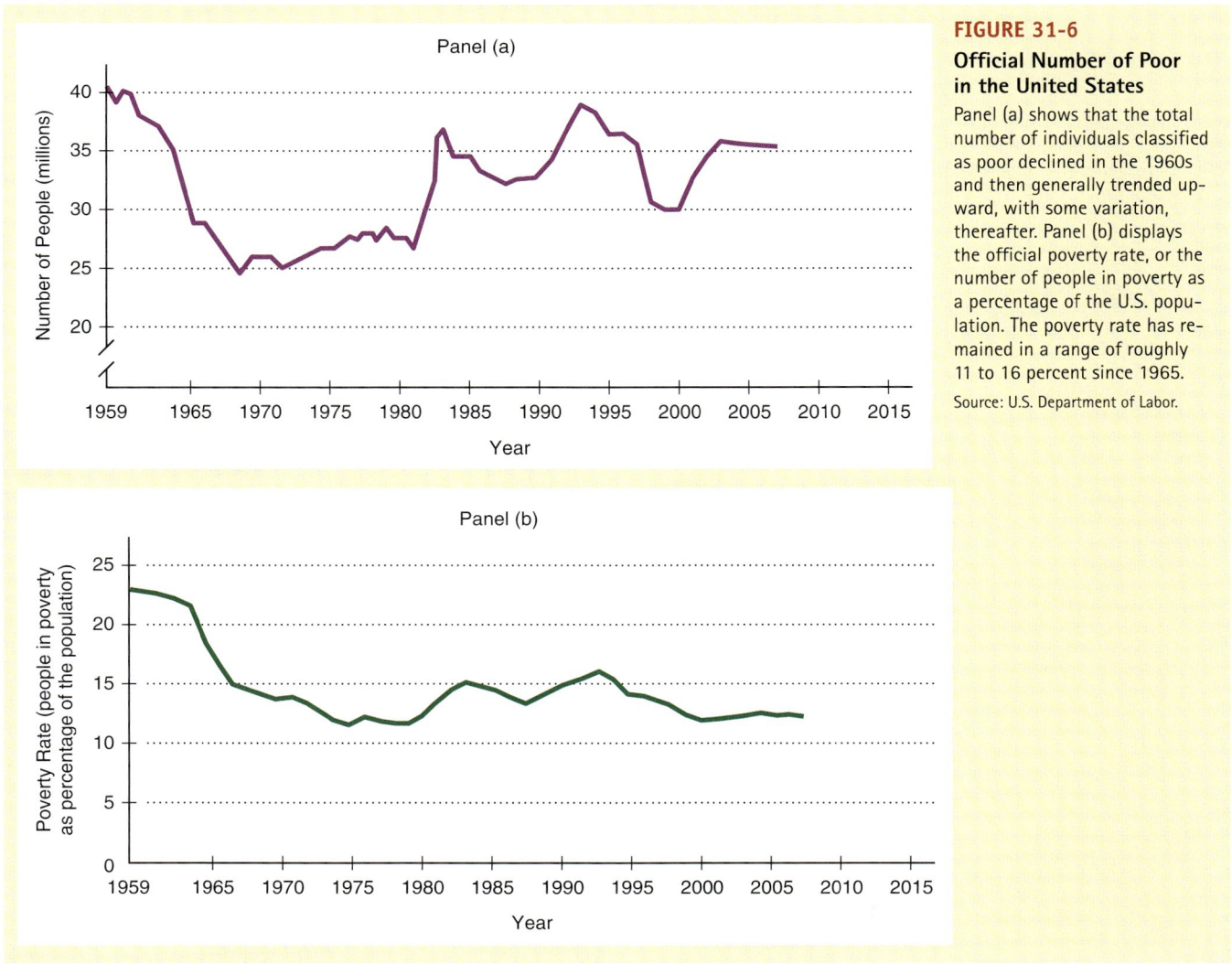

FIGURE 31-6

Official Number of Poor in the United States

Panel (a) shows that the total number of individuals classified as poor declined in the 1960s and then generally trended upward, with some variation, thereafter. Panel (b) displays the official poverty rate, or the number of people in poverty as a percentage of the U.S. population. The poverty rate has remained in a range of roughly 11 to 16 percent since 1965.

Source: U.S. Department of Labor.

Panel (b) of Figure 31-6 displays the percentage of the U.S. population determined to be in a state of poverty by the U.S. government. This percentage, called the *poverty rate*, has varied between roughly 11 percent and 16 percent during the past 40 years.

Defining Poverty

The threshold income level, which is used to determine who falls into the poverty category, was originally based on the cost of a nutritionally adequate food plan designed by the U.S. Department of Agriculture for emergency or temporary use. The threshold was determined by multiplying the food plan cost by 3 on the assumption that food expenses comprise approximately one-third of a poor family's income. Annual revisions of the threshold level were based only on price changes in the food budget. In 1969, a federal interagency committee looked at the calculations of the threshold and decided to set new standards, with adjustments made on the basis of changes in the Consumer Price Index. For example, in 2007, the official poverty level for an urban family of four was around $21,000. It goes up each year to reflect whatever inflation has occurred.

Absolute Poverty

Go to www.econtoday.com/ch31 to learn about the World Bank's programs intended to combat global poverty.

Because the low-income threshold is an absolute measure, we know that if it never changes in real terms, we will reduce poverty even if we do nothing. How can that be? The reasoning is straightforward. Real incomes in the United States have been growing at a compounded annual rate of almost 2 percent per capita for at least the past century and at about 2.5 percent since World War II. If we define the poverty line at a specific real level, more and more individuals will make incomes that exceed that poverty line. Thus, in absolute terms, we will eliminate poverty (assuming continued per capita growth and no change in income distribution).

Relative Poverty

Be careful with this analysis, however. Poverty can also be defined in relative terms; that is, it is defined in terms of the income levels of individuals or families relative to the rest of the population. As long as the distribution of income is not perfectly equal, there will always be some people who make less income than others, even if their relatively low income is high by historical standards. Thus, in a relative sense, the problem of poverty will always exist, although it can be reduced.

Transfer Payments as Income

The official poverty level is based on pretax income, including cash but not in-kind subsidies—food stamps, housing vouchers, and the like. If we correct poverty levels for such benefits, the percentage of the population that is below the poverty line drops dramatically. Some economists argue that the way the official poverty level is calculated makes no sense in a nation that redistributed over $1.3 trillion in cash and noncash transfers in 2006.

Furthermore, some of the nation's official poor partake in the informal, or underground, sectors of the economy without reporting their income from these sources. And some of the officially defined poor obtain benefits from owning their own home (40 percent of all poor households do own their own homes). Look at Figure 31-7 for two different views of what has happened to the relative position of this nation's poor. The graph shows the ratio of the top fifth of the nation's households to the bottom fifth of the nation's households. If we look

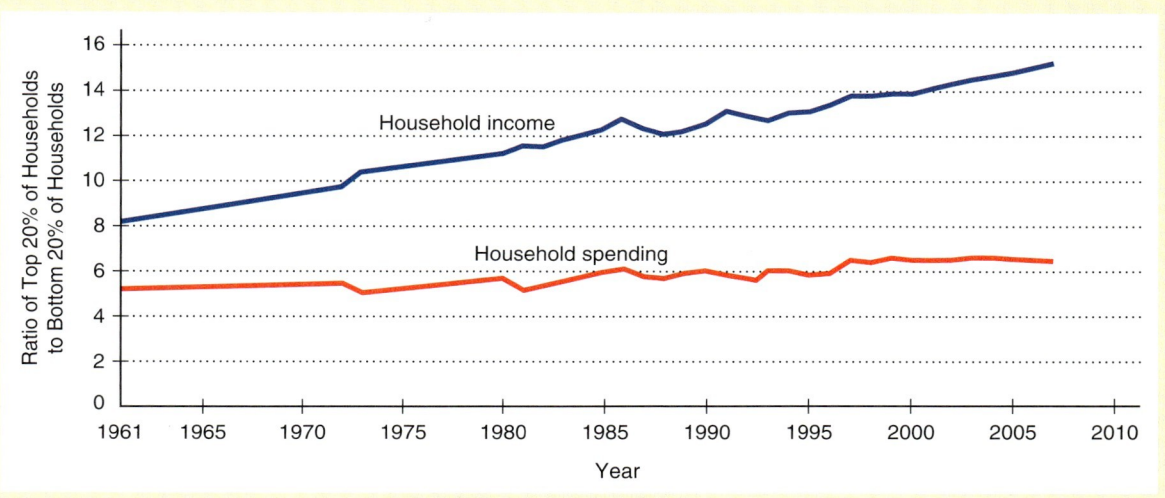

FIGURE 31-7

Relative Poverty: Comparing Household Income and Household Spending

This graph shows, on the vertical axis, the ratio of the top 20 percent of income-earning households to the bottom 20 percent. If measured household income is used, there appears to be increasing income inequality. If we look at household *spending*, though, inequality is more nearly constant.

Sources: U.S. Bureau of Labor Statistics; U.S. Bureau of the Census.

only at measured income, it appears that the poor are getting relatively poorer compared to the rich (the top line). If we compare household spending (consumption), however, a different picture emerges. The nation's poorest households are in fact holding their own.

Attacks on Poverty: Major Income Maintenance Programs

There are a variety of income maintenance programs designed to help the poor. We examine a few of them here.

Social Security. For the retired, the unemployed, and the disabled, social insurance programs provide income payments in prescribed situations. The best known is Social Security, which includes what has been called old-age, survivors', and disability insurance (OASDI). As discussed in Chapter 6, this was originally supposed to be a program of compulsory saving financed from payroll taxes levied on both employers and employees. Workers pay for Social Security while working and receive the benefits after retirement. The benefit payments are usually made to people who have reached retirement age. When the insured worker dies, benefits accrue to the survivors, including widows and children. Special benefits provide for disabled workers. Over 90 percent of all employed persons in the United States are covered by OASDI. Today, Social Security is an intergenerational income transfer that is only vaguely related to past earnings. It transfers income from U.S. residents who work—the young through the middle-aged—to those who do not work—older retired persons.

In 2007, more than 49 million people were receiving OASDI checks averaging about $960 a month. Benefit payments from OASDI redistribute income to some degree. Benefit payments, however, are not based on recipient need. Participants' contributions give them the right to benefits even if they would be financially secure without them. Social Security is not really an insurance program because people are not guaranteed that the benefits they receive will be in line with the "contributions" they have made. It is not a personal savings account. The benefits are legislated by Congress. In the future, Congress may not be as sympathetic toward older people as it is today. It could (and probably will have to) legislate for lower real levels of benefits instead of higher ones.

Supplemental Security Income and Temporary Assistance to Needy Families.

Many people who are poor but do not qualify for Social Security benefits are assisted through other programs. The federally financed and administered Supplemental Security Income (SSI) program was instituted in 1974. The purpose of SSI is to establish a nationwide minimum income for the aged, the blind, and the disabled. SSI has become one of the fastest-growing transfer programs in the United States. Whereas in 1974 less than $8 billion was spent, the prediction for 2008 is $45 billion. U.S. residents currently eligible for SSI include children and individuals claiming mental disabilities, including drug addicts and alcoholics.

Temporary Assistance to Needy Families (TANF) is a state-administered program, financed in part by federal grants. The program provides aid to families in need. TANF replaced Aid to Families with Dependent Children (AFDC) in 1996. TANF payments are intended to be temporary. Projected expenditures for TANF are $18 billion in 2007.

Food Stamps.

Food stamps are government-issued coupons (or, increasingly, electronic debit cards) that can be used to purchase food. The food stamp program was started in 1964, seemingly, in retrospect, to shore up the nation's agricultural sector by increasing demand for food through retail channels. In 1964, some 367,000 Americans were receiving food stamps. In 2007, the estimate is over 25 million recipients. The annual cost has jumped from $860,000 to more than $35 billion. In 2007, almost one in every nine citizens (including children) was using food stamps. The food stamp program has become a major part of the welfare system in the United States. The program has also become a method of promoting better nutrition among the poor.

Do people tend to value food stamps less than the amount printed on the stamps?

POLICY EXAMPLE

What Are Food Stamps Worth?

Most recipients of food stamps qualify because they have relatively low incomes. For the majority of recipients, there are times when they would rather have cash to spend on energy bills or clothing, but their billfolds contain food stamps that can only be used to purchase approved food items.

Diane Whitmore of the University of Chicago sought to determine how much value food stamp recipients place on the stamps. She found that 20 to 30 percent of recipients purchase more food with the stamps than they otherwise would if they were to receive cash instead. These individuals, she found, placed an average cash value of 80 cents on each $1 in food stamps they received.

Whitmore also measured the cash-equivalent value of food stamps in the underground market, where some recipients illegally sell their food stamps for cash. She found that food stamps trade for only about 65 percent of their face value in the underground market. This even lower market valuation of food stamps may reflect the fact that people selling them in this market put a particularly low value on the stamps. Thus, they are willing to risk breaking the law to trade them for cash.

FOR CRITICAL ANALYSIS
Who unambiguously gains from the food stamp program? (Hint: Note that many food stamp recipients buy more food than they would if they received cash transfers instead.)

The Earned Income Tax Credit Program. In 1975, the Earned Income Tax Credit (EITC) Program was created to provide rebates of Social Security taxes to low-income workers. Over one-fifth of all tax returns claim an earned income tax credit; each year the federal government grants more than $36 billion in these credits. In some states, such as Mississippi, nearly half of all families are eligible for an EITC. The program works as follows: Single-income households with two children that report income of less than about $36,000 (exclusive of welfare payments) receive EITC benefits up to about $5,000. There is a catch, though. Those with earnings up to a threshold of about $11,000 receive higher benefits as their incomes rise. But families earning more than this threshold income are penalized about 18 cents for every dollar they earn above the income threshold. Thus, on net the EITC discourages work by low- or moderate-income earners more than it rewards work. In particular, it discourages low-income earners from taking on second jobs. The Government Accountability Office estimates that hours worked by working wives in EITC-beneficiary households have consequently decreased by 15 percent. The average EITC recipient works 1,700 hours a year compared to a normal work year of about 2,000 hours.

No Apparent Reduction in Poverty Rates

In spite of the numerous programs in existence and the hundreds of billions of dollars transferred to the poor, the officially defined rate of poverty in the United States has shown no long-run tendency to decline. From 1945 until the early 1970s, the percentage of U.S. residents in poverty fell steadily every year. As panel (b) of Figure 31-6 on page 795 shows, it reached a low of around 11 percent in 1974, shot back up beyond 15 percent in 1983, fell to 13.1 percent in 1990, and has since fallen to near 12 percent. Why this pattern has emerged is a real puzzle. Since the War on Poverty was launched under President Lyndon B. Johnson in 1965, more than $12 trillion has been transferred to the poor, and yet more U.S. residents are poor today than ever before. This fact created the political will to pass the Welfare Reform Act of 1996, putting limits on people's use of welfare. The law's goal has been to get people off welfare and into jobs.

QUICK QUIZ

If poverty is defined in _____ terms, economic growth eventually decreases the number of officially defined poor. If poverty is defined in _____ terms, however, we will never eliminate it.

Although the relative position of the _____ measured by household _____ seems to have worsened, household spending by the bottom 20 percent of households compared to that of the top 20 percent has shown little change since the 1960s.

Major attacks on poverty have been made through social insurance programs, including _____ Security, _____ Security Income (SSI), Temporary Assistance to Needy Families, the _____ _____ tax credit, and _____ stamps.

See page 812 for the answers. Review concepts from this section in MyEconLab.

HEALTH CARE

It may seem strange to be reading about health care in a chapter on the distribution of income and poverty. Yet health care is intimately related to those two topics. For example, sometimes people become poor because they do not have adequate health insurance

FIGURE 31-8
Percentage of Total National Income Spent on Health Care in the United States

The portion of total national income spent on health care has risen steadily since 1965.

Sources: U.S. Department of Commerce; U.S. Department of Health and Human Services; Deloitte and Touche LLP; VHA, Inc.

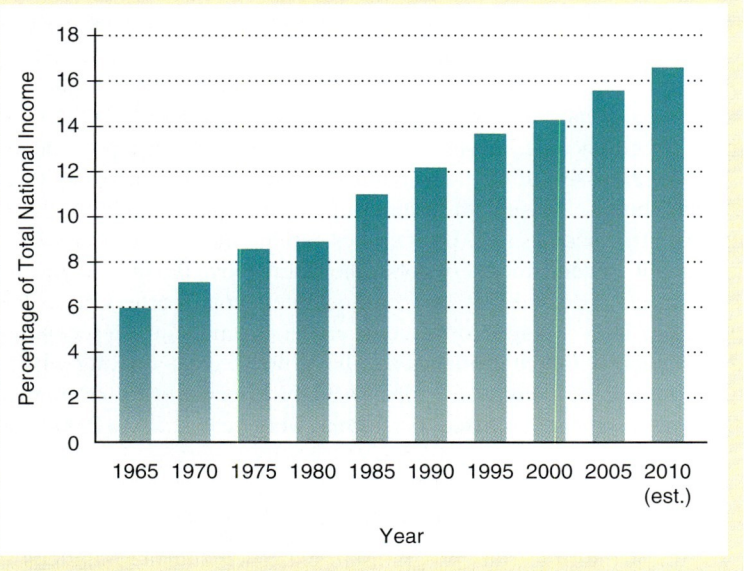

(or have none at all), fall ill, and deplete all of their wealth obtaining medical care. Moreover, some individuals remain in certain jobs simply because their employer's health care package seems so good that they are afraid to change jobs and risk not being covered by health insurance in the process. Finally, as you will see, much of the cause of the increased health care spending in the United States can be attributed to a change in the incentives that U.S. residents face.

The U.S. Health Care Situation

Spending for health care is estimated to account for about 16 percent of U.S. real GDP. You can see from Figure 31-8 that in 1965, about 6 percent of annual income was spent on health care, but that percentage has been increasing ever since. Per capita spending on health care is greater in the United States than anywhere else in the world today. On a per capita basis, we spend more than twice as much as citizens of Luxembourg, Austria, Australia, Japan, and Denmark. We spend almost three times as much on a per capita basis as citizens of Spain and Ireland.

Why Have Health Care Costs Risen So Much? There are numerous explanations for why health care costs have risen so much. At least one has to do with changing demographics: The U.S. population is getting older.

The Age–Health Care Expenditure Equation. The top 5 percent of health care users incur over 50 percent of all health costs. The bottom 70 percent of health care users account for only 10 percent of health care expenditures. Not surprisingly, the elderly make up most of the top users of health care services. Nursing home expenditures are made primarily by people older than 70. The use of hospitals is also dominated by the aged.

The U.S. population is aging steadily. More than 13 percent of the more than 300 million U.S. residents are over 65. It is estimated that by the year 2035, senior citizens will comprise about 22 percent of our population. This aging population stimulates the demand for health care. The elderly consume more than four times as much per capita health care services as the rest of the population. In short, whatever the demand for health care services is today, it is likely to be considerably higher in the future as the U.S. population ages.

New Technologies. Another reason that health care costs have risen so dramatically is advancing technology. Each CT (computerized tomography) scanner costs at least $100,000. An MRI (magnetic resonance imaging) scanner can cost over $2 million. A PET (positron emission tomography) scanner costs around $4 million. All of these machines have become increasingly available in recent decades and are desired throughout the country. Typical fees for procedures using them range from $300 to $400 for a CT scan to as high as $2,000 for a PET scan. The development of new technologies that help physicians and hospitals prolong human life is an ongoing process in an ever-advancing industry. New procedures at even higher prices can be expected in the future.

Third-Party Financing. Currently, government spending on health care constitutes over 40 percent of total health care spending (of which the *federal* government pays about 70 percent). Private insurance accounts for a little over 35 percent of payments for health care. The remainder—less than 20 percent—is paid directly by individuals. Figure 31-9 shows the change in the payment scheme for medical care in the United States since 1930. Medicare and Medicaid are the main sources of hospital and other medical benefits to 40 million U.S. residents, most of whom are over 65. Medicaid—the joint state-federal program—provides long-term health care, particularly for people living in nursing homes. Medicare, Medicaid, and private insurance companies are considered **third parties** in the medical care equation. Caregivers and patients are the two primary parties. When third parties step in to pay for medical care, the quantity demanded of those services increases. For example, when Medicare and Medicaid went into effect in the 1960s, the volume of federal government–reimbursed medical services increased by more than 65 percent.

Third parties
Parties who are not directly involved in a given activity or transaction. For example, in the relationship between caregivers and patients, fees may be paid by third parties (insurance companies, government).

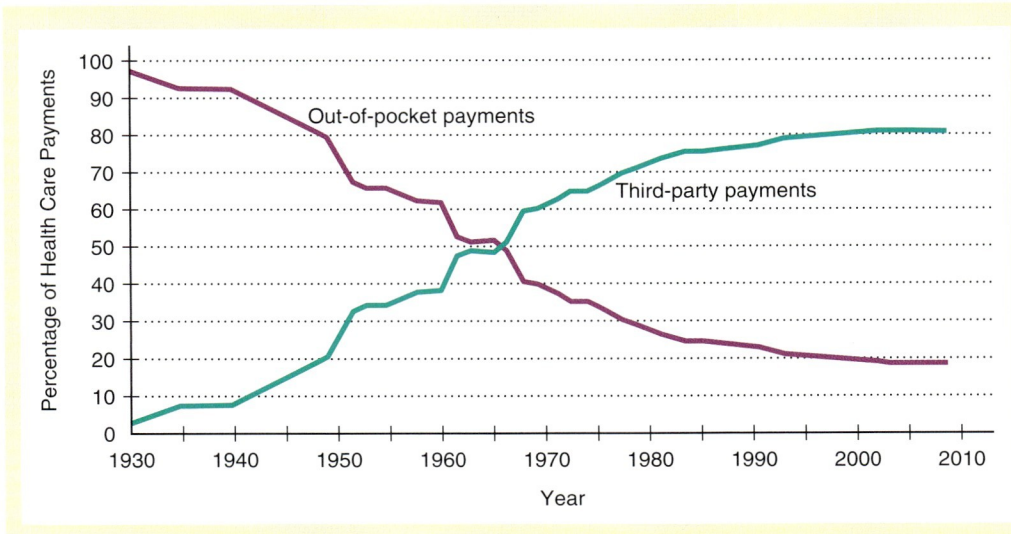

FIGURE 31-9
Third-Party versus Out-of-Pocket Health Care Payments

Out-of-pocket payments for health care services have been falling steadily since the 1930s. In contrast, third-party payments for health care have risen to the point that they account for over 80 percent of all such outlays today.

Sources: Health Care Financing Administration; U.S. Department of Health and Human Services.

The availability of third-party payments for costly medical care has generated increases in the availability of hospital beds. Between 1974 and 2007, the number of hospital beds increased by over 50 percent. Present occupancy rates are only around 65 percent.

How are present eligibility requirements for Medicaid contributing to rapid growth of this federally funded third-party program?

POLICY EXAMPLE

How "Elder Law" Fuels the Growth of Medicaid

Under the federal rules governing the Medicaid program, homes, businesses, automobiles, and term-life insurance policies are excluded from calculating whether a senior is sufficiently "poor" to qualify for Medicaid. Furthermore, an elderly individual can give most of her assets to her children and grandchildren and become eligible for Medicaid three years later with no questions asked.

Today, an entire financial-planning industry specializes in "elder law," counseling seniors about how to work within these rules to shift the costs of nursing-home care away from their family members to the federal government. At the end of the 1960s, families paid about 56 percent of the total expenditures on U.S. nursing-home care out of their own pockets, and Medicaid paid about 24 percent. Today, families pay less than 28 percent of all U.S. nursing-home costs, and Medicaid pays nearly 50 percent. (The rest is paid by private insurance benefits.)

FOR CRITICAL ANALYSIS

How does a federal rule requiring private nursing homes to accept Medicaid from a patient who has already been in residence for at least one year help higher-income seniors obtain long-term, Medicaid-sponsored care at higher-quality nursing homes? (Hint: Is a low-income person likely to be able to afford the more than $50,000 in out-of-pocket payments that is typically required by a higher-quality nursing home for a year's stay before Medicaid will finance the remaining years of care?)

Price, Quantity Demanded, and the Question of Moral Hazard. Although some people may think that the demand for health care is insensitive to price changes, theory clearly indicates otherwise. Look at Figure 31-10. There you see a hypothetical demand curve for health care services. To the extent that third parties—whether government or private insurance—pay for health care, the out-of-pocket cost, or net price, to the individual

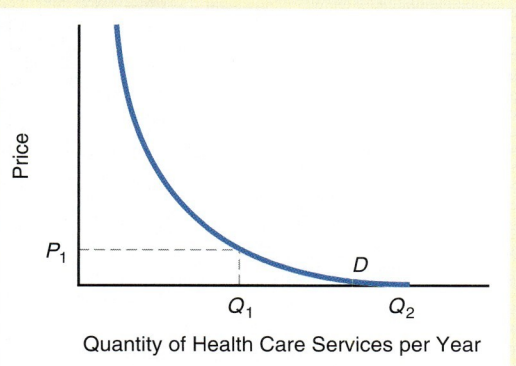

FIGURE 31-10

The Demand for Health Care Services

At price P_1, the quantity of health care services demanded per year would hypothetically be Q_1. If the price fell to zero (third-party payment with zero deductible), the quantity demanded would expand to Q_2.

decreases. If all medical expenses were paid for by third parties, dropping the price to zero in Figure 31-10, the quantity demanded would increase.

One of the issues here has to do with the problem of *moral hazard*. Consider two individuals with two different health insurance policies. The first policy pays for all medical expenses, but under the second, the individual has to pay the first $1,000 a year (this amount is known as the *deductible*). Will the behavior of the two individuals be different? Generally, the answer is yes. The individual with no deductible is more likely to seek treatment for health problems after they develop rather than try to avoid them and will generally seek medical attention on a more regular basis. In contrast, the individual who faces the first $1,000 of medical expenses each year will tend to engage in more wellness activities and will be less inclined to seek medical care for minor problems. The moral hazard here is that the individual with the zero deductible for medical care expenses may engage in a less healthful lifestyle than will the individual with the $1,000 deductible.

Moral Hazard as It Affects Physicians and Hospitals. The issue of moral hazard also has a direct effect on the behavior of physicians and hospital administrators. Due to third-party payments, patients rarely have to worry about the expense of operations and other medical procedures. As a consequence, both physicians and hospitals order more procedures. Physicians are typically reimbursed on the basis of medical procedures. Thus, they have no financial interest in trying to keep hospital costs down. Indeed, many have an incentive to raise costs.

Such actions are most evident with terminally ill patients. A physician may order a CT scan and other costly procedures for a terminally ill patient. The physician knows that Medicare or some other type of insurance will pay. Then the physician can charge a fee for analyzing the CT scan. Fully 30 percent of Medicare expenditures are for U.S. residents who are in the last six months of their lives.

How have some physicians found a way to *profit* from increasing the number of tests financed by third parties such as private insurers and the government?

EXAMPLE

To Some Physicians, the "M" in Medicaid Stands for "Markup"

One factor contributing to annual rates of growth in third-party expenses incurred by Medicaid, Medicare, and private health insurers is a physician-based moral hazard problem. Public and private third-party payment programs normally specify the rates they will pay for various types of health care services, such as tests ordered by physicians. Suppose, for instance, that a physician knows that a specific test will be covered at a $100 rate by Medicaid, but the physician also knows that he can arrange for the test to be performed by a testing center for only $30. The physician can then send a tissue sample to the testing center, pay the center $30 to perform the test, and bill Medicaid for $100. His profit is then $70 per test. Thus, if the physician can order, say, 200 tests per year and receive this amount of profit per test, he can increase his annual income by $14,000.

No one knows exactly how widespread such practices are among U.S. physicians. Nevertheless, a recent study found that when rules permit physicians to have tests performed by facilities outside their own offices, physicians order 28 percent more tests than they do when the rules of third-party payers prohibit external testing. Thus, there is at least the *appearance* that some physicians are finding ways to profit from requiring patients to undergo additional tests.

FOR CRITICAL ANALYSIS
Who provides the funds that create the profits that some physicians earn from billing Medicaid and Medicare more than they actually pay outside centers for tests?

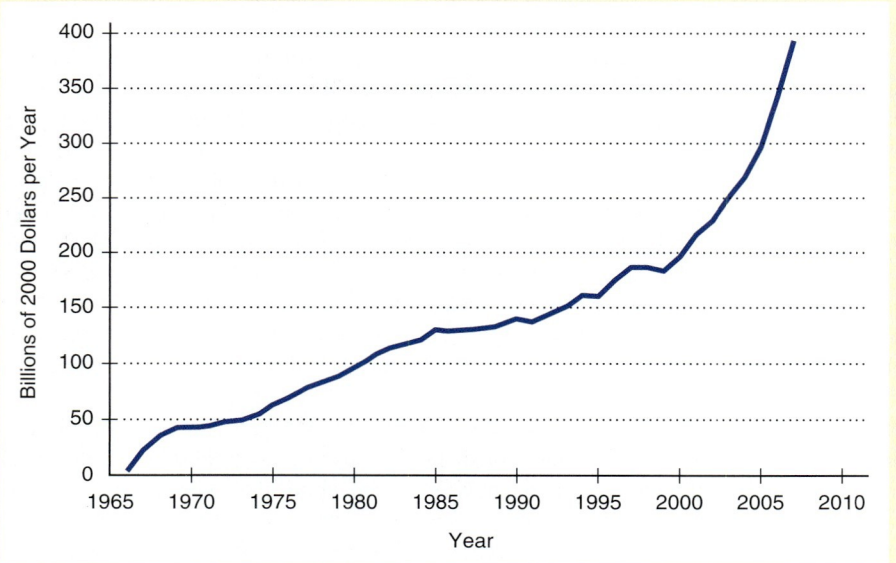

FIGURE 31-11

Federal Medicare Spending

Federal spending on Medicare has increased about 10 percent per year, after adjusting for inflation, since its inception in 1966. (All figures expressed in constant 2000 dollars per year.)

Sources: *Economic Report of the President;* U.S. Bureau of Labor Statistics.

Rising Medicare expenditures are one of the most serious problems facing the federal government today. The number of beneficiaries has increased from 19.1 million in 1966 (first year of operation) to more than 40 million in 2007. Figure 31-11 shows that federal spending on Medicare has been growing at over 10 percent per year, adjusted for inflation. The rate of growth in Medicare spending is likely to be even higher in the future as a result of the Medicare prescription drug benefit that was implemented in 2006.

Is National Health Insurance the Answer?

Proponents of a national health care system believe that the current system relies too heavily on private insurers. They argue in favor of a Canadian-style system. In Canada, the government sets the fees that are paid to each physician for seeing a patient and prohibits private practice. The Canadian government also imposes a cap on the income that any physician can receive in a given year. The Canadian federal government provides a specified amount of funding to hospitals, leaving it to them to decide how to allocate the funds. If we were to follow the Canadian model, the average U.S. resident would receive fewer health services than at present. Hospital stays would be longer, but there would be fewer tests and procedures.

Alternatives to a national health care policy involve some type of national health insurance, perhaps offered only to people who qualify on the basis of low annual income. A number of politicians have offered variations on such a program. The over 40 million U.S. residents who have no health insurance at some time during each year might benefit. The share of annual national income that goes to health care expenditures would rise, however. Also, federal government spending might increase by another $60 billion to $100 billion (or more) per year to pay for the program.

Countering the Moral Hazard Problem: A Health Savings Account

As an alternative to completely changing the U.S. health care industry, in 2003 Congress authorized **health savings accounts (HSAs).** These accounts replaced experimental *medical savings accounts* that Congress had previously permitted but had limited to 700,000 accounts nationwide. Anyone with a relatively high health insurance deductible—a minimum level of out-of-pocket expenses of $1,000 for an individual or $2,000 for a family—can open an HSA at a financial institution offering such accounts. Individuals younger than 55 can make annual deposits of up to $2,650 per person per year, and families can deposit as much as $5,250 per year. Once a person reaches the age of 55, allowable deposits can be even higher, but contributions must end once the person reaches 65 and becomes eligible for Medicare.

People with HSAs may use deposited funds and tax-free interest earnings to cover any out-of-pocket health care expenses. In addition, they can draw on HSAs to pay health insurance premiums if they become unemployed or to cover medical expenses they incur after they have retired. There is a 10 percent penalty for most withdrawals used for nonmedical purposes before retirement, but when a person retires, funds in an HSA may be used to supplement other sources of income. A single person depositing the maximum amount each year with no withdrawals will have hundreds of thousands of dollars in the account after 40 years.

Health savings account (HSA)
A tax-exempt health care account into which individuals can pay on a regular basis and out of which medical expenses can be paid.

ECONOMICS FRONT AND CENTER

To read about how developments in the use of HSAs by the insurance industry are helping combat the moral hazard problem, consider **Competing to Inform Owners of Health Savings Accounts**, on page 806.

Combating Moral Hazard. A major benefit of an HSA is that the moral hazard problem is reduced. Individuals ultimately pay for their own *minor* medical expenses. They do not have the incentive to seek medical care as frequently for minor problems. In addition, they have an incentive to engage in wellness activities. Finally, for those using an HSA, the physician-patient relationship remains intact because third parties (insurance companies or the government) do not intervene in paying or monitoring medical expenses. Patients with HSAs usually will not allow physicians to routinely order expensive tests for every minor ache or pain because they get to keep any funds saved in the HSA.

Critics' Responses. Some critics argue that because individuals get to keep whatever they don't spend from their HSAs, they will forgo necessary visits to medical care facilities and may develop more serious medical problems as a consequence. Other critics argue that HSAs will sabotage managed care plans. Under managed care plans, deductibles are either reduced or eliminated completely. In exchange, managed health care plan participants are extremely limited in physician choice. Just the opposite is true with HSAs—high deductibles and unlimited choice of physicians.

QUICK QUIZ

Health care costs have risen because (1) our population has been getting older and the elderly use _____ health care services, (2) new technologies and medicines cost more, and (3) _____-_____ financing (private and government-sponsored health insurance) _____ the incentive for individuals to decrease their spending on health care services.

_____ health insurance has been proposed as an answer to our current problems, but it does little to alter the reasons why health care costs continue to rise.

In 2003, Congress authorized _____ _____ accounts, which allow individuals to set aside funds that are tax-exempt and can be used only for medical care. Whatever is left over becomes a type of _____ account.

See page 812 for the answers. Review concepts from this section in MyEconLab.

CASE STUDY: ECONOMICS FRONT AND CENTER

Competing to Inform Owners of Health Savings Accounts

Williams is a senior executive at Consumers Mutual Insurance Company. One of the company's products is a health insurance policy that utilizes health savings accounts (HSAs). When faced with medical expenses, a policyholder pays for care by withdrawing funds from an HSA until a specified deductible is reached. Beyond this point, Consumers Mutual pays a large portion of the remaining medical expenses covered by its policies.

Williams has a problem. Many other insurers have begun offering similar health insurance plans linked to HSAs. Market clearing premium rates have fallen to a sufficiently low level that Consumers Mutual would no longer be able to earn a normal profit if it tried to attract new customers by reducing its premium rates. Thus, the company must find another way to distinguish its HSA-linked policies from those offered by its competitors.

Williams has discovered that Aetna Health Insurance has recently found a new way to compete. Aetna now provides its policyholders with information about the insurance reimbursements it pays all physicians. This information helps policyholders identify the physicians who charge the lowest fees. By choosing to utilize the services of these physicians, policyholders can thereby reduce their own deductible payments from their HSAs. By serving as an information provider as well as an insurer, Aetna has improved the quality of its plan and induced more people to buy its policies. Williams is convinced that if Consumers Mutual follows Aetna's example, it also will gain customers. He begins composing a memorandum to other senior managers suggesting that Consumers Mutual should "one-up" Aetna. The company, he writes, should immediately put a group of employees to work on setting up a system for daily Web postings of the fees the company pays when it reimburses physicians for insured services.

CRITICAL ANALYSIS QUESTIONS

1. *How do health insurance policies requiring people to pay a specified dollar amount as a deductible from their own HSAs provide incentives for people to reduce overall expenditures on medical care?*

2. *In what way might Aetna's publication of physicians' fees further contribute to lower expenditures on health care?*

Is the United States No Longer an Income-Mobile Nation?

Issues and Applications

Economists rarely use terms such as "wealthy upper class" or "lower-class poor," because the concept of class can mean different things to different observers. In contrast, incomes are measurable, allowing economists to objectively classify people into high-income groups versus low-income groups. Furthermore, economists have found evidence of considerable *mobility* within the U.S. income distribution. At one point in time, a person or a family may occupy one position within the income distribution, but at a later time the same individual or family may be at a very different location within the distribution of income.

Concepts Applied
- Distribution of Income
- Age-Earnings Profile
- Lorenz Curve

Past Evidence Supporting High U.S. Income Mobility

Traditionally, it has not been uncommon for U.S. residents who start off with relatively low incomes and fit within what some might call a "poor lower class" to end up in later years earning relatively high incomes, even fitting within what some might call a "wealthy upper class." For such individuals, often referred to as "self-made people," the age-earnings profile is very steep: Annual income is low at a young age but increases substantially by middle age.

Mobility within the U.S. distribution of income has been even more pronounced for family groups. It is not unusual, for example, for the children of unskilled, lower-income laborers to learn skills that enable them to earn much higher incomes than their parents. Hence, there has been considerable U.S. income mobility across generations as well as within generations. Estimates from the 1980s indicated that the chances that a child would end up in the same position in the income distribution as the child's parents were only 20 percent higher than the chances that children born outside that income grouping would end up there. By that measure, a low-income individual's grandchild would have only a slightly lower likelihood than the grandchild of a high-income person of attaining a place within the higher-income grouping.

Is Mobility Giving Way to a More Rigid Income-Class Structure?

Recently, some economists have questioned whether there is still as much mobility within the U.S. income distribution. Estimates in the 2000s imply that a child now is 60 percent more likely than others to end up in the same income grouping as the child's parents. These higher estimates indicate that even a great-grandfather's high income could give a child an edge in attaining a high-income classification within the U.S. income distribution. They also indicate a greater likelihood that a child born to a family in a low-income grouping will be stuck in that category. Indeed, some studies comparing income mobility across countries have concluded that there is both more income inequality and less income mobility in the United States than in most other developed countries.

Researchers who have concluded that U.S. income mobility is declining have offered various explanations. For instance, at present a key determinant of income is educational attainment. Possibly, some suggest, higher-income people are able to purchase more and better education for their children, thereby increasing the likelihood that their children will also earn higher incomes. Furthermore, in years past a U.S. family's income prospects might improve when the family moved from one U.S. region to another. Today, income differences across regions are smaller, so physical mobility may contribute less to income mobility than in years past.

Recent Immigrants Complicate Interpreting the Data

Another factor, immigration, may also be affecting the income-mobility data. For example, many new immigrants to the United States initially have low incomes. The arrival of so many immigrants in recent years has contributed to bulges in the lower-income portions of the U.S. income distribution and a more bowed U.S. Lorenz curve. Thus, one reason that there is greater observed income inequality in the United States than in other developed nations is that the United States is much more open to immigration.

The recent wave of immigration has also complicated assessing whether U.S. income mobility has truly decreased as much as recent studies have indicated. Families of immigrants often experience significant income gains during the years following their arrival in the United States. Nevertheless, most studies of income mobility track only the incomes of families that have been in the United States for generations. Many income-mobility studies exclude the families of relatively recent immigrants—which naturally biases these studies against finding as much evidence of income mobility among *all* people now residing within the United States. Thus, although U.S. income mobility may indeed have decreased, it may also be true that failing to include the income gains of recent immigrants artificially depresses measures of mobility within the U.S. distribution of income.

Log in to **MyEconLab**, click on "Economic News," and test your understanding of the chapter by answering interactive questions that relate directly to this issue.

For Critical Analysis

1. Could a nation's income mobility ever be increasing even as its Lorenz curve becomes more outwardly bowed? (Hint: Income mobility is typically measured *between* years, whereas the distribution of income summarized by a Lorenz curve is usually measured *within* a given year.)

2. Why do you suppose that some economists and policymakers advocate using income mobility within the distribution of income as a rough measure of the extent to which a merit standard prevails in a nation's economy?

Web Resources

1. For a summary of the evidence on U.S. income mobility between 1969 and 1994, go to www.econtoday.com/ch31.

2. Read a summary of some of the recent evidence indicating that there may be less U.S. income mobility at www.econtoday.com/ch31.

Research Project

Suppose that every year during a 20-year period, a nation experiences no economic growth, so its per capita real GDP remains at a very low level. Nevertheless, it has nearly perfect income equality, so its Lorenz curve is almost a straight line each year. How much income mobility will this nation experience during this interval? Now suppose that international investment in this nation has recently created businesses employing a portion of the nation's population. After observing this development, an economist makes the following argument: "Results of this business upturn will be increased economic growth, a higher level of per capita real GDP, an increase in income mobility, and, within a few years, a more unequal distribution of income." Evaluate this prediction.

WHAT YOU SHOULD KNOW		WHERE TO GO TO PRACTICE
Using a Lorenz Curve to Represent a Nation's Income Distribution A Lorenz curve is a diagram that illustrates the distribution of income geometrically by measuring the percentage of households in relation to the cumulative percentage of income earnings. A perfectly straight Lorenz curve depicts perfect income equality because at each percentage of households measured along a straight-line Lorenz curve, those households earn exactly the same percentage of income. The more bowed a Lorenz curve is, the more unequally income is distributed.	distribution of income, 784 Lorenz curve, 784 income in kind, 785 **Key figures** Figure 31-1, 785 Figure 31-2, 785 Figure 31-3, 787	• **MyEconLab** Study Plan 31.1 • Audio introduction to Chapter 31 • Animated Figures 31-1, 31-2, and 31-3
Key Determinants of Income Differences Across Individuals Because of the age-earnings cycle, in which people typically begin working at relatively low incomes when young, age is an important factor influencing income differences. So are marginal productivity differences, which arise from differences in talent, experience, and training due to different investments in human capital. Discrimination likely plays a role as well, and economists attribute some of the unexplained portions of income differences across people to factors related to discrimination.	age-earnings cycle, 789 comparable-worth doctrine, 793 **Key figure** Figure 31-5, 789	• **MyEconLab** Study Plan 31.2 • Video: The Determinants of Income Differences • Animated Figure 31-5
Theories of Desired Income Distribution Economists agree that determining how income ought to be distributed is a normative issue influenced by alternative notions of economic justice. Nevertheless, two theories of desired income distribution receive considerable attention. One is the productivity standard (also called the contributive or merit standard), according to which each person receives income according to the value of what the person produces. The other is the egalitarian principle of income distribution, which proposes that each person should receive exactly the same income.		• **MyEconLab** Study Plan 31.3
Alternative Approaches to Measuring and Addressing Poverty One approach to measuring poverty is to define an absolute poverty standard, such as a specific and unchanging income level. If an absolute measure of poverty is used and the economy experiences persistent real growth, poverty will eventually disappear. Another approach defines poverty in terms of income levels relative to the rest of the population. Under this definition, poverty exists as long as the distribution of incomes is unequal. Official poverty measures are often based on pretax income and fail to take transfer payments into account. Currently,	**Key figure** Figure 31-6, 795	• **MyEconLab** Study Plan 31.4 • Video: Defining Poverty • Animated Figure 31-6

WHAT YOU SHOULD KNOW

the U.S. government seeks to address poverty via income maintenance programs such as Social Security, Supplemental Security Income, Temporary Assistance to Needy Families, food stamps, and the Earned Income Tax Credit Program.

Major Reasons for Rising Health Care Costs Spending on health care as a percentage of total U.S. national income has increased during recent decades. One reason is that the U.S. population is aging, and older people typically experience more health problems. Another contributing factor is the adoption of higher-quality but also higher-priced technologies for diagnosing and treating health problems. In addition, third-party financing of health care expenditures by private and government insurance programs gives covered individuals an incentive to purchase more health care than they would if they paid all expenses out of pocket. Moral hazard problems can also arise because consumers may be more likely to seek treatment for insured health problems after they develop instead of trying to avoid them, and physicians and hospitals may order more procedures than they otherwise would require.

third parties, 801
Key figures
Figure 31-8, 800
Figure 31-10, 802

- **MyEconLab** Study Plan 31.5
- Animated Figures 31-8 and 31-10

Alternative Approaches to Paying for Health Care An alternative approach to funding health care would be to rely less on private insurers and more on governmental funding of care for all citizens. Under such a system, the government typically sets fees and establishes limits on access to care. Another approach would be to establish an income-based national health insurance program, in which only lower-income people would qualify for government assistance in meeting their health care expenses. Another option, which Congress authorized in 2003, is to provide incentives for people to save some of their income in health savings accounts, from which they can draw funds to pay for health care expenses in the future.

health savings account (HSA), 805

- **MyEconLab** Study Plan 31.5

Log in to MyEconLab, take a chapter test, and get a personalized Study Plan that tells you which concepts you understand and which ones you need to review. From there, MyEconLab will give you further practice, tutorials, animations, videos, and guided solutions.

Log in to www.myeconlab.com

PROBLEMS

Select problems, indicated by a blue oval , are assignable in MyEconLab.
Answers to the odd-numbered problems appear at the back of the book.

31-1. Consider the graph on page 811, which depicts Lorenz curves for countries X, Y, and Z.
   a. Which country has the least income inequality?
   b. Which country has the most income inequality?
   c. Countries Y and Z are identical in all but one respect: population distribution. The share of the population made up of children below working age is much higher in country Z. Recently, however, birthrates

have declined in country Z and risen in country Y. Assuming that the countries remain identical in all other respects, would you expect that in 20 years the Lorenz curves for the two countries will be closer together or farther apart? (Hint: According to the age-earnings cycle, what typically happens to income as an individual begins working and ages?)

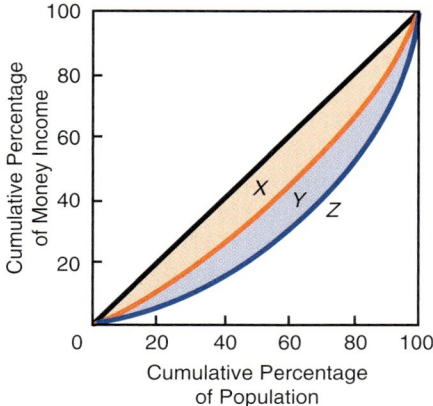

31-2. Consider the following estimates from the early 2000s of shares of income to each group. Use graph paper or a hand-drawn diagram to draw rough Lorenz curves for each country. Which has the most nearly equal distribution, based on your diagram?

Country	Poorest 40%	Next 30%	Next 20%	Richest 10%
Bolivia	13	21	26	40
Chile	13	20	26	41
Uruguay	22	26	26	26

31-3. Suppose that the 20 percent of people with the highest incomes decide to increase their annual giving to charities, which pass nearly all the funds on to the 20 percent of people with the lowest incomes. What is the effect on the shape of the Lorenz curve?

31-4. Suppose that a nation has implemented a system for applying a tax rate of 2 percent to the incomes earned by the 10 percent of its residents with the highest incomes. All funds collected are then transferred directly to the 10 percent of the nation's residents with the lowest incomes.

  a. What is the general effect on the shape of a Lorenz curve based on incomes prior to collection and redistribution of the tax?

  b. What is the general effect on the shape of a Lorenz curve based on after-tax, post-redistribution incomes?

31-5. Estimates indicate that during the early 2000s, the poorest 40 percent of the population earned about 15 percent of total income in Argentina. In Brazil, the poorest 40 percent earned about 10 percent of total income. The next-highest 30 percent of income earners in Argentina received roughly 25 percent of total income. By contrast, in Brazil, the next-highest 30 percent of income earners received approximately 20 percent of total income. Can you determine, without drawing a diagram (though you can if you wish), which country's Lorenz curve was bowed out farther to the right?

31-6. Explain why the productivity standard for the distribution of income entails rewarding people based on their contribution to society's total output. Why does the productivity standard typically fail to yield an equal distribution of income?

31-7. Identify whether each of the following proposed poverty measures is an absolute or relative measure of poverty, and discuss whether poverty could ever be eliminated if that measure were utilized.

  a. An inflation-adjusted annual income of $25,000 for an urban family of four
  b. Individuals with annual incomes among the lowest 15 percent
  c. An inflation-adjusted annual income of $10,000 per person

31-8. Some economists have argued that if the government wishes to subsidize health care, it should instead provide predetermined sums of payments (based on the type of health care problems experienced) directly to patients, who then would be free to choose their health care providers. Whether or not you agree, can you give an economic rationale for this approach to governmental health care funding?

31-9. Suppose that a government agency guarantees to pay all of an individual's future health care expenses after the end of this year, so that the effective price of health care for the individual will be zero from that date onward. In what ways might this well-intended policy induce the individual to consume "excessive" health care services in future years?

31-10. Suppose that a group of physicians establishes a joint practice in a remote area. This group provides the only health care available to people in the local community, and its objective is to maximize total economic profits for the group's members. Draw a diagram illustrating how the price and quantity of health care will be determined in this community. (Hint: How does a single producer of any service determine its output and price?)

31-11. A government agency determines that the entire community discussed in Problem 31-10 qualifies for a special program in which the government will pay for a number of health care services that most residents previously had not consumed. Many residents immediately make appointments with the community physicians' group. Given the information in Problem 31-10, what is the likely effect on the profit-maximizing price and the equilibrium quantity of health care services provided by the physicians' group in this community?

31-12. A government agency notifies the physicians' group in Problem 31-10 that to continue providing services in the community, the group must document its activities. The resulting paperwork expenses raise the cost of each unit of health care services that the group provides. What is the likely effect on the profit-maximizing price and the equilibrium quantity of health care services provided by the physicians' group in this community?

31-13. As discussed in this chapter, interest-bearing health savings accounts (HSAs) allow individuals with qualifying health insurance plans to use deposited funds to pay out-of-pocket medical expenses. Subject to penalties and taxation, holders of HSAs can use funds in the accounts and tax-free interest earnings to pay non-health-related expenses if they wish. Many people, however, participate in optional *health reimbursement accounts (HRAs)* offered alongside employer-provided health insurance plans. HRAs, into which people typically make payments via tax-free deductions from their weekly or monthly earnings, are non-interest-bearing and can be used only to pay medical expenses. Any funds in HRAs that individuals fail to use for medical expenses within a calendar year revert to the employer at the end of the year. Is an HSA or an HRA more likely to create moral hazard problems? Explain your reasoning.

ECONOMICS ON THE NET

Measuring Poverty Many economists believe that there are problems with the current official measure of poverty. In this application, you will learn about some of these problems and will be able to examine an alternative poverty measure that one group of economists has proposed.

Title: Joint Center for Poverty Research (JCPR)

Navigation: Go to www.econtoday.com/ch31 to visit the JCPR's home page. Click on *Publications*. Select the complete listing of policy briefs. Click on the *Policy Brief* titled "Measuring Poverty—A New Approach."

Application Read the article; then answer the following questions.

1. How is the current official poverty income level calculated? What is the main problem with this way of calculating the threshold income for classifying impoverished households?

2. What is the alternative conceptual measure of poverty that the authors propose? How does it differ from the current measure?

For Group Study and Analysis Discuss the two measures of poverty discussed in the article. What people would no longer be classified as living in poverty under the proposed measure of poverty? What people would join the ranks of those classified as among the impoverished in the United States? How might adopting the new measure of poverty affect efforts to address the U.S. poverty problem?

ANSWERS TO QUICK QUIZZES

p. 788: (i) income . . . equality . . . unequally; (ii) assets . . . more

p. 794: (i) age-earnings; (ii) revenue . . . revenue; (iii) talent . . . education . . . experience . . . training; (iv) human . . . opportunity; (v) Discrimination; (vi) comparable-worth . . . comparable worth; (vii) productivity . . . equality

p. 799: (i) absolute . . . relative; (ii) poor . . . income; (iii) Social . . . Supplemental . . . earned income . . . food

p. 805: (i) more . . . third-party . . . reduces; (ii) National; (iii) health savings . . . retirement

Environmental Economics

32

Since 1971, when their population had dwindled to fewer than 25,000, wild horses have been designated as a protected U.S. natural resource. A number of these wild horses are descended from horses brought to the North American continent by Spanish conquistadors in the early 1500s. Many people see the horses as a living symbol of the nation's natural beauty. Others, however, regard them as pests that have overpopulated dwindling public lands. One thing is certain: U.S. taxpayers spend more than $40 million per year on more than 50,000 wild horses and 5,000 of their cousins, wild burros that are also protected by law. In this chapter, you will learn about the economics of wild species and other natural resources.

Learning Objectives

After reading this chapter, you should be able to:

1. Distinguish between private costs and social costs
2. Understand market externalities and possible ways to correct externalities
3. Describe how economists can conceptually determine the optimal quantity of pollution
4. Explain the roles of private and common property rights in alternative approaches to addressing the problem of pollution
5. Discuss how the assignment of property rights may influence the fates of endangered species
6. Contrast the benefits and costs of recycling scarce resources

MyEconLab helps you master each objective and study more efficiently. See end of chapter for details.

Did You Know That...

a group of U.S. professors recently proposed that the U.S. government consider transplanting hundreds of African creatures—including lions, elephants, and cheetahs—to lands that the government already owns or would purchase within the Great Plains of the United States? They suggested that establishing preserves off limits to human activities would help preserve African species that are in danger of extinction and restore biodiversity in North America. A number of other scientists pointed out that previous efforts to relocate species halfway around the world, such as the introduction of rabbits and poisonous cane toads in Australia, have had negative environmental consequences. To an economist, however, an obvious question was how the social benefits of protecting African species in the United States might compare with the costs of transporting animals, buying lands, and establishing and maintaining preserves.

The economic way of thinking about endangered species requires considering the costs of protecting endangered species. Likewise, the economic way of thinking about nonrenewable resources or the environment requires taking into account the costs of resource conservation and environmental protection. What additional portion of your weekly wages are you willing to give up to purchase lands to establish preserves for endangered species? To some people, framing questions in terms of the dollars-and-cents costs of environmental improvement sounds anti-ecological. But this is not so. Economists want to help citizens and policymakers opt for informed policies that have the maximum possible *net* benefits (benefits minus costs). As you will see, every decision in favor of "the environment" involves a trade-off.

PRIVATE VERSUS SOCIAL COSTS

Human actions often give rise to unwanted side effects—the destruction of our environment is one. Human actions generate pollutants that go into the air and the water. The question that is often asked is, Why do individuals and businesses continue to create pollution without necessarily paying directly for the negative consequences?

Until now, we've been dealing with settings in which the costs of an individual's actions are borne directly by the individual. When a business has to pay wages to workers, it knows exactly what its labor costs are. When it has to buy materials or build a plant, it knows quite well what these will cost. An individual who has to pay for car repairs or a theater ticket knows exactly what the cost will be. These costs are what we term *private costs*. **Private costs** are borne solely by the individuals who incur them. They are *internal* in the sense that the firm or household must explicitly take account of them.

What about a situation in which a business dumps the waste products from its production process into a nearby river or an individual litters a public park or beach? Obviously, a cost is involved in these actions. When the firm pollutes the water, people downstream suffer the consequences. They may not want to swim in or drink the polluted water. They may also be unable to catch as many fish as before because of the pollution. In the case of littering, the people who come along after our litterer has cluttered the park or the beach are the ones who bear the costs. The cost of these actions is borne by people other than those who commit the actions. The creator of the cost is not the sole bearer. The costs are not internalized by the individual or firm; they are external. When we add *external* costs to *internal*, or private, costs, we get **social costs.** Pollution problems—indeed, all problems pertaining to the environment—may be viewed as situations in which social costs exceed private costs. Because some economic participants pay only the smaller private costs of their actions, not the full social costs, their actions ultimately contribute to higher external

Private costs
Costs borne solely by the individuals who incur them. Also called *internal costs*.

Social costs
The full costs borne by society whenever a resource use occurs. Social costs can be measured by adding external costs to private, or internal, costs.

costs on the rest of society. In such situations in which social and private costs diverge, we therefore see "too much" steel production, automobile driving, and beach littering, to pick only a few of the many possible examples.

The Costs of Polluted Air

Why is the air in cities so polluted from automobile exhaust fumes? When automobile drivers step into their cars, they bear only the private costs of driving. That is, they must pay for the gas, maintenance, depreciation, and insurance on their automobiles. But they cause an additional cost, that of air pollution, which they are not forced to take into account when they make the decision to drive. Air pollution is a cost because it causes harm to individuals—burning eyes, respiratory ailments, and dirtier clothes, cars, and buildings. The air pollution created by automobile exhaust is a cost that individual operators of automobiles do not yet bear directly. The social cost of driving includes all the private costs plus at least the cost of air pollution, which society bears. Decisions made only on the basis of private costs lead to too much automobile driving or, alternatively, to too few resources spent on the reduction of automobile pollution for a given amount of driving. Clean air is a scarce resource used by automobile drivers free of charge. They will use more of it than they would if they had to pay the full social costs.

Externalities

When a private cost differs from a social cost, we say that there is an **externality** because individual decision makers are not paying (internalizing) all the costs. (We briefly covered this topic in Chapter 5.) Some of these costs remain external to the decision-making process. Remember that the full cost of using a scarce resource is borne one way or another by all who live in the society. That is, society must pay the full opportunity cost of any activity that uses scarce resources. The individual decision maker is the firm or the customer, and external costs and benefits will not enter into that individual's or firm's decision-making processes.

Externality
A situation in which a private cost (or benefit) diverges from a social cost (or benefit); a situation in which the costs (or benefits) of an action are not fully borne (or gained) by the two parties engaged in exchange or by an individual engaging in a scarce-resource-using activity.

We might want to view the problem as it is presented in Figure 32-1 on the next page. Here we have the market demand curve, D, for the product X and the supply curve, S_1, for product X. The supply curve, S_1, includes only internal, or private, costs. The intersection of the demand and supply curves as drawn will be at price P_1 and quantity Q_1 (at E_1). We now assume that the production of good X involves externalities that the private firms did not take into account. Those externalities could be air pollution, water pollution, scenery destruction, or anything of that nature.

We know that the social costs of producing product X exceed the private costs. We show this by drawing curve S_2. It is above the original supply curve S_1 because it includes the full social costs of producing the product. If firms could be made to bear these costs, the price would be P_2 and the quantity Q_2 (at E_2). The inclusion of external costs in the decision-making process would lead to a higher-priced product and a decline in quantity produced. Thus, we see that when social costs are not being fully borne by the creators of those costs, the quantity produced is "excessive" because the price is too low.

CORRECTING FOR EXTERNALITIES

We can see here a method for reducing pollution and environmental degradation. Somehow the signals in the economy must be changed so that decision makers will take into account *all* the costs of their actions. In the case of automobile pollution, we might want to

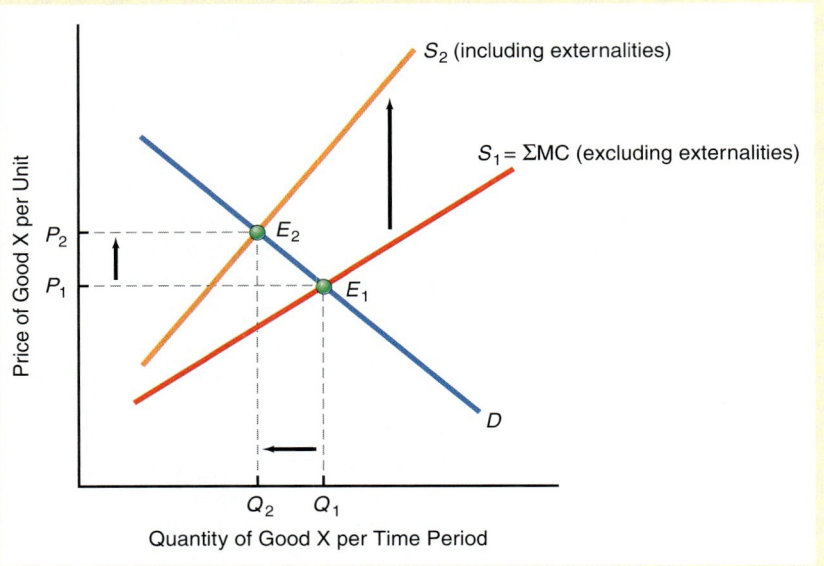

FIGURE 32-1

Reckoning with Full Social Costs

The supply curve, S_1, is equal to the horizontal summation (represented by the capital Greek letter Σ) of the individual marginal cost curves above the respective minimum average variable costs of all the firms producing good X. These individual marginal cost curves include only internal, or private, costs. If the external costs were included and added to the private costs, we would have social costs. The supply curve would shift upward to S_2. In the uncorrected situation, the equilibrium price is P_1, and the equilibrium quantity is Q_1. In the corrected situation, the equilibrium price would rise to P_2, and the equilibrium quantity would fall to Q_2.

devise some method of taxing motorists according to the amount of pollution they cause. In the case of a firm, we might want to devise a system of taxing businesses according to the amount of pollution for which they are responsible. They might then have an incentive to install pollution abatement equipment.

The Polluters' Choice

Facing an additional private cost for polluting, firms will be induced to (1) install pollution abatement equipment or otherwise change production techniques so as to reduce the amount of pollution, (2) reduce pollution-causing activity, or (3) simply pay the price to pollute. The relative costs and benefits of each option for each polluter will determine which one or combination will be chosen. Allowing the choice is the efficient way to decide who pollutes and who doesn't. In principle, just as with the use of all other scarce resources, each polluter faces the full social cost of its actions and makes a production decision accordingly.

Is a Uniform Tax Appropriate?

It may not be appropriate to levy a *uniform* tax according to physical quantities of pollution. After all, we're talking about external costs. Such costs are not necessarily the same everywhere in the United States for the same action.

Essentially, we must establish the amount of the *economic damages* rather than the amount of the physical pollution. A polluting electrical plant in New York City will cause much more damage than the same plant in Montana. There are already innumerable demands on the air in New York City, so the pollution from smokestacks will not be cleansed away naturally. Millions of people will breathe the polluted air and thereby incur the costs of sore throats, sickness, emphysema, and even early death. Buildings will become dirtier faster because of the pollution, as will cars and clothes. A given quantity of pollution will cause more harm in concentrated urban environments than it will in less dense rural environments. If we were to establish some form of taxation to align private costs with social costs and to force people to internalize externalities, we would somehow have to come up with a measure of *economic* costs instead of *physical* quantities. But the tax, in any event, would fall on the private sector and modify individuals' and firms' behavior. Therefore, because the economic cost for the same physical quantity of pollution would be different in different locations depending on population density, natural formations of mountains and rivers, and the like, so-called optimal taxes on pollution would vary from location to location. (Nonetheless, a uniform tax might make sense when administrative costs, particularly the cost of ascertaining the actual economic costs, are relatively high.)

How might imposing a uniform tax have helped save jobs at the airport in Brussels, Belgium?

INTERNATIONAL POLICY EXAMPLE

Belgian Governments Forgo a Uniform Tax and Kill Off Jobs

For years, DHL Worldwide Express has maintained its international hub for package-delivery flights at the main airport in Brussels, Belgium. In 2004, the company announced, amid considerable fanfare, plans to expand its Brussels operations and add as many as 9,000 new employees to the 6,600 people it already had on its payroll.

Expanding its operations would have required DHL to increase its late-night flights in and out of the Brussels airport from about 70 per night on average to more than 90 per night. National and regional Belgian governments objected to additional late-night flights, which they contended would add to noise pollution in the heavily populated areas close to the airport. Some observers encouraged the Belgian governments to impose a uniform tax on late-night flights by DHL planes. Such a tax, they suggested, would encourage DHL to shift some of its planned increase in flights from nighttime hours to daytime. Furthermore, funds raised from these taxes could be used to better insulate nearby houses to help protect their occupants from the higher noise levels.

Nevertheless, instead of charging DHL a tax reflecting the social costs that additional late-night flights would have imposed, the Belgian governments sought to prevent *any* additional late-night flights. These efforts to limit the quantity of flights directly were so "successful" that DHL responded by moving its international hub to Leipzig, Germany, and shifting 1,300 jobs from Brussels to Leipzig.

FOR CRITICAL ANALYSIS
In principle, could the Belgian governments have imposed a quantity limitation on late-night flights by DHL planes that would have matched the quantity of flights that DHL would have chosen to make in the face of a uniform tax? Explain.

QUICK QUIZ

_____ costs are costs that are borne directly by consumers and producers when they engage in any resource-using activity.

Social costs are _____ costs plus any other costs that are external to the decision maker. For example, the social costs of driving include all the _____ costs plus, at a minimum, any pollution caused.

When _____ costs differ from social costs, _____ exist because individual decision makers are not internalizing all the costs that society is bearing.

See page 832 for the answers. Review concepts from this section in MyEconLab.

POLLUTION

The term *pollution* is used quite loosely and can refer to a variety of by-products of any activity. Industrial pollution involves mainly air and water but can also include noise and such concepts as aesthetic pollution, as when a landscape is altered in a negative way. For the most part, we will be analyzing the most common forms—air and water pollution.

Assessing the Appropriate Amount of Pollution

When asked how much pollution there should be in the economy, many people will respond, "None." But if we ask those same people how much starvation or deprivation of consumer products should exist in the economy, many will again say, "None." Growing and distributing food or producing consumer products creates pollution, however. There is no correct answer to how much pollution should be in an economy because when we ask how much pollution there *should* be, we are entering the realm of normative economics. We are asking people to express values. There is no way to disprove somebody's value system scientifically.

Go to www.econtoday.com/ch32 to see a review by the ACCF Center for Policy Research of possible economic effects of efforts to reduce pollution.

One way we can approach a discussion of the "correct" amount of pollution is to set up the same type of marginal analysis we used in our discussion of a firm's employment and output decisions. That is to say, we should pursue measures to reduce pollution only up to the point at which the marginal benefit from further reduction equals the marginal cost of further reduction.

The Marginal Benefit of a Less Polluted Environment. Look at Figure 32-2. On the horizontal axis, we show the degree of air cleanliness. A vertical line is drawn at 100 percent cleanliness—the air cannot become any cleaner. Consider the benefits of obtaining a greater degree of air cleanliness. These benefits are represented by the marginal benefit curve, which slopes downward.

When the air is very dirty, the marginal benefit from air that is a little cleaner appears to be relatively high, as shown on the vertical axis. As the air becomes increasingly cleaner, however, the marginal benefit of a little bit more air cleanliness falls.

FIGURE 32-2
The Optimal Quantity of Air Pollution

As we attempt to get a greater degree of air cleanliness, the marginal cost rises until even the slightest attempt at increasing air cleanliness leads to a very high marginal cost, as can be seen at the upper right of the graph. Conversely, the marginal benefit curve slopes downward: The more pure air we have, the less value an additional unit of pure air. Marginal cost and marginal benefit intersect at point E. The optimal degree of air cleanliness is something less than 100 percent at Q_0. The price that we should pay for the last unit of air cleanup is no greater than P_0, for that is where marginal cost equals marginal benefit.

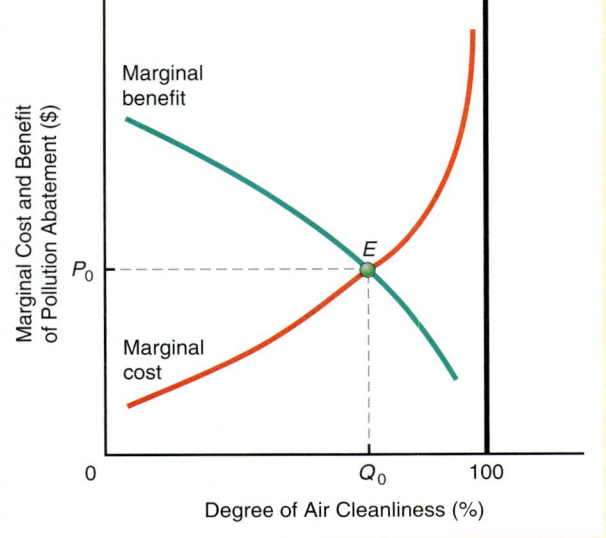

The Marginal Cost of Pollution Abatement. Consider the marginal cost of pollution abatement—that is, the marginal cost of obtaining cleaner air. In the 1960s, automobiles had no pollution abatement devices. Eliminating only 20 percent of the pollutants emitted by internal-combustion engines entailed a relatively small cost per unit of pollution removed. The per-unit cost of eliminating the next 20 percent increased, though. Finally, as we now get to the upper limits of removal of pollutants from the emissions of internal-combustion engines, we find that the elimination of one more percentage point of the amount of pollutants becomes astronomically expensive. To go from 97 percent cleanliness to 98 percent cleanliness involves a marginal cost that is many times greater than the marginal cost of going from 10 percent cleanliness to 11 percent cleanliness.

It is realistic, therefore, to draw the marginal cost of pollution abatement as an upward-sloping curve, as shown in Figure 32-2. (The marginal cost curve slopes up because of the law of diminishing marginal product.)

How have differences between the marginal costs of pollution abatement in the Netherlands and Brazil created an incentive for the Dutch government to clean up methane-gas emissions in Brazil?

> **ECONOMICS FRONT AND CENTER**
>
> For practice applying the concepts of marginal benefit and marginal cost of pollution abatement, contemplate **Reducing the Marginal Cost of Cleaning Up Nuclear Waste**, on page 826.

INTERNATIONAL POLICY EXAMPLE

A Dutch Gain from a Lower Marginal Cost of Pollution Abatement in Brazil

In 1997, in Kyoto, Japan, the government of the Netherlands joined about 130 other nations in signing a treaty, the Kyoto Protocol, committing the nations to reducing their emissions of methane gas and various other global-warming gases. Under the terms of this agreement, the Dutch government gets equal credit for battling pollution anywhere on the planet, whether inside or outside the Netherlands. In Dutch urban areas, overall air quality is better than in many Brazilian cities. Other things being equal, the marginal cost of further pollution abatement in urban areas is higher in the Netherlands than in Brazil.

Consider, for instance, the cost of eliminating a ton of methane gas from a city's atmosphere. In the Netherlands, this cost is $40 to $50, but in Brazil it is only $4 to $5. This significant marginal cost differential has given the Dutch government an incentive to de-emphasize reducing methane-gas emissions in the Netherlands. Instead, the Dutch government honors its promise to reduce pollution by cleaning up methane-gas pollution in Brazil, thereby spending much less than it would have had to spend to clean up an equal amount of pollution at home.

FOR CRITICAL ANALYSIS
What does the Kyoto Protocol assume about the marginal benefit of reducing pollution in various countries around the world?

The Optimal Quantity of Pollution

The **optimal quantity of pollution** is defined as the level of pollution at which the marginal benefit equals the marginal cost of pollution abatement. This occurs at the intersection of the marginal benefit curve and the marginal cost curve in Figure 32-2, at point E. This solution is analytically exactly the same as for every other economic activity. If we increased pollution control by one more unit greater than Q_0, the marginal cost of that small increase in the degree of air cleanliness would be greater than the marginal benefit to society.

As is usually the case in economic analysis, the optimal quantity of just about anything occurs when marginal cost equals marginal benefit. That is, the optimal quantity of pollution occurs at the point at which the marginal cost of reducing (or abating) pollution is just equal to the marginal benefit of doing so. The marginal cost of pollution abatement rises as more and more abatement is achieved (as the environment becomes cleaner and cleaner, the *extra* cost of cleansing rises). Early units of pollution abatement are easily achieved

Optimal quantity of pollution
The level of pollution for which the marginal benefit of one additional unit of pollution abatement just equals the marginal cost of that additional unit of pollution abatement.

(at low cost), but attaining higher and higher levels of environmental quality becomes progressively more difficult (as the extra cost rises to prohibitive levels). At the same time, the marginal benefits of an increasingly cleaner environment fall; the marginal benefit of pollution abatement declines as our notion of a cleaner environment moves from human life-support requirements to recreation to beauty to a perfectly pure environment. The point at which the increasing marginal cost of pollution abatement equals the decreasing marginal benefit of pollution abatement defines the optimal quantity of pollution.

Go to www.econtoday.com/ch32 to learn from the National Center for Policy Analysis about a market-oriented government program for reducing pollution.

Recognizing that the optimal quantity of pollution is not zero becomes easier when we realize that it takes scarce resources to reduce pollution. A trade-off exists between producing a cleaner environment and producing other goods and services. In that sense, environmental cleanliness is a resource that can be analyzed like any other resource, and a cleaner environment must take its place with other societal wants.

What nation is facing a potentially very high marginal cost of trying to keep its antipollution promises?

INTERNATIONAL POLICY EXAMPLE

Canada Confronts a High Marginal Cost of Pollution Abatement

Under the 1997 international pollution abatement treaty called the Kyoto Protocol, Canada promised that, by 2012, it would reduce emissions of global-warming gases to a level 6 percent below its total 1990 emissions. Nevertheless, since 1997 Canada's emissions have actually *increased* by 1.5 percent per year. One activity that has helped fuel this growth in gas emissions has been Canadian oil production. As world oil prices increased during the 2000s, Canadian oil firms ramped up production from the nation's "oil sands," vast deposits of sticky, black grit that constitute the largest single known source of oil outside Saudi Arabia. Extracting and transporting all this oil requires burning fossil fuels that create gas emissions.

Canada's government continues to promise that the nation will reach its promised level of gas emissions by 2012.

By most estimates, though, keeping this promise would require the nation's oil industry to incur hundreds of millions of dollars in costs to reduce emissions. One predicted result would be a significant reduction in Canadian oil production, requiring Canada to forgo billions of dollars in export revenues. All told, the estimated explicit and opportunity costs to the entire Canadian economy of achieving the promised emission reduction between now and 2012 would be at least $30 billion per year.

FOR CRITICAL ANALYSIS
If Canada's marginal benefit from reducing gas emissions to the Kyoto level between now and 2012 was determined to be $25 billion, would the nation be better off if it engaged in more or less pollution abatement during this interval?

QUICK QUIZ

The marginal cost of cleaning up the environment _____ as we get closer to 100 percent cleanliness. Indeed, it _____ at an _____ rate.

The marginal benefit of environmental cleanliness _____ as we have more of it.

The **optimal quantity of pollution** is the quantity at which the _____ _____ of cleanup equals the _____ _____ of cleanup.

Pollution abatement is a trade-off. We trade off _____ and _____ for cleaner air and water, and vice versa.

See page 832 for the answers. Review concepts from this section in MyEconLab.

COMMON PROPERTY

In most cases, you do not have **private property rights,** or exclusive ownership rights, to the air surrounding you, nor does anyone else. Air is a **common property,** or a nonexclusive resource. Therein lies the crux of the problem. When no one owns a particular resource, no one has any incentive (conscience aside) to consider misuse of that resource. If one person decides not to pollute the air, there will normally be no significant effect on the total level of pollution. If one person decides not to pollute the ocean, there will still be approximately the same amount of ocean pollution—provided, of course, that the individual was previously responsible for only a small part of the total amount of ocean pollution.

Basically, pollution occurs when we have poorly defined private property rights, as in air and common bodies of water. We do not, for example, have a visual pollution problem in people's attics. That is their own property, which they choose to keep as clean as they want, given their preferences for cleanliness as weighed against the costs of keeping the attic neat and tidy.

When private property rights exist, individuals have legal recourse for any damages sustained through the use of their property. When private property rights are well defined, the use of property—that is, the use of resources—will generally involve contracting between the owners of those resources. If you own land, you might contract with another person who wants to use your land for raising cattle. The contract would most likely be written in the form of a lease agreement.

Private property rights
Exclusive rights of ownership that allow the use, transfer, and exchange of property.

Common property
Property that is owned by everyone and therefore by no one. Air and water are examples of common property resources.

Voluntary Agreements and Transaction Costs

Is it possible for externalities to be internalized via voluntary agreement? Take a simple example. You live in a house with a nice view of a lake. The family living below you plants a tree. The tree grows so tall that it eventually starts to cut off your view. In most cities, no one has property rights to views; therefore, you usually cannot go to court to obtain relief. You do have the option of contracting with your neighbors, however.

Voluntary Agreements: Contracting.
You have the option of paying your neighbors (contracting) to cut back the tree. You could start out with an offer of a small amount and keep going up until your neighbors agree or until you reach your limit. Your limit will equal the value you place on having an unobstructed view of the lake. Your neighbors will be willing if the payment is at least equal to the reduction in their intrinsic property value due to a stunted tree. Your offer of the payment makes your neighbors aware of the social cost of their actions. The social cost here is equal to the care of the tree plus the cost suffered by you from an impeded view of the lake.

In essence, then, your offer of money income to your neighbors indicates to them that there is an opportunity cost to their actions. If they don't comply, they forfeit the payments that you are offering them. The point here is that *opportunity cost always exists, no matter who has property rights.* Therefore, we would expect that under some circumstances voluntary contracting will occur to internalize externalities. The question is, When will voluntary agreements occur?

Transaction Costs.
One major condition for the outcome just outlined is that the **transaction costs**—all costs associated with making and enforcing agreements—must be low relative to the expected benefits of reaching an agreement. (We already looked at this topic briefly in Chapter 4.) If we expand our example to a much larger one such as air pollution, the transaction costs of numerous homeowners trying to reach agreements with the individuals and companies that create the pollution are relatively high. Consequently, we don't expect voluntary contracting to be an effective way to internalize the externality of air pollution.

Transaction costs
All costs associated with making, reaching, and enforcing agreements.

Changing Property Rights

We can approach the problem of property rights by assuming that initially in a society, many property rights to resources are not defined. But this situation does not cause a problem as long as no one cares to use the resources for which there are no property rights or resources are available in desired quantities at a zero price. Only if and when a use is found for a resource or the supply of a resource is inadequate at a zero price does a problem develop. The problem requires that something be done about deciding property rights. If not, the resource will be wasted and possibly even destroyed. Property rights can be assigned to individuals who will then assert control; or they may be assigned to government, which can maintain and preserve the resource, charge for its use, or implement some other rationing device. With common property such as air and water, governments have indeed attempted to take over the control of those resources so that they cannot be wasted or destroyed.

Another way of viewing the pollution problem is to argue that it cannot continue to arise if a way can be found to assign private property rights for all resources. We can then say that each individual does not have the right to act on anything that is not his or her property. Hence no individual has the right to create a pollution problem using property that the individual does not specifically own.

Clearly, we must fill the gap between private costs and social costs in situations in which property rights are not well defined or assigned. There are three ways to fill this gap: taxation, subsidization, and regulation. Government is involved in all three. Unfortunately, government does not have perfect information and may not pick the appropriate tax, subsidy, or type of regulation. Furthermore, in some situations, taxes are hard to enforce, or subsidies are difficult to give out to "worthy" recipients. In such cases, outright prohibition of the polluting activity may be the optimal solution to a particular pollution problem. For example, if it is difficult to monitor the level of a particular type of pollution that even in small quantities can cause severe environmental damage, outright prohibition of activities that cause such pollution may be the only alternative.

Are There Alternatives to Pollution-Causing Resource Use?

Some people cannot understand why, if pollution is bad, we still use pollution-causing resources such as coal and oil to generate electricity. Why don't we forgo the use of such polluting resources and opt for one that apparently is pollution-free, such as solar energy? The plain fact is that the cost of generating solar power in many circumstances is much higher than generating that same power through conventional means. We do not yet have the technology that allows us the luxury of driving solar-powered cars. Moreover, with current technology, the solar panels necessary to generate the electricity for the average town would cover massive sections of the countryside, and the manufacturing of those solar panels would itself generate pollution.

What nearly pollution-free resource generates electricity in Ireland without polluting either the air or the water (albeit producing other forms of pollution)?

INTERNATIONAL EXAMPLE

Profiting by Generating Electricity from Thin Air in Ireland

The northern portion of Ireland abounds with farmland. The extreme northern tip of the country, however, is too rugged and strewn with boulders to grow crops and too full of bogs to support cattle. At one time, many farmers earned a meager living by raising sheep in this locale, but most sheep farmers barely broke even. *(continued)*

Today, numerous landowners in this part of Ireland earn millions of dollars in revenues. The source of their earnings is not the land itself, but the steady winds that blow across it. Several companies now harness the winds to power turbines that generate electricity. Although some people complain that the large windmills erected to channel wind power to turbines are eyesores that kill birds and create noise, the electricity that the turbines generate is otherwise virtually pollution free.

FOR CRITICAL ANALYSIS

Why do you suppose that Massachusetts residents owning homes with ocean views contend that the use of seaside windmills to power electricity-generating turbines would create external costs and lower property values in their part of the world?

WILD SPECIES, COMMON PROPERTY, AND TRADE-OFFS

One of the most distressing common property problems involves endangered species, usually in the wild. No one is concerned about not having enough dogs, cats, cattle, sheep, and horses. The reason is that virtually all of those species are private property. Spotted owls, bighorn mountain sheep, condors, and the like are typically common property. No one has a vested interest in making sure that they perpetuate in good health.

In 1973, the federal government passed the Endangered Species Act in an attempt to prevent species from dying out. Initially, few individuals were affected by the rulings of the Interior Department regarding which species were listed as endangered. Eventually, however, as more and more species were put on the endangered list, a trade-off became apparent. Nationwide, the trade-off was brought to the public's attention when the snail darter was declared an endangered species in the Tennessee Valley. Ultimately, thousands of construction jobs were lost when the courts halted completion of a dam in the snail darter's habitat. Then small birds, the spotted owl and marbled murrelet, were found in the Pacific Northwest, causing lumber companies to cut back their logging practices. In 1995, the U.S. Supreme Court ruled that the federal government did have the right to regulate activities on private land in order to save endangered species.

The issues are not straightforward. Today, the earth has only 0.02 percent of all of the species that have ever lived, and nearly all the 99.98 percent of extinct species became extinct before humans appeared. Every year, 1,000 to 3,000 new species are discovered and classified. Estimates of how many species are actually dying out vary from a high of 50,000 a year (based on the assumption that undiscovered insect species are dying off before being discovered) to a low of one every four years.

What costs are generated when a plant or animal is officially designated an "endangered species" by the U.S. government?

Go to **www.econtoday.com/ch32** to contemplate the issue of endangered species via a link to the National Center for Policy Analysis.

POLICY EXAMPLE

How Much Does Society Pay to Protect Endangered Species?

Of the nearly 1,300 species officially classified as endangered under the 1973 Endangered Species Act, 468 species are considered to be "stable or improving." The remaining species are continuing to die out. So far, only 10 of the species that have appeared on the endangered list have been determined to be "recovered," meaning that their numbers are sufficiently high that the species can be removed from the list. Of these "recovered" species, however, six species "recovered" because the U.S. Fish and Wildlife Service (USFWS), the primary federal agency charged with efforts to protect endangered species, originally underestimated their populations. These six species should never have been on the list in the first place.

How much does society spend on efforts to protect species on the endangered list? To begin with, the USFWS spends more

(continued)

than $12 million per year just to determine whether about 280 species not on the list should be added to it. In addition, the USFWS and other federal agencies together spend at least $800 million per year on programs intended to protect species already classified as endangered. Finally, property owners incur an estimated $1.6 billion in costs to abide by restrictions on land use imposed by the Endangered Species Act. All told, therefore, society's efforts to protect endangered species have an annual price tag exceeding $2.4 billion, or more than $18 million per species per year.

FOR CRITICAL ANALYSIS
Who finances federal spending aimed at protecting endangered species?

QUICK QUIZ

A **common property** resource is one that _____ _____ owns—or, otherwise stated, that _____ owns.

Common property exists when property rights are indefinite or nonexistent.

When no _____ _____ rights exist, pollution occurs because no one individual or firm has a sufficient economic incentive to care for the common property in question, be it air, water, or scenery.

Private costs will equal _____ costs for common property only if a few individuals or companies are involved and they are able to _____ among themselves.

See page 832 for the answers. Review concepts from this section in MyEconLab.

RECYCLING

Recycling
The reuse of raw materials derived from manufactured products.

As part of the overall ecology movement, there has been a major push to save scarce resources via recycling. **Recycling** involves reusing paper products, plastics, glass, and metals rather than putting them into solid waste dumps. Many cities have instituted mandatory recycling programs.

In what high-tech line of business has recycling proved to be a profitable enterprise?

E-COMMERCE EXAMPLE

Boom Times in Personal Computer Recycling

In a typical year, owners of more than 2 billion pounds of unwanted electronic equipment pay 400 companies nearly $1 billion to find something to do with that equipment. Personal computers account for a large and growing fraction of all this old electronic equipment. Recycling firms profit from charging businesses and individuals to collect their computers, remove any remaining proprietary and personal data, and refurbish the computers for resale at cut-rate prices. For instance, a company called Retrobox charges $40 per computer to perform these tasks. When Retrobox resells a computer, it transmits a portion of the revenues back to the original owner and keeps a portion for itself.

Today, manufacturers of new personal computers are also involved in recycling. Dell, for example, charges $15 to take an old computer off the hands of someone who buys a new Dell model. Then Dell turns the computer over to other companies, such as Retrobox, for refurbishment and recycling.

FOR CRITICAL ANALYSIS
Why do you suppose that the market clearing prices of recycled computers are typically very low?

The benefits of recycling are straightforward. Fewer *natural* resources are used. But some economists argue that recycling does not necessarily save *total* resources. For example, a study by Andrew Foster of Brown University and Mark Rosenzweig of the University of Pennsylvania suggests that recycling paper products may not necessarily save trees. Foster and Rosenzweig find that the primary factor contributing to the spread of forests is a higher demand for forest products, such as wood for fuel, wood for furniture and home construction, and pulp for producing paper. They argue that because most trees are planted specifically to produce such products, a fall in the demand for forest products generated by wood conservation programs will induce people to put certain land now used to grow trees to other uses. Thus, the end result of paper recycling and other conservation programs could well be smaller forests.

Recycling's Invisible Costs

The recycling of paper can also pollute. Used paper has ink on it that has to be removed during the recycling process. According to the National Wildlife Federation, the production of 100 tons of deinked (bleached) fiber generates 40 tons of sludge. This sludge has to be disposed of, usually in a landfill. In general, recycling creates wastes that must be eliminated.

The use of resources also involves another issue: Recycling requires human effort. The labor resources involved in recycling are often many times more costly than the potential savings in scarce resources *not* used. That means that net resource use, counting all resources, may sometimes be greater with recycling than without it.

Landfills

One of the arguments in favor of recycling is to avoid a solid waste "crisis." Some people believe that we are running out of solid waste dump sites in the United States. This is perhaps true in and near major cities, and indeed the most populated areas of the country might ultimately benefit from recycling programs. In the rest of the United States, however, the data do not seem to indicate that we are running out of solid waste landfill sites. Throughout the United States, the disposal price per ton of city garbage has actually fallen. Prices vary, of course, for the 165 million tons of trash disposed of each year. In San Jose, California, it costs about $50 a ton to dump, whereas in Morris County, New Jersey, it costs nearly $150 a ton.

Currently, municipal governments can do three things with solid waste: burn it, bury it, or recycle it. The amount of solid waste dumped in landfills is dropping, even as total trash output rises. Consider, though, that the total garbage output of the United States for the entire twenty-first century could be put in a square landfill 10 miles on a side that is 100 yards deep. Recycling to reduce solid waste disposal may end up costing society more resources simply because putting such waste into a landfill may be a less costly alternative.

Should We Save Scarce Resources?

Periodically, the call for recycling focuses on the necessity of saving scarce resources because "we are running out." There is little evidence to back up this claim because virtually every natural resource has fallen in price (corrected for inflation) over the past century. In 1980, the late Julian Simon made a $1,000 bet with well-known environmentalist Paul Erlich. Simon bet $200 per resource that any five natural resources that Erlich picked would decline in price (corrected for inflation) by the end of the 1980s. Simon won. (When Simon asked Erlich to renew the bet for $20,000 for the 1990s, Erlich declined.) From the 1980s into the 2000s, the price of virtually every natural resource fell (corrected for inflation), and so did the price of most agricultural commodities. The same was true for many forest products. Though few people remember the dire predictions of the 1970s, many noneconomists throughout the world argued at that time that the world's oil reserves were vanishing. These predictions were wrong, which is why in spite of price increases during the mid-2000s, the pretax, inflation-corrected price of gasoline is not significantly higher today than it was in the early 1980s.

In spite of predictions in the early 1980s by World Watch Institute president Lester Brown, real food prices did not rise. Indeed, the real price of food fell by more than 30 percent for the major agricultural commodities during the 1980s and by even more into the 2000s. A casual knowledge of supply and demand tells you that because the demand for food did not decrease, supply must have increased faster than demand.

With respect to the forests, at least in the United States and Western Europe, there are more forests today than there were 100 years ago. In this country, the major problems of deforestation seem to be on land owned by the U.S. Forest Service for which private timber companies are paid almost $1 billion a year in subsidies to cut down trees.

QUICK QUIZ

_____ involves reusing paper, glass, and other materials rather than putting them into solid waste dumps.

_____ does have a cost both in the resources used for recycling and in the pollution created during _____, such as the sludge from bleaching paper for reuse.

_____ are an alternative to recycling. Expansion of these solid waste disposal sites is outpacing demand increases.

Resources may not be getting scarcer. The inflation-corrected _____ of most resources has been _____ for decades.

See page 832 for the answers. Review concepts from this section in MyEconLab.

CASE STUDY — ECONOMICS FRONT AND CENTER

Reducing the Marginal Cost of Cleaning Up Nuclear Waste

Kirkwood, an economist and mid-level manager with the U.S. Environmental Protection Agency, steps into a concrete vault and peers through a 3-foot-thick window at a metal rod pulled from the radioactive depths of a nuclear waste tank. She watches as workers direct robot arms to remove a slimy transparent substance growing on the end of the rod. The robot arms smear a bit of the substance into a petri dish.

That substance, Kirkwood knows, contains a colony of bacteria, known as *extremophiles*, that can survive at least 15 times the amount of radiation that can kill a human being. Studies of the same bacteria have shown that they can also survive exposures to chemical toxins that are deadly to humans. Their ancestors are bacteria that some scientists believe either piggybacked on comets to Earth from outer space or were among the planet's first residents after the planet was born in a radioactive explosion.

Until today, Kirkwood has been interested in these bacteria mainly because they can break down herbicides, industrial solvents, and other toxic compounds to relatively harmless components. Kirkwood has already determined that using the bacteria could reduce the marginal costs of cleaning up chemical waste dumps by up to 50 percent. Now she is visiting this nuclear facility to learn how extremophiles can reduce the hazards of radioactive wastes by changing them into insoluble substances less likely to contaminate bodies of water. According to Kirkwood's initial estimates, the bacteria could help clean up each additional one-liter unit of nuclear waste at a cost 75 percent below that of conventional methods. The socially optimal amount of chemical and nuclear pollution abatement, Kirkwood muses to herself, is likely to undergo a radical change in the coming years.

CRITICAL ANALYSIS QUESTIONS

1. How is the use of extremophiles likely to affect the position of the marginal cost curves for abatement of chemical and nuclear pollution?

2. Is Kirkwood's predicted "radical change" in the optimal amount of chemical and nuclear pollution abatement likely to be upward or downward? Explain.

Issues and Applications

The Government's Climbing Costs to Protect Wild Horses

In his memoirs, Civil War general and U.S. president Ulysses Grant wrote of how, as a young officer traveling in the Southwest during the 1840s, he looked down from a peak on a panoramic view filled with herds of wild horses. During the century that followed, domestication and poaching of these herds considerably thinned the wild horse population. In the late 1950s, a Nevada woman named Velma Johnson initiated a letter-writing campaign by schoolchildren to U.S. government officials, asking for federal assistance for the wild horses. In 1971, Congress passed the Wild Free-Roaming Horses and Burros Act, which placed both wild horses and burros under the protection of the U.S. government.

Concepts Applied
- Common Property
- Transaction Costs
- Private Property Rights

The Common Property Problem

Protection from poaching and the absence of natural predators allowed the population of wild horses on U.S. government lands to more than double during the following decade. Indeed, the horse population outstripped the capacity of the open range to support its numbers, and by the 1980s many wild horses were suffering from starvation.

As common property, the wild horses were regarded as a nonexclusive resource that belonged to all the people in the United States. Consequently, no one person had responsibility for the horses. Instead, a bureau of the U.S. Department of the Interior, the Bureau of Land Management (BLM), was placed in charge of addressing the horses' plight.

Confronting Transaction Costs in Caring for Wild Horses

In an effort to ensure more humane conditions for the horses, between the mid-1980s and the early 1990s the BLM allowed individuals and companies to round up horses intended for private adoption. The government paid all costs of these roundups, which averaged about $1,400 per horse that ultimately was removed from federal lands.

Unfortunately, the BLM failed to ensure that those who removed the horses honored their agreements. As a consequence, instead of finding homes for the horses on private farms and ranches, many who had rounded up the horses profited from sending thousands of them to slaughterhouses.

827

Soon, a new letter-writing campaign by schoolchildren—supplemented this time by thousands of e-mail messages—induced another round of protections intended to stop the processing of horse meat for sale to Europe.

Turning Again to the Private Sector

Since the late 1990s, the BLM has relied on privately operated sanctuaries to look after nearly 14,000 of the federally protected horses. The agency pays ranchers in Kansas and Oklahoma a little less than $1.50 per horse per day to look after these animals. The BLM has also made onetime payments to Wyoming ranchers to take horses off taxpayers' hands, although now the BLM enforces contracts forbidding the sale of horses to slaughterhouses.

Nevertheless, each year the government finds about 600 emaciated wild horses that it sends to the two remaining U.S. horse slaughterhouses. In an effort to reduce the number of horses facing this fate, the government has also invested considerable taxpayer funds in a plan to inject wild mares with a birth-control vaccine. Implementation of this plan, the BLM hopes, will allow it to eventually cut the population of remaining horses roaming federal lands from 36,000 to closer to 25,000. Thus, after the expenditure of hundreds of millions of tax dollars, the population of wild horses may finally return to about the level it was at when the horses were first placed under federal protection in 1971.

Log in to MyEconLab, click on "Economic News," and test your understanding of the chapter by answering interactive questions that relate directly to this issue.

For Critical Analysis

1. What fundamental problem do populations of wild horses face as common property?
2. How does transfer of ownership of wild horses to private ranches potentially help to assure more humane conditions for many of these creatures?

Web Resources

1. For more information about the history of wild horses and burros and their protection as a U.S. natural resource, go to www.econtoday.com/ch32.
2. To learn more about horse sales conducted by the Bureau of Land Management's Wild Horse and Burro Program, go to www.econtoday.com/ch32.

Research Project

Consider the following statement: "The present population of wild horses would receive more humane treatment if the federal government paid ranches enough to take all the horses and got out of the business of looking after these animals." What does economic analysis tell us might happen to the wild horse population if this recommendation were adopted?

Here is what you should know after reading this chapter. MyEconLab will help you identify what you know, and where to go when you need to practice.

WHAT YOU SHOULD KNOW		WHERE TO GO TO PRACTICE
Private Costs versus Social Costs Private, or internal, costs are borne solely by individuals who use resources. Social costs are the full costs that society bears whenever resources are used. Problems related to the environment arise when individuals take into account only private costs instead of the broader social costs arising from their use of resources.	private costs, 814 social costs, 814	• **MyEconLab** Study Plan 32.1 • Audio introduction to Chapter 32

WHAT YOU SHOULD KNOW		WHERE TO GO TO PRACTICE
Market Externalities and Ways to Correct Them A market externality is a situation in which a private cost (or benefit) differs from the social cost (or benefit) associated with a market transaction between two parties or from the use of a scarce resource. Correcting an externality arising from differences between private and social costs, such as pollution, requires forcing individuals to take all the social costs of their actions into account. This might be accomplished by taxing those who create externalities, such as polluters.	externality, 815 **Key figure** Figure 32-1, 816	• **MyEconLab** Study Plan 32.2 • Video: Correcting for Externalities • Animated Figure 32-1
Determining the Optimal Amount of Pollution The marginal benefit of pollution abatement, or the additional benefit to society from reducing pollution, declines as the quality of the environment improves. At the same time, however, the marginal cost of pollution abatement, or the additional cost to society from reducing pollution, increases as more and more resources are devoted to bringing about an improved environment. The optimal quantity of pollution is the amount of pollution for which the marginal benefit of pollution abatement just equals the marginal cost of pollution abatement. Beyond this level of pollution, the additional cost of cleaning the environment exceeds the additional benefit.	optimal quantity of pollution, 819 **Key figure** Figure 32-2, 818	• **MyEconLab** Study Plan 32.3 • Animated Figure 32-2
Private and Common Property Rights and the Pollution Problem Private property rights are exclusive individual rights of ownership that permit the use and exchange of a resource. Common property is owned by everyone and therefore by no single individual. A pollution problem often arises because air and many water resources are common property, and private property rights relating to them are not well defined. Therefore, no one has an individual incentive to take the long-run pernicious effects of excessive pollution into account. This is a common rationale for using taxes, subsidies, or regulations to address the pollution problem.	private property rights, 821 common property, 821 transaction costs, 821	• **MyEconLab** Study Plan 32.4
Endangered Species and the Assignment of Property Rights Many members of such species as dogs, pigs, and horses are the private property of human beings. Thus, people have economic incentives—satisfaction derived from pet ownership, the desire for pork as a food product, a preference for animal-borne transport—to protect members of these species. In contrast, most members of species such as spotted owls, condors, or tigers are common property, so no specific individuals have incentives to keep these species in good health. A possible way to address the endangered species problem is government involvement via taxes, subsidies, or regulations.		• **MyEconLab** Study Plan 32.5
Benefits and Costs of Recycling Recycling entails reusing paper, glass, and other materials instead of putting them in solid waste dumps. Recycling has a clear benefit of limiting the use of		

WHAT YOU SHOULD KNOW

natural resources. It also entails costs, however. One cost might be lost benefits of forests, because a key incentive for perpetuating forests is the future production of paper and other wood-based products. Recycling also requires the use of labor, and the costs of these human resources can exceed the potential savings in scarce resources not used because of recycling.

recycling, 824

WHERE TO GO TO PRACTICE

- **MyEconLab** Study Plan 32.6
- Video: Recycling

Log in to MyEconLab, take a chapter test, and get a personalized Study Plan that tells you which concepts you understand and which ones you need to review. From there, MyEconLab will give you further practice, tutorials, animations, videos, and guided solutions.
Log in to www.myeconlab.com

PROBLEMS

*Select problems, indicated by a blue oval, are assignable in **MyEconLab**.*
Answers to the odd-numbered problems appear at the back of the book.

32-1. The market price of insecticide is initially $10 per unit. To address a negative externality in this market, the government decides to charge producers of insecticide for the privilege of polluting during the production process. A fee that fully takes into account the social costs of pollution is determined, and once it is put into effect, the market supply curve for insecticide shifts upward by $4 per unit. The market price of insecticide also increases, to $12 per unit. What fee is the government charging insecticide manufacturers?

32-2. A tract of land is found to contain a plant from which drug companies can extract a newly discovered cancer-fighting medicine. This variety of plant does not grow anywhere else in the world. Initially, the many owners of lots within this tract, who had not planned to use the land for anything other than its current use as a scenic locale for small vacation homes, announced that they would put all their holdings up for sale to drug companies. Because the land is also home to an endangered lizard species, however, a government agency decides to limit the number of acres in this tract that drug companies can purchase and use for their drug-producing operations. The government declares that the remaining portion of the land must be left in its current state. What will be the effect of government regulation on the market price of the acreage that is available for extraction of cancer-fighting medicine? What will be the effect on the market price of the land that the government declares to be usable only for existing vacation homes?

32-3. When a government charges firms for the privilege of polluting, a typical result is a rise in the market price of the good or service produced by those firms. Consequently, consumers of the good or service usually have to pay a higher price to obtain it. Why might this be socially desirable?

32-4. Most wild Asian tigers are the common property of the humans and governments that control the lands they inhabit. Why does this pose a significant problem for maintaining the wild tiger population in the future? (Hint: Who currently has an incentive to care about the wild tiger population?)

32-5. In several African countries where the rhinoceros was once a thriving species, the animal is now nearly extinct. In most of these nations, rhinoceros horns are used as traditional ingredients in certain medicines. Why might making rhinoceros farming legal do more to promote preservation of the species than imposing stiff penalties on people who are caught engaging in rhinoceros hunting?

32-6. Why is it possible for recycling of paper or plastics to use up more resources than the activity saves?

32-7. Examine the marginal costs and marginal benefits associated with water cleanliness in a given locale, displayed on the next page.

CHAPTER 32 Environmental Economics

Quantity of Clean Water (%)	Marginal Cost ($)	Marginal Benefit ($)
0	3,000	200,000
20	15,000	120,000
40	50,000	90,000
60	85,000	85,000
80	100,000	40,000
100	Infinite	0

a. What is the optimal degree of water cleanliness?
b. What is the optimal degree of water pollution?
c. Suppose that a company creates a food additive that offsets most of the harmful effects of drinking polluted water. As a result, the marginal benefit of water cleanliness declines by $40,000 at each degree of water cleanliness at or less than 80 percent. What is the optimal degree of water cleanliness after this change?

32-8. Examine the following marginal costs and marginal benefits associated with air cleanliness in a given locale:

Quantity of Clean Air (%)	Marginal Cost ($)	Marginal Benefit ($)
0	50,000	600,000
20	150,000	360,000
40	200,000	200,000
60	300,000	150,000
80	400,000	120,000
100	Infinite	0

a. What is the optimal degree of air cleanliness?
b. What is the optimal degree of air pollution?
c. Suppose that a state provides subsidies for a company to build plants that contribute to air pollution. Cleaning up this pollution causes the marginal cost of air cleanliness to rise by $210,000 at each degree of air cleanliness. What is the optimal degree of air cleanliness after this change?

32-9. Consider the diagram at the top of the next column, which displays the marginal cost and marginal benefit of water pollution abatement in a particular city, and answer the following questions.

a. What is the optimal percentage degree of water cleanliness?
b. When the optimal percentage degree of water cleanliness has been attained, what price will be paid for the last unit of water cleanup?

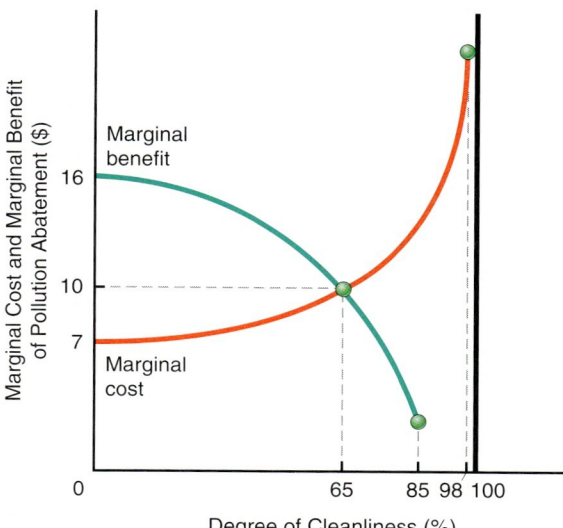

32-10. Consider the diagram in Problem 32-9, and answer the following questions.

a. Suppose that a new technology for reducing water pollution generates a reduction in the marginal cost of pollution abatement at every degree of water cleanliness. After this event occurs, will the optimal percentage degree of water cleanliness rise or fall? Will the cost incurred for the last unit of water cleanup increase or decrease? Provide a diagram to assist in your explanation.
b. Suppose that the event discussed in part a occurs and that, in addition, medical studies determine that the marginal benefit from water pollution abatement is higher at every degree of water cleanliness. Following *both* events, will the optimal percentage degree of water cleanliness increase or decrease? In comparison with the *initial* optimum, can you determine whether the price paid for the last unit of water cleanup will increase or decrease? Use a new diagram to assist in explaining your answers.

32-11. The following table displays hypothetical annual total costs and total benefits of conserving wild tigers at several possible worldwide tiger population levels.

Population of Wild Tigers	Total Cost ($ millions)	Total Benefit ($ millions)
0	0	40
2,000	25	90
4,000	35	130
6,000	50	160
8,000	75	185
10,000	110	205
12,000	165	215

a. Calculate the marginal costs and benefits.
b. Given the data, what is the socially optimal world population of wild tigers?
c. Suppose that tiger farming is legalized and that this has the effect of reducing the marginal cost of tiger conservation by $15 million for each 2,000-tiger population increment in the table. What is the new socially optimal population of wild tigers?

32-12. The following table gives hypothetical annual total costs and total benefits of maintaining alternative populations of Asian elephants.

Population of Asian Elephants	Total Cost ($ millions)	Total Benefit ($ millions)
0	0	0
7,500	20	100
15,000	45	185
22,500	90	260
30,000	155	325
37,500	235	375
45,000	330	410

a. Calculate the marginal costs and benefits, and draw marginal benefit and cost schedules.
b. Given the data, what is the socially optimal world population of Asian elephants?
c. Suppose that two events occur simultaneously. Technological development allows machines to do more efficiently much of the work that elephants once did, which reduces by $40 million the marginal benefit of maintaining the elephant population for each 7,500 increment in the elephant population. In addition, new techniques for breeding, feeding, and protecting elephants reduce the marginal cost by $10 million for each 7,500 increment in the elephant population. What is the new socially optimal population of Asian elephants?

ECONOMICS ON THE NET

Economic Analysis at the Environmental Protection Agency
In this chapter, you learned how to use economic analysis to think about environmental problems. Does the U.S. government use economic analysis? This application helps you learn the extent to which the government uses economics in its environmental policymaking.

Title: National Center for Environmental Economics (NCEE)

Navigation: Go to www.econtoday.com/ch32 to visit the NCEE's home page. Click on *Publications*. Under *other information*, select *Plain English*. Click on "Environmental Protection: Is It Bad for the Economy? A Non-Technical Summary of the Literature," and view the table of contents. Read "What Do We Spend on Environmental Protection?"

Application Read this section of the article; then answer the following questions.

1. According to the article, what are the key objectives of the EPA? What role does cost-benefit analysis appear to play in the EPA's efforts? Does the EPA appear to take other issues into account in its policymaking?
2. Back up to Table of Contents, and click on "Regardless of the Cost of Environmental Protection, Is It Still Money Well Spent?" In what ways does this discussion help clarify your answers in item 1?

For Group Study and Analysis Have a class discussion of the following question: Should the EPA apply economic analysis in all aspects of its policymaking? If not, why not? If so, in what manner should economic analysis be applied?

ANSWERS TO QUICK QUIZZES

p. 817: (i) Private; (ii) private . . . private; (iii) private . . . externalities
p. 820: (i) rises . . . rises . . . increasing; (ii) falls; (iii) marginal cost . . . marginal benefit; (iv) goods . . . services
p. 824: (i) no one . . . everyone; (ii) private property; (iii) social . . . contract
p. 826: (i) Recycling . . . Recycling . . . recycling; (ii) Landfills; (iii) price . . . falling

Comparative Advantage and the Open Economy

33

In 1990, there were a total of 50 *bilateral trade agreements*, or special treaties governing trade between a pair of countries, and *regional trade agreements*, or special treaties governing trade among a set of the world's nations. Today, there are more than 230 of these agreements. Proposals for about 70 more bilateral and regional trade agreements are under active negotiation around the globe. Why do nations enter into agreements aimed at promoting bilateral or multilateral trade of goods and services? In this chapter, you will learn about how nations can gain from engaging in international trade. You will also learn about efforts to promote international trade through the establishment of both regional and global trade agreements.

Learning Objectives

After reading this chapter, you should be able to:

1. Discuss the worldwide importance of international trade
2. Explain why nations can gain from specializing in production and engaging in international trade
3. Understand common arguments against free trade
4. Describe ways that nations restrict foreign trade
5. Identify key international agreements and organizations that adjudicate trade disputes among nations

MyEconLab helps you master each objective and study more efficiently. See end of chapter for details.

Did You Know That...

even though U.S. residents spend about $24 billion on imports from Scandinavian nations each year, or about 12 times more than the roughly $2 billion they spend on imports from Sri Lanka, they typically pay at least $10 million more in annual tariffs on Sri Lankan goods? This is because the average U.S. tariff rate on products imported from Scandinavian countries is less than 1 percent, whereas the average tariff rate on Sri Lankan imports—mostly clothing subject to particularly high tariffs—exceeds 13 percent.

What effects do tariffs have on import consumption and the prices of imported goods and services? You will learn the answer to this question in this chapter. First, however, you need to learn more about international trade.

THE WORLDWIDE IMPORTANCE OF INTERNATIONAL TRADE

Look at panel (a) of Figure 33-1. Since the end of World War II, world output of goods and services (world real gross domestic product, or world real GDP) has increased almost every year; it is now almost nine times what it was then. Look at the top line in panel (a). World trade has increased to more than 26 times what it was in 1950.

Go to www.econtoday.com/ch33 for the World Trade Organization's most recent data on world trade.

The United States figured prominently in this expansion of world trade. In panel (b) of Figure 33-1, you see imports and exports expressed as a percentage of total annual yearly income (GDP). Whereas imports added up to barely 4 percent of annual U.S. GDP in 1950, today they account for almost 17 percent. International trade has definitely become more important to the economy of the United States, and it may become even more so as other countries loosen their trade restrictions.

How has the Internet recently contributed to increased trade between the United States and Canada?

E-COMMERCE EXAMPLE

U.S. Consumers Go Online to Import Canadian Pharmaceuticals

Today, about 270 pharmacies in Canada offer services to U.S. consumers. After the pharmacies receive prescriptions from U.S. physicians, Canadian physicians review the prescriptions to verify that they comply with that nation's health care laws. Then the pharmacies ship the medications across the border. All told, more than $700 million worth of pharmaceuticals now flows southward across the U.S.-Canadian border each year.

FOR CRITICAL ANALYSIS
Some critics claim that international trade causes nations to "lose jobs." Why do you suppose that the premier of the Canadian province of Manitoba credits international trade in pharmaceuticals with creating 2,000 jobs at the province's online and mail-order pharmacies?

WHY WE TRADE: COMPARATIVE ADVANTAGE AND MUTUAL GAINS FROM EXCHANGE

You have already been introduced to the concept of specialization and mutual gains from trade in Chapter 2. These concepts are worth repeating because they are essential to understanding why the world is better off because of more international trade. The best way to understand the gains from trade among nations is first to understand the output gains from specialization between individuals.

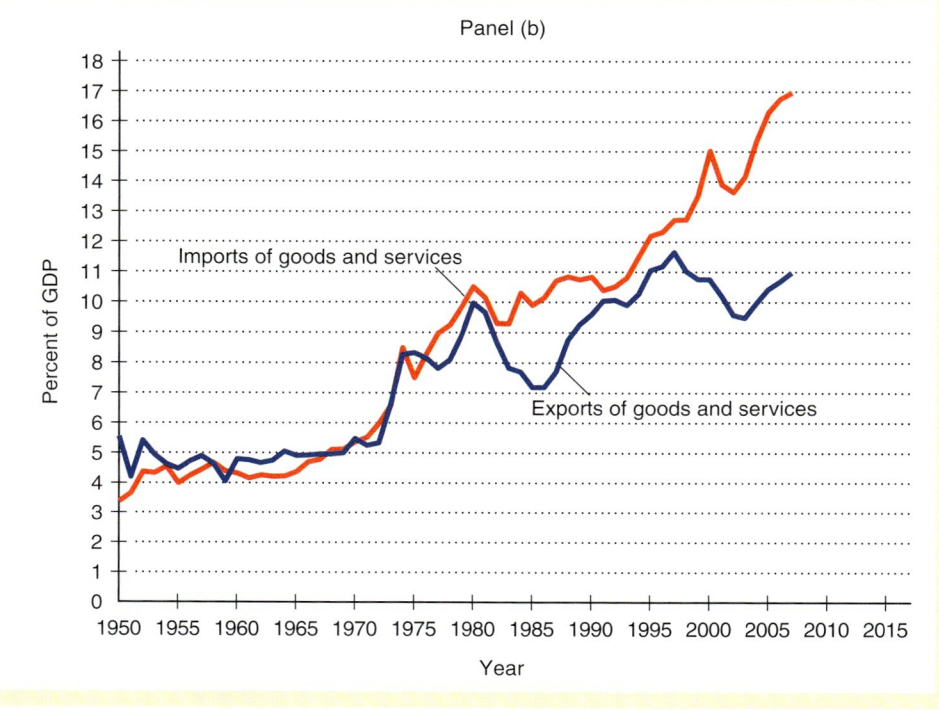

FIGURE 33-1

The Growth of World Trade

In panel (a), you can see the growth in world trade in relative terms because we use an index of 100 to represent real world trade in 1950. By the mid-2000s, that index had increased to over 2,600. At the same time, the index of world real GDP (annual world real income) had gone up to only around 900. World trade is clearly on the rise: In the United States, both imports and exports, expressed as a percentage of annual national income (GDP) in panel (b), have generally been rising since 1950.

Sources: Steven Husted and Michael Melvin, *International Economics*, 3d ed. (New York: HarperCollins, 1995), p. 11, used with permission; World Trade Organization; Federal Reserve System; U.S. Department of Commerce.

The Output Gains from Specialization

Suppose that a creative advertising specialist can come up with two pages of ad copy (written words) an hour or generate one computerized art rendering per hour. At the same time, a computer artist can write one page of ad copy per hour or complete one computerized art rendering per hour. Here the ad specialist can come up with more pages of ad copy per hour than the computer specialist and seemingly is just as good as the computer specialist at doing computerized art renderings. Is there any reason for the creative specialist and the computer specialist to "trade"? The answer is yes because such trading will lead to higher output.

Consider the scenario of no trading. Assume that during each eight-hour day, the ad specialist and the computer whiz devote half of their day to writing ad copy and half to computerized art rendering. The ad specialist would create eight pages of ad copy (4 hours × 2) and four computerized art renderings (4 × 1). During that same period, the computer specialist would create four pages of ad copy (4 hours × 1) and four computerized art renderings (4 × 1). Each day, the combined output for the ad specialist and the computer specialist would be 12 pages of ad copy and eight computerized art renderings.

If the ad specialist specialized only in writing ad copy and the computer whiz specialized only in creating computerized art renderings, their combined output would rise to 16 pages of ad copy (8 × 2) and eight computerized art renderings (8 × 1). Overall, production would increase by four pages of ad copy per day with no decline in art renderings.

The creative advertising employee has a comparative advantage in writing ad copy, and the computer specialist has a comparative advantage in doing computerized art renderings. **Comparative advantage** is simply the ability to produce something at a lower opportunity cost than other producers, as we pointed out in Chapter 2.

Why would you guess that European nations import large quantities of ready-to-eat vegetables from Kenya?

Go to www.econtoday.com/ch33 for data on U.S. trade with all other nations of the world.

Comparative advantage
The ability to produce a good or service at a lower opportunity cost than other producers.

INTERNATIONAL EXAMPLE

Kenya's Green Thumb in Exporting Green Beans

Each day, numerous flights touch down at the airport in Nairobi, Kenya, where they unload hundreds of European tourists. When the planes fly back to Europe each evening, they carry far more than weary travelers returning from African safaris. Each plane's hold is packed with an average of 25 tons of fresh green beans, okra, and about 30 other types of vegetables that were harvested in the Kenyan countryside that morning. Trucks carried this produce to air-conditioned cargo bays next to the airport, where thousands of workers washed, sorted, and packed the vegetables before rushing them to the plane's refrigerated compartments.

Average hourly wages of European agricultural and food-processing workers are more than seven times higher than the wages earned by these workers in Kenya. This factor allows Kenyan firms to grow, harvest, package, and transport vegetables for sale in Europe more efficiently than European producers. Thus, the opportunity cost of producing many packaged vegetables is lower in Kenya than in Europe, which gives Kenya a comparative advantage in producing these goods.

FOR CRITICAL ANALYSIS
If Kenyan agricultural and food-processing workers' wages were to rise somewhat relative to wages earned by European workers, would Kenya necessarily lose its comparative advantage in producing certain prepackaged vegetables?

TABLE 33-1
Maximum Feasible Hourly Production Rates of Either Commercial Software or Personal Computers Using All Available Resources

This table indicates maximum feasible rates of production of software and personal computers if all available resources are allocated to producing either one item or the other. If U.S. residents allocate all resources to producing a single good, they can produce either 90 units of software per hour or 225 PCs per hour. If residents of India allocate all resources to manufacturing one good, they can produce either 100 units of software per hour or 50 PCs per hour.

Product	United States	India
Units of software	90	100
Personal computers	225	50

Specialization Among Nations

To demonstrate the concept of comparative advantage for nations, let's consider a simple two-country, two-good world. As a hypothetical example, let's suppose that the nations in this world are India and the United States.

Production and Consumption Capabilities in a Two-Country, Two-Good World.
In Table 33-1, we show maximum feasible quantities of computer software and personal computers (PCs) that may be produced during an hour using all resources—labor, capital, land, and entrepreneurship—available in the United States and in India. As you can see from the table, U.S. residents can utilize all their resources to produce either 90 units of software per hour or 225 PCs per hour. Residents of India are able to utilize all their resources to produce either 100 units of software per hour or 50 PCs per hour.

Comparative Advantage.
Suppose that in each country, there are constant opportunity costs of producing software and PCs. Table 33-1 implies that allocating all available resources to production of 50 PCs would require residents of India to sacrifice the production of 100 units of software. On the one hand, therefore, the opportunity cost in India of producing 1 PC is equal to 2 units of software. On the other hand, the opportunity cost of producing 1 unit of software in India is 0.5 PC.

In the United States, allocating all available resources to production of 225 PCs would require U.S. residents to give up producing 90 units of software. If we continue to assume that resources are equally productive when allocated to manufacturing either software or PCs, this means that the opportunity cost in the United States of producing 1 PC is equal to 0.4 unit of software. Alternatively, we can say that the opportunity cost to U.S. residents of producing 1 unit of software is 2.5 PCs.

The opportunity cost of producing a PC is lower in the United States than in India. At the same time, the opportunity cost of producing software is lower in India than in the United States. Thus, the United States has a comparative advantage in manufacturing PCs, and India has a comparative advantage in producing software.

Production Without Trade.
Table 33-2 on the following page tabulates two possible production choices in a situation in which U.S. and Indian residents choose not to engage in international trade. In the United States, residents choose to produce and consume 30 units of software. To produce this amount of software requires producing 75 fewer PCs

TABLE 33-2
U.S. and Indian Production and Consumption Without Trade

This table indicates two possible hourly combinations of production and consumption of software and personal computers in the absence of trade in a "world" encompassing the United States and India. U.S. residents produce 30 units of software, and residents of India produce 25 units of software, so the total amount of software that can be consumed worldwide is 55 units. In addition, U.S. residents produce 150 PCs, and Indian residents produce 37.5 PCs, so worldwide production and consumption of PCs amount to 187.5 PCs per hour.

Product	United States	India	Actual World Output
Units of software (per hour)	30	25	55
Personal computers (per hour)	150	37.5	187.5

(30 units of software times 2.5 PCs per unit of software) than the maximum feasible PC production of 225 PCs, or 150 PCs. Thus, in the absence of trade, 30 units of software and 150 PCs are produced and consumed in the United States.

Table 33-2 indicates that during an hour's time in India, residents choose to produce and consume 37.5 PCs. Obtaining this amount of PCs entails producing 75 fewer units of software (37.5 PCs times 2 units of software per PC) than the maximum of 100 units, or 25 units of software. Thus, in the absence of trade, 37.5 PCs and 25 units of software are produced and consumed in India.

Finally, Table 33-2 displays production of software and PCs for this two-country world given the nations' production (and, implicitly, consumption) choices in the absence of trade. In an hour's time, U.S. software production is 30 units, and Indian software production is 25 units, so total world software production is 55 units. Thus, the total amount of software available for world consumption is also 55 units. Hourly U.S. PC production is 150 PCs, and Indian PC production is 37.5 PCs, so total world production is 187.5 PCs per hour. Consequently, the total number of PCs available for consumption in this two-country world is 187.5 PCs per hour.

Specialization in Production. More realistically, residents of the United States will choose to specialize in the activity for which they experience a lower opportunity cost. In other words, U.S. residents will specialize in the activity in which they have a comparative advantage, which is the production of personal computers. Likewise, residents of India will specialize in the area of manufacturing in which they have a comparative advantage, which is the production of commercial software.

Once the two nations have specialized, they can gain from engaging in international trade. To see why, suppose that U.S. residents allocate all available resources to producing 225 PCs, the good in which they have a comparative advantage. In addition, residents of India utilize all resources they have on hand to produce 100 units of commercial software, the good in which they have a comparative advantage.

TABLE 33-3

U.S. and Indian Production and Consumption with Specialization and Trade

In this table, U.S. residents produce 225 personal computers and no software, and Indian residents produce 100 units of software and no PCs. Residents of the two nations then agree to a rate of exchange of 1 PC for 1 unit of software and proceed to trade 75 U.S. PCs for 75 units of Indian software. Specialization and trade allow U.S. residents to consume 75 units of software imported from India and to consume 150 PCs produced at home. By specializing and engaging in trade, Indian residents consume 25 units of software produced at home and import 75 PCs from the United States.

Product	U.S. Production and Consumption with Trade		Indian Production and Consumption with Trade	
Units of software (per hour)	U.S. production	0	Indian production	100
	+ Imports from India	75	− Exports to U.S.	75
	Total U.S. consumption	75	Total Indian consumption	25
Personal computers (per hour)	U.S. production	225	Indian production	0
	− Exports to India	75	+ Imports from U.S.	75
	Total U.S. consumption	150	Total Indian consumption	75

Consumption with Specialization and Trade. U.S. residents will be willing to buy a unit of Indian commercial software as long as they must provide in exchange no more than 2.5 PCs, which is the opportunity cost of producing 1 unit of software at home. At the same time, residents of India will be willing to buy a U.S. PC as long as they must provide in exchange no more than 2 units of software, which is their opportunity cost of producing a PC.

For instance, suppose that residents of both countries agree to trade at a rate of exchange of 1 PC for 1 unit of software and that U.S. residents agree with Indian residents to trade 75 PCs for 75 units of software. Table 33-3 displays the outcomes that result in both countries. By specializing in PC production and engaging in trade, U.S. residents can continue consuming 150 PCs. In addition, U.S. residents are also able to import and consume 75 units of software produced in India. At the same time, specialization and exchange allow residents of India to continue to consume 25 units of software. Producing 75 more units of software for export to the United States allows India to import 75 PCs.

Gains from Trade. Table 33-4 on the next page summarizes the rates of consumption of U.S. and Indian residents with and without trade. Column 1 displays U.S. and Indian software and PC consumption rates with specialization and trade from Table 33-3, and it sums these to determine total consumption rates in this two-country world. Column 2 shows U.S., Indian, and worldwide consumption rates without international trade from Table 33-2. Column 3 gives the differences between the two columns.

Table 33-4 indicates that by producing 75 additional PCs for export to India in exchange for 75 units of software, U.S. residents are able to expand their software consumption from 30 units to 75 units. Thus, the U.S. gain from specialization and trade is 45 units of software. This is a net gain in software consumption for the two-country world as a whole, because neither country had to give up consuming any PCs for U.S. residents to realize this gain from trade.

TABLE 33-4

National and Worldwide Gains from Specialization and Trade
This table summarizes the consumption gains experienced by the United States, India, and the two-country world. U.S. and Indian software and PC consumption rates with specialization and trade from Table 33-3 are listed in column 1, which sums the national consumption rates to determine total worldwide consumption with trade. Column 2 shows U.S., Indian, and worldwide consumption rates without international trade, as reported in Table 33-2. Column 3 gives the differences between the two columns, which are the resulting national and worldwide gains from international trade.

Product	(1) National and World Consumption with Trade	(2) National and World Consumption without Trade	(3) Worldwide Consumption Gains from Trade
Units of software (per hour)	U.S. consumption 75 + Indian consumption 25 World consumption 100	U.S. consumption 30 + Indian consumption 25 World consumption 55	Change in U.S. consumption +45 Change in Indian consumption + 0 **Change in world consumption +45**
Personal computers (per hour)	U.S. consumption 150 + Indian consumption 75 World consumption 225	U.S. consumption 150 + Indian consumption 37.5 World consumption 187.5	Change in U.S. consumption + 0 Change in Indian consumption +37.5 **Change in world consumption +37.5**

In addition, without trade residents of India could have used all resources to produce and consume only 37.5 PCs and 25 units of software. By using all resources to specialize in producing 100 units of software and engaging in trade, residents of India can consume 37.5 *more* PCs than they could have produced and consumed alone without reducing their software consumption. Thus, the Indian gain from trade is 37.5 PCs. This represents a worldwide gain in PC consumption, because neither country had to give up consuming any PCs for Indian residents to realize this gain from trade.

Specialization Is the Key. This example shows that when nations specialize in producing goods for which they have a comparative advantage and engage in international trade, considerable consumption gains are possible for those nations and hence for the world. Why is this so? The answer is that specializing in producing goods for which the two nations have a comparative advantage allows both nations to produce more efficiently. As a consequence, worldwide production capabilities increase. This makes greater worldwide consumption possible through international trade.

Of course, not everybody in our example is better off when free trade occurs. In our example, the U.S. software industry and Indian computer industry have disappeared. Thus, U.S. software makers and Indian computer manufacturers are worse off.

Some people are worried that the United States (or any country, for that matter) might someday "run out of exports" because of overaggressive foreign competition. The analysis of comparative advantage tells us the contrary. No matter how much other countries compete for our business, the United States (or any other country) will always have a comparative advantage in something that it can export. In 10 or 20 years, that something may not be what we export today, but it will be exportable nonetheless because we will have a comparative advantage in producing it. Consequently, the significant flows of world trade shown in Figure 33-2 will continue because the United States and other nations will retain comparative advantages in producing various goods and services.

FIGURE 33-2
World Trade Flows
International merchandise trade amounts to more than $11.5 trillion worldwide. The percentage figures show the proportion of trade flowing in the various directions throughout the globe.
Sources: World Trade Organization and author's estimates (data are for 2007).

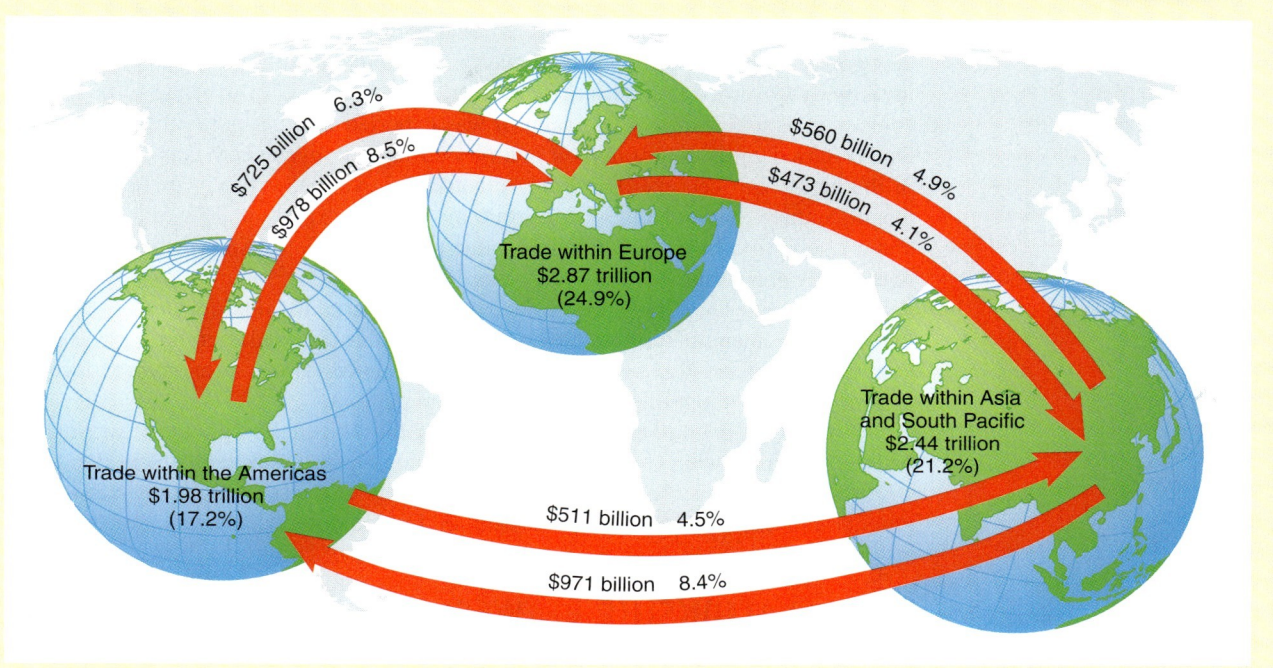

Can one nation ever lose a comparative advantage in producing certain types of products to another nation?

 **E-COMMERCE** EXAMPLE

Japan Loses Its Electronics Advantage to the United States

From the 1950s until the late 1990s, companies based in Japan—such as Sony, Panasonic, and Pioneer—made that nation a major exporter of electronic devices, including radios, stereophonic equipment, and televisions. Since the 1990s, however, U.S. companies—such as Apple Computer, Microsoft, palmOne, and Eastman Kodak—have elbowed out Japanese firms. These and other U.S. firms have greater skill in writing software for digital chips used in the latest electronic products, including downloadable-music players, videogame consoles, handheld devices, and digital cameras. In addition, U.S. electronics manufacturers have found more cost-efficient ways to design, manufacture, and distribute today's most popular devices. U.S. producers are now exporting many of these devices to Japan. Thus, the United States has developed a comparative advantage over Japan in producing a number of modern electronic products.

FOR CRITICAL ANALYSIS
If U.S. firms have a comparative advantage in producing digital electronic products, what must be true of the opportunity cost of producing these items in the United States compared with the opportunity cost in Japan?

Other Benefits from International Trade: The Transmission of Ideas

Beyond the fact that comparative advantage results in an overall increase in the output of goods produced and consumed, there is another benefit to international trade. International trade bestows benefits on countries through the international transmission of ideas. According to economic historians, international trade has been the principal means by which new goods, services, and processes have spread around the world. For example, coffee was initially grown in Arabia near the Red Sea. Around A.D. 675, it began to be roasted and consumed as a beverage. Eventually, it was exported to other parts of the world, and the Dutch started cultivating it in their colonies during the seventeenth century and the French in the eighteenth century. The lowly potato is native to the Peruvian Andes. In the sixteenth century, it was brought to Europe by Spanish explorers. Thereafter, its cultivation and consumption spread rapidly. It became part of the North American agricultural scene in the early eighteenth century.

New processes have been transmitted through international trade. One of those involves the Japanese manufacturing innovation that emphasized redesigning the system rather than running the existing system in the best possible way. Inventories were reduced to just-in-time levels by reengineering machine setup methods.

All of the *intellectual property* that has been introduced throughout the world is a result of international trade. This includes new music, such as rock and roll in the 1950s and 1960s and hip-hop in the 1990s and 2000s. It includes the software applications and computer communications tools that are common for computer users everywhere.

THE RELATIONSHIP BETWEEN IMPORTS AND EXPORTS

The basic proposition in understanding all of international trade is this:

In the long run, imports are paid for by exports.

The reason that imports are ultimately paid for by exports is that foreign residents want something in exchange for the goods that are shipped to the United States. For the most part, they want U.S.-made goods. From this truism comes a remarkable corollary:

Any restriction of imports ultimately reduces exports.

This is a shocking revelation to many people who want to restrict foreign competition to protect domestic jobs. Although it is possible to protect certain U.S. jobs by restricting foreign competition, it is impossible to make *everyone* better off by imposing import restrictions. Why? Because ultimately such restrictions lead to a reduction in employment in the export industries of the nation.

Why did U.S. exports to oil-producing nations increase during the mid-2000s even as U.S. consumers were paying more for imported oil?

INTERNATIONAL EXAMPLE

U.S. Exports Pay for More Oil Imports

The run-up in world oil prices during the 2000s contributed to an increase in U.S. import spending. It also raised the earnings of residents of oil-exporting nations, including the 11 countries that form the Organization of Petroleum Exporting Countries (OPEC). Residents of OPEC nations responded by buying more goods and services from other nations, including the United States. Imports by OPEC countries increased by more than 13 percent during 2004 and by about 15 percent during 2005. Included among those imports were U.S.-manufactured products such as digital cameras, computers, aircraft, and automobiles. These increases in U.S. exports to OPEC nations helped to pay for higher U.S. spending on oil imported from these countries.

FOR CRITICAL ANALYSIS
In the long run, how do OPEC nations ultimately pay for consumer goods that they import mainly from Japan, Europe, and the United States?

INTERNATIONAL COMPETITIVENESS

"The United States is falling behind." "We need to stay competitive internationally." Statements such as these are often heard in government circles when the subject of international trade comes up. There are two problems with such talk. The first has to do with a simple definition. What does "global competitiveness" really mean? When one company competes against another, it is in competition. Is the United States like one big corporation, in competition with other countries? Certainly not. The standard of living in each country is almost solely a function of how well the economy functions *within that country,* not relative to other countries.

Another point relates to real-world observations. According to the Institute for Management Development in Lausanne, Switzerland, the United States continues to lead the pack in overall productive efficiency, ahead of Japan, Germany, and the rest of the European Union. According to the report, the top ranking of the United States has been due to widespread entrepreneurship, more than a decade of economic restructuring, and information-technology investments. Other factors include the sophisticated U.S. financial system and large investments in scientific research.

QUICK QUIZ

A nation has a **comparative advantage** when its residents are able to produce a good or service at a _____ opportunity cost than residents of another nation.

Specializing in production of goods and services for which residents of a nation have a _____ _____ allows the nation's residents to _____ more of all goods and services.

_____ from trade arise for all nations in the world that engage in international trade because specialization and trade allow countries' residents to _____ more goods and services without necessarily giving up consumption of other goods and services.

See page 857 for the answers. Review concepts from this section in MyEconLab.

ARGUMENTS AGAINST FREE TRADE

Numerous arguments are raised against free trade. They mainly focus on the costs of trade; they do not consider the benefits or the possible alternatives for reducing the costs of free trade while still reaping benefits.

The Infant Industry Argument

A nation may feel that if a particular industry is allowed to develop domestically, it will eventually become efficient enough to compete effectively in the world market. Therefore, the nation may impose some restrictions on imports in order to give domestic producers the time they need to develop their efficiency to the point where they can compete in the domestic market without any restrictions on imports. In graphic terminology, we would expect that if the protected industry truly does experience improvements in production techniques or technological breakthroughs toward greater efficiency in the future, the supply curve will shift outward to the right so that the domestic industry can produce larger quantities at each and every price. National policymakers often assert that this **infant industry argument** has some merit in the short run. They have used it to protect a number of industries in their infancy around the world.

Infant industry argument
The contention that tariffs should be imposed to protect from import competition an industry that is trying to get started. Presumably, after the industry becomes technologically efficient, the tariff can be lifted.

Such a policy can be abused, however. Often the protective import-restricting arrangements remain even after the infant has matured. If other countries can still produce more cheaply, the people who benefit from this type of situation are obviously the stockholders (and specialized factors of production that will earn economic rents) in the industry that is still being protected from world competition. The people who lose out are the consumers, who must pay a price higher than the world price for the product in question. In any event, it is very difficult to know beforehand which industries will eventually survive. In other words, we cannot predict very well the specific infant industries that policymakers might deem worthy of protection. Note that when we speculate about which industries "should" be protected, we are in the realm of *normative economics*. We are making a value judgment, a subjective statement of what *ought to be*.

Countering Foreign Subsidies and Dumping

Go to www.econtoday.com/ch33 for a Congressional Budget Office review of antidumping actions in the United States and around the world.

Another strong argument against unrestricted foreign trade has to do with countering other nations' subsidies to their own producers. When a foreign government subsidizes its producers, our producers claim that they cannot compete fairly with these subsidized foreign producers. To the extent that such subsidies fluctuate, it can be argued that unrestricted free trade will seriously disrupt domestic producers. They will not know when foreign governments are going to subsidize their producers and when they are not. Our competing industries will be expanding and contracting too frequently.

The phenomenon called *dumping* is also used as an argument against unrestricted trade. **Dumping** is said to occur when a producer sells its products abroad below the price that is charged in the home market or at a price below its cost of production. When a foreign producer is accused of dumping, further investigation usually reveals that the foreign nation is in the throes of a recession. The foreign producer does not want to slow down its production at home. Because it anticipates an end to the recession and doesn't want to hold large inventories, it dumps its products abroad at prices below home prices. U.S. competitors may also allege that it sells its output at prices below its full costs in an effort to cover variable costs of production.

Dumping
Selling a good or a service abroad below the price charged in the home market or at a price below its cost of production.

Protecting Domestic Jobs

Perhaps the argument used most often against free trade is that unrestrained competition from other countries will eliminate jobs in the United States because other countries have lower-cost labor than we do. (Less restrictive environmental standards in other countries might also lower their private costs relative to ours.) This is a compelling argument, particularly for politicians from areas that might be threatened by foreign competition. For example, a representative from an area with shoe factories would certainly be upset about the possibility of constituents' losing their jobs because of competition from lower-priced shoe manufacturers in Brazil and Italy. But, of course, this argument against free trade is equally applicable to trade between the states within the United States.

Economists David Gould, G. L. Woodbridge, and Roy Ruffin examined the data on the relationship between increases in imports and the rate of unemployment. Their conclusion was that there is no causal link between the two. Indeed, in half the cases they studied, when imports increased, unemployment fell.

Another issue has to do with the cost of protecting U.S. jobs by restricting international trade. The Institute for International Economics examined just the restrictions on foreign textiles and apparel goods. U.S. consumers pay $9 billion a year more than they would otherwise pay for those goods to protect jobs in those industries. That comes out to $50,000 *a year* for each job saved in an industry in which the average job pays only $20,000 a year. Similar studies have yielded similar results: Restrictions on imports of Japanese cars have cost $160,000 *per year* for every job saved in the auto industry. Every job preserved in the glass industry has cost $200,000 each and every year. Every job preserved in the U.S. steel industry has cost an astounding $750,000 per year.

Emerging Arguments Against Free Trade

In recent years, two new antitrade arguments have been advanced. One of these focuses on environmental concerns. For instance, many environmentalists have suggested that genetic engineering of plants and animals could lead to accidental production of new diseases. These worries have induced the European Union to restrain trade in such products.

Another argument against free trade arises from national defense concerns. Major espionage successes by China in the late 1990s and early 2000s led some U.S. strategic experts to propose sweeping restrictions on exports of new technology.

Free trade proponents counter that at best these are arguments for the judicious regulation of trade. They continue to argue that by and large, broad trade restrictions mainly harm the interests of the nations that impose them.

> **QUICK QUIZ**
>
> The _____ industry argument against free trade contends that new industries should be _____ against world competition so that they can become technologically efficient in the long run.
>
> Unrestricted foreign trade may allow foreign governments to subsidize exports or foreign producers to engage in _____, or selling products in other countries below their cost of production. Critics claim that to the extent that foreign export subsidies and _____ create more instability in domestic production, they may impair our well-being.
>
> See page 857 for the answers. Review concepts from this section in MyEconLab.

WAYS TO RESTRICT FOREIGN TRADE

International trade can be stopped or at least stifled in many ways. These include quotas and taxes (the latter are usually called *tariffs* when applied to internationally traded items). Let's talk first about quotas.

Quotas

Under a **quota system,** individual countries or groups of foreign producers are restricted to a certain amount of trade. An import quota specifies the maximum amount of a commodity that may be imported during a specified period of time. For example, the government might

Quota system
A government-imposed restriction on the quantity of a specific good that another country is allowed to sell in the United States. In other words, quotas are restrictions on imports. These restrictions are usually applied to one or several specific countries.

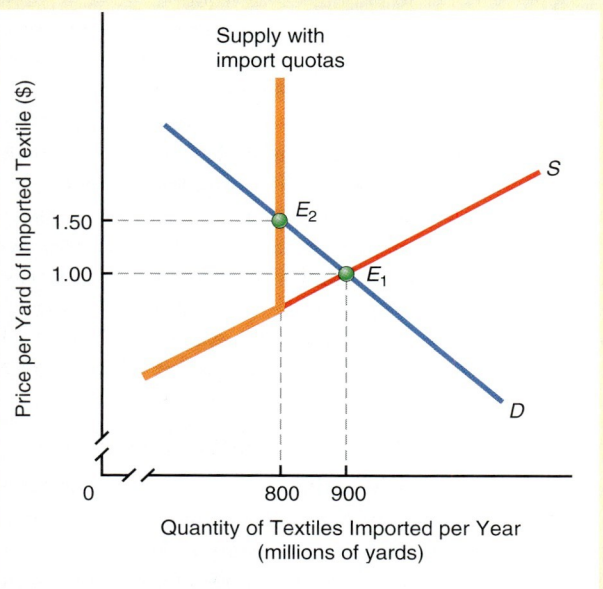

FIGURE 33-3

The Effect of Quotas on Textile Imports

Without restrictions, at point E_1, 900 million yards of textiles would be imported each year into the United States at the world price of $1.00 per yard. If the federal government imposes a quota of only 800 million yards, the effective supply curve becomes vertical at that quantity. It intersects the demand curve at point E_2, so the new equilibrium price is $1.50 per yard.

not allow more than 50 million barrels of foreign crude oil to enter the United States in a particular month.

Consider the example of quotas on textiles. Figure 33-3 presents the demand and supply curves for imported textiles. In an unrestricted import market, the equilibrium quantity imported is 900 million yards at a price of $1 per yard (expressed in constant-quality units). When an import quota is imposed, the supply curve is no longer S. Instead, the supply curve becomes vertical at some amount less than the equilibrium quantity—here, 800 million yards per year. The price to the U.S. consumer increases from $1.00 to $1.50.

Clearly, the output restriction generated by a quota on foreign imports of a particular item has the effect of raising the domestic price of the imported item. Two groups benefit. One group is importers that are able to obtain the rights to sell imported items domestically at the higher price, which raises their revenues and boosts their profits. The other group is domestic producers. Naturally, a rise in the price of an imported item induces an increase in the demand for domestic substitutes. Thus, the domestic prices of close substitutes for the item subject to the import restriction also increase, which generates higher revenues and profits for domestic producers.

Voluntary Quotas. Quotas do not have to be explicit and defined by law. They can be "voluntary." Such a quota is called a **voluntary restraint agreement (VRA)**. In the early 1980s, Japanese automakers voluntarily restrained exports to the United States. These restraints stayed in place into the 1990s. Today, there are VRAs on machine tools and textiles.

The opposite of a VRA is a **voluntary import expansion (VIE)**. Under a VIE, a foreign government agrees to have its companies import more foreign goods from another country. The United States almost started a major international trade war with Japan in 1995 over just such an issue. The U.S. government wanted Japanese automobile manufacturers voluntarily to increase their imports of U.S.-made automobile parts. Ultimately, Japanese companies did make a token increase in their imports of U.S. auto parts.

How did France seek to impose a quota of zero units on a Swiss export good?

Voluntary restraint agreement (VRA)
An official agreement with another country that "voluntarily" restricts the quantity of its exports to the United States.

Voluntary import expansion (VIE)
An official agreement with another country in which it agrees to import more from the United States.

INTERNATIONAL POLICY EXAMPLE

To the French, the Name of This Traded Good Is All Important

Near Lake Neuchâtel in western Switzerland, a number of the French-speaking residents of Champagne, Switzerland, use local Chasselas grapes to produce about 300,000 bottles of red and white wine each year. In honor of their village, since the tenth century they have marketed their relatively inexpensive wine, which is typically sold at home and abroad for about $10 per bottle, under the label "Swiss Champagne."

In 1999, however, as part of a treaty granting the Swiss airline Swissair rights to transport French goods, the government of France demanded a unique "quota" on exports of the Swiss wine. Under the treaty, the residents of Champagne, Switzerland, are no longer allowed to bottle their wine under the name "Champagne." In this way, the French government sought to prevent the Swiss village winery from incidentally competing with the nearly two-centuries-old French champagne industry, which each year sells more than 280 million bottles of sparkling wine.

FOR CRITICAL ANALYSIS
Why do you suppose that the French government wishes to prevent Swiss "champagne" from being sold, even though total worldwide sales of this product amount to only 0.1 percent of French champagne production? (Hint: What must the government of France do if its objective is to erect barriers to competition by any foreign competitors considering entry into the French champagne market?)

Tariffs

We can analyze tariffs by using standard supply and demand diagrams. Let's use as our commodity laptop computers, some of which are made in Japan and some of which are made domestically. In panel (a) of Figure 33-4 on page 848, you see the demand for and supply of Japanese laptops. The equilibrium price is $1,000 per constant-quality unit, and the equilibrium quantity is 10 million per year. In panel (b), you see the same equilibrium price of $1,000, and the *domestic* equilibrium quantity is 5 million units per year.

Now a tariff of $500 is imposed on all imported Japanese laptops. The supply curve shifts upward by $500 to S_2. For purchasers of Japanese laptops, the price increases to $1,250. The quantity demanded falls to 8 million per year. In panel (b), you see that at the higher price of imported Japanese laptops, the demand curve for U.S.-made laptops shifts outward to the right to D_2. The equilibrium price increases to $1,250, and the equilibrium quantity increases to 6.5 million units per year. So the tariff benefits domestic laptop producers because it increases the demand for their products due to the higher price of a close substitute, Japanese laptops. This causes a redistribution of income from Japanese producers and U.S. consumers of laptops to U.S. producers of laptops.

Tariffs in the United States. In Figure 33-5 on page 849, we see that tariffs on all imported goods have varied widely. The highest rates in the twentieth century occurred with the passage of the Smoot-Hawley Tariff in 1930.

Current Tariff Laws. The Trade Expansion Act of 1962 gave the president the authority to reduce tariffs by up to 50 percent. Subsequently, tariffs were reduced by about 35 percent. In 1974, the Trade Reform Act allowed the president to reduce tariffs further. In 1984, the Trade and Tariff Act resulted in the lowest tariff rates ever. All such trade agreement obligations of the United States were carried out under the auspices of

Go to www.econtoday.com/ch33 to take a look at the U.S. State Department's reports on economic policy and trade practices.

ECONOMICS FRONT AND CENTER

To consider how tariffs can present problems for international efforts to fight diseases, read **How Tariffs Complicate the Global Battle Against Malaria**, on page 851.

FIGURE 33-4

The Effect of a Tariff on Japanese-Made Laptop Computers

Without a tariff, the United States buys 10 million Japanese laptops per year at an average price of $1,000, at point E_1 in panel (a). U.S. producers sell 5 million domestically made laptops, also at $1,000 each, at point E_1 in panel (b). A $500-per-laptop tariff will shift the Japanese import supply curve to S_2 in panel (a), so that the new equilibrium is at E_2, with price increased to $1,250 and quantity sold reduced to 8 million per year. The demand curve for U.S.-made laptops (for which there is no tariff) shifts to D_2, in panel (b). Domestic sales increase to 6.5 million per year, at point E_2.

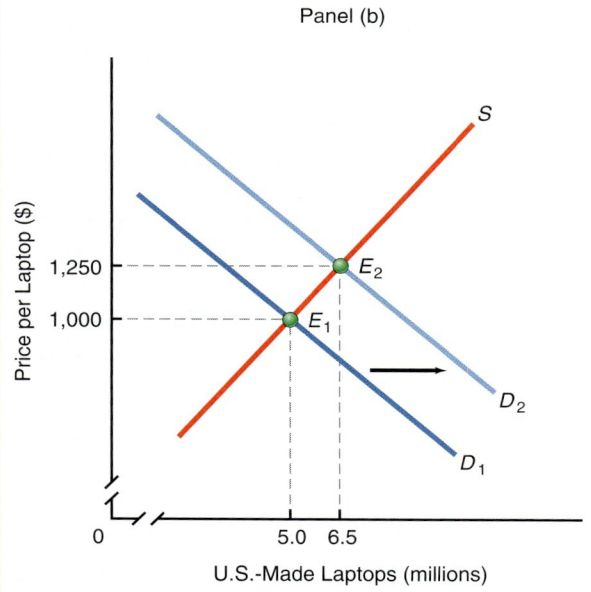

General Agreement on Tariffs and Trade (GATT)
An international agreement established in 1947 to further world trade by reducing barriers and tariffs. GATT was replaced by the World Trade Organization in 1995.

the **General Agreement on Tariffs and Trade (GATT),** which was signed in 1947. Member nations of GATT account for more than 85 percent of world trade. As you can see in Figure 33-5, there have been a number of rounds of negotiations to reduce tariffs. In 2002, the U.S. government proposed eliminating all tariffs on manufactured goods by 2015.

INTERNATIONAL TRADE ORGANIZATIONS

The widespread effort to reduce tariffs around the world has generated interest among nations in joining various international trade organizations. These organizations promote trade by granting preferences in the form of reduced or eliminated tariffs, duties, or quotas.

The World Trade Organization (WTO)

World Trade Organization (WTO)
The successor organization to GATT that handles trade disputes among its member nations.

The most important international trade organization with the largest membership is the **World Trade Organization (WTO),** which was ratified by the Uruguay Round of the General Agreement on Tariffs and Trade at the end of 1993. The WTO, which as of 2007 had 151 member nations and included 30 observer governments, began operations on January 1, 1995. WTO decisions have concerned such topics as special U.S. steel tariffs imposed in

FIGURE 33-5

Tariff Rates in the United States Since 1820

Tariff rates in the United States have bounced around like a football; indeed, in Congress, tariffs are a political football. Import-competing industries prefer high tariffs. In the twentieth century, the highest tariff was the Smoot-Hawley Tariff of 1930, which was about as high as the "tariff of abominations" in 1828.

Source: U.S. Department of Commerce.

the early 2000s, which the U.S. government removed after the WTO determined that they violated its rules. The WTO also adjudicated the European Union's "banana wars" and determined that the EU's policies unfairly favored many former European colonies in Africa, the Caribbean, and the Pacific at the expense of banana-exporting countries in Latin America. Now those former colonies no longer have a privileged position in European markets.

On a larger scale, the WTO fostered the most important and far-reaching global trade agreement ever covering financial institutions, including banks, insurers, and investment companies. The more than 100 signatories to this new treaty have legally committed themselves to giving foreign residents more freedom to own and operate companies in virtually all segments of the financial services industry.

Is there any evidence that GATT and the WTO may have promoted increased international trade around the world?

INTERNATIONAL POLICY EXAMPLE

Twin Growth Paths in World Trade

Its champions credit the WTO with boosting world trade. Doubters of this claim think it may be the other way around—that increased interest in gains from trade is fueling WTO membership. In any event, as Figure 33-6 shows, growth in world trade has taken place alongside growth in the number of nations in the WTO.

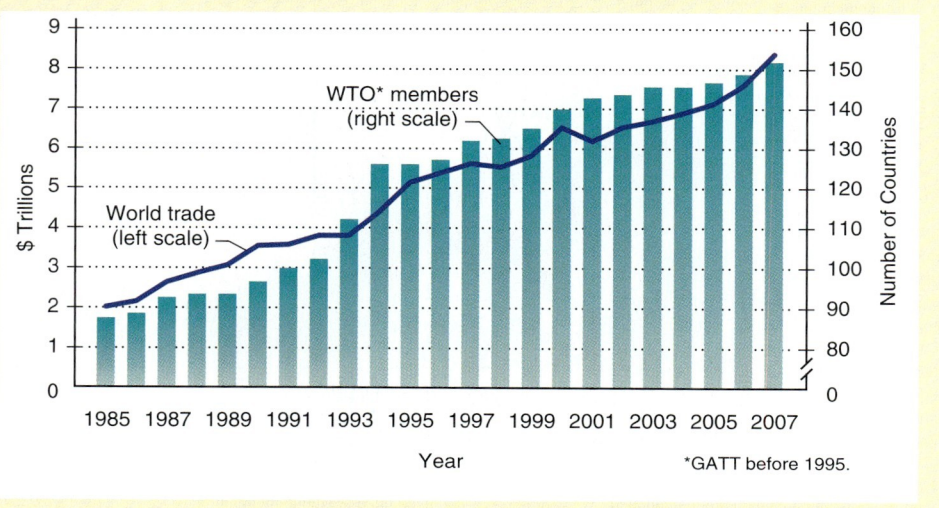

FIGURE 33-6

Growth in the World Trade Organization's Membership and in Global Trade

Both membership in the World Trade Organization and total international trade have increased considerably since the mid-1980s.

Source: World Trade Organization.

FOR CRITICAL ANALYSIS

Is it possible that the causation between WTO membership growth and growth in trade runs both directions—that the WTO really has promoted greater international trade and that more countries have joined the WTO because they wish to engage in more trade? Explain.

Regional Trade Agreements

Regional trade bloc
A group of nations that grants members special trade privileges.

Numerous other international trade organizations exist alongside the WTO. Sometimes known as **regional trade blocs,** these organizations are created by special deals among groups of countries that grant trade preferences only to countries within their groups. Currently, more than 230 bilateral or regional trade agreements are in effect around the globe. Examples include groups of industrial powerhouses, such the European Union, the North American Free Trade Agreement, and the Association of Southeast Asian Nations. Nations in South America with per capita real GDP nearer the world average have also formed regional trade blocs called Mercosur and the Andean Community. Less developed nations have also formed regional trade blocs, such as the Economic Community of West African States and the Community of East and Southern Africa.

Some economists have worried that the formation of regional trade blocs could result in a reduction in members' trade with nations outside their own blocs. If more trade is diverted from a bloc than is created within it, then on net a regional trade agreement reduces trade. So far, however, most evidence indicates that regional trade blocs have promoted trade instead of hindering it. Numerous studies have found that as countries around the world have become more open to trade, they have tended to join regional trade blocs that promote even more openness.

QUICK QUIZ

One means of restricting foreign trade is an import quota, which specifies a _____ amount of a good that may be imported during a certain period. The resulting increase in import prices benefits those who gain the right to sell the imported item and domestic _____ that receive higher prices resulting from substitution to domestic goods.

Another means of restricting imports is a **tariff**, which is a _____ on imports only. An import tariff _____ import-competing industries and harms consumers by raising prices.

The main international institution created to improve trade among nations was the General Agreement on Tariffs and Trade (GATT). The last round of trade talks under GATT, the Uruguay Round, led to the creation of the _____ _____ _____.

_____ _____ agreements among numerous nations of the world have established more than 230 _____ _____ blocs, which grant special trade privileges such as reduced tariff barriers and quota exemptions to member nations.

See page 857 for the answers. Review concepts from this section in MyEconLab.

CASE STUDY — ECONOMICS FRONT AND CENTER

How Tariffs Complicate the Global Battle Against Malaria

Benigno is the director of an organization dedicated to fighting malaria throughout the world. The mosquito-borne disease, which is caused by protozoan parasites that penetrate a victim's bloodstream, affects an estimated 350 million people around the world. Malaria claims between 1 million and 2 million lives every year.

To help reduce the number of malaria victims, Benigno's organization pays subsidies to companies that develop and distribute antimalarial drugs to developing countries most heavily affected by the disease. Sometimes Benigno's organization purchases these drugs and donates them to the poorest and hardest-hit nations.

Benigno has become increasingly frustrated, however, by the effects that many of these nations' trade policies have on his organization's efforts to promote increased availability of medications. More than 50 developing countries around the globe levy tariffs and other taxes and fees on pharmaceutical imports, which have the effect of pushing up the market clearing prices of these drugs. As a consequence, Benigno's organization must pay higher subsidies to manufacturers to induce them to produce these drugs for sale in developing nations.

Today, Benigno has received news that he can hardly believe. One African country has notified his organization that its planned *donations* of malaria-fighting drugs will be subjected to tariffs. Benigno finds himself wondering if the leaders of some developing countries really have the best interests of their nations' residents at heart.

CRITICAL ANALYSIS QUESTIONS

1. *Explain how imposing a tariff on imports of a pharmaceutical product pushes up the market clearing price of the product in the nation that assesses the tariff.*

2. *Why does Benigno's organization have to pay drug producers more subsidies to induce them to supply antimalarial drugs in countries with pharmaceutical tariffs?*

Issues and Applications

Do Regional Trade Blocs Encourage "Trade Deflection"?

Concepts Applied
- Regional Trade Blocs
- Comparative Advantage

Figure 33-7 shows that the formation of regional trade blocs is on an upswing. It also shows that the European Union and the United States are key participants in most regional trade agreements. Nevertheless, developing nations are also joining more regional trade blocs. An average African nation participates in four separate regional trade agreements. A typical Latin American country belongs to eight different regional trade blocs.

Trade Diversion versus Trade Deflection

As noted earlier, the creation of regional trade blocs might simply result in the *diversion* of trade: the shifting of trade from countries outside a bloc to nations within the bloc. Most economists now agree, however, that so far the net effect of forming regional trade blocs has been to stimulate total international trade. Although there is disagreement about how large the trade-expanding effect has been, it appears that regional trade agreements have tended to boost overall trade.

Today, a bigger issue concerns whether regional trade blocs provide an incentive for so-called *trade deflection* to occur. Trade deflection takes place when a company located in a nation outside a regional trade bloc finds a way to move goods that are not quite fully assembled into a member country, complete assembly of the goods there, and then export them to countries offering the trade preferences.

Is Trade Deflection "Bad"?

Some proponents of free trade applaud successful trade deflection. They contend that it helps to circumvent trade restrictions and thus allows nations within regional trade blocs to experience additional gains from trade.

Other free-trade-oriented economists, however, worry that trade deflection can diminish gains from trade. For instance, suppose that Peruvian auto producers were to use all Mexican-produced auto parts to assemble "Peruvian" autos for sale in other member nations of the Andean Community, such as Bolivia and Ecuador. In this way, Peruvian auto producers would benefit from an artificial advantage created by the Andean Community's special trading preferences. Engaging in this practice could help protect relatively inefficient Peruvian firms from facing open competition with Mexican automakers.

Is the Solution to Trade Deflection Worse Than the Problem?

To try to reduce incentives for trade deflection, regional trade agreements often include *rules of origin,* which are regulations that carefully define categories of products that are eligible for trading preferences under the agreements. Some rules of origin require any products trading freely among

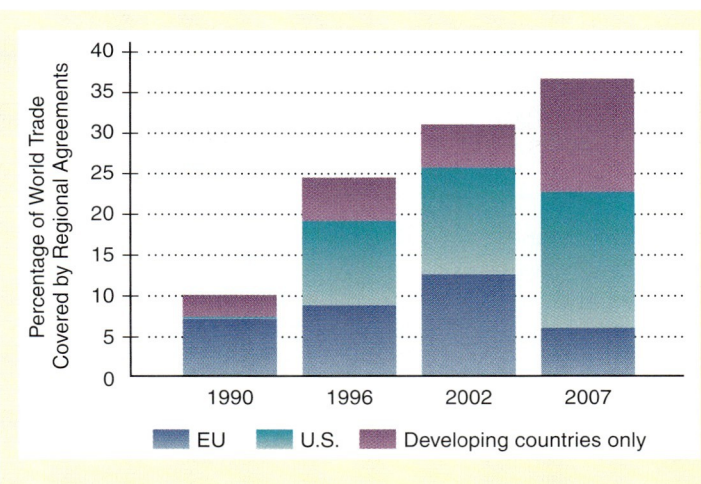

FIGURE 33-7

The Percentage of World Trade Within Regional Trade Blocs

As the number of regional trade agreements has increased since 1990, the share of world trade undertaken among nations that are members of regional trade blocs—involving the European Union (EU), United States, and developing nations—has also increased.

Source: World Bank.

members of a regional trading group to be composed mostly of materials produced within a member nation. For instance, if the Andean Community applied a rule of origin in auto trade, then an auto assembled in, say, Peru that contained more than a certain percentage of Mexican-made components would not be eligible for trade preferences in Bolivia.

Free trade advocates, however, worry that countries in regional trading blocs sometimes manipulate rules of origin in ways that turn them into barriers to trade. By making rules of origin sufficiently complex, they suggest, rules of origin can provide disincentives for countries to utilize the trading preferences that regional trade agreements are supposed to provide. Thus, it may be that this commonly utilized "solution" to the alleged trade-deflection problem is actually the greatest threat to gains from trade that regional trade agreements are supposed to engender.

Log in to **MyEconLab**, click on "Economic News," and test your understanding of the chapter by answering interactive questions that relate directly to this issue.

For Critical Analysis

1. In your own words, what is the difference between trade diversion and trade deflection?
2. In what sense do companies that succeed in engaging in trade deflection "falsely" benefit from trade preferences granted by regional trade agreements?

Web Resources

1. To learn more about rules of origin, go to www.econtoday.com/ch33.
2. To see how complicated rules of origin can be, take a look at information on rules of origin for the North American Free Trade Agreement via the link at www.econtoday.com/ch33.

Research Project

Explain why some free trade proponents worry that rules of origin aimed at limiting trade deflection can result in trade diversion. If this were definitely a result of using rules of origin to try to prevent deflection, what would happen to overall trade—other things being equal—as more regional trade blocs were formed? How might you use this prediction to try to evaluate whether the growth of regional trade blocs is helping to boost global international trade?

Here is what you should know after reading this chapter. MyEconLab will help you identify what you know, and where to go when you need to practice.

WHAT YOU SHOULD KNOW		WHERE TO GO TO PRACTICE
The Worldwide Importance of International Trade Total trade among nations has been growing faster than total world GDP. The growth of U.S. exports and imports relative to U.S. GDP parallels this global trend. Together, exports and imports now equal about one-fourth of total national production. In some countries, trade accounts for a much higher share of total economic activity.	**Key figure** Figure 33-1, 835	• **MyEconLab** Study Plan 33.1 • Audio introduction to Chapter 33 • Animated Figure 33-1
Why Nations Can Gain from Specializing in Production and Engaging in Trade A country has a comparative advantage in producing a good if it can produce that good at a lower opportunity cost, in terms of forgone production of a second good, than another nation. Because the other nation has a comparative advantage in producing the second good, both nations can gain by specializing in producing the goods in which they have a comparative advantage and engaging in international trade. Together, they can then produce and consume more than they would have produced and consumed in the absence of specialization and trade.	comparative advantage, 860 **Key figure** Figure 33-2, 841	• **MyEconLab** Study Plan 33.2 • Animated Figure 33-2 • Video: The Gains from Trade
Arguments Against Free Trade One argument against free trade is that temporary import restrictions might permit an "infant industry" to develop to the point at which it could compete without such restrictions. Another argument concerns dumping, in which foreign companies allegedly sell some of their output in domestic markets at prices below the prices in the companies' home markets or even below the companies' costs of production. In addition, some environmentalists contend that nations should restrain foreign trade to prevent exposing their countries to environmental hazards to plants, animals, or even humans. Finally, some contend that countries should limit exports of technologies that could pose a threat to their national defense.	infant industry argument, 844 dumping, 844	• **MyEconLab** Study Plans 33.3, 33.4 and 33.5
Ways That Nations Restrict Foreign Trade One way to restrain trade is to impose a quota, or a limit on imports of a good. This action restricts the supply of the good in the domestic market, thereby pushing up the equilibrium price of the good. Another way to reduce trade is to place a tariff on imported goods. This reduces the supply of foreign-made goods and increases the demand for domestically produced goods, thereby bringing about a rise in the price of the good.	quota system, 845 voluntary restraint agreement (VRA), 846 voluntary import expansion (VIE), 846 General Agreement on Tariffs and Trade (GATT), 848 **Key figures** Figure 33-3, 846 Figure 33-4, 848 Figure 33-5, 849	• **MyEconLab** Study Plan 33.6 • Animated Figures 33-3, 33-4, and 33-5 • Video: Arguments Against Free Trade

CHAPTER 33 Comparative Advantage and the Open Economy

WHAT YOU SHOULD KNOW

Key International Trade Agreements and Organizations
From 1947 to 1995, nations agreed to abide by the General Agreement on Tariffs and Trade (GATT), which laid an international legal foundation for relaxing quotas and reducing tariffs. Since 1995, the World Trade Organization (WTO) has adjudicated trade disputes that arise between or among nations. Now there are also more than 230 regional trade blocs, including the North American Free Trade Agreement and the European Union, that provide special trade preferences to member nations.

WHERE TO GO TO PRACTICE

World Trade Organization, 848
regional trade bloc, 850

- **MyEconLab** Study Plan 33.7

Log in to MyEconLab, take a chapter test, and get a personalized Study Plan that tells you which concepts you understand and which ones you need to review. From there, MyEconLab will give you further practice, tutorials, animations, videos, and guided solutions.

Log in to www.myeconlab.com

PROBLEMS

Select problems, indicated by a blue oval, are assignable in MyEconLab.
Answers to the odd-numbered problems appear at the back of the book.

33-1. To answer the questions that follow, consider the following table for the neighboring nations of Northland and West Coast. The table lists maximum feasible hourly rates of production of pastries if no sandwiches are produced and maximum feasible hourly rates of production of sandwiches if no pastries are produced. Assume that the opportunity costs of producing these goods are constant in both nations.

Product	Northland	West Coast
Pastries (per hour)	50,000	100,000
Sandwiches (per hour)	25,000	200,000

a. What is the opportunity cost of producing pastries in Northland? In Northland, what is the opportunity cost of producing sandwiches?
b. What is the opportunity cost of producing pastries in West Coast? In West Coast, what is the opportunity cost of producing sandwiches?

33-2. Based on your answers to Problem 33-1, which nation has a comparative advantage in producing pastries? Which nation has a comparative advantage in producing sandwiches?

33-3. Suppose that the two nations in Problems 33-1 and 33-2 choose to specialize in producing the goods for which they have a comparative advantage. They agree to trade at a rate of exchange of 1 pastry for 1 sandwich. At this rate of exchange, what are the maximum possible numbers of pastries and sandwiches that they could agree to trade?

33-4. Residents of the nation of Northland can forgo production of digital televisions and utilize all available resources to produce 300 bottles of high-quality wine per hour. Alternatively, they can forgo producing wine and instead produce 60 digital TVs per hour. In the neighboring country of West Coast, residents can forgo production of digital TVs and use all resources to produce 150 bottles of high-quality wine per hour, or they can forgo wine production and produce 50 digital TVs per hour. In both nations, the opportunity costs of producing the two goods are constant.

a. What is the opportunity cost of producing digital TVs in Northland? In Northland, what is the opportunity cost of producing bottles of wine?

b. What is the opportunity cost of producing digital TVs in West Coast? In West Coast, what is the opportunity cost of producing bottles of wine?

33-5. Based on your answers to Problem 33-4, which nation has a comparative advantage in producing digital TVs? Which nation has a comparative advantage in producing bottles of wine?

33-6. Suppose that the two nations in Problem 33-4 decide to specialize in producing the good for which they have a comparative advantage and to engage in trade. Will residents of both nations agree to trade wine for digital TVs at a rate of exchange of 4 bottles of wine for 1 digital TV? Why or why not?

To answer Problems 33-7 through 33-10, refer to the following table, which shows possible combinations of hourly outputs of modems and flash memory drives in South Shore and neighboring East Isle, in which opportunity costs of producing both products are constant.

South Shore		East Isle	
Modems	Flash Drives	Modems	Flash Drives
75	0	100	0
60	30	80	10
45	60	60	20
30	90	40	30
15	120	20	40
0	150	0	50

33-7. Consider the above table and answer the questions that follow.
  a. In South Shore, what is the opportunity cost of producing modems? What is the opportunity cost of producing flash memory drives in South Shore?
  b. In East Isle, what is the opportunity cost of producing modems? What is the opportunity cost of producing flash memory drives in East Isle?
  c. Which nation has a comparative advantage in producing modems? Which nation has a comparative advantage in producing flash memory drives?

33-8. Refer to your answers to Problem 33-7 when answering the following questions.
  a. Which *one* of the following rates of exchange of modems for flash memory drives will be acceptable to *both* nations: (i) 3 modems for 1 flash drive; (ii) 1 modem for 1 flash drive; or (iii) 1 flash drive for 2.5 modems? Explain.
  b. Suppose that each nation decides to use all available resources to produce only the good for which it has a comparative advantage and to engage in trade at the single feasible rate of exchange you identified in part a. Prior to specialization and trade, residents of South Shore chose to produce and consume 30 modems per hour and 90 flash drives per hour, and residents of East Isle chose to produce and consume 40 modems per hour and 30 flash drives per hour. Now, residents of South Shore agree to export to East Isle the same quantity of South Shore's specialty good that East Isle residents were consuming prior to engaging in international trade. How many units of East Isle's specialty good does South Shore import from East Isle?

33-9. Based on your answers to Problem 33-8, what is South Shore's hourly consumption of modems and flash drives after the nation specializes and trades with East Isle? What is East Isle's hourly consumption of modems and flash drives after the nation specializes and trades with East Isle?

33-10. Based on your answers to Problem 33-9, what consumption gains from trade are experienced by South Shore and East Isle?

33-11. You are a policymaker of a major exporting nation. Your main export good has a price elasticity of demand of –0.50. Is there any economic reason why you would voluntarily agree to export restraints?

33-12. The following table depicts the bicycle industry before and after a nation has imposed quota restraints.

	Before Quota	After Quota
Quantity imported	1,000,000	900,000
Price paid	$50	$60

Draw a diagram illustrating conditions in the imported bicycle market before and after the quota, and answer the following questions.
  a. What are the total expenditures of consumers before and after the quota?
  b. What is the price elasticity of demand for bicycles?
  c. Who benefits from the imposition of the quota?

33-13. The following diagrams illustrate the markets for imported Korean-made and U.S.-manufactured televisions before and after a tariff is imposed on imported TVs.

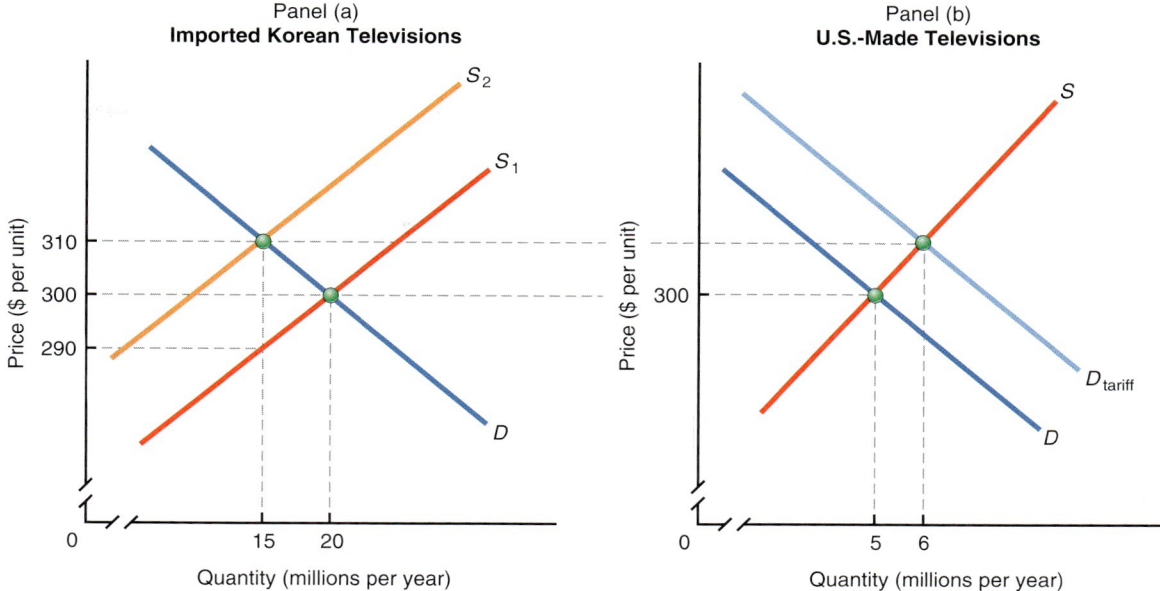

a. What was the amount of the tariff per TV?
b. Before the tariff was imposed, what were the total revenues of Korean television exporters? After the tariff was imposed?
c. What is the tariff revenue earned by the U.S. government?

33-14. Base your answers to the following questions on the graphs accompanying Problem 33-13.

a. What were the revenues of U.S. television manufacturers before the tariff was imposed?
b. What are their total revenues after the tariff?
c. Based on the available information, who has gained from the tariff, and who is worse off?

ECONOMICS ON THE NET

How the World Trade Organization Settles Trade Disputes A key function of the WTO is to adjudicate trade disagreements that arise among nations. This application helps you learn about the process that the WTO follows when considering international trade disputes.

Title: The World Trade Organization: Settling Trade Disputes

Navigation: Go to www.econtoday.com/ch33 to access the WTO's Web page titled *Dispute Settlement*. Under "Introduction to dispute settlement in the WTO," click on *How does the WTO settle disputes?*

Application Read the article; then answer the following questions.

1. As the article discusses, settling trade disputes often takes at least a year. What aspects of the WTO's dispute settlement process take the longest time?
2. Does the WTO actually "punish" a country it finds has broken international trading agreements? If not, who does impose sanctions?

For Group Study and Analysis Go to the WTO's main site at www.econtoday.com/ch33, and click on *About the WTO*. Divide the class into groups, and have the groups explore this information on areas of WTO involvement. Have a class discussion of the pros and cons of WTO involvement in these areas. Which are most important for promoting world trade? Which are least important?

ANSWERS TO QUICK QUIZZES

p. 843: (i) lower; (ii) comparative advantage . . . consume; (iii) Gains . . . consume
p. 845: (i) infant . . . protected; (ii) dumping . . . dumping
p. 851: (i) maximum . . . producers; (ii) tax . . . benefits; (iii) World Trade Organization; (iv) Regional trade . . . regional trade

34 Exchange Rates and the Balance of Payments

Learning Objectives

After reading this chapter, you should be able to:

1. Distinguish between the balance of trade and the balance of payments
2. Identify the key accounts within the balance of payments
3. Outline how exchange rates are determined in the markets for foreign exchange
4. Discuss factors that can induce changes in equilibrium exchange rates
5. Understand how policymakers can go about attempting to fix exchange rates
6. Explain alternative approaches to limiting exchange rate variability

MyEconLab helps you master each objective and study more efficiently. See end of chapter for details.

In what market do traders *daily* exchange funds equivalent in value to roughly 15 percent of U.S. real GDP—a volume of trading that is growing at a rate of 10 percent per year? The answer is the *foreign exchange market*, which is the market in which individuals, businesses, and governments buy and sell national currencies. Why are so many funds denominated in currencies from around the globe traded in this market? Which nation's currency is traded in the largest volumes each day, and why? In this chapter, you will learn the answers to these questions. You will also learn about the prices determined in this market, which are the rates at which currencies exchange for other currencies, or *exchange rates*.

Did You Know That...

a court in Thailand recently ordered the former director of the Bank of Thailand, the central bank that issues the nation's currency, the *baht*, to reimburse Thailand's government 186 billion baht ($4.6 billion) that the central bank spent buying U.S. dollars in 1997? These expenditures took place when the director ordered the Thai central bank to attempt to keep the value of its currency fixed in relation to the U.S. dollar. In its effort to maintain a fixed rate of exchange of baht for dollars, the central bank went through most of these funds in a matter of days. In the end, the Bank of Thailand failed to keep the baht's dollar value from changing.

In this chapter, you will learn about the fundamental factors that determine the dollar value of the baht and the approximately 170 other currencies in circulation around the world. First, however, you must understand how to keep track of the international financial transactions that the exchange of these various currencies helps facilitate.

THE BALANCE OF PAYMENTS AND INTERNATIONAL CAPITAL MOVEMENTS

Governments typically keep track of each year's economic activities by calculating the gross domestic product—the total of expenditures on all newly produced final domestic goods and services—and its components. A summary information system has also been developed for international trade. It covers the balance of trade and the balance of payments. The **balance of trade** refers specifically to exports and imports of goods as discussed in Chapter 33. When international trade is in balance, the value of exports equals the value of imports. When the value of imports exceeds the value of exports, we are running a deficit in the balance of trade. When the value of exports exceeds the value of imports, we are running a surplus.

Balance of trade
The difference between exports and imports of physical goods.

The **balance of payments** is a more general concept that expresses the total of all economic transactions between a nation and the rest of the world, usually for a period of one year. Each country's balance of payments summarizes information about that country's exports and imports of services as well as physical goods, earnings by domestic residents on assets located abroad, earnings on domestic assets owned by foreign residents, international capital movements, and official transactions by central banks and governments. In essence, then, the balance of payments is a record of all the transactions between households, firms, and the government of one country and the rest of the world. Any transaction that leads to a *payment* by a country's residents (or government) is a deficit item, identified by a negative sign (−) when the actual numbers are given for the items listed in the second column of Table 34-1 on the next page. Any transaction that leads to a *receipt* by a country's residents (or government) is a surplus item and is identified by a plus sign (+) when actual numbers are considered. Table 34-1 gives a listing of the surplus and deficit items on international accounts.

Balance of payments
A system of accounts that measures transactions of goods, services, income, and financial assets between domestic households, businesses, and governments and residents of the rest of the world during a specific time period.

Accounting Identities

Accounting identities—definitions of equivalent values—exist for financial institutions and other businesses. We begin with simple accounting identities that must hold for families and then go on to describe international accounting identities.

Accounting identities
Values that are equivalent by definition.

If a family unit is spending more than its current income, such a situation necessarily implies that the family unit must be doing one of the following:

1. Reducing its money holdings or selling stocks, bonds, or other assets
2. Borrowing

TABLE 34-1
Surplus (+) and Deficit (−) Items on the International Accounts

Surplus Items (+)	Deficit Items (−)
Exports of merchandise	Imports of merchandise
Private and governmental gifts from foreign residents	Private and governmental gifts to foreign residents
Foreign use of domestically owned transportation	Use of foreign-owned transportation
Foreign tourists' expenditures in this country	U.S. tourists' expenditures abroad
Foreign military spending in this country	Military spending abroad
Interest and dividend receipts from foreign entities	Interest and dividends paid to foreign residents
Sales of domestic assets to foreign residents	Purchases of foreign assets
Funds deposited in this country by foreign residents	Funds placed in foreign depository institutions
Sales of gold to foreign residents	Purchases of gold from foreign residents
Sales of domestic currency to foreign residents	Purchases of foreign currency

3. Receiving gifts from friends or relatives
4. Receiving public transfers from a government, which obtained the funds by taxing others (a transfer is a payment, in money or in goods or services, made without receiving goods or services in return)

We can use this information to derive an identity: If a family unit is currently spending more than it is earning, it must draw on previously acquired wealth, borrow, or receive either private or public aid. Similarly, an identity exists for a family unit that is currently spending less than it is earning: It must be increasing its money holdings or be lending and acquiring other financial assets, or it must pay taxes or bestow gifts on others. When we consider businesses and governments, each unit in each group faces its own identities or constraints. Ultimately, net lending by households must equal net borrowing by businesses and governments.

Disequilibrium. Even though our individual family unit's accounts must balance, in the sense that the identity discussed previously must hold, sometimes the item that brings about the balance cannot continue indefinitely. *If family expenditures exceed family income and this situation is financed by borrowing, the household may be considered to be in disequilibrium because such a situation cannot continue indefinitely.* If such a deficit is financed by drawing on previously accumulated assets, the family may also be in disequilibrium because it cannot continue indefinitely to draw on its wealth; eventually, it will become impossible for that family to continue such a lifestyle. (Of course, if the family members are retired, they may well be in equilibrium by drawing on previously acquired assets to finance current deficits; this example illustrates that it is necessary to understand circumstances fully before pronouncing an economic unit in disequilibrium.)

Equilibrium. Individual households, businesses, and governments, as well as the entire group of households, businesses, and governments, must eventually reach equilibrium. Certain economic adjustment mechanisms have evolved to ensure equilibrium. Deficit households must eventually increase their income or decrease their expenditures. They will find that they have to pay higher interest rates if they wish to borrow to finance their deficits. Eventually, their credit sources will dry up, and they will be forced into equilibrium. Businesses, on occasion, must lower costs or prices—or go bankrupt—to reach equilibrium.

An Accounting Identity Among Nations.
When people from different nations trade or interact, certain identities or constraints must also hold. People buy goods from people in other nations; they also lend to and present gifts to people in other nations. If residents of a nation interact with residents of other nations, an accounting identity ensures a balance (but not necessarily an equilibrium, as will soon become clear). Let's look at the three categories of balance of payments transactions: current account transactions, capital account transactions, and official reserve account transactions.

Current Account Transactions

During any designated period, all payments and gifts that are related to the purchase or sale of both goods and services constitute the **current account** in international trade. Major types of current account transactions include the exchange of merchandise, the exchange of services, and unilateral transfers.

Current account
A category of balance of payments transactions that measures the exchange of merchandise, the exchange of services, and unilateral transfers.

Merchandise Trade Exports and Imports.
The largest portion of any nation's balance of payments current account is typically the importing and exporting of merchandise goods. During 2007, for example, as can be seen in lines 1 and 2 of Table 34-2, the United States exported an estimated $1,002.5 billion of merchandise and imported $2,107.1 billion. The balance of merchandise trade is defined as the difference between the value of merchandise exports and the value of merchandise imports. For 2007, the United States had a balance of merchandise trade deficit because the value of its merchandise imports exceeded the value of its merchandise exports. This deficit was about $1,104.6 billion (line 3).

TABLE 34-2

U.S. Balance of Payments Account, 2007 (in billions of dollars)

Current Account			
(1)	Exports of goods	+ 1,002.5	
(2)	Imports of goods	− 2,107.1	
(3)	Balance of trade		− 1,104.6
(4)	Exports of services	+ 414.8	
(5)	Imports of services	− 300.2	
(6)	Balance of services		+ 114.6
(7)	Balance on goods and services [(3) + (6)]		− 990.0
(8)	Net unilateral transfers	− 91.2	
(9)	Balance on current account		− 1,081.2
Capital Account			
(10)	U.S. private capital going abroad	− 548.8	
(11)	Foreign private capital coming into the United States	+ 1,163.1*	
(12)	Balance on capital account [(10) + (11)]		+ 614.3
(13)	Balance on current account plus balance on capital account [(9) + (12)]		− 466.9
Official Reserve Transactions Account			
(14)	Official transactions balance		+ 466.9
(15)	Total (balance)		0

Sources: U.S. Department of Commerce, Bureau of Economic Analysis; author's estimates.
*Includes an approximately $43 billion statistical discrepancy, probably uncounted capital inflows, many of which relate to the illegal drug trade.

Service Exports and Imports. The balance of (merchandise) trade has to do with tangible items—things you can feel, touch, and see. Service exports and imports have to do with invisible or intangible items that are bought and sold, such as shipping, insurance, tourist expenditures, and banking services. Also, income earned by foreign residents on U.S. investments and income earned by U.S. residents on foreign investments are part of service imports and exports. As can be seen in lines 4 and 5 of Table 34-2 on the previous page, in 2007, estimated service imports were $414.8 billion, and service exports were $300.2 billion. Thus, the balance of services was about $114.6 billion in 2006 (line 6). Exports constitute receipts or inflows into the United States and are positive; imports constitute payments abroad or outflows of money and are negative.

When we combine the balance of merchandise trade with the balance of services, we obtain a balance on goods and services equal to −$990.0 billion in 2007 (line 7).

Because the balance on goods and services tracks *sales* of exports and imports of goods and services, it is based on the locations of producers of traded goods and services. How much different would the balance on goods and services be if it was based on the locations of the owners of the firms that produce traded goods and services?

EXAMPLE

Taking Multinational Firms into Account in Trade Statistics

The U.S. balance on goods and services tracks the net flow of international trade of goods and services based on where traded items are produced. Thus, the statisticians who tabulate this balance add only exports of goods and services *produced* within U.S. borders and subtract only U.S. imports of foreign-*produced* goods and services. But this accounting does not include all activities of U.S. firms. Consider, for example, a U.S. multinational firm that owns a plant in Mexico where it produces a good or service that it sells to Canadian residents. Because the item is produced in Mexico and purchased by Canadians, this transaction is not included in the U.S. balance on goods and services even though a U.S. firm was involved.

Recently, the U.S. Department of Commerce began reporting a measure of the balance on goods and services based on the locations of the companies that own the resources utilized to produce internationally traded goods and services. This *ownership-based* U.S. balance on goods and services adjusts exports and imports to account for purchases and sales involving foreign affiliates of U.S. firms. Annual net receipts that U.S. parent companies derive from trade conducted by their foreign affiliates are always much larger than the net receipts foreign firms receive from their U.S. affiliates that engage in international trade. Consequently, the deficit in the ownership-based balance on goods and services averages about $60 billion per year less than the deficit in the official, production-based measure of this balance.

FOR CRITICAL ANALYSIS
Why might the fact that the balance of payments accounts were designed before multinational firms were very common help explain why the balances in these accounts are not based on ownership?

Unilateral Transfers. U.S. residents give gifts to relatives and others abroad, the federal government makes grants to foreign nations, foreign residents give gifts to U.S. residents, and some foreign governments have granted funds to the U.S. government. In the current account, we see that net unilateral transfers—the total amount of gifts given by U.S. residents and the government minus the total amount received from abroad by U.S. residents and the government—came to an estimated −$91.2 billion in 2007 (line 8).

The fact that there is a minus sign before the number for unilateral transfers means that U.S. residents gave more to foreign residents than foreign residents gave to U.S. residents.

Balancing the Current Account. The balance on current account tracks the value of a country's exports of goods and services (including military receipts plus income on investments abroad) and transfer payments (private and government) relative to the value of that country's imports of goods and services and transfer payments (private and government). In 2007, it was estimated to be −$1,081.2 billion (line 9).

> *If the sum of net exports of goods and services plus net unilateral transfers plus net investment income exceeds zero, a* **current account surplus** *is said to exist; if this sum is negative, a* **current account deficit** *is said to exist. A* **current account deficit** *means that we are importing more goods and services than we are exporting. Such a deficit must be paid for by the export of money or money equivalent.*

Go to www.econtoday.com/ch34 for the latest U.S. balance of payments data from the Bureau of Economic Analysis.

Capital Account Transactions

In world markets, it is possible to buy and sell not only goods and services but also real and financial assets. These are the international transactions measured in the **capital account**. Capital account transactions occur because of foreign investments—either by foreign residents investing in the United States or by U.S. residents investing in other countries. The purchase of shares of stock in British firms on the London stock market by a U.S. resident causes an outflow of funds from the United States to Britain. The building of a Japanese automobile factory in the United States causes an inflow of funds from Japan to the United States. Any time foreign residents buy U.S. government securities, there is an inflow of funds from other countries to the United States. Any time U.S. residents buy foreign government securities, there is an outflow of funds from the United States to other countries. Loans to and from foreign residents cause outflows and inflows.

Line 10 of Table 34-2 on page 861 indicates that in 2007, the value of private capital going out of the United States was an estimated −$548.8 billion, and line 11 shows that the value of private capital coming into the United States (including a statistical discrepancy) was $1,163.1 billion. U.S. capital going abroad constitutes payments or outflows and is therefore negative. Foreign capital coming into the United States constitutes receipts or inflows and is therefore positive. Thus, there was a positive net capital movement of $614.3 billion into the United States (line 12). This net private flow of capital is also called the balance on capital account.

There is a relationship between the current account balance and the capital account balance, assuming no interventions by the finance ministries or central banks of nations.

> *In the absence of interventions by finance ministries or central banks, the current account balance and the capital account balance must sum to zero. Stated differently, the current account deficit must equal the capital account surplus when governments or central banks do not engage in foreign exchange interventions. In this situation, any nation experiencing a current account deficit, such as the United States, must also be running a capital account surplus.*

Capital account
A category of balance of payments transactions that measures flows of real and financial assets.

This basic relationship is apparent in the United States, as you can see in Figure 34-1 on the next page. As the figure shows, U.S. current account deficits experienced since the early 1980s have largely been balanced by private capital inflows, but there are exceptions, for reasons that we explain in the next section.

FIGURE 34-1

The Relationship Between the Current Account and the Capital Account

To some extent, the capital account is the mirror image of the current account. We can see this in most years since 1970. Typically, when the current account was in surplus, the capital account was in deficit. When the current account was in deficit, the capital account was in surplus. There are exceptions, such as the 1996–1998 and 2001–2003 intervals, during which the current account balance and capital account balance declined at the same time. During these periods, the official reserve transactions balance increased significantly as a result of particularly large purchases of U.S. financial assets by foreign governments and central banks.

Sources: International Monetary Fund; *Economic Indicators*.

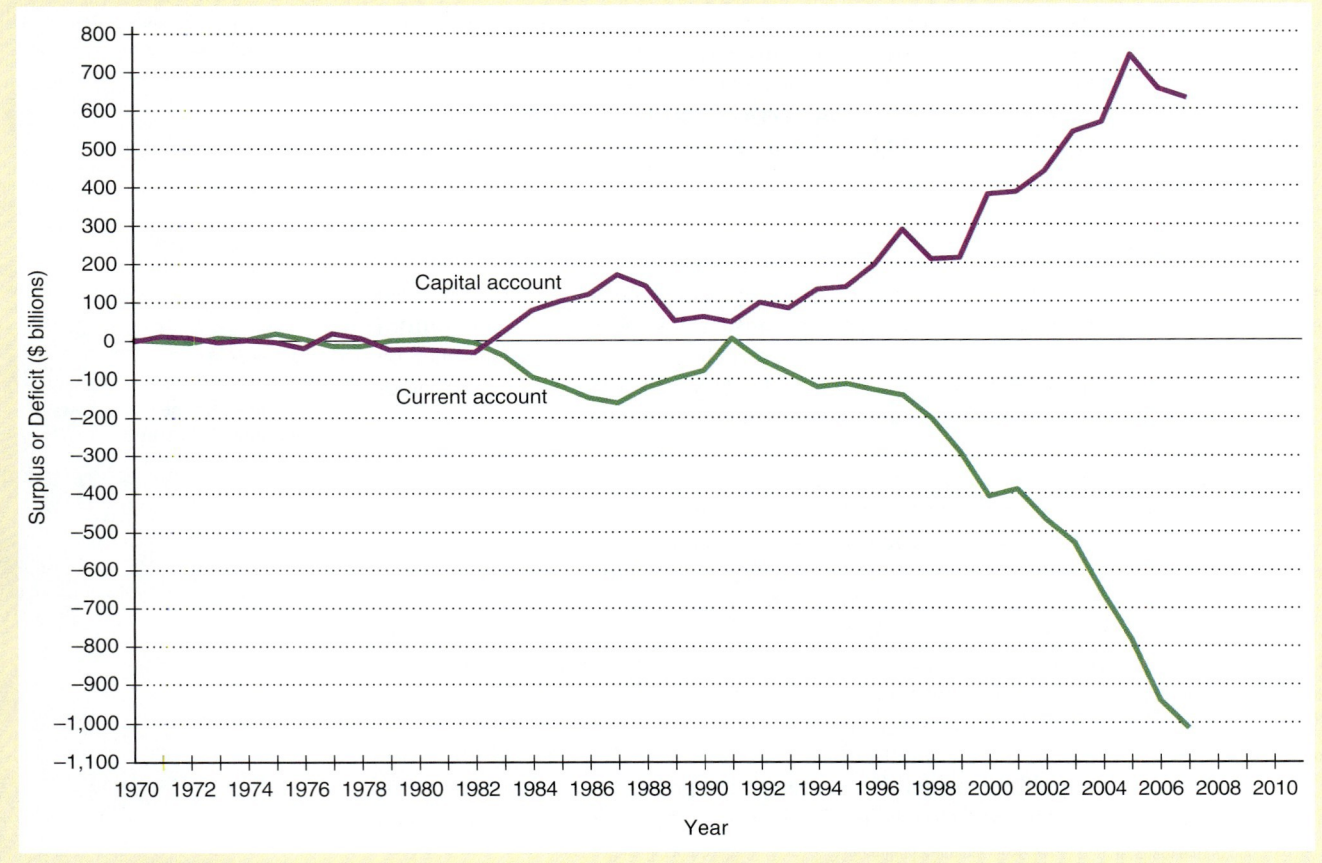

Official Reserve Account Transactions

Special drawing rights (SDRs)
Reserve assets created by the International Monetary Fund for countries to use in settling international payment obligations.

International Monetary Fund
An agency founded to administer an international foreign exchange system and to lend to member countries that had balance of payments problems. The IMF now functions as a lender of last resort for national governments.

The third type of balance of payments transaction concerns official reserve assets, which consist of the following:

1. Foreign currencies
2. Gold
3. **Special drawing rights (SDRs),** which are reserve assets that the **International Monetary Fund** created to be used by countries to settle international payment obligations
4. The reserve position in the International Monetary Fund
5. Financial assets held by an official agency, such as the U.S. Treasury Department

To consider how official reserve account transactions occur, look again at Table 34-2 on page 861. The surplus in the U.S. capital account was $614.3 billion. But the deficit in the U.S. current account was −$1,081.2 billion, so the United States had a net deficit on the combined accounts (line 13) of −$466.9 billion. In other words, the United States obtained less in foreign funds in all its international transactions than it used. How is this deficiency made up? By foreign central banks and governments adding to their U.S. funds, shown by the +$466.9 billion in official transactions on line 14 in Table 34-2. There is a plus sign on line 14 because this represents an *inflow* of foreign exchange in our international transactions.

The balance (line 15) in Table 34-2 is zero, as it must be with double-entry bookkeeping. The U.S. balance of payments deficit is measured by the official transactions figure on line 14.

The official reserve account transactions also explain why the movements in the current account balance and the capital account balance in Figure 34-1 are not exact mirror images. This is because the official reserve transactions balance has also varied over time. In recent years, there have been significant surpluses in the official reserve transactions balance. Foreign governments and central banks have purchased large volumes of U.S. financial assets, and these official capital inflows have also offset U.S. current account deficits within the overall balance of payments account.

For instance, between 1996 and 1998 and again between 2001 and 2003, the current account balance and the capital account balance declined simultaneously. During these periods, foreign governments and central banks purchased particularly large quantities of U.S. financial assets. Thus, the official reserve transactions balance increased significantly during these intervals.

What Affects the Distribution of Account Balances Within the Balance of Payments?

A major factor affecting the distribution of account balances within any nation's balance of payments is its rate of inflation relative to that of its trading partners. Assume that the rates of inflation in the United States and in the European Monetary Union (EMU)—the nations that use the euro as their currency—are equal. Now suppose that all of a sudden, the U.S. inflation rate increases. EMU residents will find that U.S. products are becoming more expensive, and U.S. firms will export fewer of them to EMU nations. At the current dollar-euro exchange rate, U.S. residents will find EMU products relatively cheaper, and they will import more. The reverse will occur if the U.S. inflation rate suddenly falls relative to that of the EMU. All other things held constant, whenever the U.S. rate of inflation exceeds that of its trading partners, we expect to see a larger deficit in the U.S. balance of trade and in the U.S. current account balance. Conversely, when the U.S. rate of inflation is less than that of its trading partners, other things being constant, we expect to see a smaller deficit in the U.S. balance of trade and in the U.S. current account balance.

Another important factor that sometimes influences account balances within a nation's balance of payments is its relative political stability. Political instability causes *capital flight*. Owners of capital in countries anticipating or experiencing political instability will often move assets to countries that are politically stable, such as the United States. Hence the U.S. capital account balance is likely to increase whenever political instability looms in other nations in the world.

QUICK QUIZ

The _____ of _____ reflects the value of all transactions in international trade, including goods, services, financial assets, and gifts.

The merchandise trade balance gives us the difference between exports and imports of _____ items.

Included in the _____ account along with merchandise trade are service exports and imports relating to commerce in intangible items, such as shipping, insurance, and tourist expenditures. The _____ account also includes income earned by foreign residents on U.S. investments and income earned by U.S. residents on foreign investments.

_____ _____ involve international private gifts and federal government grants or gifts to foreign nations.

When we add the balance of merchandise trade and the balance of services and take account of net unilateral transfers and net investment income, we come up with the balance on the _____ account, a summary statistic.

There are also _____ account transactions that relate to the buying and selling of financial and real assets. Foreign capital is always entering the United States, and U.S. capital is always flowing abroad. The difference is called the balance on _____ account.

Another type of balance of payments transaction concerns the _____ _____ assets of individual countries, or what is often simply called official transactions. By standard accounting convention, official transactions are exactly equal to but opposite in sign from the sum of the current account balance and the capital account balance.

Account balances within a nation's balance of payments can be affected by its relative rate of _____ and by its _____ stability relative to other nations.

See page 885 for the answers. Review concepts from this section in MyEconLab.

DETERMINING FOREIGN EXCHANGE RATES

Foreign exchange market
A market in which households, firms, and governments buy and sell national currencies.

Exchange rate
The price of one nation's currency in terms of the currency of another country.

When you buy foreign products, such as European pharmaceuticals, you have dollars with which to pay the European manufacturer. The European manufacturer, however, cannot pay workers in dollars. The workers are European, they live in Europe, and they must have euros to buy goods and services in nations that are members of the European Monetary Union (EMU) and use the euro as their currency. There must therefore be some way of exchanging dollars for euros that the pharmaceuticals manufacturer will accept. That exchange occurs in a **foreign exchange market,** which in this case involves the exchange of euros and dollars.

The particular **exchange rate** between euros and dollars that prevails—the dollar price of the euro—depends on the current demand for and supply of euros and dollars. In a sense, then, our analysis of the exchange rate between dollars and euros will be familiar, for we have used supply and demand throughout this book. If it costs you $1.25 to buy 1 euro, that is the foreign exchange rate determined by the current demand for and supply of euros in the foreign exchange market. The European person going to the foreign exchange market would need 0.80 euro to buy 1 dollar.

Now let's consider what determines the demand for and supply of foreign currency in the foreign exchange market. We will continue to assume that the only two regions in the world are the EMU and the United States.

Demand for and Supply of Foreign Currency

You wish to purchase European-produced pharmaceuticals directly from a manufacturer located in an EMU nation. To do so, you must have euros. You go to the foreign exchange market (or your U.S. bank). Your desire to buy the pharmaceuticals therefore causes you to offer (supply) dollars to the foreign exchange market. Your demand for EMU euros is equivalent to your supply of U.S. dollars to the foreign exchange market.

Every U.S. transaction involving the importation of foreign goods constitutes a supply of dollars and a demand for some foreign currency, and the opposite is true for export transactions.

In this case, the import transaction constitutes a demand for EMU euros.

In our example, we will assume that only two goods are being traded, European pharmaceuticals and U.S. computer printers. The U.S. demand for European pharmaceuticals creates a supply of dollars and a demand for euros in the foreign exchange market. Similarly, the European demand for U.S. computer printers creates a supply of euros and a demand for dollars in the foreign exchange market. Under a system of **flexible exchange rates,** the supply of and a demand for dollars and euros in the foreign exchange market will determine the equilibrium foreign exchange rate. The equilibrium exchange rate will tell us how many euros a dollar can be exchanged for—that is, the dollar price of euros—or how many dollars a euro can be exchanged for—the euro price of dollars.

Flexible exchange rates
Exchange rates that are allowed to fluctuate in the open market in response to changes in supply and demand. Sometimes called *floating exchange rates.*

The Equilibrium Foreign Exchange Rate

To determine the equilibrium foreign exchange rate, we have to find out what determines the demand for and supply of foreign exchange. We will ignore for the moment any speculative aspect of buying foreign exchange. That is, we assume that there are no individuals who wish to buy euros simply because they think that their price will go up in the future.

The idea of an exchange rate is no different from the idea of paying a certain price for something you want to buy. If you like coffee, you know you have to pay about 75 cents a cup. If the price went up to $2.50, you would probably buy fewer cups. If the price went down to 25 cents, you would likely buy more. In other words, the demand curve for cups of coffee, expressed in terms of dollars, slopes downward following the law of demand. The demand curve for euros slopes downward also, and we will see why.

Let's think more closely about the demand schedule for euros. Let's say that it costs you $1.25 to purchase 1 euro; that is the exchange rate between dollars and euros. If tomorrow you had to pay $1.33 for the same euro, the exchange rate would have changed. Looking at such a change, we would say that there has been an **appreciation** in the value of the euro in the foreign exchange market. But another way to view this increase in the value of the euro is to say that there has been a **depreciation** in the value of the dollar in the foreign exchange market. The dollar used to buy 0.80 euro; tomorrow, the dollar will be able to buy only 0.75 euro at a price of $1.33 per euro. If the dollar price of euros rises, you will probably demand fewer euros. Why? The answer lies in the reason you and others demand euros in the first place.

How do you suppose that significant appreciations of the currencies of Central European nations relative to the euro have affected these nations' exports of goods and services to Western European countries that use the euro?

Go to www.econtoday.com/ch34 for recent data from the Federal Reserve Bank of St. Louis on the exchange value of the U.S. dollar relative to the major currencies of the world.

Appreciation
An increase in the exchange value of one nation's currency in terms of the currency of another nation.

Depreciation
A decrease in the exchange value of one nation's currency in terms of the currency of another nation.

INTERNATIONAL EXAMPLE

Central European Currency Values Are Up, So Exports Are Down

In Central European nations such as the Czech Republic, Hungary, Poland, and Slovakia, currency values have increased by 10 to 20 percent relative to the euro since the beginning of 2004. As a consequence, buyers in Western European nations that must exchange euros for the higher-valued Czech koruna, Hungarian forint, Polish zloty, and Slovakian koruna have cut back on imports from these nations by 5 to 15 percent.

FOR CRITICAL ANALYSIS
What would you guess has happened to imports of Western European goods into the Czech Republic, Hungary, Poland, and Slovakia since the beginning of 2004?

Appreciation and Depreciation of EMU Euros. Recall that in our example, you and others demand euros to buy European pharmaceuticals. The demand curve for European pharmaceuticals follows the law of demand and therefore slopes downward. If it costs more U.S. dollars to buy the same quantity of European pharmaceuticals, presumably you and other U.S. residents will not buy the same quantity; your quantity demanded will be less. We say that your demand for EMU euros is *derived from* your demand for European pharmaceuticals. In panel (a) of Figure 34-2, we present the hypothetical demand schedule for packages of European pharmaceuticals by a representative set of U.S. consumers during a typical week. In panel (b), we show graphically the U.S. demand curve for European pharmaceuticals in terms of U.S. dollars taken from panel (a).

An Example of Derived Demand. Let us assume that the price of a package of European pharmaceuticals in the EMU is 100 euros. Given that price, we can find the number of EMU euros required to purchase 500 packages of European pharmaceuticals. That information is given in panel (c) of Figure 34-2. If purchasing one package of European pharmaceuticals requires 100 euros, 500 packages require 50,000 euros. Now we have enough information to determine the derived demand curve for EMU euros. If 1 euro costs $1.25, a package of pharmaceuticals would cost $125 (100 euros per package × $1.25 per euro = $125 per package). At $125 per package, the representative group of U.S. consumers would, we see from panel (a) of Figure 34-2, demand 500 packages of pharmaceuticals.

From panel (c), we see that 50,000 euros would be demanded to buy the 500 packages of pharmaceuticals. We show this quantity demanded in panel (d). In panel (e), we draw the derived demand curve for euros. Now consider what happens if the price of euros goes up to $1.30. A package of European pharmaceuticals priced at 100 euros in the EMU would now cost $130. From panel (a), we see that at $130 per package, 300 packages of pharmaceuticals will be imported from the EMU into the United States by our representative group of U.S. consumers. From panel (c), we see that 300 packages of pharmaceuticals would require 30,000 euros to be purchased; thus, in panels (d) and (e), we see that at a price of $1.30 per euro, the quantity demanded will be 30,000 euros.

We continue similar calculations all the way up to a price of $1.35 per euro. At that price, a package of European pharmaceuticals costing 100 euros in the EMU would cost $135, and our representative U.S. consumers would import only 100 packages of pharmaceuticals.

Downward-Sloping Derived Demand. As can be expected, as the price of euro rises, the quantity demanded will fall. The only difference here from the standard demand analysis developed in Chapter 3 and used throughout this text is that the demand for euros is derived from the demand for a final product—European pharmaceuticals in our example.

Panel (a)
Demand Schedule for Packages of European Pharmaceuticals in the United States per Week

Price per Package	Quantity Demanded
$135	100
130	300
125	500
120	700

Panel (b)
U.S. Demand Curve for European Pharmaceuticals

Panel (c)
Euros Required to Purchase Quantity Demanded (at P = 100 euros per package of pharmaceuticals)

Quantity Demanded	Euros Required (thousands)
100	10
300	30
500	50
700	70

Panel (d)
Derived Demand Schedule for Euros in the United States with Which to Pay for Imports of Pharmaceuticals

Dollar Price of One Euro	Dollar Price of Pharmaceuticals	Quantity of Pharmaceuticals Demanded	Quantity of Euros Demanded per Week (thousands)
$1.35	$135	100	10
1.30	130	300	30
1.25	125	500	50
1.20	120	700	70

FIGURE 34-2
Deriving the Demand for Euros

In panel (a), we show the demand schedule for European pharmaceuticals in the United States, expressed in terms of dollars per package of pharmaceuticals. In panel (b), we show the demand curve, D, which slopes downward. In panel (c), we show the number of euros required to purchase up to 700 packages of pharmaceuticals. If the price per package of pharmaceuticals in the EMU is 100 euros, we can now find the quantity of euros needed to pay for the various quantities demanded. In panel (d), we see the derived demand for euros in the United States in order to purchase the various quantities of pharmaceuticals given in panel (a). The resultant demand curve, D_1, is shown in panel (e). This is the U.S. derived demand for euros.

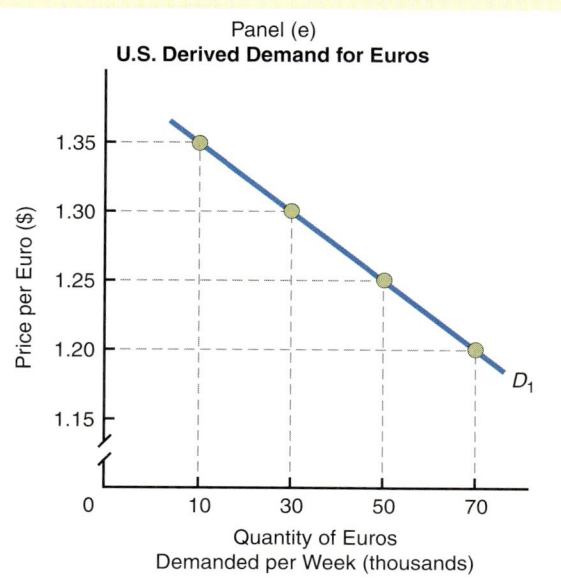

Panel (e)
U.S. Derived Demand for Euros

Supply of EMU Euros. Assume that European pharmaceutical manufacturers buy U.S. computer printers. The supply of EMU euros is a derived supply in that it is derived from the European demand for U.S. computer printers. We could go through an example similar to the one for pharmaceuticals to come up with a supply schedule of euros in the EMU. It slopes upward. Obviously, Europeans want dollars to purchase U.S. goods. European residents will be willing to supply more euros when the dollar price of euros goes up, because they can then buy more U.S. goods with the same quantity of euros. That is, the euro would be worth more in exchange for U.S. goods than when the dollar price for euros was lower.

An Example. Let's take an example. Suppose a U.S.-produced computer printer costs $200. If the exchange rate is $1.25 per euro, an EMU resident will have to come up with 160 euros (= $200 at $1.25 per euro) to buy one computer printer. If, however, the exchange rate goes up to $1.30 per euro, an EMU resident must come up with only 153.85 euros (= $200 at $1.30 per euro) to buy a U.S. computer printer. At this lower price (in euros) of U.S. computer printers, Europeans will demand a larger quantity. In other words, as the price of euros goes up in terms of dollars, the quantity of U.S. computer printers demanded will go up, and hence the quantity of euros supplied will go up. Therefore, the supply schedule of euros, which is derived from the European demand for U.S. goods, will slope upward.

We could easily work through a detailed numerical example to show that the supply curve of EMU euros slopes upward. Rather than do that, we will simply draw it as upward sloping in Figure 34-3.

Total Demand for and Supply of EMU Euros. Let us now look at the total demand for and supply of EMU euros. We take all U.S. consumers of European pharmaceuticals and all European consumers of U.S. computer printers and put their demands for and supplies of euros together into one diagram. Thus, we are showing the total demand for and total supply of EMU euros. The horizontal axis in Figure 34-4 represents the quantity of foreign exchange—the number of euros per year. The vertical axis represents the exchange rate—the price of foreign currency (euros) expressed in dollars (per euro). The foreign currency price of $1.30 per euro means it will cost you $1.30 to buy 1 euro. At the foreign

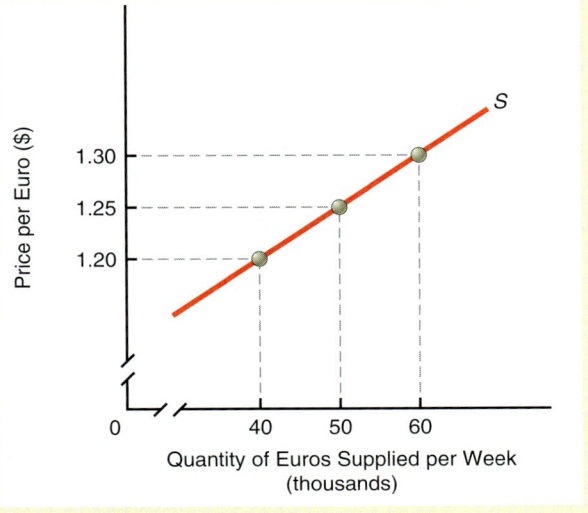

FIGURE 34-3

The Supply of European Monetary Union Euros

If the market price of a U.S.-produced computer printer is $200, then at an exchange rate of $1.25 per euro, the price of the printer to a European consumer is 160 euros. If the exchange rate rises to $1.30 per euro, the European price of the printer falls to 153.85 euros. This induces an increase in the quantity of printers demanded by European consumers and consequently an increase in the quantity of euros supplied in exchange for dollars in the foreign exchange market. In contrast, if the exchange rate falls to $1.20 per euro, the European price of the printer rises to 166.67 euros. This causes a decrease in the quantity of printers demanded by European consumers. As a result, there is a decline in the quantity of euros supplied in exchange for dollars in the foreign exchange market.

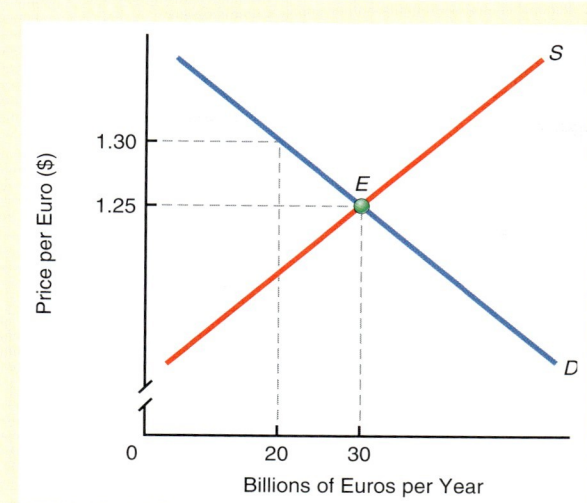

FIGURE 34-4

Total Demand for and Supply of European Monetary Union Euros
The market supply curve for EMU euros results from the total demand for U.S. computer printers. The demand curve, D, slopes downward like most demand curves, and the supply curve, S, slopes upward. The foreign exchange price, or the U.S. dollar price of euros, is given on the vertical axis. The number of euros is represented on the horizontal axis. If the foreign exchange rate is $1.30—that is, if it takes $1.30 to buy 1 euro—U.S. residents will demand 20 billion euros. The equilibrium exchange rate is at the intersection of D and S, or point E. The equilibrium exchange rate is $1.25 per euro. At this point, 30 billion euros are both demanded and supplied each year.

currency price of $1.25 per euro, you know that it will cost you $1.25 to buy 1 euro. The equilibrium, E, is again established at $1.25 for 1 euro.

In our hypothetical example, assuming that there are only representative groups of pharmaceutical consumers in the United States and computer printer consumers in the EMU, the equilibrium exchange rate will be set at $1.25 per euro.

This equilibrium is not established because U.S. residents like to buy euros or because Europeans like to buy dollars. Rather, the equilibrium exchange rate depends on how many computer printers Europeans want and how many European pharmaceuticals U.S. residents want (given their respective incomes, their tastes, and, in our example, the relative prices of pharmaceuticals and computer printers).

A Shift in Demand. Assume that a successful advertising campaign by U.S. pharmaceutical importers has caused U.S. demand for European pharmaceuticals to rise. U.S. residents demand more pharmaceuticals at all prices. Their demand curve for European pharmaceuticals has shifted outward to the right.

The increased demand for European pharmaceuticals can be translated into an increased demand for euros. All U.S. residents clamoring for European pharmaceuticals will supply more dollars to the foreign exchange market while demanding more EMU euros to pay for the pharmaceuticals. Figure 34-5 on the following page presents a new demand schedule, D_2, for EMU euros; this demand schedule is to the right of the original demand schedule. If Europeans do not change their desire for U.S. computer printers, the supply schedule for EMU euros will remain stable.

A new equilibrium will be established at a higher exchange rate. In our particular example, the new equilibrium is established at an exchange rate of $1.30 per euro. It now takes $1.30 to buy 1 EMU euro, whereas formerly it took $1.25. This will be translated into an increase in the price of European pharmaceuticals to U.S. residents and into a decrease in the price of U.S. computer printers to Europeans. For example, a package of European pharmaceuticals priced at 100 euros that sold for $125 in the United States will now be priced at $130. Conversely, a U.S. printer priced at $200 that previously sold for 160 euros in the EMU will now sell for 153.85 euros.

FIGURE 34-5
A Shift in the Demand Schedule

The demand schedule for European pharmaceuticals shifts to the right, causing the derived demand schedule for euros to shift to the right also. We have shown this as a shift from D_1 to D_2. We have assumed that the EMU supply schedule for euros has remained stable—that is, European demand for U.S. computer printers has remained constant. The old equilibrium foreign exchange rate was $1.25 per euro. The new equilibrium exchange rate will be E_2. It will now cost $1.30 to buy 1 euro. The higher price of euros will be translated into a higher U.S. dollar price for European pharmaceuticals and a lower EMU euro price for U.S. computer printers.

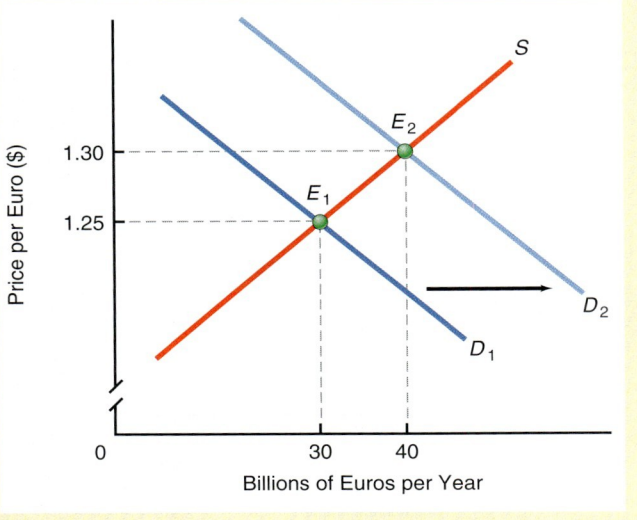

In what foreign exchange market does a single U.S. company engage in a noticeable portion of the total quantity of currency trades?

 EXAMPLE

One U.S. Firm's Key Role in the Market for Chinese Yuan

If Wal-Mart were treated as a separate "country," it would rank as the fifth-largest importer of products manufactured in China, placing it ahead of Russia and the United Kingdom. The company accounts for more than 10 percent of all U.S. imports from China. To obtain all the Chinese-made products that it sells in its stores, Wal-Mart enters the foreign exchange market and trades U.S. dollars for the Chinese currency, the yuan. Thus, Wal-Mart single-handedly generates a significant fraction of the quantity of dollar-yuan exchanges that take place in the market for this particular currency. When Wal-Mart buys the Chinese currency, its action perceptibly affects the foreign currency demand curve.

FOR CRITICAL ANALYSIS
When Wal-Mart places an order for large volumes of Chinese-manufactured toys and furniture to sell in its U.S. stores, do its actions affect the demand for or the supply of yuan?

A Shift in Supply. We just assumed that the U.S. demand for European pharmaceuticals had shifted due to a successful ad campaign. Because the demand for EMU euros is derived from the demand by U.S. residents for pharmaceuticals, this is translated into a shift in the demand curve for euros. As an alternative exercise, we might assume that the supply curve of EMU euros shifts outward to the right. Such a supply shift could occur for many reasons, one of which is a relative rise in the EMU price level. For example, if the prices of all EMU-manufactured computer peripherals went up 100 percent in euros, U.S. computer printers would become relatively cheaper. That would mean that European residents would want to buy more U.S. computer printers. But remember that

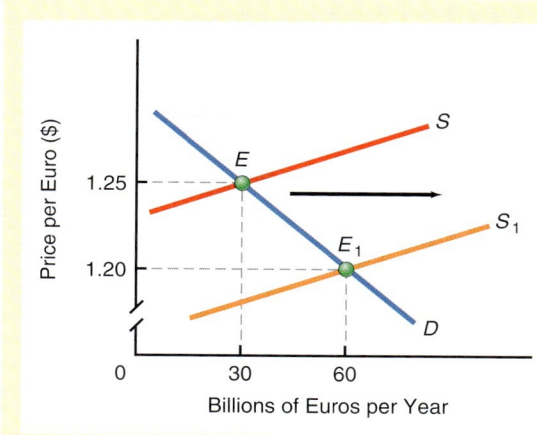

FIGURE 34-6
A Shift in the Supply of European Monetary Union Euros
There has been a shift in the supply curve for EMU euros. The new equilibrium will occur at E_1, meaning that $1.20, rather than $1.25, will now buy 1 euro. After the exchange rate adjustment, the annual amount of euros demanded and supplied will increase from 30 billion to 60 billion.

when they want to buy more U.S. printers, they supply more euros to the foreign exchange market.

Thus, we see in Figure 34-6 that the supply curve of EMU euros moves from S to S_1. In the absence of restrictions—that is, in a system of flexible exchange rates—the new equilibrium exchange rate will be $1.20 equals 1 euro. The quantity of euros demanded and supplied will increase from 30 billion per year to 60 billion per year. We say, then, that in a flexible international exchange rate system, shifts in the demand for and supply of foreign currencies will cause changes in the equilibrium foreign exchange rates. Those rates will remain in effect until world supply or demand shifts.

Market Determinants of Exchange Rates

The foreign exchange market is affected by many other variables in addition to changes in relative price levels, including the following:

- *Changes in real interest rates.* If the U.S. interest rate, corrected for people's expectations of inflation, abruptly increases relative to the rest of the world, international investors elsewhere seeking the higher returns now available in the United States will increase their demand for dollar-denominated assets, thereby increasing the demand for dollars in foreign exchange markets. An increased demand for dollars in foreign exchange markets, other things held constant, will cause the dollar to appreciate and other currencies to depreciate.
- *Changes in productivity.* Whenever one country's productivity increases relative to another's, the former country will become more price competitive in world markets. At lower prices, the quantity of its exports demanded will increase. Thus, there will be an increase in the demand for its currency.
- *Changes in consumer preferences.* If Germany's citizens suddenly develop a taste for U.S.-made automobiles, this will increase the derived demand for U.S. dollars in foreign exchange markets.
- *Perceptions of economic stability.* As already mentioned, if the United States looks economically and politically more stable relative to other countries, more foreign residents will want to put their savings into U.S. assets than in their own domestic assets. This will increase the demand for dollars.

QUICK QUIZ

The foreign _____ _____ is the rate at which one country's currency can be exchanged for another's.

The _____ for foreign exchange is a derived _____; it is derived from the demand for foreign goods and services (and financial assets). The _____ of foreign exchange is derived from foreign residents' demands for domestic goods and services.

The demand curve of foreign exchange slopes _____, and the supply curve of foreign exchange slopes _____. The equilibrium foreign exchange rate occurs at the intersection of the demand and supply curves for a currency.

A _____ in the demand for foreign goods will result in a shift in the _____ for foreign exchange, thereby changing the equilibrium foreign exchange rate. A shift in the supply of foreign currency will also cause a change in the equilibrium exchange rate.

See page 885 for the answers. Review concepts from this section in MyEconLab.

THE GOLD STANDARD AND THE INTERNATIONAL MONETARY FUND

The current system of more or less freely floating exchange rates is a relatively recent development. In the past, we have had periods of a gold standard, fixed exchange rates under the International Monetary Fund, and variants of the two.

The Gold Standard

Until the 1930s, many nations were on a gold standard. The value of their domestic currency was fixed, or *pegged,* in units of gold. Nations operating under this gold standard agreed to redeem their currencies for a fixed amount of gold at the request of any holder of that currency. Although gold was not necessarily the means of exchange for world trade, it was the unit to which all currencies under the gold standard were pegged. And because all currencies in the system were pegged to gold, exchange rates between those currencies were fixed. Indeed, the gold standard has been offered as the prototype of a fixed exchange rate system. The heyday of the gold standard was from about 1870 to 1914.

There was (and always is) a relationship between the balance of payments and changes in domestic money supplies throughout the world. Under a gold standard, the international financial market reached equilibrium through the effect of gold flows on each country's money supply. When the sum of a nation's current account balance and its capital account balance was negative, more gold would flow out than in. Because the domestic money supply was based on gold, an outflow of gold to foreign residents caused an automatic reduction in the domestic money supply. This caused several things to happen. Interest rates rose, thereby attracting foreign capital and pushing the sum of the current account balance and the capital account balance back toward zero. At the same time, the reduction in the money supply was equivalent to a restrictive monetary policy, which caused national output and prices to fall. Imports were discouraged and exports were encouraged, thereby again increasing net exports.

Two problems plagued the gold standard. One was that by varying the value of its currency in response to changes in the quantity of gold, a nation gave up control of its domestic monetary policy. Another was that the world's commerce was at the mercy of gold discoveries. Throughout history, each time new veins of gold were found, desired domestic expenditures on goods and services increased. If production of goods and services failed to increase proportionately, inflation resulted.

Bretton Woods and the International Monetary Fund

In 1944, as World War II was ending, representatives from the world's capitalist countries met in Bretton Woods, New Hampshire, to create a new international payment system to replace the gold standard, which had collapsed during the 1930s. The Bretton Woods Agreement Act was signed on July 31, 1945, by President Harry Truman. It created a new permanent institution, the International Monetary Fund (IMF). The IMF's task was to administer the agreement and to lend to member countries for which the sum of the current account balance and the capital account balance was negative, thereby helping them maintain an offsetting surplus in their official reserve transactions accounts. The arrangements thus provided are now called the old IMF system or the Bretton Woods system.

Member governments agreed to maintain the value of their currencies within 1 percent of the declared **par value**—the officially determined value. The United States, which owned most of the world's gold stock, was similarly obligated to maintain gold prices within a 1 percent margin of the official rate of $35 an ounce. Except for a transitional arrangement permitting a onetime adjustment of up to 10 percent in par value, members could alter exchange rates thereafter only with the approval of the IMF.

Par value
The officially determined value of a currency.

On August 15, 1971, President Richard Nixon suspended the convertibility of the dollar into gold. On December 18, 1971, the United States officially devalued the dollar—that is, lowered its official value—relative to the currencies of 14 major industrial nations. Finally, on March 16, 1973, the finance ministers of the European Economic Community (now the European Union) announced that they would let their currencies float against the dollar, something Japan had already begun doing with its yen. Since 1973, the United States and most other trading countries have had either freely floating exchange rates or managed ("dirty") floating exchange rates, in which their governments or central banks intervene from time to time to try to influence world market exchange rates.

FIXED VERSUS FLOATING EXCHANGE RATES

The United States went off the Bretton Woods system of fixed exchange rates in 1973. As Figure 34-7 indicates, many other nations of the world have been less willing to permit the values of their currencies to vary in the foreign exchange markets.

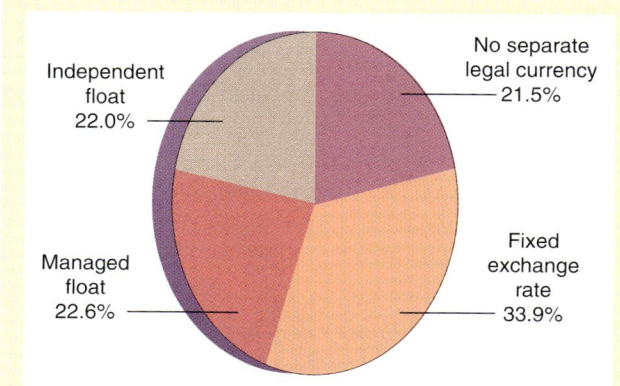

FIGURE 34-7
Current Foreign Exchange Rate Arrangements

Currently, 22 percent of the member nations of the International Monetary Fund have an independent float, and just over 22 percent have a managed float exchange rate arrangement. Among countries with a fixed exchange rate, about one-third use a fixed U.S. dollar exchange rate. Slightly over 21 percent of all nations use the currencies of other nations instead of issuing their own currencies.

Source: International Monetary Fund.

FIGURE 34-8

A Fixed Exchange Rate

This figure illustrates how the Bank of Malaysia could fix the dollar-ringgit exchange rate in the face of an increase in the supply of ringgit caused by a rise in the demand for U.S. goods by Malaysian residents. In the absence of any action by the Bank of Malaysia, the result would be a movement from point E_1 to point E_2. The dollar value of the ringgit would fall from $0.265 to $0.200. The Bank of Malaysia can prevent this exchange rate change by purchasing ringgit with dollars in the foreign exchange market, thereby raising the demand for ringgit. At the new equilibrium point, E_3, the ringgit's value remains at $0.265.

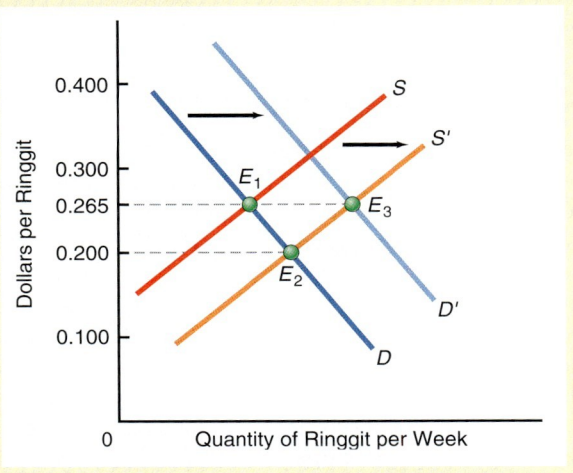

Fixing the Exchange Rate

How did nations fix their exchange rates in years past? How do many countries accomplish this today? Figure 34-8 shows the market for ringgit, the currency of Malaysia. At the initial equilibrium point E_1, U.S. residents had to give up $0.265 (26.5 cents) to obtain 1 ringgit. Suppose now that there is an increase in the supply of ringgit for dollars, perhaps because Malaysian residents wish to buy more U.S. goods. Other things being equal, the result would be a movement to point E_2 in Figure 34-8. The dollar value of the ringgit would fall to $0.200 (20 cents).

To prevent a ringgit depreciation from occurring, however, the Bank of Malaysia, the central bank, could increase the demand for ringgit in the foreign exchange market by purchasing ringgit with dollars. The Bank of Malaysia can do this using dollars that it has on hand as part of its *foreign exchange reserves*. All central banks hold reserves of foreign currencies. Because the U.S. dollar is a key international currency, the Bank of Malaysia and other central banks typically hold billions of dollars in reserve so that they can make transactions such as the one in this example. Note that a sufficiently large purchase of ringgit could, as shown in Figure 34-8, cause the demand curve to shift rightward to achieve the new equilibrium point E_3, at which the ringgit's value remains at $0.265. Provided that it has enough dollar reserves on hand, the Bank of Malaysia could maintain—effectively fix—the exchange rate in the face of the rise in the supply of ringgit.

The Bank of Malaysia has maintained the dollar-ringgit exchange rate in this manner since 1999. This basic approach—varying the amount of the national currency demanded at any given exchange rate in foreign exchange markets when necessary—is also the way that *any* central bank seeks to keep its nation's currency value unchanged in light of changing market forces.

> ECONOMICS **FRONT AND CENTER**
> To think about why foreign exchange reserves might begin to accumulate at a central bank, consider **A Big Buildup of Dollars at the Bank of Mexico**, on page 879.

Central banks can keep exchange rates fixed as long as they have enough foreign exchange reserves to deal with potentially long-lasting changes in the demand for or supply of their nation's currency.

Pros and Cons of a Fixed Exchange Rate

Why might a nation such as Malaysia wish to keep the value of its currency from fluctuating? One reason is that changes in the exchange rate can affect the market values of assets that are denominated in foreign currencies. This can increase the financial risks that a nation's residents face, thereby forcing them to incur costs to avoid these risks.

Foreign Exchange Risk.
The possibility that variations in the market value of assets can take place due to changes in the value of a nation's currency is the **foreign exchange risk** that residents of a country face because their nation's currency value can vary. For instance, if companies in Malaysia had many loans denominated in dollars but earned nearly all their revenues in ringgit from sales within Malaysia, a decline in the dollar value of the ringgit would mean that Malaysian companies would have to allocate a larger portion of their earnings to make the same *dollar* loan payments as before. Thus, a fall in the ringgit's value would increase the operating costs of these companies, thereby reducing their profitability and raising the likelihood of eventual bankruptcy.

Limiting foreign exchange risk is a classic rationale for adopting a fixed exchange rate. Nevertheless, a country's residents are not defenseless against foreign exchange risk. In what is known as a **hedge**, they can adopt strategies intended to offset the risk arising from exchange rate variations. For example, a company in Malaysia that has significant euro earnings from sales in Germany but sizable loans from U.S. investors could arrange to convert its euro earnings into dollars via special types of foreign exchange contracts called *currency swaps*. The Malaysian company could likewise avoid holdings of ringgit and shield itself—*hedge*—against variations in the ringgit's value.

The Exchange Rate as a Shock Absorber.
If fixing the exchange rate limits foreign exchange risk, why do so many nations allow the exchange rates to float? The answer must be that there are potential drawbacks associated with fixing exchange rates. One is that exchange rate variations can actually perform a valuable service for a nation's economy. Consider a situation in which residents of a nation speak only their own nation's language. As a result, the country's residents are very *immobile:* They cannot trade their labor skills outside their own nation's borders.

Now think about what happens if this nation chooses to fix its exchange rate. Imagine a situation in which other countries begin to sell products that are close substitutes for the products its people specialize in producing, causing a sizable drop in worldwide demand for the nation's goods. If wages and prices do not instantly and completely adjust downward, the result will be a sharp decline in production of goods and services, a falloff in national income, and higher unemployment. Contrast this situation with one in which the exchange rate floats. In this case, a sizable decline in outside demand for the nation's products will cause it to experience a trade deficit, which will lead to a significant drop in the demand for that nation's currency. As a result, the nation's currency will experience a sizable depreciation, making the goods that the nation offers to sell abroad much less expensive in other countries. People abroad who continue to consume the nation's products will increase their purchases, and the nation's exports will increase. Its production will begin to recover somewhat, as will its residents' incomes. Unemployment will begin to fall.

This example illustrates how exchange rate variations can be beneficial, especially if a nation's residents are relatively immobile. It can be difficult, for example, for a Polish resident who has never studied Portuguese to make a move to Lisbon, even if she is highly qualified for available jobs there. If many residents of Poland face similar linguistic or cultural barriers, Poland could be better off with a floating exchange rate even if its residents must incur significant costs hedging against foreign exchange risk as a result.

Foreign exchange risk
The possibility that changes in the value of a nation's currency will result in variations in the market value of assets.

Hedge
A financial strategy that reduces the chance of suffering losses arising from foreign exchange risk.

Splitting the Difference: Dirty Floats and Target Zones

In recent years, national policymakers have tried to soften the choice between adopting a fixed exchange rate and allowing exchange rates full flexibility in the foreign exchange markets by "splitting the difference" between the two extremes.

A Dirty Float. One way to split the difference is to let exchange rates float most of the time but "manage" exchange rate movements part of the time. U.S. policymakers have occasionally engaged in what is called a **dirty float,** the active management of flexible exchange rates. The management of flexible exchange rates has usually come about through international policy cooperation.

Is it possible for nations to "manage" foreign exchange rates? Some economists do not think so. For example, economists Michael Bordo and Anna Schwartz studied the foreign exchange intervention actions coordinated by the Federal Reserve and the U.S. Treasury during the second half of the 1980s. Besides showing that such interventions were sporadic and variable, Bordo and Schwartz came to an even more compelling conclusion: Exchange rate interventions were trivial relative to the total trading of foreign exchange on a daily basis. For example, in April 1989, total foreign exchange trading amounted to $129 billion per day, yet the U.S. central bank purchased only $100 million in deutsche marks and yen during that entire month (and did so on a single day). For all of 1989, Fed purchases of marks and yen were only $17.7 billion, or the equivalent of less than 13 percent of the amount of an average *day's* trading in April of that year. Their conclusion is that foreign exchange market interventions by the U.S. central bank or the central banks of other nations do not influence exchange rates in the long run.

Crawling Pegs. Another approach to splitting the difference between fixed and floating exchange rates is called a **crawling peg.** This is an automatically adjusting target for the value of a nation's currency. For instance, a central bank might announce that it wants the value of its currency relative to the U.S. dollar to decline at an annual rate of 5 percent, a rate of depreciation that it feels is consistent with long-run market forces. The central bank would then try to buy or sell foreign exchange reserves in sufficient quantities to be sure that the currency depreciation takes place gradually, thereby reducing the foreign exchange risk faced by the nation's residents. In this way, a crawling peg functions like a floating exchange rate in the sense that the exchange rate can change over time. But it is like a fixed exchange rate in the sense that the central bank always tries to keep the exchange rate close to a target value. In this way, a crawling peg has elements of both kinds of exchange rate systems.

Target Zones. A third way to try to split the difference between fixed and floating exchange rates is to adopt an exchange rate **target zone.** Under this policy, a central bank announces that there are specific upper and lower *bands,* or limits, for permissible values for the exchange rate. Within those limits, which define the exchange rate target zone, the central bank permits the exchange rate to move flexibly. The central bank commits itself, however, to intervene in the foreign exchange markets to ensure that its nation's currency value will not rise above the upper band or fall below the lower band. For instance, if the exchange rate approaches the upper band, the central bank must sell foreign exchange reserves in sufficient quantities to prevent additional depreciation of its nation's currency. If the exchange rate approaches the lower band, the central bank must purchase sufficient amounts of foreign exchange reserves to halt any further currency appreciation.

Dirty float
Active management of a floating exchange rate on the part of a country's government, often in cooperation with other nations.

Crawling peg
An exchange rate arrangement in which a country pegs the value of its currency to the exchange value of another nation's currency but allows the par value to change at regular intervals.

Target zone
A range of permitted exchange rate variations between upper and lower exchange rate bands that a central bank defends by selling or buying foreign exchange reserves.

In 1999, officials from the European Union attempted to get the U.S. and Japanese governments to agree to target zones for the exchange rate between the newly created euro, the dollar, and the yen. So far, however, no target zones have been created, and the euro has floated freely.

QUICK QUIZ

The International Monetary Fund was developed after World War II as an institution to maintain _____ exchange rates in the world. Since 1973, however, _____ exchange rates have disappeared in most major trading countries. For these nations, exchange rates are largely determined by the forces of demand and supply in foreign exchange markets.

Many other nations, however, have tried to fix their exchange rates, with varying degrees of success. Although fixing the exchange rate helps protect a nation's residents from foreign exchange _____, this policy makes less mobile residents susceptible to greater volatility in income and employment.

Countries have experimented with exchange rate systems between the extremes of fixed and floating exchange rates. Under a _____ float, a central bank permits the value of its nation's currency to float in foreign exchange markets but intervenes from time to time to influence the exchange rate. Under a _____ peg, a central bank tries to push the value of its nation's currency in a desired direction. Pursuing a _____ _____ policy, a central bank aims to keep the exchange rate between upper and lower bands, intervening only when the exchange rate approaches either limit.

See page 885 for the answers. Review concepts from this section in MyEconLab.

CASE STUDY

ECONOMICS FRONT AND CENTER

A Big Buildup of Dollars at the Bank of Mexico

Silva is an official at the Bank of Mexico, the nation's central bank. She is reviewing the bank's latest figures on its foreign exchange reserves. In 1996, the Bank of Mexico's foreign exchange reserves stood at $170 million. Today, the central bank's foreign exchange reserves exceed $65 *billion*.

The Bank of Mexico has purchased most of these dollars with pesos in an effort to keep the peso's exchange value from rising relative to the dollar. To prevent the total quantity of pesos in circulation from increasing rapidly, the central bank has issued peso-denominated bonds to private and public investors. In effect, the central bank has borrowed back most of the pesos it has used to buy the dollars it has accumulated.

Silva is growing concerned about the effects that this policy is having on the Bank of Mexico's net income. The central bank earns less interest on its foreign exchange reserves than it must pay on the bonds it issues. Consequently, its policy strategy with respect to its foreign exchange reserves is reducing the bank's net income. If present trends continue, the central bank may have another reason to borrow: It will require funds to pay employee wages and other expenses.

CRITICAL ANALYSIS QUESTIONS

1. *How can buying dollars with pesos enable the Bank of Mexico to prevent the peso's exchange value for the dollar from increasing, say, in response to an increase in the demand for dollars by residents of Mexico?*

2. *Other things being equal, which account in Mexico's balance of payments has been directly affected by the central bank's buildup of foreign exchange reserves?*

Issues and Applications

The Currency Most Traded in Foreign Exchange Markets

Concepts Applied
- Foreign Exchange Market
- Supply of Foreign Currency
- Demand for Foreign Currency

During the 2000s, the average daily volume of foreign exchange trading around the world has increased at an average annual rate of about 10 percent. On a typical day, the total volume of trading in the world's foreign exchange markets now exceeds $2.2 trillion. This amounts to twenty times more than daily production of world GDP and seventy times more than the volume of the daily flow of all international trade of goods and services.

The Currency of Choice

Which currencies are most commonly supplied and demanded in the world's foreign exchange markets? Figure 34-9 provides an answer to this question. It displays percentages of total foreign exchange market trading accounted for by various pairings of currencies.

As you can see, exchanges of the U.S. dollar for the European Monetary Union's euro, Japan's yen, the United Kingdom's pound, and currencies of other nations account for a total of 89 percent of all currency trades. Clearly, the dollar is the currency most commonly supplied and demanded in global foreign exchange markets.

Who Trades All Those Dollars for Other Currencies, and Vice Versa?

The bulk of foreign exchange trading involves exchanges of currencies between banks. In many cases, banks clear checks or wire funds between accounts of customers who have submitted payments to finalize import or export transactions. Such interbank currency trades reflect the fact that much of the demand for and supply of currencies is derived from the demand for and supply of goods and services in international trade.

Another source of the demand for and supply of currencies exchanged in foreign exchange markets is cross-border trading of financial assets, including stocks, bonds, deposits, and various other assets. Today, about 33 percent of all foreign exchange trading involves exchanges of currencies between banks and nonbank financial institutions such as money market mutual funds and hedge funds.

Why Dollars Are Involved in Most Trades

Why are U.S. dollars involved in payments for financial assets or for exports and imports of goods and services? There are many reasons for this. Certainly, one contributing factor is that

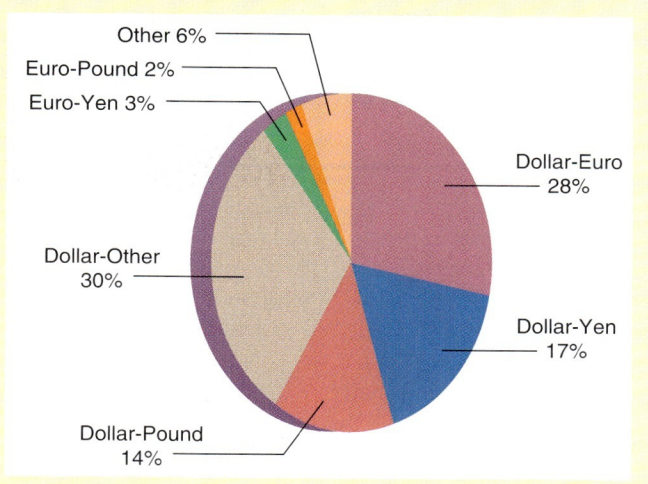

FIGURE 34-9
Currency Pairings Involved in Global Foreign Exchange Market Trades

The U.S. dollar features in almost 90 percent of the more than $2 trillion worth of currency trades that take place each day that foreign exchange markets are open.

Source: Bank for International Settlements.

the U.S. economy is the world's single largest national economy, and trades in goods, services, and assets often involve U.S. residents. Another reason is that residents of many other nations desire to hold U.S. financial assets because these assets offer returns that are both relatively high and stable due to the stability of the U.S. economic and political system.

In addition, residents of many countries outside the United States use the dollar as a "vehicle currency"—a medium of exchange for international transactions. For instance, a company in India might accept U.S. dollars in payment for delivery of exports of its product to a firm in Malaysia. Even though India's currency is the rupee and Malaysia's is the ringgit, the two firms may be willing to use U.S. dollars as a vehicle currency. Traditionally, the British pound and Japanese yen have also served as vehicle currencies, and the euro increasingly has taken on this role as well. Nevertheless, the U.S. dollar remains the most widely used vehicle currency, which is another reason why so many of the world's currency transactions involve the dollar.

Log in to **MyEconLab**, click on "Economic News," and test your understanding of the chapter by answering interactive questions that relate directly to this issue.

For Critical Analysis

1. Why does the total demand for dollars by foreign residents depend on their demand for U.S. financial assets as well as on their demand for U.S.-produced goods and services?
2. If the dollar's use as a vehicle currency were to decline, what would likely happen to the value of the dollar in foreign exchange markets, other things being equal?

Web Resources

1. To track banks' foreign-currency-denominated assets and liabilities, go to the link available at www.econtoday.com/ch34.
2. For a discussion of the U.S. dollar's use as a vehicle currency in Asia, go to www.econtoday.com/ch34.

Research Project

Identify reasons why the U.S. dollar is so widely used as a vehicle currency. Of these, which do you conclude to be most important? Why?

WHAT YOU SHOULD KNOW		WHERE TO GO TO PRACTICE
The Balance of Trade versus the Balance of Payments The balance of trade is the difference between exports of goods and imports of goods during a given period. The balance of payments is a system of accounts for all transactions between a nation's residents and the residents of other countries of the world. In addition to exports and imports, therefore, the balance of payments includes cross-border exchanges of services and financial assets within a given time interval.	balance of trade, 859 balance of payments, 859 accounting identities, 859	• **MyEconLab** Study Plan 34.1 • Audio introduction to Chapter 34
The Key Accounts Within the Balance of Payments There are three important accounts within the balance of payments. The current account measures net exchanges of goods and services, transfers, and income flows across a nation's borders. The capital account measures net flows of financial assets. The official reserve transactions account tabulates cross-border exchanges of financial assets involving the home nation's government and central bank as well as foreign governments and central banks. Because each international exchange generates both an inflow and an outflow, the sum of the balances on all three accounts must equal zero.	current account, 861 capital account, 863 special drawing rights (SDRs), 864 International Monetary Fund, 864 **Key figure** Figure 34-1, 864	• **MyEconLab** Study Plan 34.1 • Animated Figure 34-1
Exchange Rate Determination in the Market for Foreign Exchange From the perspective of the United States, the demand for a nation's currency by U.S. residents is derived largely from the demand for imports from that nation. Likewise, the supply of a nation's currency is derived mainly from the supply of U.S. exports to that country. The equilibrium exchange rate is the rate of exchange between the dollar and the other nation's currency at which the quantity of the currency demanded is equal to the quantity supplied.	foreign exchange market, 866 exchange rate, 866 flexible exchange rates, 867 appreciation, 867 depreciation, 867 **Key figures** Figure 34-2, 869 Figure 34-3, 870 Figure 34-4, 871	• **MyEconLab** Study Plan 34.2 • Animated Figures 34-2 34-3, and 34-4 • Video: Market Determinants of Foreign Exchange Rates
Factors That Can Induce Changes in Equilibrium Exchange Rates The equilibrium exchange rate changes in response to changes in the demand for or supply of another nation's currency. Changes in desired flows of exports or imports, real interest rates, productivity in one nation relative to productivity in another nation, tastes and preferences of consumers, and perceptions of economic stability are key factors that can affect the positions of the demand and supply curves in foreign exchange markets. Thus, changes in these factors can induce variations in equilibrium exchange rates.	**Key figures** Figure 34-5, 872 Figure 34-6, 873	• **MyEconLab** Study Plan 34.2 • Animated Figures 34-5 and 34-6 • Video: Market Determinants of Foreign Exchange Rates

WHAT YOU SHOULD KNOW

How Policymakers Can Attempt to Keep Exchange Rates Fixed If the current price of another nation's currency in terms of the home currency starts to fall below the level where the home country wants it to remain, the home country's central bank can use reserves of the other nation's currency to purchase the home currency in foreign exchange markets. This raises the demand for the home currency and thereby pushes up the currency's value in terms of the other nation's currency. In this way, the home country can keep the exchange rate fixed at a desired value, as long as it has sufficient reserves of the other currency to use for this purpose.

par value, 875
foreign exchange risk, 877
hedge, 877
Key figure
Figure 34-8, 876

WHERE TO GO TO PRACTICE

- **MyEconLab** Study Plans 34.3 and 34.4
- Animated Figure 34-8
- Video: Pros and Cons of a Fixed Exchange Rate

Alternative Approaches to Limiting Exchange Rate Variability Today, many nations permit their exchange rates to vary in foreign exchange markets. Others pursue policies that limit the variability of exchange rates. Some engage in a dirty float, in which they manage exchange rates, often in cooperation with other nations. Some establish crawling pegs, in which the target value of the exchange rate is adjusted automatically over time. And some establish target zones, with upper and lower limits on the extent to which exchange rates are allowed to vary.

dirty float, 878
crawling peg, 879
target zone, 879

- **MyEconLab** Study Plan 34.4

Log in to MyEconLab, take a chapter test, and get a personalized Study Plan that tells you which concepts you understand and which ones you need to review. From there, MyEconLab will give you further practice, tutorials, animations, videos, and guided solutions.

Log in to www.myeconlab.com

PROBLEMS

Select problems, indicated by a blue oval 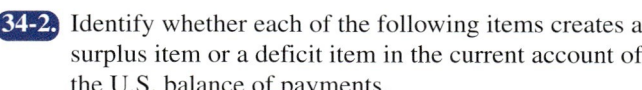, are assignable in **MyEconLab**.
Answers to the odd-numbered problems appear at the back of the book.

34-1. Over the course of a year, a nation tracked its foreign transactions and arrived at the following amounts:

Merchandise exports	500
Service exports	75
Net unilateral transfers	10
Domestic assets abroad (capital outflows)	−200
Foreign assets at home (capital inflows)	300
Changes in official reserves	−35
Merchandise imports	600
Service imports	50

What is this nation's balance of trade, current account balance, and capital account balance?

34-2. Identify whether each of the following items creates a surplus item or a deficit item in the current account of the U.S. balance of payments.

a. A Central European company sells products to a U.S. hobby-store chain.
b. Japanese residents pay a U.S. travel company to arrange hotel stays, ground transportation, and tours of various U.S. cities, including New York, Chicago, and Orlando.
c. A Mexican company pays a U.S. accounting firm to audit its income statements.
d. U.S. churches and mosques send relief aid to Pakistan following a major earthquake in that nation.

e. A U.S. microprocessor manufacturer purchases raw materials from a Canadian firm.

34-3. Explain how the following events would affect the market for the Mexican peso, assuming a floating exchange rate.

a. Improvements in Mexican production technology yield superior guitars, and many musicians around the world desire these guitars.

b. Perceptions of political instability surrounding regular elections in Mexico make international investors nervous about future business prospects in Mexico.

34-4. Explain how the following events would affect the market for South Africa's currency, the rand, assuming a floating exchange rate.

a. A rise in U.S. inflation causes many U.S. residents to seek to buy gold, which is a major South African export good, as a hedge against inflation.

b. Major discoveries of the highest-quality diamonds ever found occur in Russia and Central Asia, causing a significant decline in purchases of South African diamonds.

34-5. Explain how the following events would affect the market for Thailand's currency, the baht, assuming a floating exchange rate.

a. Market interest rates on financial assets denominated in baht decline relative to market interest rates on financial assets denominated in other nations' currencies.

b. Thailand's productivity increases relative to productivity in other countries.

34-6. Suppose that the following two events take place in the market for Kuwait's currency, the dinar: The U.S. demand for oil, Kuwait's main export good, declines, and market interest rates on financial assets denominated in dinar decrease relative to U.S. interest rates. What happens to the dollar price of the dinar? Does the dinar appreciate or depreciate relative to the dollar?

34-7. Suppose that the following two events take place in the market for China's currency, the yuan: U.S. parents are more willing than before to buy action figures and other Chinese toy exports, and China's government tightens restrictions on the amount of U.S. dollar–denominated financial assets that Chinese residents may legally purchase. What happens to the dollar price of the yuan? Does the yuan appreciate or depreciate relative to the dollar?

34-8. On Wednesday, the exchange rate between the Japanese yen and the U.S. dollar was $0.0125 per yen. On Thursday, it was $0.0110. Did the dollar appreciate or depreciate against the yen? By how much, expressed as a percentage change?

34-9. On Wednesday, the exchange rate between the euro and the U.S. dollar was $1.17 per euro, and the exchange rate between the Canadian dollar and the U.S. dollar was U.S. $0.79 per Canadian dollar. What is the exchange rate between the Canadian dollar and the euro?

34-10. Suppose that signs of an improvement in the Japanese economy lead international investors to resume lending to the Japanese government and businesses. Policymakers, however, are worried about how this will influence the yen. How would this event affect the market for the yen? How should the central bank, the Bank of Japan, respond to this event if it wants to keep the value of the yen unchanged?

34-11. Briefly explain the differences between a flexible exchange rate system, a fixed exchange rate system, a dirty float, and the use of target zones.

34-12. Consider the diagram below, which depicts the market for the baht, the currency of Thailand issued by that nation's central bank, the Bank of Thailand, and answer the following questions.

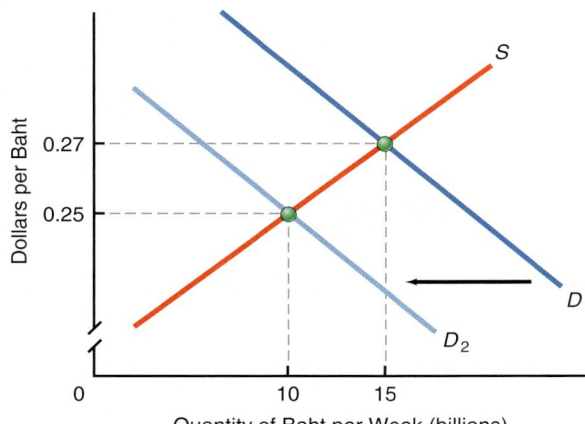

a. Which of the following events could have generated the decrease in the demand for the baht? Which could not? Explain briefly.

• A reduction in foreign purchases of Thai export goods

• An increase in foreign purchases of securities issued by Thailand's government

• A decrease in foreign purchases of financial services provided by Thai banks

- An increase in foreign purchases of Thai stocks and bonds

b. Following the decrease in the demand for the baht, has the baht appreciated or depreciated in relation to the U.S. dollar?

c. Suppose that the Bank of Thailand desires to push the equilibrium exchange rate back to a value of $0.27 per baht. How could the Bank of Thailand accomplish this objective by inducing the demand for baht to rise back to its original level? Explain.

34-13. Suppose that under a gold standard, the U.S. dollar is pegged to gold at a rate of $35 per ounce and the pound sterling is pegged to gold at a rate of £17.50 per ounce. Explain how the gold standard constitutes an exchange rate arrangement between the dollar and the pound. What is the exchange rate between the U.S. dollar and the pound sterling?

34-14. Suppose that under the Bretton Woods system, the dollar is pegged to gold at a rate of $35 per ounce and the pound sterling is pegged to the dollar at a rate of $2 = £1. If the dollar is devalued against gold and the pegged rate is changed to $40 per ounce, what does this imply for the exchange value of the pound in terms of dollars?

34-15. Suppose that the Bank of China wishes to peg the rate of exchange of its currency, the yuan, in terms of the U.S. dollar. In each of the following situations, should it add to or subtract from its dollar foreign exchange reserves? Why?

a. U.S. parents begin buying fewer Chinese-made toys for their children.

b. U.S. interest rates rise relative to interest rates in China, so Chinese residents seek to purchase additional U.S. financial assets.

c. Chinese furniture manufacturers produce high-quality early American furniture and successfully export large quantities of the furniture to the United States.

ECONOMICS ON THE NET

Daily Exchange Rates It is an easy matter to keep up with changes in exchange rates every day using the Web site of the Federal Reserve Bank of New York. In this application, you will learn how hard it is to predict exchange rate movements, and you will get some practice thinking about what factors can cause exchange rates to change.

Title: The Federal Reserve Bank of New York: Foreign Exchange 12 Noon Rates

Navigation: Go to www.econtoday.com/ch34 to visit the Federal Reserve Bank of New York's Statistics home page. Click on *Foreign Exchange 12 Noon Rates*.

Application Answer the following questions.

1. For each currency listed, how many dollars does it take to purchase a unit of the currency in the spot foreign exchange market?

2. For each day during a given week (or month), choose a currency from those listed and keep track of its value relative to the dollar. Based on your tabulations, try to predict the value of the currency at the end of the week *following* your data collections. Use any information you may have, or just do your best without any additional information. How far off did your prediction turn out to be?

For Group Study and Analysis Each day, you can also click on a report titled "Foreign Exchange 10 A.M. Rates," which shows exchange rates for a subset of countries listed in the noon report. Assign each country in the 10 A.M. report to a group. Ask the group to determine whether the currency's value appreciated or depreciated relative to the dollar between 10 A.M. and noon. In addition, ask each group to discuss what kinds of demand or supply shifts could have caused the change that occurred during this interval.

ANSWERS TO QUICK QUIZZES

p. 866: (i) balance . . . payments; (ii) physical; (iii) current . . . current; (iv) Unilateral transfers; (v) current; (vi) capital . . . capital; (vii) official reserve; (viii) inflation . . . political

p. 874: (i) exchange rate; (ii) demand . . . demand . . . supply; (iii) downward . . . upward; (iv) shift . . . demand

p. 879: (i) fixed . . . fixed; (ii) risk; (iii) dirty . . . crawling . . . target zone

ANSWERS TO ODD-NUMBERED PROBLEMS

CHAPTER 1

1-1. Economics is the study of how individuals allocate limited resources to satisfy unlimited wants.

   a. Among the factors that a rational, self-interested student will take into account are her income, the price of the textbook, her anticipation of how much she is likely to study the textbook, and how much studying the book is likely to affect her grade.

   b. A rational, self-interested government official will, for example, recognize that higher taxes will raise more funds for mass transit while making more voters, who have limited resources, willing to select replacement officials.

   c. A municipality's rational, self-interested government will, for instance, take into account that higher hotel taxes will produce more funds if as many visitors continue staying at hotels, but the higher taxes will also discourage some visitors from spending nights at hotels.

1-3. Because wants are unlimited, the phrase applies to very high-income households as well as low- and middle-income households. Consider, for instance, a household with a low income and unlimited wants at the beginning of the year. The household's wants will remain unlimited if it becomes a high-income household later in the year.

1-5. Sally is displaying rational behavior if all of these activities are in her self-interest. For example, Sally likely derives intrinsic benefit from volunteer and extracurricular activities and may believe that these activities, along with good grades, improve her prospects of finding a job after she completes her studies. Hence, these activities are in her self-interest even though they reduce some available study time.

1-7. The bounded rationality hypothesis indicates that because people cannot study every possible alternative available to them, they consider only the most obviously apparent choices. They find easy ways of deciding which of these obvious choices to select, and, according to the hypothesis, these methods are simple rules of thumb.

1-9. **a.** Yes, because Myrna is acting in her own self-interest by establishing this allocation of her time to studying economics.

   b. No, because Leonardo is leaving an important decision affecting his self-interest to random chance, potentially leaving him worse off if he fails to obtain employment.

   c. Yes, because Celeste is basing her choice on a self-interest assessment of expenditures in light of available resources.

1-11. Positive economic analysis deals with economics models with predictions that are statements of fact, which can be objectively proved or disproved. Normative analysis takes into account subjective personal or social values concerning the way things *ought* to be.

1-13. **a.** An increase in the supply of laptop computers, perhaps because of the entry of new computer manufacturers into the market, pushes their price back down.

   b. Another factor, such as higher hotel taxes at popular vacation destinations, makes vacation travel more expensive.

   c. Some other factor, such as a fall in market wages that workers can earn, discourages people from working additional hours.

APPENDIX A

A-1. **a.** Independent: price of a notebook; Dependent: quantity of notebooks

   b. Independent: work-study hours; Dependent: credit hours

   c. Independent: hours of study; Dependent: economics grade

A-3. **a.** above x axis; left of y axis

   b. below x axis, right of y axis

   c. on x axis; to right of y axis

A-2 Answers to Odd-Numbered Problems

A-5.

y	x
−20	−4
−10	−2
0	0
10	2
20	4

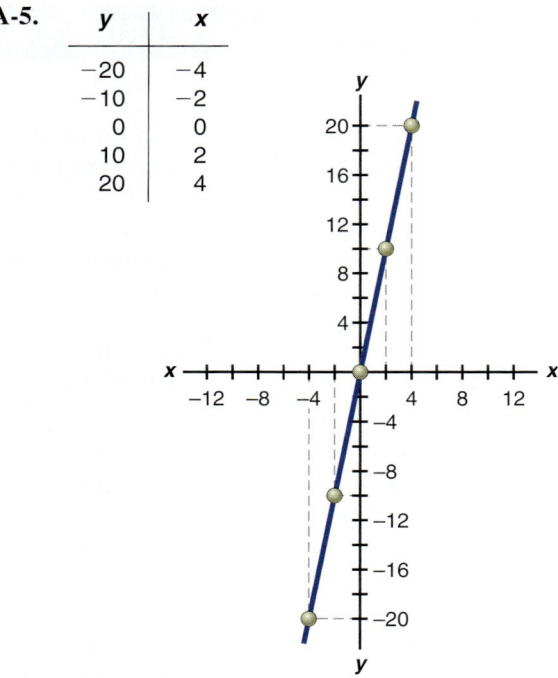

A-7. Each one-unit increase in x yields a 5-unit increase in y, so the slope given by the change in y corresponding to the change in x is equal to 5.

A-9. a. positive; each 1-unit rise in x induces a 5-unit increase in y.
  b. positive; each 1-unit rise in x induces a 1-unit increase in y.
  c. negative; each 1-unit rise in x induces a 3-unit decline in y.

CHAPTER 2

2-1. The opportunity cost of attending a class at 11:00 A.M. is the next-best use of that hour of the day. Likewise, the opportunity cost of attending an 8:00 A.M. class is the next-best use of that particular hour of the day. If you are an early riser, it is arguable that the opportunity cost of the 8:00 A.M. hour is lower, because you will already be up at that time but have fewer choices compared with the 11:00 A.M. hour when shops, recreation centers, and the like are open. If you are a late riser, it may be that the opportunity cost of the 8:00 A.M. hour is higher, because you place a relatively high value on an additional hour of sleep in the morning.

2-3. Each additional 10 points earned in economics costs 10 additional points in biology, so this PPC illustrates *constant* additional opportunity costs. It does *not* satisfy the law of increasing relative cost.

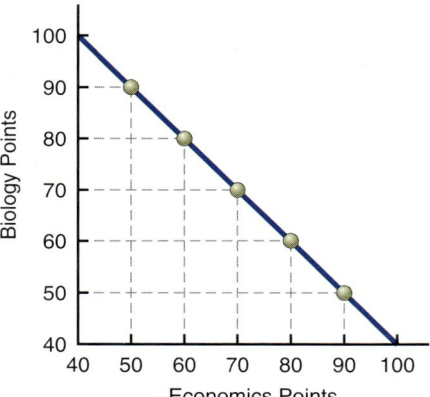

2-5. Each additional 10 points earned in economics costs a greater number of biology points. For instance, the opportunity cost to the student of increasing points earned in economics from 60 to 70 is 8 points forgone in biology, but the opportunity cost of increasing economics points from 90 to 100 rises to 20 points forgone in biology. Thus, the new PPC illustrates the law of increasing relative cost.

2-7. a. If the nation's residents increase production of consumption goods from 0 units to 10 units, the opportunity cost is 3 units of human capital forgone. If the nation's residents increase production of consumption goods from 0 units to 60 units, the opportunity cost is 100 units of human capital.
  b. Yes, because successive 10-unit increases in production of consumption goods generate larger sacrifices of human capital, equal to 3, 7, 15, 20, 25, and 30.

2-9. Because it takes you less time to do laundry, you have an absolute advantage in laundry. Neither you nor your roommate has an absolute advantage in meal preparation. You require 2 hours to fold a basket of laundry, so your opportunity cost of folding a basket of laundry is 2 meals. Your roommate's opportunity cost of folding a basket of laundry is 3 meals. Hence, you have a comparative advantage in laundry, and your roommate has a comparative advantage in meal preparation.

2-11. If countries produce the goods for which they have a comparative advantage and trade for those for which they are at a comparative disadvantage, then the distribution of resources is more efficient in each nation, yielding gains for both. Artificially restraining trade that otherwise would yield such gains thereby imposes social losses on residents of both nations.

2-13. a. If the two nations have the same production possibilities, then they face the same opportunity costs of producing consumption goods and capital goods. Thus, at present neither has a comparative advantage in producing either good.

b. Because country B produces more capital goods today, it will be able to produce more of both goods in the future. Consequently, country B's PPC will shift outward by a greater amount next year.

2-15. D

CHAPTER 3

3-1. The equilibrium price is $21 per DVD, and the equilibrium quantity is 80 million DVDs. At a price of $20 per DVD, the quantity of DVDs demanded is 90 million, and the quantity of DVDs supplied is 60 million. Hence, there is a shortage of 30 million DVDs at a price of $20 per CD.

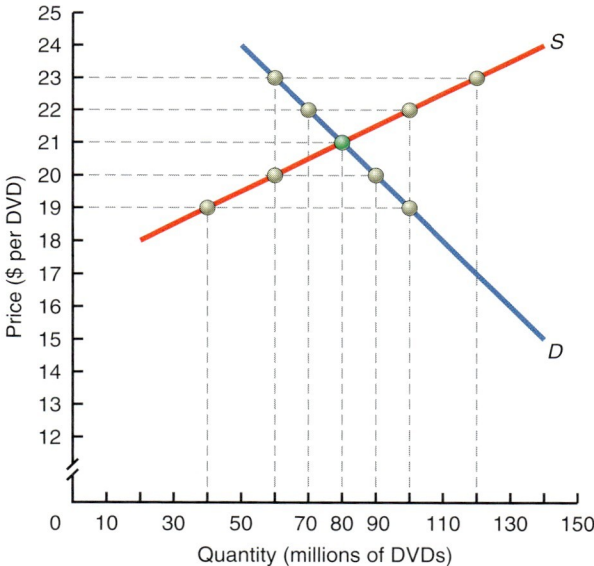

3-3. a. DSL and cable Internet access services are substitutes, so a reduction in the price of cable Internet access services causes a decrease in the demand for DSL high-speed Internet access services.

b. A decrease in the price of DSL Internet access services generates an increase in the quantity of these services demanded.

c. DSL high-speed Internet access services are a normal good, so a fall in the incomes of consumers reduces the demand for these services.

d. If consumers expect that the price of DSL high-speed Internet services will fall in the future, then the demand for these services will tend to decrease today.

3-5. a. Complement: eggs; substitute: sausage

b. Complement: tennis balls; substitute: racquetball racquets

c. Complement: cream; substitute: tea

d. Complement: gasoline; substitute: city bus

3-7. a. At the $1,000 rental rate, the quantity of one-bedroom apartments supplied is 8,500 per month, but the quantity demanded is only 7,000 per month. Thus, there is an excess quantity of one-bedroom apartments supplied equal to 1,500 apartments per month.

b. To induce consumers to lease unrented one-bedroom apartments, some landlords will reduce their rental rates. As they do so, the quantity demanded will increase. In addition, some landlords will choose not to offer apartments for rent at lower rates, and the quantity supplied will decrease. At the equilibrium rental rate of $800 per month, there will be no excess quantity supplied.

c. At the $600 rental rate, the quantity of one-bedroom apartments demanded is 8,000 per month, but the quantity supplied is only 6,500 per month. Thus, there is an excess quantity of one-bedroom apartments demanded equal to 1,500 apartments per month.

d. To induce landlords to make more one-bedroom apartments available for rent, some consumers will offer to pay higher rental rates. As they do so, the quantity supplied will increase. In addition, some consumers will choose not to try to rent apartments at higher rates, and the quantity demanded will decrease. At the equilibrium rental rate of $800 per month, there will be no excess quantity demanded.

3-9. a. Because memory chips are an input in the production of laptop computers, a decrease in the price of memory chips causes an increase in the supply of laptop computers. The market supply curve shifts to the right, which causes the market price of laptop computers to fall and the equilibrium quantity of laptop computers to increase.

b. Machinery used to produce laptop computers is an input in the production of these devices, so an increase in the price of machinery generates a decrease in the supply of laptop computers. The market supply curve shifts to the left, which causes the market price of laptop computers to rise and the equilibrium quantity of laptop computers to decrease.

c. An increase in the number of manufacturers of laptop computers causes an increase in the supply of laptop computers. The market supply curve shifts rightward. The market price of laptop computers declines, and the equilibrium quantity of laptop computers increases.

d. The demand curve for laptop computers shifts to the left along the supply curve, so there is a decrease in the quantity supplied. The market price falls, and the equilibrium quantity declines.

3-11. a. The demand for tickets declines, and there will be a surplus of tickets.
b. The demand for tickets rises, and there will be a shortage of tickets.
c. The demand for tickets rises, and there will be a shortage of tickets.
d. The demand for tickets declines, and there will be a surplus of tickets.

3-13. Ethanol producers will respond to the subsidy by producing more ethanol at any given price, so the supply of ethanol will increase, thereby generating a decrease in the price of ethanol.
a. Producers striving to supply more ethanol will consume more corn, an input in ethanol production. Hence, the demand for corn will increase, so the market price of corn will rise, and the equilibrium quantity of corn will increase.
b. A decline in the market price of ethanol, a substitute for gasoline, will cause the demand for gasoline to decline. The market price of gasoline will fall, and the equilibrium quantity of gasoline will decrease.
c. Ethanol and automobiles are complements, so a decline in the price of ethanol will cause an increase in the demand for autos. The market price of autos will rise, and the equilibrium quantity of autos will increase.

3-15. Aluminum is an input in the production of canned soft drinks, so an increase in the price of aluminum reduces the supply of canned soft drinks (option c). The resulting rise in the market price of canned soft drinks brings about an decrease in the quantity of canned soft drinks demanded (option b). In equilibrium, the quantity of soft drinks supplied decreases (option d) to an amount equal to the quantity demanded. The demand curve does not shift, however, so option b does not apply.

CHAPTER 4

4-1. The ability to produce music CDs at lower cost and the entry of additional producers shift the supply curve rightward, from S_1 to S_2. At the same time, reduced prices of substitute goods result in a leftward shift in the demand for music CDs, from D_1 to D_2. Consequently, the equilibrium price of music CDs declines, from P_1 to P_2. The equilibrium quantity may rise, fall, or, as shown in the diagram, remain unchanged.

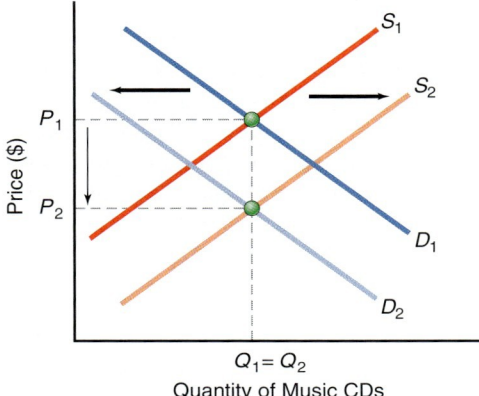

4-3. The market rental rate is $500 per apartment, and the equilibrium quantity of apartments rented to tenants is 2,000. At a ceiling price of $450 per month, the number of apartments students desire to rent increases to 2,500 apartments. At the ceiling price, the number of apartments that owners are willing to supply decreases to 1,800 apartments. Thus, there is a shortage of 700 apartments at the ceiling price, and only 1,800 are rented at the ceiling price.

4-5. At the above-market price of sugar in the U.S. sugar market, U.S. chocolate manufacturers that use sugar as an input face higher costs. Thus, they supply less chocolate at any given price of chocolate, and the market supply curve shifts leftward. This pushes up the market price of chocolate products and reduces the equilibrium quantity of chocolate. U.S. sugar producers also sell surplus sugar in foreign sugar markets, which causes the supply curve for sugar in foreign markets to shift rightward. This reduces the market price of foreign sugar and raises the equilibrium quantity in the foreign market.

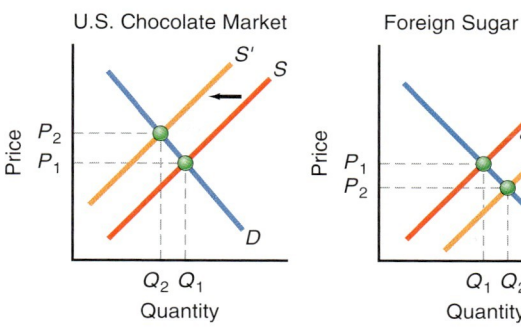

4-7. The market price is $400, and the equilibrium quantity of seats is 1,600. If airlines cannot sell tickets to more than 1,200 passengers, then passengers are willing to pay $600 per seat. Normally, airlines would be willing to sell each ticket for $200, but they will be able to charge a price as high as $600 for each of the 1,200 tickets they sell. Hence, the quantity of tickets sold declines from 1,600, and the price of a ticket rises from $400 to as high as $600.

4-9. a. Consumers buy 10 billion kilograms at the support price of $0.20 per kilogram and hence spend $2 billion on wheat.
  b. The amount of surplus wheat at the support price is 8 billion kilograms, so at the $0.20-per-kilogram support price, the government must spend $1.6 billion to purchase this surplus wheat.
  c. Pakistani wheat farmers receive a total of $3.6 billion for the wheat they produce at the support price.

4-11. a. At the present minimum wage of $9 per hour, the quantity of labor supplied is 102,000 workers, and the quantity of labor demanded by firms is 98,000. There is an excess quantity supplied of 4,000 workers, which is the number of people who are unemployed.
  b. At a minimum wage of $6 per hour, there would be nothing to prevent market forces from pushing the wage rate to the market clearing level of $8 per hour. This $8-per-hour wage rate would exceed the legal minimum and hence would prevail. There would be no unemployed workers.
  c. At a $10-per-hour minimum wage, the quantity of labor supplied would increase to 106,000 workers, and the quantity of labor demanded would decline to 96,000. There would be an excess quantity of labor supplied equal to 10,000 workers, which would then be the number of people who are unemployed.

4-13. a. The rise in the number of wheat producers causes the market supply curve to shift rightward, so more wheat is supplied at the support price.
  b. The quantity of wheat demanded at the same support price is unchanged.
  c. Because quantity demanded is unchanged while quantity supplied has increased, the amount of surplus wheat that the government must purchase has risen.

CHAPTER 5

5-1. In the absence of laws forbidding cigar smoking in public places, people who are bothered by the odor of cigar smoke will experience costs not borne by cigar producers. Because the supply of cigars will not reflect these costs, from society's perspective the market cigar supply curve will be in a position too far to the right. The market price of cigars will be too low, and too many cigars will be produced and consumed.

5-3. Imposing the tax on pesticides causes an increase in the price of pesticides, which are an input in the production of oranges. Hence, the supply curve in the orange market shifts leftward. The market price of oranges increases, and the equilibrium quantity of oranges declines. Hence, orange consumers indirectly help to pay for dealing with the spillover costs of pesticide production by paying more for oranges.

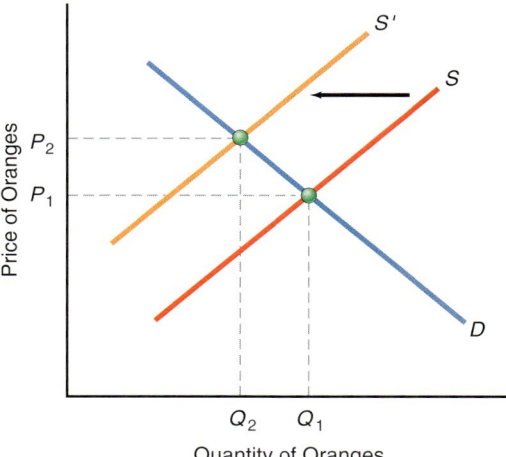

5-5. a. As shown in the figure on p. A-6, if the social benefits associated with bus ridership were taken into account, the demand schedule would be D' instead of D, and the market price would be higher. The equilibrium quantity of bus rides would be higher.

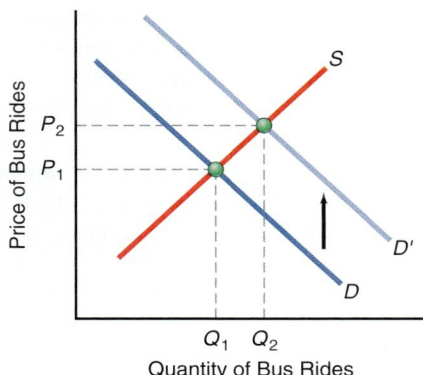

b. The government could pay commuters a subsidy to ride the bus, thereby shifting the demand curve upward and to the right. This would increase the market price and equilibrium number of bus rides.

5-7. At present, the equilibrium quantity of residences with Internet access is 2 million. To take into account the external benefit of Internet access and boost the quantity of residences with access to 3 million, the demand curve would have to shift upward by $20 per month at any given quantity, to D_2 from the current position D_1. Thus, the government would have to offer a $20-per-month subsidy to raise the quantity of residences with Internet access to 3 million.

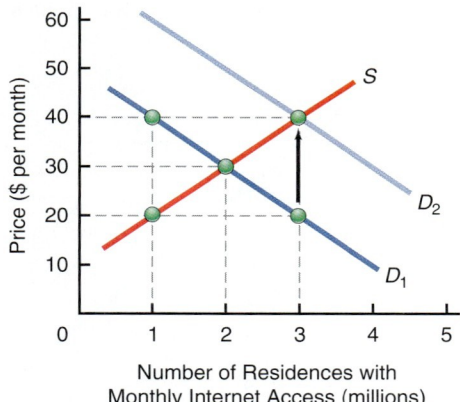

5-9. The problem is that although most people around the lighthouse will benefit from its presence, there is no incentive for people to voluntarily contribute if they believe that others ultimately will pay for it. That is, the city is likely to face a free-rider problem in its efforts to raise its share of the funds required for the lighthouse.

5-11. No, the outcome will be different. If the government had simply provided grants to attend private schools at the current market tuition rate, parents and students receiving the grants would have paid a price equal to the market valuation of the last unit of educational services provided. Granting a subsidy to private schools allows the private schools to charge parents and students a price less than the market price. Private schools thereby will receive a higher-than-market price for the last unit of educational services they provide. Consequently, they will provide a quantity of educational services in excess of the market equilibrium quantity. At this quantity, parents and students place a lower value on the services than the price received by the private schools.

5-13. a. $40 million
b. The effective price of a DVD drive to consumers will be lower after the government pays the subsidy, so people will purchase a larger quantity.
c. $60 million
d. $90 million

5-15. a. $60 − $50 = $10
b. Expenditures after the program expansion are $2.4 million. Before the program expansion, expenditures were $1 million. Hence, the increase in expenditures is $1.4 million.
c. At a per-unit subsidy of $50, the share of the per-unit $60 price paid by the government is 5/6, or 83.3 percent. Hence, this is the government's share of total expenditures on the 40,000 devices that consumers purchase.

CHAPTER 6

6-1. a. 20 percent
b. 37.5 percent

6-3. 1999: $300 million; 2001: $350 million; 2003: $400 million; 2005: $400 million; 2007: $420 million

6-5. During 2006, the tax base was an amount of income equal to $20 million/0.05 = $400 million. During 2007, the income tax base was equal to $19.2 million/0.06 = $320 million. Although various factors could have contributed to the fall in taxable income, dynamic tax analysis suggests that the higher income tax rate induced people to reduce their reported income. For instance, some people might have earned less income subject to city income taxes, and others might have even moved outside the city to avoid paying the higher income tax rate.

6-7. As shown in the diagram, if the supply and demand curves have their normal shapes, then the $2-per-month tax on DSL Internet access services shifts the market supply curve upward by $2. The equilibrium quantity of DSL access services produced and consumed declines. In addition, the monthly market price of DSL access increases by an amount less than $2 per month. Consequently, consumers and producers share in paying the tax on each unit.

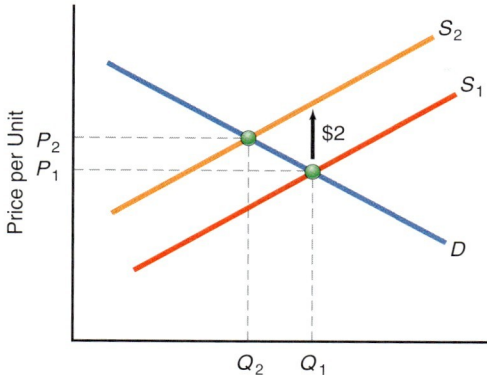

Quantity of DSL Access Services

6-9. If the market price of DSL access for businesses does not change, then as shown in the diagram below, over the relevant range the demand for Internet access services by businesses is horizontal. The quantity of services demanded by businesses is very highly responsive to the tax, so DSL access providers must bear the tax in the form of higher costs. Providers of DSL access services pay all of the tax.

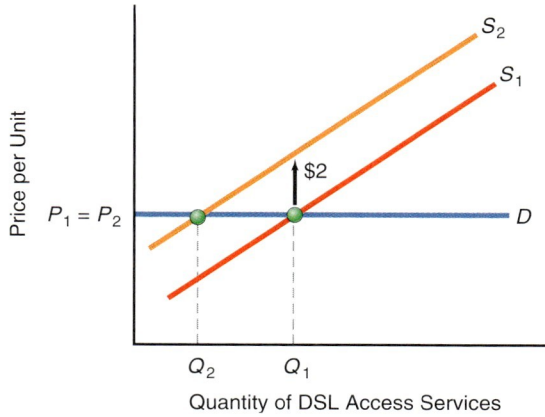

Quantity of DSL Access Services

6-11. a. 50 percent
b. −20 percent

CHAPTER 7

7-1. a. Multiplying the fraction of people who participate in the labor force, 0.7, times the adult, noninstitutionalized, nonmilitary population of 200.0 million yields a labor force of 140.0 million.

b. Subtracting the 7.5 million unemployed from the labor force of 140.0 million yields 132.5 million people who are employed.
c. Dividing the 7.5 million unemployed by the 140.0 million in the labor force and multiplying by 100 yields an unemployment rate of about 5.36 percent.

7-3. a. The labor force equals the number employed plus the number unemployed, or 152 million + 8 million = 160 million. In percentage terms, therefore, the unemployment rate is 100 times 8 million/160 million, or 5 percent.
b. These 40 million people are not in the labor force. The labor force participation rate is, in percentage terms, 100 times 160 million/200 million, or 80 percent.

7-5. a. Four of the 100 people are always continuously unemployed because they are between jobs, so the frictional unemployment rate is 4 percent.
b. Three of the 100 people are always unemployed because of a poor match of their skills with employers' requirements, so the structural unemployment rate is 3 percent.
c. The unemployment rate is the sum of the frictional and structural rates of unemployment, or 7 percent.

7-7. The overall unemployment rate is 8 percent, and the natural rate of unemployment is 5 percent.

7-9. a. 2007
b. 10 percent
c. 10 percent
d. $1,800 in 2007; $3,000 in 2011

7-11. 2 percent

7-13. a. The homeowner gains; the savings bank loses.
b. The tenants gain; the landlord loses.
c. The auto buyer gains; the bank loses.
d. The employer gains; the pensioner loses.

CHAPTER 8

8-1. a. When Juanita does all the work herself, only the materials she purchases in markets, which total to $280 per year, count in GDP.
b. She must pay the market price of $200 for the texturing, so her contribution to annual GDP from this project, including the materials, is $480.
c. Because Juanita now pays for the entire project via market transactions, her total contribution to GDP is $830 per year.

8-3. a. $16.6 trillion; NDP = $16.3 trillion; NI = $14.5 trillion.

b. GDP in 2013 will equal $15.5 trillion.
c. If the value of depreciation were to exceed gross private domestic investment in 2011, then the nation's capital stock would decline. Because capital is a productive resource, the nation's future productivity likely would decline, and this decline would worsen if the situation were to continue beyond 2011.

8-5. a. Gross domestic income = $14.6 trillion; GDP = $14.6 trillion.
b. Gross private domestic investment = $2.0 trillion.
c. Personal income = $12.0 trillion; personal disposable income = $10.3 trillion.

8-7. a. Measured GDP declines.
b. Measured GDP increases.
c. Measured GDP does not change (the firearms are not newly produced).

8-9. a. The chip is an intermediate good, so its purchase in June is not included in GDP; only the final sale in November is included.
b. This is a final sale of a good that is included in GDP for the year.
c. This is a final sale of a service that is included in GDP for the year.

8-11. Price level index for 2007: 100.0

Price level index for 2011: 127.1

8-13. The price index is (2010 nominal GDP/2009 real GDP) × 100 = ($88,000/$136,000) × 100 = 64.7.

8-15. The $1 billion expended to pay for employees and equipment and the additional $1 billion paid to clean up the oil spill would be included in GDP, for a total of $2 billion added to GDP in 2011. The rise in oil reserves increases the stock of wealth but is not included in the current flow of newly produced goods and services. In addition, the welfare loss relating to the deaths of wildlife is also not measured in the marketplace and thereby is not included in GDP.

CHAPTER 9

9-1. a. Y
b. X

9-3. The nation will maintain its stock of capital goods at its current level, so its rate of economic growth will be zero.

9-5. A: $8,250 per capita; B: $4,500 per capita; C: $21,000 per capita

9-7. 1.77 times higher after 20 years; 3.16 times higher after 40 years

9-9. 5 years

9-11. 4 percent

9-13. Per capita real GDP in 2008 was 10 percent higher than in 2007, or $2,200. The level of real GDP was $2,200 per person times 5 million people, or $11 billion.

CHAPTER 10

10-1. The amount of unemployment would be the sum of frictional, structural, and seasonal unemployment.

10-3. The real value of the new full-employment level of nominal GDP is ($14.2 trillion/1.15) = $12.35 trillion, so the long-run aggregate supply curve has shifted rightward by $0.35 trillion, in base-year dollars.

10-5. This change implies a rightward shift of the long-run aggregate supply curve along the unchanged aggregate demand curve, so the long-run equilibrium price level will decline.

10-7. There are three effects. First, there is a real-balance effect, because the rise in the price level reduces real money balances, inducing people to cut back on their spending. In addition, there is an interest rate effect as a higher price level pushes up interest rates, thereby reducing the attractiveness of purchases of autos, houses, and plants and equipment. Finally, there is an open-economy effect as home residents respond to the higher price level by reducing purchases of domestically produced goods in favor of foreign-produced goods, while foreign residents cut back on their purchases of home-produced goods. All three effects entail a reduction in purchases of goods and services, so the aggregate demand curve slopes downward.

10-9. a. At the price level P_2 above the equilibrium price level P_1, the total quantity of real goods and services that people plan to consume is less than the total quantity that is consistent with firms' production plans. One reason is that at the higher-than-equilibrium price level, real money balances are lower, which reduces real wealth and induces lower planned consumption. Another is that interest rates are higher at the higher-than-equilibrium price level, which generates a cutback in consumption spending. Finally, at the higher-than equilibrium price level P_2, people tend to cut back on purchasing domestic goods in favor of foreign-produced goods, and foreign residents reduce purchases of domestic goods. As unsold inventories of output accumulate, the price level drops toward the equilibrium price level P_1, which ultimately causes planned consumption to rise toward equality with total production.

  b. At the price level P_3 below the equilibrium price level P_1, the total quantity of real goods and services that people plan to consume exceeds the total quantity that is consistent with firms' production plans. One reason is that at the lower-than-equilibrium price level, real money balances are higher, which raises real wealth and induces higher planned consumption. Another is that interest rates are lower at the lower-than-equilibrium price level, which generates an increase in consumption spending. Finally, at the lower-than equilibrium price level P_2, people tend to raise their purchases of domestic goods and cut back on buying foreign-produced goods, and foreign residents increase purchases of domestic goods. As inventories of output are depleted, the price level begins to rise toward the equilibrium price level P_1, which ultimately causes planned consumption to fall toward equality with total production.

10-11. a. When the price level falls with deflation, there is a movement downward along the *AD* curve.

  b. The decline in foreign real GDP levels reduces incomes of foreign residents, who cut back on their spending on domestic exports. Thus, the domestic *AD* curve shifts leftward.

  c. The fall in the foreign exchange value of the nation's currency makes domestic-produced goods and services less expensive to foreign residents, who increase their spending on domestic exports. Thus, the domestic *AD* curve shifts rightward.

  d. An increase in the price level causes a movement upward along the *AD* curve.

10-13. a. The aggregate demand curve shifts leftward along the long-run aggregate supply curve; the equilibrium price level falls, and equilibrium real GDP remains unchanged.

  b. The aggregate demand curve shifts rightward along the long-run aggregate supply curve; the equilibrium price level rises, and equilibrium real GDP remains unchanged.

  c. The long-run aggregate supply curve shifts rightward along the aggregate demand curve; the equilibrium price level falls, and equilibrium real GDP increases.

  d. The aggregate demand curve shifts rightward along the long-run aggregate supply curve; the equilibrium price level rises, and equilibrium real GDP remains unchanged.

CHAPTER 11

11-1. a. Because saving increases at any given interest rate, the desired saving curve shifts rightward. This causes the equilibrium interest rate to decline.

  b. There is no effect on current equilibrium real GDP, because in the classical model the vertical long-run aggregate supply curve always applies.

  c. A change in the saving rate does not directly affect the demand for labor or the supply of labor in the classical model, so equilibrium employment does not change.

  d. The decrease in the equilibrium interest rate generates a rightward and downward movement along the demand curve for investment. Consequently, desired investment increases.

  e. The rise in current investment implies greater capital accumulation. Other things being equal, this will imply increased future production and higher equilibrium real GDP in the future.

11-3. False. In fact, there is an important distinction. The classical model of short-run real GDP determination applies to an interval short enough that some factors of production, such as capital, are fixed. Nevertheless, the classical model implies that even in the short run the economy's aggregate supply curve is the same as its long-run aggregate supply curve.

11-5. a. The labor supply curve shifts rightward, and equilibrium employment increases.

  b. The rise in employment causes the aggregate supply curve to shift rightward, and real GDP rises.

  c. Because the immigrants have higher saving rates, the nation's saving supply curve shifts to the right along its investment curve, and the equilibrium interest rate declines.

  d. The fall in the equilibrium interest rate induces a rise in investment, and equilibrium saving also rises.

  e. Capital accumulation rises, and more real GDP will be forthcoming in future years.

11-7. In the long run, the aggregate supply curve is vertical because all input prices adjust fully and people are fully informed in the long run. Thus, the short-run aggregate supply curve is more steeply sloped if input prices adjust more rapidly and people become more fully informed within a short-run interval.

11-9. This event would cause the aggregate demand curve to shift leftward. In the short run, the equilibrium price level would decline, and equilibrium real GDP would fall.

11-11. To prevent a short-run decrease in real GDP from taking place after the temporary rise in oil prices shifts the SRAS curve leftward, the central bank should increase the quantity of money in circulation. This will shift the AD curve rightward and prevent equilibrium real GDP from declining in the short run.

11-13. a. *E:* The union wage boost causes the SRAS curve to shift leftward, from $SRAS_1$ to $SRAS_3$. The reduction in incomes abroad causes import spending in this nation to fall, which induces a leftward shift in the AD curve, from AD_1 to AD_3.
b. *B:* The short-term reduction in production capabilities causes the SRAS curve to shift leftward, from $SRAS_1$ to $SRAS_3$, and the increase in money supply growth generates a rightward shift in the AD curve, from AD_1 to AD_2.
c. *C:* The strengthening of the value of this nation's currency reduces the prices of imported inputs that domestic firms utilize to produce goods and services, which causes the SRAS curve to shift rightward, from $SRAS_1$ to $SRAS_2$. At the same time, currency's strengthening raises the prices of exports and reduces the prices of imports, so net export spending declines, thereby inducing a leftward shift in the AD curve, from AD_1 to AD_3.

CHAPTER 12

12-1. The completed table, which includes the answers to parts a and b, follows (all amounts in dollars):

Disposable Income	Saving	Consumption	APS	APC
200	−40	240	−0.20	1.20
400	0	400	0.00	1.00
600	40	560	0.07	0.93
800	80	720	0.10	0.90
1,000	120	880	0.12	0.88
1,200	160	1,040	0.13	0.87

For part c, the MPS is equal to $40/200 = 0.2$, and the MPC is equal to $160/200 = 0.8$.

12-3. a. Yes, because the rate of return on the investment exceeds the market interest rate.
b. No, because the rate of return on the investment is now less than the market interest rate.

12-5. a. The completed table follows (all amounts in dollars):

Real GDP	Consumption	Saving	Investment
2,000	2,000	0	1,200
4,000	3,600	400	1,200
6,000	5,200	800	1,200
8,000	6,800	1,200	1,200
10,000	8,400	1,600	1,200
12,000	10,000	2,000	1,200

$MPC = 1,600/2,000 = 0.8$; $MPS = 400/2,000 = 0.2$.
b. The graph appears below.

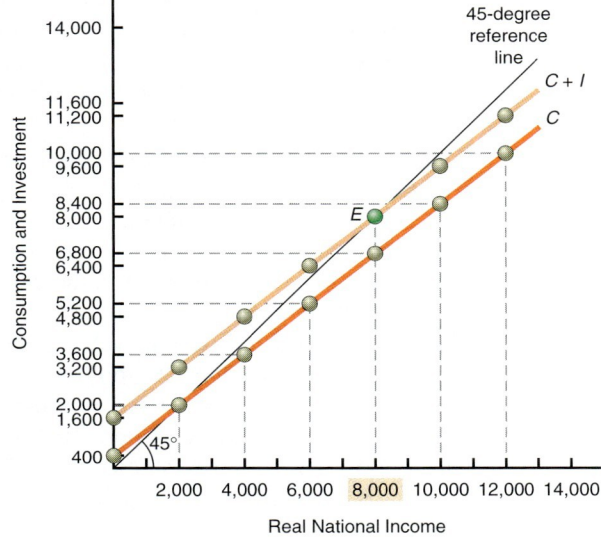

c. The graph appears below. Equilibrium real GDP on both graphs equals $8,000.

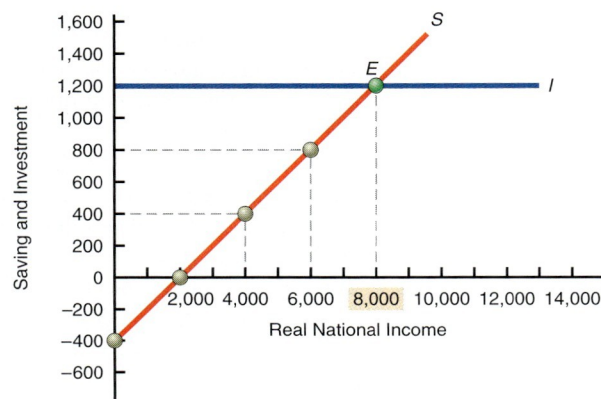

d. APS = $1,200/$8,000 = 0.15.
e. The multiplier is 1/(1 − MPC) = 1/(1 − 0.8) = 1/0.2 = 5. Thus, if autonomous consumption were to rise by $100, then equilibrium real GDP would increase by $100 times 5, or $500.

12-7. a. If $Y = 0$, autonomous consumption equals $800, which implies dissaving equal to −$800, which is the amount of autonomous saving.
b. The marginal propensity to consume is 0.80, so the marginal propensity to save is 1 − MPC = 1 − 0.80 = 0.20.
c. The multiplier is 1/(1 − MPC) = 1/0.20 = 5.0.

12-9. The multiplier is 1/(1 − MPC) = 4, so 1 − MPC = 0.25, which implies that MPC = 0.75. Thus, consumption when real GDP equals $12 trillion is $1 trillion + (0.75 × $12 trillion) = $10 trillion.

12-11. The multiplier is 1/(1 − MPC) = 1/(1 − 0.75) = 4, so the increase in equilibrium real GDP is $250 billion × 4 = $1 trillion, and the level of real GDP at the new point on the aggregate demand curve is $11 trillion.

12-13. a. The MPS is equal to 1/3.
b. $0.1 trillion

CHAPTER 13

13-1. a. A key factor that could help explain why the actual effect may have turned out to be lower is the crowding-out effect. Some government spending may have entailed direct expenditure offsets that reduced private expenditures on a dollar-for-dollar basis. In addition, indirect crowding out may have occurred. Because the government did not change taxes, it probably sold bonds to finance its increased expenditures, and this action likely pushed up interest rates, thereby discouraging private investment. Furthermore, the increase in government spending likely pushed up aggregate demand, which may have caused a short-run increase in the price level. This, in turn, may have induced foreign residents to reduce their expenditures on U.S. goods. It also could have reduced real money holdings sufficiently to discourage consumers from spending as much as before. On net, therefore, real GDP rose in the short run but not by the full amount predicted by the basic multiplier effect.
b. In the long run, as the increased spending raised aggregate demand, wages and other input prices likely increased in proportion to the resulting increase in the price level. Thus, in the long run the aggregate supply schedule was vertical, and the increase in government spending induced only a rise in the price level.

13-3. Because of the recognition time lag entailed in gathering information about the economy, policymakers may be slow to respond to a downturn in real GDP. Congressional approval of policy actions to address the downturn may be delayed; hence, an action time lag may also arise. Finally, there is an effect time lag, because policy actions take time to exert their full effects on the economy. If these lags are sufficiently long, it is possible that by the time a policy to address a downturn has begun to have its effects, real GDP may already be rising. If so, the policy action may push real GDP up faster than intended, thereby making real GDP less stable.

13-5. Situation *b* is an example of indirect crowding out because the reduction in private expenditures takes place indirectly in response to a change in the interest rate. In contrast, situations *a* and *c* are examples of direct expenditure offsets.

13-7. Situation *b* is an example of a discretionary fiscal policy action because this is a discretionary action by Congress. So is situation *d* because the president uses discretionary authority. Situation *c* is an example of monetary policy, not fiscal policy, and situation *a* is an example of an automatic stabilizer.

13-9. There is a recessionary gap, because at point A, equilibrium real GDP of $13.5 trillion is below the long-run level of $14.0 trillion. To eliminate the recessionary gap of $0.5 trillion, government spending must increase sufficiently to shift the AD curve rightward to a long-run equilibrium, which will entail a price level increase from 115 to 120. Hence, the spending increase must shift the AD curve rightward by $1 trillion, or by the multiplier, which is 1/0.20 = 5, times the increase in spending. Hence, government spending must rise by $200 billion, or $0.2 trillion.

13-11. Because the MPC is 0.80, the multiplier equals 1/(1 − MPC) = 1/0.2 = 5. Net of indirect crowding out, therefore, total autonomous expenditures must rise by $40 billion in order to shift the aggregate demand curve rightward by $200 billion. If the government raises its spending by $50 billion, the market interest rate rises by 0.5 percentage point and thereby causes planned investment spending to fall by $10 billion, which results in a net rise in total autonomous expenditures equal to $40 billion. Consequently, to accomplish its objective the government should increase its spending by $50 billion.

13-13. A cut in the tax rate should induce a rise in consumption and, consequently, a multiple short-run increase in equilibrium real GDP. In addition, however, a tax-rate reduction reduces the automatic-stabilizer properties of the tax system, so equilibrium real GDP would be less stable in the face of changes in autonomous spending.

APPENDIX C

C-1. **a.** The marginal propensity to consume is equal to 1 − MPS, or 6/7.

b. The required increase in equilibrium income is $0.35 trillion, or $350 billion. The multiplier equals $1/(1 - MPC) = 1/MPS = 1/(1/7) = 7$. Hence, investment or government spending must increase by $50 billion to bring about a $350 billion increase in equilibrium income.

c. The multiplier relevant for a tax change equals $-MPC/(1 - MPC) = -MPC/MPS = -(6/7)/(1/7) = -6$. Thus, the government would have to cut taxes by $58.33 billion to induce a rise in equilibrium real income equal to $350 billion.

C-3. **a.** The aggregate expenditure curve shifts up by $1 billion; equilibrium real income increases by $5 billion.

b. The aggregate expenditures curve shifts down by the MPC times the tax increase, or by $0.8 \times \$1$ billion = $0.8 billion; equilibrium real income falls by $4 billion.

c. The aggregate expenditures curve shifts upward by $(1 - MPC)$ times $1 billion = $0.2 billion. Equilibrium real income rises by $1 billion.

d. No change; no change.

CHAPTER 14

14-1. $0.4 trillion

14-3. A higher deficit creates a higher public debt.

14-5. The net public debt is obtained by subtracting government interagency borrowing from the gross public debt.

14-7. **a.** Previously, the small annual budget surplus had been reducing the net public debt at a slow pace. Now that Congress has reduced spending more sharply, the budget surplus will be larger this year, so the net public debt will decline at a quicker pace.

b. These are all interagency transfers that leave the amount of government bonds held by the public unchanged, so there is no effect on the net public debt.

c. The decrease in tax collections will result in a budget deficit for the present year that will cause the net public debt to increase.

14-9. **a.** Other things being equal, foreign dollar holders can be induced to hold more domestic government bonds used to finance domestic government deficits only if the domestic interest rate rises.

b. Immediately, the main source of dollars is the dollars that foreign residents otherwise would use to purchase exports.

14-11. The immediate effect would be only a change in accounting definitions. Proponents of capital budgeting argue that over time, this change would induce changes in government spending and taxation that might contribute to truly lower fiscal deficits.

14-13. As shown in the diagram below, the increase in government spending and/or tax reduction that creates the budget deficit also causes the aggregate demand curve to shift rightward, from AD_1 to AD_2. With unchanged short-run aggregate supply, a new short-run equilibrium is reached at point C. The equilibrium price level rises to a value such as 130, and equilibrium real GDP increases to a level such as $14 trillion per year. Ultimately, however, upward adjustments in wages and other input prices will induce a leftward shift in the SRAS curve to $SRAS_2$, resulting in a new long-run equilibrium at point D. In the long run, the price level will rise further, to a value such as 133, and real GDP will return to $13.5 trillion.

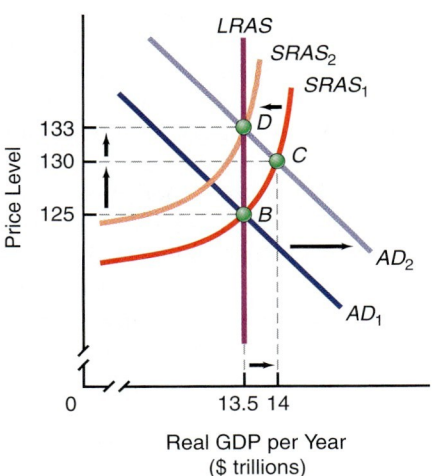

CHAPTER 15

15-1. medium of exchange; store of value; standard of deferred payment

15-3. store of value; standard of deferred payment

15-5. M1 equals demand deposits and other transactions deposits plus currency plus traveler's checks, or $625 billion + $800 billion + $25 billion = $1,450 billion; M2 equals M1 + savings deposits plus small-denomination time deposits plus money market deposit accounts plus retail (noninstitution) money market mutual funds, or $1,450 billion + $1,900 billion + $1,450 billion + $1,250 billion + $1,200 billion = $7,250 billion.

15-7.
a. neither
b. M2 only
c. M1 and M2
d. M2 only

15-9. In principle, each institution can match with each rationale; your explanations are the aspects of your answers that are most important.
a. Insurance companies limit adverse selection by screening applicants for policies.
b. Savings banks limit moral hazard by monitoring borrowers after loans have been made.
c. Pension funds reduce management costs by pooling the funds of many future pensioners.

15-11.
a. moral hazard problem
b. adverse selection problem
c. moral hazard problem

15-13. In an extreme case in which the U.S. government were to close down the Federal Reserve System, it would have to compensate holders of Federal Reserve notes for the market value of those notes.

15-15. Back in 1913, the population was centered farther to the east. Thus, congressional representation was centered farther to the east, so political concerns together with a view that the Fed districts should be designed to best serve the existing population helped determine the geographic boundaries. These have not been redrawn since.

CHAPTER 16

16-1.
a. asset
b. liability
c. liability
d. asset

16-3. The bank's reserves are its required reserves, which equal $0.10 \times \$15$ million = $1.5 million. Total assets equal total liabilities, or $15 million. Hence, its remaining loans and securities must amount to its total assets of $15 million minus its reserves of $1.5 million, or $13.5 million.

16-5. Yes, the bank holds $50 million in excess reserves. The bank's current total assets equal its $2 billion in total liabilities. It must hold 15 percent of its $2 billion in transactions deposits, or $0.30 billion as required reserves. Its total reserves equal $2 billion in total assets minus $1.65 billion in loans and securities, or $0.35 billion. Hence, the bank has $0.05 billion, or $50 million, in excess reserves.

16-7. The dealer's bank must hold 15 percent of the $1 million, or $150,000, as required reserves. Thus, the bank can lend out the excess reserves of $850,000.

16-9.
a. Total liabilities and net worth = total assets = $0.26 billion in total reserves + $3.6 billion in loans + $1 billion in securities + $0.14 billion in other assets = $5 billion.
b. The bank could lend its $10 million in excess reserves.
c. Transactions deposits equal required reserves of $0.25 billion/0.1 = $2.5 billion.

16-11.
a. Yes
b. None, because the bank has $1 billion in current transactions deposits not "swept" to money market deposit accounts, so with a required reserve ratio of 0.20 the total amount of required reserves for the bank is the $200 million in reserves it currently holds.
c. Its $1 billion in transactions deposits are currently included in M1.

16-13. When you purchase a U.S. government security, you draw on existing funds in a deposit account and thereby redistribute funds already within the banking system; by way of contrast, the Federal Reserve creates funds that had not previously existed in the banking system.

16-15. The maximum potential money multiplier is $1/0.01 = 100$, so total deposits in the banking system will increase by $5 million $\times 100 = \$500$ million.

CHAPTER 17

17-1.
a. $500/0.05 = \$10,000$.
b. Its price falls to $500/0.10 = \$5,000$.

17-3.
a. One possible policy action would be an open market sale of securities, which would reduce the money supply and shift the aggregate demand curve leftward. Others would be to increase the

discount rate relative to the federal funds rate or to raise the required reserve ratio.

b. In principle, the Fed's action would reduce inflation more quickly.

17-5. Because a contractionary monetary policy causes interest rates to increase, financial capital begins to flow into the United States. This causes the demand for dollars to rise, which pushes up the value of the dollar and makes U.S. exports more expensive to foreign residents. They cut back on their purchases of U.S. products, which tends to reduce U.S. real GDP.

17-7.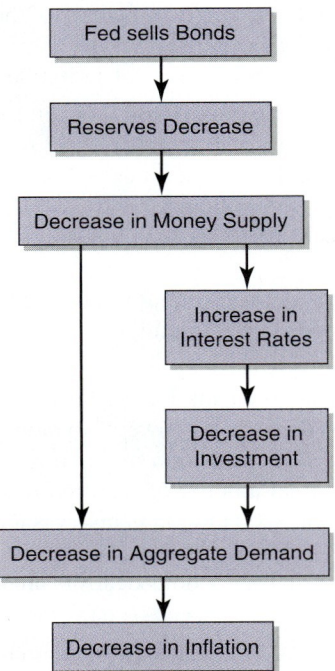

17-9. The price level remains at its original value. Because $M_s V = PY$, V has doubled, and Y is unchanged, cutting M_s in half leaves P unchanged.

17-11. a. $M_s V = PY$, so $P = M_s V/Y = (\$1.1 \text{ trillion} \times 10)/\$5 \text{ trillion} = 2.2$.
  b. 10 percent
  c. 10 percent
  d. They are equal.

17-13. Any one of these contractionary actions will tend to raise interest rates, which in turn will induce international inflows of financial capital. This pushes up the value of the dollar and makes U.S. goods less attractive abroad. As a consequence, real planned total expenditures on U.S. goods decline even further.

17-15. a. To push the equilibrium federal funds rate up to the new target value, the Trading Desk will have to reduce the money supply by selling U.S. government securities.

b. The increase in the differential between the discount rate and the federal funds rate will induce more depository institutions to borrow reserves from Federal Reserve banks. In the absence of a Trading Desk action, this would cause the equilibrium interest rate to increase. To prevent this from occurring, the Trading Desk will have to boost the money supply by purchasing U.S. government securities.

APPENDIX D

D-1. a. $20 billion increase
  b. $40 billion increase
  c. $10 billion open market purchase

D-3. Through its purchase of $1 billion in bonds, the Fed increased reserves by $1 billion. This ultimately caused a $3 billion increase in the money supply after full multiple expansion. The 1 percentage-point drop in the interest rate, from 6 percent to 5 percent, caused investment to rise by $25 billion, from $1,200 billion to $1,225 billion. An investment multiplier of 3 indicates that equilibrium real GDP rose by $75 billion, to $12,075 billion, or $12.075 trillion.

CHAPTER 18

18-1. a. The actual unemployment rate, which equals the number of people unemployed divided by the labor force, would decline, because the labor force would rise while the number of people unemployed would remain unchanged.
  b. Natural unemployment rate estimates also would be lower.
  c. The logic of the short- and long-run Phillips curves would not be altered. The government might wish to make this change if it feels that those in the military "hold jobs" and therefore should be counted as employed within the U.S. economy.

18-3. The "long run" is an interval sufficiently long that input prices fully adjust and people have full information. Adoption of more sophisticated computer and communications technology provides people with more immediate access to information, which can reduce this interval.

18-5. The natural rate of unemployment is the rate of unemployment that would exist after full adjustment has taken place in response to any changes that have occurred. In contrast, the nonaccelerating inflation rate of unemployment is the rate of unemployment that corresponds to a stable rate of inflation, which is easier to quantify.

18-7. a. The measured unemployment rate when all adjustments have occurred will now always be lower than before, so the natural unemployment rate will be smaller.

b. The unemployment rate consistent with stable inflation will now be reduced, so the NAIRU will be smaller.

c. The Phillips curve will shift inward.

18-9. No. It could still be true that wages and other prices of factors of production adjust sluggishly to changes in the price level. Then a rise in aggregate demand that boosts the price level brings about an upward movement along the short-run aggregate supply curve, causing equilibrium real GDP to rise.

18-11. a. An increase in desired investment spending induces aggregate demand, so AD_3 applies. There is an unchanged price level in the short run, and equilibrium real GDP rises from $14 trillion at point A to $14.5 trillion at point C.

b. Over time, firms perceive that they can increase their profits by adjusting prices upward in response to the increase in aggregate demand. Thus, firms eventually will incur the menu costs required to make these price adjustments. As they do so, the aggregate supply curve will shift upward, from $SRAS_1$ to $SRAS_2$, as shown in the diagram below. Real GDP will return to its original level of $14 trillion, in base-year dollars. The price level will increase to a level above 119, such as 124.

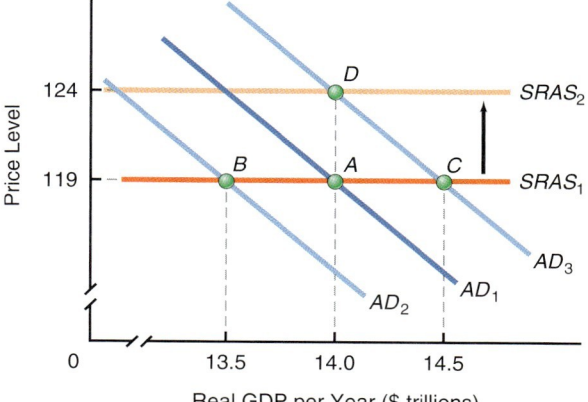

18-13. The explanation would be that aggregate demand has increased at a faster pace than the rise in aggregate supply caused by economic growth. On net, therefore, the price level has risen during the past few years.

18-15. Increasing the price of a product in response to a long-lasting increase in demand will yield higher profits for several periods. The value of this stream of future profits is more likely to be sufficiently large to outweigh a small, onetime menu cost. In this situation, it is more likely that firms will raise their prices.

CHAPTER 19

19-1. Population growth rate = real GDP growth rate − rate of growth of per capita real GDP = 3.1 percent − 0.3 percent = 2.8 percent.

19-3. a. Real GDP growth rate = rate of growth of per capita real GDP + population growth rate = 0.1 percent + 2.2 percent = 2.3 percent.

b. Rate of growth of per capita real GDP = 2.3 percent − 2.7 percent = −0.4 percent.

c. Rate of growth of per capita real GDP = 3.1 percent − 2.7 percent = +0.4 percent.

19-5. Morocco or Uruguay, then Bosnia-Herzegovina, Togo, and Angola. The cost of starting a business is slightly higher in Uruguay than in Morocco. Starting a business in Uruguay requires fewer legal steps. One of these two nations is likely to experience higher growth, other things being equal, than the others.

19-7. $10 trillion/$0.5 trillion × 0.1 = 2 percentage points.

19-9. a. Portfolio investment is equal to $150 million bonds plus $100 million in stocks representing ownership of less than 10 percent, or $250 million. (Bank loans are neither portfolio investment nor foreign direct investment.)

b. Foreign direct investment is equal to $250 million in stocks representing an ownership share of at least 10 percent. (Bank loans are neither portfolio investment nor foreign direct investment.)

19-11. a. adverse selection
b. adverse selection
c. moral hazard
d. adverse selection

19-13. a. The company had already qualified for funding at a market interest rate, so the World Bank is interfering with functioning private markets for credit. In addition, by extending credit to the company at a below-market rate, the World Bank provides an incentive for the company to borrow additional funds for less efficient investment.

b. In this situation, the World Bank effectively is tying up funds in dead capital. There is an associated opportunity cost, because the funds could instead be allocated to another investment that would yield more immediate returns.

c. In this case, the IMF contributes to a moral hazard problem, because the government has every incentive not to make reforms that will enable it to repay this and future loans it may receive.

19-15. a. There is an incentive for at least some governments to fail to follow through with reforms, even if those governments might have had good intentions when they applied for World Bank loans.

b. National governments most interested in obtaining funds to "buy" votes will be among those most interested in obtaining IMF loans. The proposed IMF rule could help reduce the number of nations whose governments seek to obtain funds to try to "buy" votes.

CHAPTER 20

20-1. The campus pizzeria indicates by its pricing policy that it recognizes the principle of diminishing marginal utility. Because a customer's marginal utility of the second pizza is typically lower than for the first, the customer is likely to value the second less and, therefore, be willing to pay less for it.

20-3. The total utility of the three, four, and five cheeseburger is 48, 56, and 60, respectively. The marginal utility of the first and second cheeseburger is 20 and 16, respectively. The total utility of one, two, and three bags of french fries is 10, 18, and 20, respectively. The marginal utility of the fourth and fifth bag of french fries is 1 and 0, respectively.

20-5. The new utility-maximizing combination is four cheeseburgers and two orders of french fries, at which the marginal utility per dollar spent is 2 units per dollar and the entire $6 is spent.

20-7. Other things being equal, when the price of soft drinks rises, the individual tends to consume fewer soft drinks and more tacos. Hence, the marginal utility of soft drinks rises, and the marginal utility of tacos falls.

20-9. a. Of all the possible one-unit increases in consumption displayed, the movement from point A to point B generates the highest marginal utility. Total utility rises by 5 units between these points, so marginal utility of the first unit consumed is 5 units.

b. Between points E and F, a one-unit increase in the quantity consumed leaves total utility unchanged at 11 units, so marginal utility is equal to zero.

c. Between points F and G, a one-unit increase in the quantity consumed causes total utility to decline from 11 units to 10 units, so marginal utility is negative and equal to -1 unit.

20-11. At these prices, the marginal utility per dollar spent on 2 fudge bars is 500 units of utility per dollar, and the marginal utility per dollar spent on 5 popsicles is also 500 units of utility per dollar. In addition, the entire budget of $9 is spent at this combination, which is the consumer optimum.

20-13. The marginal utility per dollar spent is equalized at 2.50 if 5 hot dogs and 3 baseball games are consumed, and this consumption combination just exhausts the now-available $190 in income.

20-15. The marginal utility of good Y is 9 utils.

CHAPTER 21

21-1. $|[(200 - 150)/(350/2)]/[(9 - 10)/(19/2)]|$, which is approximately equal to 2.7.

21-3. a. $|[(90 - 80)/(85)]/[(0.20 - 0.40)/(0.30)]|$, which is approximately equal to 0.32. Demand is inelastic over this range.

b. $|[(60 - 40)/(50)]/[(0.80 - 1.20)/(1.00)]| = 1.00$. Demand is unit-elastic over this range.

c. $|[(20 - 10)/(15)]/[(1.60 - 1.80)/(1.70)]|$, which is approximately equal to 5.67. Demand is elastic over this range.

21-5. $|[(80 - 120)/(200/2)]/[(\$22.50 - \$17.50)/(\$40/2)]| = 1.6$. Demand is elastic.

21-7. Because price and total revenue move in the same direction, the craftsman faces inelastic demand for his guitars.

21-9. a. More inelastic, because it represents a smaller portion of the budget

b. More elastic, because there are many close substitutes

c. More elastic, because there are a number of substitutes

d. More inelastic, because there are few close substitutes

e. More inelastic, because it represents a small portion of the budget

21-11. Let X denote the percentage change in the quantity of bacon. Then $X/10$ percent $= -0.5$. X, therefore, is -5 percent.

21-13. $[(125,000 - 75,000)/(200,000/2)]/[(\$35,000 - \$25,000)/(\$60,000/2)] = 1.5$. Supply is elastic.

21-15. The short-run price elasticity of supply is 0.5, and the long-run price elasticity of supply is 2.0.

CHAPTER 22

22-1. a. Bob earns a high economic rent. With a specialized skill that is in great demand, his income is likely to be high.
  b. Sally earns a high economic rent. As a supermodel her income is likely to be relatively high.
  c. If Tim were to leave teaching, not a relatively high-paying occupation, he could sell insurance full time. Hence, his economic rent is relatively low.

22-3. The economic rents that Michael Jordan was able to earn as a basketball player relative to those he could earn as a baseball player surely played a large role in his decision to return to basketball. Hence, they helped direct his resources (athletic talents) to their most efficient uses.

22-5. A sole proprietorship is a business entity owned by a single individual, whereas a partnership is a business entity jointly owned by more than one individual. A corporation, in contrast, is a legal entity that is owned by shareholders, who own shares of the profits of the entity. Sole proprietorships and partnerships do not face double taxation, but corporations do. The owners of corporations, however, enjoy limited liability, whereas the sole proprietor or partner does not.

22-7. Accounting profit is total revenue, $77,250, minus explicit costs, $37,000, for a total of $40,250. Economic profit is total revenue, $77,250, less explicit costs, $37,000, and implicit costs, $40,250, for a total equal to zero.

22-9. a. Physical capital
  b. Financial capital
  c. Financial capital
  d. Physical capital

22-11. a. The owner of WebCity faces both tax rates if the firm is a corporation, but if it is a proprietorship the owner faces only the 30 percent personal income tax rate. Thus, it should choose to be a proprietorship.
  b. If WebCity is a corporation, the $100,000 in corporate earnings is taxed at a 20 percent rate, so that after-tax dividends are $80,000, and these are taxed at the personal income tax rate of 30 percent, leaving $56,000 in after-tax income for the owner. Hence, the firm should be organized as a proprietorship, so that the after-tax earnings are $70,000.
  c. Yes. In this case, incorporation raises earnings to $150,000, which are taxed at a rate of 20 percent, yielding after-tax dividends of $120,000 that are taxed at the personal rate of 30 percent. This leaves an after-tax income for the owner of $84,000, which is higher than the after-tax earnings of $70,000 if WebCity is a proprietorship that earns lower pre-tax income taxed at the personal rate.
  d. After-tax profits rise from $56,000 to $84,000, or by $28,000.
  e. This policy change would only increase the incentive to incorporate.
  f. A corporate structure provides limited liability for owners, which can be a major advantage. Furthermore, owners may believe that the corporate structure will yield higher pre-tax earnings, as in the above example.

22-13. The real rate of interest in Japan is 2% − 0.5% = 1.5%. The real rate of interest in the United States is 4% − 3% = 1%. Japan, therefore, has the higher *real* rate of interest.

22-15. Ownership of common stock provides voting rights within the firm but also entails immediate loss if assets fall below the value of the firm's liabilities. Preferred stockholders are repaid prior to owners of common stock, but preferred stockholders do not have voting rights.

22-17. You should point out to your classmate that stock prices tend to drift upward following a random walk. That is, yesterday's price plus any upward drift is the best guide to today's price. Therefore, there are no predictable trends that can be used to "beat" the market.

CHAPTER 23

23-1. The short run is a time period during which the professor cannot enter the job market and find employment elsewhere. This is the nine-month period from August 15 through May 15. The professor can find employment elsewhere after the contract has been fulfilled, so the short run is nine months and the long run is greater than nine months.

23-3.

Input of Labor (workers per month)	Total Output of Flash Memory Drives	Marginal Physical Product
0	0	—
1	25	25
2	60	35
3	85	25
4	105	20
5	115	10
6	120	5

23-5. Total variable costs are equal to total costs, $5 million, less total fixed costs, $2 million, which equals $3 million. Average variable costs are equal to total variable costs divided by the number of units produced. Average variable costs, therefore, equal $3 million divided by 10,000, or $300.

23-7. **a.** TFC equals AFC, $10 per LCD screen, times the quantity produced per day, 100 LCD screens, which equals $1,000 per day.
b. The total variable costs (TVC) of producing 100 LCD screens equal AVC, $10 per unit, times the quantity produced per day, 100 LCD screens, which equals $1,000 per day.
c. The total costs of producing 100 LCD screens equal total fixed costs plus the total variable costs of producing 100 LCD screens, or $1,000 per day plus $1,000 per day, which equals $2,000 per day.
d. The average total costs (ATC) of producing 99 LCD screens equal the average fixed costs of $10.10 plus the average variable costs of $10.07, or $20.17 per LCD screen. Thus, the total cost of producing 99 LCD screens equals $20.17 times 99, or $1,996.83. The marginal cost of producing the hundredth LCD screen equals the change in total costs from increasing production from 99 to 100, or $2,000 − $1,996.83, or $3.17 per LCD screen.

23-9. **a.** Average total costs are $20 per unit plus $30 per unit, or $50 per unit, and total costs divided by average total costs equal output, which therefore is $2,500/$50 per unit, or 50 units.
b. TVC = AVC × Q = $20 per unit × 50 units = $1,000.
c. TFC = AFC × Q = $30 per unit × 50 units = $1,500; or TFC = TC − TVC = $2,500 − $1,000 = $1,500.

23-11. Hiring 1 more unit of labor at a wage rate of $20 to increase output by 1 unit causes total costs to rise by $20, so the marginal cost of the 251st unit is $20.

23-13. **a.** $2 per unit
b. 1,000 units
c. $2,000

23-15. **a.** plant size E
b. leftward movement

CHAPTER 24

24-1. **a.** The single firm producing much of the industry's output can affect price. Therefore, this is currently not a perfectly competitive industry.
b. The output of each firm is not homogeneous, so this is not a perfectly competitive industry.
c. Firms cannot easily enter the industry, so this is not a perfectly competitive industry.

24-3. **a.** For a perfectly competitive firm, marginal revenue and average revenue are equal to the market clearing price. Hence, average revenue equals $20 per unit at each possible output rate.
b. At the present output of 10,000 units per week, the firm's total revenues equal price times output, or $20 per unit times 10,000 units per week, which equals $200,000 per week. The firm's total costs equal ATC times output, or $15.75 per unit times 10,000 units per week, which equals $157,500 per week. Weekly economic profits equal total revenues minus total costs, or $200,000 − $157,500 = $42,500. The firm is maximizing economic profits, because it is producing the output rate at which marginal revenue equals marginal cost.
c. If the market clearing price were to fall to $12.50 per unit, the marginal revenue curve would shift down to this level. Average total costs would exceed the price at this output rate, but in the short run the firm would minimize its short-run economic losses by producing 8,100 units per week.
d. If the market clearing price were to fall to $7.50 per unit, the marginal revenue curve would shift down to this level. Average variable costs at an output rate of 5,000 units per week would exceed the market clearing price, so total variable costs of producing 5,000 units per week would exceed total revenues. The firm should cease production if this event takes place.

24-5. At the profit-maximizing rate of output, marginal cost equals marginal revenue, which occurs at 8 pizzas.

Total Output and Sales of Pizzas	Total Cost ($)	Marginal Cost ($ per unit)	Marginal Revenue ($ per unit)
0	5	—	10
1	9	4	10
2	11	2	10
3	12	1	10
4	14	2	10
5	18	4	10
6	24	6	10
7	32	8	10
8	42	10	10
9	54	12	10
10	68	14	10

24-7. Even though the price of pizzas, and hence marginal revenue, falls to only $5, this covers average variable costs. Thus, the shop should stay open.

24-9. Marginal revenue equals marginal cost at 1,500 units of output. The average variable cost of producing this output exceeds the market price at this output level, however, so the firm should shut down in the short run. Then it minimizes its short-run economic losses at the amount of its total fixed costs, which equal $0.50 times 1,500, or $750.

24-11. In the described situation, the firm is producing an output rate at a point on the marginal cost curve below the average total cost curve. Marginal revenue is above the minimum point of the average total cost curve, however. Hence, marginal cost at the current rate of production is less than marginal revenue. The firm is not maximizing profit, and it should increase its rate of production.

24-13. a. There was a significant increase in market supply as more firms entered the industry. A consequence for the typical firm was that the market price fell below the minimum average total cost, resulting in negative economic profits.

b. Firms will consider leaving the industry, and some firms probably *will* leave the industry.

CHAPTER 25

25-1. The demand curve faced by the firm is the downward-sloping market demand curve, so price exceeds marginal revenue at all quantities beyond the first unit produced.

25-3. a. The total revenue and total profits of the dry cleaner are as follows.

Output (suits cleaned)	Price ($ per unit)	Total Costs ($)	Total Revenue ($)	Total Profit ($)
0	8.00	3.00	0	−3.00
1	7.50	6.00	7.50	1.50
2	7.00	8.50	14.00	5.50
3	6.50	10.50	19.50	9.00
4	6.00	11.50	24.00	12.50
5	5.50	13.50	27.50	14.00
6	5.00	16.00	30.00	14.00
7	4.50	19.00	31.50	12.50
8	4.00	24.00	32.00	8.00

b. The profit-maximizing rate of output is between 5 and 6 units.

25-5. This statement is not correct. Profit maximization occurs at the output rate at which marginal revenue equals marginal cost. This rate of output may well occur at a point above and to the left of the point of minimum average total cost.

25-7. In a perfectly competitive market, price would equal marginal cost at $4.50 unit, at which the quantity is 8,000 units. Because the monopolist produces less and charges a higher price than under perfect competition, price exceeds marginal cost at the profit-maximizing level of output. The difference between the price and marginal cost is the per-unit cost to society of a monopolized industry.

25-9. a. The monopoly maximizes economic profits or minimizes economic losses by producing to the point at which marginal revenue is equal to marginal cost, which is 1 million units of output per month.

b. The profit-maximizing or loss-minimizing price of 1 million units per month is $30 per unit, so total revenues equal $30 million per month. The average total cost of producing 1 million units per month is $33 per unit, so total costs equal $33 million per month. Hence, in the short run, producing 1 million units minimizes the monopoly's loss at $3 million per month.

25-11. If price varies positively with total revenue, then the monopolist is operating on the inelastic portion of the demand curve. This corresponds to the range where marginal revenue is negative. The monopolist cannot, therefore, be at the point where its profits are maximized. In other words, the monopolist is not producing where marginal cost equals marginal revenue.

25-13. Because marginal cost has risen, the monopolist will be operating at a lower rate of output and charging a higher price. Economic profits are likely to decline because even though the price is higher, its output will be more than proportionately lower.

CHAPTER 26

26-1. a. There are many fast-food restaurants producing and selling distinguishable products. Both of these features of this industry are consistent with the theory of monopolistic competition.
   b. There are numerous colleges and universities, but each specializes in different academic areas and hence produces heterogeneous products, as in the theory of monopolistic competition.

26-3. The values for marginal cost and marginal revenue appear below. Marginal revenue equals marginal cost at approximately the fifth unit of output, so marginal analysis indicates that five units is the profit-maximizing production level.

Output	Price ($ per unit)	Total Costs ($)	Total Revenue ($)	Marginal Cost ($ per unit)	Marginal Revenue ($ per unit)	Total Profit ($)
0	6.00	2.00	0	—	—	−2.00
1	5.75	5.25	5.75	3.25	5.75	0.00
2	5.50	7.50	11.00	2.25	5.25	3.50
3	5.25	9.60	15.75	2.10	4.75	6.15
4	5.00	12.10	20.00	2.50	4.25	7.90
5	4.75	15.80	23.75	3.70	3.75	7.95
6	4.50	20.00	27.00	4.20	3.25	7.00
7	4.00	24.75	28.00	4.75	1.00	3.25

26-5. After these long-run adjustments have occurred, the demand curve will have shifted to tangency with the average total cost curve at 4 units of output. At this production level, average total cost is $3.03, so this will be the long-run equilibrium price. Because price and average total cost will be equal, the firm will earn zero economic profits.

26-7. a. mass
   b. direct
   c. mass and interactive
   d. mass

26-9. a. experience good. How well the company's employees clean a carpet can be assessed only by observing the cleanliness of the carpet after they have concluded work.
   b. credence good. The effectiveness of a new cancer treatment is difficult for a typical consumer to assess without the assistance of health care providers possessing expertise that the consumer lacks.
   c. search good. A consumer can evaluate the features of athletic socks without actually wearing them while walking, running, or participating in sports.
   d. search good. Given knowledge that the necktie is made of silk, a photo and description are sufficient to determine its characteristics.

26-11. The fact that consumers can evaluate certain aspects of a credence good in advance of purchase, as in the case of a search good, explains why ads for credence goods, such as pharmaceuticals, often have informational elements. At the same time, however, the fact that consumers cannot truly evaluate credence goods until after purchase, and even then only with assistance, explains why ads for credence goods also commonly include persuasive elements.

26-13. Typically, the fixed costs of producing an information product are relatively high, while average variable cost is equal to a very small per-unit amount. As a consequence, the average total cost curve slopes downward with increased output, and average variable cost equals marginal cost at a low, constant amount irrespective of the quantity produced.

26-15. a. Total costs of producing 300,000 units equal total fixed costs of $2,850,000 plus total variable costs of $300,000, which equals $3,150,000. If each copy is sold at a price of $1, then total revenues are $300,000, so economic losses are equal to −$2,850,000.
   b. At the profit-maximizing price of $35 per unit, the firm sells 100,000 units and earns total revenues equal to $3,500,000. Its total costs equal total variable costs of $100,000 plus total fixed costs of $2,850,000, or $2,950,000, so the maximum possible short-run economic profit is equal to $3,500,000 − $2,950,000 = $550,000.
   c. When the firm maximizes its economic profits, marginal revenue equals marginal cost, which is $1 per unit.

d. $0; in the long run, the firm earns zero economic profits, so there is no incentive for other firms to enter the industry.

CHAPTER 27

27-1. a. 15 percent + 14 percent + 12 percent + 11 percent = 52 percent.
b. 52 percent + 10 percent + 10 percent + 8 percent + 7 percent = 87 percent; or 100 percent − 13 percent = 87 percent.

27-3. a. zero-sum game
b. negative-sum game
c. positive-sum game

27-5. Bob is currently a participant in a noncooperative game, in which some people stand and block his view of the football game. His tit-for-tat strategy is to stand up as well. If he stands, however, he will block the view of another spectator. In a cooperative game, all would sit or stand up simultaneously, so that no individual's view is blocked.

27-7. This could be evidence of tacit collusion, with the university cafeteria engaging in price leadership. Nevertheless, prices also adjust across all firms under perfect competition, so it may be a coincidence that the delis' prices change just after variations in the prices at the university cafeteria.

27-9. a. This demand curve indicates that if the firm were to raise its price, other firms would not raise their prices, so the quantity demanded of the firm's product would drop significantly. If the firm were to reduce its price, however, other firms would cut their prices as well, so the quantity demanded of the firm's product would not be very responsive to the price reduction. Thus, demand is relatively more elastic at a price above the present price and relatively less elastic at a price below the present price, resulting in a kinked demand curve.
b. If consumers are willing to pay a slightly higher price for any given quantity they consume, the demand curve shifts upward by a small amount, as shown below. Because the discontinuous marginal revenue curve is derived from the demand curve, both portions of the marginal revenue curve also shift upward. The price charged by the firm does not change, however.

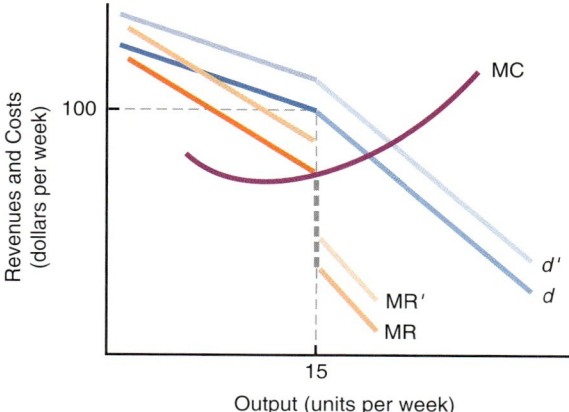

27-11. Possible examples include office productivity software, online auction services, telecommunications services, and Internet payment services. In each case, more people are likely to choose to consume the item when others do, because the inherent usefulness of consuming the item for each person increases as the number of consumers rises.

CHAPTER 28

28-1. If cable service is an industry that experiences diminishing long-run average total costs, then the city may determine that it is more efficient to have a single, large firm that produces at a lower long-run average cost. The city could then regulate the activity of the firm.

28-3. As the table indicates, long-run average cost and long-run marginal cost decline with greater output. If the firm were allowed to operate as a monopolist, it would produce to the point at which marginal cost equals marginal revenue, which is 2 units of output. The price that consumers are willing to pay for this quantity is $90 per unit, and maximum economic profits are $180 − $175 = $5.

Quantity	Price ($ per unit)	Long-Run Total Cost ($)	LRAC ($ per unit)	LRMC ($ per unit)	MR ($ per unit)
0	100	$0	—	—	
1	95	92	$92.00	$92	$95
2	90	177	88.50	85	85
3	85	255	85.00	78	75
4	80	331	82.75	76	65
5	75	406	81.20	75	55
6	70	480	80.00	74	45

28-5. Long-run average cost and price both equal $85 per unit at 3 units of output. At a price of $80 per unit, the firm's economic profits equal $255 − $255 = $0.

28-7. Lemons problems are likely to be more common in industries in which evaluating the characteristics of goods or services by simple inspection is difficult, as is true of the credence goods discussed in Chapter 26. Unaddressed lemons problems tend to depress the prices that sellers of high-quality items can obtain, which induces them to refrain from selling their high-quality items, resulting in sales of only lower-quality items. The main concern of economic regulation is to balance the trade-off between service and price, with economic regulation aiming to keep price lower than the price a profit-maximizing monopolist would charge. Social regulation seeks to improve working conditions and minimize adverse spillovers of production. The adverse incentives resulting from lemons problems are a form of market spillover, so it is arguable that social regulation is most appropriate for addressing lemons problems.

28-9. If European regulation is designed to protect domestic industries, then this is an example of the capture hypothesis. If, on the other hand, there are legitimate health concerns, then this is an example of the share-the-pain, share-the-gain hypothesis.

28-11. a. In this case, Firm 1 makes 75.0 percent of the sales in the Internet book market, and Firm 2 makes 46.7 percent of the sales in physical retail stores. By the antitrust authority's definition, there is a monopoly situation in the Internet book market.
b. In the combined market, Firm 2 accounts for 42.5 percent of all sales, and Firm 1's share drops to 7.5 percent, so under this alternative definition there is no cause for concern about monopoly.

28-13. If the Justice Department viewed Internet realtor listing services as a "relevant market" for antitrust policy, then the growing concentration of ownership within this single retailing association might be a concern. Control over Internet listings by this group could help promote cartel-type behavior. A key issue is whether the Internet marketplace for realtor listings is separate from the physical market.

28-15. This is an example of bundling. Because consumers who purchase the bundled product perceive that they have effectively paid different prices for the bundled products based on their willingness to pay, an antitrust authority might view this practice as charging consumers different prices for the same products, or price discrimination.

CHAPTER 29

29-1.

Labor Input (workers per week)	Total Physical Output (printers per day)	Marginal Physical Product	Marginal Revenue Product ($)
10	200	—	—
11	218	18	1,800
12	234	16	1,600
13	248	14	1,400
14	260	12	1,200
15	270	10	1,000
16	278	8	800

29-3. The profit-maximizing employer will hire 14 workers, because this is the level of employment at which marginal revenue product equals marginal factor cost.

29-5. a. The greater is the substitutability of capital, the more elastic is the demand for labor.
b. Because the demand for labor is a derived demand, the greater is the elasticity of demand for the final product, the greater is the elasticity of demand for labor.
c. The larger is the portion of factor costs accounted for by labor, the larger is the price elasticity of demand for labor.

29-7.

Labor Input (workers per week)	Total Physical Product	Product Price ($ per unit)	Marginal Physical Product	Total Revenue ($)	Marginal Revenue Product ($)
10	100	50	—	5,000	—
11	109	49	9	5,341	341
12	116	48	7	5,568	227
13	121	47	5	5,687	119
14	124	46	3	5,704	17
15	125	45	1	5,625	−79

29-9. a. The firm maximizes profits, so marginal revenue product (the 5-unit marginal physical product multiplied by marginal revenue) equals the wage rate of $15. Hence, marginal revenue equals $3.
b. At the profit-maximizing output, marginal revenue of $3 is less than the price of $5, so this firm does not sell its output in a perfectly competitive market.

29-11. Labor outsourcing by U.S. firms tends to push down market wages and employment in affected U.S. labor markets, but labor outsourcing by foreign firms that hire U.S. workers tends to push up market wages and employment in affected U.S. labor markets. Consequently, the overall wage and employment effects are ambiguous in the short run. In the long run, however, outsourcing enables U.S. and foreign firms to specialize in producing the goods and services that they can produce most efficiently. The resulting resource saving ultimately expands the ability of U.S. residents to consume more goods and services than they could have otherwise, which raises revenues of U.S. firms and boosts their demands for U.S. workers. In the long run, therefore, outsourcing tends to generate higher U.S. wages and employment.

29-13. The marginal physical product of labor is 2 units of output per unit of labor.

29-15. In order to maximize profits, the firm should hire inputs up to the point at which the marginal physical product per dollar spent on the input is equalized across all inputs. This is not the case in this example. The marginal physical product of labor per dollar spent on wages is 200/$10 = 20 units of output per dollar spent on labor, which is less than the marginal physical product of capital per dollar spent on capital, which is 20,000/$500 or 40 units of output per dollar spent on capital. Thus, the firm should increase the additional output per dollar spent on labor by reducing the number of labor units it hires, and it should reduce the additional output per dollar spent on capital by increasing its use of capital, to the point where these amounts are equalized.

CHAPTER 30

30-1. Individual workers can air grievances to the collective voice who then takes the issue to the employer. The individual does not run the risk of being singled out by an employer. The individual employee does not waste work time trying to convince employers that changes are needed in the workplace.

30-3. Because strikebreakers can replace union employees, they diminish the collective bargaining power of a union.

30-5. When marginal revenue is zero, the price elasticity of demand is equal to unity, and total revenue is neither rising nor falling. No additional revenues can be earned by altering the quantity of labor, so the union's revenues are maximized.

30-7. When unions in these industries attempt to bargain for higher-than-market levels of wages, the firms that employ members of these unions will not be able to readily substitute to alternative inputs. Hence these unions are more likely to be able to achieve their wage objectives.

30-9.

Quantity of Labor Supplied	Total Physical Product	Required Hourly Wage Rate ($ per unit of labor)	Total Wage Bill ($)	Marginal Factor Cost ($ per unit of labor)
10	100	5	50	—
11	109	6	66	16
12	116	7	84	18
13	121	8	104	20
14	124	9	126	22
15	125	10	150	24

30-11. At 11 units of labor, the marginal revenue product of labor equals $16. This is equal to the marginal factor cost at this level of employment. The firm, therefore, will hire 11 units of labor and pay a wage of $6 an hour.

Quantity of Labor Supplied	Required Hourly Wage Rate ($ per unit of labor)	Total Factor Cost ($)	Marginal Factor Cost ($ per unit of labor)	Total Physical Product	Product Price ($ per unit)	Total Revenue ($)	Marginal Revenue Product ($ per unit of labor)
10	5	50	—	100	3.11	311.00	—
11	6	66	16.00	109	3.00	327.00	16.00
12	7	84	18.00	116	2.95	342.20	15.20
13	8	104	20.00	121	2.92	353.32	11.12
14	9	126	22.00	124	2.90	359.60	6.28
15	10	150	24.00	125	2.89	361.25	1.65

30-13. The marginal factor cost of the last worker hired was $106,480 − $105,600 = $880, so this is the marginal product of this worker if the firms is maximizing its profits.

CHAPTER 31

31-1. a. X, because for this country the Lorenz curve implies complete income equality.
 b. Z, because this country's Lorenz curve is bowed farthest away from the case of complete income equality.
 c. Closer, because if all other things including aggregate income remain unchanged, when more people in country Y are children below working age the share of income to people this age will decline, while the reverse will occur in country Z as more of its people reach working age and begin to earn incomes.

31-3. If the Lorenz curve is based on incomes net of transfer payments, then the Lorenz curve will become less bowed. But if the Lorenz curve does not account for transfer payments, its shape will remain unaffected.

31-5. Brazil

31-7. a. Absolute. If economic growth ultimately led to inflation-adjusted annual incomes for all urban families of four rising above $25,000 per year, then by this definition poverty would be ended.
 b. Relative. By this definition, the lowest 15 percent of income earners will always be classified as being in a state of poverty.
 c. Absolute. If economic growth eventually raised inflation-adjusted annual incomes of all individuals above $10,000, then by this definition poverty would cease to exist.

31-9. First, a moral hazard problem will exist, because government action would reduce the individual's incentive to continue a healthy lifestyle, thereby increasing the likelihood of greater health problems that will require future treatment. Second, an individual who currently has health problems will have an incentive to substitute future care that will be available at a zero price for current care that the individual must purchase at a positive price. Finally, in future years the patient will no longer have an incentive to contain health care expenses, and health care providers will have no incentive to minimize their costs.

31-11. The demand for health care will increase, and the marginal revenue curve will shift rightward. Hence, the profit-maximizing price and equilibrium quantity of health care services will increase.

31-13. Because funds in HRAs earn no interest, can be used to pay only medical expenses, and revert back to the employer at the end of the year if unused, an individual faces incentives to spend all these funds on every possible health care expense. In contrast, because funds in HSAs earn interest and can be used (subject to penalties and taxation) for other types of expenses, an individual has at least some incentive to try not to spend all the funds on health care expenses. Consequently, moral hazard problems are greater with HRAs than with HSAs.

CHAPTER 32

32-1. $4 per unit, which exactly accounts for the per-unit social cost of pollution.

32-3. At the previous, lower market price, consumers failed to pay a price that reflected the social costs, including those relating to pollution, of resources that the firms use to produce the good or service.

32-5. Penalizing rhino hunting discourages most people from engaging in the activity, which reduces the supply of rhino horns and drives up their market price. This, in turn, makes illegal poaching a more lucrative activity, which can lead to an increase in illegal hunting of the few remaining rhinos. If raising rhinos as stock animals were legalized, then more rhino horns would be produced—via an increase in the number of rhinos on farms—and the market price of rhino horns would decline. This would reduce the incentive for poaching of wild rhinos.

32-7. a. 60 percent
 b. 40 percent
 c. 40 percent

32-9. a. 65 percent
 b. $10

32-11. a. The marginal costs and benefits are tabulated below:

Population of Wild Tigers	Marginal Cost ($)	Marginal Benefit ($)
0	—	—
2,000	25	50
4,000	10	40
6,000	15	30
8,000	25	25
10,000	35	20
12,000	50	10

 b. 8,000
 c. 10,000

CHAPTER 33

33-1. **a.** The opportunity cost of pastries in Northland is 0.5 sandwich per pastry. The opportunity cost of sandwiches in Northland is 2 pastries per sandwich.
b. The opportunity cost of pastries in West Coast is 2 sandwiches per pastry. The opportunity cost of sandwiches in West Coast is 0.5 pastries per sandwich.

33-3. If Northland specializes in producing pastries, the maximum number of pastries it can produce and trade to West Coast is 50,000 pastries. Hence, the maximum number of units of each good that the two countries can trade at a rate of exchange of 1 pastry for 1 sandwich is 50,000.

33-5. West Coast has a comparative advantage in producing digital TVs, and Northland has a comparative advantage in wine production.

33-7. **a.** The opportunity cost of modems in South Shore is 2 flash drives per modem. The opportunity cost of flash drives in South Shore is 0.5 modem per flash drive.
b. The opportunity cost of modems in East Isle is 0.5 flash drive per modem. The opportunity cost of flash drives in East Isle is 2 modems per flash drive.
c. Residents of South Shore have a comparative advantage in producing flash drives, and residents of East Isle have a comparative advantage in producing modems.

33-9. Residents of South Shore specialize in producing flash drives and hence produce 150 flash drives per hour. They export 30 of these to East Isle in trade for 30 modems. Thus, South Shore residents consume 120 flash drives and 30 modems. Residents of East Isle specialize in producing modems and hence produce 100 modems. They export 30 modems to South Shore in exchange for 30 flash drives. Consequently, they consume 70 modems and 30 flash drives.

33-11. A price elasticity of demand less than unity indicates inelastic demand, and, therefore, price and total revenue move in the same direction. If the nation restricts its exports, the price of the product rises and so does total revenue, even though the nation sells fewer units of output abroad.

33-13. **a.** Because the supply curve shifts by the amount of the tariff, the tariff is $20 per television.
b. Total revenue was $300 per unit times 20 million units, or $6 billion, before the tariff, and it is $310 per unit times 15 million units, or $4.65 billion, after the tariff.
c. U.S. tariff revenue is $20 per unit times 15 million units, or $300 million.

CHAPTER 34

34-1. The trade balance is merchandise exports minus merchandise imports, which equals $500 - 600 = -100$, or a deficit of 100. Adding service exports of 75 and subtracting net unilateral transfers of 10 and service imports of 50 yields $-100 + 75 - 10 - 50 = -85$, or a current account balance of -85. The capital account balance equals the difference between capital inflows and capital outflows, or $300 - 200 = +100$, or a capital account surplus of 100.

34-3. **a.** The increase in demand for Mexican-made guitars increases the demand for Mexican pesos, and the peso appreciates.
b. International investors will remove some of their financial capital from Mexico. The increase in the supply of the peso in the foreign exchange market will cause the peso to depreciate.

34-5. **a.** Investors shift their funds from Thailand to other nations where interest returns are higher, so the demand for the baht declines. The dollar-baht exchange rate falls, so the dollar appreciates. The baht depreciates.
b. The rise in Thai productivity reduces the price of Thai goods relative to goods in the United States, so U.S. residents purchase more Thai goods. This increases the demand for baht in the foreign exchange market, so the dollar-baht exchange rate increases. The dollar depreciates, and the baht appreciates.

34-7. The demand for Chinese yuan increases, and the supply of yuan decreases. The dollar-yuan exchange rate rises, so the yuan appreciates.

34-9. The Canadian dollar–euro exchange rate is found by dividing the U.S. dollar–euro exchange rate by the U.S. dollar–Canadian dollar exchange rate, or (1.17 $US/euro)/(0.79 $US/$C) = 1.48 $C/euro, or 1.48 Canadian dollars per euro.

34-11. A flexible exchange rate system allows the exchange value of a currency to be determined freely in the foreign exchange market with no intervention by the government. A fixed exchange rate pegs the value of the currency, and the authorities responsible for the value of the currency intervene in foreign exchange markets to maintain this value. A dirty float involves occasional intervention by the exchange authorities. A

34-13. When the U.S. dollar is pegged to gold at a rate of $35 and the pound at a rate of £17.50, the dollar-pound exchange rate equals $35/17.50 = 2$ ($/£).

34-15. a. The demand for yuan will decrease, which would cause the equilibrium dollar-yuan exchange rate to begin to decline. To prevent a yuan depreciation from occurring, the Bank of China can purchase yuan with dollars, thereby raising the demand for yuan to its previous level at the original exchange rate. Hence, the Bank of China should reduce its dollar reserves.

b. To purchase more U.S. financial assets, Chinese residents must obtain more dollars, so they will increase the quantity of yuan supplied at each exchange rate. This would cause the equilibrium dollar-yuan exchange rate to begin to decline. To prevent a yuan depreciation from occurring, the Bank of China can purchase yuan with dollars, thereby causing the demand for yuan to increase sufficiently to push the equilibrium exchange rate back to its original level. Thus, the Bank of China should reduce its dollar reserves.

c. U.S. residents increase the quantity of yuan demanded at any given exchange rate in order to purchase Chinese furniture, so the demand for yuan increases. This would tend to cause the equilibrium dollar-yuan exchange rate to rise, resulting in a yuan appreciation. To keep this from happening, the Bank of China can purchase dollars with yuan, thereby increasing the supply of yuan and pushing the equilibrium exchange rate back down. Consequently, the Bank of China should increase its dollar reserves.

(target zone allows the exchange value to fluctuate, but only within a given range of values.)

GLOSSARY

A

45-degree reference line The line along which planned real expenditures equal real GDP per year.

Absolute advantage The ability to produce more units of a good or service using a given quantity of labor or resource inputs. Equivalently, the ability to produce the same quantity of a good or service using fewer units of labor or resource inputs.

Accounting identities Values that are equivalent by definition.

Accounting profit Total revenues minus total explicit costs.

Action time lag The time between recognizing an economic problem and implementing policy to solve it. The action time lag is quite long for fiscal policy, which requires congressional approval.

Active (discretionary) policymaking All actions on the part of monetary and fiscal policymakers that are undertaken in response to or in anticipation of some change in the overall economy.

Ad valorem taxation Assessing taxes by charging a tax rate equal to a fraction of the market price of each unit purchased.

Adverse selection The likelihood that individuals who seek to borrow may use the funds that they receive for high-risk projects.

Age-earnings cycle The regular earnings profile of an individual throughout his or her lifetime. The age-earnings cycle usually starts with a low income, builds gradually to a peak at around age 50, and then gradually curves down until it approaches zero at retirement.

Aggregate demand The total of all planned expenditures in the entire economy.

Aggregate demand curve A curve showing planned purchase rates for all final goods and services in the economy at various price levels, all other things held constant.

Aggregate demand shock Any event that causes the aggregate demand curve to shift inward or outward.

Aggregate supply shock Any event that causes the aggregate supply curve to shift inward or outward.

Aggregate supply The total of all planned production for the economy.

Aggregates Total amounts or quantities; aggregate demand, for example, is total planned expenditures throughout a nation.

Anticipated inflation The inflation rate that we believe will occur; when it does, we are in a situation of fully anticipated inflation.

Antitrust legislation Laws that restrict the formation of monopolies and regulate certain anticompetitive business practices.

Appreciation An increase in the exchange value of one nation's currency in terms of the currency of another nation.

Asset demand Holding money as a store of value instead of other assets such as certificates of deposit, corporate bonds, and stocks.

Assets Amounts owned; all items to which a business or household holds legal claim.

Asymmetric information Information possessed by one party in a financial transaction but not by the other party.

Automatic, or built-in, stabilizers Special provisions of certain federal programs that cause changes in desired aggregate expenditures without the action of Congress and the president. Examples are the federal progressive tax system and unemployment compensation.

Autonomous consumption The part of consumption that is independent of (does not depend on) the level of disposable income. Changes in autonomous consumption shift the consumption function.

Average fixed costs Total fixed costs divided by the number of units produced.

Average physical product Total product divided by the variable input.

Average propensity to consume (APC) Real consumption divided by real disposable income; for any given level of real income, the proportion of total real disposable income that is consumed.

Average propensity to save (APS) Real saving divided by real disposable income; for any given level of real income, the proportion of total real disposable income that is saved.

Average tax rate The total tax payment divided by total income. It is the proportion of total income paid in taxes.

Average total costs Total costs divided by the number of units produced; sometimes called average per-unit total costs.

Average variable costs Total variable costs divided by the number of units produced.

B

Balance of payments A system of accounts that measures transactions of goods, services, income, and financial assets between domestic households, businesses, and governments and residents of the rest of the world during a specific time period.

Balance of trade The difference between exports and imports of physical goods.

Balance sheet A statement of the assets and liabilities of any business entity, including financial institutions and the Federal Reserve System. Assets are what is owned; liabilities are what is owed.

Balanced budget A situation in which the government's spending is exactly equal to the total taxes and other revenues it collects during a given period of time.

Bank runs Attempts by many of a bank's depositors to convert transactions and time deposits into currency out of fear that the bank's liabilities may exceed its assets.

Barter The direct exchange of goods and services for other goods and services without the use of money.

Base year The year that is chosen as the point of reference for comparison of prices in other years.

Base-year dollars The value of a current sum expressed in terms of prices in a base year.

Behavioral economics An approach to the study of consumer behavior that emphasizes psychological limitations and complications that potentially interfere with rational decision making.

Bilateral monopoly A market structure consisting of a monopolist and a monopsonist.

Black market A market in which goods are traded at prices above their legal maximum prices or in which illegal goods are sold.

Bond A legal claim against a firm, usually entitling the owner of the bond to receive a fixed annual coupon payment, plus a lump-sum payment at the bond's maturity date. Bonds are issued in return for funds lent to the firm.

Bounded rationality The hypothesis that people are nearly, but not fully, rational, so that they cannot examine every possible choice available to them but instead use simple rules of thumb to sort among the alternatives that happen to occur to them.

Budget constraint All of the possible combinations of goods that can be purchased (at fixed prices) with a specific budget.

Bundling Offering two or more products for sale as a set.

Business fluctuations The ups and downs in business activity throughout the economy.

C

Capital account A category of balance of payments transactions that measures flows of real and financial assets.

Capital consumption allowance Another name for depreciation, the amount that businesses would have to save in order to take care of the deterioration of machines and other equipment.

Capital controls Legal restrictions on the ability of a nation's residents to hold and trade assets denominated in foreign currencies.

Capital gain The positive difference between the purchase price and the sale price of an asset. If a share of stock is bought for $5 and then sold for $15, the capital gain is $10.

Capital goods Producer durables; nonconsumable goods that firms use to make other goods.

Capital loss The negative difference between the purchase price and the sale price of an asset.

Capture hypothesis A theory of regulatory behavior that predicts that regulators will eventually be captured by special interests of the industry being regulated.

Cartel An association of producers in an industry that agree to set common prices and output quotas to prevent competition.

Central bank A banker's bank, usually an official institution that also serves as a country's treasury's bank. Central banks normally regulate commercial banks.

Certificate of deposit (CD) A time deposit with a fixed maturity date offered by banks and other financial institutions.

Ceteris paribus [KAY-ter-us PEAR-uh-bus] **assumption** The assumption that nothing changes except the factor or factors being studied.

Ceteris paribus **conditions** Determinants of the relationship between price and quantity that are unchanged along a curve; changes in these factors cause the curve to shift.

Closed shop A business enterprise in which employees must belong to the union before they can be hired and must remain in the union after they are hired.

Collective bargaining Negotiation between the management of a company or of a group of companies and the management of a union or a group of unions for the purpose of reaching a mutually agreeable contract that sets wages, fringe benefits, and working conditions for all employees in all the unions involved.

Collective decision making How voters, politicians, and other interested parties act and how these actions influence nonmarket decisions.

Common property Property that is owned by everyone and therefore by no one. Air and water are examples of common property resources.

Comparable-worth doctrine The belief that women should receive the same wages as men if the levels of skill and responsibility in their jobs are equivalent.

Comparative advantage The ability to produce a good or service at a lower opportunity cost than other producers.

Complements Two goods are complements when a change in the price of one causes an opposite shift in the demand for the other.

Concentration ratio The percentage of all sales contributed by the leading four or leading eight firms in an industry; sometimes called the industry concentration ratio.

Constant dollars Dollars expressed in terms of real purchasing power using a particular year as the base or standard of comparison, in contrast to current dollars.

Constant returns to scale No change in long-run average costs when output increases.

Constant-cost industry An industry whose total output can be increased without an increase in long-run per-unit costs; its long-run supply curve is horizontal.

Consumer optimum A choice of a set of goods and services that maximizes the level of satisfaction for each consumer, subject to limited income.

Consumer Price Index (CPI) A statistical measure of a weighted average of prices of a specified set of goods and services purchased by typical consumers in urban areas.

Consumer surplus The total difference between the total amount that consumers would have been willing to pay for a good or service and the total amount that they actually pay.

Consumption Spending on new goods and services out of a household's current income. Whatever is not consumed is saved. Consumption includes such things as buying food and going to a concert.

Consumption function The relationship between amount consumed and disposable income. A consumption function tells us how much people plan to consume at various levels of disposable income.

Consumption goods Goods bought by households to use up, such as food and movies.

Contraction A business fluctuation during which the pace of national economic activity is slowing down.

Cooperative game A game in which the players explicitly cooperate to make themselves better off. As applied to firms, it involves companies colluding in order to make higher than perfectly competitive rates of return.

Corporation A legal entity that may conduct business in its own name just as an individual does; the owners of a corporation, called shareholders, own shares of the firm's profits and enjoy the protection of limited liability.

Cost-of-living adjustments (COLAs) Clauses in contracts that allow for increases in specified nominal values to take account of changes in the cost of living.

Cost-of-service regulation Regulation that allows prices to reflect only the actual average cost of production and no monopoly profits.

Cost-push inflation Inflation caused by decreases in short-run aggregate supply.

Craft unions Labor unions composed of workers who engage in a particular trade or skill, such as baking, carpentry, or plumbing.

Crawling peg An exchange rate arrangement in which a country pegs the value of its currency to the exchange value of another nation's currency but allows the par value to change at regular intervals.

Creative response Behavior on the part of a firm that allows it to comply with the letter of the law but violate the spirit, significantly lessening the law's effects.

Credence good A product with qualities that consumers lack the expertise to assess without assistance.

Cross price elasticity of demand (E_{xy}) The percentage change in the demand for one good (holding its price constant) divided by the percentage change in the price of a related good.

Crowding-out effect The tendency of expansionary fiscal policy to cause a decrease in planned investment or planned consumption in the private sector; this decrease normally results from the rise in interest rates.

Current account A category of balance of payments transactions that measures the exchange of merchandise, the exchange of services, and unilateral transfers.

Cyclical unemployment Unemployment resulting from business recessions that occur when aggregate (total) demand is insufficient to create full employment.

D

Dead capital Any capital resource that lacks clear title of ownership.

Deadweight loss The portion of consumer surplus that no one in society is able to obtain in a situation of monopoly.

Decreasing-cost industry An industry in which an increase in output leads to a reduction in long-run per-unit costs, such that the long-run industry supply curve slopes downward.

Deflation A sustained decrease in the average of all prices of goods and services in an economy.

Demand A schedule showing how much of a good or service people will purchase at any price during a specified time period, other things being constant.

Demand curve A graphical representation of the demand schedule; a negatively sloped line showing the inverse relationship between the price and the quantity demanded (other things being equal).

Demand-pull inflation Inflation caused by increases in aggregate demand not matched by increases in aggregate supply.

Demerit good A good that has been deemed socially undesirable through the political process. Heroin is an example.

Dependent variable A variable whose value changes according to changes in the value of one or more independent variables.

Depository institutions Financial institutions that accept deposits from savers and lend funds from those deposits out at interest.

Depreciation A decrease in the exchange value of one nation's currency in terms of the currency of another nation.

Depression An extremely severe recession.

Derived demand Input factor demand derived from demand for the final product being produced.

Development economics The study of factors that contribute to the economic growth of a country.

Diminishing marginal utility The principle that as more of any good or service is consumed, its extra benefit declines. Otherwise stated, increases in total utility from the consumption of a good or service become smaller and smaller as more is consumed during a given time period.

Direct expenditure offsets Actions on the part of the private sector in spending income that offset government fiscal policy actions. Any increase in government spending in an area that competes with the private sector will have some direct expenditure offset.

Direct marketing Advertising targeted at specific consumers, typically in the form of postal mailings, telephone calls, or e-mail messages.

Direct relationship A relationship between two variables that is positive, meaning that an increase in one variable is associated with an increase in the other and a decrease in one variable is associated with a decrease in the other.

Dirty float Active management of a floating exchange rate on the part of a country's government, often in cooperation with other nations.

Discount rate The interest rate that the Federal Reserve charges for reserves that it lends to depository institutions. It is sometimes referred to as the rediscount rate or, in Canada and England, as the bank rate.

Discounting The method by which the present value of a future sum or a future stream of sums is obtained.

Discouraged workers Individuals who have stopped looking for a job because they are convinced that they will not find a suitable one.

Diseconomies of scale Increases in long-run average costs that occur as output increases.

Disposable personal income (DPI) Personal income after personal income taxes have been paid.

Dissaving Negative saving; a situation in which spending exceeds income. Dissaving can occur when a household is able to borrow or use up existing assets.

Distribution of income The way income is allocated among the population.

Dividends Portion of a corporation's profits paid to its owners (shareholders).

Division of labor The segregation of a resource into different specific tasks; for example, one automobile worker puts on bumpers, another doors, and so on.

Dominant strategies Strategies that always yield the highest benefit. Regardless of what other players do, a dominant strategy will yield the most benefit for the player using it.

Dumping Selling a good or a service abroad below the price charged in the home market or at a price below its cost of production.

Durable consumer goods Consumer goods that have a life span of more than three years.

Dynamic tax analysis Economic evaluation of tax rate changes that recognizes that the tax base eventually declines with ever higher tax rates, so that tax revenues may eventually decline if the tax rate is raised sufficiently.

E

Economic freedom The rights to own private property and to exchange goods, services, and financial assets with minimal government interference.

Economic goods Goods that are scarce, for which the quantity demanded exceeds the quantity supplied at a zero price.

Economic growth Increases in per capita real GDP measured by its rate of change per year.

Economic profits Total revenues minus total opportunity costs of all inputs used, or the total of all implicit and explicit costs.

Economic rent A payment for the use of any resource over and above its opportunity cost.

Economics The study of how people allocate their limited resources to satisfy their unlimited wants.

Economies of scale Decreases in long-run average costs resulting from increases in output.

Effect time lag The time that elapses between the implementation of a policy and the results of that policy.

Efficiency The case in which a given level of inputs is used to produce the maximum output possible. Alternatively, the situation in which a given output is produced at minimum cost.

Effluent fee A charge to a polluter that gives the right to discharge into the air or water a certain amount of pollution; also called a pollution tax.

Elastic demand A demand relationship in which a given percentage change in price will result in a larger percentage change in quantity demanded. Total expenditures and price changes are inversely related in the elastic region of the demand curve.

Empirical Relying on real-world data in evaluating the usefulness of a model.

Endowments The various resources in an economy, including both physical resources and such human resources as ingenuity and management skills.

Entitlements Guaranteed benefits under a government program such as Social Security, Medicare, or Medicaid.

Entrepreneurship The component of human resources that performs the functions of raising capital, organizing, managing, assembling other factors of production, making basic business policy decisions, and taking risks.

Entry deterrence strategy Any strategy undertaken by firms in an industry, either individually or together, with the intent or effect of raising the cost of entry into the industry by a new firm.

Equation of exchange The formula indicating that the number of monetary units (M_s) times the number of times each unit is spent on final goods and services (V) is identical to the price level (P) times real GDP (Y).

Equilibrium The situation when quantity supplied equals quantity demanded at a particular price.

Excess reserves The difference between legal reserves and required reserves.

Exchange rate The price of one nation's currency in terms of the currency of another country.

Excise tax A tax levied on purchases of a particular good or service.

Exclusion principle The principle that no one can be excluded from the benefits of a public good, even if that person has not paid for it.

Expansion A business fluctuation in which the pace of national economic activity is speeding up.

Expenditure approach Computing GDP by adding up the dollar value at current market prices of all final goods and services.

Experience good A product that an individual must consume before the product's quality can be established.

Explicit costs Costs that business managers must take account of because they must be paid; examples are wages, taxes, and rent.

Externality A consequence of an economic activity that spills over to affect third parties. Pollution is an externality.

F

Featherbedding Any practice that forces employers to use more labor than they would otherwise or to use existing labor in an inefficient manner.

Federal Deposit Insurance Corporation (FDIC) A government agency that insures the deposits held in banks and most other depository institutions; all U.S. banks are insured this way.

Federal funds market A private market (made up mostly of banks) in which banks can borrow reserves from other banks that want to lend them. Federal funds are usually lent for overnight use.

Federal funds rate The interest rate that depository institutions pay to borrow reserves in the interbank federal funds market.

Fiduciary monetary system A system in which money is issued by the government and its value is based uniquely on the public's faith that the currency represents command over goods and services.

Final goods and services Goods and services that are at their final stage of production and will not be transformed into yet other goods or services. For example, wheat is not ordinarily considered a final good because it is usually used to make a final good, bread.

Financial capital Funds used to purchase physical capital goods, such as buildings and equipment, and patents and trademarks.

Financial intermediaries Institutions that transfer funds between ultimate lenders (savers) and ultimate borrowers.

Financial intermediation The process by which financial institutions accept savings from businesses, households, and governments and lend the savings to other businesses, households, and governments.

Firm A business organization that employs resources to produce goods or services for profit. A firm normally owns and operates at least one "plant" or facility in order to produce.

Fiscal policy The discretionary changing of government expenditures or taxes to achieve national economic goals, such as high employment with price stability.

Fixed costs Costs that do not vary with output. Fixed costs typically include such things as rent on a building. These costs are fixed for a certain period of time (in the long run, though, they are variable).

Fixed investment Purchases by businesses of newly produced producer durables, or capital goods, such as production machinery and office equipment.

Flexible exchange rates Exchange rates that are allowed to fluctuate in the open market in response to changes in supply and demand. Sometimes called floating exchange rates.

Flow A quantity measured per unit of time; something that occurs over time, such as the income you make per week or per year or the number of individuals who are fired every month.

FOMC Directive A document that summarizes the Federal Open Market Committee's general policy strategy, establishes near-term objectives for the federal funds rate, and specifies target ranges for money supply growth.

Foreign direct investment The acquisition of more than 10 percent of the shares of ownership in a company in another nation.

Foreign exchange market A market in which households, firms, and governments buy and sell national currencies.

Foreign exchange rate The price of one currency in terms of another.

Foreign exchange risk The possibility that changes in the value of a nation's currency will result in variations in the market value of assets.

Fractional reserve banking A system in which depository institutions hold reserves that are less than the amount of total deposits.

Free-rider problem A problem that arises when individuals presume that others will pay for public goods so that, individually, they can escape paying for their portion without causing a reduction in production.

Frictional unemployment Unemployment due to the fact that workers must search for appropriate job offers. This takes time, and so they remain temporarily unemployed.

Full employment An arbitrary level of unemployment that corresponds to "normal" friction in the labor market. In 1986, a 6.5 percent rate of unemployment was considered full employment. Today, it is assumed to be around 5 percent.

G

Game theory A way of describing the various possible outcomes in any situation involving two or more interacting individuals when those individuals are aware of the interactive nature of their situation and plan accordingly. The plans made by these individuals are known as game strategies.

GDP deflator A price index measuring the changes in prices of all new goods and services produced in the economy.

General Agreement on Tariffs and Trade (GATT) An international agreement established in 1947 to further world trade by reducing barriers and tariffs. GATT was replaced by the World Trade Organization in 1995.

Goods All things from which individuals derive satisfaction or happiness.

Government budget constraint The limit on government spending and transfers imposed by the fact that every dollar the government spends, transfers, or uses to repay borrowed funds must ultimately be provided by the taxes it collects.

Government budget deficit An excess of government spending over government revenues during a given period of time.

Government budget surplus An excess of government revenues over government spending during a given period of time.

Government, or political, goods Goods (and services) provided by the public sector; they can be either private or public goods.

Gross domestic income (GDI) The sum of all income—wages, interest, rent, and profits—paid to the four factors of production.

Gross domestic product (GDP) The total market value of all final goods and services produced by factors of production located within a nation's borders.

Gross private domestic investment The creation of capital goods, such as factories and machines, that can yield production and hence consumption in the future. Also included in this definition are changes in business inventories and repairs made to machines or buildings.

Gross public debt All federal government debt irrespective of who owns it.

H

Health savings account (HSA) A tax-exempt health care account into which individuals can pay on a regular basis and out of which medical expenses can be paid.

Hedge A financial strategy that reduces the chance of suffering losses arising from foreign exchange risk.

Horizontal merger The joining of firms that are producing or selling a similar product.

Human capital The accumulated training and education of workers.

I

Implicit costs Expenses that managers do not have to pay out of pocket and hence do not normally explicitly calculate, such as the opportunity cost of factors of production that are owned; examples are owner-provided capital and owner-provided labor.

Import quota A physical supply restriction on imports of a particular good, such as sugar. Foreign exporters are unable to sell in the United States more than the quantity specified in the import quota.

Incentive structure The system of rewards and punishments individuals face with respect to their own actions.

Incentives Rewards for engaging in a particular activity.

Income approach Measuring GDP by adding up all components of national income, including wages, interest, rent, and profits.

Income elasticity of demand (E_i) The percentage change in demand for any good, holding its price constant, divided by the percentage change in income; the responsiveness of demand to changes in income, holding the good's relative price constant.

Income in kind Income received in the form of goods and services, such as housing or medical care; to be contrasted with money income, which is simply income in dollars, or general purchasing power, that can be used to buy any goods and services.

Income velocity of money (V) The number of times per year a dollar is spent on final goods and services; equal to nominal GDP divided by the money supply.

Increasing-cost industry An industry in which an increase in industry output is accompanied by an increase in long-run per-unit costs, such that the long-run industry supply curve slopes upward.

Independent variable A variable whose value is determined independently of, or outside, the equation under study.

Indifference curve A curve composed of a set of consumption alternatives, each of which yields the same total amount of satisfaction.

Indirect business taxes All business taxes except the tax on corporate profits. Indirect business taxes include sales and business property taxes.

Industrial unions Labor unions that consist of workers from a particular industry, such as automobile manufacturing or steel manufacturing.

Industry supply curve The locus of points showing the minimum prices at which given quantities will be forthcoming; also called the market supply curve.

Inefficient point Any point below the production possibilities curve at which the use of resources is not generating the maximum possible output.

Inelastic demand A demand relationship in which a given percentage change in price will result in a less than proportionate percentage change in the quantity demanded. Total expenditures and price are directly related in the inelastic region of the demand curve.

Infant industry argument The contention that tariffs should be imposed to protect from import competition an industry that is trying to get started. Presumably, after the industry becomes technologically efficient, the tariff can be lifted.

Inferior goods Goods for which demand falls as income rises.

Inflation A sustained increase in the average of all prices of goods and services in an economy.

Inflation-adjusted return A rate of return that is measured in terms of real goods and services; that is, after the effects of inflation have been factored out.

Inflationary gap The gap that exists whenever equilibrium real GDP per year is greater than full-employment real GDP as shown by the position of the long-run aggregate supply curve.

Information product An item that is produced using information-intensive inputs at a relatively high fixed cost but distributed for sale at a relatively low marginal cost.

Informational advertising Advertising that emphasizes transmitting knowledge about the features of a product.

Innovation Transforming an invention into something that is useful to humans.

Inside information Information that is not available to the general public about what is happening in a corporation.

Interactive marketing Advertising that permits a consumer to follow up directly by searching for more information and placing direct product orders.

Interest The payment for current rather than future command over resources; the cost of obtaining credit.

Interest rate effect One of the reasons that the aggregate demand curve slopes downward: Higher price levels increase the interest rate, which in turn causes businesses and consumers to reduce desired spending due to the higher cost of borrowing.

Intermediate goods Goods used up entirely in the production of final goods.

International financial crisis The rapid withdrawal of foreign investments and loans from a nation.

International financial diversification Financing investment projects in more than one country.

International Monetary Fund An agency founded to administer an international foreign exchange system and to lend to member countries that had balance of payments problems. The IMF now functions as a lender of last resort for national governments.

Inventory investment Changes in the stocks of finished goods and goods in process, as well as changes in the raw materials that businesses keep on hand. Whenever inventories are decreasing, inventory investment is negative; whenever they are increasing, inventory investment is positive.

Inverse relationship A relationship between two variables that is negative, meaning that an increase in one variable is associated with a decrease in the other and a decrease in one variable is associated with an increase in the other.

Investment Any use of today's resources to expand tomorrow's production or consumption.

J

Job leaver An individual in the labor force who quits voluntarily.

Job loser An individual in the labor force whose employment was involuntarily terminated.

Jurisdictional dispute A disagreement involving two or more unions over which should have control of a particular jurisdiction, such as a particular craft or skill or a particular firm or industry.

K

Keynesian short-run aggregate supply curve The horizontal portion of the aggregate supply curve in which there is excessive unemployment and unused capacity in the economy.

L

Labor Productive contributions of humans who work, involving both mental and physical activities.

Labor force Individuals aged 16 years or older who either have jobs or who are looking and available for jobs; the number of employed plus the number of unemployed.

Labor force participation rate The percentage of noninstitutionalized working-age individuals who are employed or seeking employment.

Labor productivity Total real domestic output (real GDP) divided by the number of workers (output per worker).

Labor unions Worker organizations that seek to secure economic improvements for their members; they also seek to improve the safety, health, and other benefits (such as job security) of their members.

Land The natural resources that are available from nature. Land as a resource includes location, original fertility and mineral deposits, topography, climate, water, and vegetation.

Law of demand The observation that there is a negative, or inverse, relationship between the price of any good or service and the quantity demanded, holding other factors constant.

Law of diminishing marginal product The observation that after some point, successive equal-sized increases in a variable factor of production, such as labor, added to fixed factors of production, will result in smaller increases in output.

Law of increasing relative cost The fact that the opportunity cost of additional units of a good generally increases as society attempts to produce more of that good. This accounts for the bowed-out shape of the production possibilities curve.

Law of supply The observation that the higher the price of a good, the more of that good sellers will make available over a specified time period, other things being equal.

Leading indicators Events that have been found to occur before changes in business activity.

Legal reserves Reserves that depository institutions are allowed by law to claim as reserves—for example, deposits held at Federal Reserve district banks and vault cash.

Lemons problem The potential for asymmetric information to bring about a general decline in product quality in an industry.

Lender of last resort The Federal Reserve's role as an institution that is willing and able to lend to a temporarily illiquid bank that is otherwise in good financial condition to prevent the bank's illiquid position from leading to a general loss of confidence in that bank or in others.

Liabilities Amounts owed; the legal claims against a business or household by nonowners.

Limited liability A legal concept in which the responsibility, or liability, of the owners of a corporation is limited to the value of the shares in the firm that they own.

Limit-pricing model A model that hypothesizes that a group of colluding sellers will set the highest common price that they believe they can charge without new firms seeking to enter that industry in search of relatively high profits.

Liquidity The degree to which an asset can be acquired or disposed of without much danger of any intervening loss in nominal value and with small transaction costs. Money is the most liquid asset.

Liquidity approach A method of measuring the money supply by looking at money as a temporary store of value.

Long run The time period during which all factors of production can be varied.

Long-run aggregate supply curve A vertical line representing the real output of goods and services after full adjustment has occurred. It can also be viewed as representing the real GDP of the economy under conditions of full employment—the full-employment level of real GDP.

Long-run average cost curve The locus of points representing the minimum unit cost of producing any given rate of output, given current technology and resource prices.

Long-run industry supply curve A market supply curve showing the relationship between prices and quantities after firms have been allowed the time to enter into or exit from an industry, depending on whether there have been positive or negative economic profits.

Lorenz curve A geometric representation of the distribution of income. A Lorenz curve that is perfectly straight represents complete income equality. The more bowed a Lorenz curve, the more unequally income is distributed.

Lump-sum tax A tax that does not depend on income. An example is a $1,000 tax that every household must pay, irrespective of its economic situation.

M

M1 The money supply, taken as the total value of currency plus transactions deposits plus traveler's checks not issued by banks.

M2 M1 plus (1) savings and small-denomination time deposits at all depository institutions, (2) balances in retail money market mutual funds, and (3) money market deposit accounts (MMDAs).

Macroeconomics The study of the behavior of the economy as a whole, including such economywide phenomena as changes in unemployment, the general price level, and national income.

Majority rule A collective decision-making system in which group decisions are made on the basis of more than 50 percent of the vote. In other words, whatever more than half of the electorate votes for, the entire electorate has to accept.

Marginal cost pricing A system of pricing in which the price charged is equal to the opportunity cost to society of producing one more unit of the good or service in question. The opportunity cost is the marginal cost to society.

Marginal costs The change in total costs due to a one-unit change in production rate.

Marginal factor cost (MFC) The cost of using an additional unit of an input. For example, if a firm can hire all the workers it wants at the going wage rate, the marginal factor cost of labor is the wage rate.

Marginal physical product The physical output that is due to the addition of one more unit of a variable factor of production; the change in total product occurring when a variable input is increased and all other inputs are held constant; also called marginal product.

Marginal physical product (MPP) of labor The change in output resulting from the addition of one more worker. The MPP of the worker equals the change in total output accounted for by hiring the worker, holding all other factors of production constant.

Marginal propensity to consume (MPC) The ratio of the change in consumption to the change in disposable income. A marginal propensity to consume of 0.8 tells us that an additional $100 in take-home pay will lead to an additional $80 consumed.

Marginal propensity to save (MPS) The ratio of the change in saving to the change in disposable income. A marginal propensity to save of 0.2 indicates that out of an additional $100 in take-home pay, $20 will be saved. Whatever is not saved is consumed. The marginal propensity to save plus the marginal propensity to consume must always equal 1, by definition.

Marginal revenue The change in total revenues resulting from a change in output (and sale) of one unit of the product in question.

Marginal revenue product (MRP) The marginal physical product (MPP) times marginal revenue (MR). The MRP gives the additional revenue obtained from a one-unit change in labor input.

Marginal tax rate The change in the tax payment divided by the change in income, or the percentage of additional dollars that must be paid in taxes. The marginal tax rate is applied to the highest tax bracket of taxable income reached.

Marginal utility The change in total utility due to a one-unit change in the quantity of a good or service consumed.

Market All of the arrangements that individuals have for exchanging with one another. Thus, for example, we can speak of the labor market, the automobile market, and the credit market.

Market clearing, or equilibrium, price The price that clears the market, at which quantity demanded equals quantity supplied; the price where the demand curve intersects the supply curve.

Market demand The demand of all consumers in the marketplace for a particular good or service. The summation at each price of the quantity demanded by each individual.

Market failure A situation in which an unrestrained market operation leads to either too few or too many resources going to a specific economic activity.

Market share test The percentage of a market that a particular firm supplies; used as the primary measure of monopoly power.

Mass marketing Advertising intended to reach as many consumers as possible, typically through television, newspaper, radio, or magazine ads.

Medium of exchange Any item that sellers will accept as payment.

Merit good A good that has been deemed socially desirable through the political process. Museums are an example.

Microeconomics The study of decision making undertaken by individuals (or households) and by firms.

Minimum efficient scale (MES) The lowest rate of output per unit time at which long-run average costs for a particular firm are at a minimum.

Minimum wage A wage floor, legislated by government, setting the lowest hourly rate that firms may legally pay workers.

Models, or theories Simplified representations of the real world used as the basis for predictions or explanations.

Money Any medium that is universally accepted in an economy both by sellers of goods and services as payment for those goods and services and by creditors as payment for debts.

Money balances Synonymous with money, money stock, money holdings.

Money illusion Reacting to changes in money prices rather than relative prices. If a worker whose wages double when the price level also doubles thinks he or she is better off, that worker is suffering from money illusion.

Money market deposit accounts (MMDAs) Accounts issued by banks yielding a market rate of interest with a minimum balance requirement and a limit on transactions. They have no minimum maturity.

Money market mutual funds Funds obtained fron the public that investment companies hold in common and use to acquire short-maturity credit instruments, such as certificates of deposit and securities sold by the U.S. government.

Money multiplier A number that, when multiplied by a change in reserves in the banking system, yields the resulting change in the money supply.

Money price The price that we observe today, expressed in today's dollars; also called the absolute or nominal price.

Money supply The amount of money in circulation.

Monopolist The single supplier of a good or service for which there is no close substitute. The monopolist therefore constitutes its entire industry.

Monopolistic competition A market situation in which a large number of firms produce similar but not identical products. Entry into the industry is relatively easy.

Monopolization The possession of monopoly power in the relevant market and the willful acquisition or maintenance of that power, as distinguished from growth or development as a consequence of a superior product, business acumen, or historical accident.

Monopoly A firm that can determine the market price of a good. In the extreme case, a monopoly is the only seller of a good or service.

Monopsonist The only buyer in a market.

Monopsonistic exploitation Paying a price for the variable input that is less than its marginal revenue product; the difference between marginal revenue product and the wage rate.

Moral hazard The possibility that a borrower might engage in riskier behavior after a loan has been obtained.

Multiplier The ratio of the change in the equilibrium level of real GDP to the change in autonomous real expenditures; the number by which a change in autonomous real investment or autonomous real consumption, for example, is multiplied to get the change in equilibrium real GDP.

N

National income (NI) The total of all factor payments to resource owners. It can be obtained from net domestic product (NDP) by subtracting indirect business taxes and transfers and adding net U.S. income earned abroad and other business income adjustments.

National income accounting A measurement system used to estimate national income and its components; one approach to measuring an economy's aggregate performance.

Natural monopoly A monopoly that arises from the peculiar production characteristics in an industry. It usually arises when there are large economies of scale relative to the industry's demand such that one firm can produce at a lower average cost than can be achieved by multiple firms.

Natural rate of unemployment The rate of unemployment that is estimated to prevail in long-run macroeconomic equilibrium, when all workers and employers have fully adjusted to any changes in the economy.

Near moneys Assets that are almost money. They have a high degree of liquidity and thus can be easily converted into money without loss in value. Time deposits are an example.

Negative market feedback A tendency for a good or service to fall out of favor with more consumers because other consumers have stopped purchasing the item.

Negative-sum game A game in which players as a group lose at the end of the game.

Net domestic product (NDP) GDP minus depreciation.

Net investment Gross private domestic investment minus an estimate of the wear and tear on the existing capital stock. Net investment therefore measures the change in capital stock over a one-year period.

Net public debt Gross public debt minus all government interagency borrowing.

Net worth The difference between assets and liabilities.

Network effect A situation in which a consumer's willingness to purchase a good or service is influenced by how many others also buy or have bought the item.

New entrant An individual who has never held a full-time job lasting two weeks or longer but is now seeking employment.

New growth theory A theory of economic growth that examines the factors that determine why technology, research, innovation, and the like are undertaken and how they interact.

New Keynesian inflation dynamics In new Keynesian theory, the pattern of inflation exhibited by an economy with growing aggregate demand—initial sluggish adjustment of the price level in response to increased aggregate demand followed by higher inflation later.

Nominal rate of interest The market rate of interest expressed in today's dollars.

Nominal values The values of variables such as GDP and investment expressed in current dollars, also called money values; measurement in terms of the actual market prices at which goods and services are sold.

Nonaccelerating inflation rate of unemployment (NAIRU) The rate of unemployment below which the rate of inflation tends to rise and above which the rate of inflation tends to fall.

Noncontrollable expenditures Government spending that changes automatically without action by Congress.

Noncooperative game A game in which the players neither negotiate nor cooperate in any way. As applied to firms in an industry, this is the common situation in which there are relatively few firms and each has some ability to change price.

Nondurable consumer goods Consumer goods that are used up within three years.

Nonincome expense items The total of indirect business taxes and depreciation.

Nonprice rationing devices All methods used to ration scarce goods that are price-controlled. Whenever the price system is not allowed to work, nonprice rationing devices will evolve to ration the affected goods and services.

Normal goods Goods for which demand rises as income rises. Most goods are normal goods.

Normal rate of return The amount that must be paid to an investor to induce investment in a business; also known as the opportunity cost of capital.

Normative economics Analysis involving value judgments about economic policies; relates to whether things are good or bad. A statement of what ought to be.

Number line A line that can be divided into segments of equal length, each associated with a number.

O

Oligopoly A market structure in which there are very few sellers. Each seller knows that the other sellers will react to its changes in prices, quantities, and qualities.

Open economy effect One of the reasons that the aggregate demand curve slopes downward: Higher price levels result in foreign residents desiring to buy fewer U.S.-made goods, while U.S. residents now desire more foreign-made goods, thereby reducing net exports. This is equivalent to a reduction in the amount of real goods and services purchased in the United States.

Open market operations The purchase and sale of existing U.S. government securities (such as bonds) in the open private market by the Federal Reserve System.

Opportunistic behavior Actions that focus solely on short-run gains because long-run benefits of cooperation are perceived to be smaller.

Opportunity cost The highest-valued, next-best alternative that must be sacrificed to obtain something or to satisfy a want.

Opportunity cost of capital The normal rate of return, or the available return on the next-best alternative investment. Economists consider this a cost of production, and it is included in our cost examples.

Optimal quantity of pollution The level of pollution for which the marginal benefit of one additional unit of pollution abatement just equals the marginal cost of that additional unit of pollution abatement.

Origin The intersection of the y axis and the x axis in a graph.

Outsourcing A firm's employment of labor outside the country in which the firm is located.

P

Par value The officially determined value of a currency.

Partnership A business owned by two or more joint owners, or partners, who share the responsibilities and the profits of the firm and are individually liable for all the debts of the partnership.

Passive (nondiscretionary) policymaking Policymaking that is carried out in response to a rule. It is therefore not in response to an actual or potential change in overall economic activity.

Patent A government protection that gives an inventor the exclusive right to make, use, or sell an invention for a limited period of time (currently, 20 years).

Payment intermediaries Institutions that facilitate transfers of funds between depositors who hold transactions deposits with those institutions.

Payoff matrix A matrix of outcomes, or consequences, of the strategies available to the players in a game.

Perfect competition A market structure in which the decisions of individual buyers and sellers have no effect on market price.

Perfectly competitive firm A firm that is such a small part of the total industry that it cannot affect the price of the product it sells.

Perfectly elastic demand A demand that has the characteristic that even the slightest increase in price will lead to zero quantity demanded.

Perfectly elastic supply A supply characterized by a reduction in quantity supplied to zero when there is the slightest decrease in price.

Perfectly inelastic demand A demand that exhibits zero responsiveness to price changes; no matter what the price is, the quantity demanded remains the same.

Perfectly inelastic supply A supply for which quantity supplied remains constant, no matter what happens to price.

Personal Consumption Expenditure (PCE) Index A statistical measure of average prices that uses annually updated weights based on surveys of consumer spending.

Personal income (PI) The amount of income that households actually receive before they pay personal income taxes.

Persuasive advertising Advertising that is intended to induce a consumer to purchase a particular product and discover a previously unknown taste for the item.

Phillips curve A curve showing the relationship between unemployment and changes in wages or prices. It was long thought to reflect a trade-off between unemployment and inflation.

Physical capital All manufactured resources, including buildings, equipment, machines, and improvements to land that is used for production.

Planning curve The long-run average cost curve.

Planning horizon The long run, during which all inputs are variable.

Plant size The physical size of the factories that a firm owns and operates to produce its output. Plant size can be defined by square footage, maximum physical capacity, and other physical measures.

Policy irrelevance proposition The conclusion that policy actions have no real effects in the short run if the policy actions are anticipated and none in the long run even if the policy actions are unanticipated.

Portfolio investment The purchase of less than 10 percent of the shares of ownership in a company in another nation.

Positive economics Analysis that is strictly limited to making either purely descriptive statements or scientific predictions; for example, "If A, then B." A statement of what is.

Positive market feedback A tendency for a good or service to come into favor with additional consumers because other consumers have chosen to buy the item.

Positive-sum game A game in which players as a group are better off at the end of the game.

Potential money multiplier The reciprocal of the required reserve ratio, assuming no leakages into currency and no excess reserves. It is equal to 1 divided by the required reserve ratio.

Precautionary demand Holding money to meet unplanned expenditures and emergencies.

Present value The value of a future amount expressed in today's dollars; the most that someone would pay today to receive a certain sum at some point in the future.

Price ceiling A legal maximum price that may be charged for a particular good or service.

Price controls Government-mandated minimum or maximum prices that may be charged for goods and services.

Price differentiation Establishing different prices for similar products to reflect differences in marginal cost in providing those commodities to different groups of buyers.

Price discrimination Selling a given product at more than one price, with the price difference being unrelated to differences in marginal cost.

Price elasticity of demand (E_p) The responsiveness of the quantity demanded of a commodity to changes in its price; defined as the percentage change in quantity demanded divided by the percentage change in price.

Price elasticity of supply (E_s) The responsiveness of the quantity supplied of a commodity to a change in its price; the percentage change in quantity supplied divided by the percentage change in price.

Price floor A legal minimum price below which a good or service may not be sold. Legal minimum wages are an example.

Price index The cost of today's market basket of goods expressed as a percentage of the cost of the same market basket during a base year.

Price leadership A practice in many oligopolistic industries in which the largest firm publishes its price list ahead of its competitors, who then match those announced prices. Also called parallel pricing.

Price searcher A firm that must determine the price-output combination that maximizes profit because it faces a downward-sloping demand curve.

Price system An economic system in which relative prices are constantly changing to reflect changes in supply and demand for different commodities. The prices of those commodities are signals to everyone within the system as to what is relatively scarce and what is relatively abundant.

Price taker A competitive firm that must take the price of its product as given because the firm cannot influence its price.

Price war A pricing campaign designed to capture additional market share by repeatedly cutting prices.

Principle of rival consumption The recognition that individuals are rivals in consuming private goods because one person's consumption reduces the amount available for others to consume.

Principle of substitution The principle that consumers and producers shift away from goods and resources that become priced relatively higher in favor of goods and resources that are now priced relatively lower.

Prisoners' dilemma A famous strategic game in which two prisoners have a choice between confessing and not confessing to a crime. If neither confesses, they serve a minimum sentence. If both confess, they serve a longer sentence. If one confesses and the other doesn't, the one who confesses goes free. The dominant strategy is always to confess.

Private costs Costs borne solely by the individuals who incur them. Also called internal costs.

Private goods Goods that can be consumed by only one individual at a time. Private goods are subject to the principle of rival consumption.

Private property rights Exclusive rights of ownership that allow the use, transfer, and exchange of property.

Producer durables, or capital goods Durable goods having an expected service life of more than three years that are used by businesses to produce other goods and services.

Producer Price Index (PPI) A statistical measure of a weighted average of prices of goods and services that firms produce and sell.

Product differentiation The distinguishing of products by brand name, color, and other minor attributes. Product differentiation occurs in other than perfectly competitive markets in which products are, in theory, homogeneous, such as wheat or corn.

Production Any activity that results in the conversion of resources into products that can be used in consumption.

Production function The relationship between inputs and maximum physical output. A production function is a technological, not an economic, relationship.

Production possibilities curve (PPC) A curve representing all possible combinations of maximum outputs that could be produced assuming a fixed amount of productive resources of a given quality.

Profit-maximizing rate of production The rate of production that maximizes total profits, or the difference between total revenues and total costs; also, the rate of production at which marginal revenue equals marginal cost.

Progressive taxation A tax system in which, as income increases, a higher percentage of the additional income is paid as taxes. The marginal tax rate exceeds the average tax rate as income rises.

Property rights The rights of an owner to use and to exchange property.

Proportional rule A decision-making system in which actions are based on the proportion of the "votes" cast and are in proportion to them. In a market system, if 10 percent of the "dollar votes" are cast for blue cars, 10 percent of the output will be blue cars.

Proportional taxation A tax system in which, regardless of an individual's income, the tax bill comprises exactly the same proportion.

Proprietorship A business owned by one individual who makes the business decisions, receives all the profits, and is legally responsible for the debts of the firm.

Public debt The total value of all outstanding federal government securities.

Public goods Goods for which the principle of rival consumption does not apply; they can be jointly consumed by many individuals simultaneously at no additional cost and with no reduction in quality or quantity. Also no one who fails to help pay for the good can be denied the benefit of the good.

Purchasing power The value of money for buying goods and services. If your money income stays the same but the price of one good that you are buying goes up, your effective purchasing power falls, and vice versa.

Purchasing power parity Adjustment in exchange rate conversions that takes into account differences in the true cost of living across countries.

Q

Quantity theory of money and prices The hypothesis that changes in the money supply lead to equiproportional changes in the price level.

Quota subscription A nation's account with the International Monetary Fund, denominated in special drawing rights.

Quota system A government-imposed restriction on the quantity of a specific good that another country is allowed to sell in the United States. In other words, quotas are restrictions on imports. These restrictions are usually applied to one or several specific countries.

R

Random walk theory The theory that there are no predictable trends in securities prices that can be used to "get rich quick."

Rate of discount The rate of interest used to discount future sums back to present value.

Rate of return The proportional annual benefit that results from making an investment.

Rate-of-return regulation Regulation that seeks to keep the rate of return in an industry at a competitive level by not allowing prices that would produce economic profits.

Rational expectations hypothesis A theory stating that people combine the effects of past policy changes on important economic variables with their own judgment about the future effects of current and future policy changes.

Rationality assumption The assumption that people do not intentionally make decisions that would leave them worse off.

Reaction function The manner in which one oligopolist reacts to a change in price, output, or quality made by another oligopolist in the industry.

Real disposable income Real GDP minus net taxes, or after-tax real income.

Real rate of interest The nominal rate of interest minus the anticipated rate of inflation.

Real values Measurement of economic values after adjustments have been made for changes in the average of prices between years.

Real-balance effect The change in expenditures resulting from a change in the real value of money balances when the price level changes, all other things held constant; also called the wealth effect.

Real-income effect The change in people's purchasing power that occurs when, other things being constant, the price of one good that they purchase changes. When that price goes up, real income, or purchasing power, falls, and when that price goes down, real income increases.

Recession A period of time during which the rate of growth of business activity is consistently less than its long-term trend or is negative.

Recessionary gap The gap that exists whenever equilibrium real GDP per year is less than full-employment real GDP as shown by the position of the long-run aggregate supply curve.

Recognition time lag The time required to gather information about the current state of the economy.

Recycling The reuse of raw materials derived from manufactured products.

Reentrant An individual who used to work full-time but left the labor force and has now reentered it looking for a job.

Regional trade bloc A group of nations that grants members special trade privileges.

Regressive taxation A tax system in which as more dollars are earned, the percentage of tax paid on them falls. The marginal tax rate is less than the average tax rate as income rises.

Reinvestment Profits (or depreciation reserves) used to purchase new capital equipment.

Relative price The money price of one commodity divided by the money price of another commodity; the number of units of one commodity that must be sacrificed to purchase one unit of another commodity.

Rent control Price ceilings on rents.

Repricing, or menu, cost of inflation The cost associated with recalculating prices and printing new price lists when there is inflation.

Required reserves The value of reserves that a depository institution must hold in the form of vault cash or deposits with the Fed.

Required reserve ratio The percentage of total transactions deposits that the Fed requires depository institutions to hold in the form of vault cash or deposits with the Fed.

Reserves In the U.S. Federal Reserve System, deposits held by Federal Reserve district banks for depository institutions, plus depository institutions' vault cash.

Resources Things used to produce other things to satisfy people's wants.

Retained earnings Earnings that a corporation saves, or retains, for investment in other productive activities; earnings that are not distributed to stockholders.

Ricardian equivalence theorem The proposition that an increase in the government budget deficit has no effect on aggregate demand.

Right-to-work laws Laws that make it illegal to require union membership as a condition of continuing employment in a particular firm.

S

Sales taxes Taxes assessed on the prices paid on a large set of goods and services.

Saving The act of not consuming all of one's current income. Whatever is not consumed out of spendable income is, by definition, saved. Saving is an action measured over time (a flow), whereas savings are a stock, an accumulation resulting from the act of saving in the past.

Savings deposits Interest-earning funds that can be withdrawn at any time without payment of a penalty.

Say's law A dictum of economist J. B. Say that supply creates its own demand; producing goods and services generates the means and the willingness to purchase other goods and services.

Scarcity A situation in which the ingredients for producing the things that people desire are insufficient to satisfy all wants.

Search good A product with characteristics that enable an individual to evaluate the product's quality in advance of a purchase.

Seasonal unemployment Unemployment resulting from the seasonal pattern of work in specific industries. It is usually due to seasonal fluctuations in demand or to changing weather conditions, rendering work difficult, if not impossible, as in the agriculture, construction, and tourist industries.

Secondary boycott A refusal to deal with companies or purchase products sold by companies that are dealing with a company being struck.

Secular deflation A persistent decline in prices resulting from economic growth in the presence of stable aggregate demand.

Securities Stocks and bonds.

Services Mental or physical labor or help purchased by consumers. Examples are the assistance of physicians, lawyers, dentists, repair personnel, housecleaners, educators, retailers, and wholesalers; items purchased or used by consumers that do not have physical characteristics.

Share of stock A legal claim to a share of a corporation's future profits. If it is common stock, it incorporates certain voting rights regarding major policy decisions of the corporation. If it is preferred stock, its owners are accorded preferential treatment in the payment of dividends but do not have any voting rights.

Share-the-gains, share-the-pains theory A theory of regulatory behavior that holds that regulators must take account of the demands of three groups: legislators, who established and oversee the regulatory agency; firms in the regulated industry; and consumers of the regulated industry's products.

Short run The time period during which at least one input, such as plant size, cannot be changed.

Short-run aggregate supply curve The relationship between total planned economywide production and the price level in the short run, all other things held constant. If prices adjust incompletely in the short run, the curve is positively sloped.

Short-run break-even price The price at which a firm's total revenues equal its total costs. At the break-even price, the firm is just making a normal rate of return on its capital investment. (It is covering its explicit and implicit costs.)

Short-run economies of operation A distinguishing characteristic of an information product arising from declining short-run average total cost as more units of the product are sold.

Short-run shutdown price The price that covers average variable costs. It occurs just below the intersection of the marginal cost curve and the average variable cost curve.

Shortage A situation in which quantity demanded is greater than quantity supplied at a price below the market clearing price.

Signals Compact ways of conveying to economic decision makers information needed to make decisions. An effective signal not only conveys information but also provides the incentive to react appropriately. Economic profits and economic losses are such signals.

Slope The change in the y value divided by the corresponding change in the x value of a curve; the "incline" of the curve.

Small menu costs Costs that deter firms from changing prices in response to demand changes—for example, the costs of renegotiating contracts or printing new price lists.

Social costs The full costs borne by society whenever a resource use occurs. Social costs can be measured by adding external costs to private, or internal, costs.

Social Security contributions The mandatory taxes paid out of workers' wages and salaries. Although half are supposedly paid by employers, in fact the net wages of employees are lower by the full amount.

Special drawing rights (SDRs) Reserve assets created by the International Monetary Fund for countries to use in settling international payment obligations.

Specialization The organization of economic activity so that what each person (or region) consumes is not identical to what that person (or region) produces. An individual may specialize, for example, in law or medicine. A nation may specialize in the production of coffee, computers, or cameras.

Standard of deferred payment A property of an item that makes it desirable for use as a means of settling debts maturing in the future; an essential property of money.

Static tax analysis Economic evaluation of the effects of tax rate changes under the assumption that there is no effect on the tax base, meaning that there is an unambiguous positive relationship between tax rates and tax revenues.

Stock The quantity of something, measured at a given point in time—for example, an inventory of goods or a bank account. Stocks are defined independently of time, although they are assessed at a point in time.

Store of value The ability to hold value over time; a necessary property of money.

Strategic dependence A situation in which one firm's actions with respect to price, quality, advertising, and related changes may be strategically countered by the reactions of one or more other firms in the industry. Such dependence can exist only when there are a limited number of major firms in an industry.

Strategy Any rule that is used to make a choice, such as "Always pick heads."

Strikebreakers Temporary or permanent workers hired by a company to replace union members who are striking.

Structural unemployment Unemployment resulting from a poor match of workers' abilities and skills with current requirements of employers.

Subsidy A negative tax; a payment to a producer from the government, usually in the form of a cash grant per unit.

Substitutes Two goods are substitutes when a change in the price of one causes a shift in demand for the other in the same direction as the price change.

Substitution effect The tendency of people to substitute cheaper commodities for more expensive commodities.

Supply A schedule showing the relationship between price and quantity supplied for a specified period of time, other things being equal.

Supply curve The graphical representation of the supply schedule; a line (curve) showing the supply schedule, which generally slopes upward (has a positive slope), other things being equal.

Supply-side economics The suggestion that creating incentives for individuals and firms to increase productivity will cause the aggregate supply curve to shift outward.

Surplus A situation in which quantity supplied is greater than quantity demanded at a price above the market clearing price.

Sweep account A depository institution account that entails regular shifts of funds from transactions deposits that are subject to reserve requirements to savings deposits that are exempt from reserve requirements.

Sympathy strike A work stoppage by a union in sympathy with another union's strike or cause.

T

Target zone A range of permitted exchange rate variations between upper and lower exchange rate bands that a central bank defends by selling or buying foreign exchange reserves.

Tariffs Taxes on imported goods.

Tax base The value of goods, services, wealth, or incomes subject to taxation.

Tax bracket A specified interval of income to which a specific and unique marginal tax rate is applied.

Tax incidence The distribution of tax burdens among various groups in society.

Tax rate The proportion of a tax base that must be paid to a government as taxes.

Taylor rule A suggested guideline for monetary policy, in the form of an equation determining the Fed's interest rate target based on an estimated long-run real interest rate, the present deviation of the actual inflation rate from the Fed's inflation objective, and the gap between actual real GDP and a measure of potential GDP.

Technology Society's pool of applied knowledge concerning how goods and services can be produced.

Terms of exchange The conditions under which trading takes place. Usually, the terms of exchange are equal to the price at which a good is traded.

The Fed The Federal Reserve System; the central bank of the United States.

Theory of public choice The study of collective decision making.

Third parties Parties who are not directly involved in a given activity or transaction. For example, in the relationship between caregivers and patients, fees may be paid by third parties (insurance companies, government).

Thrift institutions Financial institutions that receive most of their funds from the savings of the public; they include savings banks, savings and loan associations, and credit unions.

Tie-in sales Purchases of one product that are permitted by the seller only if the consumer buys another good or service from the same firm.

Time deposit A deposit in a financial institution that requires notice of intent to withdraw or must be left for an agreed period. Withdrawal of funds prior to the end of the agreed period may result in a penalty.

Tit-for-tat strategic behavior In game theory, cooperation that continues as long as the other players continue to cooperate.

Total costs The sum of total fixed costs and total variable costs.

Total income The yearly amount earned by the nation's resources (factors of production). Total income therefore includes wages, rent, interest payments, and profits that are received by workers, landowners, capital owners, and entrepreneurs, respectively.

Total revenues The price per unit times the total quantity sold.

Trading Desk An office at the Federal Reserve Bank of New York charged with implementing monetary policy strategies developed by the Federal Open Market Committee.

Transaction costs All costs associated with making, reaching, and enforcing agreements.

Transactions approach A method of measuring the money supply by looking at money as a medium of exchange.

Transactions demand Holding money as a medium of exchange to make payments. The level varies directly with nominal GDP.

Transactions deposits Checkable and debitable account balances in commercial banks and other types of financial institutions, such as credit unions and mutual savings banks; any accounts in financial institutions from which you can easily transmit debit-card and check payments without many restrictions.

Transfer payments Money payments made by governments to individuals for which no services or goods are rendered in return. Examples are Social Security old-age and disability benefits and unemployment insurance benefits.

Transfers in kind Payments that are in the form of actual goods and services, such as food stamps, subsidized public housing, and medical care, and for which in return no goods or services are rendered concurrently.

Traveler's checks Financial instruments obtained from a bank or a non-banking organization and signed during purchase that can be used as cash upon a second signature by the purchaser.

U

Unanticipated inflation Inflation at a rate that comes as a surprise, either higher or lower than the rate anticipated.

Unemployment The total number of adults (aged 16 years or older) who are willing and able to work and who are actively looking for work but have not found a job.

Union shop A business enterprise that may hire nonunion members, conditional on their joining the union by some specified date after employment begins.

Unit elasticity of demand A demand relationship in which the quantity demanded changes exactly in proportion to the change in price. Total expenditures are invariant to price changes in the unit-elastic region of the demand curve.

Unit of accounting A measure by which prices are expressed; the common denominator of the price system; a central property of money.

Unit tax A constant tax assessed on each unit of a good that consumers purchase.

Universal banking An environment in which banks face few or no restrictions on their powers to offer a full range of financial services and to own shares of stock in corporations.

Unlimited liability A legal concept whereby the personal assets of the owner of a firm can be seized to pay off the firm's debts.

Util A representative unit by which utility is measured.

Utility The want-satisfying power of a good or service.

Utility analysis The analysis of consumer decision making based on utility maximization.

V

Value added The dollar value of an industry's sales minus the value of intermediate goods (for example, raw materials and parts) used in production.

Variable costs Costs that vary with the rate of production. They include wages paid to workers and purchases of materials.

Versioning Selling a product in slightly altered forms to different groups of consumers.

Vertical merger The joining of a firm with another to which it sells an output or from which it buys an input.

Voluntary exchange An act of trading, done on an elective basis, in which both parties to the trade are better off after the exchange.

Voluntary import expansion (VIE) An official agreement with another country in which it agrees to import more from the United States.

Voluntary restraint agreement (VRA) An official agreement with another country that "voluntarily" restricts the quantity of its exports to the United States.

W

Wants What people would buy if their incomes were unlimited.

Wealth The stock of assets owned by a person, household, firm, or nation. For a household, wealth can consist of a house, cars, personal belongings, stocks, bonds, bank accounts, and cash.

World Bank A multinational agency that specializes in making loans to about 100 developing nations in an effort to promote their long-term development and growth.

World index fund A portfolio of bonds issued in various nations whose individual yields generally move in offsetting directions, thereby reducing the overall risk of losses.

World Trade Organization (WTO) The successor organization to GATT that handles trade disputes among its member nations.

X

x **axis** The horizontal axis in a graph.

Y

y **axis** The vertical axis in a graph.

Z

Zero-sum game A game in which any gains within the group are exactly offset by equal losses by the end of the game.

INDEX

Boldface page numbers refer to figures

A

AAA (American Automobile Association), 7–8
Absolute advantage, 40–41
Absolute poverty, 796
Acceptability of money, 370
Accounting: national income. *See* National income accounting; unit of, 366, 367
Accounting identity(ies), 289, 432, 859–861; among nations, 861; defined, 859
Accounting profit(s), 616; defined, 558; economic profits versus, 559–560
AccuWeather, 683
ACHs (automated clearing houses), 596
Action time lag, 328
Active (discretionary) policymaking: challenge to, 463–465; defined, 450; passive (nondiscretionary) policymaking versus, 450–451, 469–470; rationale for, 454–456; rationalizing, modern approaches to, 465–469
Ad valorem taxation, 141–142
Adobe Acrobat, 723
Advantage: absolute, 40–41; comparative. *See* Comparative advantage
Adverse selection: defined, 376; in deposit insurance, 413; financing global growth and, 485
Advertising: brand names and, 668–671; expenses for, in U.S., 670; informational, persuasive advertising versus, 670; methods of, 669; monopolistic competition and, 664; persuasive, informational advertising versus, 670; as signaling behavior, 670–671
Aetna Health Insurance, 806
AFC (average fixed costs), 585, 587
AFDC (Aid to Families with Dependent Children), 798
Afghanistan, currency of, cutting excess zeros from, 433
AFL (American Federation of Labor): formation of, 760; merger of, with CIO, 761
AFL-CIO (American Federation of Labor-Congress of Industrial Organizations): formation of, 761; membership share in, after breakup, 778; seven unions disassociated from and formed new group, 759, 777–778
Africa: converting dollars to vouchers for use in, 368; poorer nations of, birthrate in, 478; transporting endangered species to U.S. from, 814
African Americans, education and, 792
Age: age-health care expenditure equation and, 800–801; as determinant of income, 789–790
Age-earnings cycle, 789–790
Aggregate demand: affected by weaker dollar, 278; changes in, consequences of, 274–275; decrease in. *See* Aggregate demand, decrease in; defined, 243; determinants of, 246–247; increase in. *See* Aggregate demand, increase in; in open economy, 277–279; output determination using, 270–271; total expenditures and, 243–246
Aggregate demand, decrease in: classical model and, 267; while aggregate supply is stable, 274–275
Aggregate demand, increase in: classical model and, 266–267; short-run effects of, 275
Aggregate demand curve, 243–244; $C + I + G + X$ curve and, 307–309; defined, 243; shifts in, 246–247
Aggregate demand shocks, 274
Aggregate supply: affected by weaker dollar, 277–278; defined, 240; determinants of, 274; long-run. *See* Long-run aggregate supply; in open economy, 277–279; output determination using, 270–271; short-run. *See* Short-run aggregate supply; vertical, price level, classical theory and, 266–267
Aggregate supply curve, shifts in, 272–273
Aggregate supply shocks, 274
Aggregates, 3
Agreement(s): trade. *See* Trade agreements; voluntary, 821; voluntary restraint (VRA), 846
Agriculture: economic development and, 230; price supports in, 94–97
Aid to Families with Dependent Children (AFDC), 798
Air pollution. *See* Pollution
Air transport, reducing marginal cost of, 588
Airline(s): no-frills, 698; regulation of, 707; U.S., servicing and maintenance of aircraft outsourced by, 745
Airport(s): in Brussels, Belgium versus Leipzig, Germany, DHL's plan to expand service and add employees and, 817; speedy security screening in, 642; use of, shift in, 500, 514–515
Airport Wi-Fi systems, 109
Albertsons, store closing when Wal-Mart supercenter opens nearby, 178
Alcoa (Aluminum Company of America), 635
Aldridge-Vreeland Act (1908), 381
Allamericanclassics.com, 84
Alternative minimum tax (AMT), 321
Aluminum Company of America (Alcoa), 635
Amazon.com, 697
Ambassador Bridge monopoly, 633, 653
America Online, 712
American Airlines: incentive structure and, 123; pension plan at, 153
American Automobile Association (AAA), 7–8
American Express, traveler's checks issued by, 373
American Federation of Labor. *See* AFL
American Federation of Labor-Congress of Industrial Organizations. *See* AFL-CIO
American Federation of Teachers (AFT), 763, 776
American States Water Company, 100
American Telephone & Telegraph. *See* AT&T
AMT (alternative minimum tax), 321
Amtrak, subsidies to, 135
Analysis: economic, power of, 2; graphical, 31, 502–504; marginal. *See* Marginal analysis; normative, 10, 11; positive, 10; tax, 142; utility, 501
Andean Community, 850, 852, 853
Anticipated inflation: defined, 172; unanticipated inflation versus, 172–173
Antitrust laws, 719–724. *See also* Antitrust policy; enforcement of, 113, 721–724; exemptions from, 720; key, listed, 719
Antitrust legislation, 113. *See also* Antitrust laws
Antitrust policy, 705, 719–721. *See also* Antitrust laws; goal of, 721; international discord in, 721
APC (average propensity to consume), 293
Apple Computer, 696, 841
Appreciation: defined, 867; of EMU euros, 868
APS (average propensity to save), 293
Aqua America, 100
Arabia, coffee initially grown in, 842
Arabic language, among world's ten most-used, 699, 700
Argentina, IMF's dealing with crisis in, 489
Aristotle, 366
Asset demand, 424
Assets: defined, 377; financial institution, 376–377
Association of Southeast Asian Nations, 850
Assumption(s): *ceteris paribus*, 8, 52–53; models and theories based on, 7–8; rationality, 4–5, 468–469
Astar, 684
Asymmetric information, 414; as barrier to financing global growth, 485; defined, 375, 713; product quality and, 713–714; World Bank and IMF and, 489–490
ATC. *See* Average total costs
Athearn Trains, 676
Atlas Model Railroad Company, 676
AT&T (American Telephone & Telegraph): market feedback experienced by, 697; mergers and, 705, 721, 725–726; required to open phone networks to competition, 711
AU Optronics, 67
Auctions, allocation of Army personnel and, 98
Australia: diamond industry in, 652; introduction of rabbits and poisonous cane toads in, 814; per capita spending on health care in, 800; shortage of mining workers for manufacturing industries in, 741; union membership as share of total employment in, 762
Austria, per capita spending on health care in, 800
Automated clearing houses (ACHs), 596
Automatic stabilizers, 329–330
Automobile industry: air pollution and, 815; auto safety and fuel economy and, 724; GPS (global-positioning-system) receivers and, 9; market leadership in, 693–694; as oligopoly,

I-1

683–684; shopping for auto parts on Internet and, 84
Automobiles: GPS (global-positioning-system) receivers in, 9; Japanese, restriction on imports of by U.S., 845, 846; parts for, shopping for on Internet, 84
Autonomous consumption: defined, 292; dissaving and, 291–293
Autoranch.com, 84
AVC. *See* Average variable costs
Average cost pricing, 710
Average costs: average physical product and, 592–593; relationship between marginal costs and, 588–589
Average fixed costs (AFC), 585, 587
Average physical product: average costs and, 592–593; defined, 581
Average propensity to consume (APC), 293
Average propensity to save (APS), 293
Average revenue curve, 610
Average tax rate, 136
Average total costs (ATC): defined, 587; marginal costs and, 589; minimum, perfect competition and, 624; price equals, 673–674
Average variable costs (AVC), 614; defined, 587; marginal costs and, 588
Axis: defined, 18; X, 19; Y, 19
Azclassics.com, 84

B

Bachmann Trains, 676
Bads, 29, 504
Balance of payments: defined, 859; factors affecting, 865; international capital movements and, 859–865
Balance of trade, 859
Balance sheet(s), 397–398; defined, 396; using, 399, 400
Balanced budget, 343
Balanced-budget multiplier, 340
Bank(s): of America. *See* Bank of America; central. *See* Central bank; commercial, 707; of England, 380–381; failures of, during Great Depression, 410–411; financial intermediation and, 375–379; of Malaysia, 876; megabanks and, 379; of Mexico, 879; money expansion by banking system and, 400–404; of New York, 403; online banking by customers preferred by, 376; runs on, 411; savings, 707; single, reaction of, to increase in reserves, 396–398; of Thailand, 859; throughout the world, 379–381; universal banking and, 380; World. *See* World Bank; world's largest, 379
Bank of America, 376; remote capture and, 403
Bank runs, 411
Banking structures throughout the world, 379–381. *See also* Bank(s)
Barnett Shale formation, 227
Barriers to entry: monopolistic competition and, 664; monopoly and, 634–638, 652; oligopoly and, 684
Barter, 367
Base year, 168–169
Baseball cards, 51, 75–76
Base-year dollars, 241
Battery-run backup surge protectors, 675
BEA. *See* Bureau of Economic Analysis
The Beatles, 366, 570
Beer, price of, 528
Behavior(s): models of, thought processes versus, 8–9; opportunistic, 689–690; signaling, 670–671; strategic. *See* Strategic behavior

Behavioral economics: bounded rationality and, 9–10; consumer choice theory and, 512–513; defined, 9; as a work in progress, 10
Belgium: banking in, 380; Brussels, DHL's plan to expand service and add employees at airport in, 817; per capita real GDP of, 214; retirement age in, 150
BellSouth, 725, 726
Benefits, external, 110–111
Bengali language, among world's ten most-used, 699, 700
Bentham, Jeremy, 501–502
Bernanke, Ben, 381, 423, 450
Bharti Tele-Ventures, 753
Big Board. *See* New York Stock Exchange
Bilateral monopoly, 775
Bilateral trade agreements, 833
Black market: defined, 91; price ceilings and, 90–91; rent controls and, 93
BLM (Bureau of Land Management), 827–828
BLS. *See* Bureau of Labor Statistics
B&O Railroad, 677
Bolivia, Andean Community and, 852, 853
Bomb-sniffing dogs, 74
Bond(s): defined, 566; markets for, 567–570
Bordo, Michael, 878
Botswana, diamond industry in, 652
Bounded rationality, 9–10, 468–469
Brand names: advertising and, 668–671; trademarks and, 669
Brazil: complex legal system holding back economic growth in, 477, 493–494; economic development in, 231; IMF's dealing with crisis in, 489, 493, 494; laying off a worker in, 493; marginal cost of pollution abatement in, 819; shoe manufacturing in, 844; shortage of mining workers for manufacturing industries in, 741; sugar produced in, 95; World Bank's assistance in, 493, 494
Break-even income point, 291
Breakfast food industry, 694
Bretton Woods, 875
Bretton Woods Agreement Act (1945), 875
Briggs & Stratton Corporation, 597
British Telecommunications, 721
Brown, Lester, 826
Budget(s): balanced, 343; capital, 353; deficit in. *See* Budget deficit(s); operating, 353; share of, price elasticity of demand and, 536–537
Budget constraint(s), 520, 524–525; defined, 524; government, 135; illustrated, 525; slope of, 525
Built-in stabilizers, 329–330
Bulgaria, currency of, cutting excess zeros from, 433
Bundling, 723–724
Bureau of Economic Analysis (BEA): advance estimate of GDP and, 184, 205–206; how business software purchases treated by, 185; personal consumption expenditure (PCE) index and, 170
Bureau of Engraving and Printing, 382
Bureau of Labor Statistics (BLS): categories of unemployed individuals and, 162; CPI published by, 169, 178–179; labor productivity in U.S. measured by, 219; unemployment figures published by, 160, 165
Bureau of Land Management (BLM), 827–828
Bus trip prices, rapid drop in, 606
Bush, George W., 414; Social Security proposal of, 134, 154; tax policy of, 327
Business cycles, 174. *See also* Business fluctuations; real, 463–465

Business fluctuations: changing inflation and unemployment and, 174–176; defined, 174; explaining, 175–176; idealized course of, 175
Business inventories: unplanned decreases in, 301; unplanned increases in, 300–301
Business organization, forms of, 556–558
Business receipt, 186

C

$C + I + G + X$ curve, aggregate demand curve and, 307–309
Cabibbean, nations of, U.S. public debt held by, 350
CallWave, 712
Campus, violence on, price of beer and, 528
Canada: accounting services outsourced to U.S. by, 743, 745, 746; central bank targets inflation rate in, 450; diamond industry in, 652; economic growth of, immigrants' contribution to, 233; loggers from, temporary work in U.S. and, 752; manufacturing employment in, 231; marginal cost of pollution abatement in, 820; national health insurance system in, 804; not contributing toward cost of NORAD System, 114–115; pharmaceuticals imported from, via Internet, 834; wheat farming in, 771
Canadian Wheat Board (CWB), 771
Canon, 686
Capital: allocation of, market signals and, 621; dead, 482–484; financial, 561; human. *See* Human capital; international movements of, balance of payments and, 859–865; opportunity cost of, 558–559; physical, 28; as a term, use of, 787–788
Capital account: defined, 863; relationship between current account and, 864; transactions in, 863
Capital budget, 353
Capital consumption allowance, 193, 194. *See also* Depreciation
Capital controls, 378
Capital flight, 865
Capital gain, 139
Capital goods: defined, 192, 289; economic growth and, 38–39, 482–484; growth and, 38–39; production of, reason for, 38; trade-off between consumption goods and, 38–39
Capital loss, 139
Capture hypothesis, 717
Card(s): debit. *See* Debit card(s); smart. *See* Smart cards; stored-value, 413
Carrefour, entry into Japanese discount-store industry by, 625
Cartel(s): De Beers Diamond, 652; defined, 638; economics, in Germany, 638
Catastrophe bonds, 490
Caveat emptor, 713
CDs (certificates of deposit), 374
CEA (President's Council of Economic Advisers), 167
Cellphones, 222
Cement, import restrictions on, as determinant of supply, 68
Cen Tra, 653
Central bank(s). *See also* Federal Reserve System: defined, 375; first, 380; roles of, 380–381; of the United States. *See* Federal Reserve System
Certificate of Deposit Account Registry Service, 393
Certificates of convenience, barriers to entry and, 636–637
Certificates of deposit (CDs), 374
Ceteris paribus assumption, 8, 52–53

Ceteris paribus conditions, 58, 61, 66–67, 68, 85, 618
"Chain Store Act" (Robinson-Patman Act)(1936), 719, 720
Chamberlin, Edward, 662, 667
Change to Win Federation, 759, 777–778
Check(s): clearing of, 365, 383, 386–387, 403; paper, remote capture of, 403; traveler's, 373
Check float, 5–6
Cheese prices, jump in, 86
Chemical toxins, 826
Chi Mei Optoelectronics, 67
Chile: birthrate in, 230; private property nationalized in, 231
China: aiming to duplicate Nasdaq's success, 567; economic growth has accompanied population growth in, 480; GDP of, environmental quality of life versus, 190; government-imposed birthrate in, 478; inflation in, 252; major espionage successes by, 845; manufacturing employment in, 231; measuring unemployment rate in, 166; migration of workers from rural villages to cities in, 733; per capita GDP in, 203; price ceilings on drinking water in, 99; real GDP growth in, 251, 252; Shanghai, license plates auctioned off in, 646; Shanghai Stock Exchange in, 567; Shenzhen Stock Exchange in, 567; shortage of mining workers for manufacturing industries in, 741; tungsten in, 635; U.S. public debt held by, 350; "voluntary" textile products quota and, 98; Wal-Mart as fifth-largest importer of products manufactured in, 872
Chinese language, among world's ten most-used, 699, 700
Choice(s): faced by society, 33–37; scarcity, opportunity cost and, 29–30; between two goods, 33–34
Christmas Décor, Inc., 41
Chrysler Corporation, 683
Chunghwa Picture Tubes, 67
Cigarette taxes, 532–533
CIO (Congress of Industrial Organizations): formation of, 761; merger of, with AFL, 761
Circular flow: of income, 185, 186; of product, 186; Say's law and, 263; simple, 185–187
Cisco, stock of, Nasdaq is home to, 567
Civic centers, 116
Classical model, 262–268; assumptions of, 263; decreases in aggregate demand and, 267; increases in aggregate demand and, 266–267; investment and, 264, 265; saving and, 264, 265, 290; Say's law and, 262–263; vertical aggregate supply, price level and, 266–267
Clayton Act (1914), 719, 720, 723
Close substitutes, 634–635, 642, 653
Closed shop, 761
Clothing, perfect fit and, 511
Cobb, Ty, 76
Coca-Cola, 262
Coca-Cola Company, 535; "low-carb" soft drinks and, 664–665
Coe, David, 223
COLAs (cost-of-living adjustments), 173
Colbert, Jean-Baptiste, 136
Collective bargaining, 760
Collective decision making, 122–125; defined, 122; market decision making and, differences between, 122
Colleges. *See also* Education: financial benefit of attending, 791; graduates of, minority female, 792; new building construction at, 662; tuition at, price discrimination and, 649–650

Columbus, Christopher, 7
Combination, 720
Comcast, 726
Commercial banks, 707
Common property, 821–823; defined, 821; wild horses as, 827; wild species, trade-offs and, 823–824
Common stock, 566
Community of East and Southern Africa, 850
Compaq, 596
Comparable-worth doctrine, 792–793
Comparative advantage: defined, 40; in holiday spirit, 41; international trade and, 42–43, 837; open economy and, 833–857
Competition: among bus companies, 606; government's promotion of, 113; perfect. *See* Perfect competition; in product market, 733; public-sector decision making and, 123; pure, 263
Competitiveness loans, 493
Complement(s): cross price elasticity of demand and, 539–540; defined, 60; prices of, demand shifts and, 59, 60
Compound interest, 217–218
Computer printer industry, 686
Computers: battery-run backup surge protectors for, 675; costs of producing and selling, 579; junking of, 84; personal (PCs), depreciation of, 194; recycling of, 824
Concentration ratio, 685–686
Congress of Industrial Organizations. *See* CIO
Congressional Budget Office, 353
Conspicuous consumption, 12–13
Constant dollars, 200
Constant returns to scale: defined, 594; illustrated, 595
Constant-cost industry, 622–623
Construction, rent controls and, 92
Consumer(s): choices of. *See* Consumer choice(s); cigarette, 532–533; expectations of. *See* Consumer expectations; preferences of, changes in, as market determinant of exchange rates, 873; Taxation from point of view of, 145–147
Consumer choice(s), 500–526; optimizing, 506–508; theory of, 512–513, 520–526
Consumer expectations, 60–61; supply determined by, 68
Consumer optimum, 506–508, 525–526; defined, 506; how a price change affects, 508–510; illustrated, 526; model of, 508; steps to, 508
Consumer Price Index (CPI), 200, 466; defined, 169; flaws in, 169, 179; historical changes in, 171; quality adjustments and, 178–179; Wal-Mart and, 159, 178–179
Consumer Product Safety Commission (CPSC), 708
Consumer protection: in nonmonopolistic industries, 713–714; regulation for, implementing, 714–715
Consumer surplus: defined, 659; in perfectly competitive market, 659; resulting from monopoly, 658–659
Consumption: autonomous. *See* Autonomous consumption; conspicuous, 12–13; current, forgoing, 38; defined, 38, 288; as function of real GDP, 298; investment and, 299–300; planned. *See* Planned consumption; relating to saving and income, 289; rival, principle of, 114; with specialization and trade, 839; spending on human capital and, 289–290
Consumption function, 291, 292; defined, 290; investment function and, 299–300; shifts in, causes of, 295

Consumption goods: defined, 288; tradeoff between capital goods and, 38–39
Consumption plus investment line, 299
Contraction, 174
Contributive standard, 793
Cook's, 373
Cooperative game, 687
Cooperative players, finding, 687–688
Corporation(s): advantages of, 557–558; defined, 557; disadvantages of, 558; double taxation and, 140; financing of, methods of, 566; income taxes and, 108, 140; profits of, 558; retained earnings and, 140; S, 149; separation of ownership and control in, 558; shareholders of, 557–558
Cost(s): book "overproduction" and, 599–600; economic, 817; entry, increasing, 694; explicit, 558; external, 109–110, 814; fixed. *See* Fixed costs; foregone opportunity as, 30; implicit, 558; of inputs used to produce product, as determinant of supply, 67; internal, 814; management, 376; marginal. *See* Marginal cost(s); menu. *See* Menu cost(s); minimization of, factor utilization and, 751; monopoly profit maximization and, 642–646; opportunity. *See* Opportunity cost; private. *See* Private costs; of production, 586; of regulation, 715–718; relationship between output and, 591; relative, increasing, law of, 35–37; short-run, to the firm, 584–590; small menu, 466; social. *See* Social costs; switching, 695; theft, high-tech canines and, 589; total. *See* Total costs; transaction, 83–84, 821; variable. *See* Variable costs
Cost curve(s): for an information product, 672; long-run. *See* Long-run average cost curve(s); of monopolistic competitor, 665–666; relationship of, with diminishing marginal product, 590–593; short-run average, 585–587, 673; that might lead to natural monopoly, 636
Costco, 84, 202; CPI calculations and, 178–179; entry into Japanese discount-store industry by, 625
Cost-of-living adjustments (COLAs), 173
Cost-of-service regulation, 710, 711
Cost-push inflation, 276
Council of Economic Advisers (CEA), 167
Coupons: bond payments and, 566; rationing by, 89
CPI. *See* Consumer Price Index
CPSC (Consumer Product Safety Commission), 708
Craft unions, 760, 761
Cranberries, 663
Crawling pegs, 878
Creative destruction, 231
Creative response, 716
Credence goods, 670, 714
Credit, interest and, 561–562
Credit card(s): holders of, special offer for, 562; payments preferred by McDonald's, 372–373; playing float with, 5–6
Credit market, equilibrium in, 264
Credit unions, 707
Creditors, unanticipated inflation and, 173
Cross price elasticity of demand, 539–540
Crowding-out effect(s): defined, 323; indirect, 323–324; public debt and, 349
Crude oil, price of, 261, 280–282
Cryptographic algorithm, 416
Cuba, private property nationalized in, 231
Currency drains, 406
Currency in U.S., 371–372
Currency swaps, 877

Current account: balancing of, 863; defined, 861; relationship between capital account and, 864
Current account transactions, 861–863
Curve(s): cost. *See* Cost curve(s); demand. *See* Demand curve(s); linear (slope of a line), 20–23; nonlinear, slopes of, 23; planning, 593, 594
Customer, switching costs of, 695
CWB (Canadian Wheat Board), 771
Cyberspace. *See* Internet
Cyclical unemployment, 165, 452
Czech Republic, increased value of currency in, 868

D

DaimlerChrysler, 767
Dawson, John, 242
De Beers Diamond Cartel, 652
de Soto, Hernando, 482
Dead capital, 482–484
Deadweight loss, 660
Death, regulation of, 34–35
Debit card(s): payments preferred by McDonald's, 372–373; smart cards versus, 416; as substitute for checks, 386–387; transaction using, clearance of, 377–378; use of, depository institutions offer choice in, 398
Debtors, unanticipated inflation and, 173
Decreasing-cost industry, 622, 623
Deductible, 803
Deferred payment, standard of, 366, 367–368
Deferred-compensation plans, 356
Deflation: defined, 168; goods and, 170; inflation and, 167–172; secular, 248–249; in U.S. history, 171
Dell, Inc., 412, 528, 596; computer printers and, 686; fixed costs and, 584; offered credit to customers, 563; recycling computers and, 824
Delta Airlines: operations scaled back by, 698; pension plan at, 153
Demand, 52–62; aggregate. *See* Aggregate demand; asset, 424; defined, 52; derived. *See* Derived demand; determinants of, 58–61; elastic, 530–531, 534–535; for foreign currency, 867; hair dyes and, 59; for health care services, 802; inelastic, 531, 535; law of, 52–54, 501, 510; for money, 423–424, 439; precautionary, 424; shifts in. *See* Demand shifts; supply and, 69–73; for toys, 60; transactions, 423–424; for union labor, 768–769; unit-elastic, 535
Demand curve(s), 54, 510–512; defined, 55; horizontal summation of, 56; individual, market demand curve versus, 55–57; input, 748–749; kinked. *See* Kinked demand curve; labor, shifts in, 741–742; market, individual demand curve versus, 55–57; for a monopolist, 639–641, 748–749; of monopolistic competitor, 665–666; movement along, 61; for the perfect competitor, 640; of perfect competitor, 607–608; shift in, 58
Demand for money curve, 424–425
Demand schedule(s), 54–57. *See also* Demand; defined, 55; supply schedule combined with, 69–71
Demand shifts, 57–62, 85–88; versus changes in quantity demanded, 61–62; determinants of, 58–61; effects of, 85–86; preferences and, 58–59; prices of related goods, 59–60; with shift in supply, 86–87
Demand-pull inflation, 276
Demand-side inflation, 251–252

Demerit goods, 116
Denmark: banking in, 380; GDP of, 215; per capita spending on health care in, 800
Dependent variable, 17
Deposit(s): certificates of (CDs), 374; savings, 373; time, 374; transactions, 369, 373
Deposit insurance, 410–415; adverse selection in, 413; moral hazard in, 414; objective of, 393; Promontory Interfinancial Network and, 393; rationale for, 411–412; reform and, 414; risk taking by bank managers caused by, 412–413
Deposit Insurance Fund (DIF), 414
Depository institutions: defined, 373; the Fed and, 381, 384; reserves in, 394–396. *See also* Reserve(s)
Depreciation: calculating GDP and, 196; defined, 867; of EMU euros, 868; net domestic product (NDP) and, 193; of personal computers (PCs), 194
Depression: defined, 175; Great. *See* Great Depression
Derived demand: defined, 736; for labor, 736–737
Deutsche Telecom, 721
Development economics, 228. *See also* Economic development
DHL, 684
DHL Worldwide Express, 817
Diamond industry, 652
Diamond-water paradox, 511–512
DIF (Deposit Insurance Fund), 414
Digital cash: defined, 392; how it works, 416; money multiplier and, 416–417; smart cards and, 392, 416
Digital photo printing services, 605, 627–628
Digital signature, 416
DiMaggio, Joe, 75
Diminishing marginal product, 581–584; law of, 583–584; measuring, 582–583; relationship of, with cost curves and, 590–593
Diminishing marginal utility, 505–506
Direct expenditure offsets, 325–326
Direct financing, indirect financing versus, 375
Direct marketing, 669
Direct relationship, 17
Directions, getting, 7–8
Dirty float, 878
Discount rate: borrowed reserves and, 407; changes in, 427; defined, 407; today's policy regarding, 407
Discounted present value, 552, 564, 565
Discounting, 565
Discouraged workers, 163
Discover, 562
Discrimination: economic, as determinant of income, 792–793; price. *See* Price discrimination; against women, 792–793
Diseconomies of scale: defined, 594; illustrated, 595; why firm might experience, 596
Disequilibrium, 860
Disposable personal income (DPI), 198–199
Dissaving: autonomous consumption and, 291–293; defined, 290
Distribution of income. *See* Income distribution
Dividend(s): defined, 558; from Microsoft, 563
Division of labor, 41–42
Dollar(s): base-year, 241; constant, 200; converting to vouchers for use in Africa, 368; as currency of choice, 880; as "vehicle currency," 881; weaker. *See* Dollar, weaker
Dollar, weaker: aggregate demand affected by, 278; aggregate supply affected by, 277–278; inflation and real GDP affected by, 278–279

Dollar General, 513
Dollar Tree, 513
Domestic output, 192
Dominant strategies, 688
Double coincidence of wants, 367
Double taxation, 140, 558
DPI (disposable personal income), 198–199
Dragon Lines, 606
Drought-stricken nations, 490
Drugs: government regulation and, 116; illicit, prices of, 527, 546–547; prescription, Medicare assistance and, 120, 804; sold in Malaysia, holographic labels required on, 637
Du Pont, legal work outsourced by, 745
Dumping, 844
Duopoly, 711
Durable consumer goods, 191
Dutch East India Company, 566
Dynamic tax analysis, 142

E

Earned Income Tax Credit (EITC) program, 799
Earnhardt, Dale, 570
Earnings, retained, 140
Eastern Travel, 606
Eastman Kodak, 841; digital photo printing kiosks opened by, 627
eBay, 697, 712
Eberstadt, Nicholas, 230
Ecofin (European Economic and Financial Affairs Council), 359, 360
Economic analysis, power of, 2
Economic Community of West African States, 850
Economic costs, 817
Economic damages, 816
Economic development, 228–232; keys to, 231; population growth and, 228–230; stages of, 230
Economic discrimination, as determinant of income, 792–793
Economic freedom, 480
Economic goods, 28–29
Economic growth: capital goods and, 38–39, 482–484; costs and benefits of, 217; dead capital and, 483–484; defined, 214–218; determinants of, 221–226; economic freedom and, 480; effects of, on price level, 248–249; entrepreneurship and, 227; factors accounting for, in various regions, 219, 220; global. *See* Global economic growth; government inefficiencies and, 483–484; immigration and, 226–227; labor productivity and, 219–220; long-run aggregate supply and, 241–242; new growth theory and, 221–226; open economy and, 223. *See also* Open economy; political freedom and, 480–481; population and, 226–227, 478–480; production possibilities curve (PPC) and, 37–38; property rights and, 227; rate of, importance of, 217; rate of saving and, 220–221; real per capita GDP and, 215; reduced by regulation, 242; research and development and, 222–223; secular deflation and, 248; in selected countries, 216; in United States. *See* United States, economic growth in
Economic profit(s), 613, 614; accounting profits versus, 559–560; defined, 559; zero, 616, 667
Economic regulation, 706–707, 715
Economic rent(s): allocation of resources and, 554; defined, 553; earning from beyond the grave, 570; illustrated, 554; labor and, 553–554; super, entertainment superstars make, 555
Economic stability, perceptions of, as determinant of exchange rates, 873

Economic way of thinking, 2
Economics: analysis of, power of, 2; behavioral.
  See Behavioral economics; defined, 2–3;
  development, 228. *See also* Economic
  development; environmental, 813–832;
  experimental, 687–688; nature of, 1–25;
  normative. *See* Normative economics; positive.
  See Positive economics; rationality assumption
  of, 4–5; as science, 7–10; supply-side, 326–327
The Economics of Imperfect Competition
  (Robinson), 662
Economies of scale, 673; barriers to entry and,
  635–636; defined, 594; illustrated, 595;
  oligopoly and, 684; reasons for, 595–596
Economy(ies): open. *See* Open economy;
  performance of, measurement of, 184–212. *See
  also* Economic growth; of scale. *See*
  Economies of scale; sticky-price, real GDP and
  price level in, 467–468
Economywide stability, government attempts to
  ensure, 115
Ecuador, Andean Community and, 852
Education. *See also* Colleges: access to, minorities
  and, 792; economic development and, 231;
  public. *See* Public education
EEOC (Equal Employment Opportunity
  Commission), 708
Effect time lag, 328
Efficiency: defined, 35; oligopoly and, 686;
  productive, 35, 843
Effluent fee, 111–112
Egalitarian principle of income distribution,
  793–794
E-gold, 369
Egypt, dead capital problem and, 482
EITC (Earned Income Tax Credit) program, 799
El Salvador, companies in U.S. outsource labor
  services to, 745
Elastic demand, 530–531, 534–535; perfectly, 531
Elasticity(ies): of demand. *See* Elasticity of
  demand; labeling, 533–535; monopoly and,
  641–642; of supply, price. *See* Price
  elasticity(ies) of supply; total revenues and,
  532–536, 535
Elasticity of demand: income, 540–541; price. *See*
  Price elasticity(ies) of demand; unit, 531
"Elder law," 802
E-mail, postage charges for, 11
EMI, 721
E-money, 369
Empirical science, 8
Employment: full, 166, 167; in manufacturing, 231;
  minimum wage laws' effect on, 774; under
  monopsony, 773–775; new, small-business
  entrepreneurs and, 28; outsourcing's effects on,
  743–745; real GDP and, 266
EMU (European Monetary Union), 865, 866, 867
Endangered Species Act (1973), 823–824
Endowments, 241
English language, among world's ten most-used,
  699, 700
Entitlements: defined, 356; reducing, elimination of
  federal budget deficit and, 356–358
Entrepreneur(s): role of, 556; small-business, most
  new jobs created by, 28
Entrepreneurship: defined, 28; economic growth
  and, 227
Entry: barriers to. *See* Barriers to entry; costs of,
  increasing, 694; deterring, 694–695
Entry deterrence strategy, 694
Environmental economics, 813–832
Environmental Protection Agency (EPA), 708, 826

Epson, 686
Equal Employment Opportunity Commission
  (EEOC), 708
Equality, as factor affecting income distribution,
  793–794
Equation of exchange, 432
Equilibrium: as accounting identity, 860; in credit
  market, 264; defined, 71; Keynesian, 301–304;
  labor market, 740; in labor market, 265–266;
  long-run. *See* Long-run equilibrium; market,
  individual firm and, 619–620; short-run. *See*
  Short-run equilibrium; tendency toward, 621
Equilibrium foreign exchange rate, 867–873
Equilibrium interest rate, 264
Equilibrium price, 71
Equilibrium quantity, taxes and, 146
Erlich, Paul, 825
An Essay on the Principle of Population (Malthus),
  230
Estonia, proportional income taxation in, 137
Ethiopia, setting up a business in, 478
E-Trade, 403
EU. *See* European Union
Euro, 342, 359, 372; as "vehicle currency," 881
Europe: countries in, sugar subsidies in, 95;
  horsemeat from slaughtered wild horses
  exported to, 828; labor movement in, 760; life
  insurance can be sold by banks in, 380;
  megabanks in, 379; potato brought by Spain to,
  842; ready-to-eat vegetables imported from
  Kenya by, 836; rising retirement age in, 150;
  sugar subsidies in, 95; wealthy nations of,
  birthrate in, 478
European Central bank, RFID tags and, 55
European Commission, 359
European Court of Justice, 360
European Economic and Financial Affairs Council
  (Ecofin), 359, 360
European Economic Community, 875. *See also*
  European Union
European Monetary Union (EMU), 865, 866, 867
European Union (EU): antitrust policy of, 721;
  "banana wars" of, 849; budget of, 326; China's
  "voluntary" textile products quota and, 98;
  European Commission of, 359; foreign direct
  investment to, 486; per capita real GDP in, 218;
  productive efficiency in, 843; REACH and,
  706; as regional trade bloc, 850; Stability and
  Growth Pact of, 343, 359–360; trade in
  genetically engineered plants and animals
  restrained by, 845; trade within, 42
Excess reserves, 395–396, 406
Exchange: equation of, 432; foreign. *See* Foreign
  exchange; markets and, 83; terms of, 83;
  voluntary, 83
Exchange rate. *See* Foreign exchange rate(s)
Excise taxes, 145–146
Exclusion principle, 114
Expansion, 174
Expectations: consumer, 60–61; importance of,
  456–457; inflation, 459; rational. *See* Rational
  expectations hypothesis; supply determined by,
  68
Expenditure approach: defined, 191; deriving GDP
  by, 191–195; illustrated, 197; presenting,
  192–195
Expenditures: flow of, 191; foreign, 192. *See also*
  Net exports; government. *See* Government
  spending; total, aggregate demand and,
  243–246
Experience, as determinant of marginal
  productivity, 790–791

Experience goods, 670
Explicit costs, 558
Export(s): merchandise trade, 861; net. *See* Net
  exports; relationship between imports and,
  842–843; relationship of, with imports, 192;
  service, 862
Expropriation, 124, 231
External benefits, 110–111
External costs, 109–110, 814
External shocks, 175–176
Externality(ies): correcting for, 108–112, 815–817;
  defined, 109, 815; negative, 111–112; positive.
  See Positive externalities; resource
  misallocations of, 111
Extremophiles, 826

F

Factor market, 186–187
Factors of production. *See also* Resources: defined,
  27; entrepreneurship and, 227; listed, 28;
  technology and, 222; utilization of, 750–752;
  variable, 579
Family Dollar, 513
Farm Security Act (2002), 95
Farrow, Mia, 93
FCC (Federal Communications Commission), 707,
  711, 725, 726
FDA. *See* Food and Drug Administration
FDIC. *See* Federal Deposit Insurance Corporation
FDIC Improvement Act (1991), 414
Featherbedding, 770
The Fed. *See* Federal Reserve System
Federal Aviation Administration, 707
Federal budget deficit(s): defined, 343; growing,
  U.S. economic performance and, 352–358;
  historical record of, 344–345; macroeconomic
  consequences of, 354; in open economy,
  351–352; as percentage of GDP, 345; public
  debt and, 343–344; reduction of, 354–358;
  resurgence of, 346; trade deficits and, 351–352
Federal Communications Commission (FCC), 707,
  711, 725, 726
Federal Deposit Insurance Corporation (FDIC),
  384, 707. *See also* Deposit insurance; founding
  of, 411; most employees of, are unionized,
  765–766; reform and, 414; stored-value cards
  and, 413
Federal Deposit Insurance Reform Act (2005), 414
Federal funds market, 407
Federal funds rate, 407, 422, 427, 434–439, 437;
  neutral, 440–441
Federal government: budget deficit of. *See* Federal
  budget deficit(s); debt of. *See* Public debt;
  securities of. *See* Federal government,
  securities of; spending by, 117–122; tax
  receipts of, sources of, 138
Federal government, securities of: purchase of, by
  the Fed, 400–404, 426; sale of, by the Fed,
  399–400, 425–426
Federal income tax: capital gains and, 139;
  corporate, 108, 140; personal, 138–139
Federal Insurance Contributions Act (FICA)(1935),
  141
Federal Motor Carrier Safety Administration, 707
Federal Open Market Committee (FOMC), 381,
  382, 398, 399, 437, 439, 440–441
Federal Register, 706
Federal Reserve Act (1913), 381
Federal Reserve notes, 371
Federal Reserve System (the Fed), 381–384. *See
  also* Monetary policy; ACH system of,

economies of scale in, 596; attack on Washington, DC and, 415; Board of Governors of, 381, 415; checks cleared by, 365, 383, 386–387; commercial banks regulated by, 707; current implementation of policy and, 436–439; defined, 381; depository institutions supervised by, 384; establishment of, 381; Federal Open Market Committee (FOMC), 381, 382, 398, 399, 437, 439, 440–441; Fedwire of, 383; FOMC Directive and, 437, 439; foreign exchange intervention and, 878; functions of, 382–384; illustrated, 383; as lender of last resort, 384; monetary policy target choices and, 435–436; natural rate of unemployment estimated by, 167; open market operations of, 399, 425–426, 437–438, 439, 440–441; organization of, 381, 382; personal consumption expenditure (PCE) index used by, 170; purchase by, of government security, 400–404, 426; sale by, of government security, 399–400, 425–426; Trading Desk and, 437, 438–439, 440

Federal Savings and Loan Insurance Corporation (FSLIC), 411, 412

Federal tax(es): most important, 138–141; Social Security. *See* Social Security tax; unemployment, 141

Federal Trade Commission (FTC): antitrust law enforcement and, 113, 720, 721, 725–726; charged companies with late deliveries of Internet orders, 714–715; establishment of, 719, 720; international dimensions of antitrust policy and, 721; major functions of, 708

Federal Trade Commission Act (1914 and 1938 Amendment)), 719, 720

FedEx, 627, 684

Fedwire, 383

Feedback effect, 716

FICA (Federal Insurance Contributions Act)(1935), 141

Fiduciary monetary system, 369

Final goods and services, 186

Final output, 188–189

Financial capital, 561

Financial institution liabilities and assets, 376–377

Financial Institutions Reform, Recovery and Enforcement Act (FIRREA)(Thrift Bailout Act)(1989), 414

Financial intermediaries, 375–377; assets and liabilities of, 377; defined, 375

Financial intermediation, 375–377, 375–379; across national boundaries, 378–379; defined, 375; process of, 375

Financial press, how to read, 569–570

Financial transactions, exclusion of, from GDP, 189

Finland, union membership as share of total employment in, 761, 762

Firm(s), 555–561. *See also* Business; Corporation(s); defined, 555; exit and entry of, 620–621; individual, market equilibrium and, 619–620; in industry, number of, as determinant of supply, 68; investment decision of, 323–324; legal organization of, 556–558; in monopolistic competition, number of, 662–663; multinational, taking into account in trade statistics, 862; in oligopoly, number of, 683; perfectly competitive. *See* Perfectly competitive firm; profit maximization as goal of, 560; profits of, 558; short-run costs to, 584–590; size of, reasons for diseconomies of scale and, 596

FIRREA (Financial Institutions Reform, Recovery and Enforcement Act)(Thrift Bailout Act)(1989), 414

First come, first served, 88, 89

Fiscal policy, 318–341; during abnormal times, 330; changes in taxes and, 321–322; defined, 319; discretionary, 319–322, 328; Keynesian, 331, 339–341; during normal times, 330; possible offsets to, 322–328; time lags and, 328, 332; what we know about it, 330–331

Fixed costs, 671; average (AFC), 585, 587; defined, 585; total, 584–585

Fixed exchange rate(s): floating exchange rates versus, 875–879; illustrated, 876; pros and cons of, 877

Fixed investment, 191–192, 289

Fixed-quantity price index, 169

Flexible exchange rates, 867

Float, dirty, 878

Flow(s): defined, 162; of expenditures, 191; of income, 191; international trade, 841; of production, 187–188; stocks and, 162, 289, 343–344

FOMC (Federal Open Market Committee), 381, 382, 398, 399, 437, 439, 440–441

FOMC Directive, 437, 439

Food and Drug Administration (FDA), 535, 708; regulations of, as barrier to entry, 637–638

Food for Peace, 95

Food stamps, 117, 785, 786, 798

Forbes, 555

Ford Motor Company, 683; basic auto design work outsourced by, 745; health plan and, 4; patent and, 637; pension plan at, 153

Foreign currency: demand for, 867; supply of, 867

Foreign direct investment, 484–485, 486

Foreign exchange, rate of. *See* Foreign exchange rate(s)

Foreign exchange market, 858, 866, 880–881

Foreign exchange rate(s): crawling pegs and, 878; defined, 202, 866; determining, 866–873; dirty floats and, 878; equilibrium, 867–873; fixed. *See* Fixed exchange rate(s); fixing, 876. *See also* Fixed exchange rate(s); floating, fixed exchange rates versus, 875–879; major determinants of, 873; as shock absorber, 877; target zones and, 878–879

Foreign exchange reserves, 876

Foreign exchange risk, 877

Foreign expenditures, 192. *See also* Net exports

Foreign goods, substitution of, 245–246

Foreign residents, our public debt to, 350

Forest fires, mushroom harvesting and, 67

45-degree reference line, 291, 298–299

Foster, Andrew, 825

Fractional reserve banking, 394–396

France: attempt to reduce unemployment rate in, 177; banking in, 380; coffee cultivated in colonies of, 842; contribution of, to EU, 326; EU's Stability and Growth Pact and, 343, 359–360; investment and, 265; per capita real GDP of, 214; quota agreement with Switzerland and, 847; restricting workers' hours on job in, 177; retirement age in, 150; saving and, 265

Franchises, barriers to entry and, 636–637

Free-rider problem, 114–115

Frictional unemployment, 164–165, 451

Friedman, Milton, 458

FSLIC (Federal Savings and Loan Insurance Corporation), 411, 412

FTC. *See* Federal Trade Commission

Fuji Photo Film, digital photo printing kiosks opened by, 627

Full employment, 166, 167

Full-Employment Act (1946), 115

Fuller, Ida May, 147

G

Game theory: applying to pricing strategies, 689, 690; basic notions about, 687–688; defined, 687; strategic behavior and, 687–690

Gasoline: price elasticity of demand for, 530; price of, increase in, 87; producers of, taxation from point of view of, 145–147; taxes on, 145–146

GATT (General Agreement on Tariffs and Trade), 848, 849

GDI. *See* Gross domestic income

GDP. *See* Gross domestic product

GDP deflator, 169, 170, 200, 466

Geisel, Theodor "Dr. Seuss," 570

General Accounting Office, 799

General Agreement on Tariffs and Trade (GATT), 848, 849

General Electric: fresh water treatment and, 100; health plan and, 4

General Motors Corporation, 683; basic auto design work outsourced by, 745; diseconomies of scale and, 596; market leadership and, 693–694; pension plan at, 153

Geographic market, 722

Georgia, proportional income taxation in, 137

Germany: bank borrowings in, 380; cartel of chaired economics professors in, 638; companies in U.S. outsource labor services to, 745; EU's Stability and Growth Pact and, 343, 359–360; Leipzig, DHL's decision to expand service and add employees at airport in, 817; life insurance can be sold by banks in, 380; minimum wage in, 97; per capita real GDP of, 214; productive efficiency in, 843; rate of saving in, 220; retirement age in, 150; workers from, employed in India, 753

Giambi, Jason, 76

Gifts, value of, perceived, 6

Glass industry, 845

Global Country of World Peace, 366

Global economic growth, 213–238; international institutions and policies for, 487–490; policies and prospects for, 477–499

Gold standard, 874–875

Gompers, Samuel, 760

Goods. *See also* Products: capital. *See* Capital goods; consumption. *See* Consumption goods; consumption, tradeoff between capital goods and, 38–39; credence, 670, 714; defined, 28; deflation and, 170; demerit, 116; durable consumer, 191; economic, 28–29; experience, 670; final, final services and, 186; foreign, substitution of, 245–246; government, 124; inferior, 58; inflation rate for, 170; intangible, 29. *See also* Services; merit, 115–116; nondurable consumer, 191; non-union-made, 768–769; normal, 58; political, 124; private, 113–114; public. *See* Public goods; related, prices of, demand shifts and, 59–60; search, 670; secondhand, 189; and services, all, demand for, demand for single good or service versus, 246; single supplier of, 634. *See also* Monopolist(s); two, choice between, 33–34; union-made, 768

Gould, David, 845
Government(s): civic centers funded by, 116; correction of negative externalities and, 111–112; correction of positive externalities and, 112; expenditures of. *See* Government spending; federal. *See* Federal government; financing of, spending more than tax collections and, 344, 346; financing of production by, 112; force used by, 124; functions of. *See* Government functions; funding, 134–158; goods of, at zero price, 124; individuals working for, similarities of, to individuals working in private sector, 123–124; inefficiencies in, economic growth and, 483–484; licenses and. *See* License(s); local. *See* Local government(s); paying for. *See* Tax, taxation; price controls imposed by, 90–91; public goods provided by, 113–115; quantity restrictions imposed by, 97–98; regulation by. *See* Government regulation; rents controlled by, 92–93; restrictions of, barriers to entry and, 636–638; spending by. *See* Government spending; state. *See* State government(s); United States. *See* Federal government
Government budget constraint, 135
Government budget surplus, 343
Government functions: economic, 111–115; political, 115–117
Government regulation: antitrust. *See* Antitrust laws; barriers to entry and, 637–638; benefits of, 717–718; cost-of-service, 710, 711; costs of, 715–718; drugs and, 116; economic, 706–707, 715; economic growth reduced by, 242; explaining regulators' behavior and, 716–717; of natural monopolies, 706, 707, 709–712; negative externalities and, 112; of nonmonopolistic industries, 706, 707, 713–715; positive externalities and, 112; rate-of-return, 707, 710, 711; results of, 716; social, 706, 708, 715
Government spending: changes in, fiscal policy and, 319–320, 339–340; direct expenditure offsets and, 325–326; entitlements and. *See* Entitlements; GDP calculation and, 192; Keynesian equilibrium and, 302; per capita, per day, 319; reducing, elimination of federal budget deficit and, 356–358; transfer programs and, 117–122, 147
Government transfer payments, 117, 147, 189; transmitted electronically, 386
Gramm-Leach-Bliley Act (1999), 380
Grant, Ulysses, 827
Graph(s): constructing, 18–19; of numbers in a table, 19–20; reading and working with, 17–23; working with and reading, 17–23
Graphical analysis, 31, 502–504
Great Britain. *See also* United Kingdom: labor movement in, 760; life insurance can be sold by banks in, 380
Great Depression, 147, 175, 176, 240, 269; agricultural price supports and, 94; bank failures during, 410–411; fiscal policy during, 330; government spending during, 118; Keynes' analysis of, 268, 269, 319; labor movement and, 760; private domestic investment and, 295; unemployment during, 115, 161
Great Moderation, 449, 471–472
Greece: ancient, fractional reserve banking and, 394; EU's Stability and Growth Pact and, 359–360

Greyhound, 606
Gross domestic income (GDI), 195
Gross domestic product (GDP), 187–188; China's per capita, 203; comparison of, throughout the world, 202–204; components of, 193, 195–196, 199; correcting, for price changes, 200–201; defined, 187; exclusions from, 189; final output and, 188–189; historical picture of, 192–193; limitations of, 190; measuring. *See* Expenditure approach; Income approach; nominal, 201, 202; public debt as percentage of, 348; real. *See* Real GDP; for the world, 196
Gross private domestic investment, 191
Gross public debt, 347

H

Hachette Book Group, 599
Hair dye, 59
Haiti: brain drain from, 233; registering new company in, 478
Handling charges, 561
Harrison, George, 570
Hausman, Jerry, 179
HDTV market, switching costs in, 695
Health care, 799–806; age-health care expenditure equation and, 800–801; cost of, 4; demand for, 802; medical savings accounts (MSAs) and, 805, 806; national health insurance and, 804; new technologies and, 801; publicly subsidized, 118–121. *See also* Medicaid; Medicare; situation in the United States regarding, 800–804; third-party financing and, 801–803
Hedge, 877
Heffetz, Ori, 12
Helpman, Elhanan, 223
Hewlett-Packard Corporation, 569–570; computer printers and, 686; diseconomies of scale and, 596
High-occupancy-vehicle (HOV) lanes, 716
Hilton, Paris, 1
Hindi language, among world's ten most-used, 699, 700
Hiring, general rule for, 735–737
Hispanics, education and, 792
Hobijn, Bart, 174
Holographic camera, 580–581
Homo sapiens, 26, 44–45
Hong Kong: birthrate in, 230; companies in U.S. outsource labor services to, 745; economic growth has accompanied population growth in, 480
Horizontal merger, 685
Horses, wild, 813, 827–828
Hospitals, moral hazard and, 803
Household production, 189
Housing: supply of, existing, effects of rent controls on, 92; use of, current, rationing, 92
HOV (high-occupancy-vehicle) lanes, 716
Human capital: defined, 28; importance of, 225–226; investment in, 791; spending on, 289–290
Hungary, increased value of currency in, 868
Hurricane Katrina, 530

I

Ideas: importance of, 224–225; transmission of, 842
Identity: accounting. *See* Accounting identity(ies); equation of exchange as, 432
IMF. *See* International Monetary Fund

Immigration: economic growth and, 226–227, 233–234; German minimum wage and, 97; income-mobility data and, 808; Social Security taxes and, 150
Imperfect substitutes, 642
Implicit collusion, 693–694
Implicit costs, 558
Implicit rental value, 191
Import(s): defined, 192; merchandise trade, 861; relationship between exports and, 842–843; relationship of, with exports, 192; service, 862
Import quota, 98
Incentive structure, 123–124
Incentives: defined, 2; responding to, 5
Income(s), 784–788; circular flow of, 185, 186; demand shifts and, 58; differences in, determinants of, 788–793; distribution of. *See* Income distribution; flow of, 191; higher, conspicuous consumption and, 12–13; in kind, 785; lifetime, 786; major income maintenance programs to help the poor and, 797–799; money, 785, 786; national. *See* National income; personal. *See* Personal income; of proprietors, 195; real disposable, 288, 310; redistribution of, 116–117; relating to saving and consumption, 289; total. *See* Total income; transfer payments as, 796–797; world, comparisons of, 203
Income approach: defined, 191; deriving GDP by, 195–196; illustrated, 197
Income distribution: defined, 784; desired, theories of, 793–794; measuring, 784–786; mobility within, 783, 807–808; in the United States, 786–787
Income elasticity of demand, 540–541
Income tax: capital gains and, 139; federal. *See* Federal income tax
Income velocity of money (V), 432
Increased division of tasks, 595
Increasing-cost industry, 622, 623
Independent variable, 17
India: companies in U.S. outsource labor services to, 732, 743, 744–745, 746, 747, 753–754; computer programmers from, working aboard cruise ship off California coast, 747; economic growth has accompanied population growth in, 480; economy of, outsourcing's effects on, 746; environmental quality of life and, 190; GDP of, 190, 215; labor services outsourced to other countries by, 753–754; measured full employment promoted in, 167; shortage of mining workers for manufacturing industries in, 741; sugar produced in, 95; United Kingdom's traditional ties with, 753
Indifference curve(s), 520; defined, 521; illustrated, 521, 522; properties of, 521–522; set of, illustrated, 524
Indifference map, 523–524
Indirect business taxes, 195–196
Indirect financing, direct financing versus, 375
Individual demand curve, 54, 55–57
Individual Retirement Accounts, 414
Indonesia: hit by tsunami in 2004, 239, 254–255; IMF's dealing with crisis in, 489; real GDP growth not affected by tsunami, 254–255; standard of living in, 202; wages in, boosted by tsunami relief efforts, 742
Industrial unions, 760–761
Industry(ies): airline. *See* Airline(s); automobile. *See* Automobile industry; breakfast food, 694; computer printer, 686; concentration ratio for,

685–686; constant-cost, 622–623; decreasing-cost, 622, 623; deterring entry into, 694–695; diamond, 652; digital photo printing, 605, 627–628; discount-store, 625; economic development and, 230; firms in, number of, as determinant of supply, 68; glass, 845; increasing-cost, 622, 623; infant, 843–844; long-run situation in, exit and entry of firms and, 620–623; manufacturing, shortage of mining workers for, 741; model train, 661, 676–677; monopolizing, effects of, 650; music download, 696; nonmonopolistic. *See* Nonmonopolistic industries; online auction, 697; overnight delivery, 684; perfectly competitive, supply curve for, 616–618; portable digit music player, 696; regulation of, forms of, 706–708; telecommunications, 697, 705, 711, 712, 725, 726; transistor, 623; trucking, 707
Industry concentration: measuring, 685–686; network effects and, 697
Industry concentration ratio, 685–686
Industry supply curve(s): defined, 617; derivation of, illustrated, 618; factors that influence, 618; long-run, 621–623; short-run, 617–618
Inefficient point, 35
Inelastic demand, 531, 535; perfectly, 531
Inelastic supply, 542
Infant industry argument, 843–844
Inferior goods, 58
Inflation: anticipated, unanticipated inflation versus, 172–173; causes of, 250–252; changing, business fluctuations and, 174–176; cost-push, 276; defined, 168; deflation and, 167–172; demand-pull, 276; demand-side, 251–252; effects of, 173; higher, effects of, on inflation expectations, 457; inequality of, in U.S., 174; interest rates and, 172–173; monetary policy and, 432–433; persistent, 250–251; protecting against, 173; purchasing power of money and, 168; rate of. *See* Inflation rate(s); real GDP and, affected by weaker dollar, 278–279; repricing cost of, 173; resource cost of, 173; secular, 250; supply-side, 250–251; trade-off between unemployment and, 455. *See also* Phillips curve; unanticipated, anticipated inflation versus, 172–173; in U.S. history, 171; variations in, short-run, 276–279
Inflation expectations, 459
"Inflation inequality," 174
Inflation rate(s): for goods, 170; measuring, 168–172; money supply growth versus, 394; for services, 170; in U.S., 250
Inflation targeting, 450
Inflation-adjusted return, 147–148
Inflationary gap, 275; changes in government spending and, 320; defined, 319
Inflationary premium, 172–173
Information: asymmetric. *See* Asymmetric information; incomplete, international financial crises and, 486; inside, 568–569
Information products: defined, 671; monopolistic competition and, 671–675; special cost characteristics of, 671–673
Information technology (IT): investment in, lag in, 297; new, investment in, 288
Informational advertising, 670
Infosys Technologies, Ltd., 753
Ingraham, Allan, 540
Inheritance, 791
Innovation, 223–224

Input(s): demand elasticity for, 739; relationship between output and, 580–581; used to produce product, cost of, as determinant of supply, 67; variable, 579
An Inquiry into the Nature and Causes of the Wealth of Nations (Smith), 3–4, 41–42
Inside information, 568–569
Institute for International Economics, 845
Institute for Management Development, 843
Insurers use technology to defend against accident liability and set premiums, 9
Intangible goods, 29. *See also* Services
Intel Corporation, stock of, Nasdaq is home to, 567
Intellectual property, 842
Intellifit, 511
Interactive marketing, 669
Interest, 561–565; allocative role of, 563; as component of GDP, 195; compounding, 217–218; credit and, 561–562; defined, 561; self-. *See* Self-interest; zero, for life of loan, 562
Interest rate(s): changes in, as market determinant of exchange rates, 873; equilibrium, 264; Fed's monetary policy target choice and, 435–436; induced, 323; inflation and, 172–173; money transmission mechanism based on, 434–435; nominal, 562; nominal. *See* Nominal rate of interest; present value and, 563–565; price of existing bonds and, 426; real. *See* Real rate of interest
Interest rate effect, 245
Internal costs, 814
Internal Revenue Service (IRS), 355; force used by, 124
International Brotherhood of Teamsters, 763, 777, 778
International Business Machines, 753
International competitiveness, 843
International financial crisis, 486
International financial diversification, 378
International Monetary Fund (IMF), 203, 487, 874; asymmetric information and, 489–490; Bretton Woods and, 875; creation of, 875; defined, 488; effectiveness of, 489–491, 493, 494; elimination and, 491; long-term development lending and, 490; official reserve account transactions and, 864; quota subscriptions with, 488; views on appropriate role for, 491
International trade: comparative advantage and, 42–43, 837; emerging arguments against, 845; free, arguments against, 843–845; gains from, 839–840; growth of, illustrated, 835; international competitiveness and, 843; production without, 837–838; reasons for, 834–842; transmission of ideas and, 842; ways to restrict, 845–848; worldwide importance of, 834
International trade flows, 841
Internet: online auction industry and, 697; orders on, companies charged by FTC with late deliveries of, 714–715; pharmaceuticals imported from Canada via, 834; remanufactured printer ink cartridges for sale on, 607; shopping for auto parts on, 84; taxes and, 143; telecommunications services via, 711, 712, 726
Internet Explorer, 723–724
Internet telephony, considering investment in, 309
Inventory investment, 191–192, 289
Inverse relationship, 17, 18

Investment: classical model and, 264, 265; consumption and, 299–300; defined, 191, 289; determinants of, 295–297; firm's decision to make, 323–324; fixed, 191–192, 289; foreign direct, 484–485; gross private, 191; in human capital, 791; international, obstacles to, 485–486; in Internet telephony, 309; inventory, 191–192, 289; net, 194; in new information technologies, 288; planned. *See* Planned investment; portfolio, 484–485; private, in developing nations, 484–485; saving and, 264, 265; spending on human capital and, 289–290
Investment companies, 376
Investment function: consumption function and, 299–300; planned, 295–296; shift in, cause of, 296–297
iPod, 696
Iran, earthquakes and, 277
Ireland: cellphone duopoly in, 711; per capita spending on health care in, 800; using windmills to generate electricity in, 822–823
IRS. *See* Internal Revenue Service
IT. *See* Information technology(ies)
Italy: banking in, 380; effluent-fee system to reduce restaurant smoking and, 111–112; IEU's Stability and Growth Pact and, 359–360; per capita real GDP of, 214; retirement age in, 150; shoe manufacturing in, 844
ITT Industries, 100
iTunes, 696

J

J. P. Morgan Chase, 376, 562, 694
Jackson, "Shoeless" Joe, 76
Jamaica, brain drain from, 233
Japan: banking in, 380; comparative advantage in electronics lost to U.S., 841; currency of. *See* Japanese yen; deflation is norm in, 249; discount-store industry in, 625; economic development in, 231; foreign direct investment to, 486; importation by, of U.S.-made automobile parts, 846; investment and, 265; life insurance companies can break contracts in, 385; manufacturing employment in, 231; manufacturing innovation in, 842; megabanks in, 379; per capita spending on health care in, 800; productive efficiency in, 843; real GDP in, 249; restriction on import of automobiles from, 845, 846; saving in, 220, 265; tariff on a laptops imported from, 847, 848; tax policies of, 318, 332–333; union membership as share of total employment in, 761, 762; U.S. public debt held by, 350
Japanese yen: floating against dollar, 875; as "vehicle currency," 881
JetBlue Airways, 745
Job leaver, 162
Job loser, 162
Job sharing, 743
Jobs, domestic, protecting, 844–845
Johnson, Lyndon B., 799
Johnson, Velma, 827
Jurisdictional dispute, 761
Just a Buck, 513

K

Katz, Lawrence, 451
KB Toys, 714–715
Kellogg, 694

Kenya: converting dollars to vouchers for use in, 368; ready-to-eat vegetables imported from, by Europe, 836; trying to start a business in, 492
"Key money," 93
Keynes, John Maynard, 262, 268–269, 288, 290, 319, 465–466
Keynesian cross, 317
Keynesian equilibrium, 301–304
Keynesian model, 270–271; Keynesian short-run aggregate supply curve and, 268–270; simplifying assumptions in, 288–289
Keynesian short-run aggregate supply curve, 268–270
Kinked demand curve: criticisms of, 693; illustrated, 691; nature of, 690–691; price rigidity and, 690–693
Kinko's, digital photo printing kiosks opened by, 627
Kiosk, 627
Kmart, CPI calculations and, 178–179
Knowledge: importance of, 224–225; innovation and, 223–224
Kremer, Michael, 226, 227
Kristine Travel, 606
Kroger, store closing when Wal-Mart supercenter opens nearby, 178
Kyoto Protocol, 819, 820

L

Labor. *See also* Union(s): defined, 28; derived demand for, 736–737; division of, 41–42; economic growth and, 478–481; economic rent and, 553–554; general rule for hiring and, 735–737; marginal product of, 583; market demand for. *See* Market demand for labor; outsourcing of. *See* Outsourcing; owner-provided, opportunity cost of, 559; supply of, determinants of, 743
Labor force, 160–161; defined, 160; employment, unemployment and, 161, 162; labor force participation rate and, 163–164
Labor force participation rate, 163–164
Labor Management Relations Act (Taft-Hartley Act)(1947), 761
Labor market: equilibrium in, 265–266; perfectly competitive, wage determination in, 740–743; price floors in, 96–97; price taker in, 733; in U.S., outsourcing's effects on, 744–745
Labor market equilibrium, 740
Labor productivity, 219–220
Labor unions. *See* Union(s)
Laborers International Union of North America, 763, 777, 778
Laffer, Arthur, 326
Laffer Curve, 326–327
Lagakos, David, 174
Lajoie, Lawrence "Nap," 75, 76
Lamb industry in United States, 541
Land, 27, 28
Land rent, 553
Landfills, 825
Language(s): network effects and, 699; in use today, 682, 699, 700
Larger scale, 376
Lasermonk.com, 607
Latvia, proportional income taxation in, 137
Law(s): "antigouging," 91; antitrust. *See* Antitrust laws; of demand, 52–54, 501, 510; of diminishing marginal product, 583–584; "elder," 802; of increasing relative cost, 35–37;

liability, 714–715; right-to-work, 761; rule of, per capita real GDP and, 481; Say's, 262–263; of substitution, 523; of supply, 62–69; tariff, current, 847–848
LCDs (liquid crystal displays), prices of, 67
Leading indicators, 176
Leakages, 406
Learning curve, 790
Least-cost combination of resources, 751
Legal reserves, 395
Legal system, providing, as function of government, 113
Lemons problem, 714, 715
Lender of last resort, 384
Lennon, John, 570
Levin, Andrew, 457
Lewis, John L., 761
Lexmark, 686
Liability(ies): defined, 376; financial institution, 376–377; limited, 557–558; unlimited, 557
Liability laws, 714–715
License(s): barriers to entry and, 636–637; consumer protection and, 714–715
Life-Like Products, 676
Lifetime income, 786
Limited liability, 557–558
Limit-pricing model, 694
Linux, 297
Lionel, 676
Liquidity, 368–369
Liquidity approach. *See also* M2: defined, 371; to measuring money, 373–374
Lithuania, proportional income taxation in, 137
Loan: length of, 561; life of, no interest for, 562; nonpayment of, risk of, 561–562
Local government(s): spending by, 117; tax receipts of, sources of, 138
Logging, 752
London Bullion Market Association, 369
Long run: defined, 579; short run versus, 579–580; zero economic profits and, 667
Long-run aggregate supply: decline in, 250; economic growth and, 241–242; short-run aggregate supply and, shifts in, 272
Long-run aggregate supply curve, 240–242
Long-run average cost curve(s), 593–596, 673; defined, 594; illustrated, 593; preferable plant size and, 593–594; reason behind U shape of, 594–596
Long-run equilibrium, 624, 666, 667, 674–675; price level and, 247–249
Long-run industry supply curve, 621–623
Lopez, Jennifer, 59
Lorenz, Max Otto, 784
Lorenz curve, 808; criticisms of, 784–786, 787; defined, 784; illustrated, 785
Loss(es): deadweight, 660; generated by monopoly, 660; short-run, 613–614
Lucas, Robert, 458
Lucky Star Lines, 606
Lump-sum tax, 302
Luxembourg: banking in, 380; per capita real GDP of, 214; per capita spending on health care in, 800

M

M1: composition of, 371; transactions approach to measuring money and, 371–373
M2: composition of, 371; liquidity approach to measuring money and, 373–374

Macroeconomics, 3
Maharishi Mahesh Yogi, 366
Majority rule, 124
Malaria, battle against, tariffs and, 851
Malawi, sugar produced in, 95
Malaysia: currency exchange rate maintenance in, 876; currency swaps in, 877; drug-labeling monopoly in, 637; hit by tsunami in 2004, 239, 254–255; IMF's dealing with crisis in, 489; slight falloff in real GDP growth following tsunami, 254, 255
Malthus, Thomas Robert, 230, 262
Mama Mike's, 368
Management costs, 376
Mantle, Mickey, 76
Manufacturing employment, 231
Manufacturing industries, shortage of mining workers for, 741
Marginal analysis: applying to utility, 502; using to determine profit-maximizing rate of production, 610–611
Marginal cost(s), 587–588; of air transport, reducing, 588; of cleaning up nuclear waste, 826; defined, 587; equal to marginal revenue, 611, 643; marginal physical product and, 590, 592; relationship between average costs and, 588–589
Marginal cost pricing: defined, 624–625; impracticality of, 709, 710; information products and, 673, 674; perfect competition and, 624–625
Marginal factor cost (MFC): defined, 735; monopsony and, 771–773
Marginal physical product. *See also* Marginal product: defined, 581; of labor, 733–735; marginal cost and, 590, 592
Marginal product: diminishing. *See* Diminishing marginal product; of labor, 583; production function and, illustrated, 582; specialization and, 583
Marginal productivity: determinants of, 790–791; as factor affecting income differences, 790–791
Marginal propensity to consume (MPC), 293–294
Marginal propensity to save (MPS), 293–294
Marginal rate of substitution, 523
Marginal revenue, 610–611; defined, 610; equal to marginal cost, 611, 643; for the monopolist, 639–641; for the perfect competitor, 639
Marginal revenue product (MRP), 734, 735–736, 748–749, 750
Marginal revenue product (MRP) curve, 736
Marginal tax rate(s): defined, 136; federal, 139; raising, result of, 355–356
Marginal utility(ies), 504; avoiding hassles that reduce, 514; defined, 502; diminishing, 505–506; negative, 504; relative, weighing, 514; total utility and diamond-water paradox and, 511–512
Market(s): black. *See* Black market; credit, equilibrium in, 264; defined, 52; efficient, theory of, 567–568; exchange and, 83; factor, 186–187; federal funds, 407; foreign exchange, 858, 866, 880–881; geographic, 722; labor. *See* Labor market; money, international, globalization of, 431; perfectly competitive. *See* Perfect competition; product. *See* Product market; relevant, 722, 725–726; securities, 707; size of, 61; for stocks and bonds, 567–570
Market clearing price, 71, 75–76, 619
Market decision making: collective decision making and, differences between, 124; public-

sector decision making and, similarities in, 123–124
Market demand: defined, 55; for labor. *See* Market demand for labor
Market demand curve, 55–57
Market demand for labor, 738–739; shifts in, 741–743
Market demand schedule, 57
Market failure, 108, 626, 713
Market feedback, network effects and, 696–697, 699–700
Market opportunities, 524
Market power, 686
Market price, taxes and, 146
Market share test, 722
Market signals, 621
Market structures, comparing, 697–698
Market supply curve, 63–65; taxes and, 145–146
Market system, 83. *See also* Price system
Market Velocity, 84
Marx, Karl, 793
Mass marketing, 669
Mass poverty, 794
Mays, Willie, 75
McDonald's, 202; credit and debit card payments preferred by, 372–373; long run and, 579
McGwire, Mark, 76
Medicaid, 120; as an entitlement, 356–357; coverage of psychological services and, 776; growth of, "elder law" and, 802; long-term health care provided by, 801; as third-party health care provider, 801, 803; as transfer payments, 386; as transfers in kind, 117
Medical savings accounts (MSAs), 805, 806
Medicare, 118–121; as an entitlement, 356–357; bankruptcy and, 120–121; economics of, 119; government spending on, 118, 147, 804; incentives and, 119–120; medical savings accounts (MSAs) and, 805; prescription drug assistance and, 120, 804; taxes for, 118, 120–121, 141; as third-party health care provider, 801, 803; as transfer payments, 386; as transfers in kind, 117, 147
Mediharta, 637
Megabanks, 379
Menu cost of inflation, 173
Merchandise trade transactions, 861
Mercosur, 850
Merger(s): government regulations and, 705, 721, 725–726; horizontal, 685; oligopoly by, 685; vertical, 685
Merit goods, 115–116
Merit standard, 793
MES (minimum efficient scale), 596–598
Mesopotamia, money in, 394
Mexico: Andean Community and, 852, 853; birthrate in, 230; IMF's dealing with crisis in, 489
Meyer, Bruce, 451
Microeconomics, 3
Microsoft Corporation, 841; dividend payment from boosts U.S. personal income growth, 198; incentive structure and, 123; loans to, 412; new idea discovery at, 225; paid out huge dividend, 563; software produced by, 297; stock of, Nasdaq is home to, 567; violation of antitrust law by, 720, 723–724
Microsoft Word, 723
Middle class, 788
Middlemen, role of, 84
Mill, John Stuart, 262

Minimum cost points, 589
Minimum efficient scale (MES), 596–598
Minimum wage: defined, 96; economic effects of, 96–97; in Germany, 97; laws setting, effect of, on employment, 774; monopsony's response to, 774; in United States, 83, 96
mm02, 711
MMDAs (money market deposit accounts), 373
Model(s). *See also* Theory(ies): assumptions and, 7–8; of behavior, thought processes versus, 8–9; of consumer optimum, 508; defined, 7; limit-pricing, 694; profit-maximization, 608; realism and, 7; usefulness of, deciding on, 8
Model train producers, 661, 676–677
Monetary policy: in action, 434–435; contractionary. *See* Monetary policy, contractionary; expansionary. *See* Monetary policy, expansionary; inflation and, 432–433; open economy transmission of, 430–431; tools of, 425–427; transmission mechanism of, 434–435
Monetary policy, contractionary: consequences of, 453–454; effects of, 428–429, 430–431
Monetary policy, expansionary: effects of, 428, 429, 431; impact of, 453
Monetary shock, real shock versus, 464
Monetary standards, 369–370
Money(s): acceptability of, 370; banking and, 394; defined, 366, 370–374; demand for, 423–424, 439; e-, 369; expansion of, by banking system, 400–404; functions of, 366–368; holding, 423; income velocity of (V), 432; "key," 93; liquidity and, 368–369; measuring. *See* Money, measuring; monetary standards and, 369–370; near, 373; prices and. *See* Money and prices; purchasing power of. *See* Purchasing power; special aspects of, reasons for, 423–425; types of, 366
Money, measuring: liquidity approach to, 373–374. *See also* M2; transactions approach to, 371–373. *See also* M1
Money and prices, 393–394; quantity theory of, 432
Money balances, 423
Money illusion, 263
Money income, 785, 786
Money market deposit accounts (MMDAs), 373
Money market mutual funds, 374
Money markets, international, globalization of, 431
Money multiplier(s), 405–410; defined, 405; digital cash and, 416–417; forces that reduce, 406; potential, 406; real-world, 406
Money price, 53
Money supply: changes in. *See* Money supply, changes in; defined, 370; Fed's monetary policy target choice, 435–436; growth of, inflation rate versus, 394; increase in, effects of, 428–430; regulation of, 384
Money supply, changes in: Fed's purchase of government securities and, 400–404; links with other economic variables and, 393–394; single bank's increase in reserves and, 398; ways in which Fed causes, 406–408
Monopolist(s). *See also* Monopoly(ies): defined, 634; demand curves for, 639–641, 748–749; marginal revenue for, 639–641, 749, 750; number of workers hired by, 749; pure. *See* Pure monopolist
Monopolistic competition, 661–681; compared with other market structures, 697–698; defined, 662; information products and, 671–675; long-

run equilibrium with, 666, 667; number of firms in, 662–663; perfect competition compared with, 667–668; price and output and, 665–667; short-run equilibrium with, 666
Monopolization, 720, 721
Monopoly(ies), 633–660. *See also* Monopolist(s); bilateral, 775; calculating profits for, 646–648; consumer surplus from, 658–659; defined, 113; elasticity and, 641–642; losses from, 660; natural, 635–636; perfect competition compared with, 651; perfect competition versus, 640; in product market, 743–750; social cost of, 650–651, 660
Monopoly power, 722, 724
Monopsonist, 771
Monopsonistic exploitation, 774
Monopsony, 771–775; employment and wages under, 773–775
Moral hazard: countering, 805; defined, 376; in deposit insurance, 414; financing global growth and, 485; health care and, 803, 805
Morocco, annual GDP of, 205
MPC (marginal propensity to consume), 293–294
MPS (marginal propensity to save), 293–294
MSAs (medical savings accounts), 805, 806
MTH Electric Trains, 676
Multiplier: balanced-budget, 340; defined, 304–306; graphing, 317; Keynesian cross and, 317; money. *See* Money multiplier(s); multiplier effect and, 304–305; multiplier formula and, 305–306; multiplier process and, 305; significance of, 306
Mushroom harvesting, 67
Music download industry, 696
Mutual institutions, 375

N

NAFTA (North American Free Trade Agreement), 850
NAIRU (nonaccelerating inflation rate of unemployment), 455–456
Namibia, diamond industry in, 652
Nanotechnology, 579
NASA (National Aeronautics and Space Administration), 125
Nascar, 665
Nasdaq (National Association of Securities Dealers Automated Quotations), 567
Natalucci, Fabio, 457
National Aeronautics and Space Administration (NASA), 125
National Association of Securities Dealers Automated Quotations (Nasdaq), 567
National Credit Union Administration, 384, 707
National Credit Union Share Insurance Fund (NCUSIF), 411, 412
National debt. *See* Public debt
National Governors Association, 143
National Highway Transportation Safety Administration (NHTSA), 724
National income (NI): defined, 198; percentage of, spent on health care, 800; total compensation received by workers as percentage of, 787
National income accounting, 187–190; components of, 198–199; defined, 185
National Industrial Recovery Act (1933), 760
National Labor Relations Act (NLRA)(Wagner Act)(1935), 760
National Monetary Commission, 381
National Treasury Employees Union (NTEU), 766

National Wildlife Federation, 825
NATO (North Atlantic Treaty Organization), 114
Natural gas, 227
Natural monopoly(ies): cost curves that might lead to, 636; defined, 635; economies of scale and, 635–636; future of, 710–712; regulation of, 706, 707, 709–712; unregulated, 709–710
Natural rate of unemployment, 166–167; defined, 166, 451; departures from, 452–454; in United States, 167, 451–452
Natural resources, 825–826
NCUSIF (National Credit Union Share Insurance Fund), 411, 412
NDP. *See* Net domestic product
Neanderthals, 26, 44–45
Near moneys, 373
Needs, wants versus, 29
Negative externalities, 111–112
Negative market feedback, 697, 699–700
Negative rate of return, 148, 150
Negative-sum game, 688
Net domestic product (NDP): defined, 194; depreciation and, 193
Net exports, 192; Keynesian equilibrium and, 302–303
Net investment, 194
Net public debt, 347; accumulation of, 347–348; defined, 347
Net worth, 396
Net2Phone, 712
NetBank, 403
the Netherlands: coffee cultivated in colonies of, 842; EU's Stability and Growth Pact and, 359–360; marginal cost of pollution abatement in, 819
Network effects: industry concentration and, 697; languages and, 699; market feedback and, 696–697, 699–700
Neuroeconomics, 5
Neutral federal funds rate, 440–441
New entrant, 162
New growth theory, 221–226
New Keynesian inflation dynamics, 467–468
New Keynesians: short-run aggregate supply curve and, 270; small menu costs and sticky prices and, 466
New York Bond Exchange, 567
New York Stock Exchange (NYSE)(Big Board), 368; as most prestigious stock market, 567; program trading on, 568; seat on, value of, 552, 571–572
New Zealand, central bank targets inflation rate in, 450
NHTSA (National Highway Transportation Safety Administration), 724
NI. *See* National income
Niger, negative relationship between population growth and economic growth in, 480
Nigeria: natural gas exported by, 277–278; recording a sale of land in, 478
Nixon, Richard, 875
NLRA (National Labor Relations Act)(Wagner Act)(1935), 760
Nominal GDP, 201, 202
Nominal rate of interest, 562; defined, 172; real rate of interest versus, 172–173
Nominal values, 368; defined, 199; distinguishing between real values and, 199–202; real values versus, 168
Nonaccelerating inflation rate of unemployment (NAIRU), 455–456

Noncontrollable expenditures, 356. *See also* Entitlements
Noncooperative game(s): defined, 687; strategies in, 688
Nondurable consumer goods, 191
Nonincome expense items, 196
Nonmarket production, 190
Nonmonopolistic industries, regulation of, 706, 707, 713–715
Nonprofit organizations, 553
Non-union-made goods, 768–769
NORAD (North American Aerospace Defense) System, 114–115
Normal goods, 58
Normative analysis, 10, 11
Normative economics, 844; defined, 10; positive economics versus, 10–11
North American Aerospace Defense (NORAD) System, 114–115
North American Free Trade Agreement (NAFTA), 850
North Atlantic Treaty Organization (NATO), 114
Northwest Airlines, 698, 745
Norway, workers from, employed in India, 753
NTEU (National Treasury Employees Union), 766
Nuclear power, as energy source, 742
Nuclear waste, reducing marginal cost of cleaning up, 826
Number line(s): defined, 18; horizontal, combining vertical number lines and, 18–19; scaling, 18; vertical, combining horizontal number lines and, 18–19
NYSE. *See* New York Stock Exchange

O

OASDI (old-age, survivors', and disability insurance), 797–798. *See also* Social Security
Occupational Safety and Health Administration (OSHA), 708
OECD (Organization for Economic Cooperation and Development), 544
Office of Management and Budget (OMB), 353, 355, 718
Office of the Comptroller of the Currency, 707
Office of Thrift Supervision, 384, 707
Official reserve account transactions, 864–865
Old-age, survivors', and disability insurance (OASDI), 797–798. *See also* Social Security
Oligopoly, 683–697, 684–685; characteristics of, 683–684; compared with other market structures, 697–698; defined, 683; efficiency, resource allocation and, 686; reason for, 684–685
OMB (Office of Management and Budget), 353, 355, 718
Online auction industry, 697
OPEC (Organization of Petroleum Exporting Countries), 464, 842–843
Open economy: aggregate demand and supply in, 277–279; comparative advantage and, 833–857; economic growth and, 223; federal budget deficits in, 351–352
Open economy effect, 245–246
Open market operations, 399, 425–426, 437–438, 439, 440–441
Operating budget, 353
Opportunistic behavior, 689–690
Opportunity cost: of capital, 558–559; of declaring a wrecked car a "total loss," 43; defined, 30; government regulation and, 718; of owner-provided labor, 559; of payment from voluntary agreement, 821; of planned investment, 296; public-sector decision making and, 123; scarcity, choice and, 29–30; "submit order" button and, 30; of time stuck in traffic, 32
Opportunity cost principle, 558
Optimal quantity of pollution, 818, 819–820
Ordered set of points, 18
Organization for Economic Cooperation and Development (OECD), 544
Organization of Petroleum Exporting Countries (OPEC), 464, 842–843
Origin, 19
OSHA (Occupational Safety and Health Administration), 708
Output: determination of, using aggregate demand and aggregate supply, 270–271; domestic, 192; final, 188–189; for monopolistic competitor, 665–667; prices for, 645–646; rate of, profit-maximizing, 611; relationship between costs and, 591; relationship between inputs and, 580–581; total. *See* Total output
Outsourcing, 732, 743–748; defined, 743; wage and employment effects of, 743–745
Overdraft, avoiding, 5–6
Overemployment, 163
Overnight delivery industry, 684
Ownership, transfer of, 189

P

Paige, Leroy "Satchel," 76
Pakistan, economic growth has accompanied population growth in, 480
palmOne, 841
Panasonic, 841
Par value, 875
Parallel pricing, 693
Partner, 557
Partnership, 557
Passive (nondiscretionary) policymaking: active (discretionary) policymaking versus, 450–451, 469–470; defined, 450
Patents, 222–223, 637
Payment intermediaries, 377–378
PayPal, 372–373
PCE (Personal Consumption Expenditures) Index, 169, 170, 414
Peak, 174
Peanuts, 570
Pension fund companies, 376
Pension plans, private, 153–154
People's Bank of China, real interest rate and, 430
Pepsi-Cola, 664–665
Per capita real GDP, 201; economic growth and, 215; rate of saving and, 221; rule of law and, 481; in selected countries, 216
Perfect competition, 605–632; characteristics of, 606–607; compared with other market structures, 697–698; consumer surplus in, 659; defined, 606; marginal cost pricing and, 624–625; minimum average total cost and, 624; monopolistic competition compared with, 667–668; monopoly compared with, 651; monopoly versus, 640; price determination under, 619–620
Perfectly competitive firm: defined, 606; demand curve for, 607–608, 640; labor demand for, 733–737; long-run equilibrium of, 624; marginal revenue for, 639, 748; production of, 608–610; short-run supply curve of, 616–617

Perfectly elastic demand, 531
Perfectly elastic supply, 542
Perfectly inelastic demand, 531
Perfectly inelastic supply, 542
Persistent inflation, 250–251
Personal Consumption Expenditures (PCE) Index, 169, 170, 414
Personal identification number (PIN), 398
Personal income (PI): defined, 198; disposable (DPI), 198–199
Personal rate of discount, 565
Personal saving rate, 310
Persuasive advertising, 670
Peru: Andean Community and, 852, 853; potato native to, 842
Peter Pan, 606
Phelps, E. S., 458
Phillips, A. W., 455
Phillips curve, 454–458; defined, 455; illustrated, 455; shift in, illustrated, 456; theory versus data and, illustrated, 459; U.S. experience with, 458
Physical capital, 28
Physical force, rationing and, 88
Physicians, moral hazard and, 803
PI. *See* Personal income
Piger, Jeremy, 457
Pigou, A. C., 262
PIN (personal identification number), 398
Pioneer, 841
Plane, 18
Planned consumption, determinants of, 290–295
Planned investment, actual versus, planned versus actual saving and, 300–301
Planned saving: actual versus, planned versus actual investment and, 300–301; determinants of, 290–295
Planning curve, 593, 594
Planning horizon, 593
Plant size: defined, 579; preferable, long-run average cost curves and, 593–594; reasons for diseconomies of scale and, 596
Point(s): minimum cost, 589; of saturation, 583–584
Poland, increased value of currency in, 868
Policy irrelevance proposition: defined, 461; rational expectations and, 458–463
Political freedom, 480–481
Political goods, 124
Political power, rationing and, 88
Pollution, 818–820; alternatives to, 822; costs of, 815; defined, 818; marginal benefit of abatement of, 818; marginal cost of abatement of, 819; optimal quantity of, 818, 819–820; polluters' choices and, 816; uniform tax and, 816–817
Population: economic growth and, 226–227, 478–480; educated, economic development and, 231; growth of, economic development and, 228–230; world, expected growth in, 228–229
Populism, 248–249
Portable digit music player industry, 696
Portfolio investment, 484–485
Portugal: banking in, 380; EU's Stability and Growth Pact and, 359–360
Positive analysis, 10
Positive economics: defined, 10; normative economics versus, 10–11
Positive externalities: correction of, 112; government regulation and, 112; R&D and, 222–223

Positive market feedback, 696, 699–700
Positive-sum game, 688
Potential money multiplier, 406
Poverty, 794–799; absolute, 796; attacks on, 797–799; defined, 796; major income maintenance programs to help the poor, 797–799; mass, 794; no apparent reduction in, 799; relative, 796; in the United States, 795–796; War on, 799; world, 228
Poverty rate, 795–796; no apparent reduction in, 799
PPC. *See* Production possibilities curve
PPI (Producer Price Index), 169, 170, 200, 466, 467
Precautionary demand, 424
Preferences, demand shifts and, 58–59
Preferred stock, 566
Present value(s): defined, 564; discounted, 552, 564, 565; interest rates and, 563–565; for more distant periods, 564–565
President's Council of Economic Advisers (CEA), 167
Presley, Elvis, 570
Price(s): average total cost (ATC) equals, 673–674; of beer, 528; change in, consumer optimum and, 508–510; of cheese, jump in, 86; determination of, under perfect competition, 619–620; discrimination in. *See* Price discrimination; equilibrium, 71; expectations regarding, as determinant of supply, 68; flexibility in, 263; flexibility in. *See* Price flexibility; gasoline, increase in, 87; gouging and, 91; of illicit drugs, 527, 546–547; limit-pricing model and, 694; market. *See* Market price; market clearing, 71, 75–76, 619; money, 53; money and. *See* Money and prices; for monopolistic competitor, 665–667; monopolist's marginal revenue and, 640–641; monopoly, 645, 651; for output, 645–646; parallel, 693; per constant-quality unit, 53, 54; rationing function of, 88–89. *See also* Rationing; of related goods, demand shifts and, 59–60; relative, 53; rental, 92–93; short-run break-even, 614, 615, 616; short-run shutdown, 614–615; sticky, 466–468; stock, how to read in financial press, 569–570; support. *See* Price floor(s)
Price ceiling(s): black market and, 90–91; defined, 90
Price controls: defined, 90; government-imposed, 90–91
Price differentiation, 649
Price discrimination, 648–650; in college tuitions and, 649–650; defined, 648; necessary conditions for, 649; product versioning and, 723
Price elasticity(ies): of demand. *See* Price elasticity(ies) of demand; of participation, 546–547; ranges of, 530–531; of supply. *See* Price elasticity(ies) of supply
Price elasticity(ies) of demand, 528–530; calculating, 529–530; cross, 539–540; defined, 528; determinants of, 536–539; extreme, 531; for illicit drugs, 546–547; for inputs, determinants of, 739; real-world, 538–539; for selected goods, 530, 539, 545, 546–547; total revenues and, 532–536, 535, 545
Price elasticity(ies) of supply, 542–545; classifying, 542; defined, 542; length of time for adjustment and, 543; of oil supply, 544; short-run and long-run, illustrated, 545

Price flexibility: adjustment speed and, 88; wage flexibility and, 460–463
Price floor(s): in agriculture, 94–97; defined, 90; in labor market, 96–97
Price gouging, 91
Price index(es): changes in, correcting GDP for, 200–201; computing, 168–169; defined, 168; fixed-quantity, 169; real-world, 169–170; wholesale, 169
Price leadership, 693–694
Price level(s): assumption of fixed, 341; change in, and change in real autonomous spending affects real GDP, 306–307; classical theory, vertical aggregate supply and, 266–267; effects of economic growth on, 248–249; fall in, effect of, 246; fixed versus changing, in short run, 270–271; in long run, real GDP and, 239–260; long-run equilibrium and, 247–249; real GDP and, in a sticky-price economy, 467–468; rise in, effect of, 244–246
Price rigidity: kinked demand curve and, 690–693; theory of, 692
Price searcher, 643
Price support. *See* Price floor(s)
Price system: defined, 83; function of, 108
Price taker, 639, 643; defined, 606; in labor market, 733
Price war, 692, 694
Price-earnings ratio, 570
Pricing strategy, 689, 690
Prima facie presumption, 720
Principle: exclusion, 114; of rival consumption, 114; of substitution, 510
Prisoners' dilemma, 688–689
Private costs: defined, 814; social costs versus, 814–815
Private goods, 113–114
Private pension plans, 153–154
Private transfer payments, 189
Producer durables, 192
Producer Price Index (PPI), 169, 170, 200, 466, 467
Product, circular flow of, 186
Product bundling, 723–724
Product differentiation, 663–664, 677
Product market, 186; competition in, 733; monopoly in, 743–750; relevant, 722
Product packaging, 722–724
Product quality, 713–714
Product versioning, 723
Production: of capital goods, reason for, 38; cost of, 586; defined, 27, 580; element of, destruction as, in publishing, 599; equipment used in, improved, 595–596; factors of. *See* Factors of production; flow of, 187–188; government financing of, 112; increasing, profits to be made from, 639–640; nonmarket, 190; of perfectly competitive firm, 608–610; profit-maximizing rate of. *See* Profit-maximizing rate of production; specialization in, 838; without trade, 837–838
Production function: defined, 580; marginal product and, illustrated, 582; properties of, 580–581
Production possibilities curve (PPC), 240; assumptions underlying, 33–34; being off, 35; defined, 32; economic growth and, 37–38; straight-line, 32; trade-offs and, 31
Productive efficiency, 35, 843
Productivity: changes in, as market determinant of exchange rates, 873; as determinant of supply, 67; economic growth and, 219–220; increased,

specialization and, 39–42; labor, 219–220; marginal. *See* Marginal productivity; standard of, for income distribution, 793; unions and, 768, 770
Productivity standard, 793
Products. *See also* Goods: information. *See* Information products; visible, 12
Profit(s): accounting. *See* Accounting profit(s); to be made from increasing production, 639–640; business. *See* Accounting profit(s); as component of GDP, 195; economic. *See* Economic profit(s); explanation of, 185; higher, price discrimination and, 648–650; maximization of. *See* Profit maximization; monopoly, calculating, 646–648; no guarantee of, 647–648; short-run, 612–614; total, measurement of, 612
Profit maximization: factor utilization and, 751; as goal of firm, 560; graphical depiction of, 613; illustrated, 609, 645; marginal revenue-marginal cost approach to, 643; model of, 608; monopoly, cost and, 642–646; of price and output, cost changes and, 692; total revenues-total cost approach to, 643; when achieved, 611
Profit-maximizing rate of production: defined, 610; using marginal analysis to determine, 610–611
Program trading, 568
Progressive taxation, 136, 137, 139, 326
Promontory Interfinancial Network, 393
Property: common. *See* Common property; intellectual, 842
Property rights: changing, 822; defined, 109; economic development and, 231; economic growth and, 227; private, 821
Proportional rule, 124
Proportional taxation, 136, 137, 142
Proprietors' income, 195
Proprietorship, 556–557
Protectionism, limiting, economic development and, 231
Psychologist, union "affiliation" and, 776
Public choice, theory of, 122–125
Public debt: annual interest payments on, 348; burdens of, 348–350; crowding-out effect and, 349; defined, 344; government budget deficit and, 343–344; gross, 347; held outside United States, 350; net. *See* Net public debt; paying off in future and, 349; as percentage of GDP, 348; as public enemy number one, 358; rising, evaluation of, 347–351
Public education: economic issues of, 121–122; incentive problems of, 121–122; redistribution of income and, 117; subsidies and, 122
Public goods: characteristics of, 114; defined, 114; government's providing of, 113–115
Public sector. *See* Government(s)
Public spending. *See* Government spending
Publishers, unsold books destroyed by, 578, 599–600
Purchasing power: defined, 168, 510; real income and, 510; store of, 366, 367; true, 203
Purchasing power parity: comparisons of world incomes and, 203; defined, 203
Pure competition, 263
Pure monopolist: compared with other market structures, 697–698; defined, 639

Q

Quantity: demanded, changes in, demand shifts versus, 61–62; government restrictions and, 97–98; supplied, changes in, supply shifts and, 68–69
Quantity theory of money and prices, 432–433
Queues, rationing by, 89
Quota(s), 845–847; effect of, 846; voluntary, 846
Quota subscription, 488
Quota system, 845–846. *See also* Quota(s)

R

Raam, 366
Random assignment, rationing by, 89
Random walk theory, 568
Rate of discount, 565
Rate of return, 147–148; defined, 147; negative, 148, 150
Rate-of-return regulation, 707, 710, 711
Rational expectations hypothesis: defined, 458; policy irrelevance proposition and, 458–463
Rationality, bounded, 9–10, 468–469
Rationality assumption, 4–5; bounded, 468–469
Rationing: essential role of, 89; of housing, 92; prices and, 88–89
R&D. *See* Research and development
REACH, 706
Reaction function, 687
Real disposable income, 288, 310
Real GDP: consumption as function of, 298; employment and, 266; equilibrium level of, determining, 297–301, 303; inflation and, affected by weaker dollar, 278–279; per capita. *See* Per capita real GDP; plotting, 201, 202; price level and, in a sticky-price economy, 467–468; and price level in the long run, 239–260; total, 201
Real income, 510
Real rate of interest, 562; defined, 172, 430; nominal rate of interest versus, 172–173; People's Bank of China learns about, 430
Real shock, monetary shock versus, 464
Real values: defined, 199; distinguishing between nominal values and, 199–202; nominal values versus, 168
Real-balance effect, 245
Real-income effect, 510
Realism, models and, 7
Recession: average, length of, 450; defined, 175
Recessionary gap, 274, 275; changes in government spending and, 320; defined, 319
Reciprocators, 688
Recognition time lag, 328
Recycling, 824–826; defined, 824; invisible costs of, 825; of personal computers, 824
Red Cross, 742
Reentrant, 162
Regional trade agreements, 833, 850
Regional trade blocs, 850, 852–853
Regressive taxation, 136, 137
Reinvestment, 566
Related goods, prices of, demand shifts and, 59–60
Relative cost, increasing, law of, 35–37
Relative poverty, 796
Relative price, 53
Relevant market, 722, 725–726
Remanufactured printer ink cartridges, 607
Remote capture, 403
Rent: as component of GDP, 195; defined, 553; economic. *See* Economic rent(s); land, 553
Rent control(s): defined, 92; evasion of, 92–93; gainers and losers from, 93; government policy and, 92–93

Repeat transactions, 690
Repricing cost of inflation, 173
Required reserve ratio, 395
Required reserves: changes in, 408, 427; defined, 395; sweep accounts and, 408–410
Research and development (R&D): economic growth and, 222–223; positive externalities and, 222–223; winnowing process of, 225
Reserve(s), 394–400; borrowed, discount rate and, 407; defined, 395; excess, 395–396, 406; fractional reserve banking and, 394–396; increase in. *See* Reserves, increase in; legal, 395; overall level of, Fed's direct effect on, 398–400; required. *See* Required reserves; total, 395
Reserves, increase in: single bank's reaction to, 396–398; in total banking system, 404–405
Residual claimant, 556
Resource(s). *See also* Factors of production: allocation of. *See* Resources, allocation of; defined, 3; least-cost combination of, 751; natural, 825–826; overallocation of, 111; pollution-causing, use of, 822; scarce, saving, 825–826; scarcity and, 27–28; total, 825; underallocation of, 111
Resources, allocation of: economic rent and, 554; oligopoly and, 686
Restraint of trade, 720
Retained earnings, 140
RetroBox, 84, 824
Revenue(s): marginal. *See* Marginal revenue; total. *See* Total revenue(s)
RFID tags, 55
Ricardian equivalence theorem, 324–325
Ricardo, David, 262, 325, 553
Right-to-work laws, 761
Risens Standers Bank (Sweden), 380
Risk(s): foreign exchange, 877; of nonpayment of loan, 561–562
Robinson, Joan, 662
Robinson-Patman Act ("Chain Store Act")(1936), 719, 720
Rolls Royce, 528
Romania: currency of, cutting excess zeros from, 433; proportional income taxation in, 137
Romer, Paul, 224–225
Roosevelt, Franklin D., 760
Rosenzweig, Mark, 825
Ruffin, Roy, 845
Rule of law, per capita real GDP and, 481
Rules of origin, 852–853
Rules of thumb, 10
Russia: computer programmers from, working aboard cruise ship off California coast, 747; diamond industry in, 652; IMF's dealing with crisis in, 489; as major importer of products manufactured in China, 872; proportional income taxation in, 137
Ruth, Babe, 40–41

S

S corporation, 149
Safeway, store closing when Wal-Mart supercenter opens nearby, 178
SAIF (Savings Association Insurance Fund), 411, 412
Sales, tie-in, 723
Sales promotion, 664. *See also* Advertising
Sales taxes: *ad valorem* taxation and, 141–142; defined, 141; Internet and, 143; maximixing

revenues from, 143–144; as proportional taxes, 142; states with highest and lowest, 143
Sam's Club, 84; CPI calculations and, 178–179
Santa Fe Railroad, 677
Saturation, point of, 583–584
Saudi Arabia, 820; negative relationship between population growth and economic growth in, 480; rate of saving in, 220
Saving: classical model and, 264, 265, 290; defined, 288, 289; investment and, 264, 265; measuring, 310; planned. *See* Planned saving; rate of, economic growth, 220–221; relating income and consumption to, 289; savings versus, 289; in United States, 287, 310
Saving function, 291, 292
Savings: defined, 288; saving versus, 289
Savings Association Insurance Fund (SAIF), 411, 412
Savings banks, 707
Savings deposits, 373
Say, J. B., 262–263
Say's law, 262–263
SBC, 705, 725–726
Scale, 376; constant returns to. *See* Constant returns to scale; diseconomies of. *See* Diseconomies of scale; economies of. *See* Economies of scale; minimum efficient (MES), 596–598
Scaling, 18
Scalpers, 72–73
Scandinavian nations, imports from, to U.S., 834
Scarcity, 27–29; choice, opportunity cost and, 29–30; defined, 27; resources and, 27–28; self-interest, specialization and, 41; shortage versus, 27, 72
Schulz, Charles, 570
Schumpeter, Joseph, 231
Schwartz, Anna, 878
Science: economics as, 7–10; empirical, 8
SDRs (special drawing rights), 488, 864
SeaCode, 747
Search goods, 670
Seasonal unemployment, 165
Seater, John, 242
Secondary boycott, 761
Secondhand goods, transfer of, 189
Secular deflation, 248–249
Secular inflation, 250
Securities. *See also* Bond(s); Stock(s): defined, 567; transactions in, exclusion of, from GDP, 189
Securities and Exchange Commission, 707
Securities markets, 707
Security Systems, Inc., 74
Self-interest: defined, 6; people's motivations and, 263; rational, 3–6, 41; scarcity, specialization and, 41
Separation of ownership and control, 558
Serbia, proportional income taxation in, 137
Service Employees International Union, 763, 777, 778
Services: defined, 29, 191; economic development and, 230; export of, 862; final, final goods and, 186; goods and, all, demand for, demand for single good or service versus, 246; importation of, 862; inflation rate for, 170; single supplier of. *See also* Monopolist(s)
Shanghai Stock Exchange, 567
Share-the-gains, share-the-gains theory, 717
Shenzhen Stock Exchange, 567
Sherman Antitrust Act (1890), 719–720, 721
Shock absorber, exchange rate as, 877

Shocks: external, 175–176; monetary, real shock versus, 464; real, monetary shock versus, 464
Short run: defined, 579; long run versus, 579–580
Shortage(s), 70, 71–72; defined, 69, 72; of safe drinking water, 82, 99–100; scarcity versus, 27, 72; of Super Bowl tickets, 72–73; of vaccines, 107, 126–127
Short-run aggregate supply: long-run aggregate supply and, shifts in, 272; shifts in, 272–273
Short-run aggregate supply curve: defined, 270; Keynesian, 268–270, 288; new Keynesians and, 270
Short-run break-even price, 614, 615, 616
Short-run costs to the firm, 584–590
Short-run economies of operation, 672–673
Short-run equilibrium, 666; current, 321–322
Short-run industry supply curve, 617–618
Short-run losses, minimization of, 613–614
Short-run profits, 612–614
Short-run shutdown price, 614–615
Sidak, J. Gregory, 540
Siemens, 100
Sierra Leone, establishing a business in, 478
Signal(s), 670; defined, 621
Signaling behavior, 670–671
Simon, Carly, 93
Simon, Julian, 226–227, 825
Singapore: companies in U.S. outsource labor services to, 745; economic growth has accompanied population growth in, 480; union membership as share of total employment in, 761, 762
Sixteenth Amendment, 139
Slope(s): defined, 20; of a line (linear curve), 20–23; of nonlinear curve, 23
Slovakia: increased value of currency in, 868; proportional income taxation in, 137
Small menu cost, 466
Small-denomination time deposits, 373–374, 374
Smart cards: debit cards versus, 416; defined, 392; distribution of, in world, 417; how they work, 416
Smith, Adam, 3–4, 41–42, 262, 511
Smoot-Hawley Tariff (1930), 847
Social costs: defined, 814; full, reckoning with, 816; private costs versus, 814–815
Social regulation, 706, 708, 715
Social Security: as an entitlement, 356–357; as attack on poverty, 797–798; benefits from. *See* Social Security benefits; financing, 147–151; government spending on, 118, 147; private accounts and, 134, 154; private pension plans and, 153–154; salvage options and, 148–151, 153154; taxes for. *See* Social Security tax; as transfer payments, 117, 147, 189, 386; trust fund and, 134, 154
Social Security benefits: for disability, 150; for earliest recipients, 147–148; excluded from measured wealth, 788; rate of return and, 147–148, 150–151; reducing, 149; by year of retirement, 148
Social Security contributions, 147. *See also* Social Security tax
Social Security tax: immigration and, 150; increasing, 149; rate and, 141, 149; as regressive tax, 137
Society: choices faced by, 33–37; cost of monopoly to, 650–651, 660
Sole proprietor, 556–557
Sony, 841; digital photo printing kiosks opened by, 627

Sosa, Sammy, 76
South Africa: diamond industry in, 652; gold-mining firms in, 615
South Korea: IMF's dealing with crisis in, 489; union membership as share of total employment in, 761, 762; U.S. public debt held by, 350
Soviet Union, former: GDP of, environmental quality of life versus, 190; population growth rate in, 230
Space exploration, marketplace and, 125
Spain: banking in, 380; conquistadors from, brought horses to North America, 813; manufacturing employment in, 231; per capita spending on health care in, 800; potato brought to Europe by, 842
Spam, fighting with e-mail postage charges, 11
Spanish language, among world's ten most-used, 699, 700
Special drawing rights (SDRs), 488, 864
Special taxes, 111
Specialization: among nations, 837–842; defined, 39; economies of scale and, 595; greater productivity and, 39–42; *Homo sapiens* and, 26, 45; marginal product and, 583; output gains from, 836; in production, 838; scarcity, self-interest and, 41
Spending: by government. *See* Government spending; on human capital, 289–290; public. *See* Government spending; voting versus, 124
Sports trading cards, 51, 75–76
Sprint, 697
Sri Lanka: hit by tsunami in 2004, 239, 254–255; imports from, to U.S., 834; real GDP growth not affected by tsunami, 254–255
SSI (Supplemental Security Income), 798
"Stagflation," 464
Standard(s): of deferred payment, 366, 367–368; monetary, 369–370; of value, 367
Standard Oil Trust of New Jersey, 720
State government(s): spending by, 117; tax receipts of, sources of, 138; taxes and. *See* State government tax(es); trucking fees and, 135–136
State government tax(es): decline in, combating, 152; receipts of, sources of, 138
Static tax analysis, 142
Sticky prices, 466–468
Stock(s): common, 566; defined, 162; flows and, 343–344; liquidity and, 368; markets for, 567–570; preferred, 566; price-earnings ratio and, 570; prices of, how to read in financial press, 569–570; share of, 566
Store of value, 366, 367
Stored-value cards, 413
Strategic behavior. *See also* Strategy(ies): game theory and, 687–690; with implicit collusion, 693–694; tit-for-tat, 690
Strategic dependence, 683–684
Strategy(ies). *See also* Strategic behavior: defined, 688; dominant, 688; entry deterrence, 694; limit-pricing, 694; in noncooperative games, 688; pricing, 689, 690; union, 764–769
Strike(s), 761; strikebreakers and, 764; sympathy, 761; as ultimate bargaining tool, 764
Strikebreakers, 764
Structural unemployment, 165, 451
"Submit order" button, 30
Subsidy(ies): agricultural, 94–95; to Amtrak, 135; correction of positive externalities and, 112; defined, 68; as determinant of supply, 68;

foreign, countering, 844; for public education, 122
Substitute(s): close, 634–635, 642, 653; cross price elasticity of demand and, 539–540; defined, 59; existence of, price elasticity of demand and, 536; imperfect, 642; prices of, demand shifts and, 59–60
Substitution: ease of, 739; law of, 523; marginal rate of, 523; principle of, 510
Substitution effect, 509–510
Sugar subsidies, 95
Super Bowl tickets, 72–73
Supplemental Security Income (SSI), 798
Supply: defined, 62; demand and, 69–73; of foreign currency, 867; inelastic, 542; of labor, determinants of, 743; law of, 62–69; money. *See* Money supply; shifts in. *See* Supply shifts
Supply curve(s): defined, 63; extremes in, illustrated, 543; horizontal summation of, 65; industry. *See* Industry supply curve(s); market, 63–65; for perfectly competitive industry, 616–618; shift in, 66; short-run, perfect competitor's, 616–617
Supply schedule(s), 63–65. *See also* Supply; defined, 63; demand schedule combined with, 69–71
Supply shifts, 65–69, 85–88; changes in quantity supplied versus, 68–69; determinants of, 66–68; effects of, 85–86; with shift in demand, 86–87
Supply-side economics: defined, 327; tax changes and, 326–327
Supply-side inflation, 250–251
Support price. *See* Price floor(s)
Surplus, 70; consumer. *See* Consumer surplus; defined, 69, 72
Sveriges Riksbank (Sweden), 380, 381
Sweden: companies in U.S. outsource labor services to, 745; union membership as share of total employment in, 761, 762; workers from, employed in India, 753
Sweep accounts, 408–410
Swissair, French goods imported by, 847
Switching costs, 695
Switzerland, quota agreement with France and, 847
Sympathy strike, 761

T

Table, numbers in, graphing, 19–20
Tacit collusion, 693
Taft-Hartley Act (Labor Management Relations Act)(1947), 761
Taiwan, birthrate in, 230
Talent, as determinant of marginal productivity, 790
TANF (Temporary Assistance to Needy Families), 798
Tangency point, 526
Target, CPI calculations and, 178–179
Target zones, 878–879
Tariff, 68, 223, 224, 637, 834, 845, 847–848, 851
Tastes, demand shifts and, 58–59
Tata Consultancy Services, 753
Tax, taxation: *ad valorem,* 141–142; alternative minimum (AMT), 321; business, indirect, 195–196; changes in. *See* Tax, taxation, changes in; cigarette, 532–533; of corporations, 140, 558; on demerit goods, 116; as determinant of supply, 68; double, 140, 558; equilibrium quantity and, 146; excise, 145–146; income. *See* Income tax; increasing, elimination of federal budget deficit and, 355–356; lump-sum, 302; market supply curve and, 145–146; maximizing revenues from, 143–144; Medicare, 118, 120–121, 141; of partnerships, 557; personal, 557; from point of view of producers and consumers, 145–147; progressive, 136, 137, 139, 326; proportional, 136, 137, 142; of proprietorships, 557; rate of. *See* Tax rate(s); regressive, 136, 137; sales. *See* sales taxes; Social Security. *See* Social Security tax; special, 111; system of. *See* Tax, taxation, system(s) of; tariff as, 68, 637, 834, 845, 847–848, 851; tax incidence and, 140; unemployment, 141; uniform, 816–817; unit, 145–146
Tax, taxation, changes in: fiscal policy and, 321–322, 340; supply-side effects of, 326–327
Tax, taxation, system(s) of, 136–138; as automatic stabilizer, 329
Tax base, 136
Tax bracket, 136
Tax incidence, 140
Tax rate(s): average, 136; defined, 136; marginal. *See* Marginal tax rate(s)
Tax Reform Act (1986), 139
Taylor, John, 437
Taylor rule, 437–438
Technology(ies): cellphones and, 222; defined, 34; as determinant of supply, 67; growth in, economic growth and, 221–222; health care and, 801; high-tech canines help reduce theft costs and, 589; *Homo sapiens and,* 44; information. *See* Information technology(ies); Internet telephony, 712; nanotechnology and, 579; new, *Homo sapiens and,* 44; production, 579; as separate factor of production, 222
Technovate, 732, 753
Telecommunications industry, 697, 705, 711, 712, 725, 726
Temporary Assistance to Needy Families (TANF), 798
Terms of exchange, 83
Thailand: central bank of, 859; electronic gadgets manufactured in, 67; hit by tsunami in 2004, 239, 254–255; IMF's dealing with crisis in, 489; slight falloff in real GDP growth following tsunami, 254, 255; sugar produced in, 95
Theory(ies). *See also* Model(s): assumptions and, 7–8; capital budget, 353; of consumer choice, 512–513, 520–526; defined, 7; of desired income distribution, 793–794; of efficient markets, 567–568; game. *See* Game theory; marginal product, of wage determination, 790, 793; of natural monopoly regulation, 709–710; of price leadership, 693–694; of price rigidity, 692; of public choice, 122–125; share-the-gains, share-the-gains, 717; utility, 501–502
Theory of Monopolistic Competition (Chamberlin), 662
The Theory of the Leisure Class: An Economic Study of Institutions (Veblen), 12
Third parties: defined, 109, 801; health care services paid for by, 801–803, 803
Thrift institutions, 373
Tie-in sales, 723
Time deposit, 374
Time lags, 328, 332
Time Warner, 721, 726
Tit-for-tat strategic behavior, 690
Tolkien, J. R. R., 570
Total compensation, 787
Total costs: average. *See* Average total costs; comparing total revenues with, 610, 643; defined, 584; of regulation, 718
Total income, 786; defined, 185; total output and, 185–186, 187
Total output, total income and, 185–186, 187
Total physical product (TPP), 581, 733–735
Total reserves, 395
Total resources, 825
Total revenue(s), 608–610; comparing total costs with, 610, 643; defined, 608; price elasticity of demand and, 532–536, 535
Total utility, 502; marginal utility and diamond-water paradox and, 511–512
Toyota, 671
Toys, 60
Toys "R" Us, 714–715
Trade: among regions, 42; balance of, 859; barriers to, 223, 224, 231; economic development and, 231; *Homo sapiens* and, 26, 45; international. *See* International trade; international aspects of, 42–43; interstate, 42; restraint of, 720; world. *See* International trade
Trade agreements: bilateral, 833; regional, 833
Trade and Tariff Act (1984), 847
Trade deficit, 351–352
Trade deflection, 852–853
Trade diversion, trade deflection versus, 852
Trade Expansion Act (1962), 847
Trade Reform Act (1974), 847
Trademarks, 668; brand names and, 669; model train producers pay fees for use of, 676–677
Trade-off(s): between consumption goods and capital goods, 38–39; defined, 31; between present and future, 38–39; production, 33; world of, 31–33
Trading Desk, 437, 438–439, 440
Trailways, 606
Training, as determinant of marginal productivity, 791
Transaction costs, 83–84, 821
Transactions approach. *See also* M1: defined, 371; to measuring money, 371–373
Transactions demand, 423–424
Transactions deposits, 369, 373
Transcontinental railroad, 63
Transfer(s): in kind, 117, 147; of ownership, 189; unilateral, 862–863
Transfer payments: defined, 116; government, 117, 147, 189; as income, 796–797; private, 189; stabilizing impact of, 329
Transistor industry, 623
Traveler's checks, 373
Treasury bonds, 343, 423
Trough, 174
Trucking fees, basis for, 135–136
Trucking industry, 707
Truman, Harry, 470, 875
Trump, Donald, 1
Tsunami, relief efforts following, 742
Turkey: currency of, cutting excess zeros from, 433; IMF's dealing with crisis in, 489
24/7 Customer, 732, 753
Tyco International, 100
Tyson, Cicely, 93

U

UAW (United Auto Workers), 767, 777
Uganda, converting dollars to vouchers for use in, 368

Ukraine, proportional income taxation in, 137
Unanticipated inflation: anticipated inflation versus, 172–173; defined, 172
Underground transactions and activities, 189
Unemployment, 160–167; arithmetic determination of, 161–164; categories of unemployed individuals and, 162; changing, business fluctuations and, 174–176; cyclical, 165, 452; defined, 160; discouraged worker phenomenon and, 163; duration of, 162–163; employment, labor force, and, 161, 162; frictional, 164–165, 451; major types of, 164–165; overemployment and, 163; rate of. *See* Unemployment rate(s); seasonal, 165; structural, 165, 451; trade-off between inflation and, 455. *See also* Phillips curve
Unemployment compensation, 117; stabilizing impact of, 329
Unemployment rate(s): in China, 166; during Great Depression, 115, 161; historical, 160–161; logic of, 163; natural. *See* Natural rate of unemployment; nonaccelerating inflation (NAIRU), 455–456
Uniform tax, 816–817
Unilateral transfers, 862–863
Union(s), 759–782; Congressional control over, 761; craft, 760, 761; current status of, 761; defined, 760; economic effects of, 769–770; featherbedding and, 770; goals of, 764–769; industrial, 760–761; industrialization and, 760–764; most heavily unionized occupations in U.S. and, listed, 769; productivity and, 768, 770; psychologist contemplates "affiliation" with, 776; right-to-work laws and, 761; strategies of, 764–769; strikes and, 761. *See also* Strike(s); ten largest, in U.S., listed, 763; unionization trends in U.S. and, 762–763; wages and, 765–770
Union shop, 761
Union-made goods, 768
Unit elasticity of demand, 531
Unit of accounting, 366, 367
Unit tax, 145–146
Unite Here, 777, 778
United Airlines: operations scaled back by, 698; pension plan affected by bankruptcy of, 154
United Auto Workers (UAW), 767, 777
United Brotherhood of Carpenters and Joiners of America, 777, 778
United Farm Workers of America, 777, 778
United Food and Commercial Workers International Union, 763, 777, 778
United Kingdom. *See also* Great Britain: banking in, 380; central bank targets inflation rate in, 450; contribution of, to EU, 326; India's traditional ties with, 753; as major importer of products manufactured in China, 872; pound of, as "vehicle currency," 881; U.S. public debt held by, 350
United Mine Workers, 761, 777
United Nations, 228, 229; World Food Program (WFP) of, 490
United States: advertising expenses in, 670; agricultural subsidies in, 94–95; antitrust policy in, 719–720, 721; balance of payments account in, 861; banking in, 379, 380; budget surplus in, 345; business activity in, historical picture of, 175, 176; central bank of. *See* Federal Reserve System; China's "voluntary" textile products quota and, 98; economic growth in. *See* United States, economic growth in;
economy of. *See* United States, economy of; foreign direct investment to, 486; income distribution in, 786–787; industry concentration ratios in, 685–686; inflation rates in, 250; labor movement in, 760–761; labor productivity in, 219; lamb industry in, 541; laying off a worker in, 493; life insurance can be sold by banks in, 380; manufacturing employment in, 231; minimum wage in, 83, 96; natural rate of unemployment in, 167, 451–452; net public debt as percentage of GDP in, 348; per capita real GDP in, 214, 218; per capita spending on health care in, 800; poverty rate in, 795–796; price levels in, 251, 252; productive efficiency in, 843; rate of saving in, 287, 310; real GDP growth in, 251, 252; recording a sale of land in, 478; retirement age in, 150; secular deflation in, 248–249; setting up a business in, 478; tariffs in, 847–848, 849; trade within, 42; transporting endangered species from Africa to, 814; unionization trends in, 762–763. *See also* Union(s)
United States, economic growth in: compared with various other countries, 216; historical record of, 215; immigrants' contribution to, 213, 233–234; periods of deflation during, 240; rate of, compared to European nations, 214
United States, economy of: outsourcing's effects on, 745–747; performance of, growing federal budget deficits and, 352–358
United States Constitution, 139
United States Department of Agriculture, 541; adequate food plan designed by, 796
United States Department of Commerce, 367, 862; Bureau of Economic Analysis (BEA) of. *See* Bureau of Economic Analysis; statistics from, 176, 244
United States Department of Defense, refundable commercial airline tickets purchased by and never used, 319
United States Department of Homeland Security, 74
United States Department of the Interior, 823; Bureau of Land Management (BLM) of, 827–828
United States Department of Justice: Antitrust Division of, 113; antitrust law enforcement and, 113, 720, 721, 723–724, 725–726; budget of, 343; international dimensions of antitrust policy and, 721; Microsoft antitrust case and, 720, 723–724
United States Department of Labor, 791; Bureau of Labor Statistics of. *See* Bureau of Labor Statistics; discouraged workers defined by, 163
United States Department of Transportation, 642, 724
United States Department of the Treasury, 343, 766, 864; Office of Thrift Supervision of, 384
United States Fish and Wildlife Service (USFWS), 823–824
United States Forest Service, 826
United States government. *See* Federal government
United States Patent and Trademark Office, 223, 669
United States Postal Service (USPS): incentive structure and, 123–124; share of overnight package delivery market and, 684
United States Treasury, 383, 384; currency minted by, 371
United Steelworkers of America, 777
Unit-elastic demand, 535

Unit-elastic supply, 542
Universal banking, 380
Unlimited liability, 557
UPS, 684
Uruguay Round of General Agreement on Tariffs and Trade (GATT), 848
US Airways, 698, 745
USFWS (United States Fish and Wildlife Service), 823–824
USPS. *See* United States Postal Service
Util, 501–502
Utilitarianism, 501–502
Utility, 501–502; applying marginal analysis to, 502; defined, 501; marginal. *See* Marginal utility(ies); total. *See* Total utility; utils and, 501–502
Utility analysis, 501
Utility theory, 501–502

V

Vaccines, shortage of, 107, 126–127
Vaccines for Children, 126–127
Value(s): implicit rental, 191; nominal. *See* Nominal values; par, 875; predictability of, 370; present. *See* Present value(s); real. *See* Real values; standard of, 367; store of, 366, 367
Value added, 188
Vanguard, 297
Variable costs: average. *See* Average variable costs; defined, 585; total, 585, 614
Variable factors of production, 579
Variable inputs, 579
Veblen, Thorstein, 12
Vending machines, newspaper versus candy, 505–506
Versioning, 723
Vertical merger, 685
VIE (voluntary import expansion), 846
Visible products, 12
Vodafone, 711
Voice Over Internet Protocol (VOIP), 712
VoiceGlo, 712
VOIP (Voice Over Internet Protocol), 712
Voluntary agreements, 821
Voluntary exchange, 83
Voluntary import expansion (VIE), 846
Voluntary quotas, 846
Voluntary restraint agreement (VRA), 846
Voting, spending versus, 124
VRA (voluntary restraint agreement), 846

W

Wachovia Corporation, 403
Wage(s): as component of GDP, 195; determination of. *See* Wage determination; flexibility of, 263, 460–463; minimum. *See* Minimum wage; under monopsony, 773–775; outsourcing's effects on, 743–745; unions and, 765–770
Wage determination: marginal product theory of, 790, 793; in perfectly competitive labor market, 740–743
Wagner, Honus, 75, 76
Wagner Act (National Labor Relations Act)(NLRA)(1935), 760
Waldfogel, Joel, 6
Walgreen's, digital photo printing services offered by, 627
Wall Street Journal, 569–570
Wal-Mart Stores, 202, 513; CPI calculations and, 159, 178–179; digital photo printing services

offered by, 627; entry into Japanese discount-store industry by, 625; as fifth-largest importer of products manufactured in China, 872; unions advocating boycott against, 777
Wants: defined, 3; double coincidence of, 367; needs versus, 29
War, fiscal policy during, 330
War on Poverty, 799
Waste, 667
Water, safe drinking, shortage of, 82, 99–100
Wealth: distribution of, 787–788; inherited, 791; measured, 788
Wealth effect, 245
Weather Channel, 683
Weaver Models, 676
Welfare Reform Act (1996), 799
Wendy's, long run and, 579
WFP (World Food Program), 490
Whitmore, Diane, 798
Wholesale price indexes, 169
Wild Free-Roaming Horses and Burros Act (1971), 827
Wild horses, 813, 827–828
Wild species, common property, trade-offs and, 823–824

Williams, Ted, 75
Williams Reproductions Ltd., 676
Wilson, Woodrow, 381
Wipro Technologies, Ltd., 753
Wireless and wired phone services, cross price elasticity of demand between, 540
Witherspoon, Reese, 554
Woodbridge, G. L., 845
Workers, discouraged, 163
World: comparing GDP throughout, 202–204; GDP for, 196; population of, growth in, 228–229; poverty in, 228
World Bank, 228; asymmetric information and, 489–490; defined, 487; distribution of lending by, 487; effectiveness of, 489–491, 493, 494; elimination and, 491; long-term development lending and, 490; mission of, 489; separate institutions composing, 487; views on appropriate role for, 491
World Food Program (WFP), 490
World index fund, 379
World trade. *See* International trade
World Trade Organization (WTO), 848–850; defined, 848

World War II, 175, 176, 269; government spending during, 118; private domestic investment and, 295; unemployment rate and, 160
World Watch Institute, 826
World Wide Web. *See* Internet
World-Com, 697
WTO. *See* World Trade Organization

X

X axis, 19

Y

Y axis, 19
Yahoo, 697

Z

Zambia: cellphone use in, 222; negative relationship between population growth and economic growth in, 480; sugar produced in, 95
Zero-sum game, 688
Zeta-Jones, Catherine, 59
Zimbabwe, economy of, 204

MACROECONOMIC PRINCIPLES

Cost of Holding Money

The cost of holding money (its opportunity cost) is measured by the alternative interest yield obtainable by holding some other asset.

Policy Irrelevance Proposition

Under the assumption of rational expectations on the part of decision makers in the economy, anticipated monetary policy cannot alter either the rate of unemployment or the level of real GDP. Regardless of the nature of the anticipated policy, the unemployment rate will equal the natural rate, and real GDP will be determined solely by the economy's long-run aggregate supply curve.

Natural Rate of Unemployment

The natural rate of unemployment is the rate of unemployment that exists when workers and employers correctly anticipate the rate of inflation.

Equation of Exchange

$$M_s V = PY$$

where M_s = actual money balances held by the nonbanking public
V = income velocity of money, or the number of times, on average, each monetary unit is spent on final goods and services
P = price level or price index
Y = real GDP

Potential Money Multiplier

The reciprocal of the required reserve ratio, assuming no leakages into currency and no excess reserves, is the potential money multiplier.

$$\text{Potential money multiplier} = \frac{1}{\text{required reserve ratio}}$$

Definition of Money Supply

M1 = currency + transactions deposits + traveler's checks

M2 = M1 +
1. Savings and small-denomination time deposits at all depository institutions
2. Balances in retail money market mutual funds
3. Money market deposit accounts (MMDAs)

Relationship Between Imports and Exports

In the long run, imports are paid for by exports.

Therefore, any restriction of imports ultimately reduces exports.

MICROECONOMIC PRINCIPLES

Opportunity Cost
In economics, cost is always a forgone opportunity.

Law of Demand
When the price of a good goes up, people buy less of it, *other things being equal*.

Movement Along, versus Shift in, a Curve
If the relative price changes, we *move along* a curve–there is a change in quantity demanded and/or supplied. If something else changes, we *shift* a curve–there is a change in demand and/or supply.

Income Elasticity of Demand

$$\text{Income elasticity of demand} = \frac{\text{percentage change in demand for a good}}{\text{percentage change in income}}$$

Law of Diminishing Marginal Product
As successive equal increases in a variable factor of production, such as labor, are added to other fixed factors of production, such as capital, there will be a point beyond which the extra, or marginal, product that can be attributed to each additional unit of the variable factor of production will decline.

Supply
At higher prices, a larger quantity will generally be supplied than at lower prices, *all other things held constant*.

Or stated otherwise:

At lower prices, a smaller quantity will generally be supplied than at higher prices, *all other things held constant*.

Profits

$$\text{Accounting profits} = \text{total revenues} - \text{total costs}$$

$$\text{Economic profits} = \text{total revenues} - \text{total opportunity cost of all inputs used}$$

Elasticity of Demand

$$E_p = \frac{\text{percentage change in quantity demanded}}{\text{percentage change in price}}$$

Elasticity of Supply

$$E_s = \frac{\text{percentage change in quantity supplied}}{\text{percentage change in price}}$$

Monopsony and Monopoly

		Output Market Structure	
		Perfect Competition	**Monopoly**
Input Market Structure	**Perfect Competition**	MC = MR = P W = MFC = MRP$_c$	MC = MR(< P) W = MFC = MRP$_m$ (< MRP$_c$)
	Monopsony	MC = MR = P W < MFC = MRP$_c$	MC = MR(< P) W < MFC = MRP$_m$ (< MRP$_c$)